The Glamour Girls

The Glamour Girls

**JAMES ROBERT PARISH
AND DON E. STANKE**

ARLINGTON HOUSE·PUBLISHERS
NEW ROCHELLE, NEW YORK

Library of Congress Cataloging in Publication Data

Parish, James Robert.
   The glamour girls.

   1. Moving-picture actors and actresses--United
States--Biography. I. Stanke, Don E., joint author.
II. Title.
PN1998.A2P3915   791.43'028'0922   75-5650
ISBN 0-87000-244-9

For Beulah Bondi

Who has brought her own brand of
radiant glamour to countless films.

Contents

KEY TO THE FILM STUDIOS

AA	Allied Artists Picture Corporation
AVCO/ EMB	Avco Embassy Pictures Corporation
CIN	Cinerama Releasing Corporation
COL	Columbia Pictures Industries, Inc.
EMB	Embassy Pictures Corporation
FN	First National Pictures, Inc. (later part of Warner Bros.)
FOX	Fox Film Corporation
LIP	Lippert Pictures, Inc.
MGM	Metro-Goldwyn-Mayer, Inc.
MON	Monogram Pictures Corporation
PAR	Paramount Pictures Corporation
RKO	RKO Radio Pictures, Inc.
REP	Republic Pictures Corporation
20th	Twentieth Century-Fox Film Corporation
UA	United Artists Corporation
UNIV	Universal Pictures, Inc.
WB	Warner Bros. Inc.

Acknowledgments

Research Consultant:
Doug McClelland
Manuscript Verifier:
Earl Anderson

Acknowledgments:
Jack Ano
Jack Barnich
Joan Bennett
Ralph Blase
Richard Braff
Alan Brock
Bruco Enterprises
Loraine Burdick
James Butler
Cinemabilia Book Shop
  (Ernest Burns)
Charlie Earle
Morris Everett, Jr.
Olivier Eyquem
Film Fan Monthly
Filmfacts
Films and Filming
Films in Review
Focus on Films
Pierre Guinle
Mrs. R. F. Hastings

Richard M. Hudson
Martha Hyer
Ken D. Jones
Jim King
Miles Kreuger
Albert B. Manski
Alvin H. Marill
David McGillivray
Mrs. Earl Meisinger
Jim Meyer
Peter Miglierini
Movie Poster Service
  (Bob Smith)
Movie Star News
Pat Nix
Marni Nixon
Jeanne Passalacqua
Vera Ralston
Jaces Saada
Screen Facts
  (Alan G. Barbour)
Anthony Slide
Charles Smith
Mrs. Peter Smith
Roz Starr Service
Charles K. Stumpf
Views and Reviews
Marie Windsor

And special thanks to Paul Myers, curator of the Theatre Collection at the Lincoln Center Library for the Performing Arts (New York City), and his fine staff: Monty Arnold, David Bartholomew, Rod Bladel, Donald Fowle, Maxwell Silverman, Dorothy Swerdlove, Betty Wharton; and Don Madison of Photographic Services.

Foreword

Years ago, when I was a little girl, I had a dream—probably no different from the dream of many other young girls. The dream was someday to come to Hollywood and be famous just like all those beautiful people I saw in films.

I can remember the first movie I ever saw. It was a Shirley Temple picture. I can't recall the title, but I do remember sitting on my father's lap in the theatre, and watching one particular scene where Shirley tapped her way up and down a flight of stairs, culminating her terpsichorean tricks with a grand slide down the banister, a delicate jump off its post, and a low curtsey. I can also vividly recall the perfection of every curl on Shirley's head—even when they bounced—and I wondered why my own straight locks couldn't look like hers all the time. That night I made my mother set my hair in rags, which she swore to me would give me the Shirley Temple look. And the following day I drove her crazy until she bought me a pair of Mary Jane patents—as shiny as Shirley's were. So shiny, in fact, I could see my face in them just the way Shirley had seen hers. I was only about two. *I* was going to become a dancer! The fact that I had been afflicted since birth with a muscular ailment (later to be diagnosed as an arrested case of muscular dystrophy) and couldn't walk up a step—let alone a flight of stairs—made no difference. If Shirley Temple could do it, why couldn't *I*? I couldn't. I never became a dancer. But for many years after, even though I couldn't dance like Shirley, I sure as heck tried to look like her. The closest I came was in the way my mother dressed me. She had an uncanny ability to buy outfits that looked just like Shirley Temple's, even one similar to the dress Shirley wore in that first film. I remember it had a bib collar, short ruffled sleeves, and a skirt which billowed out, to reveal yards and yards of petticoat. It was my favorite Sunday dress. I wore it till I burst its seams. Fade out.

When I reached eight my new idol became Carmen Miranda. There was something about Latin music that could get me moving like nothing else, even to this day. I am convinced that all Latins, like all blacks, are born with rhythm. And certainly my Carmen "Chiquita Banana" Miranda was no exception. I saw every movie she ever made, and after each one I'd go home to try to fashion my own personal Carmen Miranda get-up from my mother's wardrobe, or the refrigerator. Once I almost got killed for having

11

taken my mother's favorite negligee because it was the only long, flowing gown in her closet, and cutting off six inches from the hem so it wouldn't be too long. Needless to say, I never had any trouble finding bananas, grapefruits, grapes, pears and oranges. My mother believed in stocking food in our refrigerator like it was going out of style. She was always afraid, in those war years, that she would be the only person in the United States who would be rationed. At least, that's what I assumed, at age 8.

As I matured and Carmen Miranda died (leaving me to concoct my own rhumbas, sambas and tangos), I found myself shifting gears. Though I had been blessed at an early age with an overabundance of mammary development, I was not very large on exposing myself in sweaters. The few that I owned were at least five and eight times larger than I needed. Anything to hide my Leaning Tower of Pisa chest. That was until I took note of Lana Turner busting out all over. From my first recollection of Lana on the screen—until the day I met her—she has always been the epitome of womanhood to me. A body to die over, with a face to match, and blonde hair that was never out of place. And, oh yes, those bare shoulders upon which were often hung either the latest off-the-shoulder creations or strapless gowns. I dreamt nightly of becoming Lana Turner and wearing all those expensive clothes and jewelry. The closest my Clara Clutz body came to knowing what those clothes were all about was buying a Lana Turner cut-out doll book. Dreams aside, Lana Turner became *everyone's* sweater girl; *everyone's* sex symbol. It seemed whatever style she set in films was quickly emulated minutes later by every female in America. When Lana changed the rise of her eyebrow, so did everyone else.

Little did I realize, at that time, how powerful films were; how much they influenced our lives; and, more important, how they reflected our own attitudes—blatant or latent. I was to learn much later that Hollywood stars are America's answer to a Royal Family. And no matter what, our society would never really survive without such heroes and heroines.

Remember Veronica Lake in her heyday? Remember how every girl— young or old—suddenly began wearing her hair over one eye?

And what about those women who secretly yearned to be more than just housewives? Who was their idol? Why, Rosalind Russell, of course. There wasn't a working girl in the country, it seemed to me, who didn't try to look like Roz. And the uniform? A tailored suit with broad padded shoulders and hair done up in a pompadour! Of course. Remember?

And remember when the coiffure experts finally perfected do-it-yourself hair coloring kits? Overnight, every mousey brown female in America became a Rita Hayworth red. Remember?

And remember when Loretta Young, in the early 50's, became the first of the giant lady stars to come to television with her "Loretta Young Show"? Remember how she dressed? Remember how those doors swung open, and in swept Loretta, fit to kill, in some flowing, colorful chiffon—even though it was still the age of black and white TV? Remember?

12

I guess I could go on remembering forever, all the things that *made* us remember what movie stars were all about. Especially the lady ones. They had a certain, distinct something that you never forgot. A personal indelible stamp. A mark. A brand. An attitude. In one word: GLAMOUR.

I never forgot those ladies . . . Joan Crawford with her saucer eyes, her sling back pumps . . . Gloria Swanson and the draped hoods over her hair . . . Bette Davis and the mad way she puffed on a cigarette . . . Doris Day and her DA hairdo . . . or Marilyn Monroe and her puckered, whimpering lips.

When I arrived in Hollywood, I was determined that someday I would mold myself into a composite of all of them. And if not them, maybe somebody new.

May I tell you, friends—for me—the somebody new never happened on the scene. This was partly because I realized as I began to intimately know all these beautiful creatures, that Glamour Girls are really NOT Happy Girls. I didn't *want* to be one of them. But it was also partly due to the lingering death of the big film studios. Times were changing—financial times. The studio chieftains who remained no longer found it profitable to pour huge sums into the creation of illusory bubbles around new lady talent. Those bubbles, of course, had both good and bad points.

In the early years, when the girls like Lana, Ava, Rita, Kim, etc. were under contract to studios, they seemed to have been molded into roles that were not natural—lives that were not real. The unglamorous moguls, I believe, knew what they were doing. But since they were making so much money from these women who filled not only their own, but all men's fantasy desires (not to mention giving Drab Dora a pinch of faith), they weren't about to stop the flow of bucks into their Niagara bank accounts. Besides, most of these girls had been near the poverty level and were now earning more money than they ever had. Money became their narcotic. And coupled with their common quality, vulnerability (which produces a strand of weakness, not to be rejected), it trapped them. Like their mentors, they fell prey to a fear of losing it all. And finally, when the world of reality caught up with the world of fantasy, most of these ladies could not distinguish one lifestyle from the other. And so—they began to lose another of their common qualities which had made them stars: INNOCENCE!

Today, things have really changed. We are no longer producing sex symbols or glamour queens . . . and that too is a grave loss, since every man still hungers, I believe, for a glimpse and a taste of fantasy. Unfortunately, in our world of the 70's, it seems that the time it takes for fantasy to catch up with reality has drastically shortened. Again that is both good and sad.

Rona Barrett
September/October, 1974

13

Introduction:
Will the Real Glamour Girl
Please Stand Up?

René Jordan

Glamour. Also glamer. 1720. (Corruption f. GRAMMAR. Orig. *Sc;* introduced by Scott) 1. Magic, enchantment, spell. 2. A magical or fictitious
beauty attaching to any person or object; a delusive or alluring charm 1840.
3. *attrib.* as *g.-gift, might* 1805. I. When devils, wizards or jugglers deceive
the sight, they are said to cast g. o'er the eyes of the spectator—*Ramsay.*

Even such a staid, no-nonsense source as the *Oxford English Dictionary*
becomes slightly giddy when attempting to pin down the meaning of
glamour. This deceptive seven-letter word mellows the dryness of the
academic language, and, at a loss for a precise definition, the compilers
close their eyes and enter—just for a few lines—into a land of treacherous
incantations.

When categorizing glamour, this most sober of tomes resorts to com-
parisons with sorcery and magic. The philologists then step back and venture no further, like explorers in jungle movies after finding an ominous
voodoo doll. Their timorousness is justified; the essence of the word defies
analysis, and every cut of the semantic knife risks evisceration of the
romantic ideal. Conjures have a way of sounding rather repellent when
turned into recipes, from Shakespeare's witches' brew of "eye of newt,
toe of frog" to the five-dollar advice from a gypsy diviner who suggests
burning hairs and nail clippings—stolen from your beloved—as a rapid cure
for unrequited passion.

Getting to the heart of fantasy risks the danger of cardiac arrest. Once
the beat ceases one is left merely with the prosaic, so even the most
relentless of word doctors prefer to stop at the epidermis. *Glamer* cor-
rupted GRAMMAR as early as 1720; if even the purists restrain themselves and glide warily on the surface of the concept, how can one blame
the more impressionable for identifying, classifying, and deifying the
glamorous by their trappings?

Seduced by a benighted, late-show-induced madness, some fanciful nostalgia fans fall into rapture while defining a glamour queen as a woman, smothered in sable and choked in diamonds, who agitates a twelve-inch cigarette-holder like a wand and bats two-inch eyelashes like a semaphore, giving men "Stop" and "Go" signals without chromatic benefit of red and green. Such simplication is as smooth and glistening as a frozen pond, yet those who try to go deeper into the concept may sink silently and without a trace.

Glamour is much more than an iridescent and delusive surface. If it were merely a matter of accretion, a clever selection of props on which to lean, then your Aunt Maggie could be a movie queen after forty-eight grueling hours in a beauty salon. This idea of glamour as the invention of makeup men, hairdressers, and couturiers is quickly disproved by the "camp" efforts of female impersonators who sedulously imitate every trick and movement while swishing about as Dietrich, Crawford, or Hayworth. They get the quick laugh, but they will never get a gasp or a sigh. All they can achieve is parody, a parasitical form of art.

Glamour must exude from within. If it lacks the underpinnings of a steely personality, then the outer construction ends up looking ridiculous, like those satirical cartoons presenting Louis XIV as a runt of a man who contrived to look like a king, courtesy of high heels, towering peruke, silver cane, and authoritarian manner. Louis XIV had a state duty to invent himself; he could bring off the impersonation because his pretensions were supported by his birthright.

But in this democratic century, glamour queens lacked the tradition of blue blood to substantiate their claims. Some of them started as waitresses, hoofers, or worse, but an innate regal quality made up for their lack of pedigree. Possessing this quality, they could be groomed effectively for accession to the Hollywood throne.

Film work is essentially a form of collaboration, and the queen bees, in their plush cells at the studio hives, were artfully shaped by battalions of workers, from the technicians who lit their faces to the press agents who spun their legends. They were helped every step of the way, but unless the inner flame flickered, no spotlight could adequately illuminate them. Audiences would not be fooled, and the fake pretenders were soon labeled with the epithet "clothes horse" and quickly consigned to oblivion, no matter how beautiful they had managed to look.

Beauty and glamour may coincide, but they are by no means the same thing. Beauty is in the eye of the beholder; glamour is in his mind. Someone may persuade himself that his love object is beautiful, but he will seldom be able to compel anyone else to share this very private optical illusion. Blinded by passion, such a fond lover may be rash enough to try to proselytize, but his efforts will be as barren as those of a prophet in the desert. In the end, all he may get is a polite assent and a repressed snicker, for such personal feelings are noncommunicable.

Glamour is a more abstract concept than beauty, and, therefore, more susceptible to psychological manipulation. A group of anonymous people congregated in a dark movie theatre are an ideal target for the creation of a mass mentality that is independent of individual perceptions. The passive spectators can be coaxed into nurturing a superidea stronger than the sum of its component thoughts. Gustave Le Bon was not examining the star-bedazzled collective mind of moviegoers when he wrote his definitive analysis of the psychology of the masses, but these cinema visions provide an apt corollary to his theorems. The conglomerate psyche of "those wonderful people out there in the dark" was the dangerous but controllable creature that Hollywood desperately sought to tame.

If a movie mogul could convince a substantial number of spectators that a screen personality was glamorous, then the actor or actress instantly profited by the magic attribution. Call it mass delusion or mass deception—depending on whether you choose to be a romantic or a cynic—but the studios had every tool at hand to becloud the public's vision with stardust and create a dreamworld that went far beyond the mere beauty that the naked eye could see.

During the golden era of movie glamour, motion pictures often were able to hypnotize their addicts into actually believing that some shimmering figure exuded glamour. The camera invested men and women with an allure that perhaps was only partially there. Publicity would do the rest by repeating the enchanted word *glamorous* until it became second nature. In a strange symbiosis, the concept became the substance and the vicious circle was completed: these creatures had glamour because they were up there, and they wouldn't be up there unless they possessed glamour.

Producers and directors became sorcerers who foisted their own obsessions on moviegoers. The classic example is Josef von Sternberg's discovery of a rather hefty, somewhat moon-faced German girl with mercerized curls. With all the paraphernalia of the Seventh Art, Joe Stern changed the unpromising Maria Magdalena von Losch into the fascinating Marlene Dietrich. If he had introduced her to a gang of men at a company picnic, the glare of noon would have made the pair laughable. However, like a twentieth-century Pygmalion, Sternberg sculpted Dietrich in light and shadow, turning a mere mortal into a myth and offering his Galatea as a gift for the adoring audience. When Sternberg and Dietrich parted, he looked at his creation from afar, half in amazement, half in regret, and often repeated with a mischievous grin: "I am Marlene Dietrich."

Sternberg, the movie alchemist, could assess the hidden chemistry that a camera can bring out in the human face, body, and psyche. After Dietrich left his aegis, he was still able to turn Gene Tierney and Ona Munson into awesome females in *The Shanghai Gesture*. He toned down Jane Russell's harsh, deadpan vulgarity into tawdry glamour for *Macao,* and even energized the pallid Janet Leigh into a desirable, pullover-clad temptress in *Jet Pilot.*

Given the right equation, the imponderable X factor can be evoked, at least temporarily. The lasting magic depends almost entirely on the subject: several of the women analyzed in this book are living proof of the puzzling formula. Prompted by love, greed, or a combination of both, the men in their lives were determined to have the whole world agree with their particular vision. From their influential niches in the movie industry, these men spared no effort in their quest for public approval of their personal choices for admiration.

Promoters of glamour seemed to be seeking psychological assurance in a basic urge similar to that of the man who preens like a peacock while escorting a beautiful and desirable woman. In their role as movie czars they had the power to exercise this masculine pride in full, sometimes megalomaniacal, scale. It gave them pleasure to stake their property claims on goddesses of their own making.

Their stories read like tried-and-true, often remade movie scenarios. David O. Selznick falls in love with young Phyllis Isley and spends a fortune selling her as a young, highstrung Duse under the name of Jennifer Jones. Herbert Yates places the whole mini-empire of Republic Pictures at Vera Hruba Ralston's feet, the better to reaffirm his pride and her glory. Alexander Korda is so attracted to Merle Oberon that he reconstructs her into an exotic beauty capable of shackling Heathcliff and betraying Henry VIII.

These are tales of love, but there are also stories of vengeance and cruelty. When Harry Cohn was incensed by Rita Hayworth's rebellion, he took a bovine Czech-American girl called Marilyn Novak, rebaptized her Kim, and gave her the glamour treatment. With pencil-thin arched eyebrows and lavender-tinted-ash-blond hair, Cohn figured she could teach Hayworth a lesson and, with luck, even topple her. Rita and Kim did not cancel each other, but Novak made it to the top as a goddess conceived not in love but in spite.

These behind-the-scenes melodramas have been codified into Hollywood lore. For years, movie magazines parroted the apocryphal story of Lana Turner being "discovered" sipping strawberry soda at Schwab's drugstore by director Mervyn LeRoy, who launched her as the pneumatic sweater girl in a prophetically titled thriller, *They Won't Forget*. These seductive fairy tales were widely read and lured many a youngster to invade the Mecca of Moviedom, including callow Roy Fitzgerald—later known as Rock Hudson—who parked his diaper delivery truck in front of studio gates and perched himself on the fender, waiting to be spotted in an hour and glorified in a month.

Boys and girls who were pleased by what they saw in their mirrors were stung instantly by dreams of "going Hollywood." Most of them never advanced beyond the amorphous ambitions of the narcissist, but those star-struck individuals who enacted the hallucination often found there was a final truth to the shopworn cliché: "Stars are born, not made." On the reverse side of all the success stories lie the half-forgotten tales. Sometimes the willful transformation from worm to butterfly failed disastrously, and the Hollywood wizards sometimes found themselves embarrassingly reduced to mere sorcerer's apprentices.

Samuel Goldwyn, an astute producer, had a rather inglorious career as a star-maker. He imported Anna Sten from German films and fashioned her into a collage of Dietrich and Garbo. Like both of them, Sten had a solid, peasant quality that Goldwyn stylized into "Mittel-European" glamour. Sten did not respond to the experiment. She might have been a fine actress in the naturalistic vein, and her performance in *The Wedding Night* suggests her as a creditable ancestor of the Patricia Neal school of true grit, honest kitchen drama. As an object of fascination in *Nana* and *We Live Again,* she was pathetically inadequate. With the acute shyness of the displaced, she tried too hard: her fake eyelashes fluttered in a twitching desperation that belied the languor for which her directors were aiming.

Another Goldwyn mistake was Sigrid Gurie, billed as a Scandinavian import and cast as a Chinese princess in *The Adventures of Marco Polo.* Gurie was dropped by Goldwyn when the press revealed she hailed not from the frozen fjords but from downtown Brooklyn. If she had been popular or admired, her origins would not have mattered: recently Barbra Streisand has demonstrated that a very specialized kind of glamour can be found even on Flatbush Avenue. But Sigrid Gurie was not basically exotic, and Goldwyn forced her to exert the wrong type of attraction. She was enveloped in a cocoon of fakery so sheer that the audience's keen eye penetrated it and saw the larva within.

Women like Sten and Gurie were cleverly baited by Goldwyn, but they were left hanging on the hook, untouched. The public sniffed and quickly swam away. They would not bite. Studio promotion could not endow them with a spell they lacked. The attribution of glamour is so imprecise that it seems endless, but it has very constricting limits: Dolores del Rio could get away with publicity releases that announced she ate orchids for breakfast, but when Universal resurrected the gimmick and claimed flower-eating as Piper Laurie's idiosyncrasy, the readers just laughed.

These inconsistencies baffle all practitioners of the art of movie magic. Trying to reduce the abstract to the concrete, they often explain the mirage as mere photogenics. But photogenics, although an effective passkey, is not the "Open Sesame" of screen glamour. Certainly an ideal mating of the camera and its subject is immensely helpful in the realm of illusion. No one would be able to make a glamour queen out of a beautiful woman who does not photograph well, though it is possible to draw magnetism out of intrinsically bad features, i.e., Marilyn Monroe. Yet glamour transcends camera angles, interesting bone structure, and high-fashion photographer cant: top models like Suzy Parker or Jean Shrimpton registered nothing but gilded vacuums on the screen. They were photogenic but not animated. On a glossy magazine page they could sell anything from cosmetics to vodka, whereas in the movies they were unable to sell themselves.

The case for subliminal self-promotion can be further stated by a comparison between Gia Scala and Ava Gardner. In person, Gia Scala was one of the most beautiful women on earth. Unfortunately, she was painfully unsure of herself, and in her pictures she qualified, at best, as an apple-cheeked echo of the early Bergman. Her problem was not a lack of photogenics: she registered about two-thirds of her real beauty in *The Angry Hills* or *The Big Boodle,* but that was enough to make her exceptionally good looking. Yet, deep within, she was scared of her sudden preeminence. Close-ups are cruel to the doubting personality, and when Gia Scala's eyes went through a hesitation waltz the public could read her unglamorous thoughts. "What am I doing here?" she seemed to be telling herself. "Why is all this happening to me?" It was distressing for viewers to watch and proved fatal to her public image.

In person, Ava Gardner was never remotely as beautiful as Gia Scala. Delicately boned, tentatively sweet, and even a little bashful, Gardner does not project a fraction of the imposing allure she wields on the screen. But when a camera is pointed at her, Gardner truly believes she is the epitome of glamour. One can read no doubts in her eyes, not even in recent films, when time has begun to take its toll on her. The physical charm may be eroding, but the self-confidence is like a rock. Pushing fifty, in the lyrical coda to *The Life and Times of Judge Roy Bean,* she can still stir the witches' cauldron and cunningly deceive the most scrutinizing lens.

Perhaps the truest example of movie glamour was denied to American audiences at large. She is María Félix, star of dozens of Mexican, Spanish, Italian, and French films that were seldom distributed in the United States. Only Jean Renoir's *French Can Can,* with La Félix in a droll, but atypical, performance, can be cited in her readily available filmography in America. She would have been Hollywood's prize catch and remains its greatest loss in the glamour sweepstakes.

"They always offered me contracts," she once said, "but they wanted me to play Indians or peasants and, after all María Félix is María Félix." She was right! Her special allure required a sumptuous setting, and she shied away from California, where the similarly delightful María Elena Marqués was obliterated as Clark Gable's squaw in *Across the Wide Missouri,* and all the regal, middle-aged Dolores Del Rio could achieve were humiliating bits as Elvis Presley's half-breed mother in *Flaming Star* or as John Ford's displaced redskin dowager in *Cheyenne Autumn.* María Félix would not knuckle under to Hollywood chauvinism. To her, glamour was as essential as oxygen.

All through her still active career, Félix played the insatiable man-eater in mink and emeralds. Before the fifth reel of any given movie several men had shot themselves through parietals or pectorals in despair over her cast-iron disdain. In real life, she sought to maintain the same unreachable aura, and was truly shocked when informed that Montgomery Clift had been seen buying a steak at Gristede's in New York. "Montgomery Clift in a butcher shop," she moaned in anger and sorrow. "No wonder the star system is destroyed in America."

In her pictures, María Félix looks ten feet tall, appearing like a vengeful amazon. Her supreme hauteur is the impossible dream of female impersonators. As a matter of fact, Holly Woodlawn, Andy Warhol's transvestite superstar, revealed to a television talk-show audience that as a small child in his native Puerto Rico, he had modeled himself on the María Félix melodramas his mother took him to see at Saturday matinées.

In reality, María Félix is a stunning but remarkably subdued woman. Rather petite and demure, she wears little makeup and keeps her menacing dark mane well pinned under sable cloche hats. I was discouraged to find her in a suite at New York's Warwick Hotel, with a welcoming smile on her face and not a feather boa in sight. Was this the face that launched a thousand masturbatory fantasies in high school kids from Caracas to Barcelona? Was she the one who tyrannized whole generations of women into changing hairdos and lipstick shades, the better to imitate her?

Yet the icon is a very real person and, like all of us, María Félix has a consuming passion. After fifteen minutes of polite conversation, her eyes suddenly lit as she talked about her collection of a very specific style of French porcelain signed Jacob Petit. I immediately called a friend who knows the antique market to the last chink and we were off with La Félix, in search of precious dishes and tureens.

She wore a very simple tailored dress and looked like a nice Spanish lady in her early forties . . . until we reached the first store. The arrogance of antique dealers is legendary, and she failed to impress the owner as she quietly strode in. "Only to the trade, madam," he muttered, sending her away with a well-rehearsed smirk. Undaunted, María Félix walked ten paces into the shop and then turned, transmuted into a visitor from Olympus. "My good man," she whispered, "I hear you have some Jacob Petit porcelains." He had no idea who she was, had never seen any of her movies, but his knees quivered. She had him at her mercy. María Félix walked out of that shop with all she wanted, at the most reasonable prices she cunningly could haggle. When she wanted to use it, she had her own blinding, built-in spotlight.

This anecdote attests to another secret of glamour. It can be turned on and off at will. Walking down Fifth Avenue in New York with Jean Arthur, her companion wondered out loud why she was never recognized. The star replied it was merely because she did not want to be spotted. Immediately she changed her stance, her pace, her expression; on the next block, five people asked for her autograph. Jean Arthur was never a glamour girl;

a combination of common sense and sense of humor prevented it. But even such a retiring personality as Arthur's knew the mechanics of star attraction, and her sudden whim to be noticed yielded quick results.

The Hollywood saga is full of examples of this conjuring of glamour at the flick of a psychological switch. In 1931, when the young Clark Gable was little more than a struggling bit player, director Mervyn LeRoy tried unsuccessfully to convince Jack Warner to give Gable a part in *Public Enemy*. To this day, LeRoy remembers the unknown Gable as a charismatic man who could walk into a roomful of people and attract two hundred pairs of eyes with just the lifting of an eyebrow.

Others worked harder at the establishment of their charisma. In her beginnings at Universal, before she had even negotiated a contract, Maria Montez once entered the studio commissary. There was not one empty table in the room, except for half a dozen in the privileged inner sanctum reserved for the high echelon. Every eye was suddenly on this mysteriously self-assured woman who turned a deaf ear to the hostess, walked to the best table, turned a reserved sign face down, and imperiously demanded service after informing the waiter, "I am La Montez." La Montez had a well-calibrated combination of sublime chutzpah and total lack of sense of humor about her screen presence. There always seems something fishy about a siren who kids herself. Contrariwise, from the successful silent screen temptresses Montez had inherited the audacity to take herself with mortal seriousness in the most impossible of situations. From the silent era on, the history of movie glamour comprises a series of changes in style, but regardless of the differences in demeanor, all these women shared an aura of the undecipherable, the unattainable.

Glamour queens, like good strippers, must hide something to keep their audiences interested. As soon as all is revealed, they are on their way down. The public must be persuaded that there is another side to the counterfeit coin of star attraction: Susan Hayward is really hiding a marshmallow heart behind the crusty exterior; fires smoulder under Audrey Hepburn's carefully poised coolness; Yvonne De Carlo is more dangerous when she tries to be faithful than when she flaunts her deceitfulness. The glamour queen wore her question mark like a halo. She was doomed if her fans began to suspect that they knew the answers to her riddle.

This sphinxlike quality was naturally emphasized by silent films, with their dependence on pantomime and the necessity of the underlined grand gesture. Boundaries are diffuse between the vamps of the twenties and the clearly delineated glamorous ladies of the thirties. The vamp was a gluttonous devourer of heedless males: a seductive gorgon who walked around in a dazzle of sequins and a flurry of feathers, the better to attach to herself the fools who ventured into her magnetic field.

Favorite actresses of the twenties were divided sternly into "good" and "bad" girls. Not by any stretch of the imagination can enigmatic glamour be ascribed to Mary Pickford or to the soulful Lillian and Dorothy Gish. They maintained the ideal of homegrown femininity, as America's sweethearts and beleaguered sisters. With typical xenophobia, Hollywood often allotted the "dirty work" to the foreigners.

Francesca Bertini, Lyda Borelli, and La Hesperia reigned supreme in Italy, hanging for dear life to velvet curtains while their movie suppliants sipped champagne from their poisoned slippers. Pola Negri functioned as the transatlantic link that imported all this dark female foreboding to sunny California. In America, a nice Jewish girl from Cincinnati, Theodosia Goodman, had to change her name to Theda Bara, an anagram of the Arabic word for death, before she could attempt to vamp her way into a scandalous triumph. The glamour of the vampire ladies was closely associated with evil, and their sensuality was suffused in the imminent peril of the black widow spider.

Gloria Swanson had the equilibrium and good sense to vacillate between categories and alternate the "good" with the "bad." With her chameleon-like adaptability, she became the precursor of the glamour-queen style of the thirties: she lived like royalty, married a marquis, and conducted every public appearance as if an invisible camera were catching the nuances.

Then, with a further loosening of prim morality, the flapper emerged, and Clara Bow was able to project a wickedness that never became sheer evil. She was exploring a new territory in which Lana Turner would flourish in coming decades. The flapper was indigenously American, an urban woman, preferably from a big-town environment. In the henna-haired, tight-bodied persona of Miss Bow, she asserted an endearingly gauche kind of glamour, halfway between the petulant baby and the full-grown tease.

Although Swanson and Bow qualify as pioneers, it is with the thirties that the concept of glamour was fully democratized and Americanized. Dietrich and Garbo were still casting their European gossamer webs, but the local girls were now decidedly in competition. Harlow in white satin, Shearer in black tulle, the Bennett sisters in diamond earrings, Crawford wearing lamé with such unshakable assurance that one suspected her very heart was a gold ingot. They dressed sumptuously and slunk about in opulent sets. Even when they started the picture as stenographers or manicurists, the fortune wheel of a rigged plot would usually land them in the lap of luxury by the fourth reel.

The Depression was directly responsible for the emergence of glamour as Hollywood's most salable commodity. If glamour is a form of mass hypnosis, there were never more willingly mesmerized audiences than those who spared a dime to enter their chosen dream palace at the corner movie house. Hollywood catered to this hunger for the impossibly beautiful, the alluringly rich. Stars were elevated to the heights of elegance in the midst of hard times. With gowns by Adrian, coiffures by Guilaroff, and faultless skin by Max Factor, the studios could transmute these never-never women into the stuff of which Depression dreams were made.

Deprived and harassed audiences lapped up the fantasies, not with the innocence of the beguiled twenties' movie fans, but with a kind of desperation born from the need for urgent compensation against real terrors. Once the joyous cinema dream ended, nightmares awaited. A bread line and a theater line merged at some subliminal danger point, and Hollywood, like a corporate Nero, offered *panem et circenses* to the unemployed millions.

Later, as economic conditions improved slightly, the public remained hooked on the drug of escapism. In the late thirties viewers still salivated in Pavlovian response to those enameled sets and those haughty girls who adjusted their jewelry with exquisitely manicured hands, whose nails were painted Jungle Red. The Big Bad Wolf of poverty had been temporarily shooed away from the door, but clouds were gathering again. There was impending conflict in Europe, and certainly the madness would soon seep into America.

There was a mixture of euphoria and fear in the air. In this manic interregnum, audiences were titillated by the bizarre. In glamour-girl country, it was the era of the gimmick: Lamour and her sarong, Veronica Lake's peekaboo bang, Turner's mountainous sweater. These touches were all the product of unsteady transition. Moviegoers had taken one step forward but dreaded the inevitable two steps back.

Glamour thrives on difficult years, and the Second World War gave it added impetus. When the ramifications of the war finally became clear, Hollywood—like the long awaited and always dependable cavalry—was there on time. Movies distilled new doses of adrenalin for the viewer depressed by shortages, ration books, celibacy at home, Dear John letters abroad, telegrams that turned Western Union into a dot-dash-dot messenger for the Grim Reaper, or a night shift to work for victory interrupted by the insensitive milkman who wouldn't keep those bottles quiet.

This entire spectrum of woe, from mild annoyance to irreparable loss, was made more bearable by the movies. Good old reliable Hollywood again came to the rescue, and wartime pictures were as soothing and as disposable as the Kleenex that wipes away the tears at a psychiatrist's couch. Reality could be escaped by being immersed in the whirlpool of a musical or the becalming ebb tide of a romantic drama where only the achievement of true love seemed to trouble the lucky stars.

And then there was Rita Hayworth, who had the unsnappable resilience to stretch all wartime longings beyond their wildest limits. She could hoof with Astaire, glide with Kelly, or sing with a borrowed voice as if she had just reclaimed it from hock. She could be a heartless nymphomaniac in *Blood and Sand,* a disoriented fall girl in *The Lady in Question,* a whole gallery of good/bad mirrors in the shattering climax of *The Lady from Shanghai.* Above all she was *Gilda,* the supreme glamour queen who, in modern idiom, got it all together from the flightiness of Clara Bow to the cruelty of Theda Bara, interspersed with the bravado of a torch singer, the brashness of a burlesque bump-and-grind star, and the well-hidden heart of gold of the proverbial streetwalker.

Gilda is arguably the glamour movie of all time. After the reign of the vamps, screenwriters had not been able to match those ominous title cards for sheer outrageousness. However, Hayworth's Gilda could give voice to the unutterable with a demented, overt confidence that brought clichés to life by mouth-to-mouth resuscitation. "No one ever cared for me, Johnny," she told a justifiably bemused Glenn Ford. "If I'd been a ranch, they would have named me the Bar-Nothing." She taunted him mercilessly, and when she demurely thanked a Spanish admirer who respectfully complimented her for her singing, she mistranslated her equally inane "thank you" for the jealous Ford: "That means 'If a man answers, hang up.'"

Gilda crystallized the image of the forties glamour queen as the one-man woman trying to pose as a tramp to get back at a straying male. Simultaneously, she became an object of identification for her feminine audience and an arouser of desire for the masculine public. When she finally melted in Ford's arms, it was with a gasping eroticism that kept the lines from stumbling into the absurd, thus subliminating something as dangerous as a tape-recording of torrid lovemaking. "You do hate me, don't you, Johnny," she breathed heavily. "I hate you too. I hate you so much I think I'm going to die from it. Darling, I think I'm going to die from it." Gilda's emotions were illiterate, but she certainly knew how to spell O-R-G-A-S-M.

With the brazen trust of the self-deluded, Hayworth could do all this and more. She believed in all the women she portrayed, and moviegoers watched her in a trance. With the same moan, she was as vulnerable as a Gish sister and as vindictive as Pola Negri. In addition, she integrated sadomasochism and glamour by the use of breathtaking props, from a slinky, easily detached black satin sheath to a Medusa-like mane of flaming hair—each tress a ready lash to whip her lovers.

"There never was a woman like *Gilda*," the ads read in the forties. Time has projected the hyperbole into the future, for Hayworth was the apex of her type of glamour, and after her the supercharged sirens went into decline. These women were images in a dream, and dreams must end lest they prolong themselves into death. The audience woke up from the sensual reverie with a morning-after yawn. With newfound affluence after the war, the glamour of movies had begun to creep into ordinary lives and the public was ready for a change of pace.

The middle class, that longtime bastion of moviegoing, was growing increasingly sophisticated. Gourmet cooking, wine tasting, and resort vacations were no longer pleasures to be absorbed vicariously from the screen. The unattainable was within grasp, and this fact made the merchandising of glamour all the more difficult. In the early fifties, for example, European travel became accessible, and secretaries on fifteen-day package tours could stroll the Champs Elysées or pose for candid pictures on the Spanish Steps. They would no longer be fooled by blatant backdrops. With a new demand for realism, the blessed unreality of glamour was turning into a curse.

Imperceptibly but surely, glamour changed into something the stars no longer flaunted but were covertly ashamed of. Brando abandoned his "wild" image in a paroxysm of piety. Monroe expiated her billowing skirts in *The Seven Year Itch* by joining Lee Strasberg's Actors' Studio, in a Hollywood parody of the ruined girl who ran to the convent. Films were experimenting with the dangerously inverted glamour of faked truth, and *Marty* was hailed as a masterpiece because it dared call its heroine "a dog." The whole trend culminated when Elizabeth Taylor, the last of the glamour symbols, played a gray-haired, foul-mouthed harridan in *Who's Afraid of Virginia Woolf?*

Hollywood's staunchest supporters were now aspiringly glamorous, and they sought contrast in stubbornly contrary fantasies of ugliness, poverty, and sorrow. The glamour-queen torch had passed down to the suburban matron who slithered around in a carefully copied Valentino pant-suit, sipping extra-dry martinis and discreetly bumping into her Mediterranean furniture. Even the carefully resurrected dreamworld of the Lana Turner-Ross Hunter rhinestone melodramas became passé in the "serious" late sixties. Fakery had permeated the real life of the public beyond the saturation point. Blatantly glamorous movies were being rejected with a wave of the hand, like rich desserts in posh French restaurants—even when they are included in the *prix fixe* menu.

If glamour still survives in American films of the seventies, it is in the black-oriented flicks revolving around hyper-macho creatures like *Superfly* and *Shaft*. They are the prime purveyors of fantasies for a still-deprived sector of the audience who can't identify with television's consumer paradise. Whenever and wherever films can satisfy the cravings of a still unsatisfied public, there will be glamour. Around the world, in countries with high population and rampant poverty, glamour still rules with undiminished power, as proven by an Indian film industry that produces over three hundred films a year and elevates an undulating siren to box-office pinnacles as "Helen, Queen of the Nautch Girls."

Yet, despite the shrugs of the cynical, jaded, eminently practical American moviegoers of the present, the glamour of yesterday keeps feeding on itself, haunting us under the guise of nostalgia. Like very strong, well-aged liquor, it cannot be taken straight, and time is the only possible diluter. The erstwhile glamour queens, like finely crafted antiques, have tripled in value because they can no longer be reproduced in today's films. If Streisand, Minnelli, or Fonda, the favorites of the early seventies, tried to carry on like the glamorous goddesses, they would be hooted off their pinnacles of success.

We forgive the excesses of the fabulous women of the past, because they had the innocence of their assumed sophistication. They are preserved in yellowing celluloid; as years go by they become more impregnable in their sealed capsules. Glamour, that corruption of grammar, that nonword that eludes all definitions, has finally escaped even the tyranny of time and space. Contradictory as ever, pure glamour is now at its lowest ebb and, simultaneously, cresting.

People stand in line for a Dietrich double-bill. They drink four cups of coffee to stay up for a Garbo film at 3:45 A.M. on television. Eyebrows are plucked à la Harlow, sweaters are stretched à la Turner, mouths are Crawford red, foreheads reach an Oberon high. The ghosts rise again and again. They will not be exorcised. Glamour is dead! Long live glamour!

The Glamour Girls

In SHE COULDN'T TAKE IT (Col '35)

Joan Bennett

5'4"
116 pounds
Blonde hair
Blue eyes
Aquarius

Impeccable breeding and solid gold entrees into the theatre and motion-picture arenas might be heavenly delights for some people. However, for Joan Bennett, who only wanted to be a normal, upper-class American flapper, it was a devastating burden. Everyone expected her to follow her two older, more famous sisters, Constance and Barbara, into one phase or another of show business. And somehow, when marital disharmony suddenly required her as a young mother to fend for herself, Joan found acting the easiest means of livelihood.

Rarely has an actress's screen career been so clearly defined by her hair coloring. During her blonde period Joan was a pert, poised, vapid ingenue who made the transfer from bit roles in silent films to leading lady in talkies with relative ease. After all, was not her father the well-dictioned matinee idol Richard Bennett, and her mother the captivating Broadway actress Adrienne Morrison? On rare occasions, contra-casting, as in *Me and My Gal* (Fox, 1932), proved that beneath her porcelain-doll veneer the girl had a gutsy personality. Infrequent excursions into class screen dramas, such as *Little Women* (RKO, 1933) and *Private Worlds* (Paramount, 1935), substantiated the rumor that Joan was not *merely* chic Constance's magnolia-drenched little sister. But for most of the 1930s Joan was required by her studio bosses to follow a tedious course as a one-dimensional screen lovely. Like Loretta Young, she was more noted for her extravagant movie wardrobes and the quantity rather than the quality of her celluloid efforts.

Joan's movie career might have been artistically frustrating, but her social life was A-1, as she was a glittering part of the most elite movie-colony party swirl. In this ambiance she fostered a relationship with movie producer Walter Wanger, who not only guided her film career but became her husband and the father of their two children. It was because of Wanger that Joan entered her brunette period. He had cast MGM's Hedy Lamarr in *Algiers* (United Artists, 1938), and when that picture made her such a popular figure, Wanger decided that Joan might absorb some of the excessive attention directed at her look-alike, Hedy Lamarr. In *Trade Winds* (United Artists, 1938), the plot had Joan switch hair hues mid-reel. The coloring change did more than accentuate Joan's naturally good facial-bone structure. Other movie producers suddenly became aware of her untapped qualities as a meatier actress. *Man Hunt* (Twentieth Century-Fox, 1941) led to her two best 1940s films, *The Woman in the Window* (RKO, 1944) and *Scarlet Street* (Universal, 1946).

In 1951, forty-one-year-old Joan was gliding into her fourth decade as a glamorous screen star, when, at least according to Joan, a jealous act on Wanger's part nearly ended her silver-screen tenure. He shot a pistol at her business agent—good friend Jennings Lang—and went to jail on a short term for his unsuccessful manslaughter bid. Joan was already in that difficult middle-age bracket that has been so disastrous for so many cinema leading ladies. But, armed with her stage background and the example of her ex-movie-star sister Constance, Joan turned to the theatre, and then to television, for professional sustenance. The switch kept her busy and away from Hollywood, with only occasional, unmemorable forays back into film work. Her biggest success in the 1960s was in television's first Gothic soap opera, "Dark Shadows." Her autobiography, *The Bennett Playbill,* appeared in 1970.

Today, charming Joan is a respected lady of the theatre who occasionally appears in television or motion-picture outings. It was not her dream but seemingly inevitable destiny that brought her to this enviable mature status. She is still a very spunky figure to be reckoned with on many levels, from show-business celebrity to grandmother to manufacturers' representative.

Joan Geraldine Bennett was born in Palisades, New Jersey, on Sunday, February 27, 1910. She was the last child and third daughter of matinee idol Richard Bennett and stage actress Mabel Adrienne Morrison Bennett. Joan's distinguished father happened to be home for the event, resting on his day off from starring on Broadway with Maude Adams in

What Every Woman Knows. On Monday, he embarked on a five-months' tour, but left behind his eloquent description that his newborn daughter was a "rosebud blooming in the sun," and expressed no disappointment at her not being a son since, "It was love at first sight." Joan was preceded in birth by sisters Constance* and Barbara.† Constance and Joan were blue-eyed blondes, while Barbara had brown eyes and dark hair.

Ancestors on the maternal side of the family had been in the acting profession for four generations, dating back to 1789, when Joan's great-grandfather, of Welsh parentage, chose to join a group of strolling players in London. He changed his name from Wodin to Wood to conceal his identity, since in those days actors were of suspect character.

Often, when both of Joan's parents were on tour, the trio of Bennett girls were left in the care of friends, but always with a governess or housekeeper on hand to minister to their growing pains. In her book, *The Bennett Playbill* (1970), written with Lois Kibbee, Joan admits that: "I was a mother's girl and always threw a fit when she went on tour, and though I loved father, too, he scared the life out of me." She further relates that her illustrious dad was opinionated, conceited, domineering, and bombastic. When in open display, these traits sent her scurrying to the shelter of her mother's arms. Of the three girls, only extroverted Constance stood up to him and spoke his language. Barbara was an intense child who preferred Joan's playmate companionship; both were baffled by Constance's outspoken manner and sought refuge with one another. The children grew up in a household filled with talk of the theatre, and, as long as they behaved themselves, they were permitted to attend either rehearsals or actual performances.

Joan's first appearance on the stage was in Chicago in 1914. She was four. Richard Bennett directed and starred in *Damaged Goods*, adapted from Eugene Brieux's French play, *Les Avariés*, which quite openly dealt with the horrors of hereditary syphilis, a subject that was then generally mentioned—if at all—in discreet whispers behind well-closed doors. After several rejections because of its controversial theme, this preachment drama opened in New York in 1913 and later was sent on national tour for forty-two weeks. Adrienne Morrison Bennett played the feminine lead. In Chicago, it was determined by the city fathers that admission to the controversial show would be granted to no one under eighteen years of age. Bennett, a great one for defying dictatorial edicts, took it upon himself to include his daughters in the final curtain call to illustrate that he, as a family man, was convinced the subject should be brought into the open for souls of all ages to dwell upon with moral meditation. "I think that's my first remembrance of being in a theatre," Joan wrote, "though

*Born in New York City on October 22, 1904.
†Born in the Palisades, New Jersey, home on August 13, 1906.

the effect of the play's subject matter on the three of us was negligible. Constance couldn't spell it, Barbara couldn't pronounce it and I couldn't read it."

The following year, Richard Bennett directed and starred in a film version of *Damaged Goods* for American-Mutual. He considered the movies a passing fad, but could not resist the tempting offer to communicate his talent and messages to an even wider audience than the stage offered. In 1915, also for American-Mutual, he starred in *The Valley of Decision*, which explored the evils of birth control. The picture was filmed in Santa Barbara, California, and the cast contained the entire Bennett family, including Richard's sister Blanche. In the film's prelude, entitled *The Shadowland of Souls Unborn*, the Bennett children, in Grecian outfits, represented "unborn souls" and "danced around looking like refugees from a number three company of Isadora Duncan's."

The family moved in 1915 to Park Hill, New York, near Yonkers, after their Palisades home was leveled in a fire. It was a country house with wide open spaces where, in 1917, Richard Bennett benefited the war effort with a home-produced performance of *A Midsummer Night's Dream* with seven-year-old Joan as Peaseblossom. Constance and Barbara were also in the show, and Joan commented: "Whatever our merits as child Shakespearean actresses, the greatest impact of the evening on us was the excitement caused by the presence of Florenz Ziegfeld and Billie Burke, right in our own backyard."

When Joan was of school age, it was suddenly discovered that she was nearsighted. Eyeglasses were forced onto the reluctant child. She detested those glasses because: "I thought they made me look ugly, but without them, if an elephant had strolled by, I'd have missed it. I've been fumbling my way through life ever since."

In 1918, while Richard Bennett played stock in San Francisco and Los Angeles, his family visited a friend in Los Gatos, California, near San Jose. There, Joan decided to direct and star in her own play, *Timid Agnes and the Mouse*. She was the heroine of the piece, whose mouse miraculously is turned into a prince. She charged a nickel admission to children and had the nerve to commandeer a dollar from grown-ups. "I remember I was very big in Los Gatos for a time."

Late in the spring of 1918, the Bennetts quit their lives as country farmers and moved to the glitter and swank of New York City. A Victorian-styled, four-storied house on West Eighth Street near the pleasant greenery of Washington Square became their home, from which Joan set off each weekday morning as an enrollee at Miss Chandler's Day School. Mrs. Bennett, an amateur interior decorator, had already put her talents to work, first in the house at Park Hill, and later at the one in New York, all of which influenced Joan's decision, at the age of twelve, to become an interior decorator. By the time she was scholastically elevated to Miss

Hopkins School for Girls in New York City, she was positive of her goal and equally positive that she would *never* become involved in the theatre.

Rebellious, independent Constance, every bit her father's daughter, eloped in June 1921, at the age of sixteen. Her mother was immediately at her heels in order to take her home before the marriage was consummated. Quashed but unyielding, Constance was then sent on a European jaunt to cool off during the annulment proceedings, but later returned to New York where she half-heartedly entered into a moving-picture career.*

During one of Mr. Bennett's periodic filmmaking treks in the 1920s, he played a leading support role in Samuel Goldwyn's production of *The Eternal City* (Associated-First National, 1923), starring Barbara La Marr and Bert Lytell. As a lark, Joan and pal Betty Bronson (who would gain fame the next year as the screen's latest Peter Pan) were dressed as page boys and played bits in this melodrama set in 1910s-1920s Italy, and climaxing with the rise of Mussolini.

On September 30, 1923, Richard and Adrienne Bennett separated, with Richard sharing living quarters with Barbara on West Fifty-eighth Street, while Adrienne and Constance took an apartment on East Fifty-fourth. Joan was then a boarding student at St. Margaret's School in Waterbury, Connecticut. Of the separation, Mrs. Bennett explained, "You see, Mr. Bennett is a genius and geniuses should be segregated." In October 1923, at the age of seventeen, Barbara began a career as a dancer in a Broadway play with her father, called *The Dancers*.

When Joan was in her sophomore year at St. Margaret's, she devised a revue "with material lifted bodily from *Charlot's Revue*," a Broadway hit starring Gertrude Lawrence and Beatrice Lillie and co-produced by Walter Wanger. Joan specially wrote a song for her version of the show which contained the words. "Virginia, Virginia, the devil is in ya," but was not allowed to use the number because the powers at St. Margaret's considered the lyrics too risqué.

After two years of separation, Adrienne Bennett began divorce proceedings in the spring of 1925, with the charge given as "misconduct." The headmistress at St. Margaret's cautioned Joan not to discuss the matter with any of the other students. "Even then it seemed a cruel and unnecessary warning. I was too unhappy over it myself to discuss with anyone but mother." The divorce decree was issued in April 1925, which left Joan feeling very much alone in the world. She was never happy with her physical appearance, and the final breakup of her parents made her think: "I'm definitely the mess of the family. Now, if I were only as beautiful as Constance, things wouldn't be so dismal."

*Constance began with small roles in three 1922 features, *Reckless Youth*, *Evidence*, and *What's Wrong with Women?*

By June 1925, Barbara was dancing in Paris with partner Maurice Mouvet, and Adrienne was with friends in London, away from the blaring society headlines dealing with her recent divorce. Having become totally disenchanted with St. Margaret's, Joan begged her mother to allow her to change schools, and her pleas were rewarded with arrangements for her to study at Le Lierre, a finishing school near Paris. With a friend of her mother's, Countess Ina Bubna, as chaperone, she boarded the Cherbourg-bound sea-liner *Homeric* in mid-June. Constance and her gentleman friend, Philip Plant, whom she later married, saw Joan off and introduced her to John Marion Fox, also a passenger. "I thought he was the handsomest man I had ever met."

Once the ship got underway, the chaperone took to her bed due to seasickness, which permitted Fox to become better acquainted with the fifteen-year-old Bennett girl. Joan was flattered by the attentions of this older, but no wiser man, who had at one time romanced Norma Shearer. Joan chose to accompany him to London where he was scheduled to produce a musical comedy. She observed that "Jack did drink rather a good deal, but then I thought perhaps it was just a sign of his worldliness." In London, she stayed a month with her mother, who disapproved of the relationship with Fox, but, in August, she went to France to enroll at Le Lierre. It did not take her long to detest the school, however. She reasoned, "Here I am in Paris, the gayest, most wicked city in the world, and I'm living in a tomb." One night she decided to escape from the prison-like existence, literally climbing over the walls. With Fox's help she got to London, where she stayed with a friend of his family's until Le Lierre's official expulsion notice was received by her mother, who, by that time, had returned to New York.

Since it was felt that Joan's education should and must continue, Adrienne arranged, through several transatlantic telephone conversations, for her to enter L'Hermitage, a finishing school at Versailles. This institution was much more to Joan's liking since the students were treated as adults rather then irresponsible children. Jack Fox, however, had proposed marriage, an offer which Joan had no notion of ignoring. She completed the term at L'Hermitage in June 1926, and in spite of strong disapprovals from both her parents, she and Fox were married in London at St. Luke's Church in Chelsea on September 15, 1926. "I wore an ivory gown by Lanvin and carried white orchids. Mother gave away the bride, who was scared stiff and cried all the way down the aisle." Joan was then sixteen; Fox was about ten years older.

After a honeymoon in Paris and Venice, the newlyweds settled in at Fox's residence in London. Joan recalled: "Now I think I was happier there than at any other time in our marriage. Jack drank heavily, it was true, but for a while I was oblivious to anything but the fact that I was a married woman, and therefore, an adult." Things went smoothly for a while, but Fox's boozing habits got to be too much. Joan put her foot down by insisting that he quit drinking and that they return to the United States. He agreed to both requests and obtained a job on the New York Stock Exchange as a runner, but he eventually went back to London due to "pressing theatrical duties" when Joan became confined to her bed with mumps. She then visited her in-laws in Los Angeles for two months, which turned out to be a "disastrous move in every way; a grim, unhappy time."

Fox then reclaimed her and escorted her back to London. Although he now seemed different to her, and older, he was still an alcoholic. Her mind was diverted from this pressing, continuing problem when she discovered she was pregnant. She persuaded Fox that the baby should be born in the United States. They crossed the Atlantic on a non-liquor-stocked ship—chosen by Joan—and went to California, where they rented a small house in Hollywood.

Adrienne Ralston Fox was born on February 20, 1928, one week before Joan turned eighteen. She thought the baby "absolute perfection" and said: "Like my own mother, I doted on babies, mine and anyone else's, and I think if I'd been born to a more conventional, unprofessional family, I'd have doubtless grown up to be the old-fashioned one who did embroidery and minded the neighbor's babies until I had some of my own."

Although Joan had gained a daughter, she was fast losing an unemployed husband. As Fox's thirst increased in Prohibition-clad America, the family coffers emptied. His family reluctantly gave them money, and Richard and Adrienne, both of whom had married other spouses in 1927, occasionally sent them funds; but neither realized the severity of Joan's situation. Although Adrienne employed a fulltime nurse for Joan's baby, most of the dollars received as gifts went into Fox's pocket and from there into the cash registers of the local speakeasies. "My marriage was a graveyard," Joan remembers, "and I felt a little like Eliza crossing the ice, jumping from one icy dilemma to another to escape the bloodhounds of despair." Following one of their major battles, Joan had Fox put under a peace bond for her protection. When he stormed back into their apartment after learning of her legal act, she called the police, who, in turn, tossed Fox into jail. After ten days she bailed him out, but she refused to live with him again.

To support herself and her child, she obtained jobs as a movie extra.* One such role was in *Power* (Pathé, 1928), which starred William Boyd and Alan Hale as two rugged dam builders who spend as much time chasing the dames of the town as working on the construction site. Joan, along with Carole Lombard and Pauline Curley, was cast as one of the "dames" who pass in and out of the tough guys' lives.

*Joan has recollections of "appearing" in a Corinne Griffith vehicle during this period, but this film assignment has yet to be verified.

In the spring of 1928, while in San Francisco on the last lap of touring in a play, Richard Bennett telephoned his daughter in Los Angeles. Joan was not in, but he talked with the baby's nurse. Under pressure from the bombastic Bennett, the nurse confessed the truth about the Fox marriage, which sent Bennett scurrying to Los Angeles, propelled on his journey almost single-handedly by his rage. He threatened to shoot Fox if he could find him, and insisted that Joan apply for divorce (which was finalized in August 1928). He offered her the part of the ingenue, Daisy Carol, in a new play he was preparing for Broadway, entitled *Jarnegan*.

She thought over her situation and then accepted. "With all my inflexible ideas about avoiding the theatre, there I was, about to be the next one of the fifth generation to walk on a stage. Just because I was born of a theatrical family didn't mean I'd automatically turn into an actress. On the other hand, it was the only thing I knew even a little about, by osmosis if nothing else. But more important to me at the time, it was a job. I decided to give it a try until I could figure out something else." She sold her furniture, unwillingly deposited her five-month-old daughter in the care of a good friend in Los Angeles, and in late July 1928, took a train for New York.

During the period of rehearsal, she stayed with her father and his new wife. Each night Bennett coached her and worked on her capacity to project her tiny voice. "Possessed of a magnificent voice himself, he made the entire company rehearse with more voice than would ever be used in performance."

Jarnegan, which dealt with an Irish jailbird who makes good in Hollywood as a film director, was intended to be a biting indictment of the twentieth-century medium. Its subject matter, however, was considered rather old hat by then, and it required the use of some strong language on the part of the playwright to spice up the material adapted from Jim Tully's novel. The play, which opened at the Longacre Theatre on September 24, 1928, nevertheless, was greeted with respectful acceptance by the critics, as was Bennett's customary curtain-call speech (in which he lauded his own daring for presenting such an avant-garde drama). Although Wynne Gibson as the gin-partial Hollywood actress had the leading female role, Joan received good notices. "[She] took a difficult part and one none too well written and made the most of it" (*New York American*). "Joan Bennett, by the way, is both almost unbelievably beautiful and entirely moving as the ingenue ensnared by the sins of the photoplay" (Richard Watts, Jr., *New York Times*). "[Miss Bennett] played it with a pleasing clumsiness that exactly suited the character" (St. John Ervine, *New York World*).

With the success of the play assured (it would run for 138 performances) and her salary raised to $150 weekly, Joan immediately sent for her baby and the nurse, and moved into an apartment in the same building where her mother lived with her husband, Eric Pinker. Joan bolstered her income with occasional jobs as a photographic model, and Fox Films asked her to make a screentest at their Manhattan offices. "I don't remember much about it, but it must have been forgettable because the studio was mercifully silent." She dated journalist George Jean Nathan, which infuriated Richard Bennett, who considered the man his professional enemy. Through Nathan she met Walter Wanger, then general manager for Jesse Lasky of Paramount Pictures' East Coast operation. Wanger requested that Joan make a screentest at the Astoria, Long Island, studio, but afterwards confided to Joan's mother, "Your daughter is very sweet, Mrs. Pinker, but she'll never photograph."

As *Jarnegan* neared the conclusion of its New York run, Joan did double duty by performing onstage at night and matinees, and rehearsing daily for another play, *Hot Bed*. The new role was arranged by her mother, who had retired from the stage when she married Pinker and had promptly become a top New York play-broker. However, a second Broadway show was not to be Joan's destiny, for one night she was visited by Joseph Schenck and John Considine, Jr., emissaries of Samuel Goldwyn in search of a stage ingenue to play the role of Phillis Benton opposite Ronald Colman in the film version of *Bulldog Drummond* (United Artists, 1929). It was to be Colman's first talking picture.

Joan's initial reaction to a screentest offer was negative because of the nonsuccess of her previous two ventures. A short time later, she was offered the part without testing, plus a five-year contract with United Artists at $500 a week. It was a salary too attractive for a divorced mother to turn down. Despite Richard Bennett's advice to stick to the stage, Joan asked her mother to negotiate a release from *Hot Bed* as well as from *Jarnegan*, and she headed west in January 1929.

With the nurse and the baby—who was nicknamed "Ditty"—Joan moved into a small suite at the new Beverly Wilshire Hotel in Hollywood. She began work almost immediately in *Bulldog Drummond*. "Everyone knew, of course, that I was a rank beginner, and most people were kind." She received helpful tips from other cast members and from William Powell, a friend of Colman's, who explained the more technical angles of the business. "Working with Ronald was certainly a wonderful sendoff for any neophyte. I felt insecure and intimidated at the very thought of working with him. Not too long before, he'd been one of my cherished idols, and I'd gone reverently to see his movies with Vilma Banky. But he couldn't have been sweeter or more helpful, and I'll always remember his encouragement at a time when it really mattered."

Samuel Goldwyn, a co-partner at the time in the United Artists Corporation, and the director, F. Richard Jones, were not as sweet to her as the members of the cast. On one occasion, Goldwyn queried, "Where's the Bennett fire? Why don't you come across like your sister [Constance]?"

Jones gave Joan hell on one shooting day for being late on the set. "You do as you're told, young lady," he informed her. "You're new at this business." In retrospect, Joan admits, "It wasn't a particularly ego-building time, but I stuck with it because it was a matter of survival."

The British had already twice filmed silent versions of Bulldog Drummond stories,* based on the H. C. McNeile detective fiction character created in 1920, but it was not until the sound era that Hollywood became intrigued with the character, and made a picturization of the "Sapper"-Gerald Du Maurier stage play (1921). As William K. Everson in *The Detective in Film* (1972) asserts, "Colman's flawless diction, his beautiful timing, and the sense of fun he brought to the role not only dominated the film, but influenced the tongue-in-cheek playing of the rest of the cast." Unfortunately, Joan's role was rather bland. She was cast as the conventional American heroine who hires Colman, a young British army officer, to free her uncle (Charles Sellon) from an insane asylum where he is held prisoner by the diabolical, phony, physician, Dr. Lakington (Lawrence Grant), and his confederates, Montagu Love and Lilyan Tashman. Claud Allister, as Colman's confederate, Algy, supplied most of the laughs. What with this, Colman's gallantry, Tashman's vamping, and Grant's villainy, Joan was left creatively out in the cold. She photographed beautifully in her small way, and the *New York Times* found her "engaging both as to voice and appearance." However, as the girl who expresses a romantic interest in Colman, Richard Griffith retrospectively observed in his booklet, *Samuel Goldwyn* (1956), she came across "like a debutante trying to act rather than an actress playing a debutante." (Loretta Young was to suffer much the same fate in a later Colman entry, *Bulldog Drummond Strikes Back* [United Artists, 1934].)

Joan's second feature for United Artists was a comedy, *Three Live Ghosts,* dealing with three war veterans (Charles McNaughton, Claud Allister, and Robert Montgomery) who escape from a German prison camp and return to London to discover they have been listed among the dead. In the overly symmetrical plotline, each of the trio in turn comes to grief with the law, but solves his problems with the sudden discovery of unknown past facts of identity. Joan had another nondescript assignment, this time as Rose Gordon, the nice American girl Montgomery had met on his trip from America to the Continent, and the young lady he eventually weds. Joan correctly recollects that the part "didn't win me any acting awards." United Artists, which had been considering her for the lead in a remake of *Smilin' Through*, released her from her five-year contract.

She then took another "flyer into the theatre and did a costume play [*The Pirate*] with Doris Keene. We opened in Santa Barbara and played

---

*Carlyle Blackwell played the sleuth in *Bulldog Drummond* (Astra-National, 1923), and Jack Buchanan in *Bulldog Drummond's Third Round* (Astra-National, 1925).

two weeks at the Biltmore Theatre in Los Angeles, but the play was so undistinguished I've even forgotten its title."

As a freelance, Joan had the benefit of her youth, good looks, and the Bennett name to boost her along in a career that could as easily have floundered as prospered. Her sister Constance had made the transition to sound films with notable success and was already well on her way to becoming the most chic and highest paid of the early 1930s movie actresses. Producers were not unaware of the publicity value of having another Bennett girl cast in their latest silver-screen venture, and this gave Joan a push in her film career.*

It is most likely that George Arliss, the distinguished English star who was a respected actor of the 1920s American stage and screen, was attracted to Joan by her illustrious theatrical heritage. When he was casting the remake of his 1921 film success, *Disraeli,* for Warner Bros., he selected Joan to portray Lady Clarissa Pevensey,† supplying a romantic interlude with Anthony Bushell. The major portions of the feature dealt with the British Prime Minister's participation in England's acquisition of the Suez Canal. Amongst the intrigue—handled by spies Doris Lloyd and Norman Cannon—and the pretentious posturing of Arliss as the Queen's Liberal endorser, Joan was "charming" but merely tasteful set dressing. The film, itself, was declared one of the year's ten best pictures by most sources, earned Arliss an Academy Award, and when it played in London, it ran a record ten-week stretch.

Joan joyfully recalls that "Constance and I had a lot of fun in the Hollywood of the 1930's. The industry was at a peak of excitement with the advent of sound, and almost daily there was a new technical development or an exciting personality to keep things interesting." A figure who made Joan's life exciting for a time was John Considine, Jr., one of the men who had approached her in New York to test for *Bulldog Drummond.* "We became what was then called 'an item.' " But Considine divided his amorous attentions between Joan and Carmen Pantages, the beautiful brunette daughter of theatreman Alexander Pantages. After a tempestuous on-again, off-again affair, Considine would finally marry Miss Pantages in 1931, thus concluding a love triangle that had Hollywood guessing.

From late 1929 until late 1930, Joan appeared in six features, and "my career had risen enough for me to think I'd found my niche after all." She was premature in her judgment. Universal's *Mississippi Gambler* (1929) found Joseph Schildkraut rehashing his role of Gaylord Ravenal from *Show Boat* (Universal, 1929) in a romantic drama that "is so frayed a garment that figurative elbows protrude from its sleeves" (Mordaunt Hall, *New*

*Barbara was seen in *Syncopation* (RKO, 1929), filmed in New York and one of the first full-length musicals with sound. That same year she wed that film's co-player, Morton Downey, the Irish radio singer.

†In the 1921 United Artists version, Louise Huff was Clarissa.

41

York Times). As the spirited but ever so demure heroine who plays a decisive game of cards with con artist Schildkraut, Joan was once again outshone by another distaff member of the cast, this time Carmelita Geraghty, as the jealous young thing who passionately loves the southern-accented scoundrel, Schildkraut.

Puttin' on the Ritz (United Artists, 1930) was not exactly the type of vehicle in which one would have expected to find Joan cast, but it was produced-written by John Considine, Jr. Since at that time he and Joan were still dating, this explained her presence. The musical, with a Technicolor sequence, was a starring vehicle for Broadway crooner-womanizer Harry Richman, then at the height of his romance with Paramount's "It" Girl, Clara Bow. In its day, Mordaunt Hall (*New York Times*) rated the feature positively, explaining it "possesses that much sought-after ingredient—good entertainment." But when viewed today, even by an indulgent soul, *Puttin' on the Ritz* fitfully glistens with tawdriness, from its tinny script to its scrappy settings. Granted, today's scanner of the film does not have the opportunity to judge the merits of the multihued musical sequence, "Alice in Wonderland," but that apart, there is little to recommend the picture. Richman is self-indulgent and careless in his interpretation of the has-been vaudevillian who has another professional chance when he teams with Joan in a new act. Later, after success has gone to his head, he is led astray by playgirl-socialite Aileen Pringle, and then, as if a punishment from heaven, he is temporarily blinded by bad liquor. In the predictable finale, Joan and Richman have a touching reunion.

Hall of the *Times* reported to 1930 readers: "Throughout this film she reveals herself to be a wonderful young actress, but, if anything, her expression is more captivating when she is rendering this melody ["With You"] than during the other none too imaginative interludes." Joan, however, still very much in her cloche-hat period, left a good deal to be desired as the film's pivotal female. For example, near the picture's opening, Joan enters the music publishers' office, clutching her song composition, which she hopes to sell. Hotshot keyboard tinkler Richman is immediately attracted by Joan, and secondarily by her tune-for-sale. "I think the song has possibility," Richman proclaims in his hard-sell manner. Joan, attempting to register strong emotion, merely sight-reads her reply line, "Do you really?" She is equally unconvincing thereafter when Richman and pal James Gleason are fired from their jobs because of her. She feebly apologizes, "I hope I haven't caused you any trouble." As for her solo (and duet with Richman) of "With You," her singing was noticeably thin and no more agreeable than her attempts at fancy footwork in the act-within-the-show.

At least in Fox's *Crazy That Way* (1930) Joan was the plotline love-of-

life of three contrasting leading men (Kenneth MacKenna, Regis Toomey, and Jason Robards). The loosely constructed comedy was based on
Vincent Lawrence's 1923 Broadway play, *In Love with Love,* which had
starred Lynn Fontanne, Henry Hull, and Ralph Morgan, and had enjoyed
a 128-performance run. A 1928 revival ran eight performances.

In March 1930, John Barrymore was seeking a leading lady to star with
him in a remake of Warner Bros.' *Moby Dick.* He selected Joan, the
daughter of his old Broadway crony, Richard Bennett. At this point in his
career, the great profile was far more interested in the blessed event due
his actress-wife, Dolores Costello, and the outfitting of his new yacht, the
Infanta, than in going through the paces of this romanticized rendition
of Herman Melville's novel. Like Warners' 1926 version, *The Sea Beast,*
which paired Barrymore and Costello, the new scenario was a far cry
from the moralistic allegory of Melville's 1851 seafaring classic. As Faith,
a minister's daughter, demure Joan is loved by both Barrymore and his
treacherous brother (Lloyd Hughes). After a long whaling voyage in which
Barrymore loses a leg to a white whale, he returns to home port in New
Bedford, only to have Joan run away in shock from her disfigured sweetheart. Barrymore mistakes her understandable, but temporary, revulsion
to mean that she no longer loves him, and he turns into a vengeful whaler.
Both the whale (a very unconvincing rubber float) and Hughes are eventually dispatched, leaving Barrymore and Joan to be joined in a tearful
reunion. As one contemporary Manhattan reviewer noted, "The youngest of the Bennett girls fills the bill appealingly, but her part isn't awfully
important."

As for working with the legendary Barrymore, Joan would recall: "At
first I was terrified at the thought of working with one of the great actors
of the time. I'd known him since childhood, but that didn't lessen my
feelings of intimidation. His eccentric behavior and his drinking habits
were well known, and I approached the first few days of filming with a
fine case of nerves. I could have saved myself the trouble. He couldn't have
been sweeter or more considerate."

Maybe It's Love (Warner Bros., 1930) returned Joan to inconsequential
screen comedy, this time set on a college campus, and with acrobatic,
big-mouthed Joe E. Brown as the film's leading funster. She was Nan
Sheffield, the daughter of the president of Upton College. She considers it
her patriotic duty to aid the school's faltering football squad in their efforts
to overcome the Parsons varsity team. Her plan is to recruit a new crew
for Upton. To accomplish her mission, she drops her studious appearance
and reemerges with a more obviously charming deportment, which
quite rightly attracts the needed fresh blood for the squad. Will the duped
recruits forgive her and play in the big game? Yes. Does James Hall, the
spoiled son of a wealthy father, who has entered Upton under false cre-

dentials, relent in his antagonism against Joan and admit his love for her? Yes. By the way, football ace Brown and the squad do win the big game and restore Upton's honor.

With *Scotland Yard* (Fox, 1930) Joan settled down professionally to fulfill her new two-year contract at Fox Films. William Fox still headed the pioneer company, with Winfield Sheehan as chief executive in charge of studio operations on the West Coast. At this time, Fox's star roster included Will Rogers, Janet Gaynor, Elissa Landi, Warner Baxter, Charles Farrell, George O'Brien, and the new romantic team of James Dunn and Sally Eilers. In the secondary but important ranks the studio also had Joan, Victor McLaglen, John Boles, Violet Heming, Linda Watkins, Conchita Montenegro, Ralph Bellamy, Alexander Kirkland, Spencer Tracy, Minna Gombell, character actress Mae Marsh, and specialty comedian El Brendel.

Scotland Yard, based on the 1929 Denison Clift melodrama, cast Joan as the titled wife of British banker Edmund Lowe, he soon being lost in action on the French front during World War I. Meanwhile, a thief (also played by Lowe) who has encountered and fallen in love with Joan, is forced to join the army to escape Scotland Yard's clutches. When he is injured in action, he undergoes plastic surgery. He recovers to find that the doctor has remade his face to resemble the banker's (the crook had previously stolen a locket containing a photo of Joan and her weak-willed spouse). Upon returning to England, he is soon softened by his love for Joan and repents his criminal career. For her oncamera efforts, Joan was ranked "charming and efficient" (*New York Times*).

In the autumn of 1930, Joan's father offered her a part in a play he was reading for the new Broadway season. The drama was entitled *Solid South*, and the role was that of Geneva, a young southern belle. Because she was financially secure and committed to her film work, she turned it down, and the part subsequently went to Bette Davis. As it developed, Joan had decided wisely because the play, which opened at New York's Lyceum Theatre on October 14, 1930, lasted a mere three weeks.

The Frank Borzage-directed *Doctors' Wives* (1931) presented Joan as the daughter of an overworked physician who has died of a heart attack. Nevertheless, and despite her mother's warning ("the patient is the enemy of every doctor's wife"), she weds dapper healer Warner Baxter. Very soon she is experiencing her own heartache, for her husband is always on call to the needs of his flock of patients, including vampish Helene Millard. It is not too long before Joan's patience is sorely tried and she leaves Baxter to seek consolation from scientist Victor Varconi. The feature left it to the moviegoer's fertile imagination to decide just how far Joan's romantic relationship with sympathetic Varconi progresses. Nevertheless, the picture made it quite clear that Baxter welcomes her back home with open arms. Neither the drama nor its cast compared to the far superior *Arrowsmith* (United Artists, 1931) with Ronald Colman and Helen Hayes, which had parallel subject themes.

Less than three months later, the Fox flagship theatre in New York, the Roxy, had another Joan Bennett feature, *Hush Money* (1931). This film was an underworld story with a somewhat different twist. Joan is an innocent who becomes involved with an enterprising gang led by Owen Moore. When the group is eventually captured by the police and sentenced to jail, Joan is one of the first to be paroled. She turns honest, finding employment in the interior decorating field where she meets (and later weds) wealthy Hardie Albright. Moore is later released and attempts to blackmail Joan, but kindly law-enforcer Douglas Cosgrove maneuvers a cool play: he lets the other freed members of the gang know that it was Moore who squealed on them to save his own neck. In a pleasing about-face, it is the lawbreakers who eliminate their former boss, leaving the path clear for Joan and Albright to enjoy a rosy future. Spotted in a tiny role was Hollywood newcomer George Raft—playing a hood, of course.

Joan completed her 1931 releases on loan-out with Universal's *Many a Slip* (1931), a haphazard comedy devoted to detailing how a girl can be led astray by that "fatal" extra sip from a flask.* Actually, within the unsophisticated comedy, it is Joan's oncamera brother (Ben Alexander) who persuades his socialite sibling to loosen up and enjoy herself, which she does with Lew Ayres. Before the tale comes to its denouement, her family thinks she has become pregnant, and the in-laws-to-be have engaged in a madcap game of mistaken identity and musical chairs such as seen in *Up in Mabel's Room.* Although Joan was the top-billed player, it was Ayres, still being acclaimed for his performance in *All Quiet on the Western Front* (Universal, 1930), who garnered most of the publicity for the feature.

Joan's first screen role opposite fast-rising but troublesome actor Spencer Tracy was in *She Wanted a Millionaire* (Fox, 1932), in which she is Jane Miller, a poor girl who sets her sights on a man of means (James Kirkwood) only to later realize that he is a sadistic killer. She happily finds solace in the waiting arms of breezy newspaperman Tracy, the glib soul who had urged her on to enter the beauty contests which led to her almost disastrous material goals.

The inconsequential drama came and went rather quickly,† but the behind-the-scenes circumstances surrounding the feature are worth examining. The film had John Considine, Jr., a Fox associate producer, on its

---

*Universal's ad campaign for the picture read, "When the Hot Blood Runs Hot and Love Is in the Air—What's a Boy and a Gorgeous Eye-Full of a Girl to Do?"

†Mordaunt Hall (*New York Times*) tagged the photoplay "a trivial story with silly dialogue and some strangely absurd ideas." He found Joan, long a favorite of his, "lithe and attractive."

crew. At the time he was still debating between the romantic merits of Joan and Carmen Pantages, but was sufficiently interested in Joan to champion her to the studio executives as a potential star of the first magnitude. Spencer Tracy, then undergoing a rather temperamental phase of his career, was more than annoyed (1) that Joan was being showcased in nearly every scene of *She Wanted a Millionaire* at his expense, and (2) that the politic production crew was fawning over Joan to an inordinate degree. Tracy undiplomatically commented on this state of affairs to friends, and the story found its way into print, which made the actor no favorite with Joan's growing legion of fans, or with Fox executives. Compounding the tension on the set was the almost simultaneous release of invented press-fan magazine stories hinting that Considine and Tracy were rivals for Joan's affection.

Midway through this unhappy production, Joan was thrown by a temperamental horse named Gilda Grey, resulting in an injured hip and three broken vertebrae for the actress. "I was most relieved to find I hadn't broken a single fingernail," Joan later joked. The leg joined to the fractured hip was pushed up two inches shorter than the other, and, for a time, it was feared that she might never again walk correctly, but fortuitously expert medical attention remedied the impairment. Joan was confined to bed for three months and was unable to return to work for six months. The period of convalescence was made bearable by the presence of her mother, who stayed with her until the fractures mended.

The courtship conducted by MGM scriptwriter Gene Markey also helped to pass the hours of inactivity. (By this time, Considine had wed Joan's rival.) Joan had met Markey at a Hollywood party a short time before the accident, and Markey pursued the acquaintance through notes, gifts, and telephone calls. When she was in the limping stages of recovery, her doctor suggested a trip might help to make the time pass more quickly, so she took a ship bound for New York via the Panama Canal. During her absence, Markey and Joan's daughter, Ditty, became good friends. "To Ditty, Gene represented the father she'd never had," Joan says, "and their mutual affection is maintained to this day." Markey asked Joan to marry him when she returned to Hollywood in November 1931. In January, she returned to the Fox lot to complete *She Wanted a Millionaire,* which "despite all our efforts, turned out to be a bad movie."

Joan and Markey were married on Saturday, March 12, 1932, at the Town House, a luxury Hollywood apartment hotel where Joan lived while convalescing. Constance was her matron-of-honor, but Adrienne was not present due to the death of her mother in New Jersey, nor was Richard Bennett, who was busy as Cyrano de Bergerac on a Santa Barbara, California, stage. After the civil ceremony conducted by Judge Lewis R. Work of the District Court of Appeals (Los Angeles), the Markeys tossed a wedding breakfast for their fifty guests.

Her career was fast-paced in 1932 with a total of six Fox features in release, providing the quantity but not the quality to boost Joan to realistic movie stardom like her sister Constance at RKO. Along with *She Wanted a Millionaire*, Joan appeared in *Careless Lady* (Fox, 1932), a rather frivolous entertainment ("too artificial and strained to awaken much interest" said the *New York Times*) in which she loses crack golfer Weldon Heyburn because of her careless appearance, but benefits from her *faux pas* when she encounters polished John Boles (and his dog Oscar) at a speakeasy. Later, Joan, who through a series of coincidences has been passing herself off as Boles's wife, actually encounters him at a Paris hotel. He is amused by the conceit and insists that as "man and wife" they must share the same suite. Nothing too risqué transpires, but later, back in the States, Joan realizes that Boles, and not Heyburn, is *the* man for her. *Careless Lady* was directed by her once-co-star, Kenneth MacKenna.

Courtroom melodramas were still a staple of the cinema, but *The Trial of Vivienne Ware* (Fox, 1932) played a bit too fast and loose with jurisprudential proceedings. ". . . it is a spirited attempt to screw every ounce of pathos, excitement, and humour out of the trial of a woman suspected of murdering her lover while in a fit of jealousy" (*London Times*). Through a series of flashbacks, the viewer is "treated" to the case history of how Joan happened to be on trial for homicide. For diversion, there is tough prosecutor Alan Dinehart, gallant defense attorney Donald Cook, comical radio commentators ZaSu Pitts and Skeets Gallagher and, for outrageous unreality, a jury composed of both men and women. In the course of the trial, one witness is almost eliminated by a dagger, while another is shot. As the lady in the case—who is loved by Cook—Joan was rated "a pretty, if unexciting heroine" (Richard Watts, Jr., *New York Herald-Tribune*). She and her leading man, Donald Cook, years later were to enjoy a rewarding professional and personal association.

Week-Ends Only (Fox, 1932) was modest entertainment at best, with Joan again portraying a debutante type, but this time a miss whose father has been ruined in the stock market. Her former friends snub her, but the durable ex-family butler (Halliwell Hobbes), now a big shot at a local speakeasy, helps Joan find a job as a professional weekend hostess for rake John Halliday. Meanwhile, at her humble boarding house, she romantically tumbles for poor, young artist Ben Lyon. She poses for his art work, later managing to purchase his canvases without his knowledge. When he thereafter discovers her in a compromising situation with Halliday, he is horrified, but thankfully discovers her innocence in time to spare her from sailing to Europe on a loveless venture. Throughout *Week-Ends Only* it was fairly obvious that Joan was "acting" by rote rather than from any manufactured oncamera enthusiasm.

Fox's own Charles Farrell, still best known as one half of the famous *Seventh Heaven* (1927) screen love team, was without the studio-rebellious Janet Gaynor in *Wild Girl* (1932), a very offbeat outdoors drama directed by inventive Raoul Walsh. The frontier tale is set in the days immediately following the Civil War in Redwood City, somewhere in the High Sierras. While it was novel to observe a southern settlement in such alien environs, to watch Eugene Pallette, as quirky, folksy stagecoach-driver Yuba Bill, describe an outlaw holdup (complete with sound effects for his team of horses), and to see moustached Ralph Bellamy simulate a gentleman gambler, the plotline hardly merited the production mounting. (At the time it almost went unnoticed that the film boasted some fine special effects, in which, instead of using just ordinary fades or dissolves to change scenes, the action oncamera would continue as a book page [on which the scene was mounted] flipped over, and then the new scene began, all this with both sets of activities still continuing!) As *Harrison's Reports* indicated, it was "a fair entertainment for second rate theatres and down the line. The trouble with it is the fact that is too long [even at an edited eighty minutes] and the acts of the characters are either unpleasant or demoralizing." Ineffectual Farrell was miscast as the rugged ex-soldier hero who shoots the dastardly villain who had once contributed to his sister's downfall and has now propositioned forest-flower Joan. While *Harrison's Reports* further carped, "Miss Bennett is no wild girl of the woods at all, for her skin is as white as snow and her hair Broadway blonde," it was pleasant to watch liberated Joan cavort through the picture, acting tomboyish as she jumps onto a moving stage-coach and bathes in the creek (has she ever appeared before or since so *au naturel* oncamera?), and showing enthusiastic, sisterly interest in Sarah Padden's offspring.

At this juncture, Joan badly needed a professional boost. Ironically, it was to be Spencer Tracy who offered the desired chance. Tracy came up with *Me and My Gal* (Fox, 1932), a vehicle which studio story-department head Julian Johnson had initially ticketed as a possible James Dunn-Sally Eilers picture. Then Johnson thought of casting Ralph Bellamy (of *Wild Girl*) in the male lead, but Tracy persuaded the executives not only that he should play the role of Pier 13 cop Dan Dolan, but that Joan, of all people, should be cast as the gum-chewing, tough waitress, Helen Riley.

At the time of release, *Me and My Gal* was nothing more or less than a well-functioning programmer. Granted it was a "racy combination of comedy and melodrama" (*New York Times*), but it is only in recent years that the picture has taken on the aura of a minor gem. This circumstance is due to two major factors. First, Tracy, Joan, and director Raoul Walsh all had noteworthy and long film careers, and each looked back on *Me and My Gal* with particular fondness; second, in 1970, the movie was part of a Fox Films resurrection cycle on the art-house circuit. As a result, it came up for favorable reexamination, the *Village Voice*, for instance, reporting (in June 1970): ". . . it was something of a revelation. Not a masterpiece, mind you. Nothing major, but rather nice in its own vaude-ville behavioral way, well-paced, and often strangely evocative of its entire period."

Perhaps the most entertaining facet of *Me and My Gal* is its bantering good nature. Tough-mug cop Tracy admits to hashslinger Joan that he has come into the beanery so often on the pretext of wanting a cup of coffee that he could now float a battleship, and isn't it about time they began dating? At one point the movie takes potshots at MGM's *Strange Interlude* with a satirical stretch called "Strange Inner Tube" in which Tracy and Joan speak stream-of-consciousness asides. The wisecracking love scenes between the leads are far more engaging than the ostensible main plot (Tracy and Joan both become involved in the ultimate capture of escaped gangster George Walsh—the director's real-life actor brother—for whom there is a $30,000 reward). Boisterous, a bit rowdy, yet compellingly gentle, Joan's Helen Riley was a part that would have been more suited to the likes of Glenda Farrell or Claire Trevor. However, given the chance, as here, Joan demonstrated she could be much more than a bland, weak, cotton-candy screen blonde. As the bright, breezy, self-reliant heroine who finds she needs Tracy's help to save her sister (Marion Burns) from past acquaintance Walsh, hiding out in the attic, Joan received very favorable critical notices. "[She] has seldom been better than she is here . . ." (Marguerite Tazelaar, *New York Herald-Tribune*). The *Motion Picture Herald* judged Joan's performance "a sheer delight." From this point onward, Joan and Tracy were good pals.

After *Me and My Gal*, Joan might have hoped for better things at Fox. But it was the likes of *Arizona to Broadway* (Fox, 1933) which ended her studio association.* "This picture is a slapstick variation of the cheating-cheaters theme and is as unfunny as one would not wish" (*New York Times*). When Joan's brother is duped out of $20,000 by swindlers, she finds she cannot report the episode to the police. Instead, she parades about the country—as a store-window demonstrator of pancake-making—to pick up the crooked trio's trail. With the aid of Dunn, the "brains" of a fake medicine show, she eventually accomplishes her mission. Seen to good advantage in this pedestrian film are Walter Catlett with an Ed Wynn imitation, Jerry Lester doing a Jimmy Durante bit, and Herbert Mundin as the dull-witted con artist Kingfish Miller, posing as a southern colonel.

Of this year at Fox, Joan would later write in *The Bennett Playbill*, ". . . there was something vaguely dissatisfying about it. I felt as if I were just treading in one spot." In an effort to alleviate these professional misgivings, she had begged to be loaned to RKO for the role of Syd-

---

*Initially *Arizona to Broadway* was to have been a Will Rogers vehicle; then it was changed to be the sixth and final duoing of Dunn and Sally Eilers; eventually Joan was cast in the fray.

ney Fairfield, the tormented daughter in *A Bill of Divorcement* (1932). In a telephone interview with *The Glamour Girls'* co-author Don Stanke, Joan recently revealed, "Fox wouldn't let me go to RKO, and instead, they placed me in *Me and My Gal* with Spencer Tracy." Katharine Hepburn, fresh from Broadway's *Her Warrior's Husband,* was ultimately selected to portray Sydney, thereby launching her distinguished screen career.

After the dismal *Arizona to Broadway,* Joan and Fox called it quits. The studio was convinced that she was just not star material after all. Now a free agent again, Joan finally had an opportunity to work at RKO, where Constance had done so well. She won the role of Amy in Louisa May Alcott's *Little Women* (1933),* directed by George Cukor and starring Katharine Hepburn as Jo. Joan refers to this prestige picturization of the children's classic as "the long-awaited film of merit" in her career, and admits that "it is one of my favorites." Further, she says that Cukor "is one of my favorite directors. Under his direction, each character in the film leapt into life." In Gavin Lambert's book *On Cukor* (1972), the director recalls how he selected Joan for the part. "I saw her at a party and she was a little tight, and I thought, 'Oh, yes!' She was very sweet and funny, and absolutely right, so we cast her." Joan was pregnant during *Little Women* and, in one scene, was required to fall from a chest of drawers. After explaining to Cukor her reason for not wanting to comply, the script was hastily revised and Hepburn got the oncamera task.

Little Women was Joan's first prestige production since the days of *Disraeli* and *Moby Dick.*† As Amy, Joan is first seen, in the charming screen entertainment, standing on a bench in the school with a sign about her neck, "I am ashamed of myself." She is the one who loves to wrestle, to annoy Hepburn's Jo, and the March sister who revels in the display of four-syllable words like *fastidious.* It is Joan's blonde-ringlet-curled Amy who wins the heart of Douglass Montgomery, once the sweetheart of the oncamera Hepburn. For her spirited performance, Joan received excellent notices. "As vital, sympathetic and full of the joie de vivre as one could hope for" (Mordaunt Hall, *New York Times*).

Melinda Markey (nicknamed "Mims") was born on February 27, 1934, on Joan's twenty-fourth birthday. Gene Markey "loved Ditty beyond measure," Joan recalls, "but when his very own daughter came into the world, he was ecstatic."

Vanity Fair magazine, in 1934, chose Joan, along with eight other "high-priced honeys of the screen," to form the ideal feminine motion-picture

---

*In Paramount's silent version of *Little Women* (1919), Amy was played by Florence Flinn; in the 1949 MGM remake, the role was handled by Elizabeth Taylor.

†RKO was so pleased with the box-office reaction to *Little Women* that the studio tentatively planned to group players Katharine Hepburn, Joan Bennett, Edna May Oliver, and Henry Stephenson in *Pride and Prejudice* in 1934. The Jane Austen classic would be filmed in 1940 by MGM with Greer Garson, Laurence Olivier, and Edna May Oliver.

star by superimposing photographs of the nine women one on another. In the composite photo with Joan were Ruth Chatterton, Joan Crawford, Marlene Dietrich, Greta Garbo, Helen Hayes, Dorothy Jordan, Peggy Shannon, and Norma Shearer. At first glance, the end result resembles Joan more than any of the others.

It was at this crucial juncture in her career that Joan, who had already vowed not to enter into any more long-term agreements with studios, came into professional (and later social) contact with forty-year-old industry executive Walter Wanger.* He had noticed her in the successful *Little Women,* in which she had a smaller but better than usual role, and, with his perspicacity for talent-picking, signed her to a term contract. Ironically, while Joan would be quantitatively active during this period, it would be several years before Wanger's ideal image of Joan and her appropriate screen niche blended into a feasible whole.

Meantime, Wanger, as would David O. Selznick a decade later, began loaning Joan out to various companies to win her constant screen exposure and to bolster his coffers (she was earning about $2,500 weekly then). It was rumored she would play opposite Edward Arnold in Universal's *Million Dollar Ransom* (1934), based on a Damon Runyon yarn, but it was Mary Carlisle who eventually played the female lead. Instead, Joan went over to Paramount to join Czechoslovakian-born Francis Lederer in *The Pursuit of Happiness* (1934). On Broadway the period comedy had starred Peggy Conklin and Tonio Selwart and enjoyed a 248-performance run; onscreen the premise seemed very thin and the main characters less engaging. The plot revolves around the traditional colonial habit of "bundling" in which a man and woman would sleep together in the same bed, but each fully clothed. This quaint custom had potential for risqué humor, even by post-Production Code motion-picture standards, and oncamera was a diverting but mild entertainment.

The Pursuit of Happiness was set in 1776 Westville, Connecticut. Lederer, who had been forced into the Hessian army and shipped to the colonies to fight in the Revolutionary War, had deserted his comrades-in-arms, in search of "Life, Liberty and the Pursuit of Happiness." Having joined the colonial cause, he comes into contact with Joan, a rather puritanical young maiden who has flighty parents (Charlie Ruggles, Mary Boland), a boorish New England suitor (Adrian Morris), and eventually a few daring ideas of her own. Naturally the highlight of the romantic com-

---

*San Francisco-born Wanger, after graduation from Dartmouth and service in World War I, had been involved in Broadway production, then joined Paramount Pictures' East Coast office, where he participated in the launching of Rudolph Valentino's major film period with *The Sheik* (1921). He remained with the studio for a decade, bringing such diverse talent as Walter Huston, the Marx Brothers, and Kay Francis to the screen. In 1931 he was dumped from the company in a policy dispute between the firm's eastern and western divisions. Thereafter, he shuttled between the various major studios on the West Coast, via his Walter Wanger Productions. His first wife was stage actress Justine Johnstone.

edy, as in the play, occurs when Joan invites the Hessian to participate in a night of bundling, to coyly prove the old rhyme:

> Since in a bed a man and maid
> May bundle and be chaste,
> It does no good to burn out wood,
> It is a needless waste.

The film had a good send-off at Radio City Music Hall, where it was politely lauded as being "romantic comedy not ironic comment, and as such it is admirably managed" (Richard Watts, Jr., *New York-Herald Tribune*). Andre Sennwald (*New York Times*) admitted that Joan was "comely and modest," an apt description of her emoting for most of the next several pictures to come.

Joan did stop over at Universal for *The Man Who Reclaimed His Head* (1935), set in 1910s Paris and starring Claude Rains, that studio's character lead of *The Invisible Man* (1933) fame. The macabre tale, told in flashback, concerns Rains's arrival one gloomy night at the home of an old college mate, now a lawyer. Rains has a baby with him and a valise. The gruesome object in the suitcase forms the crux of the flashback. It all began, says the distraught Rains, when, as a brilliant young writer, he sold his brain power to publisher Lionel Atwill. He ghosted a series of inspired pacifist editorials prior to World War I, all in an effort to supply his wife (Joan) with the material objects she so avariciously desired. On the eve of war Atwill sells out to the munitions interests. The enraged Rains is called to arms, which is just fine for Atwill, who, by this time, is making advances to Joan. Atwill even uses his political influence to insure that Rains is saddled with dangerous military assignments far from Paris. But one day Rains returns home to find Joan and their baby in the company of Atwill. Rains's passion flares up and, within minutes, he is guilty of homicide. Of Joan's decorative performance, Andre Sennwald, writing in the *New York Times,* decided, "Miss Bennett's naive and ingenuish style of acting is of almost no assistance to a narrative which is keyed to the dark and fascinating emotionalism of Mr. Rains." A decade later, Universal would film *Pillow of Death,* a variation of *The Man Who Reclaimed His Head,* with Lon Chaney, Jr., and Brenda Joyce.

In 1935, the subject of insanity was still a daring and novel screen topic. Wanger acquired the film rights to Phyllis Bottome's popular 1933 novel *Private Worlds* and packaged a star-studded vehicle at Paramount, the new home base of the William Paley-financed Walter Wanger productions. The studio's top star, Claudette Colbert, who had won an Academy Award the previous year on loan-out to Columbia for the comedy *It Happened One Night* (1934), led the marquee names gracing the Gregory La Cava drama, in which every one of the focal figures resides in a "private world." While the message of the picture was unabashedly "physician heal thyself," one might have hoped for a more realistic study of the serious subject at hand.

The appointment of doctor Charles Boyer, an outsider, as head of a mental asylum, creates chaos among the staff members, and everyone registers antipathy to the regimen of changes the new director intends to institute. Joel McCrea, also a doctor, had hoped for the prestigious post, and in revenge for being overlooked, he makes a play for Boyer's philandering sister (Helen Vinson). Boyer, in turn, demonstrates an antipathy to female physicians, which leads to initial tensions between himself and doctor Colbert. At the same time, she finds herself attracted to the new executive head, despite her abiding ghost affair with a dead childhood lover. While these major relationships are building to a climax in the rather clubby, handsome hospital surroundings, McCrea's pregnant wife (Joan) finds herself unable to cope with her pangs of jealousy and insecurity. Within this atmosphere of insanity, she gradually loses her grip on reality and almost passes irretrievably over the brink into total irrationality, her distraught mind having associated McCrea with one of the more bizarre hospital cases.*

It was glamorous Claudette Colbert who was Oscar-nominated for *Private Worlds* (she lost to Bette Davis of *Dangerous*), but it was fourth-billed Joan who had, as she phrased it, "the glorious chance to go insane—on film." There were a few reviewers who were unimpressed with Joan's theatrics,† but the majority of the fourth estate credited her with a new dramatic power for her appearance in this "carnival of lunacy." The *New York American,* among others, commended Joan for the "chilling scene which shows her going mad before your eyes, [she] contributes what may be selected as the most terrifying climax of the drama." Joan recalls, "It was the first really challenging and the most dramatic role I'd played up to that time, and from then on, ambitions for my own career began to grow more seriously."

While ostensibly Joan and her scenarist-husband Gene Markey were still a happily married couple and very much part of the important Hollywood social set, industry observers were quick to note that Wanger had always been present on the *Private Worlds* set when Joan was on hand, but absent when she was away from the Paramount soundstages.

Like many other movie stars—and she by this point was one, even though she had no particular studio to give her that big publicity push with the public—Joan had to endure several mediocre features for every decent

---

*Ironically, McCrea had achieved great popularity co-starring with Constance Bennett in *Rockabye* (RKO, 1932) and *Bed of Roses* (RKO, 1933). During that period he and Constance had dated for a spell.

†Andre Sennwald (*New York Times*) insisted she was "Almost no assistance in the highly promising role of the doctor's wife."

role like that in *Private Worlds*. *Mississippi* (Paramount, 1935) had a hoary pedigree* long before the studio deemed it wise to team two of its faltering prize attractions, Bing Crosby and W. C. Fields, in a slapdash rendition directed by A. Edward Sutherland. *Variety* pronounced, "Paramount obviously couldn't make up its mind what it wanted to do with the film; it's rambling and hokey."

There is an abiding magnolia-and-bourbon fragrance to the semimusical *Mississippi,* which boasts an original score by Rodgers and Hart, what with cantankerous riverboat captain Fields ("Women are like elephants to me. They are all right to look at, but I wouldn't like to own one") hiring softspoken Quaker Crosby, the latter having just escaped a ticklish situation (i.e., he refused to defend his honor in a duel with hot-blooded John Miljan, which causes Crosby's lovely but cold fiancée, Gail Patrick, to reject him). Aboard the picturesque showboat, Crosby is promoted by fruity Fields as "the singing killer," a phony reputation—that is, until rowdy captain Fred Kohler, Sr., accidentally kills himself in a brawl with Crosby. Later, chance and a trite script bring Crosby once again into contact with Patrick's younger sister, blonde, sweet Joan, who has long had a crush on Crosby. Eventually the genteel troubadour finds he must use force and live up to his billing in order to win the fair hand of innocent Joan.

Within *Mississippi,* Joan had the opportunity to sing a duet with Crosby. "For the record," she says, "my singing wasn't dubbed, it was my own voice." Onscreen, Joan tells the nonchalant Crosby, "You're a man with ideals—and things!" Offscreen, she says: "I can't think of any other performer who was as easygoing as he. Even in those days when his movie career was beginning to flower, he was as relaxed as Jello and much more fun."

Evidently Crosby thought Joan was a nifty number, for she co-starred with him again, in *Two for Tonight* (Paramount, 1935), which gave both luminaries an opportunity to try their skills at madcap comedy. Crosby appears as the impecunious songwriter who crashes the estate of an ace music publisher, in the hopes of plugging some new tunes, only to discover to his dismay that the man is stone deaf. The endeavor is not a total loss, for, while on his fruitless mission, he meets Joan, a daring lady whose plane crashes into a tree on the estate. This crash injures Crosby who was ensconced in the branches. He lands in the hospital, and Joan reluctantly agrees to pay him weekly damages of $15. She also introduces him to her employer, a Broadway producer, and Crosby finds himself offered the chance to prepare a musical, but he must complete it within seven days. Tough as the challenge seems, Crosby's dizzy mother (Mary Boland) rea-

---

* Based on the 1923 Booth Tarkington play, *The Magnolia;* filmed as *The Fighting Coward* (Paramount, 1924) with Cullen Landis and Mary Astor in the leads, and then as *River of Romance* (Paramount, 1929) with Charles "Buddy" Rogers and Mary Brian.

sons: "It shouldn't be hard. A play only runs two hours, and you have a whole week to write it!"

With Crosby crooning "A Night in June," "The Top of Your Head," "Two for Tonight," and "I Wish I Were Aladdin," and the competition of two other blondes (Boland and Thelma Todd, the latter as Crosby's gal and star), Joan had a great deal of competition to keep her head above water in this venture. In fact, Frank S. Nugent (*New York Times*) ventured that Joan "should have been told by someone that *Two for Tonight* was a comedy; her performance is completely colorless."

Joan next worked for B. P. Schulberg, Wanger's old boss, in *She Couldn't Take It* (Columbia 1935), with George Raft teamed with her. Although Joan had not displayed good comedy timing in her previous screwball-comedy venture, she was asked to try again in this vehicle. "She is no less a decoration than she has ever been, nor does she wear clothes with less effect, but her natural inclinations to docility are not concealed by the amount of acting skill at her disposal in *She Can't Take It*" (John Reddington, *New York Evening Post*).

Actually, the best scenes in the film occur in the opening segment where Walter Connolly, the head of the household of the "mad Van Dykes" of Park Avenue, is sentenced to prison for wrongful manipulation of funds. Once acclimated to life in Atlanta Prison, he becomes friends with reformed criminal Raft. The older man, who realizes he has not much longer to live, makes his younger friend sole trustee of the Van Dyke estate, hoping this self-educated soul can reform his relatives, especially witless and irresponsible Joan. Raft is released from jail later on, and heads for New York, where he finds his task a tough one, especially in coping with rebellious, resentful, thoughtless Joan. Not until near the finale—a simulated Mack Sennett-Keystone Kops-type chase—in which Joan's hired abductors prove to be legitimate in their kidnap attempts, does she learn to appreciate Raft's virtues and to toe the mark. As a modern rendition of *The Taming of the Shrew, She Can't Take It* was not a success. "The film plunges back and forth between melodrama and farce so rapidly that it is difficult for a casual spectator to keep up with it. . ." (Richard Watts, Jr., *New York Herald-Tribune*).

Joan's sixth and final 1935 release, *The Man Who Broke the Bank at Monte Carlo* (Twentieth Century-Fox), was not an especially fortuitous selection. She was reteamed with Ronald Colman back at her old home studio—now merged into Twentieth Century-Fox—in a film more remembered for its lengthy thirty-three letter title than for the quality of its romantic drama. Colman, looking unusually tired and blasé, is a Russian refugee, functioning as a Parisian taxi-driver. His comrades back him in a trip to Monte Carlo where he manages to win ten million francs, which quite naturally upsets the casino syndicate. They hire Joan to romance Colman and lure him back to the gaming tables. She is successful in the Swiss interlude, causing Colman to succumb to her entreaties to return to Monte Carlo to replenish his stake and help Joan's poor, ailing "brother" (Colin Clive). As expected, Colman loses all, and dashes back to Paris to resume his cabbie career. He later locates Joan singing at a local music hall,* decides to try to snub her, but is amazed to discover—as she is too, once she learns that he is a proletarian like herself—that he really loves the small-time con artist. Colman was scolded by reviewers for his uncustomary lack of dash, while the reaction to Joan's presence ranged from "charming and straightforward" (*New York Herald-Tribune*) to "prettier than ever although somewhat lifeless in her role of unwilling adventuress . . ." (Eileen Creelman, *New York Sun*).

In January 1936, while Joan was at work on *13 Hours by Air* (Paramount, 1936),† Richard Bennett was stricken with double pneumonia while in the New York production of *Winterset*. Joan flew with Constance to New York, straight from the movie set and in her costume. Although the elder Bennett's condition was not diagnosed as extremely serious, *Winterset* was to be his last performance on the Broadway stage. Thereafter, he would reside mostly in Hollywood, where he accepted small film parts, as his failing health permitted.   •

In its slick, mechanical fashion, *13 Hours by Air* was "a sort of *Grand Hotel* of the ozone . . . it proves an implausible mesh of plots and subplots that unravel as soon as they are woven into the narrative" (Howard Barnes, *New York Herald-Tribune*). Heiress Felice Rollins (Joan) arrives at Newark Airport at the last minute, hocking a diamond ring to purchase a ticket. She boards the transcontinental plane, desperate to reach San Francisco before her younger sister weds a fortune-hunter. Aboard the flight are, among others, pilot Fred MacMurray, who falls in love with stuck-up Joan, a suspicious character named Palmer (Alan Baxter), who proves to be an escaped convict and hijacks the plane, "brain specialist" Brian Donlevy, who is really a federal agent, airsick governess ZaSu Pitts and her obnoxious ten-year-old charge, Bennie Bartlett, and, among those briefly encountered on the ground, Grace Bradley and Marie Prevost, two girls from MacMurray's past. The fact that at the time cross-country flights took fifteen to sixteen hours was not the only phony facet of this programmer in which Joan was stuck with a real nothing part.

Walter Wanger produced *Big Brown Eyes* (Paramount, 1936) and Raoul Walsh was again her director; this time out Joan had a new leading man, Cary Grant. Most of the picture's seventy-six minutes was cen-

*Joan's song-production number was deleted from the film after a West Coast preview.

†Carole Lombard, among others, had rejected the role at Paramount. In *Hollywood Director* (1973), director Mitchell Leisen tells author David Chierichetti, "Joan Bennett was a doll to work with. She was very near-sighted and she refused to wear glasses. Between scenes, she'd sit on the set doing *petit point* and she'd stick the thing about an inch from her eye to see what she was doing. I was scared to death she'd poke her eye out with the needle sometimes, but she never did."

tered around a Times Square barber shop where manicurist Joan devotes a good deal of attention to customer Danny Barr (Grant) of the metropolitan police force. Besides her ability with a cuticle scissor and a nail file, Joan's Eve Fallon has a nose for news, and she quickly deduces that customers like Walter Pidgeon are up to no good. The latter is a private detective who has been in touch with the crook trio of Lloyd Nolan, Alan Baxter, and Douglas Fowley, offering to buying their $200,000 worth of hot jewels for $30,000 (which he will then turn over to the insurance company for the reward). In the course of the inconsequential, but brisk tale Joan finds herself given the opportunity to become an overnight whiz as a newspaper editorial writer, a task which she manages in no time, dictating her essays with the ease of an experienced professional journalist. Once again, despite the preposterous nature of her screen assignment, it was a working role several cuts above her usual parts. It was something she could almost dig her teeth into, and it showed in her performance. ". . . she tosses about the smart cracks . . . with deftness that tickles the audience" (Kate Cameron, *New York Daily News*). "Miss Bennett improves constantly, offering here a knowing and sophisticated portrayal" (Marguerite Tazelaar, *New York Herald-Tribune*).

As the advertisement for *Two in a Crowd* (Universal, 1936) proclaimed: "Two strays in a city of seven million! She wanted fame! He wanted riches! Instead they got a half-ownership in each other! A story that begins with an empty purse and ends on a 'grand' note!" Translated into cinema terms, it meant actress Joan and horse-racing enthusiast Joel McCrea, both on the financial skids, find themselves each the possessor of one-half of a thousand-dollar bill. She wants to use the funds to pay off the lecherous character who intends to wed her and has put her in a financial bind. McCrea, who is about to be dispossessed by his landlord (Alison Skipworth) and whose sole horse (Hector) and jockey (Elisha Cook, Jr.) are being held for collateral by an irate coal-yard owner (Andy Clyde), has dreams of owning a stable of prize fillies. Joan does not understand or like horses, but she soon is amorously inclined towards McCrea, providing a romantic situation leading to a predictable finale. The film was handicapped both by its botched scenario (one part O. Henry, one part Damon Runyon in an unsatisfactory mix) and by the tattered dialog, none of which properly served its high-caliber cast members. It would not be unfair to observe that the likable nag Hector runs away with the picture.

Big Brown Eyes had been an amiable screen exercise, but certainly not resilient enough to warrant either the rematching of Joan and increasingly popular Cary Grant, or to indulge Joan in another round of screwball comedy. However, producer B. P. Schulberg paired the performing duo again in *Wedding Present* (Paramount, 1936), a movie which "insists on being furiously and monotonously whimsical" (William Boehnel, *New York World-Telegram*). With a very artificial and protracted élan, the comedy doggedly devotes its opening reels to demonstrating, in Hollywood fashion, just what an exceptionally brilliant team of newspaper reporters Joan and Grant are at the *Chicago News-Gazette.* In the course of one brief day, mind you, the crackerjack pair diligently scoop the town on the whirlwind wedding of an archduke (Gene Lockhart) to an American heiress, rescue a drowning gangster from an untimely end, and save the floundering survivors of a Lake Michigan steamship disaster by hijacking a plane.

When harassed city editor George Bancroft resigns his post, Grant suddenly finds himself in the office driver's seat, which soon causes prideful Joan to quit and move to New York. From this point onward, the film teeters along, struggling to survive until the promised big finale. It seems Joan has second thoughts about wedding staid Manhattan-based novelist Conrad Nagel, but she intends to carry through with the marriage. That is, until Grant, drunk and maudlin, appears in the big city to provide Joan with a very personalized wedding gift. He recalls her passion for sirens and similar noises. So he engineers a special treat for her, calling out police radio cars, emergency trucks, ambulances, fire engines, and all, to create a unique symphony beneath Joan's window. At this timely juncture, she realizes that Grant, the type who could never get serious even when they were waiting to get a wedding license, is the man for her.

Once again, as in *Big Brown Eyes,* the critics were kind to Grant's lackadaisical performance in this monkey business, but they demanded more from Joan than she was capable of, let alone willing to offer. "Joan Bennett is a pretty gracious Rusty, although her restrained screen personality hardly fits in with Rusty's wild love of adventure" (*New York Sun*). It was actually the type of film that Constance Bennett should have made (and would the next year when she paired with Grant in Hal Roach's *Topper* for MGM release).

In August 1936, Joan petitioned a law court to change her daughter Ditty's surname from Fox to Markey because "I wanted the girls to grow up as sisters and to share in everything, including the last name of Markey." The change was effected in spite of Jack Fox's feeble efforts to thwart it.

Meanwhile, Joan's marriage to Markey was falling apart at the seams. It had been announced that in the 1936-37 season, Joan would star with Fred Stone in RKO's *By the Dawn's Early Light,* based on a scenario by Markey. (The film would eventually be made at Twentieth Century-Fox as *Barricade* [1939] featuring Alice Faye.) Not only could the couple not find joint projects on which to work together harmoniously, but the reality of the rumors linking Joan with Wanger were taking their toll.* As Joan would later describe the period, her personal life had

*Hedda Hopper reported in *From under My Hat* (1952) that while on a 1936 transatlantic trip on the *Queen Mary,* Joan and England's Lord Dudley had been close companions.

become "a kind of dull, lusterless routine." She declared that "little by little some sort of erosion set in" to wear away her marital relationship with Markey. On April 29, 1937, he moved out of their home and on June 3, 1937, she filed for divorce, claiming her soon-to-be ex-husband berated her, displayed a violent temper, refused to take her to social events, and had deserted their homestead for well over a month.* In the final divorce settlement, Joan received custody of their three-year-old daughter, Melinda.

Although Joan, in conjunction with her new four-picture pact with Wanger, was to make a film in England for Gaumont British, plans did not materialize and she restricted her moviemaking to Hollywood. Wanger had now established his home base at United Artists,† where he produced the Technicolor *Vogues of 1938* (1937), Joan's only release of the year. Ostensibly Joan's role in the musical proceedings was to be another skittish heiress part, that of Wendy Van Klettering, the girl who backs out of her wedding to Alan Mowbray and seeks a job with Warner Baxter, headman at the fashionable design House of Curson. To get revenge, pompous Mowbray establishes a rival modiste firm, and the battle is on to see which company will outshine the other at the Seven Arts Ball. The convenient subplot ties together all the threads. Baxter's gold-digging wife (Helen Vinson) has theatrical ambitions, and finally she and producer Jerome Cowan talk Baxter into backing a stage show. When that production, *Vogues of '38,* flops in Boston, Baxter has a last-minute brainstorm to use the derelict scenery for his new fashion display, and finally realizes Vinson should go her own way, and that novice mannequin Joan is the girl for him.

Vogues of 1938, with its wisps of plot, was a veritable excuse for providing viewers with a colorful fashion show, and for interspersing these interludes with musical numbers, the best of the latter being the singing of Virginia Verrill ("Lovely One"), the dancing of Rocco and Saulters, and the antics of Georgie Tapps. Like the later *Cover Girl* (Columbia, 1944), Vogues of 1938 heavily publicized its bevy of beautiful mannequins, herein called the Walter Wanger Models, used to display the assemblage of chic costumes. However, the real surprise of this film was Joan. As contemporary *New York Herald-Tribune* reporter Howard Barnes acclaimed to his readers, "Much of the success of the offering as entertainment is due to the adept and agreeable performance of Joan Bennett. As a society girl turned model . . . she keeps the show weaving evenly through its multifarious incidents. Color becomes her and so do the fashions, and she

---

*Markey would later wed and divorce actresses Hedy Lamarr and Myrna Loy. In 1952 he married Mrs. Lucille Park Wright, widow-heir to the baking-powder fortune and owner of Calumet Farms racing stables.

†Among Wanger's contract personalities in 1937 were Sylvia Sidney, Charles Boyer, Madeleine Carroll, Henry Fonda, Pat Paterson, Alan Baxter, Maria Shelton, Louise Platt, and Tim Holt.

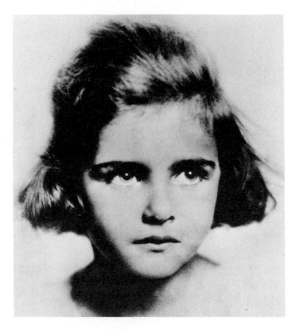

Joan Bennett as a child

With Lawrence Grant, Tetsu Komai, Lilyan Tashman, Montagu Love, and Ronald Colman in BULLDOG DRUMMOND (UA '29)

With George Arliss in
DISRAELI (WB '29)

With Lilyan Tashman, James Gleason, and Harry Richman
in PUTTIN' ON THE RITZ (UA '30)

With Lloyd Hughes and John Barrymore in MOBY DICK (WB '30)

With Warner Baxter and Helene Millard in DOCTORS' WIVES
(Fox '31)

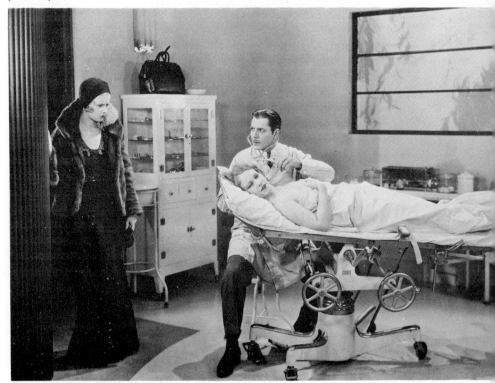

Publicity pose on the Fox lot ('31)

In SHE WANTED A MILLIONAIRE
(Fox '32)

With Spencer Tracy in ME AND MY GAL (Fox '32)

th Eugene Pallette in WILD GIRL (Fox '32)

On her wedding day (March 15, 1932) with groom Gene Markey in Los Angeles

With Spring Byington, Jean Parker, Frances Dee, and Katharine Hepburn
in LITTLE WOMEN (RKO '33)

On the set of
THE PURSUIT OF HAPPINESS
(Par '34) with Francis Lederer

With Constance Bennett at a charity polo match in Los Angeles (June 30, 1935)

With George Raft in
SHE COULDN'T TAKE IT
(Col '35)

With Vladimir Bykoff and Colin Clive in
THE MAN WHO BROKE THE BANK AT MONTE CARLO (20th '35)

handles the small situations of the small story expertly." Or as the *New York Morning Telegraph* enunciated, ". . . she is at home in a role that is blasé and cynical and the color film enhances her natural loveliness." Finally, after years of being a pleasant screen heroine, with an occasional sojourn into a meaty role, blonde Joan—thanks to Wanger—had added new luster to her screen career. She was becoming known as a chic cinema leading lady who had the ability to add bite to her assignment (e.g., recall the moment when in aiding Baxter's fashion-show ensemble, she saves the day by ripping the gown off the back of one of Mowbray's models). Thus the rather expensive color showcase proved a great boost to Joan's status on the Hollywood scene and in the public's eyes.

For a personality who initially had no desire to perform on the stage— let alone in the movies—Joan's career took a new turn when, in the winter season of 1937-38, she toured the East and Midwest in George S. Kaufman and Edna Ferber's *Stage Door,* in the role of Terry, played on Broadway previously by Margaret Sullavan and onscreen (RKO, 1937) by Katharine Hepburn. The tour, which opened in Hartford, Connecticut, and closed in Chicago, was just the distraction that she needed after her divorce from Markey.

Prior to her final breakup with Markey, Joan had purchased a piece of land on Mapleton Drive in Holmby Hills, a section of Los Angeles near Beverly Hills. While she was on tour, the builders erected a fourteen-room French Provincial house. On her return to Los Angeles, the house was nearing completion, and she devoted herself to designing the interior, something she had always dreamed of doing. At the same time, Wanger, still one of the industry's most productive and imaginative producers, continued to woo her, but neither party was anxious to leap into marriage.

Joan had three leading roles onscreen in 1938. The most substantial of the pictures was the first, *I Met My Love Again* (United Artists, 1938). Although Joan was not as felicitous a leading lady for lanky Henry Fonda as Sylvia Sidney (*You Only Live Once* [United Artists, 1937]), she proved quite adept at portraying the restless small-town Vermont girl who rushes into a whirlwind courtship with personable New York writer Alan Marshal, weds him, and only later discovers in Paris that drunken binges are his only creative efforts. The girl has spunk, though, for she endures a decade of domestic woes, before Marshal's death gives her the freedom to return home with her small daughter. Joan's wise aunt, Dame May Whitty, has some tart words for the niece's reprehensible past behavior, and is unsure of the wisdom of Joan's attempt to realign herself with taciturn biology professor Fonda, the man she jilted ten years before. Complicating matters is Louise Platt (who turns in an admirable performance) as the wealthy student nursing a crush on the passive, sensitive teacher. At the time, the critics were rather harsh on this lilting love tale, labeling it "sentimentality as sticky as a gum drop" (*Variety*), and "a hapless and witless yarn" (*New York Herald-Tribune*). But those who have caught all or parts of the feature on the late late show have come to appreciate the charm of the movie's local color, ranging from the presence of Dorothy Stickney and Florence Lake as gossipy local women, to Babbitty businessman Alan Baxter, to the beauty of the Vermont countryside. Joan and Fonda would repeat their roles on "Lux Radio Theatre" on May 30, 1938.

There were not many redeeming qualities in the would-be epic Western, *The Texans* (Paramount, 1938),* set in Texas during the post-Civil War Reconstruction period, with the opening of the Chisholm Trail, the completion of the transcontinental railroad, and the upsurge of the Ku Klux Klan as side issues. The movie was, in fact, "just another romance with unjustified pretensions to importance" (Frank S. Nugent, *New York Times*). The villainous carpetbaggers attempt to levy a tax on the ten thousand head of cattle at Joan's Boca Grande Ranch, but Joan is befriended by penniless Confederate veteran Randolph Scott, who leads a longhorn drive from Indianola, Texas, down through the Mexican border, and up north to Kansas. In the course of this fifteen-hundred-mile trek, Joan endures blizzards, brush fires, Indian raids, and dissension among the cowboys but, as was demanded by this formula picture, the trail drive is successful. Likewise, Joan and Scott, who have been arguing consistently on the wisdom of the South rising to fight again, end up in one another's arms. Fortunately, for audience diversion there were Walter Brennan as the loyal foreman, May Robson as Joan's wild and woolly grandmother, Raymond Hatton as an amusingly vengeful scout, and Francis Ford in a touching performance as a one-legged ranch hand.

If there was no real excuse for Joan acting like a debutante roughing it on a dude ranch in *The Texans,* at least Joan's relaxed performance and very attractive presence were a viable commodity in *Artists and Models Abroad* (Paramount, 1938), ostensibly a follow-up to the previous year's *Artists and Models.* Once again Jack Benny was the male lead—having lost some weight he was more credible as the Continental Casanova—and once more it was the fashion-show elements that were the big ballyhoo elements of the picture. Director Mitchell Leisen, himself a former costume designer, had the grand finale display of costuming at the Palace of Feminine Arts, a conglomerate effort of some of Paris' top couturiers, including Alix, Paquin, Lavin, Patou, Lelong, Schiaparelli, Maggy Rouff, and Worth. In this edition of the episodic revue, slapstick was a large-order substitute for the songs which had graced the original *Artists and Models,*† with the plotline focusing on Benny's efforts to get his troupe back to the States within two weeks in order to accept a forty-week booking. Meanwhile, they are holed up at a Left Bank hotel, and come into

*A remake of *North of 36* (Paramount, 1924) in which Lois Wilson was the heroine.

†Of the four musical numbers in *Artists and Models Abroad,* the Yacht Club Boys handled two of them, Benny the rest.

71

contact with divine Joan, her Texas oil millionaire father (Charley Grapewin), and the scatterbrained aunt (Mary Boland).

Joan would write in *The Bennett Playbill:* "For ten years with the exception of *Little Women* and *Private Worlds,* I'd played the insipid blonde ingenue, short on brains, long on bank accounts, the victim of love triangles, and, for some reason that now escapes me, I was often English." Early in 1939 Joan was to receive a new screen image—glamorous, tempting, throaty-voiced, and brunette.

Tay Garnett wrote and directed *Trade Winds* (1939), produced by Wanger for United Artists. Garnett, who had previously taken a yachting trip around the world on his vessel *Athene,* had shot thousands of feet of usable location footage which he intended to incorporate as process photography in one or more upcoming features. *Trade Winds* was devised to make use of this background celluloid. Once Wanger had bought the movie package, which, not only for novelty's sake, teamed Joan with Fredric March, but had Ann Sothern, the queen of the B's, as a brassy comedienne, Garnett insisted on another gimmick. Because Joan resembled Hedy Lamarr so much, except for the color of her hair, the helmer convinced Wanger that it would be a big joke to photograph Joan as a brunette.* Because everyone concerned with the feature thought of the stint as a lark, she gleefully agreed to wear a dark wig, fully intending to continue as a blonde in future pictures. "After that film," Joan remembers, "everybody liked me in dark hair so I turned my hair dark and I got much better parts. It's been that way ever since." United Artists was bombarded by fan mail after the release of *Trade Winds*, while an association of United States hairdressers predicted that the ladies of America would now become brunette-conscious because of Joan's changeover. Hollywood columnists attempted a rivalry between Joan and Lamarr, but Joan insists that none of it was true.†

As *Trade Winds* opens, Joan is a blonde San Francisco pianist.‡ She is called to the city morgue to identify the body of her sister, who committed suicide after being ditched by her lover, Sidney Blackmer. Joan, as Kay Kerrigan, then shoots—or, at least, assumes she has shot—Blackmer. She then fakes her own suicide. She escapes to Honolulu, where she dyes her hair dark and travels on to Japan, Shanghai, Singapore, Bombay, and to a remote island in the Indonesian group. Throughout the story, she is pursued by police detective March, who, of course, falls for her in a big way. Along for comedy relief are Ralph Bellamy as a dumb detective and Sothern as March's wisecracking secretary. Once back in San Francisco,

---

*Lamarr, the reigning brunette at MGM, had made her American film mark on loanout to Wanger for *Algiers* (United Artists, 1938).

†As mentioned previously, Joan's ex-husband, Markey, later wed Lamarr.

‡Several times in the course of *Trade Winds* Joan plays a Chopin Prelude.

March clears Joan of the murder rap by discovering that Blackmer had died by the gun of yet another disappointed girlfriend.

Despite the tremendous publicity and subsequent interest in *Trade Winds* because of the "new" Joan, the picture itself was not the success anticipated. "[It] is far from a heavy piece nor a particularly important one. It is just a well-turned out piece of entertainment . . ." (Eileen Creelman, *New York Sun*). Garnett's plans to utilize additional bits of local color photography in a second such film never materialized.

Nineteen hundred thirty-eight and the early part of the following year was the period of the worldwide search by David O. Selznick for an actress to portray Scarlet O'Hara in *Gone with the Wind* (MGM, 1939). Because of Joan's new, dark look, Selznick asked her to test for the part. "Because it was such a plum role I agreed at once." She worked with dialog coach Bill Price on the southern accent, and George Cukor then directed her in the test, which consisted of three scenes. The contest for the much-desired role finally narrowed down to Paulette Goddard and Joan. Then, Selznick's brother Myron, still Joan's agent, met Vivien Leigh, who was visiting in Hollywood with Laurence Olivier. Joan insists that the Academy Award-winning role would have been hers, had Leigh remained in London.

Although Joan lost the biggest opportunity of her screen career, she did not lose her growing interest in global politics. In early 1939, when Dorothy Thompson, syndicated columnist and then wife of novelist Sinclair Lewis, began a nationwide campaign to solicit the signatures of millions of Americans in a pressure drive to influence President Franklin D. Roosevelt to boycott Nazi Germany, director Herbert Biberman took up the cause in Hollywood, with Melvyn Douglas and Edward G. Robinson as his allies. They drew up a "Declaration of Democratic Independence," which was a petition to the President and Congress to break off all trade relations with Germany because of the inhumane treatment of Jews. Joan was among the first of fifty-six in the Hollywood colony to sign the document. Directly beneath her signature were those of Bette Davis, Myrna Loy, and Joan Crawford.

On April 3, 1939, Joan and Don Ameche were heard on NBC radio's "Chase and Sanborn Hour" in a dramatic sketch entitled *Society Nurse*. It was planned as the basis of a picture for Joan, to be produced by Wanger. That film never came into being, but Joan did star for producer Edward Small in *The Man in the Iron Mask* (United Artists, 1939). The adaptation of the Alexandre Dumas novel was passed off by most as a "moderately entertaining costume piece which matches the Dumas novel in its length, if not in its effectiveness" (Frank S. Nugent, *New York Times*). Louis Hayward in the dual role of King Louis XIV and his twin brother Philippe received some deserved recognition for his Errol Flynn-type swashbuckling, but Joan had a mostly passive assignment in this "slightly stuffy historical romance." This film demonstrated conclusively that Joan was not on a par with Olivia de Havilland in this genre of screenfare. As the king's (brunette-wigged) Spanish fiancée, she was strikingly gowned and coiffed, but spent her few screen moments looking more perplexed by, than in command of, her scenes.

For her next screen effort, Hal Roach's *The Housekeeper's Daughter* (United Artists, 1939), the *New York Times* discovered that "Joan Bennett is trying quite successfully to look like Hedy Lamarr." This was hardly new news. What the newspaper failed to report was that Joan was, at the time of the picture's opening (Roxy Theatre, December 1, 1939), trying her legal best to disavow herself from the production. The slapstick yarn concerned a gangster's moll (Joan) who returns to mama—housekeeper Peggy Wood—and falls in love with the rich employers' fossil-hunter son (John Hubbard). The latter takes a job as a cub reporter, which puts him on the trail of gangster Marc Lawrence, Joan's old flame, and brings onto the scene ace reporter Adolphe Menjou and veteran photographer William Gargan. Before the madcap finale, it is revealed that meek little George E. Stone, a schizoid flower peddler, had altruistically committed a series of murders. Dandy as the plot may have seemed to some —both critics and viewers—Joan was very upset to discover that Roach's publicity department was promoting the film with the catch line, "The housekeeper's daughter did things she hadn't oughter." The smoking-room overtones of the film's title and the publicity campaign so irked the actress that not only did she threaten to sue producer-director Roach, but also she wrote letters to some three thousand women's clubs explaining she was being maligned and asking them to boycott the film. As luck would have it, Joan's efforts merely made the public more curious about the film's contents, and business for the film picked up for a while.*

Joan was merely window dressing in Universal's *Green Hell* (1940), playing opposite Douglas Fairbanks, Jr. Former directing ace of horror films Jame Whale was so intent on giving the adventure yarn authentic atmosphere (the South American jungle) that plotline credibility took a back seat. An all-male expedition, led by Fairbanks, heads into the dark interior seeking a fabled Inca treasure. When one of the members, Vincent Price, is killed by a headhunter's poisoned dart, news is sent to the outpost and the man's comely widow, Joan, makes a speedy appearance on the scene. Soon the remaining members of the expedition, Fairbanks, dynamiter George Bancroft, cosmopolitan Britisher George Sanders, collegian John Howard, et al., are as intrigued by Joan's presence as by the treasure hunt. It requires little deduction to assume that Joan and Fairbanks will wed in the end. They do, and in a filmed postscript set back in civilization, Joan is told by her new spouse that he plans a new

---

*One United Artists executive is said to have told Roach of this film, which was pronounced a box-office flop, "Don't be afraid she'll sue; be afraid she won't."

74

exotic expedition. She cheerfully replies, "It's no surprise to me, Brandy. I've seen that far-away look in your eyes for months."

Wanger's own production, *The House across the Bay* (United Artists, 1940), merely served to reunite Joan with George Raft for the third time oncamera and to allow her to parade in a bedazzling Irene wardrobe. As Robert W. Dana, Jr. (*New York Herald-Tribune*) reported of this underworld melodrama, "No matter what picture Miss Joan Bennett is in these days, she is pretty certain to be the envy of the country's aspiring mannequins. From the time she was one of the mannequins on parade in *Artists and Models Abroad* she has been shown to extreme advantage in a veritable warehouse of lovely clothes." The picture may have been a fashion fan's joy, but it won no plaudits for its artistic merits.*

In January 1940, having just completed *The House across the Bay,* Joan said yes to Wanger's telephoned marriage proposal. "By then I knew I was in love with Walter and felt I could give him, at last, the settled domestic life he'd never had. . . . Most important of all, he loved Ditty and Mims." Wanger, now divorced from Justine Johnstone, was one of Hollywood's busiest and most respected citizens. Among his many official posts was the presidency of the Academy of Motion Picture Arts and Sciences (1939-45).

Joan and Wanger were married by a justice of the peace in Phoenix, Arizona, on January 12, 1940. Joan was then twenty-nine, Wanger was forty-five. On January 14, in Los Angeles, Jack Fox swallowed a few sleeping pills and called an ambulance. He muttered to the police, "I didn't like the idea of Joan being married to that other guy." His statement was a bit strange since Joan had been wed to Markey in the long interim, and Fox had married twice and had fathered two children since Joan divorced him.

Three months after her marriage to Wanger, Joan said she "was on the point of divorcing him for a romantic dereliction." When Joan became ill during one of Wanger's periodic absences, she went to her new agent, Jennings Lang, for medical arrangements and gentleness. "I turned to Jennings more often after that with feelings that went beyond our business relationship."

The year 1940 finished with two more Joan Bennett film credits. *The Man I Married* (a.k.a. *I Married a Nazi*) (Twentieth Century-Fox, 1940) is one of those efficient, topical features that has failed to retain its proper niche in cinema history. At the time it was applauded as "an extremely

*The anemic Kathryn Scola screenplay finds Joan wedding gambler George Raft, only to discover that rival racketeers want to eliminate him. To protect her beloved, she arranges—through lawyer Lloyd Nolan—to have Raft convicted of income tax evasion. But Nolan is in love with Joan, and double-crosses Raft by earning him a very healthy sentence at Alcatraz. While Raft is on the big rock, and Joan is functioning as a loyal prison widow and singing at a roadside club for her keep, Nolan makes a play for her. Raft escapes from prison, kills Nolan, and is himself shot down by the police, leaving the mourning Joan to be consoled by sympathetic airplane tycoon Walter Pidgeon.

persuasive presentation of a subject which has not been handled with much success by either stage or screen in the past" (Howard Barnes, *New York Herald-Tribune*). Within its slick seventy-seven-minute footage, the exposé detailed how an American girl on a European vacation in 1938 with her husband (Francis Lederer) is horrified to find him coming under the influence of Nazi Germany. Before the tale is completed, Lederer, now an arch Third Reich enthusiast, has learned that his pedigree is not entirely pure Aryan, so he yields to Joan's plea that she be able to take their son back to America. As she bids goodbye to her husband (she says "Heil, heel"), she takes with her a full comprehension of how Hitler's Germany is actually dealing with those who opposed his regime. *Variety* lauded the production because "it pulls no punches in displaying the ruthlessness of the Nazis in herding the populace into the swastika ranks . . ." Joan, it must be admitted, was not quite in her dramatic element in this film, especially with the acting competition of Anna Sten as a blonde fraulein, Otto Kruger as Lederer's sympathetic father, and Maria Ouspenskaya as the widow of a German philosopher (Ludwig Stossel) killed in a concentration camp. Cecilia Ager (*PM*) aptly defined Joan's histrionic problem in this film venture: "Joan Bennett has as pretty a face as anybody would want to look at on the screen, but as an actress she has her own steady tempo. It just doesn't accelerate in emotional surges, that's all. Nothing happens to her externally, of course; but nothing happens to her internally, either. And since it's her job to express what happens to a woman who marries a Nazi, she really should express something."

Joan once more performed under the aegis of Edward Small in *The Son of Monte Cristo* (United Artists, 1940), another costumer derived from the works of Alexandre Dumas. Once more she was teamed with Louis Hayward. This time her leading man portrayed the son* of Edmond Dantes in a swashbuckling tale set in the kingdom of 1865 Lichtenburg, where Grand Duchess Zona (Joan) is being controlled by commoner-dictator George Sanders. Joan's male vis-à-vis performed in the florid, grand manner, with Hayward enacting a seriallike role as the masked figure, "The Torch." However, Joan was required only to be a gracious adornment to the proceedings, standing about with wonder in her eyes, as Hayward mouthed such dialog as, "You know. You're even more beautiful when you're angry."

Joan completed the first year of her next decade as an entertainer by reenacting for "Lux Radio Theatre" (November 4, 1940) the role that brought her brunette fame, *Trade Winds*. Her co-stars were Errol Flynn, Ralph Bellamy, and Mary Astor.

Much was changing in the Bennett dynasty. Late in 1940, Constance, whose screen career had nose-dived terribly, ended another marriage, and on November 20, fifty-seven-year-old Adrienne Morrison Bennett

---

*There was no such character in Dumas's *The Count of Monte Cristo* (1844).

76

died of a heart attack in Old Lyme, Connecticut. In January 1941, Barbara Bennett would separate from Morton Downey, who would receive custody of their five children. Three days after the divorce, she wed a Western-movie player, Addison Randall, and her remaining years were a mixture of suicide attempts, alcoholism, widowhood, another marriage, and then her own untimely death in Montreal in 1958 at the age of fifty-two. Richard Bennett, who had been living on the West Coast in continually declining health, managed a few small film roles now and then, and on October 21, 1944, died at the age of seventy-one.

Joan was supposed to star for husband-producer Walter Wanger in *Sundown* (United Artists, 1941), but she declined and Gene Tierney took the role. Instead, Joan went over to Twentieth Century-Fox for *Man Hunt* (1941), directed by the second of her director favorites, Fritz Lang, whom she calls "incomparable." For her role of a Cockney whore in prewar London, she spent several weeks perfecting the accent with English music hall-Hollywood character actress Queenie Leonard.* "It was the only movie I ever made in which I knew the entire script, like a play, beforehand." Because the movie production code office objected to Lang's oncamera glamorization of a prostitute, the direction made a concession to the authorities-that-be by having a sewing machine placed in the girl's onscreen apartment, which fooled no one into believing she was a conventional home-maker.

Of Lang's several cinema espionage thrillers, *Man Hunt* is among everyone's top favorites, with its tense, terse, atmospheric production values. Then too, "from the sheerly melodramatic angle, *Man Hunt* is a stunning achievement" (Howard Barnes, *New York Herald-Tribune*). There is hardly a moment, from the opening—which finds a big game hunter with his telescopic-sighted rifle zeroing down on Hitler's woodland retreat in Bavaria—to the finish, that does not add to the relentless chase that comprises the essence of the film. The film's premise—of eliminating Hitler—adapted from Geoffrey Household's novel, *Rogue Male,* was a concept dear to the hearts of many viewers; and the fact that the movie concludes with a gratuitous epilogue is almost forgiveable.†

Within *Man Hunt,* Lang plays some stern emotional games with the audience.‡ It is more than sheer coincidence that the only person willing to help man-on-the-run Pidgeon is world-weary but kindly Joan, who pays for her patriotic good deed with her life. She has several good mo-

---

*"Joan Bennett's Cockney accent is so good that you have to look again to remind yourself that it's really Joan Bennett" (Archer Winsten, *New York Post*).

†Pidgeon is shown parachuting behind enemy lines, his telescopic rifle attached to his pack; this time intent on accomplishing the almost impossible mission—killing the Fuehrer.

‡In *Fritz Lang in America* (1969), the director told author Peter Bogdanovich, "I do not look at the oldest profession in the world with a wagging finger, as if to say, 'That is a horrible thing. . . .' And this part Joan Bennett played of the little streetwalker who falls in love with Pidgeon—a love that is doomed from the beginning—I must admit had all my heart. I think I understood her and I think Joan understood her very well."

ments in her rather small, but showy, part in *Man Hunt*. They range from the time Pidgeon comes across her in the darkened hallway and silences her with a hand over her mouth to the time where he gives her money and a chromium arrow pin (for her beret) for helping him, when all she wishes is to make love to the man who wants her as a friend, not a tool. Finally, there is the starkly frightening scene in which the doomed girl returns to her rooms to find Nazi agent George Sanders and underlings waiting for her.

For her compelling performance, Joan received some of the best reviews in her lengthy career. " . . . appealing and understanding as the child-like waif" (John Rosenfield, *Dallas Morning News*). ". . . [Miss Bennett] is not only a plausible Cockney girl but manages to do the most realistic acting job she ever hired out to pictures" (*New York Morning Telegraph*).

From this sublime grade-A programmer, she turned to class-C trivia, *She Knew All the Answers* (Columbia, 1941), a Richard Wallace-directed "comedy" that would have more suited the lesser talents of a Jinx Falkenburg. Chorine Gloria Winters (Joan) has snared wealthy John Hubbard, but the latter's stuffy uncle-guardian, Wall Street broker Franchot Tone, vetoes the union sight unseen. Determined Joan wrangles a job in Tone's office as a switchboard operator. Before she has a chance to either devastate the stock market or convince Tone that she is the girl for Hubbard, she and Tone have fallen in love. Even with Eve Arden pretending to be Joan's crippled sister in one delightful moment, and Joan giving the staid Tone eye exercises to eliminate his need for spectacles, *She Knew All the Answers* was, at best, "lightly-textured romantic farce with unsophisticated material . . ."

Joan reteamed with Henry Fonda in a somber romantic drama, *Wild Geese Calling* (1941), which emerged more as a travelog of Oregon and Alaska than a penetrating tale of a young man (Fonda) with wanderlust who weds the ex-girlfriend (Joan) of a conniving gambler (Warren William). He nearly renounces the woman before he understands that this mother-to-be never was unfaithful to him once they met. One of the kinder reviewers of the mediocre picture was Wanda Hale (*New York Daily News*) who indulgently noted, "When called for, she is as tough as any dance hall girl who has to get along, provocative when needed and a tender, understanding wife when the occasion demands." Beyond the striking nature scenes, the film's virtues consisted of Ona Munson as Clarabella, the shopworn tart, and Barton MacLane as the "pirate" who loses his Klondike hotel in a card game with William.

Joan had smartly rejected a part in Hal Roach's *Topper Returns* (United Artists, 1941) because Joan Blondell's role as the ghostly Marion Kirby was too big in comparison,* but Joan did accept the picture *Confirm or*

*Carole Landis was given the assignment that had been offered to Joan.

Deny (Twentieth Century-Fox, 1941),* opposite Don Ameche. Once again Joan was cast as a British girl, but this time as a respectable miss, one who works as a teletype operator for the Ministry of Information. One day in September 1940, during a blackout, she encounters American newspaperman Ameche, an enterprising cigarette-puffing foreign correspondent who persuades her to work for him in his London office. It was nice to see Ameche away from the stuffy roles of his past musical-biography ventures, but the Archie Mayo-directed blarney was nothing more than "a curious blend of history and commonplace fiction, the credible and the incredible" (*Brooklyn Daily Eagle*). In a rather bland assignment, Joan was reviewed more for her look-alike appearance than for her competent but uninspired performance. Wanda Hale of the *New York News* noted that she looked "more like an ethereal Ruth Hussey than an earthy Hedy Lamarr."

Like the less versatile but equally glamorous and long-enduring screen star Loretta Young, Joan found most of the early 1940s a period of professionally treading water. She performed yet again for producer Edward Small in the tinny rehash of the evergreen farce *Twin Beds* (United Artists, 1942),† in which she and oncamera spouse George Brent have the veritable limelight stolen from them by hard-working comedian Mischa Auer.

Hollywood and the world-at-large were generally offended by Ernst Lubitsch's black comedy *To Be or Not to Be* (United Artists, 1942), but that venture had the redeeming values of his best style and the solid performances of Carole Lombard and Jack Benny. The same could not be said of Columbia's *The Wife Takes a Flyer* (1942). "Kicks in the pants, belching, and exaggerated face-making are lifted from burlesque to decorate this feeble attempt" (*New York Post*). Others labeled the feeble plot as, "the height of insipidity and bad taste" (*New York World-Telegram*). Allied pilot Franchot Tone is downed in occupied Holland and is secreted in Joan's plush household. It seems that her husband (Lloyd Corrigan) is temporarily committed to an insane asylum, and Tone providentially takes his place at the hearthside. Later Joan divorces her "insane" "husband" (Corrigan), and she becomes manageress of a retired ladies' home. Meantime, Major Zellfritz (Allyn Joslyn), the Axis officer boarding in her homestead, wants to pursue a romance with Joan, leading to a finale in which Joan, Tone, and a countess (Cecil Cunningham) make a timely escape, via a stolen German plane, to England.

Joan wrapped up her streak of screen silliness with *Girl Trouble* (Twentieth Century-Fox, 1942). It teamed her yet again with Don Ameche, he as a South American (without much of an accent) in quest of a U.S. loan for a rubber plantation and finding love with Joan, who rents him her

---

* Archie Mayo replaced the uncredited Fritz Lang on this project.
† Previously filmed in 1920 and 1929 by First National.

apartment while posing as her own maid. "[It's] less than silly; it's plain stupid," was the verdict of Wanda Hale (*New York Daily News*) on this stale comedy, in which the gags were flat, the situations labored, and the performances perfunctory. Typical of the funnier moments was when flighty Billie Burke, a student of first aid, applies a tourniquet to a patient's throat to stop a bloody nose.

Meanwhile, on the homefront in 1942, Joan, along with Constance, who was then wed to Gilbert Roland, joined Hollywood's efforts to end World War II. She wore a jaunty uniform as a member of the American Women's Volunteer Service and was head of a group providing recreation to servicemen. She participated in a reception committee to greet visiting Madame Chiang Kai-shek at the Hollywood Bowl and then boarded a train on a six-week nationwide war-bond-selling trek as part of the Hollywood Caravan.

Offcamera, Joan was the authoress of *How to Be Attractive*, published by Alfred A. Knopf in 1943. Her sole film venture of the season was *Margin for Error* (Twentieth Century-Fox, 1943). Back in 1939, Clare Boothe's comedy had enjoyed a 264-performance run, but four years later, its subject matter was a bit stale. (The premise was based on New York Mayor La Guardia's political tour de force in 1938 when he named an all-Jewish police detail to guard the Manhattan Nazi consulate.) As directed by bombastic Otto Preminger, who starred in the film as the dictatorial, sinister consul,* *Margin for Error* was heavy-handed, and gave little opportunity for showcasing the comedic talents of Milton Berle as the Jewish cop who attempts to solve the VIP homicide. This caper was further complicated by the fact that the hated Nazi was poisoned, stabbed, and shot—in that order. Joan played the "wife" of the deceased villain.† She had remained with her odious spouse only because her father was in a German concentration camp. In reality, she loves Carl Esmond, Preminger's diplomatic secretary, who knows his boss has gambled with the $1 million sent him by Berlin for sabotage and propaganda in America. The film was hardly the important cinematic event anticipated by Darryl F. Zanuck's Fox studio.

Joan's screen work, along with her war efforts, halted in 1943 when, learning she was pregnant for the third time, she retired to her Holmby Hills home. On Mother's Day of that year, a fire started in the basement of the house, caused by improper wiring in the hot water furnace. Joan was the first to detect smoke and alerted other members of the household, none of whom would believe her until the flames became obvious. Everyone escaped without injury, but much of the house was damaged by smoke, water, and the firemen's axes. Because of the wartime short-

---

*Repeating his dual chores from the Broadway version.
† Her role was enacted on Broadway by Elspeth Eric.

age of construction materials, it took a year before the damaged house could be restored.

On June 26, 1943, Stephanie Wanger was born. "Walter always said he really didn't want children of his own, but he was the proudest of fathers."

Joan chose a winner in which to resume her career in 1944: *The Woman in the Window* (RKO). Written and produced by Nunnally Johnson for the newly organized International Pictures, and directed by Fritz Lang, it was, a don't-tell-your-friends-how-it-ends film. *Newsweek* magazine called it "a psychological chiller with a difference," noting that "the accumulative suspense is almost too much for normal body temperature." Despite the trick ending, which the studio realized was a shortcoming but, thereafter, tried to capitalize on, *The Woman in the Window* is a humdinger of a thriller, sizzling with misguided passion and wrongdoers running amuck. Edward G. Robinson was at his most effective as an associate professor of psychology at New York's City College who becomes embroiled in a hot and heavy romance with a beautiful artist's model (Joan), causing him to forget his family and to commit murder and endure blackmail from the deceased man's slimy bodyguard (Dan Duryea). As Lang said of the film, "This is a universal story. I mean by that, it is a story that could happen to anyone. Any man could find himself in this same situation. . . . Any story that is universal has a certain social significance." Critics and public alike, who had come to take Joan's screen presence for granted, were again shaken out of their easygoing rut by *The Woman in the Window*. It firmly demonstrated that thirty-four-year-old Joan had a few more cinematic acting tricks up her sleeve, and that her increasingly alluring curvaceous figure was not her only silver-screen asset.

Joan, Wanger, and Lang, inspired by the popularity of *The Woman in the Window*, formed Diana Productions, an independent company with distribution through Universal Studios.

Before Diana Productions got under way, Joan was used in *Nob Hill* (Twentieth Century-Fox, 1945)*, her fourth and final screen venture to date with George Raft. Originally the picture had been slated for Fred MacMurray and Lynn Bari, but since the focal points of the Barbary Coast color yarn were Vivian Blaine (as the heart-of-gold chirper) and Peggy Ann Garner (as the Irish immigrant come to find her bartender uncle, now deceased), it made little difference to director Henry Hathaway that his nominal leads were Raft and Joan. Between Blaine's several renditions of "I Don't Care" and other new and old songs, and the Margaret O'Brien-like aping of Garner, there was little occasion for Raft and

---

*A reworking of Fox's *Hello, Frisco, Hello* (1943) and the earlier, modern-dress *King of Burlesque* (Twentieth Century-Fox, 1935), both of which starred Alice Faye.

Joan to shine. Raft played the pride of the gambling casino who nearly forsakes loyal Blaine for upper-crust Joan of (S)Nob Hill. One of the film's few bright spots occurs when a very discouraged, two-timed Blaine has a confrontation with uppity Joan, and the two come to blows, vividly providing the viewer with their contrasting attachments to the mercurial male.

Scarlet Street (Universal, 1946), a remake of Jean Renoir's *La Chienne* (*The Bitch*) (1931), was the initial offering of Diana Productions. Joan was professionally reunited with Edward G. Robinson (as a henpecked married cashier) and Dan Duryea (as a pimp with a zoot suit). Joan is a woman of the streets* who gladly accepts Robinson's gifts—money he has embezzled from the company—to support her beloved Duryea in a style befitting his alleged elegance. Ungrateful Duryea may slap her in the face, which she does not mind, but Robinson's naive generosity irks her. When he volunteers to wed her, she cruelly laughs in his face. The violent, unrelenting drama, in which Robinson eventually stabs Joan to death with an ice pick and then loses his mind when Duryea is sent to the electric chair for a crime he did not commit, ran afoul of state censorship boards throughout the country. Eventually, after minor cuts here and there, a revamped release print was shown throughout America, and garnered more than $2.5 million in distributors' domestic rentals. Despite its initial profits, it is *The Woman in the Window* and not the very similar *Scarlet Street* which remains etched in viewers' memories. Bosley Crowther (*New York Times*) was prophetic when he judged the film "painfully moral . . . and, in the light of modern candor, rather tame."

Colonel Effingham's Raid (Twentieth Century-Fox, 1946) was a modest programmer held up in production release by the overload of more timely wartime dramas on the studio's completion shelf. Joan was at best decorative in the passive comedy built around Charles Coburn as retired southern colonel W. Seaborn Effingham, who militarily tries to straighten out a Georgia town of 1940 that is overwhelmed by corrupt forces. Joan was cast as the society-reporter daughter of the late editor of the Fredericksville newspaper, who appears now and again in the storyline to ask, "Isn't there anybody around here that'll stand up for what he [i.e., Coburn] thinks?" For romantic interest there was William Eythe as a reporter on the rural newspaper who joins up to fight in the war. He is the one given the patriotic lines to voice, especially at the finale: "We won't be back maybe for the next election, but we'll be back one of these days. And we're going to have something to say about what goes on around here. Too many of us have sat back like scared rabbits. . . . But maybe when we get this job done we won't scare so easily." The same subject matter, without the zealously patriotic overtones, had been han-

---

*Played by Jany Mareze in Renoir's French original.

dled much more effectively in James Cagney's *Johnny Come Lately* (United Artists, 1943).

Ernest Hemingway's literary output has generally been short-shrifted on the screen. The adaptation of his "The Short, Happy Life of Francis Macomber" was no exception, with a compromise picturization, entitled *The Macomber Affair* (United Artists, 1947). "It hints at the heated emotional conflicts, but it never brings them to a boil" (Otis L. Guernsey, Jr., *New York Herald-Tribune*). The problem lay in Zoltan Korda's too polite directorial touches, and the ending which opted for a "The Lady or the Tiger" ambiguity. In this Hemingway bastardization, American millionaire Robert Preston is displayed as a lifelong coward and weakling, facets of his personality which become all too apparent on an African big game hunt, in which he is joined by his egocentric wife (Joan) and an aloof British guide (Gregory Peck). When Preston runs away, frightened of a wounded lion on the veldt, Joan seizes on the incident as a fitting excuse to turn her loyalties and romantic interest openly towards Peck. Later, at the crucial moment, the heavy-drinking, brutal Preston unleashes a newfound manliness by downing a rampaging lion. However, at this instant of truth, Joan shoots Preston in the back of the head, with a misguided bullet ostensibly intended to eliminate the attacking beast. A tacked-on Hollywood finale to the film has the manslaughter case being aired in an African court, with the obvious implication that Joan will be cleared of the criminal charge and that she and Peck will sanctify their sexual relationship with marriage.

A goodly portion of *The Macomber Affair* was lensed in Africa and Mexico, which provided the feature with an authentic outdoors ambience, more than was evident in the generally overheated, steamy pseudodramatics. Unlike her earlier oncamera predatory females in *The Woman in the Window* or even *Scarlet Street*, Joan's Margaret Macomber is a socially affluent person, robbing her femme fatale characterization of much audience sympathy. Most viewers have at least a modicum of compassion for a self-made proletarian tart. Nevertheless, there were those who highly approved of Joan's unsubtle performance here.* Unknown to Joan or to her fans, *The Macomber Affair* was to be the apex of her screen career as a leading lady.

Woman on the Beach (RKO, 1947) gave little indication of the fine craftsmanship usually associated with director Jean Renoir, the filmmaker who was completing his Hollywood sojourn with this entry. Granted, a good one-third of the feature is supposed to have been chopped out after a disastrous preview in Santa Barbara, California, but what remains is

---

*Bosley Crowther (*New York Times*) observed, "Joan Bennett is completely hydrochloric as the peevish, deceitful dame, showing in every glance and gesture her corrosive concern for herself."

not solid drama in the acceptable sense. The film continually hints at dark, disturbed passion, but only fitfully comes alive. Within the story, Robert Ryan, a mentally ailing young coastguardsman, comes across Joan one day on the beach. She is married to Charles Bickford, once an artist of distinction but since his blindness (acquired in a drunken brawl with destructive Joan), a bitter, old recluse given over to oblique philosophizing. It is not long before Ryan, engaged to cautious, nice Nan Leslie, is making love to wanton Joan in a sinister-looking seaside wreck. Rather than being upset by this infidelity, bizarre Bickford is anxious to have the new relationship described to him in all its ramifications. Only slowly does it dawn on the distressed Ryan that Joan is a tramp, not a lady in distress, that she is being held by Bickford in a sadistic relationship, and that he (Ryan) is being exploited for nefarious reasons. Within the butchered, disjointed, seventy-one-minute narrative, there is the anticlimactic scene of Ryan leading Bickford to a cliffside abyss, hoping to prove to himself whether the man is really blind after all, and a conflagration in which Bickford's art works go up in flames.

Despite the questionable merits of any facet of *The Woman on the Beach,* Joan emerged from the proceedings almost unscathed by the critics. *Time* magazine graciously described her as "sullen-faced Joan Bennett, one of Hollywood's most efficient players of loose women," while A. Weiler of the *New York Times* said she had added "another competent portrait of a sullen and seductive dame to an ever-growing gallery."

Diana Productions' second and last film was released in January 1948 by Universal. *Secret beyond the Door* offered Britisher Michael Redgrave as Joan's murderous nemesis. She is the heiress, itchy for romance, who takes a Mexican fling and encounters charming, offbeat Redgrave. Not long after meeting her he tells her, "There's something in your face that I saw once . . . in South Dakota. Wheat country. Cyclone weather, it was." After a whirlwind courtship, the couple wed. Suddenly he becomes moody, especially after they establish themselves in his gloomy old family mansion. Quickly thereafter she discovers that her mate has a morbid fixation on death, even to the extent of having a bizarre collection of rooms in which the settings of famous murders are recreated. One locked room, she perceives, may be an untagged death chamber for her. But she is a resolute lady and is determined to see this marital crisis through to the end. Challenging her wits are a surly son from Redgrave's first marriage, a collection of closemouthed characters, and mysteriously placed lilacs. The unmotivated about-face finale did nothing to restore audience confidence in the tale.

It was quite intentional that director Fritz Lang made *Secret beyond the Door* very much in the tradition of Alfred Hitchcock's *Rebecca* (United Artists, 1940). However, "this is a dog wagon *Rebecca* with a seasoning of psychiatrics added to give it an up-to-date flavor" (Otis L. Guernsey, Jr.,

New York Herald-Tribune). This unsuccessful venture was the fourth and final association of Lang and Joan. The director would later recollect: "It wasn't my idea to make it—Wanger had some old scripts and it was jinxed from the beginning—trouble with cameramen, trouble with script. . . . I had an idea that the subconscious voice—when we hear Joan Bennett's thoughts—should be spoken by another actress. Because it *was* a different person—something in us we perhaps don't know. But Joan told me she would be *very* unhappy if I did that, so I dropped it."

Joan has different memories of *Secret beyond the Door*. For a sequence in a burning house (another copy from *Rebecca*), director Lang refused to employ doubles, and Joan and Redgrave were forced to run through flames "time and again, and it wasn't a fire for toasting marshmallows." Joan revealed that Lang "was a real Jekyll-and-Hyde character, calm and purposeful one moment, and off on a tirade the next." She further confided, "When he was in a successful period, he was impossible and Darryl Zanuck told me, 'Let him have one good resounding flop and he'll be adorable.' He got it in *Secret beyond the Door*. It flopped and Fritz was adorable at once." By this time, however, Joan was pregnant again, and Diana Productions ended on a somewhat ambivalent, but amicable, note.

Joan's fourth daughter, Shelley Wanger, was born by Caesarian section on July 4, 1948, weighing six pounds, four ounces.

Soon after, Joan was seen in Eagle-Lion's *Hollow Triumph* (1948), a picture also known as *The Scar*. It was actor Paul Henreid's first venture as a producer, a consuming task for a performer who was required to play a dual role oncamera. In the course of the eighty-three-minute black-and-white feature, Henreid plays debonair tricks with the lighting of cigarettes (a leftover stunt from his *Now, Voyager* [Warner Bros., 1942]). As he hands her one of the many lit cigarettes during the picture, he says romantically, "I'll remember you. I think I'll always take the trouble."

Garbed in a "special" wardrobe by Kay Nelson, Joan's lines in this Daniel Fuchs screenplay are often flip—"How a working girl hates Sundays" and "I'm sick of being wise. I'm tired of knowing all the answers."

As a whole, however, the film is engrossing. Henreid is a fugitive from the law who kills his look-alike, a psychoanalyst, and assumes his identity. Joan, as the doctor's secretary, is aware of the setup but loves the imposter. The surprise finale finds the carbon-copy Henreid paying the supreme penalty for the original's gambling sins. Despite the movie being "larded with bad dialogue, awkward dramatic cliches and poor direction" (*Cue* magazine), Joan received a few kind notices, with Thomas Pryor (*New York Times*), among others, thanking her "for helping out in the clinches."

While Joan's oncamera career was slowly seeping down the drain, her husband, Walter Wanger, was experiencing many financial reverses. Wanger went heavily into debt in order to finance the Ingrid Bergman color production of *Joan of Arc* (RKO, 1948), a 150-minute picturization of Maxwell Anderson's play, *Joan of Lorraine*, directed by Victor Fleming. A good deal of the epic's box-office failure could be justly blamed on the notorious romance between the actress and Italian director Roberto Rossellini. The additional fact that the costly feature was stagey and ponderous did not help matters with the critics or the public. From *Joan of Arc* onward, Wanger encountered tremendous difficulties in obtaining adequate financial backing for further film ventures, and the family went to Rome where they stayed for several months. Wanger had hopes of coaxing Greta Garbo to make a cinema comeback, but when that failed, they returned to Holmby Hills.

In July 1949, Joan became a grandmother at the age of thirty-nine, when her married daughter, Ditty, gave birth to her first child. Joan received a telegram from Hollywood's established glamorous grandmother, Marlene Dietrich, which read, "Thanks for taking the heat off."

The Reckless Moment (Columbia, 1949) was Joan's sole release of that year. Expertly directed by Max Ophuls, the setting is a spic-and-span little coastal town in California. The serenity of housewife Joan's commonplace life is suddenly shattered when her rebellious daughter (Geraldine Brooks) has sexual relations with the town libertine, who accidentally falls to his death. A blackmailer (James Mason) appears on the scene amidst the housewife's attempt to cover up her daughter's involvement with the death. The picture, which has a growing legion of admirers,* never clicked with the public.

Anxious to maintain her career in a declining motion-picture market in which the emphasis was on youth, Joan wisely moved into mother roles with *Father of the Bride* (MGM, 1950), a comedy sleeper directed by Vincente Minnelli and starring her co-lead of nearly two decades before, Spencer Tracy. The delightfully conceived picture was based on the Edward Streeter novel, and told, from the father's point of view, the "outrages" he suffers when his capricious daughter (Elizabeth Taylor) suddenly announces at midnight one night that she is going to wed Don Taylor. " . . . it packs all the satire of our modern tribal matrimonial rite that was richly contained in the original, also possesses all the warmth and poignancy and understanding that makes the Streeter treatise much beloved" (Bosley Crowther, *New York Times*).

*In *Hollywood in the Forties* (1968) Charles Higham and Joel Greenberg write that "the direction at every stage raises the level of the material, and the growing involvement of the nervous woman and the blackmailer is treated with great sympathy and understanding."

On the other hand, co-star James Mason would recall, "Walter Wanger was a man who always wanted to be European. He didn't know how to be European but he wanted to be European so this was rather the kind of film—I suppose, like *Brief Encounter*—that he was trying to make, but it wasn't very good. It was just a magazine story, not very well written. And also he was making films for his wife, Joan Bennett."

Oncamera, Joan functions as Tracy's wife and the go-between for her befuddled onscreen husband and dreamy daughter (Elizabeth Taylor). During the filming there were many marvelous moments that the moviegoer would never have a chance to witness. One day during the shooting, gossip columnist Hedda Hopper visited the set to interview Taylor. Hopper found Joan involved in a close-up scene and noted that the time was 6:30 p.m. Hedda had never forgiven the Wangers for what she considered a grave professional injustice during the filming of *Vogues of 1938* when she played Joan's dowager mother and was faced with a telling close-up late one day. She requested that Wanger allow her to take the shot the next morning when she felt more relaxed, but Wanger insisted that she perform then and there. In her syndicated column, the day after her visit to the *Father of the Bride* set, Hedda cattily wrote, "At last Miss Bennett knows how it feels to get her close-up at the end of the day and not at the beginning."

On Valentine's Day, 1950, Joan bought two full-paged advertisements, encircled by a heart, in Hollywood's daily trade papers. On one side of the ad was an excerpt from Hedda's column in which she had taken a gibe at Joan Fontaine. On the other was an excerpt from a column by Harry Crocker, a Hearst writer and frequent escort of Fontaine, which stated, "Hollywood realizes that ridiculous outbreaks are the result of her years of frustration as a jobless actress." Joan Bennett's name was signed beneath the words, "This *couldn't* be you, could it, Hedda?" Later that same day, Joan had a live, deodorized skunk delivered to Hedda's home as she said, "I've had enough of her lip." Hedda smilingly told a newsman, "I didn't think the Wangers could afford the ad—I'm completely surprised, but completely amused." Hedda christened the skunk "Joan" before giving it to the James Masons, who had been looking for one as a companion to their nine cats.

When Gene Tierney's incipient nervous breakdown forced her to bow out of Twentieth Century-Fox's *For Heaven's Sake* (1950), Producer William Perlberg cast Joan as the selfish stage actress wed to producer-director Robert Cummings. Arch Clifton Webb was the acerbic angel who materializes to help Gigi Perreau finally get born to the overly busy couple. Joan's Lydia says, "I've been waiting for only one thing—a vacation," but instead she comes under the diligent angel's spell and realizes, vaguely at first, that she wants more than fame and a vacation. The Charles LeMaire-designed gowns were a great asset to Joan's oncamera presence.

By January 1951, Wanger was close to involuntary bankruptcy, a situation forced on him by the California bank which had backed *Joan of Arc*. Joan's agent, Jennings Lang, aware that the Wangers were dangerously short of funds, sent Joan to New York to discuss a possible television series, which would be produced from Manhattan. Wanger objected to the separation and Joan returned home to California, but when Lang then suggested a video series for her to be shot in Hollywood, Wanger again objected because he considered it "a challenge to his position as head of the household." Several times Wanger threatened Joan, "If you see any more of Jennings, I'll kill him." When Wanger, desperate for industry work, was forced to take a job with poverty-row Monogram, Joan said, "the damage to his ego and pride was enormous."

In March 1951, Joan did her first television show in New York. On a variety program, NBC's "Show of Shows," she and Pat O'Brien were teamed. "So help me," she says, "we sang a song about a beanbag. It was not a particularly shining hour."

Magazine advertisements began appearing about that time proclaiming, "Happily, MGM announces a joyous new arrival, the blessed event of 1951, *Father's Little Dividend*." In this, the admirable sequel to *Father of the Bride*, Joan, Tracy, and Elizabeth Taylor repeated their key roles, as did Don Taylor, Billie Burke, and Moroni Olsen. *Variety* reported the film as number ten at the 1951 box office with distributors' domestic rentals of $3.1 million. Joan was credited as being a strong supporting asset as the "charmingly eccentric wife" (*New York Times*).

In the summer of 1951, Joan starred as Susan in the Westport, Connecticut, stock production of *Susan and God*, with her daughter Melinda in a featured role. "It was great fun for us to work together and to find Joan Bennett and Melinda Markey on the same playbill."

What was to be Joan's last big screen performance in two and a half years was *The Guy Who Came Back* (Twentieth Century-Fox, 1951), a rather pedestrian comedy in which wife and mother Joan almost loses her ex-football-player husband (Paul Douglas) to vamping Linda Darnell. Stocky ex-sports-announcer Douglas was the picture's focal point, but "sadly enough, one is only mildly intrigued, not entranced, by his case history" (A. Weiler, *New York Times*).

On December 13, 1951, Joan drove to the Beverly Hills office of her agent, Jennings Lang, and picked him up for a scheduled business luncheon. Afterwards, with Lang driving, they returned to the parking lot next to his office building across the street from the city hall and the police station. Lang got out of the car to escort Joan around to the driver's seat. Standing a few feet away was Wanger with a gun poised in his hand. Lang said, "Don't be silly, Walter, don't. . . . " But Wanger shot twice. The first bullet smashed into the car's tail fin, the second ricocheted off the pavement and hit Lang in the groin. He fell to the ground. A parking lot attendant drove Lang and Joan to the office of a doctor nearby, who, in turn, sent them to Midway Hospital in Los Angeles where an emergency operation was performed.

Wanger was escorted to the police station, where he calmly informed the arresting officers, "I've just shot the son-of-a-bitch who tried to break up my home." But Joan insists, "What even Walter didn't realize was that he wasn't shooting at Jennings so much as he was shooting at the entire motion picture industry."

Lang's recovery was speedy, and a few days thereafter he forgave Wanger publicly. "I've represented Miss Bennett for many years as her agent and can only state that Walter Wanger misconstrued what was solely a business relationship. Since there are families and children concerned, I hope this whole regrettable incident can be forgotten as quickly as possible." On April 5, 1952, on the advice of his attorney, Jerry Geisler, Wanger waived a trial on a charge of assault with a deadly weapon. On June 4, he began a four-month prison sentence at the Wayside Honor Farm at Castaic, California, fifty miles from Los Angeles, where he worked as a librarian. Joan was comforted during this period by such friends as Gene Markey, James and Pamela Mason, and Humphrey Bogart and Lauren Bacall.

Because of the highly publicized shooting incident, Joan was professionally ostracized in Hollywood. Unable to obtain screen work—she was in her early forties, a tough time for any former cinema leading lady—she agreed to replace Rosalind Russell in the role of Gillian Holroyd in the national tour of *Bell, Book and Candle.* Her leading man was first Dennis Price and then later Zachary Scott. The tour lasted from April 1952 to March 13, 1953, when the show closed in Philadelphia.

Wanger served three months and nine days of his jail sentence. On his release on September 13, 1953, he told newsmen what he thought of the American penal system, "It's the nation's number one scandal! I want to do a film about it."*

Late in 1953, Joan obtained a job in a tawdry low-budget feature, *Highway Dragnet* (Allied Artists, 1954), with Richard Conte and Wanda Hendrix. It was a petty drama "strung on a plot that will not bear close inspection" (*Variety*). In it, she is Mrs. Cummings, a suspicious-acting motorist wearing a white dress and a pearl choker, who gives a ride to hitchhiker Conte on the lam from a false murder charge in Las Vegas.

The Wangers continued living together in the Holmby Hills house, but "from then on, our lives were separate, and we preserved the amenities only for the sake of the girls [Stephanie and Shelley]." In the spring of 1954, faced with financial shortages, Joan reluctantly sold her home to Mr. and Mrs. (Louise Fazenda) Hal Wallis. Actress Martha Hyer became mistress of the house when she married widower Wallis in 1966.

On CBS-TV's "The Best of Broadway" (October 13, 1954), Joan was one of the stars in the presentation of *The Man Who Came to Dinner.* The next year, Paramount readied a screen rendition of Albert Husson's play,

---

*He actually made two films, *Riot in Cell Block 11* (Allied Artists, 1954) and *I Want to Live!* (United Artists, 1958).

*La Cuisine de Anges.** The film's star, Humphrey Bogart, stubbornly informed the studio heads that he would have nothing to do with the production unless Joan played the feminine lead in the VistaVision production. Bogart appointed himself the champion of Joan's battle for Hollywood reinstatement. Paramount's brass relented, and Joan was cast as Amelie Ducotel,† charming wife of addled Leo G. Carroll, in the Michael Curtiz-directed picturization, which received a title change to *We're No Angels*. In the faltering screen comedy she is the wife and mother (of Gloria Talbott) who plays enforced hostess to three escapees (Bogart, Aldo Ray, Peter Ustinov) from Devil's Island, who turn into her family's good-luck charm, bringing about the demise of a hated relative (Basil Rathbone) and his equally odious nephew (John Baer).

In December 1955, it was announced that Joan would star for husband Wanger in *Mother-Sir*. Wanger was back in full producer's harness, albeit at low-crust Allied Artists, with the staunch support of several influential leaders. The film, retitled *Navy Wife*, arrived on the double-bill circuit in 1956, having been largely lensed in Sasebo, Japan, with Gary Merrill as Joan's officer husband. It is a modestly appealing tiny tale of Joan's attempts to Americanize Japanese wives during the military occupation.

Joan took third billing in *There's Always Tomorrow* (Universal, 1956), a remake of that studio's 1934 feature starring Frank Morgan, Lois Wilson (in Joan's part), and Binnie Barnes. The new edition of the soaper was directed by Douglas Sirk and co-starred Fred MacMurray as an unappreciated spouse-father. He almost loses his family (including wife Joan) when he innocently seeks solace from former girlfriend Barbara Stanwyck, now a successful, and single, businesswoman. Joan was not particularly effective as a cold, bossy, shrill wife, and was clearly outdistanced in this sordid silliness by efficient, brittle Stanwyck.

In September 1956, anxious to maintain her standing in the acting field and replenish her bank account, Joan embarked on a grueling eleven-month tour as Jessica‡ in the national touring company of the comedy *Janus*. She was given cast approval and chose Donald Cook for her leading man, a decision based on having seen him onstage in past slick performances. Both had forgotten their 1932 screen work together in *The Trial of Vivienne Ware*, but Joan said, "No such memory lapse about Donald Cook would ever occur again."

With the conclusion of the *Janus* tour on March 16, 1957, Joan moved to

---

*The Bella and Sam Spewack translation of the play, *My Three Angels*—not credited in the screen version—had a 344-performance run after opening on Broadway at the Morosco Theatre on March 11, 1953.

† Played by Dorothy Adams on Broadway.

‡ Played successively on Broadway by Margaret Sullavan, Claudette Colbert, and Imogene Coca.

New York City, where most of her theatrical employment now centered. A year later, she prepared for a play that was destined, hopefully, to reach Broadway. Again Donald Cook was her co-star. John G. Fuller's *Love Me Little*, directed by Alfred Drake, did adequately on the road, but lasted a mere eight performances after its April 14, 1958 opening at Broadway's Helen Hayes Theatre. Youngish Susan Kohner, as the daughter who decides to learn about sex on a first-hand basis, received most of the kinder notices, but Whitney Bolton (*New York Morning Telegraph*) had to admit that Joan "is deliciously right for the role of the mother, [she] has never been more beautiful and has a commanding air for off-side timed comedy."

Television guesting on "Playhouse 90," "Climax," "Junior Miss," and other shows occupied much of Joan's professional time in 1959, as well as an evening video series that lasted a mere six weeks—"Too Young to Go Steady" with Donald Cook. In November 1959, she and Cook toured in *The Pleasure of His Company*, which finished in Chicago on May 28, 1960. Joan was quietly efficient as the charming mother of the household, a part played by Cornelia Otis Skinner in the Broadway original and by Lilli Palmer in the 1961 Paramount picturization.

Stephanie Wanger accompanied her mother to Baton Rouge, Louisiana, in the summer of 1960 while Joan acted the smallish part of the wife and mother who acts oddly in *Desire in the Dust* (Twentieth Century-Fox, 1960). The William F. Claxton-produced and directed feature was intended to be in the tradition of the studio's highly popular *The Long, Hot Summer* (1958), and "until it gets tangled up in its own Spanish moss, . . . [it] is an interesting little picture to watch" (Howard Thompson, *New York Times*). This time it was Martha Hyer*, not Joan, who was the lusty femme fatale dominating the action and the menfolk around her in an "essentially pointless tale of greed and lust in the backwaters of the present-day South" (*Variety*). Joan had little opportunity to shine as the deranged wife of Raymond "Perry Mason" Burr, and the excellent camerawork of Lucien Ballard could not compensate for the ludicrous plot manipulations facing the viewer onscreen.

When Joan's long-standing stage leading man, Donald Cook, died suddenly in 1961, she found a new vis-à-vis in John Emery, a friend of Cook's and the ex-spouse of both Tallulah Bankhead and actress-dancer Tamara Geva. They appeared together at Chicago's Drury Lane Theatre in *The Reluctant Debutante*, a part performed on Broadway by Adrianne Allen and in the MGM film of 1958 by Kay Kendall. In mid-1963, she re-

*Hyer recollects Joan as "a lovely lady possessed of dignity, charm and humor. One of the things I admired most about her was her professionalism. She always came to the set completely prepared—listened to the director—knew what she wanted to do in a scene, and did' it. There was no phoniness, no insecurity-covering temper tantrums or unreasonable demands or delays. She was warm and friendly with the cast and crew, but had just the right amount of reserve and mystery that a star should have."

ceived an offer to star as Edith Lambert* in *Never Too Late* at the Cocoanut Grove Playhouse in Miami for a two-week run. The show, if successful, was then to be booked to play London. On September 28, 1963, with Fred Clark as her co-star, she opened at the Prince of Wales Theatre in London for a 191-performance run.

In 1965, two years after his ill-fated, mammothly expensive fiasco *Cleopatra* (Twentieth Century-Fox, 1963) nearly closed the studio, Joan quietly obtained a Mexican divorce from Wanger.

That year, on July 26, while in a summer-stock production of *Never Too Late* in Philadelphia, Joan learned by telephone that Constance Bennett had died of a cerebral hemorrhage. "Since I knew Constance would expect it of me," Joan wrote, "I finished the show that night, then flew to Laconia, New Hampshire for the opening the following evening." Joan then planed to Washington, D.C., in time to attend her sister's funeral at Arlington National Cemetery on July 28, and then returned to Laconia in a private plane, in time for the evening show.

On June 27, 1966, Joan began what was initially supposed to be a couple of shows per week in ABC-TV's daytime soap opera series, "Dark Shadows." The Gothic-thriller chapterplay almost immediately attained enormous popularity and, before Joan quite realized it, her part was soon extended to five shows a week with the actress on the studio's stages from 8:11 A.M. to 6:30 P.M. most days. The series, set in the Victorian era, was eerie and loaded with sinister happenings in which almost daily someone was killed off or transported via "parallel time" to some other century. Joan was Elizabeth, the housekeeper. The series was on the air for five years. For several months, while performing in what became an odious oncamera duty, Joan served as consulting editor for *Girl Talk* magazine, providing a column called "Equal Time." In one of the columns, which she entitled, "From My Side of the TV Camera," she wrote: "I don't think I need tell you that television is my least favorite of the performing arts. Television—art? If *this* is regarded as *art*, I confess I do not know the meaning of the word." In the first of the two features based on "Dark Shadows," entitled *House of Dark Shadows* (MGM, 1970), lensed in Tarrytown, New York, at a cost of $750,000, Joan recreated her video part. Despite the low caliber of the screen fare, it earned over $2.1 million in distributors' domestic rentals.

With sisters Constance and Barbara and ex-husband Walter Wanger dead,† and her children grown up, Joan felt it safe and fair to write *The Bennett Playbill*, published in 1970 by Holt, Rinehart and Winston. A frank history of the illustrious Bennett acting clan, Joan honestly admits

---

*Played on Broadway in 1962 and in the 1965 Warner Bros. film by Maureen O'Sullivan.

†He died of a heart attack on November 18, 1968, at his East Fifty-seventh Street, Manhattan, apartment. He was seventy-four years old. The man, whose movie budgets often ran to multifigures, left an estate of between $10,000 and $20,000, most of which was designated for his and Joan's daughter, Shelley.

that "Lois Kibbee [daughter of Milton Kibbee] did all the dirty work, all the research. I never would have been able to do it." Charles Higham, reviewing the book in the *New York Times*, wrote, "Joan Bennett's screen personality has always been marked by a sturdy determination, a sharpness and directness and unstinting drive; not surprising, then, that her family portrait should have precisely those qualities. It is a fascinating book."

When Joan was not involved with her Puritan Dress manufacturing deal (to produce a line of women's clothes called "Forever Young") she found time to guest star on television. On *Gidget Gets Married,* an ABC-TV telefeature (January 4, 1972), she was moderately noticeable as the wife of Don Ameche, he being the dominating head of an engineering firm. The following month, in another ABC-TV telefeature (*The Eyes of Charles Sand* [February 29, 1972]) Joan had an even smaller role in the ESP-style mystery, as Aunt Alexandria.

She was more ambitious in her stage assignments. At the Pheasant Run Playhouse in Chicago in the spring of 1973, she was scheduled for a month's run as the protective mama to Jay "Dennis the Menace" North in *Butterflies Are Free*, in the role played on stage and in the 1972 Columbia film by Eileen Heckart. Virginia Graham replaced Joan when she left the show to fulfill a prior agreement with Owens-Corning Fiberglass Corporation to travel across America selling the public on the idea of fiberglass household draperies.*

Then, in November 1973, Joan returned to picture-making when she joined Stuart Whitman in the cast of *Inn of the Damned*, filmed on location in Sydney, Australia. With a $375,000 budget, the widescreen-color feature is a colonial mystery set in 1896.

When asked not too long ago what she thought of contemporary Hollywood and filmmaking, the veteran star replied: "I'm glad that when I was in it, it was *then,* not now. They're an awfully funny group now—sort of beat. These filthy films; they're all over the place. It doesn't seem to be fun any more. The spirit has changed. I don't go to films now unless it's an Audrey Hepburn picture—glamorous, beautifully mounted. She and Cary Grant still represent the Golden Age. . . . The same thing goes for plays.

"Sam Goldwyn once made a wonderful remark. He said if you have a message, send for Western Union. He didn't like message plays. Neither do I. . . . I like to go to the theater and movies to see pretty people and pretty things. Most plays today are depressing, messagey."

---

*While conducting a slide presentation at Macy's California in San Francisco, she was asked by freelance photographer Jack Barnich if she would mind his taking pictures of her, one of which was to be included in *The Glamour Girls'* chapter on her. She put her hands to her face and laughed, "Oh! I hope they won't be before and after pictures."

Feature Film Appearances

THE VALLEY OF DECISION   (American-Mutual, 1915) 5 reels

Director, Rea Berger.

Richard Bennett (Arnold Gray); Adrienne Morrison (Jane Morton); Rhoda Lewis (Blanche Hanson); George Periolat (Dr. Brainard); Constance Bennett, Barbara Bennett, Joan Bennett (Unborn Souls); Blanche Bennett (Woman).

THE ETERNAL CITY   (Associated FN, 1923) 7,800'

Producer, Samuel Goldwyn; director, George Fitzmaurice; screenplay, Ouida Bergere; camera, Arthur Miller.

Barbara La Marr (Donna Roma); Bert Lytell (David Rossi); Lionel Barrymore (Baron Bonelli); Richard Bennett (Bruno); Montagu Love (Minghelli); Joan Bennett, Betty Bronson (Boy Pages).

POWER   (Pathé, 1928) 6,092'

Producer, Ralph Block; director, Howard Higgins; story-continuity, Tay Garnett; titles, John Krafft; art director, Mitchell Leisen; assistant director, Robert Fellows; camera, Peverell Marley; editor, Doane Harrison.

William Boyd (Husky); Alan Hale (Handsome); Jacqueline Logan (Lorraine La Rue); Jerry Drew (Menace); Joan Bennett, Carole Lombard, Pauline Curley (Dames).

BULLDOG DRUMMOND   (UA, 1929) 90 M.

Presenter, Samuel Goldwyn; producer-director, F. Richard Jones; based on the play by "Sapper" and Gerald Du Maurier; screenplay, Wallace Smith, Sidney Howard; continuity, Smith; dialog, Howard; art director, William Cameron Menzies; song, Jack Yellen and Harry Akst; assistant director, Paul Jones; associate director, A. Leslie Pearce; camera, George Barnes, Gregg Toland; editors, Viola Lawrence, Frank Lawrence.

Ronald Colman (Bulldog Drummond); Joan Bennett (Phyllis Benton); Lilyan Tashman (Erma Peterson); Montagu Love (Carl Peterson); Lawrence Grant (Dr. Lakington); Wilson Benge (Danny); Claud Allister (Algy Longworth); Adolph Milar (Marcovitch); Charles Sellon (John Travers); Tetsu Komai (Chong); Donald Novis (Singer); Gertrude Short (Barmaid); Tom Ricketts (Colonel).

THREE LIVE GHOSTS   (UA, 1929) 7,486'

Producer, Max Marcin; director, Thornton Freeland; based on the play by Frederic Stewart Isham, Marcin; story, Sally Winters; screenplay, Helen Hallett; adaptor, dialog, Marcin; camera, Robert H. Planck; editor, Robert Kern.

Beryl Mercer (Mrs. Gubbins); Hilda Vaughn (Peggy Woofers); Harry Stubbs (Bolton); Joan Bennett (Rose Gordon); Nancy Price (Alice); Charles McNaughton (Jimmie Gubbins); Robert Montgomery (William Foster); Claud Allister (Spoofy); Arthur Clayton (Paymaster); Tenen Holtz (Crockery Man); Shayle Gardner (Briggs); Jack Cooper (Benson); Jocelyn Lee (Lady Leicester).

DISRAELI (WB, 1929) 89 M.

Director, Alfred E. Green; based on the play by Louis Napoleon Parker; screenplay-dialog, Julien Josephson; titles, De Leon Anthony; music arranger, Louis Silver; camera, Lee Garmes; editor, Owen Marks.

George Arliss (Disraeli); Joan Bennett (Lady Clarissa Pevensey); Florence Arliss (Lady Mary Beaconfield); Anthony Bushell (Charles/Lord Deeford); David Torrence (Sir Michael/Lord Probert); Ivan Simpson (Hugh Meyers); Doris Lloyd (Mrs. Agatha Travers); Gwendolyn Logan (Duchess of Glastonbury); Charles E. Evans (Potter); Cosmo Kyrle Bellew (Mr. Terle); Jack Deery (Bascot); Michael Visaroff (Count Bosrinov); Norman Cannon (Foljambe); Henry Carvill (Duke of Glastonbury); Shayle Gardner (Dr. Williams); Powell York (Flookes); Margaret Mann (Queen Victoria); George Atkinson (Bit).

THE MISSISSIPPI GAMBLER (Univ., 1929) 5,432'

Presenter, Carl Laemmle; director, Reginald Barker; story, Karl Brown, Leonard Fields; screenplay, Edward T. Lowe, Jr., dialog, Winifred Reeve, H. H. Van Loan; titles, Dudley Early; song, L. Wolfe Gilbert and Harry Akst; sound, Joseph R. Lapis; camera, Gilbert Warrenton; editor, R. B. Wilcox.

Joseph Schildkraut (Jack Morgan); Joan Bennett (Lucy Blackburn); Carmelita Geraghty (Suzette Richards); Alec B. Francis (Junius Blackburn); Otis Harlan (Tiny Beardsley); William Welsh (Captain Weathers).

PUTTIN' ON THE RITZ (UA, 1930) 88 M.*

Presenter, Joseph M. Schenck; producer, John W. Considine, Jr.; director, Edward Sloman; screenplay, Considine, Jr.; dialog, William K. Wells; art directors, William Cameron Menzies, Park French; songs, Irving Berlin; Harry Richman, Jack Meskill, and Pete Wendling; choreography, Maurice L. Kusell; assistant director, Jack Mintz; costumes, Alice O'Neill; sound, Oscar Lagerstrom; camera, Ray June; editor, Hal Kern.

Harry Richman (Harry Raymond); Joan Bennett (Dolores Fenton); James Gleason (James Tierney); Aileen Pringle (Mrs. Teddy Van Renssler); Lilyan Tashman (Goldie DeVere); Purnell Pratt (George Barnes); Richard Tucker (Fenway Brooks); Eddie Kane (Bob Wagner); George Irving (Dr. Blair); Sidney Franklin (Schmidt); James Bradbury, Jr. (Subway Guard); Oscar Apfel (House Manager); Budd Fine (Heckler); Lee Phelps (Listener in Audience).

CRAZY THAT WAY (Fox, 1930) 64 M.

Presenter, William Fox; associate producer, George Middleton; director, Hamilton MacFadden; based on the play *In Love with Love* by Vincent Lawrence; screenplay-dialog, MacFadden, Marion Orth; art director, Duncan Cramer; assistant director, Sam Wurtzel; costumes, Sophie Wachner; sound, Alfred Bruzlin; camera, Joseph Valentine; editor, Ralph Dietrich.

Kenneth MacKenna (Jack Gardner); Joan Bennett (Ann Jordan); Regis

*Color sequence

Toomey (Robert Metcalf); Jason Robards (Frank Oakes); Sharon Lynn (Marion Sears); Lumsden Hare (Mr. Jordan); Baby Mack (Julia).

MOBY DICK (WB, 1930) 75 M.

Director, Lloyd Bacon; based on the novel by Herman Melville; screenplay, dialog, J. Grubb Alexander; sound, David Forrest; camera, Robert Kurrle.

John Barrymore (Captain Ahab); Joan Bennett (Faith); Lloyd Hughes (Derek); May Boley (Whale Oil Rosie); Walter Long (Stubbs); Tom O'Brien (Starbuck); Nigel De Brulier (Elijah); Noble Johnson (Queequeg); William Walling (Blacksmith); Virginia Sale (Old Maid); Jack Curtis (First Mate); John Ince (Reverend Mapple).

MAYBE IT'S LOVE (WB, 1930) 74 M.

Director, William Wellman; story, Mark Canfield; screenplay-dialog, Joseph Jackson; songs, Sidney Mitchell, Archie Gottler, and George W. Meyer; camera, Robert Kurrle; editor, Edward McDermott.

Joan Bennett (Nan Sheffield); Joe E. Brown (Speed Hanson); James Hall (Tommy Nelson); Laura Lee (Betty); Anders Randolf (Mr. Nelson); Sumner Getchell (Whiskers); George Irving (President Sheffield); George Bickel (Professor); Howard Jones (Coach Bob Brown); Bill Banker (Bill); Russell Saunders (Racehorse Russell); Tim Moynihan (Tim); W. K. Schoonover (Schoony); F. N. Sleight (Elmer); George Gibson (George); Ray Montgomery (Ray); Otto Pommerening (Otto); Kenneth Haycraft (Ken); Howard Harpster (Howard); Paul Scull (Paul); Stuart Erwin (Brown of Harvard); Tom Hanlon (Tony).

SCOTLAND YARD (Fox, 1930) 65 M.

Presenter, William Fox; associate producer, Ralph Block; director, William K. Howard; based on the play by Denison Clift; screenplay-dialog, Garrett Fort; art director, Duncan Cramer; technical director, Gerald L. G. Samson; assistant directors, R. L. Hough, Ray Flynn; costumes, Sophie Wachner; sound, Al Protzman; camera, George Schneiderman; editor, Jack Murray.

Edmund Lowe (Sir John Lasher/Dakin Barrolles); Joan Bennett (Xandra, Lady Lasher); Donald Crisp (Charles Fox); Georges Renavent (Dr. Paul Deon); Lumsden Hare (Sir Clive Heathecote); David Torrence (Captain Graves); Barbara Leonard (Nurse Cecilia); Halliwell Hobbes (Lord St. Arran).

DOCTORS' WIVES (Fox, 1931) 80 M.

Director, Frank Borzage; based on the novel by Sylva Lieferant, Henry Lieferant; screenplay, Maurine Watkins; camera, Arthur Edeson.

Warner Baxter (Dr. Jode Penning); Joan Bennett (Nina Wyndram); Victor Varconi (Dr. Kane Ruyter); Helene Millard (Vivian Crosby); Paul Porcasi (Dr. Calucci); Nancy Gardner (Julia Wyndram); John St. Polis (Dr. Mark Wyndram); Cecilia Loftus (Aunt Amelia); George Chandler (Dr. Roberts); Violet Dunn (Lou Roberts); Ruth Warren (Charlotte); Louise MacKintosh (Mrs. Kent); William Maddox (Rudie).

MANY A SLIP (Univ., 1931) 64 M.

Producer, Carl Laemmle, Jr.; associate producer, Albert De Mord; director, Vin Moore; stager, Anthony Brown; based on the play by Edith Fitzgerald, Robert

Riskin; screenplay, Gladys Lehman; art director, Wallace Koessler; sound, C. Roy Hunter; camera, Jerome Ash; editors, Maurice Pivar, Harry W. Lieb.

Joan Bennett (Pat Coster); Lew Ayres (Jerry Brooks); Slim Summerville (Hopkins); Ben Alexander (Ted Coster); Virginia Sale (Smitty); Roscoe Karns (Stan Price); Vivien Oakland (Emily Coster); J. C. Nugent (William Coster).

HUSH MONEY   (Fox, 1931) 68 M.

Director, Sidney Lanfield; story-screenplay, Philip Klein, Courtney Terrett; dialog, Dudley Nichols; camera, John Seitz.

Joan Bennett (Janet Gordon); Hardie Albright (Stuart Elliott); Owen Moore (Steve Pelton); Myrna Loy (Flo Curtis); C. Henry Gordon (Jack Curtis); Douglas Cosgrove (Dan Emmett); George Raft (Maxie); Hugh White (Puggie).

SHE WANTED A MILLIONAIRE   (Fox, 1932) 80 M.

Associate producer, John Considine, Jr.; director, John Blystone; story, Sonya Levien; screenplay, William Anthony McGuire; music director, George Lipschultz; dialog director, William Collier; sound, C. Clayton Ward; camera, John Seitz; editor, Ralph Dixon.

Joan Bennett (Jane Miller); Spencer Tracy (William Kelley); Una Merkel (Mary Taylor); James Kirkwood (Roger Norton); Dorothy Peterson (Mrs. Miller); Douglas Cosgrove (Mr. Miller); Donald Dillaway (Humphrey); and: Lucille LaVerne, Tetsu Komai.

CARELESS LADY   (Fox, 1932) 74 M.

Director, Kenneth MacKenna; story, Reita Lambert; screenplay, Guy Bolton; sound, Albert Protzman; camera, John Seitz; editor, Alex Troffey.

Joan Bennett (Sally Brown); John Boles (Stephen Illington); Minna Gombell (Yvette Logan); Weldon Heyburn (Judd Carey); Nora Lane (Ardis Delafield); Raul Roulien (Luis Pareda); Fortunio Bonanova (Rodriguez); John Arledge (Hank Oldfield); Josephine Hull (Aunt Cora); Martha Mattox (Aunt Della); Maude Turner Gordon (Mrs. Cartwright); J. M. Kerrigan (Trowbridge); William Palwey (Police Captain); Richard Tucker (Captain Gerard); James Todd (Peter Towne); Howard Phillips (Jack Merrett).

THE TRIAL OF VIVIENNE WARE   (Fox, 1932) 60 M.

Director, William K. Howard; based on the novel by Kenneth Ellis; screenplay, Philip Klein, Barry Conners; art director, Gordon Wiles; costumes, David Cox; song, Ralph Freed and James Hanley; sound, Albert Protzman; camera, Ernest Palmer; editor, Ralph Dietrich.

Joan Bennett (Vivienne Ware); Donald Cook (John Sutherland); Richard "Skeets" Gallagher (Graham McNally); ZaSu Pitts (Gladys Fairweather); Lilian Bond (Dolores Divine); Alan Dinehart (Prosecutor); Herbert Mundin (William Boggs); Howard Phillips (Joe Garson); Noel Madison (Angelo Parone); J. Maurice Sullivan (Judge Henderson); Eddie Dillon (William Hardy); Jameson Thomas (Damon Fenwick); Christian Rub (Axel); Bert Hanlon (Juror); Mary Gordon (Matron); Clarence Nordstrom (Cafe Singer); Edwin Maxwell (Detective); John Elliott (Police Captain); Bob Perry (Bailiff); Ethel Wales, Dale Fuller (Listeners); Tom London (Court Officer); Ward Bond (John's Assistant); Pat Somerset (Spectator); Pat O'Malley (Broadcast Sergeant); Phil Tead (Mac, the Reporter);

Fred Kelsey (Cop); Stanley Blystone (Cop who Kills Parone); Joe King (Bailiff); Chuck Hamilton (Court Officer).

WEEK-ENDS ONLY   (Fox, 1932) 65 M.

Director, Alan Crosland; based on the novel *Week-End Girl* by Warner Fabian; screenplay, William Conselman; dialog, Fabian; sound, Eugene Grossman; camera, Hal Mohr.

Joan Bennett (Venetia Carr); John Halliday (Arthur Ladden); Ben Lyon (Jack Williams); Halliwell Hobbes (Martin); Henry Armetta (Washroom Attendant); Berton Churchill (Mr. Carr); John Arledge (Ted); John Elliott (Bartender); Walter Byron (Mr. Brigg).

WILD GIRL   (Fox, 1932) 80 M.

Director, Raoul Walsh; based on the story "Salomy Jane's Kiss" by Bret Harte and the play by Paul Armstrong; screenplay, Doris Anderson, Edwin Justus Mayer; music director, Louis de Francesco; assistant directors, Horace Hough, George Walsh; sets, Joseph Wright; costumes, Earl Luick; camera, Norbert Brodine; editor, Jack Murray.

Charles Farrell (The Stranger); Joan Bennett (Salomy Jane Clay); Ralph Bellamy (Jack Marbury); Eugene Pallette (Yuba Bill); Irving Pichel (Rufe Waters); Mina Gombell (Millie); Sarah Padden (Lize); Willard Robertson (Red Pete); Ferdinand Munier (Colonel Starbottle); Louis Beavers (Mammy Lou); Morgan Wallace (Phineas Baldwin); James Durkin (Madison Clay); Murdock MacQuarrie (Jeff Larabee); Alphonz Ethier (Sheriff); Marilyn Harris (Anna May); Carmencita Johnson (Mary Ann); Delmar Watson (Willie); Will Stanton (Bartender); Mary Gordon (Washwoman); Stanley Blystone (Deputy); George Sowards (Hangman); Jack Padjan (Possyman); Iron Eyes Cody (Indian); Robert E. Homas (Gambling Kibitzer).

ME AND MY GAL   (Fox, 1932) 79 M.

Director, Raoul Walsh; story, Barry Connors, Philip Klein; screenplay, Arthur Kober; assistant director, Horace Hough; art director, Gordon Wiles; sound, George Leverett; camera, Arthur Miller.

Spencer Tracy (Dan Dolan); Joan Bennett (Helen Riley); Marion Burns (Kate Riley); George Walsh (Duke Castege); J. Farrell MacDonald (Pat "Pop" Riley); Noel Madison (Baby Face Castenega); Henry B. Walthall (Sergeant Collins); Bert Hanlon (Jake the Tailor); Adrian Morris (Detective Al Allen); George Chandler (Eddie Collins); Will Stanton (Drunken Fisherman); Frank Moran (Frank, a Dock Worker/Wedding Guest); Roger Imhof (Down and Outer); Pat Moriarity (Priest); James Marcus (Tugboat Captain Mike Ryan); Russ Powell (Burper); Billy Bevan (Ashley); Ralph Sipperly (English Drunk); Phil Tead (Radio Salesman); Heinie Conklin (Worker); Eleanor Wesselhoeft (Wife).

ARIZONA TO BROADWAY   (Fox, 1933) 67 M.

Director, James Tinling; story-screenplay, William Conselman, Henry Johnson; sound, E. Clayton Ward; editor, Louis Loeffler.

James Dunn (Smiley Wells); Joan Bennett (Lynn Martin); Herbert Mundin (Kingfish Miller); Sammy Cohen (Morris Blitz); Theodore Von Eltz (Wayne); Merna Kennedy (Flo); Earle Foxe (Sandburg); J. Carrol Naish (Tommy); Max Wagner (Pete); Walter Catlett (Ned Flynn); Jerry Lester (Jimmy Dante).

LITTLE WOMEN   (RKO, 1933) 107 M.

Executive producer, Merian C. Cooper; associate producer, Kenneth Macgowan; director, George Cukor; based on the novel by Louisa May Alcott; screenplay, Sarah Y. Mason, Victor Heerman; art director, Van Nest Polglase; set decorator, Hobe Erwin; music, Max Steiner; costumes, Walter Plunkett; makeup, Mel Burns; assistant director, Edward Killy; sound, Frank H. Harris; special effects, Harry Redmond; camera, Henry Gerrard; editor, Jack Kitchin.

Katharine Hepburn (Jo); Joan Bennett (Amy); Paul Lukas (Professor Bhaer); Edna May Oliver (Aunt March); Jean Parker (Beth); Frances Dee (Meg); Henry Stephenson (Mr. Laurence); Douglass Montgomery (Laurie); John Davis Lodge (Brooke); Spring Byington (Marmee); Samuel S. Hinds (Mr. March); Mabel Colcord (Hannah); Marion Ballou (Mrs. Kirke); Nydia Westman (Mamie); Harry Beresford (Doctor Bangs); Marina Schubert (Flo King); Dorothy Gray, June Filmer (Girls at Boarding House); Olin Howland (Mr. Davis).

THE PURSUIT OF HAPPINESS   (Para., 1934) 75 M.

Producer, Arthur Hornblow, Jr.; director, Alexander Hall; based on the play by Lawrence Langner and Armina Marshall; screenplay, Stephen Morehouse Avery, Jack Cunningham, J. P. McEvoy, Virginia Van Upp; camera, Karl Struss.

Francis Lederer (Max Christmann); Joan Bennett (Prudence Kirkland); Charlie Ruggles (Aaron Kirkland); Mary Boland (Comfort Kirkland); Walter Kingsford (Reverend Lyman Banks); Minor Watson (Colonel Sherwood); Adrian Morris (Thad Jennings); Barbara Barondess (Meg Mallory); Duke York (Jonathan); Burr Caruth (Reverend Myles); Jules Cowles (The Drunk); Irving Bacon (Bijah); Spencer Charters (Sam Evans); John Marston (Tall Conspirator); Edward Peil, Sr. (Peddler); Paul Kruger (Orderly); Georgie Billings (Little Boy); Ricca Allen (Boy's Mother); Holmes Herbert (General Sir Henry Clinton); Boyd Irwin (Lord Pitt); Henry Mowbray (King George III); Winter Hall (Max's Uncle); Bert Sprotte (Colonel Hoffer); Colin Tapley (Aide to Sir Henry Clinton); Reginald Pasch (Colonel Hoffer's Aide); Hans Von Morhart (Corporal);Baron Hesse (Coachman).

THE MAN WHO RECLAIMED HIS HEAD   (Univ., 1934) 81 M.

Presenter, Carl Laemmle; associate producer, Henry Henigson; director, Edward Ludwig; based on the play by Jean Bart; screenplay, Jean Bart, Samuel Ornitz; editor, Murray Seldeen.

Claude Rains (Paul Verin); Joan Bennett (Adele Verin); Lionel Atwill (Henri Dumont); Juanity Quigley (Linette Verin); Bessie Barriscale (Louise, the Verins' Maid); Henry O'Neil (Fernand DeMarney); Lawrence Grant (Marchand); William B. Davidson (Charrus); G. P. Huntley, Jr. (Pierre); Valerie Hobson (Mimi, the Carnival Girl); Wallace Ford (Curly); Ferdinand Gottschalk (Baron); Hugh O'Connell (Danglas); Henry Armetta (Laurent); Doris Lloyd (Lulu); Noel Francis (Chon-Chon, Curly's Girl); Carol Coombe (Clerk); Phyllis Brooks (Secretary); Gilbert Emery (His Excellency); Walter Walker, Edward Martindel, Craufurd Kent, Montague Shaw (Dignitaries); Purnell Pratt, Jameson Thomas, Edward Van Sloan (Munitions Board Directors); Judith Wood (Margot); James Donlan (Man in Theatre Box); Rollo Lloyd (Jean, DeMarnay's Butler); Lloyd Hughes (Andre, a Secretary to Dumont); Bryant Washburn, Sr. (Antoine); Boyd Irwin (Petty Officer); Anderson Lawler (Jack); Will Stanton (Drunk Soldier); George Davis (Lorry Driver); Lionel Belmore (Train Conductor); Emerson Treacy (French Student/Attacked Pacifist); John Rutherford, Hyram A. Hoover, Lee Phelps (Soldiers); Rudy Cameron (Maitre D'Hotel); Norman Ainsley (A Steward); Russ Powell (Station Master); Harry Cording (French Mechanic); Lilyan Irene (Woman Shopper); William Ruhl (Shopper's Husband); Rolfe Sedan (Waiter); Ben F. Hendricks (Chauffeur); Maurice Murphy (Leon); William Gould (Man); Carl Stockdale (Tradesman); Tom Ricketts, Jose Swickard, William West, Colin Kenny (Citizens); Ted Billings (Newsboy); William Worthington (Attendant); Nell Craig, Grace Cunard (Women); Wilfred North (Bit); Russ Clark (French Truck Driver); John Ince (Speaker); Margaret Mann (Granny).

PRIVATE WORLDS   (Para., 1935) 84 M.

Producer, Walter Wanger; director, Gregory La Cava; based on the novel by Phyllis Bottome; screenplay, Lynn Starling; camera, Leon Shamroy; editor, Aubrey Scotto.

Claudette Colbert (Dr. Jane Everest); Charles Boyer (Dr. Charles Monet); Joan Bennett (Sally MacGregor); Joel McCrea (Dr. Alex MacGregor); Helen Vinson (Claire Monet); Esther Dale (Matron); Samuel Hinds (Dr. Arnold); Jean Rouverol (Carrie); Sam Godfrey (Tom Hirst); Dora Clement (Bertha Hirst); Theodore Von Eltz (Dr. Harding); Stanley Andrews (Dr. Barnes); Guinn "Big Boy" Williams (Jerry); Maurice Murphy (Boy in Car); Irving Bacon (Male Nurse); Nick Shaid (Arab Patient); Monte Vandergrift (Dawson); Arnold Gray (Clarkson); Julian Madison (Johnson); Harry Bradley (Johnson's Father); Eleanore King (Carrie's Nurse).

MISSISSIPPI   (Para., 1935) 80 M.

Producer, Arthur Hornblow, Jr.; director, A. Edward Sutherland; based on the play by Booth Tarkington; adaptors, Herbert Fields, Claude Binyon; screenplay, Francis Martin, Jack Cunningham; songs, Richard Rodgers and Lorenz Hart; art directors, Hans Dreier, Bernard Herzbrun; sound, Eugene Merritt; camera, Charles Lang; editor, Chandler House.

Bing Crosby (Tom Grayson); W. C. Fields (Commodore Jackson); Joan Bennett (Lucy Rumford); Queenie Smith (Alabam); Gail Patrick (Elvira Rumford); Claude Gillingwater (General Rumford); John Miljan (Major Patterson); Ed Pawley (Joe Patterson); Fred Kohler, Sr (Captain Blackie); John Larkin (Rumba); Libby Taylor (Lavinia); Harry Myers (Stage Manager); Paul Hurst (Hefty); Theresa Maxwell Conover (Miss Markham); King Baggott, Mahlon Hamilton, Al Richmond, Francis McDonald, Stanley Andrews, Eddie Sturgis, George Lloyd (Gamblers); Bruce Covington (Colonel); Jules Cowles, Harry Cody (Bartenders); Forrest Taylor, Warner Richmond, Matthew Betz (Men at Bar); Jack Mulhall (Duelist); Victor Potel (Guest); Bill Howard (Man in Auditorium); Jack Carlyle (Referee); Richard Scott (Second); Jan Duggan (Passenger on Boat); James Burke (Passenger in Pilot House); Helene Chadwick, Jerome Storm (Extras at Opening); The Cabin Kids, Molasses and January (Themselves); Dennis O'Keefe, Ann Sheridan (Extras).

TWO FOR TONIGHT   (Para., 1935) 61 M.

Producer, Douglas MacLean; director, Frank Tuttle; story, Max Lief, J. O. Lief; screenplay, George Marion, Jr.; songs, Mack Gordon and Harry Revel; camera, Karl Struss.

Bing Crosby (Gilbert Gordon); Joan Bennett (Bobbie Lockwood); Mary Boland (Mrs. J. E. Smythe); Lynne Overman (Harry Kling); Thelma Todd (Lilly Bianca);

Ernest Cossart (Hompe); James Blakeley (Buster Da Costa); Douglas Fowley (Pooch Donahue); Maurice Cass (Alexander Myers); Charles E. Arnt (Benny the Goof); Leonard Carey (Mr. Myers' Butler); Herbert Evans (Butler); Bert Hanlon (Census Taker); Arthur Housman (Warburton); Harold Minjir (Mr. Myers' Secretary); Lillian West (Nurse); Jack Mulhall (Gordon's Doctor); Charles Levison Lame (Author); Torben Meyer, Jerry Mandy (Waiters); Eddie Kane (Charlie); Hooper Atchley (Manager); Guy Usher (Police Captain); Doris Lloyd (Lady Ralston); Lionel Pape (Lord Ralston); A. S. "Pop" Byron (Jailer); John Gough (Prisoner); Edward Gargan (Taxi Driver); Beulah McDonald (Maid); Suzanne Rhodes, Irene Thompson, Jack Deery, Pat Somerset (Lord Ralston's Guests); Robert Kent, Oscar Rudolph, Jack Chapin, Toby Wing, Dorothy Thompson (College People); Monte Vandegrift, Duke York, Charles Morris, Hal Craig, Clarence L. Sherwood (Cops in Cafe); Alex Melesh (Man for Toupee Gag); Connie Emerald (Woman for Hat Gag); Phillips Smalley (Doctor in Hallway).

SHE COULDN'T TAKE IT (Col., 1935) 89 M.

Producer, B. P. Schulberg; director, Tay Garnett; story, Gene Towne, Graham Baker; screenplay, Oliver H. P. Garrett; camera, Leon Shamroy; editor, Gene Havlick.

George Raft (Spot Ricardi); Joan Bennett (Carol Van Dyke); Walter Connolly (Mr. Van Dyke); Billie Burke (Mrs. Van Dyke); Lloyd Nolan (Tex); Wallace Ford (Boston); James Blakeley (Tony Van Dyke); Alan Mowbray (Alan Hamlin); William Tannen (Cesar); Donald Meek (Uncle); Frank Conroy (Raleigh); Tom Kennedy (Slugs); Ivan Lebedeff (Count); Franklin Pangborn (Secretary); Thomas Jackson (Spieler); Huey White (Eddie Gore); Mack Gray (Ike); Peppino Dallalic (Don); Robert Middlemass (Desk Sergeant); Walter Walker (Judge); Stanley Andrews (Wyndersham); Wyrley Birch (Dr. Schaeffer); Maynard Holmes (Edgar); Maxine Lewis (Crooner); Irving Bacon (Man at Toll Gate); Ky Robinson, James Burtis, Ted Oliver (Motorcycle Cops); Eddie Gribbon (Detective); Loren Riebe (Human Fly); Olaf Hytten (Butler); George McKay (Red) Ed Dearing, Gene Morgan (District Attorney's Men); Frank Austin (Railroad Attendant); George Lloyd (Turnkey); Emmett Vogan (Reporter); John Quillian (Bellboy); Victor Potel, James B. "Pop" Kenton, Jack Duffy (Farmers); Emmett Vogan, Jimmy Harrison, Stanley Mack, Tom Costello, Antrim Short, Jack Gardner, Billy West, Charles Sherlock, Joe Clive (Reporters); Arthur Rankin, Henry Roquemore, Lee Shumway, John Webb Dillon, Arthur Stuart Hull, Paul Power (Men); Lois Lindsey, Edith Kingden, Bess Flowers, Grace Goodall, Gladys Gale, Carrie Daumery (Women); Frank Rice (Milkman); Frank LaRue, Frank Marlowe, Robert Wilber, Walter Perry, Stark Bishop, Al Ferguson (Prisoners); Nadine Dore (Girl); John Ince (Prison Official); Donald Kerr (Sailor); Harrison Greene (Spieler); Lee Phelps (Bailiff); Jack Daley (District Attorney's Man); Henry Sylvester (Stage Manager); Lon Poff (Judge); George Webb (Editor); J. Merrill Holmes (Prison Doctor); Frank G. Fanning (Warden); Mike Lally, William E. Lawrence (Photographers); Joe North (Butler); Raymond Turner (Janitor); Oscar Rudolph (Newsboy); C. A. Beckman (Traffic Cop); Kernan Cripps (Guard); Phillip Ronalde (Waiter).

THE MAN WHO BROKE THE BANK AT MONTE CARLO (20th, 1935) 67 M.

Associate producer, Nunnally Johnson; director, Stephen Roberts; based on the play by Illya Surgutchoff, Frederic Albert Swanson; screenplay, Johnson, Howard Smith; camera, Ernest Palmer.

Ronald Colman (Paul Gallard); Joan Bennett (Helen Beckeley); Colin Clive (Bertrand Beckeley); Nigel Bruce (Ivan); Montagu Love (Director); Ferdinand

Gottschalk (Office Man); Frank Reicher (Second Assistant Director); Lionel Pape (Third Assistant Director); Leonid Snegoff (Nick, the Chef); Sam Ash (Guard); Charles Coleman (Headwaiter); Vladimir Bykoff (Helen's Guide); John Percoria (Patron); Lynn Bari (Flower Girl); Charles Fallon (Croupier); Georgette Rhodes (Check Room Girl); Alphonse Du Bois (Taxi Driver); Andre Dheron (Dealer); Ramsay Hill, Milton Royce (Ushers); Harold Minjir (Man with Girl); Bruce Wyndham (Excited Man); George Beranger, Arthur Stuard Hull (Casino Assistants); Dora Clemant, Cecil Weston (Women); Rudolf Myzet (Changeur); Frederic Sullivan (Pompous Man); Anya Taranda (Girl at Bar); Francisco Maran (Doorman); Eva Dennison (Indignant Woman); Alphonse Martel (Chasseur); William Stack, John Spacey (Directors); Don Brodie (Photographer); John Miltern (First Assistant Director); Leonard Carey (Captain of Waiters); E. E. Clive, Bob De Coudic, Joseph De Stefani (Waiters); Gino Corrado (Desk Clerk); Ferdinand Munier (Maitre D'Hotel); Maurice Cass (Assistant Maitre D'Hotel); John George (Hunchback); Manuel Paris (Doorman); George Sorel (Hotel Clerk); Frank Dunn (Steward); Shirley Anderson (Telephone Girl); Frank Thornton (Guard); Jacques Vanaire, General Theodore Lodi (Captains of Waiters); Will Stanton (Drunk Waiter); Christian Rub (Gallard's Guide); Nicholas Soussanin, Alexander Melesh (Cooks); I. Miraeva (Singing and Dancing Cook); Joseph Marievsky, Norman Stengel (Singers); Art Miles, Gaston Glass (Bits); Regina Rambeau (Girl); Walter Bonn (Doorman); J. Vlaskin, V. Sabot, N. Mohoff (Dancers); A. Trevor Bland (Dancer); Tom Herbert (Man at Table).

13 HOURS BY AIR   (Par., 1936) 77 M.

Producer, E. Lloyd Sheldon; director, Mitchell Leisen; based on the story "Wild Wings" by Bogart Rogers, Frank Mitchell Dazey; screenplay, Rogers; art directors, Hans Dreier, John Goodman; set decorator, A. E. Freudeman; sound, Martin Peggi, Louis Mesenkop; special camera effects, Gordon Jennings, Farciot Edouart; camera, Theodore Sparkhul; editor, Doane Harrison.

Fred MacMurray (Jack Gordon); Joan Bennett (Felice Rollins); ZaSu Pitts (Mina Harkins); Alan Baxter (Curtis Palmer); Fred Keating (Gregorie Stephani); Brian Donlevy (Dr. Evarts); John Howard (Freddie Scott); Adrienne Marden (Ann McKenna); Ruth Donnelly (Vi Johnson); Bennie Bartlett (Waldemar Pitt III); Grace Bradley (Trixie La Brey); Dean Jagger (Hap Waller); Jack Mulhall (Horace Lander); Granville Bates (Pop Andrews); Arthur Singley (Pete Stevens); Clyde Dilson (Fat Rickhauser); Mildred Stone (Ruth Bradford); Henry Arthur (Assistant Clerk); Ed Schaefer (Harry); Dennis O'Keefe (Baker, the Co-Pilot); Bruce Warren (Tex Doyle); John Huettner (Co-Pilot); Gertrude Short, Marie Prevost (Waitresses).

BIG BROWN EYES   (Par., 1936) 76 M.

Producer, Walter Wanger; director, Raoul Walsh; based on the stories "Big Brown Eyes" and "Hahsit Babe" by James Edward Grant; screenplay, Walsh, Bert Hanlon; art director, Alexander Toluboff; set decorator, Howard Bristol; costumes, Helen Taylor; music director, Boris Morros; assistant director, David MacDonald; sound, Hugo Grenzbach; camera, George Clemens; editor, Robert Simpson.

Cary Grant (Danny Barr); Joan Bennett (Eve Fallon); Walter Pidgeon (Richard Morey); Lloyd Nolan (Russ Cortig); Alan Baxter (Carey Butler); Marjorie Gateson (Mrs. Cole); Isabel Jewell (Bessie Blair); Douglas Fowley (Benny Battle); Henry Brandon (Don Butler); Joseph Sawyer (Jack Sully); Sam Flint (Martin); Helen

Brown (Mother); Dolores Casey (Cashier); Doris Canfield (Myrtle); Edwin Maxwell (Editor); John Picorri (Defense Attorney); Eddy Conrad (Joe); Guy Usher (Judge Davis); Bert Hanlon (Farrell); Charlie Martin (Red); Francis McDonald (Malley); Frances Morris, Mary Bovard, Betty Van Auken, Dorothy Thompson, Kay Gordon, Betty Gordon, Eleanor Huntley, Janette Warren, Roberta Theiss, Gale Goodson, Helaine Moler, Beulah MacDonald, Jinx Falkenberg, Ethel Sykes (Manicurists); Phil Dunham, Francis Sayles, Mal Merrihugh, George Warren, Lloyd Taylor, Bill McGeary, Jack Dillon, Curley Wright, Bill Sullivan (Barbers); Fred "Snowflake" Toones, Eddie Hines (Shoe Shiners); Rex Moore, Hal Greene (Pages); Ray Cordell, Fred Anderson. (Elevator Boys); Geraldine Leslie, Ethel Mantell (Maids); Jack Daley (Mooney); Jack Kennedy (Mahoney); Lee Phelps (Jailer); Charles Hamilton (Clerk); Steve Strilich, John Reese (Prisoners); Lionel Pedley, George Warren (Polo Players); Allen Connor (Husband); Charles Wilson (Prosecuting Attorney); George MacQuarrie (Chief of Detectives); Homer Dickinson (Police Clerk); Don Brodie (Mah); Bud Geary (Gangster); Ed Jones (Chauffeur); Billy Arnold (Customer).

TWO IN A CROWD   (Univ., 1936) 82 M.

Executive producer, Charles R. Rogers; associate producer, E. M. Asher; director, Alfred E. Green; story, Lewis R. Foster; screenplay, Foster, Dorris Malloy, Earle Snell; art director, Albert S. D'Agostino; music director, Herman Heller; sound, Homer G. Tasker; special effects, John P. Fulton; camera, Joseph Valentine; editor, Milton Carruth.

Joan Bennett (Julia Wayne); Joel McCrea (Larry Stevens); Henry Armetta (Toscani); Alison Skipworth (Lillie "the Toad" Eckleberger); Nat Pendleton (Flynn); Reginald Denny (James Stewart Anthony); Andy Clyde (Jonesy); Elisha Cook, Mr. (Skeeter); Donald Meek (Bennett); Bradley Page (Tony Bonelli); Barbara Rogers (The Lawson Girl); John Hamilton (Purdy, the FBI Man); Tyler Brooke (Charles Brock); Douglas Wood (Ralston); Milburn Stone (Kennedy, the Cashier); Frank Layton (Bank Guard); Robert Murphy (Bartender); Matt McHugh (Taxi Driver); Ed Gargan (Policeman); Jean Rogers (Blonde at Party); Paul Porcasi (Polito, the Headwaiter); Joe Sawyer (Bonelli's Henchman); Paul Fix (Mike, Bonelli's Henchman); Eddie Anderson (Swipe); Eddie Kane (Bar Manager); Nena Quartaro (Celita, the Hat Check Girl); Alan Matthews (Taxi Driver); James C. Morton, Eddy Chandler, Henry Otho, James Flavin (Policemen); James Quinn (Ho-Head); Diana Gibson (Secretary); Evelyn Selbie (Tenement Woman); Winter Hall (Judge); Jerry Mandy (Barber); John George (Dwarf); Johnnie Morris (Balloon Vendor); Phyllis Crane, Maxine Cantway, Eloise Rozzelle (Molls); Carl Andre (Joel McCrea's Stand-In); Mary Windsor (Joan Bennett's Stand-In).

WEDDING PRESENT   (Par., 1936) 81 M.

Producer, B. P. Schulberg; director, Richard Wallace; story, Paul Gallico; screenplay, Joseph Anthony; assistant director, Ray Lissner; art directors, Hans Dreier, Earl Hendrick; sound, Jack Goodrich; camera, Leon Shamroy; editor, Robert Bischoff.

Joan Bennett [Rusty (Monica Fleming)]; Cary Grant (Charlie Mason); George Bancroft (Stagg); Conrad Nagel (Bodacker); Gene Lockhart (Arch Duke); Carl William Demarest (Smiling Benson); Edward Brophy (Squinty); Lois Wilson (Laura Bodacker); Inez Courtney (Mary Lawson); Mary Forbes (Mrs. Bodacker); Purnell Pratt (Van Dorn); Douglas Wood (Willett); George Meeker (Blaker); Damon Ford (Haley); John Henry Allen (Jonathan); George Offerman, Jr. (Sammy

Smith); Bradley Page (Givens); Torben Meyer (Winternitz); Charles Middleton (Turnbull); Clarence H. Wilson (Simmons); Katherine Perry Moore (Miss Chandler); Harry C. Bradley (Ticket Seller); Frank Darien (Cashier); Otto Hoffman (Printer); Hal K. Dawson (Furniture Salesman); Harry Tyler (Marriage License Clerk); Richard Powell (Hotel Room Waiter); George Davis (Cafe Waiter); Russ Powell (Beer Wagon Driver); Edd Russell (*Telegraph* Editor); Lee Shumway (Police Captain); Eddy Baker (Motorcycle Cop); Charles Mankin (Pompous Man); Ralph McCullough (Timid Man); Ernie Shields (Man with Key); Heinie Conklin, Billy Engle, Ray Hanson (German Band); Walter Long, Jimmie Dundee, Charles Sullivan (Gangsters); Chuck Hamilton, Jack Mulhall, Cy Ring, Marshall Ruth, Eddie Phillips, Allen Fox, Charles Williams, Eddie Borden, Ted Thompson, Charles Sherlock, Eddie Featherston, Dagmar Oakland (Reporters); Estelle Eterre, Frances Morris (Switchboard Operators); Milton Kahn, Rex Moore (Office Boys).

VOGUES OF 1938   (U. A., 1937) 108 M.

Producer, Walter Wanger; director, Irving Cummings; screenplay, Bella and Samuel Spewack; music director, Boris Morros; choreography, Seymour Felix; songs, Lew Brown and Sammy Fain; Frank Loesser and Manning Sherwin; Paul Francis Webster and Louis Alter; Alter; Alter and Webster; camera, Ray Rehnahan; editors, Otho Lovering, Dorothy Spencer.

Warner Baxter (George Curson); Joan Bennett (Wendy Van Klettering); Helen Vinson (Mary Curson); Mischa Auer (Prince Muratov); Alan Mowbray (Henry Morgan); Jerone Cowan (Mr. Brockton); Alma Kruger (Sophie Miller); Marjorie Gateson (Mrs. Lemke); Penny Singleton (Violet); Polly Rowles (Betty Mason); Marla Shelton (Miss Sims); Hedda Hopper (Mrs. Van Klettering); Roman Bohnen (Lawyer); Georgie Tapps, Virginia Verrill, Fred Lawrence, Gloria Gilbert, The Olympic Trio, The Wiere Brothers, The Four Hot Shots (Specialties); Rocco and Saulters (Cotton Club Dancers); Victor Young and His Orchestra (Themselves); Frank McGrath (Warner Baxter's Stand-In); Dick Wessel (Boxer); Jean Acker (Extra); Rosemary Theby, Harry Myers (Dress Extras); Peggy Calvin, Betty Wyman, Martha Heveran, Phyllis Gilman, Elizabeth "Libby" Harben, Ida Vollmar; Dorothy Day, Mary Oakes, Kay Aldridge, Olive Cawley, Frances Joyce, Noreen Carr, Ruth Martin, Betty Douglas (Walter Wanger Models).

I MET MY LOVE AGAIN   (UA, 1938) 77 M.

Producer, Walter Wanger; directors, Arthur Ripley, Joshua Logan; based on the novel *Summer Lighting* by Allene Corliss; screenplay, David Hertz; camera, Hal Mohr; editors, Otho Lovering, Edward Mann.

Joan Bennett (Julie); Henry Fonda (Ives); Dame May Whitty (Aunt William); Alan Marshal (Michael); Louise Platt (Brenda); Alan Baxter (Tony); Tim Holt (Budge); Dorothy Stickney (Mrs. Towner); Florence Lake (Carol); Genee Hall (Michael, the Daughter); Elise Cavenna (Agatha).

THE TEXANS   (Par., 1938) 92 M.

Producer, Lucien Hubbard; director, James Hogan; story, Emerson Hough; screenplay, Bertram Millhauser, Paul Sloane, William W. Haines; camera, Theodor Sparkuhl; editor, LeRoy Stone.

Joan Bennett (Ivy Preston); Randolph Scott (Kirk Jordan); May Robson (Granna); Walter Brennan (Chuckawalla); Robert Cummings (Alan Sanford); Raymond Hatton (Cal Tuttle); Robert Barrat (Isaiah Middlebrack); Harvey Stephens

(Lieutenant David Nichols); Francis Ford (Uncle Dud); Chris Pin Martin (Juan Rodriguez); Anna Demetrio (Rosita Rodriguez); Clarence Wilson (Sam Ross); Jack Moore (Slim); Richard Tucker (General Corbett); Edward Gargan (Sergeant Crady); Otis Harlan (Henry); Spencer Charters (Chairman); Archie Twitchell (Corporal Thompson); William Haade (Sergeant Cahill); Irving Bacon (Private Chilina); William B. Davidson (Mr. Jessup); Bill Roberts (Mustang); Richard Denning (Corporal Parker); Frank Cordell, John Eckert, Slim Hightower, Scoop Martin, Whitey Sovern, Slim Talbot (Cowboys); Jimmie Kilgannon, Edwin John Brady, Carl Harbaugh, Dutch Hendrian (Union Soldiers); Oscar Smith (Black soldier); Jack Perrin (Private Soldier); Ernie Adams, Edward J. LeSaint, James Quinn (Confederate Soldiers); Harry Woods (Cavalry Officer); Wheeler Oakman (U.S. Captain); Everette Brown (Man with Watches); Margaret McWade (Middle-Aged Lady); Vera Steadman, Virginia Jennings (Women on Street); James Kelso (Snorer); J. Manley Head (Fanatic); Philip Morris (Fen); James Burtis (Swenson); Esther Howard (Madame); James T. Mack, Lon Poff (Moody Citizens); John Qualen (Swede); Kay Whitehead (Stella); Ralph Remley (Town Lawyer); Pat West (Real Estate Man); Laurie Lane, Helaine Moler (Girls).

ARTISTS AND MODELS ABROAD   (Par., 1938) 90 M.

Producer, Arthur Hornblow, Jr.; director, Mitchell Leisen; story, Howard Lindsay, Russel Crouse; screenplay, Lindsay, Crouse, Ken Englun; art directors, Hans Dreier, Ernst Fegte; costumes, Edith Head; choreography, LeRoy Prinz; music director, Boris Morros; songs, Ralph Rainger and Leo Robin; special effects, Farciot Edouart; camera, Ted Tetzlaff; editor, Doane Harrison.

Jack Benny (Buck Boswell); Joan Bennett (Patricia Harper); Mary Boland (Mrs. Isabel Channing); Charley Grapewin (James Harper); Joyce Compton (Chickie); The Yacht Club Boys (Themselves); Fritz Feld (Dubois); G. P. Huntley (Eliot Winthrop); Monty Woolley (Gantvoort); Adrienne d'Ambricourt (Madame Brissard); Andre Cheron (Brissard); Jules Raucourt (Chaumont); Phyllis Kennedy (Marie); Mary Parker (Punkins); Sheila Darcy (Becky); Yvonne Duval (Red); Gwen Kenyon (Miss America); Joyce Mathews (Jersey); Dolores Casey (Dodie); Marie De Forest (Kansas); Alex Melesh (Count Vassily Vossilovitch); Georges Renevant, Nicholas Soussanin (Prefects of Police); Francisco Maran (Assistant to Prefect); Chester Clute (Simpson); Louis Mercier (Simpson); Louis Van den Ecker (Cabby); Charles de Ravenne (Porter); Joseph Romantini (Grocery Boy); Robert du Couedic, Eddie Davis, Alphonse Martel, Ray de Ravenne, Arthur Dulac (Waiters); Armand Kaliz (Headwaiter); George Kerebel, Saverio Rinaldo (Busboys); Gennaro Curci (Proprietor); Jean Perry, Constant Franke (Gendarmes); Paul Cremonesi, Robert Graves (Chefs); Eugene Beday (Watchman); George Davis (Leader of Guards); Paco Moreno, Jacques Vanaire, Eugene Borden, Fred Cavens, Manuel Paris (Guards); Jean De Briac, Fred Malatesta (Treasury Officials); David Mir (Attendant); Georges de Gombert (Reporter); Ferdinand Schumann-Heink (German Reporter) Ken Gibson (American Reporter); Joseph de Beauvolers, Martial de Serrand (Exposition Guards); Paul Bryar (Hotel Clerk); Peter Camlin (Assistant Manager); Andre Marsaudon Roque Guinart (Plainclothesmen); Ed Agresti (Doorman); William Emile (Secretary); Cliff Nazarro (Guide); Albert d'Arno, Harry Lamont, Maurice Brierre, Tony Merlo (Kitchen Helpers); Linda Yale (Tailor-Made Model); Donald Boucher (Page Boy); George Calliga (Keyboard Operator); Marie Burton, Paula de Cardo, Carol Parker, Helaine Moler, Evelyn Keyes, Laurie Lane, Nora Gale, Maria Doray (Girls); Ethel Clayton (Woman).

TRADE WINDS   (UA, 1938) 94 M.

Producer, Walter Wanger; director, Tay Garnett; story, Garnett; screenplay, Dorothy Parker, Alan Campbell, Frank R. Adams, music director, Alfred Newman; art directors, Alexander Toluboff, Alexander Golitzen; Joan Bennett's gowns, Irene; Ann Sothern's gowns, Helen Tayler; assistant director, Percy Ikerd; sound, Frank Maher; camera, Rudolph Mate; foreign exterior camera, James B. Shackelford; editors, Otho Lovering, Dorothy Spencer.

Fredric March (Sam Wye); Joan Bennett (Kay Kerrigan); Ralph Bellamy (Ben Blodgett); Ann Sothern (Jean Livingstone); Sidney Blackmer (Thomas Bruhme II); Thomas Mitchell (Commissioner Blackton); Robert Elliott (Captain George Faulkiner); Richard Tucker (John Johnson); Joyce Compton (Mrs. Johnson); Patricia Farr (Peggy); Wilma Francis (Judy); Phyllis Barry (Ruth); Dorothy Tree (Clara); Kay Linaker (Grace); Dorothy Comingore (Ann); Walter Byron (Bob); Wilson Benge (Martin the Butler); Harry Paine (Captain); Hooper Atchley, Lee Phelps, Franklin Parker, John Webb Dillon, Dick Rush, Jack Baxley (Detective Squad); Mrs. Sojin (Patron); Princess Luana, Marie de Forest (Hawaiian Hairdressers); Beryl Wallace, Paulita Arvizu (Hawaiian Girls); Aiko Magara (Proprietress of Tea House); Suzanne Kaaren (Russian Girl); Gloria Youngblood (Jinrikisha Girl); Lotus Liu (Shanghai Clerk); Ethelreda Leopold (Ethel); Dick Botiller (Bombay Carriage Driver); Charlie Williams (Reporter Jones); Tom Quinn (Reporter); Betty Roadman (Matron); Harry Barris (Pianist); Cyril Ring, Brooks Benedict (Party Guests); Art Baker (Voices of Various Radio [Police] Announcers); Harry Bernard (Sound Man); Beal Wong (Shanghai Cigarette Customer).

THE MAN IN THE IRON MASK   (UA, 1939) 109 M.

Producer, Edward Small; director, James Whale; based on the novel by Alexandre Dumas; screenplay, George Bruce; art director, John DuCasse Schulze; music director, Lud Gluskin; music, Lucien Moraweck; special effects, Howard Anderson; camera, Robert Planck; editor, Grant Whytock.

Louis Hayward (Louis XIV/Philippe); Joan Bennett (Maria Theresa); Warren William (D'Artagnan); Joseph Schildkraut (Fouquet); Alan Hale (Porthos); Miles Mander (Aramis), Bert Roach (Athos); Walter Kingsford (Colbert); Marian Martin (Mlle de la Valliere); Montague Love (Spanish Ambassador); Doris Kenyon (Queen Anne); Albert Dekker (Louis XIII); William Royle (Commandant of Bastille); Fred Cavens (Francois); Boyd Irwin (Royal High Constable); Howard Brooks (Cardinal); Ian MacLaren (Valet de Chambre); Dorothy Vaughan (Woman); Harry Woods (Bit).

THE HOUSEKEEPER'S DAUGHTER   (UA, 1939) 71 M.

Producer-director, Hal Roach; story, Donald Henderson Clarke; screenplay, Rian James, Gordon Douglas; art director, Charles D. Hall; music director, Lud Gluskin; orchestral score, Amedeo de Filippi; camera, Norbert Brodine; editor, William Ziegler.

Joan Bennett (Hilda); Adolphe Menjou (Deakon Maxwell); John Hubbard (Robert Randall); William Gargan (Ed O'Malley); George E. Stone (Benny); Peggy Wood (Olga); Donald Meek (Editor Wilson); Marc Lawrence (Floyd); Lilian Bond (Gladys); Victor Mature (Lefty); John Hyams (Professor Randall); Leila McIntyre (Mrs. Randall); Luis Alberni (Veroni); Rosin Galli (Mrs. Veroni).

GREEN HELL   (Univ., 1940) 87 M.

Producer, Harry Edington; director, James Whale; screenplay, Frances Marion; camera, Karl Freund; editor, Ted J. Kent.

Douglas Fairbanks, Jr. (Keith Brandon); Joan Bennett (Stephanie Richardson); George Sanders (Forrester); Vincent Price (David Richardson); Alan Hale (Doctor Nils Loren); Gene Garrick (Graham); George Bancroft (Jim "Tex" Morgan); John Howard (Hal Scott); Francis McDonald (Gracco); Ray Mala (Mala); Peter Bronte (Santos); Kay Linaker (Woman); Lupita Tovar, Yola d'Avril, Nena Quartaro, Anita Camargo (Native Girls); Eumenio Blanco (Well-Dressed Natives); Tony Paton (Bartender); Wilson Benge (Butler); Iron Eyes Cody (Indian); Franco Corsaro (Man); Noble Johnson (Indian Chief); Julian Rivero (Proprietor).

THE HOUSE ACROSS THE BAY   (UA, 1940) 88 M.

Producer, Walter Wanger; director, Archie Mayo; story, Myles Connolly; screenplay, Kathryn Scola; art directors, Alexander Golitzen, Richard Irvine; set decorator, Julie Heron; choreography, Sammy Lee; assistant director, Charles Kerr; music-music director, Werner Janssen; songs, Sidney Clare, Nick Caste, and Jule Styne; Al Siegel; George R. Brown and Irving Actman; costumes, Irene; sound, Fred Lau; special camera, Ray Binger; camera, Merritt Gerstad; editor, Dorothy Spencer.

George Raft (Steve Larwitt); Joan Bennett (Brenda Bentley); Lloyd Nolan (Slant Kolma); Walter Pidgeon (Tim Nolan); Gladys George (Mary Bogale); William Wayne (Barney); June Knight (Babe Davis); Peggy Shannon (Alice); Cy Kendall (Crawley); Max Wagner (Jim); Frank Bruno (Jerry); Joseph Sawyer (Charlie); William Halligan, Kenneth Harlan (Men in Nightclub); Mack Gray (Doorman-Lookout); Sam Finn (Head Waiter); Marcelle Corday (French Maid); Sam Ash (Broker); Norman Willis, Eddie Marr (Taresca's Henchmen); Frances Morris (Secretary to Slant); Freeman Wood (Mr. Hanson); Elsa Petersen (Mrs. Hanson); Joseph Crehan, Charles Griffin (Federal Men); Edward Fielding (Federal Judge); Paul Phillips, John Bohn (Reporters); Virginia Brissac (Landlady); Franklyn Farnum, James Farley, Martin Cichy, Pat O'Malley (Prison Guards); Dorothy Vaughan, Ruth Warren, Maxine Leslie, Helen Shipman, Kitty McHugh (Prisoners' Wives on Ferry Boat); Etta McDaniel (Lydia, the Maid); Miki Morita (Tim's Japanese House Boy); Peter Camlin (French Pilot); Georges Renevant, Jean Del Val (French Officials); Emmett Vogan (U.S. Official); Armand "Curly" Wright (Barber); Harrison Greene (Irate Customer); Allen Wood (Newsboy); Herbert Ashley (Man in Park).

THE MAN I MARRIED   (20th, 1940) 77 M.

Associate producer, Raymond Griffith; director, Irving Pichel; based on the novel *Swastika* by Oscar Schisgall; screenplay, Oliver H. P. Garrett; music director, David Buttolph; camera, Peverell Marley; editor, Robert Simpson.

Joan Bennett (Carol); Francis Lederer (Eric); Lloyd Nolan (Kenneth Delane); Anna Sten (Frieda); Otto Kruger (Heinrich); Maria Ouspenskaya (Frau Gerhardt); Ludwig Stossel (Dr. Gerhardt); Johnny Russell (Ricky); Lionel Royce (Deckhart); Fredrik Vogeding (Traveler); Ernst Deutsch (Otto); Egon Brecher (Czech); William Kaufman (Conductor); Frank Reicher (Freihof); Charles Irwin (English Newspaperman); Lillian Porter (Receptionist); Lillian West (Secretary); Harry Depp (Man); Walter Bonn (Customs Official); Glen Cavender (Petty Official); Hans Von Morhart, William Yetter (Gestapo Officers); Ragnar Quale (Freihof's Older Son); Rudy Frolich (Freihof's Son); John Stark, Tom Mizer, Hans Schumm, Rudoph Anders (Storm Troopers); Carl Freybe (Gestapo Official); Greta Meyer (Hausfrau); Albert Geigel (Boy); Eleanor Wesselhoeft (Old Lady); Diane Fisher (Young Girl); John Hiestand, Leyland Hodgson, Arno Frey, Eugene Borden (Announcers).

THE SON OF MONTE CRISTO   (UA, 1940) 102 M.

Producer, Edward Small; director, Rowland V. Lee; screenplay, George Bruce; music, Edward Ward; camera, George Robinson; editor, Arthur E. Roberts.

Louis Hayward (Count of Monte Cristo); Joan Bennett (Grand Duchess Zona); George Sanders (Gurko Lanen); Florence Bates (Mathilde); Lionel Royce (Colonel); Montagu Love (Baron Von Heuhoff); Ian MacWolfe (Conrad Stedt); Clayton Moore (Fritz Dorner); Ralph Byrd (Gluck); Georges Renevant (French Ambassador); Michael Visaroff (Pavlov); Rand Brooks (Hans Mirbach); Theodor von Eltz (Captain); James Seay (Lieutenant); Henry Brandon (Schultz); Jack Mulhall (Schmidt); Edward Keane (Turnkey); Lawrence Grant (Baron).

MAN HUNT   (20th, 1941) 105 M.

Associate producer, Kenneth Macgowan; director, Fritz Lang; based on the novel *Rogue Male* by Geoffrey Household; screenplay, Dudley Nichols; art directors, Richard Day, Wiard B. Ihnen; set decorator, Thomas Little; music, Alfred Newman; camera, Arthur Miller; editor, Allen McNeil.

Walter Pidgeon (Captain Thorndike); Joan Bennett (Jerry); George Sanders (Quive-Smith); John Carradine (Mr. Jones); Roddy McDowall (Vaner the Cabin Boy); Ludwig Stossel (Doctor); Heather Thatcher (Lady Risborough); Fred Worlock (Lord Risborough); Roger Imhof (Captain Jensen); Egon Brecher (Whiskers); Holmes Herbert (Farnsworthy); Fredrik Vogeding (Ambassador); Lucien Prival (Umbrella Man); Herbert Evans (Reeves); Edgar Licho (Little Fat Man); Eily Malyon (Postmistress); John Rogers (Cockney); Lester Matthews (Major); Arno Frey (Police Lieutenant); Keith Hitchcock (London Bobby); Otto Reichow, William Haade, Bob Stephenson (Sentries); Adolph Milar (Pigeon Man); Sven Borg (First Mate); Hans Joby (Tracker); Cyril Delevanti, Frank Benson (Cab Drivers); Douglas Gerrard (Policeman); Clifford Severn (Cockney Boy); Charles Bennett, Bobbie Hale (Coster-Mongers); Walter Bonn, Carl Ottmar (Harbor Police); Carl Ekberg (Hitler); Kurt Kreuger, Olaf Hytten (Secretaries); William Vaughn (Chief of Harbor Police); Virginia McDowall (Postmistress's Daughter); Bruce Lester (Co-Pilot).

SHE KNEW ALL THE ANSWERS   (Col., 1941) 84 M.

Producer, Charles R. Rogers; director, Richard Wallace; story, Jane Allen; screenplay, Harry Segall, Kenneth Earl, Curtis Kenyon; assistant director, Norman Deming; art director, Lionel Banks; music director, M. W. Stoloff; camera, Henry Freulich; editor, Gene Havlick.

Joan Bennett (Gloria Winters); Franchot Tone (Mark Willows); John Hubbard (Randy Bradford); Eve Arden (Sally Long); William Tracy (Benny); Pierre Watkin (George Wharton); Almira Sessions (Elaine Wingate); Thurston Hall (J. D. Sutton); Grady Sutton (Ogleby).

WILD GEESE CALLING   (20th, 1941) 77 M.

Producer, Harry Joe Brown; director, John Brahm; based on the novel by Stewart Edward White; screenplay, Horace McCoy; camera, Lucien Ballard; editor, Walter Thompson.

Henry Fonda (John Murdock); Joan Bennett (Sally); Warren William (Blackie); Ona Munson (Clarabella); Barton MacLane (Pirate Kelly); Russell Simpson (Len Baker); Iris Adrian (Mazie); James C. Morton (Mack); Paul Sutton (Manager); Mary Field (Jennie); Stanley Andrews (Delane); Jody Gilbert (Swede); Robert Emmett Keane (Head Waiter); Michael (Adman); Morris (Guide); George Watts (Mahoney); Charles Middleton (Doctor).

CONFIRM OR DENY   (20th, 1941) 73 M.

Producer, Len Hammond; director, Archie Mayo; story, Henry Wales, Samuel Fuller; screenplay, Jo Swerling; camera, Leon Shamroy; editor, Robert Bischoff.

Don Ameche (Mitch); Joan Bennett (Jennifer Carson); Roddy McDowall (Albert Perkins); John Loder (Captain Channing); Raymond Walburn (H. Cyrus Sturtevant); Arthur Shields (Jeff); Eric Blore (Mr. Hobbs); Helene Reynolds (Dorothy); Claude Allister (Williams); Roseanna Murray (M. I. Girl); Stuart Robertson (Johnny Dunne); Queenie Leonard (Daisy); Jean Prescott (Elizabeth Harding); Billy Bevan (Mr. Bindle); Alan Napier (Updyke); Lumsden Hare (Sir Titus Scott); Dennis Hoey (Duffield); Leonard Carey (Floorman).

TWIN BEDS   (UA, 1942) 85 M.

Producer, Edward Small; associated producer, Stanley Logan; director, Tim Whelan; based on story by Margaret Mayo, Edward Salisbury Field; screenplay, Curtis Kenyon, Kenneth Earl, E. Edwin Moran; art director, John DuCasse Schulze; music, Dimitri Tiomkin; camera, Hal Mohr; editor, Francis Lyons.

George Brent (Mike Abbott); Joan Bennett (Julie Abbott); Mischa Auer (Nicolai Cherupin); Una Merkel (Lydia); Glenda Farrell (Sonya); Ernest Truex (Larky); Margaret Hamilton (Norah); Charles Coleman (Butler); Charles Arnt (Butler); Cecil Cunningham (Secretary).

THE WIFE TAKES A FLYER   (Col., 1942) 86 M.

Producer, B. P. Schulberg; director, Richard Wallace; story, Gina Kaus; screenplay, Kaus, Jay Dratler; additional dialog, Harry Segall; assistant directors, William Mull, Eugene Anderson; camera, Franz F. Planer; editor, Gene Havlick.

Joan Bennett (Anita Woverman); Franchot Tone (Christopher Reynolds); Allyn Joslyn (Major Zellfritz); Cecil Cunningham (Countess Oldenburg); Roger Clark (Keith); Lloyd Corrigan (Thomas Woverman); Lyle Latell (Muller); Georgia Caine (Mrs. Woverman); Barbara Brown (Maria Woverman); Erskine Sanford (Jan); Chester Clute (Adolphe Bietjelboer); Hans Conried (Hendrik Woverman); Romaine Callender (Zanten); Aubrey Mather (Chief Justice); William Edmunds (Gustav); Curtis Railing (Mrs. Brandt); Nora Cecil (Miss Updike); Kurt Katch (Captain Schmutnick); Margaret Seddon, Kate MacKenna (The Twins); Gordon Richards (Major Wilson); Fredric Bolton (Corporal Heidne); Lloyd Bridges (German Sergeant); Gohr Van Vleck (Court Attendant); James Millican, Manart Kippen, Steven Geray, Cy Kendall (Gestapo); Erik Rolf (Gestapo Leader); Carl Ekberg (Hitler); Bert Roach (Guldschreschts); Lloyd Whitlock (Head Waiter); Collin Blair (Man); John Vosper (German Sergeant); Hallene Hill, Mary Young (Old Ladies); Gertrude W. Hoffman (Mrs. Gruyson); Mary Bertrand, Josephine Allen, Belle Johnstone, Nellie Farrell, Phoebe Rudd, Agnes Steel, Stella LeSant, Eleanor Wood, Marie Spingold, Minnie Steel, Lucille Isle, Elsie Bishop (Women); Marie Blake (Frieda); Henry Zynda, Hugh Beaumont (Officers); Joe McGuinn (Lieutenant); Wheaton Chambers (Chaplain); Vernon Downing, Leslie Denison (Enlish Officers); Max Hoffman, Jr., Max Wagner (Sergeants); Frank Alten (German Orderly); Charles Hamilton, David Newell, Arno Frey, George Turner, William Yetter, Walter Stiritz, Pat Lane, Chris Frank, John Peters (German Officers); Henry Victor (Colonel Bosch).

GIRL TROUBLE   (20th, 1942) 82 M.

Producer, Robert Bassler; director, Harold Schuster; story, Ladislas Fodor, Vicki Baum, Guy Trosper; screenplay, Fodor, Robert Riley Crutcher; camera, Edward Cronjager; editor, Robert Fritsch.

Don Ameche (Don Pedro Sullivan); Joan Bennett (June Delaney); Billie Burke (Mrs. Rowland); Frank Craven (Ambrose Murdock Flint); Alan Dinehart (Charles Barrett); Helene Reynolds (Helen); Fortunio Bonanova (Cordoba); Ted (Michael) North (George); Doris Merrick (Susan); Dale Evans (Ruth); Roseanna Murray (Pauline); Janis Carter (Virginia); Vivan Blaine (Barbara); Trudy Marshall (Miss Kennedy); Robert Greig (Fields); Joe Crehan (Kuhn); Arthur Loft (Burgess); Mantan Moreland (Edwards); John Kelly (Mug); Matt McHugh (Driver); George Lessey (Morgan); Ed Stanley (Lehman); Edith Evanson (Hulda); Lee Bennett (Tom); Bruce Warren (Jerry); Frank Coghlan, Jr. (Elevator Boy); Frances Cain, Gayne Kinsey (Dance Team); Forbes Murray (Mr. Lawson); Lois Landon (Mrs. Lawson); Arno Frey (Anton); Jeff Corey (Mr. Mooney); Ruth Cherrington (Large Woman); Henry Roquemore (Man); Eddie Acuff (Taxi Driver); Jack Stoney (Mac); Doodles Weaver (Ticket Taker); Marjorie "Babe" Kane (Cashier); Mary Currier (Secretary).

MARGIN FOR ERROR   (20th, 1943) 74 M.

Producer, Ralph Dietrich; director, Otto Preminger; based on the play by Clare Boothe; screenplay, Lillie Hayward; art directors, Richard Day, Lewis Creber; set decorators, Thomas Little, Al Orenbach; music, Leigh Harline; music director, Emil Newman; assistant director, Percy Ikerd; sound, Eugene Grossman, Harry M. Leonard; camera, Edward Cronjager; editor, Louis Loeffler.

Joan Bennett (Sophie Baumer); Milton Berle (Moe Finkelstein); Otto Premminger (Karl Baumer); Carl Esmond (Max von Alvenstor); Howard Freeman (Horst); Poldy Dur (Frieda Schmidt); Clyde Fillmore (Dr. Jennings); Joseph Kirk (Officer Solomon); Hans Von Twardowski (Fritz); Ted (Michael) North, Elmer Jack Semple, J. Norton Dunn (Saboteurs); Hans Schumm (Kurt Muller); Ed McNamara (Mulrooney); Selmer Jackson (Coroner); Eddie Dunn (Desk Sergeant); Barney Ruditsky (Policeman); Don Dillaway (Reporter); Dick French (Photographer); Ruth Cherrington (Dowager); Byron Foulger (Drug Store Clerk); Emmett Vogan (Fingerprint Expert); David Alison (Jacoby); Wolfgang Zilzer (Man); Allan Nixon, Malcolm McTaggart, Tom Seidel (Soldiers); John Wald, Gary Breckner (American Announcers); Ludwig Donath (Hitler's Voice); Bill O'Brien (Waiter); Ralph Byrd (Pete, the Dice-playing Soldier).

THE WOMAN IN THE WINDOW   (RKO, 1944) 99 M.

Producer, Nunnally Johnson; director, Fritz Lang; based on the novel *Once Off Guard* by J. H. Wallis; screenplay, Johnson; art director, Duncan Cramer; set decorator, Julia Heron; assistant director, Richard Harlan; music, Arthur Lange; sound, Frank McWhorten; camera, Milton Krasner; editors, Gene Fowler, Jr., Marjorie Johnson.

Edward G. Robinson (Richard Wanley); Joan Bennett (Alice Reed); Raymond Massey (Frank Lalor); Edmond Breon (Dr. Michael Barkstone); Dan Duryea (Heidt/Doorman); Thomas E. Jackson (Inspector Jackson); Arthur Loft (Claude Mazard [Alias Frank Howard]/Club Checkroom Clerk); Dorothy Peterson (Mrs. Wanley); Frank Dawson (Collins the Steward); Carol Cameron (Elsie Wanley); Bobby Blake (Dickie Wanley); Frank Melton, Don Brodie (Men in Front of Art Gallery); Alec Craig (Garageman); Ralph Dunn (Traffic Cop); Frank Mills (Garage Helper); Lane Watson (Man by Taxi); James Beasley (Man in Taxi); Joe Devlin (Toll Collector Sergeant); Fred Graham (Motorcycle Cop); Tom Hanlon (Radio Announcer); Calvin Emery (Newsreel Cameraman); Spanky McFarland (Boy Scout with Glasses in Newsreel); Harry Hayden (Druggist); Jack Gardner (Fred, Lalor's

Chauffeur); Arthur Space (Captain Kennedy); Harold McNulty, Joel McGinnis, Donald Kerr, Frank McClure (Elevator Operators); Ann O'Neal (Woman at Elevator); Fred Chapman (Child at Elevator); Eddy Chandler (Police Driver); Thomas P. Dillon (Officer Flynn); Iris Adrian (Street Walker); Ruth Valmy (Magazine Glamour Model); Hal Craig (News Vendor); Fred Rapport (Club Manager); Alex Pollard (William, the Head Waiter); James Harrison, Jack Gargan (Stewards); Lawrence Lathrop, William Dyer (Pageboys); Brandon Beach, Austin Bedell, Al Bensalt, Paul Bradley, James Carlisle, William Holmes, Fred Hueston, Sheldon Jett, J. W. Johnston, Charles Meakin, Harold Minjer, Ralph Norwood, Wedgewood Nowell, Louis Payne, David Pepper, Roy Saegar, Scott Seaton, Wyndham Standing, Larry Steers (Club Members); Bess Flowers (Bar Extra).

NOB HILL   (20th, 1945) C—95 M.

Producer, Andre Daven; director, Henry Hathaway; story, Eleanore Griffin; screenplay, Wanda Tuchock, Norman Reilly Raine; songs, Jimmy McHugh and Harold Adamson; music directors, Emil Newman, Charles Henderson; incidental music, David Buttolph; orchestrator, Gene Rose; art directors, Lyle Wheeler, Russell Spencer; set decorators, Thomas Little, Walter M. Scott; choreography, Nick Castle; musical settings designer, Joseph C. Wright; assistant director, Henry Weinberger; sound, W. D. Flick; special camera effects, Fred Sersen; camera, Edward Cronjager; editor, Harmon Jones.

George Raft (Johnny Angelo); Joan Bennett (Harriet Carruthers); Vivian Blaine (Sally Templeton); Peggy Ann Garner (Katie Flanagan); Alan Reed (Dapper Jack Harrigan); B. S. Pully (Joe, the Bartender); Emil Coleman (Man Playing the Piano); Edgar Barrier (Lash Carruthers); George Anderson (Rafferty); Don Costello (Fighting Bartender); Joseph J. Greene (Headwaiter); J. Farrell MacDonald (Headwaiter); The Three Swifts (Specialty); William Haade (Big Tim); Mike Mazurki (Rafferty's Fighter); Beal Wong, George T. Lee (Chinese Servants); Rory Calhoun (Jose); Robert Greig (Butler); Charles Cane (Chips Conlon); Arthur Loft (Turner); Nestor Paiva (Luigi); Jane Jones (Ruby); Otto Reichow (Swedish Sailor); Chick Chandler (Guide); Harry Shannon, Tom Dillon, Ralph Peters, Brooks Hunt, Harry Strang (Policemen); Frank Orth, Lester Dorr, Harry Harvey, Sr., Julius Tannen, Will Stanton, Syd Saylor, Marshall Ruth, Alphonse Martel, Peter Michael, Antonio Filauri, Jean De Briac (Men); Almira Sessions, Polly Bailey, Leila McIntyre, Gwen Donovan (Women); Edna Mae Jones (Dance Hall Girl); Virginia Walker, Carol Andrews, Susan Scott, Harrison Greene (Slummers); Bill "Red" Murphy (Sailor); Sven-Hugo Borg, George Blagoi (Swedish Sailors); Chief Thundercloud (Indian Chief); Ralph Sanford, Arthur Thalasso, Edward Keane, Eddie Hart, George Lloyd, Sam Flint (Politicians); Byron Foulger (Usher); Benson Fong (Chinese Boy); Olive Blakeney (Housekeeper); Joe Bernard (Printer); Lillian Salvaneschi, Mario Salvaneschi (Specialty Dance Team); George Reed (Black Man).

SCARLET STREET   (Univ., 1946) 103 M.

Executive producer, Walter Wanger; producer-director, Fritz Lang; based on the novel and play *La Chienne* by George de la Fouchardiere; screenplay, Dudley Nichols; art director, Alexander Golitzen; set decorators, Russell A. Gausman, Carl Lawrence; music, H. J. Salter; assistant director, Melville Shyer; sound, Glenn Anderson; special camera, John P. Fulton; camera, Milton Krasner; editor, Arthur Hilton.

Edward G. Robinson (Christopher Cross); Joan Bennett (Kitty); Dan Duryea (Johnny); Jess Barker (Janeway); Margaret Lindsay (Millie); Rosalind Ivan

(Adele); Samuel S. Hinds (Charles Pringle); Arthur Loft (Dellarowe); Vladimir Sokoloff (Opo Lejon); Charles Kemper (Patcheye); Russell Hicks (Hogarth); Anita Bolster (Mrs. Michaels); Cyrus W. Kendall (Nick); Fred Essler (Marshetti); Edgar Dearing, Tom Dillon, Lee Phelps, Matt Millis, Robert Malcolm, William Hall, Ralph Dunn (Policemen); Chuck Hamilton (Chauffeur); Gus Glassmire, Ralph Littlefield, Sherry Hall, Howard Mitchell, Jack Statham (Employees); Rodney Bell (Barney); Henri de Soto (Waiter); Milton Kibbee (Saunders); Tom Daly (Penny); George Meader (Holliday); Lou Lubin (Tiny); Clarence Muse (Ben); John Barton (Hurdy Gurdy Man); Emmett Vogan (Prosecution Attorney); Horace Murphy (Milkman); Will Wright (Loan Office Manager); Joe Devlin (Williams); George Lloyd (Conway); Syd Saylor (Crocker); Dewey Robinson (Derelict); Herbert Heywood (Bellboy); Charles C. Wilson (Watchman); Constance Purdy (Matron); Fritz Leiber (Evangelist); Wally Scott (Drunk); Arthur Gould Porter, Boyd Irwin, Richard Abbott (Critics); Byron Foulger (Jones); Thomas Jackson (Chief of Detectives); Edward Keane, Dick Wessel, Dick Curtis (Detectives); Richard Cramer (Principal Keeper); Reverend Neal Dodd (Priest); Kerry Vaughn (Blond Girl); Beatrice Roberts (Secretary).

COLONEL EFFINGHAM'S RAID   (20th, 1946) 70 M.

Producer, Lamar Trotti; director, Irving Pichel; based on the novel by Berry Fleming; screenplay, Kathryn Scota; art directors, Lyle Wheeler, Albert Hogsett; set decorators, Thomas Little, Ernest Lansing; music, Cyril J. Mockridge; music director, Emil Newman; assistant director, Sam Schneider; sound E. Clayton Ward; camera, Edward Cronjager; editor, Harmon Jones.

Charles Coburn (Colonel Effingham); Joan Bennett (Ella Sue Dozier); William Eythe (Al); Allyn Joslyn (Earl Hoats); Elizabeth Patterson (Emma); Donald Meek (Doc Buden); Frank Craven (Dewey); Thurston Hall (Mayor); Cora Witherspoon (Clara Meigh); Emory Parnell (Alsobrook); Henry Armetta (Jimmy Economy); Michael Dunne (Ed Bland); Roy Roberts (Captain Rampey); Boyd Davis (Bibbs); Charles Trowbridge (Tignor); Frank Orth (Wild Man); Nicodemus Stewart (Ninety-Eight); Robert Dudley (Pete); Ferris Taylor (Wishum); Oliver Blake (Bill Silk); Frank Mitchell (Major Hickock); Cyde Fillmore (Engineer); Carol Andrews (Sadie); George Melford (Park Commissioner); Harry Hayden (Box Smith); Charles Wagenheim (Young Man); Olin Howlin (Painter); Edward Fielding (Monadue); Mildred Gover (Esther); Minerva Urecal, Hallene Hill (Women); Walter Baldwin (Bus Driver); George O'Hara (Telegrapher); Edward Keane (Doctor); David Ballard (Reporter); Sam McDaniel (Janitor); George Chandler (Drummer); Ed Allen, James Adamson (Black Cab Drivers); Charles Moore (Cab Driver); Gus Glassmire, Herbert Heywood, Jim Toney, Harry Humphrey (Men); Guy Beach, Ken Christy (Motor Cops); George Reed (Janitor); Paul Burns (Man in Restaurant); Paul Kruger (Cop); Clinton Rosemond (Servant); Cecil Weston (Teacher); Phil Tead (Advertising Manager); Henry Hastings (Courthouse Janitor); Abe Dinovitch (Electrician); Marshall Ruth (Painter); Ralph Dunn (Commissioner of Streets); Alma Kruger (Mrs. Monadue); Elizabeth Williams (Guest at Tea).

THE MACOMBER AFFAIR   (UA, 1947) 89 M.

Producers, Benedict Bogeaus, Casey Robinson; director, Zoltan Korda; based on the story "The Short Happy Life of Francis Macomber" by Ernest Hemingway; adaptors, Seymour Bennett, Frank Arnold; screenplay, Casey Robinson; art director, Erno Metzer; set decorator, Fred Widdowson; music director, Miklos Rozsa; assistant director, Joseph Depwe; sound, William Lynch; African camera, O. H. Barradaile, John Wilcox, Fred Francis; camera, Karl Struss; editors, James Smith, George Feld.

Gregory Peck (Robert Wilson); Joan Bennett (Margaret Macomber); Robert Preston (Francis Macomber); Reginald Denny (Captain Smollet); Carl Harbord (Coroner Ames); Jean Gillie (Aimee); Earl Smith (Kongoni); Vernon Downing (Reporter Logan); Frederic Worlock (Clerk); Hassan Said (Abdullah); Martin Wilkins (Bartender); Darby Jones (Masai Warrior).

THE WOMAN ON THE BEACH   (RKO, 1947) 71 M.

Executive producer, Jack J. Gross; associate producer, Will Price; director, Jean Renoir; based on the novel *None So Blind* by Mitchell Wilson; adaptor, Michael Hogan; screenplay, Frank Davis, Renoir; art director, Albert S. D'Agostino, Walter E. Keller; set decorators, Darrell Silvera, John Sturtevant; technical advisor, Lt. Comdr. Charles H. Gardiner, U.S.C.G.R; music, Hanns Eisler; music director, C. Bakaleinikoff; orchestrator, Gil Grau; assistant director, James Casey; dialog director, Paula Walling; sound, Jean L. Speak, Clem Portman; montage, Harold Palmer; special effects, Russell A. Cully; camera, Leo Tover, Harry Wild; editors, Roland Gross, Lyle Boyer.

Joan Bennett (Peggy); Robert Ryan (Scott); Charles Bickford (Tod); Nan Leslie (Eve); Walter Sande (Otto Wernecke); Irene Ryan (Mrs. Wernecke); Glenn Vernon (Kirk); Frank Darien (Lars); Jay Norris (Jimmy); Hugh Chapman (Young Fisherman); Carl Faulkner (Old Fisherman); Marie Dodd (Nurse); Harry Harvey (Dr. Smith); Charles Pawley (Barton); Robert Anderson, Drew Miller, Robert Manning (Coast Guardsmen); Bill Shannon (Blacksmith); Harry Tyler (Carter); Donald Gordon (Donnie); Jackie Jackson (Johnnie); Carl Armstrong (Lenny); John Elliott (Old Workman); Bonnie Blair, Carol Donell, Kay Christopher, Nancy Saunders (Girls at Party); Martha Hyer (Mrs. Barton); Nan Leslie (Alice).

SECRET BEYOND THE DOOR   (Univ., 1948) 98 M.

Producer-director, Fritz Lang; story, Rufus King; screenplay, Silvia Richards; production designer, Max Parker; set decorators, Russell Gausman, John Austin; music, Miklos Rozsa; assistant director, William Holland; sound, Leslie I. Carey, Glenn E. Anderson; camera, Stanley Cortez; editor, Arthur Hilton.

Joan Bennett (Celia Lamphere); Michael Redgrave (Mark Lamphere); Anne Revere (Caroline Lamphere); Barbara O'Neil (Miss Robey); Natalie Schafer (Edith Potter); Paul Cavanagh (Rick Barrett); Anabel Shaw (Intellectual Sub-Deb); Rosa Rey (Paquita); James Seay (Bob Dwight); Mark Dennis (David); Virginia Brissac (Sarah); Houseley Stevenson (Andy); Marie Harmon, Kay Morley (Sub-Debs); Cran Whitley, Virginia Farmer (Lavender Falls Couple); Lucio Villegas (Priest); Eddy C. Waller (Lem); Paul Fierro (Fighter); Julian Rivero (Proprietor); Paul Scardon (Owl Eyes); Danny Duncan (Ferret-Faced Man); Frank Dae (Country Squire); Pedro Regas (Waiter); Donne Martell (Young Mexican Girl); David Cota (Small Mexican Knife Fighter); Tom Chatterton (Judge); Ralph Littlefield (Gothic Man); Nolan Leary (Station Agent); Wayne Treadway (Beefy Man); Watson Downs (Conductor); Jessie Graves (Porter); Donald Kerr (Ticket Man); Robert Espinosa, Robert Barber, Tony Rodriquez (Altar Boys); Peggy Remington (Dean of Women); Harry Denny (College President).

HOLLOW TRIUMPH* (Eagle-Lion, 1948) 83 M.

Executive producer, Bryan Foy; producer, Paul Henreid; director, Steve Sekely; basec on the novel by Murray Forbes; screenplay, Daniel Fuchs; art directors, Edward Ilou, Frank Durlauf; set decorators, Armor Marlowe, Clarence Steensen; music, Sol Kaplan; music conductor, Charles Previn; music director, Irving Friedman; assistant director, Emmett Emerson; makeup, Ern and Frank Westmore; costumes, Kay Nelson; sound, Leon S. Becker, Hugh McDowell; special effects, George J. Teague; camera, John Alton; editor, Fred Allen.

Paul Henreid (John Muller/Dr. Bartok); Joan Bennett (Evelyn Nash); Eduard Franz (Frederick Muller); Leslie Brooks (Virginia Taylor); John Qualen (Swangron); Mabel Paige (Charwoman); Herbert Rudley (March); Paul Burns (Clerk); Charles Trowbridge (Deputy); Ann Staunton (Blonde); Mack Williams (Cashier); Franklyn Farnum (Big Winner); Morgan Farley (Howard Anderson); Joel Friedkin (Williams); Rennie McEvoy (Clerk); Phillip Morris (Doorman); Tom Stevenson (Lester); Benny Rubin (Cabbie); Charles Arnt (Coblenz); Sid Tomack (Artell, the Manager); George Chandler (Aubrey, the Assistant); Alvin Hammer (Jerry); Jerry Marlowe (Hiker); Cliff Clark, Eddie Dunn (Men); Constance Purdy (Mrs. Neyhmer); Cay Forester (Nurse); Carmencita Johnson (Elevator Operator); Lucien Littlefield (Davis); Norma Varden (Mrs. Gerry); Catherine Doucet (Mrs. Nielsen); Victor Jones (Bellboy); Babe London (Lady with Orchids); Flo Wix, Lulu Mae Bohrman (Guests); Cy Ring (Croupier); Sam Finn (Patron); Joaquin Elizando (Houseman); Felice Ingersoll, Vera Marshe, Jeanne Blackford, Dulcy Day (Women); Ray Bennett (Official); Steve Carruthers, Ray Bennett, Sayre Dearing (Men); Bob Bice, Dave Shilling (Thugs); Nolan Leary (Newcomer); Tony Horton (Patron); Robert Ben Ali (Rosie); Bud Wolfe (Al); Henry Brandon (Big Boy); Tom Henry (Stansyck); Jack Webb (Bullseye); Dick Wessell (Sidekick).

THE RECKLESS MOMENT (Col., 1949) 82 M.

Producer, Walter Wanger; director, Max Ophuls; based on the story "The Blank Wall" by Elisabeth Saxnay Holding; screenplay, Henry Garson, Robert W. Soderberg; adaptors, Mel Dinelli, Robert E. Kent; art director, Cary Odell; set decorator, Frank Tuttle; music, Hans Salter; music director, Morris Stoloff; assistant director, Earl Bellamy; makeup, Newt Jones; costumes, Jean Louis; sound, Russell Malmgren; camera, Burnett Guffey; edited, Gene Havlick.

James Mason (Martin Donnelly); Joan Bennett (Lucia Harper); Geraldine Brooks (Beatrice Harper); Henry O'Neill (Mr. Harper); Shepperd Strudwick (Ted Darby); David Bair (David Harper); Roy Roberts (Nagle); Frances Williams (Sybil); Paul E. Burns (Desk Clerk); Danny Jackson (Drummer); Claire Carleton (Blonde); Billy Snyder (Gambler); Peter Brocco (Bartender); Karl "Killer" Davis (Wrestler); Virginia Hunter (Girl); Joseph Plama (Card Player); Cosmo Sardo, Holger Bendixen, Evelyn Moriarity, Al Bayne, Robert Gordon, Ed Pine, Jack Baker, John Roy, Kenneith Kendall, Richard Mickelson, David Levitt, Barbara Hatton, George Dockstader, Barry Regan, Byron Poindexter (Bits); Penny O'Connor (Liza); Bruce Gilbert Norman (Dennis); Sharon Monaghan (Bridget); Charles Marsh (Newsman); Harry Harvey, Norman Leavitt (Post Office Clerks); Boyd Davis (Tall Man); Pat Barton (Receptionist); John Butler (Pawnbroker); Kathryn Card (Mrs. Loring); Pat O'Malley (Bank Guard); Charles Evans (Bank Official); Jessie Arnold (Old Lady); Sue Moore, Dorothy Phillips, Gail Bonney (Women); Charles Jordan (Man); Celeste Savoi (Waitress); Joe Recht (Newsboy); Mike Mahoney, Glenn Thompson, John Monaghan (Policemen); William Schallert (Lieutenant).

*A.K.A. *The Scar.*

FATHER OF THE BRIDE   (MGM, 1950) 93 M.

Producer, Pandro S. Berman; director, Vincente Minnelli; based on the novel by Edward Streeter; screenplay, Frances Goodrich and Albert Hackett; music, Adolph Deutsch; art directors, Cedric Gibbons, Leonid Vasian; set decorators, Edwin B. Willis, Keogh Gleason; costumes, Helen Rose, Walter Plunkett; sound, Douglas Shearer; camera, John Alton; editor, Ferris Webster.

Spencer Tracy (Stanley T. Banks); Elizabeth Taylor (Kay Banks); Joan Bennett (Ellie Banks); Don Taylor (Buckley Dunstan); Billie Burke (Mrs. Doris Dunstan); Leo G. Carroll (Mrs. Massoula); Moroni Olsen (Herbert Dunstan); Melville Cooper (Mr. Triangle); Taylor Holmes (Warner); Paul Harvey (Reverend A. I. Galsworthy); Frank Orth (Joe); Rusty Tamblyn (Tommy Banks); Tom Irish (Ben Banks); Marietta Canty (Delilah); Willard Waterman (Dixon); Nancy Valentine (Elise); Mary Jane Smith (Effie); Jacqueline Duval (Peg); Fay Baker (Miss Bellamy); Frank Hyers (Duffy); Chris Drake, Floyd Taylor, Don Anderson, William Mahon, Walter Kelly, Peter Thompson, Carleton Carpenter (Ushers); Lucille Barnes, Erin Selwyn, Janet Fay, Wendy Waldron (Bridesmaids); Douglas Spencer (Organist); Boyd Davis, Oliver Blake (Men); William E. Green (Sad-Faced Man); Peter Thompson (Young Man); Frank Cady (Timid Guest); Roger Moore, Mickey McCardle, Sherry Hall (Bits); Ella Ethridge, William Bailey, Dorothy Phillips, Stuart Holmes, Anne Kunde (Bits in Dream Sequence); Fred Santley, Philo McCullough, Harry Stanton, Lucille Curtis, Estelle Ettere, Peggy Leon, Betty Farrington (Guests), Lillian Bronson (School Teacher); Aileen Carlyle (Woman); Thomas Browne Henry (Stranger); Mickey Golden, Gene Coogan (Barmen); Lee Phelps (Motor Cop); Patricia Miller (Wispy Girl); Frank Richards (Truck Driver); William Haade, Jeff York (Policemen); Dewey Robinson (Mover with Lamp); Ed Gargan (Mover with Door); Ralph Peters (Mover with Marquee); Dick Wessel (Mover with Chandelier); Dick Alexander (Mover with Screen); Joe Brown, Jr., Jim Hayward, Gil Perkins (Movers); Brad Hatton (Florist); John Welsh (Western Union Boy); William "Bill" Phillips (Foreman of Movers).

FOR HEAVEN'S SAKE   (20th, 1950) 92 M.

Producer, William Perlberg; director, George Seaton; based on the play *May We Come in* by Harry and Dorothy Segall; screenplay, Seaton; music, Alfred Newman; art directors, Lyle Wheeler, Richard Irvine; camera, Lloyd Ahern; editor, Robert Simpson.

Clifton Webb (Charles); Joan Bennett (Lydia); Robert Cummings (Jeff Holton); Edmund Gwenn (Arthur); Joan Blondell (Daphne); Gigi Perreau (Item); Jack LaRue (Tony); Harry Von Zell (Tex); Tommy Rettig (Joe); Dick Ryan (Michael); Charles Lane (Tax Agent); Robert Kent (Joe's Father); Whit Bissell, Ashmead Scott (Doctors); Dorothy Neumann (Western Union Woman); Perc Launders (Doorman); Gordon Nelson (Doorman); Arno Frey (Man); Albert Frey (Headwaiter); Sid Fields, Jack Daly, Bob Harlow, Richard Thorne (Waiters).

FATHER'S LITTLE DIVIDEND   (MGM, 1951) 82 M.

Producer, Pandro S. Berman; director, Vincente Minnelli; based on characters created by Edward Streeter; screenplay, Frances Goodrich and Albert Hackett; music, Albert Sendrey; music director, George Stoll; art directors, Cedric Gibbons, Leonid Vasian; set decorators, Edwin Willis, Keogh Gleason; Women's costumes, Helen Rose; camera, John Alton; editor, Ferris Webster.

Spencer Tracy (Stanley Banks); Joan Bennett (Ellie Banks); Elizabeth Taylor (Kay Dunstan); Don Taylor (Buckley Dunstan); Billie Burke (Doris Dunstan);

115

Moroni Olsen (Herbert Dunstan); Frank Faylen (Policeman); Marietta Canty (Delilah); Rusty Tamblyn (Tommy Banks); Tom Irish (Ben Banks); Hayden Rorke (Dr. Andrew Nordell); Paul Harvey (Reverend Galsworthy); Donald Clark (The Dividend); Beverly Thompson (Nurse); Dabbs Greer (Taxi Driver); Robert B. Williams (Motorcycle Cop); Frank Sully (Diaper Man); James Menzies (Mike); Thomas Menzies (Red); Harry Hines (Old Man); Janet Fay, Nancy Valentine, Wendy Waldron, Erin Selwyn, Jacqueline Duval (Bridesmaids); Paul Kruger, Joseph McGuinn, Howard Mitchell, George "Pinky" Wood (Policemen); Warren Shannon (Boy); Lon Poff (Elderly Man on Porch); George Bruggeman (Gym Instructor).

THE GUY WHO CAME BACK   (20th, 1951) 91 M.

Producer, Julian Blaustein; director, Joseph Newman; based on the story "The Man Who Sank the Navy" by William Fay; screenplay Allan Scott; art directors, Lyle Wheeler, Chester Gore; music director, Lionel Newman; camera, Joseph La Shelle; editor, William B. Murphy.

Paul Douglas (Harry Joplin); Joan Bennett (Kath); Linda Darnell (Dee); Don De Fore (Gordon Towne); Billy Gray (Willy); Zero Mostel (Boots Mullins); Edmon Ryan (Joe Demarcus); Ruth McDevitt (Grandma); Walter Burke (O'Hara); Henry Kulky (Wizard); Dick Ryan (Station Master); Robert B. Williams (Paymaster); Ted Pearson (Tom); Mack Williams (Captain of Waiters); Garnett Marks (Waiter); Shirley Tegge (Hat Check Girl); Charles Conrad (Clerk); Grandon Rhodes (Captain Shallock); John H. Hamilton (Admiral); John Close (Tufano); Tom Hanlon (Announcer); Harry Seymour (Piano Player); Lillian West (Woman); Jack Davis, J. Anthony Hughes, Rodney Bell (Men); John Smith, Warren Farlow, Wayne Farlow, Donald Gordon, Whitey Haupt, Tommie Menzies, Pat Mitchell (Boys); Thomas Browne Henry (Doctor); Emile Meyer (Police Guard); Harry Harvey (Doctor); Hal Baylor (Navy Man); Mike Marienthal, Gayle Pace (Spotters); Stanley Pinto (Referree); Robert Foulk (Fight Manager)

HIGHWAY DRAGNET   (AA, 1954) 71 M.

Executive producer, William F. Broidy; producer, Jack Jungmeyer; co-producers, A. Robert Nunes, Roger Corman; director, Nathan Juran; story, U. S. Anderson, Corman; art director, David Milton; music, Edward J. Kay; camera, John Martin; editor, Ace Herman.

Richard Conte (Jim); Joan Bennett (Mrs. Cummings); Wanda Hendrix (Susan); Reed Hadley (White Eagle); Mary Beth Hughes (Terry); Iris Adrian (Dolly); Harry Harvey (Carson); Tom Hubbard (Ben); Frank Jenks (Marine); Murray Alper (Truck Driver); Zon Murray (Officer); House Peters, Jr. (Cop); and: Joseph Crehan, Tony Hughes, Bill Hale, Fred Gabourie.

WE'RE NO ANGELS   (Par., 1955) C—103 M.

Producer, Pat Duggan; director, Michael Curtiz; based on the play La Cuisine de Anges by Albert Husson; screenplay, Ranald MacDougall; art directors, Hal Pereira, Roland Anderson; set decorators, Sam Comer, Grace Gregory; assistant director, John Coonan; costumes, Mary Grant; makeup, Wally Westmore; music, Frederick Hollander; songs, Hollander and Ralph Freed; G. Martini and Roger Wagner; assistant director, John Coonan; sound, Hugo Granzbach, John Cope; special effects, John P. Fulton; camera, Loyal Griggs; editor, Arthur Schmidt.

Humphrey Bogart (Joseph); Aldo Ray (Albert); Peter Ustinov (Jules); Joan Bennett (Amelie Ducotel); Basil Rathbone (Andre Trochard); Leo G. Carroll (Felix

Ducotel); John Baer (Paul Trochard); Gloria Talbott (Isabelle Ducotel); Lea Penman (Madame Parole); John Smith (Arnaud).

NAVY WIFE   (AA, 1956) 83 M.

Producer, Walter Wanger; director, Edward L. Bernds; based on the novel *Mother Sir* by Tats Blain; screenplay, Kay Lenard; music director, Hans Salter; song, Jack Brooks and Salter; assistant director, Ed Morey, Jr.; camera, Wilfrid Cline; editor, Richard Cahoon.

Joan Bennett (Peg Blain); Gary Merrill (Jack Blain); Judy Nugent (Debby); Maurice Manson (Arwin); Teru Shimada (Mayor Yoshida); Tom Komuro (Ohara); Shirzue Nakamura (Mitsuko); Robert Nichols (Oscar); Carol Veazie (Amelia); John Craven (Dr. Carter); Shirley Yamaguchi (Akashi); Arnold Ishii (Sato); Ziro Tenkai (Goto); Kyoko Kamo (Kimiko); Julia Katayama (Akiko); Karie Shindo (Reiko); Micko Shintani (Tomiko); Rollin Moriyama (Frock-Coated Man); Tauenko Takahashi (Mrs. Yoshida); Dona Jean Okubo (Sister Cecilia); Yoshiko Nilya (Sister Frances); Dick Tyler, Morgan Jones, Jack Bradford (Officers); Michiyo Kamo (Old Woman); Bob Okazaki (Porter); Matsukichi Kamo, John Matautani (Gardeners); Sono Shirai, Masha Kunitomi (Operators); Miyoshi Jingu (Female Attendant); Kimiko Hiroshigi (Woman); Kent Shoji (Small Boy); Karen Yamamoto (Small Girl); Jack Shintani, Kuni Morishima (Workmen); Tomiji Nagao (Man); Jim Yagi (Mr. Okato); Maudie Prickett (Nurse); Phil Arnold (Photographer); Dorothy Furamura (Geisha).

THERE'S ALWAYS TOMORROW   (Univ., 1956) 84 M.

Producer, Ross Hunter; director, Douglas Sirk; based on a story by Ursula Parrott; screenplay, Bernard C. Schoenfeld; art directors, Alexander Golitzen, Eric Orbom; music supervisor, Joseph Gershenson; music, Herman Stein, Heinz Roemheld; camera, Russell Metty; editor, William M. Morgan.

Barbara Stanwyck (Norma Miller); Fred MacMurray (Clifford Groves); Joan Bennett (Marion Groves); Pat Crowley (Ann); William Reynolds (Vinnie Groves); Gigi Perreau (Ellen Groves); Race Gentry (Bob); Myrna Hansen (Ruth); Judy Nugent (Frankie [Frances] Grover); Jane Darwell (Mrs. Rogers); Paul Smith (Bellboy); Jane Howard (Flower Girl); Helen Kleeb (Miss Walker); Frances Mercer (Ruth Doran); Sheila Bromley (Woman from Pasadena); Louise Lorimer (Chic Lady with Dog); Dorothy Bruce (Sales Manager); Hermine Sterler (Tourist's Wife); Fred Nurney (Tourist); Hal Smith (Bartender); James Rawley (Foremen); Jack Lomas (Pianist); Jean Byron (Saleswoman); Bert Holland (Clerk); Carlyle Mitchell (Mr. Carl); Mack Williams (Norma's Hotel Clerk); Richard Mayer (Customer); Pat Meller (Groom); Vonne Lester (Junior Executive); Lorelei Vitek (Bit).

DESIRE IN THE DUST   (20th, 1960) 102 M.

Producer-director, William F. Claxton; based on the novel by Harry Whittington; screenplay, Charles Lang; art directors, Ernst Fegte, John Mansbridge; assistant directors, Maurice Vaccarino, Ira Stewart; makeup, John Sylvester; sound, Jerry Trayler; camera, Lucien Ballard; editor, Richard Farrell.

Raymond Burr (Colonel Ben Marquand); Martha Hyer (Melinda Marquand); Ken Scott (Lonnie Wilson); Joan Bennett (Mrs. Marquand); Brett Halsey (Dr. Ned Thomas); Anne Helm (Cass Wilson); Jack Ging (Peter Marquand); Edward Binns (Luke Connett); Maggie Mahoney (Maudie Wilson); Douglas Fowley (Zuba Wilson); Kelly Thorsden (Sheriff Otis Wheaton); Rex Ingram (Burt Crane);

Irene Ryan (Nora Finney); Paul Baxley (Thurman Case); Robert Earle (Virgil); Patricia Snow (Nellie); Elemore Morgan (Conductor); Aubrey Moore (Frank); Joseph Sidney Phelps (Roy); Joe Paul Steiner (Deputy).

HOUSE OF DARK SHADOWS (MGM, 1970) C—97 M.

Producer, Dan Curtis; associate producer, Trevor Williams; director, Curtis; based on the television series "Dark Shadows"; screenplay, Sam Hall, Gordon Russell; assistant director, William Gerrity, Jr.; production designer, Williams; set decorator, Ken Fitzpatrick; music, Robert Cobert; costumes, Ramse Mostoller; makeup, Dick Smith, Robert Layden; main titles, Jack C. Jacobsen, Frank Hillsburg; sound, Chris Newman; camera, Arthur Ornitz; editor, Arline Garson.

Jonathan Frid (Barnabas Collins); Joan Bennett (Elizabeth Collins Stoddard); Grayson Hall (Dr. Julia Hoffman); Kathryn Leigh Scott (Maggie Evans); Roger Davis (Jeff Clark); Nancy Barrett (Carolyn Stoddard); John Carlen (Willie Loomis); Thayer David (Professor T. Eliot Stokes); Louis Edmonds (Roger Collins); Donald Brice (Todd Jennings); David Henesy (David Collins); Dennis Patrick (Sheriff George Patterson); Lisa Richards (Daphne Rudd); Jerry Lacy (Minister); Barbara Cason (Mrs. Johnson); Paul Michael (Old Man); Jumbert Astredo (Dr. Forbes); Terry Crawford (Todd's Nurse); Michael Stroka (Pall-Bearer).

GIDGET GETS MARRIED (ABC-TV, 1972) C—90 M.

Executive producer, Harry Ackerman; producer-director, E. W. Swackhamer; based on characters by Frederick Kohner; screenplay, John McGreevey; music, Mike Post, Pete Carpenter.

Monie Ellis (Gidget); Michael Burns (Jeff Stevens); Don Ameche (Otis Ramsey); Joan Bennett (Claire Ramsey); Macdonald Carey (Russ Lawrence); Paul Lynde (Louis B. Lattimer); Elinor Donahue (Medley Blaine); Corrine Camacho (Nancy Lewis); Roger Perry (Tom Blaine); Gene Andrusco (Vince Blaine); Rademas Pera (Bob Ramsey); and: Judy McConnell, Larry Delaney, Burke Byrnes, Tiger Williams, Susan Spell, Joe Bernard, Dennis Fimpfle, Victoria Meyernick, Jimmy Bracken, Nicholas Beauvy.

THE EYES OF CHARLES SAND (ABC-TV, 1972) C—90 M.

Producer, Hugh Benson; director, Roza Badiyi; story, Henry Farrell; screenplay, Farrell, Stanford Whitmore; music, Henry Mancini; camera, Ben Colman; editor, Carroll Sax.

Peter Haskell (Charles Sand); Joan Bennett (Aunt Alexandra); Barbara Rush (Katharine Winslow); Sharon Farrell (Emily Parkhurst); Bradford Dillman (Jeffrey Winslow); Adam West (Dr. Paul Scott); Gary Clarke (Raymond); Ivor Francis (Dr. Ballard); and: Owen Bush, Donald Barry, Larry Levine.

INN OF THE DAMNED (Terryrod, 1974)

Producers, Rod Hay, Terry Bourke

With: Joan Bennett, Stuart Whitman

With Ralph Bellamy and Fredric March in TRADE WINDS (UA '39)

ith George Sanders in
REEN HELL (Univ '40)

With Louis Hayward and George Sanders
in THE SON OF MONTE CRISTO
(UA '40)

With Olivia de Havilland,
David O. Selznick, and husband
Walter Wanger at the
Ambassador Hotel (March 1941)

With Franchot Tone and
Allyn Joslyn in
THE WIFE TAKES A FLYER
(Col '42)

With Don Ameche in
GIRL TROUBLE (20th '42)

With daughter Diana Markey and pet poodle Bambi in Chicago (September 1944)

In THE WOMAN IN THE WINDOW (RKO '44)

With Vivian Blaine in NOB HILL (20th '45)

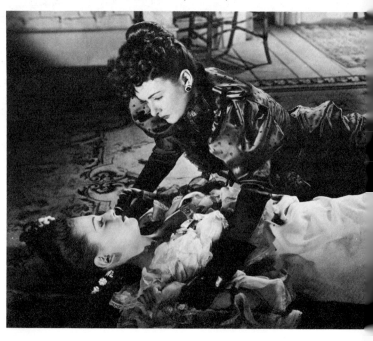

With Paul Henreid in HOLLOW TRIUMPH (*The Scar*) Eagle-Lion '48)

With James Mason in THE RECKLESS MOMENT (Col '49)

At a Beverly Hills press conference following Walter Wanger's shooting of agent Jennings Lang (December 1951)

With Don Taylor,
Spencer Tracy, and
Elizabeth Taylor in FATHER'S
LITTLE DIVIDEND
(MGM '51)

With Richard Conte and
Wanda Hendrix in
HIGHWAY DRAGNET
(AA '54)

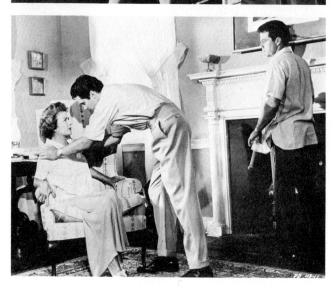

With Brett Halsey and
Ken Scott in
DESIRE IN THE DUST
(20th '60)

In San Francisco (May 1973)

Publicity pose for SALOME, WHERE SHE DANCED (Univ '45)

Yvonne De Carlo

5'4"
122 pounds
Dark brown hair
Blue-gray eyes
Virgo

Startling beauty and an enormous will to succeed have rarely been sufficient assets to insure a woman's onscreen success in Hollywood. If
young Peggy Yvonne Middleton from Vancouver, British Columbia, had
only these admirable assets to recommend her, she might have continued her quest for cinema fame over a much longer time than she did
and still not have achieved her ambitious goal. But this teenage lovely profited from a four-year struggle (1937-41) to win a film player's contract. She
replaced her original naivete with a toughened realization of life, refined
her figure and facial appearance, improved her singing, dancing, and
stage presence, and made a modest inroad into the California social
scene. Most of all, she learned the career-saving device of bending with
the wind, altering her image to suit the times.

As a member of the Paramount Pictures' stock company and now
known as Yvonne De Carlo, she spent the next two years waiting not so
patiently in the soundstage background, playing mostly bit roles oncamera, and fervently wishing for "the" break. Above all, company executives had mentioned a desire to groom her as a threat replacement and/
or successor to the lot's reigning sarong queen, Dorothy Lamour. But it
never happened.

If her fantasized aspirations to become the next Lamour could not come to fruition, then propelling herself as a more exotic reincarnation of a still thriving Maria Montez might be the next best thing. Yvonne thought so, and so did influential producer Walter Wanger and Universal Pictures, who teamed to cast her in the much-touted role of the "world's most beautiful girl," in *Salome, Where She Danced* (Universal, 1945). This Technicolor fluff was no great stuff, but Yvonne fitted very admirably into the escapist ambiance. The picture made a tidy profit, and she was on her way to knocking Montez off the company's throne. Soon Yvonne would be crowned as the studio's new queen of celluloid adventure. The fact that that Yvonne had become a proficient horsewoman and markswoman stood her in excellent stead, permitting the popular personality to assume the mantle of a distaff swashbuckler, who could parade through costumed outings or action Westerns with the greatest of apparent ease. Occasionally a straight dramatic role, as in *Criss Cross* (Universal, 1949), or a comedy assignment, as in *The Captain's Paradise* (United Artists, 1953), would demonstrate that cheesecake posing was not her sole interest.

Two of Yvonne's most fortuitous qualities have been her unpretentiousness and her zest for life. The first trait allowed her to survive the spectrum of mediocre film assignments, a precarious freelancer's status from the mid-1950s onward, and to develop a capacity for finding practical new professional horizons. Thus she could survive the down periods in her film career by turning to summer stock, nightclub tours, filming abroad, and even becoming a mock horror figure in a television series, "The Munsters." The second trait propelled her into becoming one of the world's most eligible playgirls, a status which the more glamorous Rita Hayworth might well have envied. Yvonne dated many of Hollywood's and Europe's most distinguished bachelors; yet her common sense led her to wed a hard-working movie stuntman and to survive the hazards of two decades of married life.

Yvonne achieved her ambition to star on Broadway by joining the 1971 musical *Follies,* in which she enjoyed a personal triumph with her show-stopping song, "I'm Still Here." It is just those three little words that have been the keystone of her life: past, present, and future.

She was born Peggy Yvonne Middleton on September 1, 1922, in Vancouver, British Columbia, Canada. Peggy Yvonne hardly remembered her father, a native New Zealander, who deserted her and her mother when she was scarcely three years old. Practical Mrs. Middleton, whose maiden name had been De Carlo, became a waitress to support herself and her sensitive child. If Peggy Yvonne lacked a proper homelife, Mrs. Middleton did her best to provide her creatively inclined daughter with a few of the other benefits of a normal childhood. At an early age Peggy Yvonne was enrolled at the Vancouver School of Dance, where she proved to be a most apt pupil. Later, Mrs. Middleton, who had already perceived that her offspring just might have possibilities in a show-business career, had her child study singing and dramatics.

Peggy Yvonne was not shy about entertaining the neighborhood kids with well-rehearsed divertissements. She wrote, produced, and acted in her own minidramas, charging, as she recalls, "two pennies for the boxes down front," a rather high fee for the privilege of sitting on a wooden packing crate. Peggy Yvonne first appeared as a professional in a local vaudeville skit called "Aussie the Boxing Kangaroo," but the debut performance did not lead to any notable return engagements. She later studied advanced dancing at the June Roxer School in Vancouver and was thereafter featured dancer at local playhouses, including the Vancouver Little Theatres. With so much of her daily life devoted to the pursuit of a seemingly illusive theatrical career, it was little wonder that Peggy Yvonne never had the opportunity (or inspiration) to graduate from the King Edward High School in Vancouver. One of the few highlights of her stymied education occurred when she was eleven years old and won five dollars (a big sum at the height of the Depression) in a newspaper contest. It was a landmark event that Yvonne still recalls with pride and fondness.

It was not surprising that the increasingly ambitious Mrs. Middleton should seize upon a silver-screen career as the natural outgrowth of Peggy Yvonne's professional training. In 1937, Mrs. Middleton and Peggy Yvonne made their first trip to Hollywood, the mecca of golden dreams for the girl's hopefully bright future. But the still burgeoning motion-picture town had an overload of screen-struck beautiful girls, all just waiting for the big show-business break. By the time Mrs. Middleton's visa expired, mother and daughter admitted temporary defeat and returned to Canada.

The duo were undiscouraged by the setback. Each accepted temporary jobs here and there in Vancouver to scrape together sufficient funds to launch a fresh assault on the film studios the next year. This back-and-forth procedure became an annual ritual for Mrs. Middleton and Peggy Yvonne. Usually, when in California, Mrs. Middleton would find employment as a waitress, and Peggy Yvonne would eventually rustle up a job in a minor Hollywood nightery as a chorus-line dancer.

By early 1940, seventeen-year-old Peggy Yvonne was seemingly a fixture of the Hollywood rat race, one of the many on the outer fringes of the movie business. The following year proved to be an extended season of breaks for the girl. She won the title Miss Venice Beach in a bathing beauty contest and shortly thereafter acquired a chorus-line job at Nils T. Granlund's Florentine Gardens, a Hollywood nightspot. The well-known entrepreneur of modest, moral girlie shows would later recall young Peggy Yvonne as "a shy, demure, silent brunette. . . . [She] came to Hollywood with looks, intense ambitions and nothing else. Those of us who were close to her when she first went to work for me at the Florentine Gardens said she didn't have the push and power to get herself a break. . . . When she was deported back to Canada, I got her back by giving her a contract as a featured player instead of a chorine, which made her admissible. . . . Yet she was hampered in Hollywood. She wasn't the party type, seldom went on dates, resented the wolves. She remained a sweet, unspoiled kid and continued plodding patiently instead of seeking fame overnight when she saw what happened to the gals who tried to get there the quick way."

Mrs. Middleton and Peggy Yvonne knew all the ins and outs of plodding along, suffering temporary defeats, and challenging professional obstacles. At night Peggy Yvonne kicked in the girlie line, and during the day spent all her time making the rounds of studios, with little luck. She then left the Florentine Gardens for a spot in the chorus of Earl Carroll's show at the Aquarius Theatre, but the showman fired her when she gained weight.

Frustrated Peggy Yvonne soon dieted, and at this point her casting call rounds paid dividends: she received a $100-a-week player's contract with Paramount Pictures. The Marathon Street lot was then supervised by Y. Frank Freeman, vice-president in charge of studio operations, and by B. G. De Sylva, executive producer. At the time, the big female names at the studio were Claudette Colbert, Dorothy Lamour, Paulette Goddard, and Madeleine Carroll. Ellen Drew, Mary Martin, and Susan Hayward were on lower rungs of popularity, followed by peek-a-boo hairstyled Veronica Lake, who was about to hit it big. In addition, there were Constance Moore and Martha O'Driscoll, who would soon depart for other film factories. On the minor-league players' roster were the likes of child-prodigy pianist Dolly Loehr, who would change her name to Diana Lynn and gain prominence in *The Major and the Minor* (1942). Attractive and promising Frances Gifford would soon leave Paramount to turn up later at MGM. Jean Parker was already queen of the Pine-Thomas budget film unit, and waiting in the proverbial wings were such young femme contractees as Margaret Hayes, Barbara Britton, Kay Aldridge, Jean Wallace, and Joan Marsh.

Nothing seemed to go right for Peggy Yvonne, who soon changed her name to Yvonne De Carlo. Initially she was utilized at Paramount to provide the still-picture department with cheesecake shots, and she developed a mild reputation as a prominent exponent of leg art. But this avenue of employment led nowhere for the ambitious girl. Then she was graduated to making screentests with new actors upon whom the studio had taken options. "I was the test queen at Paramount," the actress later recalled ruefully of this unproductive, thankless period.

Bandleader and womanizer Artie Shaw, who had wed and divorced Lana Turner in the early 1940s, would later remember taking Yvonne to dinner one night in 1941 and professionally advising her, "Quit. You're not in a rut, you're in a hole. In a rut, you can at least move sideways. But in a hole, you can't move at all. Quit."

Yvonne refused to heed such warnings. Like her mother, she was convinced that success was just around the corner. Yvonne tried any reasonable gambit to succeed in the film industry. For the Soundies Music Corporation, she made at least two short subjects, singing in *I Look at You* (1941) and *The Lamp of Memory* (1942). At Columbia, she joined *The Glove Slingers* series for the *King of the Campus* (1942) short entry. These stints went generally unnoticed, but finally the studio executives agreed that she might be allowed to try brief oncamera roles. Magnanimous Paramount preferred that other, lesser studios take a chance on the unproven Yvonne, and in the course of 1942, three of her appearances were made on loan-out. Chronologically, Columbia's programmer *Harvard, Here I Come* (1942) was Yvonne's first feature-film release. Don Miller in *B Movies* (1973) says of this Maxie Rosenbloom-Arline Judge quickie, "If a poll were ever taken attempting to discover the most nauseating comedy of all time, *Harvard, Here I Come* would be high on the list." Miller's evaluation is quite fair, considering the plot premise (Dumb Rosenbloom is brought to Harvard as a lab study but wangles a four-year scholarship in the process) and the revolting dialog, which has the ex-boxer personality insisting, "I'm a vulture for culture." When a professor inquires how Rosenbloom's grammar is, the brainless wonder responds, "I don't know. We haven't heard from her in a long time." In the midst of this minor melee, Yvonne was spotted as a bathing girl.

Back at Paramount, the studio turned out a magnetic picturization of Graham Greene's *A Gun for Sale*, titled for the screen as *This Gun for Hire* (1942). Alan Ladd making his reputation with this feature, was cast as a baby-faced but ruthless psychopathic killer involved in an Axis spy plot, with Veronica Lake playing the girlfriend of law-enforcer Robert Preston, who finds herself turning patriotic to help corral the espionage leaders. Yvonne was seen in a brief unbilled role as a specialty dancer in the Neptune Club sequence.

When Yvonne was hired by Paramount, there had been mild rumors that she might possibly be groomed as a replacement threat to sarong queen Dorothy Lamour, then riding the crest of her popularity. Teamed with the studio's Bing Crosby and Bob Hope, Lamour had demonstrated a pleasing comedy trait in *Road to Singapore* (1940), the first of the starring trio's *Road* pictures. In the third entry, *Road to Morocco* (1942), geared as a spoof of desert epics, Yvonne was scarcely noticeable as one of the several handmaidens to princess Lamour.* If Yvonne thought she was any

*Other "starlets" playing handmaidens were Louise LaPlanche, Theo de Voe, Brooke Evans, Suzanne Ridgway, Patsy Mace, and Poppy Wilde.

133

real competition to the top-ranking Lamour, the latter was entirely unaware of the supposed rivalry.

Yvonne then moved over to Republic Pictures for *Youth on Parade* (1942), which boasted a cast featuring John Hubbard, Martha O'Driscoll, Bruce Langley, and Ruth Terry. The best aspect of this Albert S. Rogell-directed feature was the Sammy Cahn-Jule Styne score, which contained two popular songs, "You're So Good to Me" and "I've Heard That Song Before." Yvonne was merely a coed in this musical set at Cotchatootamee College. Returning to Paramount, Yvonne was used in *Lucky Jordan* (1942), an Alan Ladd vehicle about which Joseph Pihodna (*New York Herald-Tribune*) reported, "It's still cops and robbers, no matter how you slice it." Ladd is a poolroom racketeer who is drafted into the army, later goes AWOL, and, while on the lam, forces USO hostess Helen Walker to help bait a trap for espionage agents operating in the New York City area. If a moviegoer were very observant, Yvonne could be spotted as a girl walking down the (studio) street.

Yvonne had an oncamera reunion with her Nils T. Granlund-Florentine Gardens pals in *Rhythm Parade* (Monogram, 1942). Gale Storm, later to gain more fame as television's "My Little Margie," had the female lead, bubbling forth as the vocalist who would just love to have a bandstand spot at Cliff Nazarro's little nightspot. It was all "music, legs, dancing and backstage patter, the kind of picture that doesn't get a Broadway opening because you have to stop somewhere." Game Yvonne was back in the chorus line, from whence she had sprung a year before.

Adding to her professional woes, Yvonne had been dating Paramount newcomer Sterling Hayden, but she lost out in the romantic sweepstakes as well, for, in 1942, the strapping actor wed Madeleine Carroll.

By a technicality, the first of Yvonne's seven 1943 releases was a loanout. Paramount made a deal to allow United Artists to release some of the former's produced films. *The Crystal Ball* (United Artists, 1943) offered sprightly Paulette Goddard as a resilient out-of-towner who is befriended by a shyster crystal-gazer (Gladys George) and later uses the disguise to woo upper-cruster Ray Milland away from his "unworthy" fiancée, Virginia Field. It was all "a lot of hocus-pocus" (said Bosley Crowther of the *New York Times*), but audiences were indulgently amused by the slaphappy proceedings. Yvonne and Maxine Ardell were briefly spotted as secretaries. The grade-B musical *Salute for Three* (Paramount, 1943) was yet another show-business tale set at a serviceman's canteen (this time in Manhattan) where "celebrities" act like just plain folks serving food and entertaining the armed forces. Minna Gombell was boss of the canteen kitchen, Betty Rhodes sang "There's Danger in Kissing a Stranger" and "Left Right," while benign Macdonald Carey was the wholesome soldier, almost duped by publicist Marty May in a fake romance with the vocalist. There was Dona Drake heading an all-girl band, with Marcella

Phillips, Marjorie Deanne, Yvonne, and Alice Kirby composing the Quartette Girls. Even the generally indulgent *New York Daily News* was harsh to this rationed bit of celluloid entertainment. It was slapped with a half-star rating: "The story is artificial, the dialogue insane and the cast a total loss in a morass of bad cinema."

Producer-director Sam Wood had endured great difficulties transforming Ernest Hemingway's *For Whom the Bell Tolls* into a 1943 major release. After a big talent hunt for the proper actress to play the innocent young Spanish girl, badly ravaged by the brutality of men engulfed in war, ballerina Vera Zorina was initially selected to star opposite Gary Cooper. Later she was replaced in the demanding assignment by Swedish-born Ingrid Bergman. The staunch, 168-minute color drama met with critical approval ("The screen has met the challenge of fine literature triumphantly" [Howard Barnes, *New York Herald-Tribune*]) and made the proverbial mint at the box office. Few can recall that sandwiched among the extras in a cafe sequence were contractees Maxine Ardell, Marjorie Deanne, Yvonne, Alice Kirby, Marcella Phillips, Louise LaPlanche, and other Paramount hopefuls.

For its bid as the servicewomen picture of the year, the studio offered *So Proudly We Hail!* (Paramount, 1943), which numbered Claudette Colbert, Paulette Goddard, and Veronica Lake among its major marquee assets, with a contingent of lesser players like Barbara Britton, Mary Treen, Dorothy Adams, Ann Doran, Jean Willes, and Jan Wiley portraying other military nurses involved in the desperate wartime struggle on Bataan. In the midst of this stellar cast, one had to have sharp eyes to notice Yvonne as a girl in the background of all the hubbub of this well-mounted tearjerker, which Howard Barnes (*New York Herald-Tribune*) proclaimed "an honest and valiant salute to American courage."

Let's Face It had enjoyed a 547-performance Broadway run, bolstered by the Cole Porter songs and bouncy performances by Danny Kaye, Eve Arden, Benny Baker, and others. For the Paramount cameras (1943), it was converted into a Bob Hope-Betty Hutton comedy feast that somehow lost most of its original zest in the translation. Frenetic Hutton ran a health farm for overweight women, with Hope as her rubber-spined fiancé stationed at nearby Camp Arthur, who, in the course of helping to entertain three bored middle-aged wives (Eve Arden, ZaSu Pitts, Phyllis Povah), ends up capturing a Nazi submarine prowling off Long Island Sound. The highlight of this less-than-delightful outing was Hutton's belting of "Let's Not Talk about Love." Valiant Yvonne was just a "girl" in the background, along with fellow unknowns Noel Neill, Julie Gibson, and Jayne Hazard.

True to Life (Paramount, 1943) maneuvered a wafer-thin premise (Dick Powell, the writer of a radio soap opera, gets himself into a real American home to get the flavor of actual living conditions with Mary

Martin the girl in the case, and Franchot Tone as Powell's collaborator and rival for her affections) into pleasant casualness, aided a great deal by bumbling Victor Moore as the father and addled Mabel Paige as his loving spouse. Once more Yvonne was merely among the parsley cheese-cake dressing for the airy musical.

Yvonne's first real oncamera stint was a mixed blessing, for it occurred on loan to independent producers P. S. Harrison and E. D. Derr for their skinflint version of James Fenimore Cooper's 1841 novel, *The Deerslayer*. Action-bound Republic Pictures picked up the distribution rights to this programmer, which was then packaged for double-bill engagements in lesser theatres throughout the country. "Most any gang of eight-year olds could do a better job of playing Indians," insisted the *New York Daily News*, which confessed the impoverished feature was "just like a refugee from a nickelodeon." Bruce Kellogg had the undemanding task—at least by this film's quaint acting standards—of portraying Cooper's immortal frontiersman, Natty Bumppo, better known as the Deerslayer. Demure Jean Parker was the porcelain-pretty heroine. As for Yvonne, prolific director Lew Landers let her run amuck as Wah-Tah, the Indian princess betrothed to Jingo-Good (Larry Parks). She is the object of the affections of scoundrelly Huron brave Briarthorn (Phil Van Zandt).

He not only burns her village, but kidnaps the royal squaw, leading to the "bloody" battle to the finish. Midst such abounding ineptitude in all departments of production, Yvonne's inexperienced performance in *The Deerslayer* went unadmonished by most reviewing sources that had the stomach for the child's play.

Three decades after their heyday, it may seem inexplicable to modern filmgoers just why Yvonne (or her boosters) would wish anyone to aspire to the cinema throne held jointly by Paramount's Dorothy Lamour and by contemporary Maria Montez, then ruling the tropical color-adventure-film roost at Universal. Besides, it seemed that Yvonne had appeared on the Hollywood scene too late to capture the remaining aura of popularity surrounding the exotic celluloid genres dominated by Lamour and Montez. But if one avenue of success was denied her, Yvonne was prepared to angle for another bid to success.

Interestingly, her mentor proved to be none other than megaphoned-crooner Rudy Vallee. The 1920s version of Frank Sinatra had had his share of career ups and downs, and only recently, in *The Palm Beach Story* (Paramount, 1942), had been relaunched as a stuffed-shirt cinema funnyman. When Vallee attended Earl Carroll's annual birthday party for one of Carroll's chorus girls, he was dating Howard Hughes contractee Jane Greer.* At the social affair, Vallee spotted and was introduced to Yvonne. He took an immediate shine to the radiant young woman, and in conjunction

---

*Vallee and Greer would wed on December 2, 1943; they divorced in mid-1944.

with his business manager, Ted Lesser, tried to get the actress worthwhile picture jobs. But in vain. She was "too exotic, too oriental in her features," Vallee and Lesser were told by film studios. Vallee later described his sometime-date Yvonne in his autobiography, *My Time Is Your Time* (1962), by saying "her intelligence was matched by a warm and captivating charm and personality."

While Vallee tried to make her a star, Yvonne continued to ply her craft in a minor way at Paramount. The Washington housing shortage was then America's biggest domestic war joke, and was considered fitting material to form a comedy, entitled *Standing Room Only* (Paramount, 1944). Fred MacMurray, rising young executive at Edward Arnold's midwestern toy plant, arrives in the nation's capital with secretary Paulette Goddard. When they cannot acquire lodging accommodations, they are led on a merry eighty-three-minute chase in which they become temporary domestics at Roland Young's plush digs. Yvonne was back to her old onscreen gambit, briefly appearing as a secretary.

Laraine Day, Signe Hasso, and Carol Thurston had the leading female parts in Cecil B. DeMille's patriotic wartime drama, *The Story of Dr. Wassell* (Paramount, 1944), which starred Gary Cooper as the heroic physician of Java in 1942. Yvonne had a tiny part as a native girl, but her impressive appearance made a mark in the director's memory, and more than a decade later, he would use her for a starring role in the remake of his *The Ten Commandments* (Paramount, 1956).

Yvonne's next chance to gain success came when Dorothy Lamour walked out of the lead in *Rainbow Island* (Paramount, 1944). The studio brass hastily selected Yvonne as her replacement. Then, for a variety of reasons, Lamour had a change of mind and resumed her lead assignment as Lona, the shipwrecked daughter of an American doctor who becomes the beloved sovereign of a South Pacific atoll. This jerry-built "spoof" of her previous rash of tropical romances relied more on the hapless comedy of Eddie Bracken and Gil Lamb than the exotic wiggling of Lamour, who sang "Beloved." Cast-off Yvonne was relegated to playing one of the star's assorted, stonefaced island companions. "You might have seen Gil Lamb chasing me through the bushes in it," Yvonne later recounted.

On loan-out to MGM, Yvonne was along as one of Marlene Dietrich's retinue in the color remake of *Kismet* (1944), in which Ronald Colman was the bearded Hafiz and James Craig, the handsome Caliph. Back at Paramount in *Practically Yours* (1944), Yvonne was among the employees at the Meglin Company run by Cecil Kellaway, but limelighted by worker Claudette Colbert and navy pilot Fred MacMurray. Bing Crosby had to cope with twin Betty Huttons in *Here Come the Waves* (Paramount, 1944), but only with a flash of Yvonne, minutely oncamera as a near extra. In *Bring on the Girls* (Paramount, 1945), a minor Veronica Lake entry, not even bolstered by the likes of Sonny Tufts, Eddie Bracken, or Marjorie Reynolds, Yvonne provided a momentary diversion as a hat-check girl. It proved to be the inglorious end to Yvonne's tenure at Paramount.

If Yvonne's Paramount years were generally unproductive, she did have the consolation that her untapped energies provided her with ample opportunity to practice her horsemanship, a skill which would stand her in good stead in picture-making to come. Yvonne participated in some fifteen West Coast rodeos at such places as the Los Angeles Coliseum, Hollywood's Gilmore Stadium, and the Riviera Club in Beverly Hills. She won three first prizes in the Best Old California Costume Class; three second prizes in the Trail Horse Class; and five first prizes for the "Most Beautiful Girl on Horseback."

In 1944, while Yvonne was unenthusiastically completing her Paramount contract and waiting for Rudy Vallee to make good even a few of his grandiose schemes for her, she learned about Walter Wanger's ballyhoo campaign to find "The Most Beautiful Girl in the World" to star in his forthcoming feature, *Salome, Where She Danced* (Universal, 1945). Had the film been lensed just a few years earlier, Wanger undoubtedly would have utilized Maria Montez, the intriguing star of his *Arabian Nights* (Universal, 1942). But by this juncture, that ambitious personality from the Dominican Republic was suffering a career reversal, and, engulfed in a test of wills with her studio bosses, she was unavailable for consideration in the *Salome* venture.

Meantime, Yvonne had two friends, Reginald Reid and Kenneth Ross-Mackenzie. Both of them were Royal Air Force pilot-officers, and they induced twenty of their serviceman pals to sign a petition demanding that Yvonne be chosen the contest winner. Their entry was submitted to Wanger, along with an alluring glossy photograph of Yvonne. Vallee was also prompted to suggest Yvonne for the role to Wanger—that is, after the producer had rejected Vallee's notion that Jane Greer should have the "coveted" assignment. Although Yvonne was thus the instigator of much of the outside pressure brought to bear on Wanger, it was she that had to undergo and pass an audition before Wanger himself. "I'll never forget that audition," Yvonne later recalled. "Mr. Wanger said to me, 'You're good enough so that you'll never have to cozy up to a producer.' " Perceptive Yvonne admitted she thought a good deal of her test success with Wanger was due to her superficial resemblance to the producer's current wife, glamorous Joan Bennett. After Yvonne's Universal contract was signed for the movie, Wanger told her he admired her "certain magic," which, he said, was already evident to the public. At this point he produced the RAF petition, but she impishly feigned ignorance of the whole affair.

Salome, Where She Danced proved to be one of the few major attempts Hollywood has made to produce a film that seems straightforward in its plot presentation but is really heavily tongue-in-cheek. Laurence Stallings's plot-choked screenplay, from a Michael J. Phillips story, had Viennese ballerina Salome (Yvonne)* fleeing nineteenth-century Europe during the Austro-Prussian War because she has betrayed one of Bismarck's chief officers. The harassed girl, abetted by American journalist Rod Cameron, arrives in the United States to begin a dancing tour. She lingers in the Arizona desert town of Drinkman's Wells in order to earn the remainder of her stagecoach fare to San Francisco. While there she dances for the local citizens and eventually convinces an outlaw gang to follow the straight and narrow path. Besides sashaying in rhythmic gyrations in deliberately filmy, exotic costumes, Yvonne was romanced oncamera by a quartet of leading men: Cameron, David Bruce, Albert Dekker, and Walter Slezak (not top-caliber silver-screen types but certainly a varied lot). By the end of the ninety-minute yarn, less discerning viewers had had their money's worth of entertainment, and any watcher was at least then apprised of just how the arid Arizona hamlet changed its name to that of the film's lengthy title.

The critics were not in the least won over by the Charles Lamont-directed opus. ". . . this collection of animated lantern slides, tinted in Technicolor, is probably the most fantastic horse-opera of the year" (Thomas M. Pryor, *New York Times*). Seymour Peck (*PM*) complained that "it lacks humor, suspense and pace. In a Western this is not merely unpardonable, but almost fatal." The *New York Herald-Tribune* simply tagged this $1.2 million production "a cinema curiosity."

But pulchritudinous Yvonne at least inspired Pryor of the influential *Times* to observe, "Yvonne De Carlo, a comparative newcomer, has an agreeable mezzo-soprano singing voice, all the 'looks' one girl could ask for, and moreover, she dances with a sensuousness which must have caused the Hays Office some anguish." Having given Yvonne her

---

*Oscar Wilde wrote the play *Salome* in French in 1892 for Sarah Bernhardt, but that star never played in it. It was first produced in Paris in 1896 by Lugne-Poe. The English censors banned *Salome* in their homeland until 1931, when it had its first London performance with Margaret Rawlings in the title role. In Germany, Hedwig Lachmann adapted Wilde's work for a libretto for an opera by Richard Strauss, which had its premiere performance with Marie Wittich in the title role in Dresden on December 9, 1905. The opera *Salome* was first staged at the Metropolitan with Olive Fremstad in 1907. It so shocked the staid subscription-holders that it was dropped from the repertoire and did not reappear until 1934, when it was sung by Gota Ljungberg. Mary Garden sang the operatic role in French at the Manhattan Opera House in 1909 and later on a national tour. In 1943, French mezzo-soprano Lily Djanel came from Europe to sing in the operatic *Salome* at the Metropolitan; followed six years later by Ljuba Welitch, who performed the part with Fritz Reiner conducting. Within the past decade such performers as Birgit Nilsson, Anja Silja, Grace Bumbry, and Leonie Rysanek have gained fame in the part.

Onscreen, Theda Bara was *Salome* (Fox, 1918), a performance upstaged by Nazimova's bizarre performance in her Allied Producers & Distributors rendition of 1923. That same year Diana Allen starred in a far more modest rendition of *Salome* for Malcolm Strauss Pictures. Columbia lavished a big budget on its Rita Hayworth *Salome* (1953), and in the remake of *King of Kings* (MGM, 1961) Brigid Bazlen portrayed the famed temptress.

screen due, nearly everyone agreed that it was veteran performer Marjorie Rambeau as the broken-down trouper, Madam, who stole what little there was of the *Salome, Where She Danced* show, especially when Rambeau was engulfed in black tights and rendered a tippling version of "I Dreamt I Dwelt in Marble Halls."

To Universal's face-saving surprise, *Salome, Where She Danced* emerged a box-office success. The film launched Yvonne on the path to stardom, but it was *Frontier Gal* (Universal, 1945) which solidified her position with the studio hierarchy. Originally *Frontier Gal* had been slated for tempestuous Maria Montez. But after the dismal *Sudan* (Universal, 1945), that star had declared that she would not make another picture in tandem with fading Jon Hall, and that she wanted an opportunity to display her dramatic talents in a contemporary story. While Universal's story department was dreaming up something to satisfy Montez, Cliff Work, vice-president in charge of studio production, decreed that Yvonne should inherit the *Frontier Gal* mantle. Yvonne graciously and quickly accepted, realizing that with such another popular celluloid entry she might inherit Montez's semivacant throne as queen of exotic Technicolor epics, or whatever new species of colorful adventure romances appealed to post-World War II audiences.

Universal allocated $1.4 million to this Technicolor Western, with a good deal of the budget marked for a saturation publicity campaign to sell both Yvonne and the film to the new, more demanding breed of filmgoers. Again Charles Lamont directed, this time from a script by Michael Fessier and Ernest Pagano, who also served as the film's producers. Yvonne was cast as fiery Lorena Dumont, a French saloon gal in Red Gulch, a brawling town of the West in the early 1900s. The rather rambling eighty-four-minute plot finds rugged outlaw Rod Cameron riding into town one day, just a few leagues ahead of a pursuing posse. He takes an immediate shine to self-sufficient Yvonne and at pistol-point has her wed to him. After a one-night-only honeymoon, hot-tempered Yvonne retaliates by turning Cameron over to the sheriff, and he is herded off to prison on a manslaughter charge (for killing the man who had murdered his partner). Six years later, he returns to Yvonne at her Red Horse Saloon to find that he has a five-year-old daughter, much to the dismay of his new love (Jan Wiley). Despite all the cowboy's reluctance, the expected reconciliation is finally achieved by the couple's lisping little daughter, Mary Ann (Beverly Simmons).

Backed up by a cast that included Sheldon Leonard as the chief bad guy, called Blackie, with Andy Devine and Fuzzy Knight for primary comedy relief, *Frontier Gal* was branded "slow and dull" by the *New York Times*. Despite the diversion of Yvonne's singing (including "Set 'Em up Joe" and "What Is Love?")* and dancing, *Cue* magazine was forced to admit

*Dubbed by Doreen Tryden.

she "is still no Sarah Bernhardt." *Variety* explained it more chivalrously: "[Yvonne] garners more attention as a sultry personality than as an actress, but the former is enough to assure her a following without the latter." *Newsweek* magazine observed, "Miss De Carlo, in addition to a spot of singing, contributes some striking scenic effects of her own."*Time* magazine gallantly conceded, "The picture's chief excitement is Yvonne De Carlo, a vigorous, shapely actress who looks equally luscious in sequins or a fringed deerskin skirt." In Britain, *Frontier Gal* was retitled *The Bride Wasn't Willing.*

Since Yvonne's arrival at Universal only one short year before,* she had come a long way in the film industry, but her studio bosses wisely noted that if she were to become a top-ranking screen personality,. she must learn "how to be a proper movie star." She later revealed, "I lived at the Sherry-Netherlands [in New York] for two months and I went to the John Robert Powers school. They taught me things like how to walk off a New York curb and how to enter a room in a manner befitting a bigtime movie star.

"They also tried to teach me how to eat. One day the big boss came to town and took me to dinner. I knew why he was taking me to dinner; he wanted to watch me eat. I was so nervous that when I started to lift my soup spoon to my mouth, my hand shook so much that I had to put the spoon down again. I couldn't eat soup for a whole year after that."

Eventually Yvonne returned to the West Coast to resume her film career. By this time the studio had undergone a reorganization to prevent bankruptcy. Like a well-disciplined mascot, Yvonne was told to report for costume fittings for her new starring film, *Song of Scheherazade* (Universal, 1947). Written and directed by Walter Reisch, this Technicolor absurdity claimed to tell the story of the Russian composer Nikolai Rimsky-Korsakoff (Jean-Pierre Aumont),† and how he came to write his famous music. In 1865 Rimsky-Korsakoff is a naval cadet with the Russian fleet which puts into a port in Morocco. There he finds a beautiful dancer named Cara de Talavera (Yvonne) who inspires him to write his great music. He is torn between the girl, who dances in waterfront dives to support her chic, selfish mama (Eve Arden) in the comfort to which she has become accustomed, and his music. The composer, however, comes to grips with himself and later brings Yvonne to St. Petersburg to dance at the premiere of his latest opera.

Again Universal had put Yvonne in glorious Technicolor settings with scanty costuming and much footage for sexy dancing (she had three terpsichorean turns: "Caprice Espagnole," "Fandango," and "Scheherazade").

---

*There is some indication that Universal at one point in 1944 planned to use Yvonne to play a wolfwoman character in an omnibus horror tale, rather than in *Salome, Where She Danced.*

†It was rather ironic for Yvonne to have Aumont as her leading man since he was the real-life husband of her predecessor, Maria Montez.

For reviewers like John McCarten (*New Yorker* magazine), who took the proceedings seriously, the film had a disastrous effect: "To date, this is the worst nonsense that Hollywood has cooked up about a composer." Other less-demanding members of the fourth estate, like *Time* magazine's critic, admitted it was an "amiable semi-burlesque."

In actuality, there was not much excitement to this picture, which overflowed with ornate sets and costumes. "Escapism is being provided with such a lavish and heavy hand . . . that we fervently wish there was some way of escaping all this Technicolored escapism" (Thomas M. Pryor, *New York Times*). As the focal point of the hodgepodge of color, music, and (semi)history, Yvonne did not measure up to the expectation of Universal's hotly exaggerated publicity campaign over her titillating screen presence in this extravaganza. "She brings very little color to a conventional heroine's role and her dancing is not yet up to standards one would expect from the premiere danseuse of a first-rate production." Also wasted in this divertissement was Brian Donlevy as the crusty head of the Russian fleet in which Aumont serves,* and wisecracking Arden as an anachronistic show-business mama playacting as a mantilla-clad duenna-like mother. The only legitimate interest provided by *Song of Scheherazade* was the lackluster appearance of Charles Kullman of the Metropolitan Opera Company, who sang "Song of India," "Hymn to the Sun," and "Fandango."

Film audiences were finally treated to a straight acting job by Yvonne with the June 1947 release of Universal's *Brute Force.*† It was a cagey experiment on the studio's part, since the close-up study of prison life only provided female roles in short flashback sequences. Thus Yvonne, in the company of the studio's already proven talents, Ann Blyth and Ella Raines (and with the attractive but histrionically unresourceful former model Anita Colby), could safely make a minor foray into the uncharted arena of drama without sacrificing her status as a major screen personality.

Yvonne had a very convincing cameo as Gina, the Italian girlfriend of jailbird Burt Lancaster. In a flashback scene the story of Gina is told, with Lancaster taking the prison rap when she murders her father, a black marketeer operating in Italy. A quasi-frank and deliberately brutal film,

---

*At one point, deadpan Donlevy is forced to ask Aumont, "What did posterity ever do for you?"

†*Brute Force* is generally cited in American cinema histories as a major example of Hollywood's postwar neorealistic film trend, along with such other notable entries as Louis de Rochemont's *The House on 92nd Street* (Twentieth Century-Fox, 1945), *The Killers* (Universal, 1946), and *Naked City* (Universal, 1948). The latter two pictures, along with *Brute Force,* were all produced by Mark Hellinger.

There were some contemporary critics who did not agree that *Brute Force* was an outstanding, grim landscape of reality. James Agee, in the *Nation*, snarled, "I was astounded to hear that some knowledgeable people think of *Brute Force,* a movie about men in a big jail, as a happy return to the melodramas of the early thirties. Maybe so, in some of the jabpaced, slickly sadistic action sequences. But there isn't a line in it, or a performance, or an idea, or an emotion, that belongs much later than 1915, and cheesy 1915 at that. And terrible as the movie is, that is its considerable charm."

142

Brute Force gave Yvonne her best acting role up to that time. It proved Yvonne could respond to the likes of director Jules Dassin.

It was both reasonable and possible at this juncture that Yvonne's screen career could have moved into a completely different direction than the obvious. She might have made a concerted bid as a dramatic performer, eschewing any further celluloid actioners, hoping that the public endorsement of her highly touted Maria Montez-type roles might carry her at the box office until she demonstrated her expanded histrionic mettle. This was a chancy professional avenue that neither studio, now under the production supervision of William Goetz, nor contract-bound Yvonne was willing to explore. Too much money had already been invested in her stated screen image as a fiery, exotic leading lady.

However, a concatenation of situations allowed Yvonne to initiate a new type of celluloid stardom for the sound cinema. In silent-film days, particularly in the cliffhanging serial field, it was quite common to have a Pearl White, Helen Holmes, or Grace Cunard as the athletic, daring, resourceful heroine who was a fitting match for any screen hero or villain in a Western, gangster, or espionage, etc., setting. Yet once talkies came into popularity, it was a rare occasion when an actress was allowed to be anything more than a decorative adjunct in Westerns (the Dale Evans cowgirl of the 1940s was very typical), costumed swashbucklers (à la the démure Olivia de Havilland of the Errol Flynn adventure epics), or gangster yarns (with their relatively passive molls of the Joan Blondell type).* However, by the late 1940s, Hollywood was fast abandoning the serial-making field, and decided to divert some of it standard sagebrush and pirate tales into vehicles for leading ladies. It was both a novelty and a foreshadowing of the women's liberation movement.

Universal (International) Pictures found it a natural extension of its profitable Maria Montez tropical opuses and expansive Western series lineup, to increase its share of annual product allocation to pirate, desert-and-sandal, and frilly multihued Westerns, which could be churned out with an undemanding emphasis on gaudy scenery and costumes, rather than on substantial storylines, expensive onscreen talent, or time-consuming, meticulous direction. This type of feature would become the special province of Universal (and to a lesser extent Columbia) in contrast to MGM, Paramount, Twentieth Century-Fox, and Warner Bros., which generally relegated this brand of screenfare to strictly programmer mounting.

Thirdly, at this point in Hollywood, with the major exception of Irish-born Maureen O'Hara, who would begin her own Universal association with *Bagdad* (1949), and British-born Patricia Medina (who did *The Fighting O'Flynn* [1949] and *Abbott and Costello in the Foreign Legion* [1950]

---

*In sound films, there was an occasional distaff gangster lead, as in *Madame Racketeer* (Paramount, 1932) with Alison Skipworth, *Queen of the Mob* (Paramount, 1940) with Blanche Yurka, and *Lady Scarface* (RKO, 1941) with Judith Anderson.

at Universal before moving over to the swashbuckling field at Columbia and Paramount), Yvonne was the only acknowledged leading lady on the Hollywood scene who could perform both the satisfying acrobatics and the eye-filling parading of charms required for this multifaceted species of films.*

Thus, a month after the release of *Brute Force,* Yvonne was back on the silver screen starring in another Technicolor costume picture from Universal, this one a desert epic called *Slave Girl* (1947). Produced and written by Michael Fessier and Ernest Pagano, with Charles Lamont again helming, the picture was made under the title of *Flame of Tripoli* and top-billed Yvonne over perennial leading man George Brent. Brent played a girl-happy American diplomat in the early 1800s, sent to ransom sailors held by the sinister potentate (Albert Dekker) of Tripoli. Broderick Crawford was Brent's clumsy bodyguard, prissy Arthur Treacher essayed the mirth-provoking sailor Liverpool, and Yvonne had the thankless role of Francesca, a beautiful and mysterious dancer.

At some point in the course of this production, Universal executives realized they had a holiday-sized turkey on their hands, and in desperation, they decided to turn this unintentional, flat-handed spoof into a legitimate satire. New footage was shot to introduce Lumpy, a Brooklynese-talking camel,† into the proceedings, who could deliberately focus audience attention on the picture's absurdities and grand clichés, in the hope of turning the movie's preposterous elements into money-earning belly laughs. Thus at one interval, just before Yvonne launches into her next twirling, gyrating cooch dance, Lumpy advises, "You can't have too much of this sort of thing in a picture." As *Variety* saw it, "the camel saves the picture from itself," which gives the uninitiated a rough idea of the caliber of this balderdash, filled with dancing girls, grasping potentates, torture chambers, free-for-alls, and endless talk of love and material aggrandizement.

Yvonne then played the first of several famous ladies of history in her first 1948 release, *Black Bart.* Here she was top-cast as Lola Montez,‡ who has come from Europe to California on a dancing tour. She becomes involved with the famous bandit Black Bart (Dan Duryea), who masquerades as a Sacramento rancher when he is not taking from the rich to give to himself. Yvonne's Lola discovers Duryea's true identity and tries to reform him, but she fails because of a bad twist of fate.

---

*Herbert Yates's Vera Ralston at Republic generally performed in Westerns, but most she often played a demure heroine; *Belle Le Grand* (Republic, 1951) was a rarity for her. Howard Hughes's Jane Russell was mighty distracting in *The Outlaw* (RKO, 1943), but with the exception of her Calamity Jane in *The Paleface* (Paramount, 1948) and her outlaw in *Son of Paleface* (Paramount, 1952), she mostly stuck to contemporary yarns.

†An obvious precursor of Francis, the Talking Mule, the subject of the studio's successful 1950s series.

‡Any resemblance between Yvonne's Lola and Martine Carol's memorable performance in Max Ophuls's famed 1955 feature is very slight.

The only originality to *Black Bart* was that in the finale of the flashback tale (told by deadpan Percy Kilbride), both Duryea and his one-time outlaw colleague, Jeffrey Lynn, are mowed down in an ambush, and that it develops in the fade-out that storyteller Kilbride is not a small western-town barber, as the film's opening would indicate ("Yes, I knew Black Bart well," he tells a customer), but is practicing his tonsorial art in jail.

For some strange reason, both the screenplay and director George Sherman constantly shunt Yvonne's Lola to the sidelines;* but, nevertheless, she gives a very typical performance. When she first appears, some ten minutes into *Black Bart*, she is on a California-bound stagecoach. Masked Duryea stops the coach to have an advance gander at the fabulous Lola. The other passengers are disgruntled or frightened, but Yvonne's damsel ("The emperor and I were old friends") informs coach-mate Lynn, "I can take care of myself." And that she can! With a timely kick of her booted foot, she smashes the coach door into Duryea's trigger hand, enabling herself and the coach to temporarily escape his clutches. As the tale progresses, Yvonne becomes as fond of Duryea as he is of her, but, being a self-sufficient woman, she is reluctant to admit her devotion.

Duryea: Don't you know how I feel about you, Lola?

Yvonne: That could mean any number of things.

Frankly, Yvonne is not very convincing in her few romantic intervals. At one point, she ambiguously alludes to her affection for Duryea, stating (rather blandly), "I think I like it here. It's exactly what I'm looking for." Later she rather unconvincingly advises carefree Duryea, "The whole country's looking for you. You won't have a friend when they find out who you are."

If Yvonne's dramatics were not the source of her fans' adulation for *Black Bart* or similar vehicles, her publicized dancing ability was no great shakes either. It must be noted that in this genre vehicle little effort or expense was ever devoted to properly choreographing the numbers. Nonetheless, Yvonne's two dances in *Black Bart* should have been better than they were, and the blame can only be laid at Yvonne's shapely but inexpert feet. She was required to perform two flamenco routines, each exercise noteworthy only for her spangled costuming, the clicking of heels (seemingly dubbed), castanets, and her coquettish playing with lace fans.

What was it about Yvonne, then, that inspired her studio and the public to accept so graciously her less than stellar presence? Simply her looks! Unlike Maria Montez, Yvonne never possessed that tantalizing and redeeming capacity for self-conviction and narcissistic love which made Montez movies so enticing to observe. But, Yvonne was a far better performer than Montez, which meant that she could at least emote on a

*Near the film's ending Kilbride admits, "I never did know what happened to Lola," a rather lame way of having Yvonne exit from the storyline.

satisfactory plane. Thus Yvonne was an adequate screen personality who, fortuitously, happened to be encased in a flashingly feminine frame and also was capable of handling the athletic demands of Universal's money-making commodity—upper-echelon program actioners. No one but the critics complained when Yvonne's shapely self appeared time after time oncamera. Hence, onward . . . onward . . . she went . . . into the valley of further screen mini-epics.

The film Yvonne likes the least of her Universal array of pictures is *Casbah.* Released in the spring of 1948, it was the second U.S. version of Detective Ashelbe's French novel *Pepe le Moko.* Filmed previously in France with Jean Gavin and Mireille Balin and by United Artists in 1938 with Charles Boyer, Hedy Lamarr, and Sigrid Gurie, this Technicolor adaptation added four tunes by Harold Arlen and Leo Robin.

Yvonne was badly miscast in *Casbah,* playing the role of Inez, the faithful native girl who loves jewel thief Pepe le Moko (Tony Martin). Marta Toren essayed the part of the femme fatale Gaby, performed a decade earlier by Lamarr. The part would have been much better suited for Yvonne. The Universal film, despite its slipshod aspects, was faithful to the story about the gem-stealer, Pepe le Moko, who leaves the sanctuary of the Casbah section of Algiers for the love of the beautiful and tempestuous Gaby and is killed for his famous inclinations.

James Agee (in the *Nation*) chided the filmmakers of *Casbah* for "disconcertingly straight work by Tony Martin and Yvonne De Carlo," although *Time* magazine felt that "Tony Martin and Yvonne De Carlo, who have never before seemed entirely human, are simple, likable, even believable." *Newsweek* magazine best summed up Yvonne's part by saying she "stands by looking sultry as usual." In the course of the picture, Martin sings "For Every Man There's a Woman," "What's Good about Goodbye," "It Was Written in the Stars," and the oldie, "Hooray for Love." Yvonne reprises "For Every Man There's a Woman" in the film, and duets with Martin on "Hooray for Love." But these musical interludes with crooner Martin did not disguise the fact that Yvonne was playing a mobster's Moslem moll, and doing it rather badly.

From the Casbah to the north woods was Yvonne's next trek for her final 1948 Technicolor adventure yarn, *River Lady.* She was united with brawny, but stiff, Rod Cameron in a tale of a tough gal who ambitiously wants money and love. The film is set at the headwaters of the Mississippi River with Yvonne as Sequin, the operator of the gambling boat *River Lady.* The simplistic plot finds Yvonne attempting to win the heart of lumberjack Cameron but eventually losing out to the timber boss's daughter, Helena Carter. Thrown in for good measure and a few brawls was bad guy Dan Duryea.

Time magazine said *River Lady* was "a solid little 'sleeper' in a solid set of Technicolor pajamas." Rather a far cry from Universal's publicity, which proclaimed the feature "the glory-roaring story of 1000 brawling miles of river" and Yvonne "queen of an empire of sultry romance and brawling romance."

Calamity Jane and Sam Bass (Universal, 1949) created a fictional romance between the two historical figures from the Old West, but, despite this mundane storyline ploy, the movie was an above-average rendering. Directed by George Sherman, from his story, the film covered the fairly well known facts concerning the introduction of Sam Bass (Howard Duff) into a life of crime following the murder of his "Denton mare" by dishonest citizens. A treat for the eyes was Yvonne as hard-riding, fast-shooting Calamity Jane Canary, a delightful sight in a tight buckskin suit.* Howard Barnes (*New York Herald-Tribune*) admitted, "Miss De Carlo is properly swaggering as Calamity Jane, but she always looks as though she had just come from a beauty parlor, even when she is shooting it out with the law on a craggy hillside." The *New York Times* offered a backhanded slap at Yvonne by insisting she was "playing Jane in the style of Mae West." The latter criticism was a rather unfair estimation since Yvonne instilled more verve into the role than the part warranted. Her attempts to be feminine enough to win Duff's affections from a local girl (Dorothy Hart) are amusing, and her final scene with the dying outlaw is truly touching.

A pedestrian Western came next on Yvonne's release chart. *The Gal Who Took the West* (Universal, 1949) presented the leading lady as an opera singer who arrives in the town of O'Hara, Arizona, and becomes involved in a feud between the grandsons (rancher Scott Brady and saloon-operator John Russell) of Civil War general Charles Coburn. Director Frederick de Cordova, who would later be more successful helming Johnny Carson's late-evening video talk-show, seemingly could not decide whether to make the picture a lampoon of conventional Westerns or allow the staid proceedings ("There's plenty of feudin' and fussin' but little in the way of fightin'," carped *Variety*) to sink into its own morass of wordiness† Yvonne sang "Frankie and Johnny" as well as an Irish ballad.

Undoubtedly Yvonne's best role in her seven-year Universal tenure was that of Anna in *Criss Cross* (1949). A top-flight gangster movie, written for the screen by Daniel Fuchs from Don Tracy's novel and directed by Robert Siodmak, *Criss Cross* provided Yvonne with a realistic glamorous character.

The complicated melodrama revolves around ex-criminal Burt Lancaster's return to his hometown and his becoming involved with his grasping ex-

---

*Other oncamera Calamity Janes were Jean Arthur in *The Plainsman* (Paramount, 1937) and Doris Day in the musical *Calamity Jane* (Warner Bros., 1951).

†The film is told in flashback to a modern-day writer by three old-timers (Clem Bevans, Housefly Stevenson, Russell Simpson), with each having a different opinion of the singer. One claims she was a sweet young thing, the second insists she was a drunk, and the third presents the viewpoint that she was merely a gold digger after the O'Hara fortunes.

wife (Yvonne). "You never know what you're doin'. Trouble is, you know what you want," Lancaster bitterly informs Yvonne. The materialistic tart flirts with her once-honest ex-spouse and is responsible for leading him back into crime by allowing herself to become part of an armored-car robbery, planned by her gangster-boss fiancé, Dan Duryea. At one stage in the tense picture, Lancaster tries to reassure his mother by explaining that mercenary Yvonne is the way she is because of her youth. The wise mother replies, "In some ways she knows more than Einstein." Trying to play her brutish ex-husband against her new mate (she weds Duryea during the film), Yvonne plans to stay with the man who emerges on top from the robbery and the eventual battle for her affections.

In the denouement twist, Yvonne pleads her devotion to Lancaster when it appears he has won out over Duryea. But the homicidal Duryea finds them together at the designated hideout and snarlingly kills them both, ignoring Yvonne's attempts to re-double-cross Lancaster by denouncing him.

As the girl whom Lancaster describes as one who "gets into the blood," Yvonne offered a worthy performance in *Criss Cross*, but the Universal bosses paid little attention to her budding dramatic abilities, and shoved her into more costumed celluloid fodder.

Throughout the period 1944-50, Yvonne was nearly everything for which a major studio could hope in a decorative star. She was cooperative with the studio publicity department and the global press, and she allowed Universal's still department and newspaper photographers to endlessly snap cheesecake shots of "the world's most perfect girl." In addition, she rarely, if ever, openly balked at the junk scripts her employers shoved her way. However, this is not to imply that the increasingly worldly Yvonne was anyone's fool. She had ambitions of her own, and saw that they were nurtured during this extended apprenticeship period. Professionally she was convinced that her vocal talents had not been properly exploited and, therefore, she continued to study with her voice teacher, the composer Miklos Rozsa. She felt that this regimen was not a chore but a necessity if she were to extend her entertainment activities to new forums, Socially, Yvonne had been (discreetly) linked with a wide assortment of Hollywood's more eligible bachelors, including the usual array of studio-planned dates, but she was in no rush to leap into matrimony. One of her more notable, but less publicized, escorts at the time was the bashful billionaire Howard Hughes, who, among other holdings, owned the RKO film factory. Of this iconoclastic beau, Yvonne later coyly admitted that Hughes had instructed her in many topics, in particular, how to fly. "Howard taught me to land a plane and how to take off. But he never taught me anything about flying in between. He thought that I had learned the difficult parts, and that was enough."

As would prove true throughout the years ahead, Yvonne's winning manner and stunning looks made her a great favorite among co-players, and often led male stars to request her services for their feature film projects. For example, in early 1950, Cornel Wilde's independent production company acquired the film rights to Leslie T. White's novel, *Lord Johnnie*, as its initial vehicle. Wilde intended to portray the title role, that of a highwayman, and he made it known he wished to have Yvonne signed as his leading lady. The film was to be made in England with Irving Rapper directing. Unfortunately this project came to naught, but it is to be remembered that four years hence, in RKO's *Passion*, these two vital screen players would be united oncamera.

Yvonne actually launched 1950 professionally with the second of three films she would do with director Frederick de Cordova, this one a swashbuckler called *Buccaneer's Girl*. She was Deborah McCoy, a girl from Boston who is a stowaway on a ship captured by pirate Frederic Baptiste (Philip Friend). Yvonne later becomes a New Orleans entertainer and learns that Friend, who is seeking revenge on a shipowner who ruined his father, is also the respectable Captain Kingston, a seagoing Robin Hood. As could be expected in so flimsy a tale, the secret of the dual identity is in good hands with Yvonne, especially after love conquers her Deborah and Friend's Baptiste.

In reviewing this simple-minded picture, *Christian Century* noted that it "may prove entertaining if you don't look too hard for logical motivation in plot and character." The *New York Herald-Tribune* wagered *Buccaneer's Girl* should get A for effort in "trying to get all the improbable situations into one film." While any seasoned filmgoer would vote the entertainment prize in this movie to Elsa Lanchester, a frivolous madam who takes Yvonne under her wing, Yvonne had her moments of fiery intensity, contrasted with her energetic moments of singing and dancing. Jack Brooks and Walter Scharf wrote four ditties which Yvonne sang in the guise of Deborah McCoy. They were "Here's to the Ladies," "Monsieur," "Because You're in Love," and "A Sailor Sails the Seven Seas."

After viewing Yvonne's second and last 1950 feature, *The Desert Hawk*, *New York Times* critic Bosley Crowther wryly commented, "Somehow we have the feeling we've seen this a hundred times before." Yvonne was up to her standard cinematic tricks in this colorful but crude sand saga, her final film with Frederick de Cordova. This *Arabian Nights* adventure starred Yvonne as Princess Scheherazade, who is involved with scimitar-swinging Omar (Richard Greene) and the latter's rotund but magical assistant, Aladdin (Jackie Gleason). George Macready was on hand as the villainous Prince Murad, and one of Yvonne's future co-stars, Rock Hudson, was in a small role as Captain Ras. Quite naturally Greene ends up as the Prince of Teheran and wins the fair hand of Yvonne. With such insipid dialog as Yvonne telling romance-bound Greene, "There is no precedent for action such as this," it is little wonder that Howard Barnes (*New York*

149

With Maxie Rosenbloom
and Byron Foulger in
HARVARD, HERE I
COME (Col '42)

With Bruce Kellogg in
THE DEERSLAYER
(Rep '43)

With Betty Hutton (second from left),
and Bing Crosby in HERE COME
THE WAVES (Par '44)

With Sylvia Field and Rod Cameron in SALOME, WHERE SHE DANCED

With Joe Haworth, Andy Devine, Sheldon Leonard, Jack Overman, Rex Lease, Andrew Tombes, and Jack Ingram in FRONTIER GAL (Univ '45)

Advertisement for SONG OF SCHEHERAZADE (Univ '47)

With Howard Duff in
BRUTE FORCE (Univ '47)

With Arthur Treacher,
George J. Lewis, Lois
Collier, George Brent,
Joe Haworth, Andy
Devine, and Jack Ingram
in SLAVE GIRL
(Univ '47)

With Marta Toren and
Peter Lorre in CASBAH
(Univ '48)

With Mickey Simpson
(the big man) in
RIVER LADY (Univ '48)

With Dan Duryea in
CRISS CROSS (Univ '49)

With Scott Brady, Charles Coburn, and
John Russell in THE GAL WHO TOOK
THE WEST (Univ '49)

With Philip Friend and Jay C. Flippen in BUCCANEER'S GIRL (Univ '50)

With David Tomlinson in HOTEL SAHARA (UA '51)

With Edmond O'Brien in SILVER CITY (Par '51)

With Joel McCrea in
THE SAN FRANCISCO STORY
(WB '52)

With John Ireland (rear) and
Al Kikume (standing) in
HURRICANE SMITH (Par '52)

With Vittorio Gassman in
SOMBRERO (MGM '53)

With Leonard Penn, John Dehner, Henry Corden, and Raymond Burr in
FORT ALGIERS (UA '53)

With Alec Guinness in THE CAPTAIN'S PARADISE
(Lopert '53)

With David Niven in TONIGHT'S THE NIGHT (AA '54)

Herald-Tribune) felt obliged to report, "Miss De Carlo confines her acting to being sultry and hard to get, delivering the fruity lines of the script as though they represented every-day conversation."

By the time of *The Desert Hawk's* release, Yvonne and Universal had come to a new understanding. She was obliged to make only one film a year for the Universal studio, and could accept outside assignments with other studios. In addition, and even more important for Yvonne's morale, the company gave her permission to perform in nightclubs and other musical engagements. The latter privilege came about in 1950 when she agreed to join with Donald O'Connor (star of the *Francis* series) in a Berlin nightspot engagement to promote both the stars and the studio's product. In her segment of that bill, she sang "Frankie and Johnny," "Babalu," and a selection from *Carmen*. Then, during the week of July 16, 1951, she made her operatic stage debut at the Hollywood Bowl in *Die Fledermaus* (the operetta by the Waltz King, Johann Strauss, Jr.). It was the culmination of seven years of operatic study in general, and two months in particular on this light opera, with twelve days of rehearsal with the cast. As Prince Orlovsky, lyric soprano Yvonne had to reach down to the mezzo range, which left an uncomfortable tone to her voice. The *New York Times* reviewer, who insisted she was a lyric soprano, politely admonished, "The present stage of her vocal development can scarcely be termed enchanting" and concluded that Mme. De Carlo required further polishing in the operatic field. On the other hand, Yvonne was thrilled by the opportunity *Die Fledermaus* presented, but the experience was sufficient to convince her to give up the notion of an operatic career. She admitted, ". . . you can't lead two lives. If I wanted to continue with opera, I'd have had to give up my movie career and concentrate on strengthening my voice. So I gave up opera." But Yvonne did not give up music; she recorded a single, "Take It or Leave It," for Capitol Records, and later made guest vocalist appearances on video variety shows hosted by Milton Berle, Perry Como, and Frank Sinatra. In September 1951, while picture-making abroad, Yvonne made a nine-performance singing tour of Israel's larger cities, and was a sell-out in all her stints in the Holy Land.

Tomahawk (Universal, 1951) was hardly a suitable follow-up to *Die Fledermaus,* but it was shoved into the action-film houses with hardly a complaint from exhibitors. In Technicolor, and directed by George Sherman, the film was a meandering tale set in the post-Civil War period with the government ignoring scout Jim Bridger's (Van Heflin) warning for the settlers not to move into Sioux territory. A war erupts, and caught in the fracas is Julie Madden (Yvonne), a wagon-show singer. She had little to do besides look fetching, and, at times, worried when an Indian seemed imminent. In Britain, the film was titled *Battle of Powder River*.

Offscreen, Yvonne was engaged in a most spectacular spree of romantic episodes. She was courted by a prince of Iran with whom she went hunting for big-horn sheep in the Iranian mountains while attendants served caviar in the field. She also dated Lord Lanesborough, an English peer, who gave a hunt ball in Yvonne's honor at his castle near London. "His lordship loved my new dress, a Jacques Fath original," she later said. "Little did he know that it was a gift from the Prince of Iran." She was also seen with Prince Aly Khan, Howard Hughes, Howard Duff, and bullfighter-poet Mario Cabre, the latter being her escort at the 1952 Cannes Film Festival.

With the increased competition from television and the resultant decrease in Hollywood film production, many a film star like Yvonne had to look outside California for sufficient motion-picture employment. In England, Yvonne signed with Tower Films for *Hotel Sahara*, which was released in the United States in 1951 by United Artists. The film found Yvonne as the girlfriend (wife in the U.S. version) of desert hotel-owner Peter Ustinov. As North Africa is invaded by the Germans, Italians, and British, Ustinov, Yvonne, her mother (Mireille Perrey), and the caretaker (Ferdy Mayne) comically change accents and loyalties for profit and survival.

Hotel Sahara met with a mixed critical reaction. A. Weiler in the *New York Times* lamented, "Miss De Carlo's acting . . . is as improbable as the story," while Robert Kass commented in *Catholic World*, "Miss De Carlo, who has played enough slave queens to merit charter membership in any flowing Persian harem, does a glorious take-off on herself. . . . She and the dour-faced Mr. Ustinov make *Hotel Sahara* the surprise comedy of the season." *Newsweek* magazine, however, thought the film "an international imbroglio as generally dull as a routine afternoon at the U.N." In retrospect, sweater-clad Yvonne demonstrated in *Hotel Sahara* that type-casting by Hollywood had greatly impeded the range of her film-making ventures. As Ustinov's woman, who gamely seduces a captain, a major, and a lieutenant—each of a different nationality—she displayed a refreshing charm and vitality. The picture remains one of Yvonne's all-time favorites.

Back in the United States, Yvonne discovered that the Universal regime was doing just dandy with red-headed Maureen O'Hara handling the roles that had once been her personal domain. So Yvonne signed at Paramount for the modestly budgeted color Western *Silver City* (1951). Edmund O'Brien was a mining assayer who comes to the title town to escape his past. While there he tries to help Yvonne and her father (Edgar Buchanan) develop a rich silver vein. Their attempts to mine the silver are opposed by a wealthy land-owner (Richard Arlen) who wants both Yvonne and the silver. Meantime, Yvonne is engaged in a tussle with Laura Elliot over O'Brien's affections. This Western actioner was released in Britain as *High Vermillion*.

On an almost freelance basis, Yvonne stepped up her 1952 schedule with three film releases. The first was *The San Francisco Story* (Warner Bros.,

1952), a Western in which she took second billing to Joel McCrea. Here she protrayed self-willed Adelaide McCall, the high-spirited mistress of corrupt politico Sidney Blackmer in the ramshackle San Francisco of 1856. McCrea was Rick Nelson, a wealthy mine-owner who opposes the cheap politician Blackmer and gets horsewhipped by Yvonne for his troubles. Later the girl does save McCrea from being shanghaied—a situation she had engineered—and when love hits both of them, she aids him and the vigilantes in beating Blackmer's crew in a shotgun duel at the film's climax. *Time* magazine chided, "A horse opera that tries determinedly to be rugged, *The San Francisco Story* merely succeeds in being ragged." For Yvonne De Carlo fans, the picture had one joyous moment when one character says of her Adelaide, "She's got everything. She's beautiful, smart, and democratic."

Yvonne was announced to star in *The Scarlet Flame* to be made at Warner Bros. in 1952 (after *The San Francisco Story*), a costumed drama with MGM's Fernando Lamas as her co-star. When this picture was shelved, Lamas made *The Diamond Queen* (1953) at Warner Bros. with his future wife, Arlene Dahl, as co-star. Yvonne returned to Universal to headline *Scarlet Angel* (1952), a tame remake of Marlene Dietrich's *The Flame of New Orleans* (1941). Yvonne assumed the Dietrich role of a saloon girl who rises into high society in 1865 San Francisco, where the film's locale was changed from the earlier picture.

At the outset of *Scarlet Angel*, Roxy McClanahan (Yvonne) steals $1,000 from a sea captain (Rock Hudson) and then proceeds to befriend a young widow (Bodil Miller) and her baby, who were in the captain's charge. Later, when the woman dies, Yvonne takes the baby and moves in with the woman's rich in-laws, using the dead lady's identity. Eventually her hoax is uncovered with the appearance of Hudson, but *l'amour* develops between the two and Yvonne dumps her wealthy fiancé (Richard Denning) for a more salty life with the sea captain. Howard Thompson (*New York Times*) used his review column on *Scarlet Angel* to provide a neat little essay on screen star Yvonne. ". . . the lady has an airy self-assurance that suggests, bless her heart, that the paying customer can either take or leave it . . . the ornamental Miss De Carlo, who also has the makings of a fine, brassy comedienne, is still marking time on a stereotyped leash."

Universal was so preoccupied with the likes of Maureen O'Hara, Piper Laurie, Shelley Winters, Julie Adams, Lori Nelson, Mari Blanchard, et al., that Yvonne had to look elsewhere for film work. Her last 1952 effort was Paramount's *Hurricane Smith*, labeled by one reviewer as "a flurry of low melodrama on the high seas." Yvonne was stuck with the thankless role of Luana, an exotic half-Polynesian girl in the 1850s who is involved in a treasure hunt with five leading (*sic*) men: John Ireland (in the title role), James Craig, Forrest Tucker, Lyle Bettger, and Richard Arlen. In the expected Technicolor fade-out, Ireland wins the treasure and Yvonne. If this tepid drama was attempting to resurrect the tropical-romance cycle made popular by Dorothy Lamour and Maria Montez a decade or more earlier, it failed miserably in its crusade. As for Yvonne's pagan dance on board ship, to the beat of the tom-toms conveniently provided by the Polynesian members of the crew, it is best forgotten.

Metro-Goldwyn-Mayer reportedly spent a great sum of money on *Sombrero* (1953), an episodic film which turned out to be a dud. The film was directed by former actor Norman Foster, and Yvonne was given special billing as Maria, a river girl who persuades her lover (Vittorio Gassman), who is dying of a brain tumor, to marry an aristocrat (Nina Foch). Also caught in this poor film were MGM contract players Ricardo Montalban, Pier Angeli, and Cyd Charisse. The latter performed a highly touted "Gypsy Dance." Yvonne received one of her first sympathy reviews, from the stately British *Monthly Film Bulletin*: "Miss De Carlo, clearly a jolly girl, is unfairly doomed to crouching on the floor, wrapped in a shawl, as the underprivileged Maria of the River Road; on the death of her lover, his father [Walter Hampden] sets her up as a housekeeper, and she is last seen, not surprisingly, praying in church."

Yvonne next worked for Howard Hughes in *Sea Devils* (RKO, 1953), a film directed by Raoul Walsh and very loosely based on Victor Hugo's mariner novel, *Toilers of the Sea*. The action takes place during the war between England and France. Yvonne was physically captivating as Droucette, an alluring British spy who masquerades as a countess and is held prisoner. Later, smuggler hero Rock Hudson, who had come a long way since his bit role in Yvonne's *The Desert Hawk*, rescues Yvonne and brings political stability to the situation in the Channel Islands. With stale dialog (e.g., Hudson says to Yvonne, "You call it love. I call it treachery") and a too confining budget, it was a toss-up whether the viewer was more distracted by stock shots of sailing vessels or glimpsing assorted poses of the "celebrated De Carlo charm," especially her plunging neckline gowns. One of the few tangible assets of the picture was Richard Addinsell's fine musical score.

United Artists signed Yvonne for *Fort Algiers* (1953), a double-bill entry hacked out by director Lesley Selander. It was strictly formula Foreign Legion folderol. Yvonne was cast again as an espionage agent, this time a French spy pretending to be nightclub chanteuse, Yvonne. Portly Raymond Burr appeared as the dastardly Arab chief Amir, who is plotting an attack on the French forces. At the convenient last moment, captured Yvonne is rescued from Burr's clutches by her lover-turned-agent-but-really-a-legionnaire (Carlos Thompson).* If Yvonne seemingly gave more attention to her sole song number, "I'll Follow You," it might well have been because she penned the lyrics to the Michel Michelet tune.

The Captain's Paradise, Yvonne's final 1953 release, once and for all

---

*Reportedly, Argentine singer Carlos Thompson was "discovered" by Yvonne.

proved she had a fine comic flair oncamera, and she garnered much critical acclaim as the girlfriend (second wife in the British version) of packet-
boat captain Alec Guinness, who also has a staid wife (Celia Johnson).
This well-made comedy was produced and directed in England by Anthony Kimmins for London Films with U.S. release by Lopert Films.*
Within the Alec Coppel-Nicholas Phipps screenplay, Guinness captains
a boat which plies a course between British Gibraltar, where he lives
with conventional Johnson, to Ceuta, where he abodes with Moroccan
Yvonne. For a lengthy time the captain is able to keep up the dual deception, that of a stuffy Britisher in Gibraltar and a dashing man-about-town
in Ceuta, until presents are crossed by mistake with Johnson receiving a
bikini and Yvonne getting an apron. The mix-up is further complicated
by the fact that both women are anxious to change their images and are
inspired by the gifts to switch their life-styles, much to Guinness's chagrin
and confusion.

Commonweal stated that Yvonne played the role of Nita "with lots of
what we used to call It in the twenties," and Bosley Crowther (*New
York Times*) commented, "Miss De Carlo, as the siren, 'the mate of the
tiger,' in Mr. Guinness, is wonderfully candid and suggestive. . . ."

During the production of *The Captain's Paradise*, which was originally
called *Every Port*, Yvonne convinced director Kimmins to put Guinness
in her mambo number, and she taught the British actor the dance in a
week-long series of rehearsals. "Alec may look like a one-step type, but
he has a real flair for this sort of thing," Yvonne commented.

Yvonne made her television dramatic debut in 1953 in the *Madame .44*
segment of "Ford Theatre," telecast over NBC on September 24, and on
December 29 of the same year she appeared in an episode of the "Back-
bone of America" NBC series. During the rest of the decade she would
make only four more dramatic television appearances.

She returned to Universal for a Technicolor Western called *Border River*
(1954). The film reunited her with director George Sherman and co-star
Joel McCrea. Near the end of the Civil War, McCrea of the Confederate
Army crosses the Rio Grande into Zona Libre, an independent territory
broken away from Mexico. Using gold stolen from a Colorado mint, he
seeks to purchase weapons from grasping general Pedro Armendariz.
The two men distrust one another, a situation heightened by their mutual interest in Carmelita Carias (Yvonne). McCrea, of course, captures
the arms, and wins Yvonne.

Howard Hughes's RKO pacted Yvonne for *Passion* (1954), an efficiently

---

* *The Captain's Paradise* was translated into a stage musical, which opened on Broadway
at the Alvin Theatre on February 4, 1958 for a 190-performance run under the title *Oh, Captain!* Tony Randall was the captain, Abbe Lane (later replaced by Denise Darcel) had
Yvonne's part, and Jacquelyn McKeever was Maud.

produced minor Western directed by Allan Dwan,* which found Yvonne essaying dual roles but subordinated to virile leading man Cornel Wilde and the climax in the snowy "Nevada" divide. The stormy tale was localed in old California during the land wars, with a tyrant (Raymond Burr) and his gang massacring a family, including Rosa Melo (Yvonne), the wife of Juan Obregon (Wilde). The only survivor of the hacienda wipeout is Rosa's twin sister, Tonya (also Yvonne), who teams with her brother-in-law to take vengeance on the tyrant and his men.

Thirty-two-year-old Yvonne was quite beautiful, particularly as the spiteful, vengeance-seeking sibling. In one telling scene she recognizes the ghoulish laughter she heard at the site of the massacre, which leads her and Wilde to murder one of the tyrant's henchmen, Castro, well-played by Lon Chaney. Yvonne's split performance was not of the caliber of dual roles handled by Bette Davis in *A Stolen Life* (Warner Bros., 1946) and *Dead Ringer* (Warner Bros., 1965) or by Olivia de Havilland in *The Dark Mirror* (Universal, 1946), but it was several cuts above Maria Montez's twin sisters in *Cobra Woman* (Universal, 1944) or Bonita Granville in *The Guilty* (Monogram, 1947).

Another favorite in Yvonne's canon of movies, *Tonight's the Night*, was released late in 1954. Filmed in Ireland by Associated British Corporation under the title *Happy Ever After,* it obtained American release through Allied Artists. The film with some underlying parallels (save in overall quality and box-office receipts) to the more lyrical *The Quiet Man* (Republic, 1952), was a slapstick comedy about a young lord (David Niven) taking over his ancestral home in Southern Ireland and his callous determination to milk the estate dry at the expense of the servants and villagers of Rathbarney. The townsfolk take revenge by trying to do him in one way or another. Elderly retainer Barry Fitzgerald tries to scare Niven to death by dressing up as the ghost of various ancestors and walking the halls of the great house on O'Leary Night. Villager Michael Shepley has the same idea, which leads to mayhem, unfortunately, but not to the elimination of troublesome, parsimonious Niven. Loutish Liam Redmond and Joseph Tomelty have their own schemes to blow up Niven's station wagon and/or decapitate him, but the assorted master plans all come to naught. Eventually Niven loosens up and donates his inheritance to the servants and townspeople and weds local girl Yvonne. As

*In *Allan Dwan: The Last Pioneer* (1971), the director informed author Peter Bogdanovich, "I didn't think much of the story—it was a contrived affair, but the shooting was one of our shrewd business manipulations. We rented magnificent Spanish sets Warner Bros. had built for some big picture, and then we moved over to Universal and used a lot of their sets. So we got a magnificent production for very little money."
Regarding the budget for this and other Benedict Borgeaus-produced features he directed for RKO in 1955, Dwan recalled, "Never over around 800-850 thousand. About three weeks shooting each—fifteen days . . . none of our pictures warranted a big budget—they all went out and got their money back plus a profit."

the earthy Irish lass, Yvonne had ample opportunity to display her comedic talents. The part was a precursor to her tour in *Hello, Dolly!* many years later.

During her 1953-54 sojourns abroad, Yvonne agreed to star in the Italian-French co-production *La Castiglione* (a.k.a. *La Contessa di Castiglione* and *The Contessa's Secret*). The film had Continental bookings, but was never released theatrically in America. Yvonne played a proud Italian girl who assists patriot Georges Marchal to escape from the Austrian police. After vainly waiting for Marchal's return, she agrees to wed a count. Later he takes her to Paris, where she is introduced to Napoleon III (Paul Meurisse), whom she tries to influence in favor of Italy. During her Parisian stay she again meets Marchal and plans to flee with him to England. Instead she remains to attempt a truce between the Italian terrorists and the French monarch. Marchal dies in the process, but Yvonne obtains the desired peace. When the feature was released in France in 1955, Simone Dubreuilh (*Libération*) wrote, "Badly directed by Georges Combret, badly played by Yvonne De Carlo, *La Castiglione* is a pitiful film. To choose Yvonne De Carlo, a beautiful but vulgar actress, who would only be suitable as the Prudence of *Camille*, to play Mme de Castiglione, a great lady, mistress of the emperor and for a while a rival to the splendid Eugénie is as absurd as having Eddie Constantine enact the role of George Washington."

Yvonne's recollection of this minor fiasco is rather frivolous. "Rossano Brazzi was in the picture," she later told newsmen, "playing my uncle, with a pillow-stuffed tummy and a beard. He hated the makeup—and maybe the role too. But he was well up on his lines. There was a passage when he rattled off French dialogue for a couple of minutes—and all I had to say was 'wee.' Well, wouldn't you know, I loused the whole scene up by unthinkingly barking 'yes.' . . . Yes, we're still good friends. He's a good sport."

On January 29, 1955, Yvonne returned to the United States, from her latest European business-pleasure jaunt. She confessed that if working conditions proved propitious, she was back to stay. As if news reporters and photographers who gathered to greet the well-liked celebrity could overlook the fact, Yvonne pointedly exclaimed, "Just look at me. I'm skinny and haggard, like the American clothes models you see in the slick magazines." Obviously the mature Yvonne just could not break the habits of her 1940s beauty-posing days.

By the mid-1950s, Hollywood had regained some of the confidence of its pretelevision days thanks to the box-office boosting novelties of 3-D, stereophonic sound, and widescreen processes such as CinemaScope, Cinerama, and VistaVision. Then, too, the industry had finally agreed that if it could not beat the video medium, it made good financial sense to join it by grabbing some of the producing action in the newer field. But despite the slight upswing in theatrical film production, it was still rather difficult for a personality in early middle age to obtain respectable acting assignments and proper screen billing, particularly if past success had relied to a large degree on physical beauty rather than externalized emoting. The studios were engulfed by the latest cycle of busty blondes—ranging from the multitalented sex goddess Marilyn Monroe to such lesser versions as Sheree North, Jayne Mansfield, and Mamie Van Doren. For the likes of past pedestaled celluloid cinema queens such as Hedy Lamarr or Linda Darnell, the professional descent in the 1950s was more rapid than their physical aging. Moreover, their appearance in thinly disguised programmers made in the United States and abroad dramatically demonstrated their irretrievable loss of marquee luster. However, for a cinema figure like Yvonne, despite her valiant efforts to display silver-screen talents beyond her luscious screen presence, the career decline was less obvious. She had always adorned glorified costume-action programmers; now she had to accept parts in more modestly budgeted quickies, but in essence, a mindless Western was still a mindless Western, whatever the degree of production mounting.

Yvonne accepted second billing to Sterling Hayden in the violent Western, *Shotgun* (Allied Artists, 1955), most noticeable for its colorfully rugged outdoor scenery. She was Abby, the half-breed showgirl who joins with deputy marshal Hayden, he out to avenge a killing. They are united with bounty hunter Zachary Scott, who is after the same man, when all three are welded together against rampaging Apaches. While Yvonne's river bathing might be classified as an unexpected bonus to moviegoers, only the less adept viewer could not guess that sneering Scott would be murdered by the Indians, while Hayden and De Carlo would survive to be together.

Nepotism may have a lot to do with Vera Ralston, the wife of Republic Pictures' president Herbert J. Yates, being the queen of the lot, but, on at least two occasions in 1955-56, she was unavailable for parts which Yvonne accepted. *Flame of the Islands* (Republic, 1955) was filmed on location in Nassau, Bahamas, in Trucolor. Its pedestrian plot offered Yvonne as Rosalind Dee, who is mistaken for the mistress of a murdered millionaire and is given $100,000 by the deceased man's grateful widow. She invests her bounty in a Bahamas nightspot. There she becomes involved with a quartet of men: ex-drunk-fisherman-preacher James Arness, playboy Howard Duff, club manager Zachary Scott, and gangster Kurt Kasznar. After ninety minutes of indecision she settles for Arness. It is a tossup whether the plotline was more incredible than the insipid dialog. For example, one is asked to believe that Yvonne's Rosalind actually has the muscle to land a 150-pound marlin, or that when ex-sweethearts Yvonne and Duff meet after several years, they would dare to be so clichéd as to say, ". . . it's been such a long time. . . . We have so much to say to each other, so much to explain." As the *New York Herald-Tribune* put it, "No one can say Miss De Carlo isn't trying. The odds up there on the talking screen are just too big for her."

For a glamour movie star—of whatever level—there are two fields of discussion more vital than her career potential or ambition; i.e., the state of her figure and her matrimonial status. Give or take a few excess pounds, Yvonne remained a tidy package indeed. But for years Yvonne had avoided crossing the threshold of marriage. She had glibly stated during her high-living Continental-fling period, "I collected antiques, earrings, old music— and men." Before she became amorously involved with stuntman-actor Jock Mahoney, she exclaimed, "I would never marry anyone in the business." Then she and Mahoney became engaged, but wedding plans were suddenly called off, with Yvonne explaining, "That was impossible."

Then, on the sets of *The Ten Commandments* (Paramount, 1956), Yvonne met forty-year-old stuntman Robert Morgan. They also worked together in *Raw Edge* (Universal, 1956), and on November 21, 1955, the couple drove to Reno, Nevada, and were wed in the Episcopal Chapel there. *Raw Edge* co-star Rory Calhoun was on hand to give the bride away. The six-foot-three, 200-pound Morgan had a daughter, Bari, from his first marriage to Helen Crlenkovich, a diving champion on the 1940 Olympic team, who had recently died of cancer at the age of thirty-three. In informing the press about her sudden change of heart about marrying someone in the business, let alone relinquishing her single status, Yvonne decreed, ". . . now I know what I want from life with a man who will be my life's partner."

On January 4, 1956, Yvonne appeared in *Hot Cargo* on "Screen Directors Playhouse," and on April 6 of the same year she was in *The Sainted General* segment of "Star Stage," both telecast over NBC. Much more important to Yvonne and Morgan was the birth of her first child, Bruce, born on July 8, 1956, at St. Joan's Hospital in Santa Monica, California. Newspaper reports tactfully stated that the boy was delivered two months premature.

The year 1956, qualitatively and quantitatively her last important screen year, also saw the actress starred in four films. The season led off with the release of *Magic Fire* (Republic, 1956), another colorful but empty biography of a great composer (Richard Wagner), as trite in its overall effect as Yvonne's earlier *The Song of Scheherazade*. Alan Badel impersonated the nineteenth-century German composer with Carlos Thompson as the great Franz Liszt. Yvonne was actress Minna, who, as Badel's first wife, was one of three women to inspire the classical genius to write his compositions. Rita Gam, as Thompson's daughter, and Valentina Cortesa, as Peter Cushing's spouse, were the other love interests. The only solid attribute the dull film had was the location lensing in Germany. Robert Kass commented in *Catholic World*, "*Magic Fire* should have been a good film . . . [but it is] romanticized slush . . . overloaded with pretentiousness and bad acting."

Next came Universal's tinted Western, *Raw Edge* (1956). According to the scenario, it was the unwritten law in the untamed Oregon territory of

1842 that an unattached woman belonged to the first man who claimed her. This intriguing biblical concept was gimmicky enough, but the viewer was "treated" in the course of the outdoor drama to Yvonne (or her double) being belted, bruised, clobbered, attacked, shot at, and nearly drowned in the rapids, while men left and right were tumbling for her charms and fighting and dying to win her favors. Rory Calhoun performed as the vengeance-ridden man out to eliminate the culprit who had his brother lynched. Since the skunk is stocky Herbert Rudley, the frontier-baron spouse of fetching Yvonne, the outcome is no surprise. The closing moments of stereotyped sunset chasing were quite typical of Yvonne's filmmaking ventures.

Yvonne: You going . . . where to?

Calhoun: San Antonio . . . [*long pause, much reaction*] . . . Well. What are you waiting for? [*Yvonne and Calhoun ride off together over the horizon.*]

In October 1956, Paramount proudly released its VistaVision and color roadshow-epic *The Ten Commandments,* produced and directed by Cecil B. DeMille who, thirty-three years earlier, had performed the same functions on the silent-film original. If DeMille's directing and scenario-interpreting styles could fairly be judged old-fashioned and unsubtly theatrical, his casting habits were best termed conservative, expedient, but, above all, loyal (witness his repeated use of Julia Faye throughout the years). When DeMille had been casting for *The Story of Dr. Wassell* in 1943 at Paramount, Yvonne had been briefly considered for a larger role than her very brief walk-on, but, according to reports, it was her "too blue" eyes rather than her acting inexpertise that had cost her the featured part. Although DeMille remembered his one-time bit player over the years, it was a quirk of fate that suggested to him the possibility of casting Yvonne in *The Ten Commandments.* Nina Foch was being considered for the role of Bithiah, Moses' Egyptian foster mother, and DeMille was asked by her agent to screen *Sombrero* to judge the player's acting range. While viewing the 1953 MGM picture and agreeing upon Foch's merits, DeMille was struck by Yvonne's performance as Maria, and had her considered and then signed for the role of Sephora, the warm and understanding wife of Moses (Charlton Heston).

Critics who had previously dismissed Yvonne as merely a gorgeous creature were forced to reevaluate their opinion of the actress because of her sensitive handling—given DeMille's standard black-and-white terms of directing—of the role of shepherd Jethro's (Eduard Franz) eldest daughter. It is she, in the shadow of the Holy Mount, who tells Heston that it is the Holy Tabernacle of the God of Abraham. A year later, Yvonne is called upon to heal the man's emotional wounds left by the devouring Nefretiri (Anne Baxter). Once wed to Heston, Yvonne soon gives birth to a strapping baby boy, and the two follow the leader of the Israelites on the quest to find the promise across the River Jordan. Even Bosley Crowther (*New York Times*) admitted of Yvonne that she was "notably good in a severe role."

Death of a Scoundrel (RKO, 1956) was a cinema oddity that benefited from its restricted budget and uncontrolled pacing, by giving the chronicle of the life, loves, manipulations, and death of a thoroughgoing cad, a sleazy veneer that suited its subject. At 119 minutes it was overtly over-long, but its episodic flashback structure contained many (accidentally) inspired moments of low-keyed effectiveness. Originally George Brent had been scheduled for the lead, but illness forced him out of the part (he can still be spotted in a crowd scene). Another George, Sanders, that is, took over the assignment in the Charles Martin-produced-directed-written project. In the course of con artist Clementi Sabourin's (Sanders) tawdry life-cycle, he is released from a German concentration camp, turns his brother (Tom Conway) over to the secret police to win revenge for Conway's marriage to his sweetheart (Lisa Ferraday), and then, posing as an international financial wizard, boards a ship for America. Once in New York it is not long before Sanders encounters Yvonne, a tough but good-hearted pocketbook-slinger who becomes the scoundrel's right-hand woman in his business enterprises. Along the way, Sanders takes wealthy widow Zsa Zsa Gabor for a costly fleecing, ditches Coleen Gray, who had divorced her spouse for Sanders's sake, and sweet Nancy Gates, the secretary whom Sanders claims he really loves. But in the end it is Yvonne, having risen from the gutter to respectability, who convinces Sanders to do right by his defrauded shareholders. At this point, Sanders is shot dead by his business partner (John Hoyt).

For her efforts in *Death of a Scoundrel, Films in Review* said, "Yvonne De Carlo is a thoroughly believable prostitute," while the *New York Times* opined she "does a solid and professional job as the adoring petty thief who rises to eminence."

Yvonne's co-starring role in *The Ten Commandments,* a film which went on to gross over $43 million in distributors' domestic rentals, convinced Warner Bros. and director Raoul Walsh (who had helmed Yvonne's *Sea Devils*) that she was the proper performer to play the octoroon romantic interest to Clark Gable in *Band of Angels* (1957). Not only because Gable had starred in the immortal *Gone with the Wind* (MGM, 1939) but because of many structural and atmospheric parallels to that classic, the picturization of Robert Penn Warren's novel was promoted as the new *GwtW* and had to suffer comparison to that far superior picture. *Newsweek* magazine disdained, "Here is a movie so bad that it must be seen to be disbelieved. Performances, including Gable's, make summer TV seem as dramatically powerful as the Old Vic."

One of the major problems with *Band of Angels,* beyond its timorous approach to the miscegenation issue and its inability to create an aura of credibility, was the fact that fifty-six-year-old Gable and thirty-five-year-old Yvonne were far too mature for the requirements of their roles: he as the reformed slave trader turned gentleman with a plantation outside New Orleans, she as the daughter of a debt-ridden Kentucky planter who, upon her daddy's death, discovers that her mama was a black slave and thus she can legally be sold at auction. Before the weary tale concludes, the Civil War has broken out, Gable has fallen in love with his $5,000 purchase (Yvonne), and his strong-willed ex-slave (Sidney Poitier) helps the love-bound duo to escape the Northern troops. "Fanciers of awful movies," said William K. Zinsser (*New York Herald-Tribune*), "won't want to miss this choice specimen." For Gable, who would die of a heart attack on November 16, 1960, there were still five more starring films to come. For Yvonne, *Band of Angels*, which even a far more resourceful actress probably could not have saved from the critical scalpers, marked her final bid for legitimate leading-lady stardom in major films. Onscreen, it was professionally downhill thereafter for her.

Not that Yvonne was admitting career defeat. In one of her more publicized interviews of 1957, she told note-takers: "I can't play June Allyson roles, so I don't mind doing Scheherazade or Cleopatra. But I'd like to become known, if possible as a first-class stinker. Not that I'm complaining about my former roles. After all, where would I have been without them. Hollywood's been good to me." Whatever prompted Yvonne to say the above, it was wishful thinking to assume the industry would respond with a love letter in the form of meatier, or, at that, any roles.

Yvonne lost out to Ann Blyth for the musical lead in *The Helen Morgan Story* (Warner Bros., 1957). But Yvonne did sign a recording contract with Imperial Records, hoping to resume her vocal career, which had been interrupted in the early 1950s. Meanwhile, on November 14, 1957, she gave birth to her second son, Michael, born at a Santa Monica, California, hospital.

On April 24, 1958, Yvonne appeared in the *Verdict for Three* segment on NBC-TV's "Playhouse 90." She formed a production company—then a fashionable trend—called Vancouver Productions, which planned to make a Western and also turn out *The Green Planet Sram,* an outer-space comedy she had devised with her husband. None of these projects came to fruition, so she then took a crash course in Italian for *La Spade e La Croce* (Liber, 1958), a biblical "spectacle" in which she played Mary Magdalene. The cloak-and-sandal entry was shot on location in Italy. Several female stars, from Gloria Swanson to Jayne Mansfield, had made the trek to the peninsular country to make costume films, and Yvonne's effort had the same result as the efforts of many who went before and after her. The movie was little seen outside of Europe. (When it appeared on French television in 1960, one snide reviewer—for *Telerama* magazine—chided the film for its pseudo "significant" dialog and referred to Yvonne as "that

171

ex-most beautiful girl in the world.") A dubbed version of the film got sparse bookings in the United States from Amex Productions in 1960, and is currently available for video showings.

Back from Italy, Yvonne made what was to be her last desert drama to date, beginning a four-year respite from the cinema. *Timbuktu* (United Artists, 1959), directed by Jacques Tourneur, was a complicated and heavy affair which *Variety* termed a "routine program adventure yarn," but added, "Yvonne De Carlo is beautiful." This Edward Small production involved an attempted desert revolt during World War II in the French Sudan and starred Victor Mature as a tough gun-runner who is a go-between for the French rebels and neutral Arabs. A hoax is developed between Mature and the French commandant (George Dolenz) in which Mature and Dolenz's wife (Yvonne) pretend to have an affair so Mature can win rebel confidence and gain necessary information to put down the rebellion of the urbanely wicked emir (John Dehner). The hoax works all too well, with the couple falling desperately in love. Fortunately, in the course of quelling the planned revolt, Dolenz is killed, leaving the path free for Yvonne and Mature. *Timbuktu* had a brief life on the double-bill market. When it reached England, the *Monthly Film Bulletin* allowed, "If this piece of North African fantasy were exciting and fast moving, if there were even one element of surprise in the action, one good battle, or one thrilling chase, it would be possible to forgive the leaden-footed performances, the pompous dialogue and the settings of glaring artificiality."

Because an operatic career was not to be her destiny, Yvonne thought she might try her vocal talents on Broadway. She tried to win the role of Frenchy in the musical *Destry Rides Again*, reasoning that she had played so many saloon hostesses onscreen that the role in the Harold Rome-Leonard Gershe book should be a snap. However, producer David Merrick chose Dolores Gray to play opposite Andy Griffith (Tom Destry) and Scott Brady (Kent). The show debuted at the Imperial Theatre on April 23, 1959 for a 473-performance run.

A disappointed Yvonne then turned to another forum to display her enticing combination of pulchritude and throaty rhythm. One of her first nightclub engagements was at Chadiere, an entertainment spot in Ottawa, Canada. The *Variety* reporter covering her July 1959 opening wrote: "While Yvonne De Carlo's nitery presentation is mainly songs, she has surrounded herself with a neat package that can best be described as a miniature revue. . . . The act has strong potential not only as a showcase for the screen actress but as a piece of entertainment in itself. . . . Costuming is colorful and lends impact, with Miss De Carlo's gowns bringing gasps to the audience femmes while the males gasp at what's in them. She's a top looker and garners plenty of attention by sight appeal alone. Her piping and terping are adequate, not strong, but enough to carry her through the chores."

Over the next months she embarked on an extensive nightclub tour that took her abroad on several occasions. On one of her European engagements, her act was recorded on film by director-cameraman Osvaldo Civirani for *Tentazioni Proibiti*, an anthology of musical number and striptease acts lensed in various Continental nightclubs. The so-called theme of this *Mondo Cane*-style exploitation picture was the triumph of woman in the modern world. The potpourri entertainment, which contained glimpses of such varied personalities as Brigitte Bardot and Christine Keeler, had brief European release in the early 1960s by Wonder Films.

When not on the road with her act in the following years, Yvonne dabbled in television guest-starring. She was the headliner performance on the premiere episode, *A Rose for Letta*, of "Bonanza," telecast on NBC on September 12, 1959. There followed the *Isle of Eden* segment of "Adventure in Paradise" (ABC, February 22, 1960). She guested in two segments of ABC's "Follow the Sun" series. On November 5, 1961, she was in *The Longest Crap Game in History*, and on February 11, 1962, she appeared in the *Annie Beeler's Place* episode. Plans for Yvonne to star in a pilot for a potential "Scheherazade and a Thousand and One Nights" series fell through in the 1961 season. But this disappointment was assuaged by her moral victory in finally playing the Frenchy role in *Destry Rides Again* in a stock version, which opened at the Paper Mill Playhouse in New Jersey in April 1961. It was to be one of many road versions of Broadway successes that Yvonne would undertake over the years.

Despite the amount of globe-trotting she undertook to retain some footing in show business and to assist in maintaining the family's financial well-being, Yvonne really preferred the domestic life of raising a family on a six-acre estate she and her husband had purchased in the hills above the San Fernando Valley. Among her pastimes were horse raising and showing, target practice with guns, and cooking. According to *TV Guide*, "she matches her skill in this field [cooking] with that of a Continental culinary artist."

In 1962, Yvonne's husband, Bob Morgan, was doing some vigorous stunt work on MGM's Cinerama epic, *How the West Was Won* (1962). During the George Marshall-directed segment, *The Railroad*, Morgan was clinging to a load of logs when the piling shifted, unexpectedly throwing him to the tracks. He was run over by three flatcars and his body was badly mangled; as a result he lost his left leg.* Yvonne has since called the accident "gross negligence" on the part of MGM, but several lawsuits for damages, ranging in amounts up to $1.2 million, have been dismissed on technicalities. The most recent suit was dismissed by the Arizona Supreme Court in 1967.

Morgan's convalescence was a long one and, faced with financial prob-

---

*Morgan's physical impairment was used to advantage when he was cast as the one-legged Old John in *The Culpepper Cattle Company* (Twentieth Century-Fox, 1972).

173

lems, Yvonne returned actively to work. She later admitted that some of the parts she accepted "were no good but I couldn't be fussy." Through her good friend John Wayne she returned to the cinema in a guest-star role in his Batjac production of *McLintock!* (United Artists, 1963), which found her playing second-fiddle to one-time rival Maureen O'Hara. Now forty-one, Yvonne was "attractive," as *Variety* put it, in the role of Louise Warren, a widow and the mother of a grown son (Patrick Wayne), the latter falling in love with Wayne's finishing-school-taught daughter (Stefanie Powers). Yvonne is hired as the housekeeper-cook of the McLintock ranch, and her good looks arouse jealous O'Hara. One very amusing scene had Wayne and Yvonne getting drunk together and falling in a heap at the bottom of a stairway, then looking up to find themselves under the unhappy scrutiny of a seething O'Hara.

Yvonne starred in *A Time Remembered* on "The Virginian" (NBC, December 11, 1963), and sixteen days later she appeared in a cameo on ABC's "Burke's Law." On March 10, 1964, she was in a segment of ABC's "The Greatest Show on Earth" series, which starred Jack Palance and Stuart Erwin. In it, Yvonne was miscast as a circus performer and the mother of several grown children.

Yvonne played a "global girl," one of several international beauties in the mild Bob Hope screen comedy *A Global Affair* (MGM, 1964). Also playing gorgeous "global dolls" were Lilo Pulver, Elga Andersen, Michele Mercier, and Miiko Taka, all very noticeably younger than Yvonne. In this unpopular Hope skein, he plays the head of the United Nation's Women of the World who finds himself the custodian of a fifteen-month-old girl (played by Denise and Danielle Monroe) whom 111 countries wish to adopt. The abandoned infant is so highly publicized that it creates an international upset. One of the nations wanting the child is represented by Yvonne. *Variety* graciously reported of this "lacklustre romantic comedy" that "Elga Andersen and Yvonne De Carlo etch key distaff roles with oomph."

Next Yvonne appeared in the first of three color Westerns she made for producer A. C. Lyles at Paramount. *Law of the Lawless* (1964) was very typical of the Lyles sagebrush quickies. He gorged his casts with one-time box-office names (who were thankful to be in front of the cameras again, and worked cheaply), in mediocre stories, which were churned out on the studio's idle backlot, and then profitably distributed in the lower-half of action-house double-bill programs.

Released in March 1964, *Law of the Lawless* starred a striking but matronly figured Yvonne as saloon singer (what else?) Ellie Irish, the former mistress of an accused murderer (John Agar), who is set to face trial before a hanging judge (Dale Robertson). The defense attorney (Kent Taylor) tries to use Yvonne's past in convincing the jury to disregard her damaging testimony against the accused. Nevertheless, the defendant is found guilty and sentenced to hang. During the course of the eighty-seven-minute programmer, Yvonne is manhandled by one of the accused's henchmen (Lon Chaney) and she and judge Robertson fall in love. While it was good to see Yvonne's and other veteran players' names on theatre marquees, albeit at less than prestigious film houses, the more sensitive adult filmgoer could not but sigh at the toll time had taken on a host of once so vital and youthful players.

But there were two pluses in Yvonne's declining career in 1964. In March of that year, she replaced Vivian Blaine as Angela for a two-and-a-half-month tour of Carl Reiner's comedy play *Enter Laughing*, a show which allowed Yvonne choice if not extensive stage moments as the over-ripe stock-company ingenue. Then, on September 24, 1964, CBS network debuted a new video series, "The Munsters." It was an out-and-out comedy takeoff on the old Universal horror films. Thus, nearly two decades after starring in *Salome, Where She Danced*, Yvonne returned to her old home lot to play Lily Munster, the Vampira-type monster mother, who, at the age of 156, was married to Herman Munster (Fred Gwynne), alias the Frankenstein monster. Also in the household were Lily's father, Grandpa, alias Count Dracula (Al Lewis), her son Eddie (Butch Patrick), and an ugly (she was normal to mortals) niece (Pat Priest). The series was set, of course, in a gloomy old mansion which also housed a bevy of bats, spiders, and the family pet, Spot, a dragon who resided under the stairway.

The series was an immediate success and quickly shot into the top-ten ratings with a twenty-five-point Nielsen rating. Yvonne became one of the three most celebrated "girl ghouls" of the season, along with Carolyn Jones ("The Addams Family") and Elizabeth Montgomery ("Bewitched"), the latter two both aired on ABC network. In reviewing Yvonne's performance, Jack Gould (*New York Times*) reported that "she goes along very effectively with the concept of the feminine head of the house who is perfectly adjusted to eerie surroundings and unorthodox standards of thoughtful behavior."

Although Yvonne had never appeared in horror or fright films, she "picked up the idea wonderfully fast and has given the character, Lily Munster, warmth and charm," said Bob Mosher, who produced "The Munsters" along with Joe Connelly. The show's writers often gave Yvonne amusing lines, such as her telling hubbie Herman Munster, "They don't make men like you anymore." One of the most wearisome aspects of the series was that Yvonne had to report to Universal at 6:00 A.M. on shooting days for two hours of extensive makeup. When she first tested for the series, the producers said she "was too beautiful" in the original makeup concept and more greenish tones had to be applied to give her a cadaverish look. Yvonne, thankful for the job, told newsmen that the makeup ordeal was "no worse than being made up as a glamor doll. They used to spend an hour on my hair alone." Assigned as chief makeup man for the video series was veteran Bud Westmore, who had worked on many of the famous monster makeups at Universal in the 1940s. In discussing glamour queens with *TV Guide*, Westmore said: "A great disintegration takes place in many. Some even become psychotic. But those who have developed something more than beauty are able to make a normal adjustment. Yvonne De Carlo doesn't want to be a queen again. She's a sensible woman who has learned certain skills and wants to act her age."

The success of "The Munsters" brought renewed popularity and financial security to Yvonne. By this time her husband had recovered as much as possible from his accident and had turned to television acting and running a golf-cart business. As part of the publicity for the color series, Yvonne would arrive at work each day in a black hearse. Fan magazines, anxious to find a new angle on ex-sex-symbol Yvonne, attempted to build a "feud" between her and Italian Sophia Loren. Loren was reported to have announced that Yvonne was her childhood idol, and Yvonne was reported to have retorted, "I'm not that much older than her!"

"The Munsters" returned for its second CBS season on September 16, 1965, but by this time Yvonne was becoming unhappy with the Lily Munster role. She was increasingly being overshadowed in the series by the Herman Munster character. Even though the advent of "Batman" in early 1966 on rival ABC caused "The Munsters" to drop in rating popularity, CBS planned to continue the series for a third season. But Yvonne wanted to quit and, despite the network's offer to bolster her salary with a $50,000 bonus, she remained firm. The show was canceled, but it has remained a perennial favorite on syndicated time slots around the country.

At this point (the summer of 1966) Universal rushed into release a theatrical film version of the show, called *Munster, Go Home*, hoping to capture some of the series' audience popularity while the program was fresh in prime-time viewers' minds. With the exception of the role of Marilyn Munster (now played by Debbie Watson) the series' recurring cast were all on hand to go through their polished paces. The very strung-out feature plot had the oddball family traveling to England to inherit a fortune, with devious mortal relatives (Hermione Gingold, Terry-Thomas) trying to do them in. John Carradine, who had played the semiregular TV role of Mr. Gateman, the owner of the mortuary where Herman Munster was employed, appeared as the heavily made up butler, Cruikshank. *Munster, Go Home*, as might be expected, garnered little critical or audience favor.

In the summer of 1966, Yvonne toured the summer-tent theatrical circuit in *Catch Me If You Can*. On January 17, 1967, she got special guest-star billing in *The Moulin Ruse Affair* of NBC's "The Girl from U.N.C.L.E."

Yvonne then made her second A. C. Lyles Western, *Hostile Guns* (Paramount, 1967). She was back in her standard gambit—as a dancehall hostess—this time as Laura Mannon, who had shot a man and was now one of several prisoners being transported in a prison wagon by sheriff George Montgomery and his deputy (Tab Hunter). The wagon is being stalked by an outlaw gang led by John Russell, who has a score to settle with Montgomery. *Hostile Guns*, which was produced under the working title *Huntsville*, garnered some trade publicity when former silent-screen matinee idol Francis X. Bushman, who was slated to play a saloon proprietor, died suddenly, and was replaced by former Western star Donald "Red" Barry.

While she was filming a cameo role in MGM's supernatural study, *The Power* (1968), Yvonne and her husband filed their final, and unsuccessful, damage action against that studio in the Arizona Supreme Court. At the time, Yvonne said, "there is no animosity or personal feeling—just legal technicalities" with MGM. However, her small role in *The Power* was clipped out of the feature when it played abroad,* and despite prominent fourth billing, she was hardly visible when the movie was later shown on American network television.

In press interviews at the time Yvonne admitted she would like to make more Westerns or the type of horror films done by Bette Davis and Joan Crawford. Unfortunately, *The Power* was hardly in the class of *What Ever Happened to Baby Jane?* (Warner Bros., 1962), nor were A. C. Lyles Westerns of the caliber of great outdoor dramas. On December 27, 1967, shortly before *The Power* was issued, Yvonne guest-starred on an episode of ABC-TV's "Custer" called *The Raiders*. She replaced Dolores Del Rio, who had conflicting theatrical commitments.

Yvonne's last Western to date, and her last with A. C. Lyles, was *Arizona Bushwhackers* (Paramount, 1968), a film which reunited her with director Lesley Selander, who had helmed her *Fort Algiers* and *Shotgun*. This new clinker was set during the Civil War with a portly Howard Keel as a captured Confederate riverboat gambler who is set free by the Union forces on condition he bring law and order to the town of Colton, Arizona. Keel is actually a Southern agent intent on laying hands on a cache of ammunition and arms in Colton for the Confederacy. Yvonne made her striking appearance as the town's seamstress, Jill Wyler, who proves to be a spy and an ally with Keel. Viewers were so occupied with recovering from the shock of how one former screen name after another (Brian Donlevy, Marilyn Maxwell, Scott Brady, John Ireland, et al.) had surrendered to the inroads of time, that the banal story and production values were of little importance.

---

*In the mundane (even the special effects were drab) *The Power*, Yvonne played Sally Hallson, a domestic type who turns into a lady of pleasure after the mysterious death of her scientist husband (Arthur O'Connell).

In the fall of 1968 Yvonne, not about to call it quits in show business, had a nightclub engagement in Sydney, Australia, and made some local television appearances there. During the winter of 1968-69, she toured the United States and Canada in yet another road company of *Hello, Dolly!** The tour began on December 28, 1968, in New Haven, Connecticut. *Variety* said Yvonne "has the proper verve for the role and makes the 'Hello, Dolly' number a rouser . . . her comic talents fit well." During the show's run she found time to appear on the Merv Griffin-Westinghouse talk show, and she reminisced with co-host Arthur Treacher, who had appeared with her in *Slave Girl*. She also sang a flag-waving rendition of "Until the Parade Passes by."

On January 29, 1969, NBC telecast the *Crime Wave at Buffalo Springs* segment of "The Virginian," which starred Yvonne as a saloon hostess. The program, which also featured a group called the Irish Rovers, was a pilot for a proposed series to star Yvonne and the singers, but despite a rerun in the summer of 1969, the pilot failed to sell. Resilient Yvonne returned to the nightclub field in 1969 with an act which included both singing and dancing along with comedy patter. She also made appearances on several talk shows, including those hosted by Mike Douglas, Johnny Carson, and Donald O'Connor. On the latter program, she performed "It Must Be Him," a staple in her nightclub act.

In 1970, Yvonne received special billing as Valerie in the Mickey Spillane spy melodrama, *The Delta Factor* (American-Continental). Starring Christopher George, Yvette Mimieux, Ralph Taeger, and Diane McBain, with a special appearance by Spillane's wife, Sherri, the programmer film has since received brief theatrical release in 1971 and 1973, each time with more cuts and rating changes from R to GP.

Yvonne was still determined to make her Broadway bow, and she willingly auditioned for the lead in *Follies*, a New York-bound musical with tunes by Stephen Sondheim. She lost the part to Alexis Smith.† However, the producers of the show were so impressed with her singing, dancing, and stage presence, that they purposely enlarged a minor role in the extravaganza and gave Yvonne special billing and a big production number, "I'm Still Here." The show, which co-starred Dorothy Collins, Gene Nelson, and John McMartin, along with Alexis Smith and Yvonne, opened April 4, 1971 in New York's Winter Garden Theatre to a mixed critical reaction.

Although considered a part of the nostalgia-show revival started earlier by the spectacular success of the new *No, No, Nanette* with Ruby

---

*Opened on Broadway at the St. James Theatre on January 16, 1964, for a 2,844-performance run. Carol Channing was the original Dolly, replaced first by Ginger Rogers and then by Martha Raye, Betty Grable, Bibi Osterwald, Pearl Bailey, Phyllis Diller, and Ethel Merman.

†She later said, "That wasn't really my kind of woman; it wasn't somebody I could identify with. You know, a brittle, society type dame."

178

Keeler, *Follies* was actually a bittersweet story of a group of ex-showgirls who have a special reunion. In the course of this reunion in an abandoned Broadway theatre, their lives are layed bare. Yvonne's brief role of a wisecracking queen bee who has known the depths of poverty and the heights of riches, was, perhaps, the most believable character in the show. While the critics were far from unanimous in praise of the musical, Yvonne received generally good reviews, a reaction spurred by her show-stopping "I'm Still Here" in which she appropriately belts out a parody of her own life in which she has professionally gone from vamp to camp. Walter Kerr (*New York Times*) was so impressed by Yvonne's perform-ance and striking appearance that he took space in his review to editor-ialize, "she doesn't—in all truth—look as though she'd been away any-where." Nevertheless, a contingent of destructive high-low brows, led by John Simon (*New York* magazine) and echoed by a few others, insisted that Yvonne was as vulgar and crude as in the old days, and more or less asserted that no one cared about her surviving to remind the new genera-tion of those bygone years.*

Before the grand opening of *Follies*, Yvonne matter-of-factly informed an interviewer that she was not tense about her Broadway debut.† "I'm from Hollywood. I'm too dumb to be nervous about New York."

During the show's 522-performance run,‡ Yvonne appeared with her co-stars on the Merv Griffin and David Frost programs, publicizing the show and discussing her career in general, and always performing "I'm Still Here" with great verve. Along with the others, she appeared as a guest on a segment of the syndicated video show *This Is Your Life* honor-ing Alexis Smith. The original-cast album of *Follies* was issued on Capi-tol Records (SO 761), preserving Yvonne's zingy production number for posterity. The LP was not the first for the actress, for in the 1950s she had made an album called *Yvonne De Carlo Sings* on the Master Seal label (#1669) which was later reissued on a cassette tape.

While appearing on Broadway in *Follies*, Yvonne's last big film to date was issued. *The Seven Minutes* (Twentieth Century-Fox, 1972) was produced and directed by nudie-movie-helmer Russ Meyer. This financial bomb, based on the bestselling trashy novel by Irving Wallace, was Meyer's second and last film for the studio.δ The surprisingly bland *The Seven Minutes*—the title refers to the length of time usually required

---

*Yvonne's cause with liberal intellectuals was not boosted by the fact that she openly agreed with the right-wing conservative causes tub-thumped by pal John Wayne and others, including the perpetuation of the Vietnam War. It was rumored that hawkish Yvonne, wary of the New York scene, even carried a pistol in her purse during the run of *Follies*.

†Besides *Enter Laughing, Hello, Dolly!, Destry Rides Again*, etc., Yvonne had also done stock-company versions of *Little Me* and *Pal Joey*.

‡The New York engagement of *Follies* closed with a loss of $640,000 on the $700,000 capitalization.

δThe first was *Beyond the Valley of the Dolls* (Twentieth Century-Fox, 1971).

for completion of the sex-act—dealt in juvenile terms with the obscenity trial of a sex-oriented novel written by an anonymous author. In a cast that included veteran faces (Philip Carey, Jay C. Flippen, John Carradine, David Brian, et al.) in tiny parts, Yvonne managed to walk off with the film's few acting honors. She appeared toward the end of the film in the role of Constance Cumberland, the surprise witness for the defense of the novel, and its authoress. Said the *New Yorker* magazine, "Only Yvonne De Carlo emerges unscathed, playing the lovely older movie star she happens to be."

Although *The Seven Minutes* came and went, as did a lawsuit with her ex-agent Ben Pearson concerning percentages "earned" by him on her approximately $110,000 1971 salary, Yvonne continued to appear on Broadway in *Follies*, and she became a frequent guest on the Johnny Carson "Tonight" program. For these appearances she often brought home movies she had shot over the years, which included behind-the-scenes shots from some of her films and footage she made during the 1960 production of John Wayne's *The Alamo* (United Artists) on which her husband worked as a stuntman. Yvonne also often joked with the "Tonight Show" director, Frederick de Cordova, who had helmed three of her Universal color epics.

After *Follies* folded on Broadway, the producers moved it to a brief run in St. Louis, Missouri, and then for an unsuccessful stay in Los Angeles. After the final shutdown of the beleaguered *Follies*, Yvonne returned to Australia in November 1972 to replace Cyd Charisse (who replaced an ailing Betty Grable) in the restructured lead of *No, No, Nanette.** The dance routine that had been added for Charisse was deleted, and in its place, Yvonne was given another song number, Vincent Youmans's "More Than You Know" from another Broadway show, *Great Day!* (1929).

In late 1973, Yvonne popped up at the Off Broadway Theatre in San Diego in *Ben Bagley's Decline and Fall of the Entire World as Seen through the Eyes of Cole Porter*. The three-week revue, starring Yvonne, showcased thirty-one little-known Porter songs, reflecting the flavor of three decades. The *Hollywood Reporter*'s critic, Ron Pennington, reported, "Miss De Carlo is especially not used to full advantage and while she has fun with several of her numbers only one, 'Make It Another Old Fashion, Please,' seems particularly well suited to her style. She flashes brilliant potential, however, with only a couple of bars of 'Love for Sale' during the finale."

At the end of 1973, Yvonne was back in front of the camera in *Ari-*

---

*The original version opened on Broadway on September 16, 1925, for a 321-performance run at the Globe Theatre. The revival debuted at the 46th Street Theatre on January 19, 1971, for an 861-performance run. There have been two film versions of *No, No, Nanette*, one by First National in 1930, and the other by RKO in 1940.

zona Slim (Two-Diamonds, 1975), a shot-in-New York feature about a pool hustler (Sean Walsh) and his associates. Yvonne appears as the Contessa. Produced on a $350,000 budget, the feature was lensed over a twenty-five day period, using the environs of Manhattan for scenery.

Until April 1974, Yvonne's latest dramatic television appearance was in a cameo on NBC-TV's "The Name of the Game" series. In the segment, *Island of Gold and Precious Stones* (January 16, 1970), she was a rich, eccentric beekeeper. Among the guest stars in the episode was her old beau, Rudy Vallee. Then, on April 1, 1974, Yvonne appeared in a cameo role on the telefeature *The Girl on the Late, Late Show* (NBC-TV). Although it was very ordinary ("wasn't much as a movie and was even less as a pilot," said *Variety*), it had a potentially engrossing plot premise. Video producer Don Murray searches out a movie star (Gloria Grahame) of the 1950s for a guest spot on his New York daytime TV show. Murray goes to Hollywood to find this one-time marquee name, who vanished mysteriously at the height of her fame. In his search he finds murder and blackmail. Yvonne was onscreen briefly as the former manager of the studio club where Grahame was under contract. Now a restaurant-owner, Yvonne's Lorraine tells Murray, when he asks "What went wrong for Carolyn?", "Life maybe. Life has a way of going wrong." The ex-Miss Universal looked lovely in her five-minute role and came off very well in the part.

Later that year, Yvonne accepted the small but flashy role of Isbella Vega, the wife of the ousted governor Alejandro Vega (Gilbert Roland) and the mother of Don Diego (Frank Langella), in the telefeature *The Mark of Zorro* (ABC-TV, 1974).*This swashbuckling entry was part of the new craze for cloak-and-sword entries engendered by the success of the film spoof of *The Three Musketeers* (20th Century-Fox, 1974). While Yvonne's "bit" in the telemovie was minimal, it served to keep her image in front of the public.

Now past fifty years of age, Yvonne still appears, as one writer phrased it, "more like Salome than Vampira" [referring to her "The Munsters" role]. Like many stars today, she is quite active in politics and is what *Time* magazine called "an exemplar of the John Wayne philosophy: go west and turn right." A political conservative, to say the least, Yvonne campaigned for good friend Ronald Reagan when he first ran for governor of California in 1966 and at one time she was the Honorary Mayor of Universal City. Yvonne has often expressed hawkish attitudes toward U.S. policy in Southeast Asia and is opposed to rigid gun control legislation.

*Earlier versions of the Zorro legend include Douglas Fairbanks' *The Mark of Zorro* (United Artists, 1920), three Republic serials, *Zorro Rides Again* (1920), *Zorro's Fighting Legions* (1939), and the spinoff *Zorro's Black Whip* (1944), Tyrone Power's *The Mark of Zorro* (20th Century-Fox, 1940), and the sexploitation feature *The Erotic Adventures of Zorro* (Entertainment, 1972).

Asked about her hobby of shooting guns in target practice, Yvonne informed *Time* magazine, during the run of *Follies*, "The whole company kids me. They call me the fascist right-winger of the cast. One day Hal Prince [the producer-director] and Alexis [Smith] and I were talking about how expensive things could be. I said I knew what they meant because I was buying a box of Luger bullets in Virginia City, and I was amazed at how expensive they were. There was this shocked silence. I love to shoot, a lot of people do, so what? It's just target practice. I would never shoot an animal. Only targets—or people if they were attacking my house."

Unlike most former glamour stars, Yvonne does not seem to find her past glories nostalgic.* A leading boxoffice attraction for nearly fifteen years, she was also one of the loveliest actresses ever to grace the American screen. Today she has the financial freedom to reject roles that do not interest or suit her, an option she did not enjoy a decade prior.

A film producer once described Yvonne as being like a good utility baseball player. "She can sing, dance, do comedy or straight stuff. She isn't superior in any, but is valuable for her versatility." That versatility has kept her a star for over a quarter of a century and will more than likely continue to make her a name with whom to reckon in subsequent years. She has the tenacity and temerity to consistently reemerge in one showbusiness medium or another, to remind everyone again that "I'm Still Here."

---

*Far more than discussing the past, Yvonne would soon expand on her love of flying, although she does admit, "I think the thing I fear most is having to make a parachute jump if something happened to the plane. It's a terrible thought—having to jump into space with nothing but a parachute."

Feature Film Appearances

HARVARD, HERE I COME (Col., 1942) 64 M.

Producer, Wallace MacDonald; director, Lew Landers; story, Karl Brown; screenplay, Albert Duffy; art director, Lionel Banks; music director, Morris Stoloff; camera, Franz Planer; editor, William Lyon.

Maxie Rosenbloom (Slapsie Maxie Rosenbloom); Arline Judge (Francie Callahan); Stanley Brown (Harrison Carey); Don Beddoe (Hypo McGonigle); Marie Wilson (Zella Phipps); Virginia Sale (Miss Frisbie); Byron Foulger (Professor Alvin); Boyd Davis (Professor Hayworth); Julius Tannen (Professor Anthony); Walter Baldwin (Professor MacSquigley); Tom Herbert (Professor Teeter); Larry Parks (Eddie Spellman); George McKay (Blinky); John Tyrrell (Slug); Mary Ainslee (Phyllis); Lloyd Bridges (Larry); Al Hill (Doorman); Yvonne De Carlo (Bathing Girl); Ed Emerson (Mr. Plunkett); Bobby Watson (Horace); Marion Murray (Oomphie); Dan Tobey (Master of Ceremonies); Tommy Seidel (Boy); Charles Ray, Jack Mulhall (Reporters); Harry Bailey (Guest).

THIS GUN FOR HIRE (Par., 1942) 80 M.

Producer, Richard M. Blumenthal; director, Frank Tuttle; based on the novel *A Gun for Sale* by Graham Greene; screenplay, Albert Maltz, W. R. Burnett; art director, Hans Dreier; songs, Frank Loesser and Jacques Press; camera, John Seitz; editor, Archie Marshek.

Veronica Lake (Ellen Graham); Robert Preston (Michael Crane); Laird Cregar (Willard Gates); Alan Ladd (Philip Raven); Tully Marshall (Alvin Brewster); Mikhail Rasumny (Slukey); Marc Lawrence (Tommy); Pamela Blake (Annie); Harry Shannon (Finnerty); Frank Ferguson (Albert Baker); Bernadene Hayes (Baker's Secretary); James Farley (Night Watchman); Virita Campbell (Cripple Girl); Roger Imhof (Senator Burnett); Victor Kilian (Brewster's Secretary); Olin Howland (Fletcher); Emmett Vogan (Charlie); Chester Clute (Mr. Stewart); Charles Arnt (Will Gates); Virginia Farmer (Woman in Shop); Clem Bevans (Old-Timer); Harry Hayden (Restaurant Manager); Tim Ryan (Guard); Yvonne De Carlo (Show Girl); Ed Stanley (Police Captain); Eddy Chandler (Foreman); Phil Tead (Machinist); Charles R. Moore (Dining Car Waiter); Pat O'Malley (Conductor); Katherine (Karin) Booth (Waitress); Sarah Padden (Mrs. Mason); Louise La Planche (Dancer); Richard Webb (Young Man); Frances Morris (Receptionist); Cyril Ring (Waiter); Lora Lee (Girl in Car); William Cabanne (Laundry Truck Driver).

ROAD TO MOROCCO (Par., 1942) 83 M.

Associate producer, Paul Jones; director, David Butler; screenplay, Frank Butler, Don Hartman; music director, Victor Young; songs, Johnny Burke and James Van Heusen; art director, Hans Dreier, Robert Usher; camera, William Mellor; editor, Irene Morra.

Bing Crosby (Jeff Peters); Bob Hope (Turkey Jackson); Dorothy Lamour (Princess Shahmar); Anthony Quinn (Mullay Kasim); Dona Drake (Mihirmah); Mikhail Rasumny (Ahmed Bey); Vladimir Sokoloff (Hyder Khan); George Givot (Neb Jolla); Andrew Tombes (Oso Bucco); Leon Belasco (Yusef); Monte Blue, Jamiel Hanson (Aides to Mullay Kasim); Louise La Planche, Theo de Voe, Brooke Evans, Suzanne Ridgway, Yvonne De Carlo, Patsy Mace, Poppy Wilde (Handmaidens); George Lloyd, Sammy Stein (Guards); Ralph Penney (Arabian Waiter); Dan Seymour (Arabian Buyer); Pete G. Katchenaro (Philippine Announcer); Brandon Hurst (English Announcer); Richard Loo (Chinese Announcer); Leo Mostovoy (Russian Announcer); Vic Groves, Joe Jewett (Knife Dancers); Michael Mark (Arab Pottery Vendor); Nestor Paiva (Arab Sausage Vendor); Stanley Price (Idiot); Rita Christiani (Speciality Dancer); Robert Barron (Gigantic Bearded Arab); Cy Kendall (Proprietor of Fruit Stand); Sara Berner (Voice for Female Camel); Kent Rogers (Voice for Male Camel); Edward Emerson (Bystander); Sylvia Opert (Dancer); Blue Washington (Nubian Slave); Harry Cording, Dick Botiller (Warriors).

LUCKY JORDAN   (Par., 1942) 84 M.

Associate producer, Fred Kohlmar; director, Frank Tuttle; story, Charles Leonard; screenplay, Darrell Ware, Karl Tunberg; art directors, Hans Dreier, Ernest Fegte; camera, John Seitz; editor, Archie Marshek.

Alan Ladd (Lucky Jordan); Helen Walker (Jill Evans); Sheldon Leonard (Slip Moran); Mabel Paige (Annie); Marie McDonald (Pearl); Lloyd Corrigan (Ernest Higgins); Russell Hoyt (Eddie); Dave Willock (Angelo Palacio); John Wengraf (Kesselman); Miles Mander (Kilpatrick); Charles Cane (Sergeant); George F. Meader (Little Man); Virginia Brissac (Woman with Little Man); Al M. Hill, Fred Kohler, Jr. (Killers); Jack Roberts (Johnny); Clem Bevans (Gas Station Attendant); Olaf Hytten (Charles, the Servant); William Halligan (Miller, the Gateman); Kitty Kelly (Mrs. Maggotti); George Humbert (Joe Maggotti); Dorothy Dandridge (Maid at Hollyhock School); Joseph Downing (Harrison); Carl Hughes (Girl in Back Room); Ralph Dunn, Lyle Latell (Army Guards); Edward Earle (Man); Edythe Elliott (Private Secretary); John Harmon (Big-Ears); John Hamilton, Roy Gordon (Colonels); Kirk Alyn (Pearl's Boyfriend); Arthur Loft (Hearndon); Ronnie Rondell (Florist); Terry Ray (Sentry); Sara Berner (Helen); William Forrest (Commanding Officer); Ethel Clayton (Woman); Anthony L. Caruso (Gunman); Georgia Backus (Saleslady in Toy Shop); Yvonne De Carlo (Girl).

YOUTH ON PARADE   (Rep., 1942) 72 M.

Associate producer, Albert J. Cohen; director, Albert S. Rogell; screenplay, George Carleton Brown; art director, Russell Kimball; music director, Cy Feuer; songs, Sammy Cahn and Jule Styne; camera, Ernest Miller; editor, Howard O'Neill.

John Hubbard (Professor Gerald Payne); Martha O'Driscoll (Sally Carlyle); Bruce Langley (Himself); Ruth Terry (Patty Flynn/Betty Reilly); Charles Smith (Willie Webster); Nana Bryant (Agatha Frost); Ivan Simpson (Dean Wharton); Chick Chandler (Eddie Reilly); Paul Fix (Nick Cramer); Lynn Merrick (Emmy Lou Piper); John Boyle, Jr. (The Character); Marlyn Schild (Marlyn): Eddie Acuff, Bud Jamison (Cops); Sue Robin (Bouncy); Ruth Daye (Butch); Jack Boyle (Ned); Ivan Miller (Ned); Edward Earle (Major); Betty Atkinson (Drum Majorette);

Harry Hayden (Dr. Witherspoon); Walter Soderling, Boyd Irwin, Walter Fenner, Alfred Hall, Elmer Jerome (Professors); Maurice Cass (Professor Bowilowicz); Barbara Slater (Curvy Coed); Ric Vallin (Customer); Ben Lessy (Piano Player); Warren Ashe (Clerk); Frank Coghlan, Jr. (Student); Yvonne De Carlo (Girl).

RHYTHM PARADE   (Mon., 1943) 70 M.

Producer, Sydney M. Williams; directors, Howard Bretherton, Dave Gould; story-screenplay, Carl Foreman, Charles Marion; music director, Edward Kay; songs, Dave Oppenheim and Roy Ingraham; camera, Mack Stengler.

Nils T. Granlund (Granny); Gale Storm (Sally); Robert Lowery (Jimmy); Margaret Dumont (Ophelia); Chick Chandler (Speed); Cliff Nazarro (Rocks); Jan Wiley (Connie); Florentine Gardens Revue, Candy Candido, Mills Bros., Ted Fio Rito's Orchestra (Themselves); Yvonne De Carlo (Girl).

THE CRYSTAL BALL   (UA, 1943) 81 M.

Associate producer, Richard Blumenthal; director, Elliott Nugent; story, Stevan Vas; screenplay, Virginia Van Upp; music, Victor Young; art directors, Hans Dreier, Roland Anderson; set decorator, George Sawley; sound, Gene Merritt, Don Johnson; process camera, Farciot Edouart; camera, Leo Tover; editor, Doane Harrison.

Ray Milland (Brad Cavanaugh); Paulette Goddard (Toni Gerard); Gladys George (Madame Zenobia); Virginia Field (Jo Ainsley); Cecil Kellaway (Pop Tibbets); William Bendix (Biff Carter); Mary Field (Foster); Frank Conlan (Dusty); Ernest Truex (Mr. Martin); Mabel Paige (Lady with Pekinese); Regina Wallace (Mrs. Smythe); Peter Jamieson (Brad's Secretary); Donald Douglas (Mr. Bowman); Nestor Paiva (Stukov); Sig Arno (Waiter at Stukov's); Hillary Brooke (Friend of Jo Ainsley); Tom Dugan (Plumber); Iris Adrian (Mrs. Martin); Babe London, June Evans (Tandem Riders); Reginald Sheffield (Dad in Shooting Gallery); Maude Eburne ("Apple Annie" Character); Yvonne De Carlo, Maxine Ardell (Secretaries); Christopher King, Alice Kirby, Marcella Phillips, Lorraine Miller, Lynda Grey, Donivee Lee (Garter Girls—Bazaar Sequence); Eric Alden, Donald Gallaher (Ambulance Drivers); Marjorie Deanne (Cigarette Girl); May Beatty (Dowager); Charles Irwin (Spieler).

SALUTE FOR THREE   (Par., 1943) 75 M.

Producer, Walter MacEwen; director, Ralph Murphy; story, Art Arthur; screenplay, Doris Anderson, Curtis Kenyon, Hugh Wedlock, Jr., Howard Snyder; art directors, Hans Dreier, Haldane Douglas; music director, Victor Young; songs, Jule Styne and Kim Gannon; choreography, Jack Donahue; assistant director, John Coonan; sound, Max Hutchinson, Don Johnson; camera, Theodor Sparkuhl; editor, Arthur Schmidt.

Betty Rhodes (Judy Ames); Macdonald Carey (Buzz McAllister); Marty May (Jimmy Gates); Cliff Edwards (Foggy); Minna Gombell (Myrt); Lorraine and Rognan (Themselves); Dona Drake (Dona); Charles Smith, Charles Williams, Doodles Weaver, Harry Barris, Jack Gardner, Walter Sande (Sailors); Tony Hughes (Colonel Rennick); Robert Emmett Keane (Patton); Linda Brent, Patti Brilhante, DeDe Barrington (Girls in Canteen); Frank Moran (Sleepy Soldier); Frederic Henry, Frank Wayne (M.P.s); Emmett Vogan (Radio Announcer); Eddie Dew (Marine in Broadcasting Station); Noel Neill (Gracie); Edna Bennett (Woman); Franklin Parker (Radio Official); Blanche Payson (Taxi Driver); Isabel Withers (Nurse); Frank Faylen (Soldier Friend with Buzz); Eddie Coke (Corporal); Billy Wayne, George Sherwood (Marines); Lynda Grey, Louise La Planche,

Maxine Ardell, Christopher King (Hostesses); Marcella Phillips, Marjorie Deanne, Yvonne De Carlo, Alice Kirby (Quartette Girls); Tom Seidel (Roy Ward, the Soldier); Ralph Montgomery (Sergeant in Hospital).

FOR WHOM THE BELL TOLLS   (Par., 1943) C—168 M.

Executive producer, B. G. De Sylva; producer-director, Sam Wood; based on the novel by Ernest Hemingway; screenplay, Dudley Nichols; production designer, William Cameron Menzies; art directors, Hans Dreier, Haldane Douglas; set decorator, Bert Granger; assistant directors, Lonnie D'Orsa, Joe Youngerman; music, Victor Young; orchestrators, Leo Shuken, George Parrish; sound, Harold Lewis, Don Johnson; special camera effects, Gordon Jennings, Jan Domela, Irwin Roberts; process camera, Farciot Edouart; camera, Ray Rennahan; editors, Sherman Todd, John Link.

Gary Cooper (Robert Jordan); Ingrid Bergman (Maria); Akim Tamiroff (Pablo); Arturo de Cordova (Agustin); Vladimir Sokoloff (Anselmo); Mikhail Rasumny (Rafael); Fortunio Bonanova (Fernando); Eric Feldary (Andres); Katina Paxinou (Pilar); Joseph Calleia (El Sordo); Lilo Yarson (Joaquin); Alexander Granach (Paco); Adia Kuznetzoff (Gustavo); Leonid Snegoff (Ignacio); Leo Bulgakov (General Golz); Duncan Renaldo (Lieutenant Berrendo); George Coulouris (Andre Massart); Frank Puglia (Captain Gomez); Pedro de Cordoba (Colonel Miranda); Michael Visaroff (Staff Officer); Konstantin Shayne (Karkov); Martin Garralaga (Captain Mora); Jean Del Val (Sniper); Jack Mylong (Colonel Duval); Feodor Chaliapin (Kashkin); Mayo Newhall (Don Ricardo); Michael Dalmatoff (Don Benito Garcia, the Mayor); Antonio Vidal (Don Guillermo); Robert Tafur (Don Fusatino Rivero); Armand Roland (Julian); Trini Varela (Spanish Singer); Dick Botiller (Sergeant—Elias' Man); Franco Corsaro, Frank Lackteen (Elias' Men); George Sorel (Bores Sentry); John Bleifer (Peasant—Flails Gonzales); Harry Cording (Flails the Mayor); William Edmunds, Alberto Morin, Pedro Regas (Soldiers); Soledad Jiminez (Don Guillermo's Wife); Luis Rojas (Drunkard); Manuel Paris (Officer of the Civil Guards); Ernesto Morelli, Manuel Lopez, Jose Tortosa (Civil Guards); Yakima Canutt (Young Cavalryman); Tito Renaldo (Sentry); Maxine Ardell, Marjorie Deanne, Yvonne De Carlo, Alice Kirby, Marcella Phillips, Lynda Grey, Christopher King, Louise La Planche (Girls in Cafe).

SO PROUDLY WE HAIL!   (Par., 1943) 126 M.

Producer-director, Mark Sandrich; screenplay, Allan Scott; art directors, Hans Dreier, Earl Hendrick; set decorator, Stephen Seymour; assistant director, Joe Youngerman; music, Miklos Rozsa; song, Edward Heyman and Rozsa; sound, Harold Lewis, Walter Oberst; special effects, Gordon Jennings, Farciot Edouart; camera, Charles Lang; editor, Ellsworth Hoagland.

Claudette Colbert (Lieutenant Janet Davidson); Paulette Goddard (Lieutenant Jean O'Doul); Veronica Lake (Lieutenant Olivia D'Arcy); George Reeves (Lieutenant John Summers); Barbara Britton (Lieutenant Rosemary Larson); Walter Abel (Chaplain); Sonny Tufts (Kansas); Mary Servoss (Captain "Ma" McGregory); Ted Hecht (Dr. Jose Hardin); John Litel (Dr. Harrison); Dr. Hugh Ho Chang (Ling Chee); Mary Treen (Lieutenant Sadie Schwartz); Kitty Kelly (Lieutenant Ethel Armstrong); Helen Lynd (Lieutenant Elsie Bollenbacker); Adrian Booth (Lieutenant Toni Bacelli); Dorothy Adams (Lieutenant Irma Emerson); Ann Doran (Lieutenant Betty Paterson); Jean Willes (Lieutenant Carol Johnson); Lynn Walker (Lieutenant Fay Leonard); Joan Tours (Lieutenant Margaret Stevenson); Jan Wiley (Lieutenant Lynne Hopkins); James Bell (Colonel White); Dick Hogan (Flight Lieutenant Archie McGregor); Bill Goodwin (Captain O'Rourke); James

Flavin (Captain O'Brien); Byron Foulger (Mr. Larson); Elsa Janssen (Mrs. Larson); Richard Crane (Georgie Larson); Boyd Davis (Colonel Mason); Will Wright (Colonel Clark); William Forrest (Major—San Francisco Dock); Isabel Cooper, Amparo Antenercrut, Linda Brent (Filipino Nurses); James Millican (Young Ensign); Damian O'Flynn (Young Doctor); Victor Kilian, Jr. (Corporal); Julia Faye, Hazel Keener, Frances Morris, Mimi Doyle (Nurses); Edward Earle, Byron Shores (Doctors); Harry Strang (Major Arthur); Edward Dew (Captain Lawrence); Yvonne De Carlo (Girl); Hugh Prosser (Captain); Charles Lester (Soldier).

LET'S FACE IT (Par., 1943) 76 M.

Associate producer, Fred Kohlmar; director, Sidney Lanfield; based on the musical play by Dorothy and Herbert Fields, Cole Porter, and the play *Cradle Snatchers* by Norma Mitchell, Russell G. Medcraft; songs, Porter, Sammy Cahn, Jule Styne; art directors, Hans Dreier, Earl Hedrick; set decorator, Raymond Moyer; assistant director, Lonnie D'Orsa; sound, Hugo Grenzbach, Don Johnson; camera, Lionel Lindon; editor, Paul Weatherwax.

Bob Hope (Jerry Walker); Betty Hutton (Winnie Potter); Dona Drake (Muriel); Cully Richards (Frankie Burns); Eve Arden (Maggie Watson); Zasu Pitts (Cornelia Figeson); Marjorie Weaver (Jean Blanchard); Raymond Walburn (Julian Watson); Phyllis Povah (Nancy Collister); Joe Sawyer (Sergeant Wiggins); Dave Willock (Barney Hilliard); Nicco and Tanya (Dance Team); Andrew Tombes (Judge Henry Pigeon); Grace Hayle (Mrs. Wigglesworth); Evelyn Dockson (Mrs. Taylor); Kay Linaker (Canteen Hostess); Frederic Nay (Walsh); George Meader (Justice of the Peace); Joyce Compton (Wiggins' Girl); Florence Shirley (Woman in Sun Shell Cafe); Barbara Pepper (Daisy); Robin Raymond (Mimi); Phyllis Ruth (Lulu); Lionel Royce (Submarine Commander); Emory Parnell (Colonel); Andria Moreland, Brooke Evans (Milk Maids); Don Kerr (Specialty Dancer); Edward Dew (Sergeant); Eddie Dunn (Cop); Elinor Troy (Elinor); Eleanor Prentiss (Joan, a Woman in Court); Cyril Ring (Headwaiter); William B. Davidson (Man in Boat); Yvonne De Carlo, Noel Neill, Julie Gibson, Jayne Hazard (Girls); Hal Rand, Allen Ray, Jerry James (Men); Lena Belle (Lena); Helena Brinton (Helena); Tommye Adams (Tommye); Barbara Brooks (Barbara); Ellen Johnson (Ellen); Debbra Keith (Betty).

TRUE TO LIFE (Par., 1943) 93 M.

Producer, Paul Jones; director, George Marshall; story, Ben Barzman, Bess Taffel, Sol Barzman; screenplay, Don Hartman, Harry Tugend; art directors, Hans Dreier, Earl Hedrick; set decorator, George Sawley; assistant director, Arthur Black; songs, Johnny Mercer and Hoagy Carmichael; sound, Gene Merritt, Walter Oberst; camera, Charles Lang; editor, LeRoy Stone.

Mary Martin (Bonnie Porter); Franchot Tone (Fletcher Marvin); Dick Powell (Link Ferris); Victor Moore (Pop Porter); Mabel Paige (Mom Porter); William Demarest (Jake); Clarence Kolb (Mr. Huggins); Beverly Hudson (Twips); Raymond Roe (Clem); Ernest Truex (Oscar Elkins); Harry Shannon (Mr. Mason); Charles Moore (Gabe, the Butler); Tim Ryan (Mr. Mammal; Ken Carpenter (Announcer); Nestor Paiva (Kapopolis); Betty Farrington (Mrs. Barkow); Charles Cane (Expressman); J. Farrell MacDonald, Vernon Dent, Fred Santley (Men); Grace Hayle, Esther Howard, Ethel Clayton, Gloria Williams (Women); Fred A. Kelsey (Cop); Stanley Andrews (Frank, Foreman of the Bakery); John Hiestand (Narrator); Harry Tyler (Program Director); Harry Hayden (Radio Pop); Ann Doran (Radio Kitty); Madora Keene (Radio Mom); Shirley Mills (Radio Sister);

Bill Bletcher (Radio Heavy); Bud Jamison (Radio Jake); Robert Winkler (Radio Sonny); Jack Gardner (Radio Man); Christopher King, Maxine Ardell, Yvonne De Carlo, Alice Kirby, Marcella Phillips, Marjorie Deanne, Dorothy Granger (Girls); Jack Baxley, Frank Coleman, Edna Bennett (People on Bus); Don Kerr (Guide on Bus); Dan Borzage (Beggar); Matt McHugh (Taxicab Driver); Walter Soderling (Man in Subway); Constance Purdy (Woman in Subway); Edward S. Chandler (Subway Guard); Tom Kennedy (Customer); Terry Moore (Little Girl).

THE DEERSLAYER   (Rep., 1943) 67 M.

Producers, P. S. Harrison, E. B. Derr; director, Lew Landers; based on the novel by James Fenimore Cooper; screenplay, Harrison, Derr; adaptor, John W. Krafft; assistant director, Eddie Stein; camera, Arthur Martinelli; editor, George McGuire.

Bruce Kellogg (Deerslayer); Jean Parker (Judith); Larry Parks (Jingo-Good); Warren Ashe (Harry March); Wanda McKay (Hetty); Yvonne De Carlo (Wah-Tah); Addison Richards (Mr. Hutter); Johnny Michaels (Bobby Hunter); Phil Van Zandt (Briarthorn); Trevor Bardette (Chief Rivenoak); Robert Warwick (Chief Uncas); Many Treaties (Chief Brave Eagles).

STANDING ROOM ONLY   (Par., 1944) 83 M.

Producer, Paul Jones; director, Sidney Lanfield; story, Al Martin; screenplay, Darrell Ware, Karl Tunberg; art directors, Hans Dreier, Earl Hedrick; set decorator, Ray Moyer; assistant director, Lonnie D'Orsa; music, Robert Emmett Dolan; sound, Ferol Redd, Philip Wisdom; camera, Charles Lang; editor, William Shea.

Paulette Goddard (Jane Rogers); Fred MacMurray (Les Stevens); Edward Arnold (T. J. Todd); Roland Young (Ira Cromwell); Hillary Brooke (Alice Todd); Porter Hall (Hugo Farenhall); Clarence Kolb (Glen Ritchie); Anne Revere (Major Cromwell); Isabel Randolph (Mrs. Ritchie); Marie McDonald (Opal); Veda Ann Borg (Peggy Fuller); Josephine Whittell (Miss Becker); Sig Arno (Waiter); Robin Raymond (Girl); John Hamilton (General); Regina Wallace (General's Wife); Boyd Davis (Admiral); Winifred Harris (Admiral's Wife); Roy Gordon (Commander); Mary Newton (Commander's Wife); Herbert Heyes (Colonel); Mira McKinney (Colonel's Wife); Eddie Dunn, Arthur Loft (Foremen); Lorin Raker (Hotel Clerk); Ralph Peters (Counterman); Marilynn Harris, Noel Neill, Yvonne De Carlo (Secretaries); Lal Chand Mehra (Bey); Elvira Curci (Bey's Wife); Judith Gibson, Marcella Phillips (Office Girls); Gayne Whitman (Voice over Dictograph); Rita Gould, Grayce Hampton, Ethel May Halls, Georgia Backus, Harry Hays Morgan, Forbes Murray, Edwin Stanley (Guests at Ritchie Home); Mary Currier (Additional Guest); Howard Mitchell (Conductor); Frank Faylen (Cab Driver).

THE STORY OF DR. WASSELL   (Para., 1944) 136 M.

Producer, Cecil B. DeMille; associate producer, Sidney Biddell; based on the story of Dr. Wassell, and also the story by James Hilton; director, DeMille; screenplay, Alan LeMay, Charles Bennett; art directors, Hans Dreier, Roland Anderson; set decorator, George Sawley; music, Victor Young; assistant directors, Eddie Salven, Oscar Rudolph; sound, Hugo Grenzbach; camera, Victor Milner; editor, Anne Bauchens.

Gary Cooper (Dr. Croydon M. Wassell); Laraine Day (Madeline); Signe Hasso (Bettina); Dennis O'Keefe ("Hoppy" Hopkins); Carol Thurston (Tremartini); Carl Esmond (Lieutenant Dirk van Daal); Paul Kelly (Murdock); Elliott Reid ("Andy" Anderson); Stanley Ridges (Commander Bill Goggins); Renny Mc-

Evoy (Johnny); Oliver Thorndike (Alabam); Philip Ahn (Ping); Barbara Britton (Ruth); Melvin Francis (Francis); Joel Allen (Kraus); James Millican (Whaley); Mike Kilian (Boranetti); Doodles Weaver (Hunter); Lester Mathews (Dr. Ralph Wayne); Ludwig Donath (Dr. Vranken); Richard Loo (Dr. Wei); Davison Clark (Dr. Holmes); Richard Nugent (Captain Carruthers); Morton Lowry (Lieutenant Bainbridge); George Macready (Captain Blaen); Victor Varconi (Captain Ryk); Edward Fielding (Admiral Hart); Harvey Stephens (Captain in Charge of Evacuation); Frank Wilcox (Captain's Aide for Evacuation); Minor Watson (Rear Admiral—Australia); Edmund MacDonald (Rear Admiral's Aide); William Severn (Little English Boy); Edith Barrett (Mother of Little English Boy); Catherine Craig (Mrs. Wayne); Frank Puglia (Javanese Temple Guide); Si Jenks (Arkansas Mail Carrier); Irving Bacon (Missionary); Ottola Nesmith (Missionary's Wife); Sybil Merritt (Javanese Girl); Maria Loredo (Fat Javanese Girl); Loretta Luiz (Pretty Javanese Girl); Luke Chan (Chinese Coolie—Boatman); Oie Chan (Chinese Coolie's Wife); Yu Feng Sung (Chinese Priest); Moy Ming (Chinese Tea Vendor); Hugh Beaumont (Admiral Hart's Aide); Roy Gordon (Commander USN); Ferdinand Schumann (Ensign Watch Officer USN); Charles Trowbridge, Gus Glassmire (Captains USN—Surabaya); Edward Earle, Allan Ray (Officers USN—Surabaya); Anthony Caruso (Pharmacist's Mate); Sven-Hugo Borg (Dutch Guard); Frank Lackteen (Javanese Conductor); Fred Kohler, Jr. (Bosun's Mate—Evacuation); Jack Luden (Captain Carruthers' Driver); George Eldredge (Damage Control Officer USN); Forbes Murray (Captain USN—Australia); Mary Currier (English Woman); John Mylong (Joyful Passenger); Ann Doran (Praying Woman); Stanley Price (Sobbing Man); Maxine Fife, Ameda Lambert, Carla Boehm, Phyllis Perry, Marion de Sydow (Women Evacuees); Gloria Dea, Forrest Dickson, Geraldine Fisette (Javanese Nurses); Eric Alden, Richard Barrett, John Benson, Carlyle Blackwell, John Bogden, George Bronson, Edgar Caldwell, Tony Cirillo, James Cornell, James Courtney, Clint Dorrington, Reynold DuPont, Edward Howard, Henry Kraft, Buddy Messinger, Robert Wilbur (U.S. Sailors); Yvonne De Carlo (Native Girl); Jack Norton (Man Passenger—Companionway); Mike Lally (Civilian); Sam Flint, Milton Kibbee, Hazel Keener, Cecil Weston, Frances Morris (Passengers—Janssens); Frank Elliott (English Doctor); Rodric Redwing, Roque Espiritu, Joe Dominguez, Joe Bautista (Javanese Orderlies); Russ Clark (Chief Petty Officer—*Marblehead*).

RAINBOW ISLAND   (Par., 1944) C—98 M.

Associate producer, E. D. Leshin; director, Ralph Murphy; story, Seena Owen; screenplay, Walter De Leon, Arthur Philips; art directors, Hans Dreier, Haldane Douglas; set decorator, George Sawley; music, Roy Webb; vocal arranger, Joseph J. Lilley; songs, Ted Koehler and Burton Lane; choreography, Danny Dare; assistant director, Harvey Foster; costumes, Edith Head; chants, Augie Goupil; sound, W. C. Smith; special camera effects, Gordon Jennings; process camera, Farciot Edouart; camera, Karl Struss; editor, Arthur Schmidt.

Dorothy Lamour (Lona); Eddie Bracken (Toby Smith); Gil Lamb (Pete Jenkins); Barry Sullivan (Ken Masters); Forrest Orr (Doctor Curtis); Anne Revere (Queen Okalana); Reed Hadley (High Priest Kahuna); Marc Lawrence (Alcoa); Adia Kuznetzoff (Executioner); Olga San Juan (Miki); Elena Verdugo (Moana); George Urchell (Executioner's Helper); Aggie Auld, Renee DuPuis, Iris Lancaster, Lena Belle, Virginia Lucas, Audrey Young, Louise La Planche (Native Girls); Theodore Rand, Satini Puailoa, Robert St. Angelo, Rod Redwing, Baudelio Alva, Rudy Masson, Alex McSweyn, Alex Montoya (Queen's Guards); Robert Martinez (Executioner's Assistant); Pua Kealoha (Native Man); Dan Seymour (Fat

Native Man); Hopkins Twins (Specialty Swimmers); Stanley Price (Tonto); Yvonne De Carlo, Noel Neill, Leigh Whitney, Nonny Parsons (Lona's Companions); George T. Lee, Leon Lontoc, Jimmie Lano (Japanese Pilots); Luis Alberni (Native with Laundry); Bobby Barber (Native Banana Man); Allen Fox, Frank Marlowe, Bob Stephenson (Merchant Marines); Eddie Acuff (Sailor); Larry Thompson (Lieutenant); Frank Wilcox (Captain); Paul McVey (U.S. Naval Commander); Ralph Linn (U.S.Naval Lieutenant).

KISMET (MGM, 1944) C—100 M.

Producer, Everett Riskin; director, William Dieterle; based on the play by Edward Knoblock; screenplay, John Meehan; art directors, Cedric Gibbons, Daniel B. Cathcart; set decorators, Edwin B. Willis, Richard Pefferle; assistant director, Marvin Stuart; costume supervisor, Irene; costumes executed by Karinska; songs, Harold Arlen and E. Y. Harburg; sound, Douglas Shearer; special effects, A. Arnold Gillespie, Warren Newcombe; camera, Charles Rosher; editor, Ben Lewis.

Ronald Colman (Hafiz); Marlene Dietrich (Jamilla); James Craig (Caliph); Edward Arnold (Mansur); Hugh Herbert (Feisal); Joy Ann Page (Marsinah); Florence Bates (Karsha); Harry Davenport (Agha); Hobart Cavanaugh (Moolah); Robert Warwick (Alfie); Beatrice and Evelyne Kraft (Dance Specialty); Barry Macollum (Amu); Victor Kilian (Jehan); Charles Middleton (Miser); Harry Humphrey (Gardener); Nestor Paiva (Captain of Police); Roque Ybarra (Miser's Son); Eve Whitney (Cafe Girl); Minerva Urecal (Retainer); Joe Yule (Attendant); Morgan Wallace (Merchant); John Maxwell (Guard); Walter De Palma (Detective); Jimmy Ames (Major Domo); Charles La Torre (Alwah); Noble Blake (Nubian Slave); Anna Demetrio (Proprietress of Cafe); Dan Seymour (Fat Turk); Mitchell Lewis (Sheik); Phiroz Nair Asit Ghosh (Nabout Fighters); Carmen D'Antonio (Specialty Dancer); Jessie Tai Sing, Zedra Conde, Barbara Glenz, Frances Ramsden, (Cafe Girls); Charles Judels (Rich Merchant); Dale Van Sickel (Assassin); Harry Cording, Joseph Granby (Policemen); Frank Penny, Peter Cusanelli (Merchants); Zack Williams (Executioner); Gabriel Gonzales (Monkey Man); John Merton, Eddie Abdo, Dick Botiller, Jack "Tiny" Lipson (Mansur's Aides); Lynne Arlen, Leslie Anthony, Rosalyn Lee, Sonia Carr, Carla Boehm, Yvonne De Carlo, Eileen Herric, Shelby Payne (Queen's Retinue); Paul Singh (Caliph's Valet); Eddie Abdo (Voice—Prayer in Arabic); Pedro De Cordoba (Meuzin); Paul Bradley (Magician); Louis Manley (Fire-Eater); Sammy Stein (Policeman); John Schaller, Ramiro Rivas, William Rivas (Juggling Trio).

PRACTICALLY YOURS (Par., 1944) 90 M.

Producer, Mitchell Leisen; associate producer, Harry Tugend; director, Leisen; screenplay, Norman Krasna; art directors, Hans Dreier, Robert Usher; set decorator, Stephen Seymour; music, Victor Young; assistant director, John Coonan; Miss Colbert's gowns, Howard Greer; sound, Donald McKay; special camera effects, Gordon Jennings, J. Devereaux Jennings; process camera, Farciot Edouart; camera, Charles Lang, Jr.; editor, Doane Harrison.

Claudette Colbert (Peggy Martin); Fred MacMurray (Lieutenant [s.g] Daniel Bellamy); Gil Lamb (Albert Beagell); Cecil Kellaway (Marvin P. Meglin); Robert Benchley (Judge Oscar Stimson); Tom Powers (Commander Harpe); Jane Frazee (Musical Comedy Star); Rosemary De Camp (Ellen Macy); Isabel Randolph (Mrs. Meglin); Mikhail Rasumny (La Crosse); Arthur Loft (Uncle Ben Bellamy); Edgar Norton (Harvey, the Butler); Donald MacBride (Sam); Donald Kerr (Meglin's Chauffeur); Clara Reid (Meglin's Maid); Don Barclay (Himself); Rommie (Piggy, the Dog); Charles Irwin (Patterson); Will Wright (Senator

Cowling); Isabel Withers (Grace Mahoney); George Carleton (Mr. Hardy); Frederic Nay (Michael); Stan Johnson (Pilot); James Millican (Co-Pilot); Byron Barr (Navigator); Allen Fox, George Turner, Reggie Simpson (Reporters); Ralph Lynn, Jerry James, William Meader (Cameramen); John Whitney (Pilot with Bellamy); Sam Ash, John Wald (Radio Announcers); Hugh Beaumont (Cutter); Warren Ashe (Cameraman); Roy Brent (Sound Man); Gary Bruce (Camera Operator); John James (Usher); Mike Lally (Assistant Cameraman); Jack Rice (Couturier); George Melford (Vice President—Senate); Ottola Nesmith (Hysterical Woman—Senate); Len Hendry (Naval Lieutenant—Senate); Nell Craig (Meglin's Secretary); Charles Hamilton (Guard at Prudential); Yvonne De Carlo, Julie Gibson (Girl Employees); Allen Pinson (Stimson's Chauffeur); Edward Earle (Assistant Manager—Hadley's Store); Louise Currie, Dorothy Granger (Girls); Mimi Doyle (Red Cross Worker); Helen Dickson (Woman in Subway); Jack Clifford (Subway Conductor); Gladys Blake (Brooklyn Girl in Subway); Earle Hodgins (Man with Pen Knife); Edwin Maxwell (Radio Official); Thomas Quinn (Photographer); Stanley Andrews (Official of Shipyards); Charles A. Hughes (Radio Announcer); Kitty Kelly (Wife at Newsreel Theatre); Marjean Neville (Little Girl at Newsreel Theatre); Tom Kennedy (Burly Citizen at Newsreel Theatre); Jan Buckingham (Nursemaid in Park); Michael Miller, Hugh Binyon, Sonny Boy Williams (Boys in Park); Louise La Planche (Attractive Girl); Eddie Hall, Stephen Wayne (Radio Men—PBY); Ronnie Rondell (Left Gunner—PBY; Tex Taylor (Mechanic); Anthony Marsh (Plane Captain—PBY); Larry Thompson (Right Gunner—PBY).

HERE COME THE WAVES   (Par., 1944) 99 M.

Producer-director, Mark Sandrich; screenplay, Allan Scott, Ken Englund, Zion Myers; art directors, Hans Dreier, Roland Anderson; set decorator, Ray Moyer; songs, Harold Arlen and Johnny Mercer; choreography, Danny Dare; music director, Robert Emmett Dolan; assistant directors, C. C. Coleman, George Templeton; sound, Hugh Grenzbach; special camera effects, Gordon Jennings, Paul Lerpae; process camera, Farciot Edouart; camera, Charles Lang; editor, Ellsworth Hoagland.

Bing Crosby (Johnny Cabot); Betty Hutton (Susie Allison/Rosemary Allison); Sonny Tufts (Windy); Ann Doran (Ruth); Gwen Crawford (Tex); Noel Neill (Dorothy); Catherine Craig (Lieutenant Townsend); Marjorie Henshaw (Isabel); Harry Barris (Band Leader); Mae Clarke (Ensign Kirk); Minor Watson (High-ranking Officer); Roberta Jonay, Guy Zanett (Specialty Dancers); Louise La Planche (Girl Photographer); Mona Freeman, Carlotta Jelm (Painting Girls); Jack Norton (Waiter at Cabana Club); Jimmie Dundee (Chief Petty Officer); James Flavin (Shore Patrolman); Babe London (Girl Window Washer); Oscar O'Shea (Commodore); Cyril Ring (Lieutenant Colonel); Frances Morris (WAVE); Yvonne De Carlo (Girl); Jerry James (Sailor).

BRING ON THE GIRLS   (Par., 1945) C—92 M.

Associate producer, Fred Kohlmar; director, Sidney Lanfield; story, Pierre Wolff; screenplay, Karl Tunberg, Darrell Ware; art directors, Hans Dreier, John Meehan; set decorator, Ray Moyer; music director, Robert Emmett Dolan; songs, Jimmy McHugh and Harold Adamson; choreography, Danny Dare; assistant director, Dick McWhorter; sound, Wallace Noble; camera, Karl Struss; editor, William Shea.

Veronica Lake (Teddy Collins); Sonny Tufts (Phil North); Eddie Bracken (J. Newport Bates); Marjorie Reynolds (Sue Thomas); Grant Mitchell (Uncle

191

Ralph); Johnny Coy (Benny Lowe); Peter Whitney (Swede); Alan Mowbray (August); Porter Hall (Dr. Efrington); Thurston Hall (Rutledge); Lloyd Corrigan (Beaster); Sig Arno (Joseph); Joan Woodbury (Gloria); Andrew Tombes (Dr. Spender); Frank Faylen, Huntz Hall, William Moss (Sailors); Norma Varden (Aunt Martha); Golden Gate Quartette, Spike Jones and His Orchestra (Themselves); Marietta Canty (Ida); Dorothea Kent (Myrtle); Stan Johnson (Petty Officer); Jimmie Dundee (Chief—Master at Arms); Walter Baldwin (Henry); Veda Ann Borg (Girl at Bar with Phil); Noel Neill (Cigarette Girl); Jimmy Conlin (Justice of the Peace); George Turner (Marine); Louise La Planche (Girl); Yvonne De Carlo (Hat Check Girl); Alec Craig (Stage Doorman); Barry Watkins (Rube in Comedy Skit); Kay Linaker (Commander's Wife); Frank Hagney (Flunky); Harry Hays Morgan (Waiter).

SALOME, WHERE SHE DANCED   (Univ., 1945) C—90 M.

Producer, Walter Wanger; associate producer, Alexander Golitzen; director, Charles Lamont; story, Michael J. Phillips; screenplay, Laurence Stallings; music-music director, Edward Ward; art directors, John B. Goodman, Golitzen; set decorators, Russell A. Gausman, Victor A. Gangelin; dialog director, Ernest Truex; choreography, Lester Horton; songs, Everett Carter; assistant director, Fred Frank; sound, Bernard B. Brown, William Hedgcock; camera, Hal Mohr, W. Howard Green; editor, Russell Schoengarth.

Yvonne De Carlo (Salome); Rod Cameron (Jim); David Bruce (Cleve); Walter Slezak (Dimitrioff); Albert Dekker (Von Bohlen); Marjorie Rambeau (Madam); J. Edward Bromberg (Professor Max); Abner Biberman (Dr. Ling); John Litel (General Lee); Kurt Katch (Bismarck); Arthur Hohl (Bartender); Nestor Paiva (Panatela); Gavin Muir (Henderson); Will Wright (Sheriff); Joseph Haworth (Henry); Matt McHugh (Lafe); Jane Adams, Barbara Bates, Daun Kennedy, Kathleen O'Malley, Karen Randle, Jean Trent, Kerry Vaughn (Salome Girls); Jan Williams, Doreen Tryden, Bert Dole, Emmett Casey (Specialties); Eddie Dunn (Lineman); Charles Wagenheim (Telegrapher); Gene Garrick (German Sergeant); Eric Feldary (Uhlan Sergeant); Sylvia Field (Maid); Richard Ryen (Theatre Manager); Colin Campbell (Mate); George Sherwood (Bartender); Charles McAvoy (Policeman); Al Ferguson (Deputy); Alan Edwards (Bret Harte); George Leigh (Bayard Taylor); Ina Ownbey (Girl); Eddie Cobb (Stage Driver); Jimmy Lung (Chinese Guard); Jack Clifford (Messenger); Peter Seal (Russian Chasseur); Bud Osborne (Gambler); George Morrell (Miner); Hank Bell (Cowhand); George Chesebro (Miner); Jasper Palmer (Cowhand); Budd Buster (Desert Rat); Dick Alexander (Shotgun); Cecelia Callejo (Bar Girl).

FRONTIER GAL   (Univ., 1945) C—84M.

Executive producer, Howard Benedict; producers, Michael Fessier, Ernest Pagano; director, Charles Lamont; screenplay, Fessier, Pagano; art directors, John S. Goodman, Richard H. Riedel; set decorators, Russell A. Gausman, Oliver Emert; songs, Jack Brooks and Edgar Fairchild; music-music director, Frank Skinner; vocal director, H. J. Salter; assistant director, William Tummel; sound, William Hedgcock; special camera, John P. Fulton; camera, George Robinson, Charles P. Boyle; editor, Ray Snyder.

Yvonne De Carlo (Lorena Dumont); Rod Cameron (Johnny Hart); Andy Devine (Big Ben); Fuzzy Knight (Fuzzy); Sheldon Leonard (Blackie); Andrew Tombes (Judge Prescott); Beverly Sue Simmons (Mary Ann Hart); Clara Blandick (Abigail); Frank Lackteen (Cherokee); Claire Carleton (Gracie); Eddie Dunn, Harold Goodwin (Bailiffs); Jack Overman (Buffalo); Jan Wiley (Sheila Winthrop); Rex

Lease, George Eldredge, Jack Ingram, Joseph Haworth (Henchmen); Lloyd Ingraham, Joseph E. Bernard, Douglas Carter, Lou Wood, Paul Bratti (Dealers); Edward M. Howard (Henchman at Bar); Jean Trent, Joan Shawlee, Kerry Vaughn, Karen Randle (Hostesses); Eddie Lee (Wing Lee, the Candy-Shop Proprietor); Jack O'Shea, Billy Engle (Barflies); Cliff Lyons (Brawler in Candy Shop/Double for Sheldon Leonard); Jack Rutherford (Bit at Table); Eddie Borden (Man at Table); William Desmond, Kit Guard (Extras in Saloon).

SONG OF SCHEHERAZADE (Univ., 1947) C—103 M.

Producer, Edward Kaufman; associate producer, Edward Dodds; director-screenplay, Walter Reisch; art director, Jack Otterson; music adaptator-director, Miklos Rozsa; songs by Jack Brooks for Rozsa's adaptation of Rimsky-Korsakoff music; assistant director, William Holland; choreography, Tilly Losch; sound, Bernard B. Brown; camera, Hal Mohr, William V. Skall; editor, Frank Gross.

Yvonne De Carlo (Cara de Talavera); Brian Donlevy (Captain); Jean Pierre Aumont (Rimsky-Korsakoff); Eve Arden (Madame de Talavera); Phillip Reed (Prince Mischetsky); Charles Kullman (Dr. Lin); John Qualen (Lorenzo); Richard Lane (Lieutenant); Terry Kilburn (Lorin); George Dolenz (Pierre); Elena Verdugo (Fioretta); Robert Kendall (Hassan); Res Ravelle (Sultan); Mickey Simpson (Orderly); Sol Haines (Giant); Florene Rozen (Little Sister); William Ching, Leonard East, Edward Kelly, Russ Vincent, Peter Varney, Charles Roberson, Tom Skinner, Warren W. McCollum, Ernie Mishens, Marvin Press, Fred K. Hartsook, Gordon Arnold, Bill Cabanne, Don Garner, George Holmes (Students); Milio Sheron (Basso); Audrey Young, Karen Randle (Native Girls); Joan Shawlee (French Girl); Theodora Lynch (Soprano); Dick Alexander (Attendant); Beverlee Mitchell, Matia Antar (European Girls); Mary Moore (Spanish Girl); Duke Johnson (Juggler); Chester Conklin (Sailor); Ralph Brooks (Junior Officer); Bob Barron (Ice Cream Vendor); Yussuf Ali (Cop); Emmett Vogan, Jr. (Coachman).

BRUTE FORCE (Univ., 1947) 98 M.

Producer, Mark Hellinger; associate producer, Jules Buck; director, Jules Dassin; story, Robert Patterson; screenplay, Richard Brooks; art directors, Bernard Herzbrun, John F. De Cuir; set decorator, Russell A. Gausman, Charles Wyrick; music, Miklos Rozsa; assistant director, Fred Frank; sound, Charles Felstead, Robert Pritchard; special camera, David S. Horsley; camera, William Daniels; editor, Edward Curtiss.

Burt Lancaster (Joe Collins); Hume Cronyn (Captain Munsey); Charles Bickford (Gallagher); Yvonne De Carlo (Gina); Ann Blyth (Ruth); Ella Raines (Cora); Anita Colby (Flossie); Sam Levene (Louis); Howard Duff (Soldier); Art Smith (Dr. Walters); Roman Bohnen (Warden Barnes); John Hoyt (Spencer); Richard Gaines (McCollum); Frank Puglia (Ferrara); Jeff Corey (Freshman); Vince Barnett (Muggsy); James Bell (Crenshaw); Jack Overman (Kid Coy); Whit Bissell (Tom Lister); Sir Lancelot (Calypso); Ray Teal (Jackson); Jay C. Flippen (Hodges); James O'Rear (Wilson); Howland Chamberlain (Gaines); Kenneth Patterson (Bronski); Crane Whitley (Armed Guard in Drain Pipe); Charles McGraw (Andy); John Harmon (Roberts); Gene Stutenroth (Hoffman); Wally Rose (Peary); Carl Rhodes (Strella); Guy Beach (Convict Foreman); Edmund Cobb (Bradley); Tom Steele (Machine Gunner); Alex Frazer (Chaplain); Will Lee (Kincaid); Ruth Sanderson (Miss Lawrence); Francis McDonald (Regan); Jack S. Lee (Sergeant); Virginia Farmer (Sadie); Billy Wayne, Rex Dale, Frank Marlowe, William Cozzo (Prisoners); Paul Bryar (Harry); Glenn Strange (Tompkins); Al Hill (Plonski); Peter Virgo, Eddy Chandler, Kenneth R. MacDonald, Al Ferguson, Jerry Salvail

(Guards); Rex Lease (Hearse Driver); Herbert Heywood (Chef); Blanch Obronska (Young Girl); Hal Malone (Young Inmate); Don McGill (Max); Harry Wilson (Tyrone, the Homely Prisoner); Sam Rizhallah (Convict's Son); Kippee Valez (Visitor).

SLAVE GIRL   (Univ., 1947) C—79 M.

Producers, Michael Fessier, Ernest Pagano; director, Charles Lamont; screenplay, Fessier, Pagano; art director, Abraham Grossman; set decorators, Russell A. Gausman, Edward R. Robinson; music, Milton Rosen; music arranger-orchestrator, David Tamkin; choreography, Si-Lan Chen; assistant director, Ralph Stosser; sound, Charles Felstead, Glenn E. Anderson; camera, George Robinson, W. Howard Greene; editor, Frank Gross.

Yvonne De Carlo (Francesca); George Brent (Matt Claibourne); Broderick Crawford (Chips Jackson); Albert Dekker (Pasha); Lois Collier (Aleta); Andy Devine (Ben); Carl Esmond (El Hamid); Arthur Treacher (Liverpool); Philip Van Zandt (Yusef); Dan Seymour (Telek Taurog); Trevor Bardette (Proprietor of "Sign of the Graper"); Eddie Dunn (Captain); Mickey Simpson (Head Guard); Rex Lease, George J. Lewis, Jack Ingram, Harold Goodwin, Don Turner, Phil Schumacher, Jack Shutta, Paul Bratti, Joseph Haworth (Americans); Toni Raimando (Slave Girl); June Marlowe (Mildred); Shimen Ruskin (Rug Merchant); Nancy Brinckman (Maid); Roseanne Murray (Sally); Harry Cording (Guard Captain); Nobel Johnson (Native Guard); Jack Reitzen (Auctioneer); Raman Al Amar, Yussef Ali (Guards); Jerome Groves, Rudolph Medina, Harry Lamont, Tony Del Rio (Natives in Torture Chamber); Lloyd Ingraham (Locksmith); Lacia Sonami (Native Girl); Bert Richman, Eddie Abdo, Michael Gaddis (Natives).

BLACK BART   (Univ., 1948) C—80 M.

Producer, Leonard Goldstein; director, George Sherman; story, Luci Ward, Jack Natteford; screenplay, Ward, Natteford, William Bowers; art directors, Bernard Herzbrun, Emrich Nicholson; set decorators, Russell A. Gausman, William L. Stevens; music, Frank Skinner; choreography, Val Raset; costumes, Yvonne Wood; makeup, Bud Westmore; assistant director, William Holland; sound, Leslie I. Carey, Coarson Jowett; camera, Irving Glassberg; editor, Russell Schoengarth.

Yvonne De Carlo (Lola Montez); Dan Duryea (Charles E. Boles); Jeffrey Lynn (Lance Hardeen); Percy Kilbride (Jersey Brady); Lloyd Gough (Sheriff Gordon); Frank Lovejoy (Lorimer); John McIntire (Clark); Don Beddoe (J. T. Hall); Ray Walker (MacFarland); Soledad Jimenez (Teresa); Eddy C. Waller (Mason); Anne O'Neal (Mrs. Harmon); Chief Many Treaties (Indian); Douglas Fowley (Sheriff Mix); Paul Maxey, Milton Kibbee, Ray Harper, Wayne Treadway, Earl Audet, William Norton Bailey, Kenneth Ross-MacKenzie (Men); Eddie Acuff (Elkins); Ray Teal (Pete); Bert Davidson (Blake); Marshall Ruth (Band Leader); Russ Conway (Agent Clayton); Ray Bennett (Henry); Nina Caompana (Mamasita); Bill O'Leary (Wells Fargo Man); George Douglas (Alcott); Everett Shields (Killer); Reed Howes (Bartender).

CASBAH   (Univ., 1948) 94 M.

Producer, Nat G. Goldstone; associate producer, Erik Charell; director, John Berry; based on the novel *Pepe le Moko* by Detective Ashelbe and the original screenplay by L. Bus-Fekete, Arnold Manoff; musical story, Charell; art directors, Bernard Herzbrun, John F. DeCuir; set decorators, Russell A. Gausman, Oliver Emert; music, Harold Arlen; choreography, Bernard Pearce; costumes, Yvonne

Wood; assistant director, Jack Voglin; makeup, Bud Westmore; sound, Leslie I. Carey, Jack A. Bolger, Jr.; special effects, David S. Horsley; camera, Irving Glassberg; editor, Edward Curtiss.

Yvonne De Carlo (Inez); Tony Martin (Pepe le Moko); Peter Lorre (Slimane); Marta Toren (Gaby); Hugo Haas (Omar); Thomas Gomez (Louvain); Douglas Dick (Carlo); Katherine Dunham (Odette); Herbert Rudley (Claude); Gene Walker (Roland); Curt Conway (Maurice); Andre Pola (Willem); Barry Bernard (Max); Virginia Gregg (Madeline); Will Lee (Beggar); Harris Brown (Pierre); Houseley Stevenson (Anton Duval); Robert Kendall (Ahmed); Rosita Marstini (Woman); Jody Gilbert, Kathleen Freeman (American Women); John Bagni, Bert Le Baron, Carey Harrison, Tom Tamerez (Inspectors); Antonio Pina, Jerry Pina, Abel Pina, Henry Pina (Acrobats); Paul Fierro (Policeman); Maynard Holmes (Guide); George J. Lewis (Detective); Leander De Cordova (Doorman); Maurice Navarre (Fire Eater); Basil Tellou (Blind Singer); Hassen Khayyan, Samir Rizkallah (Arabs); Major Sam Harris, Kathryn Wilson (British Tourists); Lorraine Gale (Blonde Girl); George Hyland (American Business Man); Jane K. Looffbourrow (Schoolteacher); Carmen Gonzalez, Marie Tavares (Girls in Inez's Shop); Josette Deegan (Stewardess); Barry Norton, Nick Borgani (Pilots); Elsa Walker, Tina Menard (Women); Bob Lugo (Native Man); Phil Friedman (Native); Eddie Randolph, Louise Bates, Robert L. Lorraine (Tourists); Katherine Dunham Dance Troupe with Eartha Kitt (Performers).

RIVER LADY (Univ., 1948) C—78 M.

Producer, Leonard Goldstein; director, George Sherman; based on the novel by Houston Branch, Frank Waters; screenplay, D. D. Beauchamp, William Bowers; music, Paul Sawtell; orchestrator, David Tamkin; camera, Irving Glassberg; editor, Otto Ludwig.

Yvonne De Carlo (Sequin); Dan Duryea (Beauvais); Rod Cameron (Dan Corrigan); Helena Carter (Stephanie); Lloyd Gough (Mike); Florence Bates (Ma Dunnigan); John McIntire (Mr. Morrison); Jack Lambert (Swede); Esther Somers (Mrs. Morrison); Anita Turner (Esther); Edmund Cobb (Rider); Dewey Robinson (Bouncer); Eddy C. Waller (Hewitt); Milton Kibbee (Limpy); Billy Wayne (Dealer); Jimmy Ames (Logger); Edward Earle (Executive); Paul Maxey (Mr. Miller); Dick Wessel, Charles Sullivan, Mickey Simpson, Reed Howes, George Magrill, Ray Spiker, Jack Van Zandt, Charles Morton, Don MacCracken, Carl Sepulveda (Loggers); John McGuire (Collins); Howard Negley (McKenzie); Jack G. Lee, Charles Wagenheim, Bob Wilke, Perc Launders, Kenneth Ross-MacKenzie (Men); Al Hill (Lumberjack); Harold Goodwin (Larson); Paul Fierro (Man on Deck); Beverly Warren (Girl); Jack Shutta (McGee); Jerry Jerome (Croupier); Frank Hagney (Sands).

CALAMITY JANE AND SAM BASS (Univ., 1949) C—85 M.

Producer, Leonard Goldstein; associate producer, Aaron Rosenberg; director-story, George Sherman; screenplay, Maurice Geraghty; art directors, Bernard Herzbrun, Richard Riedel; set decorators, Russell A. Gausman, Al Fields; music director-orchestrator, Milton Schwarzwald; assistant director, John Sherwood; makeup, Bud Westmore, John Holden; costumes, Yvonne Wood; sound, Leslie I. Carey, Glenn E. Anderson; camera, Irving Glassberg; editor, Edward Curtiss.

Yvonne De Carlo (Calamity Jane); Howard Duff (Sam Bass); Dorothy Hart (Katherine Egan); Willard Parker (Sheriff Will Egan); Norman Lloyd (Jim Murphy); Marc Lawrence (Dean); Houseley Stevenson (Dakota); Milburn Stone (Abe Jones); Clifton Young (Link); John Rodney (Morgan); Roy Roberts (Marshal

Peak); Ann Doran (Mrs. Egan); Charles Cane (J. Wells); Walter Baldwin (Doc Purdy); Paul Maxey (Underwood); George Carleton (Mr. Sherman); Harry Harvey (Station Agent); Jack Ingram (Mayes); Francis McDonald (Starter); Douglas Walton (Bookmaker); Nedrick Young (Parsons); Russ Conway (Baggage Man); Jimmy Ames (Blacksmith); Ezelle Poule (Woman Customer); Antony Backus, Pierce Lyden (Deputies); I. Stanford Jolley (Wilson); Stanley Blystone (Cowboy); Roy Butler, Frank McCarroll, Charles Sullavan, Bob Perry, James Linn, Bill Sundholm (Bits).

THE GAL WHO TOOK THE WEST (Univ., 1949) C—84 M.

Producer, Robert Arthur; director, Frederick de Cordova; screenplay, William Bowers, Oscar Brodney; art directors, Bernard Herzbrun, Robert Boyle; set decorators, Russell A. Gausman, John Austin; music, Frank Skinner; assistant directors, Fred Frank, George Lollier; choreography, Harold Belfer; costumes, Yvonne Wood; makeup, Bud Westmore; sound, Leslie I. Carey, Joe Lapis; camera, William Daniels; editor, Milton Carruth.

Yvonne De Carlo (Lillian Marlowe); Charles Coburn (General Michael O'Hara); Scott Brady (Lee O'Hara); John Russell (Grant O'Hara); Myrna Dell (Nancy); James Millican (Hawley); Clem Bevans (Hawley as Old Timer); Bob Stevenson (Ted); Houseley Stevenson (Ted as Old-Timer); Robin Short (Bartender); Russell Simpson (Bartender as Old-Timer); John Litel (Colonel Logan); James Todd (Douglas Andrews); Edward Earle (Mr. Nolan); Jack Ingram, Francis McDonald, Glenn Strange, William Tannen, Steve Darrell, Pierce Lyden, Ross Elliott, John James, Richard Farmer, Martin Cichy (Men); Audrey Young (Sue); Ann Pearce, June Fulton, Patricia Hall (Dance Hall Girls); Howard Negley (Potkins); Charles Cane (Grant's Man); William Haade (Lee's Man); Louise Lorimer (Mrs. Logan); Forrest Taylor (Servant); Charles Jordan (Customer); George Stern (Barber); Paul Brinegar (Salesman); William Donnelly (Cavalry Captain); Steve Crandall, Jon Riffel (Young Men); House Peters, Jr. (Trooper); Russ Whiteman (Corporal Trooper); Fraser McWinn (Sentry); Peggie Leon, Ella Ethridge, Verna Korman, William Bailey, Roger Moore, David Alison, Forbes Murray, Mildred Sellers, Louise Bates, Philip Ahlm, Helen Dickson (Guests); Harlan Hoagland (Bartender); Chalky Williams, Paul Palmer (Men in Saloon); Patrick Griffin, Gary Teague (Bits).

CRISS CROSS (Univ., 1949) 87 M.

Producer, Michel Draike; director, Robert Siodmak; based on the novel by Don Tracy; screenplay, Daniel Fuchs; art directors, Bernard Herzbrun, Boris Leven; set decorators, Russell A. Gausman, Oliver Emert; music, Miklos Rozsa; assistant director, Fred Frank; makeup, Bud Westmore; costumes, Yvonne Wood; sound, Leslie I. Carey, Richard DeWeese; special effects, David S. Horsley; camera, Frank Palmer; editor, Ted J. Kent.

Burt Lancaster (Steve Thompson); Yvonne De Carlo (Anna); Dan Duryea (Slim Dundee); Stephen McNally (Pete Ramirez); Richard Long (Slade Thompson); Esy Morales (Orchestra Leader); Tom Pedi (Vincent); Percy Helton (Frank); Alan Napier (Finchley); Griff Barnett (Pop); Meg Randall (Helen); Joan Miller (The Lush); Edna M. Holland (Mrs. Thompson); John Doucette (Walt); Marc Krah (Mort); James O'Rear (Waxie); John Skins Miller (Midget); Robert Osterloh (Mr. Nelson); Vincent Renno (Waiter); Charles Wagenheim (Waiter); Tony Curtis (Gigolo); Beatrice Roberts, Isabel Randolph (Nurses); Stephen Roberts (Doctor); Kenneth Patterson (Bently, the Guard); Gene Evans (O'Hearn, the Guard); George Lynn (Andy); Michael Cisney (Chester); Robert Winkler (Clark); Lee

Tung Foo (Chinese Cook); Ann Staunton, Dolores Castle, Jeraldine Jordan, Kippee Valez (Girl Friends); Vito Scotti (Track Usher); Diane Stewart, Jeane Bane (Girls); Timmy Hawkins (Boy); John Roy (Bartender).

BUCCANEER'S GIRL   (Univ., 1950) C—77 M.

Producer, Robert Arthur; director, Frederick de Cordova; story, Joe May, Samuel R. Golding; screenplay, Harold Shumate, Joseph Hoffman; art directors, Bernard Herzbrun, Robert F. Boyle; songs, Walter Scharf and Jack Brooks; choreography, Harold Belfer; special effects, David S. Horsley; camera, Russell Metty; editor, Otto Ludwig.

Yvonne De Carlo (Deborah McCoy); Philip Friend (Fredric Baptiste); Robert Douglas (Narbonne); Elsa Lanchester (Mme. Brizer); Andrea King (Arlene Villon); Norman Lloyd (Patout); Jay C. Flippen (Jared Hawkins); Douglass Dumbrille (Captain Martos); Henry Daniell (Captain Duval); Verna Felton (Dowager); John Qualen (Vegetable Man); Connie Gilchrist (Vegetable Woman); Ben Welden (Tom); Dewey Robinson (Kryl); Peggie Castle (Cleo).

THE DESERT HAWK   (Univ., 1950) C—77-1/2 M.

Producer, Leonard Goldstein; director, Frederick de Cordova; screenplay, Aubrey Wisberg, Jack Pollexfen, Gerald Drayson Adams; music, Frank Skinner; art directors, Bernard Herzbrun, Emrich Nicholson; camera, Russell Metty; editor, Otto Ludwig.

Yvonne De Carlo (Princess Schaharazade); Richard Greene (Omar); Jackie Gleason (Aladdin); George Macready (Prince Murad); Carl Esmond (Kibar); Marc Lawrence (Samad); Lucille Barkley (Undine); Ann Pearce (Yasmin); Lois Andrews (Maznah); Rock Hudson (Captain Ras); Frank Puglia (Ahmed Bey); Joe Besser (Sinbad); Donald Randolph (Caliph); Ian MacDonald (Yussef); Nestor Paiva (Abdul); Richard Hale (Iman); Eileen Howe, Hazel Shaw, Marian Dennish, Norma De Landa, Barbara Kelly, Vonne Lester (Harem Girls); Mahmud Shaikhaly (Akbar); Buddy Roosevelt (Baku); Virginia Hunter (Slave Girl Dancer); Lester Sharpe (Merchant); Ben Welden (Mokar); Michael Ross (Gorah); Lane Bradford (Standard Bearer); Shirley Ballard (Naga); Jack Raymond (Suif); Terry Frost, George Bruggerman (Soldiers); Michael Ansara, Fred Libby (Guards); Bob Anderson (Judah); Jan Arvan, Milton Kibbee (Merchants); Robert Filmer, Bob Wilke (Camel Drivers); Bruce Riley, Louis A. Nicoletti, Wally Walker, Mike Portanova (Sheiks); Wilson Millar, Phil Barnes, Frank Malet (Guards); Wendy Waldron, Shirley Ballard (Slave Girls); Frank Lackteen (One-Eyed Arab); George Bruggeman (Soldier); Harold Cornsweet (Arab); Lucile Barnes (Girl in Bathtub); Dale Van Sickel (Kibar Leader); Chet Brandenberg, Vic Romito (Men).

TOMAHAWK   (Univ., 1951) C—82 M.

Producer, Leonard Goldstein; director, George Sherman; story, Daniel Jarrett; screenplay, Silvia Richards, Maurice Geraghty; music, Hans J. Salter; art directors, Bernard Herzbrun, Richard H. Riedel; camera, Charles P. Boyle; editor, Danny B. Landres.

Van Heflin (Jim Bridger); Yvonne De Carlo (Julie Madden); Preston Foster (Colonel Carrington); Jack Oakie (Sol Beckworth); Alex Nicol (Lieutenant Bob Dancy); Tom Tully (Dan Castello); Ann Doran (Mrs. Carrington); Rock Hudson (Burt Hanna); Susan Cabot (Monahseetah); Arthur Space (Captain Fetterman); Stuart Randall (Sergeant Newell); John Peters (Private Osborne); Russell Conway (Major Horton); Raymond Montgomery (Blair Streeter); Dave Sharpe (Private Parr); David H. Miller (Captain Ten Eyck); John War Eagle (Red Cloud); Regis Toomey (Smith); Sheila Darcy (Woman); James A. Hermstad, Harry Peterson, Robert J. T. Simpson, Abner George, Archie N. MacVicar, Floyd Sparks, Edward Tullis, Adiel F. Wahl (Men); Chief American Horse, Chief Bad Bear (Indians).

HOTEL SAHARA   (UA, 1951) 87 M.

Producer, George H. Brown; director, Ken Annakin; assistant director, Peter Manley; story-screenplay, Patrick Kirwan, George H. Brown; music, Benjamin Frankel; art director, Ralph Brinton; sets, Betty Pierce; costumes, Julie Harris; sound, John W. Mitchell, Gordon K. McCallum; special effects, Bill Warrington; camera, David Harcourt; editor, Alfred Roome.

Yvonne De Carlo (Yasmin Pallas); Peter Ustinov (Emad); David Tomlinson (Captain Puffin Cheyne); Roland Culver (Major Bill Randall); Albert Lieven (Lieutenant Gunther von Heilicke); Bill Owen (Private Binns); Sydney Tafler (Corporal Pullar); Tom Gill (Private O'Brien); Mireille Perrey (Mme. Pallas); Ferdy Mayne (Yusef); Guido Lorraine (Capitano Guiseppi); A. C. Lewis (Suleiman the Goat); Eugene Deckers (French Spahi Officer); Rolf Richards, Henrik Jacobsen, Anton Diffring (German Soldiers); Massimo Caen, Enzo Plazzotta (Italian Soldiers); Bettina Hayes (American Woman); John Salew (American Husband); Harold Kaskett (Oriental Gentleman); Olga Lowe (Fatima).

SILVER CITY   (Par., 1951) C—90 M.

Producer, Nat Holt; director, Byron Haskin; based on the story by Luke Short; screenplay, Frank Gruber; art directors, Hal Pereira, Franz Bachelin; camera, Ray Rennahan; editor, Elmo Billings.

Edmond O'Brien (Larkin Moffatt); Yvonne De Carlo (Candace Surrency); Barry Fitzgerald (R. R. Jarboe); Richard Arlen (Charles Storrs); Gladys George (Mrs. Barber); Laura Elliot (Josephine); Edgar Buchanan (Dutch Surrency); Michael Moore (Taff); John Dierkes (Arnie); Don Dunning, Warren Earl Fisk, James Van Horn, John Mansfield, Harvey Parry, Boyd "Red" Morgan, Frank Cordell, Leo J. McMahon (Townsmen); Howard Joslin (Freed); Robert G. Anderson (Rucker); Frank Fenton (Creede); Myron O. Healey (Bleek); James R. Scott (Miner); Paul E. Burns (Paxton); Cliff Clark (Bartender); Billy House (Malone); Howard Negley (Spence Fuller); Ray Hyke (Dacy); Slim Gaut (Storekeeper).

THE SAN FRANCISCO STORY   (WB., 1952) 80 M.

Producer, Howard Welsch; director, Robert Parrish; based on the novel by Richard Summers; screenplay, D. D. Beauchamp; production designer, George Jenkins; art directors, Bernard Herzbrun, Robert Clatworthy; music, Emil Newman, Paul Dunlap; music director, Joseph Gershenson; choreography, Harold Belfaer; assistant director, Ben Chapman; camera, John Seitz; editor, Otto Ludwig.

Joel McCrea (Rick Nelson); Yvonne De Carlo (Adelaide McCall); Sidney Blackmer (Andrew Cain); Richard Erdman (Shorty); Florence Bates (Saide); Onslow Stevens (Jim Martin); John Raven (Lessing); O. Z. Whitehead (Alfey); Ralph Dumke (Winfield Holbert); Robert Foulk (Thompson); Lane Chandler (Morton); Trevor Bardette (Miner); John Doucette (Slade); Peter Virgo (Meyers); Frank Hagney (Palmer); Tor Johnson (Buck); Fred Graham (Scud).

SCARLET ANGEL   (Univ., 1952) C—80 1/2 M.

Producer, Leonard Goldstein; director, Sidney Salkow; story-screenplay, Oscar Brodney; art directors, Bernard Herzbrun, Robert Clatworthy; music director, Joseph E. Gershenson; choreography, Harold Belfer; camera, Russell Metty; editor, T. J. Kent.

Yvonne De Carlo (Roxy McClanahan); Rock Hudson (Frank Truscott); Richard Denning (Malcolm Bradley); Bodil Miller (Linda Caldwell); Amanda Blake (Susan Bradley); Henry O'Neill (Morgan Caldwell); Henry Brandon (Pierre); Maude Wallace (Eugenia Caldwell); Dan Riss (Walter Frisby); Whitfield Connor (Norton Wade); Tol Avery (Phineas Calhoun); Arthur Page (Edwards); George Hamilton (Gus); Dale Van Sickel (Jeb); Mickey Pfleger (Bobbie Caldwell); Harry Harvey (Doctor Corbin); George Spaulding (Trowbridge); Tom Browne Henry (Jason Mortimer); Fred Graham (Cass Walters); Fred Coby, Eddie Dew (Soldiers); Nolan Leary (Apothecary); Elizabeth Root (Trixie); Wilma Francis (Daisy); Betty Allen (Another Girl); Leo Curley (Sheriff Jasper); Dabbs Greer, John Roy, Martin Cichy, Jack Perry, Buddy Sullivan (Men); Sally Corner, Ada Adams (Sisters); Joe Forte (Hotel Clerk); Vera Marshe (Hotel Clerk); Fred Berest (Hamlet); Coleman Francis (Deckhand); Jack Daley (Jepson); Jean Andren (Flora); George Ramsey, Charles Horvath (Crewmen); Bud Wolfe (Bartender); Frankie Van, Carl Saxe (Waiters); Mil Patrick (Dolly); Creighton Hale (Judge Ames); Ed Hinkle (Longshoreman); Bert LeBaron (Philippe); Lila Finn (Girl); Louis G. Hart (Ad Lib Waiter).

HURRICANE SMITH (Par., 1952) C—90 M.

Producer, Nat Holt; director, Jerry Hopper; based on the story "Hurricane Williams" by Gordon Ray Young; screenplay, Frank Gruber; art directors, Hal Pereira, Walter Tyler; set decorators, Sam Comer, Bertram Granger; music, Paul Sawtell; camera, Ray Rennahan; editor, Frank Bracht.

Yvonne De Carlo (Luana); John Ireland (Hurricane Smith); James Craig (Gorvahlsen); Forrest Tucker (Dan McGuire); Lyle Bettger (Clobb); Richard Arlen (Brundage); Mike Kellin (Dicer); Murray Matheson (Dr. Whitmore); Henry Brandon (Sam); Emile Meyer (Captain Raikes); Stuart Randall (Matt Ward); Ralph Dumke (Ben Hawkins); Kim Spalding (Brown); Don Dunning (Adams); Ethan Laidlaw (Old Tom); Eric Alden, George Barton, Loren B. Brown, James A. Cornell, Clint Dorrington, Al Kikume, Leo J. McMahon, King Mojave, Fred N. Revelala, Jack Trent, Leon Lontoc (Sailors); Leon C. "Buck" Young (Guard); Cliff Clark (Australian Policeman); Anthony Warde (Bos'n); Ted Ryan, Eddie Magill (Policemen); Harvey Parry (Cook); Maiola Kalili (Malinka).

SOMBRERO (MGM, 1953) C—103 M.

Producer, Jack Cummings; director, Norman Foster; based on the novel *A Mexican Village* by Josefina Niggli; screenplay, Niggli, Foster; art directors, Cedric Gibbons, Daniel R. Cathcart; set decorators, Edwin B. Willis, Fred MacLean; choreography, Hermes Pan, José Greco; songs, Ruben Fuentes, Ruben Mendez, and Saul Chaplin; Augustin Lara and Ray Gilbert; Alfonso Esparza Oteo and A. Fernandez Bustamente; assistant director, Arvid Griffen; costumes, Helen Rose; special effects, Warren Newcombe; camera, Ray June; editor, Cotton Warburton.

Ricardo Montalban (Pepe Gonzales); Pier Angeli (Eufemia Calderon); Vittorio Gassman (Alejandro Castillo); Cyd Charisse (Lola de Torrano); Yvonne De Carlo (Maria); Rick Jason (Ruben); Nina Foch (Elena Cantu); Kurt Kasznar (Father Zacaya); Walter Hampden (Don Carlos Castillo); Thomas Gomez (Don Homero Calderon); José Greco (Gintanillo de Torrano); John Abbott (Don Daniel); Andres Soler (Little Doctor); Fanny Schiller (Doña Fela); Luz Alba (Rosaura); Rosaura Revueltas (Tia Magdalena); Alfonso Bedoya (Don Inocente); Jorge Trevino (Don Nacho); Tito Novaro (Napoleon Lopez); Manuel Arvide (Manager); Felipe De Flores (Tomas); Beatriz Ramos (Señora Inocente); Florencio Castello (Mozo); Arturo Rangel (Professor); Salvador Baquez (Bartender); Juan Duval (Bellhop); Rita Conde (Silveria); Pascual Pena (Drunk); Louise De Carlo, Gabrielle Roussellon (Girls in Cafe); Tom Hernandez, Orlando Beltran, George Derrick, Carlos Barbee, Eduardo Cansino, Miguel Contreras (Men in Cafe); Alma Beltran, Amapola Del Vando, Pilar Del Rey, Dorita Pallais, Delmar Costello (Party Guests).

SEA DEVILS (RKO, 1953) C—91 M.

Producer, David E. Rose; director, Raoul Walsh; suggested by the novel *The Toilers of the Sea* by Victor Hugo; story-screenplay, Borden Chase; art director, Wilfred Shingleton; music, Richard Addinsell; camera, Wilkie Cooper; editor, John Seabourne.

Yvonne De Carlo (Droucette); Rock Hudson (Gilliatt); Maxwell Reed (Rantaine); Denis O'Dea (Lethierry); Michael Goodliffe (Ragan); Bryan Forbes (Willie); Jacques Brunius (Fouche); Ivor Barnard (Benson); Arthur Wontner (Baron de Vaudrec); Gerard Oury (Napoleon); Laurie Taylor (Blasquito).

FORT ALGIERS (UA, 1953) 78 M.

Producer, Joseph N. Ermolieff; associate producer, Edward L. Alperson, Jr.; director, Lesley Selander; story, Frederick Stephani; screenplay, Theodore St. John; music, Michel Michelet; orchestrator, Raoul Krashaar; song, Michelet and Yvonne De Carlo; art directors, Boris Leven, Robert Peterson; gowns, Yvonne Wood; camera, Charles Lawton, Jr.; editor, Jerome Thoms.

Yvonne De Carlo (Yvette); Carlos Thompson (Jeff); Raymond Burr (Amir); Leif Erickson (Kalmani); Anthony Caruso (Chavez); John Dehner (Major Colle); Robert Boon (Mueller); Henry Corden (Yessouf); Joe Kirk (Luigi); Bill Phipps (Lieutenant Gerrier); Sandra Gale (Sandra); Charles Evans (Officer).

THE CAPTAIN'S PARADISE (Lopert, 1953) 80 M.

Producer-director, Anthony Kimmins; story, Alec Coppel; screenplay, Coppel, Nicholas Phipps; art director, Paul Sheriff; music, Malcolm Arnold; choreography, Walter Crisham, Tutte Lemkow; camera, Ted Scaife.

Alec Guinness (Captain Henry St. James); Yvonne De Carlo (Nita St. James); Celia Johnson (Maud St. James); Charles Goldner (Chief Officer Ricco); Miles Malleson (Lawrence St. James); Bill Fraser (Absalom); Tutte Lemkow (Principal Dancer); Nicholas Phipps (The Major); Walter Crisham (Bob); Ferdy Mayne (Sheikh); Sebastian Cabot (Ali); Claudia Gray (Susan Dailey); George Benson (Salmon); Joss Ambler (Professor Ebbart); Joyce Barbour (Mrs. Reid).

BORDER RIVER (Univ., 1954) C—80-1/2 M.

Producer, Albert J. Cohen; director, George Sherman; story, Louis Stevens; screenplay, William Sackheim, Stevens; assistant directors, Frank Shaw, Marshall Green; art director, Bernard Herzbrun; camera, Irving Glassberg; editor, Frank Gross.

Joel McCrea (Clete Mattson); Yvonne De Carlo (Carmelita Carias); Pedro Armendariz (General Calleja); Howard Petrie (Newlund); Erika Nordin (Annina Strasser); Alfonso Bedoya (Captain Vargas); George J. Lewis (Sanchez); Nacho Galindo (Lopez); Ivan Triesault (Baron Von Hollden); George Wallace (Fletcher); Joe Bassett (Stanton); Martin Garralaga (Guzman); Lane Chandler (Anderson); Felipe Turich (Pablo); Charles Horvath (Crowe); Salvador Baguez (General Robles); Britt Wood (Drunken American); John Verros (Ringleader); Fred Beir (Tom

Doud); Robert Tafur (Telegraph Operator); Monte Montague (Bartender); Pilar Del Rey (Spanish Girl); Orlando Beltran (Calleja's Lieutenant); Zarco Carreno (Luis); Estelita Zarco (Girl); Jarl Victor (American); Robert Hoy (Sergeant Johnson); Jack Del Rio (Dealer); Emile Avery (Bit).

PASSION (RKO, 1954) C—84 M.

Producer, Benedict Borgeaus; director, Allan Dwan; story, Joseph Leytes, Beatrice A. Dresher, Miguel Padilla; screenplay, Leytes, Dresher, Howard Estabrook; art director, Van Nest Polglase; set decorator, John Sturtevant; costumes, Gwen Wakeling; music, Louis Forbes; camera, John Alton; editor, Carlos Lodato.

Cornel Wilde (Juan Obregon); Yvonne De Carlo (Rosa Melo/Tonya Melo); Rodolfo Acosta (Salvador Sandro); Raymond Burr (Captain Rodriguez); Lon Chaney, Jr. (Castro); John Qualen (Gaspar Melo); Anthony Caruso (Sergeant Munoz); Frank De Kova (Martinez); Peter Coe (Colfre); John Dierkes (Escobar); Richard Hale (Don Domingo); Rozene Kemper (Señora Melo); Rosa Turich (Maracuita); Stuart Whitman (Bernal Vaquaro); James Kirkwood (Don Rosendo); Robert Warwick (Money Lender); Belle Mitchell (Señora Carrisa); Alex Montoya (Manuel Felipe); Zon Murray (Barca).

TONIGHT'S THE NIGHT (AA, 1954) C—88 M.

Producer, Mario Zampi; associate producer, Giulio Zampi; director, Mario Zampi; story-screenplay, Jack Davies, Michael Pertwee; assistant director, Gus Agosti; music, Stanley Black; song, Michael Carr; art director, Ivan King; camera, Stanley Pavey, Robert Walker.

David Niven (Jasper O'Leary); Yvonne De Carlo (Serena McGlusky); Barry Fitzgerald (Thady O'Heggarty); George Cole (Terence); Robert Urquhart (Dr. Michael Flynn); Eddie Byrne (Lannigan); A. E. Matthews (General O'Leary); Noelle Middleton (Kathy McGlusky); Anthony Nicholls (Solicitor); Liam Redmond (Regan); Michael Shepley (Major McGlusky); Joseph Tomelty (Dooley).

LA CASTIGLIONE (Radius-Taurus, 1954) C—89 M.

Director, Georges Combret; screenplay, Combret, Claude Boissol, Pierre Maudru; music, Paul Durand; art director, Jean Douarinou; camera, Pierre Petit; editor, Germaine Fouquet.

Yvonne De Carlo (Virginia Oldoini; later de Castiglione); Georges Marchal (Lucio Falengo); Paul Meurisse (Napoleon III); Rossano Brazzi (Cavour); Lucienne Legrand (Empress Eugenie); Lea Padovani (Princess Mathilde); Lisette Lebon (Luisa); Georges Lannes (Mocquart); Tamara Lees (Madame de Metternich); Michel Etcheverry (Pietri); Claude Roissol (Nigra); Gil Delamare (Fausto); and: Guy Cosson, Flourens, Charles Bouillaud, Robert Porte, Sylvain, Patrick Roussel, Franck Estange, Jo Dest, Charles Lemontier.

SHOTGUN (AA, 1955) C—80 M.

Producer, John Champion; director, Lesley Selander; screenplay, Champion, Clark E. Reynolds, Rory Calhoun; assistant director, Bud Andrews; music, Carl Brandt; camera, Ellsworth Fredericks; supervising editor, Lester Sansom; editor, John Fuller.

Sterling Hayden (Clay); Yvonne De Carlo (Abby); Zachary Scott (Reb); Robert Wilke (Bentley); Guy Prescott (Thompson); Ralph Sanford (Chris); John Pickard (Perez); Ward Wood (Ed); Rory Mallinson (Frank); Paul Marion (Delgadito); Harry Harvey, Jr. (Davey); Lane Chandler (Fletcher); Angela Greene (Aletha);

Robert E. Griffin (Doctor); Al Wyatt (Greybar); Bob Morgan (Sam); Peter Coe (Apache); Charles Morton, James Parnell (Cavalrymen); Richard Cutting (Holly); Fiona Hale (Midge); Frances McDonald (Dishwasher).

FLAME OF THE ISLANDS   (Rep., 1955) C—90 M.

Associate producer-director, Edward Ludwig; story, Adele Comandini; screenplay, Bruce Manning; music, Nelson Riddle; songs, Jack Elliott, Sonny Burke; assistant director, Virgil Hart; camera, Bud Thackery; editor, Richard L. Van Enger.

Yvonne De Carlo (Rosalind Dee); Howard Duff (Doug Duryea); Zachary Scott (Wade Evans); Kurt Kasznar (Cyril Mace); Barbara O'Neil (Mrs. Duryea); James Arness (Kelly Rand); Frieda Inescort (Mrs. Hammond); Lester Mathews (Gus); Donald Curtis (Johnny); Nick Stewart (Willie); John Pickard (Parks); Leslie Denison (Foster Williams); Peter Adams (Clint Johnson).

MAGIC FIRE   (Rep., 1956) C—95 M.

Producer-director, William Dieterle; based on the novel by Bertita Harding; screenplay, Harding, E. A. Dupont, David Chandler; music, Richard Wagner; choreography, Tatjana Gsovsky; assistant director, Virgil Hart; music supervisor, Erich Wolfgang Korngold; music conductor, Alois Melichar; art director, Robert Herlth; camera, Ernest Haller; editor, Stanley Johnson.

Yvonne De Carlo (Minna); Carlos Thompson (Franz Liszt); Rita Gam (Cosima); Valentina Cortesa (Mathilde); Alan Badel (Richard Wagner); Peter Cushing (Otto Wesendonk); Frederick Valk (Minister von Moll); Gerhard Riedman (King Ludwig II); Eric Schumann (Hans von Buelow); Robert Freytag (August Roeckel); Heinz Klingenberg (King of Saxonia); Charles Regnier (Meyerbeer); and: Fritz Rasp, Kurt Grosskurth, Hans Quest, Jan Hendriks.

RAW EDGE   (Univ., 1956) C—76 M.

Producer, Albert Zugsmith; director, John Sherwood; story, William Kozlenko, James Benson Nablo; screenplay, Harry Essex, Robert Hill; costumes, Bill Thomas; assistant directors, Joe Kenny, George Lollier, Ray DeCamp; song, Terry Gilkyson; art directors, Alexander Golitzen, Alfred Sweeney; music director, Joseph Gershenson; camera, Maury Gertsman; editor, Russell Schoengarth.

Rory Calhoun (Tex Kirby); Yvonne De Carlo (Hannah Montgomery); Mara Corday (Pace); Rex Reason (John Randolph); Neville Brand (Tarp Penny); Emile Meyer (Pop Penny); Herbert Rudley (Gerald Montgomery); Robert J. Wilke (Sile Doty); John Gilmore (Dan Kirby); Gregg Barton (McKay); Ed Fury (Whitey); Francis McDonald (Chief Kiyuva); Julia Montoya (Indian Squaw); Paul Fierro (Bull, the Bartender); William Schallert (Missionary); Richard James (Clerk); Robert Hoy (Five Crows).

DEATH OF A SCOUNDREL   (RKO, 1956) 119 M.

Producer, Charles Martin; associate producer, J. Herbert Klein; director-screenplay, Martin; music, Max Steiner; camera, James Wong Howe; editor, Conrad Nervig.

George Sanders (Clementi Sabourin); Yvonne De Carlo (Bridget Kelly); Zsa Zsa Gabor (Mrs. Ryan); Victor Jory (Leonard Wilson); Nancy Gates (Stephanie North); Coleen Gray (Mrs. Van Renassalear); John Hoyt (Mr. O'Hara); Lisa Ferraday (Zina Monte); Tom Conway (Gerry Monte); Celia Lovsky (Mrs. Sabourin); Werner Klemperer (Herbert); Justice Watson (Butler); John Sutton (The Actor); Curtis Cooksey (Oswald Van Renassalear); Gabriel Curtis (Max Freundlich); Morris Ankum (Captain Lafarge); George Brent (Man with Balloon at Party).

THE TEN COMMANDMENTS   (Par., 1956) C—221 M.

Producer-director, Cecil B. DeMille; based on the novels *Prince of Egypt* by Dorothy Clarke Wilson, *Pillar of Fire* by Reverend J. H. Ingraham, *On Eagle's Wings* by Reverend G. E. Southon, in accordance with The Holy Scripture, the ancient texts of Josephus, Eusebius, Philo, the Midrash; screenplay, Aeneas MacKenzie, Jesse L. Lasky, Jr., Jack Garris, Fredric M. Frank; music, Elmer Bernstein; camera, Loyal Griggs; additional camera, J. Peverell Marley, John Warren, Wallace Kelley; editor, Anne Bauchens.

Charlton Heston (Moses); Yul Brynner (Rameses); Anne Baxter (Nefretiri); Edward G. Robinson (Dathan); Yvonne De Carlo (Sephora); Debra Paget (Lilia); John Derek (Joshua); Sir Cedric Hardwicke (Sethi); Nina Foch (Bithiah); Martha Scott (Yochabel); Judith Anderson (Memnet); Vincent Price (Baka); John Carradine (Aaron); Eduard Franz (Jethro); Olive Deering (Miriam); Donald Curtis (Mered); Douglass Dumbrille (Jannes); Lawrence Dobkin (Hur Ben Caleb); Frank DeKova (Abiram); H. B. Warner (Amminadab); Henry Wilcoxon (Pentaur); Julia Faye (Elisheba); Lisa Mitchell (Jethro's Daughter); Noelle Williams, Joanne Merlin, Pat Richard, Joyce Vanderveen, Diane Hall (Jethro's Daughters); Abbas El Boughdadly (Rameses' Charioteer); Fraser Heston (The Infant Moses); John Miljan (The Blind One); Tommy Duran (Gershom); Francis J. McDonald (Simon); Ian Keith (Rameses I); Joan Woodbury (Korah's Wife); Ramsay Hill (Korah); Woody Strode (King of Ethiopia); Dorothy Adams (Hebrew at Golden Calf/Hebrew Woman at Rameses' Gate/Slave Woman); Eric Alden (High-ranking Officer/Taskmaster/Slave Man/Officer); Henry Brandon (Commander of the Hosts); Touch Connors (Amalekite Herder); Henry Corden (Sheik of Ezion); Edna May Cooper (Court Lady); Kem Dibbs (Corporal); Fred Kohler, Jr. (Foreman); Gail Kobe (Pretty Slave Girl); John Merton, Amena Mohamed (Architect's Assistants); Addison Richards (Fanbearer); Onslow Stevens (Lugal); Clint Walker (Sardinian Captain); Frank Wilcox (Wazir); Luis Alberni (Old Hebrew at Moses' House); Michael Ansara (Taskmaster); Fred Coby (Hebrew at Golden Calf/Taskmaster); Tony Dante (Libyan Captain); Frankie Darro, Carl Switzer, Edward Earle (Slaves); Franklyn Farnum (High Official); John Hart (Cretan Ambassador); Ed Hinton (Taskmaster/Flagman); Walter Woolf King (Herald); Frank Lackteen (Old Man Praying/Old Man in Granary/Hebrew at Dathan's Tent/Elder of Joseph/Old Man); Emmett Lynn (Old Slave Man/Hebrew at Golden Calf); Stanley Price (Slave Carrying Load); Robert Vaughn (Spearman/Hebrew at Golden Calf); Herb Alpert (Drum Player).

BAND OF ANGELS   (WB, 1957) C—127 M.

Director, Raoul Walsh; based on the novel by Robert Penn Warren; screenplay, John Twist, Ivan Goff, Ben Roberts; music, Max Steiner; orchestrator, Murray Cutter; costumes, Marjorie Best; assistant directors, Russ Saunders, Al Alleborn; art director, Franz Bachelin; camera, Lucien Ballard; editor, Folmar Blangsted.

Clark Gable (Hamish Bond); Yvonne De Carlo (Amantha Starr); Sidney Poitier (Rau-Ru); Efrem Zimbalist, Jr. (Ethan Sears); Rex Reason (Seth Parton); Patric Knowles (Charles de Marigny); Andrea King (Miss Idell); Torin Thatcher (Captain Canavan); William Forrest (Aaron Starr); Raymond Bailey (Mr. Stuart); Ray Teal (Mr. Calloway); Carolle Drake (Michele); Russell Evans (Jimmee); Tommie Moore (Dollie); Zelda Cleaver (Sukie); Joe Narcisse (Shad); Marshall Bradford (General Butler); Noreen Corcoran (Manty as a Child); Juanita Moore (Budge); Jack Williams (Runaway); Charles Heard (Helper); Roy Barcroft (Gillespie the Overseer); Curtis Hamilton (Jacob the Coachman); Riza Royce (Mrs. Hopewell); Mayo Loizeau, June-Ellen Anthony, Carla Merry (Girls); Jim Hayward (Sheriff); William Fawcett, Dan White, Jean G. Harvey, Alfred Meissner (Mourners); Guy Wilkerson (Minister); Larry Blake (Crier-Off Camera); Ewing Mitchell (Old

Gentleman); Forbes Murray (Younger Man); Joe Gilbert, Robert Carson (Bidders); Robert Clarke (Friend); Maurice Marsac (Young Dandy); Jeanine Grandel (Proprietor); Gizelle D'Arc (Salesgirl); Harry Fleer (Aide); Bob Steele, Zon Murray (Privates); Morgan Shaan (Corporal); X. Brands, Paul McGuire, Martin Smith, William Hughes, Myron Cook, Charles Victor, Pete Dunn, William Hudson (Officers); Ann Doran (Mrs. Morton); Walter Smith (Black Soldier); Milas Clark, Jr. (Black Boy); Carl Harbaugh (Seaman); William Schallert (Lieutenant); Charles Horvath (Soldier); Anthony Ghazlo (Driver); Robyn Faire (Little Girl); Ann Staunton (Mother); Madame Sul-Te-Wan (Flower Vendor).

LA SPADE E LA CROCE (Liber, 1958) C—105 M.

Producer, Ottavio Poggi; director, Carlo Ludovico Bragadlia; screenplay, Alessandro Continenza; music, Roberto Nicolosi; camera, Raffaele Masciocchi.

Yvonne De Carlo (Maria Maddalena); Jorge Mistral (Caio Marcello); Rossana Podesta (Marta); Massimo Serato (Anan); and: Mario Girotti, Andres Aureli, Rossano Rory, Philippe Hersent.

U.S. release: *Mary Magdalene* (Amex, 1960).

TIMBUKTU (UA, 1959) 91 M.

Producer, Edward Small; director, Jacques Tourneur; screenplay, Anthony Veiller, Paul Dudley; art director, Bill Glasgow; set decorator, Darrell Silvera; music, Gerald Fried; technical advisor, Feridun; costumes, Elva Martien; makeup, Layne Britton; sound, John Kean, Roy Cropper; special effects, Joe Zomar, Alex Weldon; camera, Maury Gertsman; editor, Grant Whytock.

Victor Mature (Mike Conway); Yvonne De Carlo (Natalie Dufort); George Dolenz (Colonel Dufort); John Dehner (Emir); Marcia Henderson (Jeanne Marat); James Fox (Lieutenant Marat); Leonard Mudie (Mohamet Adani); Paul Wexler (Suleman); Robert Clarke (Captain Girard); Willard Sage (Major Leroux); Mark Dana (Captain Rimbaud); Larry Perron (Dagana); Steve Darrell (Nazir); Larry Chance (Ahmed); Allan Pinson (Sergeant Trooper).

McLINTOCK! (UA, 1963) C—127 M.

Producer, Michael Wayne; director, Andrew V. McLaglen; screenplay, James Edward Grant; music, Frank De Vol; songs, De Vol and Dunham; Dunham; art directors, Hal Pereira, Eddie Imazu; set decorators, Sam Comer, Darrell Silvera; technical advisor, Cliff Lyons; costumes, Frank C. Beetson, Jr.; assistant director, Frank Parmenter; sound, Jack Solomon; camera, William H. Clothier; editor, Otho Lovering.

John Wayne (McLintock); Maureen O'Hara (Katherine McLintock); Yvonne De Carlo (Louise Warren); Patrick Wayne (Devlin Warren); Stefanie Powers (Becky McLintock); Jack Kruschen (Bimbaum); Chill Wills (Drago); Jerry Van Dyke (Matt Douglas, Jr.); Edgar Buchanan (Bunny Dull); Bruce Cabot (Ben Sage); Perry Lopez (Davey Elk); Michael Pate (Puma); Strother Martin (Agard); Gordon Jones (Matt Douglas); Robert Lowery (Governor); Ed Faulkner (Youngben Sage); H. W. Gim (Ching); Aissa Wayne (Alice Warren); Chuck Roberson (Sheriff Lord); Hal Needham (Carter); Pedro Gonzales, Jr. (Carlos); Hank Worden (Jeth); Leo Gordon (Jones); Mary Patterson (Beth); John Hamilton (Fauntleroy); Ralph Volkie (Loafer); Dan Borzage (Loafer); John Stanley (Running Buffalo); Kari Noven (Millie); Mari Blanchard (Camille); Frank Hagney (Bartender); Bob Steele (Railroad Engineer).

A GLOBAL AFFAIR (MGM, 1964) 84 M.

Producer, Hall Bartlett; associate producer, Eugene Vale; director, Jack Arnold;

story, Vale; screenplay, Arthur Marx, Bob Fisher, Charles Lederer; art directors, George W. Davis, Preston Ames; assistant directors, Tom Shaw, Lee Lukather; music, Dominic Frontiere; song, Frontiere and Dorcas Cochran; camera, Joseph Ruttenberg; editor, Bud Molin.

Bob Hope (Frank Larrimore); Lilo Pulver (Sonya); Michelle Mercier (Lisette); Elga Andersen (Yvette); Yvonne De Carlo (Dolores); Miiko Taka (Fumiko); Robert Sterling (Randy); Nehemiah Persoff (Sigura); John McGiver (Snifter); Jacques Bergerac (Louis Duval); Mickey Shaughnessy (Policeman); Barbara Bouchet (Girl); Billy Halop (Cabby); Adlai Stevenson (Passerby); Reta Shaw (Nurse Argyle); Henry Kulky (Charlie); Francis de Sales (U.S. Delegate); Rodolfo Hayes, Jr. (Spanish Delegate); Lester Mathews (U.K. Delegate); Booth Colman (Delegate); William Newell (Waiter).

LAW OF THE LAWLESS   (Par., 1964) C—87 M.

Producer, A. C. Lyles; director, William F. Claxton; screenplay, Steve Fisher; assistant director, Harry Hogan; art directors, Hal Pereira, Al Roelofs; set decorators, Sam Comer, Darrell Silvera; makeup, Wally Westmore; dialog coach, Jerry Buss; sound, Frank McWhorter, John Wilkonson; special camera effects, Paul K. Lerpae; camera, Lester Shorr; editor, Otho Lovering.

Dale Robertson (Judge Clem Rogers); Yvonne De Carlo (Ellie Irish); William Bendix (Sheriff Ed Tanner); Bruce Cabot (Joe Rile); Barton MacLane (Big Tom Stone); John Agar (Pete Stone); Richard Arlen (Bartender); Jody McCrea (George Stapleton); Kent Taylor (Rand McDonald); Bill Williams (Silas Miller); Rod Lauren (Deputy Tim Ludlow); George Chandler (Hotel Clerk); Lon Chaney (Tiny); Donald Barry (Tuffy); Roy Jenson, Jerry Summers, Reg Parton (Johnson Brothers); Alex Sharp (Drifter).

TENTAZIONI PROIBITI   (Wonder Film, 1964) 88 M.

Director, screenplay, Osvaldo Civirani; music, Lallo Gori; camera, Civirani.

With: Yvonne De Carlo, Dolly Bel, Alan Kemp, Helen Bugge, Dana Ghia, Nella Asaro, Francesco Ungaro, Renato Rossini, Lilli Melon, Anna Maria Mareglia, Mara Carisi, Gina Sampieri, Violetta Montenero, Gabriella De Vitto, Vivien Bocca, Graziella Rotatori, Karin Mayer, Uhti Hof, Albeert Uzan, Renato De Montis, Pino Pennese, Ottavio Possidoni, Fulvio Pellegrino, Valerio Corradi, Roberta Dominici, Bianca Pividori, Lidia Carancini, Anna Maria Bellincioni, Silvania Corsini, Claudia Maiolini, Isa Mallucci, Brigitte Bardot, Alberto Sordi, Carlo Dapporto, Christine Keeler, Carol Danell.

MUNSTER, GO HOME   (Univ., 1966) C—90 M.

Producers, Joe Connelly, Bob Mosher; director, Earl Bellamy; screenplay, George Tibbles, Connelly, Mosher; art directors, Alexander Golitzen, John Lloyd; set decorators, John McCarthy, Julie Heron; assistant director, Dolph Zimmer; music, Jack Marshall; music supervisor, Joseph Gershenson; makeup, Bud Westmore; sound, Waldon O. Watson, Corson Jowett; camera, Benny Kline; editor, Bud Isaccs.

Fred Gwynne (Herman Munster); Yvonne De Carlo (Lily Munster); Al Lewis (Grandpa); Butch Patrick (Eddie Munster); Debbie Watson (Marilyn); Hermione Gingold (Lady Effigie Munster); Terry Thomas (Freddy Munster); Jeanne Arnold (Grace Munster); Robert Pine (Roger Moresby); John Carradine (Cruikshank); Bernard Fox (Squire Moresby); Richard Dawson (Joey); Maria Lennard (Millie); Cliff Norton (Herbert); Diana Chesney (Mrs. Moresby); Arthur Malet (Alfie); Ben Wright (Hennesy).

HOSTILE GUNS (Par., 1967) C—91 M.

Producer, A. C. Lyles; director, R. G. Springsteen; story, Sloan Nibley, James Edward Grant; screenplay, Steve Fisher, Nibley; art directors, Hal Pereira, Al Roelofs; set decorators, Robert Benton, Bud Friend; assistant director, Ralph Axness; makeup, Wally Westmore; sound, John Carter, John Wilinson; special camera effects, Paul K. Lerpae; process camera, Farciot Edouart; camera, Lathrop Worth; editor, John F. Schreyer.

George Montgomery (Gid McCool); Yvonne De Carlo (Laura Mannon); Tab Hunter (Mike Reno); Brian Donlevy (Marshal Willett); John Russell (Aaron); Leo Gordon (Hank Pleasant); Robert Emhardt (R. C. Crawford); Pedro Gonzalez Gonzalez (Angel); James Craig (Ned Cooper); Richard Arlen (Sheriff Travis); Emile Meyer (Uncle Joe); Donald Barry (Johnson); Fuzzy Knight (Buck); William Fawcett (Jensen); Joe Brown (Bunco); Reg Parton (Chig); Read Morgan (Tubby); Eric Cody (Alfie).

THE POWER (MGM, 1968) C—108 M.

Producer, George Pal; director, Byron Haskin; based on the novel by Frank M. Robinson; screenplay, John Gay; music, Miklos Rozsa; art directors, George W. Davis, Merrill Pye; set decorators, Henry Grace, Don Greenwood, Jr.; assistant director, E. Darrell Hallenbeck; makeup, William Tuttle; sound, Franklin Milton; special electronic sound effects, Lovell Norman; special effects, J. McMillan Johnson, Gene Warren, Wah Chang; camera, Ellsworth Fredericks; editor, Thomas J. McCarthy.

George Hamilton (Jim Tanner); Suzanne Pleshette (Margery Lansing); Michael Rennie (Arthur Nordlund); Nehemiah Persoff (Carl Melniker); Earl Holliman (Talbot Scott); Arthur O'Connell (Henry Hallson); Aldo Ray (Bruce); Barbara Nichols (Flora); Yvonne De Carlo (Sally Hallson); Richard Carlson (N. E. Van Zandt); Gary Merrill (Mark Corlane); Ken Murray (Grover); Miiko Taka (Mrs. Van Zandt); Celia Lovsky (Mrs. Hallson); Vaughn Taylor (Mr. Hallson); Lawrence Montaigne (Briggs); Beverly Hills (Sylvia).

ARIZONA BUSHWHACKERS (Par., 1968) C—87 M.

Producer, A. C. Lyles; director, Lesley Selander; story, Steve Fisher, Andrew Craddock; screenplay, Fisher; assistant director, Dale Hutchinson; art directors, Hal Pereira, Al Roelofs; set decorators, Robert Benton, Jerry Welch; music, Jimmie Haskell; makeup, Wally Westmore; sound, Joe Edmonson, John Wilkinson; special camera effects, Paul K. Lerpae; camera, Lester Shorr; editor, John F. Schreyer.

Howard Keel (Lee Travis); Yvonne De Carlo (Jill Wyler); John Ireland (Dan Shelby); Marilyn Maxwell (Molly); Scott Brady (Tom Rile); Brian Donlevy (Mayor Joe Smith); Barton MacLane (Sheriff Lloyd Grover); James Craig (Ike Clanton); Roy Rogers, Jr. (Roy); Reg Parton (Curly); Montie Montana (Stage Driver); Eric Cody (Bushwhacker); James Cagney (Narrator).

THE DELTA FACTOR (American-Continental, 1970) C—91 M.

Producer-director, Tay Garnett; based on the novel by Mickey Spillane; screenplay, Garnett; music, Howard Danziger; art directors, Jack Collis, Ben Resella; visual consultant, Dan Fitzgerald; assistant director, Dink Templeton; stunt driving, Roger Creed, Jim Climer; wardrobe, Soni Karp; sound, Clem Portman; camera, Ted and Vince Saizis; editor, Richard Farrell.

Yvette Mimieux (Kim Stacy); Christopher George (Morgan); Diane McBain (Lisa Gordot); Ralph Taeger (Art Keefer); Yvonne De Carlo (Valerie); Sherri Spillane (Rosa); Ted De Corsia (Ames); Rhodes Reason (Dr. Fredericks); Joseph Sirola (Sal Dekker); and: Richard Ianni, George Ash, Fred Marsell.

THE SEVEN MINUTES (20th, 1972) C—116 M.

Producer, Russ Meyer; associate producers, Red Hershon, Eve Meyer; director, Russ Meyer; based on the novel by Irving Wallace; screenplay, Richard Warren Lewis; music, Stu Phillips; songs, Phillips and Bob Stone; art director, Rodger Maus; set decorators, Walter M. Scott, Raphael Bretton; costumes, Bill Thomas; makeup, Dan Striepeke, Del Acevedo, Lynn Reynolds; assistant director, David Hall; sound, Don J. Bassman, Theodore Soderberg; special camera effects, Howard A. Anderson Company; camera, Fred Mandl; editor, Dick Wormell.

Wayne Maunder (Mike Barrett); Marianne McAndrew (Maggie Russell); Philip Carey (Elmo Duncan); Jay C. Flippen (Luther Yerkes); Edy Williams (Faye Osborn); Yvonne De Carlo (Constance Cumberland); Lyle Bettger (Frank Griffith); Jackie Gayle (Norman Quandt); Ron Randell (Merle Reid); Charles Drake (Sergeant Kellog); John Carradine (Sean O'Flanagan); Harold J. Stone (Judge Upshaw); Tom Selleck (Phil Sanford); James Iglehart (Clay Rutherford); John Sarno (Jerry Griffith); Stanley Adams (Irwin Blair); Billy Durkin (George Perkins); Yvonne D'Angers (Sheri Moore); Robert Moloney (Ben Fremont); Olan Soule (Harvey Underwood); Jan Shutan (Anna Lou White); Alex D'Arcy (Christian Leroux); David Brian (Cardinal McManus); Berry Kroeger (Paul Van Fleet); Ralph Story (TV Commentator); Charles Napier (Officer Iverson); Kay Peters (Olivia St. Clair); Richard Angarola (Father Sarfatti); Baby Doll Shawn Devereaux (Yerkes' Girlfriend); Regis Cordic (Louis Polk); John Lawrence (Howard Moore); Barry Coe (Court Clerk); Mora Gray (Donna Novick); Wolfman Jack (Himself); Calvin Bartlett (Olin Adams); Ken Jones (Charles Wynter); Bill Baldwin (Commentator); Robin Hughes (Ashcroft); Vince Williams, Jim Bacon (Reporters); John Gruber (Dr. Quigley); Chris Marks (Dr. Eberhart); Stuart Lancaster (Dr. Roger Trimble); Peter Shrayder (Merle Reid's Cameraman); Lynn Hamilton (Avis); Patrick Wright (Detective); Lillian Lehman (Librarian); Judy Baldwin (Fremont's Girlfriend); Paul Stader (Thug); Henry Rowland (Yerkes' Butler); George De Normand, Jeffrey Sayre (Jurors).

THE GIRL ON THE LATE, LATE SHOW (NBC-TV, 1974) C—74 M.

Executive producer, David Gerber; producer, Christopher Morgan; director, Gary Nelson; teleplay, Mark Rogers; music, Richard Markowitz; makeup, Ben Lane; camera, Robert Morrison; editor, Richard C. Meyer.

Don Murray (William Martin); Bert Convy (F. T. Allen); Yvonne De Carlo (Lorraine); Gloria Grahame (Carolyn Porter); John Ireland (Walters); Ralph Meekers (De Biesse); Cameron Mitchell (Wilder); Van Johnson (Deverette); Mary Ann Mobley (Librarian); Joe Santis (Lieutenant Scott); Walter Pidgeon (Pahlman); Laraine Stephens (Paula); Sherry Jackson (Pat); and: Felice Orlando, Dan Tobin, Frankie Darro, William Benedict, Peter Colt.

THE MARK OF ZORRO (ABC-TV, 1974) C—90 M.

Producers, Robert C. Thompson, Rodrick Paul; director, Don McDougall; teleplay, Brian Taggert; assistant director, Joe Ellis.

Frank Langella (Don Diego/Zorro); Ricardo Montalban (Captain Estaban); Gilbert Roland (Alejandro Vega); Yvonne De Carlo (Isabella Vega); Louise Sorel (Inez); Anne Archer (Teresa); Robert Middleton (Luis); Tom Lacy (Fra Felipe).

ARIZONA SLIM (1975)

With: Sean Walsh (Arizona Slim); Yvonne De Carlo.

At New York's Idlewild Airport (December 1954)

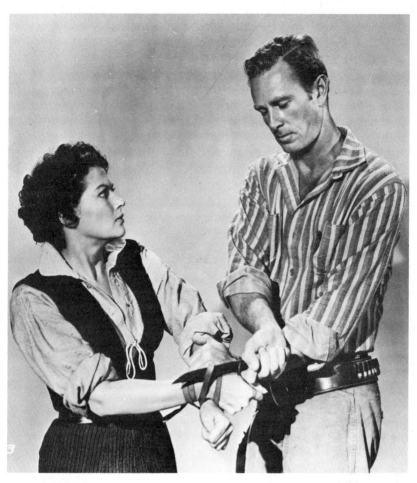

With Sterling Hayden in a publicity
pose from SHOTGUN (AA '55)

With fiancé Robert Morgan in
Hollywood (November 1955)

209

With Zachary Scott in FLAME OF THE ISLANDS (Rep '55)

With Alan Badel in MAGIC FIRE
(Rep '56)

With George Sanders in
DEATH OF A SCOUNDREL (RKO '56)

With Rory Calhoun in RAW EDGE (Univ '56)

With Sidney Poitier and Patric Knowles in BAND OF ANGELS (WB '57)

With Jorge Mistral in
LA SPADE E LA CROCE
(Liber '58)

With John Wayne in McLINTOCK! (UA '63)

In LAW OF THE LAWLESS (Par '64)

With Al Lewis, Fred Gwynne, and Butch Patrick in MUNSTER, GO HOME
(Univ '66)

With George Hamilton in THE POWER (MGM '68)

With Dorothy Collins and Alexis Smith at the opening-night party for the Broadway stage show *Follies* (April 4, 1971)

Publicity pose for COVER GIRL (Col '44)

Rita Hayworth

5'6"
120 pounds
Auburn hair
Brown eyes
Libra

"Rita Hayworth is a fraud." Words of heresy? No, a statement of blunt truth. "She's a deluxe model right out of Hollywood's glamour factory," continued this same frank-speaking studio executive. "Her breathtaking beauty, plus publicity, fame and wealth made her one of the most alluring packages ever to come out of the screen colony. But she's really just a nice dull girl who has been looking all these years for a nice guy."

In short, Rita was *Gilda* (Columbia, 1946), but Gilda is not Rita. In her cinematic heyday (1941-52), Rita was the essential movie goddess, a sparkling silver-screen image with an exquisite face, glorious hair, and the air of a conquering tigress. But offcamera she was most often meek as a house cat, interested far more in achieving domestic bliss than professional fame. It was a dichotomy of goals that had torn at her since early childhood, when her Spanish-born dancer father and American-bred actress mother molded her for a career in the family dance act.

With such an ambivalent life's ambition, it is very remarkable that Rita rose to the movie-star heights she did. Granted, a perfectionist father, a string of personality-manipulating husbands, and, most of all, a master-puppeteer movie mogul (Harry Cohn) played a huge role in her progression from Fox contractee to Columbia's queen of the movies. But if she had not been a pliable subject, capable of refining and shifting her natural assets (beauty, rhythm, verve) no one could have pushed her beyond B-picture status with a well-marked career span.

Most filmgoers were unaware of Rita's more emotional dilemmas and only cared about what they saw onscreen. She was the glorious gal who sang, danced, and romanced her way through *You Were Never Lovelier* (Columbia, 1942), *Cover Girl* (Columbia, 1944), and *Tonight and Every Night* (Columbia, 1945). Combined with her ability to be the audacious temptress in *Blood and Sand* (Twentieth Century-Fox, 1941), *Gilda*, and *The Loves of Carmen* (Columbia, 1948), Rita was more than a fitting match for her 1940s celluloid rivals: Betty Grable, Ann Sheridan, Lana Turner, and Dorothy Lamour. Few fans knew or cared that Rita's singing voice was always dubbed, that some of her intricate onscreen dancing was the footwork of another, that close-ups of her hands were sometimes those of a fill-in, or that a hair dye and electrolysis, along with padded hips to make her less leggy, had combined to provide the illusion she seemed to be. Movies were not for or about reality, and Rita was the most erotic new unreal creation since the earlier manufacturing of Marlene Dietrich.

Who was cheated in this massive deception? Certainly not the paying audiences, for she always gave them more than their money's worth. In reality, the person who was cheated was Rita herself. The on-the-ground woman was no match for the pedestaled love goddess. She knew it some of the time, Harry Cohn knew it all of the time, and the public knew it little of the time. When Manuel Puig composed his novel of life in a small Argentine town of the 1930s and 1940s, there was deliberate irony when he titled the volume *Betrayed by Rita Hayworth*. His characters play out shabby, unfulfilled, excessively passionate existences through the vicarious realms of moviegoing. One of the characters says of the onscreen Rita, "she's a pretty actress but she's always betraying somebody." That somebody was always herself.

People gleefully cite Judy Garland as the prize illustration of just how Hollywood could exploit a human being with tragic results. But the corollary was that Judy, in turn, exploited her legions of loyal fans, who, in turn, drew power from her as she grew weaker and finally expired. Rita has always been in a far more vulnerable position, for she was never capable of, or interested in, the art of exploitation. Most of the 1940s love-goddess figures have either retired or died, but Rita continues to survive in a very diminished limelight. Some say she is her own worst enemy, but the more likely truth is that her strongest foe is the cannibalistic faction that waits with bated breath for time to strip the star of her most potent weapon: her incredible beauty.

It was on October 17, 1918, on New York City's Upper West Side, that Margarita Carmen Cansino was born into a well-known family of vaudeville dancers. Her grandfather, Antonio Cansino, had been an established performer in Seville, even dancing at King Alfonso's court. Her father, Eduardo, had been part of the family in Spain with his six brothers, but at the age of seventeen he was paired with his fifteen-year-old sister, Elisa. The duo performed in Europe, England, Canada, and Australia before the blue-blood Mrs. Stuyvesant Fish, in 1913, brought the pair to New York to grace her social functions. Later Eduardo was hired for the Ziegfeld Follies. There he met Follies beauty Volga Haworth, an Irish-American descendant of Joseph Haworth (a contemporary of John Wilkes Booth), who had run away from her home in Washington, D.C., to try her luck on the stage. The love-struck couple were soon wed, and a few years later became the parents of Margarita.

Practical Eduardo, always thinking of the fate of his family-populated act, "The Dancing Cansinos," would later admit, "When I looked at Margarita— a few minutes after she was born—I was terribly disappointed. I had wanted a boy. What could I do with a girl?" Train her as a dancer, as soon as possible. On her part, Rita would later allude to her childhood with overtones of bittersweet feelings. She suggested that as an infant she had "castanets in my hands instead of a rattle" and that "From the time I was three and a half, as soon as I could stand on my own feet, I was given [dancing] lessons."

Margarita's childhood years were ostensibly spent in the environs of Brooklyn, but more often than not, the family was touring on the road and, like the proverbial girl "born in the trunk," the backstage dressing room was her most familiar surroundings, with most of her waking hours spent in dance training, watching her parents and other vaudeville acts from the wings of a theatre, or traveling to the next engagement. "Rehearse, rehearse, rehearse. That was my girlhood." The serious-faced, dark-haired, plumpish youngster would much have preferred being a "normal" child, fostering her wild dreams of being an explorer and seeing the world. She did not at all enjoy the arduous regimen imposed by her dedicated parents, "but I didn't have the courage to tell my father, so I . . . [took] the lessons." Her disciplined existence became her accepted way of life, and she began practicing very hard, hoping that maybe someday her perfectionist father might commend her dancing abilities as better than adequate.*

Between the endless tours, two sons, Vernon and Eduardo, Jr., were born to the Cansinos. But the new additions to the family did not change or detract from Margarita's obligations as the eldest child. Her terpsichorean studies continued unabated, with only occasional sojourns at Public School 69 in Jackson Heights, Long Island, where the Cansinos then resided.

Margarita made a rather inauspicious motion-picture debut. As part of "The Dancing Cansinos" she was seen very briefly in a ten-minute sound short-subject on folk dancing filmed at the Vitaphone Company's East

*Margarita learned all the fundamentals of ballet, but did no toe work, as it was feared it would make her legs ungainly for stage work.

Coast studio. The short was utilized on the supporting program at the New York premiere on August 6, 1926, of Warner Bros.,' *Don Juan*, a feature more noted for its novel use of recorded sound effects than for John Barrymore's ardent swashbuckling capers.

That same year Eduardo perceived that vaudeville was fast dying, largely due to the advent of talking pictures. He moved his family to Hollywood, opening a dance school and supplementing his income by functioning as a dance director at the Fox Studios, where the company was engaged in turning out a rash of singing-dancing-talking screen musicals. Meanwhile, Margarita's dancing lessons continued with more reason than ever before—her aunt Elisa died in 1928, and Eduardo required a new dance partner.

Probably Margarita's first real public appearance occurred in 1932 when she danced a Spanish routine (choreographed by Eduardo) in the live prologue at the premiere of *Back Street* (Universal, 1932) at the elegant Cathay Circle Theatre in Hollywood. While observing Margarita's performance from out front, Eduardo would later recall: "All of a sudden, I wake up. Wow! She has a figure! She ain't no baby any more." Fourteen-year-old Margarita was not only buxom but engagingly sultry, qualities unperceived by the theatre audience that evening.

Since the Depression had curtailed business at the dance studio, Eduardo decided that the Cansinos might have better luck if they revived the dance act. Thus "The Five Cansinos" went on tour in the United States and South America, before Eduardo decided to accept an engagement in the thriving south-of-the-border town of Tijuana, Mexico. What began as a short-term engagement at the rococo Foreign Club turned into an eighteen-month stay there. Very much a product of his Spanish background, Eduardo was greatly concerned that his maturing daughter might go astray in the company of a strange man. Thus, between shows she was locked in the dressing room, and each evening went back to the United States to join the family at Chula Vista.

Next came an engagement on the *Rex*, one of the notorious gambling ships anchored in Santa Monica Bay. Eduardo allowed himself a few hours of relaxation of fishing one day. While engaged in the sport he caught a fishhook in his body, and he went to bed with an infection.

Rita was forced to appear onstage on the *Rex* in a solo act, which flopped. "The management didn't think I had enough Spanish seductiveness. I was fifteen at the time, and the only thing that really aroused me was food."

After Eduardo recovered, the Cansinos had better luck at the Agua Caliente Hotel two miles south of Tijuana, a nightspot noted for its Hollywood clientele, all looking for more exciting diversion than Los Angeles could offer. The Cansinos were a hit there, and their four-week engagement was stretched out to seven months.

220

One of the industry executives who saw Eduardo and Rita dancing at the Agua Caliente was Winfield Sheehan, vice-president and West Coast production head of the Fox Film Corporation. He had fostered the career of protégée Janet Gaynor at the studio and was noted for his ability to spot a pretty face. He took a shine to beautiful young Margarita, and had her signed to a term contract with the studio. Eduardo was not part of the deal, but he signed the agreement on behalf of his underage daughter. Her formal education had long since been a phase of the past, for Eduardo believed, "School is nonsense for a dancer."

Her first job at Fox was an appearance in a minute dancing segment of the prologue to *Dante's Inferno* (Fox, 1935), a fabulously moralistic study of the sins of gambling and corrupt power, starring Spencer Tracy and Claire Trevor. Her routine was choreographed by Eduardo, and she was teamed with Gary Leon. At about this time she appeared with other Spanish-speaking contractees in a Fox short subject promoting Spanish-language editions of studio features.

Sheehan and other studio executives agreed that pretty Margarita had possibilities, and she was signed to a $200-a-week contract, with Eduardo hired as a home-lot dance instructor. Margarita had never previously studied acting, but as she was later to tell writer Jane Ardmore, "From the time I was twelve I was dancing for bread and butter, but in my heart I was always an actress." She had brief opportunities to test her histrionic abilities in *Under the Pampas Moon* (Fox, 1935) and *Charlie Chan in Egypt* (Fox, 1935), both released before *Dante's Inferno*.

Fox's high-priced male lead, Warner Baxter, had won an Oscar for playing the Mexican outlaw-hero, the Cisco Kid, in *In Old Arizona* (Fox, 1929), a role he repeated in *The Arizona Kid* (Fox, 1930) and *The Cisco Kid* (Fox, 1931). By 1935, Baxter was back in the saddle again in *Under the Pampas Moon,* as an irresistible gaucho who loves both racehorses and the fetching Ketti Gallian. The film, replete with phony Spanish accents and pseudo-Buenos Aires ambiance, was full of dancing. Baxter and his hefty oncamera mama (Soledad Jiminez) perform a tango in a fancy nightclub; professional specialty dancers execute a more fashionable tango, and Margarita was on hand to introduce the Zamba, an Argentine rural dance. Despite bad reviews, the picture was a moneymaker.*

In *Charlie Chan in Egypt*, the eighth Warner Oland-Fox Chan detective entry, the focus was on the blend of the Oriental with the land of the pharaohs. Sleuth Oland supplied his full quota of aphorisms,† black Stepin Fetchit added a dash of racial humor, and, in contrast to the adequate

---

*Andre Sennwald (*New York Times*) wrote, "[the film] is so bad that after a while you stop resenting it and begin to be mildly amused by its antique humor."

†Oland's Chan wisely states, "Theory, like mist on eyeglasses, obscures fact." On another occasion he remarks, "Waiting till tomorrow is waste of today." At another juncture he verbalizes, "Hasty conclusion easy to make, like hole in water."

but bland heroine (Pat Paterson), Margarita was arresting as the mysterious Nayda, one of the suspects in this caper set in Luxor, where professor Frank Conroy's scientific mission has gone awry.

Paddy O'Day (Twentieth Century-Fox, 1935) was a modestly budgeted vehicle for child actress Jane Withers, here cast as an Irish immigrant in the tradition of such screen waifs as Mary Pickford, Janet Gaynor, Marion Davies, and Wither's contemporary, Shirley Temple. Oncamera, young Withers sang and danced her way into everyone's affections, including that of Margarita Cansino, here billed as Tamara Petrovitch, the one who adopts blarney-exuding Withers. In *Human Cargo* (Twentieth Century-Fox, 1935), Claire Trevor and Brian Donlevy were rival reporters involved in an alien-smuggling racket in Southern California, with Margarita as Carmen Zoro, a minor villainess.

Before Fox Film merged with Darryl F. Zanuck-Joseph M. Schenck's Twentieth Century Pictures, Winfield Sheehan had okayed pre-production work on a remake of *Ramona*, the historical melodrama that had starred Dolores Del Rio and Warner Baxter in a popular United Artists release of 1928. Margarita was among those tested for a key role in the new film, as was Gilbert Roland. But then came the corporate merger, and Sheehan was ousted. Neither Margarita nor Roland won parts in the new *Ramona*, made for Twentieth Century-Fox release in 1936, in which Loretta Young and Don Ameche starred. In fact, Margarita, known as one of Sheehan's protégées, was dropped from the studio's performer roster.*

Because she had already been a disciplined entertainer for so many years, this professional setback did not unduly discourage Margarita. She sought screen fame on a freelance basis, with her first such assignment at Columbia Pictures. In *Meet Nero Wolfe* (Columbia, 1936), she was Maria Maringola, who makes home-brewed beer for corpulent, brew-guzzling, orchid-growing super-criminologist Edward Arnold. When Margarita reports the disappearance of her brother (Juan Toreno) to Arnold, the caper gets under way. The sleuth character was a popular *Saturday Evening Post* magazine figure, but the picturization failed to meet the same filmgoer popularity as its prototype, MGM's *Thin Man* series. The novelty of a crime detector who could solve a mystery without leaving the confines of his elaborate home, let alone his comfortable armchair, seemingly did not arouse audience curiosity.

Margarita's next four film ventures were to be Westerns. She would later say, "Those are the days I'd just as soon forget. I hate horses!" *Rebellion* (Crescent, 1936) was an unassuming programmer set in California right after the signing of the treaty with the United States guaranteeing the rights of Mexican citizens of the state. Cavalry officer Tom Keene, personal aide to the U.S. president, is sent into the disputed territory to

---

*Rita's half-minute scene in *Message to Garcia* (Twentieth Century-Fox, 1936) was deleted before the Barbara Stanwyck feature was released.

put an end to the murdering land-jumpers who have, among others, killed the father of Paula Castillo (Margarita). Her big scene occurs when she implores President Zachary Taylor (Allan Cavan) to put a stop to the lawlessness in California. Margarita had a more productive role in Tex Ritter's *Trouble in Texas* (Grand National, 1937). Since the musical Western (Ritter had three tunes) dealt with racketeers using rodeos as a cover-up for their rash of prize-money robberies, the low-budget entry had to rely on a liberal use of newsreel inserts of big-time rodeo events to pad out the feature. As Carmen, Margarita had a dance sequence besides providing the usual distaff decoration. For her efforts, Margarita received her first (prophetic) reviews. *Variety* reported: "Perhaps the best looker of any of the girls working in hoss pictures to date is Grand National's Rita Cansino. She was on the Fox lot for a while, and classes up the company she's in here." When *Trouble in Texas* was released in England in 1943 by Ambassador Films, that company took full advantage of Rita Hayworth's 1940s extreme popularity to advertise the horse opera's leads as "lovely devastating Rita Hayworth and Tex Ritter in a Musical Western." She was touted by Ambassador as "the star of the moment."

Margarita also acted with Tom Keene in *Old Louisiana* (Crescent, 1937), in which she was cast as Angela, the daughter of the Spanish governor (Carlos De Valdez) of Louisiana. Hard-riding Keene was present to represent American citizens in the Spanish colony who were outraged at the Spanish authorities' imposing a heavy duty on river traffic. Budd Buster as Kentucky supplied the comedy relief. Margarita employed her Spanish heritage to good effect here, using an accent which *Variety* termed a "tamale accent [that] fits her well for the part."* When reissued in the United States, *Old Louisiana* was retitled *Louisiana Girl* to take advantage of the Hayworth marquee name. In England, the film was retagged *Treason*.

For her fourth and final sagebrush tale of this period, Margarita moved over to Herbert Yates's Republic Pictures, where she was cast in *Hit the Saddle* (Republic, 1937), one of the earlier entries in the Robert Livingston-Ray Corrigan-Max Terhune *Three Mesquiteers* series.† As a precursor to her own change of professional name, Margarita was billed as Rita, the tough fandango dancer at the local cabaret. One member of the law-enforcing trio, Stony Brooks (Livingston), spots Margarita at the entertainment center, and they join in a duet of "Winding the Trail." His pals

---

*In his expansive career study of Rita Hayworth in *Focus on Films* (1972), cinema historian John Kobal asserts, "Underneath her American accent, softened, was the attractively melodic ring of her father's Spanish. Though she had no direct traces of an accent, indirectly she exhaled her thoughts the way Latin people speaking in English do. Words flow from her breath organically, as if she were caressing the Castilian poetry of her famous uncle Rafael Cansinos Assens, rated by Borges as one of the great writers in Spanish literature."

†Another screen star to make an early screen appearance in a *Three Mesquiteer* Western was Jennifer Jones, who as Phylis Isley appeared in *New Frontier* (Republic, 1939), which featured John Wayne, Ray Corrigan, and Raymond Hatton as the hard-riding trio.

(Corrigan-Terhune) are fearful that Livingston will be suckered by the grasping girl. Corrigan asks Livingston, "Don't you see she's not your type of girl?" Meanwhile, one of her co-workers has told Margarita, "Those boys are closer than Siamese twins." The would-be femme fatale retorts, "Oh yeah. Take a look at the baby who's going to perform the operation." She almost has her way, stating that "I'm an actress, not a washerwoman." She insists that she and Livingston will reside in New York. However, when Corrigan tells her that Livingston has no real money and offers her $1,500 plus a one-way ticket out of town, she readily agrees to the deal. *Variety's* reviewer, not very impressed with Margarita, wrote, "The girl is highly deficient in terps and as an actress . . . ."

It was at this unimpressive juncture in her life that two important events occurred which shaped the future of the budding celebrity, Rita Hayworth. One day she received a phone call from Edward Charles Judson, a foreign-car salesman, who stated that he had seen one of her films and was so impressed by her screen appearance that he wished to meet her in person. She refused the offer, saying, "I don't date . . . . Papa doesn't know you, does he?" But forty-year-old Judson was persistent and arranged an interview with Eduardo Cansino, who granted him permission to escort Margarita in public. On her part, Margarita may have been a bit surprised to find that her suitor was more than twice her age, and had both a receding hairline and the start of a double chin. Undoubtedly, he represented a friendly father figure for the girl, who obviously was flattered by the attention he showered on her.

There are conflicting reports as to whether the senior Cansino approved or disapproved of the marriage that took place between Margarita and Judson on May 29, 1937. But for Margarita, it provided an expedient exit from parental control, and incidentally led upward on her road to stardom. If Judson had been a smooth promoter of imported automobiles and Texas schemes before he met and married Margarita, he became a holy man with a cause once he decided to direct the course of his wife's professional life. In 1942, when their five-year marriage had come to a bitter conclusion, Judson would look back to the halcyon days of 1937 and recall: "The more I thought of what could be done with a girl like Rita, the more intrigued I became with the idea of being a masculine fairy godmother to this little Cinderella . . . . In the beginning I never had any idea of making her into a great film star. I merely wanted my wife to be the smartest dressed woman present."

True to his words, Judson began the almost magical transformation of Margarita Cansino into Rita Hayworth. He placed her on a rigid diet so that she would slim down to a more attractive figure; he selected the proper clothing for her to wear (often at a price that neither member of the household could afford). Bringing all his salesmanship to the fore, he brought his wife to the attention of Columbia Pictures' crude, gruff, but exceedingly perspicacious businessman, Harry Cohn, perhaps the most outrageous of the Hollywood movie moguls. She was signed to a player's contract at $75 per week. Cohn scarcely noticed his newest addition to the performer's roster, but he did suggest that Margarita Americanize her name, which was done by shortening her Christian name to Rita, and adding a *y* to her mother's maiden name of Haworth. It was Columbia's hair stylist, Helen Hunt, who suggested to Judson that Rita's hair needed definite attention. A change in color from natural black to a soft but striking auburn was a relatively easy matter; to alter her hairline, which extended too far down on her forehead, was another matter. It required the painful process of electrolysis to achieve the transformation, an unpleasant, lengthy procedure which Rita, who had a low pain threshold, reluctantly agreed to endure. Once accomplished, and with her hair flowing down her neck, Rita looked quite different, far more in the tradition of the accepted brand of Hollywoodian sex symbol.

Judson was not about to leave Rita's career dangling with these "half" measures. He hired a press agent to insure that her name would appear in the proper gossip columns, and it became a family ritual that Rita and Judson would attend as many movie premieres and industry-frequented nightspots as time and funds permitted. To make certain that Rita shone on these occasions, Judson would craftily promote a new evening gown for his wife from a publicity-hungry dress designer or fashion house, and always insisted that it was worth the expense to have Rita's hair specially groomed before she appeared at these functions.

Meanwhile, Rita launched into the next phase of her movie career, as a Columbia programmer heroine and a loan-out favorite for other low-budget producing companies. Her first appearance as Rita Hayworth was in *Criminals of the Air* (Columbia, 1937), the first of her six screen appearances with Charles Quigley. In this B-picture, Rosalind Keith was the sob-sister girl reporter who falls in love with ace government operative Quigley. He has been assigned to check into the increase of alien smuggling over the Mexico-Texas border. Cast as Rita, Rita essayed a seductive dancer who plays up to Quigley south of the border. She executed one Spanish terpsichorean routine, and regarding this effort *Variety* noted: "[It] shows her off well, even if it's nothing fancy. Gets liberal footage on it, and she seems to have possibilities for straight talking roles." As a matter of fact, the entire cast, including crime-chief Russell Hicks, performed with appropriate gusto. The finale was a minor joy for action fans, what with a dogfight in the air and a motor-car strafing sequence.

Girls Can Play (Columbia, 1937) concerned ex-convict John Gallaudet, who owns a drugstore and sells watered liquor with phony labels. He promotes the legitimate aspects of his business enterprises by sponsoring a girls' softball team, which has Jacqueline Wells as team captain, and his moll, Rita, as the catcher. While Gallaudet is busy murdering his former partner, who has broken jail, and seeing to it that Rita does not reveal all she has learned, dumb but athletic-looking reporter Charles Quigley and detective Guinn Williams are hot on the trail of solving the case. Despite the shapely competition on the diamond, Rita did not go unappreciated by filmgoers.

In *The Game that Kills* (Columbia, 1937), Rita was still in her sports-film cycle, here portraying the daughter of hockey-team manager J. Farrell MacDonald, with Charles Quigley, her vis-à-vis, as an investigator who joins the Indians and becomes its star player while unraveling the mystery of the crooked gamblers who have bought their way into the club. *Paid to Dance* (Columbia, 1937) was a low-budget exposé of the dance-hall hostess racket, with government agent Don Terry sent to smash the criminal organization. He poses as a theatrical agent and opens up an office opposite the Paradise Dance Hall, owned by Arthur Loft. Despite its suggestive title, *Paid to Dance* was not lightened by musical interludes. Rather, it relentlessly pursued its titillating theme of innocent girls lured into signing away their innocence and sometimes their lives. Jacqueline Wells was a mite too pretty and hardly convincing as a government operative posing as a dime-a-dance girl. Likewise, the other gals decorating the establishment in question—including Rita as Betty Morgan—were just too attractive for the realities of the ambiance. When shown on television, *Paid to Dance* was intriguingly retitled *Hard to Hold*.

The Shadow (Columbia, 1937) was perhaps the closest Rita ever came to appearing in a seriallike story. Written by former New York press agent Milton Raison, the film was "a fast, lurid, absorbing" (*New York Herald-Tribune*) account of murder stalking a circus owned by heroine Rita. Curly-haired Charles Quigley was reinstated as Rita's leading man, here as the inquisitive press agent who determines to find the black-caped and hooded villain who stalks the big tent with a deadly blowgun and poisoned darts. The sawdust whodunit gave Rita one of her first full-dimensional, sympathetic acting assignments.

After five 1937 film appearances, Rita sailed into 1938 with *Who Killed Gail Preston?* (Columbia, 1938), the first of four screen roles that year. Moviegoers of 1938 (or late-night-television movie viewers) who may have trouble distinguishing between Rita's assorted but basically similar pictures in this period easily remember *Who Killed Gail Preston?* For one thing, it was set in a rather novel locale: a nightclub called the Swing Swing, in which the oncamera patrons were seated in "cells" and the stage entertainers were done up in satin-striped convict garb. For another, it is hard to forget Rita's Gail Preston, a character who is beloved by none and hated by many. When she dies early in the picture—which obviously removes Rita too quickly from the limelight—police investigator Don Terry must choose among the potential suspects. There is the club's master of ceremonies, John Gallaudet, who, like her chauffeur-bodyguard (Marc

Lawrence), had a romantic interest in the vocalist. The Swing Swing Club's owner, John Spacey, was well aware that Rita knew he was an illegally domiciled alien. Temperamental Rita had even had bandleader Robert Paige fired from the nightspot because he dared to date her younger sister (Wyn Cahoon) and continued to ignore her own attentions. Then there was Rita's manager (Arthur Loft), who had appropriated $60,000 from her bank account. Since there were so many likely candidates for murderer of this volatile meanie, it took all of the sixty-one allotted minutes to uncover the actual culprit, who had utilized a special contraption to bring about the torch singer's homicide. The only person missing from the final reenactment of the killing was, of course, Rita. Even perfectionist Edward Judson must have been placated by Rita's reviews for this one. "The vivid and attractive brunette Rita Hayworth gives a nice performance" (William Boehnel, *New York World-Telegram*). "Camera makes the most of voluptuous Rita Hayworth" (*Variety*).

If one happened to blink his eyes for too long a moment, he might entirely miss Rita's remaining contributions to *There's Always a Woman* (Columbia, 1938), one of the several Melvyn Douglas-Joan Blondell pictures of this period. Initially, within this imitation *Thin Man* entry, Rita was a girl in the typing pool of district attorney Thurston Hall. She had a trio of scenes as the friend of Blondell, the latter determined to beat her private investigator husband (Douglas) in solving a murder mystery. By the time of release, all that remained of Rita in *There's Always a Woman* was her familiar figure sitting with all the other secretaries, and one small bit where she informs the district attorney of an appointment's arrival. It is reputed that within this A-feature, Rita was also the stand-in for fourth-billed Frances Drake.

Rita trekked to Canada to co-star once again with Charles Quigley in Central Films' *Convicted*, released by Columbia in 1938. It was a nimble enough programmer exercise, but hardly worth the northward trip. When Edgar Edwards, on circumstantial evidence, is accused of murdering his two-timing sweetheart (Phyllis Clare), his dancer sister (Rita) follows a trail which leads to the Night Club King, run by slick and sadistic Marc Lawrence. Police detective Quigley fortuitously comes into the case, rounding up the killer and saving curvaceous Rita from an untimely end. Despite the technical deficiencies of this quickie, which militated against Rita's screen appearance, Wanda Hale (*New York Daily News*) could write that Rita was "a competent dancer who knows how to deliver lines and how to behave in the presence of the camera."

After Samuel Goldwyn's *Dead End* (United Artists, 1937) popularized movie studies of slum youths, Hollywood producers seemed to have an insatiable urge to churn out tales about juvenile delinquency. *Juvenile Court* (Columbia, 1938) brought the genre down to the B-picture level. Young public defender Paul Kelly is determined that murderer John Tyrrell receive a life sentence for his crimes. Tyrrell's sister (Rita) and younger brother (Frankie Darro) refuse to believe there is a killer in the family. Darro, in particular, is so distrustful of well-meaning Kelly and the law in general that he does everything possible to dissuade his punky comrades from participating in the Police Athletic League's program and from following a law-abiding path. As Marcia Adams, Rita was asked to exude understanding and modest charm, but to remain firmly in the background while the film focused on the slum kids of a large city.

The Renegade Ranger (RKO, 1938), which was also filmed for Central Films in Victoria, British Columbia, had been previously lensed as *Come on Danger* (RKO, 1933) with Tom Keene and Julie Haydon and would be remade again as *Come on Danger* (RKO, 1941) with Tim Holt and Frances Neal. Rita, who still despised horse operas, was cast as Judith Alvarez, the Mexican leader of ex-ranchers whose land had been stolen by the local tax collector (William Royle) and his cohorts. In the wrap-up at Royle's hacienda, the scoundrels, including the puppet sheriff (Neal Hart), are captured, with Rita being cleared of a murder charge and then romantically united with Texas Ranger captain George O'Brien. At the same time his pal (Tim Holt) was coupled with Cecilia Callejo, the daughter of Rita's lieutenant (Lucio Villegas). As a veteran of the Columbia programmer factory, Rita handled her untaxing assignment with relative ease.

Homicide Bureau (Columbia, 1939) was Rita's first release of the new year, but there was little to distinguish it from her prior double-bill program fodder. The underworld problem at hand was the illegal shipping of scrap metal to foreign munitions-makers. Bruce Cabot played the hard-fighting G-man hero assigned to clean up the racket, who finds himself aligned with police laboratory expert (!) Rita in routing the murderous gang led by Marc Lawrence and Norman Willis. *Variety* justifiably bit down hard on this untidy entry, whose only redeeming feature was its gun-blazing finale: "Hits new low in cycle of Columbia's crime wave opuses." Rita, looking charming in a smock, was distinctly miscast, however, when peering most seriously into a microscope for a ballistics study or arduously making identification slides and memos.

Just as MGM used its *Andy Hardy* and *Dr. Kildare* series as a testing ground for its new talent, so Columbia utilized its continuing properties for like reasons. In *The Lone Wolf Spy Hunt* (Columbia, 1939),* the first of the Warren William sleuth entries, the action was set in Washington, D.C., with the espionage theme occasionally taken serious, and at times almost satirized. Enemy agent Ralph Morgan abducts ex-jewel thief William, determined to make the now law-abider lift secret anti-aircraft plans from the War Department. For diversionary entertainment purposes there are three females in the caper. Virginia Weidler had a one-shot role as William's precocious eight-year-old daughter; Ida Lupino played the sen-

---

*A remake of the part-talkie *The Lone Wolf's Daughter* (Columbia, 1929), starring Bert Lytell, Gertrude Olmstead, Lilyan Tashman, and Florence Allen.

ator's daughter who has marriage to William constantly on her mind; and Rita was cast as slinky Karen, Morgan's accomplice and the would-be seducer of suave William. As this picture proved, increasingly accomplished Rita was nearing the end of her apprenticeship. In his *New York World-Telegram* review, critic William Boehnel editorialized about "stunning brunette Rita Hayworth, whom this department would like to see in a really good part for a change."

Special Inspector (Warwick-Syndicate, 1939) was also turned out in Canada for producer Kenneth J. Bishop, with Edgar Edwards again scripting and performing in the photoplay. When her brother is killed driving a truckload of furs from Canada to San Francisco, Patricia Lane (Rita) volunteers to help spy on the syndicate running the illegal operation. In the course of the brisk little yarn,* she finds herself in a variety of difficulties with the crooks, and not until the end do she and Charles Quigley (part of the U.S. government customs forces helping the Canadian police) realize they are not only in love, but also on the same side of the law.

All during this important fledgling period, Rita, prompted, soothed, reinforced, and sometimes annoyed by her husband Judson, continued to increase her following both in the industry and the public via the most obvious gambit—publicity. Now it was not a private public-relations person who bandied Rita's name, face, and figure in the proper publication circles, but Columbia's own publicity department, headed by Lou Smith. The studio's leading actress during this period was famed Jean Arthur. As garrulous and personable as she was onscreen, Arthur was taciturn, shy, and uncooperative when not facing the cameras. She thrived on personal privacy. As if to assuage themselves for the lost chances with Arthur, Smith and his staff readily agreed to Judson's continuous suggestions about promoting photographic, pliable, and potentially potent Rita. The gambit satisfied all parties concerned. Rita and Judson were pleased with the media coverage, while Smith and his crew could document for their studio employers just how successful (and pictures of Rita in a wide variety of poses were flooding all the publications) their efforts could be when they had a cooperative subject.

It was a story torn from a fan magazine how Rita came to be discovered by producer-director-scripter Howard Hawks, who was then preparing a new Columbia picture. One night while gorgeously attired Rita was making an appearance with Judson at the lush Trocadero Club in Hollywood, she was spotted by Hawks, who thought she might be just the person for the role of the sensual Latin man-chaser Judy MacPherson in *Plane Number 4*. Columbia executives approved of Hawks's choice, since Rita's secondary part was not crucial to the box-office success of the A-picture in question.

Hawks had a penchant for helming air dramas, ranging from *The Air*

*The sixty-five-minute programmer was chopped to sixty minutes for Canadian-English release, and to fifty-three minutes for most playdates in the United States.

Circus (Fox, 1928) to *The Dawn Patrol* (First National, 1930) to *Ceiling Zero* (Warner Bros., 1936). His new aerial actioner was finally titled the ominous *Only Angels Have Wings* (Columbia, 1939). Because the pioneer phase of the plane industry was already a part of America's past, Hawks set the story in the Latin American banana port of Barranca, supposedly within the boundaries of Ecuador. Andrew Sarris, writing about "The World of Howard Hawks" for *Films and Filming* in 1962, suggested that *Only Angels Have Wings* "is the most romantic film of Hawk's career, and its pessimistic mood was the director's last gesture to the spirit of the Thirties reflected in the doomed cinema of Renoir and Carné." Sarris also noted, "once again the themes of responsibility and expiation are applied to men striving to perform the impossible for purely gratuitous reasons."

Only Angels Have Wings is structured on a pervading theme of tenseness. Cary Grant's Geoff Carter is in charge of the rickety airfield owned by Dutchman Sig Rumann, who is hoping to obtain a government franchise to fly mail. The dangers of the surrounding mountain peaks and the ever-present fog are responsible for the high mortality rate among Grant's overworked crew. The strain of the situation has taken its toll on Grant. Onto the scene pops American vaudeville entertainer Jean Arthur, stranded between engagements. Her Bonnie Lee is very much in the tradition of the wisecracking tart, but with an added dimension. The girl is on a perpetual emotional jag approaching hysteria. When woman-embittered Grant learns that part of Arthur's allergy to flying is related to her trapeze-artist father's death under the big top (he refused to use a net), a mutual bond develops between the two, enhanced by their mutual sympathy for Grant's crony, burly Thomas Mitchell, who is slowly going blind but refuses to abandon his flying profession.

Just to stir up the emotional mix of *Only Angels Have Wings* to a realistically improbable, but dramatically exciting, peak, two more characters appear on the scene. One of them is Richard Barthelmess, the cowardly pilot who had parachuted out of a disabled plane, leaving Mitchell's younger brother to die in the fiery crash. The other is Barthelmess's man-teasing wife, who, it develops, has been the temptress responsible for souring Grant on the opposite sex.

Rita's spectacular entrance in the film was enough in itself to draw gasps from filmgoers of the day and to insure that critics and patrons alike would not forget the Columbia contract player. The locale is a rowdy, man-filled bar. Suddenly the camera pans to the entrance of a high-heel-clad woman descending a staircase. Before the viewer is shown the woman's face, the film cuts to the reaction of the boisterous pub clientele, who are taken aback by the evident beauty of this provocative creature. Then the footage shifts back to the obviously predatory female strutting down upon her latest cache of victims. Then the viewer is introduced eye to eye to

Rita, the faithless wife of Barthelmess, who has been hired to work at Grant's airfield.

The outcome of *Only Angels Have Wings* is predictable to any movie-goer who has seen such entries as *Flight from Glory* (RKO, 1937) and *Test Pilot* (MGM, 1938). Grant and Arthur find a redeeming faith in one another which enables them to cope with reality—pressured or otherwise. Barthelmess proves he is not a coward. Mitchell meets a brave death in the climax. And as for Rita, she finds the courage and inspiration to remain true to a man (Barthelmess).

It was a rare soul who did not agree with *Variety* that "every facet of *Only Angels Have Wings* is big league," and that it is a "tough, terrifying melodrama . . ." (Howard Barnes, *New York Herald-Tribune*). As for Rita, *Variety's* aisle-sitter said it all: "She's a good-looking girl with an ahvoom chassis."*

Only Angels Have Wings was the turning point in Rita's movie career. Her contract option was about due, and the Columbia crowd could not decide whether to raise her weekly salary from $250 to $300, or to browbeat her into remaining at the same pay scale. According to Bob Thomas in *King Cohn* (1967), it was Rita's agents at the time, Morris Small and George Chasin, who provided a reasonable alternative, take the $50 weekly in question and use it for hiring a drama coach, Grace Fogeler, for Rita. All parties concerned were amenable to the compromise, and Rita remained with Columbia.

Obviously Harry Cohn was in no rush to push Rita into the major league, for her first two 1940 releases were merely programmers. *Music in My Heart* (Columbia, 1940) was a vehicle to showcase Tony Martin, who had left Twentieth Century-Fox where Don Ameche was ruling the musical-comedy roost. Perhaps the prime asset to this B-feature was its unpretentious qualities, which were present in the plot, the production values, and throughout most of the musical interludes. Because his family once forgot to take out citizenship papers, Broadway hopeful Martin is about to be deported. To sweeten his departure, the producers of the New York show in which he is understudying arrange for him to go on instead of the lead. Later he is rushing by taxi to board the ship which will carry him back to Europe, but his cab collides with a taxi whose passenger is none other than Rita. Martin misses his transatlantic passage, but he does commence a romance with tenement girl Rita, the latter dodging amorously inclined newspaper publisher Alan Mowbray. The plot ploy is solved with a script contrivance and all ends happily.† Martin crooned five tunes, including a finale number backed by Andre Kostelanetz and his Orchestra,

---

*For "Lux Radio Theatre," Cary Grant, Jean Arthur, Thomas Mitchell, Richard Barthelmess, and Rita repeated their *Only Angels Have Wings* assignments on May 29, 1939.

† Eccentric millionaire Mowbray takes pity on Martin, his rival for Rita's affections. He adopts the stage tenor!

while Rita had one rather uninspired dance sequence, which was marred by bad photography and abrupt editing. As was often the case, the most engaging elements of the proceedings were the comedy-relief players, including George Tobias as one of the last of the Romanoffs, who cooks in a restaurant where customers never pay, and Eric Blore as a befuddled, expressive butler.

Blondie on a Budget (Columbia, 1940) was the fourth of what would prove to be a twenty-eight-episode series starring Penny Singleton in the title role of a dilemma-prone housewife and Arthur Lake as her fumbling, trouble-addicted spouse, Dagwood P. Bumstead. Like most studio budget series, *Blondie* was a feasible testing ground for new contract performers, and Rita, as in *The Lone Wolf Spy Hunt*, found herself doing yeoman work in a thankless supporting role. In this domestic installment, which featured a drunk scene with Daisy the pooch, it seems the Bumsteads are undecided just how to spend a $200 bonus. Lake wants a trout-fishing-club membership, while Singleton favors a "chubby" fur coat for herself. Before the seventy-three minutes are up, Singleton has her coat, while Lake, hopefully, has profited from the repercussions of irritating his wife's jealous nature. Rita was drawn into the fracas as one of Lake's former sweethearts, whose mere presence is sufficient to make Singleton green with envy.

When George Cukor was preparing a new Joan Crawford vehicle at Metro-Goldwyn-Mayer, he recalled Rita, whom he had tested for the part of Katharine Hepburn's sister in *Holiday* (Columbia, 1938). "She was too young for that part, but I thought her attractive and gifted," Cukor would later remember.* He requested Columbia to loan Rita for a smallish but telling assignment in *Susan and God* (MGM, 1940)† The film revolved about the thoughtless chaos created by an indulgent Long Island socialite (Crawford) who returns from Europe imbued with a mindless do-goodism philosophy that she seeks to impose upon her neglected husband (Fredric March), her rejected daughter (Rita Quigley), and any of the hedonistic adults who happen to populate the Crawford-March estate at the moment.

As actress Leonora Stubbs, Rita appeared as the much younger spouse of aging playboy Nigel Bruce. When introduced to the new bride, "guileless" hostess Crawford exudes a greeting in a subconsciously unctuous manner, "Why, you're too, too lovely, my dear. And Hutchie [Bruce] was such a bachelor, too. But I can quite see how you did it. Hutchie, she's marvelous!" Before long, domineering, proselytizing Crawford has not only smashed Rita's budding adulterous affair with her ex-stage partner (John Carroll), but she has nearly convinced an unwilling Bruce to leave his frisky wife. Rita has a particularly delicious moment in *Susan and God* in which she is interrupted just as she launches into an undulating rumba. It

*Doris Nolan eventually assumed the role.
†The Rachel Crowthers drama, starring Gertrude Lawrence, opened on Broadway at the Plymouth Theatre on October 7, 1937, for a 288-performance run.

was a clear foreshadowing of the unbridled sensuality that would typify Rita Hayworth, the 1940s celluloid sex goddess incarnate.

Rita returned to the home lot and was rewarded—in a very minor way—by being cast with leading man Brian Aherne in *The Lady in Question* (Columbia, 1940). It was a remake of the French film *Gribouille* (1938), which starred Raimu and Michele Morgan, and had enjoyed some popularity during its American release in 1939 under the title *Heart of Paris*. Unfortunately, despite the energies of director Charles Vidor and a very game cast, the new edition did not recapture the charms of the original Gallic story. Above all, this new version was hampered unduly by the very Anglo-American players involved.

Benign, middle-aged bicycle-shop owner Aherne (with drooping eyebrows and a walrus-sized moustache) is pleased to be selected to serve on a jury. The case involves Natalie Roguin (Rita), accused of murdering her lover. Frenchman Aherne firmly believes in her innocence, and he persuades the other jurors to vote for an acquittal. Later the good soul gives the worldly girl a position in his shop, without informing his wife (Irene Rich) of her background. But his astrology-student son (Glenn Ford), who had been at the trial, recognizes Rita as the guillotine-bound defendant, and is duly shocked. However, in time he falls in love with her, just as Rich and Ford's dancer sister (Evelyn Keyes) grow to resent her presence. Aherne later becomes converted to the theory of Rita's guilt and visits the chief justice who presided at the trial. The shop owner is advised that new evidence clearly confirms Rita's innocence. Aherne returns home in time to offer his blessings to the pending marriage of Rita and Ford, who had planned to elope.

Columbia gave this arty entry little publicity and, despite a few kind reviews, it failed to generate much boxoffice interest. It did, however, demonstrate the growing prowess of Rita as a solid performer who could handle dialog with relative ease. The critics substantiated this viewpoint. "[She] reveals a winsome personality and a talent which should soon bring her recognition as one of Hollywood's more capable younger players" (Thomas M. Pryor, *New York Times*). "Miss Hayworth is, of course, stunning as the girl and her acting is quite good" *(New York World-Telegram).*

When particular Jean Arthur, the queen of the lot, rejected *Before I Die,* the film project that marked Ben Hecht's return to filmmaking, Rita was cast in the vacated female-lead role. With its sparse sets and relatively small cast, the picture—retitled *Angels over Broadway* (Columbia, 1940)—relied on the ingenuity of producer-scripter Hecht and cameraman Lee Garmes, each of whom served as co-director, to guide the elongated (eighty-minute) morality fable to its conclusion. The end-product was not very satisfying. "Picture stutters and sputters too often to carefully etch human beings, with result that it develops into an over-dramatic stage play transformed to celluloid."

This O. Henry-like fable is spun out during the course of a single rainy night in New York, and is replete with long talk-fests and few action moments. At the Aladdin Cafe on Broadway, an impoverished clerk (John Qualen) makes it known that unless he can obtain a fast $3,000 to cover the sum he "borrowed" from his firm for his spendthrift wife, he will kill himself. Thomas Mitchell, as the boozing one-time Pulitzer Prize playwright who has had three stage flops in a row and has lost his wife, overhears Qualen and offers to help. Soon out-of-work Rita (garbed in an attractive evening gown and sporty topcoat) and ex-bellboy-turned-con-artist Douglas Fairbanks, Jr.,* are dragged into Mitchell's improvised goodwill scheme. The plan is to have cardsharp Fairbanks engineer a plum poker game in his sleazy hotel where Qualen, the intended victim, can make a quick killing and then vanish before the thugs involved realize that they have been fleeced.

The higher-brow critics found some merits in *Angels over Broadway*. Theodore Strauss (*New York Times*) rated the picture "a melodramatic fantasy that is mordant, tender and quixotic, shot with ironic humor." Robert W. Dana (*New York Herald-Tribune*) approved of the "shaded, mysterious touch with which it cloaks its plot, so that the filmgoer leaves the theater with a head full of conjecture about the past and the future of its characters." Accustomed scene-stealer Mitchell garnered most of the acting limelight within the picture, but Rita's efforts did not go unappreciated. Strauss of the *Times* commented that she "responded sensitively to the demands of the script." Dana in the *Herald-Tribune* added that her performance here "is far better than anything she has ever done before." Clearly Rita's long tutorial sessions with her drama coach were paying dividends.

As the publicity campaign accelerated and intensified, and as her screen appearances verified, Rita was fast becoming one of the early-1940s most sought after and appreciated celluloid beauties. One of Rita's industry "rivals" was Warner Bros.' "oomph" girl, Ann Sheridan, who had served a very long apprenticeship both at Paramount and at her new home lot in the 1930s before success came her way. Now Sheridan was feuding with her studio bosses, demanding better roles to suit her range of acting talents. During one of her rebellious periods, she rejected, or was bypassed for, *The Strawberry Blonde* (Warner Bros., 1941).† Rita was hastily borrowed from Columbia to perform the title role in this bit of turn-of-the-century Americana, which had the play's small-town setting altered to New York. Ironically, it was in this picture that Rita's ever-changing hair color-

*The actor also functioned as associate producer on the film.

†The picture derived from James Hagen's *One Sunday Afternoon*, which opened at the Little Theatre on February 15, 1933, for a 105-performance Broadway run, with Lloyd Nolan and Francesca Bruning starred. The property was transferred to the screen with Gary Cooper. Frances Fuller, and Fay Wray featured in the 1933 Paramount release. The third picturization of Hagen's play would be *One Sunday Afternoon* (Warner Bros., 1948), with Dennis Morgan, Janis Paige, and Dorothy Malone.

ing emerged a luscious reddish hue, but *The Strawberry Blonde* was lensed in black-and-white and filmgoers could little appreciate the radiant difference it made in Rita's appearance.

Director Raoul Walsh wisely decided not to allow *The Strawberry Blonde* to marinate in nostalgia, Instead, the 1890s and 1900s serve as a wistful setting for a thin story that is sparked by an enthusiastic cast and marshaled by Walsh's firm hand into a satisfying homogeneous whole. One Sunday afternoon, correspondence-school dentist James Cagney is called into his home-office for an emergency case. The howling patient with a murderous toothache turns out to be none other than Hugo Barnstead (Jack Carson), an unscrupulous building contractor who had caused Cagney so much hardship in the past. As the doctor debates whether or not to give his noisy visitor an overdose of gas, the viewer is treated to a flashback which explains the present situation. It seems that Cagney, the son of a hearty street-cleaner (Alan Hale), has been urged by acquaintance Carson to join him on a double date. Selfish Carson arranges the privilege of escorting the neighborhood beauty (Rita) on the picnic outing, while Cagney is "stuck" with the girl's best friend (Olivia de Havilland). When grasping Rita later weds the promising Carson, envious Cagney, on the rebound, marries de Havilland. Patronizing Rita persuades Carson to give his "friend" a post in his construction firm, which Carson does, but he also insures that his "pal" is made the scapegoat for the company's corrupt schemes. Cagney is imprisoned for five years. When released he sets up a new life with Olivia, raising a family, and becoming a respected neighborhood dentist. The tale returns to the present. Cagney realizes that Carson is too worthless a foe to kill. As for Rita, she is still glamorously beautiful and sensually desirable but has turned into a nagging shrew. Cagney suddenly and laughingly realizes he has had the best breaks after all and that de Havilland is really the far better woman.

Cagney, not far away from his Academy Award-winning performance in *Yankee Doodle Dandy* (Warner Bros., 1942), was at his infectious best in *The Strawberry Blonde*, pugnacious, proud, and charming as he resourcefully portrays the sucker who emerges the champ. In contrast to second-billed de Havilland's quiet performance, Rita's appearance as the gold-digging red-haired dream, convinced quite a few, including Bosley Crowther (*New York Times*), that she was "a classic flirt." Likewise, the *New York World-Telegram* enthused, "When it comes to oomph Miss Hayworth possesses an 18-karat variety and she certainly tosses it around to good advantage here even in the pompadour hair-dos, big hats and high-necked dresses of the 1900s." Perhaps the most valuable lesson learned from Rita's work in *The Strawberry Blonde* was that she was a product of her on-screen ambiance. If she were given showcasing roles, she could rise to meet—if not overwhelm—the challenge. This fact set the tone for her peak screen period in the 1940s.

Rita remained on loan-out for the less than infectious comedy *Affection-*

ately Yours (Warner Bros., 1941), first intended for Bette Davis, and then partially reshaped to suit the particular charisma of Merle Oberon. Rita had essayed the "other woman" before onscreen, but never had she dabbled in screwball comedy. With Dennis Morgan of the twinkling eyes and broad grin as the third part of the love triangle, it was no wonder that this would-be madcap caprice emerged an entertainment dud.* It was all so pat and flat. Foreign correspondent Morgan is happily stationed in Lisbon, Portugal, enjoying the companionship of newswoman Rita and other luscious dolls. He persistently informs them that if only he were not married (to Oberon) he would wed the girl-of-the-moment in an instant. Imagine the hilarious predicament when Morgan is advised that Oberon is suing for a divorce and that she intends, perhaps, to wed well-to-do-chump Ralph Bellamy. Morgan suddenly realizes how much he will miss Oberon and hastily returns Stateside to rewoo his wife. But there are three parties who would like Morgan permanently split from Oberon: Rita, Morgan's exasperated new editor (James Gleason), who wants his star reporter to work abroad and not curl up at the American hearth of Oberon, and hayseed Bellamy. At least Hattie McDaniel and Butterfly McQueen, in their stereotyped assignments as outspoken black domestics, provided a few well-needed, if tired, laughs.

Nineteen years after the popular Rudolph Valentino version of *Blood and Sand* (Paramount, 1922), Twentieth Century-Fox decided to produce a color remake, this time starring Tyrone Power as the fame-and-love-thirsty matador, Juan Gallardo. Contract lovely Linda Darnell was assigned to play Power's dark-haired young wife, Carmen, while blonde Carole Landis was slated to play the red-haired temptress, Doña Sol. The latter, feuding with her studio at the time, refused to dye her hair, so the part was up for grabs. Rita seemed a logical choice, what with her Spanish background and her rising fame as a sultry screen figure—so she was borrowed at a salary fee five times her weekly Columbia payroll figure. Six years after she had been cast aside by Fox, she returned in glory. Her vow to make her ex-bosses eat their words of rejection had finally come true.

While this new version of Vicente Blasco Ibáñez's novel did not live up to its screen predecessor in box-office popularity, it created its own aura of fame, largely through director Rouben Mamoulian's outstanding comprehension and mastery of filmatic color composition. The 124-minute feature emerged not so much as a dramatic, emotional adventure, but as a visual treat for the eye with an array of exquisite picture-postcard settings.

Mamoulian utilized the garish hues of the three-color Technicolor process to sharp advantage throughout the costume picture. Crimson, for example, was reintroduced constantly in *Blood and Sand* as a changing

---

*Bosley Crowther (*New York Times*) said of the picture, "[It is a] pitiful imitation of frivolity more dull than lead—and heavier." Howard Barnes (*New York Herald-Tribune*) ranked it for setting "a record in synthetic showmanship."

representation: of glory (the matador's outfit), of lust (Rita's blood-red painted lips and her red evening gown in the final sequences), and of death (blood).

There is no question that the new *Blood and Sand* lost a considerable amount of the impact of the author's tale of the cruelty of the bullfighting sport, in which one day a matador is on top of his profession and the next, either supplanted by a more exciting rival or dead in the ring and quickly forgotten by the fickle crowd. However, the Fox rendition did convey Blasco Ibáñez's intended sense of the idealized glory that leads a man like Gallardo to devote his life's work to succeeding as a lustrous matador. Interspersed in the midst of his documented pursuit of career success, the film depicts the see-sawing personal struggle of the "hero," who must decide whether to remain devoted to his childlike wife (Darnell) or submit to his unquenching attraction to the vampiric femme fatale, Doña Sol (Rita).

In her low-cut gowns, cunning Rita slithers across the brocaded tapestry of *Blood and Sand* with a deliberately measured abandon that makes her protrayal a cinematic milestone of depicted temptation. Whether enticing the enamored Power with a quick smile from her ruby red lips, offering a caressing turn of her voice while serenading him on her self-played guitar, or cruelly laughing at Darnell's pitiful plea to return Power to her, reckless Rita exudes an irresistible venom which thrust her into the major leagues of screen vamping. It was almost an understatement for Robert W. Dana (*New York Herald-Tribune*) to conclude, "[She] is a devastating female menace, lovely and cruel . . ." As Rita's Doña Sol goes off with the latest matador champion (Anthony Quinn), unmindful of Power's death in the ring, one fully appreciates the wryness of an observation made earlier on the film by the effete journalist Laird Cregar, who says of her, "she is death in the evening."

After three films away from the Gower Street lot, Rita returned to home base for a musical comedy, *You'll Never Get Rich* (Columbia, 1941). It was persistently typical of Hollywood executives to ignore a performer's basic talents in the mad search to transform the person into a totally new screen persona. Rita was no exception. She had hardly turned a dance step on-screen since her earliest Fox days,* and filmgoers generally knew her only as the veteran of scores of forgettable B-films and the "other woman" of major productions. Thus, when Fred Astaire was contracted for a Columbia picture and the studio selected Rita as his new co-star, moviegoers waited with great anticipation to view the "new" Rita.

Astaire had not fared too well since he and his oncamera dance partner, Ginger Rogers, had gone their separate professional paths. He had teamed with Eleanor Powell in *Broadway Melody of 1940* (MGM, 1940) and with

---

*When her role demanded it, Rita had on occasion broken into dance, as in *Susan and God* or her erotic dance bit in *Blood and Sand*, whereby she weaves her destructive spell over an agog Power. But none of these screen moments was of the typical song-and-dance variety.

Paulette Goddard in *Second Chorus* (Paramount, 1940), but the results were less than spectacular. Initially Astaire was apprehensive about being paired with Rita. He was nearly twenty years her senior,* she was almost his height,† and he was a perfectionist. However, Columbia's Harry Cohn persuaded the dancing star to take the role. Cole Porter was hired to contribute the songs, Rita was placed under the training of choreographer Robert Alton, and for a Columbia picture, the production values were of considerable merit.

After completing *You'll Never Get Rich*, the demanding Astaire had an entirely different attitude towards Rita. He would later admit: "She learned steps faster than anyone I've ever known. I'd show her a routine before lunch. She'd be back right after lunch and have it down to perfection. She apparently figured it out in her mind while she was eating."

Creating Rita's performance for *You'll Never Get Rich* may not have been as smooth sailing as Astaire would like to recall, but moviegoers of the day were entranced with Rita's newest screen image. Herein she was cast, for a change, as a very honorable young lady, displaying a litheness of characterization and movement. It little mattered—even if the general public had been aware of the deception—that her onscreen singing voice was supplied by the offcamera Nan Wynn. What did count was that Rita radiated an infectious enthusiasm, combined with her pervading grace and consistently breathtaking beauty. The *Dallas Morning News* reviewer's bemused and entranced feeling would be echoed by the general public: "Miss Hayworth is a blitz, a bombshell, and a wow."

The plot for *You'll Never Get Rich* is a slight affair at best, and outwardly the second part of the film too closely resembles an Abbott and Costello service comedy. To help his woman-chasing producer (Robert Benchley) maintain a shaky marriage, Broadway dance director Astaire pretends that a bracelet Benchley purchased for showgirl Rita is actually his gift for the chorine. Benchley is taken off the domestic hook, but Astaire finds himself confronting a romantically inclined Rita, who takes his pretense as real. To escape her attentions, bachelor Astaire joins the army (recall the chorus girls' sendoff for their ex-boss at Grand Central Station?), only to find himself stationed as a private at Camp Weston, with colonel's daughter Rita bivouacking at her aunt's (Marjorie Gateson) nearby farm. Later, Astaire reluctantly agrees to direct the camp show, with Rita as his leading lady. Their mutual distrust turns to love, and in the finale they are wed.

There is a rich potpourri of dance and song blended into *You'll Never Get Rich*. While in jail for having gone AWOL, nimble-footed Astaire performs an amazing gymnastic dance to the "Boogie Woogie Barcarolle" backed by the vocals of a black quartet (The Four Tones). Rita and Astaire engage in the ballroom rhythms of "Dream Dancing," the jazzier "Wedding Cake-

---

*Some thirty years before, Astaire and Rita's father had shared the same vaudeville bills.
† Rita was provided with very low heeled shoes.

238

walk," and others. In all her light-footed scenes, Rita seems to float through the routines, her lustrous red hair flowing in the wind of her movements, and her countenance effervescent with delight.

It was little wonder, what with the screen exposure provided by her four 1941 releases, that Rita climbed to second spot in a poll tabulation of United States exhibitors conducted by *Motion Picture Herald* and *Fame* publications to select the Stars of Tomorrow. (MGM's Laraine Day was in number-one spot.) Crowning Rita's lofty status as a very hot screen property was her appearance in the August 11, 1941, issue of *Life* magazine. On the publication's cover she was unglamorously shown munching a hamburger, but the inside feature story contained a Robert Landry photograph of a luscious Rita clad in a tight-fitting black filmy negligee kneeling on a satin-sheeted prop bed. The shot has become a cheesecake classic. The almost superfluous accompanying text proclaimed Rita's future: "This sultry young lady is developing rapidly from an ornamental but small-time starlet into a big-time actress."

When *You'll Never Get Rich* debuted in New York at the Radio City Music Hall on October 23, 1941, Rita was on hand for the festivities. Harry Cohn now considered her among the most valuable of his female contract players and had the publicity department go all out for the event.* Rita was asked to tour Manhattan accompanied by a member of each branch of the armed forces. The gimmick received tremendous press coverage.

Rita was then announced for a variety of projects for the 1942 film season, including *Holiday Inn* (Paramount, 1942), *My Sister Eileen* (Columbia, 1942), and *She Knew All the Answers* (Columbia, 1942), but for one reason or another she was replaced, respectively, by Marjorie Reynolds, Janet Blair, and Joan Bennett. Instead, she returned to Twentieth Century-Fox for two films and then back at Columbia starred with Fred Astaire in another musical.

When Alice Faye rejected *My Gal Sal* (Twentieth Century-Fox, 1942) Rita was substituted. The color musical purported to be a song-and-dance biography of composer Paul Dresser (1857-1911), with a screenplay that claimed to be derived from the songwriter's story as recollected by his real-life brother, novelist Theodore Dreiser. But there was little resemblance between the actual 300-pound, girl-chasing tunesmith and leading man Victor Mature, or in the substance of his "life" as shown onscreen.

But as diversionary entertainment, *My Gal Sal* was smashing. It had something for nearly everyone. For women filmgoers there was Mature, labeled as that "beautiful hunk of man." For the male contingent, there was bustled Rita, who was, in the words of Wanda Hale (*New York Daily News*), "nothing less than sensational. She's a soldier's or sailor's

*The distaff contract roster at the time included Jean Arthur, Joan Bennett, Janet Blair, Joan Blondell, Virginia Bruce, Kay Harris, Rochelle Hudson, Evelyn Keyes, Patti McCarty, Eileen O'Hearn, Penny Singleton, Claire Trevor, and Loretta Young.

dream in color. . . . In a word, she's a wow." Twentieth Century-Fox had a penchant for Tin Pan Alley musicals, and director Irving Cummings helmed the film in the best of this gaudy tradition.

The picture loosely traces Mature's emergence from the Indiana small-town world into the excitement of New York living. He had run away from home when his father suggested he become a preacher. He joins an itinerant medicine show, where he first encounters the scorning Rita, who mocks his hickish clothes. He swears she will sing a different tune when he becomes rich and famous. He enjoys an abortive romance with sweet, blonde Carole Landis, then makes his way eastward to Manhattan, where the banjo-and-piano-playing songwriter is aided by one-time music publisher James Gleason. Meantime, Mature and musical-comedy performer Rita cross paths again. In true movie tradition he alternately is attached to and repulsed by the enchanting but frivolous onscreen Rita. When she appears bent on wedding her manager-beau (John Sutton) Mature and she squabble and he turns to an exotic countess (Mona Maris). However, by the finish, the screen leads are joyfully reunited. No wonder that within the picture, Mature's composer creates the title melody, "My Gal Sal," to describe his amore: "They call her frivolous Sal. A peculiar sort of a gal."

As the top-billed performer in *My Gal Sal*, there was no question about Rita holding forth stage front and center. She is gorgeously displayed in a variety of music-hall production numbers including "Come Tell Me What's Your Answer, Yes or No," "On the Banks of the Wabash," "Mr. Volunteer (You Don't Belong to the Regulars, You're Just a Volunteer)," and the finale reprise of "My Gal Sal."* The combination of Hermes Pan's choreography, Gwen Wakeling's period costumes, and Ernest Palmer's tinted camerawork provided Rita with a devastating showcase. "She is divine, she is distracting, she is altogether charming in the modish, lavish ensembles of the not-so-long-ago period. She sings prettily. She dances gracefully" (Archer Winsten, *New York Post*).

Rita remained at Darryl F. Zanuck's studio for *Tales of Manhattan* (Twentieth Century-Fox, 1942). Director Julien Duvivier, attempting to give the moviegoer something different,† created a five-ring circus with each of the segments garnished with an intriguing selection of stars.‡ Despite the marquee value of the assembled cast, the picture never measured up to a satisfying whole, nor were the individual parts very believable. The thin plot-thread holding the segments together was the fate of a gentleman's dress suit as it passed from one person to another. In story

*Interestingly, Fox's publicity made no attempt to hide the fact that Nan Wynn provided Rita's soundtrack singing voice.

†*If I Had a Million* (Paramount, 1932) had offered a similar gimmick.

‡John T. McManus (*PM*) wrote, "It has more big names than Heinz has pickles; and each gives generously of his vaunted best." One of the co-stars was Ginger Rogers, whose mother's sister was married to Rita's mother's brother (performer Vinton Haworth).

number one, a charming matinee idol (Charles Boyer) has a passion for lovely Rita, the chameleonish wife of staid, jealous Thomas Mitchell. Rita photographed well but generated little conviction to her anemic, tailor-made part.

You Were Never Lovelier (Columbia, 1942) was packaged in color to exploit the favorable past public response to Rita and Fred Astaire.* In the new vehicle, Jerome Kern and Johnny Mercer supplied the songs, with William A. Seiter directing. The production values were a little more elaborate and the ambiance a touch more exotic. Argentine hotel tycoon Adolphe Menjou insists that his two younger daughters (Leslie Brooks and Adele Mara) cannot marry till their stubborn older sister (Rita) is wed. Lovely but bored Rita is just not interested in matrimony till her imaginative father strikes her romantic chord. He sends her flowers and love notes, signed by an unknown admirer. Chance causes Rita to assume that unemployed, American playboy-dancer (Astaire) is the man in question, a situation which vain Menjou finds both irritating and embarrassing, but expedient.

For the South American beat there was Xavier Cugat and his Orchestra, with vocalist Lina Romay performing "Chiu Chiu." Most of the emphasis, however, quite naturally was on Astaire's musical courtship of the reluctant, old-fashioned Rita. Once again Nan Wynn supplied Rita's soundtrack vocals, while an unknown double was utilized to bolster Rita's duet footwork (with Astaire) of the elaborately tricky "Shorty George." As the doubtful senorita of Buenos Aires, generally clad in diaphanous evening wear,† tantalizing, nimble-footed Rita was a sensation. She was worth every bit of her new salary rate at the home studio, which by the mid-1940s would escalate to $6,500 weekly. She had become Columbia's biggest box-office attraction.

As might be expected, Rita's rapidly advancing movie career meant that she had a decreasing need for reliance on her husband's professional advice. She soon realized that one of the few areas of mutual interest was their fourteen-room Westwood home, which they had purchased in 1941. By the time of filming *My Gal Sal*, Rita realized that she was no longer in love with Judson, and she indulged in an imprudent romance with co-star Victor Mature that would eventually terminate when he joined the Coast Guard.

Harry Cohn and the Columbia executives fostered this domestic separation, believing that the less influence Edward Judson had on their prize property, the better. In September 1942, Rita filed for divorce from Judson, with the decree becoming official on September 7, 1943. Regarding this marriage dissolution, Rita would later admit, "I married him for love, but

*On Andre Kostelanetz's CBS radio show on July 12, 1942, Rita and Astaire did a half-hour of patter talk to provide listeners with a preview of the forthcoming *You Were Never Lovelier*.
†In the "Shorty George" number she wore form-revealing shorts.

241

he married me for an investment. . . . I got a divorce to be myself again." On another occasion, she explained more fully: "From the first he told me I couldn't do anything for myself. 'You're such a child,' he'd say. I didn't have any fun those five years we were married. I was never permitted to make any decisions. He robbed everything of excitement. He was husband-nursemaid."

Meantime, the Columbia hierarchy was busy at work hushing up a potentially scandalous divorce situation. It seemed that in February 1942, when Rita and Mature had been seeing one another frequently, she had signed an agreement to pay Judson the sum of $12,000, part of the inducement that he would "not imply, directly or indirectly, that she had committed an offense involving moral turpitude under federal, state or local laws, or that she had conducted herself in any manner which would cause her to be held in scorn, or which would damage her career." After making four monthly payments of $500 each, Rita stopped payment, which led to a lawsuit in November 1943. Columbia finally had to make a settlement with Judson, some say to the tune of $30,000, to insure his future silence. In turn, Rita was informed that in the future she must be far more discreet and realize the obligations attached to being a full-fledged movie star.

Before the war and Harry Cohn brought an end to Rita's attachment to Mature, she met Orson Welles at a dinner party given by Joseph Cotten. The boy genius of show business had been brought to Hollywood by RKO in 1940 on a fabulous contractual agreement. The production and various ramifications of *Citizen Kane* (RKO, 1941), *The Magnificent Ambersons* (RKO, 1942), and *Journey into Fear* (RKO, 1943) had soured RKO on Welles, and he was now biding his time between radio broadcasts and other assorted entertainment ventures by performing his magic acts for USO shows. The pre-bulbous, twenty-eight-year-old Welles was as magnetically drawn to Rita's beauty as she was to his renowned intellect.* The "enfant terrible" persuaded his new conquest to participate in his sleight-of-hand show by serving as the girl who is sawed in half.† Rita and Welles were married on September 7, 1943—the same day her divorce became final—in a civil ceremony at the Bay City Building in Santa Monica, California.

Like other celebrated screen beauties (Lana Turner, Ava Gardner, Marilyn Monroe) over the years, uneducated Rita was tremendously impressed by the intellectual reputation of her new spouse, and she attempted to remold herself by a tedious process of accelerated education supervised by Welles. She dearly wanted to please her quixotic, iconoclas-

---

*He had been previously married to Virginia Nicholson (1934-40), by whom he had a son, Christopher. One of Welles's more celebrated romances in the pre-Rita period was actress Dolores Del Rio.

†Mature, who might be termed a sore loser, is said to have quipped, "A hell of a way to woo a girl."

tic, and very broke husband, but it was a tough, near-impossible challenge, as Rita was to discover in the following years.

Rita's only 1943 film appearance was in special footage shot for *Show Business at War*, a Twentieth Century-Fox short subject for *The March of Time* series. Other celebrities guesting in the entry were Ethel Barrymore, Jack Benny, Errol Flynn, Kay Francis, Myrna Loy, Ginger Rogers, Lana Turner, Orson Welles, and Colonel Darryl F. Zanuck.

Rita, prompted by her new husband's suggestions, rejected a role in *Once Upon a Time* (Columbia, 1944) in which she would have played opposite Cary Grant,* but did agree to reunite with director Charles Vidor for *Cover Girl* (Columbia, 1944). It is perhaps Rita's best-remembered musical feature. Gene Kelly was borrowed from MGM to be Rita's dancing partner in this color tribute to luscious magazine mannequins. Balancing the inventive choreography of Val Raset-Seymour Felix-Kelly-Stanley Donen, was the score by Ira Gershwin-Jerome Kern-E. Y. Harburg. Aesthetically, the major flaw of *Cover Girl* was the picture's excessive length (107 minutes) in which scenarist Virginia Van Upp struggled to properly bridge the more than eight musical interludes.

The gimmicky plot-server of searching for a new cover girl among unknowns had been, and would continue to be, a favorite device among the makers of Hollywood movie musicals, but here the ploy is complicated by *Vanity* magazine publisher Otto Kruger searching for a young beauty to match the visual delight of a girl from his past, the Gay Nineties entertainer Maribelle Hicks (Rita). As predicted, when he and his wisecracking assistant (Eve Arden) come across Rusty Parker (Rita), and Kruger later learns she is his lost love's granddaughter, the story has found its basis of resolution. To complicate the mixture even further, Rita cannot decide romantically between Kelly, her dance partner from her Brooklyn nightclub days, and slick Lee Bowman, Kruger's playboy production man, who stars her on Broadway.

Stylistically, Kelly's solo spot, the "Alter Ego" dance, in which he "duets" with his own reflection via double exposure filming, is the most catchy element in *Cover Girl*, but it remains just a novelty turn. "Put Me to the Test," as first performed by Rita and Kelly, provides a semiparallel to the Ginger Rogers-Fred Astaire romance-and-challenge team dancing in their 1930s musicals. Rita and Kelly are their most ingratiating selves in this segment. The "Make Way for Tomorrow" number foreshadows Kelly's rendition of "Singin' in the Rain" from the 1952 MGM movie of the same title. In the *Cover Girl* version, Rita and Kelly are joined by their zany show-business comrade Phil Silvers in a nighttime street dance in which they disrupt the flow of traffic and leave the procession of passersby dumbstruck. Most Rita Hayworth fans focus on the "Long Ago and Far

*Janet Blair was substituted as Grant's leading lady.

With Warner Baxter in UNDER THE PAMPAS MOON (Fox '35)

With Thomas Beck, Pat Paterson, Frank Conroy, and Warner Oland in
CHARLIE CHAN IN EGYPT (Fox '35)

With Ray Corrigan, Oscar Gahan (musician), Max Terhune, Robert Livingston, Jack Kirk, Wally West (with bandana), and George Morrell (third from right) in HIT THE SADDLE (Rep '37)

Publicity pose (c. 1937)

With George O'Brien in
THE RENEGADE RANGER (RKO '38)

With Cary Grant and Jean
Arthur in ONLY ANGELS
HAVE WINGS (Col '39)

With Joey Ray, Edith Fellows,
Tony Martin, George Tobias,
Robert Frazer, Joseph Crehan,
George Humbert, Alan
Mowbray, and Eric Blore in
MUSIC IN MY HEART
(Col '40)

Publicity pose for SUSAN AND GOD (MGM '40)

With Nigel Bruce, Joan Crawford, and John Carroll in SUSAN AND GOD

With Jack Carson in
THE STRAWBERRY
BLONDE (WB '41)

Publicity pose with Tyrone Power for BLOOD AND SAND (20th '41)

With Frank Ferguson and Fred Astaire in YOU'LL NEVER GET RICH (Col '41)

With Charles Boyer and Thomas Mitchell in
TALES OF MANHATTAN (20th '42)

With Adolphe Menjou and Fred Astaire in
YOU WERE NEVER LOVELIER (Col '42)

With Otto Kruger and Eve Arden in COVER GIRL

happily employed at the West End theatre run by dowager-type Florence Bates. Then, in a bomb shelter, she meets RAF pilot Lee Bowman, who soon develops a crush on her. Meanwhile, a new show recruit (Platt) from Manchester arrives on the scene and promptly falls in love with Rita, who only thinks of him in a brotherly way. While all this is transpiring, Rita's confrere on stage, Blair, has romantically tumbled for Platt, but he only thinks of her in a sisterly manner.

With the above as a plot basis, *Tonight and Every Night* leaves ample opportunity for Rita to shine photographically, romantically, and above all in a dancing capacity.* (Her songs were here dubbed by Martha Mears.) In the army camp scene Rita and Janet duet the comic skit, "The Boy I Left Behind"; "You Excite Me" is a torchy number highlighted by a Brazilian-rhythmed samba; the extended "Cry and You Cry Alone" segment features Rita in a diaphanous Grecian outfit with Platt her agile dance partner in a mixture of classical and modern steps; in a nurse-maid's outfit she handles "What Does an English Girl Think of a Yank?" and in the finale, she "croons" the title tune previously rendered by Blair.

Whatever trepidations Harry Cohn may have suffered about the effects of Rita's marriage to Welles on her professional life, her career seemed to be running relatively smoothly. She had won the *Look* magazine Achievement Award as 1944's best actress for her performance in *Cover Girl. Tonight and Every Night* had made an impressive dent at the box office. Besides, also in 1945, American G.I.s had been urged to vote Rita "Number One Back Home Glamour Girl." At a well-publicized ceremony at Walter Reed Hospital she received her special "Oscar," which was inscribed with the words, "Her willingness to share such loveliness through the medium of the screen with millions of war-sick and lonely G.I.s has contributed immeasurably to the morale of the fighting men." Cohn lost no time in rushing Rita back to Hollywood, where his still photographers snapped a new pinup pose of her in a clinging chiffon negligee. When asked the obvious question of how she enjoyed being a glamour symbol, Rita admitted she liked it very much. "After all, a girl is . . . well, a girl. It's nice to be told you're successful at it."

Rita's next film, *Gilda* (Columbia, 1946), proved to be the high-water mark of her career, providing her with the ultimate femme-fatale

---

*However, Rita was not very adept at handling a Jean Arthur-type sequence. For instance, Bowman induces her to return to his apartment under the pretext of meeting a fellow American, who conveniently does not show up. She retorts to his confession of a romantic set-up, "I'm glad this is not an example of British strategy, or I'd be very wary of the outcome of the war."

Near the flashback's climax, the local pub is bombed out. Platt and Blair are missing. Rita's dramatic response is not very convincing. She rushes out of the theatre, tearfully approaching the rubble: "Dear God, please save Judy, save Tommy." When her friends' bodies are found, Rita returns to the theatre, and in the best *42nd Street* movie tradition, she bravely tells Bates, "Don't cut Judy's number. I'll do it," and she launches into "Tonight and Every Night."

screen role and bringing in over $3.75 million in distributors' domestic rentals. It was produced and structured by Virginia Van Upp,* directed by Charles Vidor, who knew how to best present Rita's talents onscreen, and co-starred Glenn Ford, who had recently returned from World War II duty in the Marines.

Everyone seemed to have a different explanation for the popularity of the black-and-white feature, *Gilda*. Howard Barnes (*New York Herald-Tribune*) reasoned, "this newest screen offering has so much cinematic sense that it almost denies a bad story in treatment." *Variety* had a fuller explanation: "when things get trite and frequently far-fetched, somehow, at the drop of a shoulder strap, there is always Rita Hayworth to excite the filmgoer. When story interest lags, she's certain to shrug a bare shoulder, toss her tawny head in a intimately revealing closeup, or saunter teasingly through the celluloid. She dissipates the theories, if any, that sex has its shortcomings as a popular commodity. Miss Hayworth will do business." Rita would later provide her own (haphazard) rationale: "That strip I did—'Put the Blame on Mame, Boys.' Remember it? Just with those long white gloves, but I took 'em off—wow! And there were great scenes with Glenn Ford, slappin' each other, kissin' each other. It was a marvelous big mess!"

On many levels, *Gilda* is a tremendously erotic picture.† The deliberate contradictions between the visuals (supplied by cinematographer Rudolph Mate) and the dialog (credited to Marion Parsonnet) force even the casual viewer to realize the dichotomy between appearance and reality within the film. Sometimes the contrast is almost too blatant, as when Ford's Johnny Farrell is led upstairs to meet the new wife (Rita) of his boss (George Macready).

Macready: [*calling*] Are you decent?
Rita: [*her head popping into camera range for the first time*] Me . . . sure I'm decent.

Immediately thereafter, the situation becomes more subtle, as the viewer perceives, while Rita's passionate possessor (Macready) only

---

*Rita is supposed to have confided to Van Upp that she was to blame for some of the star's romantic complications. " . . . you wrote *Gilda*. And every man I've known has fallen in love with Gilda and wakened with me."

†Sadomasochistic overtones run rampant throughout the relationship between the characters played by Glenn Ford and George Macready. Near the very opening of *Gilda*, Macready, with his phallic knife-concealing cane, rescues Ford from three toughs who want to roll him for his gambling winnings. Macready says to Ford about his weapon, "It is silent when I wish it to be silent. It talks when I wish it to."

Ford: Is that your idea of a friend?
Macready: Yes.

When being hired to work in Macready's casino, Ford states, "You have no idea how faithful I can be for a salary."

Further pointing up the homosexual ambiance between the two men is Macready's statement to Ford on the night Rita appears at Macready's home: "You never thought I'd have a woman in the house."

senses, the past stormy relationship between Rita and Ford. When Macready introduces his protégé-assistant to Rita, she retorts, "Johnny. That is such a hard name to remember and such an easy one to forget."

It is an accepted dramatic principle that if the playwright tells an audience anything often enough, they will accept it. Throughout *Gilda*, the characters are constantly admitting their unbridled emotional reaction to the captivating Rita, forcing even the recalcitrant moviegoer to finally accept that Rita's Gilda is the most exciting female in the world. At one point Macready insists, "I'm mad about her, mad." As for the likes of Gerald Mohr and Robert Scott, they are mere putty in Rita's beguiling hands. Ford has a different emotional response to Rita, that of a love-hate relationship.

Ford: I hated her so, I couldn't get her out of my mind for a minute.

Rita: [*re Ford at a later juncture*] I hate you so much, I'd like to take you down with me.

Rita: [*speaking to Ford at a still later point*] Hate is a very exciting emotion. Haven't you noticed? . . . I hate you so. I think I'm going to die from it.

As if the steamy intensity of their expressions of emotion is not enough to kindle their perverse passions, Rita and Ford engage in actual physical brutality (modified oncamera to slapping one another in anger), as well as anticipated sadistic pleasures (just before leaving for the costume ball, Rita menacingly toys with a whip).

To clinch *Gilda*'s thematic premise that Rita's character is the most sensual creature walking the earth, she is made to sing and dance the erotic striptease number, "Put the Blame on Mame, Boys."* Even though post-World War II industry censorship prevented the disrobement number from proceeding beyond the removal of her long white gloves, filmgoers got the point and their imaginations did the rest.

For those rare souls who preferred not to indulge in the erotic fantasies running rampant in *Gilda*, the film was also geared on a very simplistic level as an espionage-adventure story, with casino-owner Macready the secret head of an international cartel, operating in tungsten, which is sponsored by the Nazis. After Germany's surrender, the situation takes a political turn, and Macready finds it necessary to flee Argentina and fake an ocean plane crash. His "widow" Rita is left in control of a business empire, but she soon becomes a virtual prisoner of retaliatory Ford, who thereafter weds her. Near the finale, Macready makes a surprise appearance on the scene, but just as he is about to shoot the double-crossing Rita and Ford, washroom attendant Steven Geray stabs him to death with

---

*Anita Ellis dubbed Rita's singing segments of the number. Rita would later recall: "Harry [Cohn] always liked that big band sound in his musicals, and he claimed my voice wasn't loud enough. Except for the bar scene in *Gilda* where I sang [sic] "Put the Blame on Mame" and one song in *Pal Joey*, he always used someone else's voice. Fine thing, I had studied singing since I was a little girl."

Macready's own omnipresent cane. Police inspector Joseph Calleia refuses to arrest anyone for Macready's death, for after all, a man cannot die twice. Now the girl from New York with the mysterious background and her equally elusive spouse (Ford) have a new future ahead. The picture concludes with her saying, "Johnny, let's go home [Manhattan]. Let's go home."

It is almost needless to say that the expensively mounted (by Columbia's standards) *Gilda* was a smash hit when it opened at Radio City Music Hall (March 14, 1946).

But Harry Cohn's delight with the financial success of *Gilda* was marred by his concern over Rita's private life. Columnist Louella Parsons had once written of her: "There is no star in Hollywood who has such a genius for getting herself in a mess as Rita Hayworth. Ever since the day she married Ed Judson, she's let her heart rule her life. Never has her head entered into her romance." Cohn was to learn the full meaning of these words the hard way.

Cohn had worried that the birth of Rita's child (Rebecca Welles—born December 17, 1945) might damage her reputation as a sex symbol, but her popularity continued undiminished, and her pregnancy hardly caused a delay in the star's filmmaking schedule. But Rita's marriage to Welles was beginning to deteriorate. During a period of separation in 1945, Rita had begun dating Tony Martin. Before their romance cooled,* Cohn was in an emotional state near shock. He was relatively pleased when Rita and Welles reconciled. In fact, when the latter, unable to pick up the pieces of his film directorial career, went east to direct and star in Mike Todd's stage version of *Around the World in 80 Days* (1946), Cohn agreed to put $50,000 into the floundering Broadway show on condition that Welles write and direct a picture for Columbia. *Around the World* was a box-office failure, and Welles returned to Hollywood to fulfill his Columbia commitment. By this point, Cohn was fired with enthusiasm over the project and insisted that Rita should star in *The Lady from Shanghai*,† filmed in 1946, but not released in the United States until 1948. It was a decision Cohn would long regret.

While the fate of *The Lady from Shanghai* was hanging in moratorium, Cohn scheduled Rita to appear in *Down to Earth* (Columbia, 1947), a musical-fantasy sequel to the very popular *Here Comes Mr. Jordan* (Columbia, 1941). To insure the box-office appeal of the project, Columbia's leading man, Larry Parks, who had made such a hit in *The Jolson Story* (Columbia, 1946), was cast opposite Rita. By this point, Rita had been convinced that Cohn and Columbia Pictures were exploiting her mar-

---

*On a later occasion, Martin would say of Rita: "Have you any conception of how perfect she is? There's her sweetness as well as her beauty, her simplicity as well as her glamour. I've never been in love like this with anyone. I never knew I could be."

† Rita had already starred with Welles in some radio dramas, including *Break of Hearts* (September 11, 1944) on CBS's "Lux Radio Theatre."

quee value, and that she was not receiving a fair share of the bounty. She had been guided by her William Morris Agency mentors in the formation of her own corporation, Beckworth Productions, and she now demanded that, via her company, she receive twenty-five percent of the profits from her films. When Rita carried out her threat to be "unavailable" for shooting and thus delay the production of *Down to Earth*, the movie mogul finally consented to her financial wishes.

The box-office pull of Rita and Larry Parks in a color musical was sufficient to insure a profitable return on *Down to Earth*, even though the actress and some critics were not pleased with the outcome.* Director Alexander Hall and cast members James Gleason and Edward Everett Horton repeated their *Here Comes Mr. Jordan* assignments in this new tale of the heavenly Grecian queen of dance, Terpsichore (Rita), who from her vantage point on Mount Parnassus is unhappy about the Broadway musical about the nine muses being done in jazz by producer Parks. She requests permission to come to earth to clean up the show, and soon finds herself replacing Adele Jergens in Parks's musical, spurred on by the knowledge that if the show fails on Broadway, gangsters have threatened to kill money-owing Parks. There were moments when Rita was breathtakingly gorgeous, as when she lets down her red hairdo and, swathed in mink, walks into Parks's rehearsal, but everything about the picture had the devastating touch of prefabrication.

After the success of *Gilda*, in which one reviewer compared her to a "bombshell with a delayed action fuse," the army took due note and pasted her *Life* magazine bed pose shot onto the Bikini atomic bomb. Her popularity endorsement after the opening of *Down to Earth* was equally ecstatic, if less dramatic. Timed to coincide with the premiere of *Down to Earth* was the November 10, 1947, issue of *Life* magazine, containing a cover feature story by Winthrop Sargent on "The Cult of the Love Goddess in America." The piece was devoted entirely to Rita! The author postulated in his piece: "It has remained for Americans of the hard-boiled 20th Century to enthrone Aphrodite as the supreme deity of their popular religion, to portray her rather dubious machinations as the most exalting and satisfying of human experiences and to subscribe with unquestioning faith to her incessant litany that sex is the most important thing in the world." In relating this definition to Rita, Sargent explained: "Though the idea of doing anything for its own sake is completely foreign to her, she will accomplish prodigies to please others. Few women have more willingly and deftly submitted to becoming the passive material out of which a myth can be created, and this fact, added to her rather remarkable physical qualifications, goes a long way toward explaining her success." Crowning this glowing endorsement, which put her at the top of the heap in Hollywood, a full print of *Down to Earth*, along with various

---

Variety complained of the "slow, tiresome and unacceptable plot."

other examples of twentieth-century Americana, was placed in a time capsule to be opened in the year 2047. Rita had been truly immortalized.

By the time *The Lady from Shanghai* had its delayed American release in May 1948, Rita and Orson Welles had divorced, with Rita retaining custody of Rebecca. When proceeding through the marital-dissolution legalities on November 10, 1947, Rita admitted, "I couldn't take his genius twenty-four hours a day any longer. I was married and yet I didn't have a husband." Rita's father was a little more emotional in his statements about the divorcement. "Whadda you expect? I am personally very sorry. Welles is a fine man. But you can't leave a young girl like Rita alone while you sit up all night working. You can't go to New York for three months and produce plays." After Rita and Welles went their separate paths, she moved out of their elaborate home and took up residence in a more modest Brentwood home.

The divorce of "beauty and the beast" generated some public interest in *The Lady from Shanghai*, but once word-of-mouth spread about this entertainment dud, nothing could save the picture from box-office failure. At the start of the film, Welles, as the young Irish sailor Michael O'Hara, tells the viewer, "When I start out to make a fool of myself, very little can stop me." This film certainly proved that! In his unyielding attempt to mold Rita into a new image of his own conceit, Welles nearly destroyed every aspect of her legendary charisma. Before he would allow Rita to portray the role of conscienceless Elsa Bannister, he insisted that her famed red locks be dramatically altered in color and style. A near-apoplectic Cohn fumed, "Everyone knows that the most beautiful thing about Rita is her hair." Eventually Cohn conceded to Welles's persistent demands, and with news photographers on hand to record the historic event, Rita's famed mane of red hair was chopped to a far shorter style and her remaining locks dyed topaz blonde.

If Rita was fully aware of how the physical change in her looks (and the necessary accompanying alterations in wardrobe and makeup) would besmirch her screen image, she seemed then—and to this day—to be convinced of the soundness of Welles's idea to reshape her already successful celluloid persona. She would later say, with more misguided seriousness than flippancy, "Orson taught me to act and I taught him to direct."

In *The Lady from Shanghai*, Rita's character is not just another femme fatale with a shady past as in *Gilda*. Viewers are told that Elsa Bannister was born of Russian parents in Chi-Ful, and that she worked in Macao and Shanghai ("You need more than luck in Shanghai"). But it requires the full eighty-six minutes for Rita's character as a treacherous murderess to become apparent. She is as spiritually unredeemed at the finish when she dies as when the stagy picture opens. Audiences just might have accepted the novelty of the "new look" Rita, but they could hardly like such an unsavory person as the grasping young blonde wife of a crippled criminal lawyer (Everett Sloane), particularly when her emoting left such a great deal to be desired.

It was no accident on Welles's part that Rita in *The Lady from Shanghai* presided over a yacht named *The Circle*, that she sang such a dispassionate song as "Please Don't Kiss Me,"* or that she had a fatalistic approach to life.† It was all part of Welles's grand concept to out-Gilda *Gilda*.

The crushing blows to the box-office fate of *The Lady from Shanghai* were the insistence of the already cherubic Welles on playing her leading man (imagine Humphrey Bogart in the role?),‡ and Welles's initial refusal to keep the project within a reasonable budget § or to accept the advice of other creative talents who were more familiar with the requisite ingredients for a successful Rita Hayworth screen vehicle. Only after the film had undergone a disastrous preview in Santa Barbara, California, would Welles admit he had gone astray and allow a horrified Columbia to intervene. By then it was too late either to make lowbrow sense out of Welles's original lofty concepts or to restructure the existing footage into an acceptable melodrama. What emerged onscreen was one of the decade's most murky plotlines, equaled perhaps only by Howard Hawks's *The Big Sleep* (Warner Bros., 1946), which, however, unlike Welles's venture, proved profitable.

It would be unfair to deny the brilliant moments in *The Lady from Shanghai*,δ the sterling performance of Sloane as Rita's physically and mentally twisted spouse, or the fact that the picture has been mildly canonized by Wellesian disciples and is now a standard item on the programs of art-film houses. However, in the progression of Rita's movie career, the venture was a near-fatal experiment.

As a successor to *Down to Earth* and a picture that would dissipate the bad taste left by *The Lady from Shanghai*, studio executives agreed that Rita should be reshifted back into the mold that she played best—the role of a fiery but repentant temptress. The vehicle selected, *The Loves of Carmen* (Columbia, 1948), had several built-in ingredients to insure a profit:

---

*Anita Ellis dubbed Rita's song.

†Rita's character says that "everything's bad. . . . Everything. You can't escape it or fight it. You've got to get along with it, deal with it, make terms."

‡Rita had been scheduled to appear with Bogart in *Dead Reckoning* (Columbia, 1947), but she was feuding with the studio and Lizabeth Scott was substituted.

§The original $1.2 million budget pushed up to $2 million before the film's completion, caused by Welles's demands for on-location shooting in Acapulco, the building of sets that were hardly used, and the constant changes in the screenplay, which threw the production schedule way off kilter.

δE.g., Rita seen through a telescope swimming in the shimmering water or sitting in profile on a big rock with the striking contrast of her white blonde hair and the black bathing suit; the abortive love-making in front of the squirming sea creatures at the aquarium; the hazy Chinatown ambiance; or the stunning finale in the fun-house room of mirrors.

Hayworth-experienced Charles Vidor would produce-direct, increasingly popular Glenn Ford would again be her leading man, and Rita would portray a sultry character well known to the general public—Carmen.

The advertisements for *The Loves of Carmen* proudly announced of Rita's new picture, "This is Carmen . . . creature of a thousand moods . . . whose arms were kind . . . whose lips were maddening . . . whose story is immortal." The publicity posters carefully mentioned that the new picture was musically unrelated to Georges Bizet's famed opera, and that it was actually a dramatic version of Prosper Mérimée's story, unfolded in the glories of Technicolor.

When *The Loves of Carmen* debuted at Loew's State Theatre in New York on September 2, 1948, Howard Barnes *(New York Herald-Tribune)* would report, "It is a gaudy and colorful period horse opera marked by pompous dialog and random direction." Set in 1820s Seville, the tale opens at the cigarette factory, Fabrica de Tabacos, and soon depicts the arrival of Don Jose (Ford), a dragoon corporal who, despite warnings that she is a thief, a liar, and has had many lovers, falls madly in love with the tempestuous Carmen (Rita). At the same time, Rita is furious at her uncontrollable, passionate attraction for Ford, since a fortuneteller has told her that she will one day be killed by the man she loves. As events fall into place, Rita is responsible for Ford's having to desert his duty and flee as a wanted man to her gypsy camp. There he discovers she is already wed to Garcia (Victor Jory); in the ensuing bouts of jealous rivalry, Ford kills Jory, weds Rita, and assumes command of the gypsy outlaws. Later she returns to Seville, where she consummates a romance with a famed bullfighter (John Baragrey). The enraged Ford follows, demands her return, and, when she refuses, stabs her to death just as the police arrive. He is shot down, and dies with the body of Rita still clutched in his arms.

Over the years many performers had played Carmen,* but few were as shapely as Rita, who might have been born to play the woman who drove men mad with each rustle of her skirts. The combination of her athletic scuffle with Veronica Pataky, her seduction of the various leading men, her interpretive dancing to the bulerias, zambra, fandanguillo, shufla, etc., and her enticing singing of "The Love of a Gypsy,"† easily should have created the impression of a tidy bundle of erotica; " . . . but her undisciplined histrionics never allowed her to be quite as heartless a femme fatale as she would like to pretend. Even when she is intent upon driving men mad, she tends to look as innocent as a girl who would regard an unchaperoned trip to Bear Mountain as devilish" (John Mc-

---

*Among the actresses playing Carmen onscreen have been Theda Bara, Geraldine Farrar, Raquel Meller, Pola Negri, Dolores Del Rio, and Viviane Romance. In 1915, Charlie Chaplin made his own spoof of the Carmen legend. Dorothy Dandridge starred in the picturization of the 1943 stage musical *Carmen Jones,* and Uta Levka was the title figure in the sexploitation feature *Carmen, Baby* (Audubon, 1967).

†Anita Ellis dubbed for Rita.

Carten, *New Yorker* magazine). The blame could not entirely be placed on Rita's lovely personage, for none of the picture's dramatic scenes had enough fluency or credibility to successfully cover the bridges to the musical or romantic interludes. *The Loves of Carmen* was not the costumed *Gilda* Columbia had intended.

At the time Rita divorced Orson Welles, she had told the press, with a tinge of acidity to her voice: "Mr. Welles showed no interest in establishing a home. Mr. Welles told me he never should have married in the first place, as it interfered with his freedom in his way of life." Obviously, once the aura of his intellectual splendor had worn off, Rita had been shocked by the humiliating realization that she held such little power over this creative wizard. Men around the world would have paid dearly to enjoy the company of the real-life Gilda, but Welles seemingly took his famous wife for granted. He showed his apparent romantic disinterest in startling ways. For example, he would frequently hold all-night project conferences in their home bedroom. Rita had the option of either vacating the environs or falling asleep in the midst of the gathered underlings.

Now that Welles was physically if not entirely emotionally in the past, Rita volunteered an answer to the most frequently asked question, "Would she remain a free woman?" Her answer was, "Certainly I'm going to marry again." A perturbed Harry Cohn could only sit back, wondering whom his prize property would next wed and just when the next round of emotional chaos would commence.

It all happened sooner and far more dramatically than anyone could have expected, even from Rita. With her family sufficiently well provided for,* Rita decided to pamper her own fondest dream: "Just to roam, to live for a year like the natives in each country." More specifically, she had decided upon a European jaunt. Since she would be making public appearances on behalf of the studio while abroad, and since Columbia had no immediate film project readied for Rita, Cohn agreed to her travel plans. He was concerned when she announced the vacation might extend to three or four months. However, she was a very determined thirty-one-year-old woman and won her way. She bid goodbye to her latest series of escorts, which included Tony Martin and David Niven, and crossed the Atlantic. In Cannes, famed party-giver Elsa Maxwell invited her to a dinner party. As Maxwell would later write to a friend of that fateful social gathering, "I don't know whether I did well or not but I placed the beautiful Rita next to the Prince at dinner the other night." The royal personage in question was Aly Khan, the son of the Aga Khan, who was Imam, or hereditary head, of the vast Ismailian sect of Mos-

---

*Vernon Cansino had had bits in both *The Lady from Shanghai* and *The Loves of Carmen*, with Jose Cansino also in the latter film. Rita's brother Eduardo, Jr., was working as a taxi-driver, and her father still ran a dance studio in Hollywood.

lems. Aly would have no official status till he succeeded his father, but meantime he was accorded the courtesy title of "Prince." Aly's mother, the second of the Aga's four wives, was Theresa Magleano, an Italian noblewoman-sculptress, and the first of the Aga's Caucasian spouses. At the time Aly was still married to Joan Yorde-Buller, the ex-wife of brewing heir Thomas Loel Guinness.

When Rita first met Aly at Maxwell's gathering she claimed she was intrigued by the charming, slick man, but that she had no idea of his claim to enormous power and future wealth. As the romance proceeded during a joint tour that extended from the Riviera to Spain's Toledo and Madrid, on to Lisbon, and back to Cannes, the inordinate amount of press coverage given to the royal romance had its influence on Rita. Her heart had been lost to this most royal of playboys, and she was convinced that here at last was a man who did not want to guide her career or manipulate her fame in artistic experiments, but a suitor who was enthralled just by her very feminine being. Rita returned to Hollywood aglow with love.

Cohn was very well aware that when Rita was a woman in love, she would listen to no business sense. She proved true to form. Columbia had a new film project lined up for her. She was to play the title role in *Lona Hanson,* based on the Thomas Savage novel, about a girl who inherits a Montana cattle ranch. Her leading man was to be the very-much-in-demand William Holden. The director was to be Norman Foster. Rita rejected the project, and joined by Aly, who had flown to Hollywood to be with his beloved, she flew to Mexico City. There, to avoid the barrage of reporters following them everywhere, they barricaded themselves in their suite at the Hotel Reforma. One of the few people to be admitted to their sealed-off rooms was Virginia Van Upp, a person whom Rita greatly respected. As Cohn's emissary, Miss Van Upp politely inquired what Rita's career intentions were and then sat back at a special conference between them to learn all the details of Rita's love for Aly.

Rita and Aly then flew on to Cuba, where again persistent newsmen were constantly at their heels. Finally, the ever-cool Aly turned to one reporter and said, "Look here, old boy, I'd like to answer your questions, but how can I when they are so embarrassing?"

The couple next returned to California, where on December 1, 1948, she acquired her final divorce papers in the Welles suit. Two days later the adamant Rita failed to show up at the Nogales, Arizona, site for the planned Western movie. Columbia placed her on suspension, with Rita forfeiting her $248,000 yearly salary.* To make the frustrated Cohn even more perturbed, the Hollywood Women's Press Club named Rita the "Least cooperative actress of the year."

*Under the terms of her contract via Beckworth (of which Rita was a little less than fifty-percent stockholder; Columbia held the majority share) with the studio, she had a seven-year agreement of two pictures annually, with a $248,000 yearly remuneration.

Rita was indifferent to the turn of events in her career. She packed her trunks, and with daughter Rebecca in town, departed with Aly on the ship *Britannia* for London. The British were not very gracious about having Rita conduct her headlined affair in their midst. The *London Sunday Pictorial* editorialized, "Does she imagine that by trailing Rebecca after her, she lends an air of domesticity . . . to her irresponsible jaunt?" Back in California, the influential *Hollywood Reporter* declared that the industry should "wash its hands of Rita Hayworth."

On the surface at least, Rita seemed blissfully unaffected by the public denunciations. After visiting with Aly's two sons, Karim Aga and Amyon Mohammed, the contingent departed for Aly's County Kildare estate near Dublin, and then on to the Riviera. Even though Aly's divorce from his wife of thirteen years would not be final for some months to come, he and Rita announced their engagement in the spring of 1949. Rita broke her persistent silence with the press and admitted: "I'm so excited. I can hardly think. I'm sort of lost in a dream world. When someone asks me a question, I bring myself to and grunt."

Even though the Grace Kelly and the more recent Princess Anne weddings might be thought to supersede it in grandeur, the 1949 planned Rita Hayworth-Aly Khan nuptials were considered the international marriage ceremony of the century. The media relegated global news events to secondary spots in order to headline the latest bit of new detail revealed about the pending nuptials. To be among the exclusive VIP guest list was considered the honor of a lifetime. Hedda Hopper was livid to learn that her newspaperwoman rival, Louella Parsons, long a confidant of Rita, was among the select few scheduled to attend. One of the rare individuals to reject an invitation was Harry Cohn. What was the momentary personal happiness of Rita compared to the losses she was inflicting on Columbia shareholders?

Initially it was announced that the wedding ceremony would be held at L'Horizon, Aly's Cannes estate. Then the French government announced that there must be a proper civil ceremony and the wedding site was switched to the Vallauris mayoral office, where on May 27, 1949, the Communist mayor, Paul Derigon, wed Rita and Aly. She wore—as all the world was soon informed—an ankle-length light-blue crepe dress by Jacques Fath, with a matching, blue-veiled hat, and carried a white lace handkerchief in her black-gloved hand. Rita acknowledged her wedding vows with a French *oui*. Aly placed a twelve-karat wedding ring on Rita's extended finger. After the ceremony, Aly donated the sum of $1,587 to the local poor. Then the couple stepped into his cream-colored, chauffeur-driven Cadillac and led the procession of guests back to L'Horizon for the festivities set by the orange blossom-scented pool. Typical of the lush catering were the fifteen bottles of champagne earmarked for each guest. Aly capped the occasion by leaning forward at one point when Rita was seated, and kissing her slipper. The next day, the couple went through a Moslem wedding ceremony. Among Aly's many gifts to the bride were a cash dowry, a quartet of racehorses, an Alfa-Romeo car, and assorted diamonds and rubies.

Now that Rita and her dream man had finally been wed, speculations turned to the couple's future. The most discussed point was how could an American Catholic girl become, one day, the Begum, the distaff spiritual leader, of millions of Moslems? Columnist Igor Cassini had a hopeful theory: "Of course, Rita is pretty lucky at that since Aly Khan, though a Moslem, was brought up very much as a Western gentleman. Aly's father, the Aga, and his entire family have spent most of their lives on the European continent. The Aga seemed to care much more about his racing stables and the Riviera than living the life of the powerful Oriental potentate he is."

By the winter of 1949, it was evident to everyone that Rita was quite pregnant. When she was tactfully asked when the child was expected, she said on December 20 in Lausanne, Switzerland, "I don't expect to have a baby until February, and why everybody seems to think it's going to happen earlier beats me." Well, eight days later on December 28, at the Montchoisi Maternity Clinic in Lausanne, Rita gave a premature but normal* birth to a five-and-one-half-pound princess, who was named Yasmin. The couple then retreated to their chateau, L'Horizon, but only for a short while, as Aly was a very social creature who had a passion for the race tracks, the casinos, and for villa-hopping. At a later date, Aly's chauffeur would detail the inherent problems in the Rita-Aly Khan relationship. "One of the first causes of Miss Hayworth's unhappiness, in her role as Princess Aly, stemmed from the fact that she nearly always felt like a fish out of water with the Prince's friends. My boss lived for horses, and enjoyed nothing more than the company of trainers, owners, and jockeys." It did not help matters that most of Aly's pals could not speak English and that Rita had difficulty learning fluent French. In essence, Moslem Aly did not want an equal marital partner, and was emotionally unequipped to be the devoted groom to the domesticity-inclined Rita.

Meanwhile, worried Harry Cohn was wondering whether his chief onscreen attraction would ever return to Hollywood and moviemaking. He made a special trip to France, hoping to induce Rita to return to California and accept the responsibilities of a screen star. He offered her solid financial inducements to split her existence into part-time princess and sometime movie queen, but Rita refused to budge in her decision to abandon the cinema. Cohn tried to appeal to her vanity by a threat scare, and he started a massive campaign to build up Rita-look-alike Mary Castle as Rita's successor. Princess Aly seemed unperturbed by it all.

However, she was quite concerned about the obvious problems in her

*Rebecca Welles had been born by Caesarian section.

wedded life. Aly had been a womanizer before their marriage, as she well knew. Her belief that she could change all this was ill-founded, and the dissension between the couple grew. To appease Rita, Aly suggested a second honeymoon, with Africa as the locale. What was to be an intimate reconciliation trip for Rita and Aly turned into a highly publicized champagne safari.* The retinue on the trek included four Moslem millionaires who came along to play bridge with Aly, two cooks, one valet, two pilots, two aides, three secretaries, and assorted French socialites. One of the trucks used for the excursion carried only a load of champagne, another was jammed with refrigerators. It all proved to be too much for Rita, and she returned to France, gathered together her two children, and in July 1951, after two and one half years away, returned to Hollywood. A few days later she went to Lake Tahoe in Nevada in order to establish six-weeks residence for her divorce. When she spoke to the press, she displayed a recently acquired Oxford accent, and told of her reasons for breaking with Aly: " . . . various factors, including my husband's extensive social obligations and interests, make it impossible to establish or maintain the kind of home I want and my children need. . . . He is a playboy. He doesn't understand family life. He thinks only of gambling, horse racing, big game hunting."

On the past two occasions when Rita had separated from a spouse, the break, once announced, had been permanent. But there were two new guiding factors concerning the Prince: (1) she wanted a huge $3 million settlement for Yasmin (nothing for herself), and (2) she professed that she still loved Aly. She admitted: "I am still friendly with Aly and his family. It is better that way. I always want Yasmin to feel that her father loves her. I don't want her to feel neglected as Rebecca often has."

In Hollywood, Rita lived in seclusion with her two daughters, but soon made it known to Harry Cohn that she was ready to return to work. The reason—she was flat broke! Her nearly $300,000 savings was gone. Cohn was caught a bit off guard, but he soon came up with *Affair in Trinidad* (Columbia, 1952), a Virginia Van Upp story that was geared to be in the *Gilda* tradition. Vincent Sherman was contracted to helm the picture, and Glenn Ford was added to the package for shrewd good luck. Rita consented to the project, but demanded that rewrites and revisions in the production schedule be made to bolster the film's values. Cohn and the New York board of directors were incensed at Rita's demands, but they acceded. They all remembered the box-office grosses of *Cover Girl, Tonight and Every Night, Gilda,* and even *The Loves of Carmen.* They also knew full well that Columbia's talent department had yet to come up with a new sex symbol to match Rita. Judy Holliday was fine for comedy, and the likes of Donna Reed, Marta Toren, Gale Robbins, and even Caro-

---

*Jackson Leighter produced and photographed a sixty-minute documentary entitled *Champagne Safari* (a.k.a. *Safari So Good*) detailing some of Rita and Aly's treks to various bastions of the Moslem world. It was initially distributed in 1951 by Defense Films.

lina Cotton or Gail Davis for Programmers, but they had no one to compete with MGM's Lana Turner or Twentieth Century-Fox's Betty Grable and Marilyn Monroe. Rita was a necessary adjunct to the sustaining success of Columbia's feature-film production, or so everyone thought.

While the studio was ironing out the problems in Rita's new picture and finalizing her latest revised contract,* she took the opportunity to speak to the public via her usual mouthpiece, Louella Parsons. In conversations with the columnist, reported at great length in Parson's syndicated pieces, Rita confessed: "I feel I have so much to live for in my two little girls. I'm going to keep working hard to take care of them and give them the advantages they should have." Regarding her alleged conversion to the Moslem faith: " . . . religion is not just something with a *name*. It is something inside you that you carry all your life, no matter what outside influences come along. I have never forgotten my vows as a Catholic. The important thing about religion is not what the world may label you— but what you feel in your heart. I want to feel that I am right within my heart—and then no further explanation is needed."

Rita then asked Parsons the ultimate question (which was duly printed with the gossip collector's prize reply): "Do you think the fans will be glad to have me back, Louella?"

Parsons's grand response was: "Yes, Rita. I think they will be glad to have you back as soon as they begin to know that you are the same sweet, unaffected person you were before you left to be a Princess. And I'm proud to be the one to tell them that our own Rita Hayworth is back with us again."

Columbia had its own ostentatious way of announcing Rita's screen return. The gaudy picture advertisements brazenly proclaimed, "She's back! I do what I love and I love what I do!" Although the magic of having Rita back oncamera was enough to lure patrons into theatres, the picture turned out to be a pale copy of *Gilda*, both in ambiance and storyline.†

Rita sported a $25,000 wardrobe, had two provocative dances choreo-

---

*The new agreement provided Rita with a $252,000 annual salary and, through the Beckworth Company, a twenty-five percent cut of the profits of her films.

†When the body of Ross Elliott, a young American artist and a dupe in the hands of international crook Alexander Scourby, is found adrift in a sailboat off Port-of-Spain, Trinidad, the police insist it is a case of suicide. Elliott's wife (Rita) is cavorting at the Club Caribbee when informed of her husband's death, and does not seem much concerned. Then the dead man's older brother (Ford) arrives in Trinidad, and is soon convinced that Elliott was murdered. He begins to tie together the pieces when he recognizes one of Scourby's house guests (George Voskovec) as a leading authority on V-2 rockets in World War II. Soon Ford is as openly resentful of Scourby's attentions to wanton Rita, as is Voskovec's drunken wife (Bettis). Several killings later, it develops that Scourby had stolen plans for a super-rocket from the U.S., which he has then sold to Karel Stepanek, a representative of a foreign power. The turgid drama concludes with Rita and Ford on the afterdeck of a passenger ship heading to America and happiness.

graphed by co-player Valerie Bettis,* did some singing,† and engaged in several torrid love-hate scenes with Ford (including the *de rigueur* face slapping and kissing).

All in all, *Affair in Trinidad* was "the kind of affected, static cat-and-mouse drama that pulls smiles in the wrong places" (Otis L. Guernsey, Jr., *New York Herald-Tribune*). Bosley Crowther (*New York Times*) was even less complimentary: "Outside of its celebration of the return of Rita Hayworth to the screen—an occurrence almost as momentous as the birth of a new camel at the zoo—there is little to endow with distinction that lady's and Columbia's new film."

Columbia had lavished $1.2 million on *Affair in Trinidad*; for *Salome* (Columbia, 1953) the studio lavished a higher budget to insure that the direction (William Dieterle), the co-players (ranging from MGM's Stewart Granger to Charles Laughton, to Judith Anderson, Sir Cedric Hardwicke, and Maurice Schwartz), and the biblical ambiance (with sets by John Meehan and cinematography by Charles Lang) would combine to make the period epic the most successful of Hollywood's new rash of costume dramas.

There had been many screen Salomes before, ranging from Theda Bara to Nazimova to Yvonne De Carlo's modern version, but none had captured either the legendary grandeur of the lady as derived from her scant mention in the Bible, or the decadent spirit as detailed by playwright Oscar Wilde and later translated into an opera by Richard Strauss. Rita's Salome was no improvement on past presentations. It was in many ways "the movie mixture presented many times before, a combination of musical comedy lavishness, dime novel melodrama and Biblical passion, with the stock characters dusted off once again for a vaudeville show of production" (Otis L. Guernsey, Jr., *New York Herald-Tribune*).

Although she was already in her mid-thirties, Rita still looked ravishingly beautiful in front of the Technicolor cameras. Visually she was just right as the temptress who defies King Herod (Laughton) and nearly leads Roman commander Claudius (Granger) astray. As had always been the case, Salome's famed dance was the highlight of the proceedings. Valerie Bettis was on tap again to choreograph Rita's erotic dance of the seven veils. Clad in a clinging, diaphanous gown, Rita swirled around an agog Laughton, shedding one colored chiffon after another, taunting her stepfather into agreeing to spare John the Baptist (Alan Badel) from decapitation.‡ Her dance was sufficient to arouse any male viewer, but it failed

*Rita performed a barefoot calypso to "Trinidad Lady" and did a sophisticated and sultry time-step to "I've Been Kissed Before."

†Jo Ann Greer dubbed Rita's singing.

‡In the Oscar Wilde play, and the opera by Strauss, decadent Salome wants the head of John the Baptist, and when she kisses the severed head, Herod orders his soldiers to kill her. The 1953 Columbia version is a complete distortion.

to save the religious figure's head. In an anticlimactic finale, Rita departs the scene in pursuit of Christianity and her beloved Granger.

Rita's second 1953 release was also geared to exploit her famed body. *Miss Sadie Thompson* (Columbia, 1953) was based on Somerset Maugham's short story, which had been adapted for the stage by John Bolton as *Rain*. It had already provided the basis for many actresses to play the harlot stranded on Pago-Pago who falls temporarily under the spell of religious conversion.* The new edition was partially filmed on location in Hawaii and was entirely lensed in 3-D color. Although the emphasis was vulgarly placed on crudely staged songs and dances,† the ninety-one-minute feature did require some strong dramatics on Rita's part. Considering that she had to contend with an unrealistic plot (due to the need to conform to industry censorship codes) and a most hammy co-star (Jose Ferrer as the repressed, puritanical reformer, Alfred Davidson—a layman in this version), Rita acquitted herself quite respectably. However, the critics were too busy lambasting the film's deficits and alluding to Rita's decidedly mature looks, to appreciate any of the finer points of her acting, while any filmgoer was, most likely, concentrating on each and every lascivious movement made by Rita. *Miss Sadie Thompson* was not the anticipated box-office smash hit.

While Columbia was busily pondering the best way to restore Rita's diminished marquee luster, the star was busily engaged in a series of romantic interludes that were a full-time career in themselves. Back in August 1952, Aly Khan had flown to Hollywood to talk with Rita. Their first meeting was at the house of director Charles Vidor and lasted five hours. Their second get-together over luncheon went on for two hours. Aly's only comment to the press was that "everything is going fine." But

---

*Jeanne Eagels starred in the original New York production, which opened at the Maxine Elliott Theatre on November 7, 1922, and enjoyed a 648-performance run. It was revived in 1924 on Broadway, then had its London premiere in 1925, starring Olga Lindo. Tallulah Bankhead, who had been rejected for the West End version by Somerset Maugham, starred in a short-lived 1935 Broadway revival. The Vernon Duke-Howard Dietz-Rouben Mamoulian musical version starred June Havoc, and opened at the Alvin Theatre on November 16, 1944, but closed on Broadway after sixty performances. Onscreen Gloria Swanson starred in *Sadie Thompson* (United Artists, 1928), Joan Crawford in *Rain* (United Artists, 1932), and Kim Novak in *Jeanne Eagels* (Columbia, 1957). In 1946, there appeared *Dirty Gertie from Harlem, U.S.A.*, which, despite a screen crawl credit that the original story and adaptation were by True T. Thompson, was actually a takeoff on the Sadie Thompson tale. Francine Everette was the black Gertie, with Don Wilson (no relation to Jack Benny's one-time announcer) as Diamond Jim. The picture was directed by Spencer Williams, best known for being Andy on television's "Amos 'n Andy."

†Rita's four songs, dubbed by Jo Ann Greer, were "The Heat Is On," "Hear No Evil, See No Evil," "A Marine, a Marine, a Marine," and "Blue Pacific Blues." Some critics carped heavily about the production numbers performed by Rita's floozie. John McCarten (*New Yorker*) reported, "As the new-day Sadie, Rita Hayworth switches about with the healthy muscularity of a drum major-ette in a Legion parade and lines out songs. . . . as if she were the song leader on an old-fashioned hay ride."

no reconciliation was forthcoming, and much of 1953 was devoted to proposed terms for a divorce settlement; the biggest questions at hand were how much money was to be put aside for Yasmin, and who would have custody of the child. Finally, on January 26, 1953, Rita attained a Reno, Nevada, divorce, but the settlement was far longer in being reached, with threats by Aly not to return Yasmin when she made her annual visits to him.

Meanwhile, Rita had been conducting a romantic twirl with actor Kirk Douglas, followed by a brief relationship with newcomer-singer Bob Savage (he alleged a passionate courtship but she denied it all). Then thirty-year-old singer Dick Haymes entered her life.* He had enough problems to keep a television soap opera in continuous plotline for years. His second wife (actress Joanne Dru) was suing him for back alimony and support for their three children, his third wife (Nora Eddington, the ex-spouse of Errol Flynn) was in the process of divorcing him, the Internal Revenue Service claimed he had been negligent with back taxes, and the U.S. Immigration Service had a deportation case against him because he had skirted the military draft by claiming to be an Argentine citizen. Rita seemed oblivious to the problems plaguing Haymes, and blithely accompanied him to New York, where they sought shelter at the Plaza Hotel from gossip mongers and process servers. Rita discreetly registered in a suite several floors above Haymes's room.

Then Columbia ordered Rita to Hawaii for the filming of *Miss Sadie Thompson*. Haymes followed in pursuit, later returning to the States with Rita. However, he had failed to notify the immigration authorities about either his exit or his return to this country. This provided more than sufficient grounds for another deportation order against the singer. Because of, or despite, his harrowing problems, Rita remained loyal to her constant companion. She insisted, "I'll stand by him even if he is deported." Haymes told the press: "I owe this girl so much that I will do anything in the world to protect her. I intend to stand on my own two feet and take care of all my own troubles. I only thank God that I have her and her love to inspire me enough to work and fight my own battles."

On September 23, 1953, Haymes and Rita were domiciled in Las Vegas, Nevada, where he obtained his divorce decree from Nora Eddington.

---

*Haymes was born in Argentina in 1918; he was schooled in Switzerland, later attending Loyola University in Montreal. He formed a band, which failed, and later was vocalist with groups headed by Johnny Johnston, Bunny Berigan, Harry James, and Tommy Dorsey. He had made his film debut in a small part in *Dramatic School* (MGM, 1938) and then was oncamera again as a Tommy Dorsey band vocalist in *DuBarry Was a Lady* (MGM, 1943). As a recording artist, he hit the big time in the mid-1940s, when he was considered a big threat to leading crooner Frankie Sinatra. He made four Twentieth Century-Fox musicals and then two box-office duds for Universal. By the early 1950s his promising career was on the rocks.

The following day at eleven o'clock in the Gold Room of the Sands Hotel in Las Vegas they were married by District Judge Frank McNamee.* What with the gambling continuing unabated around the wedding group, it was a rather ludicrous setting. Yasmin and Rebecca were both attendees at the ceremony. In the midst of the three-minute civil service, Yasmin was heard to yell out, "I want a ring, too, mommy." As *Life* magazine reported the union, "For Rita, the girl who four years ago starred in a diamond-studded matrimonial production staged by Prince Aly Khan, this was a skid into the rhinestones." Thereafter the couple and the children temporarily retired to a lakeside cabin in a deserted stretch of Nevada.

At this juncture Rita was financially and professionally in great peril. She frankly admitted that she was flat broke and that Haymes had to support her, a rather difficult situation since he was already in debt to the tune of $100,000 to the Internal Revenue Service. A month after their marriage, Haymes was arrested (but freed on bail) for being behind in payments to ex-wife Dru. A few days later a deputy marshal served him with a bill for $1,071.37 owed various men's clothing stores, and a gas station sued him for an $80 bill. When and if Haymes could find singing engagements, the government promised to attach his earnings.

Rita, caught in the morass of her new husband's problems, could not concentrate on her career. By mutual consent with Columbia, a planned starring vehicle based on Frank G. Slaughter's *The Galileans*, in which she would play Mary Magdalene, was shelved. She was to star with Glenn Ford in Fritz Lang's *Human Desire* (Columbia, 1954), but she pleaded emotional stress and Gloria Grahame was substituted in the role. The distraught Rita finally persuaded Cohn to allow her a professional moratorium in order to repair her domestic scene. Cohn reluctantly agreed, even advancing Rita and Haymes some funds in order to lessen their embarrassing financial situation.

With the sums advanced by Columbia, plus Rita's share of the modest profits from *Salome* and *Miss Sadie Thompson*, the couple first rented a Malibu Beach cabin and later moved into an unostentatious Wilshire Boulevard apartment in West Los Angeles. Their Nevada legal residence was maintained for the sake of Rebecca and Yasmin. Then, in early 1954, Rita and Haymes went to New York, where they barricaded themselves in at the Hotel Madison on East Fifty-eighth Street, avoiding the pursuing sheriffs who were after Haymes for defaulting on payments to Dru. The next month the Los Angeles court ordered Haymes deported to Argentina, but his attorneys appealed the case to the Board of Immigration in Washington. Rita insisted, "I will stand by Dick. There is something rotten in this procedure."

*Rita had been persuaded to require Haymes to sign a premarital agreement regarding any assets she might have or later acquire.

Perhaps the low-point of the decade in Rita's life occurred in April, 1954. Rita and Haymes had gone to Key West, Florida, allegedly to have a meeting with representatives of Aly Khan regarding a financial settlement for Yasmin. Rebecca and Yasmin had been left in the care of Dorothy Chambers of Central Avenue, White Plains. While Rita and Haymes were away, the Westchester Society for Prevention of Cruelty to Children charged the star with neglect and brought a court case that made headlines around the world. Both Aly Khan and Orson Welles came to her defense, and in a private settlement, Aly agreed to take technical custody of both girls. Later he only grudgingly allowed Yasmin to return to her mother's side.

By 1954, Harry Cohn and the Columbia board of directors were fast losing patience with Rita. They had offered her a musical, *Enchanting Rebel,* based on the Allen Lesser novel about the life of stage performer Adah Isaacs Menken (1835-68), who created a sensation in *Mazeppa* (1862) when, at the terrific climax of the show, she, clad in pink tights and thus looking nude, appeared strapped to the back of a horse. The project fell apart, and then Cohn came up with *Joseph and His Brethren.* He had not been so enthusiastic about a film project in a long time. Not even the highly profitable and Oscar-winning *From Here to Eternity* (Columbia, 1953) and *On the Waterfront* (Columbia, 1954) had intrigued him so much. Clifford Odets was hired to prepare a script for the high-budgeted biblical epic, and Rita, of course, was to play Zuleika, wife of Potiphar (a part already cast with Lee J. Cobb). Because this was *the* production for Cohn, he was taking great pains in casting the title role. Among those tested and/or considered for Joseph were Tony Curtis, John Cassavetes, Peter Finch, Alan Badel, Gerard Philipe, Jack Lemmon, Steven Hill, Robert Francis, and Kerwin Matthews. Finally, in December 1954, it seemed that the project was finalized and Rita and Columbia signed a new agreement. The contract was reputed to be geared to net her a $1 million plus $300,000 for two films. A special proviso insured that the studio would create special screen parts for Haymes.

As it developed, Haymes thought he would be ideal as Joseph, a feeling not shared by Cohn or his executives.* The March 8, 1955, shooting date for *Joseph and His Brethren* arrived with Cohn having determined once and for all who the leading man would be; Rita insisted she would not begin work on such an unsettled production.† On April 13, 1955, she walked

---

*Cohn would later reveal, "That crooner told me that either he played Joseph or his wife was out of the cast." According to industry reports, when Orson Welles was up for a role in *Joseph,* Haymes said, "[I am sure] she would not want to appear with Orson."

†The picture had to be finished by a particular date so she could go to Paris with Yasmin to see her father. Rita feared that if she remained behind Aly might carry out his threats to permanently kidnap the girl.

off the film altogether. This was the final straw for Cohn, who eventually had to shelve permanently the biblical picture. The indignant studio boss blasted forth at Rita. "When you came here," he told her, "you were nothing, a nobody. All you had was a beautiful body and Harry Cohn. Now you just have the body." Cohn was determined to prove to Rita, to Hollywood, and to himself that he could manufacture a new star. Kim Novak, who had already scored in *Pushover* (Columbia, 1954), was given the big build-up with *Picnic* (Columbia, 1955) and *The Eddy Duchin Story* (Columbia, 1956), solidifying her spot as the studio's new sex goddess.

An offended Rita had her attorneys institute a suit against Columbia Pictures, demanding full payment for the role, which she claimed she had been ready to essay. The studio counterclaimed for assorted damages, including restitution of $98,000 they had advanced Rita on the *Joseph* project, plus the $50,000 handed to Haymes to settle his debts. When Rita, under Haymes's "management," formed her own film company, Crystal Bay Productions, and made plans with United Artists for several projects, Columbia threatened United Artists, or any other studio considering hiring her, that Rita's contractual obligations to Columbia took precedence over any other agreement.* A stymied Rita found herself legally unable to seek employment in the film industry.

By mid-1955 there were already strong rumors in Hollywood that a hard-drinking Haymes was being physically abusive to Rita. As was her custom with past husbands, Rita would never openly criticize Haymes. However, on August 29, 1955, she announced her separation from him;† on November 3, 1955, while in Paris with Yasmin, she filed for divorce, and on December 12 of that year, the decree was granted in absentia in Reno, Nevada (neither she nor he was in court).

In the course of early 1956, Rita and Columbia reached a compromise, with the star agreeing to make two final films for the studio at an overall salary of $300,000. The first was *Fire Down Below* (Columbia, 1957), filmed largely on location in Trinidad by a London company with American stars backed up by a top English supporting cast. As in days of old, Rita was cast as a woman with a shady, mysterious past, and a very uncertain future. Again, she was a *femme fatale* who set men's blood boiling. Having been buffeted from port to port, in Puerto Rico she hires two roughnecks (Robert Mitchum and Jack Lemmon) to transport her in their tub to the French isle of Santa Nada. Quite predictably the two men fight over rights to Rita. At first, Lemmon appears the victor and announces that he and Rita will return to the States as man and wife. But in the cli-

*Rita had already received a $100,000 advance from United Artists.

†At the time Haymes moaned publicly, "I don't know what I'll do without Rita. She's wonderful. I can't go on without her. I'm in love with her. A man is only in love once. If she divorces me, I don't know what I'll do!" Haymes would later marry and divorce singer Fran Jeffries. For the past decade he has been wed to English model Wendy Smith. After publicly renouncing drinking in 1965, he has made a vocal-career comeback.

max to a tense subplot, which has Lemmon being rescued from a sinking cargo vessel, he realizes Rita belongs with Mitchum and bows out of the scene.

Fire Down Below was budgeted at $2.4 million, but hardly made back its costs. "No need to call the Fire Department to handle *Fire Down Below*," wrote Bosley Crowther (*New York Times*), "it has its own built-in cold water . . . " As for Rita, she enjoyed one inspired sequence in the picture, in which she launched into a frenzied limbo dance at a noisy West Indian festival. Her gusto here brought back memories of *Gilda* and the erotic samba she performed in that famed film. But for the most part, the Rita of *Fire Down Below* was a sadly worn-out creature. Her character's revealing statement had quite a bit of self-truth in it, "I'm no good for you. No good for anyone. Armies have marched over me." Her comeback picture had been a fizzle.

Harry Cohn and Columbia had long owned the screen rights to *Pal Joey* and at last turned it into a screen musical for the 1957 film season.* Cohn was insistent that Frank Sinatra play the lead and eventually had to pay the crooner $125,000 plus twenty-five percent of the profits. To insure a healthy return on this investment, Cohn hired George Sidney to direct the color musical, and placed Rita and Kim Novak, his old and new sex goddesses, in the starring line-up.

Pal Joey turned out to be a popular blockbuster, grossing $4.7 million in distributors' domestic rentals.† Although Rita received top billing in the musical, it was Sinatra as the goodnatured louse, Joey Evans, who stole the show, with Novak as the "innocent" chorine, Linda English, running in second place. Once again Rita's role was a slice of reality. She was cast as the mature woman who discovers that money and experience are not enough to keep the interest of a younger man (Sinatra) from wandering to a fresh-blooming young woman (Novak). For any viewer who appreciated Rita's real-life situation, the final sequence of *Pal Joey* was enough to bring tears to the eyes. Rita's character offered Sinatra a choice: either he could have her and her backing for his nightclub, Chez Joey, or he could take the broke but loving Novak. Rita already knows the answer, but waits in her chauffeur-driven car for the final tabulation. She then stoically watches the love-exhilarated Sinatra and Novak walk off hand in hand into the sunset.

Rita had three musical scenes in *Pal Joey:*‡ a rendering of the ballad "Bewitched, Bothered and Bewildered," performed in a magnificently

---

*The Richard Rodgers-Lorenz Hart musical based on the John O'Hara story opened on Broadway at the Ethel Barrymore Theatre for a 374-performance run. Vivienne Segal, Gene Kelly, and June Havoc were in the leads. A 1952 Broadway revival starred Segal and Harold Lang.

† Rita's *Salome* had grossed $4.75 million in distributors' domestic rentals.

‡While Rita expertly provided her own talk-sing introductions to each of the songs, Jo Ann Greer dubbed the actual vocals.

appointed bedroom with a glass shower ensemble; the dynamic-witty (despite a laundering of the lyrics) strip number, "Zip";* and the garish dream sequence dance with wisecracking Sinatra and moony Novak. The latter segment very clearly revealed just how physically mature and uncertain of her former sex-goddess status Rita had become.† Both she and Novak were clothed in form-clinging leotard outfits, and each wore unbecoming hair falls. While radiant blonde Novak merely appeared gawky in the under-choreographed routine, Rita seemed downright frightened, tentative, and awkward. Her fabled terpsichorean grace had evidently vanished from lack of practice and the natural onset of advanced years. *Pal Joey* was indeed a swansong for the star—as Harry Cohn would say when the contracts of William Holden, Glenn Ford, and Rita expired, "There go my three kids. It's the end of an era." Rita was less sentimental about the departure from her home studio after two decades. "I don't look back. I did what I had to. I was the property of Columbia Pictures and they kept me busy. Since I could sing, dance and act, I never felt like one of those movie queens they used to manufacture in Hollywood. I had sexy genes, I guess, and that helped. I was held back by what the studio thought I could do. But I made some good films, though never a lot of money.‡ I have no head for business. My one pursuit is acting and I'm dedicated to it."

Just from the tenor of her statements to the press, it was evident that the nearly forty-year-old Rita was taking stock of what the future had to offer her professionally. When asked her feelings about the popularity of Marilyn Monroe and Jayne Mansfield as celluloid sex objects, Rita remarked: "Marilyn and Jayne can have the headlines. I've had enough! From now on the only headlines I want are on my acting!" On another occasion she announced: "I'm in a new phase of my career. I'm a freelance actress. I could have stayed under a studio contract; by not staying, I gave up a lot of money. But I felt that at some point in my life I had to choose my own roles. I looked at all the parts I had done and realized that, no matter how they were sliced, it was still Salome."

In 1956 Rita had been dating producer Ramon Hakim, a romance that did not last. While attending a party for *Fire Down Below*, she met producer James Hill; their mutual admiration was of a personal and professional nature. He was a partner in Hecht-Hill-Lancaster Productions, which was then preparing a screen version of Terence Rattigan's London

*Bosley Crowther (*New York Times*) commented, "[She will] undoubtedly be the envy of all women—She has the occasion to sing 'Zip' with the uninhibited eclat of any burlesque queen."

†Rita, evidently very sensitive about the critics' slamming of her present looks ("[she] seems almost a shell of her former self. Her hair is hennaed beyond reasonable demand" said Justin Gilbert of the *New York Mirror*), snapped back, "I was supposed to be the older woman—and Frank Sinatra happened to be older than I was."

‡Columbia was reported to have grossed about $20 million from worldwide distribution of *Cover Girl, Tonight and Every Night,* and *Gilda.*

and Broadway success, *Separate Tables* (United Artists, 1958).* When Laurence Olivier and Vivien Leigh dropped out of the pending filmization, David Niven was cast as Major Pollock, and Rita, still a very stunning woman, was selected to play Ann Shankland, the former wife of an American writer (Burt Lancaster). In the course of the expanded screen plot, she arrives at the Hotel Beauregard in Bournemouth, England, to beg for a reconciliation with Lancaster. In a tearful scene, that failed to garner respect from the critics or admiration from enough filmgoers,† a hysterical Rita confesses that she has been vain and neurotic most of her life, but that being an unattached, middle-aged socialite in New York was more lonely than she could bear. The movie was rather popular, with David Niven and Wendy Hiller (as the hotel proprietress who is Lancaster's mistress) winning Academy Awards and co-star Deborah Kerr being Oscar-nominated. Despite the conspicuous lack of comments on Rita's performance, the actress has a fond regard for *Separate Tables*.‡

On February 2, 1958, Rita and James Hill were married at his Beverly Hills home, with both of Rita's daughters in attendance. It was her fifth marriage, his first. She was thirty-nine, and he was forty-one years old.

She then returned to Columbia Pictures to co-star with top-billed Gary Cooper in *They Came to Cordura* (Columbia, 1959). The old home studio was not the same, for on February 27, 1958, sixty-six-year-old Harry Cohn had died. But then, Rita was not the same in this widescreen color Western budgeted at $4.5 million. For the first time in her screen career, the most glamorous of the glamour sex queens was appearing onscreen without benefit of much makeup.§ She was cast as the haggard Adelaide Geary, who has been accused of consorting with Pancho Villa's forces and is under the guarded escort of Major Thomas Thorn (Cooper) on the harrowing trek to Cordura, where fellow journeyers (Van Heflin, Tab Hunter, Richard Conte, Michael Callan) are to be given U.S. governmental decorations of honor for valor in action (medals which none of them deserves, and each knows it). For a change, Rita received some good notices. "[She] acts almost human in a stained and dusty riding costume" (Bosley Crowther, *New York Times*). However, the offbeat Western was not the commercial success anticipated.

Rita finally had an opportunity to perform in a Clifford Odets screenplay

*The 1954 London drama opened at the Music Box Theatre in New York City on October 25, 1956, for a 332-performance run. In the stage version, Margaret Leighton and Eric Portman played both sets of lead characters.

†The *London Times* insisted, "Miss Hayworth totally fails to suggest the pathetic weaknesses that lie at the heart of the woman who was once so cruelly beautiful and who now needs drugs to ward off the vision of old age."

‡Rita would later explain, "I liked the role of Ann because she had great depth and the part permitted a good deal of variation. . . . With many roles, an actress is either one sort of person or another—but in Ann there were many variables."

§There was a good deal of publicity about the "efforts" of the makeup man at making Rita look worn-out, dirty, sun-blistered, and, in short, a harridan.

when she played Jo Morris in *The Story on Page One* (Twentieth Century-Fox, 1959). Odets directed this stark, black-and-white courtroom drama of a conventional middle-class housewife (Rita) who has an affair with an apron-strung mama's boy (Gig Young) and is accused of killing her policeman husband (Alfred Ryder). Once again Rita appeared onscreen with only the least traces of camera makeup. The ex-glamour star turned in another sterling, low-keyed performance. "If she had as stinging a vehicle as Susan Hayward had in *I Want to Live,* she might well have turned in the performance of her career" (Paul V. Beckley, *New York Herald-Tribune*). Unfortunately, despite the publicity hoopla surrounding the rushing of theatre prints of *The Story on Page One* onto the market in time to qualify for the Oscar races, the picture never garnered proper momentum to insure financial success.

For nearly a decade, trouble-prone Rita had been engulfed in various law suits and personal struggles with Aly Khan over the future of their daughter, Yasmin. In November 1954, Rita had won legal approval of her 1953 divorce settlement, in which the proud woman only accepted pittances.* But at least she retained custody of Yasmin, who, as the fourth person in line of ascent to the Aga Khan's throne, was of vital importance to the millions of Ismaili Moslems. Then, on July 10, 1957, the Aga died in Geneva at the age of seventy-nine, and Prince Karim was appointed Aga Khan IV. On May 22, 1957, Aly obtained a Swiss divorce from Rita so that he could wed model Bettina (his constant companion since his romances with Gene Tierney and Yvonne De Carlo had evaporated). The divorce† nullified the requirement for Aly to post a $100,000 bond each time Yasmin left her mother's custody to visit with him. In July 1959, Rita's husband (James Hill) arranged a new settlement between Rita and Aly regarding Yasmin, by which Rita gave up any claim on Yasmin's behalf to the millions of dollars in the Aga's and Aly's control. It was a sensible compromise, since Aly, as the Pakistani ambassador to the United Nations, was under diplomatic immunity, which prevented Rita from serving him with any more legal suits.

Then, on May 12, 1960, Aly Khan was killed in an auto accident in France. A shocked Rita, who had collapsed upon hearing the news, later told the press: "For both Yasmin and myself, I can only say at this time how deeply moved we are at the news of Aly's death. It will be a tremendous loss to Yasmin, who has always been most attached to her father." Two years later a Paris court would award Yasmin $30,000 in damages for Charles Bichaton's negligence, which caused the road fatality.

---

*She was to receive $15,000 for past legal expenses; $8,000 for Aly's arrears in child support, and thereafter $8,000 a year for the support of Yasmin and $1,000 a month when the child was with Rita and not in boarding school.

†Aly once said of Rita, "All that she ever wanted to do was slip into something comfortable and stay around the fireside. Excitement? She was just a homebody."

When she recuperated from the trauma of Aly's death, a financially needy Rita went to Spain to appear in the hastily conceived *The Happy Thieves* (United Artists, 1962). Her leading man was dapper Rex Harrison. This tale of two middle-aged art thieves who plan the heist of a Goya painting from the Prado Museum was dismal in all areas of production, even to the murky black-and-white photography. It sat on the shelf for nearly a year before United Artists tossed it into domestic distribution. *Time* magazine chided of the stars, "[They] are both old enough to know better." A serious-looking Yasmin (she had braces on her teeth and could not smile) had a bit as an extra.

When Rita returned from Spain, she and Hill separated and in September 1961 they were divorced in a Santa Monica, California, court. She said: "My husband was more concerned with his own career than his family life with me. When he would come home he would be very distant, very aloof and go off by himself for hour after hour." In the court testimony Rita admitted that Hill "said I was not a nice woman in too loud a voice."

Hardly had Rita exited from the Hill ruckus, than she flew back into the frying pan again, this time in the company of Gary Merrill, the fifty-one-year-old actor ex-husband of Bette Davis. The decorous elements in the movie colony were aghast that Rita and Merrill, in an evident bid for hippiedom, would walk barefoot and, wearing the most casual of garb, enter supermarkets and restaurants in sedate Beverly Hills. The press reports were most unfriendly and unimpressed by Rita's explanation of her unladylike bohemian behavior: "At last I am free." As one film producer snidely remarked of the relationship, "Bette Davis she ain't."

In February 1962, Rita and Merrill were in Manhattan preparing for the Broadway debut of Bernard Evslin's play, *Step on a Crack*. Rita was studying voice control with Alfred Dixon in order to better portray the role of a vaudeville performer whose marriage to a small-town doctor is on the verge of disintegration. Rita confided about her new-vista acting ambition: "I'm not doing this simply to show I can. It's just that I have confidence. I feel I have changed." However neither Rita nor the play made it to Broadway. She checked into Flower Fifth Avenue Hospital with physical fatigue, and Nancy Kelly was substituted in her part, but the show closed on the road. The trade press insisted she had been forced to withdraw from the production because of stage fright and overweight. Rita countered: "Apart from anemia and fatigue, there is nothing wrong with my health or outlook. It is ridiculous for anyone to say I am at the end of my rope."

Rita's romance with Merrill faded soon therafter, and it was another two years before she again appeared onscreen. Her part in *Circus World* (Paramount, 1964), a John Wayne actioner directed by Henry Hathaway, could not be considered anything but a glorified cameo part. She was Lilli

Alfredo, the aerial performer, who had mothered his child (Claudia Cardinale). A brave Rita informed reporters of her casting: "It's marvelous . . . I can't play sex symbols all my life. I'm not a glamour girl anymore. I'm a mature woman." However, as the still curvaceous, but faded big-top performer, it was quite evident that Rita was doing her darnedest to muster the old charisma to compete with the far younger Cardinale oncamera. Besides a large fire at the Madrid soundstages of producer Samuel Bronston, rumor had it that the production was plagued by problems engendered by Rita's acquired habit of hard-drinking.

She was among the collection of "names" who appeared for near-charity wages (expense-paid trips to exotic locales was the inducement) in the telefeature *The Poppy Is Also a Flower* (ABC, April 22, 1966), which had twenty minutes restored to the eighty-minute tale when it was theatrically released in Europe. Princess Grace of Monaco narrated this naive tale of a United Nations team's hunt for a narcotics smuggling ring, with Rita on tap briefly as the junkie wife of Gilbert Roland. The project was warmly panned by the critics. Rita received some pathetic publicity over an incident that occurred in Nice, France, where she was filming her bit. At dinner one night a waiter, with all good intentions, said to her, "My mother loved all your pictures." Rita took umbrage at this unintentional slap, and the scene received global press coverage.

When *Affair in Trinidad* was released, Rita had been the big star, but now, in *The Money Trap* (MGM, 1966), Glenn Ford was the marquee name, Elke Sommer was his vis-à-vis, and Rita was reduced in this programmer to playing a guest spot as the blowsy waitress from corrupt law-enforcer Ford's past. "Everyone in *The Money Trap* is contemptible but Rita Hayworth, and she gets pushed off a building" (*Newsweek* magazine). Archer Winsten (*New York Post*) enunciated: " . . . in her comparatively small role, as an alcoholic slatter, Miss Hayworth is entirely convincing, from slurred speech to wobbly walk. The middle-aged actress has been more fair—but never more admirable." It was hard to decide whether the latter comment was a complimentary tribute or a requiem testimonial.

At one point, Anthony Quinn had announced that he and Rita, who had played together in *Blood and Sand*, would appear in a feature about an aging bullfighter and a dancer who have each outlived their career peaks. That project never materialized, but the two performers did join together for *L'Avventuriero* (*The Rover*), which was filmed at Rome's Cinecitta studio and on the island of Elba in late 1966. Quinn was a pirate adventurer in the 1810s, with Rita as the aunt of Rosanna Schiaffino, the girl who shelters the hounded buccaneer. The picture had scanty European playdates in 1967, with even spottier American distribution by Cinerama in 1971.

It is not easy for a world-famous sex symbol to grow old gracefully, let alone retain any semblance of a film career.* This point was made brutally clear on a "First Tuesday" network interview in November 1968, which labeled Rita, for all intents and purposes, as washed up. Certainly her next three films did nothing to alter this staggering viewpoint. She replaced Joan Crawford as the very middle-aged mother of a group of jewel thieves in the Spanish-lensed *I Bastardi* (*Sons of Satan*) (Warner Bros., 1969), which has yet to have full American release. The most bizarre film assignment of her career to date was *The Naked Zoo* (Haven, 1970), which was lensed in Miami. Apparently after Rita's completed scenes were viewed, it was decided to bolster the quickie picture with two very plotwise unrelated sexploitation scenes. The picture opened and closed in New York in three days, but not quickly enough to escape being reviewed. *Cue* magazine's Donald J. Mayerson reported of this farrago, "Miss Hayworth—older, wrinkled, and edematous—is seen to such disadvantage that it would be a kindness to her to avoid the film." She played the role of a wheelchair-ridden woman and has an affair with an LSD-addicted pimp (Stephen Oliver).

Rita returned to Europe for *Sur la Route de Salina* (*Road to Salina*) Avco-Embassy, 1971), which found her playing the hysterical operator of a roadside gas station, who insists that young hitchhiker Robert Walker, Jr., is her long-lost son. The film came and went, but Rita garnered some touching reviews. Vincent Canby (*New York Times*) noted: "Most affecting, for reasons that have little to do with her performance as the mother (which is perfectly all right), is Miss Hayworth. Her magnificent former beauty acts as a kind of camera filter. It softens but never denies the passage of time, which could only end in defeat."

While her screen career was dribbling down the drain, Rita made a few other media appearances. On February 1, 1971, she made her first real television performance on, of all things, "The Carol Burnett Show." On this CBS-TV variety show, Rita appeared alternately very calm and quite nervous, particularly when she joined the comedienne in the charwoman mop-and-pail routine. That fall, Rita was back in Manhattan on a professional assignment. When it was announced that Lauren Bacall was going to California with the national company of her Tony-winning Broadway musical *Applause*,† Rita, Anne Baxter, and Lizabeth Scott were all under consideration for the star's New York replacement. Rita was considered to have the most marquee draw among the trio and was signed for the part. After five weeks of rehearsal, the producers fired her,

---

*A laudatory chapter of NBC-TV's "Hollywood and the Stars," entitled *The Odyssey of Rita Hayworth* (April 13, 1964), made it seem that the actress was at the height of her career. The half-hour show used a good many film clips from Rita's Columbia pictures, as well as including a specially lensed new interview with the star.

†The musicalized version of *All about Eve* (Twentieth Century-Fox, 1950) opened at the Palace Theatre on March 30, 1970, for a run of 896 performances.

claiming she was a "slow study." She returned to California, but not before sounding off, "I withdrew when I realized that I couldn't have been ready by July. I couldn't get to rehearse on the stage of the theatre because it wasn't made available to me. . . . I wasn't allowed to keep my three dachshunds. . . . I wasn't comfortable in my hotel and I'd forgotten that I hate elevators." The management made no counterclaims, and Anne Baxter assumed the part.

After a few months of inactivity in California, Rita received a telephone call from her former co-star and still good friend Robert Mitchum, offering her a part in his new picture *The Wrath of God* (MGM, 1972). After much persuasion, the now screen-timorous Rita accepted the role of a stately Mexican señora who joins with a revolutionary priest (Mitchum) against her power-crazed son (Frank Langella). From the Guanajuato, Mexico, location site, Rita exclaimed: "It's great to be filming again. I'm never bored, but one movie a year would be just right for me. I've made a couple in the last three years which nobody ever saw. This is the most important thing I've done in a long time." Rita was amazed to find, when she arrived at the south-of-the-border airport, that local citizenry appeared in great numbers to greet her with cries of "Geel-da, Geelda!" She ruminated; "Funny isn't it. They still remember me for that. Film makers too. They'd have me playing Gilda today and still talk about a remake. But, of course, I wouldn't do it."

The $2.5 million *The Wrath of God* did not live up to the expectations of producer-director Ralph Nelson. The *Los Angeles Herald-Examiner* for one, labeled the picture "old-fashioned glorious nonsense . . . salty plot-sensational scenery." Rita's reviews were polite, with more attention given to her well-preserved looks than to her emoting (which was out of tune with the other players). She had been scheduled to make a national publicity tour on behalf of the film, but the campaign was altered without official explanation.

In the summer of 1972 it was announced Rita would appear in *The Deadly Species*, a ninety-minute television pilot for a series to be lensed in Rome. She was to play Helena Modjeska (1844-1909), the famed Polish actress. That unrealistic project vanished, but Rita did go to England in October 1972 to play the role of an Auntie Mame-type literary agent in the Grand Guignol five-part picture, *Tales that Witness Madness* (Paramount, 1973). Filming had barely gotten under way for the Freddie Francis-directed horror film when Rita withdrew for reasons of health. Ironically, coincidentally, or intentionally, her replacement was Kim Novak. Rita was later sued for $1 million for performing in "an unprofessional, undiligent, and improper manner." The case had an out-of-court settlement. When that venture ended so badly for Rita, projected plans for her to reunite with Glenn Ford in *Mia*, a film to be directed by Ida Lupino in London, were dropped.

Rita returned to California, more subdued but unbeaten. In later October of that year, she appeared at the San Francisco International Film Festival at the Palace of Fine Arts. In the course of her Tribute Evening, she was subjected to some rather crude questioning from the gathered crowd.* She returned to her Beverly Hills home ("my only shelter in the world"), which is around the corner from Glenn Ford's abode. In early 1973, she was among the guests on the syndicated "This Is Your Life" show segment devoted to subject Glenn Ford (NBC, February 3, 1973). It was her last professional appearance to date.

Now that her daughter Rebecca is married and residing near Vancouver, Washington, Yasmin is based in New York preparing for a vocal career, and her brother Eduardo is dead.† Rita is very much alone, familywise. But, she insists, "I don't live alone. I love people. I'm always going out. I love being around people. A celebrity like I am, sort of, if she's not out every night, people say she's a recluse." In mid-1972, Rita's constant escort was fifty-six-year-old William Gilpin, a Los Angeles furniture dealer. That association was terminated when Rita became professionally and emotionally involved with twenty-nine-year-old Curtis Roberts, her new business manager.

Although she is out of the motion-picture limelight, Rita is still considered very newsworthy. She is constantly asked a barrage of questions on a whole spectrum of subjects. Some of her recent replies have been:

On matrimony: "I didn't want five husbands. But it happened that way, and that's all there is to it. I meant what I said about a sixth. I'd like to get married again, and I'd like to go on working.

"But falling in love doesn't happen overnight. It never happened overnight with me. I always had to know somebody pretty well before I married them.

"Why should I be criticized for being married five times? I know a lot of people are shocked by it, or pretend to be. But a lot of people also marry once and have dozens of lovers on the side. Is that any better?

"When I look back on my marriages, on the break-ups, sure I know the pain I went through. But that's part of life, and it has its own value.

" . . . If I marry again I could never live with somebody without a sense of humor. Looks hasn't anything to do with it—none of my husbands looked the same, did they? I'd be happier with someone with an artistic nature."

When queried about her husbands in particular, Rita has remarked, recently, " . . . [Orson Welles] was tormented, possessive, insecure . . . a

*One rude audience participant inquired, "How do you feel seeing your beautiful face on the screen as opposed to seeing it in the mirror when you wake up in the morning?"
A startled, angry Rita retorted, "I don't have to look at it in the morning. I don't wake up until the afternoon."
†He died on March 11, 1974 of cancer at the age of 54. He was buried at Hollywood Cemetery. He was survived by his widow, Teresa, and three sons, Eduardo III, Raul, and Raymond.

genius, crazy like a horse, and a marvelous man, completely unaware of reality." As for Aly Khan, "He was upset by the fact that my character was becoming more definite. Perhaps for him I should have been and remained something like one of his horses."

What have her many marriages taught her? "Basically, I am a good, gentle person but I am attracted to mean personalities."

On nudity: "Everybody else does nude scenes, but I don't. I never made nude movies. I didn't have to do that. I danced. I was provocative, I guess, in some things. But I was not completely exposed."

Re interviews: "Why do they want to peel them [the subjects] down to the very marrow?"

About freedom of will: "Nobody makes up my mind for me. They used to at Columbia."

Concerning an autobiography: "A book! Me? Why? I have nothing to be ashamed of and, in today's market, if you've got nothing to be ashamed of, nobody would buy it. How do people write a whole book about themselves, anyway?"

Of life's bounties: "I haven't had everything from life. I've had too much."

Regarding her personality: "Some people mistake my shyness for snobbishness. It just isn't so."

About the past: "I don't sit and think about it. It's what is happening now—it's today—not yesterday."

If any small grouping of words can best sum up the Rita Hayworth of today, it is her own recent statement: "Honey, I've no regrets. I made mistakes, and I paid for them. But I wouldn't change one hour of my life, because it's made me what I am."

Feature Film Appearances

As Rita Cansino:

UNDER THE PAMPAS MOON (Fox, 1935) 72 M.

Producer, B. G. De Sylva; director, James Tinling; story, Gordon Morris; screenplay, Ernest Pascal, Bradley King; songs, De Sylva and Walter Samuels; Paul Francis Webster and Lew Pollack; Arthur Wynter-Smith; Cyril J. Mockridge and Miguel De Zarraga; choreography, Jack Donahue; camera, Chester Lyons.

Warner Baxter (Cesar Campo); Ketti Gallian (Yvonne LaMarr); Frank Veloz and Yolanda (Dancers); John Miljan (Gregory Scott); J. Carrol Naish (Tito); Soledad Jiminez (Pepita Campo); Jack LaRue (Bazan); George Irving (Don Bennett); Blanca Vischser (Elena); Rita Cansino (Carmen); Armida (Rosa); Ann Codee (Madame LaMarr); Phillip Cooper (Little Jose); Paul Porcasi (Pierre); Max Wagner (Big Jose); Chris-Pin Martin (Pietro); Lona Andre (Dolores); Princess Mural Sharado (Bit); Tito Guizar (Singer).

CHARLIE CHAN IN EGYPT (Fox, 1935) 65 M.

Producer, Edward T. Lowe; director, Louis King; based on the character created by Earl Derr Biggers; screenplay, Robert Ellis, Helen Logan; music arranger-conductor, Sammy Kaylin; art director, William Darling; sound, E. H. Hansen; camera, Daniel B. Clark; editor, Alfred DeGaetano.

Warner Oland (Charlie Chan); Pat Paterson (Carol Arnold); Thomas Beck (Tom Evans); Rita Cansino (Nayda); Jameson Thomas (Dr. Anton Racine); Frank Conroy (Professor John Thurston); Nigel De Brulier (Edfu Ahmad); Paul Porcasi (Soueida); Arthur Stone (Dragoman); Stepin Fetchit (Snowshoes); James Eagles (Barry Arnold); Frank Reicher (Dr. Jaipur); George Irving (Professor Arnold); Anita Brown (Snowshoes' Friend); John Davidson (Daoud Atrash, the Chemist); Gloria Roy (Bit); John George (Dwarf Egyptian Helper).

DANTE'S INFERNO (Fox, 1935) 91 M.

Producer, Sol M. Wurtezl; director, Harry Lachman; screenplay, Philip Klein, Robert M. Yost; music director, Arthur Lange; music, Hugo Friedhofer, Samuel Kaylin, R. H. Bassett, Peter Brunelli; choreography, Sammy Lee; allegorical set designs, Willy Pogany; camera, Rudolph Mate; editor, Al De Gaetano

Spencer Tracy (Jim Carter); Claire Trevor (Betty McWade); Henry B. Walthall (Pop McWade); Scotty Beckett [Alexander (Sonny) Carter]; Alan Dinehart (Jonesy); Astrid Allwyn, Ruthelma Stevens (Girls in Stoke-Hold); Joe Brown (Baseball Concessionaire); George Humbert (Tony, the Hamburger-Stand Proprietor); Robert Gleckler (Dean); Maidel Turner (Mme. Zucchini); Nella Walker (Mrs. Hamilton); Lita Chevret (Mrs. Martin); Richard Tucker (Mr. Hamilton); Edward Pawley (Clinton, the Ship's Officer); Morgan Wallace (Captain Morgan);

Harry Woods (Second Officer Reynolds); Gary Leon, Rita Cansino (Specialty Dancers); Ruth Clifford (Mrs. Gray); Dorothy Dix (Ticket Seller); Hal Boyer, J. Lloyd (College Boys); Jayne Regan (College Girl); Gardner James (Radio Operator); Jerry Gamble (Speiler); Edward McWade (Professor of Anatomy); Patricia Caron (Sailor's Girl); John George (Andrew, the Hunchback Speiler); Ronald Rondell (Ticket Buyer); Harry Schultz, John Carpenter, George Chan (Concessionaires); Gertrude Astor, Tiny Jones (Concessionaires' Wives); Frank Austin (Photographer); Frank Moran (Mike, the Stoker); Kenneth Gibson (Assistant Purser); Harold A. Miller, Barrett Whitelaw, Jean Fenwick (Group in Boiler Room); Warren Hymer (Bozo, the Stoker); Ray Corrigan, Paul Schwegeler, Noble Johnson (The Devils); Lorna Lowe (Cleopatra); Elinor Johnson (Sappho); Andre Johnsen (Salome); Constantine Romanoff, Harry Wilson (Stokers); Paul McVey (Assistant); Charlie Sullivan (Drunken Sailor); Leona Lane (Borgia); Juana Sutton (Catherine de Medici); Marion Strickland (Eve); Gale Goodson (Little Bo Peep); Eve Kimberly (Oriental Maid); Margaret McCrystal, Dorothy Stockmar (Trumpeters); Jay Eaton, Reginald Sheffield (Bidders); Maude Truax (Fat Dowager); Oscar Apfel (Williams); Willard Robertson (Inspector Harris); Aloha Porter (Devil); Charles C. Wilson (Police Inspector); John H. McGuire (Wireless Operator); Bob Reel McKee (Wireless Operator's Assistant); Hale Hamilton (Wallace); George Meeker, Barbara Pepper, Lloyd Pantages (Drunks at Ship's Cafe); Eddie Tamblyn (Page Boy); Jack Norton, Robert Graves (Drunks in Cabin); Harry Holman (Jolly Fat Man); Harry Strang, George Magrill, Paul Palmer (Ship's Officers); Bud Geary (Park Attendant); Billie Huber, Paddy O'Flynn (Married Couple); Andrea Leeds (Anna, Maid to Betty); Mary Ashcraft, Paul Power, Marion Ladd (Bits—New Inferno); Robert Ross (Court Clerk); Russell Hicks (Prosecuting Attorney); Frank Conroy (Defense Attorney); George Irving (Judge); Cliff Lyons, Yakima Canutt (Stokers on the *Paradise*); Dennis O'Keefe (Extra—Ship's Fire).

PADDY O'DAY   (20th, 1935) 73 M.

Producer, Sol M. Wurtzel; director, Lewis Seiler; story-screenplay, Lou Breslow, Edward Eliscu; songs, Sidney Clare, Eliscu, and Harry Akst; camera, Arthur Miller; editor, Al De Gaetano.

Jane Withers (Paddy O'Day); Rita Cansino (Tamara Petrovitch); Pinky Tomlin (Roy Ford); Jane Darwell (Dora); Michael S. Visaroff (Popushka Petrovitch); Nina Visaroff (Momushka Petrovitch); Vera Lewis (Aunt Flora Ford); Louise Carter (Aunt Jane Ford); Russell Simpson (Benton); Francis Ford (Immigration Officer); Pat O'Malley (Wilson); Robert Dudley (Chauffeur); Selmer Jackson, Ruth Clifford, Larry Steers (First Class Passengers); Harvey Clark (Ship's Doctor); Jessie Pringle, Evelyn Selbie (Immigrant Women); Myra Marsh (Matron); Jane Keckley (Maid); Tommy Bupp, Sherwood Bailey, Harry Watson (Street Boys); Russ Clark (New York Traffic Policeman); Larry Fisher (Truck Driver); Hal K. Dawson (Motorist); Egon Brecher, Leonid Snegoff, Demetrius Alexis (Russian Musicians); Clarence H. Wilson (Brewster); Richard Powell (Taxi Driver).

HUMAN CARGO   (20th, 1936) 66 M.

Producer, Sol M. Wurtzel; director, Allan Dwan; based on the novel *I Will Be Faithful* by Kathleen Shepard; screenplay, Jefferson Parker, Doris Malloy; art director, Duncan Cramer; costumes, William Lambert; camera, Daniel B. Clark; editor, Louis R. Loeffler.

Claire Trevor (Bonnie Brewster); Brian Donlevy (Pack Campbell); Alan Dinehart (Lionel Crocker); Rita Cansino (Carmen Zoro); Ralph Morgan (District Attorney Carey); Morgan Wallace (Fender); Helen Troy (Susie); Ralf Harolde (Tony); John McGuire (Spike); Wade Boteler (McSweeney); Harry Woods (Conklin); Stanley Blystone, Ivan "Dusty" Miller, Pat Hartigan, Tom O'Grady (Detectives); Herman Bing (Schultz); Paul McVey (Ship's Officer); Tom Ricketts (Reporter); Harry Semels (Baretto); Wilfred Lucas (Detective Lieutenant); Edward Cooper (Butler); Frederick Vogeding (Captain); John Rogers (Foreigners' Agent); Arno Frey (German Husband); Rosalie Hegedus (German Mother); Hans Fuerberg, Milla Davenport (German Characters); Otto H. Fries (German Cook); Alphonse Martell (Frenchman); Hector V. Sarno (Italian); Eddie Buzard (Copy Boy); Claudia Coleman (Sob Sister).

MEET NERO WOLFE (Col., 1936) 73 M.

Producer, B. P. Schulberg; director, Herbert Biberman; based on the novel *Fer de Lance* by Rex Stout; screenplay, Howard J. Green, Bruce Manning, Joseph Anthony; camera, Henry Freulich; editor, Otto Meyer.

Edward Arnold (Nero Wolfe); Lionel Stander (Archie Goodwin); Joan Perry (Ellen Barstow); Victor Jory (Claude Roberts); Nana Bryant (Sara Barstow); Dennie Moore (Mazie Gray); Russell Hardie (Manuel Kimball); Walter Kingsford (E. J. Kimball); Boyd Irwin, Sr. (Professor Barstow); John Qualen (Olaf); Gene Morgan (O'Grady); Rita Cansino (Maria Maringola); Frank Conroy (Dr. Bradford); Juan Toreno (Carlo Maringola); Martha Tibbetts (Anna); Eddy Waller (Golf Starter); George Offerman, Jr. (Mike); William Benedict (Johnny); Raymond Borzage (Tommy); William Anderson (Bill); Henry Roquemore, Arthur Rankin (Men); Eric Wilton (Butler); Arthur Stuart Hull, Jay Owen (Men); Al Matthews (Attendant); David Worth (Kimball's Chauffeur); Roy Bloss (Messenger Boy).

REBELLION (Crescent, 1936) 60 M.

Producer, E. B. Derr; director, Lynn Shores; story-screenplay, John T. Neville; music director, Abe Meyer; art director, Edward C. Jewell; costumes, Lou Brown; assistant director, Fred Spencer; sound, J. S. Westmoreland; camera, Arthur Martinelli; editor, Donald Barrat.

Tom Keene (Captain John Carroll); Rita Cansino (Paula Castillo); Duncan Renaldo (Ricardo Castillo); William Royle (Harris); Gino Corrado (Pablo); Roger Gray (Honeycutt); Robert McKenzie (Judge Moore); Allan Cavan (President Zachary Taylor); Jack Ingram (Hank); Lita Cortez (Marquita); Theodore Lorch (General Vallejo); W. M. McCormick (Dr. Semple).

TROUBLE IN TEXAS (Grand National, 1937) 63 M.

Producer, Edward F. Finney; supervisor, Lindsley Parsons; director, R. N. Bradbury; screenplay, Robert Emmett; camera, Gus Peterson; editor, Fred Bain.

Tex Ritter (Tex); Rita Cansino (Carmen); Earl Dwire (Barker); Yakima Canutt (Squint); Dick Palmer (Duke); Hal Price (G-Man); Fred Parker (Sheriff); Horace Murphy (Lucky); Charles King (Pinto); Tom Cooper (Announcer); Glenn Strange (Sheriff); Jack Smith (Bix).

OLD LOUISIANA (Crescent, 1937) 64 M.

Producer, E. B. Derr; director, Irvin V. Willat; story, John T. Neville; camera, Arthur Martinelli; editor, Donald M. Barratt.

Tom Keene (John Colfax); Rita Cansino (Angela Gonzales); Robert Fiske (Gilmore); Ray "Raphael" Bennett (Flint); Allan Cavan (President Thomas Jefferson);

Will Morgan (Steve); Budd Buster (Kentucky); Carlos De Valdez (Governor Gonzales); Wally Albright (Davey); Ramsey Hill (James Madison).

HIT THE SADDLE   (Rep., 1937) 57 M.

Producer, Nat Levine; director, Mack V. Wright; based on characters created by William Colt MacDonald; adaptors, Oliver Drake, Maurice Geraghty; screenplay, Drake; songs, Drake and Sam H. Stepf; camera, Jack Marta.

Robert Livingston (Stony Brooks); Ray Corrigan (Tucson Smith); Max Terhune (Lullaby Joslin); Rita Cansino (Rita); J. P. McGowan (Rance McGowan); Edward Cassidy (Sheriff Miller); Sammy McKim (Tim Miller); Yakima Canutt (Buck); Harry Tenbrojok (Joe Harvey); Robert Smith (Hank); Ed Boland (Pete); George Plues (Hechman); Jack Kirk, Russ Powell, Bob Burns (Ranchers); Volcano (Stallion); Allan Cavan (Judge); George Morrell, Wally West (Patrons); Budd Buster (Drunk); Kernan Cripps (Bartender).

As Rita Hayworth:

CRIMINALS OF THE AIR   (Col., 1937) 61 M.

Associate producer, Wallace MacDonald; director, C. C. Coleman, Jr.; story, Jack Cooper; screenplay, Owen Francis; camera, George Meehan; editor, Dick Fantl.

Rosalind Keith (Nancy Rawlings); Charles Quigley (Mark Owens); Rita Hayworth (Rita); John Gallaudet (Ray Patterson); Marc Lawrence (Blast Reardon); Patricia Farr (Mamie); John Hamilton (Captain Wallace); Ralph Byrd (Williamson); Walter Soderling (Camera-Eye Condon); Russell Hicks (Kurt Feldon); Johnny Tyrrell (Bill Morris); Lester Dorr (Trigger); Frank Sully (Contact); Herbert Heywood (Hot-Cake Joe); Lucille Lund (Ruby); Crawford Weaver (Ronnie); Ruth Hilliard (Ronnie's Wife); Matty Kemp (Arnold); Robert Fiske (Groom); Martha Tibbetts (Bride); Howard C. Hickman (Harrison); Sam Flint (Chafin); Eddie Fetherston (Simmons); Jay Eaton (Harry, the Actor); Jane Weir (Actor's Wife); Norman Pabst (Field Porter); Sammy Blum (Bartender); Richard Botiller (Mike).

GIRLS CAN PLAY   (Col., 1937) 58 M.

Producer, Ralph Cohn; director, Lambert Hillyer; story, Albert DeMond; screenplay, Hillyer; women's costumes, Kalloch; art director, Stephen Goosson; music, Morris Stoloff; sound, John Livadary; camera, Lucien Ballard; editor, Byron Robinson.

Jacqueline Wells [later Julie Bishop] (Ann Casey); Charles Quigley (Jimmy Jones); Rita Hayworth (Sue Collins); John Gallaudet (Foy Harris); George McKay (Sluggy); Patricia Farr (Peanuts); Guinn Williams (Lieutenant Flannigan); Joseph Crehan (Brophy); John Tyrrell (Danny Maschio); Richard Terry (Cisto); James Flavin (Bill O'Malley); Beatrice Curtis, Ruth Hilliard (Infielders); Lee Prather (Coroner); Harry Tyler (Dugan); Beatrice Blinn (Mae); George Lloyd (Blater); Michael Breen (Man); Fern Emmett (Anna); Richard Kipling (Mr. Raymond); Bruce Sidney (Doctor); Lucille Lund (Jane Harmon); Evelyn Selbie (Fortuneteller); Lee Shumway (Captain Curtis); Ann Doran (Secretary).

THE GAME THAT KILLS   (Col., 1937) 56 M.

Director, D. Ross Lederman; story, J. Benton Cheney; screenplay, Grace Neville, Fred Niblo, Jr.; music director, Morris Stoloff; camera, Benjamin Kline; editor, James Sweeney.

Charles Quigley (Alec Ferguson); Rita Hayworth (Betty Holland); John Gallaudet (Sam Erskine); J. Farrell MacDonald (Joe Holland); Arthur Loft (Rudy Maxwell); John Tyrrell (Eddie); Paul Fix (Dick Adams); Max Hoffman, Jr. (Bill Drake); Dick Wessel (Leapfrog Soule); Maurice Black (Jeff); Clyde Dilson (Steve Moran); Harry Strang (Walter); Dick Curtis (Whitey); Lee Prather (Bronson); Jack Dougherty, Edmund Cobb (Cops); Ralph Dunn (Detective); Ethan Laidlaw, Eddie Fetherston (Cab Drivers); George Chesebro (Waiter); Bud Weiser, Lloyd Ford (Motor Cops); Sammy McKim (Jack).

PAID TO DANCE   (Col., 1937) 55 M.

Associate producer, Ralph Cohn; director, C. C. Coleman, Jr.; story, Leslie T. White; screenplay, Robert E. Kent; camera, George Meehan; editor, Byron Robinson.

Don Terry (William Dennis); Jacqueline Wells [later Julie Bishop] (Joan Bradley); Rita Hayworth (Betty Morgan); Arthur Loft (Jack Miranda); Paul Stanton (Charles Kennedy); Paul Fix (Nifty); Louise Stanley (Phyllis Parker); Ralph Byrd (Nickels Brown); Beatrice Curtis (Frances Mitchell); Bess Flowers (Suzy); Beatrice Blinn (Lois); Jane Hamilton (Evelyn); Dick Curtis (Mike Givens); Al Herman (Joe Krause); Thurston Hall (Governor); John Gallaudet (Barney Wilson); Horace McMahon (LaRue); George Lloyd (Sanders); Ruth Hilliard (Ruth Gregory); Ann Doran (Rose Trevor); Bud Jamison (Lieutenant); Bill Irving (Salesman); Eddie Fetherston (Skipper); Edward LeSaint (Magistrate); Ernest Wood (Francine); Lee Prather (McDonald); Jay Eaton, Stanley Mack, Ethan Laidlaw, Arthur Stuart Hull (Men); Georgie Cooper (Mrs. Daniels); Edward Hearn (Butler); Bill Lally, Dan Wolheim, Dick Rush, Bruce Mitchell (Cops); George Lollier (Sailor); Jack Cheatham (Radio Cop); Bud McTaggart (Newsboy); Edward Peil, Sr. (Conductor); Walter Lawrence (News Vendor); Nell Craig (Woman); Harry Strang (Attendant).

Television Title: *Hard to Handle*

THE SHADOW   (Col., 1937) 59 M.

Director, Charles C. Coleman; story, Milton Raison; screenplay, Arthur T. Horman; camera, Lucien Ballard; editor, Byron Robinson.

Rita Hayworth (Mary Gillespie); Charles Quigley (Jim Quinn); Marc Lawrence (Kid Crow); Arthur Loft (Sheriff Jackson); Dick Curtis (Carlos); Vernon Dent (Dutch Schultz); Marjorie Main (Hannah Gillespie); Donald Kirke (Señor Martinez); Dwight Frye (Vindecco); Bess Flowers (Marianne); Bill Irving (Mac); Eddie Fetherston (Woody); Sally St. Clair (Dolores); Sue St. Clair (Rosa); John Tyrrell (Mr. Moreno); Beatrice Curtis (Mrs. Moreno); Ann Doran (Miss Shaw); Beatrice Blinn (Miss Shaw); Bud Jamison, Harry Strang (Ticket Sellers); Francis Sayles (Mr. Shaw); Edward Hearn (Circus Doctor); Edward J. LeSaint (Bascomb); Mr. and Mrs. Clemens (Knife-Throwing Act); Ted Mahgean (Masked Figure); Harry Bernard (Watchman); George Hickman (Messenger Boy); Ernie Adams (Roustabout).

WHO KILLED GAIL PRESTON?   (Col., 1938) 61 M.

Director, Leon Barsha; story-screenplay, Robert E. Kent, Henry Taylor; songs, Milton Drake and Ben Oakland; camera, Henry Freulich; editor, Byron Robinson.

Don Terry (Inspector Tom Kellogg); Rita Hayworth (Gail Preston); Robert Paige (Swing Traynor); Wyn Cahoon (Ann Bishop); Gene Morgan (Cliff Connolly); Marc Lawrence (Frank Daniels); Arthur Loft (Jules Stevens); John Gallaudet (Charles Waverly); John Spacey (Patsy Fallon); Eddie Fetherston (Mike); James Millican (Hank); Mildred Gover (Maid); Dwight Frye (Mr. Owen); John Dilson (Curran); Bill

Irving (Arnold); Vernon Dent (Bill, Watchman); Ruth Hilliard (Cigarette Girl); Jane Hamilton (Hat-Check Girl); Allen Brook, Jack Egan (Radio Technicians); James Burtis (Headwaiter); Nell Craig (Society Woman); Hal Craig (Motor Cop); Larry Fisher, Charles Hamilton, George Magrill, Billy Lally, E. L. Dale (Cops); Ralph McCullough (Marshall); Nick Copeland (Louis); Bruce Sidney (Society Man); Broderick O'Farrell (Doctor); Malcolm McTaggart (Elevator Boy); Lee Shumway (Police Announcer); Dick Curtis (Jake).

THERE'S ALWAYS A WOMAN   (Col., 1938) 82 M.

Producer, William Perlberg; director, Alexander Hall; story, Wilson Collison; (uncredited) screen treatment, Joel Sayre, Philip Rapp; screenplay, Gladys Lehman, (uncredited) Morrie Ryskind; art directors, Stephen Goosson, Lionel Banks; gowns, Kalloch; music director, Morris Stoloff; camera, Henry Freulich; editor, Viola Lawrence.

Joan Blondell (Sally Reardon); Melvyn Douglas (William Reardon); Mary Astor (Lola Fraser); Frances Drake (Anne Calhoun); Jerome Cowan (Nick Shane); Robert Paige (Jerry Marlowe); Thurston Hall (District Attorney); Pierre Watkin (Mr. Ketterling); Walter Kingsford (Grigson); Lester Matthews (Walter Fraser); Rita Hayworth (Ketterling's Secretary); Wade Boteler (Sam, Radio-Car Driver); Arthur Loft (Radio Patrolman); William H. Strauss (Rent Collector); Marek Windheim (Headwaiter); Bud Jamison (Jim, the Bartender); George Davis (Waiter); Robert Emmett Kean (*Dispatch* City Editor); John Gallaudet (Reporter); Eddie Fetherston (Photographer); Josef De Stefani (Cigar Stand Clerk); Ted Oliver (Cop); Gene Morgan (Officer Fogarty); Tom Dugan (Detective Flannigan); Bud Geary (D. A.'s Assistant); Billy Benedict (Bellhop); Lee Phelps (Police Broadcaster); Eddie Dunn, George McKay (Cops).

CONVICTED   (Col., 1938) 56 M.

Producer, Kenneth J. Bishop; director, Leon Barsha; based on the story "Face Work" by Cornell Woolrich; screenplay, Edgar Edwards; camera, George Meehan; editor, William Austin.

Charles Quigley (Burns); Rita Hayworth (Jerry Wheeler); Marc Lawrence (Milton Miltis); George McKay (Kane); Doreen MacGregor (Mary Allen); Bill Irving (Cobble-Puss Coley); Eddie Laughton (Berger); Edgar Edwards (Chick Wheeler); Phyllis Clare (Ruby Rose); Bob Rideout (Rocco); Michael Heppell (Pal); Noel Cusack (Aggie); Grant MacDonald (Frankie); Don Douglas (District Attorney).

JUVENILE COURT   (Col., 1938) 58 M.

Director, D. Ross Lederman; story-screenplay, Michael Simmons, Robert Kent, Henry Taylor; music director, Morris Stoloff; assistant director, Wilbur McCaugh; sound, Lodge Cunningham; camera, Benjamin Kline; editor, Byron Robinson.

Paul Kelly (Gary Franklin); Rita Hayworth (Marcia Adams); Frankie Darro (Stubby Adams); Hally Chester (Lefty); Don Latorre (Mickey); David Gorcey (Pighead); Dick Selzer (Ears); Allan Ramsey (Davy); Charles Hart (Squarehead); Howard Hickman (Governor Stanley); Joseph DeStefani (Judge); John Tyrrell (Dutch Adams); Dick Curtis (Detective); Kane Richmond (Bradley); James Blaine, Lee Shumway, Edmund Cobb, Tom London, George Chesebro, Eddie Hearn (Cops); Edward LeSaint (Mr. Lambert); Lee Prather (Mr. Allen); Gloria Blondell (Gary's Secretary); Stanley Andrews (Mayor); Harry Bailey, Steve Clark,

Stanley Mack, Dan Wolheim (Men); Cleo Ridgley, Dorothy Vernon, Eva Mc-Kenzie (Women); Kernan Cripps, Charles Hamilton, Ethan Laidlaw (Radio Cops); Al Herman (Postman); Bud Osborne (Driver); Lester Dorr (Druggist); Harry Bernard (Hick); Vernon Dent (Schultz); Tina Marshall (Davey's Mother); Jack Long (Truck Driver); Buster Slaven (Joe); George Billings (Kid); Cy Schindell (Referee); Helen Dixon (Matron); Reggie Streeter, John Fitzgerald (Boys); Bob Perry (Bartender); Nick Copeland (Drunk); Reginald Simpson, Sam Ash, Don Reed (Reporters).

THE RENEGADE RANGER   (RKO, 1938) 59 M.

Producer, Bert Gilroy; director, David Howard; story-screenplay, Bennett Cohen; camera, Harry Wild; editor, Frederick Knudtson.

George O'Brien (Captain Jack Steele); Rita Hayworth (Judith Alvarez); Tim Holt (Larry Corwin); Ray Whitley (Happy); Lucio Villegas (Juan Capillo); William Royle (Ben Sanderson); Cecilia Callejo (Tonio Capillo); Neal Hart (Sheriff Joe Rawlings); Monte Montague (Monte); Bob Kortman (Idaho); Charles Stevens (Manuel); Jim Mason (Hank); Tom London (Red); Guy Usher (Major Jameson); Chris-Pin Martin (Felipe); Hank Bell (Barfly); Jack O'Shea (Henchman).

HOMICIDE BUREAU   (Col., 1939) 56 M.

Director, C. C. Coleman, Jr.; story-screenplay, Earle Snell; music director, Morris Stoloff; camera, Benjamin Kline; editor, James Sweeney.

Bruce Cabot (Jim Logan); Rita Hayworth (J. G. Bliss); Marc Lawrence (Chuck Brown); Richard Fiske (Hank); Moroni Olsen (Captain Raines); Norman Willis (Briggs); Gene Morgan (Blake); Robert Paige (Thurston); Lee Prather (Jamison); Eddie Fetherston (Specks); Stanley Andrews (Police Commissioner); John Tyrrell (Employee in Poolroom); Charles Trowbridge (Henly); George Lloyd (Boat Captain); Ann Doran (Nurse); Joseph De Stefani (Miller); Beatrice Curtis (Stewardess); Beatrice Blinn (Woman); Dick Curtis (Radio Broadcaster); Stanley Brown (Police Photographer); George De Normand (Trigger); Harry Bernard (Joe); Nell Craig, Georgia Cooper (Committee Women); Kit Guard (Mug); Gene Stone (Man); Ky Robinson (Casey); Dick Rush (Cop); Lee Shumway (Police Switchboard Operator); Wedgwood Nowell (Committee Man); Lester Dorr (Gangster).

THE LONE WOLF SPY HUNT   (Col., 1939) 67 M.

Associate producer, Joseph Sistrom; director, Peter Godfrey; based on a story by Louis Joseph Vance; screenplay, Jonathan Latimer; art director, Lionel Banks; music director, M. W. Stoloff; camera, Allen G. Siegler; editor, Otto Meyer.

Warren William (Michael Lanyard); Ida Lupino (Val Carson); Rita Hayworth (Karen); Virginia Weidler (Patricia Lanyard); Ralph Morgan (Gregory); Tom Dugan (Sergeant Devan); Don Beddoe (Inspector Thomas); Leonard Carey (Jameson); Ben Welden (Jenks); Brandon Tynan (Senator Carson); Helen Lynd (Marie Templeton); Irving Bacon (Sergeant); Marek Windheim (Waiter); Jack Norton (Charlie Fenton, the Drunk); Dick Elliott (Little Cop); Alec Craig (Marriage Bureau Clerk); Alec Craig, Dick Curtis, Lou Davis, John Tyrrell (Heavies); Marc Lawrence (Heavy-Leader); Stanley Brown, Beatrice Curtis, Lola Jensen, James Craig (Guests); Tony Hughes, Bud Jamison (Bartenders); Eddie Laughton (Footman); Forbes Murray (Angus Palmer); James Blaine (Cop); Frank Baker (Doorman); Russ Clark (Evans); Landers Stevens (Thatcher); Lee Phelps (Police Broadcaster); Vernon Dent (Fat Man at Party); Adrian Booth (Girl Whom Lanyard Meets in Club); Eddie Fetherston (Man); Jim Millican (Cab Driver); Jack Hill, George DeNormand, Ed Brandenberg, Dick Jensen, Ed Randolph (Doubles); Eddie Hearn (Police Sergeant); Eddie Cobb (Police Clerk); I. Stanford Jolley (Doorman).

SPECIAL INSPECTOR (Warwick-Syndicate Exchange, 1939) 65 M.

Producer, Kenneth J. Bishop; director, Leon Barsha; screenplay, Edgar Edwards; camera, George Meehan; editor, William Austin.

Charles Quigley (Tom Evans); Rita Hayworth (Patricia Lane); George McKay (Silver); Edgar Edwards (Bill); John Spacey (David Foster); Bob Rideout (Dapper); Grant MacDonald (Skip); Bill Irving (Pete); Vivian Coombs (Mother Jones); Fred Bass (Ralph Collins); Vincent McKenna (Hendricks); Don Douglas (Williams).

ONLY ANGELS HAVE WINGS (Col., 1939) 121 M.

Producer-director-story, Howard Hawks; screenplay, Jules Furthman; music, Manuel Maciste; music director, M. W. Stoloff; art director, Lionel Banks; aerial stunts, Paul Mantz; aerial camera, Elmer Dyer; camera, Joseph Walker; editor, Viola Lawrence.

Cary Grant (Geoff Carter); Jean Arthur (Bonnie Lee); Richard Barthelmess (Bat MacPherson); Rita Hayworth (Judy MacPherson); Thomas Mitchell (Kid Dabb); Allyn Joslyn (Les Peters); Sig Rumann (Dutchy); Victor Kilian (Sparks); John Carroll (Gent Shelton); Donald Barry (Tex Gordon); Noah Beery, Jr. (Jeb Souther); Manuel Maciste (The Singer); Melissa Sierra (Lily); Lucio Villegas (Dr. Lagorio); Pat Flaherty (Mike); Pedro Regas (Pancho); Pat West (Baldy); Candy Candido (Musician); Charles Moore (Servant); Ines Palange (Lily's Aunt); Rafael Corio (Purser); Lew Davis, Jim Millican, Al Rhein, Ky Robinson, Eddie Foster, Curly Dresden, Ed Randolph, Bud Wolfe (Mechanics); Cecilia Callejo (Felice, the Spanish Blonde Girl); Forbes Murray (Hartwood); Stanley Brown (Hartwood, Jr.); Francisco Maran, Victor Travers (Planter Overseers); Wilson Benge (Assistant Purser); Vernon Dent (Boat Captain); Elana Duran (Spanish Blonde Girl); Budd Fine (First Mate); Jack Lowe, Tex Higginson (Banana Foremen); Enrique Acosta, Raoul Lechuga, Dick Botiller, Harry Bailey, Amora Navarro, Tessie Murray (Tourists).

MUSIC IN MY HEART (Col., 1940) 70 M.

Producer, Irving Starr; director, Joseph Santley; story-screenplay, James Edward Grant; songs, Chet Forrest and Bob Wright; dialog director, William Castle; camera, John Stumar; editor, Otto Meyer.

Tony Martin (Robert Gregory); Rita Hayworth (Patricia O'Malley); Andre Kostelanetz and Orchestra (Themselves); Edith Fellows (Mary); Alan Mowbray (Charles Gardner); Eric Blore (Griggs); George Tobias (Sascha); Joseph Crehan (Mark C. Gilman); George Humbert (Luigi); Joey Ray (Miller); Don Brodie (Taxi Driver); Julieta Novis (Leading Lady); Eddie Kane (Blake); Phil Tead (Marshall); Marten Lamont (Barrett).

BLONDIE ON A BUDGET (Col., 1940) 73 M.

Director, Frank R. Strayer; based upon the comic strip created by Chic Young; story, Charles Molyneux Brown; screenplay, Richard Flournoy; camera, Henry Freulich; editor, Gene Havlick.

Penny Singleton (Blondie); Arthur Lake (Dagwood); Larry Simms (Baby

Dumpling); Daisy (Himself); Rita Hayworth (Joan Forrester); Danny Mummert (Alvin Fuddle); Don Beddoe (Marvin Williams); John Qualen (Mr. Fuddle); Fay Helm (Mrs. Fuddle); Irving Bacon (Mailman); Thurston Hall (Brice); William Brisbane (Theatre Manager); Emory Parnell (Dempsey); Willie Best (Black Boy); Hal K. Dawson (Bank Teller); Chester Clute (Ticket Agent); Dick Curtis (Mechanic); George Guhl (Platt); Janet Shaw, Claire James (Usherettes); Mary Currier, Rita Owin (Salesladies); Gene Morgan (Man); Jack Egan (Elevator Man); Ralph Peters (Bartender).

SUSAN AND GOD (MGM, 1940) 117 M.

Producer, Hunt Stromberg; director, George Cukor; based on the play by Rachel Crothers; screenplay, Anita Loos; art director, Cedric Gibbons; music, Herbert Stothart; costumes, Adrian; sound, Douglas Shearer; camera, Robert Planck; editor, William H. Terhune.

Joan Crawford (Susan Trexel); Fredric March (Barry Trexel); Ruth Hussey (Charlotte); John Carroll (Clyde Rochester); Rita Hayworth (Leonora Stubbs); Nigel Bruce (Hutchins Stubbs); Bruce Cabot (Michael O'Hara); Rose Hobart (Irene Burrows); Rita Quigley (Blossom Trexel); Romaine Callender (Oliver Leeds); Marjorie Main (Mary); Aldrich Bowker (Patrick); Constance Collier (Lady Wiggam); Herbert Evans (Bronson); Cece Broadhurst (Cowboy Joe); Richard O. Crane (Bob); Don Castle (Attendant); Henryetta Yates (Fifi); Oscar O'Shea (Sam, the Bartender); Claude King (J. F.); Jane Drummond (Rose); Dan Dailey (Homer); Louis Payne (Dave); Sam Harris (Amos); Bobby Hale (Tom); Keith Hitchcock (Scotchman); Edward Paysen (Athlete); Phil Tead (Customer); Edward Gargan (Cab Driver); Eleanor Soohoo, Rama Bai (Native Women); Harold Landon (Christopher); David Oliver (Man at Bar); Gloria De Haven (Enid); Joan Leslie, Susan Peters, William Lechner, David Tillotson (Guests).

THE LADY IN QUESTION (Col., 1940) 81 M.

Director, Charles Vidor; story, Marcel Achard; screenplay, Lewis Meltzer; art director, Lionel Banks; music, Lucien Moraweck; music director, M. W. Stoloff; camera, Lucien Andriot; editor, Al Clark.

Brian Aherne (Andre Morestan); Rita Hayworth (Natalie Roguin); Glenn Ford (Pierre Morestan); Irene Rich (Michele Morestan); George Coulouris (Defense Attorney); Lloyd Corrigan (Prosecuting Attorney); Evelyn Keyes (Francoise Morestan); Edward Norris (Robert LaCoste); Curt Bois (Henri Larette); Frank Reicher (President); Sumner Getchell (Fat Boy); Nicholas Bela (Nicholas Farkas); William Stack (Marinier); Dorothy Burgess (Antoinette); Hamilton MacFadden, Allen Marlow (Guards); Leon Belasco (Barber); Eddie Laughton (Man); Julius Tannen (Judge); Philip Van Zandt (Court Clerk); Fern Emmett (Nathalie Roguin); James B. Carson (Wine Salesman); Jack Rice (Newly Married Juror); Harrison Greene (Jury Foreman); William Castle, Earl Gunn (Angry Jurors); Frank Hilliard, Carlton Griffin, Ronald Alexander, Alexander Palasthy, Ted Lorch, Frank Pharr (Jurors); Fred Rapport (Alternate Juror); Louis Adlon (Clerk); Mary Bovard (Miss Morlet); Emma Tansey (Flower Woman); Ralph Peters (Pedestrian); George Davis (Customer); Jack Raymond (Expressman); Vernon Dent (Gendarme).

ANGELS OVER BROADWAY (Col., 1940) 80 M.

Producer, Ben Hecht; associate producer, Douglas Fairbanks, Jr.; directors, Hecht, Lee Garmes; story-screenplay, Hecht; assistant director, Clifton Broughton; art director, Lionel Banks; camera, Garmes; editor, Gene Havlick.

293

Douglas Fairbanks, Jr. (Bill O'Brien); Rita Hayworth (Nina Barona); Thomas Mitchell (Gene Gibbons); John Qualen (Charles Engle); George Watts (Hopper); Ralph Theodore (Dutch Enright); Eddie Foster (Louie Artino); Jack Roper (Eddie Burns); Constance Worth (Sylvia Marbe); Richard Bon (Sylvia's Escort); Frank Conlan (Joe); Walter Baldwin (Rennick); Jack Carr (Tony); Al Seymour (Jack); Jimmy Conlin (Proprietor); Ethelreda Leopold (Cigarette Girl); Edward Earle (Headwaiter); Catherine Courtney (Miss Karpin); Al Rhein, Jerry Jerome, Roger Gray, Harry Strang (Gamblers); Bill Lally (Doorman); Tommy Dixon (Checkroom Boy); Fred Sweeney (Hugo); Carmen D'Antonio (Specialty Dancer); Carlton Griffin (Waiter); Stanley Brown (Master of Ceremonies); Patricia Maier (Girl); Lee Phelps (Police Lieutenant); Harry Antrim (Court Clerk); Blanche Payson (Large Woman); Caroline Frasher (Streetwalker); Billy Wayne (Taxi Driver); Walter Sande (Lunch Wagon Waiter); Art Howard (Night Court Judge); Ben Hecht (Bit).

THE STRAWBERRY BLONDE   (WB, 1941) 97 M.

Producers, Jack L. Warner, Hal B. Wallis; associate producer, William Cagney; director, Raoul Walsh; based on the play *One Sunday Afternoon* by James Hagan; screenplay, Julius J. Epstein; Philip G. Epstein; art director, Robert Haas; costumes, Orry-Kelly; assistant director, Russ Saunders; music, Heinz Roemheld; orchestrator, Ray Heindorf; dialog director, Hugh Cummings; sound, Robert E. Lee; camera, James Wong Howe; editor, William Holmes.

James Cagney (Biff Grimes); Olivia de Havilland (Amy Lind); Rita Hayworth (Virginia Brush); Alan Hale (Old Man Grimes); George Tobias (Nick Pappalas); Jack Carson (Hugo Barnstead); Una O'Connor (Mrs. Mulcahey); George Reeves (Harold); Lucile Fairbanks (Harold's Girlfriend); Edward McNamara (Big Joe); Herbert Heywood (Toby); Helen Lynd (Josephine); Peter Ashley (Young Man); Roy Gordon (Bank President); Tim Ryan (Street Cleaner—Foreman); Eddy Chandler, Jack Mower, John Sheehan, David Thursby (Street Cleaners); Addison Richards (Official); Frank Mayo, Max Hoffman, Jr., Pat Flaherty (Policemen); Peggy Diggins, Susan Peters, Ann Edmonds, Margaret Carthew (Girls); Jack Daley (Bartender); Bob Perry, Harrison Greene (Hangers-On); Dick Wessel, Billy Newell, Frank Melton, Harry Seymour (Men); Dorothy Vaughan (Woman); Richard Clayton (Dandy); Herbert Anderson (Boy); Frank Orth (Baxter); James Flavin (Inspector); George Campeau (Sailor); Abe Dinovitch (Singer); Paul Phillips (Fellow); George Humber (Guiseppi); Creighton Hale (Secretary); Carl Harbaugh (Workman); Lucia Carroll (Nurse); Russell Hicks (Treadway); Wade Boteler (Warden).

AFFECTIONATELY YOURS   (WB, 1941) 90 M.

Executive producer, Hal B. Wallis; associate producer, Mark Hellinger; director, Lloyd Bacon; story, Fanya Foss, Aleen Leslie; screenplay, Edward Kaufman; dialog director, Robert Foulk; art director, Anton Grot; music, Heinz Roemheld; choreography, Matty King; music director, Leo F. Forbstein; camera, Tony Gaudio; editor, Owen Marks.

Merle Oberon (Sue Mayberry); Dennis Morgan (Richard Mayberry); Rita Hayworth (Irene Malcolm); Ralph Bellamy (Owen Wright); George Tobias (Pasha); James Gleason (Chester Phillips); Hattie McDaniel (Cynthia); Jerome Cowan (Cullen); Butterfly McQueen (Butterfly); Renie Riano (Mrs. Snell); Frank Wilcox (Tom); Grace Stafford (Miss Anderson); Pat Flaherty (Harmon); Murray Alper (Blair); William Haade (Matthews); James Flavin (Tomassetti); Carmen Morales (Anita); George Meeker (Anita's Escort); Creighton Hale

(Hotel Manager); Charles Wagenheim (Bystander); Gino Corrado (Lisbon Head-waiter); Antonio Filauri (Portuguese); Irene Colman (Barmaid); William Hopper (Air Line Attendant); Frank Faylen (Ambulance Driver); Garrett Craig (Field Guard); Nat Carr (Delicatessen Proprietor); Ed Brian (Copy Boy); Ann Edmonds (Stenographer); Charles Marsh (City Editor); Billy Wayne (Bell Captain); Wedgwood Nowell (Judge); Peggy Diggins, Alexis Smith (Bridesmaids); Garry Owen (Taxi Driver); Ed Gargan (Traffic Cop); Dorothy Adams (Hospital Attendant); Henry Blair (Little Boy); Charles Drake (Interne); Faye Emerson (Nurse); Mary Field (Mrs. Collins).

BLOOD AND SAND   (20th, 1941) C—124 M.

Producer, Darryl F. Zanuck; associate producer, Robert T. Kane; director, Rouben Mamoulian; based on the novel *Sangre y Arena* by Vicente Blasco Ibáñez; screenplay, Jo Swerling; assistant directors, Robert Webb, Sidney Bowen, Henry Weinberger; art directors, Richard Day, Joseph C. Wright; set decorator, Thomas Little; costumes, Travis Banton; toreador costumes, José Dolores Perez Martinez; gypsy theme music, Vicente Gomez; sound, W. D. Flick, Roger Heman; camera, Ernest Palmer, Ray Rennahan; editor, Robert Bischoff.

Tyrone Power (Juan Gallardo); Linda Darnell (Carmen Espinosa); Rita Hayworth (Doña Sol); Nazimova (Señora Augustias); Anthony Quinn (Manolo de Palma); J. Carrol Naish (Garabato); John Carradine (Nacional); Lynn Bari (Encarnacion); Laird Cregar (Natalio Curro); Monty Banks (Antonio Lopez); George Reeves (Captain Pierre Laurel); Vicente Gomez (Guitarist); Pedro de Cordoba (Don Jose Alvarez); Victor Kilian (Priest); Adrian Morris (La Pulga); Charles Stevens (Pablo Gomez); Ann Todd (Carmen as a Child); Cora Sue Collins (Encarnacion as a Child); Russell Hicks (Marquis); Rex Downing (Juan as a Child); Maurice Cass (El Milquestoast); John Wallace (Francisco); Jacqueline Dalya (Gachi); Cullen Johnson (Manolo as a Boy); Ted Frye (La Pulga as a Boy); Schuyler Standish (Nacional as a Boy); Paco Moreno (Conductor); Elena Verdugo, Mariquita Flores (Specialty Dancers); Rosita Granada (Singer); Julian Rivero, Andre Cuyas, Michael Visaroff, Thornton Edwards, Rafael Corio, Francisco Maran (Men); Kay Linaker (Woman); Racquel Verria (Girl); Francis McDonald (Man); Fred Malatesta (Waiter); Cecilia Callejo, Esther Estrella (Gachis); Paul Ellis (Ortega); Alberto Morin (Attendant); Harry Burns (Engineer).

YOU'LL NEVER GET RICH   (Col., 1941) 88 M.

Producer, Samuel Bischoff; director, Sidney Lanfield; screenplay, Michael Fessier, Ernest Pagano; songs, Cole Porter; choreography, Robert Alton; music director, M. W. Stoloff; art director, Lionel Banks; camera, Philip Tannura; editor, Otto Meyer.

Fred Astaire (Robert Curtis); Rita Hayworth (Sheila Winthrop); John Hubbard (Tom Barton); Robert Benchley (Martin Cortland); Osa Massen (Sonya); Frieda Inescort (Mrs. Cortland); Guinn Williams (Kewpie Blain); Donald MacBride (Top Sergeant); Cliff Nazarro (Twivel Tongue); Marjorie Gateson (Aunt Louise); Ann Shoemaker (Mrs. Barton); Boyd Davis (Colonel Shiller); Mary Currier (Costume Designer); Robert Homans (Stage Doorman); Sunnie O'Dea (Marjorie); Martha Tilton, Gwen Kenyon (Singers); Frank Ferguson (Justice of Peace); Emmett Vogan (Jenkins); Jack Rice (Jewelry Clerk); Hal K. Dawson (Information); Harry Burns (Foreigner); Patti McCarty (Young Girl); Edward McWade (Army Doctor); Lester Dorr (Photographer); Tim Ryan (Policeman); Frank Sully, Garry Owen (Robert's Guards); Paul Irving (General Trafscott); Harry Strang (Colonel's Orderly); Eddie Laughton (Lieutenant); Dorothy Vernon (Kewpie's

Mother); Stanley Brown (Draftee); Monty Collins (Sleeper); Paul Philips (Captain Nolan); Harold Goodwin (Captain Williams); Jack O'Malley (Sentry); Eddie Coke (Chauffeur); Larry Williams, James Millican (Privates); Forrest Prince (Soloist); Frank Wayne, Tony Hughes (Prisoners); Rudolph Hunter, John Porter, Lucius Brooks, Leon Buck (The Four Tones).

MY GAL SAL (20th, 1942) C—102 M.

Producer, Robert Bassler; director, Irving Cummings; screenplay, Seton I. Miller, Darrell Ware, Karl Tunberg; songs, Paul Dresser, Leo Robin and Ralph Rainger; music director, Alfred Newman; choreography, Hermes Pan, Val Raset; art directors, Richard Day, Joseph C. Wright; set decorator, Thomas Little; makeup, Guy Pearce; costumes, Gwen Wakeling; sound, Alfred Bruzlin, Roger Heman; camera, Ernest Palmer; editor, Robert Simpson.

Rita Hayworth (Sally Elliott); Victor Mature (Paul Dreiser); John Sutton (Fred Haviland); Carole Landis (Mae Collins); James Gleason (Pat Hawley); Phil Silvers (Wiley); Walter Catlett (Colonel Truckee); Mona Maris (Countess Rossini); Frank Orth (McGuinness); Stanley Andrews (Mr. Dreiser); Margaret Moffat (Mrs. Dreiser); Libby Taylor (Ida); John Kelly (John L. Sullivan); Curt Bois (De Rochement); Gregory Gaye (Garnier); Andrew Tombes (Corbin); Albert Conti (Henri); Charles Arnt (Tailor); Chief Thundercloud (Murphy); Hermes Pan (Specialty Dancer); Robert Lowery, Dorothy Dearing, Michael (Ted) North, Roseanne Murray (Sally's Friends); Harry Strang (Bartender); Milton Kibbee, Luke Cosgrave, Ernie Adams, Joe Bernard, John "Skins" Miller, Gus Glassmire, Tom O'Grady, Frank Ferguson, Cyril Ring (Men); Billy Wayne (Delivery Man); Edward McNamara, Ed Dearing (Policemen); Rosina Galli (Maid); Larry Wheat (Stage Door Man); Eddy Waller (Buggy Driver); Terry Moore (Carrie); Barry Downing (Theodore); Tommy Seidel (Usher); Billy Curtis (Midget Driver); Tommy Cotton (Midget Footman); Paul Burns (Ferris Wheel Man); George Melford (Conductor); Charles Tannen (Hotel Clerk); Clarence Badger, Kenneth Rundquist, Delos Jewkes, Gene Ramey (Quartette).

TALES OF MANHATTAN (20th, 1942) 118 M.

Producers, Boris Morros, S. P. Eagle; director, Julien Duvivier; stories-screenplay, Ben Hecht, Ferenc Molnar, Donald Ogden Stewart, Samuel Hoffenstein, Alan Campbell, Ladislas Fodor, Laslo Vadnay, Laszlo Gorog, Lamar Trotti, Henry Blankfort; assistant director, Robert Stillman; music, Sol Kaplan; music director, Edward Paul; songs, Leo Robin and Ralph Rainger; Paul Francis Webster and Saul Chaplin; art directors, Richard Day, Boris Leven; sound, W. D. Fleck, Roger Heman; camera, Joseph Walker; editor, Robert Bischoff.

Sequence A: Charles Boyer (Paul Orman); Rita Hayworth (Ethel Halloway); Thomas Mitchell (John Halloway); Eugene Pallette (Luther); Helene Reynolds (Actress); Robert Greig (Lazar the Tailor); Jack Chefe (Tailor); William Halligan (Oliver Webb); Charles Williams (Paul's Agent); Eric Wilton (Halloways' Butler).

Sequence B: Ginger Rogers (Diane); Henry Fonda (George); Cesar Romero (Harry Wilson); Gail Patrick (Ellen); Roland Young (Edgar the Butler); Marian Martin (Squirrel); Frank Orth (Second-Hand Clothes Dealer); Connie Leon (Mary).

Sequence C: Charles Laughton (Charles Smith); Elsa Lanchester (Mrs. Smith); Victor Francen (Arturo Bellini); Christian Rub (Wilson); Adeline deWalt Reynolds (Grandmother); Sig Arno (Piccolo Player); Forbes Murray (Dignified Man); Buster Brodie (Call Boy); Frank Jaquet (Musician); Will Wright (Skeptic); Frank

Dae (Elderly Man); Rene Austin (Susan); Frank Darien (Grandpa); Dewey Robinson (Bar Proprietor); Tom O'Grady (Latecomer); Curly Twyfford (Bird Man); Gino Corrado (Spectator).

Sequence D: Edward G. Robinson [(Larry) Avery L. Browne]; George Sanders (Williams); James Gleason (Father Joe); Harry Davenport (Professor Lyons); James Rennie (Hank Bronson); Harry Hayden (Soupy Davis); Morris Ankrum (Judge Barnes); Don Douglas (Henderson); Mae Marsh (Molly); Barbara Lynn (Mary); Paul Renay (Spud Johnson); Alex Pollard (Waiter); Joseph Bernard (Postman); Don Brodie (Whistler); Esther Howard (Woman); Ted Stanhope (Chauffeur).

Sequence E: Paul Robeson (Luke); Ethel Waters (Esther); Eddie "Rochester" Anderson (Reverend Lazarus); J. Carrol Naish (Costello); Hall Johnson Choir (Themselves); Clarence Muse (Grandpa); George Reed (Christopher); Cordell Hickman (Nicodemus); Blue Washington (Black Man); Johnny Lee (Carpenter); John Kelly (Monk); Lonnie Nichols (Brad); Phillip Hurlic (Jeff); Charles Gray (Rod); Archie Savage (Bit); Rita Christiani, Laura Vaughn, Ella Mae Lashley, Olive Ball, Maggie Dorsey (Women); Alberta Gary (Black Girl); Charles Tannen (Pilot).

YOU WERE NEVER LOVELIER   (Col., 1942) 97 M.

Producer, Louis F. Edelman; director, William A. Seiter; story, Carlos Olivari, Sixto Pondal Rios; screenplay, Michael Fessier, Ernest Pagano, Delmer Daves; songs, Jerome Kern and Johnny Mercer; choreography, Val Raset; camera, Ted Tetzlaff; editor, William Lyon.

Fred Astaire (Robert Davis); Rita Hayworth (Maria Acuna); Adolphe Menjou (Edwardo); Leslie Brooks (Cecy Acuna); Adele Mara (Lita Acuna); Isobel Elsom (Mrs. Maria Castro); Gus Schilling (Fernando); Barbara Brown (Mrs. Delfina Acuna); Douglass Leavitt (Juan Castro); Catherine Craig (Julia Acuna); Kathleen Howard (Grandmother Acuna); Mary Field (Louise); Larry Parks (Tony); Stanley Brown (Roddy); Xavier Cugat and His Orchestra (Themselves); Kirk Alyn (Groom); George Bunny (Flower Man); Ralph Peters (Chauffeur).

COVER GIRL   (Col., 1944) C—107 M.

Producer, Arthur Schwartz; director Charles Vidor; story, Erwin Gelsey; adaptation, Marion Parsonnet, Paul Gangelin; screenplay, Virginia Van Upp; art directors, Lionel Banks, Cary Odell; set decorator, Fay Babcock; assistant directors, Jack Voglin, Bud Boetticher; music director, M. W. Stoloff; music arranger-orchestrator, Carmen Dragon; choreography, Val Raset, Seymour Felix, Gene Kelly, Stanley Donen; songs, Ira Gershwin and Jerome Kern; Gershwin, Kern, and E. Y. Harburg; sound, Lambert Day; camera, Rudolph Mate, Allen M. Davey; editor, Viola Lawrence.

Rita Hayworth (Rusty Parker/Maribelle Hicks); Gene Kelly (Danny McGuire); Lee Bowman (Noel Wheaton); Phil Silvers (Genius); Jinx Falkenburg (Jinx); Leslie Brooks (Maurine Martin); Eve Arden (Cornelia Jackson); Otto Kruger (John Coudair); Jess Barker (Coudair as a Young Man); Anita Colby (Anita); Curt Bois (Chem); Ed Brophy (Joe); Thurston Hall (Tony Pastor); Jean Colleran, Francine Counihan, Helen Mueller, Cecilia Meagher, Betty Jane Hess, Dusty Anderson, Eileen McClory, Cornelia B. von Hessert, Karen X. Gaylord, Cheryl Archibald, Peggy Lloyd, Betty Jane Graham, Martha Outlaw, Susann Shaw, Rose May Robson (Cover Girls); Jack Norton (Harry, the Drunk); Robert Homans (Pop, the Doorman); Eddie Dunn (Mac, the Cop); Sam Flint (Butler); Shelley Winters (Girl); Kathleen O'Malley (Cigarette Girl); William Kline (Chauffeur); Victor

Travers (Bartender); Robert F. Hill (Headwaiter); John Tyrrell (Electrician); Frank O'Connor (Cook); Eugene Anderson, Jr. (Bus Boy); Sam Ash (Assistant Cook); Vin Moore (Waiter); Ralph Sanford, Ralph Peters (Truckmen); Barbara Pepper, Grace Leonard (Chorus Girls); Gwen Seager, Sally Cairns, Eloise Hart, Diane Griffith, Wesley Brent, Lucille Allen, Virginia Gardner, Helene Garron, Muriel Morris, Patti Sacks, Marion Graham (Cover Girl Contestants) Frances Morris (Coudair's Secretary); Billy Benedict (Florist Boy); William Sloan (Naval Officer); Grace Hayle, Fern Emmett (Women Columnists); Rudy Wissler, Glenn Charles, Jackie Brown (Boys); Ilene (Betty) Brewer (Autograph Hound); Warren Ashe (Rusty's Interviewer); John Dilson (Rusty's Photographer); Jack Rice (Reporter); Sam Flint (Coudair's Butler); Ed Allen (Best Man); George Lessey (Minister); Miriam Lavelle, Miriam Franklin, Ronald Wyckoff (Specialty Dancers); Grace Gillern, Eddie Cutler, Randolph Hughes, Jack Bernett, George Dobbs, Al Norman, Larry Rio, Jack Boyle, Virginia Wilson, Betty Brodel (Dancers); Johnny Mitchell (Pianist-Maribelle's Love); Patti Sheldon (Girl).

TONIGHT AND EVERY NIGHT (Col., 1945) C—92 M.

Producer-director, Victor Saville; based on the play *Heart of a City* by Lesley Storm; screenplay, Lesser Samuels, Abem Finkel; art directors, Stephen Goosson, Rudolph Sternad, Lionel Banks; set decorator, Frank Tuttle; music director, M. W. Stoloff; choreography, Jack Cole, Val Raset; songs, Jule Styne and Sammy Cahn; orchestrator, Marlin Skiles; assistant director, Louis Germonprez; sound, Lambert Day; special effects, Lawrence W. Butler; camera, Rudolph Mate; editor Viola Lawrence.

Rita Hayworth (Rosalind Bruce); Lee Bowman (Paul Lundy); Janet Blair (Judy Kane); Marc Platt (Tommy Lawson); Leslie Brooks (Angela); Professor Lamberti (The Great Waldo); Dusty Anderson (Toni); Stephen Crane (Leslie Wiggins); Jim Bannon (*Life* Photographer); Florence Bates (May Tolliver); Ernest Cossart (Sam Royce); Philip Merivale (Reverend Gerald Lundy); Patrick O'Moore (David Long); Gavin Muir (Group Captain); Shelley Winters (Bubbles); Marilyn Johnson (Pamela); Mildred Law (Frenchie); Elizabeth Inglise (Joan); Aminta Dyne (Mrs. Peabody); Joy Harrington (Mrs. Good); Ann Codee (Annette); Cecil Stewart (Bert); Dagmar Oakland, Victor Travers, Charles Meakin (Jolly Trio); Gary Bruce, Fred Graff (American Soldiers); Edward Cooper, William Lawrence (Waiters); David Thursby (Scotch Soldier); Jeanne Bates (WAC); Robert Williams (U.S. CPO); John Bleifer (Russian Sailor); Adele Jergens (Show Girl); Tom Bryson, Nigel Horton (English Sailors); Donald Dewar (Boy); P. J. Kelly, Keith Hitchcock (ARP Men); Charles McNaughton (Peters); Stuart Nedd (Petty Officer); Russell Burroughs (Orderly); George Kirby (Father); John Heath, Tony Marsh (Sailors); Dick Woodruff, Richard Deane (Soldiers); Wilson Benge (News Vendor); Nelson Leigh (British Army Officer); C. Montague Shaw (Old Bobby); Alec Craig (Englishman); Dave Clyde (Police Sergeant); Queenie Leonard (Cockney Woman); Sheilah Roberts (Barmaid); Frank Leigh (Air Warden).

GILDA (Col., 1946) 110 M.

Producer, Virginia Van Upp; director, Charles Vidor; story, E. A. Ellington; adaptation, Jo Eisinger; screenplay, Marion Parsonnet; art directors, Stephen Goosson, Van Nest Polglase; set decorator, Robert Priestly; music directors, M. W. Stoloff, Marlin Skiles; songs, Allan Roberts and Doris Fisher; choreography, Jack Cole; costumes, Jean Louis; assistant director, Art Black; sound, Lambert Day; camera, Rudolph Mate; editor, Charles Nelson.

Rita Hayworth (Gilda); Glenn Ford (Johnny Farrell); George Macready (Ballin

Mundson); Joseph Calleia (Obregon); Steven Geray (Uncle Pio); Joe Sawyer (Casey); Gerald Mohr (Captain Delgado); Robert Scott (Gabe Evans); Ludwig Donath, Lionel Royce (Germans); Don Douglas (Thomas Langford); Saul Z. Martel (Little Man); George J. Lewis (Huerta); Rosa Rey (Maria); Jerry DeCastro (Doorman); Robert Kellard, Ernest Hilliard, Frank Leigh, Rodolfo Hoyos, Jean Del Val, Paul Regas, Phil Van Zandt (Men); Fernanda Eliscu (Bendolin's Wife); Frank Leyva (Argentine); Forbes Murray, Sam Flint (Americans); Oscar Lorraine, Jean DeBriac (Frenchmen); Herbert Evans (Englishman); Eduardo Cianelli (Bendolin); Robert Tafur (Clerk); Russ Vincent (Escort); Erno Verebes, Eugene Borden (Dealers); Alphonse Martell, Leon Lenoir (Croupiers); Soretta Raye (Harpy); J. W. Noon, Nobel G. Evey (Bunco Dealers); George Sorel, Jack Chefe, Albert Pollet, Lou Palfy (Assistant Croupiers); Sam Appel (Black Jack Dealer); Jack Del Rio (Cashier); Julio Abadia (Newsman/Waiter); Cosmo Sardo, Paul Bradley, Nina Bara, Ruth Roman, John Tyrrell (Bits); Ted Hecht (Social Citizen); Leander DeCordova (Servant); Fred Godoy (Bartender); Lew Harvey, John Merton (Policemen); Herman Marks, Carli Elinor, Joseph Palma, Alfred Paix, Herman Marks, Ralph Navarro (Waiters); Ramon Munox (Judge); Argentina Brunetti (Woman); Sam Ash (Gambler).

DOWN TO EARTH (Col., 1947) C—101 M.

Producer, Don Hartman; director, Alexander Hall; based on characters from the play *Heaven Can Wait* by Harry Segall; screenplay, Edward Blum, Don Hartman; art directors, Stephen Goosson, Rudolph Sternad; set decorator, William Kiernan; music, George Duning, Heinz Roemheld; music director, M. W. Stoloff; songs, Allan Roberts and Doris Fisher; choreography, Jack Cole; gowns, Jean Louis; assistant director, Wilbur McGaugh; sound, George Cooper, Philip Faulkner; camera, Rudolph Mate; editor, Viola Lawrence.

Rita Hayworth (Terpsichore); Larry Parks (Danny Miller); Marc Platt (Eddie); Roland Culver (Mr. Jordan); James Gleason (Max Corkle); Edward Everett Horton (Messenger 7013); Adele Jergens (Georgia Evans); George Macready (Joe Mannion); William Frawley (Police Lieutenant); Jean Donahue (Betty); Kathleen O'Malley (Dolly); William Haade (Spike); James Burke (Kelly); Fred Sears (Orchestra Leader); Lynn Merrick, Dusty Anderson, Doris Houck, Shirley Molohon, Peggy Maley, Dorothy Brady, Jo Rattigan, Lucille Casey (Muses); Lucien Littlefield (Escort 3082); Myron Healey (Sloan); Harriette Ann Gray (Dancer); Rudy Cameron (Stage Manager); Arthur Blake (Mr. Somerset); Wilbur Mack (Messenger); Cora Witherspoon (Woman on Street); Kay Vallon (Rosebud); Ernest Hilliard, Fred Howard, Forbes Murray, Cecil Weston, Mary Newton, Ottola Nesmith (Bits); Jean Del Val (Croupier); Billy Bletcher (Conductor); Nicodemus Stewart (Porter); Boyd Irwin (Man); Raoul Freeman, Bob Ryan (Policemen); Matty Fain (Henchman); Frank Darien (Janitor); Jack Norton (Sleeping Man); Tom Hanlon (Announcer); Mary Forbes (Dowager); Grace Hampton, Winifred Harris (Women); Edward Harvey (Man); Count Stefanelli (Frenchman); Eddie Acuff (Stage Hand); Alan Bridge (Police Sergeant); Tom Daly (Reporter); Francine Kennedy (Chorine); Virginia Hunter (Muse).

THE LADY FROM SHANGHAI (Col., 1948) 86 M.

Executive producer, Harry Cohn; associate producers, Richard Wilson, William Castle; director, Orson Welles; based on the novel *If I Die Before I Wake* by Sherwood King; screenplay, Welles; assistant director, Sam Nelson; art directors, Stephen Goosson, Sturges Carne; set decorators, Wilbur Menefee, Herman Schoenbrun; music, Heinz Roemheld; music director, M. W. Stoloff; orchestrator,

Herschel Burke Gilbert; song, Allan Roberts, Doris Fisher; sound, Lodge Cunningham; special effects, Lawrence Butler; camera, Charles Lawton, Jr.; editor, Viola Lawrence.

Rita Hayworth (Elsa Bannister); Orson Welles (Michael O'Hara); Everett Sloane (Arthur Bannister); Glenn Anders (George Grisby); Ted de Corsia (Sidney Broome); Erskine Sanford (Judge); Gus Schilling (Goldie); Carl Frank (District Attorney); Louis Merrill (Jake); Evelyn Ellis (Bessie); Harry Shannon (Cab Driver); Wong Show Chong (Li); Sam Nelson (Yacht Captain); Tiny Jones (Woman); Edythe Elliott (Old Lady); Peter Cusanelli (Bartender); Joseph Granby (Police Lieutenant); Al Eben, Norman Thomson, Harry Strang, Steve Benton, Milton Kibbee, Edward Coke (Policemen); Gerald Pierce (Waiter); Maynard Holmes (Truck Driver); Jack Baxley (Guard); Dorothy Vaughan (Old Woman); Philip Morris (Port Stewart/Policeman/Peters); Phil Van Zandt (Toughie/Cop); William Alland, Alvin Hammer, Mary Newton, Robert Gray, Byron Kane (Reporters); Ed Peil, Heenan Elliott (Guards); Charles Meakin (Jury Foreman); John Elliott (Clerk); Jessie Arnold (Schoolteacher); Doris Chan, Billy Louie (Chinese Girls); Joe Recht (Garage Attendant); Jean Wong (Ticket Seller); Mabel Smaney, George "Shorty" Chirello, Vernon Cansino (Bits); Grace Lem (Chinese Woman); Preston Lee (Chinese Man); Joseph Palma (Cab Driver); Artarne Wong (Ticket Taker).

THE LOVES OF CARMEN   (Col., 1948) C—99 M.

Producer-director, Charles Vidor; based on the story *Carmen* by Prosper Merimee; screenplay, Helen Deutsch; art directors, Stephen Goosson, Cary Odell; set decorators, Wilbur Menefee, William Kiernan; music, Mario Castelnuovo-Tedesco; music director, M. W. Stoloff; choreography, Robert Sidney, Eduardo Cansino; costumes, Jean Louis; assistant director, Earl Bellamy; makeup, Clay Campbell; sound, Frank Goodwin; camera, William Snyder; editor, Charles Nelson.

Rita Hayworth (Carmen Garcia); Glenn Ford (Don Jose); Ron Randell (Andres); Victor Jory (Garcia); Luther Adler (Dancaire); Arnold Moss (Colonel); Joseph Buloff (Remendado); Margaret Wycherly (Old Crone); Bernard Nedell (Pablo); John Baragrey (Lucas); Philip Van Zandt (Sergeant); Anthony Dante (Groom); Veronika Pataky (Bride); Rosa Turich (Bride's Mother); Leona Roberts (Ancient Old Gypsy); Vernon Cansino, Peter Virgo (Soldiers); Fernando Ramos, Roy Fitzell, Jose Cansino (Specialty Dancers-Gypsies); Joaquin Elizonda, Paul Bradley, Lala DeTolly, Marie Scheue, Barbara Hayden (People on Stagecoach); Wally Cassell (Dragoon); Nenette Vallon (Woman with Broom); Kate Drain Lawson (Woman Relative); Inez Palange, Eula Morgan (Women in Crowns); Peter Cusanelli (Man in Crown); Joseph Malouf (Orderly); George Bell, Rosita Delva, Lucille Charles, Thomas Malinari, Delores Corral, Andrew Roud, Al Caruso, Roque Ybarra, Dimas Sotello, Julio Rojas (Bits); Frances Rey, Roselyn Strangis (Girls); Claire DuBrey (Woman in Window); Tessie Murray, Angella Gomez, Lulu Mae Bohrman, Virginia Vann (Women); David Ortega, Cosmo Sardo, Alfred Paix, Jerry De Castro, Paul Fierro, John J. Verros (Men); Celeste Savoi (Ad Lib Bit); Alma Beltran, Florence Auer (Trinket Sellers); Lupe Gonzalez, Nina Campana (Chestnut Sellers); Robert Sidney (Specialty Dancer); Francis Pierlot (Beggar); Juan Duval (Toreador); Trevor Bardette (Footman); Paul Marion (Sergeant of Dragoons).

AFFAIR IN TRINIDAD   (Col., 1952) 98 M.

Producer-director, Vincent Sherman; story, Virginia Van Upp, Berne Giler; screenplay, Oscar Saul, James Gunn; art director, Walter Holscher; set decorator,

William Kiernan; music, Morris Stoloff, George Duning; choreography, Valerie Bettis; camera, Joseph Walker; editor, Viola Lawrence.

Rita Hayworth (Chris Emery); Glenn Ford (Steve Emery); Alexander Scourby (Max Fabian); Valerie Bettis (Veronica); Torin Thatcher (Inspector Smythe); Howard Wendell (Anderson); Karel Stepanek (Walters); George Voskovec (Dr. Franz Huebling); Steven Geray (Wittol); Walter Kohler (Peter Bronec); Juanita Moore (Dominique); Gregg Martell (Olaf); Mort Mills (Martin); Robert Boon (Pilot); Ralph Moody (Coroner); Ross Elliott (Neal Emery); John Parlow, Albert Szabo (Butlers); Don Kohler (Mr. Peters the Reporter); John Sherman (Englishman); Calvin Emery (Newspaper Reporter); Fred Baker (Airport Clerk); Kathleen O'Malley (Stewardess); Leonidas Ossetynski, Franz Roehn (Refugees); Don Blackman (Bobby); Ivan Browning, Roy Glenn, Joel Fluellen (Fishermen).

SALOME   (Col., 1953) C—103 M.

Producer, Buddy Adler; director, William Dieterle; story, Jesse L. Lasky, Jr., Harry Kleiner; screenplay, Kleiner; choreography, Valerie Bettis; music for dances, Daniele Anfitheatrof; art director, John Meehan; camera, Charles Lang; editor, Viola Lawrence.

Rita Hayworth (Princess Salome); Stewart Granger (Commander Claudius); Charles Laughton (King Herod); Judith Anderson (Queen Herodias); Sir Cedric Hardwicke (Caesar Tiberius); Alan Badel (John the Baptist); Basil Sydney (Pontius Pilate); Maurice Schwartz (Ezra); Rex Reason (Marcellus Fabius); Arnold Moss (Micha); Sujata and Asoka (Oriental Dance Team); Robert Warwick (Salome's Servant); Michael Granger (Captain Quintus); Karl "Killer' Davis (Slave Master); Joe Shilling, David Wold, Ray Beltram, Joe Sawaya, Anton Northpole, Carlo Tricoli, Franz Roehn, William McCormick (Advisors); Mickey Simpson (Herod's Captain of the Guards); Eduardo Cansino (Roman Guard); Lou Nova (Executioner); Fred Letuli, John Wood (Sword Dancers); William Spaeth (Fire Eater); Abel Pina, Jerry Pina, Henry Pina, Henry Escalante, Gilbert Maques, Richard Rivas, Miguel Gutierez, Ramior Rivas, Ruben T. Rivas, Hector Urtiaga (Acrobats); Duke Johnson (Juggling Specialty); Earl Brown, Bud Cokes (Galilean Soldiers); George Khoury, Leonard George (Assassins); Eva Hyde (Herodia's Servant); Charles Wagenheim (Simon); Italia De Nublia, David Ahdar, Charles Soldani, Dimas Sotello, William Wilkerson, Mario Lamm, Tina Menard (Extras); Leslie Denison (Court Attendant); Henry dar Boggia, Michael Couzzi, Bobker Ben Ali, Don De Leo, John Parrish, Eddy Fields, Robert Garabedion, Sam Scar (Politicians); Tris Coffin, Bruce Cameron, John Crawford (Guards); Michael Mark (Old Farmer); David Leonard, Maurice Samuels, Ralph Moody, Saul Martell (Old Scholars); Paul Hoffman (Sailmaster); Stanley Waxman (Patrician); Franz Roehn, Jack Low, Bert Rose, Tom Hernandez (Townsmen); Trevor Ward (Blind Man); Barry Brooks (Roman Guard); Roque Barry (Slave); George Keymas, Fred Berest, Rick Vallin (Sailors).

MISS SADIE THOMPSON   (Col., 1953) C—91 M.

Producer, Jerry Wald; associate producer, Lewis J. Rachmil; director, Curtis Bernhardt; based on the story "Rain" by W. Somerset Maugham; screenplay, Harry Kleiner; art director, Carl Anderson; music, George Duning; songs, Lester Lee and Allan Roberts; Lee and Ned Washington; choreography, Lee Scott; gowns, Jean Louis; assistant director, Sam Nelson; makeup, Caly Cambell; sound, George Cooper; camera, Charles Lawton; editor, Viola Lawrence.

Rita Hayworth (Sadie Thompson); Jose Ferrer (Alfred Davidson); Aldo Ray

(Sergeant Phil O'Hara); Russell Collins (Dr. Robert MacPhail); Diosa Costello (Ameena Horn); Harry Bellaver (Joe Horn); Wilton Graff (Governor); Peggy Converse (Mrs. Margaret Davidson); Henry Slate (Griggs); Rudy Bond (Hodges); Charles Bronson (Edwards); Frances Morris (Mrs. MacPhail); Peter Chong (Chung); John Grossett (Reverend); Billy Varga, Teddy Pavelec, Frank Stanlow, Harold Tommy Hart, Charles Horvath, Ben Harris, Ted Jordan, Eduardo Cansino, Jr., John Duncan (Marines); Erlynn Mary Botelho, Elizabeth Bartilet, Dennis Medieros (Children); Joe McCabe (Native); Robert G. Anderson (Dispatcher); Al Kikume (Native Secretary); Fred Letuli (Native Messenger).

FIRE DOWN BELOW   (Col., 1957) C—116 M.

Producers, Irving Allen, Albert R. Broccoli; associate producer, Ronald Kinnoch; director, Robert Parrish; based on the novel by Max Catto; screenplay, Irwin Shaw; assistant director, Gus Agnosti, Bluey Hill; choreography, Tutte Lemkow; music, Arthur Benjamin; harmonica theme, Jack Lemmon; music director, Muir Matheson; gowns, Balmain, Berman; camera, Desmond Dickinson; editor, Jack Slade.

Rita Hayworth (Irena); Robert Mitchum (Felix); Jack Lemmon (Tony); Herbert Lom (Harbor Master); Bonar Colleano (Lieutenant Sellers); Bernard Lee (Doctor Sam); Edric Conner (Jimmy Jean); Peter Illing (Captain); Joan Miller (Mrs. Canaday); Anthony Newley (Miguel); Eric Pohlmann (Hotel Owner); Vivian Matalon, Gordon Tanner, Maurice Kaufmann (U. S. Sailors); Lionel Murton (American); Murray Kash (Bartender); Maya Koumani (Waitress); Philip Baird (Young Man); Keith Banks (Drunken Young Man); Sean Moster, Greta Remin, Lorna Wood, Barbara Lane, Brian Blades, Gina Chare, Shirley Rus (Dancers); Stretch Cox Troupe (Limbo Dancers).

PAL JOEY   (Col., 1957) C—111 M.

Producer, Fred Kohlmar; director, George Sidney; based on the play by John O'Hara, Richard Rodgers, Lorenz Hart; screenplay, Dorothy Kingsley; songs, Rodgers and Hart; music supervisor-conductor, Morris Stoloff; music arranger, Nelson Riddle; music adaptors, George Duning, Riddle; orchestrator, Arthur Morton; art director, Walter Holscher; set decorators, William Kiernan, Louis Diage; gowns, Jean Louis; assistant director, Art Black; makeup, Ben Lane; sound, Franklin Hansen; camera, Harold Lipstein; editors, Viola Lawrence, Jerome Thoms.

Rita Hayworth (Vera Simpson); Frank Sinatra (Joey Evans); Kim Novak (Linda English); Barbara Nichols (Gladys); Bobby Sherwood (Ned Galvin); Hank Henry (Mike Miggins); Elizabeth Patterson (Mrs. Casey); Robin Morse (Bartender); Frank Wilcox (Colonel Langley); Pierre Watkin (Mr. Forsythe); Barry Bernard (Anderson); Ellie Kent (Carol); Mara McAfee (Sabrina); Betty Utey (Patsy); Bek Nelson (Lola); Henry McCann (Shorty); John Hubbard (Stanley); James Seay (Livingstone); Hermes Pan (Choreographer); Ernesto Molinari (Chef Tony); Jean Corbett (Specialty Dance Double); Robert Rietz (Boyfriend); Jules Davis (Red-Faced Man); Judy Dan (Hat Check Girl); Gail Bonney (Heavy-Set Woman); Cheryl Kubert (Girl Friend); Tol Avery (Detective); Robert Anderson (Policeman); Genie Stone (Girl); Raymond McWalters (Army Captain); Bob Glenn (Sailor); Sue Boomer (Secretary); Helen Eliot (Traveler's Aid); Hermie Rose (Bald Club Owner); Jack Railey (Hot Dog Vendor); Frank Wilimarth (Sidewalk Artist); Roberto Piperio (Waiter); Bobbie Lee, Connie Graham, Bobbie Jean Henson, Edith Powell, Jo Ann Smith, Ilsa Ostroffsky, Rita Barrett (Strippers); Howard Sigrist (Sidewalk Photographer); Paul Cesari (Pet Store Owner); Maurice Argent (Tailor); Frank Sully, Eddie Vartell, Albert Nalbandian, Joseph Mikask, Sydney

Chatton (Barkers); Everett Glass (Pet Store Owner); Andrew Wong (Chinese Club Owner); George Chan (Chinese Pianist); Allen Gin (Chinese Drummer); Barbara Yung, Pat Lynn, Jean Nakaba, Elizabeth Fenton, Lessie Lynne Wong, Nellie Gee Ching (Chinese Dancers); George DeNormand, Oliver Cross, Bess Flowers, Franklyn Farnum (Bits); Giselle D'Aro (Vera's Maid); Leon Alton (Printer Salesman); Michael Ferris (Tailor); Jane Chung (Flower Lady); George Ford (Electrician); Ramon Martinez (Headwaiter); Steve Benton (Electrician).

SEPARATE TABLES   (UA, 1958) 98 M.

Producer, Harold Hecht; director, Delbert Mann; based on the play by Terence Rattigan; screenplay, Rattigan; production designer, Harry Horner; art director, Edward Carrere; set decorator, Edward G. Boyle; assistant director, Thomas F. Shaw; costumes, Mary Grant; Miss Hayworth's gowns, Edith Head; makeup, Harry Maret; sound, Fred Lau; title song, Harry Warren and Harold Adamson; camera, Charles Lang, Jr.; editors, Marjorie Fowler, Charles Ennis.

Rita Hayworth (Ann Shankland); Deborah Kerr (Sibyl Railton-Bell); David Niven (Major Pollock); Burt Lancaster (John Malcolm); Wendy Hiller (Miss Cooper); Gladys Cooper (Mrs. Railton-Bell); Cathleen Nesbitt (Lady Matheson); Felix Aylmer (Mr. Fowler); Rod Taylor (Charles); Audrey Dalton (Jean); May Hallatt (Miss Meacham); Priscilla Morgan (Doreen); Hilda Plowright (Mabel).

THEY CAME TO CORDURA   (Col., 1959) C—123 M.

Producer, William Goetz; director, Robert Rossen; based on the novel by Glendon Swarthout; screenplay, Ivan Moffat, Rossen; music, Elie Siegmeister; music conductor, Morris Stoloff; orchestrator, Arthur Morton; assistant director, Milton Feldman; art director, Cary Odell; set decorator, Frank A. Tuttle; makeup, Clay Campbell; technical advisor, Col. Paul Davison, U.S.A. (Ret.); second unit director, James Havens; sound, John Livadary; camera, Burnett Guffey; editor, Milton Feldman.

Gary Cooper (Major Thomas Thorn); Rita Hayworth (Adelaide Geary); Van Heflin (Sergeant John Chawk); Tab Hunter (Lieutenant William Fowler); Richard Conte (Corporal Milo Trubee); Michael Callan (Private Andrew Hetherington); Dick York (Private Renziehausen); Robert Keith (Colonel Rogers); Carlos Romero (Arreaga); James Bannon (Captain Paitz); Edward Platt (Colonel DeRose); Maurice Jara (Mexican Federale); Sam Buffington, Arthur Hanson (Correspondents).

THE STORY ON PAGE ONE   (20th, 1959) 122 M.

Producer, Jerry Wald; director-screenplay, Clifford Odets; art directors, Lyle R. Wheeler, Howard Richmond; set decorators, Walter M. Scott, G. W. Berntsen; assistant directors, Jack Gertsman; makeup, Ben Nye; music, Elmer Bernstein; orchestrator, Edward B. Powell; sound, Alfred Bruzlin, Harry M. Leonard; camera, James Wong Howe; editor, Hugh S. Fowler.

Rita Hayworth (Jo Morris); Anthony Franciosa (Victor Santini); Gig Young (Larry Ellis); Mildred Dunnock (Mrs. Ellis); Hugh Griffith (Judge Nielsen); Sanford Meisner (Phil Stanley); Robert Burton (Nordau); Alfred Ryder (Lieutenant Mike Morris); Katherine Squire (Mrs. Brown); Raymond Greenleaf (Judge Carey); Myrna Fahey (Alice); Leo Penn (Morrie Goetz); Sheridan Comerate (Francis Morris); Biff Elliot (Eddie Ritter); Tom Greenway (Detective Captain Kelly); Jay Adler (Lauber); Carol Seflinger (Avis Morris); Theodore Newton (Dr. Kemper); James O'Rear (Hauser); Richard Le Pore (Calvin Lewis); Dan Riss (Court Clerk); Joe Besser (Gallagher); Joseph McGuinn (Lieutenant Morris); Leonard George (Jury Foreman); Miranda Jones (Miss Monroe, the Secretary);

George Turley (Court Stenographer); Jerry Sheldon (Quiet Man at Bar); Art Salter (Bartender); Bru Danger (Cook); Valerie French (Liz, the Waitress); William Challee (Lemke); Virginia Carroll (Police Matron).

THE HAPPY THIEVES (UA, 1962) 88 M.

Director, George Marshall; based on the novel *The Oldest Confession* by Richard Condon; screenplay, John Gay; art director, Ramiro Gomez; music, Mario Nascimbene; Miss Hayworth's wardrobe, Pierre Balmain, Pedro Rodrigues; camera, Paul Beeson; editor, Oswald Hafenfichter.

Rex Harrison (Jim Bourne); Rita Hayworth (Eve Lewis); Joseph Wiseman (Jean Marie Calbert); Gregoire Aslan (Dr. Munoz); Alida Valli (Duchess Blanca); Virgilio Texiera (Cayetano); Peter Illing (Mr. Pickett); Brita Ekman (Mrs. Pickett); Julio Pena (Señor Elek); Gerard Tichy (Antonio); Lou Weber, Antonio Fuentes (Guards); George Rigaud (Inspector); Barta Barri (Chern); Karl-Heinz Schwerdtfeger (Police Official); Princess Yasmin (Girl).

CIRCUS WORLD (Par., 1964) C—135 M.

Producer, Samuel Bronston; executive associate producer, Michael Wasynski; director, Henry Hathaway; story, Philip Yordan; screenplay, Ben Hecht, Julian Halvey; production designer, John DeCuir; second unit director, Richard Talmadge; first unit assistant director, Jose Lopez Rodero; second unit assistant director, Terry Yorke; co-ordinator of circus operations, Frank Capra, Jr.; makeup, Maria Van Riel; costumes, Renie; titles, Dong Kingman; music, Dmitri Tiomkin; title song, Tiomkin and Ned Washington; camera, Jack Hildyard, Claude Renoir; editor, Dorothy Spencer.

John Wayne (Matt Masters); Rita Hayworth (Lilli Alfredo); Claudia Cardinale (Toni Alfredo); Lloyd Nolan (Cap Carson); Richard Conte (Aldo Alfredo); John Smith (Steve McCabe); Henri Dantes (Emile Schuman); Wanda Rotha (Mrs. Schuman); Katharyna (Giovana); Kay Walsh (Flo Hunt); Margaret MacGrath (Anna); Kathrine Ellison (Fritzi); Miles Malleson (Billy Hennigan); Katharine Kath (Hilda); Franz Althoff (Bartender); Robert Cunningham, Francois Calepides (Ringmasters).

THE MONEY TRAP (MGM, 1966) 91 M.

Producers, Max E. Youngstein, David Karr; director, Burt Kennedy; based on the novel by Lionel White; screenplay, Walter Bernstein; assistant director, Hank Moonjean; art directors, George W. Davis, Carl Anderson; set decorators, Henry Grace, Robert R. Benton; makeup, William Tuttle; music, Hal Schaefer; sound, Franklin Milton; camera, Paul C. Vogel; editor, John McSweeney.

Glenn Ford (Joe Baron); Elke Sommer (Lisa Baron); Rita Hayworth (Rosalie Kenny); Joseph Cotten (Dr. Horace Van Tilden); Ricardo Montalban (Pete Delanos); Tom Reese (Matthews); James Mitchum (Detective Wolski); Argentina Brunetti (Aunt); Fred Essler (Mr. Klein); Eugene Iglesias (Father); Teri Lynn Sandoval (Daughter); Bill McLean (Delivery Man); Parley Baer (Banker); Robert S. Anderson (Police Inspector); Than Wyenn (Phil Henny); Ted DeCorsia (Police Captain); Helena Nash (Madame); Marya Stevens, Charlita, Stacey King (Women); Fred Scheweiller (Bartender); Ward Wood (Man); William Campbell (Jack Archer); Walter Reed, Budd Landreth (Detectives); Paul Todd (Interne); Herman Boden (Parking Lot Attendant); George Sawaya (Angelo); Jo Summers (Dead Mother); Stacy Harris (Drunk); Cleo Tibbs, Sallie H. Dornan (Nurses).

THE POPPY IS ALSO A FLOWER   (ABC-TV, 1966) C—105 M.

Executive producer, Edgar Rosenberg; producer-director, Terence Young; story idea, Ian Fleming; screenplay, Jo Eisinger; music, Georges Auric.

E. G. Marshall (Collie Jones); Trevor Howard (Sam Lincoln); Angie Dickinson (Linda Benson); Senta Berger (Addict-Stripper); Stephen Boyd (Benson); Yul Brynner (Colonel Salem); Georges Geret (Roche); Hugh Griffith (Chieftain); Jack Hawkins (General Bahar); Rita Hayworth (Monique Marco); Jocelyn Lane (Photographer); Trini Lopez (Himself); Marcello Mastroianni (Mosca); Amedeo Nazzari (Captain Dinnono); Jean-Claude Pascal (Tribe Leader); Anthony Quayle (Captain Vanderbilt); Laya Raki (Stripper in Shower); Luisa Rivelli (Miss Hatif); Gilbert Roland (Serge Marco); Harold Sakata (Martin); Omar Sharif (Rad); Silvia Sorente (Virgia); Barry Sullivan (Chasen); Nadja Tiller (Dr. Brunovska); Eli Wallach (Happy Locarno); Robert Cunningham (Fred-Marco's Aide); Violette Marceau (Bit); Grace Kelly (Special Introduction); and: Howard Vernon, Marilu Tolo, Gilda Daheberg, Morteza Kazerouni, Ali Ovelsi.

THE ROVER (L'AVVENTURIERO)   (Cinerama, 1967) C—103 M.

Producer, Alfredo Bini; director, Terence Young with the collaboration of Giancarlo Zagni; based on the novel by Joseph Conrad; screenplay, Luciano Vincenzoni, Jo Eisinger; director of fight sequences, Franco Fantasia; art director, Gianni Polidori; set decorators, Dario Micheli, Luciano Spadoni; costumes, Veniero Colasanti; makeup, Otello Fava; music, Ennio Morricone; music conductor, Bruno Nicolai; camera, Leonida Barboni; editor, Peter Thornton.

Anthony Quinn (Pyerol); Rosanna Schiaffino (Arlette); Rita Hayworth (Aunt Caterina); Richard Johnson (Real); Ivo Garrani (Scevola); Mino Doro (Dussard); Luciano Rossi (Michel); Mirko Valentin (Jacot); Gianni Di Benedetto (Lieutenant Bolt); Anthony Dawson (Captain Vincent); Franco Giornelli (Simmons); Franco Fantasia (Admiral); Fabrizio Jovine (Archives Officer); John Lane (Captain of the Port); Vittorio Venturoli (French Officer); Gustavo Gionni (Sans-Colette); Lucio De Santis (Fisherman); Raffaela Miceli (Arlette as a Child); Ruggero Salvadori (Hoodlum); Paola Bassalino, Rita Klein, Cathy Alexander (Girls).

SONS OF SATAN (I BASTARDI)   (WB, 1969) C—102 M.

Producer, Turi Vasile; director, Duccio Tessari; story, Mario Di Nardo; screenplay, Ennio De Concini, Di Nardo, Tessari; art director, Luigi Scaccianoce; set decorator, Dante Feretti; music-music director, Michel Magne; costumes, Danda Ortone; sound, Claudio Maielli; camera, Carlo Carlini; editor, Mario Morra.

Giuliano Gemma (Jason); Rita Hayworth (Martha); Klaus Kinski (Adam); Margaret Lee (Karen); Claudine Auger (Barbara); Serge Marquand (Jimmy); Umberto Raho (The Doctor); and: Karl Cik, Paola Natale, Hans Thorner, Mirella Pamphili, Detlev Uhle.

ROAD TO SALINA (SUR LA ROUTE DE SALINA)   (Avco-Embassy, 1971) C—96 M.

Producers, Robert Dorfmann, Yvon Guezel; director, Georges Lautner; based on the novel by Maurice Cury; screenplay, Lautner, Pascal Jardin, Jack Miller; art director, Jean D'Eaubonne; music-songs, Bernard Berard, Christophe, and Ian Anderson; music conductor, Gerard; assistant directors, Claude Vital, Robert Davis Israel; second unit director, Paul Nuyttens; camera, Maurice Fellous; editors, Michelle David, Elizabeth Guido.

Mimsy Farmer (Billie); Robert Walker (Jonas); Ed Begley (Warren); Bruce Pecheur (Charlie); David Sachs (The Sheriff); Sophie Hardy (Linda); Marc Porel (Rocky); with: Ivano Staccioli, Albane Navizet; and: Rita Hayworth (Mara).

THE NAKED ZOO   (R & S Film Enterprises, 1971) C—105 M.

Producer, William Grefe; associate producer, Stuart Merrill; director, Grefe.

With: Rita Hayworth, Fay Spain, Steven Oliver; Ford Rainey, Fleurette Carter, Willie Pastrano, Joe E. Ross.

THE WRATH OF GOD   (MGM, 1972) C—111 M.

Executive producer, Peter Katz; associate producer, William S. Gilmore, Jr.; director, Ralph Nelson; based on the novel by James Graham; screenplay, Nelson; production designer, John S. Polin, Jr.; set decorator, William Kiernan; music, Lalo Schifrin; action co-ordinator, Everett Creach; assistant directors, Mario Cisneros, Jerry Ziesmer; camera, Alex Phillips, Jr.; editors, J. Terry Williams, Richard Bracken, Albert Wilson.

Robert Mitchum (Van Horne); Frank Langella (Tomas de la Plata); Rita Hayworth (Señora de la Plata); John Colicos (Colonel Santilla); Victor Buono (Jennings); Ken Hutchison (Emmet Keogh); Paula Pritchett (Chela); Gregory Sierra (Jurado); Frank Ramirez (Moreno); Enrique Lucero (Nachito); Jorge Russek (Cordona); Chano Urueta (Antonio); José Luis Parades (Pablo); Aurora Clavell (Señora Moreno); Victor Eberg (Delgado); Pancho Cordova (Tacho); Guillermo Hernandez (Diaz); Ralph Nelson (Executed Prisoner).

Advertisement for GILDA (Col '46)

With Sam Ash and Joseph Calleia in GILDA

In GILDA

With James Gleason in
DOWN TO EARTH (Col '47)

With Orson Welles in
THE LADY FROM SHANGHAI (Col '48)

With Glenn Ford and Victor Jory in
THE LOVES OF CARMEN (Col '48)

With groom, Prince Aly Khan,
in Monte Carlo (May 27, 1949)

On the set of AFFAIR IN TRINIDAD
(Col '52) with hairdresser Helen Hunt and
photographer Robert Coburn

With Glenn Ford and George Voskovec in
AFFAIR IN TRINIDAD

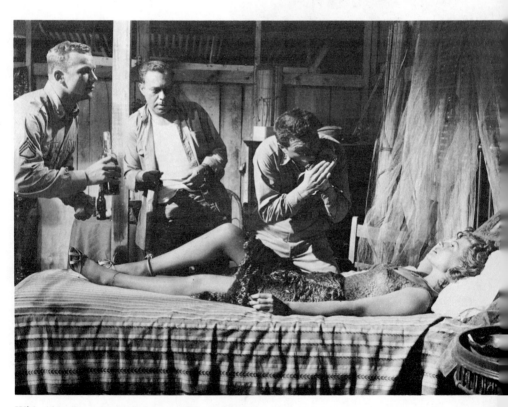

With Aldo Ray, Rudy Bond, and Henry Slate in
MISS SADIE THOMPSON (Col '53)

New York with Princess Yasmin and Rebecca Welles (October 1955)

In PAL JOEY (Col '57)

With Deborah Kerr and Gladys Cooper in
SEPARATE TABLES (UA '58)

Rehearsing for the Broadway-
bound STEP ON A CRACK
with Gary Merrill (1962)

HE STORY ON PAGE ONE (20th '59)

313

With Rex Harrison in
THE HAPPY THIEVES (UA '62)

With Claudia Cardinale and John Wayne in
CIRCUS WORLD (Par '64)

With Glenn Ford in THE MONEY TRAP (MGM '66)

With Anthony Quinn in THE ROVER (Cinerama '67)

In 1968

With Stephen Oliver in
THE NAKED ZOO
(R & S Films '71)

Publicity pose (1971)

In MY FAIR LADY

Audrey Hepburn

5'7"
101 pounds
Brown hair
Brown eyes
Taurus

Like most top-notch international cinema superstars, Audrey Hepburn conveyed her own unique charisma on the screen. Granted, in her fledgling film period she was often compared to contemporaries Leslie Caron and Maggie McNamara, but she soon skyrocketed far above and beyond these "similar" waifish movie types. During a fifteen-year span (1953-67), Audrey entranced the moviegoing public with her oncamera depictions of the piquant, elfish Cinderella, who usually, in the course of her feature films, met Prince Charming, and in the most ladylike manner suddenly awoke to romantic maturity and waltzed off into the glorious sunset draped in a divine Hubert de Givenchy wardrobe.

There were occasions when five-time-Oscar-nominated Audrey was not typecast as the elegant gamin per her Oscar-winning characterization in *Roman Holiday* (Paramount, 1953). Producers, with Audrey's gracious permission, saw fit to cast her as the rebellious cloistered Belgian girl in *The Nun's Story* (Warner Bros., 1959), providing her with a fitting dramatic showcase. As the sensitive, unknowing object of lesbian adoration in *The Children's Hour* (United Artists, 1961), or as the frightened blind wife in the thriller *Wait until Dark* (Warner Bros., 1967), Audrey was technically adept but emotionally at sea, as in the box-office fiasco *Paris When It Sizzles* (Paramount, 1964), which forced her to be a lifelike mannequin in a dead script.

If any creative fault can be found with Audrey's onscreen career, it is

319

that she too frequently allowed executive pressure for creating "sure box office" to turn potentially rich, offbeat portrayals into yet "another Audrey Hepburn part." Thus her Rima the Bird Girl in *Green Mansions* (MGM, 1959), Holly Golightly in *Breakfast at Tiffany's* (Paramount, 1961), and Eliza Doolittle in *My Fair Lady* (Warner Bros., 1964) were too akin in character delineation to her trend-setting *Sabrina* (Paramount, 1954), when each of these challenging new parts begged for a freshly conceived, individualistic interpretation.

Within a year of Audrey's arrival in America, she had won both an Oscar and a Tony Award (for *Ondine,* 1954), insuring her an immediate and lucrative niche in the changing entertainment world of the 1950s and 1960s. But just as she had kept herself remote from the social ambiance of her early career years in the British theatre-cinema, so she never truly became part of the Hollywood or international filmmaking play set. Whether under contract to England's Associated British Pictures or later to William Wyler-Paramount Pictures, Audrey remained a very private person, insisting upon being the straight-lined, unobtrusive figure she was. Her legion of movie fans forgave this eccentricity of form, and remained faithful to the ladylike, glamorous creature with the *Funny Face* (Paramount, 1957).

Although Audrey was not a studio-manufactured movie star, she certainly "owed" much of her cinema career direction to her husband-mentor Mel Ferrer, an enigmatic actor-producer-director who guided Audrey's private and professional life with hawklike totalitarianism. She would reject plum movie assignments if it meant leaving his side or if the project had no suitable "spot" for his particular brand of talent. Conversely, she indulged in some feature-making, especially *Green Mansions,* which only the whim of pleasing her spouse could conceivably have led her to accept as feasible projects.

By the time of the technically mod *Two for the Road* (Twentieth Century-Fox, 1967), Audrey's life was in total flux. Her marriage to Ferrer was overtly disintegrating, and oncamera she could no longer disguise her distinctly young-matronish looks. Perforce, thereafter, as in *Wait until Dark,* she would have to delve far afield for viable screen projects.

The now semiretired Audrey, residing in Rome, remains her charming, graceful self, exuding élan as before. It has yet to be demonstrated on film whether the elusive child-woman can or will in the future reveal new mature dimensions of the fascinating and bewitching personality so well known to moviegoers of past decades.

Audrey was born Edda van Heemstra Hepburn-Ruston on Saturday, May 4, 1929, in Brussels, Belgium. Her mother, wealthy Dutch Baroness

Ella van Heemstra, had two sons from the first of her two previous marriages, both of which had ended in divorce. Edda's father, Joseph Hepburn-Ruston, was an Irish businessman and manager of his wife's finances and holdings through the Bank of England branch in Brussels.

Edda's early childhood years were spent on the van Heemstra ancestral estate, where she grew up learning to speak French, English, and Italian. She was a thin, sickly little girl, unhappy with her looks, especially her nose. Admittedly, she was "quite miserable about my prospects." Edda's parents were constantly quarreling, largely over the Baroness's money matters, and Edda became a very introverted youngster. She rarely made acquaintances with children her own age, much preferring the company of her two older half-brothers.

In 1935 her parents separated and three years later divorced, one of the decree's stipulations being that Edda be placed in a school near London in order that her father might visit her with sufficient frequency. The girl was "terrified at first about being away from home, but it turned out to be a good lesson in independence."

The Baroness was on holiday with relatives in Arnhem, Holland, when England declared war against Germany in September 1939. She persuaded Hepburn-Ruston that Holland was probably a safer place for their daughter. After joining the Baroness, Edda's hyphenated surname was shortened. At first Edda encountered difficulties when she was enrolled in a Dutch school without knowing the language, but this scholastic problem was soon overcome because of her propensity for languages.

Early in 1940, when she was eleven, Edda decided she wanted to become a dancer, and she entered the Arnhem Conservatory of Music. A few weeks later, in May 1940, the Germans invaded and occupied Holland. In the four years of Nazi rule in the Netherlands, Edda attended day school only irregularly and only sporadically practiced her dancing.* Because there was never sufficient food, milk, or vitamins, she grew extremely thin and developed minor anemia. One account has it that at one point, when the German invaders were rounding up the children in the area to work in the Nazi officers' kitchen, lithe Edda escaped from her captors and went into a month's hiding, during which period the Arnhem area was the locale for Allied-Axis crossfire. Edda emerged alive, but badly shaken from the ordeal.

One of Edda's half-brothers was dragged away to a German labor

---

*Quite naturally, Edda (Audrey) has been reticient to discuss this grueling phase of her childhood. "Interviewers try to bring it up so often, but it's painful to think about. It was a long time ago, and I'm sure other people have been through much worse. I dislike talking about it because I feel it's not something that should be linked to publicity. The superficial things aren't interesting—the deeper things are. That's what it really comes down to. I wouldn't have missed it for the world. Anything that happens to you is valuable."

camp, while an uncle and a cousin were executed as enemies of the Third Reich. The van Heemstra estate, along with much of the family's money, was confiscated, and the Baroness, whose ancestry was part Jewish, actively joined the underground by staging fund-raising amateur shows behind locked church doors. Edda appeared in several of these "musicales," although at this time she had little stamina for this type of stage performing under such harrowing conditions. Of this bleak period, she once said, "Unfortunately people basically learn little from war. We needed each other so badly that we were kind, we hid each other, we gave each other something to eat. When it was over, people were just the same—gossipy and mean."

After the liberation, Edda studied ballet most diligently for three years in Amsterdam with Holland's famed Sonja Gaskell. In 1948 Edda made her motion-picture debut in a British-Dutch co-production, *Dutch at the Double (Nederlands in Zeven Lessen),* produced, directed, and scripted by Huguenot van der Linden and H. M. Josephson.* The documentary-style travelog concerned a young man who discovers Holland, its people, and its traditions. Edda had a very brief bit, appearing quite gauche as an air hostess at the beginning and at the end of the forty-minute film.†

That same year the Baroness and Edda returned to England. Mr. Hepburn-Ruston was then living in Ireland, and although Edda saw him occasionally, father and daughter were unable to resume a close relationship. In London Edda enrolled in advanced ballet classes under the direction of the noted British teacher, Marie Rambert, an instructress noted for whacking her students' knuckles with a stick when they were discovered with folded arms or slouched shoulders. To help pay her expenses, Edda doubled as a high-fashion photographer's model. In this part-time endeavor she learned the importance of clothes and found that she wore them quite well. It was the beginning of a lifelong desire (almost compulsion) to be meticulously dressed. For professional reasons, she anglicized her first name to Audrey and took her father's name of Hepburn as her last name.

Since part-time modeling jobs were not always available in postwar London, she signed up with the motion-picture casting offices, being hopeful but, realistically, not very optimistic. She did some cabaret dancing and in 1949, at the age of nineteen, secured a minor spot in the second chorus of the London production of *High Button Shoes.*‡ Her weekly salary was eight pounds. She had an alternate professional offer at just about the same time, that of joining a touring ballet company planning a South American engagement. She picked the musical job because, "I had found that my height [five feet, seven inches] was a handicap in ballet

---

*The cast included Wam Heskes, Han Bents van den Berg, Koos Koon, and Edda.
†Originally seven ten-minute segments.
‡Opened at the Hippodrome Theatre on December 22, 1948, for a 291-performance run.

and I might have to slave for years to achieve only limited success. I couldn't wait years; I needed money badly."*

When *High Button Shoes* embarked on a national tour of England, she chose to leave the show, and a short time later was hired for a part in Cecil Landeau's twenty-seven segment musical revue, *Sauce Tartare,* which debuted at the Cambridge Theatre in London's West End on May 18, 1949.† Then came a better role in Landeau's follow-up venture, *Sauce Piquante.‡* Audrey was once again in the dancing chorus of this show, but she had a spotlighted turn with a solo dance spot. Her appearance attracted the attention of screenwriter-director Thorold Dickinson, who jumped at the idea of screentesting her for a major supporting role in his upcoming film, *Secret People* (1952). However, negotiations were still in progress to cast Lea Padovani in the lead female part, and production was held up for several months.

Meanwhile, Audrey, who had been studying acting with Felix Aylmer, British performer and drama coach, gained an unbilled bit part in the Eros-Coronet Film, *One Wild Oat* (Eros, 1951), based on the sex-innu-endo-ridden stage farce by Vernon Sylvaine.§ The carbon-copy screen rendition retained the Romeo and Juliet theme, with Robertson Hare and Stanley Holloway as the heads of two opposing households, and June Sylvaine and Andrew Crawford their respective children who fall in love. Meanwhile, Audrey tested for the lead part of a beauty queen in Associated British's *Lady Godiva Rides Again* (British Lion, 1951), but the assignment went to the unknown Pauline Stroud. At the time, Audrey had been receiving a good deal of publicity for her nightclub work. *Picturegoer* magazine reported: "God's gift to publicity men is a heart-shattering young woman with a style of her own, no mean ability, and a photogenic capacity for making the newspaper pages among the first-nighters. The name is Audrey Hepburn; and the fact that some people have been twenty-four times to Ciro's to see her cabaret performance is a good enough start for . . . [Associated British] to talk of signing her for the screen."

Then Continental producer Mario Zampi, who was planning a comedy, *Laughter in Paradise* (Associated British, 1951), convinced Associated British to hire her for a tiny role, that of a nightclub cigarette girl.δ She

---

*She was then living in a cold-water flat, and most anxious to become independent, financially at least, of her mother's influence.

†The song-dance-comedy-sketch show debuted at the West End theatre for a 433-performance run. It starred Renee Houston, Claude Hulbert, Muriel Smith, Jack Melford, and Ronald Frankau.

‡The follow-up opened April 27, 1950, at the Cambridge Theatre for a scant 67-performance run. The revue starred Douglas Byng, Moira Lister, Muriel Smith, Marcelle Bon, Norman Wisdom, and Bob Monkhouse.

§Opened at the Garrick Theatre on December 8, 1948, for a 508-performance West End run.

δZampi claimed he had been to see Audrey's performance in *Sauce Piquante* some fourteen times.

appeared in a few scenes with a cigarette tray and had just one line, "But, I'm not a lady—I'm a girl." In this picture about an eccentric old practical joker who dies leaving 50,000 pounds to each of four relatives (including Alastair Sim) on various conditions, Audrey's name in the special screen billing, along with Veronica Hurst's, was prefaced with the word "Introducing." The film, acclaimed as one of the era's most hilarious British comedies, was a top moneymaker in England.

At this point Associated British thought enough of the "budding" actress to sign Audrey to a contract, and she was next loaned out for a minuscule part in *The Lavender Hill Mob* (General Film Distributors, 1951), the joyous Alec Guinness comedy of an innocuous little London bank clerk who engineers a grand gold theft from his stodgy employers. Audrey, as Chiquita, appears very briefly in one scene near the film's opening. In the Rio de Janeiro hotel-cafe setting, where Guinness is apparently the wealthy man of the hour, she is seen wearing a chic white suit with a black scarf. As she walks over to the munificent Guinness, he hands her a roll of bills. She says, "Oh—but I—how sweet of you," and leans down and kisses him on the right temple. This General Film Distributors' release was named the Best British Film of 1951 according to the British Film Academy.*

Guinness, who had been initially introduced to Audrey by Aylmer, liked the young actress and later suggested to producer-director Mervyn LeRoy that she be considered for a lead in MGM's pending epic production, *Quo Vadis* (MGM, 1951), then being readied for European filming. LeRoy, however, demanded an established name, and Deborah Kerr was later selected.

Back at Associated British, Audrey was called upon to enact a sizable role in the comedy, *Young Wives' Tales* (Associated British, 1951), based on the Ronald Jeans play.† In this domestic-romantic comedy, she is a single girl forced to share living quarters with two married couples because of the postwar housing shortage. She becomes infatuated with one of the husbands (Nigel Patrick), leading to the expected complications. The British *Monthly Film Bulletin* commented: "The high pitched playing of the actors give the film movement, so that it rarely drags. Situations follow quickly upon one another, and it is from this rather than from the not very witty dialogue that the comedy springs." Audrey received scant mention in the British reviews of the picture, but when the film opened in New York (Paris Theatre, November 3, 1952), Bosley Crowther *(New York Times)* berated the production for being a "dismal situation [comedy] as ever leaked from an uninspired brain." But he did make particular mention of "that pretty Audrey Hepburn."

*When *The Lavender Hill Mob* played Manhattan (October 1951), Bosley Crowther *(New York Times)* judged the picture a "jolly trifle."

†Opened at the Savoy Theatre for a 374-performance West End run, commencing July 7, 1949.

By now Thorold Dickinson had given up hopes of wooing Padovani for his *Secret People* for General Film Distributors, and he instead cast Valentina Cortese in the demanding assignment of a perceptive but life-exhausted refugee who is pressured into assisting her lover (Serge Reggiani) with a political assassination. Audrey was handed the part of Nora, Cortese's young sister, a dancer who finds herself drawn into Reggiani's circle of intrigue. She has one telling scene near the finale, when she suffers the trauma of seeing her stabbed sister die in front of her eyes, which leads her to break with Reggiani's organization. *Variety* rated the black-and-white picture a "hackneyed story of political agents working against a tyrannical dictator, dressed up with all the familiar clichés to make a dull and rather confusing offering." The trade paper did observe, however, that "[Audrey Hepburn] combines beauty with skill, shining particularly in two short dance sequences."

In the summer of 1951, Audrey was on the French Riviera filming *Nous Irons à Monte Carlo* (Hoche, 1951).* Her part was that of a film star whose baby is erroneously given to someone else during the confusion of a measles epidemic. Her plight was generously interspersed with endless interludes designed to exploit the virtues of Europe's Ray Ventura and his musicians. The film was lensed in French and English *(Monte Carlo Baby* [General Film Distributors, 1953]), with Audrey acting in both versions.

During the shooting of a scene at the Hotel Paris, seventy-eight-year-old novelist Sidonie-Gabrielle Colette, a guest at the hotel, was wheeled past the company of actors as they rested between takes. She spotted Audrey and knew at once that she had found the English-speaking girl to portray Gigi in the forthcoming Broadway production of her famous work.† Colette later confessed: "The moment I saw her I could not take my eyes away. 'There,' I said to myself incredulously, 'is Gigi.'" Colette learned Audrey's name, and later the authoress had her husband, Maurice Goudeket, offer the girl the plum acting part. Audrey's initial reaction was, "I simply couldn't do it. Why, I've never said more than one or two lines on the stage in my life." Colette ignored all protests and cabled news of her find to Anita Loos, then based in New York. Miss Loos had adapted Colette's novel for the stage. She, in turn, telephoned Gilbert Miller, the show's producer.

In the meantime, with the completion of *Nous Irons à Monte Carlo,*‡ Audrey returned to London where a young trucking-company executive

---

*The only excuse for this picture being made was that its predecessor, *Nous Irons a Paris* (Unidex, 1949), starring Ventura with a guest appearance by George Raft, had done enough box-office business to warrant Ventura producing this new celluloid exploit.

†Danielle Delorme had previously enacted the role in a French screen version in 1948.

‡*Nous Irons à Monte Carlo* was released in France in November 1951, garnering mediocre reviews. The critic for *Cinematographie Française,* despite Audrey's very small part in the film, prophetically observed that she is "destined to a brilliant future." The English-language version, *Monte Carlo Baby,* reached British shores in 1953, with less than enthusiastic reviews.

325

named James Hansen was waiting for her. Hansen, whom she had met several months earlier, wanted to marry her, but it had not been possible to come up with a definite decision because of Audrey's erratic work schedule.

Veteran Broadway producer Miller was anxious to meet this girl about whom Colette was so persistently enthusiastic. He flew to London and was convinced too, after a brief meeting, that Audrey was exactly what they wanted—an unknown who could sing, dance, and act the difficult role of the spirited French girl. Encouraged by the strong belief of Colette and Miller, Audrey signed a contract. The news was released to the press almost before the ink was dry. An elaborate coverage appeared in all British newspapers and rotogravures.

Before leaving for New York with the ever-present Baroness, Audrey underwent a screentest for director William Wyler at Paramount's London headquarters.* Wyler was then seeking an English actress to portray a sleeping princess in a film he was preparing, based on a story by Ferenc Molnár, the Hungarian writer. Her test was enthusiastically received, and she was selected more for her class than for her appearance. "She's a real aristocrat in every way," Wyler announced. With the participation of her employer, Associated British, Audrey was signed to an exclusive four-picture deal, the terms of the contract to be fulfilled after the run of *Gigi*.

Audrey, still a very much unknown commodity, arrived unheralded in New York. This status changed overnight when *Gigi* made its Broadway bow at the Fulton Theatre on Saturday, November 24, 1951. Most critics agreed with William Hawkins *(New York World-Telegram)* that the show's sexual ambiance was "more cool than tantalizing." But the reviewers were ecstatic over Audrey as the leggy, boisterous, graceless Parisian lass of fifteen who lives with her joyous grandmother (Josephine Brown). In the play Gigi is instructed in the art of being a coquettish young woman by her aunt (Cathleen Nesbitt), but really awakens through the amorous interest of Gaston (Michael Evans). "The delightful Miss Hepburn obviously is not an experienced actress," observed Richard Watts, Jr. *(New York Herald-Tribune)*, "but her quality is so winning and so right that she is the success of the evening. . . . [She] is as fresh and frisky as a puppy out of a tub. She brings a candid innocence and a tomboy intelligence to a part that might have gone sticky, and her performance comes as a breath of fresh air in a stifling season." The *Brooklyn Daily Eagle*'s aisle-sitter was most perceptive in discerning the qualities that would

---

*In *William Wyler* (1973), an authorized biography by Axel Madsen, Wyler recalls that he ordered a British test director to have the cameras continue rolling long after the "cut" signal had been given, so that he could observe a relaxed Audrey. "She was absolutely delightful. First, she played the scene from the script, then you heard someone yell 'Cut!' but the take continued. She jumped up in bed relaxed now, and asked, 'How was it? Was I any good?' She looked and saw that everybody was so quiet and that the lights were still on. Suddenly, she realized the camera was still running and we got *that* reaction too. Acting, looks, and personality! She was absolutely enchanting and we said, 'That's the girl!' The test became sort of famous and was once shown on TV."

soon be endearing Audrey to moviegoers around the world. "Audrey Hepburn, a fresh young beauty with a grave manner, in spite of her tomboyish role, is a thoroughgoing joy as the child-woman who grows up suddenly. She makes the transition persuasive and vivid, and her final scene is genuinely touching."

At the age of twenty-two, elfin Audrey was the toast of Broadway as the pert, naive girl in turn-of-the-century Paris who outwits her family's efforts to raise her in a life of fashionable sin. Audrey captured the hearts of the most jaded of theatregoers.

A few performances after the opening, British-born stage star Gertrude Lawrence came backstage after witnessing the show and expressed the wish that *if ever* her life were recorded, she wanted Audrey to play the part.* Like Miss Lawrence, Audrey possessed the triple-threat talents of singing, dancing and acting—a rare combination. Of herself, Audrey perceived, "I'm halfway between a dancer and an actress. I've got a lot to learn." She gave all credit to her dance training, explaining, "Ballet is the most completely exhausting thing I have ever done, but if I hadn't been used to pushing myself that hard, I could never have managed the tremendous amount of work necessary to learn in three weeks how to play a leading role in my first real acting job." Actor-director Alfred Lunt remarked upon meeting Audrey, "She has authentic charm. Most people simply have nice manners."

James Hansen showed up in New York, and on November 28, 1951, he made the official announcement that he and Audrey would be wed. He lingered on in the States for as long as his business could possibly permit, but finally returned to England when Audrey was still unable (or unwilling) to make positive matrimonial plans. She informed eager reporters about Hansen's departure, "We decided we weren't meant for each other. It was a mutual decision and a very personal matter about which I have nothing more to say."

Despite her critical and popular acclaim (she was now being referred to as "that other Hepburn," the reference being to Katharine Hepburn), Audrey remained calm about her success and refused to participate in the glittering New York after-hours social life. She continued her acting lessons with Cathleen Nesbitt, insisting that her one life's ambition was "to become a truly great actress."

On April 13, 1952, Broadway's newest attraction took time away from her daily study schedule to make a special appearance in an episode on CBS Network Television's "TV Workshop." She starred in a poignant story entitled *Rainy Day in Paradise Junction.*

After a successful six-month run in New York,† during which time it

---

*When Twentieth Century-Fox filmed the Gertrude Lawrence story, entitled *Star!* (1968), it was Julie Andrews who had the title role.

†Jan de Hartog's *The Fourposter* and Julie Harris (of *I Am a Camera*) won Tony Awards that Broadway season as best play and best actress.

played to 217 audiences, *Gigi* closed on May 31, 1952.* During the summer of 1952 Audrey was in Rome to film *Roman Holiday* (Paramount, 1953), a comedic story by Ian McLellan Hunter which William Wyler had acquired from director Frank Capra, as an on-location Italian production for Paramount release. After the European filming, Audrey returned to the United States and starred in the national tour of *Gigi,* which opened at the Nixon Theatre in Pittsburgh on October 13, 1952. It traveled for eight months, closing on May 16, 1953, at the Alcazar Theatre in San Francisco, following a Los Angeles run. Among those to see *Gigi* in San Francisco was film historian Earl Anderson, who recently recalled: "She was superb, as well as the play and the production, and it was unfortunate that there were rows of empty seats. It was already mentioned here that the previous summer she had made the film and Paramount expected when it was released that she would prove the sensation she did."†

Gordon Gow in *Hollywood in the Fifties* (1971) has said of *Roman Holiday*'s uniquely popular qualities, "Wyler imparts both humour and a delicate charm, slightly out of fashion but much appreciated by contrast to realistic essays or coarser comedies on the subject of love embattled by convention." In *Roman Holiday,* Audrey appears as Princess Anne, the lovely but lonely heiress apparent of a mythical European nation who becomes fed up with the dull routine of her royal post and flees to Rome, where, on a twenty-four-hour lark, she meets a very couth American newspaper correspondent (Gregory Peck). Together they take a light-hearted tour of the city, including swimming in the Tiber, driving a motor scooter, starting a minor riot, eating ice cream cones, and escaping the police. Through it all, the AWOL princess believes she is incognito, what with a chopped haircut and a new name (Anne Smith), but the diligent reporter discovers her identity early in the game. She does not realize that he knows because he keeps mum, figuring that his news editor will be elated by a personal feature article on the "real" princess. Naturally his professional interest soon turns to romantic aspiration. However, when the fun is done, the girl obediently returns to the royal court, with she and Peck sharing a touching farewell in the midst of a regal reception.

The Ruritanian romance opened at New York's Radio City Music Hall on August 27, 1953, to qualified but substantial reviews. "[It is] composed

---

Gigi would be turned into a Vincente Minnelli-directed musical film in 1958. It was Oscar-awarded as Best Picture of the Year and garnered $7.74 million in distributors' gross rentals, with Leslie Caron in the lead role. In 1973, *Gigi,* with additional Alan Jay Lerner-Frederick Loewe tunes, turned up as a Broadway musical with Karen Wolfe in the title part.

†In a January 1954 *Photoplay* magazine interview with Mike Connolly entitled "Who Needs Beauty!", Connolly said of Audrey: "I reminded her that only a few months previously, while she was appearing here in Los Angeles in *Gigi* and prior to the release of *Roman Holiday,* Hollywood columnists and reporters had not been too eager to meet her. As a matter of fact, Paramount had had to beg a number of newspaper people to take free tickets to see her in the play. She laughed, 'It's not very nice of you to remind me of that!' "

almost entirely of cliches that turn out to be fun" *(New Yorker).* Co-star Peck was commended for being handsome and resilient, and Eddie Albert as the bearded expatriate photographer received his share of the laurels, but it was Audrey who wowed the critics. "She is a piquant find, and the pretty young lady knows how to act. I don't know how tough it is to behave like a princess, but she behaves like one all right" (Hollis Alpert, *Saturday Review).* "Miss Hepburn (Audrey, that is) is a thing of beauty—in comedy, romance, drama and farce" *(Cue).* The *New York Herald-Tribune's* Paul Beckley recorded, "A remarkable young actress, Audrey Hepburn carries off the finale with a nicety that leaves one a little haunted." However, there were some who thought that Audrey's limitations in the area of the bosom would deflect audiences away from the film. A theatre-owner in Berkeley, California, promoted the feature with a composite photo of Terry Moore's shapely torso topped by Audrey's face. He declared that the gimmick was a boon to business, and Terry, flattered by such a tribute, said, "I only hope it does as much for me as it did for Audrey."

Coincidental with the release of *Roman Holiday,* England's Princess Margaret surprised the world by falling for a commoner, and the public immediately identified the film with the real happening. Aided by this, the motion picture became a favorite with ticket-buyers.

At a gala party following the splashy London premiere,* Gregory Peck introduced Audrey to Mel Ferrer,† who was then appearing onscreen in *Lili* (MGM, 1953), co-starring with Audrey's Gallic counterpart, Leslie

---

Punch magazine enthused, "Such is the fresh charm of Audrey Hepburn in *Roman Holiday* . . . that it is hard not to decide that her personality and ability are the film's most important qualities. . . . Miss Hepburn is good: she is not merely young and charming, that happens to all sorts of people—she can, at least within the limited range provided here, act." *Picturegoer* was even more charmed, "So flowers, please, for the enchanting Audrey—for the girl that has shown that real stars are still to be found."

†Melchior Gaston Ferrer was born in Elberon, New Jersey, on August 25, 1917. He quit Princeton University in his sophomore year to try his luck in summer stock; later he was an editor for a publishing house in Brattleboro, Vermont, and wrote a children's book, *Tito's Hat.* He made his Broadway bow as a dancer in two musicals, *You Never Know* and *Everywhere I Roam,* both 1938 productions. After appearing onstage in the Otto Preminger-directed *Cue for Passion* (1940), he was forced to spend a year recuperating from a bout with polio. After a spell as a radio disc-jockey and newscaster, NBC hired him as a producer-director for some of its better audio programs. In 1945, Columbia Pictures offered him a job with wide-ranging capacities, as actor, director, or story consultant. After the failure of his directing a "C" celluloid remake of *The Girl of the Limberlost* (1945) the studio dropped him. He made his Broadway in *Strange Fruit* (1945), and the next year had the title role in a revival of *Cyrano de Bergerac,* directed by José Ferrer (no relation). David O. Selznick-RKO hired Mel Ferrer on terms similar to his Columbia deal, and he worked on John Ford's *The Fugitive* (RKO, 1947) and was one of several directors that RKO's new owner, Howard Hughes, assigned to *Vendetta,* an expensive fiasco finally released in 1950.

Ferrer, who had been performing at the La Jolla Playhouse in California, made his cinema acting debut in *Lost Boundaries* (Four Continents, 1949), directed Claudette Colbert in RKO's *The Secret Fury* (1950), and performed in *Born to Be Bad* (RKO, 1950), *The Brave Bulls* (Columbia, 1951), and *Rancho Notorious* (RKO, 1952), which concluded his studio pact. MGM then hired Ferrer as an actor, and he played in *Scaramouche* (1952), *Lili, Saadia* (1953), and *Knights of the Round Table* (1953).

Caron. Audrey and the twelve-year-older Ferrer liked each other immediately and found that they had many interests in common. She promptly agreed to his suggestion that they work together if a suitable stage play could be found.

Paramount, extraordinarily pleased by Audrey's American film debut, once again maneuvered to purchase her Associated British movie contract, but with no success. They were forced to undergo the ignominy of paying an increasingly larger loan-out fee to the British movie company for her continued oncamera services. At this time, Paramount, like the other Hollywood film factories, was undergoing the repercussions of the tremendous transitions necessitated by both the postwar governmental antitrust suits, which separated studio distribution from national theatrical exhibition, and, of course, the devastating financial effects of the competing television medium. Y. Frank Freeman, vice-president in charge of production and studio operations at Paramount, had a rather limited stable of performers with which to balance out his production schedule. The hold-over greats from the 1940s (Bing Crosby, Bob Hope, Betty Hutton, Dorothy Lamour, special pactee Joan Fontaine, and Lizabeth Scott of Hal Wallis's independent-production studio unit) were on their way out. There was Wallis's extremely popular comedy team of Dean Martin and Jerry Lewis making studio features, and in mid-1954 Wallis would sign young Broadway musical-comedy hopeful Shirley MacLaine to a pact which would bolster Paramount's performer lineup, as did a later Wallis employee, Elvis Presley. But in 1953, in the area of female players, the studio had to be content with the like of Arlene Dahl, Rhonda Fleming, Patricia Medina, Rosemary Clooney, Polly Bergen, Jan Sterling, and Dorothy Malone. Thus Paramount was most grateful, under whatever conditions it had to endure, to have Audrey's services to garnish its plum film projects.

Freeman cast her in the title role of *Sabrina* (Paramount, 1954), based on Samuel Taylor's sophisticated stage success, *Sabrina Fair.** Producer-director-co-scripter Billy Wilder, who was completing his Paramount tenure with this production, filmed on location between September and November 1953 at the Long Island Sound estate of studio president Barney Balaban, and at Glen Cove, Long Island. He zealously described his new leading lady, "After so many drive-in waitresses in movies—it has been a real drought—here is class, somebody who went to school, can spell and possibly play the piano. . . . She's a wispy, thin little thing, but you're really in the presence of somebody when you see that girl. Not since Garbo has there been anything like it, with the possible exception

*The stage comedy, starring Margaret Sullavan, Joseph Cotten, and Scott McKay, opened at the National Theatre on November 11, 1953, and enjoyed a 318-performance Broadway run.

of [Ingrid] Bergman."* The male screen roles were given to Humphrey Bogart (who replaced the originally scheduled Cary Grant) and a blond William Holden.

Within the film, Audrey is Sabrina, the gamine daughter of a staid chauffeur (John Williams) to a wealthy Long Island family. She has a crush on the younger, playboy son (Holden), which the older, staunch, career-businessman son (Bogart) squelches, but in so doing he falls for her himself. Although cynical Wilder twisted some of the original import of playwright Taylor's dramatic intentions, *Sabrina* remained a Cinderella tale, with Audrey literally undergoing a drastic transition in looks, charm, and philosophy once she returns from her stay in Paris, where she was sent to a haute-cuisine cooking school. Bosley Crowther *(New York Times)* rated *Sabrina* the "most delightful comedy-romance in years," and while admitting that the picture equally belonged to dour-faced Bogart, he applauded Audrey as "a young lady of extraordinary range of sensitive and moving expressions within such a frail and slender frame. She is even more luminous as the daughter and pet of the servants' hall than she was as a princess last year, and no more than that can be said." *Time* magazine could offer a back-handed compliment: "Actress Hepburn's appeal, it becomes clearer with every appearance, is largely to the imagination; the less acting she does the more people can imagine her doing, and wisely she does very little in *Sabrina.* That little she does skillfully." But it was Otis L. Guernsey, Jr. *(New York Herald-Tribune)* who pegged Audrey's true acting forte and her special cinema niche: "Fairy tales are her natural element."

During the filming of *Sabrina,* Audrey enlisted the fast-becoming-famous Hubert de Givenchy to design her personal wardrobe for the picture. It was the beginning of a lasting relationship.† Also, production on this picture provided Audrey with a professional introduction to Frank McCoy, who was to become her hairdresser on most of her future pictures. With the combined assistance of these and other creative technical talents, Audrey demonstrated in *Sabrina* a pixie, yet authoritative, chic that was to become her special professional trademark, a happening which must have surprised the very outspoken Wilder, who before the filming of *Sabrina* had remarked of Audrey's countenance, ". . . that curious, ugly face of that dame."

---

*Post filming *Sabrina,* Wilder, who had a difficult time working with co-star Bogart, was still enthused about Audrey's potential. "She's like a salmon swimming upstream. She can do it with very small bozooms. Titism has taken over this country. This girl single-handed may make bozooms a thing of the past. The director will not have to invent shots where the girl leans way forward for a glass of Scotch and soda."

†Audrey would say of de Givenchy: "He's my great love. He made the first dresses I ever wore from a good fashion house, and designed that wonderful ball gown I wore in *Sabrina.* . . . I consider him one of my best and most important friends."

Meantime, Mel Ferrer had found a play in which to co-star with Audrey. After securing Alfred Lunt as director, and the Playwrights Company as producer, he hurried to Hollywood to discuss with the much-in-demand Audrey the possibility of appearing in Jean Giraudoux's *Ondine* (1939), adapted from the French by Maurice Valency. While Hollywood observers were noting the "togetherness" of Audrey and Ferrer, the Baroness also appeared on the Hollywood scene and carefully advised the press that her daughter was in no way romantically aligned with the three-time divorced Ferrer.*

Ferrer proved persuasive in convincing Audrey of the stage venture's worth, and the lyric allegory *Ondine,* with music by Virgil Thomson, costumes by Richard Whorf, and lighting by Jean Rosenthal, opened at the 46th Street Theatre on February 18, 1954. It proved to be one of the season's most gala events. With her hair cropped close to her head and dyed blonde to make her look more nymphlike, Audrey was a sweet-tempered sprite who lives in a lake and promptly falls in love with the first young man she has ever seen (Ferrer). In a sprite's costume especially designed for her by Valentina, Audrey was an enchanting sight to behold. The show was declared "a pastry, all air and light, a confection of foam-like texture. Its writing is graceful, its humors are delicious, its performances are of the jewel variety" (Whitney Bolton, *New York Morning Telegraph*). Vis-à-vis Ferrer was passed off by the press as "a trifle too mundane" *(Variety),* but Audrey received a full bouquet of accolades. "Miss Hepburn moves with the fleet freedom that testifies to her ballet training, and she speaks with a voice of strange and vibrant beauty. She makes Ondine the image of the ageless nymph whose wisdom, like her innocence, is drawn from the lore of sprites and supernatural beings," *Variety* decided. "The girl really has the magic; she's tremendous. Largely because of her personal incandescence and quicksilver performance, *Ondine* is a resounding hit, adding lustre to an already distinguished season."

A few days later, Audrey was nominated for an Academy Award for her performance in *Roman Holiday.* Her four competitors were Leslie Caron for *Lili,* Ava Gardner for *Mogambo,* Deborah Kerr for *From Here to Eternity,* and Maggie McNamara for *The Moon Is Blue.* Audrey was considered the favorite to win, and a month later, wearing her *Ondine* costume and garish eye and mouth makeup, she rushed across midtown Manhattan—with the Baroness at her side—to a theatre where the Academy Award ceremonies were being televised from Hollywood. She bit her fingernails through an interminable build-up, until she was announced

*Ferrer had been previously wed to sculptress Frances Pilchard, by whom he had a son and a daughter. After divorcing her, he wed Barbara C. Tripps, by whom he had another son and daughter. When that union failed, he rewed and then redivorced Pilchard.

the Oscar winner for Best Actress of the Year. (She had already won the New York Film Critics and the *Film Daily* awards in the same category for *Roman Holiday.)* The next day, she said: "I never lost consciousness all night. I just lay there in a sort of wakeful dream with pretty pictures in my head. It's difficult to say what the nicest things that ever happened to me are. But, this, surely is one of them." A week later she won a Tony Award for *Ondine*, which earned her the right to take solo curtain calls thereafter.

At the age of twenty-four, Audrey's star was high in the heavens, but she sensibly reflected to the press, "When I've made about seventy films and the public still wants to see me—then I shall think of myself as a star."

To capitalize on her popularity, Collier Young's Filmakers Company acquired the United States rights to *Monte Carlo Baby* and released it in May 1954. Oscar Godbout *(New York Times)* reported: "It is rather astonishing how she stands out in that seared desert of mediocrity. Miss Hepburn saves *Monte Carlo Baby* from being completely worthless."

When *Ondine* closed on July 3, 1954, after 157 performances, Audrey flew to Switzerland with Ferrer. They were married on Saturday, September 24, 1954, at 1:00 P.M., at the Burgenstock Mountain Chapel, overlooking Lake Lucerne. Sir Neville Bland, a former diplomat, gave the white-dress-clad bride away. Ferrer's sister Terry was also among the wedding party. After an Italian honeymoon, Audrey and Ferrer flew to Amsterdam, where Audrey made a personal-appearance tour to help raise money for Dutch war veterans.

In October 1954, *Variety* reported that *Sabrina,* with distributors' domestic rentals of $4 million, was the number-three moneymaker of the year. In February 1955, the film gained Audrey her second Academy Award nomination, but she lost to Grace Kelly of *The Country Girl.* Meanwhile, early in 1955, at the small wooden chalet rented by the Ferrers at Burgenstock, Switzerland, Audrey suffered the first of several miscarriages.

For months, director King Vidor had been hounding Audrey to star for him in the projected Dino De Laurentis production of *War and Peace* (Paramount, 1956).* Vidor finally cornered the star at Burgenstock and convinced her to portray the heroine, Natasha. Ferrer had earlier been tabbed to portray the character's first love, Andrei. Since much of the $6 million epic filmed in color and widescreen VistaVision was to be lensed near Rome, the Ferrers rented a pink farmhouse twenty miles

---

*Prior to Vidor-Paramount-De Laurentis-Associated British agreeing on their plans for *War and Peace,* David O. Selznick announced that he had a Ben Hecht screenplay for the Tolstoy novel and would start lensing in June 1955. At about the same time, producer Mike Todd insisted that his rendition of *War and Peace,* based on a Robert Anderson screenplay, would be shot in Todd-AO widescreen in Europe in May 1955; and MGM, not to be left out of the act, publicized that its edition of *War and Peace,* possibly with Audrey as Natasha, would commence lensing in August 1955.

outside the city. The abode was stocked with three servants and a menagerie of cats and dogs.

Work began in mid-July 1955 on Leo Tolstoy's 650,000-word novel (1865-69), which had required six credited writers to adapt it into a reasonable movie format. Henry Fonda was added to the cast as the bespectacled, sensitive Pierre; other members were John Mills (Platon) and Herbert Lom (Napoleon Bonaparte) of Britain, Tullio Carminati (Kuragine) and Vittorio Gassman (Anatole) of Italy, Helmut Dantine (Dolokhov) and Oscar Homolka (General Kutuzov) of Austria, and Sweden's Anita Ekberg (Helene), plus 8,000 horses, 2,876 cannons, and 15,000 Italian soldiers impersonating Russian and French troops in scenes depicting the battles of Borodino, Berezina, and Austerlitz, the burning of Moscow, and Napoleon's retreat. A portion of 1812 Moscow was reconstructed in a bend of the Tiber River while ninety tailors were kept busy for seven months making buttons for the costumes. Most of the scenes depicting the Russian winter were actually shot beneath the July sun of Italy. In one scene, wearing heavy winter clothing, Audrey was required to sit atop a sweating mount. The animal collapsed from heat prostration and had to be retired, but Audrey went on to put in a full day's work. About her characterization of Natasha, the beautiful daughter of Count Rostov (Barry Jones), who is engaged to wealthy, handsome Ferrer, but ruins the proposed marriage by her scandalous attempt to elope with rakish Gassman and eventually weds Fonda after Ferrer is mortally wounded in battle, Audrey has said that the role, which required her to age through three years of war, was "the toughest job I've had to do."

The original 33,000 feet of recorded film was cut to 18,700 feet, or three hours and twenty-eight minutes of screen fare—just twelve minutes shorter than the longest film made to that time, *Gone with the Wind* (1939). When Audrey finished work on the marathon picture, she said happily, "Anything good happening to me from now on will be surplus."

War and Peace premiered at New York's Capitol Theatre on August 21, 1956. *Time* magazine judged that it "is one of the industry's best. Visually, it could scarcely be improved." Bosley Crowther *(New York Times)* fairly represented the intellectual set when he complained of the film, "This tireless and changeless progression through the episodes of Tolstoy's cluttered tale makes for an oddly mechanical and emotionally sterile air." Or, as England's *Manchester Guardian* would sum up the epic, it "has length without depth." But the public was sufficiently impressed by the sweep of Vidor's film to earn it $6.25 million just in distributors' domestic rentals, a figure much increased on its international release. As for Audrey's pivotal role, William K Zinsser *(New York Herald-Tribune)* was in the majority when he proclaimed, "she is very beautiful and she has a shining exuberance. . . . A fleeting look in her eyes can express all the pain of growing up." *Time* observed: "Of the film's three stars, only

Audrey Hepburn, with her precocious child's head set upon a swanlike neck, looks the part. She is perfectly the Natasha described by Tolstoy."*

Audrey had been paid $350,000 for her three months' acting stint in *War and Peace,* with a $500 weekly expense account, making her one of the highest paid film performers both in the United States and abroad.†

Ironically, in 1956 Audrey was not among the top-ten box-office attractions, according to the *Motion Picture Herald-Fame* poll,‡ nor would she ever make an appearance in this particular survey's winner's circle.

Having completed their exhausting chores in *War and Peace,* Audrey and Ferrer repaired to their Burgenstock chalet for a rest. In the simple, quiet setting of their favorite spot in the world, they settled down for a few months' solitude, which gave Audrey's mother, the Baroness, further ammunition for her claim that Ferrer was doing his best to sabotage Audrey's budding screen career. Audrey was forwarded several scripts for consideration, one of which was *The Diary of Anne Frank* (eventually produced by Twentieth Century-Fox in 1959 with Millie Perkins in the key role). But she turned down any offer that would have meant her having to leave her husband's side.

Meantime, MGM had been toying with a variation of *Funny Face,* "based" on a 1927 Broadway show which had starred Fred Astaire.§ The studio wanted to borrow Audrey for the screen musical, but Paramount refused, and eventually the entire production package was moved over to Paramount. Audrey accepted the role because *Funny Face* (Paramount, 1957) was to be lensed in Hollywood and Paris, and Ferrer would also be in the French capital at that time making *Paris Does Strange Things* (Warner Bros., 1957) with Ingrid Bergman. Astaire persisted with the project through the complex negotiations because, "This could be the last and only opportunity I'd have to work with the great and lovely Audrey and I was not missing it."δ

As it developed, the Stanley Donen-directed *Funny Face,* beyond its title, had next to nothing to do with the old Astaire stage show. The Leonard Gershe screenplay was tailor-made for Audrey,γ casting her as Jo Stockton, a Greenwich Village bookshop bookworm who is transformed into the world's most glamorous mannequin with "pazaaz" by fashion photographer Astaire. Inspired by the career of renowned camera-clicker

---

*In the eight-hour Russian version of *War and Peace* (1966), actress Ludmila Savelyeva, as Natasha, bore a remarkable resemblance to Audrey.

†Ferrer was paid $100,000 for his participation in the film.

‡The top ten of 1956 were (1) William Holden, (2) John Wayne, (3) James Stewart, (4) Burt Lancaster, (5) Glenn Ford, (6) Dean Martin and Jerry Lewis, (7) Gary Cooper, (8) Marilyn Monroe, (9) Kim Novak, (10) Frank Sinatra.

§Alvin Theatre, November 22, 1927, with a run of 244 performances.

δAstaire had previously danced oncamera with Leslie Caron, still considered Audrey's "type," in Twentieth Century-Fox's *Daddy Long Legs* (1955).

γGershe had originally prepared the script for a Broadway project entitled *Wedding Day.*

With Guy Middleton in LAUGHTER IN PARADISE
(Associated British Pictures '51)

With Joan Greenwood and Nigel Patrick in YOUNG WIVES' TALE
(Associated British Pictures '51)

Relaxing on the set of THE LAVENDER HILL MOB
(General Film Distributors '51)

In SECRET PEOPLE (General Film Distributors '52)

With Gregory Peck in
ROMAN HOLIDAY
(Par '53)

With William Holden and Humphrey Bogart in SABRINA (Par '54)

In WAR AND PEACE (Par '56)

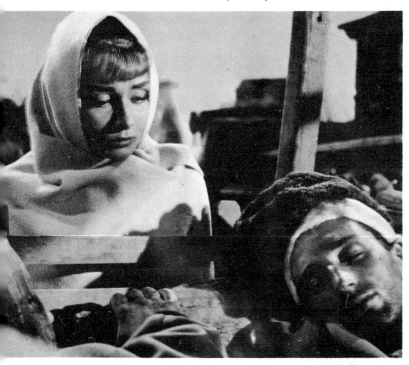

In FUNNY FACE (Par '57)

With Maurice Chevalier in
LOVE IN THE AFTERNOON (AA '57)

In BREAKFAST AT TIFFANY'S (Par '61)

With George Peppard and Martin Balsam in BREAKFAST AT TIFFANY'S

With Fay Bainter, Shirley MacLaine, Karen Balkin, and James Garner in
THE CHILDREN'S HOUR (UA '62)

With William Holden on location in Paris (April 1962) for
PARIS WHEN IT SIZZLES (Par '64)

Richard Avedon, it contains many exciting shots of Audrey in stunning Givenchy creations against dramatic Parisian settings. As the erudite drab who is told that she has certain good physical qualities, she coldly replies, "I see no functional advantage in having a marvelous mouth," but changes her mind when informed that, as a high-fashion model, she would be whisked off to Paris. Because she knows that is where the bearded intellectuals of the world are reputed to live, she consents to the job, hoping to have ample opportunity to discuss life's convoluted philosophies with her soul mates.

In the course of the well-executed 103-minute color and VistaVision feature, Audrey shares several song-dance sequences with mature Astaire, including "Funny Face," "He Loves and She Loves," and "S'Wonderful." With the delightful Kay Thompson, Audrey duets "On How to Be Lovely," and in a fascinating split-screen trio with Astaire and Thompson, she performs "Bonjour Paris." Audrey had an opportunity to exhibit her dancing acumen in "Basal Metabolism," performed in a Left Bank cellar setting with two male dancers. Her solo song, "How Long Has This Been Going On?" while setting no new highs in vocal renditions, revealed that the star had a pleasing, if thin and languorous, singing voice.*

Despite the many versatile virtues of *Funny Face,* it was never the popular hit it rightly deserved to become. *Look* magazine did report, "*Funny Face* is exceptional not so much for its story as for the warm performances of Hepburn and Astaire and the bold brilliance of its color." Critic-personality Rex Reed would later herald the movie as "the best fashion show ever recorded on film." But only in recent years has the neglected motion picture, containing Audrey's musical-comedy cinema debut performance, received its just due, leading many authorities to agree that it is a far more cogent, inventive, and less cliched study of 1950s celluloid musical comedy than the far overrated study of the Parisian scene, *An American in Paris* (MGM, 1951).†

In January 1957, the Ferrers went into rehearsal for one of the most elaborate of that or any year's television productions. Budgeted at $620,000, the ninety-minute, color "Producer's Showcase" offering of *Mayerling* (NBC-February 4, 1957) told the famous story of Austria's Crown Prince Rudolph (Ferrer), who, on January 30, 1889, executed a death pact with his seventeen-year-old mistress, Maria Vetsera (Audrey).‡ The video

---

*In *The Musical Film* (1967), author Douglas McVay points out one of the film's few flaws as being Audrey's "over-mannered pronunciation of 'sen-ses' and, particularly, 'defences,' at the start of [this number]."

†McVay, in *The Musical Film,* observes that *Funny Face* "is not merely one of the most melodious and rhythmically exciting of all film musicals, but arguably the most pictorially ravishing of all Hollywood musicals—and all American pictures."

‡The cast also included Diana Wynyard as the Empress, Raymond Massey as the Prime Minister, Judith Evelyn as Countess Larische, and Basil Sydney as the Emperor; and boasted costumes by Dorothy Jenkins.

project was directed by Anatole Litvak, who had also helmed the French movie version of 1937, which starred Charles Boyer and Danielle Darrieux.* In a cover feature story for *Life* magazine, Continental Litvak informed a reporter how it was to work with actors who were married to each other in real life. "When Audrey plays Maria, speaking to the prince, she is also Audrey speaking to her husband. It is very difficult to get Mel to treat her roughly. I had to work with him to get him to do it." The television "epic" proved to be one of the big flops of the season. "It was a spectacular on all counts except one, the drama. A more pallid or elementary version of *Mayerling* would be difficult to imagine" (Jack Gould, *New York Times*). Audrey's reviews were equally anemic. "She was called on to do little more than look beautiful and to be smitten with maidenly adoration, an assignment which gave her no trouble at all" (Jay Nelson Tuck, *New York Post*). The dismal *Mayerling* was later released theatrically in Europe.

"The Elegant Gamine," as Audrey was labeled by one writer at the time, then accepted Billy Wilder's offer to co-star with Gary Cooper in a romantic comedy taken from Claude Anet's novel, *Ariane*.† The film became *Love in the Afternoon* (Allied Artists, 1957).‡ The black-and-white feature was shot at the Studios de Boulogne and on location in outlying districts of Paris, and at the Chateau de Vitry. Ferrer was then (August-December 1956) involved in two European-based films, *The Vintage* (MGM, 1957) and *The Sun Also Rises* (Twentieth Century-Fox, 1957), thus making it possible for them to visit each other on their days off from shooting.

Love in the Afternoon, a delicately shaped frou-frou in the finest tradition of the best Ernst Lubitsch screen comedies, deals with an aging American roué (Cooper) who becomes fascinated with an uninhibited Parisian cellist (Audrey) whose father is a private detective (ably portrayed by a seemingly ageless bon vivant, Maurice Chevalier). Within the leisurely 125-minute photoplay, Cooper overcomes his inhibitions about courting a much younger girl, and, at the end, he and the romantically awakened girl depart from Paris aboard a train.

Cooper, who looked excessively tired and all of his fifty-six years in the film, paid young Audrey a supreme compliment at the outset of filming

---

*MGM was to film a 1969 version of *Mayerling,* a fiasco starring Omar Sharif and Catherine Deneuve as the star-crossed lovers.

†The story had been filmed twice before under its book title, *Ariane*. Elisabeth Bergner appeared as the heroine in both versions: in the 1931 German edition, Rudolf Forster played the Gary Cooper role; in the English remake (1934), Percy Marmont undertook the Cooper part.

‡In rerelease, a few years later, it was retitled *Fascination*. When the picture was shown in Spain, a few scenes had to be revised to be less "offensive" to the general public. In France, the movie was called *Ariane*, as the American movie title was considered too suggestive.

when he said, "I've wanted to act with Miss Hepburn ever since seeing her in *Gigi.*"* Wilder, having enjoyed his *Roman Holiday* association with Audrey, was eager to be realigned professionally with the star. He later stated, "I had a chance of getting Audrey Hepburn and I thought the picture could be good, with feelings, humour and everything."

Sophisticated and piquant as *Love in the Afternoon* was, it did not stir up much public enthusiasm in America, doing better box-office business abroad. Like *Funny Face,* it involved Audrey in a May-December romance, an amorous set-up in much disfavor with 1950s audiences. Audrey had to accomplish two difficult acting feats in *Love in the Afternoon.* One was mastering the finger movements for the cello part of Haydn's Eighty-eighth Symphony; the other involved an island picnic scene in which she was required to eat chicken, which was always prepared with garlic, to which she is allergic. "So, I stick a piece of pear to a chicken leg with toothpicks," she confessed to a *McCall's* magazine writer. "When the public sees me biting into the chicken, what I really will be chewing is pear."

Audrey next accompanied Ferrer to Mexico, where he was required for additional scenes for *The Sun Also Rises* (Twentieth Century-Fox, 1957).† There, Ferrer read, for a second time, the famed W. H. Hudson novel *Green Mansions* (1904), a fantasy about a mystical and delicate girl-child of the forest. He hit on an idea for a motion picture that would construe the story not as fantasy, but as potential reality. MGM found Ferrer's interpretation viable and gave an affirmative reply to his directorial proposal after learning that Audrey would be available to star as the ethereal Rima the bird girl, who, fate had decreed, could not leave her jungle sanctuary.‡

With a company of thirty, Ferrer spent two months wandering through Venezuela, British Guiana, and Colombia filming outdoor background scenes. In Brazil he contracted Heitor Villa-Lobos, age seventy-one, to compose special music, his first for a film. Anthony Perkins, then, like Audrey, under Paramount commitments, was chosen to play Abel, a Venezuelan who flees a revolution by going into the wilds in search of gold. Instead he finds Rima, becomes entranced with her, but loses her when local Indians destroy her with fire because of their belief that she

---

*After the release of *Love in the Afternoon* Audrey facetiously (?) commented to the press that she thought the film might have worked better had Cooper and Chevalier switched roles!

†It was Audrey who suggested to producer Darryl F. Zanuck that her friend, singer Juliette Greco, would be perfect in the role of Georgette.

‡Back in 1932, RKO had bought the screen rights to *Green Mansions* for $12,000 as a potential Dolores Del Rio project. Because that studio later decided it was unmarketable in the Depression era, it was sold in 1943 to independent producer James B. Cassidy for $15,000. In 1945, Cassidy, in turn, resold the vehicle to MGM for $82,500. From time to time, Metro experts took a crack at it; in fact, in 1953 MGM had Alan Jay Lerner prepare a *Green Mansions* script and then sent director Vincente Minnelli, unit manager William Kaplan, and art director Preston Ames to South America to film some background footage for the project, which was tentatively agreed upon to star Pier Angeli in the title role.

possesses an evil spirit. As the bird girl, Audrey wore a long brown wig and semidiaphanous costumes designed by Dorothy Jenkins. The film was completed in November 1958 and released during Easter Week, 1959, with a big send-off at the Radio City Music Hall. When asked by friends how it was to be directed by her husband, Audrey replied, "As natural as brushing my teeth." Ambiguous Ferrer, on the other hand, told the press: "I'll admit that some of my delight over directing *Green Mansions* may have come from my being on one side of the camera and Audrey on the other. But we always intended to have two very separate careers."

Moviegoers did not find many virtues to *Green Mansions* (MGM, 1959) above and beyond the sharp photography of Franz Planer or the nostalgic sight of seeing former silent-film star Sessue Hayakawa perform in the near-silent role of an aged Indian. The sound of Perkins singing "Song of Green Mansions," or of Audrey's Rima wandering through the forest, communing with her mother ("Oh mother, hear me, it's about this young man in the forest"), or the finale, which has Perkins seeing a vision of the dead bird girl beckoning to him from a nearby misty ridge, were no assets to the production. At least Audrey made no bird calls. As *Variety* aptly summed it up, "This is one of those screen versions that is likely to confuse those who haven't read the book and irritate those who have." *Cue* magazine was more biting, "[The film] makes this neoclassic seem like a mawkishly absurd burlesque of a jungle *al fresco* romance." *Variety* complained that star Audrey showed "no particular depth." One of her few critical champions was Arthur Knight *(Saturday Review),* who decided, "Audrey Hepburn's doe-like grace probably comes closer to a real-life Rima than we have any reason to expect . . ."

At this juncture more than just Audrey's mother, the Baroness, were questioning the professional alliance of the Oscar-winning star and Ferrer, a couple often referred to as Hollywood's latest Trilby and Svengali. Paramount, even before *Green Mansions,* had rejected Audrey's bid to star in versions of Thomas Wolfe's *Look Homeward, Angel* and Jean Anouilh's *The Lark* if Ferrer were the male lead, or to headline a film version of Edmond Rostand's *L'Aiglon* if Ferrer directed her. When, having already rejected *The Diary of Anne Frank,* she later rejected *The Inn of the Sixth Happiness* (Twentieth Century-Fox, 1958),* industry observers wondered where her once bright career was heading.

However, professionally things took a good turn for Audrey. Within weeks, she went from nymph to nun, from South America to the Belgian Congo. Kathryn C. Hulme's 1956 biographical novel, *The Nun's Story,* sold over three million copies in the United States alone and was later translated into twelve languages. Adapted for the screen by Robert Anderson and directed by Fred Zinnemann, a Jew, it was an intellectual

---

*Ingrid Bergman was substituted.

examination of one aspect of the Roman Catholic religion. Before departing for a three-month shooting schedule in Stanleyville in the Belgian Congo, Audrey met with the woman whose real-life experiences she would depict onscreen. "She really didn't want to meet me," Sister Luke later said. "She felt the story was too much of my private life. She just sat there and didn't ask any questions."*

Cast and crew members alike at Stanleyville certified that Audrey, in the confining robes of a nun, was calm and sweet-tempered through the dank tropic heat. She did not complain when a monkey bit into her right arm, and she refused (to no avail) to have publicity made of the accident. Nevertheless, she did not attempt to conceal her glee when Zinnemann announced the completion of Congo location work. Because the movie company was moving on to Belgium for further scenes, this also meant that Audrey would have a chance to visit with relatives.

The Nun's Story (Warner Bros., 1959), which begins in 1927, has Audrey as Gabrielle Van Der Mal, who agrees to relinquish all her material goods, friends, and worldly attachments in order to serve God. As she proceeds from a novitiate through the prescribed indoctrination into Holy Orders, she mistakes the quality of her sacrifices as coming from love of God, when in reality it derives from pride. She studies at the School of Tropical Medicine in Antwerp and then embarks, as Sister Luke, for the Belgian Congo, where she works tirelessly under the harsh direction of an atheistic surgeon (Peter Finch). Not only does he brutishly suggest that he is sexually interested in her ("Don't ever think for an instant your habit will protect you") but, later on, his iconoclastic philosophy, in conjunction with her growing doubts, causes her to reexamine the stringent demands put upon her by the Order. When she finds she is no longer able to resist her rebellious instinct, she returns to her native Belgium, where she is allowed to be released from her vows (this element being the most shocking part of Sister Luke's real-life experience).

The 149-minute color feature premiered in Los Angeles in May 1959, at the Egyptian Theatre.† Both Sister Luke and Miss Hulme were delighted with the results. The former said, after viewing it three times, "I could just sit there and cry my eyes out, not with regret or anything, but because of the beauty of it." *Life* magazine termed *The Nun's Story* "a movie masterpiece" and "a hauntingly, beautiful, tragic account." Critics and public alike were rather amazed that Zinnemann's tasteful feature did not pander to the usual Hollywoodian concept of cloistered nuns, and as Hollis Alpert *(Saturday Review)* perceived, "While there are moments of humor,

* On another occasion, Audrey admitted to the press, "I have come to know the woman on whose life the book was based—she lives quietly here [California]. I know what parts of the story have been dramatized. But the story remains basically true. It is not pro-Catholic, nor is it anti-Catholic. It is simply a story and a very warm and interesting one."

† The picture had its New York bow at Radio City Music Hall (July 18, 1959).

350

terror, and tragedy in this nun's tale, which keep it alive with interest, it is the more religious aspect that sets the film apart and makes it fascinating."

However, there were some who believed, as did *Time* magazine, that "although a sensitive performance, the leading lady seems unable to express strong feelings of any kind. She is too cool; and so is the picture. She has the presence of the sprite, not the presence of the spirit. Calm and exquisite in her habit, she looks most of the time like nothing more troubled or troubling than (if such a thing were possible) a recruiting poster for a convent." Nevertheless, *The Nun's Story* took in $5.75 million in distributors' domestic rentals, and *Variety* affirmed that Audrey, she of the almond-shaped, wide-eyes, "has her most demanding film role and she gives her finest performance." She was selected as best actress of 1959 by the New York Film Critics and received her third Academy Award nomination, but lost to Simone Signoret of *Room at the Top* (Continental). Although *The Nun's Story* received a total of six Oscar nominations, it failed to win one.*

In June 1959, it was announced that, after five years of marriage, thirty-year-old Audrey was expecting a child sometime in January 1960. "If it's a boy, I'm sentimental about my brother's name—which is Ian," she confided. "If it's a girl, we're thinking of naming her Kathleen."

Her pregnancy was not discovered until after she had accepted a $300,000 job with producer James Hill and director John Huston as Burt Lancaster's co-star in *The Unforgiven* (United Artists, 1960). Filmed in the badlands of central Mexico, the picture's theme focused on the Zachary family in the Texas Panhandle of the late 1860s. The household consists of the mother (Lillian Gish), three sons (Lancaster, Audie Murphy, Doug McClure), and a dark-skinned daughter (Audrey). Audrey is revealed to be an adopted Kiowa Indian girl, and the sister of the chief, who now wants her returned. The Zacharys' neighbors and one brother (Murphy) desert the family and the Kiowas ravage the Zacharys' land, while the whites huddle inside their sod hut† holding off the attackers. Gish is killed, Audrey is forced to kill her Indian brother, and Murphy returns to single-handedly rout the Indians. The ending, even by Hollywood and Audie Murphy cultist standards, is quite unbelievable. Perhaps a line of Audrey's Rachel Zachary near the story's beginning, best describes the final action, "I'm dreamin', ain't I?"

About midway through the shooting of *The Unforgiven,* Audrey was thrown from a horse, resulting in four fractured vertebrae, and a badly

---

*MGM's blockbuster, *Ben-Hur,* was stiff competition to all other 1959 contenders, garnering a total of eleven Oscars. Rumor has it that Audrey, as a gag, appeared in a *Ben-Hur* mob scene, but this has not been factually substantiated.

†It cost $300,000 to construct.

sprained foot. Learning of the accident, Sister Luke (of *The Nun's Story)* flew to Durango, Mexico, and persuaded Audrey to return to California, which she did on February 2, 1959. For three weeks the devoted nurse attended to the star's injury as well as salving her conscience for holding up the $5,550,000 film production. By dint of inner energy, Audrey was back on the set by March 10.

When *The Unforgiven* debuted in April 1960, the critics immediately noted strong similarities to the George Stevens-directed *Shane* (Paramount, 1953), but unlike the latter picture, *The Unforgiven* proved to be no classic. Although it attempted to be an "adult Western" in a day when this term seemed ridiculous, it did delve into the area of miscegenation (i.e., Caucasian Lancaster's affection for half-breed Audrey), but at heart it was just an overblown sagebrush tale. *Time* magazine credited it with being a "massive and masterful attempt to gild the oat," and the picture did much to restore director Huston's sagging professional reputation. But European-born Audrey, despite the attempts to give her "a look of buckskin toughness," emerged in the picture as "a bit too polished, too fragile and civilized among such tough and stubborn types as Burt Lancaster, Lillian Gish and Audie Murphy" (Bosley Crowther, *New York Times).*

Meanwhile, Audrey joined Ferrer at their Burgenstock retreat to await the birth of her child, but the physical damage had been done. She collapsed and miscarried in July 1959. Late the following month, in order to counteract her despondency, Ferrer convinced Audrey that she should do a mad fashion spread in Paris for *Harper's Bazaar.* Under the photographic direction of her pal from *Funny Face,* Richard Avedon, she appeared with Ferrer, Zsa Zsa Gabor, and Buster Keaton in a story done with photographs in which she wore the latest creations of designers Goma, Laroche, Cardin, Balmain, Paton, and Dior. She starved herself for a day to fit into a beaded Dior dress with a very tight band around the knees, then feasted on champagne and caviar at 3:30 A.M. in an empty Maxim's.

Finding, in December 1959, that she was again pregnant, Audrey placed herself in the care of a doctor, who recommended scheduled hormone injections and ordered complete rest at the villa the Ferrers had recently purchased at Tolochenaz, Switzerland. Under the physician's regimen she was not permitted to go to Rome while Ferrer starred in *Blood and Roses* (Paramount, 1961). She declined invitations from Hollywood to attend the April 1960 Academy Awards ceremony and from the New York Film Critics to accept in person their award to her as Best Actress of the Year for *The Nun's Story.*

On Sunday, July 17, 1960, Audrey gave birth to a nine-and-one-half-pound son, who was born at Lucerne Maternity Clinic not far from Tolochenaz. A few weeks later, in a Givenchy-designed christening outfit, Audrey beamed proudly as she cradled the baby for a Richard Avedon photograph. Named Sean, the Irish version of Ian, the boy cried briefly during the ceremony, prompting the omnipresent Baroness to remark, "A good cry at the christening lets the devil out." Henry Taylor, Jr., the American ambassador to Switzerland at the time, presented young Sean with his first American passport and an American flag. Audrey said: "Like all mothers, I couldn't believe at first he was really for me, and I could really keep him. I'm still filled with the wonder of being able to go out and come back and find he's still there!" As for his future, she added to the press: "I would like him to mix in every country with all kinds of people, so that he will learn what the world is all about. If he's the right kind of person, he should take his own small part in making the world a better place."

Two months later, Audrey and Sean went to New York where she began location filming for *Breakfast at Tiffany's* (Paramount, 1961), directed by Blake Edwards. The George Axelrod screenplay of Truman Capote's popular 1958 novel was considerably different from the original in order to placate the Motion Picture Production Code and audience tastes of the 1960s. In Capote's book, the amoral heroine, Holly Golightly, is a weed-smoking hippie-type who is about to have an illegitimate child. In the film she winds up with a man (George Peppard) instead of leaving Manhattan alone. Capote apparently did not mind the alterations and commented, "The screenplay seems to me excellent, but more as a creation of its own than an adaptation of my book—no complaints, however . . . and, anyhow, Holly is still Holly, except once or twice."*

Within the 114-minute color feature, Audrey's Holly earns her living through $50 powder-room money received from her escorts and $100-a-visit trips to Sing Sing Prison for chats with an ex-mobster. Determined to wed a South American millionaire, she at first denies any feelings she has for upstairs neighbor Paul Varjak (Peppard). However, when the millionaire bids her goodbye after he learns that she has unwittingly been carrying narcotic-ring information to Sing Sing, she experiences a traumatic change of heart and suddenly decides she really loves Paul, who has recently concluded his sojourn of being kept by an older woman (Patricia Neal).

In essence, and in spite of the screenplay's alterations, Holly is a kookie kook, a screen part that would seemingly have been ideal for the like of

*In 1968, two years after the abortive Broadway musical version of *Breakfast at Tiffany's* starring Richard Chamberlain and Mary Tyler Moore, Paramount planned a television series based on the original Truman Capote property, but the mercurial Capote pooh-poohed it, stating, "They [the studio] made a big, boring Audrey Hepburn thing out of it. My lawyers have advised them they have no authority to make a tv series of the story."

Shirley MacLaine, who had rejected the movie role.* With a $4.2 million distributors' domestic-rental intake, no one could deny that *Breakfast at Tiffany's* was a commercial commodity, especially with so many built-in publicity ingredients: Oscar-winner Audrey, rising new sex symbol Peppard, a chic, bizarre, and well-exploited party sequence, a guest appearance by Mickey Rooney as the iconoclastic upstairs tenant, Mr. Yunioshi, and, of course, all the lush production-mountings imaginable.

Audrey was probably most amazed of all that the bulk of the critics, and the public, fully accepted her as the semilegendary beatnik, Holly Golightly. Richard L. Coe (*Washington Post*) noted "a new and wondrously mature look to Miss Hepburn. Her baby face, through living, I imagine, shows a lovely unique beauty of experience in living." A. H. Weiler (*New York Times*) complimented, "[The film] has the overpowering attribute known as Audrey Hepburn, who despite her normal, startled fascinating exterior, now is displaying fey, comic talent." Audrey received her fourth Academy Award nomination, and although she lost to Sophia Loren for *Two Women,* she was delighted to have introduced, in *Breakfast at Tiffany's,* the Johnny Mercer-Henry Mancini song "Moon River," which did win the Oscar as the Best Song of the Year.

In 1961, William Wyler decided to produce and direct, for United Artists, a faithful rendering of the Lillian Hellman play, *The Children's Hour.*† It was unlike Wyler's 1936 picturization, which the Hays Office forced him to retitle to *These Three* (United Artists), with the main theme changed from lesbianism to adultery. Audrey, fulfilling her Wyler contract terms, was cast in the role of Karen Wright, which was previously acted by Katherine Emery on Broadway in 1934, by Merle Oberon in the 1936 Samuel Goldwyn movie, and by Kim Hunter in a 1952 Broadway revival. The part of Martha Dobie, played onstage in 1934 by Anne Revere and in 1952 by Patricia Neal, was taken by Shirley MacLaine. An interesting bit of casting was that of Miriam Hopkins, who played Martha in *These Three* and was now relegated to the supporting part of Martha's shallow Aunt Lily.

In the story of *The Children's Hour,* Audrey and MacLaine head a small private school for girls whose major disciplinary problem is the granddaughter of the town's most influential citizen (Fay Bainter). When the child is justly punished for telling a fib, she retaliates by telling granny an even bigger one—that her teachers are having an unnatural relationship.

---

*At one point, Audrey publicly confessed: "I read the book and liked it very much. But I was terribly afraid I was not right for the part. I thought I lacked the right sense of comedy. . . . This part called for an extroverted character. I am not an extrovert. I am an introvert. It called for the kind of sophistication that I find difficult. I did not think I had enough technique for the part. But everyone pressed me to do it. So I did. I suffered through it all. I lost weight. Very often while I was doing the part I was convinced I was not doing the best possible job."

†The drama opened at the Maxine Elliott Theatre on November 20, 1934, and had a 691-performance Broadway run.

The townspeople, led by granny, remove their girls from the school, and the teachers lose a slander suit against the old woman. The scandal arouses in MacLaine the sudden thought that she really does have a sexual yen for Audrey, and she confesses her love before hanging herself. Left alone, Audrey leaves town, rejecting the passive support of her doctor fiancé, James Garner.

The Children's Hour was hurried into a December 1961 release in Los Angeles in order to qualify for that year's Academy Awards. It received nominations in five categories, but won none. Not only was it felt, by 1961 standards, that Hellman's original play concept was no longer novel (except to censorship boards), but also that the filming might have been more plausible had Audrey and MacLaine switched roles. It certainly did not aid the picture's ambiance to have bewildered Garner, the former star of television's "Maverick" Western series, meandering about the premises, looking as if he wished he were back astride a horse rather than coping with the delicate situation at hand. *Time* magazine criticized Audrey for giving "her standard, frail, indomitable characterization, which is to say that her eyes water constantly (frailty) and her chin is forever cantilevered forward (indomitability)."

Although *The Children's Hour* was a financial fizzle, Audrey, after almost a decade of Hollywood-oriented filmmaking, was an established superstar. Along with Doris Day, Elizabeth Taylor, Marilyn Monroe,* Shirley MacLaine, and the European-based Sophia Loren, Audrey was considered among the top distaff box-office lures in America. The key to Audrey's success had always been her elfinlike, gamine charms; but on the surface what appealed most to her staunchest admirers (matronly suburban housewives and wistful young men) was Audrey's capacity to create an aura of chic glamour, not only with her internal ability to make Cinderella screen tales ring true, but in her position as a leading fashion plate. Audrey was constantly being asked about her role as a designer's dream. Early in 1962, she expressed the notion: "Although I am no authority on fashion, I do feel I have learned over a period of years of trial and error what clothes suit me best. Such beautifully dressed women as Mrs. John F. Kennedy and Mrs. Noel Guinness have a personal style of their own, a style they've developed as being best for themselves. It seems to me that it is within the reach of every woman to develop a similar individuality of style by learning to know herself." It was this very modest outlook of the onscreen vulnerable (but offscreen so apparently retiring) Audrey that endeared her so much to the public.

Having found her working relationship with producer-director Stanley Donen *(Funny Face)* so satisfying, Audrey was pleased to have the opportunity to again work under his aegis in *Charade* (Universal, 1963), filmed

---

*When Monroe died on August 5, 1962, one European director noted, "The American cinema is now left with only the smile of Audrey Hepburn."

in Paris. The seemingly indestructible "Mr. Debonair," Cary Grant, was top-billed in this Peter Stone-Marc Behm murder yarn, which Donen helmed as a fast-paced comedy-mystery. With the added technical talent of Charles B. Lang, Jr. (cinematography), Henry Mancini (music), and Hubert de Givenchy (Audrey's admirable wardrobe, especially in the opening sequences), Donen produced a winner wherein a quartet of crooks (James Coburn, .George Kennedy, Ned Glass, and duplicitous Walter Matthau) endeavor to locate $250,000 in American gold coins buried behind the German lines during the war by Audrey's recently deceased spouse. Since the husband absconded with the money, the CIA tells her to find it and return it to the United States government. One by one, the crooks are killed off, and Grant, supposedly one of the gang, but actually a CIA employee, saves Audrey from death at the hands of the only remaining gang member. The displaced loot is found in the obvious but ingeniously located place, clues to which are presented throughout the film for the more discerning mystery-film addicts.

Universal released *Charade* in December 1963, accompanied by a vast magazine ad campaign exclaiming that the picture was "a game of danger and delight." As the Donen-helmed picture zoomed along to its conclusion, audiences found themselves confronted with a swiftly changing set of moods (mystery, romance, brutality, comedy), but with each alteration of ambiance always handled deftly either with a zing of suspense or surprise, or dialog delivered with élan. For example, when the police quiz Grant about a particular murder and ask where he was at the time, he states he was in his hotel room, in fact, in bed. The lawman turns to onlooker Audrey and asks her the same question. She promptly answers, "The same for me . . . in my room . . . in bed." The defeated inquisitor shrugs his shoulders, admitting, "It must be true. Nobody could possibly invent a lie like that."

Richard L. Coe *(Washington Post)* thought *Charade* was a "fine example of making a silk purse out of thin air." With a distributor's domestic-rental intake of $6.15 million, *Charade* was its own box-office bonanza, and provided Audrey—who, like Grant, had a participation deal in the film—with bonus deferred revenue. Judith Crist *(New York Herald-Tribune)* favored this tongue-in-cheek exercise and happily observed, "Miss Hepburn has emerged from her Tom Sawyer gamine stage as a breathtakingly beautiful woman"; *Look* magazine stated that "Grant, Hepburn and Paris never looked better." Back in Hollywood in December, Grant said, "All I want for Christmas is another movie with Audrey Hepburn," a wish that has yet to be granted.

Back in 1961, after making *Breakfast at Tiffany's* and *The Children's Hour,* Audrey had returned home to Europe. She spent a brief holiday at the villa with her husband and son and then went on to Paris to perform in *Paris When It Sizzles* (Paramount, 1964). With William Holden co-starred as a cynical, veteran screenwriter, the Richard Quine-directed feature was "intended" to be a lively spoof on moviemaking, but the *New York Times* summed it up as a "Technicolor cliche." Movies about a movie were old hat by this time, and Audrey, as Holden's admiring secretary, could do little with the lumbering George Axelrod dialog (e.g., "Depravity can be boring if you don't drink or smoke"). There were brief silent, guest appearances by Marlene Dietrich and Ferrer, and a long guided tour of Paris highspots, but the film was a near total fizzle. Apparently, Paramount executives agreed when they saw the completed film, for it was shelved for more than two years before being publicly unveiled in April 1964. It suffered a quick death on the exhibition circuit. Audrey was politely complimented for her fetching, if already dated, oncamera wardrobe.

My Fair Lady! Three words that generate delightful memories. George Bernard Shaw's 1912 play, entitled *Pygmalion,* was first offered on Broadway in 1914 when forty-nine-year-old Mrs. Patrick Campbell recreated her London (April 1914) role of Eliza Doolittle, a part written especially for her by Shaw. It was revived in New York in 1926 with a mature Lynn Fontanne, again in 1945 with a fortyish Gertrude Lawrence, and on national tour with a late-fortyish Ruth Chatterton. It was transformed into a popular British movie in 1938 with twenty-six-year-old Wendy Hiller (and Leslie Howard). Then, on March 15, 1956, the Alan Jay Lerner-Frederick Loewe musical extravaganza opened at the Mark Hellinger Theatre for what proved to be an astounding six-and-one-half-year run, through 2,717 performances. The show made a star of Britisher Julie Andrews, then just twenty-two years old and probably the correct age for Eliza. Jack L. Warner bought the film rights to *My Fair Lady* for a record $5.5 million and soon announced that Rex Harrison would repeat his stage characterization of Professor Henry Higgins.* It was expected that Warner would hire Julie Andrews for Eliza, but he rocked the profession by casting Audrey, who, he figured, was far better known to screen audiences. Audrey's salary was $1 million for six months work, which officially began on August 13, 1963.

For six weeks prior to that, Audrey worked diligently, practicing Cockney with a phonetics expert, learning dances, and importing her own New York vocal coach, although, under her contract with Warner Bros., the studio was not obligated to use her singing voice on the final soundtrack. Audrey spent hours posing for publicity shots in gowns created by Cecil Beaton. Without being disloyal to Givenchy, who heartily approved of Beaton's period costumes, she said, "He makes you look the way you have always wanted to look." By August 13, under the direction of elite George Cukor,

---

*Cary Grant had been offered the screen part first.

an expert at "women's pictures" and the director of the much underrated *Les Girls* (MGM, 1957), the movie edition of *My Fair Lady* (Warner Bros., 1964) got under way.

The $1 million sets occupied a majority of the twenty-six Warner Bros. studio soundstages. On that first day, with Vaseline and fuller's earth in her hair, grease and grime on her face, and black clay embedded beneath her fingernails, Audrey danced on nonskid-rubber cabbage leaves while mouthing the words to "Loverly." She later informed newsmen: "I believe this is the most difficult role I've ever undertaken. In some ways, Eliza is the first real character I've attempted on the screen. In others there has almost always been a little of me; in this one, there is none."

Her singing voice was recorded on the soundtracks until a day in September when the corporate decision was handed down that the original tracks were to be discarded. It was then announced that the voice of Marni Nixon was to be inserted. On hearing of this sudden technical change, Audrey uttered one word, "Oh!", and walked proudly out of the studio. The next day, she returned and apologized to everyone for her "outrageous behavior."

Miss Nixon has this to say of Audrey: "I have only a good feeling about her. She was kind, thoughtful, almost aristocratic in manners, and, as such, was very gentle. Hers was an iron will, but she was extremely sensitive to others. She was a hard worker and conscientiously strived for a better and better performance. Although I adored her, I never saw the real, spontaneous side of her. I felt that she respected me, and we worked very well and very closely together."

Everyone involved with the long-in-production film became Audrey's pal. She knew them all by name, from the electricians down to the "nice cigarette man" who kept her supplied with filtered cigarettes. For the tenth anniversary of her marriage to Ferrer, she threw an elaborate cocktail party for the cast and crew at the end of the September workday. (Ferrer, who had been in Hollywood with her up until then, was not present; he was at work in Europe on *The Fall of the Roman Empire* [Paramount, 1964].)

A few weeks later, Universal asked her to bring friends to a preview showing of *Charade,* and she wrote personal invitations to all the *My Fair Lady* people, which began, "Would you like to see *Charade,* a new picture with Cary Grant and Eliza Doolittle?" On November 22, 1963, the company was between scenes on the Covent Garden stage set when word came through that President John F. Kennedy was dead. "I'm incapable of telling them," Cukor told an assistant. "I'll do it, if you'd like," Audrey said softly and promptly borrowed a microphone from head electrician Frank Flanagan. "The President of the United States is dead," she began, and informed the cast and crew what little was then known of the assassination. "Shall we have two minutes of silence to pray or do whatever you feel is appropriate. May he rest in peace." Flanagan later recalled, "She had tears in her eyes, but it was done with great dignity."

By December 1963, Audrey's work as Eliza Doolittle was completed. Warner and Cukor gave her a farewell party, and she handed out individual gifts to cast and crew. To her hairdresser, she gave a Yorkshire terrier puppy named "Henry Higgins." She retired to her Continent-based villa weighing some eight pounds less than when she started the film.

The $17 million *My Fair Lady,* running 170 minutes, was released in October 1964 at road-show prices. To date, the film is one of the ten all-time grossers in motion-picture history, having earned Warners over $33 million.* While several members of the *My Fair Lady* screen cast and technical talent were nominated for Oscars, Audrey was snubbed by the Academy of Motion Picture Arts and Sciences; many said this was because of the Julie Andrews situation, and others insisted it was because Marni Nixon had had it very well publicized that she did the actual soundtrack singing for Audrey. But Audrey registered only ladylike happiness at the Santa Monica Auditorium the night of April 5, 1965, when she presented a Best Actor Oscar to Rex Harrison for his admirable, if overaged, Henry Higgins portrayal. Minutes later, Julie Andrews was named Best Actress of the Year for her starring role in Walt Disney's musical film *Mary Poppins.* When accepting the Oscar, Andrews pointedly told the auditorium and television audiences, "My thanks to Mr. Jack L. Warner, who made all this possible."

In retrospect, *My Fair Lady* is less a movie musical than a too-faithful rendering of a stage production, with only the Ascot Race Track scene, with its gray-white-black monotone decor, and the ballroom sequences bringing new vitality to a too well known property. Harrison, by virtue of his aging in the interval between the stage musical's debut and the film-making, and Audrey, being too patrician in look and performance, were both miscast performers, each determined for different reasons to prove him or herself to screen audiences. As Andrew Sarris *(Village Voice)* dissected her characterization: "Audrey has always been the gamine, relying more on charm than character, her eyes flirting shamelessly with coy flutters of regal helplessness. Unfortunately, *Pygmalion* is not concerned with a sleeping beauty who is awakened in time for the Royal Ball. . . . [She] suggests nothing so much as a Vogue model masquerading as a flower girl."

In April 1965, Audrey (who could hardly be accused of being career-conscious) was touted as being signed to play Queen Isabella of Spain in

---

*In August 1972, the NBC Network paid nearly $3 million for the rights to televise *My Fair Lady* twice, the first showing on Thanksgiving Day (November 22) 1973. NBC was aghast when its costly feature was outranked in the November 22 ratings by the competing CBS network showing of an episode of "The Waltons" and a repeat of the movie *Duel at Diablo* (United Artists, 1966).

Columbia's projected *The Castles and the Crown,* based on Townsend Miller's 1963 novel. Mel Ferrer was to produce the screen epic. That project came to naught, but Audrey did return to filmmaking in *How to Steal a Million* (Twentieth Century-Fox, 1966), directed by William Wyler. Shot entirely in Paris, the sophisticated comedy boasted scenic photography (by Charles Lang) and a smart Givenchy wardrobe for Audrey. Peter O'Toole, more at ease in significant drama than fey comedy, was signed as her co-star, playing a private detective who she thinks is a crook. She hires him to steal her father's (Hugh Griffith) donation of Cellini's *Venus* to a Paris art museum before the authorities discover that it is a forgery. Fox promoted the movie with a special Parke-Bernet New York gallery exhibition of forty fake paintings created for the movie, and showcased the comedy at the Radio City Music Hall. Taken as a whole— it does not bear dissection—*How to Steal a Million* is a crafty deception, trying every trick in the book of witty, romantic screen comedy, and foisting a high tone on the proceedings by dealing with the world of art. If one found Griffith's performance hammy, and the theft sequence endless and inferior to the robbery in *Topkapi* (United Artists, 1964), there was a certain amount of elegance to the tender romancing of O'Toole and Hepburn as they crouched hidden in the museum's broom closet and found the physical proximity enhancing their budding romantic inclinations to the point of an eventual declaration of mutual love. For pleasant diversion, charming Charles Boyer was oncamera briefly as an art dealer, while, for annoying distraction, there was Eli Wallach as Audrey's crude American millionaire fiancé.*

While *How to Steal a Million* earned $4.4 million in distributors' domestic rentals, the film and Audrey were not invulnerable to critical barbs of the most justified nature. Richard Schickel *(Life* magazine) complained: "they have her repeat her characterization of the *jeune fille* undergoing romantic awakening, a role in which she is now expert to the point of ennui—a kind of upper class Debbie Reynolds. But she has become a sophisticated, even worldly, woman and it's high time she be allowed this new image."

In 1966 it was announced that Audrey and Richard Burton, each for a salary of $1 million against ten percent of the picture's gross profit, would star in MGM's musical remake of *Goodbye, Mr. Chips.* (When the film was eventually made and released in 1969, Peter O'Toole and Petula Clark were the stars.) Then it was stated that Audrey would star, with George Cukor directing, and Ferrer producing, in a new rendition of *Peter Pan,* but Walt Disney, who had made a full-length cartoon version in 1953 for RKO release, instituted a court injunction, and the project fell

---

*Actor George C. Scott had been fired during production, and Wallach was hired as his replacement.

into limbo. In her personal life, Audrey suffered another miscarriage in July 1966.

At this vital juncture in her career and depressing time in her private life, Stanley Donen came up with a new film project, *Two for the Road* (1967), which Twentieth Century-Fox would release. It was on a script by Frederic Raphael, the author of *Nothing But the Best* (Royal, 1964) and *Darling* (Embassy, 1965). Raphael's new plot was the analysis of a twelve-year-old marriage in which both partners are adulterous. Audrey read the script and said, "It is inconceivable that it could have been submitted to me ten years ago, even five." Unsure in her mind, she requested Ferrer's opinion. He read it through and advised her, "Take it right away." She signed for the bittersweet comedy venture, with Britisher Albert Finney, several years her junior, as her male lead.

Ferrer accompanied Audrey to Paris where shooting was to commence. The first order of business was her film wardrobe, and when Donen informed her that it would be strictly Mod—no Givenchy—she cried, "Why? Hubert makes me feel so sure of myself. I'll give a better performance in his clothes." Donen was firm. "We will find your wardrobe in boutiques," he said, and they selected twenty-nine youthful outfits for the first part of the film—the present. Midwesterner Ken Scott was called in to design her clothes for the other dozen years covered in the film, but only a few of his ideas were accepted. Scott said: "From the outset, Audrey had very firm, not to say rigid, ideas about how she should be dressed. No bright colors. Above all, no prints. She said they would take away from her face. Can you imagine—Audrey Hepburn, with her head, worried about a dress upstaging her?" Scott further admitted to padding the swimsuits, with Audrey's permission. Lady Rendlesham of London was contracted to provide the remainder of the wardrobe. "I've never seen anything like her professionalism," she revealed of Audrey. "She's not all that easy to dress, either. The lines have to be just so. She likes all the sweaters and blouses taken in almost like skin. It was very new for her, wearing an outfit that came straight off the peg for only seventeen guineas."

As the *Two for the Road* company moved to the French Riviera, Ferrer went to Italy to star in *El Greco* (Twentieth Century-Fox, 1966). It was then that Audrey really cut loose, frugging in discotheques and dashing in and out of boutiques during her offcamera hours. Her almost constant companion was Albert Finney. Audrey's friend, novelist Irwin Shaw, explained the relationship: "She and Albie have this wonderful thing together, like a pair of kids with a perfect understanding and a shorthand of jokes and references that close out everybody else. It's like a brother-sister in their teens." Audrey had this to say of "Albie": "He makes me laugh like no one else can. And you can talk to him. Really *talk*. He's serious, too, about acting. Albie's just plain wonderful, that's all there is to it."

Richard Schickel *(Life* magazine), a very ardent observer of the Audrey Hepburn mystique, in reviewing *Two for the Road,* analyzed: "It is possible to describe . . . [the film] as just another Audrey Hepburn picture. You know, a romantic comedy in which the star is dressed in beautiful and charming clothes, photographed against a series of beautiful and charming backgrounds, and placed in a succession of [stereotyped] b and c situations which lead, ultimately, to her passage from the innocence of girlhood to the maturity of womanhood. It is a ritual for those of us who are, without quite knowing why, her devoted admirers."

For the first time oncamera, Audrey's characterization gives the viewer a peek five years into the future of the girl she constantly plays onscreen. Within the course of *Two for the Road,* Audrey, an American student on a Continental tour, meets young architect Finney; they romance, marry, and do not live happily ever after. He asks her, "Why do we keep on with this bloody farce?" At another point she observes, "When we married you were a disorganized, egotistical failure. Now you are a disorganized, egotistical success." Likewise, there is the moment when she insists, "There are two of us," and he retorts, "Two of us—that's the basis of the whole trouble." Perhaps Audrey's most touching moment in the film occurs when she returns to Finney after her adulterous love affair has turned sour, and she says with forced cheerfulness and an attempt at naturalness, "I'm back." The film concludes with what is rather shocking dialog for an Audrey Hepburn picture.

He: You bitch.

She: You bastard.

They embrace and go off on another trip together. It was something of a milestone for the "elegant gamine of the silver screen."

Although Eleanor Bron and William Daniels and their brattish child (Gabrielle Middleton) nearly stole the show as Audrey and Finney's traveling companions in one sequence, the critics agreed that Audrey was offering her most considered performance in years. "Miss Hepburn, all eyes and sensitivity, transcends changing hair styles and chic to span the twelve years with subtlety, growing before our eyes from romantic girlhood to fact-facing womanliness" (Judith Crist, *New York World Journal Tribune).* With all its fancy telescoping of time and unmarked flashbacks and mod camera techniques, *Two for the Road* may have baffled some viewers, but it pleased the smart set and won the Golden Shell Prize at the San Sebastian Film Festival in July 1967.

Frederick Knott's thriller, *Wait until Dark,** had clicked well on Broadway and earned a Tony nomination for its star, Lee Remick. Therefore, the trade announcement that the project was to become a motion picture came

*The drama opened at the Ethel Barrymore Theatre on February 2, 1966, for a 373-performance Broadway run. The later London edition starred Honor Blackman.

as no great surprise, but those closest to the Ferrers were startled on hearing that Ferrer would produce the feature, with Audrey as his $1 million star. For some months, there had been rumors of discord in their marriage, and Ferrer's name had been linked romantically with that of a young Spanish singer.

Nevertheless, the filming of exteriors for this Warner Bros.-Seven Arts production, directed by Terence Young, began in New York City in April 1967, and Audrey became preoccupied with studying for her role as a fashion photographer's blind wife. She visited the Lighthouse for the Blind many times to observe and talk with the sightless. She also learned to read a few basic sentences in Braille. The remainder of the feature was lensed in Hollywood at Warners' Burbank studio, where technicians who had worked with Audrey on *My Fair Lady* were touched by her tired and gaunt appearance.

Neither her physical condition nor her emotional status prevented Audrey from offering an excellent performance as Suzie Hendrix, "world's champion blind lady," who becomes the object of pursuit within her own Greenwich Village apartment by a trio of crooks (Alan Arkin, Richard Crenna, Jack Weston) who are after a doll stuffed with a cache of heroin. The scene where she discovers that her telephone cord has been cut, thus blocking off her warning system with the little girl upstairs (Julie Herrod), is one of her best oncamera moments. "Miss Hepburn does very well by the role with her special way of being femininely fragile, yet independent. More important, she never lets one feel sorry for the character" (Kathleen Carroll, *New York Daily News).* Audrey gained her fifth Oscar nomination for this role, but lost out this time to the other Hepburn for *Guess Who's Coming to Dinner* (Columbia, 1967). The film itself, despite objections to Arkin's too comical approach to his sinister role, proved a hefty box-office attraction, pulling in $7.8 million in distributors' domestic rentals.

In September 1967, Audrey went through another miscarriage. A few weeks later, she and Ferrer were separated after thirteen years of marriage. Two months later she filed for divorce at Morges, Switzerland, on the standard grounds of "incompatibility."

Although she led a respectable life in Europe after the divorce, living alone with Sean and servants, the paparazzis of the world attempted to devise a love affair between her and every eligible man with whom she was seen. Even Givenchy was suspect, as was Yul Brynner, the ex-husband of her best friend, Doris.

Audrey looked beautiful at the Tony Awards on NBC-TV in April 1968 when she was presented with a "special" Tony, along with Pearl Bailey, Carol Channing, David Merrick, Marlene Dietrich, and Maurice Chevalier. It was not made clear just why Audrey was selected for the honor, and, as Rex Reed put it, "Anyway you look at it a Tony Award to Audrey

Hepburn for deserting the theatre for more money in Hollywood is still preposterous."

That summer, Audrey accepted the invitation of Princess Olympia Torlonia and her husband, Paul Annik Weiller, son of the French petroleum magnate, to cruise the Greek isles aboard a chartered yacht. Also on board was Andrea Mario Dotti, a wealthy Italian jet-setter and psychiatric assistant to Professor Giancarlo Reda at the University of Rome. Along the way they fell in love. "It happened somewhere between Ephesus and Athens," Dotti told friends. "We were playmates on a cruise ship with other friends, and slowly, day by day, our relationship grew into what it is." He went on to say that "Big, buxom women never did especially appeal to me."

On December 5, 1968, Audrey's divorce became final. She received custody of Sean and a reported $1 million settlement plus the Tolochenaz villa.* On Christmas Eve, Dotti gave her a large diamond ring as a gift and, on Saturday, January 18, 1969, they were wed in a simple ceremony at the eighteenth-century town hall in Morges, Switzerland. The civil service was conducted by Morges' registrar, Denise Rattaz. The witnesses were Doris Brynner and French actress Capucine. Among the forty guests attending the event was Audrey's son, Sean.

Whereas Ferrer had been thirteen years her senior, Audrey's new husband, at thirty, was nine years her junior. They honeymooned in Switzerland and then took up residence in Rome in an apartment overlooking the Gianicola and Castel Sant'Angelo. "I'm in love and happy again," she said. "I never believed it could happen to me. I had almost given up." She stated flatly that she did not want to continue her acting career. "Now Mia Farrow will get my parts." More seriously, she added: "I worked nonstop from when I was twelve until I was thirty-eight. I feel a need to relax, sleep in the morning, take care of my child. Why should I resume work and the life I rejected when I married a man I love, whose life I want to live?"

Audrey's second son, weighing seven pounds, eight ounces, was delivered by Caesarean section on February 8, 1970, in Lausanne, Switzerland. Named Luca, in honor of Andrea's brother, the male child represented the final signal to the large Dotti clan† that the marriage was running smoothly, even though the actress was a lady who had been divorced.

Thereafter, at various times, Dotti was seen and photographed at Roman nightspots with several different female companions. Often his club partner was Daniela Ripetti, a local model-actress who had been

---

*Ferrer later wed Belgian Elizabeth Soukutine, who is an editor of children's books and is some twenty years younger than he.

†Another member of the family was Mario Bandini, uncle to Andrea, and one-time romantic escort to Kim Novak.

released from nine months of imprisonment on drug charges. Dotti's meanderings with other women were explained as "research" for a book he was compiling about the use of drugs by women.

Suddenly, Audrey, who had performed a guest spot reading a children's story on a UNICEF television special, did four one-minute television commercials for a Japanese wig manufacturer. She then expressed a desire to star in the screen version of *Forty Carats* (Columbia, 1972), but lost out to Liv Ullmann when she refused to leave Rome for the filming.

While spending a few weeks in 1972 on the Côte d'Azur with Andrea and Luca, Audrey received word from California that Sean, who was then vacationing with Ferrer, had been mauled by a lion at a "jungle park" while standing beside the animal's cage for souvenir photos. As it developed, the twelve-year-old's wounds were not extensive and did not warrant Audrey's leaving Europe.

In November 1972, producer Ross Hunter broadly hinted in Hollywood that he had a perfect middle-aged love story lined up for Audrey and Peter Finch. It was titled *The Marble Arch,* and Hunter advised Audrey that all exteriors would be filmed in Italy, "with only a few weeks of interiors to film in Hollywood." The project was later shelved. Then, in mid-1973, it seemed that after six filmless years, Audrey would actually come out of retirement for Terence Young, who had directed her in *Wait until Dark.* With the title of *The Survivor,* the new feature was described as "a romantic suspense film in the Hitchcock tradition." A condition in Audrey's contract was that it be lensed in Rome, close to home, with the exception of seven days, and no more, for shooting in London. However, nothing came of this rumored comeback. A much more likely Audrey Hepburn project was Luchino Visconti's new film project to co-star Burt Lancaster. But in the long run, Audrey balked at the deal.

When, in November 1973, Audrey and her husband arrived in New York, speculation ran high that her return to the States might auger a new movie project, but she insisted that her visit was only in conjunction with Dr. Dotti's planned attendance at a medical conference in Washington, D.C. As for any film work, the very charming Audrey advised, "If there's a picture that can be done in Rome and I like it, I might do it." During their brief Manhattan stay, Audrey did not even find time to attend one of the stage performances of the musical *Gigi.*

In mid-1974 it seemed that finally Audrey had found that Rome-based feature suitable to her demands. The project was Terence Young's *Jackpot,* and Richard Burton was to co-star. But within a month Audrey had "broken" her pledge to director Young. The film was later postponed indefinitely. Audrey's reason was a surprise: she was expecting her third child (her second by Dotti). To guard against a possible miscarriage, the actress put herself under the care of the same Swiss gynecologist who counseled Sophia Loren through her two touch-and-go pregnancies.

Audrey once said of herself: "I know my body well. I am not a beauty. Taken one by one, my features are not really good. When I work, I rely on my studio hairdresser and makeup man. When you look at yourself professionally, you must see yourself objectively, as though you were some kind of tool." Obviously, Audrey's special brand of wide-eyed professional reserve, in combination with her domestic insecurity, has created this career stagnation of her mid-forties. It is a sad waste of a fertile acting talent.

Feature Film Appearances

ONE WILD OAT (Eros, 1951) 78 M.

Producer, John Croydon; director, Charles Saunders; based on the play by Vernon Sylvaine; screenplay, Sylvaine, Lawrence Huntington; music, Stanley Black; camera, Robert Navarro; editor, Marjorie Saunders.

Robertson Hare (Humphrey Proudfoot); Stanley Holloway (Alfred Gilbey); Sam Costa (Mr. Pepys); Andrew Crawford (Fred Gilbey); Vera Pearce (Mrs. Gilbey); June Sylvaine (Cherrie Proudfoot); Robert Moreton (Throstle); Constance Lorne (Mrs. Proudfoot); Irene Handl (Audrey Cuttle); Ingeborg Wells (Gloria Samson); Charles Groves (Charles); Joan Rice (Annie); Audrey Hepburn (Extra).

LAUGHTER IN PARADISE (Associated British Pictures Corp., 1951) 93 M.

Producer-director, Mario Zampi; screenplay, Michael Pertwee, Jack Davies; art director, Ivan King; music, Stanley Black; camera, William McLeod; editor, Giulio Zampi.

Alastair Sim (Deniston Russell); Fay Compton (Agnes Russell); Beatrice Campbell (Lucille Grayson); Veronica Hurst (Joan Webb); Guy Middleton (Simon Russell); George Cole (Herbert Russell); A. E. Matthews (Sir Charles Robson); Joyce Grenfell (Elizabeth Robson); Anthony Steel (Roger Godfrey); John Laurie (Gordon Webb); Eleanor Summerfield (Sheila Wilcott); Ronald Adam (Mr. Wagstaffe); Leslie Dwyer (Sergeant); Ernest Thesiger (Endicott); Hugh Griffith (Henry Russell); Michael Pertwee (Stuart); Audrey Hepburn (Cigarette Girl).

YOUNG WIVES' TALE (Associated British Pictures Corp., 1951) 79 M.

Producer, Victor Skutezky; director, Henry Cass; based on the play by Ronald Jeans; screenplay, Ann Burnaby; art director, Terence Verity; assistant director, Jack Martin; music, Philip Green; music director, Louis Levy; makeup, Bob Clark; sound, Cecil Thornton; camera, Erwin Miller; editor, E. Jarvis.

Joan Greenwood (Sabina Pennant); Nigel Patrick (Rodney Pennant); Derek Farr (Bruce Banning); Guy Middleton (Victor Manifold); Athene Seyler (Nanny Gallop); Helen Cherry (Mary Banning); Audrey Hepburn (Eve Lester); Fabia Drake (Nurse Blott); Irene Handl, Joan Sanderson (Nurses—Regent Park); Jack McNaughton (Taxi Driver); Carol James (Elizabeth); Brian Oulton (Man in Pub).

THE LAVENDER HILL MOB (General Film Distributors, 1951) 78 M.

Producer, Michael Balcon; associate producer, Michael Truman; director, Charles Crichton; screenplay, T. E. B. Clarke; art director, William Kellner; music, Georges Auric; camera, Douglas Slocombe; editor, Seth Holt.

Alec Guinness (Holland); Stanley Holloway (Pendlebury); Sidney James (Lackery); Alfie Bass (Shorty); Marjorie Fielding (Mrs. Chalk); John Gregson

(Farrow); Clive Morton (Sergeant); Ronald Adam (Turner); Sydney Tafler (Clayton); Edie Martin (Miss Evesham); Jacques Brunius (Official); Meredith Edwards (PC Edwards); Gibb McLaughlin (Godwin); Patrick Barr (Inspector); Marie Burke (Señora Gallardo); Audrey Hepburn (Chiquita).

NOUS IRONS À MONTE CARLO   (Hoche, 1951) 89 M.

Producer, Ray Ventura; director, Jean Boyer; screenplay, Boyer, Alex Joffe; dialog, Serge Veber; music, Paul Misraki; art director, Robert Giordani; sound, A. Archimbault; camera, Charles Suin; editor, Fanchette Mazin.

Ray Ventura and His Orchestra (Themselves); Max Elloy (Max); Henri Genes (Antoine); Philippe Lemaire (Philippe); Andre Luguet (Chatenay-Maillart); Georges Lannes (Private Detective); Marcel Dalio (Poulos); Jeannette Batti (Marinette); Danielle Godet (Jacqueline); Audrey Hepburn (Melissa Walter); John Van Dreelen (Rudy Walter); Y. Orrigo (Baby); and: Edmond Audran, Madame Guemard, Jackie Rollin.

SECRET PEOPLE   (General Film Distributors, 1952) 96 M.

Producer, Sidney Cole; director, Thorold Dickinson; story, Dickinson, Joyce Carey; screenplay, Dickinson, Wolfgang Wilhelm, Christianna Brand; music, Robert Gerhard; camera, Gordon Dines; editor, Peter Tanner.

Valentina Cortesa (Maria); Serge Reggiani (Louis); Audrey Hepburn (Nora Brent); Charles Goldner (Anselmo); Megs Jenkins (Penny); Irene Worth (Miss Jackson); Reginald Tate (Inspector Eliot); Michael Shepley (Manager); Athene Seyler (Mrs. Kellick); Geoffrey Hibbert (Steenie); Sydney Tafler (Syd Burnett); John Ruddock (Daly); Michael Allan (Rodd); John Field (Fedor Luki); Norman Williams (Sergeant Newcome); Bob Monkhouse (Barber); Charles Cairoli and Paul (Specialty).

MONTE CARLO BABY   (General Film Distributors, 1953) 79 M.*

Producer, Ray Ventura; directors, Jean Boyer, Lester Fuller; screenplay, Alex Joffe, Boyer, Fuller; art director, Robert Giordani; music, Paul Misraki; songs, Misraki and Geoffrey Parsons; camera, Charles Suin; editor, Fanchette Mazin.

Audrey Hepburn (Linda Farrel); Jules Munshin (Antoine); Michele Farmer (Jacqueline); Cara Williams (Marinette); Philippe Lemaire (Philippe); Russell Collins (Max); Ray Ventura and His Orchestra (Themselves).

ROMAN HOLIDAY   (Par., 1953) 119 M.

Producer, William Wyler; associate producer, Robert Wyler; director, William Wyler; story, Ian McLellan Hunter; screenplay, Hunter, John Dighton; art directors, Hal Pereira, Walter Tyler; music, Georges Auric; assistant director, Herbert Coleman; makeup, Wally Westmore; sound, Joseph De Bretagne; camera, Franz F. Planer, Henri Alekan; editor, Robert Swink.

Gregory Peck (Joe Bradley); Audrey Hepburn (Princess Anne); Eddie Albert (Irving Radovich); Hartley Power (Mr. Hennessy); Laura Solari (Hennessy's Secretary); Harcourt Williams (Ambassador); Margaret Rawlings (Countess Vereberg); Tullio Carminati (General Provno); Paolo Carlini (Mario Delani); Claudio Ermelli (Giovanni); Paolo Borboni (Charwoman); Heinz Hindrich (Dr. Bonnachoven); Gorella Gori (Shoe Seller); Alfredo Rizzo (Taxi Driver); John Horne (Master of Ceremonies); Count Andrea Eszterhazy, Col. Ugo Ballerini, Ugo

*The English-language version of *Nous Irons à Monte Carlo.*

De Pascale, Bruno Baschiera (Embassy Aides); Princess Alma Cattaneo, Diane Lante (Ladies-in-Waiting); Giacomo Penza (H. E. The Papal Nuncio, Monsignor Altomonto); Eric Oulton (Sir Hugo Macy de Farmington); Rapindranath Mitter, Princess Lilamani (H.R.R. the Maharajah and The Raikuuari of Khanipur); Cesare Viori (Prince Istvar Barossy Nagyavaros); Colonel Nichola Konopleff, Baroness Teresa Gauthier (Ihre Hoheit Der Furst und die Furstin von und zu Luchten-stichenholz); Hari Singh, Kmark Singh (Sir Hari Singh and Kmark Singh); Luigi Bocchi, Helen Fondra (Count and Countess Von Marstrand); Mario Lucinni, Gherdo Fehrer (Senhor y Senhora Joaquin de Capoes); Luis Marino (Hassan El Din Pasha); Armando Annuale (Admiral Dancing with Princess); Luigi Moneta (Old Man Dancing with Princess); Marco Tulli (Pallid Young Man Dancing with Princess); Maurizio Arena (Young Boy with Motorcar); John Fostini, George Higgins, Alfred Browne, John Cortay, Richard McNamara, Sidney Gordon (Correspondents at Poker Game); Richard Neuhaus (Embassy Guard Reporting); Alcide Tico (Sculptor); Tania Weber (Irving's Model); Armando Ambrogi (Man at the Telephone); Patricia Varner (Schoolmarm at Fontana di Trevi); Gildo Bocci (Flower Seller); Giustino Olivieri (Cafe Waiter); Dianora Veiga, Dominique Rika (Girls at Cafe); Gianna Segale (Girl with Irving); Carlo Rizzo (Police Official); Mimmo Poli (Workman Hugging Three outside Police Station); Octave Senoret, Pietro Pastore (Faceless Men on Barge); Giuliano Raffaelli (Faceless Man on Gangplank); Hank Werbe, Adam Jennette, Jan Dijkgraaf (Correspondents); Piero Scanziani, Kurt Klinger, Maurice Montabre, Sytske Galema, Jacques Ferrier, Otto Gross, J. Cortes Cavanillas, Friedrich Lampe, Julio Moriones, Stephen House, Ferdinando De Aldisio (Themselves); Edward Hitchcock (Head of Foreign Correspondents); Desiderio Nobile (Embassy Official at Press Conference).

SABRINA (Par., 1954) 114 M.

Producer-director, Billy Wilder; based on the play *Sabrina Fair* by Samuel Taylor; screenplay, Wilder, Taylor, Ernest Lehman; art directors, Hal Pereira, Walter Tyler; set decorators, Sam Comer, Ray Moyer; music, Frederick Hollander; songs, Wilson Stone; Richard Rodgers and Lorenz Hart; Harold Lewis and John Cope; assistant director, C. C. Coleman, Jr.; costumes, Edith Head; makeup, Wally Westmore; sound, Harold Lewis, John Cope; special effects, John P. Fulton, Farciot Edouart; camera, Charles Lang, Jr.; editor, Arthur Schmidt.

Humphrey Bogart (Linus Larrabee); Audrey Hepburn (Sabrina Fairchild); William Holden (David Larrabee); Walter Hampden (Oliver Larrabee); John Williams (Thomas Fairchild); Martha Hyer (Elizabeth Tyson); Joan Vohs (Gretchen Van Horn); Marcel Dalio (Baron); Marcel Hillaire (The Professor); Nella Walker (Maude Larrabee); Francis X. Bushman (Mr. Tyson); Ellen Corby (Miss McCardle); Marjorie Bennett (Margaret, the Cook); Emory Parnell (Charles, the Butler); Kay Riehl (Mrs. Tyson); Nancy Kulp (Jenny, the Maid); Kay Kuter (Houseman); Paul Harvey (Doctor); Emmett Vogan, Colin Campbell (Board Members); Harvey Dunn (Man with Tray); Charles Harvey (Spiller); Marion Ross (Spiller's Girl Friend); Gray Stafford (Man with David); Bill Neff (Man with Linus); Otto Forrest (Elevator Operator); David Ahdar (Ship Steward).

WAR AND PEACE (Par., 1956) C—208 M.

Producer, Dino De Laurentis; director, King Vidor; based on the novel by Leo Tolstoy; screenplay, Bridget Boland, Robert Westerby, Vidor, Mario Camerini, Ennio De Concini, Ivo Perilli; art director, Mario Chiari; music director, Franco Ferrara; music, Nino Rota; assistant directors, Piero Musetta, Guidarino Guidi; costumes, Maria De Matteis; camera, Jack Cardiff, Aldo Tonti; supervising editor, Stuart Gilmore; editor, Leo Cattozzo.

Audrey Hepburn (Natasha); Henry Fonda (Pierre); Mel Ferrer (Andrei); Vittorio Gassman (Anatole); John Mills (Platon); Herbert Lom (Napoleon); Oscar Homolka (General Kutuzov); Anita Ekberg (Helene); Helmut Dantine (Dolokhov); Barry Jones (Count Rostov); Anna Maria Ferrero (Mary Bolkonsky); Milly Vitale (Lise); Jeremy Brett (Nicholas Rostov); Lea Seidl (Countess Rostov); Wilfred Lawson (Prince Bolkonsky); Sean Barrett (Petya Rostov); Tullio Carminati (Kuragin); May Britt (Sonya); Patrick Crean (Denisov); Gertrude Flynn (Peronskaya); Teresa Pellati (Masa); Maria Zanoli (Mayra); Alberto Carlo Lolli (Rostov's Major-Domo); Mario Addobati (Young Servant at Rostov's); Gualtiero Tumiati (Pierre's Father); Clelia Matania (Mlle. Georges); Gianni Luda, Eschilo Tarquini, Alex D'Alessio, Alfredo Rizzo (Soldiers During the Rostovs' Exile); Mauro Lanciani (Young Prince Nicolai Bolkonsky); Ina Alexeiva (His Governess); Don Little (Young Dancing Partner of Natasha); John Horne (Old Gentleman Dancing with Natasha); Sdenka Kirchen (Old Maid at Rostov's); Nando Gallai (Count Bezukhov's Servant); Michael Tor (Pope); Piero Pastore (Andre Bolkonsky's Servant); Vincent Barbi (Balaga, Dolokhov's Coachman); John Douglas, Robert Stephens (Officers Talking with Natasha During Exile); Luciano Angelini (Young Soldier at Borodino); Charles Fawcett (Russian Artillery Captain); Piero Palermini (Russian Artillery Lieutenant); Angelo Galassi, David Crowley, Patrick Barrett, Michael Billingsley (Russian Soldiers); Aldo Saporetti, Dimitri Konstantinov, Robin White Cross, Lucio de Santis (Young Officers at Orgy); Robert Cunningham (Pierre's Second at Duel); Andrea Eszterhazy (Dolokhov's Second); Marianne Leibl (Servant at Bolkonsky's); Marisa Allasio (Matriosa, Dolokhov's Servant); Stephen Garrett (Coachman/Doctor); Micaela Giustiniani (Woman); Cesare Barbetti (Young Boy); Francis Foucaud (French Soldier); Savo Raskovitch (Alexander I); George Brehat (French Officer at Execution); Gilberto Tofano (Young Dying Soldier); Umberto Sacripante (Old Man); Paole Quagliero (Young Girl Protected by Pierre); Christopher Hofer (French Officer During Retreat); Carlo Delmi (Young Guard); Enrico Olivieri (French Drummer); Eric Oulton, Archibald Lyall, John Stacey, Mino Doro (Russian Generals); Alan Furlan, Joop van Hulsen (Russian Officers); Giovanni Rossi-Loti (Young Russian Officer at Austerlitz); Giacomo Rossi-Stuart (Young Cossack); Guido Celano (Napoleon's Officer); Jerry Riggio, Geoffrey Copplestone, Mimmo Palmara, Giorgio Constantini (French Officers); Richard McNamara (De Beausset); Andrea Fantasia (Constand—Napoleon's Valet); Stephen Lang (Tichon, Old Servant at Bolkonsky); Carlo Dale, Paul Davis (Young French Officers).

FUNNY FACE   (Par., 1957) C—103 M.

Producer, Roger Edens; director, Stanley Donen; screenplay, Leonard Gershe; art directors, Hal Pereira, George W. Davis; set decorators, Sam Comer, Ray Moyer; songs, George and Ira Gershwin; music adaptor, Adolph Deutsch; additional songs, Edens; orchestrators, Conrad Salinger, Van Cleave, Alexander Courage, Skip Martin; choreography, Eugene Loring, Fred Astaire; assistant director, William McGarry; costumes, Edith Head; Paris wardrobe, Hubert de Givenchy; makeup, Wally Westmore; sound, George and Winston Leverett; special camera effects, John P. Fulton; process camera, Farciot Edouart; camera, Ray June; editor, Frank Bracht.

Audrey Hepburn (Jo Stockton); Fred Astaire (Dick Avery); Kay Thompson (Maggie Prescott); Michel Auclair (Professor Emile Flostre); Robert Flemyng (Paul Duval); Dovima (Marion); Virginia Gibson (Babs); Suzy Parker, Sunny Harnett (Specialty Dancers—"Think Pink" Number); Sue England (Laura); Ruta Lee (Lettie); Jean Del Val (Hairdresser); Alex Gerry (Dovitch); Iphigenie Castiglioni (Armande); Albert D'Arno (Beautician); Nina Borget (Assistant Hairdresser); Marilyn White, Dorothy Colbert (Receptionists); Louise Glenn, Heather Hopper, Cecile Rogers (Junior Editors); Nancy Kilgas (Melissa); Emilie Stevens (Assistant Beautician); Don Powell, Carole Eastman (Specialty Dancers); Bruce Hoy (Assistant Dance Director); Paul Smith (Steve); Diane Du Bois (Mimi); Karen Scott (Gigi); Gabriel Curtiz (Man Next to Hand Stand); Peter Camlin (Man Buyer); Elizabeth Slifer (Madame La Farge); Donald Lawton (Airport Clerk); Karine Nordman (French Girl); Genevieve Aumont (French Actress); Nesdon Booth (Southern Man); George Dee, Marcel de la Brosse, Albert Godderis (Seedy Men); Jerry Lucas (Bruiser); Jack Chefe (Frenchman); Jan Bradley (Crying Girl); Jerry Chiat (Man on Head); Elsa Peterson (Woman Buyer); Fern Barry (Southern Wife).

LOVE IN THE AFTERNOON   (AA, 1957) 125 M.

Producer, Billy Wilder; associate producers, William Schorr, Doane Harrison; director, Wilder; based on the novel *Ariane* by Claude Anet; screenplay, Wilder, I. A. L. Diamond; art director, Alexander Trauner; songs, F. D. Marchetti and Maurice de Feraudy; Charles Trenet; Henri Betti and Andre Hornez; music adaptor, Franz Waxman; assistant director, Paul Feyder; sound, Jo De Bretagne; camera, William Mellor; editor, Leonid Azar.

Gary Cooper (Frank Flannagan); Audrey Hepburn (Ariane Chevasse); Maurice Chevalier (Claude Chevasse); Van Doude (Michel); John McGiver (Monsieur X); Lise Bourdin (Madame X); Bonifas (Commissioner of Police); Audrey Wilder (Brunette); Gyula Kokas, Michel Kokas, George Cocos, Victor Gazzoli (Gypsies); Olga Valery (Lady with Dog); Leila and Valerie Croft (Swedish Twins); Charles Bouliaard (Valet at the Ritz); Minerva Pious (Maid at the Ritz); Filo (Flannagan's Chauffeur); André Priez, Gaidon (Porters at the Ritz); Gregory Gromoff (Ritz Doorman); Janine Dard, Claude Ariel (Existentialists); François Moustache (Butcher); Gloria France (Client at Butcher's); Jean Sylvain (Baker); Annie Roudier, Odette Charblay, Jeanne Charblay (Clients at Baker's); Gilbert Constant, Monique Saintey (Lovers on Left Bank); Jacques Preboist, Anne Laurent (Lovers Near the Seine); Jacques Ary, Simone Vanlancker (Lovers on Right Bank); Richard Flagy (Husband); Jeanne Papier (Wife); Marcelle Broc, Marcelle Praince (Rich Women); Guy Delorme (Gigolo); Olivia Chevalier (Little Girl in the Gardens); Solon Smith (Little Boy in the Gardens); Eve Marley, Jean Rieubon (Tandemists); Christian Lude, Charles Lemontier, Emile Mylos (Generals); Alexander Trauner (Artist); Betty Schneider, Georges Perrault, Vera Boccadoro, Marc Aurian (Couples Under Water Wagon); Bernard Musson (Undertaker); Michele Selignac (Widow).

GREEN MANSIONS (MGM, 1959) C—104 M.

Producer, Edmund Grainger; director, Mel Ferrer; based on the novel by William Henry Hudson; screenplay, Dorothy Kingsley; art directors, William A. Horning, Preston Ames; set decorators, Henry Grace, Jerry Wunderlich; costumes, Dorothy Jeakins; makeup, William Tuttle; assistant director, Robert E. Relyea; special music, Heitor Villa-Lobos; music, Bronislau Kaper; title song, Kaper and Paul Francis Webster; marake dance choreography, Katherine Dunham; primitive music, Pierre Gaisseau, Alan Lomax; special effects, A. Arnold Gillespie, Lee LeBlanc, Robert R. Hoag; camera, Joseph Ruttenberg; editor, Ferris Webster.

Audrey Hepburn (Rima); Anthony Perkins (Abel); Lee J. Cobb (Nuflo); Sessue Hayakawa (Runi); Henry Silva (Kua-Ko); Nehemiah Persoff (Don Panta); Michael Pate (Priest); Estelle Hemsley (Cla-Cla); Bill Saito, Yoneo Iguchi (Native Guides).

THE NUN'S STORY   (WB, 1959) C—149 M.

Producer, Henry Blanke; director, Fred Zinnemann; based on the novel by Kathryn C. Hulme; screenplay, Robert Anderson; art director, Alexander Trauner; set decorator, Maurice Barnathan; music-music conductor, Franz Waxman; assistant director, Piero Mussetta; costumes, Marjorie Best; makeup, Alberto De Rossi; sound, Oliver S. Garretson; camera, Franz Planer; editor, Walter Thompson.

Audrey Hepburn [Sister Luke (Gabrielle Van Der Mal)]; Peter Finch (Dr. Fortunati); Dame Edith Evans (Mother Emmanuel); Dame Peggy Ashcroft (Mother Mathilde); Dean Jagger (Dr. Van Der Mal); Mildred Dunnock (Sister Margharita); Beatrice Straight (Mother Christophe); Patricia Collinge (Sister William); Rosalie Crutchley (Sister Eleanor); Ruth White (Mother Marcella); Barbara O'Neil (mother Katherine); Margaret Phillips (Sister Pauline); Patricia Bosworth (Simone); Colleen Dewhurst (Archangel); Stephen Murray (Chaplain); Lionel Jeffries (Dr. Goovaerts); Niall MacGinnis (Father Vermeuhlen); Eva Kotthaus (Sister Marie); Molly Urquhart (Sister Augustine); Dorothy Alison (Sister Aurelie); Jeanette Sterke (Louise Van Der Mal); Errol John (Illunga); Diana Lambert (Lisa); Orlando Martins (Kalulu); Richard O'Sullivan (Pierre Van Der Mal); Marina Wolkonsky (Marie Van Der Mal); Penelope Horner (Jeanette); and: Frank Singuineau, Juan Aymerich, Giovanna Galletti.

THE UNFORGIVEN   (UA, 1960) C—120 M.

Producer, James Hill; director, John Huston; based on the novel by Alan Le May; screenplay, Ben Maddow; art director, Stephen Grimes; wardrobe, Dorothy Jeakins; assistant director, Thomas F. Shaw; music-music conductor, Dmitri Tiomkin; makeup, Frank McCoy, Frank Larue; sound, Basil Fenton Smith; special effects, Dave Koehler; camera, Franz Planer; editor, Hugh Russell Lloyd.

Burt Lancaster (Ben Zachary); Audrey Hepburn (Rachel Zachary); Audie Murphy (Cash Zachary); John Saxon (Johnny Portugal); Charles Bickford (Zeb Rawlins); Lillian Gish (Mattilda Zachary); Albert Salmi (Charlie Rawlins); Joseph Wiseman (Abe Kelsey); June Walker (Hagar Rawlins); Kipp Hamilton (Georgia Rawlins); Arnold Merritt (Jude Rawlins); Carlos Rivas (Lost Bird); Doug McClure (Andy Zachary).

BREAKFAST AT TIFFANY'S   (Par., 1961) C—114M.

Producers, Martin Jurow, Richard Shepherd; director, Blake Edwards; based on the novel by Truman Capote; screenplay, George Axelrod; art directors, Hal Pereira, Roland Anderson; set decorators, Sam Comer, Ray Moyer; costume supervisor, Edith Head; Miss Hepburn's wardrobe, Hubert de Givenchy; Miss Neal's wardrobe, Pauline Trigere; makeup, Wally Westmore; assistant director, William McGarry; music, Henry Mancini; song, Johnny Mercer and Mancini; special camera effects, John P. Fulton; process camera, Farciot Edouart; camera, Franz F. Planer; editor, Howard Smith.

Audrey Hepburn (Holly Golightly); George Peppard (Paul Varjak); Patricia Neal ("2 E"); Mickey Rooney (Mr. Yunioshi); Buddy Ebsen (Doc Golightly); Martin Balsam (O. J. Berman); Jose-Luis De Villallonga (Jose); Dorothy Whitney (Mag Wildwood); Alan Reed (Sally Tomato); John McGiver (Tiffany Salesman); Stanley Adams (Rusty Trawler); Beverly Hills (Nightclub Dancer); Claude Stroud (Sid Arbuck); Elvia Allman (Librarian); Michael Quinn (Man with Eye Patch); James Lanphier (The Cousin); Gil Lamb, Robert Patten, Nicky Blair, Miriam Nelson, Henry Barnard, Thayer M. Burton, Roy Clark, Marian Collier,

Tom Curtis, James Field, Frank Marsh, Bill Neff, Peggy Lloyd Patten, Towyna Thomas, Wilson Wood, Tommy Farrell, Hanna Landy, Fay McKenzie, Helen Spring, Sue Casey, Florine Carlan, Jacqueline Green, Barbara Kelly, Frank Kreig, Mary E. LeBow, Joyce Meadows, Hollis Morrison, John Perri, Michael Quinlivan, Joe Scott, Richard Wyler (Party Guests); Linda Wong, Annabella Soong (Chinese Girls at Party); William Benegal Rau (Hindu at Party); Joan Staley (Girl in Low Cut Dress at Party); Christina Corbin (Woman Visiting Sing Sing Prison); Chuck Niles (Sing Sing Guard); Kate-Ellen Murtagh (Policewoman); Henry H. Beckman, Bill Hampton (Detectives); Joseph H. Greene (Mr. O'Shaunessey); Mike Mahoney (Desk Sergeant); Glen Vernon, Bill Bradley (Reporters); Alfred Avallone (Spieler at Stripjoint); Nino Tempo (Customer); Paul Lees (Floorwalker); Leatrice Leigh (Telephone Operator); Mel Leonard, Dick Crockett (Cab Drivers).

THE CHILDREN'S HOUR   (UA, 1961) 107 M.

Producer, William Wyler; associate producer, Robert Wyler; director, Wyler; based on the play by Lillian Hellman; screenplay, John Michael Hayes; art director, Fernando Carrere; set decorator, Edward G. Boyle; assistant director, Robert E. Relyea; wardrobe, Bert Henrikson, Irene Caine, Ruth Stell; dialog coach, Leon Charles; makeup, Emile La Vigne, Frank McCoy; music, Alex North; sound, Fred Lau, Don Hall; camera, Franz F. Planer; editor, Robert Swink.

Audrey Hepburn (Karen Wright); Shirley MacLaine (Martha Dobie); James Garner (Dr. Joe Cardin); Miriam Hopkins (Mrs. Lily Mortar); Fay Bainter (Mrs. Amelia Tilford); Karen Balkin (Mary Tilford); Veronica Cartwright (Rosalie); Jered Barclay (Grocery Boy); and: Gene Gannon, Bob Karnes, Byron Morrow, Arthur Peterson, Sally Winn, Leon Charles.

CHARADE   (Univ., 1963) C—113 M.

Producer, Stanley Donen; associate producer, James Ware; director, Donen; screenplay, Peter Stone, Marc Behm; music, Henry Mancini; title song, Mancini and Johnny Mercer; art director, Jean D'Eaubonne; Miss Hepburn's Clothes by Hubert de Givenchy; assistant director, Marc Maurette; sound, Jacques Carrere, Bob Jones; camera, Charles Lang, Jr.; editor, James Clark.

Cary Grant (Peter Joshua); Audrey Hepburn (Reggie Lampert); Walter Matthau (Hamilton Bartholomew); James Coburn (Tex); George Kennedy (Scobie); Ned Glass (Gideon); Jacques Marin (Grandpierre); Paul Bonifas (Felix); Dominique Minot (Sylvie); Thomas Chelimsky (Jean-Louis).

PARIS WHEN IT SIZZLES   (Par., 1964) C—110 M.

Producers, Richard Quine, George Axelrod; associate producers, Carter De Haven, John R. Coonan; director, Quine; story, Julien Duvivier, Henri Jeanson; screenplay, Axelrod; art director, Jean D'Eaubonne; set decorator, Gabriel Bechir; music, Nelson Riddle; orchestrator, Arthur Morton; Miss Hepburn's wardrobe and perfume, Hubert de Givenchy; makeup, Frank McCoy; assistant director, Paul Feyder; sound, Jo De Bretagne, Charles Grenzbach; special camera effects, Paul K. Lerpae; camera, Charles Lang, Jr.; editor, Archie Marshek.

William Holden (Richard Benson); Audrey Hepburn (Gabrielle Simpson); Gregoire Aslan (Police Inspector); Noel Coward (Alexander Meyerheimer); Raymond Bussieres (Gangster); Christian Duvallex (Maitre d'Hotel); Marlene Dietrich, Tony Curtis, Mel Ferrer (Guest Stars); Fred Astaire, Frank Sinatra (Singing Voices of).

MY FAIR LADY (WB, 1964) C—170 M.

Producer, Jack L. Warner; director, George Cukor; based on the play *Pygmalion* by George Bernard Shaw and the musical play by Alan Jay Lerner and Frederick Loewe; screenplay, Lerner; costumes-scenery-production designer, Cecil Beaton; art director, Gene Allen; songs, Lerner and Loewe; additional music, Loewe; vocal arranger, Robert Tucker; music supervisor-conductor, Andre Previn; orchestrators, Alexander Courage, Robert Franklyn, Al Woodbury; choreography, Hermes Pan; assistant director, David Hall; sound, Francis J. Scheid, Murray Spivack; camera, Harry Stradling; editor, William Ziegler.

Audrey Hepburn (Eliza Doolittle); Rex Harrison (Henry Higgins); Stanley Holloway (Alfred P. Doolittle); Wilfred Hyde-White (Colonel Hugh Pickering); Gladys Cooper (Mrs. Higgins); Jeremy Brett (Freddy Eynsford-Hill); Theodore Bikel (Zoltan Karpathy); Isobel Elsom (Mrs. Eynsford-Hill); Mona Washbourne (Mrs. Pearce); John Alderson (Jamie); John McLiam (Harry); Marni Nixon (Singing Voice of Eliza); Bill Shirley (Singing Voice of Freddie); Ben Wrigley, Clive Halliday, Richard Peel, Eric Heath, James O'Hara (Costermongers); Kendrick Huxham, Frank Baker (Elegant Bystanders); Walter Burke (Main Bystander); Queenie Leonard (Cockney Bystander); Laurie Main (Hoxton Man); Maurice Dallimore (Selsey Man); Owen McGiveney (Man at Coffee Stand); Jack Raine (Male Member); Marjorie Bennett (Cockney with Pipe); Britannia Beatey (Daughter of Elegant Bystander); Beatrice Greenough (Grand Lady); Hilda Plowright (Bystander); Dinah Anne Rogers, Lois Battle (Maids); Jacqueline Squire (Parlor Maid); Gwen Watts (Cook); Eugene Hoffman, Kai Farrelli (Jugglers); Raymond Foster, Joe Evans, Marie Busch, Mary Alexander, William Linkie, Henry Sweetman, Andrew Brown, Samuel Holmes, Thomas Dick, William Taylor, James Wood, Goldie Kleban, Elizabeth Aimers, Joy Tierney, Lenore Miller, Donna Day, Corinne Ross, Phyllis Kennedy, Davie Robel (Cockneys); Iris Briston, Alma Lawton (Flower Girls); Gigi Michel, Sandy Steffens, Sandy Edmundson, Marlene Marrow, Carol Merrill, Sue Bronson, Lea Genovese (Toffs); Jack Greening (George); Ron Whelan (Algernon); John Holland (Butler); Roy Dean (Footman); Charles Fredericks (King); Lily Kemble-Cooper (Lady Ambassador); Grady Sutton, Orville Sherman, Harvey Dunn, Barbara Morrison, Natalie Core, Helen Albrecht, Diana Bourbon (Ascot Types); Moyna MacGill (Lady Boxington); Colin Campbell (Ascot Gavotte); Marjory Hawtrey, Paulle Clark, Allison Daniell (Ad Libs at Ascot); Betty Blythe (Ad Lib at Ball); Buddy Bryan (Dancer); Tom Cound, William Beckley (Footmen); Alan Napier (Ambassador); Geoffrey Steele (Taxi Driver); Jennifer Crier (Mrs. Higgins' Maid); Henry Daniell (Prince Gregor of Transylvania); Pat O'Moore (Man); Victor Rogers (Policeman); Michael St. Clair, Ron Whelan (Bartenders); Brendon Dillon (Leaning Man); Olive Reeves Smith (Mrs. Hopkins); Miriam Schiller (Landlady); Barbara Pepper, Ayllene Gibbons, Elzada Wilson, Jeanne Carson, Buddy Shea, Jack Goldie, Sid Marion, Stanley Fraser, George Pelling, Colin Kenny, Phyllis Kennedy, LaWana Backer, Monika Henried, Anne Dore, Pauline Drake, Shirley Melline, Wendy Russell, Meg Brown, Clyde Howdy, Nicholas Wolcuff, Martin Eric, John Mitchum (Ad Libs at Church); Major Sam Harris (Guest at Ball).

HOW TO STEAL A MILLION (20th, 1966) C—127 M.

Producer, Fred Kohlmar; director, William Wyler; story, George Bradshaw; screenplay, Harry Kurnitz; production designer, Alexander Trauner; music, Johnny Williams; orchestrator, James Harbert; main titles, Phill Norman; Miss Hepburn's clothes, Hubert de Givenchy; makeup, Alberto De Rossi; assistant director, Paul Feyder; sound, Joseph De Bretagne, David Dockendorf; camera, Charles Lang; editor, Robert Swink.

Audrey Hepburn (Nicole Bonnet); Peter O'Toole (Simon Dermott); Eli Wallach (David Leland); Hugh Griffith (Charles Bonnet); Charles Boyer (De Solnay); Fernand Gravey (Grammont); Marcel Dalio (Señor Paravideo); Jacques Marin (Chief Guard); Moustache (Guard); Roger Treville (Auctioneer); Eddie Malin (Insurance Clerk); Bert Bertram (Marcel); Louise Chevalier (Cleaning Woman in Museum); Remy Longa (Young Man); Gil Delamare (Stunt Double for Audrey Hepburn).

TWO FOR THE ROAD   (20th, 1967) C—112 M.

Producer, Stanley Donen; associate producer, Jimmy Ware; director, Donen; screenplay, Frederic Raphael; music, Henry Mancini; art directors, Willy Holt, Marc Frederic; set decorator, Roger Volper; wardrobe coordinator, Sophie Issartel Rochas; Miss Hepburn's clothes, Ken Scott, Michele Rosier, Paco Rabanne, Mary Quant, Foale and Tuffin; Mr. Finney's wardrobe, Hardy Amies; makeup, Alberto De Rossi, Georges Bouban; assistant director, Jacques Corbel; special effects, Gilbert Manzon; aerial camera, Guy Tabary; camera, Christopher Challis; editors, Richard Marden, Madeleine Gug.

Audrey Hepburn (Joanna Wallace); Albert Finney (Mark Wallace); Eleanor Bron (Cathy Manchester); William Daniels (Howard Manchester); Claude Dauphin (Maurice Dalbret); Nadia Gray (Francoise Dalbret); George Descrieres (David); Gabrielle Middleton (Ruth); Kathy Chelimsky (Caroline); Carol Van Dyke (Michelle); Karyn Balm (Simone); Mario Verdon (Palamos); Roger Dann (Gilbert); Irene Hilda (Yvonne de Florac); Dominique Joos (Sylvia); Libby Morris (American Lady); Yves Barsacq (Police Inspector); Helene Tossy (Madame Solange); Jean-Francoise Lalet (Boat Officer); Albert Michel (Customs' Officer); Jackie Bisset, Joanna Jones, Judy Cornwell, Sofia Torkeli, Patricia Viterbo, Olga Georges Picot, Clarissa Hillel (Joanna's Touring Girl Friends).

WAIT UNTIL DARK   (WB-7 Arts, 1967) C—107 M.

Executive producer, Walter MacEwen; producer, Mel Ferrer; director, Terence Young; based on the play by Frederick Knott; screenplay, Robert and Jane-Howard Carrington; music, Henry Mancini; song, Mancini, Jay Livingston and Ray Evans; art director, George Jenkins; set decorator, George James Hopkins; makeup, Gordon Bau; assistant director, Jack Aldworth; sound, Everett Hughes; camera, Charles Lang; editor, Gene Milford.

Audrey Hepburn (Susy Hendrix); Alan Arkin (Roat); Richard Crenna (Mike Talman); Efrem Zimbalist, Jr. (Sam Hendrix); Jack Weston (Carlino); Samantha Jones (Lisa); Julie Herrod (Gloria); Frank O'Brien (Shatner); Gary Morgan (The Boy); Jean Del Val (The Old Man).

With husband Mel Ferrer and son Sean in 1962

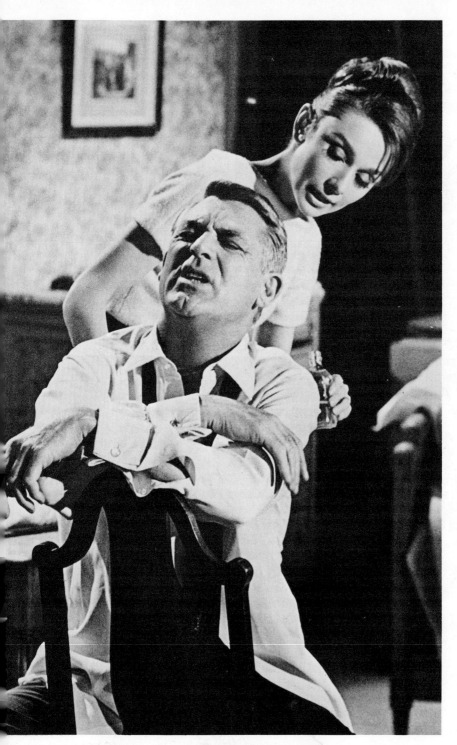

With Cary Grant in CHARADE (Univ '63)

Preparing for the bath scene in PARIS WHEN IT SIZZLES

With William Holden in PARIS WHEN IT SIZZLES

With Rex Harrison in MY FAIR LADY (WB '64)

With Gladys Cooper at the 37th Annual Academy Awards in Santa Monica,
California (April 5, 1965)

With Peter O'Toole in HOW TO STEAL A MILLION (20th '65)

With Albert Finney in TWO FOR THE ROAD (20th '67)

With Richard Crenna in WAIT UNTIL DARK (WB-7 Arts '67)

With Maurice Chevalier at the Tony Awards ceremony in New York City
(April 1968)

In a candid moment (c. 1968)

Following her wedding to Dr. Andrea Dotti on January 18, 1969, at Morges, Switzerland

Shopping in Rome (1971)

In INDISCRETION OF AN AMERICAN WIFE (Col '54)

Jennifer Jones

5'8"
120 pounds
Brown hair
Gray-green eyes
Pisces

With her first major screen role, *The Song of Bernadette* (Twentieth Century-Fox, 1943), Jennifer Jones won an Academy Award and "overnight" became an important motion-picture star. Thereafter she was dogmatically guided, goaded, and protected in her professional and domestic spheres by dynamic film producer David O. Selznick, who later became her husband. When he lost his Hollywood power base in the late 1950s, Jennifer's industry standing promptly fizzled, and after his death in 1965, she was a lost soul both in the movie business and in her private world. She indiscriminately selected inferior parts in bad films and made a splash in the newspapers with a grandiose suicide bid. It seemed that few people took her seriously anymore or even cared about her past and her lofty dramatic achievements. Then, in storybook fashion, along came a mature Prince Charming in the form of multimillionaire Norton Simon, and with her latest marriage, she attained the material and emotional cushioning needed for her survival.

In the rather sparse canon of Jennifer Jones films—twenty-three features and one serial—she was undeniably radiant and quietly intense on many occasions, as evidenced in the trashy epic Western *Duel in the Sun* (Selznick Releasing, 1946) and the diffuse soap opera *Love Is a Many Splendored Thing* (Twentieth Century-Fox, 1955). Offscreen, she was undeniably shy and excessively introverted. This duality of nature was compounded by Selznick's twenty-year campaign to elevate his actress discovery to the ranks of saintliness and/or love goddess. It was a heady emotional challenge that Jennifer as a performer was not always equipped to handle (who could?), as in *Portrait of Jennie* (Selznick Releasing, 1948) or *Carrie* (Paramount, 1952). At other times, particularly when Selznick was forced to remain discreetly in the production background, Jennifer surprised even her more ardent fans by offering a fully-shaded performance that capitalized on her oversensitive nature. Then too, had Selznick allowed her to expand her pleasant facility for film comedy—*Cluny Brown* (Twentieth Century-Fox, 1946), *Beat the Devil* (United Artists, 1954)—she might well have developed an entirely new vista to her inbred, mannered screen emoting.

At present, Jennifer's status in cinema history is badly in need of re-evaluation. Her persistent antipathy to close-at-hand fan adulation resulted in the loss of her public following long before she had ceased to be a viable screen leading lady. With no legion of champions, most current movie chroniclers ignore her impressive acting qualities and brand her as a one-film "star." More realistically, an appreciation of Jennifer's film persona is an acquired taste, requiring patience, open-mindedness, and a willingness to explore the visually and emotionally offbeat. Such experimentation, however, is worth the effort, and will pay viable dividends to the viewer.

Phylis Lee Isley entered the world in Tulsa, Oklahoma, on Sunday, March 2, 1919. She was the only child of Phil and Flora Mae (née Suber) Isley, owners, managers, and stars of the Isley Stock Company, a summer tent show transported by truck to rural communities of the south-central states.

A traveling show provided a most unusual proving ground for an imaginative youngster. At each designated stop the same routine was followed: a tent was pitched, and for a 10-cent admission charge (20 cents for front-row seats) the entertainment-hungry inhabitants were treated to an Isley-conceived stage production, occasionally accompanied by a projector-worn vintage film. The company's itinerary did not vary much from year to year, but the stage offerings did. The audience that witnessed a comedy one year would sit through a drama the following season. Most of the Isley company was composed of stage veterans who were masters of the art of timing; all were rugged individuals who worked quite hard for their weekly $25. When not performing, the actors hung around or slept in musty rural hotels or in the trucks amongst their props. Because of their tent-show affiliations, the group was unacceptable to their peers of the legitimate theatre. Other than their immediate cohorts, they made few friends en route.

The Isleys spent the off-season months in Oklahoma City, where the father operated his own movie theatre and where Phylis attended the Edgemere Public School. Her summer vacations were spent acquiring a quite different type of education on tour with the family's theatrical troupe. At the age of ten Phylis was already promoted to the job of the outfit's ticker-taker and candy-seller. She was encouraged to actively participate onstage whenever a role came along requiring a juvenile. Her father believed that such experiences might help to rid her of her inordinate shyness.

Despite her extremely quiet nature and the fact that she kept to herself a great deal, Phylis was popular among her high school classmates. Because of her acting background, it was natural that she should be selected to perform in school plays. On stage, having the security of "being" someone else, she was a new person, taking on the identity of the character she was portraying at the moment. Her less creatively oriented contemporaries found this facility hard to comprehend.

Later, at Monte Cassino Junior College, a school of the Benedictine Sisters in Tulsa, she starred in every possible student production, while at the same time she was heard in minor roles on Tulsa radio. She continued to tour with her parents in the summer months, until September came around and it was time to return to school. By this juncture, through the acquisition of several motion-picture theatres in Texas, Phil Isley had become a prominent film distributor. With some reluctance, he conceded to his daughter's pleadings that he provide tuition for her to study dramatics at Northwestern University. It was Mr. Isley's contention that studying to act, without remuneration, was a darn waste of time. He believed that his daughter was ready for Hollywood movies and offered to get her started in that direction through certain industry connections of his.

Nevertheless, and greatly to her credit, Phylis remained steadfast in her desire and belief that a proper educational background was essential. In fact, she wrote to Broadway star Katharine Cornell and asked whether a young beginner should get started at once or should first go to college. Miss Cornell's emphatic reply was to obtain a "cultural background" and then pursue a career. Who was Phil Isley to argue with the great Cornell!

After a summer of stock with a group called the Mansfield Players, Phylis departed for Evanston, Illinois. One year was spent at the Northwestern University School of Speech. She then returned home to inform her father that she was not returning to college, but instead wanted to study at the American Academy of Dramatic Arts in New York City. Phil and Flora Mae had many discussions over the wisdom of this latest proposition from their daughter, but finally agreed. Phil shook his head, sighing, "It's cheaper to hire an actress than to raise one."

In September 1937, Phylis entered the American Academy of Dramatic Arts. Diana Barrymore was a classmate, as was a solemn, baby-faced boy of Salt Lake City origin named Robert Walker. His demonstrated stage abilities, while at the San Diego Military Academy, had influenced the financial support for his Academy studies by a wealthy aunt, Hortense Odlum, a Bonwit Teller magnate.

Phylis portrayed Elizabeth Barrett to Walker's Robert Browning in a January 1938 Academy production of *The Barretts of Wimpole Street*. In the beginning it was acting, but after several love-scene rehearsals they discovered that it might be love for real. Their offstage relationship blossomed through mutual interests and identical pecuniary situations; neither of them had much money of his/her own. On long walks or 5-cent trolley rides through Manhattan, they held hands and dreamed aloud of the day when they would be famous performers.

Phylis returned to Oklahoma that summer and worked with her father's tent show. Her favorite role under the hot canvas was that of Moonyean in *Smilin' Through*. She returned to New York and the Academy that autumn, but dropped out of classes after only a few sessions. Walker had induced her to join him in his search for a gainful stage job so that they could be married. She wrote of her latest momentous decision to her parents, who lost no time in boarding a New York-bound train to learn for themselves exactly what was happening with their sole offspring. They found their daughter and Walker working variety with Paul Gilmore's Cherry Lane troupe in Greenwich Village, each earning 50 cents a performance. At once Phil Isley saw the seriousness of their feeling for each other and ominously advised Phylis, "Don't marry an actor. I know actors—they're hard to raise."

The elder Isleys returned home where Phil immediately arranged with a local radio-station executive to contract his daughter for a recurring part in a daytime soap opera at $25 a week for thirteen weeks. Phylis responded to the news with a telegram tersely stating that she would accept the post *only* if a job were also provided for Walker. A few weeks later, Phil sent money for two train tickets to Tulsa.

Phylis and Walker performed on the same radio show for the alloted thirteen-week contract. At the end of this time, Phil consented to their being married. He found that he liked Walker in spite of the boy's acting ambitions. As a wedding gift he presented them with a new, blue 1939 Buick car. In a church ceremony in Tulsa, Phylis Isley became Mrs. Robert Walker. The date was January 2, 1939, the anniversary of their first meeting, and she was then nineteen, while he was twenty.

When no further job opportunities in Tulsa materialized, the newlyweds decided to return to New York, but Phil insisted that they try Hollywood instead. With their savings of $200 crunched inside Phylis's purse, the Walkers drove west in their new car.

Through a talent-scout friend of her father's the Walkers obtained screentests at Paramount. The couple made a joint oncamera screentest, with Phylis playing Walker's mother. The studio was unimpressed by the youngsters' emoting, and no contract evolved. However, through another connection of her father's, Phylis obtained a six-month contract with Herbert Yates's Republic Studios, while Robert made repeated rounds of all the studios' casting calls.

Using her maiden name, Phylis's initial screen appearance was in *New Frontier* (1939), the twenty-fifth in the fifty-two-entry *Three Mesquiteers* Western series. The star of the film was John Wayne, and this proved to be his final performance in the long-running *Mesquiteers* adventures. Even the amiable Wanda Hale of the even more amiable *New York Daily News* was strongly critical of the film, complaining that the fifty-six-minute programmer "lacks the action and honesty that goes to make a western amiable entertainment. The story is a little forced." (The tale was no great shakes, but it did move right along: the community of New Hope is celebrating its fiftieth anniversary when the townsfolk learn that their valley settlement is to be condemned because a neighboring city is badly in need of water. The Mesquiteers come to their rescue.) As a settler's demure sister, Phylis successfully wielded a rifle when the time came to defend the family's land. She and Wayne had a slight hint of a romance, but, since it would be heresy to break up the horse-riding trio by introducing a marriage into the situation, Wayne and his pals remain their own men when the gunfire and the film have faded from sight. *Variety* rightfully acknowledged that "the part has little enough to give her a good chance," but Miss Hale (*Daily News*) used her woman's intuition to point out that Phylis was "a cute new girl."

Phylis next was utilized at Republic in the fifteen-chapter serial, *Dick Tracy's G-Men* (1939).* Unlike fellow studio worker Carole Landis, who had a sizable part in that year's chapterplay, *Daredevils of the Red Circle,* Phylis had relatively scant oncamera footage in this actioner, which was mostly devoted to Dick Tracy (Ralph Byrd) of the FBI combating sinister international spy Zanoff (Irving Pichel), who seemingly had more lives than a cat. Alan G. Barbour in *Days of Thrills and Laughter* (1970) ranks these *Dick Tracy* cliffhangers as "creative masterpieces, filled with location photography and imaginative action sequences." Whatever their intrinsic value, the serial did little to advance Phylis's career. Both she and the studio seriously wondered whether her two weeks' work in the fisticuffs marathon (at $75 per week) was worth it. As Gwen Andrews, she was hardly noticeable or memorable in the helter-skelter proceedings.

In the meantime, Walker had wangled a two-line bit in Ann Sheridan's *Winter Carnival* (United Artists, 1939), as well as less important

---

*This was the third of four *Dick Tracy*-Republic serials, each starring Ralph Byrd: *Dick Tracy* (1937), *Dick Tracy Returns* (1938), *Dick Tracy's G-Men* (1939), and *Dick Tracy vs. Crime, Inc.* (1941).

jobs in two Lana Turner-featured B-pictures at MGM, *These Glamour Girls* (1939) and *Dancing Co-Ed* (1939), and a bit in a Jack Randall cheapie Western, *Pioneer Days* (Monogram, 1940). When Phylis's Republic option was not renewed, the couple admitted failure in Hollywood, sold their car, and bought train tickets for New York.

From an $18-a-month furnished room in Greenwich Village, they set out each day in search of theatrical work. But there came a point when Phylis could no longer hide her pregnancy, and she had to remain behind to sew, clean, and cook. Robert had no luck with stage casting calls, but did land some work on various daytime soap operas, usually cast in the role of a juvenile. On April 14, 1940, Robert Hudson Walker, Jr. was born.

The new parents took turns babysitting while one or the other went job hunting. Through the renowned Powers Agency, Phylis found employment modeling hats, and various photographs of her appeared in *Harper's Bazaar* magazine. This newfound career had to be put aside, however, for she became pregnant a second time and another son, Michael Ross Walker, was born on March 17, 1941. By then, Walker, who had been heard on CBS radio's "Maudie's Diary," was a regular on the same network's long-running "Myrt and Marge," in which he assumed the role of Ted Smith. By this time the Walkers had moved to a six-room apartment in Garden City, Long Island. They had repeatedly refused financial help from the Isleys, but Phylis's mother insisted on sending them Henrietta, a family servant, to assist with the children. At the same time Phylis won a few radio jobs and the Walkers' luck seemed to have switched for the good.

Having studied Rose Franken's popular novel *Claudia* and having seen Dorothy McGuire in the title role on Broadway,* Phylis learned, in July 1941, that Hollywood producer David O. Selznick was planning to film it. She loved the story and thought she would be good in the lead role of the young wife who has yet to grow to emotional maturity. She contacted a local talent scout she had met while employed in Paul Gilmore's variety shows and inquired whether he could possibly arrange something with Selznick's New York office. The scout talked with Katharine Brown, Selznick's East Coast representative, who suggested that the girl come around for a line reading. Phylis read, and, in her own words, she "was very, very bad." She burst into tears at the same moment that the lofty producer of *Gone with the Wind* (MGM, 1939) walked into the office. The thirty-nine-year-old Hollywood genius was instantly impressed by Phylis's good looks—especially her "big eyes"—and by her acting potential. He had pretty well decided to cast Dorothy McGuire in the projected film since she was then sparkling as the onstage Claudia, but thought of Phylis

---

*The show opened at the Booth Theatre on February 12, 1941, for a 453-performance run, and then reopened on May 24, 1942, at the St. James Theatre for a 265-performance engagement.

as a possible candidate for the part of Nora in his proposed screen version of the A. J. Cronin novel, *The Keys of the Kingdom*. An appointment was made for her to return to the Selznick office the following day, but she thought it nothing more than a polite ruse to stop her flow of tears. She promptly forgot about the appointment. When she failed to appear the next day, Miss Brown phoned and caught a much-surprised Phylis shampooing her hair. She grabbed a towel and a taxi and raced into town from Long Island.

A contract, drawn up after this second meeting, was formally signed two weeks later. Phylis subsequently commented, "I pushed my way into pictures and thought I'd have to keep on pushing all my life, but all of a sudden everything seemed to be taken out of my hands."

Despite her enthusiastic wish to start film work immediately, Selznick insisted that she remain in New York for extensive training, including correct posture and diction, with dramatic and voice coaches. There were times when Selznick reconsidered utilizing her for *Claudia* after all, and she was permitted to replace McGuire in one performance onstage. Not only was she given the cold shoulder by the other cast members, but the author also disapproved of her in the pivotal role.

As Phylis progressed in her training, Selznick made periodic screen-tests with her and continued his search for a new name for Phylis. He considered the name of Phylis Walker too undistinguished and too similar to that of Phyllis Thaxter, who had also played *Claudia* onstage and who was well on the way to launching a film career (eventually at MGM).

In January 1942, Selznick, recovering from his shock at learning that she had previously worked in films, decided on one of his favorite feminine names, Jennifer. For the surname he wanted a short one that would blend well with Jennifer. He selected Jones.

Jennifer Jones was then "chosen" to star for several weeks in a summer-stock company sponsored by Selznick in Santa Barbara, California, at the Lobrero Theatre. It was a season of plays designed to utilize the off-camera talents of Selznick's growing stable of contract personalities, who were either between films, as in the case of Ingrid Bergman, who did *Anna Christie,* or who were awaiting the propitious time to make their (real) cinema bow, as with Jennifer.* She appeared opposite Harry Bratsberg in a one-act play which had never before been staged, *Hello, Out There* by William Saroyan. John Houseman was the group's director. Although Jennifer played the part to favorable reviews, she was sent back to New York for further study under the tutelage of Sanford Meisner and Constance Collier.

*Since the release of *Gone with the Wind,* independent producer Selznick had been augmenting his company's coffers by signing up promising new talent and/or reestablished stars and loaning their services to other studios at a hefty profit to himself, but not the players. Among the Selznick brood were Joan Fontaine, Ingrid Bergman, Joseph Cotten, Shirley Temple, Dorothy McGuire, and Jennifer.

In a Selznick-staged interview, a reporter asked how she had acquired the name of Jennifer Jones. "My mother must have been reading an English novel," the coached actress shyly replied, "but I suppose they'll change it once I get to Hollywood." And she got there in December 1942 when Twentieth Century-Fox announced the end of their six-month search for an unknown to star in *The Song of Bernadette* (1943). *Producer William Perlberg had claimed he wanted no preconceived audience reactions to the girl who would portray St. Bernadette onscreen. For that reason he insisted on an unknown, or, at least, an unestablished cinema beginner. More than two thousand applicants had supposedly been processed and/or tested, one of whom was Fox contractee Anne Baxter,† when Selznick sent his newest actress employee to the auditioning hall, but not before she spent two weeks at Elizabeth Arden's health farm in Maine to guarantee her resemblance to a fourteen-year-old virgin.

The competition narrowed down to six finalists when director Henry King waved a long stick in the air and asked each to imagine that the stick was a vision. "Only Jennifer saw a vision," King later said, and it was decided to borrow her from Selznick to enact the difficult role of the half-starved French peasant girl who saw the beautiful Blessed Virgin Mary looking down at her from a grotto in the rocks. Written by German refugee Franz Werfel and based on the supposed actual experiences of Bernadette Soubirous in 1858, the novel had been an outstanding best seller of 1942.

With her sons, Jennifer set up California headquarters in a colonial home in Bel Air. Walker remained in New York until a few days before Christmas when MGM called him to Hollywood to play Sailor Purckett in *Bataan* (1943). The dreams shared on nickel trolly rides through New York City were magically materializing.

As Jennifer delved into *Bernadette's* 329-page script by George Seaton and learned camera techniques by testing with candidates for other roles in the costly feature, Twentieth Century-Fox initiated a publicity campaign to herald the supreme virtues of the future star. It was an operation keyed exclusively towards her more goodly virtues and serious drama, avoiding the usual leg-and-bosom-art buildup. An image was soon created of a very ethereal and untouchable celebrity, and it was this special image that was to be hers throughout her career. No public mention was made of her motherhood or wifely devotion, and a clause in the Fox contract forbade her to be photographed with her husband or sons. Walker's career at MGM skyrocketed through his performances in *Bataan* and *Madame*

---

*Selznick sold the rights to *The Keys to the Kingdom* to Twentieth Century-Fox. When that studio produced the feature in 1944, it was Jane Ball who played the role that Selznick had once considered for Jennifer.

†Baxter did play in *The Song of Bernadette* on "Lux Radio Theatre" on April 11, 1949, with Charles Bickford as one of her co-stars.

Curie (1943), however, and the couple became too newsworthy to ignore.* The contractual clause was quietly dismissed. The public became very aware of the handsome Walkers with their tow-headed sons. It was only some time after *The Song of Bernadette* debuted that some astute film-goers recalled that Jennifer and Phylis Isley were one and the same, at which point the studio dropped the notion that this was Jennifer's screen bow.

The final cast chosen for *The Song of Bernadette* comprised such competent actors as Gladys Cooper, Anne Revere, Charles Bickford, Vincent Price, Roman Bohnen, and Lee J. Cobb. Linda Darnell, a Fox star(let) dissuaded from coveting the plum role of Bernadette, was photographed, without billing, as the Virgin. Bickford, playing the priest who eventually comes to believe in Bernadette's vision, befriended the tyro Jennifer and offered her valuable advice on movie acting. This was the beginning of a friendship that endured more than twenty-four years.

The film was completed in the summer of 1943 and released in Los Angeles in December in order to qualify for that year's Academy Awards. The $2 million production was conceived on a grand scale and dedicated to the commercial, but also idealistic, notion that a paean to religious devotion would capture the hearts of World War II audiences.† (It did. The film grossed over $5 million in distributors' domestic rentals.) With a running time of 156 minutes, *Newsweek* magazine observed, "[it] is easily half an hour too much of a very good thing." The overly embroidered final product could well have benefited from further judicious footage shearing, just as Ivan Butler in *Religion in the Cinema* (1969) fairly assesses: ". . . visual beauty (the whole thing is stunningly photographed) is no substitute for emotional depth, and there is little sense of mystery or 'revelation.' The scenario is based on a very sentimentalised best-selling novel and this is, perhaps, a pity." But on the whole, the contemporary filmgoing public was of the same mind as the *New York Time*'s Bosley Crowther, who acclaimed the picture as a "hymn to the everlasting beauty of innocence and faith."

Jennifer's role as Bernadette Soubirous was a difficult histrionic challenge, one that might well have stymied a far more experienced screen performer.‡ She was required not only to capture and convey the various aspects of a sensitive fourteen-year-old girl who grows to physical maturity in the course of the story, but also to create strong audience empathy for the picture's reverent point of view. As *The Song of Bernadette* opens,

*At one point Selznick himself had considered placing Walker under contract.
†The film's pious foreword stated, "For those who believe in God no explanation is necessary. For those who do not believe in God, no explanation is possible." Wisely, the film made no effort to proselytize the audience one way or the other.
‡In the 1960, Robert Darene-directed *Il Suffit d'Aimer* (*Bernadette of Lourdes*), actress Daniele Ajouret offered a remarkable portrayal of the French girl who, on December 8, 1933, was canonized a saint.

the viewer encounters Jennifer, the elder daughter of a poverty-stricken family, existing in an abandoned jailhouse in Lourdes, a small village on the River Gave in southern France. One day, while gathering firewood with her sister Marie (Ermadean Walters), Jennifer is frightened. A woodsman lifts the girl across the stream. Then she hesitates at the grotto of Massaroses, and there she sees a vision of "a lady all in white with a blue girdle and gold roses on her feet." This day that she experienced the wondrous encounter was February 11, 1858, and thereafter, at the "lady's" request, she returns for fifteen consecutive days. Later the girl digs a hole in the ground with her hands, from which pours forth a spring. Just as her classmates previously had scorned Jennifer as being a sickly, strange child, so now the townsfolk, and especially the local political and church officials, scoff at her insistence that she actually saw the Blessed Virgin Mary, who told her, "I am the Immaculate Conception." As the film progresses, the viewer finds himself succumbing to the girl's overwhelming persistence that her encounter was authentic. The story's credibility is heightened by the presence of such counter-belief figures as the prosecutor, Dutour (Vincent Price), and, especially, the jealous, vindictive Sister Vauzous (Gladys Cooper), the latter dogging the girl's steps through her years at the nunnery and right up to her deathbed. Even at the very end, the faithful believer Jennifer utters, "I did see the Lady."

While there were critics who rightly carped that Jennifer conveyed neither the appearance nor the feel of a frail youngster, most of the reviewers were enchanted with this "new" screen find.* ". . . through Jennifer Jones, a new actress who plays the difficult role of Bernadette, it achieves a rare quality of sweetness that lifts it above its common faults" (Bosley Crowther, *New York Times*). *Variety* called her "wistful, naive and at times angelic," while James Agee (*Time*) reported that "newcomer Jennifer Jones makes one of the most impressive screen debuts in many years." *Newsweek* insisted that "the outstanding feature of an elaborate production is the fine acting of a hand-picked cast. . . . But isolated from the rest—less by the trying demands of the titular role than by the luminous spirituality and simplicity she brings to Bernadette—is the cinematic cinderella who has been cautiously publicized as Jennifer Jones." It was Kate Cameron in her four-star *New York Daily News* review who prophetically observed, "she not only reaches stardom, but she must be counted a phenomenon, and I doubt if she will ever equal, or come close to the perfection of her first [*sic*] performance."

Despite the tremendous publicity the onscreen Jennifer was receiv-

---

*Among the fence-sitting reviewers was the *New Yorker*'s critic, who noted, "I won't say that Jennifer Jones, the young discovery who plays Bernadette, is the greatest find of the decade, the role of a simple, pious child is one of the easiest of the decades, but she is unquestionably appealing and makes no noticeable mistakes. I will say, incidentally, that she has been given one of the worst screen names in the business."

ing, Selznick was forced to admit that, offcamera, his newest star was excessively shy and projected little color for the press. He hired beauty consultant Anita Colby to tutor Jennifer in the arts of dress, makeup, and conversation. Colby taught her, among other essential qualities, to look directly at people when talking with them, rather than to lower her eyes or to look away.

In September 1943, production began on Selznick's *Since You Went Away* (United Artists, 1944), which the producer determined to make into a contemporary epic equal to *Gone with the Wind.** The novel by Margaret Buell Wilder derived from the author's true-life experience, and was in the form of letters written by one Anne Hilton, an American housewife and mother, to her soldier husband, Tim. Selznick slaved over the screenplay, which he dedicated "to that fortress—the American home." For a time it was rumored that Katharine Cornell might appear as the young wife, but Paramount's Claudette Colbert became the final selection for that role, with a supporting cast that rivaled another past Selznick production, *Dinner at Eight* (MGM, 1933). Twenty-four-year-old Jennifer was given the second lead role, one that Selznick especially enlarged for her. The 172-minute feature presented her as the elder Hilton daughter in the first bloom of womanhood. Selznick chose this type of part for her second movie so that the public would not forever regard her as (in his words) "a sort of Bernadette in real life, an eminently worthy character, but lacking variety." Other members of the cast included Joseph Cotten as the serviceman ex-beau of Colbert, Shirley Temple as the skittish younger Hilton daughter, Monty Woolley as the irascible Hilton boarder and owner of the beloved dog Soda, Hattie McDaniel as the jovial, loyal family servant, Agnes Moorehead as the acerbic "friend" of Colbert, Lionel Barrymore as the clergyman who delivers an uplifting oration, and Robert Walker, borrowed from MGM, as Woolley's grandson, whom Jennifer loves but loses to the war. The music, written around the theme "Together," was composed by Max Steiner, who won an Oscar for his contribution to this movie.

It was while they were at work on their soundstage love scenes that Jennifer and Walker decided that they could no longer stand each other. He moved out of their home; three of Hollywood's major studios—MGM (Walker's home base), Twentieth Century-Fox (owners of *The Song of Bernadette*), and United Artists (releasers of *Since You Went Away*)— all attempted to patch up the domestic shambles, but the situation was apparently hopeless. The Walkers agreed to announce that they had decided upon an "amicable separation," the statement of which a press agent managed to bury in the Sunday sections of Los Angeles newspapers. "It won't make any difference in our acting [in *Since You Went*

---

*One slogan of the publicity campaign for *Since You Went Away* proclaimed the title, "The four most important words since *Gone with the Wind.*"

Away]. Bob and I are both troupers," Jennifer told studio heads as she continued her emotional oncamera sequences with him as dictated by the Selznick script.

Although Selznick, by this time, was openly madly in love with Jennifer,* he, too, preferred that the Walkers remain "happily married," at least until both *The Song of Bernadette* and *Since You Went Away* were well into national release. The expected storm of public protests over the marital breakup did not materialize, however, and Jennifer's fan mail continued to flow at a heavy rate.

In November 1943, Selznick discovered several flaws in Jennifer's professional personality, which he took immediate steps to rectify. Her readings in the dressing room or on the rehearsal set differed vastly from what she offered in front of the camera. She was seemingly unable to project her thin voice beyond its normal tone, even though the sound-recording engineer on *Since You Went Away* screamed for more voice volume, which she was just incapable of giving. It affected her performance to the point where the studio was losing time and money on continual retakes. She had not had this problem while working on *The Song of Bernadette* because director Henry King permitted her to talk in natural tones and informed his sound department to pamper the girl in this area. Selznick took care of the pressing matter through his habitual means of expression, the memo,† to his production manager, Raymond Klune. Also, since she was constantly nervous while acting, everyone was ordered away from the set except the minimum necessary crew. (In this respect of creative endeavor, at least, Jennifer followed the tradition of the equally shy and self-conscious Greta Garbo.)

The award nominations by the Academy of Motion Picture Arts and Sciences for achievement during 1943 were announced in January 1944. To few people's surprise, Jennifer was nominated as best actress for *The Song of Bernadette*. Her four rivals were Jean Arthur for *The More the Merrier,* Ingrid Bergman (also on Selznick's payroll and Jennifer's friend) for *For Whom the Bell Tolls,* Joan Fontaine (another Selznick employee and a good pal to Jennifer over the years) for *The Constant Nymph,* and Greer Garson for *Madame Curie. Bernadette* received a nomination as Best Picture as well as for both Supporting Actor (Charles Bickford), and Actresses (Gladys Cooper, Anne Revere), and in several technical categories.

March 2, 1944, was Jennifer's twenty-fifth birthday. It was also the date of the Oscar ceremony, which, for the first time, took place in a

---

*On April 29, 1930, Selznick had wed twenty-two-year-old Irene Gladys Mayer, daughter of MGM mogul Louis B. Mayer. The Selznicks had two sons, Jeffrey born in 1932 and Daniel born in 1936. At this point (1943) the Selznicks maintained a marriage of convenience.

†For further illumination on the Selznick memo mania and for amplification on the Selznick-Jennifer Jones professional relationship, there is available Rudy Behlmer's *Memo from David O. Selznick* (1969).

theatre. On the stage of Grauman's Chinese Theatre on Hollywood Boulevard, she received a gold-colored plaster statuette for her first major screen performance. (Normally the Oscar is composed of metal, but during the war years, he went patriotic. After the war the plaster statuettes were exchanged for metal ones.) *Bernadette* received a total of five awards the most for any picture in 1943, but it did not win the Best Picture prize, which went to Warner Bros.' *Casablanca*. Oscar-winner Jennifer was also accoladed by *Look* magazine and was presented with its Achievement Award.

The following day, Jennifer officially announced her intention to proceed with a divorce suit against Robert Walker.

Since You Went Away was released in July 1944. The film captured the emotions of some critics, like the *New York Herald-Tribune* reviewer, who penned, "it has heart and a curious simplicity which permits each and every spectator to identify himself with a screen fable." Other professional viewers were more cautious in their praise, as was Bosley Crowther *(New York Times)*, who reported, "Its humors are frequent and cheerful; its spirit is hopeful and brave. But it does come off, altogether, as a rather large dose of choking sentiment." With its built-in audience of the folks at home and G.I.s. at war, it was quite natural that *Since You Went Away*, under John Cromwell's overall direction, would emerge as a financial success, garnering over $4.95 million in distributors' domestic rentals on a $2 million production investment. If anyone was disappointed by the final public response to *Since You Went Away*,* it was Selznick himself, who had fervently hoped that this smashing production would equal or top *Gone with the Wind* in critical and public acclaim.

With so much screen footage there was ample opportunity for each member of the cast to shine in some distinct individual spotlight throughout the course of the picture. Jennifer was blessed with two particularly memorable sequences. The first took place during the picnic that she and Walker enjoy in the country, which is interrupted by a sudden rainstorm, forcing them to take shelter in a farmyard barn where they indulge in gentle romancing. The other sequence was a tearjerking scene of farewell, which surely must have evoked immediate response from countless thousands of moviegoers who had undergone similar, if less dramatic, departures from their loved ones. In this scene, Jennifer accompanies serviceman Walker to the train station, for he is shipping out to eventual overseas duty. By this point they are deeply in love, and their separation is heartbreaking to both parties. As his train slowly moves out of the crowded terminal, the teary-eyed Jennifer runs after the moving coaches,

*Selznick was not very pleased to have his "modern masterpiece" labeled "the American *Mrs. Miniver*."

401

waving a brave goodbye to the man she adores and may never see again. (She does not, for he is killed in action in Italy.)

Louella Parsons, in her syndicated entertainment column, boldly announced, "Jennifer Jones belies the whisper that she is a 'one-picture' girl. In the beginning of the picture I was afraid that might be true. But gradually Jennifer, who starts as a gangly, sentimental girl, develops into a fine dramatic actress." It may have been difficult for some viewers to accept Jennifer as the adult daughter of Colbert (still extremely attractive at age thirty-eight), or to balance the real-life Jennifer, who was divorcing Walker, from the oncamera Hilton girl, who refuses to attend college in order to work in a munitions factory. Nevertheless, as the *New York Herald-Tribune* summed it up, "The erstwhile Bernadette is quietly convincing as a bereaved adolescent." Crowther of the *Times* cheered, "[She is] surpassingly sweet as a well-bred American daughter in the first bloom of womanhood and love."

Selznick allowed the Academy to place Jennifer's name among those nominated as Best Supporting Actress, but took careful measures, thereafter, to insure that her career would take no other avenue but that of a top-flight star. She lost the 1944 Oscar contest to Ethel Barrymore of *None But the Lonely Heart* (RKO). Twentieth Century-Fox invited Jennifer to play the title role in *Laura* (1944), but Selznick declined the invitation and the part went to Gene Tierney. He did allow his protégée to be heard on Cecil B. DeMille's "Lux Radio Presents Hollywood" with Van Johnson and Jean Hersholt in *Seventh Heaven* on October 16, 1944. According to the Gallup Poll, Johnson was the fastest rising male star in 1944, and Jennifer ranked as his female counterpart. A remake of *Little Women* was considered, with Jennifer as Jo March, a part previously handled oncamera in 1919 by Dorothy Bernard and in 1933 by Katharine Hepburn, but the project was eventually dropped by Selznick.* In addition, Selznick thought that film fan magazines were too frivolous an interview outlet for an actress of Jennifer's caliber and status, and most were studiously avoided.

In the autumn of 1944, production began on what Selznick hoped was to be his greatest success, *Duel in the Sun.* He wrote the screenplay, based on the Niven Busch novel, and chose as his stars a trio of top box-office attractions: Jennifer, Gregory Peck, and Joseph Cotten. For her role as Pearl Chavez, the Mexican half-breed, Jennifer spent hours each workday applying Indian makeup over her entire body.

In between filming scenes for the protracted production of *Duel in the Sun*—Selznick was even more of a perfectionist than Howard Hughes with his Western, *The Outlaw* (RKO, 1943)—Jennifer and Cotten, in 1945, worked together in Paramount's *Love Letters,* produced by Hal B.

*When the project was sold to MGM, Jo was played by June Allyson in that studio's 1949 release.

Wallis, directed by William Dieterle, and with an unnecessarily grandiloquent screenplay by the eminent Ayn Rand. The picture's basic theme was a contemporary offshoot of *Cyrano de Bergerac* twisted into a romantic yarn that leaned too heavily towards the bizarre. Jennifer appeared as Singleton, the recipient of lofty, romantic letters she believed to have been written by her soldier lover (Robert Sully) on the Italian war front, but actually composed by G.I. Alan Quinton (Cotten).* Britisher Jennifer makes the fatal error of wedding the bogus letter-writer while he is on leave, only to become disillusioned with the egocentric chap. Later, he becomes drunk and viciously beats her. To save her life, Jennifer's foster mother (Gladys Cooper) stabs the brutish husband to death. Because Cooper suffers a stroke and becomes speechless, she can be of little help to Jennifer when the girl is tried for murder and sentenced to a year in prison on a manslaughter charge. During the traumatic episode, Jennifer's heroine develops amnesia, and it is not until she is later freed, then meets and weds Cotten, that she regains her memory and is able to enjoy her newfound happiness.

It was apparent to even the more generous moviegoer that *Love Letters* was more neurotic than romantic. *Variety,* for industry reasons, leaned over backwards to find kind words for the production, labeling it "warm and appealing, sentimental and emotional," but it was Bosley Crowther *(New York Times)* who took a firmer, more realistic stand: "A worse script or less expert direction has seldom been tossed at an innocent star's head." James Agee in *The Nation* was even more emphatically annoyed by the film's structure: "A story so inconceivably factitious that only a poet-moralist or a romancer of genius could have been wisely attracted by it, or could have brought it above the sill of absurdity." With the major exceptions of Victor Young's music score and Ann Richards's performance of Jennifer's protective friend, the psychological thriller had little solid entertainment value to offer moviegoers. (Ironically, the picture was a box-office success.) *The Song of Bernadette* had found Jennifer emoting with spiritual-visionary overtones, and in *Since You Went Away* she had gained adult womanhood through her hysteria at losing the man she loved. However, in *Love Letters,* there were few redeeming qualities to her performance. ". . . she behaves like a tipsy, high-school girl who has smelled the cork once too often and is all giggly and loose at the joints" (Bosley Crowther, *New York Times*). It was the first real oncamera indication of the neurotic qualities that would infect Jennifer's film performances in the years to come. Nevertheless, for the third time, Jennifer was Oscar nominated, but on this occasion she lost to Joan Crawford of *Mildred Pierce* (Warner Bros.).

*Typical passages of the letters were, "I think of you, my dearest, as a distant promise of beauty untouched by the world," and "Thank you for seeing life not as a burden or a punishment, but as a dream made beautifully real."

In the final year of World War II, when not in front of the camera in one production or another, Jennifer devoted what spare time she had to visiting hospitalized servicemen, launching Red Cross drives for nurses aides, and speaking at bond rallies.

On June 28, 1945, her divorce from Robert Walker was finalized. She was twenty-six, and he was twenty-seven. Walker entered into a lengthy period of what columnists called "torch carrying" and, due to an enormous consumption of alcohol, was often jailed as a public nuisance.*

Two months later, Selznick's wife, Irene, left her husband and relocated in New York. Industry observers were blunt in their predictions that it would only be a matter of (a short) time before Selznick and Jennifer formalized their long-standing liaison.

In February 1946, Selznick made grandiose plans, which were later abandoned, to bring to the screen a large-budgeted Technicolor film with Jennifer as *Joan of Arc*.† He also bought the book *Mary Magdalene*, re-titled it *The Scarlet Lily*, and proposed to star Jennifer in the vehicle.‡ Nevertheless, this idea failed to see fruition under the Selznick banner. There were persistent rumors that Jennifer and Tyrone Power would star in *The Dark Wood*, an Otto Preminger project for Twentieth Century-Fox. Because of scripting problems this screen property withered.

Meanwhile, *Duel in the Sun* still had not yet been publicly shown, but *Cluny Brown* (1946), shot at Twentieth Century-Fox under the direction of Ernst Lubitsch, debuted in June of that year at New York's Rivoli Theatre. For once the renowned past master of sophisticated screen comedy did not turn to a Hungarian or even a Middle-European source for his script. Instead he chose Margery Sharp's penetrating novel of English class snobbism for his storyline basis. What emerged may not have been top-notch Lubitsch, but it was pretty close to a vintage product. As Howard Barnes *(New York Herald-Tribune)* indicated, "it has a rich fund of humor and a wealth of superior cinematic detail." A. H. Weiler *(New York Times)* labeled the picture a "delectable and sprightly lampoon."

Cluny Brown opens in 1939 London on a quiet Sunday when a pert young miss (Jennifer) substitutes for her plumber uncle (Billy Bevan) and quite innocently finds herself in a compromising position with improvident, charming Czechoslovakian refugee Charles Boyer. Almost immediately, impish Jennifer is packed off as a maid to the Devon country estate of Sir Henry Carmel (Reginald Owen), where, it is hoped, she will learn her proper place in English society. However, fortunately for the

*In 1948, Walker would wed one of John Ford's daughters; the marriage lasted less than five months.

†Ingrid Bergman later appeared in *Joan of Arc* (RKO, 1948), based on the Maxwell Anderson drama in which she had starred on Broadway.

‡Among the many acrresses to portray Mary Magdalene oncamera was Yvonne De Carlo in *La Spade e la Croce*, a 1958 Italian-made feature.

machinations of the script, she does not. Once established at the rural castle she encounters none other than Boyer, now a guest of Owen's son (Peter Lawford) and romantically indolent enough to make passes at the latter's fiancée (Helen Walker). It is almost a foregone conclusion that saucy Jennifer will soon ditch prissy, mother-dominated pharmacist Wilson (Richard Haydn) and build her on-again-off-again flirtation with Boyer into a legally consummated union of marriage. Within the slick but indulgent comedy,* Boyer was at his most charming, the British actor contingent (Lawford, Reginald Gardiner, Owen, Sir C. Aubrey Smith, et al.) efficient as always, and Haydn quite hilarious in his caricature of the meticulous, effeminate chemist. However, it was Jennifer who provided the picture's surprise with her first oncamera comedy role. As a self-liberated miss in pre-World War II England, she proved to be the most delightful component of the film, giving the production the needed lightness and bounce.

Contemporary audiences found *Cluny Brown* a mirth-provoking light satire, and the picture made its financial mark at the box office. The critics had to agree that the ex-Bernadette was "artful and attractive for the most part, even in the expedient ending . . ." (Howard Barnes, *New York Herald-Tribune*).† Unfortunately, it was to be Jennifer's last celluloid comedy for eight years, largely because her mentor, Selznick, had grandiose visions of his beloved as the Duse of the screen, capable of portraying heavy romantic drama for the glory of Selznick and the edification of the public. This mistaken belief was a pity for, as Herman G. Weinberg would point out in *The Lubitsch Touch* (1968), ". . . delectable Jennifer . . . [displayed] just the right fey edge to her playing." As it turned out, this would be Lubitsch's final full feature, for the great director died on November 30, 1947.

Meanwhile, *Duel in the Sun* continued its production saga. Director King Vidor resigned midway through filming after a fierce quarrel with Selznick, the latter persisting in haunting the Arizona location sites with critical demands aimed at an unheard of perfectionism. The picture had a $4 million budget ceiling, but the ultimate cost was estimated to be nearly $7 million. William Dieterle was the replacement director although release credit was given to Vidor through an appeal to the Screen Directors Guild.

There are many intriguing production parallels between Howard Hughes's *The Outlaw* starring Jane Russell and Selznick's *Duel in the*

*The British evidently did not find Lubitsch's comments on English class smugness so funny. The *London Observer* labeled the picture "an affront to common sense, intelligence, and good taste."

†In the final scene, Jennifer and Boyer, now wed, are walking on a crowded London street. She faints, a policeman comes by, but Boyer indicates that it is nothing serious, his wife is merely pregnant.

Sun. Like the former, the latter underwent a steamy conflict with the censorial authorities in Hollywood. Unlike the even more sensuously oriented Hughes, Selznick had worked closely with Joseph L. Breen of the Production Code Office regarding this colossal Western. When Breen disapproved of a dance routine that had taken Jennifer several weeks to learn, on the grounds that it was too suggestive, it was agreed that a new variation should be substituted, and Jennifer was forced to start from scratch and perfect a second routine.

By mid-1946, trade papers and the lay press were already carrying facets of Selznick's expansive publicity campaign for his newest, grandest, most epic production. However, as the time for trade screening approached, the maestro decided the film required additional retakes, and with "deep regret" the unveiling of the film was delayed until December of that year (the latest date by which the picture could qualify for the Oscars). By that time, Selznick and United Artists had severed their working relationship, and Selznick had formed Selznick Releasing Organization in order to distribute his own product. A last-minute delay of the processing of *Duel in the Sun* at the Technicolor laboratories prevented the new releasing company from previewing the picture for the West Coast Legion of Decency. When the Western opened in Los Angeles without benefit of the religious organization's scrutiny, Archbishop Cantwell, the head of the Los Angeles Archdiocese, stated that until the motion picture was viewed by the Legion of Decency and classified, Roman Catholics would do well to refrain from seeing it. After much diplomatic interchange, the Legion was invited to screen *Duel in the Sun,* at which point *Tidings,* the official newspaper of the Los Angeles Archdiocese, reported, "It shows Jennifer Jones as unduly, if not indecently, exposed, and it shows a character [The Sin Killer, played by Walter Huston, who had also been in *The Outlaw*] acting as a minister of religion, who parodies prayer and thus becomes a comical character." However, the National Legion of Decency Office labeled the film with a B-rating, and all parties were pacified by the end results.

As to *Duel in the Sun* itself, Charles Higham and Joel Greenberg in *Hollywood in the Forties* (1968) have fittingly described the feature as "large of gesture, florid and monumental, . . . [it has] an almost operatic quality, each bravura set-piece shot, edited and scored for maximum kinetic effect. . . . This was film-making in the grand manner, utterly self-confident and self-sufficient, its plastic splendor ultimately cancelling out its colossal lack of taste."

Unfortunately, the film opens with a most pretentious, stentorian prolog, spoken ominously by Orson Welles. It sets the tone for the earthy, elongated dramatics about to be unfolded onscreen. "For more than half a century, over the great and rolling plains of the cattle country . . . a legend has lingered, like dust particles in the sunlight, up-flung by long-vanished herds of Texas longhorns . . . a strange story of a young outlaw and a half-breed Indian girl, a tale told on nights when there's a heavy ground mist and the moon's behind a distant ridge, for it is there, some say, you can glimpse the shadowy figure of Pearl Chavez on her horse, still following her lover; Pearl, who came from down along the Border, and who was like a wildflower sprung from the hard clay, quick to blossom, early to die."

In its basic theme, *Duel in the Sun* was much like a sagebrush Cain and Abel tale, with Gregory Peck as the rebel and Joseph Cotten as the goodly worker, both the sons of fierce Senator McCanles (Lionel Barrymore) and his faded southern-belle wife (Lillian Gish). Then, along comes Jennifer, the mixed-blood offspring of righteous Herbert Marshall and wild, amoral Tilly Losch. Jennifer's Pearl is a sensual half-breed and attractive troublemaker, who yearns for sexual and material gratification. Her entrance pushes the tragedy into full play and ends with Jennifer turning on Peck after she witnesses him shooting down Cotten without giving him a chance to draw his gun. The final sequence of the motion picture has become a classic of perverse sexuality, with Jennifer and Peck engaging in their own gun duel, and the wounded Jennifer crawling (endlessly) over rocks and dusty expanses finally to die in her lover's arms.

On May 7, 1947, *Duel in the Sun* had its New York premiere at the Capitol Theatre and thirty-eight other Loew's theatres in the metropolitan area, as well as in 261 additional cinema palaces around the country. Industry sources reasoned that Selznick wanted the public to rush in to see this much-heralded horse opera before the critics or the general public could comment adversely on the picture. Nevertheless, the critics did roast the film, with Howard Barnes *(New York Herald-Tribune)* judging it a "munificent muddle . . . it is more ponderous and tasteless than cumulatively entertaining." Jessie Zunser *(Cue)* was even less indulgent, calling it an "absurdly overblown emotional steam bath . . . frequently and comically reminiscent of the 1890 school of panting passion and asthmatic melodrama."

Selznick had promoted the film with a million-dollar publicity campaign, labeling the movie "The Picture of a Thousand Memorable Moments." The public preferred another appellation for the 138-minute epic: "Lust in the Dust," a phrase which most fittingly summed up the overriding pseudoerotic tone that Selznick had coaxed into the basic tale of an imperious rancher (Barrymore) in post-Civil War Texas fighting the encroaching railroad and grazing, land-stealing settlers. Both Bob Thomas in *Selznick* (1970) and Behlmer in *Memo from David O. Selznick* offer elaborate details of just how the almost obsessed producer-director slaved over this tremendously personal film venture to transform his Jennifer into the ultimate 1940s love goddess-femme fatale.* Selznick demanded that Dmitri Tiomkin's soundtrack score fully reflect the orgasms of passion between Jennifer and Peck. Moreover, for ultimate realism in the climactic sequence, Jennifer was covered with excessive fake blood and scratches and had to endure constant reshootings of her very painful, lingering, and agonizing crawl to her beloved (Peck).

Selznick's outrageous ballyhoo tactics paid off richly at the box office, for *Duel in the Sun* garnered, through its initial release and in the 1959 national reissue, over $11.3 million in distributors' domestic rentals, making it the most profitable Western of its time. For the fourth consecutive year, Jennifer was Oscar-nominated. She lost to Olivia de Havilland *(To Each His Own),* but Selznick had the slight consolation that he had succeeded with moviegoers, if not the critics,† in forcing the public into buying his new concept of his paramour. The actress Jennifer emerged oncamera from the sanctified and demure cocoon of her previous roles to a new genre as a supposedly fiery, glamorous, sensual, beautiful creature. For her change of character, she won the *Look* magazine Achievement Award for 1946.

On Selznick's advice, Jennifer rejected the proffered role of the unsettled girl who marries a Minnesota judge in *Cass Timberlane,* and Lana Turner inherited the part to be played opposite Spencer Tracy. Dentists in convention at New London, Connecticut, chose Jennifer as their "Enamel Girl" while the Hollywood Women's Press Club voted her the year's Most Uncooperative Actress. Meantime, Jennifer embarked on the first of several soul-searching trips to India, where she hoped to find answers to life's many questions through meditation, and thereafter she sojourned in Switzerland for a visit with the noted analytical psychologist, Carl Jung.

Her next picture added great diversification to her acting. *Portrait of Jennie* (1948), distributed through the Selznick Releasing Organization, was a dramatic fantasy of two people displaced in time and space. Eban Adams (Joseph Cotten) is an unsuccessful artist who meets Jennie (Jen-

---

*In his forced, overdone use of symbolism, Selznick had Jennifer's Pearl constantly falling to the ground, clawing and clinging to any object in sight, which was his unsubtle way of depicting the character's earthy, passionate, unbridled nature. Nothing that Selznick could do for Jennifer, however, displaced Rita Hayworth and Betty Grable as the top-level sex symbols of American cinema throughout the 1940s.

†"[Jennifer] gives occasional glints of the pathos of loneliness and heartbreak, but mostly she has to pretend to be the passion-run child of nature in loosest theatrical style" (Crowther, *New York Times*). "She over-acts at every turn of the plot, bringing a minimum of modulation to a part which finds her dishonored, the instrument of a man's murder and eventually the slayer of her lover" (Barnes, *Herald-Tribune*). Obviously, such scenes as the heated Jennifer throwing a slab of bread and jelly into lewd Peck's face, her "nude" bathtub scene, her seduction by Peck, and her symbolic use of the rifle to shoot down Peck in the finale, did not convince critics of the day that she possessed an irresistibly sensual nature.

nifer), a lonely little girl playing hopscotch in Central Park in New York City in the 1930s. "I know a song," she tells him and sings:*

Where I come from
Nobody knows;
And where I'm going
Everything goes.
The wind blows,
The sea flows—
Where I come from
Nobody knows.

Eban encounters the girl five times during the lapse of a few days or a week. Each time Jennie is older, more mature, more beautiful. Haunted and inspired by her, Eban captures the girl's ethereal beauty on canvas, thereby earning himself a place of honor in the Metropolitan Museum.†

Photographed by Joseph August, some of the film's scenes were lensed in color, some in sepia, some in black-and-white. Selznick, sensing that this offbeat drama required some gimmick to sell it to the discriminating public, decided upon a spectacular ending for the picture and rewrote the final portion of the tale told in Robert Nathan's novel, on which his film was based. In Selznick's newly conceived finale, Cotten loses the girl in a hurricane and tidal wave near a New England lighthouse. Two technical innovations were dredged up from past experimentation to be used in all first-run engagements of *Portrait of Jennie*. In the "spectacular" climax, the picture and sound effects were expanded through the utilization of a cycloramic green-tinted screen, thirty by thirty feet, and a multisound system. Hopefully the audience would feel engulfed and overwhelmed by thunder and wind. For these innovations, the film received an Oscar for special effects. However, despite these gimmicky special effects, the onlocation New York City shooting, and the Dmitri Tiomkin score (relying somewhat on Debussy's "Afternoon of a Faun"), the $2.5 million picture did not catch on with moviegoers. As *Cue* magazine perceived, "Snaring elusive fantasy is difficult under the best of conditions." (This was particularly true of the second half of the film, which was excessively episodic and rambling and could not be salvaged by the fine supporting cast: Ethel Barrymore as an art dealer, Lillian Gish as the mother superior of the convent that the young Jennifer attended, Henry Hull as a Cape Cod seadog, Albert Sharpe as a Third Avenue, Manhattan, saloon-keeper, and landlady Florence Bates.) *Variety* pinpointed the film's aesthetic faults on another level: ". . . its very spiritual quality, no matter how tastefully done, lacks the earthy warmth needed to spellbind."

*Dubbed by Martha Mears.
† The actual portrait of Jennie, painted by Robert Brackman, did hang for a time in the Metropolitan Museum in New York.

With Ray Corrigan, John
Wayne, and Sammy McKim
(right) in NEW FRONTIER
(Rep '39)

With Ralph Byrd in the serial
DICK TRACY'S G-MEN
(Rep '39)

With William Eythe and Anne Revere in
THE SONG OF BERNADETTE (20th '43)

With fellow Oscar-winner Paul Lukas at the Academy Award Ceremonies
in Los Angeles (March 1944)

With Robert Walker and Guy Madison in
SINCE YOU WENT AWAY (UA '44)

With Joseph Cotten and Cecil Kellaway in LOVE LETTERS (Par '45)

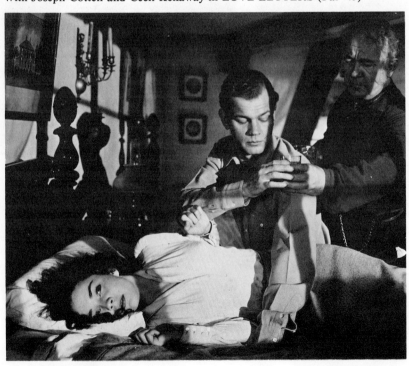

With Charles Boyer in CLUNY BROWN (20th '46)

In DUEL IN THE SUN

With Joseph Cotten in
DUEL IN THE SUN

With producer David O. Selznick at the Hollywood premiere of
DUEL IN THE SUN (Selznick Releasing '46)

414

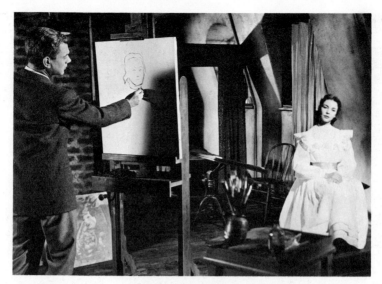

With Joseph Cotten in PORTRAIT OF JENNIE (Selznick Releasing '48)

With Wally Cassell, Gilbert Roland, and David Bond in WE WERE STRANGERS (Col '49)

With Frederic Tozere and Van Heflin in MADAME BOVARY (MGM '49)

In GONE TO EARTH *(The Wild Heart)* (British Lion '50)

On a hospital tour in Korea (June 1951)

As for Jennifer's interpretation of the elfinlike Jennie, the major reviewers qualified their endorsements of her performance. "There is a grave sincerity about her portrayal which gives a bit of plausibility to a drama of the spirit" (Howard Barnes, *New York Herald-Tribune*). "[She] is beaming and breathless most of the time as this oddly literal wraith" (Bosley Crowther, *New York Times*). The lukewarm critical reaction to Jennifer was indeed off, for most sources consider this performance to be one of her best jobs onscreen. Although she was ignored by the Academy in the Oscar race, Spain's Triunfo Award was bestowed on her, as was *Photoplay* magazine's Gold Medal. The readers of *Cine Monde,* a French film publication, voted her the most popular and best foreign actress of the year.

At this time, a number of Selznick's contract stars were regular performers at the La Jolla Playhouse in La Jolla, California. After completion of *Portrait of Jennie,* Jennifer appeared there in the title role of *Serena Blandish* with Selznick's enthusiastic advice and encouragement.* While the once masterful executive was dallying with Jennifer's involvement in this minor-league stage production, his recently organized film company, Selznick Releasing Organization, was promptly falling to shreds.†

In need of ready capital, and perhaps sensing that she might do better under another producer's aegis, Selznick loaned Jennifer to Columbia for John Huston's *We Were Strangers* (1949), which was based on bits from Robert Sylvester's novel *Rough Sketch*. In the film, as China Valdes, a Cuban patriot in 1933 Havana, Jennifer hopes to avenge her brother's murder by joining dedicated anarchists John Garfield and Gilbert Roland in a daring plot to dig a tunnel into a cemetery. The valiant group hope to assassinate corrupt, high-ranking Cuban government officials when they visit the grave of a compatriot whom the rebels have already murdered. The whole outlandish plan backfires when the dead official is buried elsewhere. A fierce, climactic gun battle with the police concludes the picture, hopefully leaving the viewer with the "optimistic" thought that from the tragedy of isolated revolutionary failures comes long-run success.

Unlike Huston's *The Treasure of the Sierra Madre* (Warner Bros., 1948), *We Were Strangers* did not find its proper niche in the post-World War II film market. "All that is wanting in the production," observed Howard Barnes *(New York Herald-Tribune),* "is genuine meaning in the midst

*Ruth Gordon and Hugh Sinclair had appeared on Broadway in this sophisticated comedy in 1929.

†During this crucial period, Selznick had rejected Howard Hawks's *Red River* (1948), which grossed United Artists $4.35 million, and almost botched the deal with Carol Reed's British production, *The Third Man,* which did go out under the Selznick Releasing Organization banner and made a tidy profit.

It was also at this time that Selznick planned to make joint ventures with the British-based Sir Alexander Korda; one project was to be a new version of Thomas Hardy's *Tess of the D'Urbervilles,* to be filmed in color and directed by Carol Reed.

of violence and pictorial beauty." With her dark hair cut short for the first time onscreen, Jennifer managed to look beautiful even when well smudged from the tunnel digging. However, the mixture of her unconvincing native accent and the obtrusive love affair between her and Garfield mangled her characterization and detracted from the picture's effectiveness as stark drama. "There is neither understanding nor passion in the stiff, frigid creature she achieves. And instead of making apparent some plausible reasons for a tragic romance amid all this strain and mortification she makes the idea repulsive and absurd" (Bosley Crowther, *New York Times*). Furthermore, the film's best performances were those of the supporting cast, especially Gilbert Roland as the peasant-poet and Pedro Armendariz as the sinister, foppish chief of police. There was an especially effective interlude in which slant-eyed Jennifer proceeds to allow the villainous Armendariz to make love to her while she plies him with liquor, eventually succeeding in making the greedy brute pass out. Plaudits also went to cinematographer Russell Metty, who did a superlative job of creating an aura of claustrophobia within the tunnel where so much of the story took place.

MGM had long considered filming its own rendition of Gustave Flaubert's 1857 novel, *Madame Bovary*.* At one point it was considered a potential vehicle for Greta Garbo, but in the end it was Jennifer who portrayed the famed role in a shiny 1949 Metro production directed by Vincente Minnelli, a technician celebrated for his handling of screen musicals. It was well known that Flaubert's daring romantic novel had caused a scandal upon publication in France and that the writer had had to defend his work in court against charges of "contributing to public immorality." Although mores had greatly changed in the intervening ninety-two years, cautious MGM still felt it obligatory to cloak the salacious account within the framework of Flaubert (James Mason)† on trial for having penned the book and defending his work of art by relating the novel's content.

As Madame Bovary, Jennifer, for the first time, was required to come to grips with a famous literary character whose qualities were well known to a relatively large segment of the public. As depicted by Flaubert, Emma Bovary is an overly sentimental young woman whose unrealistic romantic fantasies on life and love cause her to become dissatisfied with her dull husband and to fall into two hopeless love affairs, and,

---

*Pola Negri had starred in a 1934 French film version directed by Jean Renoir, one of several adaptations of the illustrious romance.

† Mason had first been offered the Rodolphe Boulanger role, but declined it as not suitable for his nature, agreeing instead to be the Flaubert character. In retrospect, Mason has said, "it was absolutely impossible to make that story, as one had always thought . . . particularly if you have a rather disjointed American cast, and if you do it at MGM studios where there was no individual style. . . . it's always been impossible and it remains impossible to translate a story with a French background into English speaking terms."

finally, to die from a self-administered dose of arsenic. In the Walter Plunkett-designed costumes, Jennifer was lovely, enhancing the nineteenth-century surroundings created by Cedric Gibbons and Jack Martin Smith. However, as the impressionable "heroine" yearning for a Prince Charming in a Norman village, Jennifer emerged more willful than tortured. Part of the blame goes to Robert Ardrey's conventional script and to Minnelli's bland direction. Equally debilitating was the fact that she was surrounded by three extremely competent leading men: Van Heflin as the doltish country-doctor spouse unable to cope with his temperamental, yearning wife; Louis Jourdan as the slick patrician who is too shrewd, suave, and quick-witted to retain interest in the country lady once he has made a conquest; and Christopher Kent as the impoverished, pitiful law clerk, a weakling who is too passive to declare his love for her. Like Metro's other oversized adult-classic picturization of the year, *That Forsyte Woman, Madame Bovary* failed to impress the average movie attendee.

While *Madame Bovary* was Jennifer's third straight misfire on the American film market, she did receive some recognition from abroad for her celluloid histrionics. She was selected as Best Foreign Actress of the Year by the Paris Film Festival and was presented with the Film Francais Grand Prix des Directeurs de Cinema by theatre managers of France and North Africa. She also received a special Accomplishment Award from *Fortune* magazine.

In January 1949, it was announced in New York that Irene Mayer Selznick's divorce had become final. Irene Selznick, who had never approved of Jennifer even when the latter was still wed to Robert Walker, was totally different from Jennifer in that she was independent, with, as Hedda Hopper observed: "a brain like a man, plus sound business sense and an instinct for the theatre. She was also bossy like her father."

While Selznick had succeeded in shedding a spouse, he was occupied in early 1949 with clearing up his snowballing business incumbrances. Hard-pressed for funds, he leased the services of several of his star stable (Jennifer, Joseph Cotten, Shirley Temple, Gregory Peck, Louis Jourdan, Betsy Drake, Rory Calhoun) to Warner Bros., and also turned over reissue rights to many of the Selznick classics (but not *Gone with the Wind,* which MGM controlled) to Eagle-Lion. In March 1949, Jennifer left for Europe, preparatory to beginning work on a new film, *Gone to Earth* (1950). When she landed at Shannon Airport in Ireland, accompanied by Anita Colby, she was in a state of collapse, and was diagnosed as suffering from fatigue. By mid-summer, Selznick had completed liquidation of his corporate accounts, and he joined the recuperated Jennifer in Zurich. He had already told the press, "I don't know exactly when or where we will be married, but it will be some time before the end of summer, when we can get a breather from our work."

Jennifer, having known the high-pressure Selznick for several years, was not sure that marriage between them was the best idea. But Selznick was not a man easily shaken, particularly when the entire film industry and the fan-magazine-reading public were fully aware of his devotion to Jennifer. He continued his courtship aboard a thirty-three-ton yacht, *Manona,* while cruising in the Mediterranean, and finally convinced Jennifer to say yes to his persistent marriage proposal. On July 13, 1949, Jennifer (age thirty) was married to Selznick (age forty-seven) aboard the yacht by the British captain of the ship. The couple's witnesses were Mr. and Mrs. Louis Jourdan and Mr. and Mrs. Leland Hayward. Later that day, to make sure that the marriage was legal, the couple was remarried at the Genoa city hall. They honeymooned aboard the *Manona* and a week later arrived in London to begin work on *Gone to Earth.* As they debarked from their plane, British reporters elbowed in to question them, but got no more than polite smiles for their efforts. Selznick placed his arm around her waist and guided her through the crowd. Jennifer had always detested interviews, and even now, when she was a full-fledged star, she flinched even at routine questions. She left the talking up to her number-one press agent—her husband and mentor. Her attitude can perhaps best be explained in her own words; in 1962 she said: "Why must I talk about myself? Why must I play the game? When they make actors or actresses they should give them that other ingredient—the one that enables them to cope with publicity. They left that out of me." When asked if shyness had anything to do with her reluctance to talk, she retorted, "No, I'm not shy. To be in this business, you have to have basic self-confidence. Just call me eccentric." After they were wed, Selznick sent her fresh flowers every day as a gesture of his devotion to her. His monthly florist bill was said to be $1,000.

Gone to Earth, based on the Mary Webb novel, was written, produced, and directed by Michael Powell and Emeric Pressburger, with Selznick and Alexander Korda serving as executive producers. It was completed in time for the Selznicks to spend Christmas of 1949 in Hollywood with Jennifer's sons.

The 110-minute *Gone to Earth* received abysmal trade notices when screened in England, and the picture was not distributed in the United States until 1952, and then by RKO, under the title of *The Wild Heart.* By this time, Selznick, aided by director Rouben Mamoulian, had made several alterations, including the deletion of twenty-eight minutes, hoping to make it more appetizing to American audiences. (For first-run engagements in the United States the widescreen effect was utilized for the hunt scenes.) It still was no go, and the movie was labeled as "an exasperating brew of dank melodrama and shimmering picture loveliness." Once again, Jennifer was given a rather incredible part to portray: the elfin daughter of a Shropshire beekeeping coffin-maker (Esmond Knight) who also plays the harp. Since the death of her Gypsy mother, her father has paid little attention to her, and she has grown up somewhat wild, with rabbits, a jackdaw, a one-eyed cat, and other lost or maimed animals as her only friends. Fate brings the superstitious girl into contact with the notorious local squire, Jack Reddin (David Farrar), and even after she weds virtuous minister Edward Marston (Cyril Cusack), she hankers so much for the squire-huntsman that she runs off with Farrar to satisfy her animal passions. Eventually the untutored girl realizes her error and returns to Cusack. Nevertheless, in the tradition of morality-prone films, she must be punished for her transgressions, and she pays for her behavior with her life, dying with her pet fox (Foxy) in her arms. Photographed in glorious Technicolor, Jennifer never appeared more appealing oncamera, but the combination of the tattered storyline, her phony Welsh accent, and the slow pacing detracted from the possible merits of her performance. As Selznick learned to his dismay, pretty scenery was not enough to engender audience interest in a clinker.

Paramount had long owned the screen rights to *Sister Carrie,* Theodore Dreiser's controversial novel of 1900. In the early 1930s, when Sylvia Sidney was starring in picturizations of Dreiser's *An American Tragedy* (1931) and *Jennie Gerhardt* (1933), both at Paramount, it had been rumored that she would headline the movie version of *Sister Carrie.* A decade later, the studio planned to film the property with Ginger Rogers, but the star's platinum-blonde mother, Mrs. Lela E. Rogers, forbade her obedient daughter to participate in a film whose theme was "Communistic." Shortened to *Carrie* (so no potential filmgoer would think it was a nun story), the William Wyler-produced-directed feature went before the cameras in August 1950. Only at this juncture did Wyler learn that Jennifer was pregnant and that she had hid the news for fear of losing the prize part.* Laurence Olivier, who had recently been knighted, was selected instead of such other possible choices as Kirk Douglas, Gary Cooper, James Stewart, and Cary Grant (who rejected the role) because Wyler felt that only a Britisher could convey the oily-smooth sophistication demanded for the character of George Hurstwood. Olivier accepted the part largely because his wife, Vivien Leigh, would be in Hollywood at the same time to film *A Streetcar Named Desire* (Warner Bros., 1951). Although he was to be top-billed over Jennifer, Olivier insisted that his title not be used in the film's publicity or onscreen credits. What made *Carrie* a unique Jennifer Jones screen venture was that Selznick gave Wyler his solemn word not to interfere in this production, a film in which he had no direct connection. Surprisingly, the usually omnipresent producer kept his promise.

*In Axel Madsen's *William Wyler* (1973), the director recalls that he told Jennifer that she would only have to wear the period corsetry in long or medium shots. "But she always had herself strapped in. Just watching her made me uncomfortable. She lost the baby after the picture. How much the strapping of her waist had to do with it, I don't know."

Translated to the screen by Ruth and Augustus Goetz,* *Carrie* emerged "smooth, if superficial" *(New Yorker)*. The storyline finds Jennifer a poor turn-of-the-century farmgirl who journeys to Chicago to find a respectable husband. Instead, she encounters and lives with good-time Charley Drouet (Eddie Albert) until she falls in love with a "proper gent," restaurant manager Hurstwood (Olivier). Olivier, however, is weak-kneed and henpecked by his wife (Miriam Hopkins). He steals money and takes Jennifer to New York, and, when he fails in his endeavors, she becomes a moderately successful stage actress. Near the film's beginning, Olivier inquires of her whether she really loves the man with whom she is currently living. Her reply is prophetic: "When you're poor it gets all mixed up. You like the people who are good to you."

As with the previous *Madame Bovary*, Jennifer was not at her best coping with a "heroine" from a literary classic. In addition, The Goetzs' screenplay transformed Carrie Meeber into a weak, sentimentalized shadow of Dreiser's original concept, and made her too sympathetic (e.g., when she rejects Olivier at the finale it is made to seem an act of sacrifice rather than a display of selfish whimsy). Wyler, who had urged solid performances from such cinema stars as Merle Oberon *(These Three—* United Artists, 1936), Bette Davis *(Jezebel—*Warner Bros., 1938; *The Letter—*Warner Bros., 1940), and Myrna Loy *(The Best Years of Our Lives—* RKO, 1946), could not seem to coax a convincing performance from Jennifer. "Miss Jones," said one annoyed critic, "seems to spend a good deal of her time leaning against door frames, a prey to doubts and fighting back tears." The fact that Jennifer was stunning in her Edith Head costumes was hardly adequate consolation. *Carrie* was not released until the summer of 1952, almost two years after its completion, and a year after another Theodore Dreiser venture had been very successfully picturized (George Steven's remake of *An American Tragedy*, entitled *A Place in the Sun*). The latter film received the lion's share of publicity from Paramount and garnered all the accolades from critics and public.

Meanwhile, in 1951, at Selznick's urging, Jennifer took what he prescribed as a rest, but she quietly made a tour to South Korea to visit with over four thousand wounded American soldiers near the front lines. Her unselfish and unpublicized mission earned her an award from *Stars and Stripes*, a special citation from the American Red Cross, and a gold medal from General James Van Fleet, field commander of the United Nations forces.

At 8:30 P.M. on August 29, 1951, a fire rescue squad was summoned to the Hollywood home of Robert Walker. His housekeeper had telephoned the psychiatrist who had been treating him for eighteen months. She said that the MGM actor was so drunk and out of control of his faculties

---

* The scenarist couple had prepared the equally difficult screenplay of *The Heiress* (Paramount, 1949) for Wyler.

that she did not know how to cope with him. Walker was injected with sodium amytal to calm him down, but minutes later his breathing failed. The firemen were unable to revive him and he was pronounced dead at 10:00 P.M.* Jennifer flew in from Europe, where she was vacationing with Selznick, to be with her sons. She thought it best that they not attend the Utah funeral because she wanted them "to remember their father as he was."

Later in 1951, Jennifer resumed work with a loan-out to Twentieth Century-Fox as *Ruby Gentry* (1952). The trade ads proclaimed that in this King Vidor-directed feature she was "A Siren Who Wrecked a Whole Town—Man by Man—Sin by Sin." Jennifer was never more tantalizing oncamera than as the sexy swamp girl from Braddock, North Carolina, who seeks revenge when her muscular boyfriend (Charlton Heston) weds a more respectable girl (Phyllis Avery). As the flashback tale continues, the movie audience witnesses Jennifer becoming "friends" with Karl Malden and his bedridden wife (Josephine Hutchinson). When the latter dies, Jennifer and the self-made, wealthy Malden wed. Later Malden is accidentally killed in a boating accident, and Jennifer has the bittersweet joy of foreclosing on one of Heston's mortgages. Still further on in the hoary tale, her mentally disturbed religious-fanatic brother (James Anderson) murders Heston in a swamp clash-out, and Jennifer thereafter is forced to kill Anderson.

The love scenes in *Ruby Gentry* between Jennifer and Heston were some of the most torrid ever set on film, helped a great deal by Russel Harlan's upshot-angled cinematography, which accentuated Jennifer's sensuality. Whether in skin-tight Levi's or occasionally viewed in Valentina-designed gowns, Jennifer conveyed all the sexuality that Selznick had endeavored (somewhat in vain) to inject into *Duel in the Sun*. The musical score for the picture was composed by Heinz Roemheld who utilized a single harmonica to emphasize the love theme, a technique responsible for the emergence of "Ruby" as a popular recording hit. Later, when lyrics were added, the song was recorded by more than twenty best-selling vocalists.

Co-producer-director Vidor later offered his opinion of Jennifer's screen persona: " . . . it was necessary to start her in the right mood every day by telling her the story of her part up to that moment. . . . Whenever she played a scene with a feeling of insecurity, it showed in some strange tricks she did with her mouth. It was the director's responsibility to make certain that this didn't happen . . . "

In Rome, Selznick found a more economical base of operations and negotiated with Vittorio De Sica, in 1953, to direct a picture for him called *Terminal Station*. Selznick, who was now only concerned with promul-

---

*At the time Walker was in the midst of filming Leo McCarey's *My Son, John* (Paramount, 1952).

gating Jennifer's career, believed that De Sica, one of the best of the neo-realist Italian directors, could accomplish with Jennifer what Roberto Rossellini had failed to do with his own protégée (and wife), Ingrid Bergman; that is, create an arty, commercial film success. Needless to say, the mixture of the highly organized, bureaucratic-oriented Selznick and the inspirational, off-the-cuff De Sica did not blend, leading to a badly mishmashed drama. After the film's fitful debut in Italy, Selznick stepped into the situation to a far fuller extent than before. He demonstrated his salesmanship of old by convincing Columbia to pay him $500,000 for the celluloid project. Thereafter he excised the film of what he considered to be excess footage. When the restructuring brought the film to a brief sixty-three minutes, it was decided that a specially Rome-lensed interlude, hostessed-sung by Patti Page, should be added to the picture to increase its running time.*

Indiscretion of an American Wife, the U.S. release title for *Terminal Station,* premiered in America at New York's Astor Theatre on June 25, 1954. The internationally famous De Sica received few critical plaudits for his stark study of a dramatic farewell in Rome's crowded railroad station. Despite Selznick's careful cutting, it was obvious that the Italian director was far more interested in capturing vignettes of local color than in the main story. The plot concerned Philadelphia matron Jennifer, who is concluding her Italian holiday and finding it difficult to conclude her passionate romance with an overly intense Italian (Montgomery Clift). When the police catch the couple in a deserted railroad coach in a compromising position, and the lovers are dragged off to the police station, it seems that fate may be deciding their future. But they obtain their freedom and after a protracted farewell, bid one another a turgid goodbye.

Considering the inadequacies of this film, Jennifer, surprisingly, received rather good reviews. "Miss Jones makes it look as though a female with decent and generous instincts is trying to work herself out of a tough spot. In the course of an hour, she makes a woman of little sympathy look much better" (Bosley Crowther, *New York Times*). *Variety* applauded her courage in shedding her glamorous image to suit the role, "managing to be just a bit dowdy and matronly in her Christian Dior costumes, as would be the character she portrays."

Jennifer remained in Italy for her next role as a blonde in *Beat the Devil* (United Artists, 1954), shot in the remote Italian town of Ravello. The initial script for the John Huston-directed feature was so bad that Bogart, who had long owned the screen rights to the James Helvick novel, stated in his own concise way that, "It stinks." At Selznick's bidding, Huston, who had assisted Anthony Veiller and Peter Viertel in drafting the initial scenario, called in Truman Capote for a rewrite job. Capote

*The songstress, shown on a Roman balcony, sang two songs, "Autumn in Rome" and "Indiscretion," while oncamera were interspersed scenic shots of Italy's famed metropolis.

later claimed that when filming began, only he and Huston knew what the story was all about, "And I have a suspicion that John wasn't too clear about it."

In this elaborate shaggy-dog tale, Bogart, Robert Morley, and Peter Lorre (in a parody of Bogart's *The Maltese Falcon* [Warner Bros., 1941] and several other of his screen gangster capers) are after uranium; Jennifer is after Bogart; Gina Lollobrigida is after Jennifer's dour, prim husband (Edward Underdown); and the police are after them all. Upon initial release, the $1 million picture was a box-office dud, but most critics found it delightful. *Time* magazine called it a "sort of screwball classic." Howard Thompson *(New York Times)* rated it "a pointedly roguish and conversational spoof."

After a rash of portraying oversexed, neurotic screen ladies, Jennifer was in her element essaying a charming, habitual liar, who finds that she has a mad crush on freewheeling Bogart. At one point, the supreme prevaricator, who casually tells one whopper after another, confesses to her would-be lover (Bogart), "I was falling in love with you and couldn't let you think I was a nobody." When she later informs Bogart, "I am experiencing something rare and beautiful. I shall not deny it," both he and the viewer are at a loss to know whether the lady of untruths is finally being honest. Interestingly, Jennifer, the pure Bernadette of the 1940s, and Lollobrigida, the Italian sexpot of the 1950s, displayed good rapport on-camera. When the motley group is captured by Arab police, nervous Lollobrigida asks Jennifer, "Do you think they'll torture us?" Jennifer replies, "Just let them try. *I'm* a British subject." At the finale it is dimwitted, bogus Underdown who has grabbed title to the uranium holdings in British East Africa. He telegraphs to bewildered Jennifer that he is willing to overlook her extraordinary past behavior if she immediately joins him in Africa *and* if she arrives with a hot water bottle.

As *Time* magazine aptly noted, Jennifer "does the best with the best part—she manages to catch the mystic fervor of the truly creative liar." *Variety* commended the actress for "a vivacious study."

Over the years, *Beat the Devil* has gained a special spot in cinema history as one of the more artful examples of screen satire. Perhaps *Punch* magazine back in 1954 expressed it best when, in reviewing the film, it decided, "Not a thought-out-picture or a very important one, but intelligent, refreshing, unusual and extremely entertaining."

On August 12, 1954, some six months after *Beat the Devil* had opened simultaneously in New York and around the country, Jennifer gave birth to a seven-pound, eight-ounce girl, in Santa Monica, California. Named Mary Jennifer Selznick* she was to be the couple's first and only child,

*Using only the name Mary Jennifer, she is now studying acting at the Uta Hagen-Herbert Berghof School of Acting in Manhattan.

but each were parents for the third time. Jennifer was thirty-five and Selznick was fifty-two.

Jennifer encountered a bad professional setback on December 21, 1954, when she made her New York stage debut as Isabel Archer in the ANTA production, *Portrait of a Lady*. In a badly conceived three-act dramatization of Henry James's novel, William Archibald attempted to convey in theatrical terms what James had written of expatriate Americans in 1870s Europe. With settings by William and Jean Eckart, gowns by Cecil Beaton, staging by Jose Quintero, and a cast that included Cathleen Nesbitt, Douglas Watson, Barbara O'Neil, Eric Fleming, and Halliwell Hobbes, the show seemingly had everything going for it, except for a good, solid script. "Miss Jones does her level best to pump something besides gilly water and lavender flowers into this work and it must be a tremendous task. She has life, she has color and warmth and desperation. But the vehicle burdens her" (Whitney Bolton, *New York Morning Telegraph*). Louis Sheaffer of the *Brooklyn Daily Eagle* was a bit more severe in his judgment, "Not that she is complete mistress of the stage or rises with much force to her dramatic moments, but her lyrical vulnerable quality is suited to the role and, of course, her radiant looks don't hurt any." The show folded after only seven performances, and Selznick abandoned plans to film the venture. Jennifer confirmed that the project had been an exhausting disaster, "I was bleeding from every pore. I wanted to run off to Tahiti and hide."

Obviously, Jennifer's career badly needed a shot in the arm at this point. Selznick cornered director Joshua Logan at a Hollywood party and suggested strongly that he use Jennifer for the role of Madge Owens in *Picnic* (Columbia, 1955). Logan replied firmly that his film was going before the cameras in a very few days and that Columbia contractee Kim Novak was definitely slated for the part at Harry Cohn's orders. Besides, he felt that it was too late to make such a major cast change.

Then, through industry manipulation, Selznick convinced Twentieth Century-Fox executive Buddy Adler to hire Jennifer on a three-film deal. Her first assignment proved her most effective. It was an adaptation of Dr. Han Suyin's *Love Is a Many Splendored Thing* (1955), directed by Henry King, who had helmed *The Song of Bernadette*. As contrived for the screen by scenarist John Patrick, the 102-minute color and CinemaScope feature was nothing more than "dew-dappled romance" (*New York Times*), but thanks to splendid photography by Leon Shamroy and a pop-hit title song by Sammy Fain and Paul Francis Webster, the movie went on to become a $4-million-grossing entry. This film helped to give Jennifer true status at the studio where blonde Marilyn Monroe was queen.

Within the story, Jennifer appears as Dr. Han Suyin, a Eurasian widow living in Hong Kong who meets sun-tanned, fingernail-biting war correspondent Mark Elliot (William Holden). She falls in love with him, but cannot wed him because his wife refuses to grant him a divorce. When Holden is sent to Korea to cover the war action, Jennifer is sustained by his many letters of love. After his death she receives his last letter, containing the words, "Life's greatest tragedy is not to be loved."

Despite, or perhaps because of, the film's banality, which weakened the real essence and impact of the original novel, Jennifer made a strong impression as the mixed-blood professional woman, who not only must cope with an illicit romance, but come to terms with her racial origins and her loyalties to her "people" behind the Bamboo Curtain. "Her transformation from efficient doctor to passionate woman has the proper hesitancy and never for one moment hints a wrong note. Miss Jones' accomplishment in a very difficult part is quite remarkable. . . . Her love scenes with Holden sizzle without ever being cheap or awkward" (*Variety*).

Love Is a Many Splendored Thing, paired with another Fox Cinema-Scope travelog-romance hit, *Three Coins in a Fountain* (1954), would be reissued at least three times before being leased for television showings. In 1966, Sidney Glazier, Han Suyin's son-in-law, announced that the property would become a Broadway musical. It never did, but in 1967 the title showed up as the basis of a short-lived CBS-TV soap opera. None of these offshoots detracted from or supplanted the memory of Jennifer standing on the lofty hillside overlooking Hong Kong harbor, waiting for the real (and later the dream-fulfillment) image of Holden to appear racing up the incline to embrace her.

The tearjerker *Good Morning, Miss Dove* was Jennifer's second 1955 release for Twentieth Century-Fox. With Frances Gray Patton's novel as a basis, and bearing in mind the success MGM had in 1939 with *Goodby Mr. Chips*,* director Henry Koster set out to create a sentimental image of a middle-aged frump of a teacher with whom any filmgoer could immediately identify as a peer figure from his/her own past. By the use of constant flashbacks the viewer learns that Jennifer had been a boarding-school-bred girl all set to wed Marshall Thompson, when it was discovered that her late banker father had embezzled over $10,000 from the savings institution of which he was then president. She immediately decides that she must save the family honor and repay the theft. In so doing she loses her beau and finds herself ensnared in a life of teaching, an occupation which she initially finds distateful. As the years pass, she becomes set in her staid ways, but gains pleasure in watching the maturing of her former pupils. As the fifty-two-year-old present-day Miss Dove, Jennifer lies in her hospital bed awaiting a crucial operation. She en-

---

*Twentieth Century-Fox had some degree of success with Claudette Colbert's *Remember the Day* (1941) about a self-sacrificing teacher; while MGM had created a dud in *Her Twelve Men* (1954) about prep-school teacher Greer Garson.

counters many former students, including Robert Stack (now a doctor), Peggy Knudson (now a nurse), Kipp Hamilton (Stack's wife, who is about to give birth to a child), Chuck Connors (currently a police officer), Jerry Paris (presently a playwright), and Edward Firestone (a small-time crook who breaks out of jail just to see how his old teacher is doing).

In the tradition of well-constructed soap opera, *Good Morning, Miss Dove* ends on a cheery note. Jennifer's operation is a success and she can look forward to at least thirteen more years of shaping youngsters' personalities before she retires. The picture concludes with a holiday at Cedar Grove School to celebrate Miss Dove's good luck. As the film finishes, physician Stack turns to leave her hospital room, bows, and says, "Good morning, Miss Dove."

Jennifer retorts, "Good morning, Thomas." For the first time, the severe, conservative schoolmarm has smiled.

" . . . her performance is a solid rock in a sea of jello," reported William K. Zinsser (*New York Herald-Tribune*). "If her performance lacks variety this is perhaps in part due to the apparent determination of Mr. Koster and his associates that Miss Dove leave no problem unresolved."

Just as Martha Scott had undergone an aging process as the midwestern teacher in *Cheers for Miss Bishop* (United Artists, 1941), Jennifer's role encompasses the great contrast of her as the young, carefree rich man's daughter and later, thanks to a sterling makeup job, as the stolid, disciplined, middle-aged citizen of Liberty Hill, who is the type of teacher who believes that trips to the water fountain during class periods are unnecessary. As she explains, "The camel is not a pretty beast, but it can go many days without water." For her performance in this sentimental, maudlin romantic drama, Jennifer was presented with the California Federation of Women's Clubs Motion Picture Award.

The following year Jennifer was reteamed with her *Duel in the Sun* co-star in *The Man in the Gray Flannel Suit,* a Darryl F. Zanuck production based on the popular Sloan Wilson novel. In director Nunnally Johnson's very commercial but bland pro-Establishment screen adaptation, Jennifer plays a success-craving suburban wife to a slick Madison Avenue businessman, Gregory Peck. In his struggle to get ahead at United Broadcasting, a New York corporation headed by power-hungry Fredric March, Peck soon finds himself burdened with phantoms from his past. Discovering that Peck had sired another woman's child during his World War II tour of duty in Italy, Jennifer becomes hysterically upset,* and a good deal of subsequent screen footage is required for a reconciliation to occur. By the finale, Jennifer has reconciled herself to the fact that no one, including her husband, is perfect, that her drive to win her relative's estate is a

---

*When that scene was shot, producer Johnson sent his own memo to Selznick, "In case your wife is too modest to tell you, I want you to know that she did a scene today that was absolutely marvelous."

mean and material goal, and that her spouse's decision to both support his illegitimate child in Rome and devote more time to his Connecticut family is sound.

In retrospect *The Man in the Gray Flannel Suit* emerges as a banal, compromising, and consistently undistinguished film. "[It] has quite a few scenes that aren't at all badly constructed, and if it were an old-fashioned serial, I'm sure we might be able to tolerate it. In one massive dose, though, it's just too damned much and I think you'd be better off taking a tranquilizer pill than going through all this just for the sake of escaping the world and its woes" (John McCarten, *New Yorker*). As for Jennifer's performance, the same reviewer observed, "As played by Jennifer Jones, the lady is so persistently surly that it's hard to imagine why the fellow [Peck] does not clear out."

Nineteen years after playing the role opposite the hopeful Robert Walker, Jennifer was again Elizabeth Barrett in MGM's plush remake of its 1934 *The Barretts of Wimpole Street*.* Both films were directed by Sidney Franklin, and it was apparent that both cinematic techniques and Franklin's directorial techniques had improved in the twenty-three years since Norma Shearer, Fredric March, and Charles Laughton starred in the steamy drawing-room drama. Filmed in England, the entire cast, save for couch-bound Jennifer, consisted of British talent, a grouping highlighted by Sir John Gielgud as the tyrannical father who has an incestuous love for his invalid poetess-daughter. Howard Thompson (*New York Times*) reported, "That rarity—a remake of an established Hollywood classic that is exceptionally fine in every respect. Jennifer Jones is a far healthier invalid heroine than was Norma Shearer and Bill Travers a bit more boyish than Fredric March, but both are excellent." Despite the fine sets and costumes, and the sturdy emoting for the widescreen camera, this time-worn drama held little general interest for the dwindling filmgoing audience at large.

By negotiating and trading with Warner Bros., plus a cash payment of $25,000, Selznick acquired the property rights to one of his favorite novels, *A Farewell to Arms,* Ernest Hemingway's World War I Romeo and Juliet

---

*Katharine Cornell first starred in Rudolf Besier's drama on February 9, 1931, at the Empire Theatre on Broadway with Brian Aherne as her co-lead. The show ran for 372 performances. She then took it on national tour with Aherne again her leading man. During the 1933-34 season she performed the show in repertoire, along with *Romeo and Juliet* and *Candida*, giving 225 performances in seventy-five cities. On this tour, Basil Rathbone played Robert Browning. At the end of the tour the company played twenty-three performances in New York. During 1944, Cornell and Aherne headed a company which toured for six months abroad, completing its engagement with an eighty-seven-performance run at the Ethel Barrymore Theatre on Broadway. The actress recorded her opening scene from the play with Aherne for Decca Records; years later she and Anthony Quayle did excerpts of the show for the Caedmon label. On April 2, 1956, Cornell was headlined in the "Producers Showcase" rendition of *The Barretts of Wimpole Street* on NBC-TV.

story.* He accepted a bid from Twentieth Century-Fox to finance and distribute the picture, and production began on a lavish scale in Italy in 1956. Universal's very popular leading man, Rock Hudson, was borrowed for the role of the American ambulance driver, while Jennifer was cast as Catherine Barkley, the ill-fated nurse who loves him.†

It was not long before demanding Selznick, thoroughly convinced that only he knew how to present his wife properly oncamera, clashed with director John Huston. With the latter's departure, Selznick blithely told the press, "In Mr. Huston, I asked for a first violinist and instead got a soloist." While a new director was being selected, second-unit helmer Andrew Marton handled the expansive mountain sequences, which utilized some 8,500 soldiers from the Italian army, and Art Fellows was promoted to directing the location scenes, which Huston had already outlined for the film. Finally, Charles Vidor was hand-picked by Selznick to take over the directorial reins, although it was Selznick who remained firmly in charge via his presence and his continual rash of demanding, meticulous, annoying memos. It must be remembered, however, that this was his first real film production since the late 1940s, and in the intervening years he had stored up a lot of excess energy concerning both the shape of Jennifer's motion-picture career and just how a film should be made.

Asked if he thought himself a severe executive, Selznick the moviemaker retorted: "Sure I am. Who the hell doesn't insist on having his own way if he is in charge. Why is this a criticism? I have a different concept of producing than other producers. Some producers are simply money men, others entrepreneurs, and others just lieutenants. But to me to produce is to make a picture. . . . There is no mystery to directing. I don't have time. Frankly it's easier to criticize another man's work than to direct myself."

When asked whether he felt he was being unduly protective of his wife, Jennifer, in this epic vehicle, he replied, "I have always protected my stars and I make no difference between her and any other star."

Another, more blunt reporter (Lloyd Shearer of *Parade* magazine) cornered the busy executive with this query: "I wonder if you would tell me what sort of girl [Jennifer] she really is?"

Selznick: "It's nobody's business what sort of woman my wife is. If I didn't think she was a fascinating woman, I wouldn't have married her and remained married to her for eight years. Jennifer is extraordinarily sensitive. I have a feeling that she was born out of her time. She has nothing in common with modern women. There is about her an almost

*It was originally filmed by Paramount in 1933 with Helen Hayes and Gary Cooper, and again in 1951, by Warner Bros., as *Force of Arms* with Nancy Olson and William Holden.
†Part of the tasteless (i.e., desperate) publicity campaign for this remake stated of Jennifer's character, "She made his temperature go down by day, and up by night."

Victorian quality, and she has a strange mystical sixth sense about things. She is extremely ambitious but for reasons completely different than those of other actresses.

"She has no interest in fame or money. All her awards, including the Oscar, have mysteriously disappeared from our house. She acts because she must act. It's a compulsion."

Regarding her well-known aversion to any sort of publicity, Selznick explained, "She has a deep, ingrained feeling that the press wants to talk about her personal life. She just doesn't like being probed. Members of the press who stick to professional topics have no trouble with Jennifer."

As the shooting time on *A Farewell to Arms* at the Cinecitta Studios in Rome lengthened inordinately, Selznick became more determined than ever that the film's love scenes (as well as the "realistic" childbirth sequence) had to be restructured and elongated to give more emphasis to the oncamera romance between Jennifer and Hudson, even at the expense of the war mood and battle scenes. By the time Selznick and Jennifer returned to the States in August 1957, Twentieth Century-Fox was in such dire financial straits that they pleaded with Selznick to rush the film into release by Christmas of that year, enticing the producer with the notion that in this manner his "masterpiece" would be eligible for the Oscars. When the 152-minute feature was premiered in Los Angeles, and later in New York City, the critics tore into the roadshow-style production with a vengeance. "If there were a supreme Bad Taste Award for Movies, *A Farewell to Arms* would win it hands down. This smutty version of Ernest Hemingway's novel will set thousands of stomachs to turning" (William K. Zinsser, *New York Herald-Tribune*).

The press and moviegoers alike were astounded that Hemingway's fondly-remembered love story had been transformed into a protracted demonstration of keyhole drama in which the viewer had to suffer through embarrassing intimacies between the lovers. The Ben Hecht screenplay, as it evolved on the wide screen, was awkward at best. For example, when Lieutenant Frederick Henry (Hudson), an American who volunteered to serve with an Italian ambulance unit during World War I, meets and romances British nurse Catherine Barkley (Jennifer), and the two soon go to a hotel room together, the seemingly prim Jennifer utters, "I never felt like a whore before." Later Jennifer expectedly becomes pregnant, but at this point she refuses to wed Hudson, for she believes the ceremony would not be a proper one while she is with child and, besides, she feels that they are already married. As reel after reel unwinds, there are presented assorted sequences of the couple (im)patiently awaiting the blessed event, almost totally ignoring the catastrophic war around them. "Little Catherine is turning cartwheels," Jennifer informs Hudson and asks him to feel for himself. After Hudson has deserted his regiment during the retreat from Caporetto, he rejoins

Jennifer at Stresa and rows his loved one across Lake Como to Switzerland. When it comes times for Jennifer to give birth to her child, Hudson takes her to the hospital and thereafter the moviegoer is punished with what has been described as "an obstetrical orgy," providing in minute clinical detail all the agonies of delivery. The final clinker occurs when, after Jennifer's stillborn son has been delivered by Caesarian section, she dies and Hudson wonders aloud: "Why, I felt him kick inside Catherine. Except that last week. Maybe he was dead then. Poor kid. Maybe this is the price you pay for sleeping together?"

As was expected, Jennifer was lambasted by the critics for being much too old for the role of the dreamy but sensual nurse, and Hudson was cursed as appearing too lethargic as her soldier-lover. The supporting cast in their thankless assignments received some praise: Vittorio De Sica as the army doctor overcome by exhaustion, Alberto Sordi as the priest who abhors the war but moves with compassion among the dying soldiers, Elaine Stritch and Mercedes McCambridge stereotype cast as tough nurses, and Oscar Homolka trying to come to grips with the one-dimensional role of a Swiss physician. It was a long distribution road before the ill-fated feature earned back some of its exorbitant production costs.*

Not only was Selznick shattered that his executive-artistic acumen had so obviously failed at the box office, but he was distraught that he had not been able to achieve for Jennifer what he had accomplished for Vivien Leigh with *Gone with the Wind*. As fate would have it, the disastrous *A Farewell to Arms* proved to be Selznick's final feature as an official producer.

However disillusioned and heartbroken Selznick may have been, and no matter what the sad status of his finances after this debacle, he continued living in the grand tradition. He, Jennifer, and their children (including Mary Jennifer and the two Walker sons) resided in the palatial Hollywood home once owned by John Gilbert. While Selznick continued to attend industry parties alone or gave out lengthy interviews on the current ills of the industry, Jennifer went deeper into seclusion. She babysat at home with a book or applied herself to yoga. She took an occasional trip to India for meditation and paid a second visit to Carl Jung in Switzerland. However, she was too late, for he was then too ill to see anyone. "If I had pressed it, I might have seen him," she wistfully admitted. "I shall always regret that I didn't try harder." In defense of her closeted studying, she states: "When Hollywood first sent out the call, I didn't have enough character to refuse. Now I really want to develop."

*It was Jennifer who had persuaded Selznick to offer Hemingway, who had no further legal rights in screen versions of this novel, some compensation for the new picturization. In a grandiose bid for publicity, Selznick granted the author $50,000 from the film's anticipated profits. Hemingway, no fan of the producer, and irate that Jennifer should be (mis)cast for the much younger heroine, dictated an obscene reply to Selznick concerning the so-called largesse.

As far back as 1951, Selznick had plans for putting F. Scott Fitzgerald's 1934 novel, *Tender Is the Night*, on film, with Vivien Leigh and Cary Grant or Laurence Olivier. Not until 1961, after he had sold the property to Twentieth Century-Fox with retention of certain approval rights, did the plans materialize, with Jennifer as Nicole Warren, the fabulously rich American who as a young girl had an incestuous relationship with her father and thereafter suffered a mental breakdown. Jason Robards, Jr., was finally selected as Dick Diver, the brilliant young psychiatrist who weds Jennifer and is destroyed in the process. Selznick had wanted Richard Burton or Peter O'Toole for Jennifer's co-star, while the actress had opted for William Holden. Fox at the time was undergoing the rumblings of an organizational shakeup due to the financial dilemma caused by the ever-mounting production costs on Elizabeth Taylor's *Cleopatra* (1963). Other films, including *Tender Is the Night*, suffered severe budget cuts to compensate for the monetary drain of that costume spectacle. It was a small miracle that producer Henry Weinstein and director Henry King were allowed to undertake some location shooting in Zurich, Switzerland, and then on the French Riviera.

If Fox contract performers Tom Ewell as an alcoholic songwriter, Jill St. John as the sparkling movie star, and Cesar Danova as the war hero gave empty performances, the 1920s set production was fortunate in having ex-Selznick stable star Joan Fontaine as Jennifer's arrogant older sister, Baby, Paul Lukas as the wise, elder psychiatrist, and, surprisingly, Jennifer and Robards in the leads. Director King had coped rather better than expected with *The Sun Also Rises* (1957), which also had key performers much too old for the portrayals of the main characters, and here he utilized the stars' maturity to good advantage. As *Time* magazine blatantly diagnosed: "King faced his biggest problem in Actress Jones, and the problem wasn't only age: in recent films the lady has limited her expressions largely to a toneless hysterical laugh and an alarming sick tic. But in *Night* she is well cast as a neurotic, and does her best work in a decade."

Although Selznick remained behind in Hollywood while the production crew and cast went abroad to capture the magnificent scenery for the widescreen, color production, he conversed with Jennifer nightly on the transatlantic telephone, as well as communicating to King and others his suggestions for the filming and, in particular, on the handling of Jennifer in the pivotal role of the woman who gathers strength while her husband (Robards) emotionally falls apart, unable to cope with his empty existence as a playboy doctor.

While *Tender Is the Night* never became a major moneymaker, the studio, like many others, was pleasantly surprised that the picture garnered so many respectable notices.* " . . . on its own filmic terms [it is]

*Some sources, such as Stanley Kauffmann *(New Republic)*, branded the film "not even an honest failure, it is a vulgarization."

a thoughtful, disturbing, and at times absorbing romantic drama" (*Variety*). Jennifer, already in her forties, and making her first film appearance in five years, received, on the whole, more laudatory critiques than could have been expected for a star whose last major acting successes were in the 1940s. Bosley Crowther (*New York Times*) judged, "Jennifer Jones is quite proficient as the mercurial Nicole, proceeding from a state of mental anguish to one of rigid and heartless self-control." Others were a bit condescending toward the actress's mannered performance, even while granting that she obtained little assist from Ivan Moffat's fuzzy screenplay or from Robards. The latter certainly did not personify the usual cinematic romantic type nor, seemingly, was he always in control of his rather ambiguous characterization. "Jennifer Jones has it a little easier with Nicole, who is meant to seem incomprehensible because psychotic, but she looks more comfortable in the last half hour when some shred of a sane dilemma confronts her" (Paul V. Beckley, *New York Herald-Tribune*). Nearly everyone, however, had to admit that in the course of the over-lengthy 146-minute production, which covered over a decade in time span, Jennifer and Fontaine were knockouts in the period costumes designed by Pierre Balmain and Marjorie Best, and in the appropriate hairstyles created by Helen Turpin and George Masters. Ironically, it was the film's saccharine title song, by Sammy Fain and Paul Francis Webster, that was nominated for an Oscar. However, it failed to win.

Selznick had suffered five heart attacks between April 1964 and June 22, 1965, when he was stricken in the Beverly Hills offices of his lawyer, Barry Brannen. He was rushed to Mount Sinai Hospital, accompanied by Jennifer, who was with him at the time. He died that day of an acute coronary. Suddenly the motion-picture industry, which had branded the man a has-been, changed its tune and, at least briefly, took time out to pay tribute to the once important film executive. At a memorial service held at Forest Lawn cemetery on June 25, Katharine Hepburn, Cary Grant (reading a speech prepared by CBS-TV head William S. Paley), and Joseph Cotten were among those who eulogized Selznick.* Jennifer was the sole beneficiary of his million-dollar insurance policy.

In September 1965, when Kim Stanley suddenly exited Joseph E. Levine's English-lensed production, *The Idol* (Embassy, 1966), Jennifer flew to London to take over the part of a medical student's (John Leyton) provocative mother who is willingly seduced on New York's Eve by her son's friend (Michael Parks).† The son, on learning of his mother's sexual experiences, accidentally drowns the seducer. The whole tawdry cellu-

---

*Prior to this event, more than two hundred persons, including Jennifer, attended the funeral service in the small Church of the Recessional at Forest Lawn that morning. Among the pallbearers were Alfred Hitchcock, William Wyler, Sam Spiegel, Samuel Goldwyn, Christopher Isherwood, and William S. Paley.

† In 1964, Shelley Winters had been mentioned to play the role.

loid affair was amply described by Judith Crist on television's "Today" show: "This maudlin tale of mommy's romance with sonny's beatnik pal doesn't even qualify for worst picture of the year, missing the perfection and purity of that category by the sheer ineptness of script, direction and performance."

What inner drive prompted Jennifer to accept the bizarre role in *The Idol* is anyone's guess. At least the film was not an overt Grand Guignol programmer like many of her contemporaries were being forced to accept in order to stay active in the film business. Just as Leyton had too strong a face and demeanor to portray a mother-dominated youth, and Parks, then riding his crest as the 1960s James Dean, was too laconic and mumbling as the American art student, so Jennifer as the near divorcée was too healthy in looks and too neurotic in mannerism to portray the carefree, subconscious temptress.* As Leo Mishkin (*New York Morning Telegraph*) deciphered the situation, "It's not the years that have exacted their toll. It's the lamentable choice of the vehicle in which Miss Jones may now be seen."

Jennifer's second try at the New York stage was eighteen performances more successful than her first. She was Georgie Elgin in the City Center Drama Company's production of Clifford Odets's *Country Girl* from September 29 to October 16, 1966.† Directed by Martin Fried, the cast included Rip Torn as the sympathetic director, Joseph Anthony as the alcoholic husband, and, in a small part, Richard Beymer, who many years before had been in the cast of *Indiscretion of an American Wife*. Jennifer, as the patient spouse of a disillusioned, drunken actor who has a chance for a big Broadway comeback, did not impress the critics. " . . . although it is a good decent country-girlified performance, it lacks the clinching opposite spark at critical moments, especially in the last act and half, when the much-abused lady is supposed to be flickering back to life" (Jerry Talmer, *New York Post*). "Miss Jones read most of her lines in a dull, listless fashion and appeared to be unconscious of the fact that she was playing with other actors" (Chauncey Howell, *Women's Wear Daily*). Other reviewers noted that the exceedingly nervous Jennifer relied too heavily on outer manifestations to convey her characterization, as when she puts on her reading glasses to show herself in an intellectual mood, and then vice versa. Perhaps Vincent Canby (*New York Times*) best summed up the situation: "It's difficult to discern which has been more unkind—time or

---

*As the nymphomania-inclined mama, Jennifer has one particularly perverse and intriguing sequence with Parks. As she nervously tugs at her blouse front, she coyly asks the blase young man, "Ever been to Corsica? . . . The sun beats on you like a hammer . . . delicious . . . frightening."

† The drama had first opened on Broadway on November 10, 1950, at the Lyceum Theatre for a 235-performance run with Uta Hagen in the title role. Grace Kelly won an Oscar for her portrayal of the part in the 1954 Paramount picture, and Maureen Stapleton later tackled the role in another Broadway revival.

this production. There is no problem about Miss Jones's looks, but her performance is cool when it should be vital and petulant when it should be angry."

Jennifer remained out of the news for over a year. Then, on November 10, 1967, after being notified of the death of her old friend, Charles Bickford, she checked into a Malibu Beach, California, motel under the name of Phylis Walker, and took four Seconal pills accompanied by several long swigs of wine. She then telephoned her psychiatrist, Dr. William Molley, at 8:45 P.M. and informed him of what she had done and, very distraught, said that she intended taking more. Police searched the Malibu area and found her late-model car parked at the top of a four-hundred-foot cliff. She lay unconscious on the beach below, her body partly submerged in the churning surf. She was pulled from the water by police sergeant Eldon Loken and given mouth-to-mouth resuscitation, and then was rushed to Mount Sinai Hospital, where her stomach was pumped. No official explanation for her attempted suicide was offered then or later. She was released from the hospital on November 12.

Obviously, without the guiding professional or personal hand of Selznick, Jennifer was losing all sense of proportion about her career at work, and her decision to appear in Sam Katzman's "major" production for American International Pictures verifies that contention. *Angel, Angel, Down We Go* was first released in the summer of 1969, heralded by the studio as the initial intellectual entry from a company that had once specialized in beach party, horror, and motorcycle pictures. Its reception was so bad that it never found its way to a major movie theatre. Then, in February 1971, it was released with a new title, *Cult of the Damned*, on the bottom half of a double horror show in Manhattan. In this incomprehensible tale involving drugs, ritual murder, perversion, and cannibalism, Jennifer played the mother of a thrill-seeking pudgy eighteen-year-old girl (Holly Near). Mama is one of the world's most beautiful women and the reputed star of more than twenty-five stag movies. She is seduced by a predatory rock singer (Jordan Christopher) and later falls to her death from an airplane piloted by her dream-world daughter. The *New York Daily News* asked, "Jennifer Jones—how did she ever get mixed up in such a weird production?" Kevin Thomas (*Los Angeles Times*) commented, "All the principals give wildly uneven performances, with Jennifer Jones perhaps faring the best. (Her fear of aging rings with decided conviction)." This farrago was to be Jennifer's last professional appearance for some time.*

In 1970, Jennifer became involved with the Los Angeles-based Manhattan Project, an organization devoted to setting up a series of Salvation Army-type residential treatment facilities for young people

---

*Jennifer was not part of the NBC-TV special *Hollywood: The Selznick Years* (March 21, 1969) narrated by Henry Fonda.

strung out on narcotics. Jennifer was a weekly volunteer worker with the charity, often having fifteen or more drug-addicted youths at her home on weekends for therapy sessions. The star was an active worker in achieving the funds and construction of a new branch near Salt Lake City, Utah.

In Los Angeles, on May 5, 1971, guests at a dinner hosted by a *Newsweek* editor included Jennifer and Norton Simon, millionaire industrialist, art collector, and unsuccessful 1970 candidate in the California senate race.* An immediate courtship began, and later Simon persuaded Jennifer to join him on a trip to Europe where he proposed to her at seven o'clock one morning in Paris. They were married at four in the morning on May 30—twenty-five days after their initial meeting—on a launch in the English Channel with a Unitarian clergyman performing the services. Jennifer was fifty-two; Simon was sixty-four. He explained their whirlwind romance by telling newsman: "There was a soul communication— great simpatico between us right from the start. I found her soul much more beautiful than her face, and her face is pretty nice." Jennifer told reporters after their wedding, "He walked me around Paris and London until I was so exhausted I couldn't resist him anymore." When asked about the impromptu wedding, Jennifer replied, "It was the most romantic thing that's ever happened to me."

In California, the Simons presently divide their residency between a Malibu beach house, once owned by director John Frankenheimer, and a more sedate Pasadena mansion. They entertain often, and the recipients of their hospitality include, along with film people, such high-ranking political figures as Henry Kissinger. While Jennifer remains distinctly out of the limelight, Simon continues to garner tremendous attention with his lavish spending on his art collection. In 1973, for example, he paid $1 million for a bronze sculpture of a Hindu deity which he freely admitted had been stolen from a temple in southern India. Proud of that acquisition, Simon also informed reporters that in the past two years he had allocated approximately 15-16 million dollars for the purchase of Asian artwork.

As for Jennifer's children by Walker, Robert Jr. made his New York stage debut in 1961 in *The Magic Weave* at the Sullivan Street Playhouse, and two years later appeared in his first film, *The Hook* (MGM). Since then he has been seen in such features as *The Ceremony* (United Artists, 1963), *Ensign Pulver* (Warner Bros., 1964), and the recent *And God Bless Grandma and Grandpa*. Once asked what his mother, Jennifer, thought of his being an actor, he replied: "She never said anything either way. She was just pleased that I was doing what I want." He made minor headlines in late 1973 when he "quit" his show-business career to

*Simon in 1970 had divorced his wife, Lucille, after thirty-seven years of marriage. One of their two sons had only recently committed suicide.

work as a $200-a-week chauffeur for a Los Angeles rental limousine company. He told the press, "For the first time I really feel like a useful person instead of a show business commodity trying to make a fortune by whatever means possible." A few weeks later he quietly returned to the world of entertainment. Jennifer's son Michael had a brief acting fling, appearing in a small role in Ivan Tors's *Namu, the Killer Whale* (United Artists, 1966).

Until May 1974, it seemed highly unlikely that the financially and emotionally well protected Jennifer would ever return to her acting craft. Then lo and behold, when Irwin Allen was assembling his star-studded cast for *The Towering Inferno* (1974), a co-production of Twentieth Century-Fox and Warner Bros., Jennifer was signed on for the co-starring role of Lisolette, the widow. The John Guillermin-directed action spectacle concerns a sudden fire which engulfs a 132-story skyscraper in San Francisco, with the crux of the fiery tale concerning the assorted types of humanity caught in the blazing structure. The fact that Norton Simon is among the biggest independent stockholders in Twentieth Century-Fox may well have had something to do with Jennifer's surprise screen return to her old studio.

In the midst of the deluge of giant disaster films, *The Towering Inferno,* which debuted in late December 1974, struck the proper response with the thrilled public. Even the picky Vincent Canby *(New York Times)* had to admit, "Movies like *The Towering Inferno* appear to have been less directed than physically constructed. This one is overwrought and silly in its personal drama, but the visual spectacle is first rated." As for Jennifer, she looked anything but matronly as the widow Lisolette, who has more of a function in the feature than higher-billed Faye Dunaway (as architect Paul Newman's mistress). One could scarcely believe Jennifer when her character remarks to charming con artist Fred Astaire, "These days I don't worry what time a man shows up [for a date] but if he arrives at all." Garbed in a diaphanous white outfit, Miss Jones ran through her paces with far less nervousness than she had exhibited in most of her recent screen experiences. In fact, not since *Duel in the Sun* has Jennifer had such a physically demanding part. Within the contrived storyline, she is forced to crawl midst the burnt-out wreckage of the skyscraper in her bid to stay alive after the holocaust. When, after surmounting this obstacle course, she later meets her grisly demise, there is genuine sympathy from a shocked audience. The *Hollywood Reporter* noted of her efforts, "Jennifer Jones, looking fit and attractive, not only gets to play romantic scenes . . . but also struggles gamefully through tough physical ordeals."

Even if Jennifer had not elected to return to face the cameras in *The Towering Inferno,* it is unlikely that her contributions to the cinema would or could be forgotten. Her films still grace TV's late, late shows, and many of her Selznick ventures are currently in theatrical re-release.

Moreover, a sketched scene from *Duel in the Sun* has been utilized by a New York-based custom wallcovering firm as part of a new design, "the first wallcovering dedicated to Hollywood's Golden Years—the Forties." In the section devoted to the Western film, there is David Croland's childlike drawing of a cowboy (apparently Gregory Peck) standing over a feminine form on the ground (apparently Jennifer). Behind them, just so there will be no doubt as to the film depicted, the sun is shown large and aglow. Jennifer, thus represented, will apparently adorn the walls of all those who buy this wallcovering, at least for a time—a dubious tribute to one of the most radiant, enigmatic screen figures of the 1940s.

Feature Film Appearances

As Phylis Isley:

NEW FRONTIER (Rep., 1939) 56 M.

Associate producer, William Berke; director, George Sherman; screenplay, Betty Burbridge, Luci Ward; music, William Lava; production manager, Al Wilson; camera, Reggie Lanning; editor, Tony Martinelli.

John Wayne (Stony Brooke); Raymond Hatton (Rusty Joslin); Ray Corrigan (Tucson Smith); Phylis Isley (Celia); Eddy Waller (Major Braddock); Sammy McKim (Stevie); LeRoy Mason (Gilbert); Harrison Greene (Proctor); Reginald Barlow (Judge Lawson); Burr Caruth (Doc Hall); Dave O'Brien (Jason); Hal Price (Sheriff); Jack Ingram (Harmon); Bud Osborne (Dickson); Charles (Slim) Whitaker (Turner); Bob Burns (Fiddler); Bob Reeves, Frank Ellis, Walt LaRue (Dance Extras); Jody Gilbert (Woman at Dance); Oscar Gahan (Musician); Charles Murphy (Zeke, the Mailman); Herman Hack (Jim, the Construction-Wagon Driver); George Plues (Henchman); Wilbur Mack (Dodge).

DICK TRACY'S G-MEN (Rep., 1939) 15 chapters

Associate producer, Robert Beche; directors, William Witney, John English; based on the comic strip by Chester Gould; screenplay, Barry Shipman, Franklyn Adreon, Rex Taylor, Ronald Davidson, Sol Shor; music, William Lava; camera, William Nobles.

Ralph Byrd (Dick Tracy); Irving Pichel (Nicholas Zarnoff); Ted Pearson (Steve Lockwood); Phylis Isley (Gwen Andrews); Walter Miller (Robal); George Douglas (Sandoval); Kenneth Harlan (FBI Chief Clive Anderson); Robert Carson (Scott); Julian Madison (Foster); Ted Mapes (G-Man Dan Murchison); William Stahl, Robert Wayne (G-Men); Joe McGuinn (Tommy, a Henchman); Kenneth Terrell (Ed, a Henchman); Harry Humphrey (Warden Stover); Harrison Greene (Baron); Jack Roberts (Lennie Slade); Lloyd Ingraham (Judge Stoddard); Charles K. French, Stanley Price (Doctors); Tristram Coffin, Perry Ivans (Three Powers Representatives); Joe Forte (Stanton, the Weatherman); Lee Shumway (Commissioner Burke); Edmund Cobb (Lieutenant Reynolds); Charles Murphy (Stokes); Al Taylor, Wally West, Bud Wolfe, Ed Parker (Henchmen); Frank O'Connor (Captain); Budd Buster (Sailor-Henchman); Tom Steele (Yacht Captain); Josef Swickard (President Mendoza); Reed Howes (Slim, a Pilot); Jack Ingram (Al, a Mechanic); Bob Terry (Gas Station Attendant); Ed Brady (Injured Mine Worker-Decoy); Ethan Laidlaw (Pete); Edward Hearn (Forest Ranger); Milton Frome (Police Driver-Car 42); Jack Raymond (Sawmill Foreman); Bud Geary (Gunman); Forrest Taylor (Stevens, an Engineer); Broderick O'Farrell

(Russell, a Furrier); Merrill McCormick (Assistant Cameraman); Jerry Frank (Jake, the Driver); George Cleveland (Gramps); Sammy McKim (Sammy Williams); Reginald Barlow (Dr. Alfred Guttenbach); Charles Sullivan (Brodie, a Cabby); Allan Cavan (Warden); Tom Steele (Henchman/Irving Pichel's Double); Dave Sharpe (Ralph Byrd's Double-Early Chapters); George DeNormand (Ralph Byrd's Main Double); Carey Loftin (Cop).

CHAPTERS: (1) *The Master Spy;* (2) *Captured;* (3) *The False Signal;* (4) *The Enemy Strikes;* (5) *Crack-Up!* (6) *Sunken Peril;* (7) *Tracking the Enemy;* (8) *Chamber of Doom;* (9) *Flames of Jeopardy;* (10) *Crackling Fury;* (11) *Caverns of Peril;* (12) *Fight in the Sky;* (13) *The Fatal Ride;* (14) *Getaway;* (15) *The Last Stand.*

As Jennifer Jones:

THE SONG OF BERNADETTE (20th, 1943) 156 M.

Producer, William Perlberg; director, Henry King; based on the novel by Franz Werfel; screenplay, George Seaton; music, Alfred Newman; orchestrator, Edward Powell; art directors, James Basevi, William Darling; set decorators, Thomas Little, Frank E. Hughes; assistant director, Joseph Behm; sound, Roger Heman; special camera effects, Fred Sersen; camera, Arthur Miller; editor, Barbara McLean.

Jennifer Jones (Bernadette Soubirous); William Eythe (Antoine); Charles Bickford (Peyremale); Vincent Price (Dutour); Lee Cobb (Dr. Dozous); Gladys Cooper (Sister Vauzous); Anne Revere (Louisa Soubirous); Roman Bohnen (François Soubirous); Mary Anderson (Jeanne Abadie); Patricia Morison (Empress Eugenie); Aubrey Mather (Lacade); Charles Dingle (Jacomet); Edith Barrett (Croisine); Sig Rumann (Louis Bouriette); Blanche Yurka (Bernarde Casterot); Ermadean Walters (Marie Soubirous); Marcel Dalio (Callet); Pedro de Cordoba (Le Crampe); Jerome Cowan (Emperor Napoleon); Charles Waldron (Bishop of Tarbes); Moroni Olsen (Chaplain); Nana Bryant (Convent Mother Superior); Manart Kippen (Charles Bouhouhorts); Merrill Rodin (Jean Soubirous); Nino Pipitone, Jr. (Justin Soubirous); John Maxwell Hayes (Father Pomian); Jean Del Val (Estrade); Tala Birell (Mme. Bruat); Eula Morgan (Mme. Nicolau); Frank Reicher (Dr. St. Cyr); Charles La Torre (Duran); Linda Darnell (Blessed Virgin); Nestor Paiva (Baker); Dorothy Shearer (Mother Superior); Nino Pipitone, Sr. (Mayor's Secretary); Edwin Stanley (Mr. Jones); Lionel Braham (Baron Massey); Ian Wolfe (Minister of the Interior); Andre Charlot (Bishop); Irina Semochenko, Marie Carrozza, Joyce Miller, Alicia Diaz (Bernadette's Schoolmates); Ruth Robinson (Nun); Alan Napier (Psychiatrist); Eugene Borden (Gendarme); Edward Clark (Hospital Attendant); Frank Leigh (Cleric); Charles Bates (Bouhouhorts' Boy at Seven Years of Age); Claudine LeDuc, Margaret Hoffman, Connie Leon, Edythe Elliott, Elvira Curci, Adrienne d'Ambricourt, Belle Mitchell, Mae Marsh, Fernanda Eliscu, Ruth Warren, Lucille Ward, Minerva Urecal, Cecil Weston, Marie Pope, Marjorie Copley (Women); Alex Papana, Alphonse Martell, Muni Seroff, Frank Lackteen, Stephen Roberts, Frank Dae, Louis Pacigalupi (Men); Harry Denny (Priest); Curt Furberg, Armand Cortez, Louis Arco, George Sorel (Franciscan Monks); Jean De. Briac, Davison Clark, Antonio Filauri, Julian Rivero (Dominican Monks); Charles Wagenheim (Peasant); Edward Keane, Hooper Atchley (Policemen); Edward Van Sloan, Edward Fielding, John Dilson, Tom Stevenson (Doctors); Fred Essler (Minister of Justice); Harry Cording (Stone Mason); Pat Dillon (Bouhouhorts' Boy); Louis Mercier (Huckster); Dickie Moore (Adolar); Fritz Leiber, Arthur Hohl (Monks); Geraldine Wall (Nun).

SINCE YOU WENT AWAY   (UA, 1944) 172 M.

Producer, David O. Selznick; director, John Cromwell; based on the novel by Margaret Buell Wilder; adaptor, Wilder; screenplay, Selznick; production designer, William L. Pereira; set decorator, Victor A. Gangelin, music, Max Steiner; associate music director, Louis Forbes; art director, Mark Lee Kirk; assistant director, Lowell Farrell; sound, Percy Townsend; special effects, Jack Cosgrove, Clarence Slifer; camera, Stanley Cortez, Lee Garmes; editor, Hal C. Kern.

Claudette Colbert (Anne Hilton); Jennifer Jones (Jane Hilton); Joseph Cotten (Anthony Willett); Shirley Temple (Bridget "Brig" Hilton) Monty Woolley (Colonel Smollett); Lionel Barrymore (The Clergyman); Robert Walker (William G. Smollett II); Hattie McDaniel (Fidelia); Agnes Moorehead (Emily Hawkins); Guy Madison (Harold Smith); Keenan Wynn (Lieutenant Solomon); Lloyd Corrigan (Mr. Mahoney); Gordon Oliver (Marine Officer); Jane Devlin (Gladys Brown); Ann Gillis (Becky Anderson); Nazimova (Zosia Koslowska); Dorothy Garner ("Sugar"); Andrew McLaglen (Former Plowboy); Jill Warren (Waitress); Terry Moore (Refugee Child); Warren Hymer (Patient at Finger Ladder); Robert Johnson (Black Officer); Dorothy Dandridge (His Wife); Johnny Bond (AWOL); Irving Bacon (Bartender); George Chandler (Cabby); Jackie Moran (Johnny Mahoney); Addison Richards (Major Atkins); Barbara Pepper (Pin Girl); Byron Foulger (Principal); Harry Hayden (Conductor); Edwin Maxwell (Businessman); Florence Bates (Dowager); Theodore Von Eltz (Desk Clerk); Adeline de Walt Reynolds (Elderly Woman); Doodles Weaver (Convalescent); Eilene Janssen (Little Girl); Jonathan Hale (Conductor); Albert Basserman (Dr. Sigmund Gottlieb); Craig Stevens (Danny Williams); Ruth Roman (Envious Girl); William B. Davidson (Taxpayer); Jimmy Clemons, Jr. (Boy Caroler); Neil Hamilton (Tim Hilton in Photograph).

LOVE LETTERS   (Par., 1945) 101 M.

Producer, Hal B. Wallis; director, William Dieterle; based on the novel by Chris Massie; screenplay, Ayn Rand; art directors, Hans Dreier, Roland Anderson; set decorator, Ray Moyer; assistant director, Richard McWhorter; music, Victor Young; song, Young; dialog director, Victor Stoloff; technical adviser, Lieutenant Geoffrey Steele, R.A.R.O.; sound, Don McKay, Don Johnson; special camera effects, Gordon Jennings; process camera, Farciot Edouart; camera, Lee Garmes; editor, Anne Bauchens.

Jennifer Jones (Singleton); Joseph Cotten (Alan Quinton); Ann Richards (Dilly Carson); Anita Louise (Helen Wentworth); Cecil Kellaway (Mack); Gladys Cooper (Beatrice Remington); Byron Barr (Derek Quinton); Robert Sully (Roger Morland); Reginald Denny (Defense Attorney); Ernest Cossart (Bishop); James Millican (Jim Connings); Lumsden Hare (Mr. Quinton); Winifred Harris (Mrs. Quinton); Ethel May Halls (Bishop's Wife); Matthew Boulton (Judge); David Clyde (Postman); Ian Wolfe (Vicar); Alec Craig (Dodd); Arthur Hohl (Jupp); Conrad Binyon (Boy in Library); Nina Borget (Barmaid in Italian Inn); Louise Currie (Clara Foley); Mary Field, Connie Leon (Nurses); George Humbert (Proprietor of Italian Inn); Clifford Brooke (Cart Driver); Constance Purdy (Old Hag); Ottola Nesmith (Attendant); Helena Grant (Attendant); Catherine Craig (Jeanette Campbell); Harry Allen (Farmer); Anthony Marsh (Young Man at Party).

CLUNY BROWN   (20th, 1946) 100 M.

Producer-director, Ernst Lubitsch; based on the novel by Margery Sharp; screenplay, Samuel Hoffenstein, Elizabeth Reinhardt; assistant director, Tom Dudley;

art directors, Lyle Wheeler, J. Russell Spencer; set decorators, Thomas Little, Paul Mockridge; music director, Emil Newman; orchestrator, Maurice de Packh; sound, Arthur L. Kirbach, Roger Heman; special camera effects, Fred Sersen; camera, Joseph La Shelle; editor, Dorothy Spencer.

Charles Boyer (Adam Belinski); Jennifer Jones (Cluny Brown); Peter Lawford (Andrew Carmel); Helen Walker (Betty Cream); Reginald Gardiner (Hilary Ames); Reginald Owen (Sir Henry Carmel); Sir C. Aubrey Smith (Colonel Duff-Graham); Richard Haydn (Wilson); Margaret Bannerman (Lady Alice Carmel); Sara Allgood (Mrs. Maile); Ernest Cossart (Syrett); Florence Bates (Dowager); Una O'Connor (Mrs. Wilson); Queenie Leonard (Weller); Billy Bevan (Uncle Arn); Michael Dyne (John Frewen); Christopher Severn (Master Snaffle); Rex Evans (Guest Pianist); Ottola Nesmith (Mrs. Tupham); Harold DeBecker (Mr. Snaffle); Jean Prescott (Mrs. Snaffle); Al Winters (Rollins); Clive Morgan (Waiter); Charles Coleman (Constable Birkins); George Kirby (Latham); Whitner Bissell (Dowager's Son); Bette Rae Brown (Girl at Party); Philip Morris (New York Policeman); Betty Fairfax (Woman in Chemist's Shop); Norman Ainsley (Mr. Tupham); Brad Slaven (English Boy on Bike); Billy Gray (Boy in Shop).

DUEL IN THE SUN (Selznick Releasing Organization, 1946) C—138 M.

Producer, David O. Selznick; director, King Vidor; based on the novel by Niven Busch; adaptor, Oliver H. P. Garrett; screenplay, Selznick; second unit directors, Otto Brower, B. Reeves Eason; art directors, James Basevi, John Ewing; production designer, J. McMillan Johnson; set decorator, Emil Kuri; music-music director, Dmitri Tiomkin; song, Allie Wrubel; assistant directors, Lowell Farrell, Harvey Dwight; solo dances, Tilly Losch; group dances, Lloyd Shaw; sound, James Stewart, Richard DeWeese; special camera effects, Clarence Slifer, Jack Cosgrove; camera, Lee Garmes, Hal Rosson, Ray Renahan; additional camera, Charles P. Boyle, Allen Davey; editors, Hal C. Kern, William Ziegler, John D. Faure, Charles Freeman.

Jennifer Jones (Pearl Chavez); Joseph Cotten (Jesse McCanles); Gregory Peck (Lewt McCanles); Lionel Barrymore (Senator McCanles); Lillian Gish (Laura Belle McCanles); Walter Huston (The Sin Killer); Herbert Marshall (Scott Chavez); Charles Bickford (Sam Pierce); Joan Tetzel (Helen Langford); Harry Carey (Lem Smoot); Otto Kruger (Mr. Langford); Sidney Blackmer (The Lover); Tilly Losch (Mrs. Chavez); Scott McKay (Sid); Butterfly McQueen (Vashti); Francis McDonald, Victor Kilian (Gamblers); Griff Barnett (The Jailer); Frank Cordell (Frank); Dan White (Ed); Steve Dunhill (Jake); Lane Chandler (Captain, U.S. Cavalry); Lloyd Shaw (Barbecue Caller); Bert Roach (Eater); Si Jenks, Hank Worden, Rose Plummer (Dancers); Guy Wilkerson (Barfly); Lee Phelps (Engineer); Al Taylor (Man at Barbecue); Orson Welles (Narrator).

PORTRAIT OF JENNIE (Selznick Releasing Organization, 1948) 88 M.*

Producer, David O. Selznick; associate producer, David Hempstead; director, William Dieterle; based on the novel by Robert Nathan; adaptor, Leonardo Bercovici; screenplay, Paul Osborn, Peter Berneis; production designer, J. McMillan Johnson; art director, Joseph B. Platt; set decorator, Claude Carpenter; music-music director, Dmitri Tiomkin; assistant director, Arthur Fellows; makeup, Mel Berns; costumes, Lucinda Ballard, Anna Hill Johnstone; sound, James G.

*Special Color Sequence.

Stewart; special effects, Clarence Slifer; camera, Joseph August; editor, William Morgan.

Joseph Cotten (Eben Adams); Ethel Barrymore (Miss Spinney); Cecil Kellaway (Mr. Matthews); Jennifer Jones (Jennie Appleton); Florence Bates (Mrs. Jekes, the Landlady); Esther Somers (Mrs. Bunce, Her Friend); David Wayne (Gus O'Toole); Albert Sharpe (Mr. Moore); John Farrell (The Policeman); Felix Bressart (The Old Doorman); Maude Simmons (Clara Morgan); Lillian Gish (Mother Mary of Mercy); Clem Bevans (Captain Caleb Cobb); Robert Dudley (Old Mariner); Henry Hull (Eke); Anne Francis (Teenager).

WE WERE STRANGERS   (Col., 1949) 106 M.

Producer, S. P. Eagle; associate producer, Jules Buck; director, John Huston; based on the novel *Rough Sketch* by Robert Sylvester; screenplay, Peter Viertel, Huston; art director, Cary Odell; set decorator, Louis Diage; music, George Antheil; music director, M. W. Stoloff; assistant director, Carl Hiecke; makeup, Robert Shiffer; costumes, Jean Louis; sound, Lambert Day; camera, Russell Metty; editor, Al Clark.

Jennifer Jones (China Valdes); John Garfield (Tony Fenner); Pedro Armendariz (Armando Ariete); Gilbert Roland (Guillermo); Ramon Novarro (Chief); Wally Cassell (Miguel); David Bond (Ramon); Jose Perez (Toto); Morris Ankrum (Bank Manager); Tito Renaldo (Manolo); Paul Monte (Roberto); Leonard Strong (Bombmaker); Robert Tafur (Rubio); Alexander McSweyn, Alfonso Pedroza (Sanitation Men); Ted Hecht (Enrico); Santiago Martinez (Waiter); Joel Rene (Student); Argentina Brunetti, Mimi Aguglia (Mamas); Robert Malcolm (Priest); Roberta Haynes (Lolita); Lelia Goldoni (Counsuelo); Paul Marion (Truck Driver); Felipe Turich (Spy); Fred Chapman (Altar Boy); Julian Rivero (Flower Vendor); Rod Redwing, Charles Granucci, Herschel Graham, Abdullah Abbas, Gertrude Chorre, Thomas Quon Woo, Spencer Chan, Edwin Rochelle, Rodolfo Hoyos, Billy Wilson, Tina Menard, Joe Sawaya (Bits); Harry Vejar (Watchman); Fred Godoy (Contreras); Peter Virgo (Contreras' Chauffeur).

MADAME BOVARY   (MGM, 1949) 115 M.

Producer, Pandro S. Berman; director, Vincente Minnelli; based on the novel by Gustave Flaubert; screenplay, Robert Ardrey; art directors, Cedric Gibbons, Jack Martin Smith; set decorators, Edwin B. Willis, Richard A. Pefferle; music, Miklos Rozsa; assistant director, Al Raboch; makeup, Jack Dawn; choreography, Jack Donohue; costumes, Walter Plunkett; sound, Douglas Shearer, Standish J. Lambert; special effects, Warren Newcombe; camera, Robert Planck; editor, Ferris Webster.

Jennifer Jones (Emma Bovary); James Mason (Gustave Flaubert); Van Heflin (Charles Bovary); Louis Jourdan (Rodolphe Boulanger); Christopher Kent (Alf Kjellin) (Leon Dupis); Gene Lockhart (J. Homais); Frank Allenby (L'hereux); Gladys Cooper (Mme. Dupuis); John Abbott (Mayor Tuvache); Henry (Harry) Morgan (Hippolite); George Zucco (Dubocage); Ellen Corby (Felicite); Eduard Franz (Roualt); Henri Letondal (Guillaumin); Esther Somers (Mme. Lefrancois); Frederic Tozere (Finard); Paul Cavanagh (Marquis D'Andervilliers); Larry Simms (Justin); Dawn Kinney (Berthe); Edith Evanson (Mother Superior); Edward Keane (Presiding Judge); Paul Bryar (Bailiff); Ted Infuhr (Boy); Florence Auer (Mme. Petree); Constance Purdy (Mme. Foulard); Harold Krueger (Harelip Youth); Karl Johnson (Drunken Guest); Bert Le Baron (Young Man); Phil Schumacher, Jack Stoney, Anne Kunde, Sailor Vincent, Dick Alexander, Helen Thurston, Lon Poff, Stuart Holmes, Fred Cordova (Guests); Eula Morgan, Gracille La-Vinder (Women); Jeanine Caruso (Berthe at Fifteen Months); Ed Agresti, Charles Bancroft, Mayo Newhall, David Cavendish (Men); Andre Charisse (Young Man); Manuel Paris (Servant); Victor Kilian (Monsieur Canivet); Angie O. Poulos (Porter); John Ardizoni (Lagandy); Dickie Derrel (Urchin); Charles De Ravenne (Pimply-Faced Youth); George Davis (Innkeeper); Jac George (Opera Conductor); Helen St. Rayner (Opera Singer).

GONE TO EARTH   (British-Lion, 1950) C—110 M.*

Executive producers, Alexander Korda, David O. Selznick; producers-directors, Michael Powell, Emeric Pressburger; based on the novel by Mary Webb; music-music conductor, Brian Easdale; production designer, Jein Heckroth; art directors, Arthur Lawson, Ivor Beddoes; assistant director, Sydney S. Street; sound, Charles Poulton, John Cox; process camera, W. Percy Day; camera, Christopher Challis; editor, Reginald Mills.

Jennifer Jones (Hazel Woodus); David Farrar (Jack Reddin); Cyril Cusack (Edward Marston); Sybil Thorndike (Mrs. Marston); Edward Chapman (Mr. James); Esmond Knight (Abel Woodus); Hugh Griffith (Andrew Vessons); George Cole (Albert); Beatrice Varley (Aunt Prowde); Frances Clare (Amelia Comber); Raymond Rollett (Elder/Landlord); Gerald Lawson (Elder/Roadmender); Joseph Cotten (Narrator).

CARRIE   (Par., 1952) 118 M.

Producer-director, William Wyler; based on the novel *Sister Carrie* by Theodore Dreiser; screenplay, Ruth and Augustus Goetz; art directors, Hal Pereira, Roland Anderson; camera, Victor Milner; editor, Robert Swink.

Laurence Olivier (George Hurstwood); Jennifer Jones (Carrie Meeber); Miriam Hopkins (Julia Hurstwood); Eddie Albert (Charles Drouet); Basil Ruysdael (Fitzgerald); Ray Teal (Allen); Barry Kelley (Slawson); Sara Berner (Mrs. Oransky); William Reynolds (George Hurstwood, Jr.); Harry Hayden (O'Brien); Walter Baldwin (Carrie's Father); Dorothy Adams (Carrie's Mother); Royal Dano (Captain); Albert Astar (Louis, the Headwaiter); William Bailey (Man at Bar); James Flavin (Mike, the Bartender); Harry Denny (Elderly Man); Harlan Briggs (Joe Brant); Martin Doric (Maitre D'); Jack Gargan, Eric Alden, Donald Kerr, Jerry James (Bartenders); Len Hendry (Frank); Jean Debriac (Wine Steward); Melinda Plowman (Little Girl); Margaret Field (Servant Girl); Nolan Leary, F. Patrick Henry (Cabbies); Jerry James (Boy Friend); Jasper D. Weldon (Porter); Mike P. Donovan, Roy Butler (Conductors); Irene Winston (Anna); Anitra Sparrow (Factory Worker); Charles Halton (Parson, a Factory Foreman); Bob Foulk (Sven); Jacqueline de Wit (Minnie); Raymond Russell Roe (Boy); Leon Tyler (Connell); Ralph Sanford (Older Waiter); G. Raymond Nye, Bruce Carruthers, James Davies, Ethan Laidlaw (Waiters); George Melford, Al Ferguson (Patrons at Slawson's); John Alvin (Stage Manager); Gail Bonney (Older Chorus Girl); Lois Hall (Lola); Bill Meader, Allen Ray (Stage Door Johnnies); Don Beddoe (Goodman); Bill Sheehan (Assistant Stage Manager); Sherry Hall (Theatre Cashier); Richard Kipling (Farmer); Howard Mitchell (Business Man); Herman Nowlin (Hack Driver); Lester Sharpe (Blum); Charles B. Smith (Young Man/Job Seeker); Jim Hayward (Hirer); Dulce Daye, Jay K. Eaton (Bride's Parents); Kenneth Patterson (Reporter); Mike Mahoney (Call Boy); Judith Adams (Bride); Mary Murphy (Jessica Hurstwood); Harry Hines (Floorman); Ralph Moody, Slim

*U.S. Release: *The Wild Heart* (RKO, 1952) C—82 M.

Gaut, Kit Guard (Bums); Daria Massey (Carrie's Sister); Edward Clark (Ticket Agent); Gerry Ganzer (Showgirl); Julius Tannen (John); Oliver A. Cross (Host); Jack Roberts (Bum at Hofer's); Harper Goff, Chalky Williams, Snub Pollard, Jack Low (Men); Charley McAvoy, Cliff Clark (Policemen); Frank Wilcox (Maitre D'); Allen D. Sewall (Clerk); Paul E. Burns (Coachman); Edward J. Marr (Necktie Salesman); Douglas Carter (Businessman); Frances Morris (Maid); Start Holmes, Franklyn Farnum (Restaurant Patrons); James Cornell (Brakeman)

RUBY GENTRY   (20th, 1952) 82 M.

Producers, Joseph Bernhard, King Vidor; director, Vidor; story, Arthur Fitz-Richard; screenplay, Silvia Richard; music, Heinz Roemheld; music supervisor, David Chudnow; art director, Dan Hall; set decorator, Ed Boyle; sound, Jean L. Speak; camera, Russell Harlan; editor, Terry Morse.

Jennifer Jones (Ruby Gentry); Charlton Heston (Boake Tackman); Karl Malden (Jim Gentry); Tom Tully (Jud Corey); Bernard Phillips (Dr. Saul Manfred); James Anderson (Jewel Corey); Josephine Hutchinson (Letitia Gentry); Phyllis Avery (Tracy McAuliffe); Herbert Heyes (Judge Tackman); Myra Marsh (Ma Corey); Charles Cane (Cullen McAuliffe); Sam Flint (Nell Fallgren); Frank Wilcox (Clyde Pratt).

INDISCRETION OF AN AMERICAN WIFE   (Col., 1954) 63 M.

Producer-director, Vittorio De Sica; based on the story "Terminal Station" by Cesare Zavattini; screenplay, Zavattini, Luigi Chiarini, Giorgio Prosperi; dialog, Truman Capote; music, Alessandro Cicognini; songs, Paul Weston and Sammy Cahn; art director, Virgillo March; camera, G. R. Aldo; editors, Eraldo De Roma, Jean Barker.

Jennifer Jones (Mary); Montgomery Clift (Giovanni); Gino Cervi (Commissioner); Dick Beymer (Paul).

BEAT THE DEVIL   (UA, 1954) 93 M.

Associate producer, Jack Clayton; director, John Huston; based on the novel by James Helvick; screenplay, Huston, Truman Capote; art director, Wilfred Shingleton; music, Franco Mannino; music director, Lambert Williamson; sound, George Stephenson, E. Law; camera, Oswald Morris; editor, Ralph Kemplen.

Humphrey Bogart (Billy Dannreuther); Jennifer Jones (Gwendolen Chelm); Gina Lollobrigida (Maria Dannreuther); Robert Morley (Petersen); Peter Lorre (O'Hara); Edward Underdown (Harry Chelm); Ivor Barnard (Major Ross); Bernard Lee (C.I.D. Inspector); Marco Tulli (Ravello); Mario Perroni (Purser); Alex Pochet (Hotel Manager); Aldo Silvani (Charles); Guilio Donnini (Administrator); Saro Urzi (Captain); Juan de Landa (Hispano-Suiza Driver); Manuel Serano (Arab Officer); Mimo Poli (Barman).

LOVE IS A MANY SPLENDORED THING   (20th, 1955) C—102 M.

Producer, Buddy Adler; director, Henry King; based on the novel *A Many Splendored Thing* by Han Suyin; screenplay, John Patrick; art directors, Lyle R. Wheeler, George W. Davis; music, Alfred Newman; orchestrator, Edward B. Powell; Sammy Fain and Paul Francis Webster; assistant director, Hal Herman; costumes, Charles Le Maire; camera, Leon Shamroy; editor, William Reynolds.

William Holden (Mark Elliot); Jennifer Jones (Han Suyin); Torin Thatcher (Mr. Palmer-Jones); Isobel Elsom (Adeline Palmer-Jones); Murray Matheson (Dr. Tam); Virginia Gregg (Ann Richards); Richard Loo (Robert Hung); Soo Yong

(Nora Hung); Philip Ahn (Third Uncle); Jorja Curtright (Suzanne); Donna Martell (Suchen); Candace Lee (Oh-No); Kam Tong (Dr. Sen); James Hong (Fifth Brother); Herbert Heyes (Father Low); Angela Loo (Mei Loo); Marie Tsien (Rosie Wu); Barbara Jean Wong, Hazel Shon, Jean Wong (Nurses); Kei Chung (Interne); Henry S. Quan (Officer); Ashley Cowan (British Sailor); Marc Krah (Wine Steward); Joseph Kim (General Song); Salvador Basquez (Hotel Manager); Edward Colmans (Dining Room Captain); Leonard Strong (Fortune Teller); Aen Ling Chow, Stella Lynn, Irene Liu (Wives); Beulah Kwoh (Aunt); Howard Soo Hoo (Second Brother); Walter Soo Hoo (Third Brother); Keye Luke (Elder Brother); Lee Tung Foo (Old Loo); John W. T. Chang (Gate Keeper); Weaver Levy (Soldier).

GOOD MORNING, MISS DOVE   (20th, 1955) C—107 M.

Producer, Samuel G. Engel; director, Henry Koster; based on the novel by Frances Gray Patton; screenplay, Eleanore Griffin; art directors, Lyle Wheeler, Mark-Lee Kirk; set decorators, Walter M. Scott, Paul S. Fox; wardrobe director, Charles Le Maire; costumes, Mary Wills; makeup, Ben Nye; assistant director, Ad Schaumer; music, Leigh Harline; orchestrator, Bernard Mayers; sound, Eugene Grossman, Harry M. Leonard; special camera effects, Ray Kellogg; camera, Leon Shamroy; editor, William Reynolds.

Jennifer Jones (Miss Dove); Robert Stack (Tom Baker); Kipp Hamilton (Jincey Baker); Robert Douglas (Mr. Porter); Peggy Knudsen (Billy Jean); Marshall Thompson (Mr. Pendleton); Chuck Connors (Officer Bill Holloway); Biff Elliot (Alex Burnham); Jerry Paris (Maurice); Mary Wickes (Miss Ellwood); Ted Marc (David Burnham); Dick Stewart (Dr. Temple); Richard Deacon (Mr. Spivey); Than Wyenn (Mr. Levine); Leslie Bradley (Alphonso Dave); Edward Firestone (Fred Makepeace); Cheryl Callaway (Annabel); Mark Engel (Marks); Tim Cagney (Bobsie); Bill Walker (Henry); Robert Lynn, Sr. (Dr. Hurley); Kenneth Osmond (Tommy Baker at Age Nine); Paul Engle (Alex Burnham at Age Nine); Tiger Fafara (Fred Makepeace as a Child); Martha Wentworth (Gramdma Holloway); Virginia Christine (Mrs. Rigsbee); Junius Matthews (Mr. Pruitt); Reba Tassell (Polly Burnham); Gary Diamond (Harrison); Myna Cunard (Mrs. Aldredge); A. Cameron Grant (Mr. Prouty); Janet Brandt (Mrs. Levine); Linda Brace (Jacqueline Wood); Ann Tyrell (Mrs. Makepeace); Nan Dolan (Mrs. Wood); Betty Caulfield (Mother); Elmore Vincent (Mailman); Vincent Perry (Principal); Steve Darrell (Police Captain); Milas Clark, Leonard Ingoldsby, Cary Savage, Tim Haldeman, Michael Gainey (Boys); Ernest Dotson (Boy at Fountain); Mary Carroll, Sarah Selby (Teachers); Jo Gilbert (Young Matron); Pamela Beaird, Carol Sydes, Lydia Reed (Girls); Jean Innes (Night Nurse); Maude Prickett, Catherine Howard (Nurses); John Hiestand (Prison Guard); Edward Mundy (Hearse Driver); Tim Johnson (Freshman); Jean Andren (Secretary to Mr. Dove); Jane Crowley, Eleanore Vogel (Women); Mae Marsh (Woman in Bank); Virginia Carroll (Ann); Elizabeth Flournoy (Mildred); George Dunn (Janitor); Herb Virgran (Police Surgeon); Charles Webster, Richard Cutting (Husbands); Sam McDaniel (Man); William Hughes (Bit).

THE MAN IN THE GRAY FLANNEL SUIT   (20th, 1956) C—152 M.

Producer, Darryl F. Zanuck; director, Nunnally Johnson; based on the novel by Sloan Wilson; screenplay, Johnson; art directors, Lyle Wheeler, Jack Martin Smith; set decorators, Walter M. Scott, Stuart A. Reiss; assistant director, Hal Herman; music, Bernard Herrmann; sound, Alfred Bruzlin, Harry M. Leonard; camera, Charles G. Clarke; editor, Dorothy Spencer.

Gregory Peck (Tom Rath); Jennifer Jones (Betsy Rath); Fredric March (Hopkins); Marisa Pavan (Maria); Lee J. Cobb (Judge Bernstein); Ann Harding (Mrs. Hopkins); Keenan Wynn (Caesar Gardella); Gene Lockhart (Hawthorne); Gigi Perreau (Susan Hopkins); Portland Mason (Janie); Arthur O'Connell (Walker); Henry Daniell (Bill Ogden); Connie Gilchrist (Mrs. Manter); Joseph Sweeney (Edward Schultz); Sandy Descher (Barbara); Mickey Maga (Pete); Kenneth Tobey (Mahoney); Geraldine Wall (Miriam); Jack Mather (Police Sergeant); Frank Wilcox (Dr. Pearce); Nan Martin (Miss Lawrence); Phyllis Graffeo (Gina); Dorothy Adams (Mrs. Hopkins' Maid); Dorothy Philips (Maid); John Breen (Waiter); Mario Siletti (Carriage Driver); Roy Glenn (Master Sergeant Mathews); Robert Boon, Jim Brandt, Otto Reichow (German Soldiers); Harry Lauter, Paul Glass, William Phipps (Soldiers); Alfred Caiazza, Raymond Winston, John Crawford (Italian Boys); De Forrest Kelley (Medic).

THE BARRETTS OF WIMPOLE STREET   (MGM, 1957) C—105 M.

Producer, Sam Zimbalist; director, Sidney Franklin; based on the play by Rudolf Besier; screenplay, John Dighton; art director, Afred Junge; assistant director, D. Middlemas; costumes, Elizabeth Haffenden; makeup, Charles Parker; sound, Gerald Turner; camera effects, Tom Howard; camera, Freddie A. Young; editor, Frank Clarke.

Jennifer Jones (Elizabeth Barrett); John Gielgud (Mr. Barrett); Bill Travers (Robert Browning); Virginia McKenna (Henrietta); Susan Stephen (Bella); Vernon Gray (Captain Surtees Cook); Jean Anderson (Wilson); Maxine Audley (Arabel); Leslie Phillips (Harry Bevan); Laurence Naismith (Dr. Chambers); Moultrie Kelsall (Dr. Ford-Waterlow); Michael Brill (George); Kenneth Fortescue (Octavius); Nicholas Hawtrey (Henry); Richard Thorp (Alfred); Keith Baxter (Charles); Brian Smith (Septimus).

A FAREWELL TO ARMS   (20th, 1957) C—152 M.

Producer, David O. Selznick; director, Charles Vidor; based on the novel by Ernest Hemingway; screenplay, Ben Hecht; art director, Mario Garbuglia; music, Mario Nascimbene; music conductor, Franco Gerrara; camera, Piero Portalupi, Oswald Morris; editors, Gerald J. Wilson, John F. Foley.

Rock Hudson (Lieutenant Frederick Henry); Jennifer Jones (Nurse Catherine Barkley); Vittorio De Sica (Major Alessandro Rinaldi); Alberto Sordi (Father Galli); Mercedes McCambridge (Miss Van Campen); Oscar Homolka (Dr. Emerich); Elaine Stritch (Helen Ferguson); Leopoldo Trieste (Passini); Franco Interlenghi (Aymo); Georges Brehat (Captain Bassi); Memmo Carotenuto (Nino); Victor Francen (Colonel Valentini); Joan Shalwee (Nurse); and: Guido Martufi, Umberto Spadaro, Umberto Sacripanti, Alberto D'Amario, Giacomo Rossi Stuart, Carlo Pedersoli, Alex Revides, Franco Mancinelli, Patrick Crean, Guidarino Guidi, Diana King, Clelia Matania, Eduard Linkers, Johanna Hofer, Luigi Barzini, Carlo Licari, Angiolo Galassi, Carlo Hintermann, Tiberio Mitri, Eva Kotthaus, Gisella Mathews, Vittorio Jannitti, Peter Illing, Sam Levine.

TENDER IS THE NIGHT   (20th, 1962) C—146 M.

Producer, Henry T. Weinstein; director, Henry King; based on the novel by F. Scott Fitzgerald; screenplay, Ivan Moffat; music, Bernard Herrmann; title song, Sammy Fain and Paul Francis Webster; art directors, Jack Martin Smith, Malcolm Brown; set decorators, Walter M. Scott, Paul S. Fox; costumes, Pierre Balmain, Marjorie Best; makeup, Ben Nye; assistant director, Eli Dunn; sound,

Bernard Freericks, Warren B. Delaplain; special effects, L. B. Abbott, Emil Kosa, Jr.; camera, Leon Shamroy; editor, William Reynolds.

Jennifer Jones (Nicole Diver); Jason Robards, Jr. (Dick Diver); Joan Fontaine (Baby Warren); Tom Ewell (Abe North); Cesare Danova (Tommy Barban); Jill St. John (Rosemary Hoyt); Paul Lukas (Dr. Dohmler); Bea Benadaret (Mrs. Mc-Kisco); Charles Fredericks (Mr. McKisco); Sanford Meisner (Dr. Gregorovious); Mac McWhorter (Colis Clay); Albert Carrier (Louis); Richard De Combray (Francisco); Carole Mathews (Mrs. Hoyt); Alan Napier (Pardo); Leslie Farrell (Topsy Diver); Michael Crisalli (Lanier Diver); Earl Grant (Piano Player); Maurice Dallimore (Sir Charles Golding); Carol Veazie (Mrs. Dunphrey); Arlette Clark (Governess); Marcel de la Brosse (Proprietor); Art Salter (Photographer); Armand Largo (Reporter); Michael Korda (Italian Gentleman); George Clark (Young Roman Aristocrat); Eric Feldary (Headwaiter); Joe La Cava (Bartender); Con Convert (Female Impersonator); Jacques Gallo (Gendarme); Florene Williams (Girl); Tom Hernandez (Nobleman); Vera de Winter, Katherine Berger, Renee Godfrey (Nurses); Orrin Tucker (Musician); Nora Evans (Singer); Bruno Della Santana (Reception Clerk); Jean de Briac (Dr. Faurore); Louis Mercier (Concierge); Jean Bori (Barber); Carl Princi (Assistant Manager); Gilbert Paol (Maitre D'); Linda Hutchins, Maggi Brown, John Richardson (Bits).

THE IDOL   (Embassy, 1966) 107 M.

Executive producer, Joseph E. Levine; associate producer, Robert Porter; director, Daniel Petrie; story, Ugo Liberatore; screenplay, Millard Lampell; art director, George Provis; assistant director, Bryan Coates; makeup, Wally Schneiderman; costumes, Yvonne Blake; music-music conductor, John Dankworth; camera, Ken Higgins; editor, Jack Slade.

Jennifer Jones (Carol); Michael Parks (Marco); John Leyton (Timothy); Jennifer Hilary (Sarah); Guy Doleman (Martin Livesy); Natasha Pyne (Rosalind); Caroline Blakiston (Woman at Party); Jeremy Bulloch (Lewis); Fanny Carby (Barmaid); Vernon Dobtcheff (Man at Party); Michael Gordon (Boy); Gordon Gostelow (Simon); Ken Haward (Policeman); Renee Houston (Woman at Party); Priscilla Morgan (Rosie); Edna Morris (Mrs. Muller); Peter Porteous (Tommy); Terry Richards, Derek Ware (Laborers); Jack Watson (Police Inspector); Tina Williams (Dorothea).

ANGEL, ANGEL, DOWN WE GO   (American International, 1969) C—93 M.*

Executive producer, Sam Katzman; producer, Jerome F. Katzman; associate producer, Arthur Dreifuss; director-screenplay, Robert Thom; music-music conductor, Fred Karger; songs, Barry Mann and Cynthia Weil; art director, Gabriel Scognamillo; set decorator, Don Greenwood; costumes, Renee; makeup, William Reynolds; assistant director, John Wilson; choreography, Wilda Taylor; collage effects, Shirley Kaplan; camera, Jack Warren; editor, Eve Newman.

Jennifer Jones (Astrid Steele); Jordan Christopher (Bogart Peter Stuyvesant); Roddy McDowall (Santoro); Holly Near (Tara Nicole Steele); Lou Rawls (Joe); Charley Aidman (Willy Steele); Davey Davison (Anna Livia); Marty Brill (Maitre D'); Hiroko Watanabe (Masseuse); and: Carol Costello, Sandrine Gobet, Rudy Battaglia, Ron Allen, Danielle Aubry, Joan Calhoun, George Ostos, Romo Vincent.

*Reissued as: Cult of the Damned (1971).

450

THE TOWERING INFERNO (20th, 1974) C—

Producer, Irwin Allen; associate producer, Sidney Marshall; director, John Guillermin; based on the novels *The Tower* by Richard Martin Stern and *The Glass Inferno* by Frank Robinson and Tom Scortia; art director, Ward Preston; set designer, Rafael Bretton; production designer, William J. Creber; costume designer, Paul Zastupnevich; mechanical effects. A. D. Flowers; makeup, Monte Westmore; technical advisor for Los Angeles, Pete Lucarelli; technical advisor for San Francisco, Jack Cavallero; special camera effects, L. B. Abbott; camera, Fred Koenekamp, Joseph Biroc; editor, Harold Kress.

Steve McQueen (O'Hallorhan); Paul Newman (MacAllister); William Holden (Duncan); Fay Dunaway (Susan); Fred Astaire (Harlee); Richard Chamberlain (Simmons); Jennifer Jones (Lisolette); O. J. Simpson (Jernigan); Robert Wagner (Bigelow).

In RUBY GENTRY (20th '52)

With husband
David O. Selznick in
Los Angeles (August 1951)

A publicity pose with Laurence
Olivier for CARRIE (Par '52)

In INDISCRETION OF AN
AMERICAN WIFE (Col '54)

With Edward Underdown in
BEAT THE DEVIL (UA '54)

With William Holden in LOVE IS A MANY SPLENDORED
THING (20th '55)

On the set of GOOD MORNING, MISS DOVE (20th '55)

With Robert Stack and Biff Elliot in GOOD MORNING, MISS DOVE

With Gregory Peck in THE MAN IN THE GRAY FLANNEL SUIT (20th '56)

With Virginia McKenna and John Gielgud in THE BARRETTS OF WIMPOLE STREET (MGM '57)

With David O. Selznick and their daughter, Mary Jennifer, aboard H.M.S. *Queen Elizabeth* in New York harbor (August 1957)

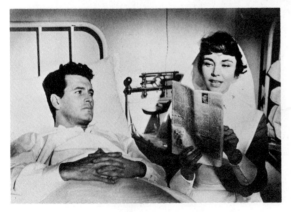

With Rock Hudson in A FAREWELL TO ARMS (20th '57)

456

With Vittorio De Sica in A FAREWELL TO ARMS

With Jason Robards, Jr., in TENDER IS THE NIGHT (20th '62)

With John Leyton in THE IDOL (Embassy '66)

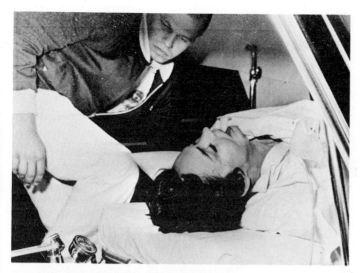

Transfer to Mt. Sinai Hospital in Los Angeles after
suicide bid (November 10, 1967)

With Holly Near, Lou Rawls, and Jordan Christopher in
ANGEL, ANGEL, DOWN WE GO (American International '69)

With husband Norton Simon in Los Angeles (June 1971)

THE TOWERING INFERNO (20th-WB '74)

Maria Montez in 1944

Maria Montez

5'7"
125 pounds
Reddish-brown hair
Brown eyes
Gemini

As a character in the play *The Boys in the Band* so aptly phrased it, "Maria was a good woman." She had a short, happy life and a short, mostly happy film career, and rarely, if ever, wished even her most ardent detractors any serious harm.

Undoubtedly, Maria was one of filmdom's least expert thespians; nonetheless, she rose to stardom in a series of Universal-produced tropical-island, jungle, and desert films. At a time when the public was eager for enticing movie escapism, Maria was offering filmgoers exactly what they needed—a chance to forget the global problems of the World War II years.

Besides her obvious sensual appeal, Maria possessed another rare silver-screen asset, a unique and blatant relish for playing "pretend" oncamera. Like today's South American sexploitation cinema queen, Isabel Sarli, Maria's narcissistic revelry is always fascinating to behold, riveting the viewer's attention to her flickering image as surely as the bravura dramatics of a Bette Davis or a Glenda Jackson.

Bombastic, fiery, foreign-accented Maria was always her own best publicity agent, a pinup beauty of the early 1940s who freely admitted, in the days when it was rash to do so, that she abhorred wearing a brassiere. Often accused of being a brash phony, she generally had a witty, accented retort for her would-be oppressors, who in the long run could not fault her strongest asset. She passionately believed in each and every thing she wanted to do and say, and her wildest statements emerged from her well-shaped lips as sincere gospel.

Over two decades have passed since this most delightful woman expired, but thanks to the aid of television's late shows, she continues to weave her charismatic charms and achieves for viewers many impossible dreams.

It all began for her on Sunday, June 6, 1920,* in tropical Santo Domingo on the shores of the Caribbean. Her father, Ysidoro Gracia, was Spanish consul and embassy delegate to the Dominican Republic in the period when that country's government was militarily supervised, by "mutual" consent, by the United States Marines. Her mother, Teresa, was the daughter of political refugees.

In the Cathedral of Santa Maria la Menor, in which are entombed the remains considered to be those of Christopher Columbus, she was christened Maria Antonia Vidal de Santo Silas y Gracia. Señor and Señora Gracia had nine other children, providing Maria with four sisters and five brothers.

Except for the youngest sister, Lucita, the Gracia children were born in rapid succession. They grew up together and delighted in pursuing their favorite pastime—baseball. Maria's chief family responsibility was to watch over baby Lucita, and when Maria discovered that by blowing her breath into the baby's eyes, the child would quickly fall asleep, she employed the tactic constantly in order to free herself to take up her position as pitcher on the Gracia ball team.

The family's homestead was situated on the island of Tenerife, the largest of the Canary group in the Atlantic Ocean off the northwest coast of Africa. The islands have been a Spanish province since the fifteenth century. During one of the Gracias' rare visits to Tenerife, it was decided that Maria should remain and obtain a proper education at the Sacred Heart Convent in Santa Cruz, the island's capital city. She did not take to this idea, but her father's word was law and she dared not directly defy him. Several times during her enrollment she rebelled at the rigid discipline demanded by the nuns, and she ran away. But Maria always returned to the convent school since there were few places in the vicinity where she could hide for very long. By the time her basic education was completed, her father had earned a consular assignment to France, and Maria was at last permitted to rejoin her family. From there she took frequent trips to all the major

*Some sources suggest Maria was born in 1917.

464

European cities, and she learned to speak French as well as Italian with considerable proficiency.

When Maria was in her mid-teens, the Spanish consulship in Belfast, Northern Ireland, was delegated to Señor Gracia, and the family once again had to reestablish their headquarters. It was in Belfast that Maria experienced her first taste of acting. She joined a local amateur theatre group established for the Spanish-speaking colony there and later became a member of a nonprofessional Irish stage company. Because of her decided accent, Maria was always assigned minor parts requiring little dialog.

In 1937, at the age of seventeen, Maria was courted in grand style by wealthy Irishman William McFeeters, an officer in the British army. Recognizing the young man's genuinely sincere intentions, Ysidoro Gracia granted permission for them to wed in spite of the short time the couple had known one another. During the summer of their marriage, the newlyweds resided on the estate of McFeeters's parents, where they rode to the hounds by day and played auction bridge nightly with his parents. For the winter months, the couple rented a flat in Belfast and spent many evenings going to the movies. Maria would later claim that it was from following the plots and dialog of the imported American and British films, that her English improved.

It was not long, however, before Maria became restless and bored with her rather empty existence. Whenever young McFeeters was away on military duty, the skittish Maria would flee to London or Paris in search of excitement. She also made periodic visits to Liverpool, where her consular father had been restationed. On one particularly devilish spree, she landed in New York City, where several of her European friends had recently taken up residence. The home of a Bavarian duke and duchess became her headquarters, and she settled in for a lengthy stay. Through her friends, Maria met the most dashing and eligible men of New York and was seen with them in all of the city's best clubs and restaurants.

Husband McFeeters, meanwhile, having received no replies to his many cables requesting his wife to return to the auction-bridge routine, boarded a New York-bound ship. Maria met him at the dock and promptly advised him that his transatlantic voyage had been in vain. She explained that she had no intention of renewing their marital relationship. McFeeters lingered for a week in Manhattan but then bowed to the inevitable and returned to Ireland, consoled by the firm belief that headstrong Maria was intent on ruining her promising life. A quick divorce was arranged, much to the dismay of her staunch Catholic family. Maria's father, ill in Liverpool, was especially hard hit by the news. Maria tossed her marriage aside with the lightest of care. She later told the press, "He was a very nice fellow, but it was one of

465

those things you do when you are seventeen and you don't know very much."

Manhattan newspaper photographers found a very willing subject in the well-dressed, beautiful auburn-haired girl, and soon Maria's picture was appearing regularly in the society columns. Artist McClelland Barclay saw some of these snapshots and decided that she was indeed the girl he had been seeking as his model of "the complete cosmopolitan woman."* She promptly accepted Barclay's tempting professional offer. Once Barclay's oil painting was finished and on display, innumerable job requests came her way from illustrators, photographers, modeling agencies, and other local artists. Maria accepted a few jobs, but she was far too energetic and vivacious to spend hours sitting almost motionless in one pose. Privately, her goal was to star in Hollywood movies because the manager of a New York nightclub had repeatedly told her that that was where she truly belonged.

One morning in 1940, Maria received word from an informant that George J. Schaefer, president of RKO-Radio Pictures, was in New York and that he had reserved a table for luncheon at "21." She dressed meticulously and went to the restaurant, slipped a discreet tip to the maître d'hotel, who was also her pal, and was soon seated at a table next to Schaefer's. The studio head was midway into his lunch at this juncture. To attract his attention, Maria went into her standard coquettish act: smiling prettily, tilting her head kittenishly, and laughing merrily as she placed her order with the waiter. Schaefer could not but help notice the foreign-accented beauty, and soon sent his business card over to her table. Introductions were made and she graciously invited the powerful industry figure to take his coffee at her table. As she anticipated. Schaefer eventually got around to the subject of screentests and asked Maria if she might consider it. She "naively" answered, "Moov-ing peec-tures?", then shrugged and added, "What ha-rm can eet do?"†

After viewing her screentest, RKO officials informed New York-based Maria that a contract would be drawn up for her signature, but she would *first* be required to take a three-month course in "corrective" speech in the hope of softening her accent. It was indicated that her weekly salary would be $100. In the meantime, however, a Universal talent scout, a flunkie for that studio's prize producer, Joe Pasternak, managed to see Maria's test and immediately offered her a $150

---

*Maria was blessed with a spectacular 36-inch bust and 36½-inch hip measurements.

†Mexican-born Lupe Velez (1909-1944), the Latin bombshell who had hit Hollywood in the late 1920s and made her fame with her peppery, volatile nature, was in 1940 at RKO making her *Mexican Spitfire* series of pictures with Leon Errol. Schaefer, no doubt, had thoughts of hiring Maria as a stand-by/successor to the maturing Velez.

contract, plus a studio-paid trip to Hollywood. She accepted Universal's offer.*

Before she signed the Universal term deal, Maria's father died. A few weeks later, her mother passed away. Maria's share of the family heirlooms included a set of Goya prints and some antique jewelry of inestimable value, claimed to have originated in the fifteenth century from the gem collection of Spanish Queen Isabella. Her inheritance also consisted of lesser jewels of topaz and aquamarine.

In Hollywood, Universal's vice-president and general manager, Cliff Work, consigned Maria to the professional hands of studio publicity director John E. Joseph. It was assumed that she would receive the standard production-line ballyhoo handed to any new contractee. But no one had counted on Maria's fiery determination to put her natural and cultivated assets to their best use. It was obvious to her, as to her bosses, that with her striking five-foot, seven-inch figure, dark skin, and long, reddish hair, there would be no problem feeding publicity poses of her to the fan magazines and columnists. Maria solved the task of providing herself with a new professional name, choosing the surname Montez after the famous adventuress-dancer of the nineteenth century, Lola Montez, who, Maria believed incorrectly, had also been a daring Spaniard.† Unlike most starlets-in-the-making, Maria was intelligent, well traveled, and a very knowing novice. She was ambitious and knew exactly what she wanted, that is, to be a star, not just another contract player.

Despite Maria's bravura, her first screen assignment was an unbilled appearance in *Lucky Devils* (Universal, 1941), the sixth in a series of inexpensive Richard Arlen-Andy Devine programmers. This entry, directed by Lew Landers, cast the duo "leading" men as newsreel photographers, allowing for a legitimate use of excessive library stock footage. In this film, filled with what *Variety* termed "trite situations," Maria was very briefly seen as a bathing-beauty contestant privileged within the sixty-minute footage to have one close-up shot and a few terse lines of inconsequential dialog. It must have infuriated her when another "starlet," Janet Shaw, received billing status although she had less to do in *Lucky Devils*.

Maria publicly predicted, in English spoken with something akin to a Castilian lisp, "Three mawnths time een Holleey-wood and eevery-body

---

*Maria would later state that she had chosen the Universal deal because, in her estimation, it was the only Hollywood film company without a complement of glamour-girl stars. Universal's female roster at the time included postadolescent singing luminary Deanna Durbin, and such other term contractees as Dorothy Darrell, Jane Frazee, Anne Gwynne, Gloria Jean, Kay Leslie, Peggy Morgan, Anne Nagel, Helen Parrish, and Baby Sandy. They also maintained, on special picture deals, the Andrews Sisters, Carol Bruce, Virginia Bruce, Marlene Dietrich, Irene Dunne, Barbara O'Neil, and Loretta Young.

†Her real name was Eliza Gilbert, and she was born in Ireland.

knows mee." She set her forecast into motion on one of her first days at Universal by entering the studio commissary promptly at noon wearing a tall hat of mink and a spectacularly lowcut dress. She sat by herself at a table situated in the center of the room, opened a movie trade paper, and proceeded to "read" it ever so intently. On one page she seemed so disturbed by an item that she grimaced and moaned. A bit of trade news on another page caused her to laugh merrily and she intermittently gurgled and made odd cries of pleasures or throaty chuckles over other paragraphs. An understanding waitress whispered to her that she was wasting her time, that none of the important studio executives lunched until one o'clock or later.

Without a word, Maria rose and swept majestically out of the commissary. Promptly at one, she reappeared, now decked out in a complete change of wardrobe, from shoes to hat. Again, she strode imperiously to a centrally located table and went into her emotional act of perusing the trade news. Within an hour, everyone in the place knew she was there and knew her name. One observer of the occasion later remarked, "When she left, the dining room lost its sparkle; the food lost its zest."

In August 1940, Maria was given the opportunity to act with benefit of a camera in one of the quickie, low-budgeted, but profitable Johnny Mack Brown Universal Westerns. These entries ran from fifty-six to sixty-three minutes of onscreen time and were intended for the action-house and kiddie-matinee exhibition market. Invariably directed at this time by Ray Taylor, the sagebrush yarns contained the standard supporting cast of Fuzzy Knight and Nell O'Day. This particular assembly-line production was originally titled *Trail to Paradise Valley*. It was later shortened to *Paradise Valley* and was finally given its release title of *Boss of Bullion City* (Universal, 1941). In the undemanding role of Linda Calhoun, Maria was supposed to be virtuous and God-fearing, and she spent considerable footage gazing worshipfully at the righteous, girth-expanding hero Brown.

With sixty feature releases planned for 1941, Universal was not about to allow even a self-proclaimed star-in-the-making to sit about idly, and Maria found herself quickly changing from wardrobes befitting the Western American frontier to contemporary dress of the early 1940s for *The Invisible Woman* (1941), a further spin-off from the studio's very successful *The Invisible Man* (1933).* This one had Virginia Bruce in the title role as a model who is turned invisible by screwball scientist John Barrymore. With the still lovely Bruce forced to sublimate her physical charms through much of the film, the aging John Barrymore aping the mannerisms of brother Lionel, and comedy relief by Donald MacBride and Edward Brophy as two bungling gangster henchmen, it was little wonder that the *New York Times* passed off the venture as "silly, banal and repetitious." Among

*United Artists had *Topper Returns* and Columbia provided *Here Comes Mr. Jordan* as 1941 entries in the invisible-ghost gimmick sweepstakes.

the several decorous young ladies who appeared as models in this film were Maria (with one line of dialog) and Kay Leslie. *The Invisible Woman* went into release three days before *Boss of Bullion City.*

Because of her lead role in *Boss of Bullion City,* Maria assumed she was worthy of more demanding celluloid roles than one-line parts and spoke out boldly to the Universal hierarchy. They told her to be patient and continue gathering experience. While the studio continued to search for roles that coincided with her un-American accent, Maria was busily forming her "Montez for Stardom Club," finding a goodly number of supporters from the cheesecake-photograph contingent.

Then, Twentieth Century-Fox put out a casting call for a Latin—with accent—to portray a Brazilian showgirl in a film they were concocting with the working title *Road to Rio.* The call came at a propitious time. By loaning Maria to Twentieth (at a small profit, of course), Universal had a moratorium during which to dig further for material of their own for this demanding new player.

That Night in Rio, as the Fox picture was retitled, was a reworking of Maurice Chevalier's *Folies Bergere* (United Artists, 1935), a plotline which would be used yet again in a later Danny Kaye vehicle, *On the Riviera* (Twentieth Century-Fox, 1951). Not only was *That Night in Rio* intended as a showcase for the studio's reigning blonde singing star, Alice Faye, but it was devised to make use of the bizarre talents of specialty-star contractee Carmen Miranda, the Brazilian Bombshell. Then too, studio mogul Darryl F. Zanuck hoped that the Good Neighbor-policy flavor of *That Night in Rio* would make amends for *Down Argentine Way* (1940), which, with its condescending attitude to south-of-the-border citizens, had offended the very Latin Americans that United States-Hollywood circles wanted most to placate in the critical pre-Pearl Harbor days.

The picture, directed by Irving Cummings, was lensed in Fox's delightfully garish Technicolor hues, which flattered Maria's reddish-tinged hair. She was cast as Inez, the ex-girlfriend of airline magnate Baron Duarte (Ameche). Torso-twitching Miranda is the paramour of the Baron's lookalike, nightclub entertainer Larry Martin (also Ameche), who finds Maria cozying up to the Baron in the mistaken belief that he is Larry, thus igniting a momentary blaze of jealousy. While most of the critical attention went to Faye as the languorous Brazilian countess and to fruit-bedecked Miranda, Maria did not go unnoticed in her short-skirted costume, which revealed her very shapely legs.*

By this point in her blossoming career, Maria was being heavily promoted in the cheesecake sweepstakes by assorted poses meant for fram-

---

*That Night in Rio, which caused Bosley Crowther (*New York Times*) to note "[it has] enough gorgeous girls in stunning dresses to knock the eyes out of a strick misogynist," boasted the presence of such John Powers models as Marion Rosamond, Bunny Hartley, and Roseanne Murray.

ing or taping to the inside cover of the footlockers of GIs. Her name turned up frequently in the gossip columns, and she became an ardent exponent of the fad of the day—tight-clinging sweaters. While college girls were generally still wearing their sweaters several sizes too large, the motion-picture girls chose to wear sensationally form-fitting types, onscreen as well as off.

On April 2, 1941, the Hays censorship office lowered the boom with a disquieting letter from Joseph L. Breen, the chief arbiter of motion-picture morals, to every Hollywood producer.*

Life magazine covered the Breen admonition in a two-page feature spread with enticing photographs of some of the major offenders, one of whom was Maria Montez. In the utilized shot, her sweater clung to her bosom, clearly revealing that she was not wearing a brassiere. The caption read, "Maria Montez, Latin American starlet, is prominent member of Hollywood's so-called Sweater Set."

And then, perhaps in search of a new dimension of her personality or talents, the studio had Maria go blonde for *Raiders of the Desert* (Universal, 1941), one more installment in the seemingly endless adventure saga of the 1940s Rovers Boys, Richard Arlen and Andy Devine. In this John Rawlins-directed mini-opus, Arlen and Devine, two "soldiers of fortune," find themselves in the Arabian country of Libertahd, a far cry from the sunny shores of California where they had hoped to disembark. Once on dry ground, they soon size up the situation: duplicitous Hassen Mohammed (Turhan Bey) is actually in league with Sheik Talifah (Ralf Harolde) to oppose the modernization program of Jones (George Carleton). While "vigorous" Arlen is gallantly courting Carleton's secretary (Linda Hayes), bulbous Devine has romantic eyes for the paramour (Maria) of Abdullah (Lewis Howard). While *Raiders of the Desert* offered Maria her first screen chance at Near Eastern costumed adventure, with diaphanous veils flowing from her chalky hair, the highlight of the black-and-white feature was the scene in which a determined Devine attempts to romance a resistant Montez—his mode of courtship, singing in his gravel-voiced tones, strains of "I'm a Big Bad Bagdad Daddy," while accompanying himself on the ukelele. Vampish Maria amused filmgoers by looking decidedly unimpressed with her oncamera suitor.

Remaining light-haired, her next film appearance was a sorry "B," *Moonlight in Hawaii* (Universal, 1941). Theodore Strauss (*New York*

---

*The epistle read, "In recent months we have noticed a marked tendency to inject into motion pictures shots of low-cut dresses which expose women's breasts, as well as sweater shots—shots in which the breasts of women are clearly outlined and emphasized. All such shots are in direct violation of the Production Code which states clearly that the more intimate parts of the human body must be fully covered at all times, and that they should not be clearly and unmistakably outlined by the garment. In the future, any shots in which women's breasts are partially or wholly exposed or any sweater shots in which the breasts are clearly defined will be rejected. This is important."

Times) called it "the sort of desperate drivel that turns contented movie-goers into fanatics thirsting for vengeance." The reviewer might have done action-house movie addicts more of a service had he advised them that this sixty-minute musical was a remake of the studio's *Hawaiian Nights* (Universal, 1939), which had also featured Johnny Downs. At least there was a new score for the rehashed plotline in which sixth-billed Maria was a civilized island native named Ilani, who is captivated by the charms of Downs but fails to permanently distract his affections away from lovely Jane Frazee. Others along for the moonlight were Leon Errol, Mischa Auer, and the Merry Macs.

While Maria was doing yeoman service oncamera, she was energetically devising new means of gaining the public's attention. In October 1941, the Harvard Student Union invited her to its annual Halloween dance. She was paired with a freshman who was reportedly cut out on the dance floor by as many as 999 other students. The university's newspaper, the *Harvard Crimson,* was all set editorially to burn Maria to a crisp, but after meeting her the editors reversed their plan and pledged unwavering devotion.

Meanwhile, Maria got far more attention that month when, on October 27, it was announced that Lt. Commander Claude Strickland, an RAF pilot, was listed as missing in action. Maria suddenly announced that he was indeed more than just another battle casualty serviceman, since he was her fiancé. She claimed they had first met in 1939 when Maria was still residing in London, and that they had been engaged since early 1941. An allegedly bereaved Maria informed one reporter: "I just know he's alive, even if he is in a prison camp. I know he's alive somewhere. He just sent me this picture a few weeks ago. Look at the words Claude wrote on it. 'All my love. I adore you.' That's the way we felt about each other." On November 12, Strickland was discovered to be a prisoner of war in a German detention camp. Somehow, for whatever reasons, the Maria-Strickland liaison soon thereafter disappeared from the realities of life.

Maria's seventh 1941 release, *South of Tahiti* (Universal) was the film that established her as *the* exotic beauty of jungle, desert, and tropical isle, a province formerly reigned over by Paramount's Dorothy Lamour. For *South of Tahiti,* Universal decided that Maria's past film assignments were so minuscule and/or unimportant that only in this movie did her cinema career really begin. Thus, in the cast credits it is stated, "and introducing Maria Montez." Universal clad her in a slendang, which their publicity department insisted was the proper Malayan word for the garment popularly known as a sarong. Back with dark hair, Maria was Melahi, white girl of the jungle, who is smitten with hard-boiled Brian Donlevy, one of a trio (the others: Andy Devine, Broderick Crawford) of pearl hunters shipwrecked on a tropical isle. In true Lamouresque tradition, she had a leopard for her household pet, and even "sang" a song, "Melahi."*

*Probably dubbed by Martha Tilton.

While the more demanding critics lambasted the modestly budgeted feature ("You cannot create a satire about something which is already low burlesque"—Archer Winsten, *New York Post*), moviegoers were enthusiastic about this escapist-type fare, and especially about Maria. Billed in the film as "The Daughter of Eve with a Soul of Satan," Maria's special charisma caught on with film audiences, and soon her fan mail tripled and she was dubbed by many as "The Dorothy Lamour of San Fernando Valley" (the site of Universal's home lot). Maria was delighted with the comparison. She rhetorically queried, "They talk, eh? They mention my name?"

Before *South of Tahiti,* her last 1941 release, was in general distribution, Universal had plunked her in two conventional-type mysteries. She was back in street clothes in *Bombay Clipper* (Universal, 1942), an unassuming "B" programmer, greatly enhanced by Stanley Cortez's craftsmanlike photography. The film's slim premise concerned $4 million worth of diamonds, gift of India's government to Great Britain, which the latter intended to use for precision tools to bolster wartime industrial production. Aboard the Bombay-to-San Francisco flight are newsman William Gargan, his would-be fiancée, Irene Hervey, a swarthy doctor, and ex-pilot with a bad record, a businessman from Cleveland, Ohio, a sweater-knitting matron, a cardsharp, and, among others, slinky Maria. She, of course, turns out to be a pistol-carrying agent for Axis spies. The best the *New York Times*'s Theodore Strauss could say of this actioner was, "The singular fascination . . . is the flawless precision with which it uses nearly every cliche known to the science of grade-B movies." Maria's unimaginative portrayal was not even of the caliber of exotic Ilona Massey's espionage agent in *International Lady* (United Artists, 1941).

Next on Maria's production schedule at Universal was *The Mystery of Marie Roget* (1942),* very loosely based on Edgar Allan Poe's tale of one hundred years ago. Poe had based his detective whodunit on a true incident in New Jersey in which Mary Cecilia Rogers's torso was found floating in the Hudson River off Hoboken. The rather flimsy film plot conventionally depicted Marie Roget (Maria) as a flirtatious Parisian musical star who plots with Edward Norris to murder her younger sister (Nell O'Day). In the course of the pedestrian tale set in 1889 Paris, two corpses are pulled from the Seine, Maria vanishes at a crucial point, and police chemist-detective Patrick Knowles, who fancies himself a Sherlock Holmes, proves to be a gallant but rather ineffectual culprit guesser. Maria's big number was "Mama Dit Moi," a song dubbed offcamera by vocalist Dorothy Triden. Up until this juncture, Maria had been demanding serious dramatic parts, but her performance in this bit of gaslight-era skulduggery proved she was not yet equipped to handle them. Most critics found her

*Reissued later by Realart as *Phantom of Paris.*

emoting rather embarrassing and preferred to focus their attention on the overdone but engaging performance of Maria Ouspenskaya as the peppery grandmother.

In early 1942, producer Walter Wanger, president of the Academy of Motion Pictures Arts and Sciences, and then married to actress Joan Bennett, was based on the Universal lot. He was anxious to produce an Arabian fantasy film, something more alluring than his *Shanghai* (Paramount, 1935), more gaudy than his very popular *Algiers* (United Artists, 1938), and certainly more exotic than his *Sundown* (United Artists, 1940). While generally quite conservative in its picture-budgeting, Universal agreed with Wanger's belief that World War II-weary film audiences would be pleased by a colorful, adventurous bit of escapism. The studio therefore agreed to his impressive concept for *Arabian Nights* (Universal, 1942), very thinly conceived from the popular English translation of the fabled tales by Sir Richard Burton in 1885-88.

When the eighty-six-minute color feature debuted at the Rivoli Theatre on Christmas Day, 1942, *PM's* reporter was quick to report that this film was "probably the gaudiest and most cynical transformation of a classic since the Ritz Brothers played the *Three Musketeers* [Twentieth Century-Fox, 1939]." But the public went wild over the gorgeously hued, swashbuckling account in the tradition of a Douglas Fairbanks, Sr., epic. It was Kate Cameron (*New York Daily News*) who properly caught the flavor of the picture in her three-star review: " . . . there are times when the picture moves with the swiftness and melodramatic excitement of a good old western horse opera."

Arabian Nights sets the mold for Maria's most successful Universal ventures. It represented her first co-starring vehicle with Jon Hall and Sabu, two desperate types who added much versatility to the juvenile shenanigans of the Near Eastern sagebrush tale. If anyone expected to find traces of Sinbad's magical voyages or Aladdin and his wonderful lamp, they were sadly disappointed. For in this comic-strip-like romance tale, these famous characters from the *Tales of a Thousand and One Nights* were reduced to comic relief, as handled in hammy style by John Qualen (Aladdin), Shemp Howard (Sinbad), and especially by Billy "The Sneezer" Gilbert as Almad, head of the traveling circus in which Maria and Sabu perform.

Hall, often tagged the poor man's Errol Flynn, or, as Samuel Goldwyn's publicity had previously referred to him, "Goldwyn's gift to women," was not exactly the most virile, or energetic, male lead to portray Maria's vis-à-vis. However, he could handle the rather idiotic dialog with a straight face, looked reasonably at ease in robes and sandals, and wielded a scimitar adequately. Sabu, who had made such an indelible impression on filmgoers as *The Elephant Boy* (United Artists, 1937) and in a co-starring role in *The Thief of Bagdad* (United Artists, 1940), functioned as the young mascot-matchmaker-jokester-plot maneuverer in *Arabian Nights* and in the new love team's major subsequent vehicles.

As for Maria, *Arabian Nights* provided her with a world all her own, and she entered the mystical chambers with the conviction of a true believer. Thus she imbued her one-dimensional characterization as the vain dancing girl, Sherazad, with a captivating conviction—no small task, considering that she had to cope with, and overcome, such amazingly inept dialog. At one point, her slave rushes into her tent to advise her that the circus audience is eagerly, indeed impatiently, awaiting her specialty turn. Her disdainful reply to her maid's entreaties is a scornful, "Fools! Let them wait!" Later in the wild and very woolly tale, Maria is forced to perform (with the dynamic aid of a double) a dance of the single veil, hoping to stave off the evil stepbrother (Leif Erikson) of Hall. In the course of the film, Maria finds herself held prisoner in a harem guarded by leopards, escaping with Hall in a thrilling two-on-a-horse sequence, and parading through the meretricious venture with assorted turbans bedecking her lovely head. (With the latter, she set an international wartime fashion mode for women.)

Despite or, more likely, because of the cotton-candy texture of *Arabian Nights,* which grossed over $2 million, Maria was suddenly important news to the critics (who felt obliged to discover what the bulk of the girlie-conscious public already knew). "Maria Montez's streamlined chassis will be the chief attraction [in *Arabian Nights*] . . . after her performance in this opus, Miss Montez climbs several steps in everybody's estimation" (Lee Mortimer, *New York Daily Mirror).* There would be an occasional pan from a less indulgent reviewer, such as Bosley Crowther (*New York Times*) who carped that she "plays the beauteous dancer with the hauteur of a tired night-club showgirl." But most of the fourth estate had to agree with Leo Mishkin (*New York Morning Telegraph*), who, in analyzing Maria's screen charms, had two words of evaluation: "woo-woo!"* Maria herself, after viewing the completed *Arabian Nights,* said of her Technicolored image: "When I look at myself, I am so beautiful. I scream with joy."

Maria was then scheduled to appear in support of moneymaking comedians Bud Abbott and Lou Costello in *Pardon My Sarong* (Universal, 1942), but because of her sudden *Arabian Nights* popularity, the Universal regime decided (after some prodding from Maria) that it was unwise to reduce her lustrous new image in a lesser motion picture role. She was replaced in the slapstick comedy by another M.M., Marie "The Body" McDonald.

Time magazine, in reviewing this opus, a film deliberately spotted with scantily clad harem girls, stated, "The New Year will be a Technicolor year and in Technicolor Miss Montez will help make it happy." The magazine was further impressed by the multihued color photography and continued, "The Technicolor Motion Picture Corporation which processes color film for all the studios, is turning out some 7,000,000 feet a month. [All strictly rationed by wartime restrictions.] But not many of the feet will be as pretty as Miss Montez."

In one of her many interviews in 1943, Maria was quoted as making the rather audacious (even for her) statement that she was now determined to capture an Oscar within the next five years and that she was accustomed to getting what she wanted because, "I am veree stubborn—and when I am stubborn, I scream." She further admitted, "Each time I look in mirror, I vant to scream I am so beautiful."

Such remarks made good copy, and she was well aware of it. The people of the press enjoyed Maria's self-enchantment publicizing and went out of their way to interview or photograph her. Once, when a photographer failed to obtain sufficient pictures of her by daylight, she cooperatively suggested that she be lensed at night. "Veree pretty, the moonlight." She was completely aware of the great power of the press and, assisted by her personal publicity man, engendered goodwill by stopping at any time to talk or pose. She explained, "I never put up a front with newspaper pip-ple. They vant to do a good story, and I vant a good story about me, too. So that makes two of us." Whenever she was sent on personal-appearance tours she became a fast friend of all theatre managers to the point of later establishing a running correspondence with them. It was also revealed to the eager public that her collection of hats was the largest in Hollywood and that her vast wardrobe contained countless pairs of shoes and only the lowest of lowcut gowns. Perhaps the crowning achievement of her self-engendered publicity was the announcement that her poem "Crepúsculo" ("Twilight") had appeared in the South American literary magazine *Baho Rueo*; the poem was awarded a special prize by a writers group, the Manuscripters.

Maria, who, in her own exotic way, rivaled the pinup popularity of Betty Grable, Rita Hayworth, Lana Turner, and Hedy Lamarr, proved to be just as romantically determined about love as she was in the pursuit of her hedonistic Hollywood dream wishes. At 5:00 P.M. on October 1, 1942, while in Chicago on a personal appearance tour, she changed trains at bustling Dearborn Street Station. There, for the first time, she encountered Jean-Pierre Aumont, a six-foot, blue-eyed, blond, Parisian actor.* She later confided, "I even tell you to the second when I see heem; it vas the same second I fall in love vith heem—boom."

Meanwhile, anxious to keep the public interested in its new brand of

---

*Born Jean-Pierre Salomons on January 5, 1913, in Paris, France, Aumont made his stage debut as Oedipus in Jean Cocteau's *La Machine Infernale* at the Comédie Champs-Elysées in Paris in April 1934. He later played in *Le Coeur* (1937), *Pelleas et Melisande* (1938), and in *As You Like It*. His film debut occurred in *Echec et Mat*, a 1931 French-made feature, and he appeared in twenty-five more Gallic motion pictures (including *L'Equipage* [1936] and *Bizarre Bizarre* [1939]) before leaving the show-business scene to fight for his country. Awarded the Croix de Guerre in 1940, he fled his homeland when it fell to the Germans and thereafter made his way to the United States in 1941. His American stage debut occurred in San Francisco as part of Katharine Cornell's company of *Rose Burke* (1942). His Hollywood movie bow was in *Assignment in Brittany* (MGM, 1943).

Anne Nagel (black dress), Virginia Bruce (center), and Maria Montez
(silver gown) in THE INVISIBLE WOMAN (Univ '41)

With Leon Errol and Johnny Downs in
MOONLIGHT IN HAWAII (Univ '41)

476

With Peter George Lynn,
Truman Bradley,
Turhan Bey, Mary
Gordon, Charles Lang,
Lloyd Corrigan, Philip
Trent, Irene Hervey, and
William Gargan in
BOMBAY CLIPPER
(Univ '42)

With Broderick Crawford, Andy Devine, Brian Donlevy,
and Henry Wilcoxon in SOUTH OF TAHITI (Univ '41)

With John Litel,
Nell O'Day, and
Maria Ouspenskaya in
THE MYSTERY OF
MARIE ROGET
(Univ '42)

Publicity pose with Jon Hall for ARABIAN NIGHTS (Univ '42)

With Edgar Barrier, Jon Hall, Kermit Maynard, Leif Erikson, and
Shemp Howard in ARABIAN NIGHTS

With Anne Gwynne in front of a
portrait of Maria Montez painted by
artist Frederick L. Sprague (c. 1943)

With beau Jean-Pierre Aumont at
the Hollywood Bowl in 1943

With husband Jean-Pierre Aumont at the Los Angeles Airport (1943)

Publicity pose with Jon Hall for WHITE SAVAGE (Univ '43)

adventure thriller, Universal put scripter Richard Brooks to work on a tale that would again involve the starring trio of *Arabian Nights* and duplicate that film's special escapist ambiance. Long before the film debuted at New York's Rivoli Theatre, Maria gleefully informed the devoted press, "My peectures are getting nakeder and nakeder. In zee last one, *White Savage,* I wear less than ever."

Eileen Creelman *(New York Sun)* might criticize the Technicolor *White Savage* (Universal, 1943), "[It] has a plot like a comic strip and characters no more subtly drawn," but the public was pleased to have such simple-minded diversion from the war news and rationing. Director Arthur Lubin, realizing the dramatic limitations of his star trio and the wispiness of the fantasy-land scenario, allowed his players free reign to indulge their screen personae to the fullest. Set in the South Seas on the imaginary Temple Island, *White Savage* found Maria parading about with aloof delight as Princess Tahia, who reigns contentedly over indulgent native subjects. Unlike the sinister German (Thomas Gomez) who thirsts for the wealth of the fabled, jeweled-encrusted pool on Temple Island, or the Australian fisherman (Jon Hall), who seeks the rights to shark-hunt in the lush water beds near Temple Island,* Maria's royal character is far more concerned with primping her exotic personage and maintaining a watchful eye over her white man-corrupted brother (Turhan Bey). Hall, who for novelty's sake wore both shoes and long hair and smoked a pipe in this entry, naturally proved to be the jocular hero who wins Maria's reluctant admiration. In her first oncamera kissing scene, she informs Hall, the delighted recipient, "Kaloe *you* no need Vitamin A."

Within the film's seventy-five minutes, there was a succession of pagan rituals, sinister villains, and a climactic cave-in to provide the plot with poetic justice, but the entire proceedings were just a well-engineered excuse to dangle Maria's special charms in front of filmgoers. "Mlle Montez in a sarong knows how to throw all the curves and display all the features that one could possibly ask for . . . " (Leo Mishkin, *New York Morning Telegraph*).

White Savage proved to be another box-office bonanza. Universal had its "perfect" formula: the new love team of Maria and Jon Hall, Sabu for innocent comedy relief, exotic backdrops with turquoise waters, lush vegetation, and burgeoning blossoms, and a plotline that would whet the adventurous appetite of any indulgent, action-hungry film-viewer. Keen observers might point out that these MM-South Seas entries were more akin to Westerns in disguise than Dorothy Lamour-oriented tropical offerings. Nevertheless, in swift order, Maria had demonstrated conclusively to her studio bosses and the public alike, that when it came to wearing filmy

---

*Hall wants to kill the sharks for their vitamin-valuable livers, and persuades Sabu, the son of Maria's chief handmaiden, to present his cause to the reluctant Princess.

clothing, play-acting the regal heroine, or arching her back provocatively from a prone position, she had no contemporary peers. Seemingly, male moviegoers everywhere dreamed of future days when they, too, might wind up in a sun-drenched land with valuables and an attractive partner like Maria.

Now safely ensconced in her special star position at Universal,* Maria took time off from her career to wed Aumont on Tuesday, July 13, 1943. He was thirty-four, she was twenty-three. The ceremony, in Hollywood, was well attended by representatives of Southern California's newspapers and magazines. Maria would later estimate for the press that she had kissed her new husband oncamera 112 times that eventful day.

A handful of filmland's skeptics, eager to put her down, then spread the word that Maria Montez was a phony and that her pedigree was as fake as that of the much-publicized "import" of the 1930s, Sigrid Gurie. They insisted she was probably born in Brooklyn of questionable parentage, that her collection of jewels were glass imitations, that her accent was a clever part of the act. The bit about coming from Brooklyn "always wake my foony bone," she said. "I went to Brooklyn once to see the aquarium. Only I was not sure I was there. I ask pipple, 'where is it, thees Brooklyn?' and they look at me coldly. I find out later that all time while I am asking them, I am een Brooklyn. Instead of Brooklyn adopting me, I theenk I weel adopt eet." She further elucidated, "My legs are so good pipple theenk they must be American. Maybe that is why they theenk I am from the city weeth the loving-bums baseball team."

When two of Maria's sisters came to the United States to spend some time with her in Hollywood, Mrs. John Alexander, an instructress in Romance languages at the University of Pennsylvania, was hired to provide them with English lessons. The authoritative Mrs. Alexander cleared the accent question by stating, "There is no reason to doubt that the sisters, and Maria, are exactly what they claim to be."

As for the jewels, a Beverly Hills expert "happened" to be at Universal one day and visited the set where Maria was emoting. Quietly, but with many curious eyes watching him, he gave an appraisal of a bracelet she was wearing with, "You could easily duplicate that for about sixty thousand."

The final squelch to the accusations that she was not "for real" came in November 1943 from Flor Trujillo, the daughter of the President of the Dominican Republic, who presented Maria with the Order of Juan Pablo Duart and the Order of Trujillo. The awards were made for promoting friendly relations between the United States and the Dominican Republic and for Maria's outstanding feminine achievements. Maria was the first

*Her salary, even by Universal's parsimonious standards, was not extravagant; a mere $250 weekly as late as early 1943.

woman of her country to be so honored. It was highly unlikely that the Trujillos would have selected a Brooklyn-born American to wear the republic's medals of distinction.

Very calmly, Maria had the last say about those members of the sex she considered to be largely responsible for the attempted defamation. "I like women. I like them for the good they can do for you if they want to. On the other hand, there are some women who don't like you, no matter what you do. I theenk if somebody would open a school to teach women to love, there would be fewer divorces. I have talked to American girls about these theengs, and their ideas of love-making are very strange. Like dry ice."

In the autumn of 1943, Aumont, who had been featured in MGM's *The Cross of Lorraine*, left Hollywood to serve with De Gaulle's Free French Army in Africa. Maria hung a service star in a window of her home, and, in a well-circulated interview with *Saturday Evening Post* writer Pete Martin, explained her remedies for her solitary domestic state. She exercised strenuously and took very cold showers to help pass the time. In addition to such curatives for loneliness, she resumed her career with five 1944-released films.

The first was *Ali Baba and the Forty Thieves* (Universal, 1944) with Jon Hall, but with Sabu replaced by the coming studio contractee, exotic Turhan Bey. Advertised as an "original story," the sketchy plot, with its modern World War II message, focused on Ali Baba, Caliph of Baghdad (Hall), forced into exile by the Mongol Hulagu Khan (Kurt Katch).* Maria was presented as the tempestuous Princess Amara, betrothed to Ali since childhood. Bulky Andy Devine waddled about as a Moslem, and, with the legendary forty thieves, aids Caliph Ali to regain his rightful throne. In one scene, the cinema-history-making words "Open sesame" were uttered and forthwith the side of a mountain magically swung open to reveal a spacious studio-soundstage cave.

Newsweek magazine aptly summed up this blend of fairyland operetta-adventure and serial-actioner: "[The picture] calls for fanciful sets, swashbuckling sword play, wild riding and several documentary glimpses of Princess Amara splashing happily in her bath. The final honors for eye appeal are pretty evenly divided between the photogenic Miss Montez and the dazzling Technicolor photography." Or, as the piercing Otis L. Guernsey, Jr. (*New York Herald-Tribune*) reported, "The swordplay is more notable for quantity than savagery—in fact, the film is never anything more than a big game being played by a lot of actors dressed up in very fancy costumes." Regarding Maria's characterization,† *PM* buttonholed her spe-

---

*Since China was then America's wartime ally, the villain's nationality was diplomatically altered accordingly.

†Maria engineered some fresh publicity for herself at the start of the picture's shooting by announcing that according to her latest horoscope, the combination of letters in her character's name was unlucky for her. The studio obligingly came up with the name Amara, which she readily accepted.

cial cinema allure: "[She] will undoubtedly do as every man's Scheherazade as long as her selling message is physical and not verbal." *Ali Baba and the Forty Thieves*, which cost a reputed $750,000 to produce, proved a lucrative grosser for the Universal corporation.

Follow the Boys (1944) was Universal's World War II entry into the allstar, all-variety, all-skits category. In it, Maria was very briefly seen as herself, attending a Hollywood Victory Committee meeting with a contingent of studio contract performers. The committee's aim, like the film's, was to spread cheer through the armed forces. Highlights of the film included George Raft dancing the Charleston to "Sweet Georgia Brown," the Andrews Sisters' version of "Shoo-Shoo Baby," and W. C. Fields's comic exhibition of playing pool with a warped cue. The *Hollywood Citizen-News* said, "it's a good picture in spite of itself." Heard for the first time in this film was the Sammy Cahn-Jule Styne song "I'll Walk Alone," which was Oscar-nominated and became a wartime hit.

"That *Cobra Woman* was a steenker," Maria once said of her next multihued feature (1944). The ads enticed audiences with promises of viewing a "Pagan Witch—No Man Could Resist or Subdue!" The *New York Times* inquired, "Do you want to know that Miss Montez plays dual roles—those of the good twin and the bad twin—without a trace of distinction between?" Leo Mishkin (*New York Morning Telegraph*) was more discerning when he realized what Universal producer George Waggner's intent was: "Two Maria Montezes in the same picture, cavorting all over the landscape with gowns that fit down to here, and sometimes not even that. Zowie!"

The Gene Lewis-Richard Brooks screenplay offered Maria as two physically identical but personality-contrasting siblings, similar to Bette Davis in *A Stolen Life* (Warner Bros., 1946), Olivia de Havilland in *Dark Mirror* (Universal, 1946), and Bonita Granville in *The Guilty* (Monogram, 1947). The good twin, Nadja, a lithe South Sea islander—what else!—is about to wed Jon Hall when she is suddenly abducted by the Cobra People, a tribe of fanatic snake worshippers ruled on Cobra Island by the bad twin, High Priestess Tollea, who grows progressively more tyrannical as the film unwinds.* The natives' hope that Nadja will save them from race suicide is well-founded, except that once they are saved from Tollea and her demands for human sacrifice, the naive, good-natured twin deserts her people for the love of Hall.

Maria's enticing wardrobe by Yvonne Wood extended from simple slendangs to glittering, bejeweled head and face adornments and the dazzling gowns of the evil high priestess. *Time* magazine pointed out, "As if cinemactress, Maria Montez, in her strenuously unclad dual role, did not

*Hava the mute, played by the studio's new horror star, Lon Chaney, Jr., was ordered by the Queen (Mary Nash) to kidnap Nadja from her island innocence and save the simple souls of Cobra Island from Tollea and her henchman Martok (Edgar Barrier).

provide enough cheesecake, there is also Sabu in a pair of trim bathing trunks." The film's director, Robert Siodmak, in a *Sight and Sound* magazine interview some years later, analyzed: *"Cobra Woman* was silly but fun. You know, Maria Montez couldn't act from here to there, but she was a great personality and believed completely in her roles. If she was to play a princess you had to treat her like one all through lunch, but if she was a slave girl you could kick her around and she wouldn't object."

At the time, Alton Cook (*New York World-Telegram*) suggested that *Cobra Woman* "is the kind of picture you measure by the number of whistles it gets." Today the film is regarded by Maria Montez devotees as the apogee of high camp, a story resplendent with exotic music, solemn gongs booming here and there, the rumbling of a great fire mountain, and most of all a bizarre Maria (as the self-gratifying Tollea) performing the hypnotizing snake dance. Her honky-tonk gyrations—or interpretive dancing, if you will—as she demoniacally whips herself into a frenzy of passion, pointing here and there in the temple room to the next sacrificial victims to be thrown into the mouth of the volcano, is a sight to be long cherished. Just how hokey a film could be is demonstrated by the fact that it is not baggy-pants Hall who rescues Nadja from her vicious sister, but Hall's pet chimp!

The settings and the characters changed slightly for her offering of October 1944, *Gypsy Wildcat*. Universal was having great success with its series of horror films set in Transylvanian Balkan Europe and decided to place its tropical star, Maria, in this "in" locale. Here she is Carla, an energetic gypsy dancer who is actually, of course, a long-lost countess and heiress to a sizable castle. At one point she is discovered and taken captive by the avaricious Douglass Dumbrille, but she is eventually rescued by her perennial celluloid Lochinvar, Jon Hall. The *New York Times*'s Bosley Crowther wrote of Maria, "She does yawn and stretch eloquently." Of the whole ball of colored wax, *Newsweek* magazine reported: "Maria Montez and Jon Hall's latest adventures in cuckoo land make a popular pill for escapists. . . . It's all as wholesome as bran for breakfast: the villainy is deep-dyed, the heroism opera bouffe, and the dialogue somewhat out of a rational world." For action-film fans, *Gypsy Wildcat* did provide an excellently staged climactic carriage chase, while for cheesecake devotees, Maria was permitted one change of costume from her form-concealing gypsy skirts and blouses, when she is presented in a décolleté black-lace nightgown. And if anyone should be foolish enough to tire of Maria's fiery-flirtatious-fickle Carla, there was Oscar-winner Gale Sondergaard and hammy Leo Carrillo as gypsy-camp leaders, and Nigel Bruce as an outrageously scenery-chewing high sheriff. *Cue* magazine correctly predicted, "the picture's so bad, it's bound to make money."

Maria's cinematic year ended with the November release of a black-and-white film with modern costumes, modern sets, and a very flimsy story. *Bowery to Broadway* (Universal)—the three-word title told it all—dealt with two competitive beer-garden showmen, Jack Oakie and Donald Cook, who move their respective Bowery musical shows up to Forty-second Street and the big time. It provided another musical showcase for several of Universal's contract players, especially sopranos Ann Blyth and Susanna Foster. In the role of Marina, Maria was a showgirl who makes it big as a songstress. Her lavish production number, "Montevideo," had her voice again dubbed on the soundtrack by Martha Tilton. The role certainly did not enhance Maria's acting career, but it did reconfirm the fact that she knew how to wear clothes.*

In 1944, the high priestess of cinema gossip columnists, Louella Parsons, observed in print, "The always unpredictable and exciting Maria Montez never fails to come through with some unexpected and dramatic episode. . . . I'm always fascinated with the Montez girl. There's never a dull moment when you talk to her. Her life as she tells it is far more romantic than any fiction." Maria, who was then known to the G.I.s as the "Bra Woman," would have been the first to agree with Parsons. Maria had already stated that year, "Nobody can be a beeg star unless she gets her name in the newspaper . . . " And Maria did everything possible to keep herself in the news. She "wrote" an article, "Hollywood Wolves I Have Tamed," in which she said of Orson Welles, "He makes a woman feel very beautiful and desirable, and besides, he is every bit as spectacular as I am."

Maria pontificated that same year: "I am very easy to get along with. I am very nice. I have changed a lot during this last year. I have outgrown my old publicity. I used to do and say things to shock people. That was how I became famous. But now it is different. First the public likes you because you're spectacular. But after it thinks you are a star, it wants you to be nice. Now I am a star. Now I am nice. I am more ladylike—and I don't like it." As for her screen roles: "I am tired of being a fairy-tale princess all the time. In every picture I have royal blood. I told the studio I wanted to do something else. I thought everything was fixed when they put me in *Gypsy Wildcat*. But do you know what happened in the end of that picture? I turn out to be a countess." As for her cheesecake pinup fame, she had tired of the whole business. "They make me look like a smouldering fire."

Maria could also be something of a philosopher. "Whatever happens to me good or bad, I am somewhat of a spectator. I'm always able to sit outside myself and to a certain degree I'm able to watch my happiness or sorrow. I remember the day Jean-Pierre left for Europe. I couldn't have been more miserable and yet as he said good-by I said to him, 'Remember this

---

*Maria portrayed an European import, but her character did not enter the story scene till well after the first hour. With Andy Devine as a priest, twelve song turns by the cast, and the scene-stealing novelty number, "He Took Her for a Sleigh Ride," performed by Donald O'Connor and Peggy Ryan, Maria took a decided back seat in this screen venture.

day, because we shall probably never experience anything more beautiful.' Maybe he thought I was a little crazy, but in his letters later on, he has reminded me of that particular moment many a time, and agreed that I was right."

One more dramatic event happened to Maria in 1944, but she was seemingly unaware of it. She had passed her box-office peak; her cinema novelty was wearing out, and as World War II was drawing to a close, so were her days of stardom at Universal. With V-E Day a reality and V-J Day not that far away, there was no longer any need for fostering the belabored Pan-American Good Neighbor policy and the studios could and would turn to other locales for striking settings. It may have been a coincidence that the "Mexican Spitfire," Lupe Velez, committed suicide in 1944, thus ending her cinema career, but it was no accident that by 1945 south-of-the-border exponents Maria and Carmen Miranda were rapidly falling into career slumps. Paramount had already realized that their Dorothy Lamour's jungle-princess days were numbered and put her into a spoof of the genre, *Rainbow Island* (1944). Perhaps the most telling indication of Maria's forthcoming professional downfall was that when Walter Wanger cast his *Salome, Where She Danced* (Universal, 1945) it was star-in-the-making Yvonne De Carlo who had the lead, not Maria. The picture may have turned out to be a costumed bore, but it set De Carlo onto the path of fame, as she eclipsed Maria from the studio-luminary glamour scene.

Meanwhile in 1945, the unsuspecting Maria confessed that in her spare time, along with steam baths to maintain her weight at 125 pounds, she was preparing a novel called *Forever Is a Long Time* about a passionate and wild Spanish girl who falls in love with a ghost. "The love scenes are done with such delicacy," she admitted. "Eet is all very spiritual. There are no bulging stomachs. My style is poetic. I have three hundred pages done, and it may run to three-fifty or four hundred." Further, she revealed: "I was a very strange leetle girl myself, very much like the girl in thees book. I went to a convent, too, like the girl in my book. As a matter of fact, eet was the same convent." A publicity photograph of Maria in deep concentration at the keyboard of a piano was released to the press with the caption that another of her hobbies was songwriting. It stated that she had completed two tunes for distribution, "Doliente" and "Midnight Mem'ries."

A widely read interview with Maria occurred in 1945 with columnist Earl Wilson. He inquired, "How many baths have you taken? In pictures, I mean." Her reply: "Out of feefteen peectures, in about thirteen I have been in a bath or a sweem. My studio gives the public their money's worth. Mr. Hays watches me close, and I can never kees the guy, he says, 'too hawt.' " When Wilson asked her opinion of brassieres, she said, "My dear fellow, I never have used them. I have no need for them, tank Gawd!" At another time, she explained her motion-picture success with one succinct sentence: "Eet ees because I look sexy—but sweet."

Maria's only 1945 release was *Sudan* (Universal), originally entitled *Queen of the Nile*. The studio pulled out all the costume stops, which resulted in one of the most expensively elegant wardrobes ever to rest on the well-formed body of any Universal actress. The tale, however, was more than empty, and director John Rawlins, who had helmed her *Raiders of the Desert* and *Arabian Nights*, was hard-pressed to work some enthusiasm into the lackluster happenings. Princess Naila (Maria) is forced into exile by evil prime minister George Zucco. Her life is saved—after a frenetic, veiled dance in an Arab village—and her throne is restored by the leaders of the liberated slaves, Jon Hall and Turhan Bey. She gives her love in the final scenes, however, not to Hall, whose career was waning faster than Maria's, but to Bey.

Sudan was the finish of her co-star liaison with Jon Hall. She stated at the time: "I never pay much attention to my leading men. I call them 'my leetle men.' I would rather play third feedle to Boyer than first feedle to one of them. I have nothing against Jon Hall. I have a deep, warm feeling for heem. Theengs have come to such a pass that if I am in a peecture without Jon Hall, pipple weel say, 'Are they keeding?' "

At this point, Maria decided that she had truly outgrown the adventure-film gambit and expressed a vehement desire to do something highly dramatic oncamera at a much larger salary. "I need an awful lot of money," she said. "I have a lot of pipple on my shoulder. Every month I sign checks for ten or eleven pipple. I've got a business manager, but he is tight with me. I give away more than four hundred dollaire a month." Her demands were countered by the studio's casting her in *Frontier Gal* (1945) as a saloon queen. She stood her ground and staunchly refused to have anything to do with such casting.

Maria became more vocal in scorning her past cinema efforts. "Every time I begin to emote, I look up and there is a horse—stealing my scene. I never like my peectures. I have quit one hundred and forty-eight times." Then, in a spurt of self-pity, she admitted: "I have nothing against twelve-year-olds, but I wish somebody else would come to see my peectures. I read a screenplay recently about a bad girl who dies, but Grable will probably get it. Me, I would like to play Lucrezia Borgia or Joan of Arc in Spanish."

Universal, despite Maria's persistent wails, had no intention of making the switch from a strong box-office attraction in adventure yarns to something for which they knew she had no aptitude. She was placed on suspension, and the role in *Frontier Gal* (Universal, 1945) went to ambitious Yvonne De Carlo, who was given one of the biggest publicity buildups ever bestowed on a player at the studio.

Frontier Gal turned out to be no more than mildly successful, however, and Universal carefully reconsidered Maria's requests for serious roles. It was decided to put her back to work—and fast—lest the fickle public forget her. Scripters hurried to the task of creating a story "especially" geared to her exotic beauty and one which, they hoped, might bring out her dramatic qualities if, indeed, they existed. Adhering further to her wishes, the setting had to be contemporary, as did her costumes. The late summer days of 1945 were turning into autumn when Maria entered the soundstage that was to be the site of the major professional mistake of her life. Before starting the screen drama, she grandly announced: "To date, I have given the movie audiences sex. From now on, I weel combine sex with drama."

By using a faraway locale with a strange-sounding name as the title, it was hoped that the public would buy the notion that the film was another *Sudan*. But it wasn't. It was *Tangier* (Universal, 1946). As a Spanish dancer named Rita, Maria spent seventy-five screen minutes searching for the fifth columnist who had killed her next of kin. Pudgy Robert Paige was cast as a discredited American war correspondent, with Louise Allbritton as Maria's stand-in, and Kent Taylor as the star's dance partner. Sabu appeared as a native troubadour and stole the show with his renditions of "Polly Wolly Doodle" and "She'll Be Comin' Round the Mountain."

If Preston Foster summed up *Tangier* fittingly when his character says, "There seems to be an element of confusion here," the *New York Times*'s A. H. Weiler was more incisive, "Miss Montez's array of clothes is far more impressive than the picture's plot and the people involved in it." Granted, even a far more versatile actress would have been hard put to cope with the trite dialog,* but, as Joe Pihodna (*New York Herald-Tribune*) admitted: "The role of sorceress of a group out to avenge Nazi brutalities is a bit too much for Maria Montez. A handsomely mounted girl, who can swish as engagingly as any one in a negligee, Miss Montez finds the road to Tangier a tough one." By 1946, spy melodramas, even of superior caliber, were old hat to weary moviegoers.

With the cessation of the European portion of the war in May 1945, Jean-Pierre Aumont, then an attache on General Eisenhower's staff, returned home on leave. Maria announced that she no longer needed cold showers or steam baths to calm her down since Jean-Pierre was at home. By Thanksgiving, he was back in Hollywood to stay. To show the public that Maria and Jean-Pierre were now very American, Universal released a publicity photograph of uniformed Aumont smilingly posed with carving tools placed against a well-browned turkey. Beautiful Maria stood beside him to tuck a protective napkin into the front of his shirt collar. The photo caption read: "Maria Montez is having her best Thanksgiving holiday since pre-World War II. The Universal Picture star has just rushed her

---

Maria: You are protecting me. Why?
Paige: We had a date. Remember?

490

latest film, *Tangier*, to completion since she and Aumont are expecting and will welcome their first-born in the spring."

Their daughter, Maria Christina, was born on Thursday, February 14, 1946, in Hollywood.

Maria returned to the screen in *The Exile* (Universal, 1947), based on Cosmo Hamilton's novel, *His Majesty, the King*. Douglas Fairbanks, Jr., wrote the screen adaptation, produced the film, and starred. Maria's appearance as the Countess was no more than an oversized cameo although she was given second billing (top in some advertisements). Fairbanks was seen as Charles II on the lam in Holland prior to his restoration to the English throne in 1660. The purpose of Maria's twenty-minute role was to establish her relationship as Fairbanks's mistress, whom he shed for Dutch girl Paula Corday—until duty calls him back to London. Despite being directed by the international film master, Max Ophuls, *The Exile* emerged as a plodding swashbuckling entry and was not bolstered very much by its sepia coloring.

In an obvious attempt to assuage the Montez fans who felt cheated for having seen so little of her in *The Exile*, Maria was next starred in *Pirates of Monterey* (Universal, 1947) in glorious Technicolor and lavishly costumed by Yvonne Wood. Universal proclaimed the film "Bold Adventure . . . wild, exciting! sultry lips . . . warm, enticing!" but as *Cue* magazine discovered, it was instead an "elaborately undistinguished drama of Mexico-ruled California in the 1840s."

Maria's role as Marguerita found her arriving in the far western territory to wed dashing Spanish soldier Philip Reed. However, she fairly reels at the sight of American soldier Rod Cameron. The latter, in the course of the tale, hustles a wagon-train-load of the latest-type rifles from Mexico City to the Mexican army detachment at the presidio in old Monterey. *Modern Screen*'s reviewer wrote: "*Pirates of Monterey* has beautiful Technicolor, beautiful Maria Montez and a plot of which I was able to make neither head nor tail. Maybe you'll be luckier . . . " In past years, Maria had been berated for her sparse display of thespian talents, but 1947 found her under critical fire for her accent, which once had been considered quite endearing. Regarding *The Exile, Variety* had complained that as the French titled lady she "is not always understandable." Now, regarding *Pirates of Monterey*, Howard Barnes (*New York Herald-Tribune*) carped, "Maria Montez exaggerates a Spanish accent to a ludicrous degree."

Pirates of Monterey was to be her last film in color. Her seven-year Universal contract expired upon the film's completion* and with her husband backing her up,† she embarked on a freelance arrangement.

*Production was completed July 15, 1946, after seventy-nine days of work.
†Aumont fared little better at Universal in *Song of Scheherazade* (1947) cast opposite his wife's studio successor, Yvonne De Carlo.

In May 1947, Maria and Jean-Pierre agreed to star for producer Seymour Nebenzal in a new version of his previous, European-made epic, *L'Atlantide* (1931). Arthur Ripley was hired as director, with Karl Struss as cinematographer, Jean Schlumberger as costume designer, and Lionel Banks in charge of designing some forty sets which occupied all of the largest stage on a rented Samuel Goldwyn soundstage. The suite of rooms in which most of the action was to occur included a terrace, a reception room, and a boudoir with a bed ten feet long and seven feet high, built in the shape of a conch shell and lined with coral silk.

The film's amazing story was based on the fabled lost island continent of Atlantis, which supposedly sank thousands of years ago. Nebenzal's theory was that it did not disappear at all, but rose up out of the Sahara Desert. His Atlantis was inhabited by alluring queens descended from gods and goddesses and was ruled by the sultriest of them all, Antinea, played by Maria. Two soldiers of the French Foreign Legion (Aumont and Dennis O'Keefe) stumble onto the majestic desert land and fall in love with its queen, who eventually destroys them both.

At the outset of filming, when Maria was informed that she was to impersonate the most amorous woman in history, she threw herself into character by kissing her leading man—Aumont—a reputed total of 551 times in twenty-eight days of oncamera work. Her explanation: "After the first day of shooting I forgot that Jean-Pierre was my husband and that I was his wife. I became the most cruel siren in history, the seductive Queen Antinea of Atlantis. Eet is our practice at home that makes our screen love scenes so perfect." There were other scenes that called for her to treat Aumont's Andre St. Avit like a dog. "I would be most apologetic to heem, later, and pour tenderness at heem. Of course, at home, I would do my best to make it up to heem." One of the new screen team's oncamera embraces, on a fifteen-foot oval lounge, consumed two minutes of film. Because it was a sequence considered too suggestive for the Production Code censors, it eventually landed on the cutting-room floor.

United Artists had agreed to release the "epic," but upon screening a rough cut, insisted that director John Brahm be hired to liven up the sluggish proceedings. Film editor Gregg Tallas was employed to add desert footage from the 1931 version. Ultimately, Brahm refused to have his name connected with something he considered so artistically inferior, and most sources today give directorial credit to Tallas. Ripley had quit during the early months of production.

As *Siren of Atlantis*, the picture was finally released in August 1949, almost two years after it was begun. The trade ads pronounced that Maria was "The Queen Who Out-Ambered Amber" (referring to Linda Darnell's marathon role in Twentieth Century-Fox's *Forever Amber* [1947]), but that was not enough to induce an uncaring public into theatres showing the film. Joe Pihodna (*New York Herald-Tribune*) warned his readers, "That little number at the Globe Theatre . . . is making a bid for two annual prizes for the year—the worst picture and the worst acting." The age of Maria Montez in Hollywood had come to a close.

Months before *Siren of Atlantis* was shown on any theatre screen, the Aumonts had moved to France. Maria had often said that one day she wanted a hilltop palace of her own, similar to that of Queen Antinea's, but with more than just a false front. Jean-Pierre fulfilled her wish by presenting her with a three-story, five-bedroom home surrounded by pine trees, located in Suresnes, some six miles from the center of Paris.

Professionally, since Aumont was still a favorite with Parisian audiences, it was thought a winning idea to combine her talents with his on-camera. Their initial film abroad was in French. Entitled *Hans le Marin* (*Hans the Sailor*) (1949), it was directed by Aumont's brother, Francois Villiers. Maria portrayed an unscrupulous nightclub entertainer who becomes involved with a Canadian sailor (Aumont) suffering from loss of memory. Aumont soon loves her, but later kills the duplicitous creature. Maria was physically captivating in the film, but the Parisian critics were quick to note that she seemed to be struggling with the French dialog. The kindly critic from *Carrefour* admitted that Maria seems "more than willing to get rid of the kind of pin-up girls and male-tamers roles she has essayed until now." The film was distributed for a brief time in the United States in 1950 with English dubbing, under the title *The Wicked City*.

Maria was far more seductive and successful in her second French film, *Portrait d'un Assassin* (1949) with Erich von Stroheim and Pierre Brasseur. The latter was called in at the last minute to replace Orson Welles, who claimed to have had more urgent business elsewhere. Some claimants insist Welles was hired to direct Maria's scenes. The film was considered a "big" production, if only for its international cast and the inclusion of such well-known character actors as Marcel Dalio and Jules Berry. Although Maria was top-billed in the production, the rather bizarre storyline and the in-depth study of the carnival and circus world took front and center.* André Bazin (*Ecran Français*) insisted that Maria's voice was dubbed on the French soundtrack, but that her presence was "not so bad." Henry Magnan (*Le Monde*) reported, "Maria Montez is beautiful and still doesn't

*The plot of *Portrait d'un Assassin* is as follows: Fabius (Pierre Brasseur), a stunt motorcyclist, is engaged by talent manager Lucienne (Maria) to perform a double-looping stunt in a show. Maria is a sadistic woman who has already destroyed several lovers and only gives herself to men in exchange for their promise to take part in dangerous stunts. One of these unfortunates is Eric (Erich von Stroheim), a former trapeze artist who was injured in a fall and now must wear an iron brace. One evening Brasseur, who wished to murder his wife, Martha (Arletty), accidentally fires at Maria. Under these circumstances he comes to know Maria and soon leaves his wife for her. The night of the first carnival show he learns that Arletty has tried to perform his stunt and died in the try. Brasseur comprehends that he has been a puppet in the hands of Maria, and he murders her. He then accomplishes his daring stunting act, convinced that he will die in the process. By chance he survives and then gives himself up to the police.

know what an intonation is but glances with talent." This motion picture has not been shown commercially in the United States.

Meanwhile, Aumont, long known for his artistic creativity, was on the Paris stage in a play of his own authorship, *L'Empereur de Chine*. After a moderately successful run there, it was adapted for Broadway by Philip Barry. Known as *My Name Is Aquilon*, it opened at New York's Lyceum Theatre on February 9, 1949, starring Aumont, Phyllis Kirk, and Lilli Palmer.

Maria sojourned in New York with her husband while he performed on stage. She commented to Manhattan newsmen, "In Paris, I can do no wrong. They love me there." As it turned out, the Aumonts' stay in New York was brief; *My Name Is Aquilon* folded on March 7, 1949, after only thirty-one performances.

Maria immediately went to Italy to star in *Il Ladro di Venezia*, which would later be released in the United States as *The Thief of Venice* (Twentieth Century-Fox, 1952). The cast included Paul Christian, Faye Marlowe, and Massimo Serato, with John Brahm functioning as director. Set around 1575 and filmed in, on, and around the canals of Venice, it offered Maria as the proprietress of a tavern who assists naval captain Christian, the Robin Hood of Venice, to free the Renaissance city of its unconscionable grand inquisitor (Serato). Several sources acknowledged that Maria gave the best performance of her film career in this swashbuckling picture.*

Maria was again in Italy in 1950 for the costumer *Amore e Sangue* (*Love and Blood*), in which she was a cafe singer who unwittingly sets off a feud between the police of Naples and a well-organized gang of thugs known as la Camora. Massimo Serato enacted the part of her lover, whom she eventually stabs to death. Also in the cast was Alan Curtis, another displaced American. The film reached France in 1953 where it engendered some interest as the last released motion picture of the actress. André Bazin (*Radio Cinema*) noted: "Direction is on a par with the script and is as sparing of means as the screenwriter of his imagination. The poor Maria Montez is seemingly lost in this adventure play; a lady of little virtue and with a big heart." The reviewer for *Ecran Français* observed: "A ridiculous melodrama where the fine Italian countryside is badly put to use. The only emotion comes out of seeing beautiful Maria Montez in her last role." *Amore e Sangue* was shown on American television in 1955, dubbed into English and under the title tag, *City of Violence*.

On January 2, 1951, Maria's legal representatives won a $38,000 law suit in Los Angeles Superior Court against Seymour Nebenzal, concerning alleged unpaid salary on *Siren of Atlantis*. The proceedings described the film as a "calamity from a financial standpoint." Nebenzal, who had

---

*The British *Monthly Film Bulletin* complained: "The playing uninspired and the plot confusingly developed, but the Venetian setting is well used; the final scene of the Grand Canal with the procession of river-crafts escorting the giant state gondola, is particularly effective."

seen no profits on the box-office dud, claimed that he had already loaned Maria sums as advances on her $100,000 salary. Although a technical victory for Maria, reportedly she never saw a penny of her court-approved claim.

Meanwhile, back in Paris, Maria made her stage debut in January 1951 in *L'Ile Heureuse* (*Happy Island*), a divertissement written by Aumont, concerning a young G.I. who comes to Hollywood after the war to sell a studio producer his meaningful drama. The ex-soldier refuses to be cowed by the big-shot producer—an ex-masseur—or by the tempestuous film star, Carlotta Goya (Maria). In the end, the novice writer becomes the hero of the day with everyone at his beck and call. Robert Kemp, in reviewing the production for *Le Monde*, was rather unpersuaded by the play's structure. As for Maria, he noted, "one looks at Maria Montez and even listens to her funny accent: she has almost the accent and the dash of Elvire Popesco,"* and concluded by noting that Maria's diction was very hard to understand. The play had a short run.

Later in 1951, Maria and Aumont appeared together oncamera in an Italian film entitled *La Vendetta del Corsaro* (*The Pirate's Vengeance*), also called *La Donna del Corsaro* (*The Pirate's Woman*). Aumont was cast as the daring leader of a band of pirates who, upon boarding a Spanish ship at sea, encounters the noble and beautiful Consuelo (Maria), with whom he falls in love. Later he learns that her chambermaid (Milly Vitale) is none other than his long-lost half-sister.

A few days after returning to Suresnes from the Italian filmmaking, Maria complained of pains near her heart and remarked jokingly, "I'd better watch that because eet might end up playing me a dirty trick." On Friday night, September 7, 1951, the Aumonts dined at a fashionable restaurant in Paris with their houseguests, Maria's sisters, Anita and Teresita. The following day, before lunch, Maria adjourned to her bath of extremely hot water mixed with reducing salts. This was a habit that had become a daily ritual because of her growing anxiety about retaining her standard weight of 125 pounds.

The sisters, waiting downstairs, became worried when she seemed to be taking longer than usual. Anita went upstairs and knocked at the bathroom door. When there was no answer, she opened the door and found Maria submerged, with just her forehead above water. The two sisters, although in a state of semi-hysterics, managed to carry her to her bedroom and then called a doctor. Firemen were summoned to apply artificial respiration. After almost three hours of efforts to revive her, Maria Montez was declared dead of a heart seizure. Jean-Pierre, who had been called home from the movie set where he was at work, collapsed in grief. His deceased wife was only thirty-one years old.

*A Rumanian actress noted for her extravagantly heavy accent.

The Roman Catholic funeral for Maria was held in the local church of Saint Pierre de Chaillot on Tuesday, September 11. It was not until February 10 of the following year that Aumont came upon Maria's will, tucked away in some papers stored over the garage. She left the bulk of her $200,000 estate to Aumont and their five-year-old daughter, with special provisions for her sisters.*

Up until 1957, the Montez films were occasionally reissued at neighborhood theatres in larger U.S. cities. That year, all of Maria's Universal features were leased to television, and now, for the most part, her movies, very badly edited, haunt the late, late shows. A few years later, certain underground-movie moguls devised parodies of her features, but none of them was sufficiently imaginative to generate a Montez cult. In the mid-1960s, a female impersonator appeared on the drag scene known as Mario Montez, but the imitation was a far cry from the authentic Maria of 1940s filmdom.

Maria Christina, the Aumonts' daughter, married successful French actor-director Christian Marquand in 1963.† Known professionally as Tina Marquand (sometimes as Tina Aumont), she made a small dent in celluloid history in the late 1960s by lending support to the stars of *Modesty Blaise*, *Texas across the River*, *The Game Is Over*, *Excuse Me, Are You For or Against It*, and *Il Sergente Klems*. In the midst of her modest film career, Tina was occasionally interviewed, with the most frequent question being, "Do you remember your mother?" The candid actress replied: "Actually I don't know. You know how it is with small children. I have a vivid mental picture of her which I might have gotten from seeing her photographs, hearing my father, her sister and friends often speak of her. But I like to think I remember her."

In the summer of 1972, news photographers covering the San Sebastian Film Festival in Madrid were desperate to find newsworthy material until a dusky, eighteen-year-old starlet calling herself Maria Montez showed up on the scene. She claimed to be a niece of the late star and stated, "Why should I change my name?" when someone inquired why she had chosen that name tag. "It's the name I was born with. . . . She [her aunt] died in September. I was born in October. My father was her brother and he named me in remembrance of her." She had played a small part in *Valdez Is Coming* (United Artists, 1971).

It is generally agreed that it would be impossible for Maria Montez to find a proper niche in today's Hollywood. Fortuitously she lived in the right places at the right time and left an indelible mark for generations to come.

*On March 27, 1956, Aumont wed Marisa Pavan, the actress sister of Pier Angeli. The couple have two sons. Aumont has continued to be very active in films, television, and stage work both in Europe and the United States.

†When Marquand met actress Dominique Sande, he and Tina separated, and later divorced.

Feature Film Appearances

LUCKY DEVILS (Univ., 1941) 60 M.

Associate producer, Ben Pivar; director, Lew Landers; story, Sam Robins; screenplay, Alex Gottlieb; camera, Charles Van Enger.

Richard Arlen (Dick); Andy Devine (Andy); Dorothy Lovett (Norma); Janet Shaw (Gwendy); Gladys Blake (Secretary); Vinton Haworth (Bradford); Gus Schilling (Grimshaw); Tim Ryan (Momser); Ralf Harolde (Ritter); Edwin Stanley (Official); Walter Soderling (Cordall); Mildred Shay (Agnes); Dora Clement (Duchess); Frank Mitchell (Foreigner); Hugh Huntley (Duke); William Forrest (Chandler); Eddie Bruce (Myers); Robert Winkler (Mopey); Dick Terry (Berko); Kathryn Sheldon (Malinda); Arthur O'Connell (Pilot); Dick Wessel (Simmons); James Morton (Exposition Guard); Lew Kelly (Process Server); Frank Brownlee (Farmer); Charles Smith (Copy Boy); Jack Smith (Dam Guard); J. Paul Jones (Cassidy); David Oliver (Carter); Victor Zimmerman (Guard); Roger Haliday (Policeman); Guy Kingsford (Lab Man); Ed Peil, Sr. (Jail Guard); Maria Montez (Bathing Beauty Being Interviewed).

THE INVISIBLE WOMAN (Univ., 1941) 72 M.

Associate producer, Burt Kelly; director, A. Edward Sutherland; story, Kurt Siodmak, Joe May; screenplay, Robert Lees, Fred Rinaldo, Gertrude Purcell; art director, Jack Otterson; camera, Elwood Bredell; editor, Frank Gross.

John Barrymore (Professor Gibbs); Virginia Bruce (Kitty Carroll); John Howard (Richard Russell); Charles Ruggles (George); Oscar Homolka (Blackie); Donald MacBride (Foghorn); Edward Brophy (Bill); Shemp Howard (Frankie); Margaret Hamilton (Mrs. Jackson); Anne Nagel (Jean); Kathryn Adams (Peggy); Maria Montez (Marie, the Model); Kay Leslie (Model); Thurston Hall (Hudson); Charles Lane (Growley); Eddy Conrad (Hernandez); Kay Linaker, Sarah Edwards (Buyers); Kitty O'Neil (Mrs. Patten); Mary Gordon (Mrs. Bates); Harry C. Bradley (Want Ad Man); Kernan Cripps (Postman).

BOSS OF BULLION CITY (Univ., 1941) 61 M.

Director, Ray Taylor; story, Arthur St. Claire; screenplay, St. Claire, Victor McLeod.

John Mack Brown (Tom Bryant); Fuzzy Knight (Burt Penneycracker); Nell O'Day (Martha Hadley); Maria Montez (Linda Calhoun); Harry Woods (Sheriff Salter); Melvin Lang (Fred Wallace, the Deputy); Richard Alexander (Steve Hogan); Earle Hodgins (Mike Calhoun); Karl Hackett (Tug Crawford, the Deputy); Frank Ellis (Deputy); George Humbert (Mario Frenandez); Tex Terry, Kermit Maynard, Bill Nestell (Cowboys).

THAT NIGHT IN RIO (20th, 1941) C—90 M.

Associate producer, Fred Kohlmar; director, Irving Cummings; based on a play by Rudolph Lothar, Hans Adler; adaptor, Jessie Ernst; screenplay, George Seaton, Bess Meredyth, Hal Long; additional dialog, Samuel Hoffenstein; choreography, Hermes Pan; music director, Alfred Newman; songs, Mack Gordon and Harry Warren; costumes, Travis Banton; art directors, Richard Day, Joseph C. Wright; set decorator, Thomas Little; sound, W. D. Flick, Roger Heman; camera, Leon Shamroy, Ray Rennahan; editor, Walter Thompson.

Alice Faye (Baroness Cecilia Duarte); Don Ameche (Larry Martin/Baron Duarte); Carmen Miranda (Carmen); S. Z. Sakall (Arthur Penna); J. Carrol Naish (Maghado); Curt Bois (Felicio Salles); Leonid Kinskey (Pierre Dufont); Banda Da Lua (Carmen Miranda's Orchestra); Frank Puglia (Pedro, the Valet); Maria Montez (Inez); Georges Renavent (Ambassador); Eddy Conrad (Alfonso); Fortunio Bonanova (Pereira, the Headwaiter); Flores Bros. (Specialty Singers); Lillian Porter (Luiza, the Maid); Fred Malatesta (Butler); Alberto Morin (Eca, the Pilot); Fredrik Vogeding (Trader); Jean Del Val (Man); Charles de Ravenne (Page Boy); Gino Corrado (Clerk); Eugene Borden (Official at Airport); Andre Cuyas (Waiter); George Bookasta (Bell Boy); Mary Ann Hyde, Vivian Mason, Barbara Lynn, Jean O'Donnell (Secretaries); Bettye Avery, Bunny Hartley, Marion Rosamond, Mary Joyce Walsh, Lillian Eggers, Roseanne Murray, Poppy Wilde, Dorothy Dearing, Bonnie Bannon, Monica Bannister (Models).

RAIDERS OF THE DESERT (Univ., 1941) 66 M.

Associate producer, Ben Pivar; director, John Rawlins; screenplay, Maurice Tombragel, Victor I. McLeod; music director, H. J. Salter; camera, John Boyle; editor, Maurice Wright.

Dick Arlen (Dick Manning); Andy Devine (Andy McCoy); Linda Hayes (Alice Evans); Lewis Howard (Abdullah Ibn el Azora el Karim); George Carleton (Jones); Turhan Bey (Hassen Mohammed); John Harmon (Ahmed); Maria Montez (Zuleika); Ralf Harolde (Sheik Talifah); Neyle Marx (Moviow) (Zeid); Jamiel Hasson (Knife-Throwing Warrior); Charles Regan (Warrier); Stanley Price (Gate Cop); Sig Arno (Suliman); Ralph Peters (Max); Harry Cording (Rawlins); Armand "Curley" Wright (Waiter); Pat Gleason (Sailor); Evelyn Selbie (Flower Woman); Sheila Darcy, Suzanne Ridgway, Rose Burich, Mayta Palmera (Arab Girls); Bob Wilbur (Caravan Leader); Nick Shaid (Patriarch); Dave Sharpe (Double for Turhan Bey).

MOONLIGHT IN HAWAII (Univ., 1941) 61 M.

Associate producer, Ken Goldsmith; director, Charles Lamont; story, Eve Greene; screenplay, Morton Grant, James Gow, Erna Lazarus; art director, Jack Otterson; music director, Charles Previn; songs, Don Raye and Gene DePaul; camera, Stanley Cortez; editor, Arthur Hilton.

Johnny Downs (Pete); Jane Frazee (Toby); Joe McMichael (Beans); Ted McMichael (Red); Judd McMichael (Ollie); Mary Lou Cook (Mary Lou); Leon Errol (Spencer); Richard Carle (Lawton); Marjorie Gateson (Mrs. Flote); Mischa Auer (Clipper); Sunnie O'Dea (Gloria); Maria Montez (Ilani); Elaine Morey (Doris); Charles Coleman (Butler); Jean De Briac (Headwaiter); Ernie Stanton (Truck Driver); Eddie Lee (Charlie); Jim Spencer (Chief Kikhanoui).

SOUTH OF TAHITI (Univ., 1941) 75 M.

Associate producer-director, George Waggner; story, Ainsworth Morgan;

screenplay, Gerald Geraghty; art director, Jack Otterson; music director, Charles Previn; song, Frank Skinner and Waggner; camera, Elwood Bredell.

Brian Donlevy (Bob); Broderick Crawford (Chuck); Andy Devine (Moose); Maria Montez (Melahi); Henry Wilcoxon (Captain Larkin); Abner Biberman (Tahawa); Frank Lackteen (Besar); Ignacio Saenz (Kuana); Armida (Putara); John Merton, Dave Wengren (Sailors); H. B. Warner (High Chief); Barbara Pepper (Julie); Belle Mitchell (Taupa); Al Kikume (Policeman); Frank Brownlee (Harbor Master); Mayta Palmera (Dancer); Victor Groves, Jerry Seri Groves (Sword Dancers); Tom Steele, George Magrill (Sailors in Brawl).

BOMBAY CLIPPER   (Univ., 1942) 60 M.

Associate producer, Marshall Grant; director, John Rawlins; screenplay, Roy Chanslor, Stanley Rubin; music director, Hans J. Salter; camera, Stanley Cortez; editor, Otto Ludwig.

William Gargan [Jim (James Montgomery) Wilson]; Irene Hervey (Frankie Gilroy Wilson); Lloyd Corrigan (George Lewis); Mary Gordon [Abigail (Mag) MacPherson]; Truman Bradley (Dr. Gregory Landers); Maria Montez (Sonya Dietrich Landers); Philip Trent (Tom Hare); Turhan Bey (Captain Chundra); Charles Lang (Tex Harper); John Bagni (Paul, the Purser); Riley Hill (Steward); Peter Lynn (Bland); Warren Ashe (R. C. Bradford, the Airline Manager); Wade Boteler (Ruggles); Billy Wayne (Jeremiah Lamb); Keith Kenneth (Hotel Clerk); Connie Leon (Chambermaid); Mel Ruick (Submarine Commander); Harold Daniels (Sam); John Picorri (Waiter); Pat O'Malley (Chief Inspector); C. Montague Shaw (Captain Caldwell, Commander of the Port); Paul Dubov (News Photographer); Harry Strang (Submarine Officer); Jack Lee (Sub-Inspector); Shuran Singh (Singapore Policeman); Philip Ahlm, Tom Schamp, Lal Chan Mehra (Submarine Gun Crew); Beatrice Roberts (Miss Kane, the Secretary).

THE MYSTERY OF MARIE ROGET   (Univ., 1942) 61 M.

Producer, Paul Malvern; director, Phil Rosen; screenplay, Michael Jacoby; music, H. J. Salter; songs, Everett Carter and Milton Rosen; camera, Elwood Bredel; editor, Milton Carruth.

Patric Knowles (Dr. Paul Dupin); Maria Montez (Marie Roget); Maria Ouspenskaya (Mme. Cecile Roget); Lloyd Corrigan (Gobelin, the Prefect of Police); John Litel (Henri Beauvais); Nell O'Day (Camille Roget); Edward Norris (Marcel Vignon); Frank Reicher (Magistrate); Clyde Fillmore (Monsieur De Luc); Norma Drury (Madame De Luc); John Maxwell, Bill Ruhl, Paul Bryar (Detectives); Paul Burns (Gardener); Charles Middleton (Curator of the Zoo); Reed Hadley (Naval Officer); Paul Dubov (Pierre, the News Vendor); Joe Bernard, Frank O'Connor (Men); Ray Bailey (Gendarme); Charles Wagenheim, Lester Dorr (Subordinates to Prefect); Alphonse Martel (Vegetable Cart Driver); Francis Sayles, Jimmie Lucas (Parisians); Beatrice Roberts (Wife on Street); Caroline Cooke (Woman).

ARABIAN NIGHTS   (Univ., 1942) C—86 M.

Producer, Walter Wanger; director, John Rawlins; story-screenplay, Michael Hogan; additional dialog, True Boardman; technical adviser, Jamiel Hasson; music, Frank Skinner; assistant director, Fred Frank; production designer, Jack Otterson, Alexander Golitzen; set decorator, R. A. Gausman, Ira S. Webb; women's costumes, Vera West; music director, Charles Previn; camera, Milton Krasner; editor, Philip Cahn.

Sabu (Ali Ben Ali); Jon Hall (Haroun al Raschid); Maria Montez (Sherazad); Leif Erikson (Kamar); Billy Gilbert (Almad); Edgar Barrier (Hadan); Richard

Lane (Corporal); Turhan Bey (Captain); John Qualen (Aladdin); Shemp Howard (Sinbad); Wee "Willie" Davis (Valda); Thomas Gomez (Hakim, the Slave Trader); Jeni Le Gon (Sherazad's Dresser); Robert Greig (Eunuch-Story Teller); Charles Coleman (Eunuch); Adia Kuznetzoff (Slaver); Emory Parnell (Harem Sentry); Harry Cording (Blacksmith); Robin Raymond (Slave Girl); Carmen D'Antonio, Virginia Engels, Nedra Sanders, Mary Moore, Veronika Pataky, Jean Trent, Frances Gladwin, Rosemarie Dempsey, Patsy Mace, Pat Starling, June Ealey (Harem Girls); Andre Charlot, Frank Lackteen, Anthony Blair, Robert Barron, Art Miles, Murdock MacQuarrie (Bidders); Elyse Knox (Duenna); Burno Acquanetta (Ishya); Ernest Whitman (Nubian Slave); Eva Puig (Old Woman); Ken Christy (Provost Marshal); Johnnie Berkes (Blind Beggar); Cordell Hickman, Paul Clayton (Black Boys); Phyllis Forbes, Peggy Satterlee, Helen Pender, Eloise Hardt (Virgins); Alaine Brandes (Street Slave Girl); Jamiel Hasson, Crane Whitley, Charles Alvarado (Officers); Duke York (Archer); Mickey Simpson (Hangman); Amador Gutierrez, Ben Ayassa Wadrassi, Edward Marmolejo, Daniel Barone (Tumblers); Kermit Maynard (Soldier); Dave Sharpe (Double for Sabu).

WHITE SAVAGE   (Univ., 1943) C—75 M.

Producer, George Waggner; director, Arthur Lubin; story, Peter Milne; screenplay, Richard Brooks; music, Frank Skinner; music director, Charles Previn; assistant director, Charles Gould; art directors, John B. Goodman, Robert Boyle; set decorators, R. A. Gausman, Ira S. Webb; sound, Charles Carroll; camera, Lester White, William Snyder; editor, Russell Schoengarth.

Maria Montez (Tahia); Jon Hall (Kaloe); Sabu (Orano); Thomas Gomez (Sam Miller); Sidney Toler (Wong) Paul Guilfoyle (Erik); Turhan Bey (Tamara); Don Terry (Gris); Constance Purdy (Blossom); Al Kikume (Guard); Frederick Brunn (Sully); Pedro de Cordoba (Candlemaker); Anthony Warde (Clark); Jim Mitchell, Bella Lewitzky (Specialty Dancers); John Harmon (Williams); Minerva Urecal, Kate Lawson (Native Women).

ALI BABA AND THE FORTY THIEVES   (Univ., 1944) C—87 M.

Producer, Paul Malvern; director, Arthur Lubin; screenplay, Edmund L. Hartmann; art directors, John B. Goodman, Richard H. Riedel; set decorators, R. A. Gausman, Ira S. Webb; music-music director, Edward Ward; song, J. Keirn Brennan and Ward; choreography, Paul Oscard; assistant director, Charles Gould; technical adviser, Jamiel Hasson; dialog director, Stacy Keach; sound, Bernard B. Brown, Robert Pritchard; special camera, John P. Fulton; camera, George Robinson, W. Howard Green; editor, Russell Schoengarth.

Jon Hall (Ali Baba); Maria Montez (Amara); Turhan Bey (Jamiel); Andy Devine (Abdullah); Kurt Katch (Hulagu Khan); Frank Puglia (Cassim); Fortunio Bonanova (Baba); Moroni Olsen (Caliph); Ramsey Ames (Nalu); Chris-Pin Martin (Fat Thief); Scotty Beckett (Ali as a Boy); Yvette Duguay (Amara as a Girl); Noel Cravat, Robert Barron (Mongol Captains); Jimmy Conlin (Little Thief); Harry Cording (Mahmoud); Ethan Laidlaw, Hans Herbert, Dick Dickinson, Joey Ray, John Calvert, David Heywood, Pedro Regas (Thieves); Eric Braunsteiner, Jerome Andrews, Alex Goudovitch, Ed Brown, George Martin, Dick D'Arcy (Dancers); Rex Evans (Arab Major Domo); Belle Mitchell (Nursemaid); Harry Woods, Dick Alexander, Art Miles (Mongol Guards); Alphonse Berge (Tailor); Charles Wagenheim (Barber); Wee Willie Davis (Arab Giant); Norman Willis, Pierce Lyden, Don McGill (Guards); James Khan (Persian Prince); Theodore Patay (Arab Priest); Angelo Rossitto (Arab Dwarf).

FOLLOW THE BOYS (Univ., 1944) 122 M.

Producer, Charles K. Feldman; associate producer, Albert L. Rockett; director, A. Edward Sutherland; screenplay, Lou Breslow, Gertrude Purcell; art directors, John B. Goodman, Harold H. MacArthur; set decorators, Russell A. Gausman, Ira S. Webb; assistant director, Howard Christie; music director, Leigh Harline; choreography-stagers, George Hale, Joe Schoenfeld; songs, Sammy Cahn and Jule Styne; Kermit Goell and Walter Donaldson; Billy Austin and Louis Jordan; Dorothy Fields and Jimmy McHugh; Sheldon Brooks; Inez James and Buddy Pepper; Phil Moore; Leo Robin, W. Franke Harling and Richard Whiting; Roy Turk and Fred Ahlert; Dick Charles and Larry Markes; sound, Robert Pritchard; special camera, John P. Fulton; camera, David Abel; editor, Fred R. Feitshans, Jr.

George Raft (Tony West); Vera Zorina (Gloria Vance [Bertha Lindquist]); Charles Grapewin (Nick West); Grace McDonald (Kitty West); Charles Butterworth (Louie Fairweather); George Macready (Walter Bruce); Elizabeth Patterson (Annie); Theodor von Eltz (William Barrett); Regis Toomey (Dr. Jim Henderson); Ramsey Ames (Laura); Spooks (Junior); Jeanette MacDonald, Orson Welles, Marlene Dietrich, Dinah Shore, Donald O'Connor, Peggy Ryan, W. C. Fields, The Andrews Sisters, Artur Rubinstein, Carmen Amaya and Her Company, Sophie Tucker, Delta Rhythm Boys, Leonard Gautier's Bricklayers, Agustin Castellon Sabicas, Ted Lewis and His Band, Freddie Slack And His Orchestra, Charlie Spivak and His Orchestra, Louis Jordan and His Orchestra, Louise Beavers, Clarence Muse, Maxie Rosenbloom, Maria Montez, Susanna Foster, Louise Allbritton, Robert Paige, Alan Curtis, Lon Chaney, Jr., Gloria Jean, Andy Devine, Turhan Bey, Evelyn Ankers, Noah Beery, Jr., Gale Sondergaard, Peter Coe, Nigel Bruce, Thomas Gomez, Lois Collier, Samuel S. Hinds, Randolph Scott, Martha O'Driscoll, Elyse Knox, Philo McCullough (Themselves); Mack Gray (Lieutenant Reynolds); Molly Lamont (Miss Hartford, the Secretary); John Meredith (Blind Soldier-MacDonald Number); John Estes (Patient); Ralph Gardner (Patient in Leg Cast-MacDonald Number); Doris Lloyd (Nurse); Charles D. Brown (Colonel Starrett); Nelson Leigh (Bull Fiddler); Lane Chandler (Ship's Officer); Cyril Ring (Laughton, the *Life* Photographer); Emmett Vogan (Harkness, the *Life* Reporter); Addison Richards (MacDermott, the *Life* Editor); Frank LaRue (Mailman); Tony Marsh (Officer); Stanley Andrews (Australian Officer); Leslie Denison (Reporter); Leyland Hodgson (Australian Reporter); Bill Healy (Ship's Officer); Frank Jenks (Chick Doyle); Ralph Dunn (Loomis); Billy Benedict (Joe, a Soldier); Grandon Rhodes (George Grayson-Guild Member); Edwin Stanley (Taylor, the Film Director); Roy Darmour (Eddie, the Assistant Director); Carl Vernell (Terry Dennis, the Dance Director); Tony Hughes (Man); Wallis Clark (HVC Committee Man); Richard Crane (Marine Officer); Frank Wilcox (Captain Williams, the Army Doctor); Jimmy Carpenter, Bernard Thomas, John Whitney, Walter Tetley, Joel Allen, Carlyle Blackwell, Mel Schubert, Stephen Wayne, Charles King (Soldiers); Carey Harrison, William Forrest (Colonels); Steve Brodie (Australian Pilot); Clyde Cooke (Stooge); Bobby Barber (Soldier in W. C. Fields's Routine); Tom Hanlon (Announcer); Odessa Lauren, Nancy Brinckman, Janet Shaw, Jan Wiley (Telephone Operators); Bob Ashley, Lennie Smith (Jitterbugs); Duke York (M.P.); Don Kramer, Allan Cooke, Luis Torres, Nicholai, John Duane, Ed Browne, Clair Freeman, Bill Meader, Eddie Kover (Soldiers); Daisy (Fifi); Lee Bennett (Acrobat); Baby Marie Osborne (Nurse); George Shorty Chirello (Orson Welles' Assistant); Nicodemus Stewart (Lieutenant Reynolds, USAF); George Eldredge (Submarine Officer); Janice Gay, Jane Smith, Marjorie Fectean, Doris Brenn, Rosemary Battle, Lolita Leighter, Mary Rowland, Eleanor Counts, Linda Brent (Magic Maids); Bill Wolfe (Man in Zoot Suit in W. C. Fields's Routine).

COBRA WOMAN   (Univ., 1944) C—71 M.

Producer, George Waggner; director, Robert Siodmak; story, W. Scott Darling; screenplay, Gene Lewis, Richard Brooks; assistant director, Mack Wright; dialog director, Gene Lewis; art directors, John B. Goodman, Alexander Golitzen; music, Edward Ward; sound, Joe Pais; special effects, John Fulton; camera, George Robinson, Howard Greene; editor, Charles Maynard.

Maria Montez (Tollea/Nadja); Jon Hall (Ramu); Sabu (Kado); Lon Chaney, Jr. (Hava); Edgar Barrier (Martok); Mary Nash (The Queen); Lois Collier (Veeda); Samuel S. Hinds (Father Paul); Moroni Olsen (MacDonald); Robert Barron (Chief Guard); Vivian Austin, Beth Dean, Paulita Arvizu (Handmaidens); Fritz Leiber (Venreau); Belle Mitchell (Native Woman); John Bagni (Native); Dale Van Sickel, Eddie Parker, George Magrill (Guards).

GYPSY WILDCAT   (Univ., 1944) C—77 M.

Producer, George Waggner; director, Roy William Neill; story, James Hogan, Ralph Stock; screenplay, Hogan, Gene Lewis, James M. Cain; additional dialog, Joseph Hoffman; assistant director, Melville Shyer; music director, Edward Ward; song, Ward and Waggner; choreography, Lester Horton; dialog director, Emory Horger; art directors, John B. Goodman, Martin Obzina; sound, Glenn E. Anderson; special effects, John Fulton; camera, George Robinson, W. Howard Greene; editor, Russell Schoengarth.

Maria Montez (Carla); Jon Hall (Michael); Leo Carrillo (Anube); Gale Sondergaard (Rhoda); Peter Coe (Tonio); Nigel Bruce (High Sheriff); Douglass Dumbrille (Baron Tovar); Curt Bois (Valdi); Harry Cording (Captain Marver).

BOWERY TO BROADWAY   (Univ., 1944) 95 M.

Producer, John Grant; director, Charles Lamont; story, Edmund Joseph, Bart Lytton; screenplay, Joseph, Lytton, Arthur T. Horman; art directors, John B. Goodman, Martin Obzina; set decorators, Russell A. Gausman, Ted von Hemert; assistant director, Mack Wright; music director, Edward Ward; musical numbers stagers, Carlos Romero, Louis Da Pron, John Boyle; songs, Everett Carter and Edward Ward; Don George and Dave Franklin; Kim Gannon and Walter Kent; dialog director, Edward Colebrook; sound, Charles Carroll; camera, Charles Van Enger; editor, Arthur Hilton.

Maria Montez (Marina); Jack Oakie (Michael O'Rourke); Susanna Foster (Peggy Fleming); Turhan Bey (Ted Barrie); Ann Blyth (Bessie Jo Kirby); Donald Cook (Dennis Dugan); Louise Allbritton (Lillian Russell); Frank McHugh (Joe Kirby); Rosemary DeCamp (Bessie Kirby); Leo Carrillo (P. J. Fenton); Andy Devine (Father Kelley); Evelyn Ankers (Bonnie Latour); Thomas Gomez (Tom Harvey); Richard Lane (Walter Rogers); George Dolenz (George Henshaw); Mantan Moreland (Alabam); Ben Carter (No-More); Maude Eburne (Madame Alda); Robert Warwick (Cliff Brown); Donald O'Connor, Peggy Ryan (Specialty Number); Joe Mole (Bicycle Specialty); Jack Frost, Art Smith, Chick Madden, Jack Barbee (Rainbow Four); George Meeker, Emmett Vogan (Dandies); Harry Bradley (Reformer); Jimmy Kelly, Tim Taylor (Horse Act); Terry Adams, Karen Raven, Katherine Yorke (Showgirls); Robert Homans (Policeman); Harold DeGarro (Stilt Walker); Beverlee Mitchell (Chewing Gum Girl); Buz Buckley, Teddy Infuhr (Small Boys); Ronnie Rondell, Milton Kibbee, Donald Kerr (Reporters); Virginia Brissac (Sophie); Walter Tetley (Attendant); Jerry Shane (Elevator Boy); Mary Eleanor Donahue (Bessie Jo); Frank Darien (Hot Dog Vendor); Marguerita Padula (Singer); Roy Butler, Jack Rice, Nelson McDowell, Jimmy Lucas

(Quartette); Billy Newell, Howard Mitchell, John Elliott, Clyde Fillmore (Reformers); Ralph Dunn, Harry Strang, Edgar Dearing, Eddie Dunn, Charles McAvoy (Cops); Walter Clinton (Minstrel Man); John Pearson (Minstrel Dancer); William Desmond (Barfly); Joe Kirk (Sign Man); Harry Semels (Drunk); Larry Steers (Van Damm, the Theatre Patron Who Gets Garter); Brooks Benedict (Tammany Hall Representative); Howard Hickman, Snub Pollard, Charles K. French (Lambs Club Members); Jac George (Violinist).

SUDAN   (Univ., 1945) C—76 M.

Producer, Paul Malvern; director, John Rawlins; screenplay, Edmund L. Hartmann; art directors, John B. Goodman, Richard H. Riedel; set decorators, Russell A. Gausman, Leigh Smith; assistant director, William Tummel; dialog director, Stacy Keach; music, Milton Rosen; songs, Rosen and Everett Carter; sound, Bernard B. Brown, William Hedgcock; camera, George Robinson; editor, Milton Carruth.

Maria Montez (Naila); Jon Hall (Merab); Turhan Bey (Herua); Andy Devine (Nebka); George Zucco (Horadef); Robert Warwick (Maatet); Phil Van Zandt (Setna); Harry Cording (Uba); George Lynn (Bata); Charles Arnt (Khafra, the Horse Trader); Ray Teal (Slave Trader); Hans Herbert, Dick Dickinson (Buyers); Bob Barron (Jailer); Gene Stutenroth, Art Miles (Executioners); Charles Morton (Soldier); Tor Johnson (Slaver); Ed Hyans (Master of Ceremonies); James Dime, George Magrill (Guards); Art Foster (Wrestler); Jimmy Lucas, Byron Ruggles, Charles McAvoy (Bettors); Dave Kashner (Crack Bull Whip); Artie Ortego (Starter); Dink Trout (Potter); Duke Johnson (Juggler); Phil Dunham, Alix Nagy, Dan White (Men); Joe Bernard (Horse Owner); Shirley Hunter (Herita); Kay Yorke (Nephytis); Jack Chefe (Mestat); Roy Darmour (Horse Owner); Mary O'Brien (Nephytis); Ann Roberts, Maxine Leeds, Kathleen O'Malley, Rita Benjamin, Rosemarie Babbick, Vivian Mason (Girls); June Pickrell (Old Woman); Belle Mitchell (Woman); Clarke Stevens, Robert Strong (Sentries); Al Ferguson (King); Lloyd Ingraham (Elderly Man).

TANGIER   (Univ., 1946) 76 M.

Executive producer, Joe Gershenson; producer, Paul Malvern; director, George Waggner; story, Alice D. G. Miller; screenplay, M. M. Musselman, Monty F. Collins; assistant director, Charles S. Gould; art directors, John B. Goodman, Sturges D. Carne; set decorators, Russell A. Gausman, Ted Von Hemert; music-music director, Milton Rosen; song, Waggner, Jose Antonio Zorrill, and Gabriel Ruiz; choreography, Lester Horton; sound, Charles Carroll; special camera, D. S. Horsley; camera, Woody Bredell; editor, Edward Curtiss.

Maria Montez (Rita); Robert Paige (Paul Kenyon); Sabu (Pepe); Preston Foster (Colonel Jose Aritego); Louise Allbritton (Dolores); Kent Taylor (Ramon); J. Edward Bromberg (Alec Rocco); Reginald Denny (Fernandez); Charles Judels (Dmitri); Francis McDonald (Sanchez); Erno Verebes (Captain Cartiaz); George Lynn (Lieutenant); Rebel Randell (Rocco's Girl); Dorothy Lawrence (Maid); James Linn (Servant); Billy Greene (Mike); Phil Garris (Elevator Boy); John Banner (Ferris Wheel Operator); Charles Wagenheim (Hadji); Joe Bernard, Dick Dickinson (Men); Charles Stevens (Juan); Eddie Ryans, Jerry Riggio, Parker Garvie, Wheaton Chambers (Vendors); Billy Snyder (Barker); Margaret Hoffman (Police Matron); Jack Chefe (Hotel Clerk); Abel Pina, Henry Pina, Jerry Pina, Jr., Antonio Pina (Tumbling Act); Bobby Barber (Sergeant); Crystal White (Barber Maid); Murray Parker (Juggler); Roxanne Hilton, Karen Raven (Girls); Pierre Andre, Maurice St. Clair, Crystal White (Dance Doubles).

THE EXILE (Univ., 1947) 95 M.*

Producer, Douglas Fairbanks, Jr.; director, Max Ophulus; based on the novel *His Majesty, the King* by Cosmo Hamilton; screenplay, Fairbanks, Jr.; art directors, Bernard Herzbrun, Hilyard Brown; set decorators, Howard Bay; assistant directors, Ben Chapman, George Lollier; sound, Charles Felstead, William Hedgcock; camera, Franz Planer; editor, Ted J. Kent.

Douglas Fairbanks, Jr. (Charles Stuart); Maria Montez (The Countess); Paula Corday (Katie); Henry Daniell (Colonel Ingram); Nigel Bruce (Sir Edward Hyde); Robert Coote (Pinner); Otto Waldis (Jan); Eldon Gorst (Seymour); Milton A. Owen (Wilcox); Colin Keith-Johnston (Captain Bristol); Ben H. Wright (Milbanke); Colin Kenny (Ross); Peter Shaw (Higson); Will Stanton (Tucket); C. S. Ramsey Hill (Cavalier Officer); Gordon Clark (Cavalier Guard); Lumsden Hare (Roundhead General); Lester Mathews (Robbins); Thomas P. Dillon (Jasper); William Trenk (Footman); Fred Cavens (Coachman); Alla Dunn (Marie); Torben Meyer (Sea Captain); Grayce Hampton, Mary Forbes (Court Ladies); Charles Stevens (Painter); James Logan (Thurber); Art Foster (Jessop); Harry Cording, Bruce Riley (Roundheads); Erich Von Schilling, Garry Watson, Joe Ploski, Lillian Castle (Servants); Reginald Sheffield (Commanding Officer); Colin Campbell (Old Secretary); James Craven, Leonard Carey, Pat O'Moore (Cavaliers); Lotte Stein (Fat Dutch Woman); Michael Mark (Drunk); Edwin August (Burger); David Cavendish (Pigeon Keeper); Norbert Schiller (Messenger); John Meredith (Trumpeter); Richard Abbott (Dutch Berger); Keith Hitchcock (Military Man); Daniel de Jonghe (Working Man); Charles Knight (Ingram's Aide); Edith Clinton (Cavalier's Wife); Perc Launders (Guitar Player); Mary Bye (Waitress); Sheldon Jett, Frank Austin, Jack Curtis (Card Players); Pat Griffin (Small Boy); Eddie Cregar (Young Boy); Joseph Kamaryt (Man at Inn); Elinor Vandivere (Woman); Diane Stewart (Girl).

PIRATES OF MONTEREY (Univ., 1947) C—75 M.

Producer, Paul Malvern; director, Alfred Werker; story, Edward T. Lowe, Bradford Ropes; screenplay, Sam Hellman, Margaret Buell Wilder; art directors, Jack Otterson, Richard H. Riedel; set decorators, Russell A. Gausman, Leigh Smith; music, Milton Rosen; assistant director, William Holland; sound, Bernard B. Brown, Charles Carroll; camera, Hal Mohr, W. Howard Greene, Harry Hallenberg; editor, Russell Schoengarth.

Maria Montez (Marguerita); Rod Cameron (Phillip Kent); Mikhail Rasumny (Pio); Philip Reed (Lieutenant Carlos Ortega); Gilbert Roland (Major De Roja); Gale Sondergaard (Senorita de Sola); Tamara Shayne (Filomena); Robert Warwick (Governor); Michael Raffetto (Sergeant Gomara); Neyle Morrow (Manuel); Victor Varconi (Captain Cordova); Charles Wagenheim (Juan); George J. Lewis (Pirate); Joe Bernard (Doctor); George Navarro (Lieutenant); Victor Romito, Don Driggers (Thugs); George Magrill (Pirate); Lucius Villegas (Padre); Chris-Pin Martin (Caretta Man); Julia Andre (Young Woman); Lilo Yarson, Fred Cordova (Sentries); Dick Dickinson (Jailer).

SIREN OF ATLANTIS (UA, 1949) 75 M.

Producer, Seymour Nebenzal; associate producer, Roman I. Pines; director, Gregg Tallas; based on the novel *L'Atlantide* by Pierre Benoit; screenplay, Roland

*Sepia

Leigh, Robert Lax; additional dialog, Thomas Job; music, Michel Michelet; music supervisor, David Chudnow; music director, Heinz Roemheld; assistant director, Milton Carter; makeup, Lee Greenway; choreography, Lester Horton; production designer, Lionel Banks; set decorator, George Sawley; costumes, Jean Schlumberger; sound, Corson Jowett; special effects, Rocky Cline; camera, Karl Struss; editor, Tallas.

Maria Montez (Antinea); Jean-Pierre Aumont (Andre St. Avit); Dennis O'Keefe (Jean Morhange); Henry Daniell (Blades); Morris Carnovsky (Le Mesge); Alexis Minotis (Cortot); Milada Mladova (Tanit Zerga); Allan Nixon (Lindstrom); Russ Conklin (Eggali); Herman Boden (Cegheir); Margaret Martin (Hand Maiden); Pierre Watkin (Colonel); Charles Wagenheim (Doctor); Jim Nolan (Major); Joseph Granby (Expert).

HANS LE MARIN (Discina, 1949) 95 M.*

Supervisor, Marcel Cravenne; director, Francois Villiers; based on the novel by Edouard Peysoon; screenplay, Villiers Cravenne, Michel Arnaud; dialog, Jean-Pierre Aumont; art director, Jean d'Eaubonne; music, Joseph Kosma; costumes, Choumansky; camera, Jean Bourgoin; editor, Henri Taverna.

Maria Montez (Dolores); Jean-Pierre Aumont (Eric, alias Hans); Lilli Palmer (Tania); Marcel Dalio (Marcel); O'Brady (Gypsy Leader); and: Gregoire Aslan, Roger Blin, Roland Toutain, Pierre Bertin, Catherine Damet, Lita Reccio, Roger Hubert, Jean Roy, Georges Jamin.

PORTRAIT D'UN ASSASSIN (S.E.L.F., 1949) 100 M.†

Director, Bernard Roland; screenplay, Marcel Rivet; adaptor, Henri Decoin; dialog, Charles Spaak, Francois Chalais; art director, Roland J. Quignon; music, Maurice Thriet; technical advisor, Serge T. Laroche; sound, Jacques Lebreton; editors, Rene Le Henaff, Germaine Arthus.

Maria Montez (Lucienne); Erich von Stroheim (Eric); Arletty (Martha); Pierre Brasseur (Fabius); Jules Berry (Pfeiffer); Marcel Dieudonné (Prosper); Marcel Dalio (Fred); Edy Debray (Barker); Julien Maffre (Helper); and: Gisele Preville, Natol, the Frotellini Troupe, Marcel Rouzé.

IL LADRO DI VENEZIA (Fox, 1950) 100 M.‡

Producer, Robert Haggiag; director, John Brahm; story, Michael Pertwee; screenplay, Jesse L. Lasky, Jr.; music, Allessandro Cicognini; art directors, Otto Scotti, Louis Scacciandoci; camera, Anchise Brizzi; editors, Terry Morse, Renzo Lucidi.

Maria Montez (Tina); Paul Christian (Alfiere Lorenzo Contarini); Massimo Serato (Scarpa, the Inquisitor); Faye Marlowe (Francesca Disani); Aldo Silvani (Captain Von Sturm); Louis Saltamerenda (Alfredo); Guido Celano (Polo); Humbert Sacripanti (Derro); Ferinand Tamberlani (Lombardi); Camillo Pilotto (Admiral Disani); Liana Del Balzo (Duenna); Paolo Stoppa (Marco); Mario Tosi (Mario); Vinicio Sofia (Grazzi); Leon Menoir (Sharp Eye).

*U.S. release title: The Wicked City (1951).
†A.k.a. Portrait of a Murder.
‡U.S. release title: The Thief of Venice (20th, 1952).

AMORE E SANGUE   (A.B. La Querica, 1951) 86 M.

Producer, William Szekely; director, Marino Girolami*; screenplay, Ernst Marischka; music, Renzo Rossellini; production supervisor, G. B. Bigazzi; camera, Anchise Brizzi.

Maria Montez (Dolores); Massimo Serato (Beppe); and: Alan Curtis, Folco Lulli, Mirella Uberti, Clelia Matania, Hans Schnker, S. Reuer.

A.k.a. *Love and Blood.* U.S. television title: *City of Violence.*

LA VENDETTA DEL CORSARO   (Athena Cinematografica, 1951) 88 M.

Producer, Pietro Bigerna; director, Primo Zeglio; screenplay, E. Sabi; art director, Alfredo Montori; music, Carlo Rustichelli; camera, Gabor Pogany; editor, A. Guftuni.

Jean-Pierre Aumont (Enrico de Roquebrune); Maria Montez (Consuelo); Milly Vitale (Luela); and: Roberto Risso, Franca Mazi, Saro Urzi, Paul Muller, Enrico Glori, Mario Castellani, F. Tamahtin, J. Myhers.

A.k.a. *The Pirates' Revenge.*

*Some sources list John Wolff as the director.

With Jon Hall in WHITE SAVAGE

With Frank Puglia and Kurt Katch (foreground) in ALI BABA AND THE FORTY THIEVES (Univ '44)

On the set of ALI BABA AND THE
FORTY THIEVES with Jon Hall

In COBRA WOMAN

With Lois Collier in
COBRA WOMAN (Univ '44)

With Jon Hall in
GYPSY WILDCAT (Univ '44)

In BOWERY TO BROADWAY
(Univ '44)

With Jean-Pierre Aumont, Thanksgiving, 1945

With daughter Maria Christina and
Jean-Pierre Aumont in 1946

With Douglas Fairbanks, Jr., in THE EXILE (Univ '47)

With Jean-Pierre Aumont and Lilli Palmer in HANS LE MARIN (Discina '49)

With Aldo Silvani in IL LADRO DI VENEZIA (20th '52)

In THE NOTORIOUS LANDLADY (Col '62)

Kim Novak

5'6"
125 pounds
Blonde hair
Green eyes
Aquarius

In the mid-1950s, with the accelerated decay of the Hollywood studio-star system, one of the most impressive twentieth-century American myths was mouldering—i.e., that any good-looking young miss (if sufficiently ambitious, pliable, naive, etc.) could be magically transformed into a Hollywood silver-screen celebrity. One of the last authentic manufactured celluloid love goddesses was Columbia's Kim Novak, who possessed more than a fair share of viable beauty and sex appeal. Between 1955 and 1960, she rivaled Marilyn Monroe and Elizabeth Taylor as the most sensually desirable domestic film personality on the California scene.

When the very raw talent known as Marilyn Pauline Novak was pushed through the Columbia star-making production line in 1954, she was saddled with a veneer of cosmetics, hair styles, costuming, diction, and "acting" mannerisms that combined to give her that special big screen look. The public bought the specially packaged merchandise and Kim Novak, the new blonde bombshell, became the superstar successor to Columbia's 1940s empress, Rita Hayworth. But unlike a goodly number of her forerunners, competitors, or hopeful successors, Kim was far more rational about her sudden rise to fame and riches; she could and did differentiate between soundstage fantasy and real-life actualities. After all, she once admitted: "I never wanted to be a movie star. It was an accident. You know why I came to Hollywood in the first place? Some fellow in Chicago was bugging me to marry him, so I ran away."

Whether it was Columbia's grasping mogul Harry Cohn, now dead, or vulnerable-tough Kim, now semiretired, who was most responsible for perceiving, creating, and perpetuating the commodity known to millions as Kim Novak the silver-blonde love muse, is now largely academic.* In her prime, she demonstrated an inborn ability to convey frosty sensuality combined with passionate openness, qualities which brought to a peak the viewer's panting interest in her sexual allure.† She was constantly berated by the elite critics as being a non-actress of the highest order, yet in her best features, *Picnic* (Columbia, 1955), *The Eddy Duchin Story* (Columbia, 1956), and *Vertigo* (Paramount, 1958), she displayed subtleties of human frailty that might well have been a springboard for a dramatic versatility of sorts.

However, once Kim became a freelance screen notable of the 1960s, her career floundered. Some of the obvious causes were her advancing age, changing styles of sexual fantasies, a frozen disregard for challenging histrionic tutelage, and her general ineptness in selecting proper vehicles.

While Kim's legendary glamour is now better preserved on past films than in present reality, she, unlike many other overripe glamour girls, seems far better able to cope with "ordinary" life on a very private, naturalistic, simple level in which sophistication of any sort has no part.

Joseph and Blanche Novak became parents of their second daughter at St. Anthony's Hospital in Chicago, Illinois, on Monday, February 13, 1933, in Room 313 at 3:13 A.M. The Novaks, positive the baby would be a boy, were quite unprepared with a girl's name. They hastily settled for Marilyn Pauline. A Catholic christening followed. Marilyn and her three-year-old sister, Arlene, were the only children in the modest Novak home at 1910 Springfield Avenue. The residence, in the midst of a mixed Jewish-Bohemian neighborhood, was owned by the maternal grandmother. Joseph Novak was a transit clerk with the Chicago-Milwaukee

---

*The great Cohn once said: "Great parts make great pictures! Great pictures make great parts! This girl [Kim Novak] has had five hit pictures. If you wanna bring me your wife or your aunt, we'll do the same for them."

Kim once countered: "I resent people saying that it was Mr. Cohn who made me what I am today. After all, you can't make a star out of somebody just because you say you're going to. The person has to have something to start with."

†One of Kim's directors observed: "You don't have a casting problem with this girl. If you've got a woman character who's losing a lover, dying of an incurable disease, going to prison or being swindled out of her life savings then you need Novak. She doesn't have to act. She can just turn on her own worries and frustrations."

Director George Sidney has observed: "She has the facade and the equipment of a bitch in the long shot. And yet when you look in Kim's eyes in a close-up, she's like a baby. She's a dual personality. You can't tell whether she's an angel or a bitch."

Life magazine described Kim thus: "Her face is the sort of face that looks as if the rest of the body is making love. She just laps you up with her eyes and lips and tongue. Her face is like a sponge that can soak you up."

Railroad, while Blanche Kral Novak had been a history teacher before her marriage. Both were of Czechoslovakian descent.

One strict house rule when Marilyn was an infant was to never pick her up when she cried. Years later, in searching for a reason for her seeming independence as an adult, she offered: "Perhaps this had an effect on me. Perhaps I didn't have a normal feeling of love, and so I learned to be on my own—and not to fear being a loner."

As a young man, Joseph Novak had moved to Chicago from Oregon, where he, too, had been a teacher as well as a devout lover of nature and the wide open spaces. He felt claustrophobic in crowded Chicago and never seemed at ease in his mother-in-law's house, where his opinions were generally ignored by his wife and her stern parent. Many times he tried to convince his wife to return to Oregon, where he hoped to live out his life on a ranch, but she adamantly refused to leave her mother and resorted to a continual routine of tears and arguments.

Of her parents, Marilyn was more drawn to her father, overlooking his profound sense of life failure, and instead focusing on his more admirable trait of sensitivity. She was determined to please him in every way, but somehow never managed to win his much-sought-after approval. As if to compensate for his own frustrations, he was constantly trying to alter her into new images, never satisfied with her natural progression as a youngster. For example, when she developed as a left-handed penwoman, he nagged after her, to no avail, to be "normal" and write with her right hand.

Even more instrumental in the emotional development of Marilyn was her growing up in the shadow of her sister. Arlene was the favored one because she took an avid interest in domestic subjects, learning to sew and cook, and offering to help the mother with the chores. As Mrs. Novak would later say: "How could you expect Kim to have a personality of her own, with Arlene there all the time? Arlene was a leader type. Kim was never a leader. She was very quiet. She listened more than she spoke." Marilyn, plain-looking, timid, and moody, regularly locked herself in her room. There, she talked softly to her dolls and made them characters in imaginary stories. She avoided the other neighborhood children, who thought of her only as "Arlene's sister."

At the William Penn Elementary School, Marilyn was insecure and indifferent to her teachers and studies. Arlene earned good grades, but Marilyn apparently did not even try to compete in this arena. Mrs. Novak once recalled: "Marilyn never excelled at anything. She never made an effort at anything unless I pressed her."

Marilyn was thin and much taller than her classmates, which made her feel self-conscious to the point of wearing a doleful expression much of the time, thus earning her the name of "Sad Eyes." Her only companion for a time was a paper figure of a woman she had drawn with pencil and named Mickey, a nickname sometimes applied to herself as well. The hours spent talking to her paper friends worried the Novaks, who sent her to a clinic specializing in emotional disturbances. For months a battery of child psychologists analyzed her, but "It didn't do much good to see the doctors, I guess. They told me I was jealous of Arlene, but that wasn't really true. I was never envious of someone who had reason to be better than I. My sister was prettier, and talented and by far the better girl. I just couldn't get along with other kids. There is such a thing as being very lonely, but liking to be alone."

Mrs. Novak pitched in with her own brand of Czech home psychology by forcing Marilyn to stand in front of a mirror each night and repeat, "You can, you will, you must conquer your shyness." When possible, Marilyn rode her bicycle into the nearest wooded suburban area and hid out for hours. Often, she took home sick or wounded birds or stray dogs as pets. She cried if she found a dead bird, and she refused to step on an earthworm or a leaf for fear of hurting them. All dead animals were given a solemn burial service by the taciturn Marilyn.

Teachers at Chicago's Farragut High School had problems disciplining the non-conformist Marilyn because, "I never liked people telling me 'do this' or 'do that.' I was also perfectly willing to cheat at exams to get by." Although she was outgrowing her physical gawkiness, Marilyn remained tremendously self-conscious about her appearance. As her best high school friend, Barbara Mellon, remembers: "Marilyn was just as attractive as Arlene but she worried about her figure and her weight. On the beach we'd always walk away from each other because she didn't like the contrast of my skinny legs and her fat legs. And she'd always be brushing her hair in the girls' room at the beach."

Probably the first crucial turning point in Marilyn's life occurred when her mother persuaded her to join a young girls' social group called the Fair Teens Club, hoping she might gain poise and self-confidence through association with people her own age. Sponsored by a Chicago department store, the club members—girls from all over Chicago—were encouraged to model teen fashions, for which they were paid a nominal fee. Marilyn's family was overjoyed to find that she enjoyed modeling, for up until that time she had had serious thoughts of becoming a nun or a veterinarian. But through the combination of doing well in her modeling chores and winning a beauty contest as Queen of Lake Michigan (due no doubt to the help of her vote-procuring mother, who promoted her daughter's new robust shapeliness), Marilyn began to blossom into her own, even daring now to "advise" sister Arlene on the proper art of makeup.* Marilyn then won a $400 scholarship to Chicago's Patricia Stevens Modeling

*At one point, when sister Arlene enrolled at the Art Institute in Chicago, Marilyn followed suit, with the girls calling themselves Lyn and Lee Kavon. Marilyn dropped out of the courses rather precipitously, once again haunted by the fear that she could not match her elder sister's level of competence in this arena.

School, along with the title "Miss Rhapsody in Blue." She modeled part time—which brought additional revenue into the Novak household and gave Marilyn new-won respect in her family—and then she enrolled for a year and a half at the local Wright Junior College, where she casually aimed at a major in dramatics. She joined the Alpha Beta Mu Sorority, which intrigued her more than a role in the class production of *Our Town,* in which she had a quick walk-on, uttering "Hello" and exiting.

Marilyn's first "adult" romance was with a student from Northwestern University whom she half-heartedly agreed to wed, but "when we went to buy the engagement ring, I couldn't stand it. I cried so hard that the boy brought me home. He wisely decided that I didn't really want to marry him." Then, out of twisted spite at her lack of "normalcy," Marilyn promised to marry a German-accented Chicagoan who claimed to be a baron, but she sensibly called off the whole relationship before it could be legally consummated.

Her haphazard junior college days ended abruptly in the spring of 1953 when twenty-year-old Marilyn accepted a summer-long job with Thor Appliances.* Along with three other models she was contracted for a nationwide tour as "Miss Deep Freeze," a demonstrator of washing machines and refrigerators. The five-week tour concluded in San Francisco, but Marilyn, already wise in the ways of professional modeling, was reluctant to return to the restraining atmosphere of Chicago and her parents, and had her transportation ticket rerouted to Los Angeles. With fellow model Peggy Dahl and the latter's mother, who rushed out to California to watch over her daughter, she rented a room at the Beverly Hills Hotel; later Marilyn moved to the YWCA-sponsored Studio Club at $19.50 a week.

Marilyn thrived on the Los Angeles climate and decided to extend her stay in town. Registered with the Caroline Leonetti Modeling Agency, five-foot, six-inch, 37-23-37 Marilyn found herself somewhat busy, posing for a magazine illustration here, or appearing in a television commercial on another occasion, and, according to *unconfirmed* reports, joining a crowd of model-extras as a harem girl in the Victor Mature costumer *The Veils of Bagdad* (1953), released by Universal Pictures.

With her inbred sense of inferiority, Marilyn might well have drifted out of the highly competitive Hollywood scene, but early on in her tinseltown sojourn, she encountered thirty-three-year-old Mac Krim, a Beverly Hills businessman, who promptly fell in love with her and soon pro-

---

*In 1955, Marilyn (by then Miss Kim Novak) would recall: "I became a model when I first went to work. Everyone just snapped my picture and didn't care what I thought or felt. I decided to try other jobs. I became a dentist's receptionist and was really good at the job. At last I felt I was doing something useful. Then the dentist's wife said I was too pretty to have around and the dentist fired me. Next I worked in a five-and-dime store. Pretty soon there was a crowd of boys just hanging around but not buying anything, and I was asked to leave. I went back to modeling because it seemed the only thing I could succeed at . . ."

posed marriage. He never got as far as the altar with Marilyn, but for the next several years he remained her faithful escort-confidant-booster, providing her with some of the emotional security that she had missed as a youth.

Through the Leonetti Agency, Marilyn was among fifteen models shipped over to mogul Howard Hughes's RKO lot in Culver City to provide additional background-cheesecake appeal for the Jane Russell 3-D musical *The French Line* (RKO), made in 1953, but not released until mid-1954 due to Hughes—engineered publicity with the Production Code Office regarding the rather salacious display of Russell's double-barrelled assets in startling stereoscopic exploration. Hughes, more concerned with promoting this 102-minute color musical as the box-office successor to Russell's *Gentlemen Prefer Blondes* (Twentieth Century-Fox, 1953), paid no heed to the presence of Marilyn among the bevy of girls strung throughout the movie.* Even sharp-eyed filmgoers today have a difficult time spotting Marilyn as one of the models who decorously stroll down a staircase while star Russell and raucous comedienne Mary McCarty perform a pistol-packin'-mama type of duet, "Any Gal from Texas."

However, Billy Daniel, choreographer on *The French Line,* did take notice of Marilyn, and through him she was introduced to talent agent Wilt Melnick, who found her "extremely attractive" but "a little overweight." The next day she signed an agency contract, which Melnick tucked inside a desk drawer, explaining, "It stays there until you take off weight." Ten days later and fifteen pounds lighter, Marilyn was introduced to Columbia's casting director, Max Arnow. At that juncture, every Hollywood studio was seeking a match for Twentieth Century-Fox's goldmine blonde, Marilyn Monroe, an actress whom Columbia had once allowed to slip through their contract grasp. Max Arnow had a hunch that Marilyn Novak might be Columbia's candidate. He ordered a screentest consisting of two scenes, directed by former actor Richard Quine.† For the first, she wore a full-skirted pink dress with a demure Peter Pan col-

---

*In February 1954, Marilyn would return to RKO to play one of the harem "raiders" in *Son of Sinbad,* which was not released until 1955 because studio boss Hughes again used a censorship ploy to boost the potential revenue on this Dale Robertson-Sally Forrest-Vincent Price tongue-in-cheek swashbuckling color entry. The Victor Young score was considered the best asset of this SuperScope production. Once again Marilyn was bypassed by womanizer Hughes and his girl-hunting staff, for it was Susan Ames, Dorothy Van Dyke, Andrea Cleve, and Yvonne White who were singled out from among the female set dressing to later promote the picture. By that time, of course, Marilyn was a Columbia hot property, and the slight could not have mattered less to her or her career.

†Quine, who would play such an important role in Kim's professional and personal life, was born November 12, 1920, in Detroit, Michigan. He was on Broadway in *Counsellor at Law* (1931), became a film player in Hollywood in 1933, then returned to stage-vaudeville-Broadway work and later became a radio announcer. He rejoined the movies in such features as *Babes on Broadway* (MGM, 1941), served with the U.S. Coast Guard during World War II, and in 1948 co-produced and co-directed his first movie, *Leather Gloves* at Columbia, the studio where he mainly functioned during the subsequent decades. Quine had been married in 1943 to MGM starlet Susan Peters, but they were divorced in 1948, four years after she was crippled in a hunting accident.

lar and read a passage from the *The Moon Is Blue*. Next, wearing Rita Hayworth's slinky, black gown from *Affair in Trinidad* (Columbia, 1952), which had been altered to Marilyn's dimensions and 125-pound frame,* she read a passage from *Devil Passes*. Inexperienced Marilyn had no idea what to do with her cumbersome hands until Quine patiently suggested that she back up to a fake fireplace and place her arms behind her along the mantel. This telling posture accentuated her ample bosom.

Iconoclastic, shrewd, gross, demanding Harry Cohn, the sixty-three-year-old master of Columbia, appeared to be unimpressed when Arnow asked him to watch the Novak rushes. "What can I do with her?" cigar-chomping Cohn asked. "She can't act. I can't hear what she's saying." Realizing that he was being baited by astute Cohn, who could not help but recognize the physical potential of this candidate, Arnow replied; "A lot of stars in pictures can't act, but they're great personalities. That's what this kid is. She'll never be star quality." Through Arnow, Cohn proposed a six-month starlet contract at $100 a week. Agent Melnick accepted on Marilyn's behalf.

Then began a crash glamorization campaign by Columbia's team of specialists. Ever-present in Cohn's cash-register mind was the hope of finding a replacement for thirty-six-year-old love goddess Rita Hayworth, the studio princess whose globe-trotting love affairs and assignment refusals were giving him a permanent migraine. Cohn and Columbia had failed to turn Mary Castle into the new Hayworth of the 1950s, nor were "newcomer" May Wynn, or established contractees Donna Reed, Barbara Hale, Gloria Grahame, Mary Murphy, Martha Hyer, Karin Booth, or Joan Vohs filling the void in the star roster, in which Hayworth and Academy Award-winning comedienne Judy Holliday were the studio's biggest female assets.

Perhaps "that fat Polack," as Cohn called Marilyn behind her back, was just that replacement. She was rushed into acting lessons (for which she paid), her teeth were straightened and capped, and she was placed on a stringent diet. All of Columbia's executives were ordered to suggest a suitable name since the too-familiar tag "Marilyn" was simply out of the question for Columbia's new screen hope. The New York office came up with Kit Marlowe, a name that was to Cohn's liking, but detested by the girl who was to bear it. She preferred Lynn or Lisa Novak, which added up to nine letters and was divisible by three (because of the many threes connected with her birth, she superstitiously believed it to be her lucky number). She complained to George Lait, Columbia's publicity director, who discussed the "vital" matter with autocratic Cohn. Cohn's immediate reply was, "Whoever heard of a glamor girl named Novak?† But I like it, it's reverse English." When she learned that her name was

---

*Rita Hayworth was five feet, six inches in height; weighed 120 pounds; and measured 36-26-35.

†Cohn obviously had forgotten about the two attractive Novak sisters, Eva and Jane, of silent-screen prominence.

521

to be Kit Novak, she complained that she still was not satisfied since she did not like the name Kit. Lait arranged for her personally to take up the matter with Cohn in his office. She said, during a discussion of a wide range of professional and social matters, "I like Kim. It's close to Kit and it's got three letters, too." Cohn refused. When she turned on full-force tears, he allegedly conceded just to get her to quiet down and leave his inner sanctum.

Further drastic steps were taken toward creating a marketable image to go along with the new name, so that Kim Novak might become to Columbia what Monroe was to Fox. A makeup was concocted to soften her features, her ash-blonde hair became silvery with a tint of lavender and haut couturier Jean-Louis was summoned to create an appropriate wardrobe that would emphasize her bust, which she adamantly refused to cover with a brassiere except for fittings. Reams of biographical information and stacks of glossy cheesecake photos were issued to the press and fan magazines. Inspired by the lavender tint in her hair, an imaginative press agent came up with the gimmick of dressing her in shades of purple and lavender and decorating her living quarters in the same colors. The rumor was widely circulated that she had been discovered while pedaling her lavender bicycle through Beverly Hills. Splashy articles with colored pinups appeared in all the fan magazines. One story told the fans that "the sheets in Kim's hope chest are tinted a delicate shade of lavender, Kim's favorite color." Because of this constant, saturation magazine exposure, she had a large following of eager fans even before she appeared onscreen in a major role.

Kim's initial studio acting assignment was in the black-and-white melodrama *Pushover* (Columbia, 1954) directed by Richard Quine and starring perennial leading man Fred MacMurray. It was a modest B-production, in which MacMurray rehashed his *Double Indemnity* (Paramount, 1944) success, here portraying an honest police enforcer who turns corrupt, involving himself in murder before the lurid, but obvious finale. Kim had a rather undemanding role as a bank robber's moll who holds the key to the whereabouts of the $200,000 loot.

Despite the free-form, stereotyped nature of her role as Lona McLane in *Pushover*, Kim, understandably was overwrought about handling the major female part. Her co-workers mistook her tremendous self-consciousness about her screen acting inexperience as a manifestation of conceit. In the best Marilyn Monroe method, she was late for rehearsals, muffed lines, and seemed at a loss to cope with the regimen required for turning out a low-budget production on schedule. Quine was required to work exceptionally closely with her for each scene. Benno Schneider, the studio drama coach, advised: "Be yourself. Say the lines naturally. You don't study acting, you feel a thought and then you express it." For the worldly wise but intellectually and emotionally undeveloped Kim, this seemed a difficult conception to put into proper execution.

But as if by some magic of fate, *Pushover* augered well for Kim. The film came and went rather quickly on the action market, but Kim attracted some brief notice. *Newsweek* magazine labeled her "a purry blonde," and Howard Thompson (*New York Times*) noted that she was "wide-eyed, undulating." What worked best for Kim within *Pushover* were the several sequences in which she is the subject stalked by the police, who trace her actions through binoculars and tape recorders, thus making her an object for physical and vocal observation rather than emotional interaction with fellow performers. It indicated the special brand of enticing isolationism that would become a trademark of the better Kim Novak film roles in the years to come. Director Quine analyzed the situation thus: "Kim has a ladylike quality, but it goes a step further. She has a combination of that with sex appeal and a childlike quality. It is most unusual. Although she had no acting training—she had never even read the funnies out loud—she brought a childlike pathos to her first role. It was something inherent—the little girl-woman personality."

Cohn and Columbia perceptively realized that Kim's cinema future had a certain potential, and they decided to boost her career (and at the same time save on the budget) by canceling a deal to use Sheree North—Twentieth Century-Fox's second-string Monroe rival—for the role of the empty-headed blonde sexpot in *Phffft!* (Columbia, 1954).* Based on an unproduced comedy by George Axelrod (author of *The Seven Year Itch*), this was the second Columbia vehicle to team comedienne Judy Holliday with Cohn's contract protégé, Jack Lemmon. † The film's modest premise finds Holliday and Lemmon divorcing after eight years of conventional wedlock, each now eager to learn what kinds of promiscuous fun they have been missing. While Holliday is innocently and nervously flirting with stolid ham actor Jack Carson, Lemmon's best friend, Lemmon is cavorting with Kim. Wildly eager to be sexually adolescent again, Lemmon strains and sweats to make his rendezvous with Kim sexually stimulating, but the girl is too addled to appreciate either his animal drives or his embarrassment at being so rusty in the game of "putting on the make." Director Mark Robson opted to handle Kim in a Monroe-imitation manner, making her a breathless, nonsense-expostulating, curvaceous chick, who naively admits, "Sometimes I think I should have gone to college. There's a lot a person can pick up at college." Or later, the higher-education-prone Kim remarks, "I almost went to college and majored in music. I was a drum majorette." Lemmon and Kim share a mambo-dance scene, more athletic than amusing. *Phffft!* made a splash at the box office, and while Holliday and Lemmon were the focus of critical interest, Kim's participation in the comedy did not go unnoticed. Bos-

---

*Columbia's publicity department got a good deal of mileage out of the unusual title *Phffft!*, with television comedians having a field day making double entendres on its real meaning. In the film, it is Kim who explains how the word is pronounced.

†The first film was *It Should Happen to You* (Columbia, 1954).

ley Crowther (*New York Times*) tagged her a "ravishing blonde," the *New York Herald-Tribune* approved of her "zesty show," the *New York Journal-American* named her "best discovery of 1954," and the grande dame of the gossip columnists, Louella Parsons, ever ready to please Harry Cohn, acknowledged, "The sexy newcomer steals the show."

Now that Kim was no longer just another fringe member of the motion-picture industry, but a definite, if manufactured, personality on the upswing in the land of make-believe, her parents were forced to cope with the changing status of their increasingly famous younger daughter. Mrs. Novak announced: "I was not in favor of Hollywood. I didn't see any sense to it. I figured, well, she'd get enough of it and come home. But that was the beginning of the end of my supervision." For his part, Mr. Novak admitted: "Neither one of us disapproves. I'm satisfied as long as she lives an upright life. When she left home I said I don't mind you coming home in a mink coat but be sure you earn it honestly, because so many girls come home in mink coats but you know how they got it." As for sister Arlene, she had married a telephone company lineman in Chicago and would be the mother of two children, all hopes of any sort of artistic career sublimated to domesticity.

As a result of *Pushover* and *Phffft!*, fan mail began pouring into the Gower Street Studio addressed to Kim Novak. Convinced now that he had a likely winner in the starter's circle, Harry Cohn determined that she would not be permitted to make the same mistakes as Rita Hayworth—i.e., enjoy too much personal freedom, since this might interfere with her proper cycle of filmmaking and studio publicity-money making. Cohn insisted that she continue to reside at the Studio Club and dictated, rather naively, that she not date except on weekends. This order did not concern Kim because, as she innocently expressed her feeling: "I loved it there; it was my second home. I saw the sad side of Hollywood there. All those young girls, few with real talent, trying to crash the big time. Even those with talent still had to have the luck. Watching all those girls struggling to achieve something kept me in touch with the realities." Possessive Cohn went so far as placing a guard outside the residence to make certain, as much as possible, that she was obeying his orders. Her weight was carefully checked, and when the scales revealed that she had gained a telltale pound, she was forced to live in her studio dressing room and to partake rigidly of slimming foods prepared especially for her by the studio chef. None of this discipline bothered Kim, however, because: "When I started getting parts in pictures I took them seriously, worked hard at them. I went along with the studio, worked at my publicity. I didn't mind. When you're just starting, you don't care."

Not that Kim remained a complete recluse during her period of stardom grooming. She continued to date theatre-owner, real-estate investor Mac Krim, even when the amour on her part had cooled. "We were inseparable for a while," said Kim. "We'd joke about what a funny name Kim Krim would be. Mac and I were in love, but he didn't understand me when I wanted to be serious. I'd mention a poem or an article I'd read, and he'd stop listening. I realized suddenly that we didn't have as many interests in common as we had thought. He wanted to see the sunny side of everything. I didn't—and don't." Cohn was delighted to hear such words. It had been his strongest advice that she not become involved in a difficult love affair or contemplate marriage during the early years of her career.

Kim, the looker, the more earthy Grace Kelly type, the less kookie Shirley MacLaine of the mid-1950s, the more desirable love object than brasher Sheree North or more endowed Jayne Mansfield or Mamie Van Doren, was now a definite asset to the Columbia production schedule. Opera singer-TV commercials girl Mary Costa had been cast for the female lead in the Phil Karlson-directed *Five against the House* (Columbia, 1955), but she was replaced by Kim in this modest black-and-white production filmed largely on location in Reno, Nevada. It was a strange bit of substitute assignment, for the part of Kay Greylek required Kim to be a nightclub songstress, and it was necessary to have Jo Ann Greer dub in Kim's vocal numbers.* On its own, *Five against the House* is a far sturdier gambling-casino caper than such later entries as *Ocean's Eleven* (Warner Bros., 1960), *Seven Thieves* (Twentieth Century-Fox, 1960), and *They Came to Rob Las Vegas* (Warner Bros., 1969). The eighty-four-minute Columbia entry focuses on a quartet of army-veteran college men (psychotic Brian Keith, level-headed Guy Madison, intellectually challenged Kerwin Mathews, and fun-seeking Alvy Moore) who decide to rob the seemingly impregnable gambling palace known as Harold's Club. Once again, Kim's screen role required her to be an object of adoration, either to the nightclub patrons, her beau, Madison, or the audience watching the proceedings. In this advantageous capacity, her appearance won the endorsement of A. H. Weiler (*New York Times*), who wrote, "[She] is as tempting a dish as any to have been set before a viewer this season." *Variety* substantiated that Kim in *Five against the House* showed "considerable s[ex] a[ppeal] voltage."

Before *Five against the House* went into national release in mid-1955, Columbia negotiated for Kim to appear on television opposite her film co-star, Madison, on the "Light's Diamond Jubilee" special (ABC, CBS, NBC—October 24, 1954) in an episode entitled *A Kiss for the Lieutenant*. It served its designed purpose to sufficiently alert the entertainment-conscious public of the Novak-Madison starring combination in the forthcoming *Five against the House.*

"Gorgeous Novak" with the hazel-green eyes and the sultry voice,

*"They Call Me the Life of the Party" and "I Hadn't Anyone Till You."

525

which she purposely learned to modulate to a low, husky, purring tone, was then given a solid term contract with Columbia, with the usual promises of salary raises in the months and years to come. The salary raise to $250 weekly came early in 1955 when Cohn slated her as one of the stars of the studio's prestige picture of the year, *Picnic* (Columbia, 1955). At the same time she was named as the top motion-picture discovery of the year by six national fan magazines, by the Hollywood Foreign Press Association, and as a final—almost superfluous—accolade, both Hedda Hopper and Louella Parsons reconfirmed that Kim was the girl of the year.

Picnic was an award-winning Broadway play of the 1952-53 season when Columbia purchased the motion-picture rights.* Originally authored by William Inge, it was adapted for the screen by Daniel Taradash in a literate fashion which preserved the original blend of poetry and reality. Anxious to make this production a hit with intellectuals as well as the mass audience, Cohn enticed Joshua Logan from the New York stage to repeat his directorial chores, and assigned veteran actors William Holden, Rosalind Russell,† and Betty Field in key roles. Cohn then shocked the Hollywood set by decreeing that Kim Novak would take on the part of Madge Owens, the role played on Broadway by Janice Rule. Those who had seen the stage production wondered how Kim "no talent" Novak could cope with the role of the naive, small-town Kansas girl who had never known the sadness of love. When Logan strongly objected to directing an inexperienced newcomer in one of the key roles, Cohn replied with finality, "Take her or I'll get a new director." Logan relented and tested her several times in various scenes from the script, but still was dissatisfied with her ability until Columbia contractee Aldo Ray was told to test a love scene with her. Ray was ordered to "get some emotion from her any way you can, short of rape." The result was a torrid celluloid scene. Logan found the test completely acceptable and was ready to go ahead with her in the part, on condition that her hair style be remodeled. He did not consider her short coiffure feminine enough. Thus in the color film she wears a shoulder-length red wig.

When the *Picnic* company moved on location to Hutchinson, Kansas, Kim took with her a small suitcase filled with good-luck charms, including a toy clown, a stuffed teddy bear, holy medals, and dolls. At the Catholic church in Hutchinson she prayed daily for help while oncamera. On the first day of shooting, she was required to cry in a scene but could not

---

Picnic opened at the Music Box Theatre for a run of 477 performances. A musical version, entitled *Hot September*, tried out in Boston in September-October 1965, but closed before its Broadway bow. In 1972-73, not too long before his death, author Inge rewrote *Picnic* as *Summer Brave*.

†Russell received special billing "and co-starring Rosalind Russell as Rosemary," a situation which prevented her performance from being nominated for Best Actress in the Academy Award race that year. She declined to be suggested for the Best Supporting Actress category.

muster up the proper tears. Exasperated, and sweltering in the burning summer sun, temperamental Logan punched her twice and she promptly burst into tears. The scene, as required, was lensed. Production went along smoothly after that and Logan commented when *Picnic* was completed: "She is a sensitive and creative girl. She is as gifted as she is exquisite and can handle anything from boredom to terror with impact."

Picnic has emerged as a classic film of the 1950s, equally enhanced by James Wong Howe's expansive CinemaScope camerawork and by George Duning's score.* Critics may have carped that William Holden, at a very mature thirty-seven, was too old to provide the proper physical delineation to the part of sensual drifter Hal Carter, or that stylized Russell, in her anxiousness to dominate the screen proceedings, overly dominated the scenery in her face cream and drunk scenes. However, on the whole, the Academy Award-nominated feature (*Marty* won) pleased most levels of moviegoers and garnered a rich $6.3 million in distributors' domestic rentals.

Within *Picnic*, Kim's character suffers from the classic beautiful-girl syndrome, a situation emphasized by having Susan Strasberg as the poetically inspired, plain-Jane younger sister. As Kim informs her insensitive country-club beau (Cliff Robertson), "It's no good just to be pretty." This point is made clear when carefree man-of-the-road Holden drifts into the sleepy small town and Kim, through her attraction to the newcomer, awakens to the possibility that she possesses more than good looks, that she can be a warm, nice, giving individual. During the course of the elongated Labor Day picnic and its intertwined aftermath, she discovers that "I'm real too."

Director Logan graciously provides Kim with two telling screen sequences in the movie. She has been crowned Queen of the Picnic, a fact which bores her, and later drifts through the day's events of games and food-tasting with all the enthusiasm of a distracted sleepwalker. But then, as dusk nears, she and Holden find themselves off from the crowd, continuing their badinage of the day; suddenly it becomes clear that she is slowly awakening to the tantalizing charms of devil-may-care stud Holden. The theme tune "Moonglow" builds on the soundtrack, and in a deserted pavilion Kim and Holden move toward one another in a bit of choreographed sexual undulation that sets the proper tone for Kim's burgeoning potential. As she and Holden caress and dance, no longer is she the unawakened princess or the emotionally suffocated miss. Now with Holden she suddenly perceives a fulfilling future. Even the distasteful exhibition of a soused Russell tearing off Holden's shirt with animalistic abandon cannot break the spell, nor does the warning of Kim's weather-beaten mother (Betty Field) prevent her from reaching the logical roman-

*It was cited by the Composers Guild of America in cooperation with *Down Beat* magazine as "the best original underscore for a non-musical film."

527

tic conclusion. She must follow after Holden wherever he may go. Thus, in the artistically composed final shot, a dewy-eyed but determined Kim is seen boarding a bus for Tulsa. The widescreen camera pans back and upward, showing the bus and the freight train (which Holden has hopped) both traveling in a parallel direction—heading off into the sunset. The poetic fantasy is erotically complete.

Despite her occasional lapses with the complex characterization of Madge Owens and the insistence of director Logan on molding her performance along the lines of the far-different Janice Rule stage original, Kim received more than adequate acknowledgment from critical circles. *Newsweek* magazine might flippantly remark that she "portrays dumb but beautiful girls better and better all the time," but more somber souls, like A. H. Weiler (*New York Times*), acclaimed: "[Kim] is a joy to behold. Although the role is not expansive, she manages to convey the confusion and yearning of a maid who is weary of being called beautiful and is soulfully seeking something more substantial."

Released in Los Angeles in late 1955 in time for Academy Award consideration, *Picnic* garnered Oscars for art-set decoration and editing.

Prior to its release, Otto Preminger asked for the loan of Kim as the second feminine lead in *The Man with the Golden Arm* (1955) for United Artists release. Across the bargaining table, Preminger agreed to pay Cohn-Columbia's coffers $100,000 for her services, a neat profit for the studio, since Kim's salary, even after her *Picnic* chore, was only $750 per week.

The Man with the Golden Arm was just as important a career step for Otto Preminger as for Kim. The Continental director, who has always thrived on high controversy and Prussian autocratic behavior, had found himself cast out of the industry limelight with his two most recent pictures—both for Twentieth Century-Fox—*River of No Return* (1954), with Marilyn Monroe, and the tame, black-cast musical *Carmen Jones* (1954). Preminger smartly decided to return to his former daringness, as exemplified by his sex comedy *The Moon Is Blue* (United Artists, 1953). For his new venture he selected Nelson Algren's widely read 1949 novel, *The Man with the Golden Arm*. Preminger rightly guessed that its "hot" subject matter (the avidly debated topic of drugs) would cause the Motion Picture Production Code enforcers to deny this major feature picture Code approval, which they did, a fact which could only boost the box-office potential of the 119-minute black-and-white feature. Combined with an innovative, jazzy Elmer Bernstein score and Sam Leavitt's penetrating camera work *The Man with the Golden Arm* lived up to its potential as a major contender for attention from all avenues of the industry and the public, and amassed a $4.35 million distributors' domestic gross in its playoff engagements.

Once again, fate worked well with Kim's cinema rise, for although she

528

had only the second-lead female role, established actress Eleanor Parker turned in an uncharacteristically shrill, rancid performance as Zosh, the supposedly crippled wife of card dealer-dope addict Frankie Machine (Sinatra). It proved to be Kim as Molly, the couple's downstairs neighbor who works as a B-girl at the sleazy Club Safari, who grabbed audience interest and sympathy. The life-hardened soul who has retained a streak of kindness, she offers Sinatra the encouragement to fulfill his dream to be a drummer and to finally kick his heroin habit. Not that she is a tenement angel, for when married Sinatra is unavailable she turns to Drunky (John Conte), reasoning, "I got lonely . . . 'n' he's a poor beat guy who needs someone too."

As the sad-faced, world-weary, but loyal trollop, Kim's satisfying performance in *The Man with the Golden Arm* is far exceeded by her beauty. She is exquisite in a black-sequined gown as she tiredly leaves the Club Safari at 5 A.M., and in a simple, V-neck gray sweater over a black skirt as she watches Sinatra lose his battle against drug addiction. Much of Kim's softly spoken dialog consists of "Great, Frankie" or "That's swell, Frankie," but in one scene she describes her existence with, "All my life has been one day—on and on and on," and the viewer believes she means it. The *New York Herald-Tribune's* scribe said that she "was firm and sensible" in the part, with Arthur Knight (*Saturday Review*) describing her as "decorative and appealing." As the authentic new love goddess of the 1950s cinema, Kim was fulfilling all the professional requirements.

During the lensing of *The Man with the Golden Arm*, Kim was frequently escorted about Hollywood by hot-shot Sinatra, but to queries whether there was a possible romance between them, she said, "We're just friends." From Sinatra, so Hollywood observers noted, Kim learned much more about the importance of being independent, and through him she found greater self-confidence.

She was then put onto her first public-appearance tour to coincide with the New York opening of *Picnic* at the Radio City Music Hall (December 15, 1955). Accompanied by a studio publicity aide, she paid a quick stopover visit to her family in Chicago and arrived in New York where she was greeted by the expected hordes of photographers and news-hungry reporters. She cooperated fully with the press in answering questions (with spontaneity rather than perception), but refused to pose for cheesecake shots, which she generally felt—or so the studio had her say—would dampen her attempts to be known as a dramatic actress.* On New York tele-

---

*Columnist Earl Wilson (an amateur photographer by avocation), in his *The Show Business Nobody Knows* (1971), relates a long anecdote about how Kim, earlier in her career, had cooperatively posed for him. "[She] adored the way her bare body was revealed in pictures and was willing, even eager, to cheat a little so that there'd be more than a flash of her bosom." Wilson sold some of the shots to a girlie magazine; Cohn exploded, and years later a weary Novak wrote Wilson, "Don't you think you should take those horrid pictures of me off the market?"

vision, she was first upstaged by J. Fred Muggs, the chimp on the Dave Garroway-hosted "Today" show on NBC. Then she was booked to appear on the CBS "Ed Sullivan Show" in a revealing and clinging dress while cueing Susan Strasberg in a scene from *Picnic*. Kim insisted that her talents were being belittled by emcee Sullivan and pleaded with Columbia Studio executives to intercede on her behalf. Her complaints were futile, and she finally solved the situation by tossing a vase of flowers against a wall in her TV studio dressing room and crying pitifully while a handy photographer snapped away. Sullivan eventually gave in to her wishes.

In January 1956, Kim was instructed to return to Hollywood to take over Rita Hayworth's role in the long-delayed biblical epic, *Joseph and His Brethren*. As she departed the Sherry-Netherland Hotel, where she stayed during her Manhattan visit, a *Newsweek* reporter inquired how she felt about her status as the "new Rita Hayworth." Kim replied, "I wouldn't want to fill her shoes. I've admired her work for so many, many years." Kim arrived in Hollywood to find that the sword-and-sandal picture had been shelved for an indefinite time.

Kim's next film, *The Eddy Duchin Story* (Columbia, 1956), could have been considered box-office duty for Columbia's pace-setting star, but it provided her with her most exquisitely photographed role, creating visual images that remained burned into filmgoers' minds for decades to come. Universal had already turned out *The Glenn Miller Story* (1954) and *The Benny Goodman Story* (1955) with enormous box-office results, particularly from the former picture, which starred James Stewart and June Allyson. Columbia producer Jerry Wald rightly reasoned that a fictionalized biography of society pianist Eddy Duchin (1910-1951) would appeal to moviegoers, particularly with Tyrone Power as the country's former top piano-playing maestro, whose secret for dazzling success was, "I close my eyes, hum to myself, and then play what I happen to feel inside of me."

After witnessing the completed CinemaScope-Technicolor production directed by George Sidney, the reviewer for the elite *Saturday Review* inquired in print: "Can anyone—I mean anyone—believe that the life of that stricken man was so beautiful? Does anyone really want to believe it?" Obviously so, for *The Eddy Duchin Story* took in $5.3 million in distributors' domestic grosses. Within the gloriously decorated 123 minutes of the tear-drenched drama, the film traces Duchin's arrival in New York, fresh from pharmacy school in Boston, and hoping to join Leo Reisman's orchestra at the Central Park Casino, then Manhattan's poshest dancing spot. By 1931 he has taken over Reisman's spot as leader at the Casino, and through the decade he continues to fascinate the luxury-craving crowds with his flashy piano-playing (dubbed in the movie by veteran pianist Carmen Cavallaro). Kim was assigned the comparatively small role of his first wife, interior designer Marjorie Oelrichs, who dies in childbirth on Christmas Eve part way through the film. However, her demise did not come before she and Power enjoyed some heavy romantic scenes, particularly one in which the couple walk through a rainstorm in Central Park. The Samuel Taylor screenplay also provided fitting opportunities for Kim to model stunning Jean Louis period outfits, each one geared to accentuate the ethereal, untouchable beauty of the silver-blonde screen star. It is Kim as this society lady who informs Power that "you produce happiness." After they are wed he tells her he wants to buy her a diamond as big as the Ritz Hotel, but she says, "I want just you; the things you can give me of you." Many viewers noted that once Kim's character departed the story, the film took a downhill course, becoming overmaudlin as the picture traces the pianist's World War II service, his eventual reconciliation with his young son (Rex Thompson), his second marriage (to Victoria Shaw—a new Columbia contractee), and the downbeat ending which has Power's Duchin dying of leukemia to the strains of his theme song, Chopin's E-Flat Nocturne. The *New York World-Telegram and Sun* critic said that Kim "puts a flavor of foreboding doom into her playing," while Bosley Crowther (*New York Times*) more enthusiastically proclaimed that she "is slumberous but lovely."

Offscreen, star Power was not in the least anxious to buy coplayer Kim any gifts. He was disgusted with the many delays in shooting, many of which were caused by Kim, who often lingered in her dressing room, checking and rechecking her face. One of her major insecurities in the business of making motion pictures was her almost constant fear that her makeup was bad or that she did not look her best. Power's angry comment was, "Confusion between temperament and bad manners is unfortunate." Director Sidney, who would helm three additional Novak outings, let it be known that he was greatly disturbed by the "hopeless poison that gets into actresses when they become big stars."

In 1956, Kim's cinema popularity reached an all-time high. Her fan mail ran as high as 3,500 letters a month, which was considerable, taking into account the inroads television and changes in fan club habits had made in the Post-World War II era. Kim was named by *Boxoffice* magazine as one of the ten most popular movie stars and was presented with an annual Mark of Achievement Award by the amusement industry division of the Federation of Jewish Philanthropies. An article in *Life* stated that she had "naturalness, pliability and boundless energy" in the $11 million worth of films in which she had appeared to date. *Parade* magazine called her ambitious and quoted her as telling them, "I have no social life. I work sixteen hours a day," but fashion designer Don Loper reportedly sold her $100,000 worth of new wardrobe because "she felt badly dressed." Paradoxically, in interviews—and the studio worried greatly what the natural Kim might next say—she insisted that she was most comfortable in men's shirts worn outside a pair of Levi's. Catty columnist Dorothy Kilgallen spotted her with her matching platinum-blonde poodle and wrote that they "stop traffic wherever they go when both sport matching pink pearl earrings three inches long." Yet Kim avowed publicly that she disliked wearing jewelry of any kind. She claimed that her favorite pastimes were horseback riding, bicycling, tennis, and listening to music. Al Capp, creator of the "L'il Abner" comic strip, introduced a cameo character into his work called Kim Goodnick, who bore a strong resemblance to Miss Novak. It seemed that Kim, with half the effort of the more driving Jayne Mansfield or the lesser Mamie Van Doren, had capitalized on all potential means of becoming the personification of Hollywood's latest, and perhaps last, genuine studio-created major star.

In June 1956, Kim was sent to New York for the Radio City Music Hall premiere of *The Eddy Duchin Story*. As her bags were unpacked, it was discovered that her favorite good-luck charm was missing, a miniature clown whose stomach contained a music box that played Brahms' "Lullaby." It went everywhere with her and was her best nonhuman friend. She wept and brooded for days when she failed to find it. The studio vainly suggested replacing it, but she refused a substitute. "I don't know what I'll do when I start a picture without him," she moaned. "He had a little tinkling sound, and I wrote a prayer to go with the Brahms music. He had been with me in every trouble, and every day when I worked I'd wind up his nose and he'd sing. I'm sick about it. He knows me and I know him."

Kim did manage to appear on television guest shots in New York with Perry Como and Steve Allen, and was a "mystery guest" on "What's My Line?" On June 24, she was one of those who helped Ed Sullivan celebrate his eighth year on the tube.

She then vacationed in Europe, where Elsa Maxwell, limping along as the duenna of the dying rich-life set, introduced her to Count Mario Bandini, an aristocratic Roman. Of their reputed romance, Kim revealed: "It was my first trip abroad and Mario asked if he could show me around. We went boating. I liked him, but with the kind of publicity I get, there are too many strikes against me. Everyone's out to make a sizzling love affair out of the smallest romance, and consequently nothing develops."

Back in Hollywood, she received a pay increase, bringing her weekly salary to $1,000, and was given the title role in *Jeanne Eagels* (Columbia, 1957), the purported biography of the talented, tempestuous actress of the early twentieth century (1894-1929), who fell victim to alcohol and drugs. Happily, Kim bore a slight physical resemblance to the woman she was to portray; she read everything she could locate on Miss Eagels and plastered her dressing-room walls with her pictures. To further establish the proper mood, Kim insisted upon playing music of the 1920s on her studio phonograph.

From the garish opening credits, *Jeanne Eagels*, directed by George

Sidney, was off to a bad start. The blurb popped onto the screen: ". . . all events in this photoplay are based on fact and fiction." As the fabricated tale unreels, one follows the actress's rise from a midwestern carnival-side-show cooch-dancing act to being a noted legitimate performer on Broadway, famed for her interpretation of Sadie Thompson in *Rain.* Kim's inability to cope with the growing complexities of the screen characterization became more apparent as the Jeanne Eagels personality split into a woman fighting herself on every level. Kim's histrionic interpretation was not bolstered by co-star Jeff Chandler as the carnival-owner who loves but misunderstands her (he was even more passive in his raw performance than Kim), or by Agnes Moorehead as an imperious dramatic coach who snappishly judges, "This girl has talent." One subtle note in the film was provided by Virginia Grey as the washed-up performer who is done out of her comeback chance by an overambitious Kim. The overly banal film concludes with a remorseful Chandler visiting a movie theatre to watch a posthumously released film in which his late amour warbles "I'll Take Romance" (dubbed by Eileen Wilson).

"Whatever possessed Columbia to cast this comparative fledgling, with her nice light comedy flair, as one of Broadway's immortals, remains a studio secret." The studio had no retort for *New York Times* critic Howard Thompson's query, and *Jeanne Eagels* played off to minimal financial results, only salvaged by a saturation publicity campaign. Adding insult to the matter, Mrs. Elaine Eagels Nicklas sued Columbia for $950,000, claiming the expensive picture depicted her relative as a "dissolute and immoral person" and a "woman of low character." The case was eventually settled out of court. Years later Kim would say, "I know most people don't agree with me, but I think I got what I saw in the character. It was a big hit in Japan and Latin America."

Kim was now ready to display some of the independence gained during her few short years in Hollywood. When she learned that her *Jeanne Eagels* co-star, Jeff Chandler, was being paid $200,000 for his contribution as leading man as opposed to her meager $13,000 for thirteen weeks work, she fired her agent and signed with the powerful William Morris Agency. They immediately demanded more money and residual benefits for their new client, claiming she was now one of filmdom's biggest box-office attractions and was worthy of at least $3,000 weekly. Quite naturally, Cohn vehemently disagreed and placed Kim on suspension, a ploy he regularly used to force members of his star stable to crawl back to him when their bank accounts ran dry. But in Kim's case, the Morris Agency subsidized her all the while her Columbia salary was withheld. Cohn was furious!

In December 1956, Kim's growing importance was emphasized by her keenly watched appearance on Edward R. Murrow's CBS-TV network show, "Person to Person." From his New York-based studio Murrow interviewed Kim at her parents' rather modest home in Chicago, with the star displayed beside the family Christmas tree. She even consented to wear a brassiere for the event since she figured she would be required to carry a microphone in her bosom.

Harry Cohn finally came to terms with Kim's powerful agents with a compromise weekly payroll figure of $2,750. "I have never met a grateful performer in the picture business," he grumbled. "I'm only afraid she'll ask me to make Kim Novak pictures instead of Columbia pictures. We've got twelve to fifteen million dollars invested in her. She's the number one woman star in Hollywood. Audrey Hepburn is the only one else. The public has accepted this girl."

The first order of business after the salary settlement was for Kim to move from the Studio Club to a $240-a-month Beverly Hills apartment, furnished, of course, in lavender. She then traded in her bicycle for a white Corvette car and discovered, so the press releases went, the writings of novelist Thomas Wolfe and Sigmund Freud.

The first thing Cohn did was to cast her in a film with the star she was replacing as queen of the lot, Rita Hayworth. In May 1957, the ladies and Frank Sinatra went oncamera for *Pal Joey* (Columbia, 1957) for director George Sidney. Reportedly, Kim and Rita avoided each other on the set and spoke to each other only when it was absolutely required, but Kim later told the *New York Times*, "I didn't have any trouble with Rita—she was sweet."

Pal Joey was adapted by Dorothy Kingsley from the stage musical based on John O'Hara's novel.* The male lead in the picture version was switched from a dancer to a singer (to accommodate Sinatra's talents), and the locale was changed from Chicago to San Francisco. Kim was in third billing, following Hayworth and Sinatra, as Linda English, an innocent but shapely showgirl who loves Joey Evans (Sinatra) and gets in the way of his business relationship with ex-stripper-cum-socialite Vera Simpson (Hayworth), who has set him up in his own club Chez Joey, in return for his "escort" services.

Those who remembered the stage original or the revival were disappointed that so many of the Rodgers and Hart tunes, like "What Is a Man," "In Our Little Den of Iniquity," "Take Him" "Do It the Hard Way," and "Plant You Now" were either missing altogether or reduced to snatches of background music. Obviously the rather tough nightworld tale had to be laundered for the general filmgoing public, but there were strong arguments against making heel Joey Evans turn out to be such a good-natured schnook in the cinema version.

Pal Joey opened on Broadway at the Ethel Barrymore Theatre on December 25, 1940, for a 270-performance run, and then was revived at the Shubert Theatre on September 1, 1941, for a 104-performance swing, with Gene Kelly, Vivienne Segal, and June Havoc. In 1952, there was a major Broadway revival of the production with Harold Lang and Vivienne Segal in the top roles.

Kim said of her *Pal Joey* role, "I just never cared for the part . . . I can't stand people like that girl Linda—I can't even stand the name." Evidently her lack of interest in the role, coupled with her inability to find a working rapport with director George Sidney, led her to admit defeat before she even began work on the musical. Granted her part as a knowing chorus girl, who is supposed to be innocent and optimistic in contrast to the world-weary, weathered Vera (Hayworth), was an ambiguous, passive role at best, but there just was no life in Kim's interpretation. William K. Zinsser of the *New York Herald-Tribune* decided, "[She] has reduced her acting technique to the process of rolling her huge eyes back and forth like pinballs, in the manner of silent film stars, and since she says almost nothing she might as well be in a silent film."

Her big solo number in *Pal Joey* was "My Funny Valentine," a Rodgers and Hart tune added to the film. In a wide gold skirt and bustle made of some twenty-five yards of gold cloth with a flaring tiered underskirt of seventy-five yards of pleated white organza, she made her entrance through the center of a huge heart. The premise of the number was that Sinatra insists she do a strip (Hayworth has demanded that Novak leave the club or she will withdraw her backing). Kim, within the film, naturally misinterprets Sinatra's order, but then, getting drunk, she calls his game and agrees to do the strip, saying she will "take it off and let it lay." Two factors ruined this potentially dynamite sequence. Kim, who could talk-sing through some of the film's opening chorus-girl numbers, had to rely on dubber Carole Richards for this vocally demanding song, making her performance one part ghost. To compound the unfortunate scene, during the song-strip Sinatra cannot bear seeing his loved one publicly disrobe herself, and calls off the routine. Kim, while mouthing words of anguish at the whole situation, gives no inner indication that the disrobement proceedings bother her character one iota. Thus, audience sympathy and all credibility for her role dribbled down the drain. However, the film ends on an upbeat, with Sinatra and Kim walking off toward the sun rising over San Francisco Bay, and even receiving the blessings of ex-stripper Hayworth.

Pal Joey grossed $4.7 million in distributors' domestic rentals, which offset the bad reviews Kim received for her contribution to the film. *Photoplay* magazine insisted she "has no personality beyond a publicity handout, and has outstripped her meagre talent." Cohn and Columbia evidently did not feel so, for Kim inherited the departing Hayworth's star dressing room and was finally, once and for all, queen of the studio lot.

Kim's honors in 1957 were diverse. Liggett and Myers Tobacco Company named her Chesterfield's calendar girl for the year, and the *Harvard Lampoon* cited her as the year's worst actress. She attended art courses at Los Angeles City College and on October 18 appeared on Frank Sinatra's ABC-TV debut series show along with Bob Hope and Peggy Lee. After

At the age of eleven in 1944

With Fred MacMurray in
PUSHOVER (Col '54)

Cheesecake, Columbia Pictures
style (1954)

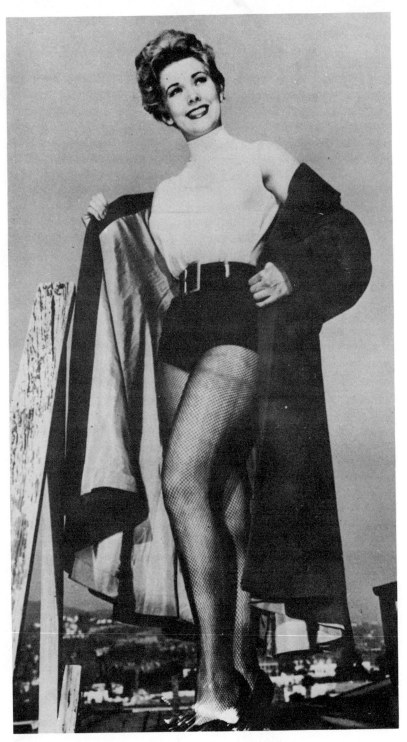

Publicity pose (1954)

With Jack Lemmon in PHFFFT! (Col '54)

With Guy Madison in
FIVE AGAINST THE HOUSE (Col '55)

With Susan Hayward, Egyptian Tahia Carioca, and Ginger Rogers at
the Cannes Film Festival (May 1956)

With Eleanor Parker in
THE MAN WITH THE GOLDEN ARM (UA '55)

Publicity pose with Victoria Shaw and Tyrone Power for
THE EDDY DUCHIN STORY (Col '56)

With Larry Gates and Agnes Moorehead in JEANNE EAGELS (Col '57)

Tub-side in 1957

In PAL JOEY (Col '57)

With Elsa Lanchester and
Jack Lemmon in BELL, BOOK
AND CANDLE (Col '58)

With General Rafael Trujillo
in 1958

With Fredric March in
MIDDLE OF THE NIGHT
(Col '59)

544

With Kirk Douglas in STRANGERS WHEN WE MEET (Col '60)

witnessing Kim's "unrehearsed" appearance, Harry Cohn issued two new edicts: *first,* that she not be permitted to do further television guesting because of her obvious ineptness on the Sinatra outing, and *second,* for publicity reasons, that she make an earnest effort to socialize more in the accepted Hollywood circles and be seen more often by the trade press who count. She obeyed her boss's strictures, and at a party in December, met thirty-two-year-old black performer Sammy Davis, Jr.* They dated secretly several times and met for a Christmas holiday in Aurora, Illinois, where Kim's sister then lived. The story goes that when Cohn learned about the rendezvous he placed a telephone call from his California office to a mobster in Las Vegas, where Sammy was performing. What actually transpired may never be publicly known, but soon after the telephone call, Sammy announced his pending marriage to Lorena White, a black showgirl in Vegas. Fifteen months later they were divorced, but the Novak-Davis dating game had officially ended.

Prior to incurring the wrath of Cohn, Kim managed, through her agents, to obtain a special seven-percent-interest loan based on her established salary. With this, she bought a $95,000, eight-room house on Tortuosa Drive in Bel Air, which had an all-blue bedroom, an all-purple study, a gray living room and sleeping porch, and a pool, where she swam—at least for the press—wearing a straw hat. Sharing the house was her secretary, Barbara Mellon, a friend from Chicago about whom she volunteered: "She has her own personal life, and it never interferes with mine. The older I get, the fussier I am about privacy. When I study a script or paint, I have to be alone. I can't express my deep feelings in front of a lot of people. I can't let go." Clearly Marilyn Pauline Novak was maturing into her own kind of person, coping internally with her fame and fortune on a different level than, say, Marilyn Monroe, Doris Day, or Elizabeth Taylor, all of whom owed their boost in prominence to the studio star system of the 1940s and early 1950s.

At Paramount, producer-director Alfred Hitchcock was readying a Technicolor mystery film with the working title *Among the Dead,* based on a French novel, *D'entre les Mortes.* It was announced that James Stewart would perform the lead role of a retired police detective suffering from acrophobia, which gave him vertigo. Hitchcock wanted Vera Miles to work opposite Stewart as a San Francisco shopgirl who is paid by a shipbuilder (Tom Helmore) to impersonate his wife, who thinks she is pos-

*According to Sammy Davis's discreet autobiography, *Yes I Can* (1965), written with Jane and Burt Boyar, he claims that after their initial party meeting caused industry gossip (e.g., "Guess which sepia entertainer's attentions are being whispered as The Kiss of Death to guess which blonde movie-star's career?"), he phoned Kim to apologize and she, in turn, invited him to dinner that very evening. Davis's further summarizing of their subsequent liaison then dissolves into a tactful statement that he soon comprehended that the slurmongers were causing a "deep insult to me and to all Negro people." Kim's presence in the Davis chronicle ends at this juncture.

sessed by the spirit of her great-grandmother. Helmore murders his wife, using the unsuspecting Stewart for his alibi, and the latter, who has fallen in love with the girl, suffers a nervous breakdown. Later, Stewart re-encounters the I. Magnin department-store girl, quite rightly convinced that she is the spitting image of his recent lost love. He becomes freneti-cally in love with the look-alike only to lose her in the film's surprise finish.

When Miles, whom Hitchcock had employed in *The Wrong Man* (Paramount, 1957), announced that she was unavailable for the new pic-ture due to advanced pregnancy, the director turned to Kim, whom he had previously thought of casting in *The Trouble with Harry* (Paramount 1956) before he settled on actress Shirley MacLaine as being more appro-priate to the country-lass part.

Although Hitchcock has stated in interviews that he was not overjoyed working with Kim,* on this new production—released as *Vertigo* (Para-mount, 1958)—she proved to be in the best tradition of the director's famed line of ice-cool blondes,† with her developed screen persona admirably suited to the dual-role assignment. With costumes by Edith Head, makeup by Wally Westmore, hair styles by Nellis Manley,‡ and VistaVision camerawork by Robert Burks, Kim had every physical advan-tage to delineate her dual part. First, she played Madeleine Elster, the bogus wealthy woman whom ex-detective Stewart drags from San Francisco Bay after a "planned" suicide attempt ordered by Helmore as part of the scheme. The viewer first glimpses the sultry, aloof Kim lying in Stewart's bed where he takes her after the drenching; the impassive look on her countenance combined with her apparent nudity provides an engaging ambiance of vulnerability and impenetrability, all of which excites both Stewart and the viewer. Later, it is a deliberate setup on the part of Hitchcock that when Stewart and Kim-Madeleine visit the art museum, the painting of the girl's "great-grandmother" seems more vibrantly alive than this unreal living descendant. In the later part of the film, when Kim has become plain Judy Barton again, the filmgoer shares Stewart's almost maniacal desire to transform this shopgirl into the replica of his lost amour. The convoluted plot twists work both for and against the strange attraction-love that develops between Stewart and Kim-Judy, with the latter conveniently killed before the plotline would require her to suffer the legal consequences for her part in the murder

---

*As the director informed François Truffaut in *Hitchcock* (1966): "Miss Novak arrived on the set with all sorts of preconceived notions that I couldn't possibly go along with. You know, I don't like to argue with a performer on the set; there's no reason to bring the elec-tricians in on our troubles. I went to Kim Novak's dressing room and told her about the dresses and hairdos that I had been planning for several months. I also explained that the story was of less importance to me than the over-all visual impact on the screen, once the picture is completed."

†Madeleine Carroll, Joan Fontaine, Grace Kelly, Vera Miles, Tippi Hedren.

‡Hitchcock insisted that Kim not wear lavender hair.

of Helmore's real wife. Thus, both of Kim's characters (Madeleine, Judy) disappear from the mystery film, each an enticing, confounding creature for very different reasons.

Vertigo, with exteriors shot on location in northern California, did not prove to be one of Hitchcock's or Paramount's biggest box-office attractions, but the reviewers were in favor of Kim's performance. "Kim Novak behaves like an actress in *Vertigo*" (*Toronto Globe and Mail*). "Miss Novak is really quite amazing" (Bosley Crowther, *New York Times*). C. A. Lejeune (*London Observer*) was even more penetrating in detailing the rationale for Kim's success in this Hitchcockian exercise. "Miss Novak plays both girls with a lovely, unrevealing face; not a line of character can be distinguished behind the smooth, eggshaped mask; the heavy make-up suggests something from the old German school of cinema." Moreover, it worked to Kim's advantage, if not always for the story's credibility factor, that the "other" woman in *Vertigo,* Stewart's old girlfriend, Midge (Barbara Bel Geddes), is presented as a well-meaning, but mousey, bespectacled conventionalist who is unable to fathom the extent of Stewart's drive to fashion some reality out of his sexual fantasies.

Back on the home lot, Kim was immediately put to work, as a modern sorceress who purrs rather than cackles, in *Bell, Book and Candle* (Columbia, 1958), based on John Van Druten's Broadway comedy of 1950.* James Stewart, as part of the Kim-*Vertigo* production package, owed Columbia two pictures, and he was assigned the part of the mortal Manhattan publisher with whom Gillian Holroyd (Kim), the blonde witch, falls in love. Constance Bennett in *Topper* (MGM, 1937) and Veronica Lake in *I Married a Witch* (United Artists, 1942) may have been more adroitly insouciant as chic apparitions in those respective features, but Kim with her twenty-three costume changes, the flattering color-camera work of James Wong Howe, and the sympathetic cooperation-guidance of director Richard Quine,† emerged quite an ethereal sight, perfectly in keeping with the role. ". . . such a delightful witch as Kim Novak should happen to all of us," remarked Paul V. Beckley (*New York Herald-Tribune*). Bolstering the storyline a great deal was the presence of a wide variety of madcap actor-comics, ranging from Ernie Kovacs (an alcoholic author), Elsa Lanchester (a zany witch), and Hermione Gingold (the high priestess of witchdom), to a more subdued Jack Lemmon (as Kim's war-

---

**Bell, Book and Candle,* starring Rex Harrison and Lilli Palmer, opened at the Ethel Barrymore Theatre on November 14, 1950, for a 233-performance run. David O. Selznick originally purchased the screen rights to the property, planning to film it in London with Jennifer Jones starring. In 1955, producer Julian Blaustein and writer Daniel Taradash acquired the screen rights from Selznick for a $150,000 price.

†Quine, at the time, was supposedly serene in his marriage to the granddaughter of one-time matinee idol Francis X. Bushman. Although Kim and Quine had professionally worked together five years earlier, they now viewed each other from a romantic angle.

lock brother) and the film's big scene-stealer, a Siamese feline named Pyewacket.

As in *Vertigo*, a good deal of Kim's overall success with her characterization was the result of her pedestaled screen presence matching the demands of the role.* As *Time* magazine analyzed, "The part is almost perfectly written for Actress Novak. The script quickly announces that as a witch she is not supposed to blush, cry, or indeed have very much expression at all." *Films in Review*'s Henry Hart went closer to the truth: "Miss Novak's usual lifelessness was an asset in this film and Director Quine got an effective performance out of her (she even read the lines as though she understood their purport)."

While *Bell, Book and Candle* made some box-office coin, it was the second Kim Novak film in a row to gross under $4 million in distributors' domestic receipts. Some industry observers blamed the box-office slump on the hard-to-accept romantic combination of a twenty-five-year-old Kim making love oncamera to fifty-year-old Stewart. Then too, the film's premise was based on a one-joke affair—that zany witches could exist in contemporary Manhattan, a premise which proved to be much more commercially suited to macabre exorcism delineation, as in the later box-office powerhouse, *Rosemary's Baby* (Paramount, 1968).

On February 27, 1958, the respected but feared chief of Columbia Pictures, Harry Cohn, died of heart failure at the age of sixty-six. Almost at once, as though she were thumbing her nose at Cohn, Kim involved herself in an international affair with Lieutenant General Rafael "Ramfis" Trujillo, son of the Dominican dictator. They first met at a party given by Zsa Zsa Gabor and, said Kim, "we saw a great, great deal of each other" until the blonde star discovered that he had a wife and five children stashed away. She then returned his gifts—an $8,700 Mercedes convertible and $5,000 in jewelry—but the scandal news leaked out along with the juicy information that Zsa Zsa had also accepted his tokens of esteem —a $5,800 sports car and a $17,000 chinchilla coat. Representative Charles Porter of Oregon suggested in Congress that since Trujillo spent $1 million a year, the $1.3 million aid given by the United States to the Dominican Republic be dovetailed directly to the taxable movie stars in question. Kim's standing reputation as the pure, sweet, home-loving girl was threatened, and Columbia's board of executives ordered her to promptly end the affair. Members of the studio's publicity staff worked in shifts inside and outside her home to make certain that she behaved. One time, she managed to elude them and gave "Ramfis" thirty minutes of farewell in his private railway car before he departed Hollywood.

*Within *Bell, Book and Candle*, Kim's performance retreats to a languid, unsatisfying level when she suddenly finds that love has made her human, and that she can now blush, cry, and see her reflection in the mirror. Thus, once her character becomes mortal, Kim the actress seems at a loss to invest her part with needed warmth and conviction, artistic shortcomings that have marred her celluloid appearances throughout her career.

She later told George Christy of the *Ladies' Home Journal*: "Everybody wants to make 'Ramfis' out to be a wild, love-'em-and-leave-'em playboy but all I know is that he reached me. He wrote me a poem every day . . ."

An honor was extended Kim in 1958 at the Brussels World Fair when, in a demonstration of the American voting machine, a poll was taken in several categories, one of which was "the favorite all-time actress in the world." Kim won with the greatest number of votes—far ahead of other names placed in contention.

Paddy Chayefsky's *Middle of the Night* was an hour-long television drama in 1954 starring E. G. Marshall and Eva Marie Saint.* In 1956 it became a two-act Broadway drama with Edward G. Robinson and Gena Rowlands starred,† and in 1959 it was a 118-minute black-and-white feature with Fredric March and Kim Novak. It is the story of a fifty-six-year-old Jewish clothing manufacturer who believes he has fallen in love with his not-too-bright twenty-four-year-old divorced receptionist. Against all advice from relatives and friends, he eventually weds her, knowing full well the potential consequences of this May-December romance. March was not as Jewish as Robinson in his character delineation, but he offered what is considered one of the best modulated performances of his long and varied career. Dramatically, Kim could not quite keep pace with him, although the Chayefsky screenplay aided her a good deal by making her Betty Preisser a confused young lady, not quite certain whether she is seeking a father figure, a substitute for her unreliable ex-husband (Lee Philips), or an honest avenue of romantic involvement. As *Time* magazine recorded, "Amazingly, Actress Novak shows up not too badly, despite the distinguished company, and credit for that seems to belong chiefly to director Delbert Mann . . ."

Once again, Kim's role in the film required her to be the passive figure, but in *Middle of the Night* (Columbia, 1959), it was on a much more refined, intellectualized level. In the course of the picture, March wavers back and forth between being a middle-aged man certain that this young woman is his key to a new lease on life, and, on other occasions, shaken to the core by realistic doubts as to whether she can be the tonic for his existence. Most importantly, and considerately, he worries about his ability to offer her the compatibility he feels she rightly deserves. With such a mercurial, complex character with whom to interact, Kim was pushed to offer more than just simple reactions and mumbled dialog. To her credit, she tried her darndest, but as *Variety* observed: "there is a static, shallow approach in the scripting that prevents Miss Novak from obtaining conviction except from her staunch admirers. Others may

*"Philco Playhouse" (NBC-TV, September 19, 1954).
†It opened at the ANTA Theatre on Broadway on February 8, 1956, for a 477-performance run.

find Miss Novak hopelessly lost and inadequate in attempting to give even surface value to her role." For many viewers—and this art-house-type feature did not attract mass audiences—the sight of Kim and March huddled together on a Central Park bench or romantically entangled in the front seat of his car, was a chilling, foreboding sight, too depressingly realistic for conventional screenfare entertainment.*

Artistically though, *Middle of the Night*, which had been shot on location in New York in January 1958, was selected in May 1959 as the United States entry at the 1959 Cannes Film Festival. Officially chosen to represent Columbia at Cannes, Kim embarked, with her parents, on a thirty-day tour of Europe. Newsmen had a field day with her and the famous men she encountered. In France, she met Prince Aly Khan, who invited her to spend an afternoon with him, the Aga Khan, and the Begum at their Cannes villa. It was a publicity affair with photographers on hand to record the "historic" meeting but later, after Kim and the Prince became better acquainted, she admitted of the ex-spouse of Rita Hayworth: "I could never get serious about him, although he talked about marriage. I liked him, but you never really knew what he felt. I doubt if any woman would ever feel secure with him as a husband. He just loved women too much."

Kim had become friends with Cary Grant the previous year at Paramount when she was involved with *Vertigo* and he was doing *Houseboat* (Paramount, 1958) with Sophia Loren. Fifty-four-year-old Grant, already three times wed, showed up at Cannes and escorted Kim to the Russian Embassy ball, where they danced until dawn. They made such a hit with the Russians that they were invited to the next Moscow Film Festival. "I adore him," Kim said of Grant, "we speak the same language." When reminded of his mature age, she said in seeming surprise, "Good heavens, is he really? I thought he was under forty." Next, she was kissed feelingly in a Paris marketplace by globe-trotting actor Anthony Quinn, who claimed to be overwhelmed by the "wonderful smells and the feel of life." When questioned about her husband's unpremeditated whirl with Kim, Katherine DeMille Quinn replied rather vaguely, "I know nothing of it." Leaving France, Kim took her parents to Rome, where Mario Bandini laid aside his work as an engineer to escort the celebrated blonde star about town. Kim's official remark on her date was, "I think he is divine." The Novaks wound up their heady trip with a visit to relatives in Prague, thus concluding a romantic—real or otherwise—conquest of Europe.

Twentieth Century-Fox had already examined extramarital shenani-

---

*Since *Middle of the Night*, there have been Jack Lemmon's *Save the Tiger* (Paramount, 1973), which on different terms examines the same career and love frustrations experienced by March in the former picture, and, of course, *Forty Carats* (Columbia, 1973), which in sugary, more palatable terms reverses the situation (i.e., older woman, young man).

gans in American suburbia in its modest but effective *No Down Payment* (1957). Nevertheless, producer-director Richard Quine joined with producer-star Kirk Douglas to translate Evan Hunter's novel *Strangers When We Meet* into Columbia's more expansive and hopefully more daring study of adultery among the upper-class suburban set. Kim was second-billed to Douglas in this 1960 account of an ambitious but intellectual architect (Douglas) who, feeling abused by his too mundane wife (Barbara Rush), enters into a love affair with a sexually neglected housewife (Kim). No matter how grandiose the production values—with Kim and Douglas cooing in and out of motels and beaches and through an ultra-modern two story mansion in Bel-Air Canyon built especially for the film at the cost of $250,000—the picture was just overpuffed pulp-magazine nonsense—"A pictorially attractive but dramatically vacuous study of modern-style infidelity" (*Variety*).

Despite the puerile, self-congratulatory approach of *Strangers When We Meet*, there are many who feel this film represents the best joint screen work achieved by director Quine and star Kim, in which she lives up to her established brand of screen exotica; "a dreamy and ruminative type," as stated by A. H. Weiler (*New York Times*).

During the filming of *Strangers When We Meet*, it was well known in Hollywood that dimpled-chin Douglas and Kim disliked each other off-screen, and Mike Connolly, in his *Hollywood Reporter* column, suggested a title change to *Stranglers When We Meet*. Quine's divorce was decreed by the time the film was completed, and, as a marriage inducement, Columbia offered Kim and Quine the specially built mansion in Bel-Air Canyon.

Whatever plans Kim might have had for marrying were not formulated. She was whisked off to Mexico City to help exploit the Cantinflas film *Pepe* (Columbia, 1960), in which she appeared briefly as herself along with thirty-five other guest stars whom director George Sidney corraled into the 195-minute roadshow-style film, which bombed with the public.*

From Mexico, Kim went to Rio de Janeiro, where she donned a black wig, an old shirt, and torn Levi's and danced in the streets with the local celebrants of Carnival. Next, she flew to London to attend a Royal Command Performance of Columbia's Paul Muni picture, *The Last Angry Man* (1959). Since director Quine was already there helming scenes for *The World of Suzie Wong* (Paramount, 1961), Kim indicated to Louella Parsons the possibility of a British Isles wedding. Although Kim and Quine saw London together, the wedding never materialized, and

---

*Among the tedious interludes and gratuitous cameo-star-studded bits within *Pepe*, Kim's appearance attracted special attack. Bosley Crowther (*New York Times*) reported that within the picture Cantinflas "has to stand by while Kim Novak oozes one of the most tastelessly patronizing bits of bathos we have ever beheld."

Quine moved on to Hong Kong for additional local shooting. Kim returned to New York, where she was hospitalized for two weeks at Doctors Hospital with a minor case of hepatitis. She was advised by doctors to slow down and did so by developing her hobby of painting. In an interview with *Newsweek* she revealed: "Acting is very frustrating. I like it, but you have no control over the direction it takes. In movies, I just let the script take me. But as far as just plain old fulfillment goes, it's not satisfying. That's why I have to paint. It's the only place I get my satisfaction."

Meanwhile, the fan magazines were flooded with pointed articles concerned with Kim's lack of marital status, such as "Will Kim Novak Be a Spinster?" and "Kim Novak: Afraid of Marriage." Louella Parsons jumped to her defense by issuing statements that such tales seemed "to be writing her off pretty fast. She's only twenty-eight." Parsons further rationalized for her readers that it was a matter of religious principle that prevented Kim from wedding a divorced man (Quine).

Although Kim was still much in the news in 1961, it was fast becoming apparent that professionally she had to expand in new directions or be left behind in the competitive lurch among the top personalities of the movie industry. Doris Day, Elizabeth Taylor, and Sandra Dee were among the top-ten box-office stars in the United States in 1960-62, with Kim, like the fading Marilyn Monroe, falling fast into the background. Granted, thousands of teenaged girls across America were still wearing the "Kim Novak look" with short, blonde hair, dark eye liner, and a splash of lavender, but Kim was no longer the "big" commodity in the movie industry. Since the death of Harry Cohn, Columbia had been undergoing its own corporate shakeup and reorganization, with A. Schneider as company president and Samuel J. Briskin as vice-president in charge of West Coast activities. Kim's love-hate, professional-social relationship with the late Harry Cohn had been a mixed bag for Kim the private person, but it was Cohn who had craftily engineered her build-up as a major motion-picture personality, and since his demise, her career was floundering without direction. The 1960s demanded a new breed of screen celebrities to persuade viewers to leave their television-saturated homes and come back to the theatres. In the course of eight years, Kim had appeared and/ or starred in sixteen features. Her screen presence had been saturated in a variety of good to mediocre projects, always attuned to demonstrating that, physically, Kim the love goddess was nigh on unimpeachable. But the public was more demanding now. If they were to continue their adoration of Kim the mature movie star, they now wanted a new, up-to-date Kim, a personality who would be more earthily sexy, more dramatically penetrating, or more comically lighthearted—anything, but just something different to compensate for the lost blush of youth from aging Kim.

Thus, on August 21, 1961, it was announced in the trade papers that

Kim had joined forces with Filmways Productions, an independent company headed by Martin Ransohoff. The new association was called Kimco Filmways Picture Corporation, and the first production began in October 1961 at MGM, entitled *Boys' Night Out* (1962), a presentation of the 1950s-1960s wildest film showman, Joseph E. Levine. The rather arch Ira Wallach screenplay revolved around the premise that Kim, a graduate sociology student studying the sexual behavior of the adult male, allows herself to be set up in a plush Manhattan apartment by three married commuters (Tony Randall, Howard Duff, Howard Morris) and a bachelor (James Garner). The picture was devised to have the same double-entendre, glossy look as the Doris Day-Rock Hudson vehicles, but somehow the proper momentum and flavor never caught on with this well-appointed imitation. Throughout the 115-minute multihued sex-farce proceedings, everyone talks so much about sex and about what might happen if it did happen, that nothing ever does, leaving the baited viewer totally frustrated. Randall-Duff-Morris-Garner gave stock-reaction performances, which was hardly fair to the quintet of intriguing supporting female players (Janet Blair, Jessie Royce Landis, Patti Page, Anne Jeffreys, Zsa Zsa Gabor). And, most sadly, Kim just could not carry the slim, cold-cream-slapping vehicle on her shoulders. She wore leotards, bulky sweaters, and scuttled about the sets with a minimum of enthusiasm, leading Bosley Crowther (*New York Times*) to decry, "Her inclination to ardor appears no more powerful than her passion for a doctor's degree."

Although Kim was now an independent film producer, she still had a contractual obligation to Columbia and had reached the zenith of choosing her own scripts.* She selected *The Notorious Landlady* (Columbia, 1962) with Richard Quine as her director, and Jack Lemmon and Fred Astaire as her co-stars. Although the murder-mystery story is set in Britain, the film was made 250 miles north of Hollywood in the Big Sur country near Monterey on the same estate that was used in 1939 for the exteriors of *Rebecca*.

Kim was cast as Carlye Hardwicke, a house-owner suspected of murdering her husband. She rents a room to a young American State Department official (Lemmon) who soon decides to find out the truth about her. Lemmon's departmental superior (Astaire) finds himself involved in the mystifying caper. In the film's final hectic scenes, Kim is required to be disguised as a Cockney maid, battling it out near perilous cliffs with the real murderess, played by oversized Philippa Bevans. Not only was it Kim's first movie fight, but the first time oncamera that she did not look as though she had just stepped out of an Elizabeth Arden beauty parlor.

*Kim got $600,000 for *The Notorious Landlady*, which proved to be her last Columbia Picture, although there have been negotiations for two additional Kimco-Columbia releases, and a potential television series entitled "Emmy Lou."

Kim described the novel experience thus: "I love physical scenes like this, in which I can throw myself without any self-consciousness. It's great not to care how your hair and face are looking every minute. This wasn't just an ordinary hair-pulling and scratching match, either. We fought like men, with our fists. A woman fighter is much dirtier, without any rules." (Kim trained for the fight sequence with a stuntman and a gym punching bag.)

The Notorious Landlady premiered in New York on July 26, 1962, a little over a month after the Manhattan debut (June 21, 1962) of *Boys' Night Out*. These were Kim's first film releases in two years, and their public reception was vital to the future of her movie career. *Boys' Night Out* had neither impressed nor unduly offended the critics in their regard for the Kim Novak living legend. However, *The Notorious Landlady,* which received far less of a ballyhoo sendoff by Columbia, had a short-lived box-office record. Not that the reviewers were averse to the picture's mixed comedy-mystery potential: "This suspense comedy runs along blithely enough . . . " (*New York Herald-Tribune*); "Beguiling if hokey mystery-comedy" (*Time* magazine). In fact, the bulk of the fourth estate praised Lemmon's refined antic performance as salvaging the picture, aided by Astaire and Lionel Jeffries. But Kim, in the title role as the lonely, scared sole occupant of a stately London house, was no longer allowed by the critics to pass muster solely on her "opulent looks." Arthur Knight (*Saturday Review*) sniped, "Miss Novak may be decorated enough in the series of costumes she designed for herself [executed by Elizabeth Courtney], but her fixed expression of gloomy seductiveness hardly sets a key for sprightly comedy." Stanley Kauffmann (*New Republic*), who reviewed both *Boys' Night Out* and *The Notorious Landlady* in one overall review, sizzled, "In both films Miss Novak is the same: a voice like an improperly closed gas jet, the poise of a novice doing her first striptease at a conclave of longshoremen, the artistic endowments of a Broadway backer's girl friend who has been given a two-line part as tit for tat. . . . [In *The Notorious Landlady*] her efforts arouse compassion." Rounding out the roasting of the 1950s love goddess was Bosley Crowther (*New York Times*): "Miss Novak is one of those performers who have cast so many drab and saggy palls over good motion pictures that one shudders to see her name in a cast. . . . In short, Miss Novak is a flat tire."

While Kim's movie career was drifting into limbo, her private life continued to command news space. In March 1963 she had gone to Moscow, and upon her return to the United States she announced: "I want to make a movie in Russia. . . . This is very important. I mean. I just feel—well the way to help things, to ease tensions is through communications—I mean, a film could do the trick—a love story—two people having an understanding and closeness despite the society. And there's just never been a better time than now to make this picture. Serious pictures can be appetizing too." Kim was a bit more precise when questioned about her relationship abroad with Prince Alfonso Hohenlohe, "We are old friends. There is no romance."

Hollywood still buzzed about her status with director Richard Quine, but Kim had fallen in love with a new object, a house. She had found a turreted house set on a jagged ocean cliff at Big Sur. A tidal wave had swept through it a few weeks before, which she considered a good omen. "I feel as if that wave was meant to clear the house for me." She bought the hideaway, which was called "Gull House," for $90,000. "I'll live here, look at the ocean, and paint. It's the peaceful haven I've always wanted—and the most romantic place in the world. You can almost hear music as you approach." She joined the inhabitants of Big Sur-Monterey-Carmel in picnics, nude communal baths, musicales, and folk dancing. She was accepted as a painter, not a movie star. She preferred bare feet, and said, "I like loose-fitting clothes that mold to my body softly, but allow me freedom." She further revealed: "Most of the time I sleep in the nude, but it depends on my mood. Sometimes I wear flannel nightgowns or sexy negligees. But freedom is the thing."

Marilyn Monroe's suicide on August 5, 1962, left Kim the undisputed junior-matron queen of Hollywood glamour and one of the last of the classic blonde prototypes, along with aging Jayne Mansfield and Britain's Diana Dors. On hearing of Marilyn's passing, Kim stated: "With Marilyn it's so sad because she didn't have a family, really. I think you need roots. You certainly don't get them in this business."

Kim left her oceanside Utopia in the winter of 1962 to go to Ireland for the filming of *Of Human Bondage* (MGM, 1964) for MGM. The resultant production was a fiasco from the start. Somerset Maugham's novel (1915) had first been picturized in 1934 with Leslie Howard and Bette Davis, winning its own distinctive place in cinema history, more for Davis's bravura performance as the slatternly Cockney waitress, Mildred Rogers, than for the film's faithfulness to the very popular British novel. Warner Bros. made the error of refilming the story in 1946 (with Paul Henreid and Eleanor Parker) to negligible artistic and commercial results. The property might have remained dormant, but in 1953, director Henry Hathaway, having found his professional association with Marilyn Monroe on *Niagara* so satisfying, perceived that Monroe would be ideal to portray Mildred Rogers in a new version of *Of Human Bondage*, possibly with Montgomery Clift as the sensitive, club-footed Philip Carey. Hathaway acquired the screen rights, but then Twentieth Century-Fox studio boss Darryl F. Zanuck nixed Hathaway's project, and the property was later sold to Seven Arts Productions, which thereafter joined with MGM for the newly packaged edition of the Maugham classic. Because of Hathaway's prior interest in the story, he was hired to direct the film, although he made it clear that he did not want Kim for the part of Mildred, but a younger blonde, someone like Tuesday Weld.*

Kim was nervous about this film because she had never before worked on a motion picture outside the United States and, too, she had great difficulty coping with Mildred's Cockney accent, which, she insisted, was the crux to capturing the proper characterization. From the start, the latest *Of Human Bondage* was a jinx. There were British union squabbles, and after about one day of actual shooting, Hathaway withdrew from the production, claiming he was unable to cope with Kim's nervous interpretation. In the following hectic interim period, scripter Bryan Forbes took over the directorial reins, but he eventually relinquished them to Ken Hughes. Adding further to the chaos on the *Of Human Bondage* set was co-star Laurence Harvey, whose sense of professionalism did not match up with hers, making for tenseness between them. At one point presumptuous Harvey departed the production location to fly to Nice to confer with ninety-year-old Somerset Maugham on the progress of the new film.† Meanwhile, Kim's hysteria in coping with the demanding role increased, and in April 1963 the production was halted. For a time there was talk of Elizabeth Taylor taking over the part, but eventually Kim and Harvey returned to the soundstages, and the necessary footage was finally shot.

One of the other publicized aspects of *Of Human Bondage* was the fact that Kim was required to play an in-bed scene in the nude. When asked if she minded, she said, "I . . . guess not. Just as long as it gives something to the picture, helps the story." Yousuf Karsh, the famous portrait photographer from Ottawa, Canada, was contracted to "capture" Kim in her waitress outfit to show the world that she was turning really dramatic in *Of Human Bondage*. After the session, Karsh gleefully proclaimed: "She's magnificent. Not at all what I expected. They made her out to be just another stereotyped Hollywood glamour girl. She has great sensitivity. She's warm, human. I think she has been misrepresented, caricatured. She has humility, like most women. Only men are vain. Men are the vainest of all creatures."

Of Human Bondage, which went some five weeks over production schedule at an additional cost of $1 million, debuted in the fall of 1964 to unanimous pans. The tale of a bitchy, whorish London waitress who inflicts mental anguish on a club-footed young physician had too little cogency for 1960s filmgoers. As A. H. Weiler (*New York Times*) explained: "the current adaptation merely evolves as a stoic old-fashioned tale in

---

*Referring to this misadventure, Hathaway has said, "Later on Seven Arts took it and they made it with Stupid—what's her name, Kim Novak."

†The presence of Joan Cohn, Harry's widow, visiting beau Harvey on the *Of Human Bondage* set caused additional friction between the co-stars.

which lip service substitutes for the truly poignant, self-revelatory story from which it stems. . . . These are not classically tortured people who emerge whole and alive on film but are, instead, artificially quaint Edwardians who are simply play acting and speaking lines that seem alien to them and the viewer."

None of the fourth estate had kind words for Harvey's surface interpretation of the haunted Philip Carey, and although many denounced Kim's performance as the worst case of cinema miscasting of the 1960s, there were a few champions for her interpretation of the grasping working girl. "[She] comes up with a performance which, though uneven, reveals some unexpected flashes of depth" (*Variety*). *Newsweek* offered a backhanded compliment to her portrayal, which at least gave her credit for acting: " . . . if there is any fault to find with the way she plays the round-heeled love of the lame but game medical student, that fault is her excess of verisimilitude. She clasps the squalor of Maugham's famed novel so tightly to her bosom that the film sometimes seems like Person to Person."

Of Human Bondage, denied a Production Code approval because of the "nude" scene, flitted through national distribution very quickly. The public scarcely had an opportunity to judge for itself the precise nature of Kim's latest attempt to play a screen tramp, some six years after her chaotic try at portraying Sadie Thompson in the *Rain* excerpt within *Jeanne Eagels*.

Producer-director-scripter Billy Wilder, who had made a reputation for increasingly smutty cinema yarns, hit the bottom (or the top?) of the barrel with *Kiss Me, Stupid* (Lopert, 1964). The dirty-joke premise concerns pop singer Dino (Dean Martin), who is driving through Nevada and stops off in the town of Climax. His car is sabotaged by amateur songwriter Orville J. Spooner (Ray Walston—who replaced an ailing Peter Sellers) and his crony (Cliff Osmond), who intend to interest Martin in one of their tunes. Martin is invited to spend the night at Walston's home, and to insure that the vocalist has proper companionship for the night, Walston gets his wife, Zelda (Felicia Farr), out of the way and substitutes Polly the Pistol (Kim Novak) from the Belly Button Bar to be the proxy wife and accommodating hostess. Walston, however, becomes jealous, tosses Martin out, and while Walston and Kim spend the evening together, Martin finds solace at Kim's lodgings, where a drunken Farr is resting. All ends well when, sometime later, Martin sings one of Walston's tunes on television. When the baffled Walston asks his knowing wife how this came about, she replies, "Shut up and kiss me, stupid."

Needless to say, in 1964 much of this raw subject matter was offensive to segments of the film industry and to community organizations at large throughout America. The film was given a C (condemned) rating by the Catholic Legion of Decency and denied a seal of approval from the Motion Picture Association of America. United Artists was forced to turn the picture over for release to its subsidiary, Lopert Pictures. (While standards of decency have greatly eased up in the past decade, *Kiss Me, Stupid* is still not considered fit television fare.)

Kiss Me, Stupid, which was generally branded "pitifully unfunny" (*New York Times*), "a jape that seems to have scraped its blue-black humor off the floor of a honky-tonk nightclub" (*Time*), did provide Kim with her definitive exposure as the cinema broad. As the displaced "cocktail waitress" from New Jersey, who is stranded in the desert town's sleazy nightspot, she has endured most of life's hard knocks (e.g., being raffled off at a local cookout for $83 and ending up the loser with no money and a case of poison ivy). As she readily admits to her Belly Button Club customers, "Around here I'm just someone the barman recommends." Wilder directed Kim to be a lusty-voiced, dim-witted realist rather than a wistful optimist (the way Marilyn Monroe, no doubt, would have handled the tailor-made part). In her scenes with raunchy Martin, Kim revealed a natural ease with the tough-as-nails dialog, belting out the distasteful repartee with no sense of shame or thought. Martin inquires why she is called "Lambchops," to which she hastily answers, "Perhaps it's because I wear paper panties." In what seems like a bit of accidental thoughtfulness, it is Kim's Polly who has the one sympathetic moment, for when she and Walston couple for the night, he informs her, "Tonight you're not Polly—you're Mrs. Orville J. Spooner." At long last—if only for a brief spell— she has a chance to perform her services on a "moral" basis.

If 1964 was not Kim's prime cinema year, she still retained her stake in the show-business world. NBC-TV's "Hollywood and the Stars" devoted a half-hour episode, *In Search of Kim Novak* (March 9, 1964), to the notion that the blonde star lives in two diverse worlds, one as a prime Hollywood movie star, and the other as a recluse in a small stone castle near Monterey. In September 1964, Vernon Scott of the *Saturday Evening Post* revealed that Kim had formed a music company, Spindrift Corporation, intended to publish several of the thirty songs she had written with her Big Sur boyfriend, Al Schackman. Sample song titles were: "Somewhere in December," "Tides," "Starfish," and "Sea Shell." She informed Scott: "Right now I'm hung up on song writing. I don't know where I'm going and I'm not concerned about it." In discussing marriage and the fact that, at thirty-one, she was still single, she said, huskily: "Marriage is unnatural. Sex has never been limited to marriage, despite our moral code. And it is just as unnatural for a woman to mate for life as it is for a man. In other species, it's not just males who switch mates; the female does too."

Soon after these remarks, Kim was at Shepperton Studios in London for the filming of *The Amorous Adventures of Moll Flanders* (Paramount, 1965), the distaff view of *Tom Jones*, the 1963 British feature which had garnered over $17.2 million in distributors' domestic rentals. Producer Marcel Hellman reasoned that there was a goldmine to be made in translating Daniel Defoe's 1722 novel of the famed English adventuress into a picaresque, risqué screen tale, laden with heavy doses of costumed pageantry, double-entendre dialog, compromising situations, and racy pacing. Included in an international cast was British actor Richard Johnson as the lovable thief Jemmy, the final object of Moll's amour.* An orphan, Moll is first engaged as a maid by an eighteenth-century English family chiefly composed of sex-starved males. She marries the imbecilic second son, who prefers booze to copulation. Too embarrassed to speak the truth of him, she demurely tells friends, "Modesty forbids me to reveal the secrets of the marriage bed." She then meets a banker (George Sanders), becomes maid-companion to a count (Vittorio De Sica) and his lady (Angela Lansbury), and finally weds Sanders, but leaves him on their first night together. She then joins a group of thieves and becomes their number-one asset, goes to prison, finds Jemmy, and, in the end, everyone is on an America-bound boat except Sanders, who fortuitously dies of a heart attack before he has had an opportunity to alter his will. The film is colorful, long, and mildly amusing. Kim's hair is plentiful and red; her eye makeup is heavy and dark; her acting is enthusiastic and she looks as though she is having fun. " . . . she has entered into the spirit of the film with a gusto and rowdiness that is unusual for her" (*New York Daily News*). "She wears her flouncy costumes well, in all stages of dress and undress, and whatever may be lacking in her acting is more than recompensed by a gusty presence" (*Variety*). Unfortunately, *The Amorous Adventures of Moll Flanders*, considering its steep production costs, was not the anticipated big-money-earner envisioned. (Even the fact that the Catholic Legion of Decency called it "morally objectionable in parts for all" did not stir up the necessary big business.)

*Johnson was born July 30, 1927, in Upminster, Essex, the son of Keith Holcombe Johnson and Frances Louisa Olive (Tweed). He studied for the stage at the Royal Academy of Dramatic Arts, first appearing at the Opera House, Manchester, England, in a small role in *Hamlet* (July 1944), and later playing the same part on the West End. After serving in the Royal Navy (1945-48) he returned to acting in repertory. He joined the Old Vic Company for the 1953 season, worked in television in 1954. He specialized in Shakespearian drama, playing both in England and abroad. He was a member of the Royal Shakespeare Company. He made his first New York stage appearance in *The Complaisant Lover* (1961). In 1969 he formed Pageant Entertainment Ltd., producing *Brief Lives* on the British stage; more recently he has returned as actor to the Royal Shakespearian Company in *Antony and Cleopatra* and *Julius Caesar*. Johnson made his film bow in *Captain Horatio Hornblower* (Warner Bros., 1951) and has appeared in such movies as *Never So Few* (MGM, 1959), *Cairo* (MGM, 1962), *The Haunting* (MGM, 1963), *Eighty Thousand Suspects* (Rank, 1963), *The Pumpkin Eater* (Columbia, 1964), *Operation Crossbow* (MGM, 1965), *Khartoum* (United Artists, 1966), *Deadlier than the Male* (Universal, 1966—as Bulldog Drummond), *Danger Route* (United Artists, 1967), *La Strego in Amore* (Italian, 1967), *Oedipus the King* (Universal, 1968), *A Twist of Sand* (United Artists, 1968), *Lady Hamilton* (Rank, 1968), *Some Girls Do* (Rank, 1968), *Julius Caesar* (American International, 1970), and the unreleased *The Beloved* (c. 1970).

His first wife, whom he later divorced, was Sheila Sweet.

Kim, at thirty-two, and Johnson, at thirty-seven, found that they shared many interests, such as poetry, hot sulphur baths, skiing, nature, good food, deep breathing, and a hippie way of life.* Their publicized courtship and their marriage on March 15, 1965, put an end to overt conjectures regarding Kim's spinsterhood. At exactly 3:13 P.M., in keeping with her superstition, the ceremony took place in a snowy meadow called Beaver Dam near the Aspen, Colorado, ski resort. Pitkin County Judge William R. Shaw officiated, and Mr. and Mrs. Hollee Kasell (he was Kim's business manager) were in attendance. When asked by reporters why she chose an outdoor wedding, Kim replied: "We couldn't be married in church, since he'd been married before. I thought outdoors would be the next closest thing to God—He being part of nature and all." Kim's wedding ring, fashioned by an Aspen silversmith, was intertwined with gold and silver bands and was called "Slalom."

As newlyweds, they divided their lives between London and Big Sur, never reaching a satisfactory agreement on where they wanted to make a permanent joint home. In September 1965, Kim went to Paris to begin on-location work in a new suspense film, *13*, produced by Martin Ransohoff for MGM release. Her co-star was elite David Niven. Production progressed in the Bordeaux country of rural France at a slower-than-expected pace, due to scripting problems with the modern exorcism tale, and then, in November of that year, Kim developed a "back" injury from her on-the-set work. While she recuperated in London for two weeks, the $3 million film hung in the balance, and it was finally decided, by "mutual consent," to release Kim and substitute Niven's often leading lady, Deborah Kerr, in the role of the Marquis's wife who learns that her spouse is doomed under a family witchcraft curse. The trouble-prone feature, retitled *Eye of the Devil*, did not see release until mid-1967, and then died a quick box-office death.

Meanwhile, Kim's marriage to Johnson was rapidly disintegrating, and after a joint appearance on the April 1966 televised Oscarcasts, they were hardly seen together. She finally withdrew to Big Sur, where she

---

*Johnson, who had been dating actress Geraldine Chaplin before meeting and romancing Kim, expostulated at great length on the future of the couple. "Kim and I are very much in accord about the way we want to live our lives. She isn't happy in cities and neither am I. I hope we can find a cottage in England where it's wild. . . .

"My intention is not to be separated for long periods of time. If it entails my giving up a picture to avoid it I will consider it—provided it doesn't involve too much sacrifice. I don't ever want to be in the position of saying, 'I gave this up because of you.'"

About his bride-to-be, Johnson offered, "She's a very emotional girl and I'm not emotional enough. I tend to think things out and intellectualize. She can make me feel more—and I can make her think more. I think she's a frightfully good actress and people don't appreciate her. She's tremendously sensitive. She reacts instantly to the slighest change in a scene. Of course, she's a marvelous looking girl and I don't think she should really worry about acting—but she does."

In publicly declaring her affection for Johnson, Kim explained, "Richard is the right man for me. Love without understanding and friendship would not have been enough. Now I have all of this and more."

refused to answer her telephone or respond to letters. After fourteen months of marriage, she obtained a divorce on May 26, 1966, and isolated herself at "Gull House," surrounded by two horses, a snake, several cats, a dog, a goat, and a mynah bird.* She insisted: "I'll never, never go back to Hollywood to live. Nor will I ever live in a city again. It would be like going back to slavery, living a regimented life, breathing polluted air and listening to the lies and insincerities of human society."

On another occasion, she expostulated on her life-style thus: "I spend as much time in the woods with my dogs as I do in this house. I've had a few really good pictures, some good ones. But I can't dive into a shallow pool again. I've got to have some depth. You've got to be true to yourself. If not, who's going to be your authority? I play hard and I work hard. I drink very little, usually only wine with dinner. I don't smoke. I'm rather a religious person. When I get tensed up, I go out in the woods and dance, dance, and then take a mineral bath. With my dogs I sleep until sunrise and then drive home. At this stage of life, I'm not looking for anything—if it happens I'm receptive."

Although Kim attempted to remain a private individual, her name continued to crop up in the news. On December 7, 1966, she was involved in an automobile crash when her station wagon spun out of control on a rainy West Los Angeles street, and two women passengers in the other vehicle were slightly injured. A few days later, the press reported in detail how Kim was forced to flee the sanctity of her home when a mudslide buried much of her yard and threatened the structural stability of the house.

In 1968, three years after her last film, thirty-five-year-old Kim returned to civilization to star† in MGM's *The Legend of Lylah Clare*, a drama based on the "DuPont Show of the Week" teleplay (NBC, May 19, 1963), which had starred Tuesday Weld and Alfred Drake. Having been away from the screen for nearly three years, Kim seemed rather indifferent to this "comeback" opportunity, brought about by a prior contract commitment. She casually told the press, "I'm not really wild about working, anyway, never have been. Oh, I know some performers worry if they are not working all the time, and they'll take anything that comes along. I can't do that. It would be like being a prostitute."

By its very nature, *The Legend of Lylah Clare,* released by MGM, was a bizarre film project for the late 1960s movie market. It dealt with a dictatorial film director (Peter Finch) who hires an unknown actress (Kim) to portray the lead role in a planned movie biography of a late, great Hollywood star. In the course of recreating the legendary actress's

*Johnson would later explain re the break-up, "It was just that Kim didn't find it easy to adjust to the relationship of being married. She felt she had lost freedom. I took issue with her on this."

†Jeanne Moreau had been director Aldrich's first choice for the part.

oversized life on film, details of the lady's mysterious death are revealed, proving that her former associates, friends, lovers, and enemies have harbored dark secrets about her these many years.

Probably no other producer-director but iconoclastic Robert Aldrich would have considered lensing such a potentially limited subject (after all, by now Hollywood was almost a ghost town, and the public was interested in television, the Mets, and Vietnam, not *Sunset Boulevard*-type mad nostalgia). However, Aldrich had always been fixated with tales of Hollywood on Hollywood,* and he saw in *The Legend of Lylah Clare* an opportunity to mix the still commercial genres of Grand Guignol with exotic romanticism. Somewhere during the course of the expensive color production, Aldrich and/or the distributor realized that the 130-minute movie had gone badly astray. As *Time* magazine reasoned, "the decision to spoof it up [particularly in the subsequent publicity ad campaign] was the only course possible, short of dropping the whole project." Hollis Alpert (*Saturday Review*) tore into the film, branding it "unpalatable," while *Newsweek* magazine opined, "In terms of its intentions, the film fights cliches with cliches." One of the picture's few mini-champions—beyond the Robert Aldrich student cultists—was critic Judith Crist (*New York*), who waspishly enthused, "[The film] is about as schmaltzy and wonderful and well acted and cliche-ridden and stereotype-filled a piece of contrived entertainment as ever kept you enthralled and didn't make you feel foolish an hour later."

Back in 1958, Kim had portrayed a dual role in *Vertigo*, and once again in *The Legend of Lylah Clare*, she was required to perform a double assignment of sorts. As Elsa Brinkmann, the Chicago actress, she is brought to Hollywood only to find that it is her resemblance to the late, great silver-screen star Lylah Clare that intrigues director Finch so greatly. Before long, she is saturated with the unsavory background of the legendary celluloid personality who mysteriously fell to her death on the night of her wedding to director Finch. Elsa's transformation into Lylah soon is so complete that she is possessed by the spirit of the dead woman, and even finds herself talking with the German-accented voice of the late celebrity. The denouement reveals that Finch had allowed Lylah to fall to her death down a long flight of stairs on their nuptial night after he discovered that she was a lesbian. And just as in *Vertigo*, where the dual female character suffers the same fate, Kim's Elsa also plummets to her own death at the movie's finish.

The Legend of Lylah Clare, despite MGM's heavy publicizing, was a commercial bust. It was quickly relegated to hasty play-off dates, and soon forgotten by the public, i.e., those who bothered to see the film. However, because of the picture's outrageous ambiance and implications, it soon

---

The Big Knife (United Artists, 1955), *What Ever Happened to Baby Jane?* (Warner Bros., 1964).

ʃ

became a favorite point of intellectualization among cinema critics. It was easy enough to dismiss Finch's one-dimensional performance as a Josef von Sternberg-Erich von Stroheim amalgam figure, or to scoff at the comic-strip caricatures provided by Coral Browne (as a Hedda Hopper type), Ernest Borgnine (a watered-down Harry Cohn figure), or Sidney Skolsky (the columnist playing himself). But what of Kim in the title role? Everyone agreed that even at thirty-five, she was a stunner in her Renie wardrobe, and that although the likes of Elke Sommer could have handled the character's German dialog without the necessity of dubbing, Kim had made a concerted effort to bring some dimension to a patently ridiculous role.

Throughout the filming of *Lylah Clare*, drama coach Benno Schneider was at Kim's side, offering advice and encouragement as to her interpretation of this Marlene Dietrich-Greta Garbo-type figure who stalks through the preposterous screenplay. While the reviewers of the finished product could laughingly say, "One way of dealing with Kim Novak's acting is to pretend that it was meant to be that way" (*Time*), *Variety* admitted that she was "only intermittently given a challenging scene or two." But it remained for Judith Crist (in *New York* magazine) to perceptively observe, if not to cogently communicate, that Kim's prize assets for a picture were her own natural brand of aloofness, mixed with vulnerability and a fear of dependency on others.* Kim could hardly be blamed for having to deal with (let alone react oncamera to) such trivial dialog as stone-faced Finch mumbling, "I'll rummage through your soul like a pickpocket through a stolen purse," or "You're an illusion. Without me, you don't exist." If it was embarrassingly puerile to observe theatrical Rossella Falk parading through the movie as a possessive, intense lesbian on the make for Novak, it was more discomfiting to endure the childish heterosexual sequence in which Kim is forced to parade "nonchalantly" through Finch's elaborate back gardens, clad in a bra and slacks, while being ogled in the most tasteless manner by the gardener (Gabriele Tinti). Maturity and subtlety have never been part of director Aldrich's canon of operations, and Kim's focal role suffered most from the helmer's guiding gaucheries.

Following the *Lylah Clare* fiasco, Kim retreated to her private world, occasionally being seen in the company of bearded Joel Thomas, who owned the El Matador restaurant. In April 1969, she was in court in Salinas, California, combating a suit by the Monterey County Board of Supervisors, who demanded that she be refrained from keeping a young

*Crist wrote: "Kim Novak, who indeed seems to bring natural talent to the dumb-actress portrait, is in good shape and fine to watch in or out of wigs and decolletage; her performance might even be termed unconscious camp. (And this is no denigration of Miss Novak, who gave good accounts of herself in *Jeanne Eagels* and *Middle of the Night*.) She is just fine as an impassive slightly bovine victim-of-circumstance type."

Arabian colt on her 1.9-acre castle grounds because the animal disturbed the neighbors. Kim won her case.

When Melina Mercouri proved unavailable to appear in *The Great Bank Robbery* (Warner Bros.-Seven Arts, 1969), the company negotiated for Kim to substitute as Zero Mostel's co-star (!) in a would-be Western spoof lensed in Sonora, California. The tinny premise had Kim and an assortment of buddies pose as leaders of the only church in Friendly, Texas, their intention being to rob the fortresslike bank built by the Brothers James, Dalton, and Younger to house their ill-gotten gold. Arriving in town on dust-covered feet, Kim is introduced by the phony evangelist (Mostel) as "my cousin" and she promptly opens her dress with "I've just gotta get my clothes off," thereupon displaying all but the nipples of the famous Novak bosom. Director Hy Averback never came to grips with what makes the essence of a sagebrush spoof, leading Archer Winsten (*New York Post*) to decry, "It is a picture that tries too hard, and everyone in it tries too hard too. They cancel each other almost completely out, and you too, if you're still there for the finale." At one point in *The Great Bank Robbery*, Kim's character is made to wisecrack, "Sister Lyda's ass is draggin'," and so it was, and so was she throughout this shambles of a Western.

On the film's completion—and after performing some half-hearted promotional touring for *The Great Bank Robbery* (she usually turned up late for interviews and was rather taciturn), Kim returned to her cliffside hideaway where she was known as "The Hermit of Big Sur." Curious tourists were kept off the property by a fierce goat named "Creature" (which also upset her sensitive neighbors), and a Great Dane named "Paloosa." Kim seldom saw anyone and went into the nearest town, Carmel-by-the-Sea, only to purchase needed provisions. Her financial interests included real property other than Gull House and she was a silent partner in Joel Thomas's El Matador restaurant-nightclub.

Often, Kim would drive to New Mexico or Texas in her pickup truck with several animals beside her and a trailer containing two horses. "As often as not," she said, "I sleep in the back of the pickup parked by the road. It's not always possible to find a motel where they will take horses for the night." Her friends worried about her behavior, and Richard Johnson, who claimed "I still love her," paid an occasional visit to Gull House or sent an emissary to check up on her. Kim's reaction to all the worry was, "The simple truth is that I finally am leading a very beautiful, normal life." In the summer of 1972 she placed a $195,000 price tag on Gull House in the hope of finding a buyer because she wanted to move where it was less crowded.

In September 1972, she was persuaded by television executives Aaron Spelling and Leonard Goldberg to come off her private mountain to appear in an ABC-TV "Movie-of-the-Week," entitled *Home for the Holidays*. At the last minute, though, she was called to the Florida bedside of her mother, who had suffered a stroke. She was replaced in the telefeature by Eleanor Parker, her former *The Man with the Golden Arm* costar.

A few weeks later, Kim suddenly showed up at Shepperton Studios in England as one of the stars of the horror feature film *Tales that Witness Madness* (Paramount, 1973). She took over the role of a theatre agent from Rita Hayworth, who had "stalked" off the production after five days work, allegedly a victim of the London flu. Kim's salary for this quickie film venture was reported to be $100,000 as compared to the $60,000 salary provided for Miss Hayworth. Again, Kim had replaced Rita, and this time Harry Cohn had nothing to do with it.

Kim was then signed by Playboy Productions for the lead, along with guest star Tony Curtis, in that organization's initial effort in the television arena, an ABC-TV "Movie-of-the-Week" (October 16, 1973), *The Third Girl from the Left*, scripted by Dory Previn. The plot has her in the title role as an aging chorus girl in pursuit of a Las Vegas comedian-singer (Curtis). It was originally announced that, for her first telefilm, Kim would be professionally reunited with Richard Quine as director, but he voluntarily left the project while it was still in the planning stages and was replaced by Hungarian-born British director Peter Medak. On this, his first picture in the United States, Medak was amazed to find that he was allotted a mere three weeks for completion. Kim worked feverishly with choreographer Miriam Nelson until she had perfected the high-kicking dance sequences with chorus girls far younger and much more experienced than she. Kim's fortieth birthday, on February 13, 1973, was observed on the telefeature set with the filming of a birthday-party scene. It was later reported that Kim, the renowned loner, mingled congenially with other cast members and the crew during her free time. There was no display of star temperament. On completing the film, she admitted: "I loved doing it, and I was so nervous. Everyone told me we had to work so much faster than in feature movies—but it's not that way at all." She was delighted to the point of asking the producer to be on the lookout for another telefilm for her.

Meanwhile, another "film" featuring Kim was making the circuit of museums and educational institutions. The Franklin Mint, a commemorative coin company which annually presents a short-subject movie for numismatic conventions and other subsidiary-rental users, sponsored the Modern Talking Picture Service eleven-minute short *Celebrity Art*, dealing with screen personalities whose hobby is painting. Among those shown at their artistic endeavors were Kim, Dinah Shore, Richard Chamberlain, Candice Bergen, Red Skelton, Henry Fonda, and Tony Bennett.

Although *The Third Girl from the Left* had the rating misfortune to air directly opposite the World Series game, there was more than usual interest in Kim's official return to big-time entertainment performing. In true telefeature fashion, the storyline was badly padded, thinly written, and overdosed with sleep-inducing pacing. Many another former love goddess would have shrunk from tackling a role which constantly emphasized that the bloom of youth had long since passed her by (e.g., one character says of Kim's Gloria, "When the face goes, you go"), but Kim in her rather touching performance gave no visible indication that the too-close-to-life premise had penetrated her famed emotional fortress.

Within the telefeature's tattered scenario, Kim had four particularly telling sequences. One occurred on a bus with her co-player Michael Brandon (as the twenty-three-year-old intellectual drop-out), in which a toughened but still wistful Kim admits to the youth who wants to date her, "I never dream . . . never." Later, Kim's Gloria, who has been Broadway's famous chorus girl for *too* many years, suddenly finds that her crass employers have decided to fire her. Rather than perform the onerous task directly, they cruelly announce at a dress rehearsal that henceforth Kim will be relegated to the back row. The look of shame, embarrassment, fear, and resignation that crossed over Kim's face during this bit was all the more valid when one recalled the reverse situation in *Pal Joey*, when within the film, she had been moved up from the back line to the featured chorus spot. Near the conclusion of the bittersweet tale, Kim has a confrontation sequence with egotistical Joey (Curtis), the show-business performer who has postponed their marriage for some thirteen years. He discovers her in a compromising situation with Brandon and berates her for her lack of morals. She, suddenly sensing that her dream man is perhaps just a windbag of selfishness and double standards, screams out to him that not once in their relationship has he ever bothered to really look at the paintings she had done, particularly her cherished canvas hanging in the bedroom. But most of all, in remembering *The Third Girl from the Left*, sadly one of the video season's weakest offerings, one is left with the haunting vision of Kim in the precredit opening moments of the program, as she applies makeup to her face, preparatory to joining the other chorus girls in their tawdry nightclub routine.*

Some weeks later Paramount released *Tales That Witness Madness*, yet another omnibus horror picture in the current trend-tradition of *Tales from the Crypt* (1972), *Asylum* (1972), and *The Vault of Horror* (1973). Production values for this Freddie Francis-directed feature were exceptionally superior, but the five jumbled yarns unreeled within the ninety minutes were so amateurishly scripted that theatre audiences howled when Jack Hawkins as the story-linker said, "But this is all so preposterous."

Kim appeared in *Luau*, the fourth and longest episode. Perhaps the re-

*Kay Gardella (*New York Daily News*) deplored the telefeature, labeling it a "collector's item" and stating that Kim's talents "lie in the area between her neck and her knees."

placed Rita Hayworth might have handled the nontaxing assignment more appropriately, but Kim, by temperament, was in no way qualified to essay the role of Auriol, an effervescent Auntie Mame-like British literary agent who is the gallivanting mother of gawky twenty-one-year-old Ginny (Mary Tamm).* Kim was physically alluring in her gaudy six-costume-change wardrobe,† but she seemed stumped by the framework of the ludicrous voodoo plot premise and was barely able to cope with the horrendously inept dialog (e.g., "I'm giving the most dee-vine party. You must come, won't you"). Kim may be many things to many people, but she is not the bon-vivant Rosalind Russell type. As in *The Third Girl from the Left*, there were script lines which reminded Kim Novak fans that the star's Madge Owens (*Picnic*) days were far away in the dim past.

Kim: I forgot we don't talk how old we are.

Tamm: Either of *us.*

The gothic horror film, even of the multipart variety, had long since passed its vogue, causing *Tales That Witness Madness* to receive very perfunctory critical attention. Vincent Canby (*New York Times*) said that "it takes a special kind of optimism to continue seeing them," As for this particular example of the species, Canby ranked it director Freddie Francis's "glossiest, most absurd, almost all-star horror film yet," and found Kim's appearance to be "ın her most inept Lylah Clare [*sic*] style." *Variety* was more scalding in its assessment of Kim's vignette: "Novak's acting is awful, never in command of the role in which she must be giddy but man-hungry at the same time. But the plot gimmick sort of carries the ball to conclusion."

Before the critical reaction and public inaction demonstrated that Kim's professional return was not only unheralded but undesired, she announced that she would accept a cameo role (with star billing and "star money") in *The Hot-Cold War Man* to be produced by Jerry Epstein in England with Oliver Reed starring. Kim explained, "I like keeping my hand in the acting field by accepting an occasional role I feel is special— my real interests still revolve around my home and my animals." In early 1974, it was announced that *The Hot-Cold War Man* project had been (permanently) shelved.

In late 1974, Kim emerged from her retreat yet again for an ABC-TV "Movie of the Week," this time, one entitled *Satan's Triangle* (January 14, 1975). With Doug McClure and Alejandro Rey as her co-stars, Kim went on location to Oxnard, California, to film this tale of the sole survivor (Kim) of a damaged boat. While the rescuing Coast Guard insists

---

*Whether by accident or intentionally, Tamm was, in contrast to Kim, far less attractive and even more gauche in the proceedings.

† Kim's face, via soft-focus photography, lensed well, but even with her moo-moo outfits, there was a telltale roll of flab about her waist.

that the deaths of her fellow passengers were due to explainable causes, she says that they were the doings of the Devil. Before she returned to to her hideaway home, Kim told the press, "I have fond memories of this place [Hollywood]. . . . Now it's a real turn-on for me to visit the big city!" As to the possibility of future job acceptances, she maintains, "Only when I like the subject matter."

Ensconced on her estate overlooking the Pacific at Big Sur, Kim's frequent companion is still Michael Brandon, her twenty-five-year-old co-star from *Third Girl from the Left*. According to the reports, publicity-conscious Brandon said: "[Kim] is the first older woman I've ever gotten involved with. It's working, because Kim's a realist, a giving woman, who's given up playing little games with people she cares about."

Whatever the outcome of this romantic interlude which still continues it is a cinch that Kim will continue to be a loner in the years to come. As she views herself: "I no longer believe in goals. But if there was any one thing I could say I truly seek now, it would be to achieve the really simple life—even to the extent of living without electricity."

Unlike such other love goddesses as Marilyn Monroe and Sophia Loren, who each underwent traumatic difficulties in attempting to fulfill their roles as a woman by becoming a mother, Kim has said on the subject: "At least by not having children I've made some positive contribution towards the problem of the world's population explosion. I love children, really I do—but as long as they belong to someone else. . . . Even if I did have children of my own, who is to say they would be better than any others? . . . It really hasn't worried me. It's more the loss of an ego trip in not having had children, isn't it?"

On yet another occasion, the resilient, iconoclastic Kim reasoned her mode of existence: "Storms come, houses are wiped out, people drown, but every last little palm is there after the storm. Man is always saying, 'I will overwhelm.' Why can't he bend like the little palms and rise again? Isn't that better than being broken and washed away?"

Feature Film Appearances

THE FRENCH LINE (RKO, 1954) C—102 M.

Producer, Edmund Grainger; director, Lloyd Bacon; story, Matty Kemp, Isabel Dawn; screenplay, Mary Loos, Richard Sale; art directors, Albert S. D'Agostino, Carroll Clark; songs, Josef Myrow, Ralph Blane, and Robert Wells; music, Walter Scharf; choreography, Billy Daniel; camera, Harry J. Wild; editor, Robert Ford.

Jane Russell (Mary Carson); Gilbert Roland (Pierre); Arthur Hunnicutt ("Waco" Mosby); Mary McCarty (Annie Farrell); Joyce MacKenzie (Myrtle Brown); Paula Corday (Celeste); Scott Elliott (Bill Harris); Craig Stevens (Phil Barton); Laura Elliot (Katherine Hodges); Steven Geray (François); John Wengraf (First Mate); Michael St. Angel (George Hodges); Barbara Darrow (Donna Adams); Barbara Dobbins (Kitty Lee); Jean Moorhead, Mary Rodman, Charmienne Harker, Dolores Michaels, Suzanne Alexander, Eileen Coghlan, Rosemary Colligan, Millie Doff, Jane Easton, Helene Hayden, Ellye Marshall, Jarma Lewis, Kim Novak, Pat Sheehan, Maureen Stephenson, Shirley Tegge, Beverly Thompson, Doreen Woodbury, Devvy Davenport, Barbara Lohrman, Dolly Summers, Phyllis St. Pierre, Shirley Buchanan (Models); Ray Bennett (Foreman); Lane Bradford (Cowboy); Al Cavens, Jo Gilbert, Frank Marlowe, Nick Stuart, Charles Smith, Allen Ray, Jeffrey Sayre, Ralph Volkie, Carlos Albert, Robert Dayo, Donald Moray, Joseph Rubino, Renald Dupont (Reporters); Bess Flowers (Saleslady); Theresa Harris (Clara); Peggy Leon, Leoda Richards (Customers); Ramona Magrill (Seamstress); John Mooney, George Wallace (Cowboys); Edward Short (Willie); Edward Coch, Wayne Taylor (French Bellhops); Pierre Chandler, Frederick Stevens, Arthur Dulac (French Stewards); Jack Chefe (Wine Steward); William Forrest (Sam Baker); Louis Mercier (Steward); Buck Young (Photographer); Sue Casey, Mary Ellen Gleason, Mary Langan, Bobette Bentley, Gloria Watson, Dede Moore, Helen Chapman, Gloria Pall, Dawn Oney, Joyce Johnson, Lonnie Pierce (Showgirls); Mary Jane Carey (American Nurse); Toni Carroll (Toni); Sandy Drescher (Girl); Joi Lansing (Showgirl); Wanda Ottoni (French Nurse); Shirley Patterson (Elsie); Lucien Plauzoles (Boy); Lomax Study (French Waiter); Billy Daniel (Andre); Jack Boyle, Joel Friend (Actor-Dancers); Suzanne Ames, Babs Cox (Maids); Anne Ford, Virginia Bates, Katherine Cassidy (Paris Models); Lizz Slifer (French Woman); Stanley Farrar (French Man); Marina Cisternas (Customer at Paris Salon); Dan Bernaducci, Fritz Feld (French Cabbies); Marie Rabasse (Flower Woman); Bert Le Baron (Doorman).

PUSHOVER (Col., 1954) 88 M.

Producer, Jules Schermer; associate producer, Philip A. Waxman; director, Richard Quine; based upon the serialized story "The Killer Wore a Badge" and the novel *The Night Watch* by Thomas Walsh and the novel *Rafferty* by William S.

Ballinger; screenplay, Roy Huggins; art director, Walter Holscher; assistant director, Jack Corrick; music, Arthur Morton; camera, Lester H. White; editor, Jerome Thoms.

Fred MacMurray (Paul Sheridan); Kim Novak (Lona McLane); Phil Carey (Rick McAllister); Dorothy Malone (Ann); E. G. Marshall (Lieutenant Carl Eckstrom); Allen Nourse (Paddy Dolan); Phil Chambers (Briggs); Alan Dexter (Fine); Robert Forrest (Billings); Don Harvey (Peters); Paul Richards (Harry Wheeler); Ann Morriss (Ellen Burnett); Dick Crockett (Young Man); Marion Ross (Young Woman); Kenneth L. Smith (Bank Guard); Joe Bailey (Hobbs); Hal Taggart (Bank Executive); John De Simone (Assistant Bank Manager); Ann Loos (Girl Teller Who Screams); Mel Welles, Jack Wilson (Detectives); Walter Beaver (Schaeffer); John Tarangelo (Boy); Richard Bryan (Harris); Paul Picerni (Dapper Man); Tony Barrett (Man); Mort Mills, Robert Carson (Barkeeps); James Anderson (Berry).

PHFFFT! (Col., 1954) 91 M.

Producer, Fred Kohlmar; director, Mark Robson; story-screenplay, George Axelrod; assistant director, Carter De Haven, Jr.; music, Frederick Hollander; art director, William Flannery; camera, Charles Lang; editor, William Kiernan.

Judy Holliday (Nina Tracy); Jack Lemmon (Robert Tracy); Jack Carson (Charlie Nelson); Kim Novak (Janis); Luella Gear (Mrs. Chapman); Donald Randolph (Dr. Van Kessel); Donald Curtis (Rick Vidal); Arny Freeman (Language Teacher); Merry Anders (Marcia); Eddie Searles (Tommy); Wendy Howard (Artist's Model); William Lechner (Boy); Sue Carlton (Girl); Olan Soule (Mr. Duncan); Geraldine Hall (Nina's Secretary); Harry Cheshire (Lawyer); William Newell (Workman); Eugene Borden, Alphonse Martell (Maitre D's); Jerry Hausner (Radio Actor); Charlotte Lawrence (Radio Actress); Patrick Miller, George Hill (Pages); Tom Kingston (Manager); Fay Baker (Serena); Sally Mansfield (Miss Comstock); Vivian Mason, Maxine Marlowe, Shirlee Allard, Joyce Jameson (Secretaries); Hamil Petroff, Mylee Andreason (Dance Teachers); Charles Heard, Virgil Johansen (Doormen); Jimmie Dodd (Taxi Driver); Frank Arnold (Art Teacher); Richard Gordon, Edwana Spence, Joe Karnes (Extras Converted to Bits); Walter Hastings, Gil Warren, Ted Thorpe (Ad Lib Bits).

SON OF SINBAD (RKO, 1955) C—88 M.

Producer, Robert Sparks; director, Ted Tetzlaff; screenplay, Aubrey Wisberg, Jack Pollexfen; art directors, Albert S. D'Agostino, Walter E. Keller; set decorator, Darrell Silvera; music director, C. Bakaleinikoff; camera, William Snyder; editors, Roland Gross, Frederick Knudtson.

Dale Robertson (Sinbad); Sally Forrest (Ameer); Lili St. Cyr (Nerissa); Vincent Price (Omar); Mari Blanchard (Kristina); Leon Askin (Khalif); Jay Novello (Jiddah); Raymond Greenleaf (Simon); Nejla Ates (Dancer in Market); Kalantan (Dancer in Desert); Ian MacDonald (Murad); Donald Randolph (Councillor); Larry Blake (Samit); Edwina Hazard (Lota); Fred Aldrich (Torturer); John Merton, George Sherwood, M. U. Smith, Woody Strode (Guards); George Barrows (Khalif Officer); Marilyn Bonney (Veronica); Janet Comerford (Latisse); Alyce Cronin (Helena); Mary Ann Edwards (Rosine); Dawn Oney (Alicia); Marvleen Prentice (Zaza); Joan Pastin (Camilla); Judy Ulian (Dalya); Suzanne Alexander, Randy Allen, Jane Easton, Jeanne Evans, Helene Hayden (Harem Girls); Joanne Jordan (Ghenia); Wayne Berk (Gondra); James Griffith (Arab Guide); Bette Arlen, Joann Arnold, Gwen Caldwell, Anne Carroll, Carolea Cole, Claire De Witt,

Nancy Dunn, Marjorie Holliday, Judy Jorell, Joi Lansing, Diane Mumby, Jonni Paris, Jeanne Shores, Maureen Stephenson, Libby Vernon, Doreen Woodbury, Betty Onge, Dee Gee Sparks, DeDe Moore, Sue Casey, Carol Brewster, Chris Fortune, Helen Chapman, Barbara Drake, Bobette Bentley, Joan Whitney, Dolores Michaels, Barbara Lohrman, Zanne Shaw, Gloria Watson, Ann Ford, Donna Hall, Pat D'Arcy, Charlotte Alpert, Roxanne Arlen, Eleanor Bender, Evelyn Bernard, Shirley Buchanan, Roxanne Delman, Mary Ellen Gleason, Diane James, Keith Kerrigan, Mary Langan, Gloria Laughlin, Vonne Lester, Nancy Neal, Gloria Pall, Lynne Forrester, Audrey Allen, Nancy Moore, Phyllis St. Pierre, Evelyn Lovequist, Gerri Patterson, Kim Novak, Rosemary Webster, Laura Carroll, Penny Sweeny, Trudy Wroe, Joyce Johnson (Raiders); Tom Monroe, Peter Ortiz (Cutthroats); Virginia Bates, Katherine Cassidy, Honey King, Sally Musik (Trumpeters); Leonteen Danies, Elaine Dupont, Gilda Fontana, Joy Lee, La Rue Malouf, Anna Navarro, Paula Vernay (Slave Girls); Michael Ross (Palace Guard); Michael Mark (Caravan Merchant); Bob Hopkins (Slave Auctioneer); Gus Schilling (Jaffir); Max Wagner (Merchant at Market Place); Nancy Westbrook (Wench); Elizabeth Smith, Wanda Barbour, Irene Bolton, Joy Langstaff, Betty Sabor, Eileen Maxwell, Louise Von Kories, Annabelle Thiele, Arlene Hunter (Tartar Girls); Naji Gabby, Laura Carroll (Arabs).
A. k. a. *Night in a Harem.*

FIVE AGAINST THE HOUSE   (Col., 1955) 84 M.

Producers, Stirling Silliphant, John Barnwell; associate producer, Helen Ainsworth; director, Phil Karlson; story, Jack Finney; screenplay, Silliphant, William Bowers, Barnwell; art director, Robert Peterson; music director, Morris Stoloff; assistant director, Milton Feldman; gowns, Jean Louis; music, George Duning; camera, Lester White; editor, Jerome Thoms.

Guy Madison (Al Mercer); Kim Novak (Kay Greylek); Brian Keith (Brick); Alvy Moore (Roy); William Conrad (Eric Berg); Kerwin Mathews (Ronnie); Jack Dimond (Francis Spieglebauer); Jean Willes (Virginia).

PICNIC   (Col., 1955) C—115 M.

Producer, Fred Kohlmar; director, Joshua Logan, based on the play by William Inge; screenplay, Daniel Taradash; art director, William Flannery; music director, Morris Stoloff; music, George Duning; orchestrator, Arthur Morton; gowns, Jean Louis; assistant director, Carter De Haven, Jr.; camera, James Wong Howe; editors, Charles Nelson, William A. Lyon.

William Holden (Hal Carter); Rosalind Russell (Rosemary Sydney); Kim Novak (Madge Owens); Betty Field (Flo Owens); Susan Strasberg (Millie Owens); Cliff Robertson (Alan); Arthur O'Connell (Howard Bevans); Verna Felton (Mrs. Helen Potts); Reta Shaw (Linda Sue Breckenridge); Nick Adams (Bomber); Raymond Bailey (Mr. Benson); Elizabeth W. Wilson (Christine Schoenwalder); Phyllis Newman (Juanita Badger); Don C. Harvey, Steven Benton (Policemen); Henry P. Watson (President of Chamber of Commerce); Floyd Steinbeck, Paul R. Cochran, Harold A. Beyer, Adlai Zeph Fisher, Harry Sherman Schall (Chamber of Commerce Men); Abraham Weinlood (Trainman); Wayne R. Sullivan (Foreman); Warren Frederick Adams (Stranger); Carle E. Baker (Grain Elevator Worker); Henry Pegueo (Mayor); Flomanita Jackson (Committee Woman); George E. Bemis (Neighbor).

THE MAN WITH THE GOLDEN ARM   (UA, 1955) 119 M.

Producer-director, Otto Preminger; based on the novel by Nelson Algren;

screenplay, Walter Newman, Lewis Meltzer; music-music conductor, Elmer Bernstein; orchestrator, Frederick Steiner; titles, Saul Bass; art director, Joseph Wright; set decorator, Darrell Silvera; costume supervisor, Mary Ann Nyberg; men's wardrobe, Joe King; women's wardrobe, Adele Parmenter; makeup, Jack Stone, Bernard Ponedel, Ben Lane; assistant directors, Horace Hough, James Engle; sound, Jack Solomon; camera, Sam Leavitt; editor, Louis R. Loeffler.

Frank Sinatra (Frankie Machine); Eleanor Parker (Zosh Machine); Kim Novak (Molly); Arnold Stang (Sparrow); Darren McGavin (Louie); Robert Strauss (Schwiefka); John Conte (Drunky); Doro Merande (Vi); George E. Stone (Markette); George Mathews (Williams); Leonid Kinskey (Dominowski); Emile Meyer (Bednar); Shorty Rogers, Shelly Manne (Themselves); Frank Richards (Piggy); Will Wright (Lane); Tommy Hart (Kvorka); Frank Marlowe (Antek); Joe McTurk (Meter Reader); Ralph Neff (Chester); Ernest Raboff (Bird Dog); Martha Wentworth (Vangie); Jerry Barclay (Junkie); Lennie Bremen (Taxi Driver); Paul E. Burns (Suspenders); Charles Seel (Landlord).

THE EDDY DUCHIN STORY   (Col., 1956) C—123 M.

Producer, Jerry Wald; associate producer, Jonie Taps; director, George Sidney; story, Leo Katcher; screenplay, Samuel Taylor; art director, Walter Holscher; music supervisor-conductor, Morris Stoloff; piano recordings, Carmen Cavallaro; incidental music, George Duning; gowns, Jean Louis; assistant director, Seymour Friedman; camera, Harry Stradling; editors, Viola Lawrence, Jack W. Ogilvie.

Tyrone Power (Eddy Duchin); Kim Novak (Marjorie Oelrichs); Victoria Shaw (Chiquita); James Whitmore (Lou Sherwood); Rex Thompson (Peter Duchin at the Age of Twelve); Mickey Maga (Peter Duchin at the Age of Five); Shepperd Strudwick (Mr. Wadsworth); Frieda Inescort (Mrs. Wadsworth); Gloria Holden (Mrs. Duchin); Larry Keating (Leo Reisman); John Mylong (Mr. Duchin); Gregory Gay (Philip); Warren Hsieh (Native Boy); Jack Albertson (Piano Tuner); Carlyle Mitchell (Doctor); Richard Sternberg, Andy Smith (Boys); Lois Kimbrell (Nurse); Oliver Cliff (Man); Ralph Gamble (Mayor Walker); Richard Walsh (Young Man); Howard Price (Range Recorder Operator); Richard Cutting (Captain); Richard Crane, Brad Trumbull (Seamen); Gloria Ann Simpson (Mrs. Rutledge); Arline Anderson (Guest); Michael Legend, Rick Person (Bits); Butler Hixson (Butler); Peter Norman (Walter); Betsy Jones Moreland, Joan Raynolds, Jacqueline Blanchard (Girls); Kirk Alyn (Young Man).

JEANNE EAGELS   (Col., 1957) 109 M.

Producer-director, George Sidney; story, Daniel Fuchs; screenplay, Fuchs, Sonya Levien, John Fante; art director, Ross Bellah; music director, Morris Stoloff; music, George Duning; orchestrator, Arthur Morton; assistant director, Charles S. Gould; gowns, Jean Louis; camera, Robert Planck; editors, Viola Lawrence, Jerome Thoms.

Kim Novak (Jeanne Eagels); Jeff Chandler (Sal Satori); Agnes Moorehead (Mme. Neilson); Charles Drake (John Donahue); Larry Gates (Al Brooks); Virginia Grey (Elsie Desmond); Gene Lockhart (Equity Board President); Joe de Santis (Frank Satori); Murray Hamilton (Chick O'Hara); Will Wright (Marshal); Sheridan Comerate (Actor-Confederate Officer); Lowell Gilmore (Reverend Dr. Davidson); Juney Ellis (Mrs. Davidson); Beulah Archuletta (Mrs. Horn); Jules Davis (Mr. Horn); Florence MacAfee (Mrs. McPhail); Snub Pollard (Quartermaster Bates); Joseph Novak (Patron); Johnny Tarangelo (Private Griggs); Bert Spencer (Dr. McPhail); Richard Harrison (Corporal Hodgson); Ward Wood (Stage Manager); Myrtle Anderson (Jeanne's Maid); Michael Dante (Sergeant O'Hara); Joseph Turkel (Eddie); George Neise (Jerry, the Traveling Salesman); Charles Couch, William Couch, Sammy Finn, Wallace Ross, Walter Ridge (Barkers); Richard Gaines (Judge); Patricia Mowry (Hefty Bathing Beauty); Junius Matthews (Court Clerk); George de Normand (Police Sergeant); Tom McKee (Police Lieutenant); Eleanor Audley (Sob Sister); Bill Suiter (Dancer-Sailor); Myna Cunard (Neilson Maid); Bob Hopkins (Reporter); Judd Holdren (Actor); John Celentano, Tommy Nolan (Satori's Sons); Raymond Greenleaf (Elderly Lawyer); Doris Lloyd (Mrs. Corliss); Carlyle Mitchell (Equity Spokesman); James Gonzales (Equity Man); Joe Mell (Kevin); Jennie Lea (Young Ingenue at Equity Trial); Helen Marr Van Tuyl (Great Lady on Equity Board); Bradford Jackson (Young Man on Equity Board); Lillian Culver (Equity Board Woman); Alyn Lockwood (Rosalie Satori); Deon Robb, Rebecca Godinez (Satori's Daughters); Irving Mitchell (Lawyer); George J. Lewis (Foreman); Frances Driver (Maid); Joan Harding, Reita Green, Myrna Fahey, Joy Stoner (Girls); Hal Le Sueur (Disgruntled Man); Leon Tyler (Bellhop); Ted Marcuse (Dr. Richards); Giselle D'Arc (French Maid); Lee Trent (Leading Man on Equity Board); Kenneth Gibson (Middle-Aged Man); Jean Vachon (Middle-Aged Woman); Whitey Haupt, Paul De Rolf, Larry Larson, Gary Pagett (Wise Teenagers); Nanette Fabares, Brenda Lomas (Teenage Girls); Eugene Jackson (Piccaninny); Jimmy Murphy (Assistant Director); Cosmo Sardo, Larry Blake, Walter Conrad, Eugene Sherman (Reporters); William "Tex" Carr (Specialty Fire Eater); Frank Borzage (Director); Lou Borzage (Assistant Director); Jack Ano (Soldier).

PAL JOEY   (Col., 1957) C—111 M.

Producer, Fred Kohlmar; director, George Sidney; based on the play by John O'Hara, Richard Rodgers, Lorenz Hart; screenplay, Dorothy Kingsley; songs, Rodgers and Hart; music supervisor-conductor, Morris Stoloff; music arranger, Nelson Riddle; music adaptors, George Duning, Riddle; orchestrator, Arthur Morton; art director, Walter Holscher; set decorators, William Kiernan, Louis Diage; gowns, Jean Louis; assistant director, Art Black; makeup, Ben Lane; sound, Franklin Hansen; camera, Harold Lipstein; editors, Viola Lawrence, Jerome Thoms.

Rita Hayworth (Vera Simpson); Frank Sinatra (Joey Evans); Kim Novak (Linda English); Barbara Nichols (Gladys); Bobby Sherwood (Ned Galvin); Hank Henry (Mike Miggins); Elizabeth Patterson (Mrs. Casey); Robin Morse (Bartender); Frank Wilcox (Colonel Langley); Pierre Watkin (Mr. Forsythe); Barry Bernard (Anderson); Ellie Kent (Carol); Mara McAfee (Sabrina); Betty Utey (Patsy); Bek Nelson (Lola); Henry McCann (Shorty); John Hubbard (Stanley); James Seay (Livingstone); Hermes Pan (Choreographer); Ernesto Molinari (Chef Tony); Jean Corbett (Specialty Dance Double); Robert Rietz (Boyfriend); Jules Davis (Red-Faced Man); Judy Dan (Hat Check Girl); Gail Bonney (Heavy-Set Woman); Cheryl Kubert (Girl Friend); Tol Avery (Detective); Robert Anderson (Policeman); Genie Stone (Girl); Raymond McWalters (Army Captain); Bob Glenn (Sailor); Sue Boomer (Secretary); Helen Eliot (Traveler's Aid); Hermie Rose (Bald Club Owner); Jack Railey (Hot Dog Vendor); Frank Wilimarth (Sidewalk Artist); Roberto Piperio (Waiter); Bobbie Lee, Connie Graham, Bobbie Jean Henson, Edith Powell, Jo Ann Smith, Ilsa Ostroffsky, Rita Barrett (Strippers); Howard Sigrist (Sidewalk Photographer); Paul Cesari (Pet Store Owner); Maurice Argent (Tailor); Eddie Vartell, Albert Nalbandian, Joseph Mikask, Sydney Chatton, Frank Sully (Barkers); Everett Glass (Pet Store Owner); Andrew Wong (Chinese Club Owner); George Chan (Chinese Pianist); Allen Gin (Chinese Drummer); Barbara Yung, Pat Lynn, Jean Nakaba, Elizabeth Fenton, Lessie Lynne Wong, Nellie Gee Ching (Chinese Dancers); George DeNormand, Oliver Cross, Bess Flowers,

Franklyn Farnum (Bits); Giselle D'Aro (Vera's Maid); Leon Alton (Printer Salesman); Michael Ferris (Tailor); Jane Chung (Flower Lady); George Ford (Electrician); Ramon Martinez (Headwaiter); Steve Benton (Electrician).

VERTIGO   (Par., 1958) C—123 M.

Producer, Alfred Hitchcock; associate producer, Herbert Coleman; director, Hitchcock; based on the novel *D'Entre les Morts* by Pierre Boileau, Thomas Narcejac; screenplay, Alex Coppel, Samuel Taylor; art directors, Hal Pereira, Henry Bumstead; set decorators, Sam Comer, Frank McKelvy; assistant director, Daniel McCauley; titles, Saul Bass; costumes, Edith Head; special sequences designer, John Ferren; music, Bernard Herrmann; makeup, Wally Westmore; sound, Harold Lewis, Winston Leverett; special camera effects, John P. Fulton; process camera, Farciot Edouart, Wallace Kelley; camera, Robert Burks; editor, George Tomasini.

James Stewart (John "Scottie" Ferguson); Kim Novak (Madeleine Elster/ Judy Barton); Barbara Bel Geddes (Midge); Tom Helmore (Gavin Elster); Henry Jones (Coroner); Raymond Bailey (Doctor); Ellen Corby (Manageress); Konstantin Shayne (Pop Leibel); Lee Patrick (Older Mistaken Identity); Paul Bryar (Captain Hansen); Margaret Brayton (Saleswoman); William Remick (Jury Foreman); Sara Taft (Nun); Julian Petruzzi (Flower Vendor); Fred Graham (Policeman); Mollie Dodd (Beauty Operator); Don Giovanni, Buck Harrington, John Benson (Salesmen); Roxann Delmar (Model); Bruno Santina (Waiter); Dori Simmons (Middle-Aged Mistaken Identity); Ed Stevlingson (Attorney); Joanne Genthon (Girl in Portrait); Nina Shipman (Young Mistaken Identity); Rolando Gotti (Maitre D'); Carlo Dotto (Bartender); Jean Corbett (Acting Double for Kim Novak); Jack Richardson (Man Escort); June Jocelyn (Miss Woods); Miliza Milo (Saleswoman); Jack Ano (Extra).

BELL, BOOK AND CANDLE   (Col., 1958) C—103 M.

Producer, Julian Blaustein; director, Richard Quine; based on the play by John Van Druten; screenplay, Daniel Taradash; assistant director, Irving Moore; gowns, Jean Louis; music, George Duning; art director, Cary Odell; set decorator, Louis Diage; native primitive art, Carlesbach Gallery; makeup, Ben Lane; sound, Franklin Hansen, Jr.; camera, James Wong Howe; editor, Charles Nelson.

James Stewart (Shephard Henderson); Kim Novak (Gillian Holroyd); Jack Lemmon (Nicky Holroyd); Ernie Kovacs (Sidney Redlitch); Hermione Gingold (Mrs. De Pass); Elsa Lanchester (Queenie); Janice Rule (Merle Kittridge); Philippe Clay (French Singer); Bek Nelson (Secretary); Howard McNear (Andy White); The Brothers Candoli (Musicians); Wolfe Barzell (Proprietor); Joe Barry (Exterminator); Gail Bonney (Merle's Maid); Monty Ash (Herb Store Owner); Ollie O'Toole (Elevator Operator); John Truax, Don Brodie (Cab Drivers); James Lanphier (Waldo); William Bloom, Maurice Marks, Joe Palma, Dick Crockett, Ted Mapes (Bits).

MIDDLE OF THE NIGHT   (Col., 1959) 118 M.

Producer, George Justin; director, Delbert Mann; based on the play by Paddy Chayefsky; screenplay, Chayefsky; music-music conductor, George Bassman; assistant director, Charles H. Maguire; art director, Edward S. Haworth; set decorator, Jack Wright, Jr.; costumes, Frank L. Thomson; clothes for Miss Novak, Jean Louis; technical advisor, Lionel Kaplan; makeup, George Newman; sound, Richard Gramaglia, Richard Vorisek; camera, Joseph Brun; editor, Carl Lerner.

Kim Novak (Betty Preisser); Fredric March (Jerry Kingsley); Lee Philips (George); Glenda Farrell (Mrs. Mueller); Albert Dekker (Lockman); Martin Balsam (Jack); Lee Grant (Marilyn); Edith Meiser (Evelyn Kingsley); Joan Copeland (Lillian); Betty Walker (The Widow); Rudy Bond (Gould); Effie Afton (Mrs. Carroll); Jan Norris (Alice Mueller); Anna Berger (Caroline); David Ford (Paul Kingsley); Audrey Peters (Elizabeth Kingsley); Lou Gilbert (Serman); Dora Weissman (Lockman's Wife); Alfred Leberfeld (Ellman); Lee Richardson (Lockman's Son); Nelson Olmsted (Erskine).

STRANGERS WHEN WE MEET   (Col., 1960) C—117 M.

Producer-director, Richard Quine; based on the novel by Evan Hunter; screenplay, Hunter; art director, Ross Bellah; set decorator, Louis Diage; music, George Duning; music supervisor, Morris Stoloff; orchestrator, Arthur Morton; assistant director, Carter De Haven, Jr.; gowns, Jean Louis; makeup, Ben Lane; sound, Charles J. Rice, Lambert Day; camera, Charles Lang, Jr.; editor Charles Nelson.

Kirk Douglas (Larry Coe); Kim Novak (Maggie Gault); Ernie Kovacs (Roger Altar); Barbara Rush (Eve Coe); Walter Matthau (Felix Anders); Virginia Bruce (Mrs. Wagner); Kent Smith (Stanley Baxter); John Bryant (Ken Gault); Roberta Shore (Linda Harder); Nancy Kovak (Marcia); Carol Douglas (Honey Blonde); Paul Picerni (Gerandi); Ernest Sarracino (Di Labbia); Harry Jackson (Bud Ramsey); Bart Patton (Hank); Robert Sampson (Bucky); Ray Ferrell (David Coe); Douglas Holmes (Peter Coe); Timmy Molina (Patrick Gault); Betsy Jones Moreland (Mrs. Gerandi); Audrey Swanson (Mrs. Baxter); Cynthia Leighton (Mrs. Ramsey); Judy Lang (Ad Lib Girl); Sharyn Gibbs (Girl at Beach); Charles Victor, Joe Palma, Tom Anthony, Sheryl Ellison, Mark Beckstrom (Bits); Sue Ane Langdon (Daphne); Ruth Batchelor (Waitress); Dick Crockett (Charlie); Lorraine Crawford (Redhead).

PEPE   (Col., 1960) C—195 M.

Producer, George Sidney; associate producer, Jacques Gelman; director, Sidney; based on the play *Broadway Zauber* by Ladislaus Bus-Fekete; screen story, Leonard Spigelgass, Sonya Levien; screenplay, Dorothy Kingsley, Claude Binyon; assistant director, David Silver; art director, Ted Haworth; set decorator, William Kiernan; music supervisor-background score, Johnny Green; special musical material, Sammy Cahn, Roger Eden; songs Andre Previn, Dory Langdon; Hans Wittstatt, Langdon; Previn; Augustin Lara, Langdon; choreography, Eugene Loring, Alex Romero; makeup, Ben Lane; gowns Edith Head; camera, Joe MacDonald; editors, Viola Lawrence, Al Clark.

Cantinflas (Pepe); Dan Dailey (Ted Holt); Shirley Jones (Suzie Murphy); Carlos Montalban (Auctioneer); Vicki Trickett (Lupita); Matt Mattox (Dancer); Hank Henry (Manager); Suzanne Lloyd (Carmen); Carlos Rivas (Carlos); Stephen Bekassy (Jewelry Salesman); Carol Douglas (Waitress); Francisco Reguerra (Priest); Joe Hyams (Charro); Joey Bishop, Michael Callan, Maurice Chevalier, Charles Coburn, Richard Conte, Bing Crosby, Tony Curtis, Bobby Darin, Sammy Davis, Jr., Jimmy Durante, Zsa Zsa Gabor, the voice of Judy Garland, Greer Garson, Hedda Hopper, Ernie Kovacs, Peter Lawford, Janet Leigh, Jack Lemmon, Dean Martin, Jay North, Kim Novak, Andre Previn, Donna Reed, Debbie Reynolds, Edward G. Robinson, Cesar Romero, Frank Sinatra, Billie Burke, Ann B. Davis, William Demarest, Jack Entratter, Col. E. E. Fogelson, Jane Robinson, Bunny Waters (Guest Stars); Shirley DeBurgh (Señorita Dancer); Steve Baylor, John Burnside (Parking Lot Attendants); James Bacon (Bartender); Jimmy Cavanaugh (Dealer); Jeanne Manet (French Woman); Robert B. Williams (Immigration Officer); Bonnie Green (Dancer); Lela Bliss (Dowager); Ray Walker (Assistant Director); David Landfield (Announcer's Voice); Margie Nelson (Patron); Dorothy Abbott, Kenner C. Kemp, Steve Carruthers, Jim Waters, Billy Synder (Bits); Fred Roberto (Cashier).

BOYS' NIGHT OUT (MGM, 1962) C—115 M.

Producer, Martin Ransohoff; associate producer, James Pratt; director, Michael Gordon; based on the story by Marvin Worth, Arne Sultan; adaptation, Marion Hargrove; screenplay, Ira Wallach; music, Frank De Vol; songs, James Van Heusen and Sammy Cahn; art directors, George W. Davis, Hans Peters; set decorators, Henry Grace, Jerry Wunderlich; assistant director, Ivan Volkman; sound, Franklin Milton; camera, Arthur E. Arling; editor, Tom McAdoo.

Kim Novak (Cathy); James Garner (Fred Williams); Tony Randall (George Drayton); Howard Duff (Doug Jackson); Janet Blair (Marge Drayton); Patti Page (Joanne McIllenny); Jessie Royce Landis (Ethel Williams); Oscar Homolka (Dr. Prokosch); Howard Morris (Howard McIllenny); Anne Jeffreys (Toni Jackson); Zsa Zsa Gabor (The Girlfriend); Fred Clark (Mr. Bohannon); William Bendix (Slattery); Jim Backus (Peter Bowers); Larry Keating (Mr. Bingham); Ruth McDevitt (Beaulah Partridge).

THE NOTORIOUS LANDLADY (Col., 1962) 123 M.

Producer, Fred Kohlmar; director, Richard Quine; based on the story by Margery Sharp; screenplay, Larry Gelbart, Blake Edwards; music, George Duning; orchestrator, Arthur Morton; art director, Cary Odell; set decorator, Louis Diage; Miss Novak's gowns designed by herself; executed by Elizabeth Courtney; assistant director, Carter De Haven, Jr.; makeup, Ben Lane; sound, Charles J. Rice, Josh Westmoreland; camera, Arthur Arling; editor, Charles Nelson.

Kim Novak (Carlye Hardwicke); Jack Lemmon (William Gridley); Fred Astaire (Franklyn Ambruster); Lionel Jeffries (Inspector Oliphant); Estelle Winwood (Mrs. Dunhill); Maxwell Reed (Miles Hardwicke); Philippa Bevans (Mrs. Brown); Henry Daniell (Stranger); Ronald Long (Coroner); Doris Lloyd (Lady Fallott); Richard Peel (Dillings); Florence Wyatt (Ambruster's Secretary); Frederic Worlock (Elderly Colonel); Dick Crockett (Carstairs); Scott Davey (Henry); Jack Livesey (Counsel); Tom Dillon (Coroner's Officer); Benno Schneider, Clive Halliday, Antony Eustrel (Men); Carter De Haven, Sr., David Hillary Hughes, Nelson Welch (Old Men); Cecil Weston, Mavis Neal, Cicely Walper, Queenie Leonard (Women); Betty Fairfax (Woman in Bathrobe); Clive Morgan (Man in Smoking Jacket); Julie Scott (Flousy); Eric Micklewood (Man with a Hangover); Mary Burke (Little Girl); Ottola Nesmith (Flower Lady); Milton Parsons (Mysterious Man); Bru Mysak (Ambruster's Driver); Iris Bristol (Girl); Ross Brown (Boy); Gwen Watts (Wife); James Logan (Bobby); Bryan Herbert (Husband); Michael St. Clair (Fire Chief); Mary Scott (Waitress); Tudor Owen (Farmer); Tom Symonds (Alf); Laurence Conroy (Clerk); Barry Bernard (Attendant); Mary O'Brady (Mrs. Oliphant); Towyna Thomas (Dowager); Harold Innocent (Young Escort); Marjorie Bennett (Autograph Seeker); Alex Finlayson, Jackson Halliday, Ogden Dangerfield, Joe Palma (Reporters); Jacqueline Squire (Woman Reporter); Brian Gaffikin (TV Reporter); George Pelling (Ticket Agent).

OF HUMAN BONDAGE (MGM, 1964) 99 M.

Producer, James Woolf; associate producer, Ernest Holding; director, Ken Hughes; additional scenes directed by Henry Hathaway; based on the novel by W. Somerset Maugham; screenplay, Bryan Forbes; production designer, John

Box; music-music conductor, Ron Goodwin; makeup, George Frost; costumes, Beatrice Dawson; camera, Oswald Morris; additional camera, Denys Coop; editor, Russell Lloyd.

Kim Novak (Mildred Rogers); Laurence Harvey (Philip Carey); Robert Morley (Dr. Jacobs); Siobhan McKenna (Norah Nesbitt); Roger Livesy (Thorpe Athelny); Jack Hedley (Griffiths); Nanette Newman (Sally Athelny); Ronald Lacey (Mathews); Anthony Booth (Martin); Anna Manahan, Derry O'Donovan (Waitresses); Jacqueline Taylor (Cook); Helen Robinson (Manageress-Cashier); Michael Doolan (Man with Club Foot); John Sutton (Kingsford); Leo McCabe (Elderly Man in Railway Carriage); Olive White (Griffiths' Girl Friend); Blanaid Irvine (Distinguished Girl); Eamonn Morrisey (Bespectacled Student); Ann Manceer (Girl Patient); Peter Moray (Student); Martin Crosbie (Porter); Robert Lepler (Jeweler); Evelyn McNeice (Mrs. Harding); Norman Smythe (Attendant in Dissecting Theatre); Caroline Swift (Nurse); Cecil Nash (Father of Boy with Club Foot); Peter Nash (Young Boy); May Cluskey (Sister I); Terry Clinton (Barmaid); Danny O'Shea (Headwaiter); Brendan Mathews (Technician); Alex Dignam (Porter).

KISS ME, STUPID   (Lopert, 1964) 126 M.

Producer, Billy Wilder; associate producers, I. A. L. Diamond, Doane Harrison; director, Billy Wilder; based on the play *L'Ora Della Fantasia* by Anna Bonacci; screenplay, Wilder, Diamond; songs, George and Ira Gershwin; music, Andre Previn; choreography, Wally Green; costume designer, Bill Thomas; wardrobe, Wes Jeffries, Irene Caine; art director, Robert Luthardt; set decorator, Edward G. Boyle; assistant director, C. C. Coleman, Jr.; sound, Robert Martin, Wayne Fury; special effects, Milton Rice; camera, Joseph LaShelle; editor, Daniel Mandell.

Dean Martin (Dino); Kim Novak (Polly the Pistol); Ray Walston (Orville J. Spooner); Felicia Farr (Zelda Spooner); Cliff Osmond (Barney Millsap); Barbara Pepper (Big Bertha); James Ward (Milkman); Doro Merande (Mrs. Pettibone); Howard McNear (Mr. Pettibone); Bobo Lewis (Waitress); Tommy Nolan (Johnny Mulligan); Alice Pearce (Mrs. Mulligan); John Fiedler (Reverend Carruthers); Arlen Stuart (Rosalie Schultz); Cliff Norton (Mack Gray); Mel Blanc (Dr. Sheldrake); Eileen O'Neill, Susan Wedell (Showgirls); Bern Hoffman (Bartender); Henry Gibson (Smith); Alan Dexter (Wesson); Henry Beckman (Truck Driver).

THE AMOROUS ADVENTURES OF MOLL FLANDERS
(Par., 1965) C—126 M.

Producer, Marcel Hellman; director, Terence Young; based on the novel by Daniel Defoe; screenplay, Denis Cannon, Roland Kibbee; production designer, Syd Cain; assistant director, David Adderson; music, John Addison; camera, Ted Moore; editor, Frederick Wilson.

Kim Novak (Moll Flanders); Richard Johnson (Jemmy); Angela Lansbury (Lady Blystone); Vittorio De Sica (The Count); Leo McKern (Squint); George Sanders (The Banker); Lilli Palmer (Dutchy); Peter Butterworth (Grunt); Dandy Nichols (Orphanage Superintendent); Noel Howlett (Bishop); Barbara Couper (Mayor's Wife); Daniel Massey (Elder Brother); Derren Nesbitt (Younger Brother); Ingrid Hafner (Elder Sister); June Watts (Younger Sister); Judith Furse (Miss Glowber); Anthony Dawson (Officer of Dragoons); Roger Livesey (Drunken Parson); Jess Conrad (Muhock).

THE LEGEND OF LYLAH CLARE   (MGM, 1968) C—130 M.

Producer, Robert Aldrich; associate producer, Walter Blanke; director, Aldrich; based on the teleplay by Robert Thom, Edward De Blasio; screenplay, Hugo Butler, Jean Rouverol; music, Frank De Vol; song, De Vol and Sibylle Siegfried; art directors, George W. Davis, William Glasgow; set decorators, Henry Grace, Keogh Gleason; makeup, William Tuttle, Robert Schiffer; assistant director, Cliff C. Coleman; costumes, Renie; recording supervisor, Franklin Milton; camera, Joseph Biroc; editor, Michael Luciano.

Kim Novak (Lylah Clare/Elsa Brinkmann); Peter Finch (Lewis Zarkan); Ernest Borgnine (Barney Sheean); Milton Selzer (Bart Langner); Rossella Falk (Rossella); Gabriele Tinti (Paolo); Coral Browne (Molly Luther); Valentina Cortesa (Countess Bozo Bedoni); Jean Carroll (Becky Langner); Michael Murphy (Mark Peter Sheean); George Kennedy (Mat Burke in *Anna Christie*); Lee Meriwether (Young Girl); James Lanphier, Hal Maguire (Legmen); Robert Ellenstein (Mike); Nick Dennis (Nick); Dave Willock (Cameraman); Peter Bravos (Butler); Ellen Corby (Script Girl); Michael Fox (Announcer); Vernon Scott (Himself); Queenie Smith (Hairdresser); Sidney Skolsky (Himself); Barbara Ann Warkmeister, Mel Warkmeister (Aerialists); Tom Patty (Bedoni's Escort).

THE GREAT BANK ROBBERY   (WB-7 Arts, 1969) C—98 M.

Producer, Malcolm Stuart; associate producer, Richard Freed; director, Hy Averback; based on the novel by Frank O'Rourke; music, Nelson Riddle; music supervisor, Sonny Burke; songs, Sammy Cahn and James Van Heusen; vocal arranger, Ken Darby; orchestrator, Gil Grau; production designer, Jack Poplin; set decorator, William L. Kuehl; titles, Don Record; choreography, Miriam Nelson; costumes, Moss Mabry; makeup, Al Greenway; assistant director, Jack Cunningham; sound, Everett A. Hughes; special effects, Ralph Webb; aerial camera, Jack Willoughby; camera, Fred J. Koenekamp; editor, Gene Milford.

Zero Mostel (Pious Blue); Kim Novak (Lyda Kabanov); Clint Walker (Ben Quick); Claude Akins (Slade); Akim Tamiroff (Papa Pedro); Larry Storch (Juan); John Anderson (Kinkaid); Sam Jaffe (Brother Lilac); Mako (Secret Service Agent Fong); Elisha Cook, Jr. (Jeb); Ruth Warrick (Mrs. Applebee); John Fiedler (Brother Dismas); John Larch (Sheriff); Peter Whitney (Brother Jordan); Norman Alden (The Great Gregory); Grady Sutton (Reverend Sims); Homer Garrett (Square Dance Caller); Byron Keith (Deputy); Bob Steele, Ben Aliza, Mickey Simpson (Guards); Guy Wilkerson, Burt Mustin (Glaziers); Royden Clark (Commandant); Janet Clark (Lady); Jerry Brown (Driver); Chuck O'Brien, Philo McCullough, Fred Krone, Dick Hudkins, Emile Avery, Everett Creach, William Zuckert, Jerry Summers (Stunt Men); Bob Mitchell Boys Choir (Vocalizers).

THE THIRD GIRL FROM THE LEFT   (ABC-TV, 1973) C—90 M.

Producer, Ron Roth; director, Peter Medak; screenplay, Dory Previn; songs, Previn; music supervisor, Nikolas Venet; music arranger, James E. Bond, Jr.; choreography, Miriam Nelson; art director, Frank Arrigo; Miss Novak's wardrobe, Bill Thomas; camera, Gayne Rescher; editor, Jim Benson.

Kim Novak (Gloria); Michael Brandon (David); George Furth (Zimmy); Tony Curtis (Joey); Michael Conrad (Hugh); Bern Hoffman (Len); Jenifer Shaw (Gaye); Louis Guss (Murray); Barbi Benton (Melanie); Anne Ramsey (Madeline); Larry Bishop (Bedford).

TALES THAT WITNESS MADNESS   (Par., 1973) C—90 M.

Producer, Norman Priggens; director, Freddie Francis; screenplay, Jay Fairbank; art director, Roy Walker; music-music conductor, Bernard Ebbinghouse; assistant director, Peter Saunders; makeup, Eric Allwright; wardrobe supervisor, Bridget Sellers; sound, Ken Ritchie, Nolan Roberts; camera, Norman Warwick; editor, Bernard Gribble.

Clinic Link Episodes: Jack Hawkins (Nicholas); Donald Pleasence (Tremayne).

Mr. Tiger: Georgia Brown (Fay); Donald Houston (Sam); Russell Lewis (Paul); David Wood (Tutor).

Penny Farthing: Suzy Kendall (Ann Beatrice); Peter McEnery (Timothy); Neil Kennedy, Richard Connaught (Removal Men); Beth Morris (Polly); Frank Forsyth (Uncle Albert).

Mel: Joan Collins (Bella); Michael Jayston (Brian).

Luau: Kim Novak (Auriol); Michael Petrovitch (Kimo); Mary Tamm (Ginny); Lesley Nunnerley (Vera); Leon Lissek (Keoki); Zohra Segal (Malia).

SATAN'S TRIANGLE   (ABC-TV, 1975) C—90 M.

Executive producers, Paul Junger Witt, Tony Thomas; producer, James Rokos; director, Sutton Roley; teleplay, William Reed Woodfield; music, Johnny Pate; director of photography, Leonard J. South; special effects, Gene Griff.

Kim Novak (Eva); Doug McClure (Haig); Alejandro Rey (P. Martin); Ed Lauter (Strickland); Jim Davis (Hal); Michael Conrad (Pagnolini); Titos Vandis (Salao); Zitto Kazann (Juano); Peter Bourne (Swedish Captain); Hank Stohl (Coast Guard Captain); Tom Dever (Miami Rescue Radio Officer); Trent Dolan (Miami Rescue Lieutenant).

Movie star, 1960 style

With Tony Randall in
BOYS' NIGHT OUT (MGM '62)

With Laurence Harvey in
OF HUMAN BONDAGE
(MGM '64)

With Alan Dexter and
Henry Gibson in KISS ME,
STUPID (Lopert '64)

On the set of THE AMOROUS ADVENTURES OF MOLL FLANDERS (Par '65) with a football player from the South Ruislip U.S. Air Force Base

With George Sanders in
THE AMOROUS ADVENTURES OF
MOLL FLANDERS

With Richard Johnson at Aspen,
Colorado on the day of their wedding
(March 15, 1965)

In THE LEGEND OF LYLAH CLARE (MGM '68)

At the Grauman's Chinese Theatre
(Hollywood) premiere of
THE LEGEND OF
LYLAH CLARE
(August 21, 1968)

Horseback-riding with beau Joel Thomas in Burbank, California (1969)

With Zero Mostel in THE GREAT BANK ROBBERY

In THE GREAT BANK ROBBERY (WB-7 Arts '69)

In THE THIRD GIRL FROM THE LEFT (ABC-TV, October 16, 1973)

In TALES THAT WITNESS MADNESS (Par '73)

In FOLIES BERGÈRE (UA '35)

Merle Oberon

5'2"
112 pounds
Black hair
Brown eyes
Pisces

It requires a bit of audacity to pity the likes of elegant, incandescent Merle Oberon, who in a five-decade screen career has maintained an avid following of civilized movie fans. More importantly, for her at least, she has almost always luxuriated in the rarefied social mode befitting an affluent, eternally youthful princess. One might legitimately ask whether these rewards are satisfying substitutes for an unrealized onscreen potential?

In the annals of motion-picture achievement, Merle stands somewhere between Marlene Dietrich and Loretta Young. The former is more consistently exotic and carefully sophisticated; the latter is a more fashionable mannequin with a more ingratiating, if forced, public personality. All three female stars offer contrasting variations of the personification of the Fountain of Youth.

The unfortunate aspect of Merle's filmmaking years is that they have been filled with "almosts." Her mentor-producer-director-husband Alexander Korda never found the proper vehicle of enduring worth to showcase Merle's many oncamera attributes. *The Private Life of Henry VIII* (United Artists, 1933) revolved around bulbous Charles Laughton, while *The Divorce of Lady X* (United Artists, 1938) was only a pleasant divertissement without much comic substance. Merle might have met her greatest professional aid in Josef von Sternberg, but by the time of *I, Claudius* (London Films, 1937), neither party was able to cope with production shambles or to exert a sound influence on the other. Samuel Goldwyn offered Merle in *The Dark Angel* (United Artists, 1935) as a warmup to the gigantic *Wuthering Heights* (United Artists, 1939), which proved to be her chef d'oeuvre. But that poetic tearjerker is more noted for its resplendent settings and creative photography than for the actress's histrionics. Warner Bros. had definite plans to transform Merle into Bette Davis's rival, but abandoned their ambitions after two shallow features failed to click, *'Til We Meet Again* (1940) and *Affectionately Yours* (1941).

Some point to *Lydia* (United Artists, 1941) as an indication of Merle's inability to properly emote in sensitive romantic drama. Perhaps. But what of her impressive hysterics in *Dark Waters* (United Artists, 1944) or her valiant perseverance in the inferior *This Love of Ours* (Universal, 1945)? Ironically, Merle's most indelible celluloid appearance to date occurs in *Desiree* (Twentieth Century-Fox, 1954), which cast her as an aging courtesan delicately clinging to shreds of lost youth and power. At the time it had a great deal of similarity to her own reality. That Merle later deluded herself by starring in the embarrassing *Of Love and Desire* (Twentieth Century-Fox, 1963) or the half-baked *Interval* (Avco-Embassy, 1973) is a display more of human frailty than acting limitations.

The problem of how to rate a big-name star whose (hopefully) better acting self has yet to grace the silver screen is a dilemma. Above all, it is a pity.

Tasmania, Australia's only offshore state, lies one hundred and fifty miles south of the Australian mainland. There, in the city of Port Arthur, Estelle Merle O'Brien-Thompson was born on Sunday, February 19, 1911.* Her heritage, chiefly of French, Irish, and Dutch ancestry, accounted for her black hair, ivory skin, high cheekbones, and sloping hazel eyes. Her father, Major John Thompson of the British army, had taken his pregnant wife, Constance Charlotte, to Tasmania on a holiday to visit with his sister. Three weeks before the birth of his only child, the major died, leaving his small family with only moderate means of support.

Estelle spent the first six years of her life on the 24,450-square-mile expanse and once claimed, "A little girl's life in Tasmania is much as it is anywhere else." In 1918, no longer wishing to impose on her stiff in-laws, Estelle's proper middle-class mother unhesitatingly accepted an invitation from friends in Bombay, India, to visit them for an indefinite period. Therefore, at the age of seven, Estelle's environment became

---

*Merle has always been femininely coy about her actual age and many of the circumstances surrounding her parentage and early years.

one that was exclusively tropical and comprised families affiliated with the British Colonial Office.

A few months after arriving in Bombay, Mrs. Thompson succumbed to a money-making scheme proposed to her by a gentleman acquaintance. She was led to believe that by investing her capital in the man's American automobile agency, she would become an instant millionairess through the demand for U.S. automobiles. The entire Thompson savings were turned over to the sharp promoter, who immediately left town, never to be heard of again. After his hasty departure, it was discovered that Mrs. Thompson was but one of several people who had been cleverly fleeced by the con artist. Without any visible means of support, Mrs. Thompson then took her daughter on a trip across India to Calcutta, where they were made welcome as unexpected additions to the household of Mrs. Thompson's brother.

The children of British families in Calcutta were generally sent to England for schooling, but since Mrs. Thompson desired her daughter to remain close at hand, Estelle was enrolled at La Martinere School in Calcutta. Her classmates nicknamed her Queenie because she was the prettiest and most regal girl in the school. Estelle studied a standard curriculum and, as well, she learned French and Hindustani. In her early teens she added shorthand and typing to her skills, abilities which were put to use in her uncle's government office. He took her on his payroll as a part-time employee. In her spare time she danced in programs staged by the Calcutta Amateur Theatrical Society and, in her fifteenth year, she was considered to be one of the most stunning girls in all of Calcutta. She could easily have had her pick of any of the dashing young English officers there, but she yearned to go to London to pursue a dance career. Everyone told her that she ought to be in motion pictures because of her beauty, and she decided they were, perhaps, right.

Propitiously, in 1929 her uncle took a leave of absence in order to enjoy a few weeks of holiday in London, and Estelle asked to go with him. Mrs. Thompson gave permission, but the uncle refused. No amount of pleading could make him change his mind. He boarded his ship for England on schedule and when the vessel was well at sea, Estelle appeared on deck. She had purchased a passage ticket with the money she had saved while working in his office. The uncle had to accept her as his traveling companion because there was no way of putting her ashore.

In London, the ambitious, independent Estelle soon enrolled in a dancing school and, using the name Merle O'Brien, applied for work as an extra with all the local film companies. When the uncle was ready to return to India, she begged him to let her stay to complete the dance course, which had two months remaining. She faithfully promised to follow him just as soon as the instruction period was completed. Reluctantly, he agreed, gave her $100 to support her through the eight weeks, and purchased her return boat ticket. As soon as he was beyond London's city limits, she cashed in the ticket and bought a new coat. She completed the dance course since it had been paid for in advance, but she literally haunted the casting offices in her spare time.

Finally, with the depletion of her funds, she took a night job as a dance hostess at the Cafe de Paris, near London's West End theatrical district. Although she felt the position was beneath her, she thought of it merely as a temporary measure until she was able to break into the movies. Besides, in addition to the weekly salary of 2 pounds, 10 shillings (approximately $12) she received her dinners at the club. "It was the dinner that turned the scales," Merle later admitted. Finally, while making a daily visit to one of the casting offices, she received work as an extra in *Alf's Button* (Gaumont, 1930), the second of three versions of a 1917 stage comedy. This was followed by occasional walk-ons in other British features, such as *Never Trouble Trouble* (Producers Distributing Corp., 1931), starring Lupino Lane, and *Fascination* (Wardour, 1931) with Madeleine Carroll. Merle verbally fattened her list of actual screen credits with nonexistent ones and years later confided that not only had she never been in many of the films, she had never even seen them.*

Along the way, industrious Merle became acquainted with a young cameraman who spoke on her behalf to movie executive Harry Lachman, who was then looking for a young woman to portray an oncamera vamp. Lachman agreed to talk with Miss O'Brien, but, at the outset of the interview, he neglected to tell her that the meeting was also to be a test. She was rushed onto a set where actor Carl Brisson grabbed her without warning and kissed her. She screamed, slapped him in the jaw, and stomped out in righteous indignation. Lachman decided she was not right for the seductive part.

A few days later, however, she was given a real screentest at British Paramount Studios, and this proved more successful. She received work as an extra in the comedy *Service for Ladies* (Paramount British, 1932), produced and directed by the thick-accented Hungarian, Alexander Korda. The film, a variation of Adolphe Menjou's *The Grand Duchess and the Waiter* (Paramount, 1926), is notable for the screen debut of Leslie Howard. Merle was then used as an extra in *Ebb Tide* (1932), also for British Paramount, and allegedly remained at the same studio to appear in several crowd scenes of *Aren't We All?* (Paramount British, 1932), a sophisticated Gertrude Lawrence comedy directed by Harry Lachman. Her salary was $10 a day, which prompted Merle to quit her odious job at the Cafe de Paris. It was at this same time that she officially met Alexander Korda.

The thirty-nine-year-old Hungarian noticed her in the canteen at the British and Dominion Studios, where he was lunching with his wife,

*It has as yet been impossible to verify even the three extra appearances by Merle that are listed here.

594

Hungarian actress Maria (Farkas) Corda, by whom he had a son, Peter. Maria Corda spotted the attractive girl eating a sandwich and observed aloud, "That's the most interesting face I've seen in a long time." Korda, who was currently directing a film other than the one in which Merle was working as an extra, wandered onto the set of *Aren't We All?* Merle recalled the incident to Katharine Roberts of *Collier's* magazine a few years later: "He did a good piece of acting. I thought he was just another producer chap come to talk to .my producer. On the way out he bumped into me, said he was sorry, took a look at me and remarked, 'we're starting a new company soon. Come on over and I'll give you a test.' "* She made the test, which Korda himself directed. He then noted on her studio file card, "In good demand for special crowd work. A. K. interested."

Nothing happened for three weeks, until she read in a London trade paper that Korda had signed up a new actress named Stella Merle. In the meantime, Mrs. Thompson had arrived in London to personally transport her errant daughter back to India. However, she quickly changed her mind when London Films did, in fact, sign Merle to a seven-year contract. The new contractee immediately voiced her displeasure at being called Stella Merle and insisted that she be professionally known as Merle O'Brien. Korda objected, "Everybody in New York is called O'Brien." He considered the surname too undistinguished for her exotic looks and chose Auberon, which also happened to be the name of a noted Bond Street hairdresser. When the stylist loudly protested sharing his commercial name with the likes of an unproven film player, Merle's last name was changed to Oberon.

Merle's initial screen appearance under contract was a top-featured role in *Wedding Rehearsal*, released by Ideal in 1932. The comedy starred Roland Young, Wendy Barrie, John Loder, and Joan Gardner. Young appeared as the footloose bachelor who does his best to outwit his grandmother (Kate Cutler), who is determined to see him married and properly settled. He eventually weds his secretary (Merle). That same year Korda hired Leontine Sagan, who had made quite a reputation directing the German-made *Maedchen in Uniform* (1931), to helm *Men of To-morrow* (Paramount British, 1932), a study of Oxford graduates. In particular, the drama focuses on Maurice Braddell, as a moody youth expelled from the English university for writing a scathing article about thè school. After he fails to pursue a successful literary career in London, he eventually returns to Oxford, where his wife (Joan Gardner) is working on scientific experiments. Merle, in spite of her first screen "test," was cast as Ysobel D'Aunay, a Myrna Loy-type vamp who does her best to lead distraught Braddell down the primrose path. Robert Donat, in his motion-picture debut, was seen as the student who attempts to corrupt Gardner's morals. Neither Merle nor Donat had much of a part, and it

---

*The new company referred to was London Films.

595

was only after each had become well known in the cinema that the picture was distributed in the United States in 1935, where it served to show reviewers and filmgoers just how much each star had improved histrionically (especially in diction) since that entry was produced.

Meanwhile, Merle read in a newspaper that she had been chosen to portray Anne Boleyn in *The Private Life of Henry VIII* (United Artists, 1933), to be produced and directed by Korda. She was intrigued by the historical part and proceeded to read everything available on Anne (1507-1536), the second wife of the much-married monarch. She felt a strange closeness to the doomed queen, but on reading the draft script of the film, found that Anne's story occupied only two pages. This was a distinct disappointment, after recently playing lead roles, but she still had a hunch that the part would be good for her career.

Most British film authorities considered a motion picture about Henry VIII (1491-1547) a lunatic idea, and Korda found it difficult to get financial backing for his project. The cast and crew agreed to share in the profits or losses, and the film was rushed to completion in the record time of five weeks, leading the star, Charles Laughton, on leave from his Hollywood Paramount contract, to call it "one of the least expensive big productions ever made." The actual beheading scene of Catherine Howard (Binnie Barnes), the fifth wife of the Tudor king, was deleted from the final print, not as a result of Merle's complaint to Korda that a second decapitation would detract from her scene, but because Binnie delivered her last line in an unmistakable Cockney accent.

With the ninety-six-minute film completed, Korda's next problem was to find a major distributor. Since the English firms were leary of a film that treated a past ruler so jocularly, and especially with Laughton as a marathon-style lover, an American distributor was required. United Artists took it on, and *The Private Life of Henry VIII* had its world premiere at Radio City Music Hall on October 12, 1933 (with subsequent openings in Paris and London).

From the start, it is quite obvious that the Arthur Wimperis screenplay is not a reverent study of the gluttonous king, for a foreword states that because Laughton's first wife, Catherine of Aragon, was so respectable, the film will have no part of her. In the course of the chronicle, which covers the ruler's life from the age of thirty-seven to forty-five, the film presents Laughton's interaction with the five women who became his wives (and queens) numbers two through six. Merle, well appointed in the John Armstrong costumes, was front and center as the adulterous Anne, who gives birth to the future Elizabeth I, and then goes to the block for her extramarital relations. Wendy Barrie plays the childlike Jane Seymour, who dies in childbirth. Elsa Lanchester (Laughton's real-life wife) as the fourth spouse, Anne of Cleves, stole the limelight with her comic portrayal of a plain lady who was witty enough to bring her gross husband to task. Binnie Barnes is the imperious Catherine Howard,* who dallies with Thomas Culpeper (Robert Donat) and goes to the block for her indiscretions, and Laughton's final wife, the children's nurse, Catherine Parr, is played by Everley Gregg.

The American critics, who up to this point had only barely acknowledged the British cinema as a viable commercial industry, were forced to reevaluate their opinion. Thornton Delehanty (*New York Post*) cheered that *The Private Life of Henry VIII* was "perhaps the first historical film that doesn't look as if it had been unpacked from a cedar chest." John S. Cohen, Jr. (*New York Sun*) enthused, "It is so right in its collection of types, in its pageantry . . ." Although Laughton, who was to win an Academy Award for his royal performance, received the lion's share of critical and audience attention, each of the five leading ladies was given her due by the fourth estate. Richard Watts, Jr. (*New York Herald-Tribune*) described Merle as "lovely and pathetic," while *Variety* devoted more space to its appreciation of the relative newcomer: "Miss Oberon is a British edition of Fay Wray. Her beauty is conceivably the cause of Korda's lone error in that the director has lingered too long over the execution of Anne Boleyn (Miss Oberon), the second wife upon which the story opens."

When the celluloid tapestry of British history reached England (Leicester Square Theatre, London, October 24, 1933), the *London Daily Mail* labeled it "the Greatest British film triumph." In its first world run, the feature grossed $2.5 million, and it was periodically rereleased until sold to television in 1957.

Merle's hunch about playing Anne Boleyn proved correct. Almost "overnight" she established her name and face with global filmgoing audiences as the gallant, mistreated mother of a future queen. Most everyone who saw the picture was mystified and intrigued by the moment when imprisoned Anne Boleyn looks at her reflection in a hand mirror and wistfully observes, "It's such a *little* neck," before going bravely to her death under the axe of a French executioner.

The dark-haired girl, who stood five feet, two inches tall, and weighed 112 pounds, with a hint of the Oriental in her face, was on her way cinematically.

Although *The Private Life of Henry VIII* was nominated for an Academy Award for the Best Picture of 1933, it lost to *Cavalcade* (Fox). The film was named by the National Board of Review and other sources as one of the ten best foreign films of that year.

Like *Henry VIII* co-stars Wendy Barrie, Binnie Barnes, and Elsa Lan-

---

*In this picture, Barnes photographed even more beautiful than Merle, and, moreover, she enjoyed some smart dialog. When Laughton knocks at her bedroom chambers, she haughtily inquires who is there. Taken aback, he announces, "Henry." She retorts, "Henry who?"

chester, Merle found herself in much greater professional demand after that film's release. Korda loaned her first to producer Leon Garganoff for the English-language version of *The Battle* (Gaumont, 1934), shot in Paris simultaneously with the French edition, which also starred Charles Boyer, but had Annabella in the female lead assignment.

Unlike the more elaborate but inferior *Madame Butterfly* (Paramount, 1932), starring Sylvia Sidney and Cary Grant, *The Hatchet Man* (First National, 1932), with Edward G. Robinson and Loretta Young, or such other Hollywood entries as *Son-Daughter* (MGM, 1932), with Helen Hayes and Ramon Novarro, *The Battle* was a picture set in the Far East in which the Occidental players gave rather convincing, restrained performances as Orientals. When *The Battle* (a.k.a. *Thunder in the East*) reached New York in November 1934, Andre Sennwald (*New York Times*) felt justified in reporting that it "is tragedy in the proper technical sense, and it represents an exalting experience." Based on the 1912 French novel, the plot has Boyer as the captain of a Japanese battleship which is victorious in a naval engagement. He realizes that the victory was due largely to the enemy's frailties. When he learns that John Loder, the British naval attaché on his ship, is to make a secret report to his home government, Boyer is anxious to learn the document's contents, so that he can understand his countrymen's military flaws and help his nation in further wartime encounters. To accomplish this aim, he forces himself to assume a responsive attitude to the loathsome Britisher and his customs, while, at the same time, urging his uncomprehending wife to be especially receptive to Loder's needs. Merle soon finds herself falling in love with the man, a member of a society she has been trained to despise. Later, in a battle at sea, Loder is killed, and, as the victorious Japanese fleet returns to Nagasaki harbor, the distraught Boyer, who knows all, retires to his chambers and commits hara-kiri. While Boyer had the pivotal role, Merle received very complimentary reviews for her performance. "Miss Oberon acts the part of the Marquise with an Oriental delicacy and originality of performance new to the screen. It is chiefly in her deft pantomime that she packs so much of the ·artistry which reverberates back to the audience with such emotion" (Marguerite Tazelaar, *New York Herald-Tribune*). The London *Picturegoer* magazine praised her for playing her part "with conviction and sensitive understanding."

When Merle returned from Paris to London, Olympic Films borrowed her for the second female lead in *The Broken Melody* (1934), a hurly-burly tale of a struggling composer (John Garrick) who weds a temperamental opera singer (Margot Grahame), murders her lover, is sentenced to Devil's Island, escapes, and finds eventual happiness with the girl (Merle) who has loved him all along. Grahame received most of the viewer attention in this clumsy, slow-moving melodrama. Merle was rated as "competent" in her pedestrian, passive assignment.

Having dealt so successfully with a historical figure, Korda decided to repeat the formula with *The Private Life of Don Juan* (United Artists, 1934), this time debunking the legendary lover-rogue of the thirteenth century. At first glance it must have seemed that the casting of Douglas Fairbanks, Sr., in the title role was inspired thinking. However, by this point, the fifty-one-year-old personality was no longer the limber, swash-buckling figure who had delighted moviegoers in *The Mark of Zorro* (United Artists), *Robin Hood* (United Artists, 1922), *The Thief of Bagdad* (United Artists, 1924), and *The Iron Mask* (United Artists, 1929).* The screenplay, based on Henri Bataille's play, was by Frederick Lonsdale and Lajos Biro and employed the dramatic device of the play within a play.

This "elaborate and unimportant, pretentious and prolix romantic fable" *(New York World-Journal)* finds Fairbanks's Don Juan exhausted from living up to his reputation as the century's greatest lover, dualist, and bon vivant. During his absence from Seville, an imposter is killed by an outraged husband, and when the deceased is taken to be Don Juan, Fairbanks is content to let his legend die. He even goes so far as to attend (à la Tom Sawyer) his own funeral. However, time marches on; the man hankers once again to be in the center of the limelight, but is aghast to discover that the fair señoritas of Seville now consider him an antiquated buffoon. When the aging Lothario attends a play based on his own life and jumps up on the stage to denounce it as a charade, he is booed off the platform by the audience, and his wife (Benita Hume) refuses to acknowledge his true identity.

The Private Life of Don Juan premiered at the International Cinema Exhibition at Venice (August 27, 1934), then opened at the London Pavilion Theatre on September 5, 1934, and made its New York bow at the Rivoli Theatre on December 10, 1934. Richard Watts, Jr. (*New York Herald-Tribune*) suggested that "the production might well have contained a greater share of vitality." Other reviewers and the public were less kind to this tongue-in-cheek exercise. Among the gallery of women who appeared in the film as Fairbanks's actual and would-be conquests were Binnie Barnes, Joan Gardner, Patricia Hilliard, Diana Napier, and, finally, Merle, cast as Antonia, an exotic cafe dancer who becomes famous because Don Juan once kissed her. She is the figure who later rebuffs the bedraggled Casanova. Andre Sennwald *(New York Times)* was among those who credited Merle with being "an enormously decorative young woman, who combines a unique talent and personal charm." In recalling this "costume prank," most viewers almost immediately remember the pictorially stunning segment in which Merle floats through the air on a

---

*During the filming of *Don Juan* in London, Fairbanks, then still wed to America's Sweetheart, Mary Pickford, was romantically linked with ex-chorus girl Lady Sylvia Ashley. *Don Juan* would prove to be the star's last film. He died on December 12, 1939 in Hollywood.

swing in the orchard, with the lovely Spanish sky as the impressive backdrop.

By this time, Korda had a working arrangement with Samuel Goldwyn in Hollywood, who handled the American distribution of Korda's pictures through the services of United Artists. *The Scarlet Pimpernel* (United Artists, 1935) was such a venture. Baroness Emmuska Orczy (1865-1947), a prolific novelist, had written this French Revolution-period spy-thriller in 1905, the same year in which she dramatized the tale with her husband, Montagu W. Barstow. Leslie Howard, who had gone to America to work on Broadway and in Hollywood, was brought back to England to portray the heroic English gentleman Sir Percy Blakeney, who masquerades his bravery behind the guise of a fop at the court of King George III. Like the tyrannical Robespierre (Ernest Milton), Howard's wife (Merle), a French girl of dubious background, has no idea as to the gallant Pimpernel's real identity. Along with the sinister Chauvelin (Raymond Massey), the revolutionists' unofficial ambassador to the Court of St. James's, Merle finds herself baffled by the dual nature of Howard. In fact, through Massey's chicanery, Merle is duped into betraying Howard. At the memorable Lion d'Or Inn finale, the plot evolves into a battle of wits between Massey and Howard, with the former being outwitted by the latter, who escapes with Oberon to continue the noble gesture of rescuing French nobility from the blade of the guillotine.

Once again, producer Korda was reaching into history to find his motif for screen entertainment, and, as with *The Private Life of Henry VIII,* he succeeded admirably. The film was approved for being "stirring to the pulse and beautiful to the eye" (Andre Sennwald, *New York Times).* Howard, who, the previous year, had been engaged in the Russian Revolution espionage picture *British Agent* (First National, 1934), was lauded for adding the proper balance to this "gallant, straightforward melodrama" *(New York American).* In actuality Merle had a relatively minor, decorative role, cast in a part that required her to be soulful and sad throughout much of the exciting proceedings. Nevertheless, Edwin Schallert *(Los Angeles Times)* was able to praise her because "she manages to blend diversified emotions effectively." *Variety* labeled her "the slant-eyed knockout," and Richard Watts, Jr. *(New York Herald-Tribune)* tagged her as "devastating." Clearly Merle had already become, in three years, one of the most desirable beauties of the British cinema, and, because several of her films had attained global popularity, her likeness and name were known to moviegoers nearly everywhere.

During the lensing of *The Scarlet Pimpernel,* in late 1934, there were discreet rumors that forty-one-year-old Howard, a husband and father, and twenty-three-year-old Merle were seeing one another off the soundstage sets. While that liaison came to nothing, her previous romance with fifty-two-year-old Joseph M. Schenck, the film executive who was chairman of the board of directors of United Artists, later its president, and thereafter, in 1933, the co-founder with Darryl F. Zanuck of Twentieth Century Pictures, had beneficial repercussions on her career, if not her domestic life. In August 1934, Merle announced from her Monte Carlo headquarters that she and he were engaged. Schenck, then divorced from actress Norma Talmadge, denied the official linkage, but did admit to the press that it "would give me great happiness if she became my wife." The legalized union that each party seemingly desired never came to pass,* but it did expedite the signing of an agreement between Korda and Samuel Goldwyn that Merle's filmmaking contract should be shared between them, and that her first American-made motion picture would be for United Artists' new Twentieth Century Pictures unit.†

It was first announced that Merle would join George Arliss's cast of *Cardinal Richelieu* (United Artists, 1935), but the role of Lenore went to Maureen O'Sullivan, and Merle instead joined Twentieth Century's splashy musical *Folies Bergère* (United Artists, 1935).‡ Merle went to Hollywood in the winter of 1934 and was quickly discovered by makeup artists, who converged on her with "Oh, baby! What we can do with *your* face." She emerged with a rosette mouth, thinly penciled eyebrows, cosmetically slanted eyes, and lacquered hair.

In *Folies Bergère,* Maurice Chevalier is the male star in dual roles as an entertainer asked to substitute for his look-alike, a society financier. Merle is Genevieve, the stately wife of the banker, while Ann Sothern is Mimi, the girlfriend of the Folies Bergère's comic-mimic. Although the film suffered from having its song numbers stuffed into the opening and closing sections with the storyline shoved in between, the film was greeted as a saucy song-and-dance divertissement of the highest order, and proof that producer Zanuck (of *Forty-Second Street* [Warner Bros., 1933] fame) and Chevalier (of MGM's *The Merry Widow* [1934]) had not lost their box-office touch.§ While Ann Sothern was technically the second female lead, she received most attention in this film, next to Chevalier, both as his oncamera dueting partner ("Rhythm in the Rain") and as the romantically inclined music-hall doll.

Merle, looking exquisite in her Omar Kiam gowns, had a rather passive assignment in *Folies Bergère. Variety* unabashedly stated in its review column, "This girl, the strongest femme luminary in England, makes her first Hollywood appearance in this film, and it seems curious that she

*The engagement ring Merle returned to Schenck was later purchased by Douglas Fairbanks, Sr., for Lady Sylvia Ashley.
†At one point, it was rumored that Merle had signed a four-year pact with producer Edward Small to make two pictures a year. Her first project in Hollywood was to be *The Count of Monte Cristo* (United Artists, 1934) with John Barrymore in the title part.
‡The musical derived from the play *The Red Cat,* which Twentieth Century co-produced on Broadway in 1934. It had a short, fourteen-performance run. The premise of *Folies Bergère* was reutilized by Twentieth Century-Fox in *That Night in Rio* (1941), with Alice Faye in Merle's role, and again in 1951 as *On the Riviera,* with Gene Tierney in the part.
§In the simultaneously lensed French-language version of *Folies Bergère,* Chevalier repeated his dual role, but Natalie Paley inherited Merle's part, and Sim Viva played Mimi.

should have been brought clear across the ocean and continent for the assignment. She doesn't fit in. Her respect-compelling chassis and her smart gowning will get attention, but it just isn't a happy assignment. It's a bit too light for her, and the camera isn't as kind to her as it might be, either." Thorton Delehanty *(New York Post)* confirmed that the musical comedy "offers Merle Oberon little exercise for her ability, and the Hollywood beauticians have turned her into an impeccable store-window model."

After viewing the film, Merle was of the same opinion as the critics, and she began to seriously question the wisdom of having come to Hollywood. "I didn't seem to have anything they wanted," she later explained, "and when they designed the new face for me, I thought it was fine. It's incredible—but I did." She then spent a week in New York where she contemplated returning to London, but, instead, signed an agreement with top talent agent Myron Selznick. She was in good company with Selznick, who represented such other luminaries as Mary Astor, Gary Cooper, Ruth Chatterton, Kay Francis, Charles Laughton, Fredric March, Laurence Olivier, Ginger Rogers, and Margaret Sullavan.

The next question was what to do with and for Merle. Goldwyn's contention was that she looked like an English girl in real life, and therefore should play that type of role onscreen. He proposed a remake of *The Dark Angel* (United Artists, 1935) in which Merle would portray the lovestruck Kitty Vane, minus the exotic makeup. United Artists officials were not so sure, reasoning that a girl whose background included Tasmania and India was best qualified to play only a Hindu or other equally exotic, sloeeyed roles. Via cablegram and overseas telephone, Goldwyn communicated with Korda, and the two of them agreed that Merle should do *The Dark Angel.* Thus the actress's request "to play a normal, natural person like myself" was finally granted and she expressed her gratitude that "Mr. Goldwyn has a great deal of foresight."

The London *Times,* in reviewing this production, would be quick to point out, "It is not a story which anyone could take very seriously by itself, but the film makes a systematic and often very skillful appeal to those untrustworthy emotions which may suddenly cause the most hardened intellect to dissolve before the most obvious sentimentality." The teary tale, based on a Guy Bolton play, deals with Fredric March, Herbert Marshall, and Merle as three childhood friends who grow up at the time of World War I.* Both men cherish Merle, but she picks March, with whom she spends the night before he is shipped off to war duty in France. (They had been unable to secure the marriage license in time.) When Marshall, March's commanding officer at the front, learns of his pal's ungentlemanly conduct, they argue, and March is sent on a dangerous

*In Goldwyn's silent version of the story (First National, 1925), Ronald Colman and Vilma Banky were teamed together onscreen for the first time, with Wyndham Standing in the role of Gerald Shannon.

mission from which he does not return. Later, back in England, Marshall and Merle plan to wed, although she still loves March. At this juncture she learns that her beloved is still alive, and she and Marshall go to visit him. Unknown to them, March is blind, but he has memorized every detail of his room, so as to prevent his love and once best friend from discovering the truth. The ruse almost works until it is time to say goodbye and March cannot see Merle's offer of a handshake. Suddenly the truth is out, and the two lovers are reunited.

The star trio all received critical praise for their sensible handling of this lachrymose silver-screen study, each making his/her particular on-camera persona effective amidst the superior Goldwyn production values.* Everything for which Merle, Goldwyn, and Korda had hoped in this movie came true. She was greeted by reviewers and public alike as a fresh, new personality. "Merle Oberon—no longer an exotic but a fresh and appealing English girl—is not only the most fetching eyeful to hit the screen in some time but gives a performance of blended warmth and restraint that marks her for a glittering future" *(Liberty* magazine). ". . . abandoning the Javanese slant of the eyes for the occasion, [she] plays with skill and feeling" *(New York Times).* "As for Miss Oberon, everything America says of her is true. Half-a-dozen pictures have been enough to place her among the first half-dozen actresses on the screen" *(London Daily Telegraph).* Merle and Marshall would recreate their popular *The Dark Angel* roles on "Lux Radio Theatre" on June 22, 1936. Later, on the "Screen Guild Theatre," sponsored by Gulf Oil, she again played Kitty Vane while Ronald Colman and Donald Crisp were the friends who loved her. Merle was Oscar-nominated for Best Actress for *The Dark Angel* but lost the competition to Bette Davis of *Dangerous* (Warner Bros.).

Goldwyn, who by this point had given up his dreams of converting European import Anna Sten into a great Hollywood star,† now focused on Merle and ex-Paramount star Miriam Hopkins as the two feminine focal points in his star-stable roster. The iconoclastic producer decided to star Merle with Gary Cooper, Joel McCrea, and Miriam Hopkins in *Maximilian of Mexico.* So far as Goldwyn was concerned, there was but one man qualified to portray Maximilian, and when Paramount's production schedule prevented the loan-out of their popular leading man, the epic picture was called off.‡ Instead, the indefatigable Goldwyn decided to put a Broadway property he owned onto film.

---

*Merle had one unfortunate scene in *The Dark Angel*—a fox hunt in which she is dislodged from her mount in a manner which came across unfortunately comic in tone.

†The Russian-born would-be rival to Greta Garbo was starred by Goldwyn in *Nana* (1934), *We Live Again* (1934), and *The Wedding Night* (1935), all United Artists releases and each a box-office dud.

‡When Warner Bros. filmed *Juarez* (1939), Brian Aherne was Maximilian von Hapsburg with Bette Davis as his wife, Carlotta, and Paul Muni in the title role.

The project was *The Children's Hour,* based on Lillian Hellman's play.‡ The drama's theme revolved around a lesbian relationship, which was then a taboo screen subject. As the *New York Times* economically described the situation when the picturization opened at New York's Rivoli Theatre on March 18, 1936: "we are fairly sure that if you listen attentively you may hear Mr. Goldwyn laughing up his sleeve. The picture carefully refrains from mentioning its parent work, cheerfully limiting itself to the word that its screenplay is by Miss Hellman. And while Miss Hellman might concede, under duress, that she has plagiarized her play, she might argue, too, that her theme is quite changed and that the resemblance of *These Three* to 'The Children's Hour' is merely superficial. It wouldn't be much of an argument, of course, but you must admit that it satisfied Mr. Hays' watchdogs."

Having already paid Hellman $50,000 for the screen rights to the drama, Goldwyn hired the playwright to translate her work into acceptable screen terms. *These Three* became a heterosexual study of two young women (Merle and Hopkins) who, upon graduation from college, find themselves without any future prospects. They decide to take the Connecticut home left to Merle and convert it into a private school for young girls. Merle falls in love with the local physician (Joel McCrea), unaware that Hopkins also hankers for the handsome doctor. One willful girl (Bonita Granville) learns from a cowardly classmate (Marcia Mae Jones) that Hopkins had been reprimanded by her aunt (Catherine Doucet) for having allowed McCrea into her bedroom. Although the Hopkins-McCrea situation was quite innocent, it soon gets blown out of proportion by the vindictive Granville, and the school is forced to close. McCrea loses his hospital post and returns to Vienna, where eventually he and Merle are reunited. As for the lovelorn Hopkins, she is "content" that her best friend has saved her romance, although more perceptive filmgoers were aware that, contrary to the script, Hopkins's romantic interest was more closely fastened onto Merle than on the wholesome but bland McCrea.

While most of the critics and audience attendees were so preoccupied with discovering how close a parallel to the stage original the film was, or marveling at the waspish qualities of young performer Granville, there were those who took time out to make note of the star trio's emoting. "Miss Merle Oberon brings her personal attractiveness, her increasing expertise as an actress and her excellent voice to the role" (Richard Watts, Jr., *New York Herald-Tribune).*

In keeping with her new image as a subdued, glamorous, very Occidental leading lady, Merle was next cast by Goldwyn in *Beloved Enemy*

‡It opened at the Maxine Elliott Theatre on November 20, 1934, for a 691-performance run with Katherine Emery as Karen Wright. In a 1952 New York stage revival, the part would be played by Kim Hunter, and in William Wyler's remake, entitled *The Children's Hour* (United Artists, 1961), it would be handled by Audrey Hepburn.

(United Artists, 1936), with Brian Aherne as her co-star. Set against the bleeding streets of 1921 Dublin with the Irish and British at one another's throats, Merle appeared as Helen Drummond, the aristocratic daughter of Lord Athleigh (Henry Stephenson), who has come to Ireland to investigate the rebellion. It is not long before well-bred Merle has encountered Dennis Riordan (Aherne), the gallant young rebel leader who is gaining victories over the English. Unthinkingly Merle turns informer on Aherne and reveals his identity to the British. Nevertheless, the reckless patriot still loves her and brooks many dangerous obstacles to rendezvous with the intriguing titled lady. Through their relationship of growing love, they begin to respect one another's political viewpoint, eventually leading Aherne to urge his followers to accept the British compromise terms at a London peace talk. When Merle convinces Aherne to cast his vote for a cessation of the hostilities, a number of his old friends believe he is now a traitor, and it is his best friend-bodyguard O'Rourke (Jerome Cowan) who shoots down Aherne. But this finale is not unmitigated tragedy, for Aherne has accomplished what he set out to do, bringing the two opposing forces to a closer understanding. (A happy ending for *Beloved Enemy* had also been filmed, but was discarded as inappropriate to the flavor of the story.)

While *Beloved Enemy* was not in the same league as the powerful *The Informer* (RKO, 1935) or the lyrical *The Plough and the Stars* (RKO, 1936), both directed by John Ford, it could be fairly ranked "a fine and mature and dignified drama" (Frank S. Nugent, *New York Times*). As the film's foreword points out, the picture is not meant to be a historical documentary, but rather a dramatic representation of the mood and personalities of those troubled times. Merle, who was becoming renowned as the gorgeous living embodiment of the best 1936 fashions that Omar Kiam could create, again received superior acting notices, demonstrating that she was not being judged by viewers on her beauty alone.* "[She] is afforded an opportunity . . . to pour forth her histrionic ability in what is perhaps the greatest profusion of her movie career" (Wanda Hale, *New York Daily News*). One might find it difficult to believe, as the script indicates, that it was solely through Merle's inspired instigation that the Black and Tan combat was halted for a while, but she imparted conviction to a heroine's role that might easily have become mere set dressing in the hands of a less accomplished actress.

Within *Beloved Enemy* there are some memorable moments, such as when Merle and Aherne are passionately discussing the futility of bloodshed, while being surrounded by angered Irishmen ready to kill, or the situation which finds Merle engaged in a languid shipboard discus-

*In the film's histrionic footrace, Merle received sturdy competition from Karen Morley, cast as Aherne's widowed sister, the one person who sympathizes with the couple's romance.

sion with her worldly father (Stephenson). Her performance led Howard Barnes *(New York Herald-Tribune)* to acclaim, "she brings beauty and a sensitive understanding to the part of the English girl."

While Merle's star status in the film industry was rising under Goldwyn's aegis, she was eager to expand her professional stamping grounds, and agreed to star in David O. Selznick's *The Garden of Allah* (United Artists, 1936), based on the 1904 Robert Hichens novel, a stage version, and the 1927 Metro-Goldwyn-Mayer feature with Alice Terry. Charles Boyer was selected as her leading man in this Technicolor desert drama with Richard Boleslawski as director. Before production had actually gone very far, Selznick had a change of heart and decided that Merle was not right for the part of Domini Enfilden, a young woman who encounters and falls in love with Boyer at the desert city of Beni-Mora, not realizing that he is actually a Trappist monk who has fled his order. Selznick fastened on the belief that Marlene Dietrich was the proper screen figure for the exotic role and made arrangements for her to assume Merle's part. To assuage Merle's artistic and emotional hurt, her lawyers instituted a law suit against Selznick, seeking the balance of her full $136,000 salary plus damages for this professional humiliation. Eventually the suit was dropped and settled out of court, with Merle receiving a $90,000 compensation plus promises of additional film projects from the United Artists production line-up. As it developed, *The Garden of Allah* was not the smash hit Selznick had foreseen.

Meanwhile, Merle, who had been seriously dating young David Niven, the Goldwyn contractee who played the staff officer and third part of the romantic triangle in *Beloved Enemy*, embarked for New York with plans to set sail for England. Korda was anxious to have Merle return to London for both professional and romantic reasons. He had abandoned plans for Merle to star in a version of George Bernard Shaw's *Caesar and Cleopatra* with Cedric Hardwicke,* and dropped the notion of reteaming Merle with Charles Laughton in a screen adaptation of *Cyrano de Bergerac.*† Instead, he came upon the novels *I, Claudius* (1934) and *Claudius the God* (1934) by the poet-novelist Robert Graves, and immediately decided to pair Merle with Laughton in this study of Emperor Tiberius Claudius Nero Germanicus (10 B.C.-A.D. 54) and the royal intrigue instigated by his third wife (Valeria) Messalina (Merle), who betrays her ambitious husband and is eventually sentenced to execution by him.

With Graves commissioned to prepare the screenplay, shooting on *I, Claudius* began at the Denham Studios on February 8, 1937. Problems arose from the start because Laughton was unsure of how best to portray

---

*When the Shaw play was picturized (United Artists, 1946), Claude Rains and Vivien Leigh had the title roles.
†In the 1950 United Artists version, Jose Ferrer had the lead part with Mala Powers as Roxane.

the humble, stumbling autocrat. He was convinced he was losing his talent, and neither Korda nor authoritarian director Josef von Sternberg could persuade him otherwise. Behind his dressing-room door, Laughton chose Merle as his sounding board and confided his darkest fears to her. Meanwhile, the totalitarian von Sternberg, understandably concerned about his ability to tackle such an ambitious, actionful feature after his series of Paramount mood studies with Marlene Dietrich, clashed with cast members, and actors like Raymond Massey began to leave the production.

On the elaborate sets, Laughton spent hours replaying the abdication speech of King Edward VIII, hoping to attain some synthesis of the noble humility required for the screen role. The more Laughton tried to come to grips with the part, the more it eluded him, leading him to forget lines, and to constantly alter the physical aspects of his characterization, which required him to limp, stutter, and twitch. By March 11, the perturbed Laughton announced to the trade press that when his contract with London Films expired on April 21, he was leaving the soundstages of *I, Claudius* no matter what.

Then, on March 16, 1937, with two-thirds of the 150,000-pound budget already spent and not even one-half of the picture completed, Merle was involved in a London car accident.* She was rushed to Middlesex Hospital with a slight concussion of the brain and a severe cut on the right side of her face, which required cosmetic surgery. Contemporary reports differ as to the seriousness of her injuries, but at the time her physician estimated that she would require at least three months to recuperate. Korda, who despaired of the film ever being completed, suspended production on the day of Merle's accident, and three days later shut down production on *I, Claudius* completely. The footage was shelved, and Korda was able to obtain some 80,000 pounds recompense from the Prudential Insurance Company.

The saga of *I, Claudius* was not to end at this point, for in 1966 the British Broadcasting Corporation discovered all the cans of printed film from the unfinished picture stored at the Denham studios of London Films. Deciding to make a documentary entitled *The Epic That Never Was,* the network interviewed Dame Flora Robson, Emlyn Williams, Josef von Sternberg, and others for the video special. John Baxter in *The Cinema of Josef von Sternberg* (1971) reported on the television probe: "Unfortunately, simplifications necessary to make the documentary more lively as well as changes in the original version demanded by Miss Oberon robbed the film of much historical value. Audiences were asked to

---

*In a suit later instituted by Edward J. Bundy, driver of the other vehicle, Oberon's chauffeur, Sidney J. Dignby, was charged with negligence, but the court, holding that while Dignby was somewhat at fault, Bundy had an improper cause of action, dismissed his complaint.

accept that *I, Claudius* was 'built around' Miss Oberon, an absurd statement as the plot synopsis indicates. . . . As for the view that it would have been impossible to re-shoot Miss Oberon's material after her accident [one of Korda's excuses for abandoning the film], a close examination of her few scenes suggests that replacement by another actress would have been simple."

It was a bizarre situation for a performer such as Merle to have snatches of previously unseen screen emoting reviewed thirty years after the fact, but such was the case with her scenes from *I, Claudius* as displayed in *The Epic That Never Was*. One sequence has her traipsing down a colonnaded hallway, her figure in its shimmering costume coming in and out of focus amidst the streaks of sunlight. Another completed section shows Merle, having completed an abandoned dance (footage that was apparently lost), causing the avaricious, depraved Caligula (Williams) to turn to Laughton and evilly state, "Isn't she fantastically beautiful, just as you, uncle, are fantastically ugly." There were also a series of close-ups of Laughton's pathetic character and of Merle's waspish Messalina, the latter filmed in diffused shadow, with the results unflattering to the star. Peter John Dyer *(Sight and Sound* magazine) complained of Merle's "performance," "[She] has all the panache of a wayward debutante."

While Merle was recuperating from her accident, her mother, age fifty-six, died on April 23, 1937. To cheer up his favored actress, Korda then cast her in a color comedy, *Over the Moon* (United Artists, 1937—released in the United States in 1939-40). Scripted by Anthony Pelissier, Arthur Wimperis, and Alec Coppel, and based on a Robert Sherwood story, the film presented Merle as June Benson, the niece of an eccentric old man who dies, leaving no indication of his actual state of enormous wealth. A local young doctor (Rex Harrison) takes an interest in her, and withdraws his small savings from the bank to provide her with a wish-fulfillment chance to enjoy the splendors of Monte Carlo. The couple are prepared to wed, but then Merle learns she is a $90 million heiress; Harrison becomes prideful and refuses to marry her. Subsequent reels are devoted to a multihued travelog as Merle, accompanied by self-appointed parasites, runs off to the playgrounds of the Continent, including stopovers in Monte Carlo, Switzerland, and Italy. Harrison, who disappears from the film for a big chunk of the proceedings, is reintroduced in time to patch up his relationship with Merle, who has learned a thing or two about the value of human kindness and sincerity. The unsubstantial comedy was not a big success, and when it played engagements in the States, most critics (especially distaff members) noted that Merle's facial contours were not enhanced by the color photography.

Returning to London after paying a visit to Hollywood in June 1937, Korda proudly announced that he now intended to produce a full roster of features, one of which was to be *Tempest Within* with Merle as the star. This plan did not materialize and Korda then decided on a remake of *Counsel's Opinion,* a low-budget feature he had done in 1933 with Binnie Barnes and Henry Kendall. The 1938 rendition was lavishly mounted in color and filled with imposing British screen names.

The illustrious project emerged as *The Divorce of Lady X* (United Artists, 1938), a sparkling bedroom comedy in the finest sense of the genre. The plot has Merle attend a costume ball at the Royal Park Hotel. Because of the inevitable London fog, she is forced to spend the night at the hotel. Since there is a shortage of rooms, she finds herself cajoling an "impertinent" young barrister (Laurence Olivier) out of his suite, his bed, his pajamas, and his reading matter. The next day, after she has mysteriously departed, he is hired by a titled classmate (Ralph Richardson) to handle a divorce suit. Olivier mistakenly believes Merle to be the woman in question, which would make him the co-respondent to his own suit. In reality, however, it is Richardson's much-divorced, frivolous spouse, Binnie Barnes. As Olivier finds himself falling more deeply in love with the enigmatic, fickle Merle, he subconsciously begins to alter his philosophy on the subject of divorce, causing much confusion in the courtroom, presided over by Merle's grandfather (Morton Selden).

Olivier offers a polished, lighthearted characterization as the smitten barrister, but it is Richardson, as the slowburning, dull-witted peer, who garners the bulk of the adulation, especially for his droll drunk scene. Once again, because this was a color feature, most critics chose to review Merle's array of Rene Hubert outfits, rather than her performance.* This was a pity, for she had indeed learned a great deal about handling Noël Coward-style comedy in her onscreen years. As Frank S. Nugent *(New York Times)* concluded, "[She] enjoys comedy, and vice versa." Merle is especially effective in the opening reels as the brash young debutante who cons intellectual Olivier out of his possessions, without resorting to the cloyingly coquettish posing that many another actress would have utilized in such a scene.

Other Hollywood actresses had sojourned in England for a picture-making spree, including Sylvia Sidney in *Sabotage* (Gaumont British, 1936), Ann Harding in *Love from a Stranger* (United Artists, 1937), Miriam Hopkins in *Men Are Not Gods* (United Artists, 1937), and Ruth Chatterton in *The Rat* (RKO, 1938). However, none of their careers profited particularly from these overseas filmmaking excursions. On the other hand, Merle had not lost any ground by her stay in England: two above-par

---

*It was a toss-up whether Merle was more fetching in the blazer-striped pajamas; the black fur-trimmed suit, with a blue blouse and halo tam; or at the costume ball (in which all the women attempt to be Empress Eugénie) with Merle bedecked in a winterhalter ball dress in white with blue blows on the hoops, and a huge ostrich fan in shades of blue.

comedies that received good distribution in the States, and an abortive epic called off because of her sympathy-gathering automobile accident. Thus, when Goldwyn asked her to come back to America, she returned in the full blossom of stardom, a front-ranking celebrity ready to continue her picture-making activity in Hollywood while not slighting her always ardent and politic socializing.

The picture Goldwyn had in mind for Merle was *Graustark,* and it was to co-star her with Gary Cooper and Sigrid Gurie.* Massive sets were constructed on the Goldwyn backlot, but the day before shooting was to begin on the costume drama, Goldwyn canceled the vehicle. But the iconoclastic producer had a substitute project ready for the Paramount-loaned Cooper and for Merle, who had London commitments to Korda to fulfill.

The idea for *The Cowboy and the Lady* (United Artists, 1938) originally derived from an idea Leo McCarey had about wealthy playgirl Doris Duke (hypothetically) romancing a radio cowboy. McCarey and his collaborator, Frank R. Adams, sold the premise to Goldwyn, who put S. N. Behrman and Sonya Levien to work on a screenplay. Not satisfied with the script, which was called variously, *Spring in My Heart* and *A Kiss in the Sun,* Goldwyn hired Dorothy Parker and Alan Campbell, and then Frederick Lonsdale to doctor the storyline. Finally, coincident with the demise of *Graustark,* a "workable" shooting script was at hand, with William Wyler set to direct. The latter, after a few days on the production, admitted to himself and others an inability to cope with this contemporary cowboy comedy and, in order to be relieved of his duties, he picked a fight with Goldwyn. Wyler was replaced by H. C. Potter, who had directed Merle's *Beloved Enemy.*

By the time the actual shooting on *The Cowboy and the Lady* commenced, Thomas Mitchell had been replaced by Henry Kolker, Benita Hume as Merle's mother had been written out of the story, and in the course of production, David Niven's footage as a representative of the British diplomatic corps was excised from the release print, because his part as an unsuccessful suitor might offend the British filmgoing market. Finally the $1.7 million feature was completed and on November 24, 1938, it debuted at Radio City Music Hall.

"... a moth-eaten tale has received a good deal more than it deserves in this offering," was the verdict of Howard Barnes *(New York Herald-Tribune).* The premise cast Merle as the daughter of presidential candidate Kolker. Because her father is in the political limelight she must live a very decorous existence. When she and her uncle (Harry Davenport) are caught in a nightclub raid, her father orders the rebellious socialite to the family's Palm Beach estate. Once there, she becomes bored, and,

---

*This highly touted Goldwyn discovery, hailed as a Norwegian import, was actually born in the Flatbush section of Brooklyn, New York.

joined by the cook (Patsy Kelly) and the maid (Mabel Todd), she goes out on a triple date with rodeo cowboy Cooper and his two sidekicks (Walter Brennan, Fuzzy Knight). Predictably, it is not long before Merle has tumbled for this prairie knight, but she cannot bring herself to tell him the truth about her identity, even after he has tossed her into the estate swimming pool, she has been spattered in the face with mud, and become entangled with fly paper. Before he returns to Galveston, Texas, he proposes marriage. However, she puts him off, only to discover, after he leaves, that she really loves him. She races to the ship, rushes aboard, and the couple are wed on the high seas. She later returns to Florida to hostess an important political dinner party for her dad, an event interrupted by the unexpected arrival of Cooper. In the tradition of his best all-American everyman crusading, he is shocked to learn the truth of Merle's pedigree, and before barging out of the banquet, he proceeds to tell the gathering "to get off their high horses" and learn to act human. Eventually Davenport makes his brother realize that Merle's happiness means more than a stab at the presidency, and it is Kolker who brings the warring couple together for a happy fade-out.

While Barnes *(Herald-Tribune)* justifiably blasted the film's paucity of entertainment substance, he had a few kind words for Merle's performance: "[She] is properly reticent and properly romantic as the heroine." This description covers some aspects of Merle's emoting in the ninety-one-minute film, but it remained for the British magazine *Country Life* to report, "[She] is handicapped by lighting and costumes which do her face and figure less than justice, and fails moreover to bring to her part that modicum of warmth and liveliness which it so badly needs." In short, Merle and laconic Cooper were not the romantic screen couple of the year, and the comedy antics of Kelly, Todd, Brennan, and Knight could not salvage the slow-as-molasses pacing of director Potter or the predictability of the old-hat storyline. Merle would rehash this less than successful venture on "Lux Radio Theatre" on January 20, 1941 with Gene Autry as Cooper's stand-in.

After the relative debacle of *The Cowboy and the Lady,* Goldwyn was eager to push ahead with another major project of great importance. Not since *Dead End* (United Artists, 1937) had his company enjoyed an artistic success, and while the likes of *The Adventures of Marco Polo* (United Artists, 1938), *The Goldwyn Follies* (1938), and *The Real Glory* (United Artists, 1939) were guaranteed to earn profits for Goldwyn Pictures, the entrepreneur wanted to bedazzle his fellow industry workers and the public with a stunning classic cinema venture.

For over two years, Goldwyn's contract director, William Wyler, had been imploring his boss to venture a screen adaptation of Emily Brontë's 1847 novel, *Wuthering Heights.* As it happened, Walter Wanger owned a screenplay of the brooding novel, turned out by Ben Hecht and Charles

MacArthur, which he planned to use as a starring vehicle for contractees Sylvia Sidney and Charles Boyer. But Sidney balked at the project as unsuitable for her. While Wyler was at Warner Bros. directing Bette Davis in *Jezebel* (1938), there was talk of her starring as Cathy Linton in the projected film, but Jack Warner was too slow in purchasing the screen adaptation, for once Goldwyn heard that there was competition for the vehicle, he relinquished his objections, and *Wuthering Heights* (United Artists, 1939) was announced as a Samuel Goldwyn Production to be directed by William Wyler and starring Merle.

It was Wyler's contention, and one agreed upon by Goldwyn, that the film's cast should all be British. With this notion in mind, Wyler, while vacationing in Europe, met with Laurence Olivier about reteaming with Merle in the picture. The British actor rather reluctantly agreed, although displeased that his wife, Vivien Leigh, was only offered the secondary part of Isabella.*

With the usual lavish Goldwyn production touch, the mounting of *Wuthering Heights* was sumptuous. Above and beyond the meticulously built sections of indoor and outdoor sets on the Goldwyn soundstages, the producer approved the special re-creation of Yorkshire moors, assembled by the studio at Chatsworth in Ventura County, California, resplendent with miles of hot-house heather. But most importantly for the film's artistic well-being, director Wyler's aim was not so much to recapture the actual locales as to create an ambiance situated in the "wilderness of the imagination."

During the course of the lengthy shooting schedule for *Wuthering Heights,* Merle and Olivier, who had worked so compatibly together during the making of *The Divorce of Lady X,* fell into disharmony. It began—on the surface at least—when the director was rehearsing a run-through of the romantic idyll at Penniston Crag. When Olivier happened to sputter somewhat while reciting a line, Merle frigidly demanded, "Please don't spit at me!" The scene was replayed, and again, when the same expectoration occurred, Merle stated icily, "You spat again!" Olivier lost his temper and made some ungentlemanly statement, and before long both stars had stomped off the set. They were eventually recalled by Wyler, and the passionate love scene was shot for the cameras, with the director, if not the co-leads, quite satisfied with their seeming display of emotional fervor.

Adding to the friction on the sets was the fact that Goldwyn soon became disenchanted with Olivier. If it had not been for Wyler's insistence, the mercurial producer might well have shut down the production until Olivier was replaced. Then there was the problem of David Niven, a Goldwyn contractee, who disliked the idea of working with Wyler again

*Geraldine Fitzgerald was eventually hired for the part.

after the actor's miserable experience on *Dodsworth* (United Artists, 1936), and felt uncomfortable portraying Merle's cuckolded husband (Edgar Linton) when it was well known in the film colony that he and Merle had been romantically involved on and off for the past few years. Niven eventually acceded to Goldwyn's and Wyler's implorings to take the role.

Wuthering Heights was finally completed at a cost of about $1.8 million, edited, and made ready for its premiere at Manhattan's Rivoli Theatre on April 13, 1939.* The critics seemed more insistent on displaying to their readers a thorough knowledge of Brontë's original book and how it had been altered for the screen, than in judging the film on its own merits. There was a hue and cry that the story's setting had been transformed from the Regency to the Georgian period (because Goldwyn thought Merle would look better in Georgian costumes), that the tale was now framed by the old housekeeper (Flora Robson) telling a snow-bound stranger of the strange myth of romantic tragedy hovering about the estate of Wuthering Heights, and that the second generation of characters in the novel had been omitted from the screenplay.

Despite the criticisms of the film, there was a general degree of hosannas, with some reviewers even daring to prefer the movie to the book original. ". . . a strong and somber film, poetically written as the novel not always was, sinister and wild as it was meant to be, far more compact dramatically than Miss Brontë had made it" (Frank S. Nugent, *New York Times*). At the time, Olivier's performance, which in retrospect is the sturdiest aspect of the film, was questioned for being so brooding, scowling, churlish, with bouts of temperament (as the book indicates) as if demon-possessed, and then suddenly so brimming over with wild tenderness. Nevertheless, he was Oscar-nominated, but he lost to Robert Donat of *Goodbye, Mr. Chips* (MGM).

On the other hand, Merle's performance was considered to be more in keeping with the tenor of cinema-leading-lady playing. "She has perfectly caught the restless, changeling spirit of the Brontë heroine who knew she was not meant for heaven and broke her heart and Heathcliff's in the synthetic paradise of her marriage with gentle Edgar Linton" (Nugent, *New York Times*). "Miss Oberon gives an immensely versatile characterization of Cathy and rises to a fine pitch of intensity in her final death scene" (Howard Barnes, *New York Herald-Tribune*). There is no denying that Merle was at her most attractive in this film, whether rushing across the wind-swept heather moors to cling in Olivier's arms, splashing in her copper bath tub, or being properly flirtatious with the swain Niven. However, in her dramatic moments, Merle leaves a good deal to be desired in her performance: whether in a panic as Niven's estate

*Merle was heard in a condensation trailer of *Wuthering Heights* on the "Kate Smith Hour" (March 30, 1939) with Santos Ortega as Heathcliffe.

With John Garrick in THE BROKEN MELODY
(Associated Producers & Distributors '34)

With Emlyn Williams
in MEN OF
TOMORROW (Par. '32)

With Douglas Fairbanks in **THE PRIVATE LIFE OF DON JUAN** (UA '34)

h Herbert Marshall in THE DARK ANGEL (UA '35)

With Joel McCrea, Alma Kruger, and Miriam Hopkins in THESE THREE
(UA '36)

With Brian Aherne in BELOVED ENEMY (UA '36)

With Rex Harrison in
OVER THE MOON
(UA '37)

With Laurence Olivier
in WUTHERING
HEIGHTS (UA '39)

With Doris Lloyd and
Geraldine Fitzgerald
in 'TIL WE MEET
AGAIN (WB '40)

With Reginald Gardiner, Anna Neagle, and Mary Pickford at a Hollywood radio broadcast for the benefit of the Canadian Red Cross (September 29, 1940)

With husband Sir Alexander Korda at Shrine Auditorium, Los Angeles (1941)

With George Reeves in LYDIA (UA '41)

With Clyde Cook and Robert Cummings in FOREVER AND A DAY (RKO '43)

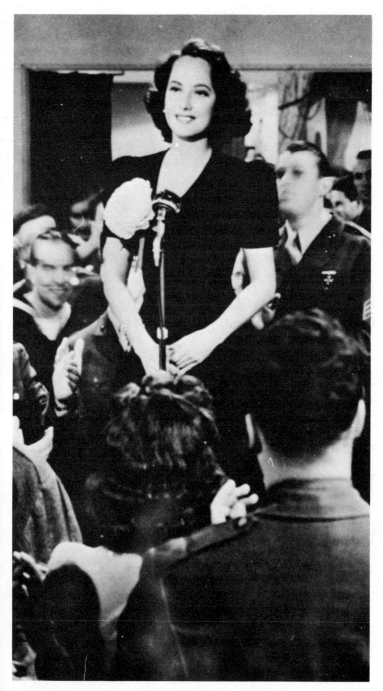

In STAGE DOOR CANTEEN (UA '43)

dogs growl at her feet, or countering Olivier's statement that she is "a vain cheap worldly fool" by calling him " a stable boy," or, most of all, failing to convey credibility in the finale where she must convince the audience, "I am Heathcliff!" and later dies in Olivier's arms. As Richard Griffith judged in his booklet *Samuel Goldwyn* (1956): "Miss Oberon shows early in the film that she understands very completely that everything pivots on her ability to show herself linked to Heathcliff by an intangible bond which sets the two apart from all the world, but as her performance progresses she seems less and less able to realize the 'wild Cathy' whom Ellen [Flora Robson] laments at the end. Torn and dying on her pillow, she is unbelievably beautiful and touching but the character has lost its tone of other-worldliness." Merle's performance as the fiery, impetuous girl who loves the strong-willed gypsy stable boy was not Oscar-nominated.* It must have given Olivier some moments of ironic amusement that his wife, Vivien, who had been refused the key role of the ambitious girl who wants to be "the finest lady in the county," should win the Academy Award that year for her performance in *Gone with the Wind* (MGM, 1939).

While 1939 was certainly a year for tearjerkers, with Bette Davis's *Dark Victory*† and Donat's *Goodbye, Mr. Chips, Variety* predicted tough sledding for *Wuthering Heights* with rural audiences: "Its general sombreness and psychological tragedy is too heavy for general appeal." It was not until 1963, when Goldwyn nationally reissued *Wuthering Heights,* before leasing the televison rights, that the picture made some actual profit.‡

Almost immediately after completing *Wuthering Heights,* Merle took ill and a medicine was prescribed to which she was allergic. "I got a sulphanilamide infection. It went all over my face. I was blessed with beautiful skin up until then, but this scarred my face. I wouldn't go out for the longest time. I lost a year—from my work too."

Over a five-year period, the very professionally successful and socially popular Merle had been romantically linked with a variety of men on two continents. Usually the relationship would terminate, however,

*In a 1973 interview, Merle admitted that this "was my favorite film. She's like me, Cathy. Maybe I'm not as wild, but I can be quite wild, you know. Give me a walk on the beach or a lovely sunrise and I'm happy."

In Wyler's original shooting script, the ill-fated lovers are not reunited until after death. After the movie was completed, Goldwyn decided he did not like the notion of Olivier's final scene being his frozen body slumped over Oberon's grave, so he added a new finale in which the couple's ghostly figures meet at their favorite hiding place on the moors and walk off together into the heavenly mist. The ghosts were enacted by stand-ins, as the stars had gone off to other work.

†The film rights to this property, based on a shortlived Broadway drama starring Tallulah Bankhead, had originally been purchased by Goldwyn as a vehicle for Merle.

‡*Wuthering Heights*, on a far more pedestrian scale, would be remade in 1971 by American International Pictures with Timothy Dalton as Heathcliff and Anna Calder-Marshall as Cathy.

when Merle made it quite clear that her film career was more important than marriage. Then, on Saturday, June 3, 1939, she was quietly married to Alexander Korda in a civil ceremony at the town hall in the French city of Antibes. Mayor Jules Grec presided, with Henri Guenot of Juan-les-Pins, and Mme. Suzanne Blum, a Paris lawyer, as witnesses. Merle was then twenty-eight; Korda was forty-six.

In September 1939, the newlyweds were in Korda's London offices when the announcement was made that Great Britain was at war with Nazi Germany. Merle wept, but Korda, anxious to serve the country which had so graciously adopted him, borrowed on his life insurance policy to produce a British documentary, *The Lion Has Wings* (United Artists, 1939). Four days after the declaration of war by Prime Minister Neville Chamberlain, the film went into production at the Denham Studios and twelve days later, the $150,000 project was completed. It was the first of the official British propaganda pictures to reach America. In this part-documentary, part-dramatic film, there is a good deal of footage devoted to justifying Britain's war stand; while the second segment weaves a slight story around the development and activities of the Royal Air Force.* Within the story section, Merle appears as the nurse-wife of a Royal Air Force officer (Ralph Richardson). Her most effective moment occurs when she and another girl sit silently listening to Chamberlain's declaration of war on the radio, and then, as the news makes its impact on the two women, "God Save the King" is played on the soundtrack.

Not only did Korda feel that Merle ought to return to America for safety now that England was at war, but she had been offered a new studio home base at Warner Bros. That studio's boss, Jack L. Warner, was well aware that Merle and Goldwyn had reached an impasse regarding her future status with Samuel Goldwyn Productions, and that she and Goldwyn had not been able to reach an agreement for her to portray Lily Langtry in *The Westerner* (United Artists, 1940).† With her Goldwyn tenure ended, Warner invited Merle to join the Burbank roster, which then included such diverse distaff talent as Bette Davis, Miriam Hopkins (another ex-Goldwyn star), Olivia de Havilland, Priscilla Lane, and such fast-rising Warner actresses as Ida Lupino, Ann Sheridan, Jane Bryan, and Jane Wyman.

Warner offered to give Merle the red-carpet treatment, and Hollywood observers were insistent that the movie mogul was indicating that Bette Davis's days as queen of the lot were numbered. Merle accepted the picture pact and departed for Hollywood. Korda followed a few months later.

*Herbert Cohn (*Brooklyn Daily Eagle*) complained, "We expected something more entertaining to spice Lowell Thomas' factual sound track than a few well-directed sequences of exciting air action [referring to the restaged RAF raids on the German armada at the mouth of the Kiel Canal]."
†Lillian Bond was given the part.

By the time Merle reached California she discovered that the shifting star-status situation at Warner Bros. was not quite what she had pictured it would be. She was handed two projects which Davis had already rejected. The first was *'Til We Meet Again* (Warner Bros., 1940), a remake of the well-remembered *One Way Passage* (Warner Bros., 1932), which had featured Kay Francis and William Powell. As with many rehashes of past cinema successes, the new edition did not, and could not, live up to its glorious predecessor.

As Joan Ames, Merle is the restless socialite who encounters Dapper Dan Hardesty (George Brent) in the Bar of All Nations in Hong Kong. The newly introduced couple drink a Paradise cocktail together, acknowledging that it is an ambrosia "for everyone who knows that every second is important." It then develops that each is to be a passenger on a vessel docked in the harbor, which is leaving Hong Kong for San Francisco, However, neither party realizes that this is a one-way passage: Merle is suffering from a fatal heart condition, Brent is being escorted back to San Quentin by law-enforcer Pat O'Brien and is to be executed on a murder charge. Aboard ship, the doomed couple engage in a passionate romance, with Brent passing up a chance to escape during the Honolulu stopover because Merle suddenly succumbs to a fainting spell. Once docked in the Northern California harbor, they bid each other goodbye, making plans to meet on New Year's Eve at the Palace Bar in Mexico, but each knows he/she will not be able to keep the appointment. As in the original (but handled in a far more pragmatic, unspiritual manner), when the designated time comes, the viewer sees two glasses at the bar rise in a toast, and then break. Neither Merle nor Brent imparted sufficient conviction to their ill-fated romance, robbing the drama of its potential four-handkerchief status. Rather it was Frank McHugh (repeating his role from the original film) as the good-natured con artist, Binnie Barnes as the phony countess, and Geraldine Fitzgerald as the little-seen, but engagingly enthusiastic tourist, who gave this Edmund Goulding-directed effort its major entertainment value. Merle, Brent, and O'Brien repeated their roles on "Lux Radio Theatre" (June 10, 1940).

Between contract commitments at Warners, Merle joined with Melvyn Douglas and Burgess Meredith in *That Uncertain Feeling* (United Artists, 1941), directed by Ernst Lubitsch, who had helmed an earlier version of the marital tale (*Kiss Me Again* [Warner Bros., 1925]). It was a "pinprick satire on psychoanalysis" (*New York Times*) made in the days before that subject became passé, and it should have been much funnier than it was. After six years of marriage, Merle finds it rather strange that she has trouble sleeping nights, while her insurance-executive spouse (Douglas) can snore blithely right through the dark hours. She consults Dr. Vengard (Alan Mowbray), a rather melodramatic psychoanalyst who proceeds to make Merle marriage-conscious and insists that her hiccups are a manifestation of her discontent. Adding to her domestic woes, she meets wacky concert pianist Meredith, another of Mowbray's patients, who not only proceeds to move into Merle's Park Avenue household but almost succeeds in gaining a permanent foothold in her romantically confused heart. One of the more amusing aspects of this frou-frou is the repeated use of offbeat word sounds by the starring trio. Merle is constantly mumbling "whoosh" in competition with her husband's snoring, Douglas always taps Merle in the ribs and utters "keeks" every time he wants to make a point, and the madcap Meredith is continually berating everything with a definitive "phooey."

Variety unhappily reported of *That Uncertain Feeling,* "The famed Lubitsch touch is there but the entertainment value isn't." Merle appeared appropriately beautiful in her Irene wardrobe, and she even sparkled in one deft comedy sequence in which she bounds into Douglas's hotel room, convinced that she will find his secretary (Eve Arden) there in a compromising position. However, as Theodore Strauss (*New York Times*) related, "[Merle] still has something to learn as a comedienne . . ."

It was rather unfortunate for the welfare of Merle's screen career that the same day *That Uncertain Feeling* opened at Radio City Music Hall (May 1, 1941), *Affectionately Yours* (Warner Bros.) debuted at the nearby Strand Theatre. More than three years after the screwball-comedy movie cycle had died, this weak entry attempted to revive it. But said Howard Barnes (*New York Herald-Tribune*), "[It] sets something of a record in synthetic showmanship." Merle was badly miscast as the distraught wife of war correspondent Dennis Morgan, who decides a Reno divorce trip would be more appropriate than waiting for her errant, globe-trotting husband to make another brief appearance on the homefront. When Morgan hears the unwanted news, he sets out to re-court Merle, meeting obstacles on three fronts: from the disbelieving Merle, who is now dating a hayseed, wealthy Romeo (Ralph Bellamy); from Morgan's harassed city editor (James Gleason), who would prefer Morgan to remain matrimonially unattached so he will return to the European theatre of war; and from Rita Hayworth, a fellow journalist who would now like to pin down Morgan's promise that everything would be different between them if only he were single. For much needed, if stereotyped, comedy relief, there are Hattie McDaniel and Butterfly McQueen as two black household domestics, George Tobias as a befuddled Turkish photographer, and an occasional moment when Merle and Morgan go wacky à la Carole Lombard-William Powell of *Mr. and Mrs. Smith* (RKO, 1941) or Myrna Loy-William Powell of *Love Crazy* (MGM, 1941). Merle received some of the worst film reviews of her career. "[She] seems unequal to the task of essaying a type of role so skillfully handled in the past several years by Carole Lombard and more lately by Rosalind Russell" (*Variety*). " . . .

the dignity she tries to bring to the part coupled with her precise British accent tends to throw the film out of kilter" (Gilbert Kanour, *Baltimore Evening Sun*). It just seemed that it was not Merle's cup of tea to join forces oncamera with an unmitigated heel (Morgan) and engage in such unbecoming shenanigans as falling off a pier into the cold water.*

Her agent Myron Selznick, obtained Merle's release from her Warners contract, leaving Joan Fontaine to play the heroine of *The Constant Nymph* (1943), a property that had been purchased with Merle in mind. She then joined in a filmmaking venture with Korda, entitled *Lydia* (United Artists), directed by Julien Duvivier and based on the Frenchman's story, which had formed the basis of his earlier, very well received *Un Carnet de Bal* (French, 1937).† This was Merle's first opportunity to work with Korda as his wife, and she suddenly became very aware of production costs. In September 1941, she told Kyle Crichton of *Collier's* magazine: "I am a star—and what do I get? I get into a stew because too much time is being taken up with shooting. I'm a nut."

As Lydia, Merle ages from sixteen to sixty within the course of the 144-minute black-and-white feature. Three hours a day were required for the elderly-woman makeup, which meant that Merle rose every workday at 5:30 A.M. and labored in front of the camera until ten at night. But, since it was for a family cause, she seemingly did not mind too terribly. After all, it was a different type of screen role that afforded her a glorious opportunity to jump out of the confining glamour-girl mold.

Within *Lydia*, Merle is first displayed as an elderly spinster who is the honored guest at the opening of a new orphanage, one of her pet charities. At the gathering, she encounters a physician suitor (Joseph Cotten) from the past. He asks how she has spent the intervening years. She wistfully replies, ". . . [with] work . . . and some memories of you, Bob, Frank and Michael—and a ghost." Two days later Cotten invites her to a special reunion, to become reacquainted with her swains from four decades ago. As the group reminisce at Cotten's Central Park West penthouse apartment, the viewer is afforded a flashback memory book of Merle's carefree courtship years. She had lived in Boston's Back Bay, her upbringing supervised by her crusty grandmother (Edna May Oliver), the widow of a sea captain. There was Bob Willard (George Reeves) a Harvard football hero—1897 style—who had proposed that they elope—only he became drunk on their Quincy outing, and she finds herself going back to Oliver's home. Cotten was the thoughtful son of the family butler (John Halliday) and Oliver's favorite choice for Merle's hand in marriage; certainly a more likely prospect than blind musician Frank Audry (Hans Yaray). But Merle had the

---

*At one point in the helter-skelter proceedings, Merle turns to Morgan and Bellamy and implores, "Will you two stop acting like children?"

†Marie Bell had the focal role as the woman looking back on a life filled with romantic wrong moves.

misfortune to meet and fall instantly in love with seafaring Richard Mason (Alan Marshal) with whom she spent two heavenly weeks at Macmillansport, before he sailed away, leaving her a note that implies there is another woman in his life. As the lachrymose tale is brought up to date, the expected climactic event occurs—Marshal makes his appearance. The nosegay story ends with an ironic twist, for the aged Marshal has completely forgotten her, leaving Merle and the viewer pondering her foolishness in staking so much of her unfulfilled life on such a scapegrace.

In a year that saw Greer Garson age and mature magnificently in *Blossoms in the Dust* (MGM) and schoolteacher Martha Scott gain insight with the passing, unselfish years in *Cheers for Miss Bishop* (United Artists), Merle's handling of this romantic chronicle lacked the definition of characterization required for her pivotal role. ". . . only occasionally [does she] show the strength and conviction that such a task requires" (Leo Mishkin, *New York Morning Telegraph*). Or, as Bosley Crowther (*New York Times*) phrased it, "Miss Oberon is lively and beguiling in her countless costumes as an Eighteen-Nineties girl and she pleasantly conveys a spirit of rapture and innocence. As an old woman she is disappointing." Merle would repeat her *Lydia* assignment, along with Oliver and Marshal, on "Lux Radio Theatre" (September 22, 1941). It has remained a particularly favorite part with her. As she said at the time, "I never really acted until now. I just said those words and let it go at that. Korda makes me give out."

By the end of 1941, Merle was busily involved with radio work on behalf of the USO and the British War Relief. Whatever proceeds she gained from her appearances were reinvested in funds aimed at shortening the war. Over CBS radio, she was heard on the Conrad Nagel-hosted "Silver Theatre" in a specially written, patriotic episode, *I Love Thee*. She was often a guest on radio's "Stage Door Canteen" for which a studio was remodeled to resemble an actual servicemen's canteen, where Bert Lytel was the congenial emcee.

Korda, who in 1942 was knighted, thus making Merle Lady Korda, commuted back and forth between America and England during the early 1940s by whatever transportation means were available to him, usually in a bomber plane. From London in mid-1942, he announced plans to film Leo Tolstoy's *War and Peace* in Canada, with Merle in the role of Natasha.* These plans were abandoned, however, due to the monumental task of adapting the marathon epic novel into script form and conforming to wartime production strictures.

After an absence of a year and a half from the screen, Merle joined seventy-eight other British performers who worked without pay in *Forever and a Day* (RKO, 1943). In gratitude for American contributions to British War Relief, seven directors and producers and twenty-one writers of Holly-

---

*In Paramount's *War and Peace* (1956), Audrey Hepburn played Natasha, while in the Russian-made version (1969) Lyudmila Savelyeva had the part.

wood's English colony, along with the many actors, put together an episode chronicle of a stately London house built in 1804 by Sir. C. Aubrey Smith and depicted its various inhabitants down through the years until its near destruction in 1943 by a Nazi bomb. All U.S. profits on the feature went to the National Foundation for Infantile Paralysis and the American Red Cross. Merle appeared in the film as a desk clerk. The highlight of the 104-minute film proved to be Buster Keaton's near-pantomime bit as a plumber's assistant having the devil of a time with a newfangled bathtub.

Merle played herself in a brief scene in the film *Stage Door Canteen* (United Artists, 1943), most of the proceeds of which went to furthering the cause of the American Theatre Wing School for young actors. Katharine Hepburn was the ostensible marquee lure in this all-star variety entry, hooked around a loose tale of romance at the Forty-fourth Street social retreat for servicemen. "This may not be the picture to arouse the sophisticates," reported Bosley Crowther (*New York Times*), "but it will fetch honest thrills, tears and laughter from millions throughout the land." There were enough contrasting star luminaries to trip over one another, with such specialty acts as Yehudi Menuhin performing "Ave Maria" and "Flight of the Bumblebee" on the violin, Ethel Waters singing "Quick Sands," George Jessel recreating his evergreen telephone routine, Xavier Cugat and his Orchestra with Lina Romay executing "She's a Bombshell from Brooklyn," Katharine Cornell in a bit from *Romeo and Juliet*, and Kenny Baker vocalizing "Good Night, Sweetheart." Merle was seen greeting some Chinese visitors at the canteen.

Merle finished out the year by reteaming with her *Beloved Enemy* co-star, Brian Aherne, in *First Comes Courage* (Columbia, 1943), a threadbare espionage adventure tale, originally called *Attack by Night*. By this time during the years of World War II, the global cinema had delved into almost every conceivable (commercial) variation of the commando-spy drama, and what had not been unreeled onscreen in 1942 in *The Adventures of Tartu* (MGM) and *The Commandos Strike at Dawn* (Columbia) was presented in 1943 with *This Land Is Mine* (RKO), *Assignment in Brittany* and *The Edge of Darkness* (Warner Bros.), and *The Moon Is Down* (Twentieth Century-Fox). This situation did not leave much room for a wearisome B-formula drama like *First Comes Courage*, whose "authors and director have failed to stamp it with any distinction or depth of conviction" (Theodore Strauss, *New York Times*).

Under Dorothy Arzner's pedestrian handling, Merle offered an indifferent performance as a seeming Norwegian quisling who, in reality, is pandering to Nazi garrison commandant Carl Esmond in order to obtain information for forthcoming RAF bombing raids. When she weds Esmond, the townfolk of Stravig ostracize her, leaving her to her own devices to sneak out the invaluable information to Allied contacts. As fate would have it, Aherne, her former lover, is a British commando sent to the occupied land to make preparations for an invasion. After he has killed Esmond, Aherne offers her the chance to find safety in England, but she nobly chooses to remain behind to become the paramour of Esmond's successor.

In March 1943, Korda resumed a full-time career in London after negotiating a merger between London Films and MGM's British interests, which involved a $10 million production schedule. Merle chose to maintain her residence in California, with infrequent visits to London by any available transportation. She lived quietly in the Kordas' tastefully furnished Bel Air home, where she served tea every afternoon to her guests. She saw few people except the wives of Fred Astaire, David O. Selznick, and Darryl F. Zanuck.

During this time she embarked on a freelance status and starred in *The Lodger* (Twentieth Century-Fox, 1944)* as an 1889 London music-hall can-can dancer named Kitty. The John Brahm-directed feature is not a whodunit thriller because almost from the start one is aware that Laird Cregar, as the psychopathic Jack the Ripper figure, is the mad fiend whom Scotland Yard is doing its best to capture. Instead, the film becomes a tale of suspense, hopefully making the viewer wonder just where or when Cregar, the new boarder in the Sara Allgood-Cedric Hardwicke home, will attack and try to kill the latter's attractive niece (Merle). By the time bulky Cregar has set his sights on Merle, her Scotland Yard beau (George Sanders) has deduced the villain's identity and is on hand to pump the maniac full of bullets. Cinematographer Lucien Ballard, who would become Merle's second husband, was lauded for his camera work in capturing the shadowy eeriness of fog-bound London during the gas-light era. In one sequence it is Ballard's camera which becomes the Ripper as Cregar determinedly pursues a shaking, gasping victim (Doris Lloyd).

As the coquette, Merle had her most attractive screen role in some time, appearing most tantalizing in her abbreviated stage costumes, and performing a few rowdy French-type music-hall numbers. It was quite apparent that Merle was more at ease in her dramatic-romantic moments than in the musical-comedy sequence, in which her singing was dubbed. (The following year, Fox would turn out *Hangover Square*, a variation on *The Lodger*, with contract players Laird Cregar and George Sanders again co-starred under John Brahm's direction, but with studio favorite Linda Darnell in the female lead.)

Next on Merle's agenda came *Dark Waters* (United Artists, 1944), another Gothic thriller, but this time set in the lurking Louisiana swamps. It was one of the mild sleepers of the year and received sturdy notices. Merle is Leslie Calvin, an emotionally shaken survivor of a torpedoed ship on which her parents were drowned. She arrives at her musky home in bayou country to learn that a quartet of guardians have taken over: an aunt

*Previously filmed twice in England, in 1926 and 1932, both times starring Ivor Novello.

(Fay Bainter) and uncle (John Qualen) who are strangers to her, and their friends, Mr. Sydney (Thomas Mitchell) and Cleeve the overseer (Elisha Cook, Jr.). Through a series of well-staged "hallucinations" and a timed recording of an eerie voice calling her from the misty distance, Merle is soon convinced she is losing her sanity. With the conviction of a doomed soul, she moans, "Under the water, that's where I belong—Under the water with my mother and father." With the help of a black plantation hand (Rex Ingram), she unravels the truth that her actual relatives are dead in the bayou, and that the imposters are clearly after her valuable property. With the aid of country doctor Franchot Tone, the culprits (those who survive) are apprehended. Merle repeated her well-modulated characterization on "Lux Radio Theatre" (November 27, 1944) with Preston Foster and Mitchell as her co-players.

George Sand (pseudonym of Amandine Aurore Lucile Dudevant, née Dupin, 1804-1876) was a famous nineteenth-century novelist-poetess and one of the forerunners of the women's lib movement.* She often wore men's clothing, which coincided with her passion for dominating whatever man happened to be her lover. She was depicted by Merle in *A Song to Remember* (Columbia, 1945), directed by Charles Vidor. Sidney Buchman, who produced the Technicolor film, was also responsible for the unsatisfactory screenplay, giving little intrinsic support to this overblown entry in the 1940s music-composer biopic cycle.† Cornel Wilde is the Polish patriot, pianist, and composer Frédéric Chopin (1810-1849), while Paul Muni—in the key role—is his old professor, Joseph Elsner. The real stars of the pseudocultural picture were José Iturbi (unbilled because of his MGM contract), who provided the offcamera piano playing for Wilde, and cinematographers Tony Gaudio and Allen Davey, who successfully captured the multi-hued richness of mid-nineteenth-century Paris.

In this *very* fictionalized film, Wilde encounters the pants-clad young authoress Merle soon after his arrival in Paris. She advises him to "discontinue that so-called Polonaise jumble you've been playing for days" and write pretty waltzes that will sell. When, during the course of their decade-long romance, she advises him against going on tour to raise money for Poland, he goes against her wishes and she is finished with him. She later attempts a reconciliation, but he refuses. As he lies dying of con-

---

*William Wyler had tried to interest Samuel Goldwyn back in 1938 in filming a biography of George Sand-Frédéric Chopin, with Marlene Dietrich, but Goldwyn was not interested, and Wyler's negotiations with Columbia's Harry Cohn fell through, although the latter acquired the screen rights to the story, which became on film *A Song to Remember*.

†Cary Grant as Cole Porter (*Night and Day*, Warner Bros., 1944); Robert Alda as George Gershwin (*Rhapsody in Blue*, Warner Bros., 1945); Robert Walker as Jerome Kern (*Till the Clouds Roll By*, MGM, 1946); Paul Henreid as Robert Schumann and Robert Walker as Johannes Brahms (*The Song of Love*, MGM, 1947); Jean-Pierre Aumont as Rimsky-Korsakoff (*Song of Scheherazade*, Universal, 1947); and Mickey Rooney and Tom Drake as Lorenz Hart and Richard Rodgers (*Words and Music*, MGM, 1948).

sumption, having hemorrhaged vividly across the white keyboards, he sends for her, but she is too preoccupied posing for a portrait and cannot be bothered. "Continue, Monsieur Delacroix," she orders the artist.

A Song to Remember only comes alive as film entertainment during the early sections in which Wilde is struggling for recognition in Warsaw and then in Paris. Thereafter it bogs down into a purposeful picture of patriotism (tied in with parallels to the mid-1940s world situation), and is further overweighed by Muni's scene-stealing as the rascally old instructor who demands that Wilde use his music to aid Poland's liberation from tyranny. Wilde was to be commended for controlling his performance as the overly romantic composer so easily controlled by others, but Merle was not at her histrionic best playing a villainous (rather than the inspirational force she was in reality) life innovator. She did have one very effective scene, best described by contemporary reporter Thomas Pryor (*New York Times*): ". . . the parting with Chopin, which she plays to perfection. The audience burst into spontaneous applause upon the conclusion of that scene, a unique tribute."

The majority of reviewers preferred commenting on Merle's array of unique costumes in *A Song to Remember*, in which she struts about in pants, tailcoat, vest, and bow tie, and smokes cigars. *Life* magazine discovered that "[she] has a nineteenth century face, and the garb of a Parisienne of the 1840s suits her well." *Newsweek* magazine reported, "Despite the handicap of her own photogenic qualities, Merle Oberon bears a reasonable resemblance to the novelist . . ."* Merle claimed that she enjoyed playing the role of George Sand but that it drained her emotionally. "Sand is not what I am," she informed *Life*. "I am not a predatory woman." She went on to describe herself as "just a sentimental slob." Ironically, despite the "vague, soulless and often dull" (*New York Times*) aspects of *A Song to Remember*, the film made a profit for Harry Cohn's Columbia Pictures.

In December 1944, soon after completing her work as George Sand, Merle announced to the press that she was separating from Sir Alexander, because, among other reasons, she had only seen him for brief visits since he returned to England in 1943. "I feel so awful," she claimed, "Alex and I have been friends for such a long time. I hope everything will be all right with us as friends." On June 26, 1946, she obtained a divorce from Korda in Juarez, Mexico.† The same day she wed Lucien Keith Ballard

---

*In fact, the actress was far more attractive than the stark, if striking, real-life personality. Thus Otis L. Guernsey, Jr. (*New York Herald-Tribune*) noted that Merle's "doll-like face is undoubtedly an improvement over that of the famous author." In 1960, Patricia Morison was an equally striking George Sand in Columbia's *Song without End*, the story of Franz Liszt. In the 1974 BBC-TV special *George: Portrait of a Woman*, Rosemary Harris portrayed George Sand.

†Korda would wed Alexandra Irene Boycun in 1953; the producer-director died on January 23, 1956, in London, at the age of sixty-two.

by proxy, as he was then at work in Hollywood.* Merle was then thirty-four (although she gave her age as thirty); Ballard was thirty-seven.

Merle then signed for a trio of pictures at Universal, the home base of Deanna Durbin, Maria Montez, and the upcoming Yvonne De Carlo. Merle's first assignment was *This Love of Ours* (1945), adapted by Bruce Manning from Luigi Pirandello's play, *Come Prima Meglio de Prima.* William Dieterle directed and, not surprisingly, Ballard was cinematographer on the tearjerker tale, a morose soap opera that Thomas M. Pryor (*New York Times*) insisted was "about as captivating as a funeral dirge, but is exquisitely acted by Merle Oberon and Charles Korvin, once you accept the fact that their behavior is more juvenile than adult." Told through flashback, the somber romance relates how Parisian musical-comedy star Merle sprains her ankle at the club and is treated in her dressing room by handsome French interne Korvin. When her troupe moves on, she remains behind to become the poor but happy housewife of the young physician. Thereafter, they have a daughter and life seems complete, that is (and herein lies the weakest point of the plotline), until Korvin pays heed to the malicious gossip of some shoppers in a bakeshop. He becomes convinced that Merle has been unfaithful, grabs their daughter, and rushes out of her life. Ten years pass, and Korvin finds himself in Chicago at a medical convention. While slumming on the town, whom does he encounter but Merle, now the diverting assistant of wise and witty caricaturist Claude Rains. There is the obvious reconciliation after he saves her from a suicide attempt, but then arises the "insurmountable" problem of how to introduce Merle into Korvin's household, for their teenaged daughter (Sue England) believes mama is dead. In fact, she has built a garden shrine to the dear lady's memory. Through trauma, heartache, and faith, the trio manage to rebuild a happy household. If the story seems familiar, it was more recently utilized for Universal's remake, entitled *Never Say Goodbye* (1956), with Rock Hudson, Cornell Borchers, and George Sanders in the pivotal roles.

In the course of her already lengthy film career, Merle had transcended her Korda period, followed by her Goldwyn years, the brief Warners era, and now a new span as a freelancer. From *This Love of Ours* onward, it became apparent that Merle was more intent on preserving the illusion on-camera (and off) of her youthful looks than on extending the range and depth of her acting. Otis L. Guernsey, Jr. (*New York Herald-Tribune*) offered what was to become a fairly typical review for Merle's onscreen emoting, "Though she is always poised and attractive, Miss Oberon's performance is accented on posing with her face, a white mask to cover her emotion, with very few changes of pace."

*Ballard was assistant to Lee Garmes on Josef von Sternberg's *Morocco* (Paramount, 1930), with the director giving Ballard his big break as co-cinematographer on *The Devil Is a Woman* (Paramount, 1935) and as cameraman on *Crime and Punishment* (Columbia, 1935).

In the mid-1930s, producer Walter Wanger had planned to film a Technicolor version of George S. Hellman's novel *Peacock's Feather,* with silverblonde RKO star Ann Harding. It was not until a decade later that the project came into being, lensed at Universal in April 1945 and released a year later as *A Night in Paradise.* Wanger, who always had a yen for exotic Far Eastern tales, had enjoyed great success with his *Arabian Nights* (Universal, 1942), which launched Maria Montez's rise to fame at that studio, where she would be teamed again with handsome, if wooden, Jon Hall in other tropical erotica. However, by the mid-1940s, audience tastes had changed, as Wanger's *Salome, Where She Danced* (Universal, 1945) with Yvonne De Carlo unfortuitously demonstrated. But Wanger was not to be thwarted in his ambitions, and *A Night in Paradise* came into being, with Merle as the Persian queen, Delerai.

Even the mild-mannered Dorothy Masters of the *New York Daily News* had to admit that this would-be epic was the "spoofingest artistry of the season." It was difficult to take anything seriously in this fable of love and adventure in the court of King Croesus (Thomas Gomez) in the year 580 B.C. Gale Sondergaard made an overwrought, campy appearance as the sorceress Attossa, who seeks revenge when Merle, and not she, is chosen to wed Gomez. But none of the parties concerned had counted on the arrival of Aesop (Turhan Bey), the ambassador from Samos, who is hopeful of preventing Gomez's Lydians from invading his country. First disguised as an old man, Bey fails to arouse Merle's interest, but when he sheds his makeup, she is first shocked and then aroused by his handsomeness.

The Ballards were professionally reunited for *Temptation* (Universal, 1946), yet another screen rendition of Robert Hichens's *Bella Donna,* which had been a Broadway play in 1912 with Nazimova as the star.* In this version, Merle is presented as an unprincipled, impeccably gowned temptress with an hourglass figure in 1900s wardrobe. She convinces staid archeologist George Brent to marry her. She then travels with him to Egypt, where, while he is excavating the tomb of Rameses V, she takes a blackmailer (Charles Korvin) as her lover. She then sets out to slowly poison Brent, but midway through her evil task she decides that he is the man whom she really loves, and thereupon feeds the poisoned powder to Korvin. To pacify the Production Code Office, Merle meets a tragic fate shortly after she and Brent are reconciled. Universal's advertising campaign asked, "Who Was She . . . this woman called Ruby?" But any seasoned filmgoer knew it was merely Merle in a new situation premise which would allow her to display an enticing (Victorian) wardrobe, while going through rather one-dimensional paces.

John Cromwell directed Merle's only 1947 release, RKO's *Night Song.* The soggy premise asked the question whether a wealthy San Francisco music lover (Merle) can provide sufficient love rather than pity for an em-

*One of the more notable picturizations was Pola Negri's version for Paramount in 1923.

bittered blind composer (Dana Andrews) who has a great concerto roaming around his brain? Of course! To accomplish her noble aim, she pretends to him that she is also poor and blind, and the sap falls for her. When his genius comes to the fore and he wins the $5,000 prize in the music contest Merle has created, he has an operation that restores his sight. But he cannot bring himself to return to his poor, blind girlfriend. Merle then goes to him, revealing herself as the girl she really is, and the situation is resolved when she performs a piece of music which they shared when each was "blind." The redeeming aspects of the film were Ethel Barrymore as Merle's advice-giving grandmother, Hoagy Carmichael as Andrews's seeing-eye friend who is a deft hand at the keyboard, and Artur Rubinstein and the New York Philharmonic Orchestra under Eugene Ormandy's direction, performing Leith Stevens's specially composed piece, Concerto in C Minor.* *Cue* magazine branded the film a "completely unbelievable drama." However, since the picture was produced by master movie columnist Louella Parsons's daughter, Harriet, *Night Song* received far more attention than it rightfully deserved.

Meanwhile, Merle, with Ballard as her husband-escort, was becoming well known as one of Hollywood's most resourceful party givers. Louella Parsons told the world, via her fan-magazine-style column: "Maybe it's a hangover from her days as Lady Korda, but Merle lives in great luxury. Even when she is entertaining twenty or thirty, it's usually a formal 'sit down' dinner." Those in the cinema city who were well acquainted with Merle called her "Princess," and knew that she hated to answer telephones and never wrote letters. Her greatest wish at this time was to have children, and she underwent several operations in the hope of correcting her physical impairment, but the surgery proved unsuccessful.

The staggering realism and authenticity of shell-shattered Frankfurt and Berlin was the real highlight of Merle's next film, *Berlin Express* (RKO, 1948) directed largely on location by Jacques Tourneur with stark photography by Lucien Ballard. ". . . a practical and immensely entertaining demonstration of the screen's capacity for dealing with important subjects" (Otis L. Guernsey, Jr., *New York Herald-Tribune*). It was part of the neorealist wave to hit post-World War II Hollywood. The film capital discovered that in concepts and lensing, it could no longer afford to be insularly confined to the California soundstages.

Merle, fast approaching the age of forty, could no longer hide her middle-aged appearance, and this realization seemed to inhibit her onfilm performance here. In *Berlin Express*, a slick programmer, she was but one of the many assorted characters, thrust together on a Paris-Berlin train, who must cope with the murder of a government official on the crack express. There is talkative American agricultural expert Robert Ryan, British teacher Robert Coote, distrustful Russian officer Roman Toporow, mys-

---

*The *New York Herald-Tribune's* music critic, Jay S. Harrison, analyzed the composition as "slick as ice and just about as stable."

terious French businessman Charles Korvin, German statesman Paul Lukas, and Merle, his French secretary. Before the espionage thriller has played out its plotline, Ryan and Merle have become good friends, but there is a scant hint of any romantic involvement between the two. Obviously, Hollywood was growing up.

On February 10, 1949, Merle revisited Juarez, Mexico, where she obtained a divorce from Ballard. She informed newsmen, "I have no plans to marry again." Following the split-up, she embarked on a European tour. On the Riviera she was hosted by Lord Beaverbrook, whose impressive guest list included Sir Winston Churchill. When she and Churchill compared their amateur painting talents, he told her, "You have a nice eye for color." In August of that year, on the 31st, her current enamorata, wealthy thirty-one-year-old Italian Count Giorgio Cini, was preparing to fly his private light plane from Cannes to Venice on business. With Merle watching from the ground, he buzzed the Cannes airstrip in a farewell salute. His plane went out of control and crashed. With the Count dead, Merle broke down and sobbed, "My life is finished. There's no point in going on."

But she did, and in 1950 she made two films in France. The first, *Pardon My French* (United Artists, 1951),* cast her as a prudish but romantic Boston schoolmarm who inherits a French chateau. On claiming the inheritance, she finds the building occupied by a charming music composer (Paul Henreid) and five orphaned children. "There's not much to recommend, entertainment-wise," was *Variety*'s verdict on this technically inferior product. In the second film, *24 Hours of a Woman's Life* (Associated British Pictures, 1952),† one of the several film versions of Stefan Zweig's novel,‡ director Victor Saville offered a mellow drama of a story within a story as a novelist (Leo Genn) tells a group of tourists the account of a young widow staying on his yacht before World War II, who became romantically involved with an inveterate gambler (Richard Todd). She tried to reform him and save him from himself, but she failed and he committed suicide. As the picture concludes, Genn introduces his wife who is, as expected, the ex-widow (Merle). The British *Monthly Film Bulletin* criticized "the three stars [who] perform with unusual woodenness . . ." Each of the two features, on reaching the United States, wound up on the bottom half of double bills.

In the year that followed, Merle devoted her full energies to international socializing in jet-set fashion, but in 1953 she turned to American television on three occasions. On February 12, she rallied to David Niven's need for well-known guest stars to appear on the CBS anthology series "Four Star

*Originally titled *The Lady from Boston*.
†When the color feature was distributed in the United States in 1953, fifteen and one-half minutes were chopped from the running time.
‡Ingrid Bergman offered a marvelous performance in a television special (CBS, March 20, 1961) based on the novel.

Playhouse," the show (and its related production company) which he had formed with Charles Boyer and Dick Powell. Merle starred in an episode entitled *Sound Off.* On April 16, she was on NBC-TV in the *Allison, Ltd.* segment of "Ford Theatre," and on July 17, she again starred for "Four Star Playhouse" in *The Journey.* That same year, while in Madrid, she co-starred in *Todo Es Possible en Granada* (Chapalo, 1954), an inconclusive love story in which she is an American who intends to purchase a particular property in Granada, believing that a fabulous Mussulman treasure is buried there. She never unearths the fortune, but she does find romance with free-booter Francisco Rabal.

At a time when Hollywood was undergoing drastic retrenchments due to the repercussions both from competing television and the government's antitrust suits against the major film companies, it was difficult at best for young players to make a start in the faltering industry. For mature glamour stars, such as Merle, there was little opportunity to find proper roles in major vehicles. In 1954, much to the amazement of some industry executives and of her loyal fans, Merle appeared in two features.

Desiree (Twentieth Century-Fox) is only memorable for its gaudy display of color CinemaScope and for Marlon Brando's mannered interpretation as a British-accented Napoleon Bonaparte. The Henry Koster-directed feature emerged as a giant-sized soap opera, which was not unfitting since it was based on a sudsy best-selling novel. Britisher Jean Simmons, who, unlike more ethereal, elfinlike Audrey Hepburn, had never become a major American screen personality, had the title role as the young millinery clerk in 1794 France who becomes infatuated with Brando, but winds up wedding General Jean-Baptiste Bernadotte (Michael Rennie), the latter an aide to Brando who later joins the forces that bring about the Emperor's downfall.

One can only wonder how Merle actually reacted to being cast in the important, but obviously subordinate, role of the mature Josephine Beauharnais, the worldly courtesan who marries Brando, becomes Empress of France, but then is cast aside by her spouse when she proves unable to produce an heir to the throne. Granted, Merle gave elegance and style to her comparatively small part, displaying what the *Saturday Review* termed "the most effective of the brilliant costumes created by Rene Hubert for the production, and she wears them with superb chic." However, the limelight was clearly fastened on Brando and flighty Simmons, as each dipped in and out of fastidiously recreated historical scenes, filled with name-dropping figures. In its own very quiet way, Merle's subdued portrayal of the pitiful, aging mistress-wife could be compared favorably to Gloria Swanson's shedding of her glamorous image in *Sunset Boulevard* (Paramount, 1950) or Bette Davis's devastating image-dissection in *All about Eve* (Twentieth Century-Fox, 1950).

Merle then went over to MGM in Culver City for *Deep in My Heart*

(1954), which purported to be a biography of composer Sigmund Romberg (1887-1951). Jose Ferrer, in the title role, offered an energetic but very schmaltz-filled vaudevillian-style performance as the immigrant European who arrives in pre-World War I America, takes a piano-playing job at Helen Traubel's New York cafe, and then is launched onto his career as a leading operetta composer. Merle, smartly clothed and coiffed, appeared as Romberg's "discovery" and lyricist, Dorothy Donnelly, who, in the course of the 132-song-and-dance story, becomes ill, withers away, and dies on an elegant living-room sofa while Ferrer plays the piano and Traubel belts out "Auf Wiedersehen." The lengthy celluloid offering ("This is a good deal of Romberg to take straight," *New Yorker*) allowed ample opportunity for Metro to throw in a mixed bag of guest-star turns, ranging from Tony Martin singing numbers from *New Moon*, to Ann Miller as the It Girl, gyrating in an orange dress to a tune from *Artists and Models*, to Vic Damone and Jane Powell crucifying "Will You Remember?" from *Maytime*.

Merle was a frequent television guest star in 1954-55, ranging from her portrayal of Monty Woolley's secretary in *The Man Who Came to Dinner* (CBS, October 13, 1954) to tackling the difficult part as Jane Marryot in a video condensation of Noël Coward's nostalgic chronicle, *Cavalcade,* on ABC's "Twentieth Century-Fox Hour" (October 5, 1955). Critics remembered all too well the well-turned performance of Diana Wynyard in the original Fox film (1933), and criticized Merle's performance for being "so placid that the years seemed to roll over her with little toll at all" (Jack Gould, *New York Times*).

She returned to moviemaking in a Universal B-entry, *The Price of Fear,* directed by former actor Abner Biberman. The modest suspense yarn opened with narrator Charles Drake describing Merle's Jessica Warren as "beautiful, successful, above reproach—heading toward a fateful decision." As it develops, she is a hit-and-run driver who kills Gia Scala's father. Her car is later stolen by Lex Barker, on the run from Warren Stevens's henchmen, and as the couple dodge their pursuers, the film's interest-level quickly deteriorates.

Merle could find no further theatrical film work, and accepted a post as hostess of a syndicated British video series, "Assignment, Foreign Legion," which debuted on America's CBS network on September 15, 1957. Earlier in the year, she had guested on the *I Will Not Die* episode of "G.E. Theatre" (CBS, April 28, 1957).

Then in Rome, on Tuesday, July 28, 1957, at the age of forty-six, Merle wed the Italian-born Mexican industrialist Bruno Pagliai (age fifty-three), one of Mexico's wealthiest citizens.* It was Pagliai's fourth marriage, and the ceremony was performed by Monsignor Quirino Paganuzzi, secretary

*Pagliai later told Merle that he had met her a decade earlier, and that if she had even noticed him then, "he would have dropped everything and followed her."

of the Vatican's Office of the Master of the Chamber to Pope Pius XII at the fourth-century Church of the Four Crowned Martyrs.

After selling her Bel Air home, Merle commuted with her new husband between their three abodes (Beverly Hills, Mexico City, and Cuernavaca, Mexico). Merle freely admitted that she could not possibly reside in Mexico "for longer than a week because the altitude makes me sick." The vicinity of their Beverly Hills manse was shared by the Jack L. Warners, Ned Washington, Hedda Hopper, and Kurt Frings. One would have supposed that Merle, the eternal party-giver, thoroughly enjoyed her hostessing duties, but she once disclosed: "Parties are lonely things. I really don't like them—the small talk—and walking into a room in the beginning makes me feel very uncomfortable. I'd rather be alone with some good music or a book than be at a party."

In 1959, the Pagliais adopted a boy and a girl, who were named Bruno and Francesca. For the next four years, Merle devoted herself to the children, but during this period, she managed rather ingeniously to always remain in the limelight, never letting the public at large forget that she was very much a part of the world's most luxurious social set.

In early 1963, film director Richard Rush visited Merle in Mexico and convinced the actress to star in his projected screen drama, *Of Love and Desire* (Twentieth Century-Fox, 1963). Commenting on her decision to return to the cinema after a seven-year absence, Merle revealed, "I have refused to do quite a few pictures offered to me. They're not up to the standards I would like. . . . If I'm going to leave my husband and children for a film, the part ought to be exceptionally good."

Well, for *Of Love and Desire*, Merle did not have to leave her family for very long, for the widescreen, color story was lensed almost entirely at the Pagliais' white-brick home in Mexico City, and the part-sixteenth-century house in Cuernavaca. After it was over, Merle reported, "It was all done in five weeks, not counting rehearsals. Great fun!"

The film, which debuted in New York in September 1963, was a clinker of the highest order. In the neurotically conceived scenario, Merle is Katharine, a beautiful, unstable nymphomaniac in search of a lost passion. She is accused of indulging in a "comparison shopping spree from man to man" and asks one of the men for whom she is on the prowl: "What's the matter, was I too fast? Should I have said 'no' two more times and 'would you like another drink?' What do you need to feel like you've made a conquest?" Merle was handicapped, along with a bad script, by being cast with the American cinema's greasiest-looking bloated actor (Steve Cochran,) the Continent's most solemn performer (Curt Jurgens), and 1940s Hollywood's candidate for leading nonactor (John Agar).

The kindest of critics called the fiasco a "sticky, maudlin glob of nonsense" (Leo Mishkin, *New York Morning Telegraph*). Less generous reviewers unleashed their most scathing words of comment on Merle's comeback project. Bosley Crowther (*New York Times*) led the pack, reporting: "What you will see in this picture is a sadly worn Merle Oberon playing a coy, bright-eyed, come-hither, race-you-cross-the-swimming pool co-quette. . . . More than her writers and director have been cruel to Miss Oberon. Her cameraman, too, has caused her to look downright pitiful. And like the rest of the picture, which was made in Mexico, he has let his color filters bathe her in a sickly green. It's too bad, because what fond memories we have of Miss ·Oberon! Who can forget the vital beauty of her Cathy in *Wuthering Heights*! Well, she shouldn't have let herself be tempted to do such a meretricious film, for which no one deserves a bit of credit."

Upon reading Crowther's review, Merle sent the critic a telegram. As she told newsmen: "I feel that artists must be good sports about bad reviews, as long as they stick to the performance. But personal slashing is unfair and cruel, like shooting at a sitting duck." As to the contents of her Western Union missive, Merle alluded, "I said more or less what I just told you, but not so politely."

As fate would have it, less than a month later the two feuding personalities came face to face at the New York premiere of the revival of *Wuthering Heights*. Crowther, embarrassed that his newspaper review had caused such a furor on Merle's part, attempted to apologize, but the irate star returned his apologies with icy indignity.

Also in 1963, construction began on a fourth Pagliai house, this one in Acapulco on the coastline with "huge rocks and a tiny beach." Merle collected pre-Columbian figures (she pronounced it "figgers") in pottery and obsidian and found delight in showing houseguests the Aztec and Mayan ruins. "Chichen Itza is a dream," she said. The house in Acapulco required two full years to build and when completed was christened "Ghalal" (Love). Together with Merle, it became one of the area's major tourist attractions. Frequent guests included Frank Sinatra, attorney Louis Nizer, Henry Ford, John Wayne, Lynda Bird Johnson, George Hamilton, and Merle's personal costumer, Luis Estevez.

She was among the guest celebrities on the "Hallmark Hall of Fame" November 30, 1964, NBC-TV salute, *The Other World of Wines*. Two years later, *The Oscar* (Embassy, 1966) brought Merle back to the screen as herself, the presenter of the Best Actor Award to Frank Sinatra, while the film's heel, Frank Fane (Stephen Boyd), goes into temporary shock over losing the coveted award. The tenor of the mediocre study of Hollywood on Hollywood was expressed by Tony Bennett as Boyd's friend-valet. On two occasions in the course of the Russell Rouse screenplay, he philosophizes, "When you lie down with garbage, you get up smelling like a pig."

The following year, director Richard Quine helmed the picturization of Arthur Hailey's best-selling *Hotel* (Warner Bros., 1967). In this meretricious, cut-rate variation of *Grand Hotel* (MGM, 1932), Merle was paid a $50,000 salary (which she donated to charity) to portray the arrogant, domineering British duchess who has her jewels stolen in the New Orleans hostelry.* She was stunningly costumed by Edith Head, with hairstyles by Jean Burt Reilly that accentuated the miraculous vitality of her presence. She and Michael Rennie, he as the weak-willed duke, who is guilty of a hit-and-run homicide, were a handsome couple. The film received less than polite reviews, but made a healthy box-office profit. Critics granted that Merle was "sincere" and amply successful in displaying "icy ambition." At the time of a special Miami preopening screening of the film, Merle attended and expressed displeasure to newsmen that so little of her part remained in the final print. More cynical sources insisted that her role had never been any larger.

When the press inquired into the inevitable, how she preserved her beauty at her time of life, she responded: "It boils down to the fact that I like to do the things that are good for me. I eat very carefully and I don't smoke or drink." She expressed her thoughts on the benefits derived from exercise and explained that each of her four homes had a swimming pool, which she used constantly because "I owe it to myself, to God, and to those who have to look at me."

Vogue magazine had Merle as a guest travel columnist in its January 15, 1967 issue. She related the joys one discovers in Cuernavaca, along with revealing the mystery that existed in the Pagliai home: "Our house has a ghost—according to our caretaker, who is apparently a perfectly normal person apart from the fact that for years he has insisted that a man in a shroud appears to him. A guest, the late David Selznick, once said he was awakened every night at midnight by a knocking at his door. My husband tells me that some years ago he had an outside wall broken into, in order to find out what prevented a vine from covering it. When the bricks were removed, a skeleton was discovered. To add to the mystery, when the skeleton was taken out and the wall bricked up again, the vine grew with no difficulty."

In the autumn of 1971, Merle attended the annual San Francisco Film Festival wearing a smart beige silk suit. As one of those honored in a retrospective glance at past films, she submitted to a brief question-and-answer period. She informed the audience that she would like to have seen excerpts from *Desiree,* which she considered one of her best acting jobs, and said she was terrible in *The Lodger,* claiming she had taken the role to "get away from duchess parts," which seems strange, since she was seldom cast as a titled figure. Someone inquired why she had never portrayed a servant onscreen, to which she replied, "If you can speak

*Merle wore $500,000 worth of her own baubles, including a brooch reputed to have once belonged to Marie Antoinette.

properly you get upper class parts; if you have a regional accent you usually play working class roles."

From time to time, after *Hotel,* various film companies sent scripts to Mexico for Merle's perusal. In 1969, it was reported that she would go to London to make *The Private War of Mrs. Darling,* for Avco-Embassy, but nothing came of the project. Then MGM asked Churubasco Studios of Mexico to produce two features. It was agreed, on the condition that one of the pictures star Merle. Scripts were again submitted to her, but apparently none was to her liking. On a flight between New York and London she read the film pages of several newspapers and later exclaimed, "I was shocked to see what kind of pictures were playing. I thought if this was the only kind of pictures being made, I wanted none of it."

In an interview conducted by Gene Shalit on NBC-TV's "The Today Show" on June 11, 1973, Merle revealed, "So I said to Gavin Lambert, who is a friend of mine and a marvelous writer, 'Gavin, why don't you try to write a story for me?' Lambert wrote a screenplay of a love affair between a woman past middle age and a younger man. He called it *Interval.*" Merle sent the script to her friend, Noël Coward, who called it "fantastic," and "that pushed me into producing the thing—putting it all together." Shooting began in Yucatán, Mexico, in early 1972 under the auspices of Churubasco Studios. There were production problems, one director went, and Daniel Mann came in as a replacement. Robert Wolders, a thirty-seven-year-old Dutch actor, best known for his two-year stretch on American television's "Laredo" series, was selected as Merle's leading man. Merle enthusiastically described the picture's theme: "It's about a woman of my age—mature, to say the least—who is self-reliant; she's come to terms with life; she's had a terrible tragedy in her past and she manages to overcome it. She has no idea of romance in her mind. She meets this man who 'invades' her—invades her life—and—then comes the love story." She termed it "an old, new love story."

When the film was completed, Merle rented a beach house at Malibu in Southern California, claiming that she was in the midst of editing the feature and needed to be near Hollywood facilities. She denied rumors that she was maritally separated from Pagliai, although she admitted that loneliness was a contributing reason for her leaving Mexico. "I realized my children are of an age where they don't need me. And Bruno's work is in Mexico City. Bruno's like Niarchos; they're tycoons. I'm sure if he could get away from his business there, he'd come to Acapulco."

In November 1972, Merle donated a theatre facility to the Actors' Studio West in Los Angeles, to be known as the Merle Oberon Playhouse. The event was celebrated in Hollywood with a black-tie supper.

Also in November, the Pagliais' Acapulco mansion was up for sale at a $2 million price, or for rent at $1,000 a day, including a full servant staff. "It's a bargain because we're in a hurry to sell it," Merle said. In December, Pagliai appeared on the Malibu scene and preceded Merle to Acapulco, where they spent Christmas with the children.

Interval finally premiered on February 28, 1973, at the Diana Theatre in Mexico City for the benefit of the American Red Cross. Among those attending were the first lady of Mexico, Maria Esther Zuno de Echeverría, Cary Grant, Ricardo Montalban, Lex Barker, and Joseph E. Levine; the latter had agreed to handle the film's distribution outside Latin America through his Avco-Embassy Picture Corporation. Grant commented to the press on Merle's courage in returning to the screen: "She didn't have to come back, and when she did, she came back with a romantic picture at a time when everybody else is making films about sex and violence. The film has values you don't see around anymore." Levine added, "Merle and I are old friends; she could no more stay out of this business than I could." Of the film, the *Hollywood Reporter*'s Marvene Jones recommended, "When it opens in the States I strongly suggest you see it. It's beautiful."

After the premiere and a round of formal parties in her honor, Merle flew back to California, with a stopover in Cuernavaca where she filed for a legal separation from her husband of fifteen years. "There has been a difficulty with the marriage," she admitted. "At the moment, I really don't know what my future is, where I'll live or even where I'll be in a year's time." As for the romantic rumors concerning herself and Wolders, who had also taken a Malibu Beach house, she quipped: "All of this talk of Robert and me is a natural outcome of both my situation and my doing a picture with someone who's attractive, nice and intelligent. This business of Robert and me—it's very much overplayed. Why don't people mind their own bloody business?" Wolders commented, "She's got the body of a twenty-five year old woman. Wait until you see her in a bathing costume."

On March 27, 1973, Merle was in the presenter lineup at the forty-fifth annual Awards Ceremony of the Academy of Motion Picture Arts and Science at the Dorothy Chandler Pavilion at the Los Angeles Music Center. Impeccably dressed in white, she presented the Oscar for special effects to *The Poseidon Adventure* (Twentieth Century-Fox, 1972). It was her fifth appearance on an Oscar show.

She accepted the Woman of the World award at the International Orphans Century Plaza, Inc., in Los Angeles on May 7, 1973. Dressed in a Fabiani pink and white suit, she addressed the luncheon group with: "Aren't we lucky to be living in a country where people have the opportunity to make money and be able to help the less fortunate? People should appreciate this country. I get awfully tired of putting down America."*

Merle announced in June 1973 that she would marry Wolders. She explained the matter of age difference, "I think it depends on the people,

*Merle is still a British subject, never having opted for American citizenship.

really. You can be a very old twenty-five and you can be a very young one hundred and two." On another occasion Merle, who "admitted" to being fifty-six years old, said, "Actually I never thought I'd fall in love with anybody or have anything serious in my life again." As for her almost ex-husband: "I'm very affectionate and loyal, and because I've fallen in love with somebody else doesn't mean I don't love Bruno anymore. We haven't fought. . . . I'm still his friend and I think he feels the same way."

Interval had its United States premiere on June 13, 1973, at Manhattan's 34th Street East Theatre. Rex Reed observed in the *New York Daily News* that Merle "has a body of a girl and the face of an angel," but "what this movie celebrates is a hymn to clean living and the wonders of modern cosmetology and what Merle Oberon needs is a better vehicle to celebrate it in." As for the film's old-fashioned romantic flavor, Archer Winsten *(New York Post)* reported, "Let's say it's probably right for Merle Oberon but not geared for today's audiences." The *New York Times*'s Roger Greenspun parried, "It is one of those ecstatic affairs, full of wonder and discovery, and yet it doesn't work. . . . But truth to tell, Merle Oberon is well over 60, and from time to time it shows. . . . Such uncanny freedom from wrinkles has not been achieved without a certain cost, and at this stage in her career Miss Oberon seems to have only two or three facial expressions left." Doris Duke, on hand for the premiere, said, "This is the first picture I've seen in fifteen years and I adored it."

The newspaper and magazine publicity accompanying Merle's return to the screen was nationwide, but after a three-week engagement in New York, the film quietly disappeared from sight. Merle as both star and producer admitted that she would never undergo the joint-capacity ordeal again. "If all stars only knew what agony is involved in putting a picture together they would be gentler with producers."

Since then, ever-radiant Merle has traveled to different parts of the world, always accompanied by faithful Robert Wolders. If she allows anything to publicly bother her, it is remarks concerning her relationship with Wolders. "I know people are talking about Rob and me. I know people are making jokes about us." But, she insists: "Rob really knows me and after really knowing me he loves, admires and respects me. . . . I feel very peaceful at this moment with my new life ahead of me. That's how Rob makes me feel." As an afterthought, she explained, "He fell in love first." And to prove that this is not just a regressional kittenish flirtation on her part, she insists, "At my age my standards are high. I feel a man must be able to give tenderness, kindness, intellectual stimulation and, what's very important to me, companionship."

In a recent United Press interview, Merle expressed her particular views on the uses of wealth. "I used to buy land whenever I saw good property for sale. I still own acreage in Mexico, the United States and Spain. But I don't want everyone to think I am rich. I'm not. [It has been estimated that Merle's emerald collection is second only to that of England's Queen

Elizabeth II.] But I did buy five post offices and then leased them to the government. I still own three of them. I guess that makes me a landlady to the U.S. government."

Now, some forty-five years after she first entered the cinema business, Merle is trying to remain active at her craft. When pal Joseph E. Levine was still head of Avco-Embassy Pictures in late 1973 there was talk of Merle accepting a guest-starring role as the wife of Mahatma Gandhi in Robert Bolt's screenplay of *Gandhi,* to be directed by Richard Attenborough. Now that this project is in abeyance, Merle has been talking recently with Doug Cramer and MGM-TV of tackling again the role of George Sand in a new film based on that woman's noteworthy life. As for opting the path chosen by Bette Davis, Joan Crawford, and Ann Sothern, among others: "I would not be a freak in those horror films as others have and I would not disrobe. I'd rather get a job selling stockings if I had to and keep my pride."

As amazing as Merle's career longevity, her unique vitality, and her recent May-October romance, is her circumspect evaluation of herself. Not long ago, she confessed: "I never thought I had any sex appeal. I just want to look my best. I truthfully find sex appeal hard to define, and I am really not sure it is connected with physical beauty."

Feature Film Appearances

ALF'S BUTTON (Gaumont, 1930) 96 M.*†

Producer, L'Estrange Fawcett; director, W. P. Kellino; based on the play by W. A. Darlington; screenplay, Fawcett.

Tubby Edin (Alf Higgins); Alf Goddard (Bill Grant); Nora Swinburne (Lady Isobel Fitzpeter); Polly Ward (Liz); Humberston Wright (Eustace); Gypsy Rhouma (Lucy); Annie Esmond (Mrs. Gaskins); Peter Haddon (Lieutenant Allen); Cyril McLaglen (Sergeant-Major); Bruce Winston (Mustapha); Spencer Trevor (Lord Dunwater); and: Anton Dolin and Anna Ludmilla, Nervo and Knox, Merle Oberon.

NEVER TROUBLE TROUBLE (Producers Distributing Corp., 1931) 75 M.*

Director, Lupino Lane; story, Laur Wylie; screenplay, George Dewhurst.

Lupino Lane (Oliver Crawford); Renee Clama (Pam Tweet); Jack Hobbs (Jimmie Dawson); Wallace Lupino (Mr. Tweet); Iris Ashley (Gloria Baxter); Dennis Hoey (Stranger); Wally Patch (Bill Hainton); Lola Hunt (Mrs. Hainton); Barry Lupino (Tompkins); George Dewhurst (Inspector Stevens); and: Merle Oberon.

FASCINATION (Wardour, 1931) 70 M.*

Producer, Clayton Hutton; director, Miles Mander; based on the play by Eliot Crawshay-Williams; screenplay, Victor Kendall.

Madeleine Carroll (Gwenda Farrell); Carl Harbord (Larry Maitland); Dorothy Barlan (Vera Maitland); Kay Hammond (Kay); Kenneth Kove (Bertie); Louis Goodrich (Colonel Farrington); Roland Culver (Ronnie); Freddie Bartholomew (Child); Merle Oberon (Extra).

SERVICE FOR LADIES (Paramount British, 1932) 93 M.

Producer-director, Alexander Korda; based on the novel *The Head Waiter* by Ernst Vajda; screenplay, Eliot Crawshay-Williams, Lajos Biro.

Leslie Howard (Max Tracey); George Grossmith (Mr. Westlake); Benita Hume (Countess Ricardi); Elizabeth Allan (Sylvia Robertson); Morton Selten (Mr. Robertson); Cyril Ritchard (Sir William Carter); Ben Field (Breslmeyer); Annie Esmond (Duchess); Martita Hunt (Aline, a French Maid); Merle Oberon (Extra).

U.S. release title: *Reserved for Ladies*

EBB TIDE (Paramount British, 1932) 74 M.

Producer, Walter Morosco; director, Arthur Rosson; based on the novel *God Gave Me 20 Cents* by Dixie Wilson; screenplay, Basil Mason, Reginald Denham.

Dorothy Bouchier (Cassie); Joan Barry (Mary); George Barraud (Steve); Vanda

*Unverified credit.

†Some sequences filmed in color.

Greville (Millie); Alexander Field (Barney); Annie Esmond (Landlady); Merle Oberon (Girl).

AREN'T WE ALL? (Paramount British, 1932) 80 M.*

Producer, Walter Morosco; director, Harry Lachman; based on the play by Frederick Lonsdale; screenplay, Basil Mason, Gilbert Wakefield.

Gertrude Lawrence (Margot); Hugh Wakefield (Lord Grenham); Owen Nares (Willie); Harold Huth (Karl van der Hyde); Marie Lohr (Lady Frinton); Renee Gadd (Kitty Lake); Emily Fitzroy (Angela); Aubrey Mather (Vicar); Rita Page (Dancer); Merle Oberon (Extra).

WEDDING REHEARSAL (Ideal, 1932) 84 M.

Producer-director, Alexander Korda; story, Robert Vansitt; art, Lajos Biro, George Grossmith; screenplay, Arthur Wimperis.

Roland Young (Reggie Candysshe); George Grossmith (Lord Stokeshire); John Loder (Bimbo); Maurice Evans (Tootles); Lady Tree (Lady Stokeshire); Edmund Breon (Lord Fleet); Wendy Barrie (Lady Maryrose Wroxbury); Joan Gardner (Lady Rosemary Wroxbury); Merle Oberon (Miss Hutchinson); Kate Cutler (Marchioness of Buckminster); Diana Napier (Mrs. Dryden); Morton Selten (Major Harry Wroxbury).

MEN OF TOMORROW (Paramount British, 1932) 88 M.

Producer, Alexander Korda; director, Leontine Sagan; based on the novel *Young Apollo* by Anthony Gibbs; screenplay, Arthur Wimperis, Gibbs.

Maurice Braddell (Allan Shepherd); Joan Gardner (Jane Anderson); Emlyn Williams (Horners); Robert Donat (Julian Angell); Merle Oberon (Ysobel d'Aunay); John Traynor (Mr. Waters); Esther Kiss (Maggie); Annie Esmond (Mrs. Oliphant).

THE PRIVATE LIFE OF HENRY VIII (UA, 1933) 96 M.

Producers, Alexander Korda, Ludovico Toeplitz; director, Korda; story, Lajos Biro, Arthur Wimperis; screenplay, Wimperis; art director, Vincent Korda; costumes, John Armstrong; music, Kurt Schroeder; camera, Georges Perinal; editors, Harold Young, Stephen Harrison.

Charles Laughton (Henry VIII); Robert Donat (Thomas Culpeper); Lady Tree (Henry's Old Nurse); Binnie Barnes (Catherine Howard); Elsa Lanchester (Ann of Cleves); Merle Oberon (Anne Boleyn); Franklin Dyall (Cromwell); Miles Mander (Wriothesley); Wendy Barrie (Jane Seymour); Claud Allister (Cornell); John Loder (Thomas Peynell); Everley Gregg (Catherine Parr); Lawrence Hanray (Cranmer); William Austin (Duke of Cleves); John Turnbull (Holbein); Judy Kelly (Lady Rochford); Frederick Culley (Duke of Norfolk); Gibb McLaughlin (French Executioner); Sam Livesey (English Executioner).

THE BATTLE (Gaumont, 1934) 85 M.

Producer, Leon Garganoff; director, Nicolas Farkas; based on the novel *La Bataille* by Claude Farrere; screenplay, Farkas, Bernard Zimmer, Robert Stevenson.

Charles Boyer (Marquis Yorisaka); John Loder (Fergan); Merle Oberon (Marquise Yorisaka); Betty Stockfeld (Betty Hockley); Valery Inkijinoff (Mirata); Miles Mander (Felze); Henri Fabert (Admiral).

U.S. release title: *Thunder in the East*
British reissue title: *Hara-Kiri* (1943)

*Unverified credit.

THE BROKEN MELODY   (Associated Producers and Distributors, 1934) 84 M.

Producer, Julius Hagen; director-story, S. Bernard Vorhaus; screenplay, Vera Allinson, Michael Hankinson, H. Fowler Mear.

John Garrick (Paul Verlaine); Margot Grahame (Simone St. Clair); Merle Oberon (Germaine); Austin Trevor (Pierre); Charles Carson (Dubonnet); Harry Terry (Henri); Andrea Malandrinos (Brissard); Tonie Edgar Bruce (Vera).

THE PRIVATE LIFE OF DON JUAN   (UA, 1934) 80 M.

Producer-director, Alexander Korda; based on the play by Henri Bataille; screenplay, Lajos Biro, Frederick Lonsdale; song "Don Juan's Serenade" by Michael Spolianski; song, Arthur Wimperis and Arthur Benjamin; costumes, Oliver Messell; settings, Vincent Korda; camera, George Perinal; editor, Stephen Harrison.

Douglas Fairbanks (Don Juan); Merle Oberon (Antonia); Benita Hume (Dolores); Binnie Barnes (Rosita); Joan Gardner (Carmen); Melville Cooper (Leporello); Athene Seyler (Theresa); Owen Nares (Actor); Patricia Hilliard (Girl in Castle); Gina Malo (Pepita); Heather Thatcher (Actress); Claud Allister (Duke); Barry MacKay (Roderigo); Lawrence Grossmith (Guardian); Edmund Breon (Author); Clifford Heatherley (Pedro); Diana Napier (Would-Be Wife); Gibson Gowland (Don Ascanio); Hay Petrie (Manager of the Golden Pheasant); Natalie Paley (Wife); Bruce Winston (Cafe Manager); Edmund Willard (Prisoner); Hindle Edgar (A Husband); Florence Wood (A Cook at the Inn); Annie Esmond (Dolores' Dueña); Morland Graham (The Cook in Don Juan's Kitchen); William Heughan (Statue); Veronica Brady (One of Don Juan's Early Loves); Betty Hamilton (An Actress); Margaretta Scott (Tonita, a Dancer); Natalie Lelong, Rosita Garcia (Wives of Tired Business Men); Nancy Jones (Woman); Elsa Lanchester (Maid).

THE SCARLET PIMPERNEL   (UA, 1934) 98 M.

Producer, Alexander Korda; director, Harold Young; based on the novel by the Baroness Orczy; screenplay, Robert E. Sherwood, Sam Berman, Arthur Wimperis, Lajos Biro.

Leslie Howard (Sir Percy Blakeney); Merle Oberon (Marguerite Blakeney); Raymond Massey (Chauvelin); Nigel Bruce (Prince of Wales); Bramwell Fletcher (Priest); Anthony Bushell (Sir Andrew Ffoulkes); Joan Gardner (Suzanne de Tournay); Walter Rilla (Armand St. Just); Mabel Terry-Lewis (Countess de Tournay); O. B. Clarence (Count de Tournay); Ernest Milton (Robespierre); Edmund Breon (Winterbottom); Melville Cooper (Romney); Gibb McLaughlin (Barber); Morland Graham (Treadle); Allan Jeayes (Lord Greville); William Freshman (Lord Hastings); Hindle Edgar (Lord Wilmot); Lawrence Hanray (Burke); Edmund Willard (Bibot, the Republican Officer); Gertrude Musgrove (Sally, Jellyrand's Daughter).

FOLIES BERGÈRE   (UA, 1935) 83 M.

Executive producer, Darryl F. Zanuck; associate producers, William Goetz, Raymond Griffith; director, Roy Del Ruth; based on the play *The Red Cat* by Rudolph Lothar, Hans Adler; screenplay, Bess Meredyth, Hal Long; music arranger-conductor, Alfred Newman; choreography, Dave Gould; art director, William Darling; songs, Jack Meskill and Jack Stern; Harold Adamson and Burton Lane; Victor Young, Ned Washington, and Bing Crosby; Andre Christien and Albert Willemetz, English lyrics by Herbert Reynolds; costumes, Albert M. Levy; Miss Oberon's gowns, Omar Kiam; sound, E. H. Hansen; camera, Barney McGill, Peverell Marley; editors, Allen McNeil, Sherman Todd.

Maurice Chevalier (Eugene Charlier/Fernand the Baron Cassini); Merle Oberon (Baroness Genevieve Cassini); Ann Sothern (Mimi); Walter Byron (Rene); Lumsden Hare (Gustave); Robert Grieg (Henri); Eric Blore (François); Halliwell Hobbes (Paulet); Philip Dare (Victor); Frank McGlynn, Sr. (Joseph); Ferdinand Munier (Morizet); Ferdinand Gottschalk (Ferdinand); Barbara Leonard (Josephine); Georges Renavent (Premier); Olin Howland (Stage Manager); Sailor Vincent (Bit Rubber); Robert Graves, Paul Kruger (Doormen); Olga Borget, Irene Bentley, Vivian Martin, Jenny Gray, Doris Morton (Usherettes); Joseph E. Bernard (Butler); Albert Pollet (Secretary); Perry Ivins (Airport Official); Mario Dominici (Doctor); Paul Toien (Page Boy); Lew Hicks, Leon Baron (Attendants); Nam Dibot (Ticket Man); Harry Holman (Cafe Waiter); Leonard Walker (Assistant Stage Manager); Albert Pollet, Max Barwyn (Waiters in Box); Ed Reinach, Joe Mack, Pop Garson, Bruce Covington, Charles Hagen, Adolph Faylauer, Harry Milton, Conrad Seidermann, Austin Browne (Bearded Men); Marbeth Wright, Lucille Lund, Jeanne Hart, Joan Woodbury, Bernadene Hayes, Marie Wells, Fay Worth, Maryan Dowling (Girls in Bar); Pauline Rosebrook, Shirley Hughes, Dixie McKinley, Libby Marks, Rosa Milano, Zandra Dvorak (Girl Models); Roy Seagus, Eugene Beday, Harry Semek, Hans Schumm, Alex Chevron, Luis Hanore, Rene Mimieux, Dick Allen, Henri Runique (Bartenders); Bob Von Dobeneck, Al Mazzola, Bill O'Brien, Al Constance, Jack Raymond (Waiters); Audrey Hall, Pokey Champion, Rita Dunn, Claudia Fargo, Myra Jones, Billie Lee, Mary Jane Hodge (Girls in Shell); Helen Mann, Joan Sheldon, Jill Evans, Barbara Roberts, Angela Blue, Nell Rhoades, June Gale, Mae Madison (Girls in Secretary Number); Jenny Gray, Thaya Foster, Ruth Day, Barbara Beall, Gail Goodson, Virginia Dabney (Girls in Hat Store); Wedgwood Nowell, Barlowe Borland, Anders Van Haden, John Ince, Wilson Millar, Yorke Sherwood, Cyril Thornton, Vesey O'Davoren, Robert Cody (Principals in Montage).

THE DARK ANGEL (UA, 1935) 105 M.

Producer, Samuel Goldwyn; director, Sidney Franklin; based on the play by Guy Bolton; screenplay, Lillian Hellman, Mordaunt Sharp; music, Alfred Newman; assistant director, Hugh Boswell; camera, Gregg Toland; editor, Sherman Todd.

Fredric March (Alan Trent); Merle Oberon (Kitty Vane); Herbert Marshall (Gerald Shannon); Janet Beecher (Mrs. Shannon); John Halliday (Sir George Barton); Henrietta Crosman (Granny Vane); Frieda Inescort (Ann West); Claud Allister (Lawrence Bidley); George Breakston (Joe); Fay Chaldecott (Betty); Dennis Chaldecott (Ginger); Douglas Walton (Roulston); Sarah Edwards (Mrs. Bidley); John Miltern (Mr. Vane); Olaf Hytten (Mills); Lawrence Grant (Mr. Tanner); Helena Byrne-Grant (Hannah); Ann Fielder (Mrs. Gallop); David Torrence (Mr. Shannon); Cora Sue Collins (Kitty as a Child); Jimmie Butler (Gerald as a Child); Jimmy Baxter (Alan as a Child); Randolph Connolly (Lawrence as a Child); Edward Cooper (Martin, the Butler); Andy Arbuckle (Mr. Gallop); Colin Campbell (Vicar); Silvia Vaughan (Landlady at Inn); Murdock MacQuarrie (Waiter at Inn); Holmes Herbert (Major in Dugout); Robert Hale (Orderly in Dugout); Douglas Gordon (Porter at Station); Gunnis Davis (News Vendor at Station); Harold Howard (Jarvis, the Station Attendant); Bud Geary, Jack Deery, Roy Darmour, Walt Voegeler, Carol Voss, Colin Kenny (Officers at Station); Montague Shaw (Train Passenger); Clare Verdera, Vesey O'Davoren (Voices at Station); Albert Russell (Innkeeper); Vernon P. Downing, Charles Tannen, Frederick Sewall, Robert Carlton, Philip Dare (Men in Dormitory); Claude King

(Sir Mordaunt); Phillis Coghlan (Shannon Maid); Francis Palmer Tilton (Chauffeur); Tom Moore, Major Sam Harris, Doris Stone, Louise Bates, Audrey Scott (Hunt Guests).

THESE THREE (UA, 1936) 93 M.

Producer, Samuel Goldwyn; director, William Wyler; based on the play *The Children's Hour* by Lillian Hellman; screenplay, Hellman; assistant director, Walter Mayo; music, Alfred Newman; art director, Richard Day; costumes, Omar Kiam; sound, Frank Maher; camera, Gregg Toland; editor, Danny Mandell.

Miriam Hopkins (Martha Dobie); Merle Oberon (Karen Wright); Joel McCrea (Dr. Joseph Cardin); Catherine Doucet (Mrs. Mortar); Alma Kruger (Mrs. Tilford); Bonita Granville (Mary Tilford); Marcia Mae Jones (Rosalie); Carmencita Johnson (Evelyn); Mary Ann Durkin (Lois); Margaret Hamilton (Agatha); Mary Louise Cooper (Helen Burton); Walter Brennan (Taxi Driver).

BELOVED ENEMY (UA, 1936) 90 M.

Producer, Samuel Goldwyn; associate producer, George Haight; director, H. C. Potter; story, John Balderston; screenplay, Balderston, Rose Franken, William Brown Meloney, David Hart; camera, Gregg Toland; editor, Sherman Todd.

Merle Oberon (Helen Drummond); Brian Aherne (Dennis Riordan); Karen Morley (Cathleen); Jerome Cowan (O'Rourke); David Niven (Gerald Preston); Henry Stephenson (Lord Athleigh); Donald Crisp (Burke); Ra Hould (Jerry); Granville Bates (Ryan); P. J. Kelly (Rooney); Leo McCabe (Connor); Pat O'Malley (Callahan); Jack Mulhall (Casey); Claude King (Colonel Loder); Wyndham Standing (Thornton); Robert Strange (Perrins); Lionel Pape (Crump); John Burton (Hall); Leyland Hodgson (Hawkins); David Torrence (Alroyd); Theodore Von Eltz (O'Brien).

I, CLAUDIUS (London Films, 1937) (Unfinished)

Producer, Alexander Korda; director, Josef von Sternberg; based on the novel *I, Claudius* by Robert Graves; screenplay, von Sternberg; costumes, John Armstrong; choreography, Agnes de Mille; settings, Vincent Korda; camera, Georges Perinal.

Charles Laughton (Tiberius Claudius Drusus); Merle Oberon (Messalina); Flora Robson (Livia, the Empress Dowager); Emlyn Williams (Caligula); and: Ralph Richardson, Robert Newton, John Clements, Basil Gill, Everley Gregg.

OVER THE MOON (UA, 1937) C—78 M.

Producer, Alexander Korda; directors, Thornton Freeland, William K. Howard; story, Robert E. Sherwood, Lajos Biro; screenplay, Anthony Pelissier, Arthur Wimperis, Alec Coppel; music, Michael Spolianski; songs, Spolianski and Desmond Carter; camera, Harry Stradling.

Merle Oberon (June Benson); Rex Harrison (Dr. Freddie Jarvis); Ursula Jeans (Lady Millie Parsmill); Robert Douglas (John Flight); Louis Borell (Count Pietro d'Altamura); Zena Dare (Julie Deethorpe); Peter Haddon (Lord Petcliffe); David Tree (Journalist); Mackenzie Ward (Lord Guy Carstairs); Carl Jaffe (Michel); Elisabeth Welch (Singer); Herbert Lomas (Ladbrooke); Wilfred Shane (Frude); Gerald Nodin (Cartwright).

THE DIVORCE OF LADY X   (UA, 1938) C—92 M.

Producer, Alexander Korda; director, Tim Whelan; based on the play *Counsel's Opinion* by Gilbert Wakefield; screenplay, Lajos Biro, Arthur Wimperis, Ian Dalrymple, Robert Sherwood; costumes, Rene Hubert; art director, Lazare Meerson; camera, Harry Stradling.

Merle Oberon (Leslie Steele); Laurence Olivier (Logan); Binnie Barnes (Lady Mere); Ralph Richardson (Lord Mere); Morton Selten (Lord Steele); J. H. Roberts (Slade); Gertrude Musgrove (Saunders); Gus McNaughton (Waiter).

THE COWBOY AND THE LADY   (UA, 1938) 91 M.

Producer, Samuel Goldwyn; director, H. C. Potter; story, Leo McCarey, Frank R. Adams; screenplay, S. N. Behrman, Sonya Levien; art director, Richard Day, James Basevi; set decorator, Julie Heron; assistant director, Eddie Bernoudy; songs, Lionel Newman, Arthur Quenzer, L. Wolfe Gilbert; music, Alfred Newman; costumes, Omar Kiam; sound, Paul Neal; special camera effects, Ray Binger; camera, Gregg Toland; editor, Sherman Todd.

Gary Cooper (Stretch); Merle Oberon (Mary Smith); Patsy Kelly (Katie Callahan); Walter Brennan (Sugar); Fuzzy Knight (Buzz); Mabel Todd (Elly); Henry Kolker (Mr. Smith); Harry Davenport (Uncle Hannibal Smith); Emma Dunn (Ma Hawkins); Walter Walker (Ames); Berton Churchill (Henderson); Charles Richman (Dillon); Fredrik Vogeding (Captain); Arthur Hoyt (Valet); Mabel Colcord (Old Woman); Billy Wayne, Ernie Adams, Russ Powell, Jack Baxley, Johnny Judd (Rodeo Riders).

WUTHERING HEIGHTS   (UA, 1939) 103 M.

Producer, Samuel Goldwyn; director, William Wyler; based on the novel by Emily Brontë; screenplay, Ben Hecht, Charles MacArthur; music director, Alfred Newman; art director, James Basevi; assistant director, Walter Mayo; set decorator, Julie Heron; costumes, Omar Kiam; makeup, Blagoe Stephanoff; sound, Paul Neal; camera, Gregg Toland; editor, Daniel Mandell.

Merle Oberon (Cathy Linton); Laurence Olivier (Heathcliff); David Niven (Edgar Linton); Donald Crisp (Dr. Kenneth); Flora Robson (Ellen Dean); Hugh Williams (Hindley); Geraldine Fitzgerald (Isabella Linton); Leo G. Carroll (Joseph); Cecil Humphreys (Judge Linton); Miles Mander (Lockwood); Sarita Wooton (Cathy as a Child); Rex Downing (Heathcliff as a Child); Douglas Scott (Hindley as a Child); Romaine Callender (Roubert, the Butler); Helena Grant (Miss Hudkins); Susanne Leach (First Guest); Tommy Martin, Schuyler Standish (Little Boys); Diane Williams (Little Girl); Harold Entwistle (Beadle); Frank Benson (Heathcliff's Servant); Philip Winter (Cathy's Partner); William Stelling (Dancer); Mme. Alice Ahlers (Frau Johann, the Harpsichordist); Vernon Downing (Giles); Eric Wilton (Linton Servant); Major Sam Harris (Wedding Guest).

THE LION HAS WINGS   (UA, 1939) 76 M.

Producer, Alexander Korda; directors, Michael Powell, Brian Desmond Hurst, Adrian Brunel; story, Ian Dalrymple; screenplay, Adrian Brunel, E. V. H. Emmett.

E. V. H. Emmett (Narrator);* Merle Oberon (Mrs. Richardson); Ralph Richardson (W. C. Richardson); June Duprez (June); Robert Douglas (Briefing Officer); Anthony Bushell (Pilot); Derrick de Marney (Bill); Brian Worth (Bobby); Austin Trevor (Schulemburg); Ivan Brandt (Officer); G. H. Mulcaster (Controller); Herbert Lomas (Holveg); Milton Rosmer (Observer); Robert Rendel (Chief of Air Staff); and: John Longden, Bernard Miles.

*In U.S. version, Lowell Thomas supplied the narration.

650

'TIL WE MEET AGAIN   (WB, 1940) 99 M.

Producers, Jack L. Warner, Hal B. Wallis; associate producer, David Lewis; director, Edmund Goulding; story, Robert Lord; screenplay, Warren Duff; camera, Tony Gaudio; editor, Ralph Dawson.

Merle Oberon (Joan Ames); George Brent (Dan Hardesty); Pat O'Brien (Steve Burke); Geraldine Fitzgerald (Bonnie Coburn); Binnie Barnes (Countess de Vaubert); Frank McHugh (Achilles Peddicord); Eric Blore (Sir Harold Landamuir); George Reeves (Jimmy Coburn); Henry O'Neill (Dr. Cameron); Frank Wilcox (Assistant Purser); Doris Lloyd (Louise, the Maid); John Ridgely (Junior Officer); Marjorie Gateson (Mrs. Hestor); Regis Toomey (Freddy); William Halligan (Barman); Victor Kilian (McGillis); Wade Boteler (Stoddard); Charles Sherlock (Master-at-Arms); Frank Orth (Bartender); Maris Wrixon, Jane Gilbert, Mary Anderson (Girls); Chester Gan (Hong Kong Policeman); Frank Mayo, William Hopper (Men); Hal Brazealeo (Lemmy); Sol Gorss (Sailor); Mary MacLaren (Woman); Jeffrey Sayre, Jack Mower (Stewards); Grace Hayle (Fussy Woman Passenger); Lynn Merrick (Her Daughter); David Tillotson (Boy); Nat Carr, David Newell (Assistant Pursers); Ed Keane (Officer); William Gould (Chief of Police); Robert Homans (Dock Policeman); Robert Elliott, Edwin Parker (Detectives); Walter Miller (American Bartender); Frank Puglia, George Regas (Mexican Bartender).

THAT UNCERTAIN FEELING   (UA, 1941) 84 M.

Producer-director, Ernst Lubitsch; based on the play *Divorcons* by Victorien Sardou, Emile de Najac; adaptor, Walter Reisch; screenplay, Donald Ogden Stewart; art director, Alexander Golitzen; music, Werner Heymann; gowns, Irene; camera, George Barnes; editor, William Shea.

Merle Oberon (Jill Baker); Melvyn Douglas (Larry Baker); Burgess Meredith (Sebastian); Alan Mowbray (Dr. Vengard); Olive Blakeney (Margie Stallings); Harry Davenport (Attorney Jones); Eve Arden (Sally); Sig Rumann (Mr. Okfka); Richard Carle (Butler); Mary Currier (Maid); Jean Fenwick (Nurse).

AFFECTIONATELY YOURS   (WB, 1941) 90 M.

Executive producer, Hal B. Wallis; associate producer, Mark Hellinger; director, Lloyd Bacon; story, Fanya Foss, Aleen Leslie; screenplay, Edward Kaufman; dialog director, Robert Foulk; art director, Anton Grot; music, Heinz Roemheld; choreography, Matty King; music director, Leo F. Forbstein; camera, Tony Gaudio; editor, Owen Marks.

Merle Oberon (Sue Mayberry); Dennis Morgan (Richard Mayberry); Rita Hayworth (Irene Malcolm); Ralph Bellamy (Owen Wright); George Tobias (Pasha); James Gleason (Chester Phillips); Hattie McDaniel (Cynthia); Jerome Cowan (Cullen); Butterfly McQueen (Butterfly); Renie Riano (Mrs. Snell); Frank Wilcox (Tom); Grace Stafford (Miss Anderson); Pat Flaherty (Harmon); Murray Alper (Blair); William Haade (Matthews); James Flavin (Tomassetti); Carmen Morales (Anita); George Meeker (Anita's Escort); Creighton Hale (Hotel Manager); Charles Wagenheim (Bystander); Gino Corrado (Lisbon Headwaiter); Antonio Filauri (Portuguese); Irene Colman (Barmaid); William Hopper (Air Line Attendant); Frank Faylen (Ambulance Driver); Craig Stevens (Field Guard); Nat Carr (Delicatessen Proprietor); Ed Brian (Copy Boy); Ann Edmonds (Stenographer); Charles Marsh (City Editor); Billy Wayne (Bell Captain); Wedgwood Nowell (Judge); Peggy Diggins, Alexis Smith (Bridesmaids); Garry Owen (Taxi Driver); Ed Gargan (Traffic Cop); Dorothy Adams (Hospital Attendant); Henry Blair (Little Boy); Charles Drake (Interne); Faye Emerson (Nurse); Mary Field (Mrs. Collins).

LYDIA (UA, 1941) 144 M.

Producer, Alexander Korda; associate producer, Lee Garmes; director, Julien Duvivier; story, Duvivier, Laslo Bus-Fekete; screenplay, Ben Hecht, Samuel Hoffenstein; production designer, Vincent Korda; associate art director, Jack Okey; costumes, Marcel Vertes, Walter Plunkett; makeup, House of Westmore; set decorator, Julie Heron; assistant director, Horace Hough; music, Miklos Rozsa; sound, William Wilmarth; special effects, Lawrence Butler; camera, Garmes; editor, William Hornbeck.

Merle Oberon (Lydia Macmillan); Edna May Oliver (Granny); Alan Marshal (Richard Mason); Joseph Cotten (Michael Fitzpatrick); Hans Yaray (Frank Audry); George Reeves (Bob Willard); John Halliday (Butler); Sara Allgood (Johnny's Mother); Billy Roy (Johnny); Frank Conlan (Old Ned).

FOREVER AND A DAY (RKO, 1943) 104 M.

Producers-directors, Rene Clair, Edmund Goulding, Cedric Hardwicke, Frank Lloyd, Victor Saville, Robert Stevenson, Herbert Wilcox; screenplay, Charles Bennett, C. S. Forrester, Lawrence Hazard, Michael Hogan, W. P. Lipscomb, Alice Duer Miller, John Van Druten, Alan Campbell, Peter Godfrey, S. M. Herzig, Christopher Isherwood, Gene Lockhart, R. C. Sheriff, Claudine West, Norman Corwin, Jack Hartfield, James Hilton, Emmett Lavery, Frederick Lonsdale, Donald Ogden Stewart, Keith Winters; art directors, Albert D'Agostino, Lawrence P. Williams, Al Herman; music director, Anthony Collins; camera, Robert De Grasse, Lee Garmes, Russell Metty, Nicholas Musuraca; editors, Elmo J. Williams, George Crone.

Anna Neagle (Miriam [Susan]); Ray Milland (Bill); Claude Rains (Pomfret); C. Aubrey Smith (Admiral Trimble); Dame May Whitty (Mrs. Trimble); Gene Lockhart (Cobblewick); Ray Bolger (Sentry); Edmund Gwenn (Stubbs); Lumsden Hare (Fitts); Stuart Robertson (Lawyer); Claud Allister (Barstow); Ben Webster (Vicar); Alan Edmiston (Tripp); Patric Knowles (Courier); Bernie Sell (Naval Officer); Halliwell Hobbes (Doctor); Helene Pickard (Maid); Doris Lloyd, Lionel Belmore, Evelyn Beresford, Charles Irwin, Eric Snowden, Gerald Smith, Herbert Evans, Gerald Hamer, Leslie Francis, Vivi Steele, Mary Gordon, Helene Grant, Irene Denny, Moyna MacGill, Viola Moore, Barbara Everest, Harry Allen, Cecil Kellaway, Doreen Munroe, Arthur Treacher, Anna Lee (Bits); Louis Bissinger (Infant Baby); Clifford Severn (Nelson Trimble); Charles Coburn (Sir William); Alec Craig (Butler); Ian Hunter (Dexter); Jessie Matthews (Mildred); Charles Laughton (Bellamy); Montagu Love (Sir John Bunn); Sir Cedric Hardwicke (Dabb); Reginald Owen (Mr. Simmons); Colin Campbell (Mr. Wickes); Ernest Cossart (Mr. Blinkinsop); Peter Godfrey (Mr. Pepperdish); Buster Keaton (Dabb's Assistant); Wendy Barrie (Edith); Ida Lupino (Jenny); Brian Aherne (Jim Trimble); Edward Everett Horton (Sir Anthony); Isobel Elsom (Lady Trimble-Pomfret); Wendell Hulett (Augustus); June Duprez (Julia); Eric Blore (Selsby); Mickey Martin (Boy); Queenie Leonard (Housemaid); May Beatty (Cook); Merle Oberon (Marjorie); Una O'Connor (Mrs. Ismay); Nigel Bruce (Major Garrow); Anita Bolster (Mrs. Garrow); Marta Gale (Miss Garrow); Roland Young (Mr. Barringer); Gladys Cooper (Mrs. Barringer); Robert Cummings (Ned Trimble); Herbert Evans (Bobby); Kay Deslys, Vangie Beilby (Women Drunks); Richard Haydn (Mr. Fulcher); Emily Fitzroy (Mrs. Fulcher); Hugh Harrison (Soldier); Odette Myrtil (Mrs. Dallas); Elsa Lanchester (Mamie); Sara Allgood (Cook-1917); Clyde Cook (Taxi Driver); Dorothy Bell (W.A.A.C. Girl); Joan Prescott (A.T.S. Girl); Robert Coote (Blind Officer); June (V.A.D. Girl); Art Mulliner, Ivan Simpson (Elderly Bachelors); Pax Walker, Lola Vanti (Housemaids); Bill Cartledge (Telegraph Boy); Bill Cartledge, Charles Hall, Clyde Cook, Aubrey Mather, George Kirby, Walter Kingsford, Dennis Hoey, Reginald Gardiner, Alec Craig (Men); Donald Crisp (Captain Martin); Sylvia Logan, May Beatty, Connie Leon (Women); Ruth Warrick (Leslie); Kent Smith (Gates Pomfret); June Lockhart (Daughter); Lydia Bilbrook (Mother); Billy Bevan (Cabby); Stuart Robertson (Air Raid Warden); Herbert Marshall (Curate); Victor McLaglen (Spavin); Harry Allen (Cockney Watcher); Ethel Griffies (Wife); Gabriel Canzona (Man with Monkey); Joy Harrington (Bus Conductress); Ernest Grooney (Clerk); Dorothy Bell (Flower Girl); Roger Steele, Ernest Severn, Radford Allen (Boys); Paula Allen (Girl); Daphne Moore (Nurse); Philip Ahlin, Barry Norton, Barry Heenan, Stuart Hall (Card Players).

STAGE DOOR CANTEEN   (UA, 1943) 132 M.

Producer, Sol Lesser; associate producer, Barnett Briskin; director, Frank Borzage; screenplay, Delmer Daves; art director, Hans Peters; set decorator, Victor Gangelin; music, Freddie Rich; music director, C. Bakaleinikoff; assistant directors, Lew Borzage, Virgil Hart; songs, Lesser, Al Dubin, and Jimmy Monaco; Lorenz Hart and Richard Rodgers; Dubin and Monaco; production designers, Harry Horner, Clem Beauchamps; costumes, Albert Deano; sound, Hugh McDowell; camera, Harry Wild; editor, Hal Kern.

Cheryl Walker (Eileen); William Terry (Ed "Dakota" Smith); Marjorie Riordan (Jean); Lon McCallister ("California"); Margaret Early (Ella Sue); Michael Harrison (Sunset Carson) ("Texas"); Dorothea Kent (Mamie); Fred Brady ("Jersey"); Marion Shockley (Lillian); Patrick O'Moore (The Australian); Ruth Roman (Girl); Francis Pierlot (Man); Judith Anderson, Henry Armetta, Benny Baker, Kenny Baker, Tallulah Bankhead, Ralph Bellamy, Edgar Bergen and Charlie McCarthy, Ray Bolger, Helen Broderick, Ina Claire, Katharine Cornell, Lloyd Corrigan, Jane Cowl, Jane Darwell, William Demarest, Virginia Field, Dorothy Fields, Gracie Fields, Lynn Fontanne, Arlene Francis, Vinton Freedley, Billy Gilbert, Lucile Gleason, Vera Gordon, Virginia Grey, Helen Hayes, Katharine Hepburn, Hugh Herbert, Jean Hersholt, Sam Jaffe, Allen Jenkins, George Jessel, Roscoe Karns, Virginia Kaye, Tom Kennedy, Otto Kruger, June Lang, Betty Lawford, Gertrude Lawrence, Gypsy Rose Lee, Alfred Lunt, Bert Lytell, Aline MacMahon, Harpo Marx, Elsa Maxwell, Helen Menken, Yehudi Menuhin, Ethel Merman, Ralph Morgan, Alan Mowbray, Paul Muni, Elliott Nugent, Merle Oberon, Franklin Pangborn, Helen Parrish, Brock Pemberton, George Raft, Lanny Ross, Selena Royle, Martha Scott, Cornelia Otis Skinner, Ned Sparks, Bill Stern, Ethel Waters, Johnny Weissmuller, Arleen Whelan, Dame May Whitty, Ed Wynn (Guest Players); Count Basie and His Band, Xavier Cugat and His Orchestra with Lina Romay, Benny Goodman and His Orchestra with Peggy Lee, Kay Kyser and His Band, Freddy Martin and His Orchestra, Guy Lombardo and His Orchestra (Guest Performers).

FIRST COMES COURAGE   (Col., 1943) 88 M.

Producer, Harry Joe Brown; director, Dorothy Arzner; based on the novel *The Commandos* by Elliott Arnold; screenplay, Lewis Meltzer, Melvin Levy; adaptor, George Sklar; art directors, Lionel Banks, Rudolph Sternad; set decorator, Fay Babcock; music, Ernst Toch; music director, M. W. Stoloff; assistant director, William Mull; sound, Lambert Day; camera, Joseph Walker; editor, Viola Lawrence.

Merle Oberon (Nicole Larsen); Brian Aherne (Captain Allan Lowell); Carl Esmond (Major Paul Dichter); Fritz Leiber (Dr. Aanrud); Erville Alderson (Soren);

Erik Rolf (Ole); Reinhold Schunzel (Colonel Kurt Von Eiser); Isobel Elsom (Rose Lindstrom); William Martin (Hans, Dichter's Chauffeur); Richard Ryen (Dr. Hoff); Lewis Wilson (Dr. Kleinich); John H. Elliott (Norwegian Patient); Greta Granstedt (Girl Assistant); William Phillips (Edward, Aanrud's Assistant); Peitro Sosso (Janitor); Conrad Binyon (Small Boy); Arno Frey (Sergeant); Eric Feldary, Henry Rowland (Privates); Hans von Morhart (German Guard); Ethel Griffies (Nurse); Walter Thiel (Orderly); John Royce (German Orderly); Frederick Brunn (German Guard); Lloyd Ingraham (Elderly Norwegian Man); Duke Louis Adlon (Nazi Lieutenant); Niels Bagge (Thorsten); Rex Williams, Otto Reichow (Young Nazi Officers); Hans Von Twardowski (Nazi Captain); Fern Emmett (Dress Designer); Robert McKenzie (Justice of the Peace); Guy Kingsford (Sub Commander); Louis Jean Heydt (Norwegian); George O'Flaherty (Cipher Expert); Nelson Leigh (Blake); Tom Stevenson (Blakeley); Emerson Fisher-Smith (Cipher Expert); Miles Mander (Colonel Wallace); Evan Thomas (Ship's Captain); Larry Parks (Captain Langdon); Marten Lamont (Lieutenant Colonel); Byron Foulger (Norwegian Shopkeeper); Rolf Lindau (Junior Officer); Charles Irwin (Captain Lungden); Paul Langton, Gordon Clark (Commandos); Sven-Hugo Borg (Schmidt); Paul Power (English Officer); J. Pat Moriarity (Irish Top Sergeant); Leslie Denison (English Officer).

THE LODGER   (20th, 1944) 84 M.

Producer, Robert Bassler; director, John Brahm; based on the novel by Marie Belloc Lowndes; screenplay, Barre Lyndon; art directors, James Basevi, John Ewing; set decorators, Thomas Little, Walter M. Scott; music, Hugo W. Friedhofer; music director, Emil Newman; assistant director, Sam Schneider; choreography, Kenny Williams; sound, E. Clayton Ward, Roger Heman; special camera effects, Fred Sersen; camera, Lucien Ballard; editor, J. Watson Webb.

Merle Oberon (Kitty); George Sanders (John Garrick); Laird Cregar (The Lodger); Sir Cedric Hardwicke (Robert Burton); Sara Allgood (Ellen); Aubrey Mather (Superintendent Sutherland); Queenie Leonard (Daisy); David Clyde (Jennie); Helena Pickard (Anne Rowley); Lumsden Hare (Dr. Sheridan); Frederick Worlock (Sir Gerard); Olaf Hytten (Harris); Colin Campbell (Harold); Anita Bolster (Wiggy); Billy Bevan (Publican); Forrester Harvey (Cobbler); Skelton Knaggs (Costermonger); Charles Hall (Comedian); Edmund Breon (Manager); Harry Allen (Conductor); Raymond Severn (Boy); Heather Wilde (Girl); Colin Kenny, Bob Stephenson, Les Sketchley, Clive Morgan (Plainclothesmen); Craufurd Kent, Frank Elliott (Aides); Stuart Holmes (King Edward); Walter Tetley (Call Boy); Boyd Irwin (Policeman); Herbert Clifton (Conductor); Jimmy Aubrey (Cab Driver); Will Stanton (Newsboy); Gerald Hamer (Milkman); Montague Shaw (Stage Manager); Cyril Delevanti (Stage Hand); Connie Leon (Woman); Kenneth Hunter (Mounted Inspector); Donald Stuart (Concertina Player); John Rogers (Down and Outer); Wilson Benge (Vigilante); Alec Harford (Conductor); Yorke Sherwood, Colin Hunter (Policemen); Dave Thursby (Sergeant); John Rice (Mounted Police); Herbert Evans (Constable); Charles Knight (Vigilante); Douglas Gerrard (Porter); Ruth Clifford (Hairdresser).

DARK WATERS   (UA, 1944) 88 M.

Executive producer, James Nasser; director, Andre De Toth; based on the novel by Frank Cockrell, Marian Cockrell; screenplay, Joan Harrison, Marian Cockrell; additional dialog, Arthur Horman; art director, Charles Odds; set decorator, Maurice Yates; music-music director, Miklos Rozsa; choreography, Jack Crosby; assistant director, Joseph De Pew; sound, Frank Webster; special effects, Harry Redmond; camera, Archie Stout, John Mescall; editor, James Smith.

Merle Oberon (Leslie Calvin); Franchot Tone (Dr. George Grover); Thomas Mitchell (Mr. Sydney); Fay Bainter (Aunt Emily); John Qualen (Uncle Norbert); Elisha Cook, Jr. (Cleeve); Rex Ingram (Pearson Jackson); Odette Myrtil (Mama Boudreaux); Eugene Borden (Papa Boudreaux); Eileen Coghlan (Jeanette); Nina Mae McKinney (Florella); Alan Napier (The Doctor); Rita Beery (The Nurse); Gigi Perreau (Girl).

A SONG TO REMEMBER   (Col., 1945) C—113 M.

Producer, Lou Edelman; director, Charles Vidor; story, Ernst Marischka; screenplay, Sidney Buchman; art directors, Lionel Banks, Van Nest Polglase; set decorator, Frank Tuttle; music supervisor, Mario Silva; music director, M. W. Stoloff; musical recordings, William Randall; assistant director, Abby Berlin; sound, Lodge Cunningham; camera, Tony Gaudio, Allen M. Davey; editor, Charles Randall.

Paul Muni (Professor Joseph Elsner); Merle Oberon (George Sand); Cornel Wilde (Frederic Chopin); Stephen Bekassy (Franz Liszt); Nina Foch (Constantia); George Coulouris (Louis Pleyel); Sig Arno (Henri Dupont); Howard Freeman (Kalbrenner); George Macready (Alfred DeMusset); Claire Dubrey (Madame Mercier); Frank Puglia (Monsieur Jollet); Fern Emmett (Madame Lambert); Sybil Merritt (Isabelle Chopin); Ivan Triesault (Monsieur Chopin); Fay Helm (Madame Chopin); Dawn Bender (Isabelle Chopin at Age Nine); Maurice Tauzin (Chopin at Age Ten); Roxy Roth (Paganini); Peter Cusanelli (Balzac); William Challee (Titus); William Richardson (Jan); Alfred Paix (Headwaiter); Charles Wagenheim, Paul Zaeremba (Waiters); Charles LaTorre (Postman); Earl Easton (Albert); Gregory Gaye (Young Russian); Walter Bonn (Major Domo); Henry Sharp (Russian Count); Zoia Karabanova (Countess); Michael Visaroff (Russian Governor); John George (Servant); Ian Wolfe (Pleyel's Clerk); Lucy Von Boden (Window Washer); Norma Drury (Duchess of Orleans); Alfred Allegro, Cosmo Sardo (Lackeys); Al Luttringer (De La Croux); Darren McGavin (Man).

THIS LOVE OF OURS   (Univ., 1945) 90 M.

Associate producer, Edward Dodds; director, William Dieterle; based on the play *Come Prima Meglio De Prima* by Luigi Pirandello; screenplay, Bruce Manning, John Klorer, Leonard Lee; art directors, John B. Goodman, Robert Clatworthy; set decorators, Russell A. Gausman, Oliver Emert; music, H. J. Salter; assistant director, Fred Frank; sound, Charles G. Carroll; camera, Lucien Ballard; editor, Frank Gross.

Merle Oberon (Karin); Charles Korvin (Tuzac); Claude Rains (Targel); Carl Esmond (Uncle Robert); Sue England (Susette); Jess Barker (Chadwick); Harry Davenport (Dr. Wilkerson); Ralph Morgan (Dr. Lane); Fritz Leiber (Dr. Bailey); Helene Thimig (Tucker); Ferike Boros (Housekeeper); Howard Freeman (Dr. Barnes); Selmer Jackson (Dr. Melnik); Dave Willock (Dr. Dailey); Ann Codee (Anna); Andre Charlot (M. Flambertin); Doris Merrick (Vivian); William Edmunds (Jose); Barbara Bates (Mrs. Dailey); Leon Tyler (Ross); Cora Witherspoon (Woman); Maris Wrixon (Evelyn); Robert Raison (Call Boy); Evelyn Falke (Nanette); Joanie Bell (Susette as a Small Child); Beatrice Roberts (Surgical Nurse); Daun Kennedy (Receptionist); Jane Adams, Kathleen O'Malley, Jean Trent, Joan Shawlee, Karen Randall, Kerry Vaughn (Chorus Girls); Frank Arnold (M. Labrot); Loulette Sablon (Nurse); Ralph Littlefield (Comic); George Davis (Character Man); Constance Purdy (Character Woman); Simone La Brousse (Mme. Rigaud); Irving Greines, Peter Miles, Billy Ward, Diane Miller, Kay Smith, Robert Cole, Vicki Benedict, Olivia West (Children); Andre Marsauden (Dr. Fessier); Georges Renavent (Dr. Lebreton); Jacques Catelain (Dr. Robichaux);

Eve Garrick, Nanette Vallon, Francesca Waskowitz (Guests); Rosita Marstini (Mme. Flambertin); Marcelle Corday (Woman); Adrienne D'Ambricourt (Mme. Rocheville); Ian Wolfe (Dr. Straus); Tony Ellis (Anaesthetist); Nolan Leary (Waiter); Vangie Beilby (Irish Mother); Louise Long (Stout Woman); Richard Ryen (Chabon); Cyril Delevanti (Man Secretary); Herbert Heywood (Gardener); Joel Fluellen (Porter); Ruth Brennan (Maid); Pearl Early (Cook); Bobby Dillon, Dickie Love, Bonnie Henjum, Hugh Maguire, Pamela Peyton, Mickey Kuhn, Sewell Shurtz, Loretta Cunningham, Eleanor Taylor, Ian Bernard, Edna Mae Wonacott, Jane Eckland (Youngsters).

A NIGHT IN PARADISE   (Univ., 1946) C—84 M.

Producer, Walter Wanger; associate producer, Alexander Golitzen; director, Arthur Lubin; based on the novel *Peacock's Feather* by George S. Hellman; adaptor, Emmet Lavery; screenplay, Ernest Pascal; dialog director, Joan Hathaway; art director, John B. Goodman; set decorators, Russell A. Gausman, E. R. Robinson; music-music director, Frank Skinner; assistant director, Fred Frank; sound, William Hedgcock; special camera, John P. Fulton; camera, Hal Mohr, W. Howard Greene; editor, Milton Carruth.

Merle Oberon (Delerai); Turhan Bey (Aesop [Jason]); Thomas Gomez (King Croesus); Gale Sondergaard (Attossa); Ray Collins (Leonides); George Dolenz (Frigid Ambassador); John Litel (Archon); Ernest Truex, Jerome Cowan, Marvin Miller (Scribes); Douglass Dumbrille, Moroni Olsen, Francis McDonald (High Priests); Paul Cavanagh (Cleomenes); Richard Bailey (Lieutenant); Wee Willie Davis (Salabaar); Roseanne Murray (Marigold); Hans Herbert (Priest); Ruth Valmy, Karen X. Gaylord, Kathleen O'Malley, Karen Randle, Kerry Vaughn, Daun Kennedy, Julie London, Audrey Young, Barbara Bates (Palace Maidens); Eula Morgan, Art Miles, Al Chosis, Myrtle Ferguson, Frank Hagney (Townspeople); James Hutton (Delerai Messenger); Juli Lynne (Song Specialty); Jean Trent (Iris); Jane Adams (Lotus); John Merton (Sailor); Don Stowell (Sentinel); Pedro de Cordoba (Magus); Harry Cording (Captain); Ann Everett, Dorothy Tuomi, Marguerite Campbell, June Frazer (Flower Girls); Colin Campbell (Goatman); Nikki Kerkes, Mercedes Mockaitis (Special Water Girls); Harlan Miller (Slave); Denny Burke (Contortionist); Neal Young (Nobleman); Joe Bernard (Old Man); John Berkes, Al Ferguson, Pietro Sosso (Beggars); Earle Ozman, Dick Alexander (Temple Guards); Rex Evans (Chef); Jack Overman (Man); Wade Crosby (Rough Man); Charles Bates, Clyde Flynn, Joel Goodkind, Jimmy Fresco, Mickey Fresco, Juan Estrada, Robert Espinosa, Louis Montoya (Boys); Kit Guard (Man in Crowd).

TEMPTATION   (Univ., 1946) 92 M.

Producer, Edward Small; director. Irving Pichel; based on the novel *Bella Donna* by Robert Hichens and the play by James Bernard Fagan; screenplay, Robert Thoeren; art director, Bernard Herzbrun; set decorator, Hugh Hunt; music, Daniele Amfitheatrof; assistant director, Frank Shaw; sound, Glenn Anderson; camera, Lucien Ballard; editor, Ernest Hunt.

Merle Oberon (Ruby); George Brent (Nigel); Charles Korvin (Bareudi); Paul Lukas (Isaacson); Lenore Ulric (Marie); Arnold Moss (Ahmed); Ludwig Stossel (Dr. Mueller); Gavin Muir (Smith-Barrington); Ilka Gruning (Frau Mueller); Robert Capa (Hamza); John Eldredge (Don Gibbs); Andre Charlot (Professor Dupont); Suzanne Cloutier (Yvonne Dupont); Gloria Lloyd (Jean McCormick); Mary Young (Mrs. McCormick); Aubrey Mather (Dr. Harding); Samir Rizkallah (Abdullah); Egon Brecher (Ibrahim); Reginald Sheffield (Wickersham); Fred

Essler (Pepito); George Humbert (Mustapha Pasha); George Carleton (Mr. McCormick); Tom Stevenson (Photographer); Eddie Abdo (Egyptian Policeman); Rouhia Bey (Oriental Dancer); Lane Watson (Guest); Nick Thompson (Native Waiter); George David (Conductor); Bobby Hale (Coachman); Jean Ransome (Receptionist).

NIGHT SONG   (RKO, 1947) 101 M.

Executive producer, Jack J. Gross; producer, Harriet Parsons; director, John Cromwell; story, Dick Irving Hyland; adaptor, DeWitt Bodeen; screenplay, Frank Fenton, Hyland; art directors, Albert S. D'Agostino, Jack Okey; set decorators, Darrell Silvera, Joseph Kish; music, Leith Stevens; music director, C. Bakaleinikoff; songs, Jack Brooks and Leith Stevens; Fred Spielman, Janice Torres, and Hoagy Carmichael; assistant director, Maxwell Henry; sound, John Tribby, Clem Portman; special effects, Russell A. Cully; camera, Lucien Ballard; editor, Harry Marker.

Dana Andrews (Dan); Merle Oberon (Cathy); Ethel Barrymore (Miss Willey); Hoagy Carmichael (Chick); Artur Rubinstein (Himself); Eugene Ormandy (Himself); Jacqueline White (Connie); Donald Curtis (George); Walter Reed (Jimmy); Jane Jones (Mamie); Whit Bissell (Ward Oates); Lennie Bremen (Headwaiter—Chez Mamie); Jack Gargan, Alex Melesh (Waiters); Vic Romito, Charles Cirillo (Sailors); Eva Mudge, Angela Clarke (Women); Hercules Mendez (Headwaiter); Harry Harvey (Postman); Suzi Crandall (Girl on Street); George Cooper (Bellboy); Luis Alberni (Flower Vendor); Howard Keiser (Newsboy); Herbert Evans (Butler); George Chandler (Bartender); Antonio Filauri (Chef); Hector Sarno (Proprietor); Ervin Richardson (Artist).

BERLIN EXPRESS   (RKO, 1948) 86 M.

Executive producer, Dore Schary; producer, Bert Granet; director, Jacques Tourneur; story, Curt Siodmak; screenplay, Harold Medford; art directors, Albert S. D'Agostino, Alfred Herman; set decorators, Darrell Silvera, William Stevens; music, Frederick Hollander; music director, C. Bakaleinikoff; assistant director, Nate Levinson; makeup, Gordon Bau; choreography, Charles O'Curran; costumes, Orry-Kelly; sound, Jack Grubb, Clem Portman; special effects, Harry Perry, Russell A. Cully, Harold Stine; camera, Lucien Ballard; editor, Sherman Todd.

Merle Oberon (Lucienne); Robert Ryan (Robert Lindley); Charles Korvin (Perrot); Paul Lukas (Dr. Bernhardt); Robert Coote (Sterling); Reinhold Schunzel (Walther); Roman Toporow (Lieutenant Maxim); Peter Von Zerneck (Hans Schmidt); Otto Waldis (Kessler); Fritz Kortner (Franzen); Michael Harvey (Sergeant Barnes); Tom Keene (Major); Jim Nolan (Train Captain); Arthur Dulac (Dining Car Steward); Ray Spiker, Bruce Cameron (Huskies); Charles McGraw (Colonel Johns); Buddy Roosevelt (M.P. Sergeant); David Clarke (Army Technician); Roger Creed (M.P.); Gene Evans (Train Sergeant); Robert Shaw (R.O.T. Sergeant); Eric Wyland (Clown); Norbert Schiller (Saxophone Player); Marie Hayden (Maja); Bert Goodrich, George Redpath (Acrobatic Team); Richard Flato (Master of Ceremonies); Jack Serailian (Cigarette Maker); Lisl Valetti (German Waitress); Eva Hyde (Ticket Taker); Allan Ray (Corporal); Taylor Allen (Fraulein); David Wold, George Holt, Bill Raisch, Carl Ekberg, Hans Hopf (Germans); Willy Wickerhauser (Frederich); Will Allister (Richard); William Yetter, Jr., Robert Boon (German Youths); Ernest Brengk (Artist); Hermine Sterler (Frau Borne); Rory Mallinson (M.P. Guard); Fernanda Eliscou (German Woman); Curt Furburg (German Bystander); Larry Nunn, Jim Drum (G.I.s); Fred Spitz (German Civilian); Hans Moebus (Clerk); Jack G. Lee (Captain); Frank Alten (German

Steward); Leonid Snegoff (Russian Colonel); James Craven (British Major); Fred Datig, Jr. (American Jeep Driver); William Stelling (American Sergeant); Al Winters (German Peasant).

PARDON MY FRENCH   (UA, 1951) 81 M.

Producers, Peter Cusick, Andre Sarrut; director, Bernard Vorhaus; screenplay, Roland Kibbee; music, Guy Bernard; art director, Emile Alex; sound, Richard Smith; camera, Gerald Gibbs; editors, Derek Armstrong, Gordon Hales.

Paul Henreid (Paul Rencourt); Merle Oberon (Elizabeth Rockwell); Maximilienne (Mme. Bleubois); Paul Bonifas (Bleubois); Jim Gerald (Poisson); Martial Rebe (Mobet); Dora Doll (Yvette); Lauria Daryl (Mme. Mobet); Lucien Callemand (Inspector); Victor Merenda (Francois); Gilberte Defoucault (Marie-Claire); Marina (Jacqueline); Gerard Rosset (Michel); Albert Cullaz (Andre); Andre Aversa (Pierrot); Nicole Monnin (Marcella).

24 HOURS OF A WOMAN'S LIFE   (Associated British Picture Corp., 1952)
C—90 M.

Producer, Ivan Foxwell; director, Victor Saville; based on the novel by Stefan Zweig; screenplay, Warren Chetham Strode; art director, Terence Verity; camera, Christopher -Challis.

Merle Oberon (Linda Venning); Richard Todd (Young Man); Leo Genn (Robert Stirling); Stephen Murray (Abbe Benoit); Peter Reynolds (Peter); Joan Dowling (Mrs. Barry); June Clyde (Mrs. Rohe); Peter Illing (Monsieur Blanc); Jacques Brunius (Francois); Isabel Dean (Miss Johnson); Peter Jones (Bill); Yvonne Furneaux (Henriette); Mara Lane (Alice Brown); Robert Ayres (Frank Brown).

U.S. release title: *Affair in Monte Carlo* (AA, 1953)

TODO ES POSSIBLE EN GRANADA   (Chapalo, 1954) 80 M.

Director, J. L. Sáenz de Heredia; screenplay, de Heredia, Carlos Blanco; art directors, Ramiro Gomez, José Caballero; camera, Ted Pahle; editor, Julio Pena.

Merle Oberon (Margaret Fobson); Francisco Rabal (Fernando); Antonio (Shoeshine Boy); Peter Damon (Robey); Rafael Bardem (Mr. Taylor); Felix Dafauce (Mr. Olivier); Gustavo Re (Storekeeper).

DESIREE   (20th, 1954) C—110 M.

Producer, Julian Blaustein; director, Henry Koster; based on the novel by Annemarie Selinko; screenplay, Daniel Taradash; music, Alex North; assistant director, William Eckhardt; art directors, Lyle Wheeler, Leland Fuller; camera, Milton Krasner; editor, William Reynolds.

Marlon Brando (Napoleon Bonaparte); Jean Simmons (Desiree Clary); Merle Oberon (Josephine); Michael Rennie (Bernadotte); Cameron Mitchell (Joseph Bonaparte); Elizabeth Sellars (Julie); Charlotte Austin (Paulette); Cathleen Nesbitt (Mme. Bonaparte); Evelyn Varden (Marie); Isobel Elsom (Madame Clary); John Hoyt (Tallyrand); Alan Napier (Despereaux); Nicolas Koster (Oscar); Richard Deacon (Etienne); Edith Evanson (Queen Hedwig); Carolyn Jones (Mme. Tallien); Sam Gilman (Fouche); Larry Craine (Louis Bonaparte); Judy Lester (Caroline Bonaparte); Richard Van Cleemput (Lucien Bonaparte); Florence Dublin (Eliza Bonaparte); Louis Borell (Baron Morner); Peter Bourne (Count Brahe); Dorothy Neumann (Queen Sofia); David Leonard (Barras); Siw Paulsson (Princess Sofia); Lester Mathews (Caulaincourt); Gene Roth (Von Essen); Colin Kenny (General Becker); Leonard George (Pope Pius VII); Richard Garrick (Count

Reynaud); Violet Rensing (Marie Louise); Bert Stevens (Man at Chaumiers); George Brand (Servant); Kay Kuter (Lacky); Sven Hugo Borg (Aide); Jac George (Piano Teacher); Jack Mather (Sergeant); J. Ellis (Swedish Instructor); Harry Carter (Coachman); Marina Koshetz (Singer); A. Cameron Grant (Montel).

DEEP IN MY HEART   (MGM, 1954) C—132 M.

Producer, Roger Edens; director, Stanley Donen; based on the book by Elliott Arnold; screenplay, Leonard Spigelgass; assistant director, Robert Vreeland; choroegraphy, Eugene Loring; orchestrators, Hugo Friedhofer, Alexander Courage; art directors, Cedric Gibbons, Edward Carfango; set decorators, Edwin B. Willis, Arthur Krams; music conductor, Adolph Deutsch; choral arranger, Robert Tucker; makeup, William Tuttle; special effects, Warren Newcombe; camera, George Folsey; editor, Adrienne Fazan.

Jose Ferrer (Sigmund Romberg); Merle Oberon (Dorothy Donnelly); Helen Traubel (Anna Mueller); Doe Avedon (Lillian Harris Romberg); Walter Pidgeon (J. J. Shubert); Paul Henreid (Florenz Ziegfeld); Tamara Toumanova (Gaby Deslys); Paul Stewart (Bert Townsend); Isobel Elsom (Mrs. Harris); David Burns (Berrison, Sr.); Jim Backus (Ben Judson); Rosemary Clooney, Gene and Fred Kelly, Jane Powell, Vic Damone, Ann Miller, William Olvis, Cyd Charisse, James Mitchell, Howard Keel, Tony Martin, Joan Weldon (Guest Stars); Douglas Fowley (Harold Butterfield); Robert Easton (Cumberly); Suzanne Luckey (Arabella Bell); Russ Tamblyn (Berrison, Jr.); Ludwig Stossel (Mr. Novak); Else Neft (Mrs. Novak); Norbert Schiller, Torben Meyer (Card Players); Reuben Wendorff, Franz Roehn (Men); Laiola Wendorff (Woman); Henri Letondal (Francois); Lane Nakano (Japanese Butler); John Alvin (Mr. Mulvaney); Jean Vander Pyl (Miss Zimmerman); Mary Alan Hokanson (Miss Cranbrook); Maudie Prickett (Lady); Henry Sylvester (Judge); Bob Carson (Orchestra Leader); Robert Watson (Florist); Marjorie Liszt (Waitress); Gail Bonney, Jean Dante (Women Guests); Dulce Daye, Margaret Bacon, Gloria Moore, Lulumae Bohrman, Tailor Boswell, Richard Beavers (Bits); Gordon Wynne (Treasurer); Mitchell Kowall (Oscar Hammerstein); Joe Roach (Groom); Dee Turnell (Bride).

THE PRICE OF FEAR   (Univ., 1956) 79 M.

Producer, Howard Christie; director, Abner Biberman; story, Dick Irving Hyland; screenplay, Robert Tallman; art directors, Alexander Golitzen, Robert Clatworthy; music director, Joseph Gershenson; assistant directors, Marshall Green, Jimmie Welch; gowns, Jay A. Morley, Jr.; camera, Irving Glassberg; editor, Ray Snyder.

Merle Oberon (Jessica Warren); Lex Barker (Dave Barrett); Charles Drake (Pete Carroll); Gia Scala (Nina Ferranti); Warren Stevens (Frankie Adair); Mary Field (Mrs. McNab); Tim Sullivan (Lou Belden); Phil Pine (Vince Brady); Dan Riss (Lieutenant Walsh); Stafford Repp (Johnny McNab); Konstantin Shayne (Bolasny).

OF LOVE AND DESIRE   (20th, 1963) C—97 M.

Producer, Victor Stoloff; director, Richard Rush; story, Stoloff, Jacquine Delessert; screenplay, Laslo Gorog, Rush; music, Ronald Stein; art director, Robert Silva; assistant directors, Henry Spitz, Mario Cisneros; sound, Manuel Topete; camera, Alex Phillips; editor, Harry Gerstad.

Merle Oberon (Katherine Beckman); Steve Cochran (Steve Corey); Curt Jurgens (Paul Beckman); John Agar (Gus Cole); Steve Brodie (Bill Maxton); Edward

Noriega (Mr. Dominguez); Rebecca Iturbide (Mrs. Renard); Elsa Cardenas (Mrs. Dominguez); Tony Carbajal (Dr. Renard); Aurora Munoz (Maria, the Housemaid); Felix Gonzalez (Engineer); Felipe Flores (Julio).

THE OSCAR (Embassy, 1966) C—119 M.

Executive producer, Joseph E. Levine; producer, Clarence Greene; director, Russell Rouse; based on the novel by Richard Sale; screenplay, Harlan Ellison, Rouse, Greene; songs, Leo Robin and Ralph Rainger, Sammy Cahn and James Van Heusen; music supervisor, Irving Friedman; orchestrators, Leo Shuken, Jack Hayes; music, Percy Faith; art directors, Hal Pereira, Arthur Lonergan; set decorators, Robert Benton, James Payne; gowns, Edith Head; women's wardrobe, Glenita Dinneen; Mr. Boyd's wardrobe, Robert Magahay; assistant director, Dick Moder; dialog coach, Leon Charles; choreography, Steven Peck; sound, Harry Lindgren, John Wilkinson; camera, Joseph Ruttenburg; editor, Chester W. Schaeffer.

Stephen Boyd (Frank Fane); Elke Sommer (Kay Bergdahl); Milton Berle (Kappy Kapstetter); Eleanor Parker (Sophie Cantaro); Joseph Cotten (Kenneth H. Regan); Jill St. John (Laurel Scott); Tony Bennett (Hymie Kelly); Edie Adams (Trina Yale); Ernest Borgnine (Barney Yale); Ed Begley (Grobard); Walter Brennan (Orrin C. Quentin); Broderick Crawford (Sheriff); James Dunn (Network Executive); Peter Lawford (Steve Marks); Jack Soo (Sam); Jean Hale (Cheryl Barker); Edith Head, Hedda Hopper, Frank Sinatra, Bob Hope, Merle Oberon, Nancy Sinatra (Themselves).

HOTEL (WB, 1967) C—124 M.

Producer, Wendell Mayes; director, Richard Quine; based on the novel by Arthur Hailey; screenplay, Mayes; art director, Cary Odell; set decorator, George James Hopkins; music, Johnny Keating; assistant director, Mickey McCardle; costumes, Howard Shoup; makeup, Gordon Bau; gowns, Edith Head; sound, M. A. Merrick; camera, Charles Lang; editor, Sam O'Steen.

Rod Taylor (Peter McDermott); Catherine Spaak (Jeanne Rochfort); Karl Malden (Keycase); Melvyn Douglas (Warren Trent); Richard Conte (Dupere); Merle Oberon (The Duchess); Michael Rennie (Duke of Lanbourne); Kevin McCarthy (Curtis O'Keefe); Carmen McRae (Christine); Alfred Ryder (Captain Yolles); Roy Roberts (Bailey); Al Checco (Herbie); Sheila Bromley (Mrs. Grandin); Harry Hickox (Sam); William Lanteau (Mason); Ken Lynch (Laswell); Clinton Sundberg (Morgan); Tol Avery (Kilbrick); Davis Roberts (Dr. Adams); Jack Donner (Elliott); Lester Dorr (Elevator Operator); Dee Carroll (Mother); Judy Norton (Daughter).

INTERVAL (Avco-Embassy, 1973) C—84 M.

Producer, Merle Oberon; director, Daniel Mann; screenplay, Gavin Lambert; music, Armando Manzanero, Ruben Fuentes; costume designer, Luis Estevez; camera, Gabriel Figueroa; editor, Howard S. Deane.

Merle Oberon (Serena Moore); Robert Wolders (Chris); Claudio Brook (Armando Vertiz); Russ Conway (Fraser); Charles Bateman (Husband); Britt Leach (Leonard); Peter Von Zerneck (Broch); Fernando Soler, Jr. (Waiter); Gloria Mestre (Rosalia); Cristina Moreno (Jody); Betty Lyon (Ellie); Anel (Jackie); Barbara Ranson (Susan).

With Carl Esmond in FIRST COMES COURAGE (Col '43)

With Sir Cedric Hardwicke and George Sanders in THE LODGER (20th '44)

With Fay Bainter and Thomas Mitchell in DARK WATERS (UA '44)

With Cornel Wilde in A SONG TO REMEMBER (Col '45)

With Charles Korvin and
Sue England in THIS
LOVE OF OURS
(Univ '45)

With Lenore Ulric in
TEMPTATION (Univ '46)

With Hoagy Carmichael and
Dana Andrews in NIGHT SONG
(RKO '47)

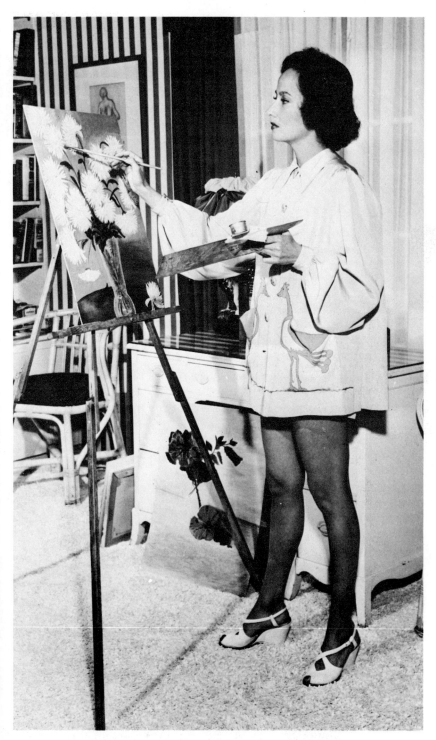

Painting at home (1948)

With Richard Todd in 24 HOURS OF A
WOMAN'S LIFE *(Affair in Monte Carlo)*
(Associated British Pictures '52)

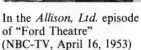

In the *Allison, Ltd.* episode
of "Ford Theatre"
(NBC-TV, April 16, 1953)

With Marlon Brando and Jean Simmons (center, behind train bearer) in
DESIREE (20th '54)

Monty Woolley, Buster Keaton, Bert Lahr, ZaSu Pitts, and Joan
ett in *The Man Who Came to Dinner* episode of "Best of Broadway"
-TV, October 13, 1954)

With Helen Traubel and Jose Ferrer in DEEP IN MY HEART (MGM '54)

With husband Bruno Pagliai
(c. 1960)

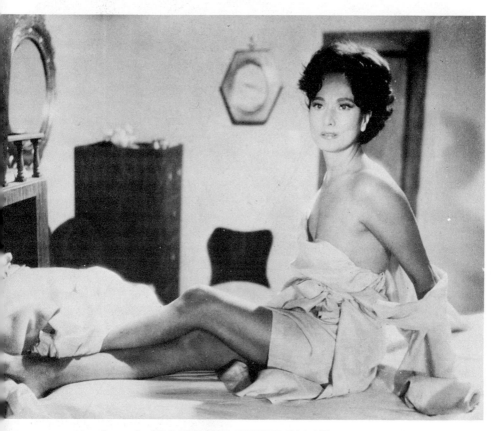

In **OF LOVE AND DESIRE** (20th '63)

With Rod Taylor in HOTEL (WB '67)

With Noel Coward at the
National Theatre, London
(December 14, 1969)

With Robert Wolders in **INTERVAL** (Avco-Embassy '73)

With Robert Wolders at the New York premiere
of **INTERVAL** (June 15, 1973)

In LAKE PLACID SERENADE (Rep '44)

Vera Ralston

Almost two decades have passed since Vera Hruba Ralston starred in her last motion picture, a programmer thriller called *The Man Who Died Twice* (Republic, 1958). Yet even today, the merest mention of her imposing name brings instant smiles to faces of movie "camp" followers everywhere, hampering any serious effort to assess fairly her personal merits as a screen actress.

Vera was certainly not a grand movie thespian in the flamboyant manner of Gale Sondergaard, nor did she reach the acting level of another East European, charming Ilona Massey. However, like the equally exotic but more obviously alluring Maria Montez and Yvonne De Carlo, Vera possessed an amazing self-confidence that carried her through years of making mediocre motion pictures and often through some very un-polished performances on her part.

It is now fashionable to sympathize with the plight of actress Marion Davies, who, because of her millionaire mentor-lover, William Randolph Hearst, was forced to continue a film career long after she wished to retire, urged on by him to star in antiquated, unflattering ve-hicles that pleased only his highly unique fantasies about her charisma. On a similar, if less grandiloquent, level, it was Vera's (mis)fortune to have at-tracted the attention of senior citizen Herbert J. Yates, head of low-bud-get Republic Pictures. It was he who envisioned in his "protégée" Vera, whom he later wed, a totally alluring femme fatale of the screen.

If Vera had not encountered Yates, she might well have continued her spectacular ice skating career, which first brought her to America as a new Sonja Henie type. But having been lured to Hollywood by "Pappy" Yates, she fell in with his master plan to convert her into a glamorous silver-screen lady equal to the best product of any other Hollywood film factory. Unfortunately, Yates's tastes, like his studio's quickie movies, were geared to the cultural level of *Spy Smasher* serials and Roy Rogers-Dale Evans-Gabby Hayes Westerns. Thus, while David O. Selznick was showcasing his mistress-later-wife Jennifer Jones (who had herself debuted at Republic Pictures) in the well-mounted *Since You Went Away* (United Artists, 1944) and *Portrait of Jenny* (Selznick Releasing, 1948), Yates, with fewer aesthetic standards to go by, was displaying Vera's sundry charms in such tepid sagebrush adventures as *Plainsman and the Lady* (Republic, 1946) and such contemporary-set rubbish as *Angel on the Amazon* (Republic, 1948) and *Accused of Murder* (Republic, 1956). Even when the very aged Yates threw the stockholders' financial assets to the wind with the recklessly elaborate *Jubilee Trail* (Republic, 1954), it was the second female lead, Joan Leslie, and *not* his wife, Vera, who had the focal emphasis.

In short, as a notable (and scoffed at) example of studio nepotism, Vera suffered the scorn of the film industry, but in return she rarely gained the benefits of proper display in pictures that would accentuate her intriguing Continental personality. Had Yates allowed her to occasionally be loaned to more opulent, resourceful studios, her movie career just might have turned out differently. However, he jealously guarded her, oncamera and off, with all the foresight of a miser sifting through his hoarded pot of gold.

If the progression of Vera's screen presence in the course of her twenty-six features (all made at Republic) is studied, remarkable strides in her acting acumen can be noted. Habitués of the small-town movie theatres and the big-city double-bill action houses had a seventeen-year span to become accustomed to Vera's svelte figure, changing hair color and style, foreign-accented speech, and particular onscreen bearing. There is no reason to doubt that many of these filmgoers readily accepted Vera at face value. Given her special Republic Pictures level, she represented for them a variation of the Hollywood glamour girl, as alluring and enticing as a Jennifer Jones or Ilona Massey, or the more elaborate big-studio glamour stars, Joan Crawford, Marlene Dietrich, and Hedy Lamarr. It is only a matter of relativity. As with Yates's own special, if often ludicrous, vision of Vera's silver-screen potential, beauty, as always, is in the eyes of the beholder.

Until January 1973, Vera Ralston had always assumed her correct birth-date was July 12, 1920, but suddenly, after more than four years of waiting for Communist bureaucracy to unravel yards of red tape, she received an official copy of her Prague, Czechoslovakia, birth certificate. The attested date of her birth was Thursday, July 12, 1923. She was, to say the least, jubilant over the difference of three years in her favor. "I took that paper, had all kinds of copies made, and stuck it in my bank vault." Laughingly, she added, "If I were a heavy drinker, I'd have gotten drunk."*

Vera's father, Rudolf Hruba, was a wealthy jeweler and president of the Jewels Association, a society composed of Prague's better retail jewelers. Her mother, Marie, according to Vera, "was just a mother, and a good one, too." There was one other child in the Hruba family, Rudolf, Jr., born two years before Vera.

Blonde, blue-eyed Vera Helena Hruba received a Roman Catholic christening and devoted most of her first four years to discovering, inside and out, the comfortable Hruba home and grounds set on the banks of the Berounka River on the outskirts of Prague. An inquisitive, intelligent, and certainly precocious child, she reveled in everything she encountered.

In the winter of 1927, while brother Rudy was busily playing late-afternoon hockey on the frozen Berounka River, four-year-old Vera was enrolled in ballet classes. Not long after she began classes, she insisted upon demonstrating to the teacher that she was double-jointed. Although this physical uniqueness made her basically more nimble than her contemporaries, she proved to be only a better than adequate student. In grade school, she exhibited a special adeptness for reading and writing and by her eighth year she had written poems and short stories, some of which were published by local Prague newspapers.

Of her early youth, Vera particularly remembers Rudy's German shepherd dog, a large, bounding animal which fascinated more than intimidated her. At the same time, her pet was a goat which she named Suzie. "I didn't speak English. Where I picked up the name of Suzie," Vera said, "I don't know." At any rate, with her pet goat on its leash, she and Suzie followed everywhere after Rudy and his dog.

Because her parents thought it imperative for a girl of Vera's background to learn additional languages in order to be more well balanced in her education, she was sent to a German convent in Doksi, Czechoslovakia, for the 1932 summer vacation away from regular schooling. "I didn't like it," Vera recalls of that sojourn at the convent, where institutional austerity was the order of the day. Even the recreational activities had a solemn tone to them, "[in which] you have to play tennis with black up to your neck and long sleeves and when you have to swim in long bathing suits. It's no fun for a young kid." Vera did everything possible to be expelled. "I was nasty, I was naughty, I was horrible." Nothing seemed to upset the supervisors, that is, until Vera was caught smoking cigarettes.†

---

*This quotation and most of the first-person statements in this chapter are from an interview with Miss Ralston at her home in Santa Barbara, California, conducted on March 10, 1973, by this book's co-author, Don E. Stanke.

†Vera, 1973-style, recalling those long-ago days, added, "And, do you know, I've been smoking ever since."

Then "they threw me out. I was a bad influence on everyone else. That was fine with me! All the other kids were having summer fun at home, why not me, too?"

That winter, Vera learned to ice skate, with brother Rudy providing her with the basic instruction. Because of her prior ballet training, Vera caught on quickly to the new sport and soon found that she enjoyed it far better than the more formalized discipline of classical dancing. From this point onward, she devoted every available moment through the remainder of that memorable winter to skating on the portion of the river nearest her home, which Rudy always kept cleared of snow.

Rudolf Hruba, above and beyond being a good businessman and a devoted husband and father, was extremely politically minded. He instilled in his children an understanding and appreciation of Czech history. In 1933 he predicted what the Germans under their new "saviors," Adolf Hitler and the National Socialist Party, hoped to gain from neighboring countries like Czechoslovakia. This foreboding of his country's impending doom encouraged Hruba in his decision that each and every Czech must now do his part to bolster the Czech sense of national pride. He perceived that Vera, if she pursued her ice skating with great diligence, could be a living symbol of the best that their country had to offer. Thus he arranged for her to spend the summer vacation of 1934 in London, where, unlike Czechoslovakia, there were indoor rinks and she could continue her lessons during the warm months when lessons in Prague would have been impossible.

Vera did well with her accelerated skating instruction, and she returned to England the following summer to win the British gold medal, one of the highest awards an amateur figure skater can receive. It was a double honor in that, as a relative beginner, she was in competition with girls who had skated for many years longer than herself. By September 1935, when she returned to Prague, she not only had her well-publicized medal, but also had a speaking knowledge of the English language as pronounced by the "ver-ee" British. Photographs of Vera from this period reveal that the pert adolescent, who had been born with light yellowish-brown hair, was now a natural "brownette" (a color somewhere between medium and dark brown).

The skating portions of the 1936 Olympics took place at Garmisch-Partenkirchen in Germany.* At "sixteen"† Vera was her country's entry in the competition for the Gold Medal. Since the German Fuehrer, Adolf Hitler, was host to the Olympics, he was naturally anxious for Ger-

*Much of the 1936 Olympics was filmed in an expansive, imaginative documentary by Leni Riefenstahl. The edited footage, in various formats, has been shown over the years, as recently as 1972 on American network television.

†Vera's parents, wanting their daughter to be "mature" and eligible for skating events, had by this point induced her to believe she was now sixteen.

many to make a superlative showing by winning as many medals as possible in all conceivable categories. However, he was advised that Germany lacked a woman figure-skater who was sufficiently expert to capture a trophy in this area. He sent for Vera and requested her to represent Germany by skating in the Olympics under his country's flag. According to Vera and substantiated by those present at this meeting, she looked the little man straight in the eyes and replied, "I would rather skate *on* it than *for* it." Hitler glared at her and said out of the corner of his mouth, "That is a shame, isn't it?" Vera insulted the German leader even further by not acknowledging his presence with a salute when she later skated past his reviewing box. Such audacity by a young girl gained her widespread publicity as a heroine of the day.

In the final tally of judges' votes, it was Sonja Henie of Norway who won the Gold Medal for the women's figure-skating competition.* Vera skated a very close second and took the Silver Medal. Vera says of Henie: "She was one of the greatest skaters. There will never be another like her. I was never jealous of her because I always admired her. It made me feel good to lose to her."

The following year (1937) Rudolf Hruba accompanied his daughter to the United States, where she performed with distinction in ice revues in several major eastern cities and in Canada. She was contracted to skate in Madison Square Garden, where she hit upon the idea of skating to the popular dance, "The Big Apple." "I saw people were dancing it in restaurants and I thought 'why not put it on ice' and when I did, Madison Square Garden went wild for it. I had one encore after another." Because Vera and her father were in the States on special visitors' visas, it was established that they would be able to take home with them whatever American currency she earned during the stay. "I made a lot of money," Vera now recalls. "I was paid like $1,000 a minute."

Before Vera left Manhattan to continue the skating tour in Boston and Philadelphia, RKO. Studio scouts arranged for her to be screentested. When a term contract was offered, she proudly said, "Oh, no, I'm going home. I'm getting married." She considered herself engaged to a "very nice rich boy who was studying to be an engineer." However, when she

---

*Henie was born on April 8, 1912, in Oslo, Norway. At the age of fourteen she won the Norwegian skating championship and in 1927 acquired her first world's figure-skating prize. In 1928, 1932, and 1936 she won the Olympic women's figure-skating events. She had made her film debut in *Syv Dager for Elisabeth* (1927), a Norwegian silent movie, but it was not until 1936 that she decided first to give up her amateur standing and turn professional, and then also, hopefully, to pursue a motion-picture career. As the dimpled, blonde Henie phrased it, "I want to do with skates what Fred Astaire is doing with dancing." By mid-1936, Henie was in America. She went to the West Coast, scheduled a special three-day ice show at the Polar Ice Palace in order to give movie executives a chance to observe her special talents, and within a short time had signed a lucrative cinema contract with Darryl F. Zanuck, mogul of Twentieth Century-Fox Films. Henie's first American picture was *One in a Million* (Twentieth Century-Fox, 1936).

677

returned to Prague five and one-half months later, all hopes she had of a forthcoming marriage had been dissolved by both families. The half-Jewish boy's parents would not consent to his wedding a Catholic, while the Hrubas did not want Vera to marry anyone who was not a Catholic.

In 1938 and early 1939, Hitler made hysterical pronouncements that Czechoslovakia rightfully belonged to his people, and because the Germans required "lebensraum," German troops moved in and occupied Prague on March 15, 1939. Vera and her mother embarked on the last plane to leave the city before the Nazi takeover. They flew to France and then, several weeks later, boarded a ship for New York.

Once in America, Vera experienced no difficulty in obtaining employment. She joined a skating show called the Ice Vanities, which toured the United States. "Now, that show was just about the finest show that will ever be put on ice because it had every kind of a champion from all over the world—English, Canadian, Norwegian. It was the greatest show as far as skating talent was concerned." Occasionally, between breaks in the show's tour schedule, Vera would return to New York, as she did in late 1939 when she joined the on-ice revue at the Hotel New Yorker's Terrace Room. The club revue was staged by Katie Schmidt, with Nate Walley and Edith Dustman receiving top billing. Vera performed two specialty numbers, a rumba on ice and a ballet dance on skates to the melody of "Deep Purple."

Later, while performing with the Vanities in New Orleans, she broke an ankle and went with her mother to Miami Beach to wait for the bone to mend. Six weeks later she was able to resume skating and practiced daily at a Miami arena. She was asked to do a benefit show and, while so doing, was spotted by an agent from the Ice Capades who signed her up for the 1940 season. In colorful and spectacular costumes she skated as one of the stars in the elaborately staged production numbers for which the Ice Capades has always been famous. Her roommate for the entire time she was with the show was Bobbie Dorree, a skater in the chorus whom Vera had first met in England.

In January 1941, while in Chicago with the Ice Capades, Vera expressed to a friend her concern over what might happen to her when her U.S. visitor's permit expired in March. She was convinced Hitler would remember with vehemence her act of independence and that it would mean great problems for her should she be forced to return to occupied Czechoslovakia. Someone advanced the notion that her problem would be solved if she were to wed an American citizen. Shortly thereafter her photograph appeared in a Chicago newspaper along with the story of her plight, in which she said that she would be agreeable to accepting an American suitor. "I got something like 2,400 offers to get married. I had a full trunk of letters. One man, for instance, was in jail and he wrote saying, 'I will be out in a year and will be most happy to marry you.' Oh ya," the Vera of today laughed in recalling this episode. "I even had jail-birds writing." It did not become necessary to accept any of the marriage proposals, however, because the United States Immigration Service intervened, due to the tremendous publicity, and quickly arranged for Vera to travel to Canada and then to reenter the United States under a special Czech quota.

In the early summer of 1941, the Ice Capades troupe was stationed in Atlantic City performing a special engagement. Donna Atwood of California, who had won the national seniors pair championship with Gene Turner, was the show's top star, with Vera again billed as a special featured attraction. Upon completing their New Jersey engagement, the company headed for California, for they had already received and agreed to accept a special bid from Herbert J. Yates, president of Republic Pictures, to appear in a musical movie which was to be written around their ice-skating acts.*

Legend has it that Yates, on one of his frequent cross-country sales tours, had stopped off in Kansas City and, finding himself with a free evening, purchased a ticket to the Ice Capades. He was so enthralled by the performance that he hastily determined to have the troupe utilized in one of his film company's upcoming productions.† On the surface, Yates's notion seemed sound enough, for Republic's celluloid output was especially geared to the lucrative small-town theatre bookings where Americans had thoroughly endorsed the studio's annual output of Westerns, serials, actioners, and bucolic, homey tales. Yates evidently reasoned that if traveling ice-skating revues were still big business in America, it did not matter that Twentieth Century-Fox had suffered great reversals in the sales of Sonja Henie movies since 1939, the same year MGM buried a Joan Crawford movie bomb entitled *Ice Follies of 1939*.

By the time the Ice Capades troupe arrived in Hollywood, they found

---

*Yates was born in Brooklyn, New York, on August 24, 1880. He graduated from Columbia University and thereafter joined the American Tobacco Company, rising through the ranks to become eastern regional sales manager. He later was made vice-president in charge of sales, and before retiring from the field, was also involved with the Liggett & Myers tobacco Company.

Back in 1910, Yates had had his first brush with motion pictures when he agreed to underwrite Roscoe "Fatty" Arbuckle in a film series. In 1915, Yates joined Hedwig Film Laboratories, Inc., and three years later organized Republic Film Laboratories. The next year he formed Allied Film Laboratories, and three years later emerged with Consolidated Film Industries, Inc. In May 1935, under Yates's auspices, four independent producing companies, including Mascot and Monogram Pictures, were merged into Republic Pictures Corporation, at first utilizing rented space at the Mack Sennett Studios in North Hollywood. Consolidated Laboratories remained a key ingredient of the Republic Pictures Corporation setup.

At this time Yates was married; he and his wife, Petra, had a daughter, Elissa, and three sons, Richard, Douglas, and Herbert, Jr.

†According to some accounts, Yates first became interested in the Ice Capades, and Vera Hruba in particular, when James Johnston, Madison Square Garden impresario, introduced her to him around 1939. It has been alleged that at this time Yates advised Vera that she should both slim down to more American figure standards and learn to speak English better.

that a $50,000 skating rink—a half-block square—had been constructed on the studio backlot, and that Yates had five scriptwriters busy at work concocting some thread of a tale to surround the skating talent in this film, to be called *Ice-Capades* (Republic, 1941).

As it developed, the eighty-nine-minute feature had the slimmest of storyline plots. Newsreel cameraman James Ellison neglects to follow up an assignment to photograph a top Swedish skating star (Renie Riano) at Lake Placid, and in order to paste together some footage to please his boss, he goes to Central Park and there photographs Dorothy Lewis skating about the pond. Impresario Phil Silvers views Lewis on film and wants to sign her for a stage revue, but it turns out that she is an immigrant illegally in the United States. The big show does go on, Lewis's passport problems are clarified, and Ellison wins her affection.

Young Lewis, then a big name in ice revue circles, had the major share of the screen time, both on and off the ice in *Ice-Capades,* while the other members of the skating group were merely spotted briefly with their specialty numbers. Lois Dworshak led a jitterbug session on the frozen water, Belita performed ballet dances on ice, Megan Taylor executed figure-skating feats, Jackson and Lynam did comedy sketches. Although Yates was already deeply interested in Vera, she received no special attention within *Ice-Capades,* being just one of the many "internationally known skating stars" as she shared screen footage with Belita. The big-city critics who bothered to review this Republic "extravaganza" on ice insisted that "the little bit of ice and skating which are shown in the Republic picture of the same name give it about as much claim to the title as one icicle would have to the name of iceberg" (Bosley Crowther, *New York Times*). The reviewers were far more impressed, to a limited extent, with the eyeball-rolling comedy of Jerry Colonna and the shenanigans of ex-radio performer Barbara Jo Allen (cast as Vera Vague, a name she would subsequently adopt professionally). As for skating "star" Dorothy Lewis, the reviewers were decidedly unimpressed by her dry-land dramatics.

Evidently theatre patrons in Middle America were less critical than the Broadway reviewers, or Herbert J. Yates was just a determined soul, for the following year he produced a follow-up venture entitled *Ice-Capades Revue* (Republic, 1942). Ten minutes shorter than its predecessor, this black-and-white entry benefitted from a much stronger leading cast of dramatic performers, particularly Ellen Drew as the New England farmgirl who inherits a bankrupt ice show, and Richard Denning and Harold Huber as the two men out to fleece country-girl Drew. Because they had worked well together in *Ice-Capades,* Jerry Colonna (as a bogus backer) and feather-brained Barbara Jo Allen were on hand for comedy relief. *Ice-Capades* had had one semipotent "big" number, the "Legend of the Falls" finale, but *Ice-Capades Revue,* according to *Variety,* was "strong on music and in spectacular production numbers."

Within *Ice-Capades Revue,* there are sufficiently well handled ice skating chorus numbers involving the melodies of "Tequila" and "The Guy with the Polka Dot Tie," and to add the proper patriotic note for those World War II times, the film's finale provided a V-for-Victory formation, using the melodies of "Anchors Aweigh," "The Caissons Go Rolling Along," "The Marines' Hymn," and the "Army Air Corps Song." Vera was given a much more prominent role in *Ice-Capades Revue.* She performed a hula dance on ice to the tune of "Song of the Islands," and in another scene, playing herself, was given dialog describing her escape from Prague.

Of her "dramatic" motion-picture debut Vera remembers: "Nervous? Yes. I had goose pimples and was shaking like a leaf. I had butterflies in my stomach. It was awful."

Once again the movie critics were not particularly aware of Vera's presence on the Hollywood scene. Nevertheless, Yates advised her to make a concerted effort to Americanize her British-accented English.

Meanwhile, through Czech authorities in the United States working in cooperation with the underground in Prague, Vera's brother, Rudy, was snatched out of Czechoslovakia and was eventually flown to New York. After a few weeks of relaxation with his sister, he joined the United States Army in 1942 and served with General Patton overseas. Rudolf, Sr., chose to remain in his native land to do whatever he could from within to rout the hated Germans.

In 1943, Vera left the Ice Capades when Yates offered her a long-term Republic contract.* She requested that her roommate Bobbie Dorree, be hired too, as her stand-in. The stipulation was granted, and Bobbie remained in that job throughout Vera's screen career.†

Vera then went to work studying under the tutelage of drama and voice coach Josephine Dillon, whose most famous student had been her ex-husband, Clark Gable. Among her other pupils had been Gary Cooper, Lupe Velez, and Lydia Roberti. Vera's most difficult task was altering her speech pattern to acceptable "Yankee" English. Miss Dillon worked diligently with the novice actress until Yates was satisfied that she was now ready to emote oncamera in a starring role.

Because her name was already established as that of a figure-skating

---

*In 1940, Yates had signed Judy Canova, the vaudeville-stage-radio-motion-picture yokel-comedienne to a long-term contract. While at the studio (1940-43) she proved enormously successful with her slapstick rural comedies. Canova later admitted that she left Republic in 1943 (although she returned there again from 1951 to 1955) because Yates had taken a too "personal" interest in her, and when she rebuffed him, he had deliberately sabotaged her career. In the serial-making division of Republic, Linda Stirling, Kay Aldridge, and Lorna Gray were the prime figures; and in Westerns, Dale Evans, who joined the studio in 1942, became Queen of the Cowgirls and in 1947 the wife of Republic's cowboy star, Roy Rogers.

†Bobbie Dorree died in January 1974. Vera, making one of her rare appearances in Los Angeles, attended the memorial services held at the Wee Kirk of the Heather in Forest Lawn.

star, it was decided to retain it and to add something distinctively American to it. Vera chose "Ralston" for the simple reason that she liked the breakfast cereal bearing that name. Yates agreed readily since it was a well-known word in millions of households from coast to coast. Vera's mother also adopted Ralston as her surname, as did Rudy when he was eventually released from military duty at the end of World War II.

For Vera's initial nonskating melodrama, Yates chose to embellish Curt Siodmak's 1943 novel, *Donovan's Brain*.* It became *The Lady and the Monster* (Republic, 1944), set in a castle on the Arizona desert.† The name Vera Hruba Ralston was given prominent billing, almost eclipsing that of Erich von Stroheim, the famed director-actor who had fallen on such hard times that he was taking pick-up acting assignments wherever and whenever he could find them in Hollywood.

Although *The Lady and the Monster* was minus any elaborate production values, associate producer-director George Sherman managed to engender a lot of eerie values from his limited budget. The film script had "mad" doctor von Stroheim removing the undamaged brain of a financial genius, W. H. Donovan, who died in a plane crash near the scientist's castle laboratory. The organism is kept alive in a murky glass-tank enclosure, and gradually comes to dominate the actions of von Stroheim's junior associate, Richard Arlen. Vera portrayed Janice, a medical assistant to chain-smoking von Stroheim, the eccentric doctor who insists, "When you're trying to solve the mysteries of nature it doesn't matter whether you experiment with humans or guinea pigs." Whenever the somewhat deranged physician orders Vera to "get the Gigli saw," she knows that it means another head is about to be opened and its brain extracted. The words cause her to freeze with astonishment. Naturally, as the tale unfolds and her boyfriend (Arlen) comes under the evil influences of the self-generating brain, she finds herself cut off more and more from any contact with rationality.‡

Vera's coach, Josephine Dillon, was offered the small part of a grandmother in the film, so she could be present on the set and instill confidence in Vera. Actually, the movie newcomer required all the assistance she could muster because the Dane Lussier-Frederick Kohner screenplay did little to give her character any dimension or rationale.§ She was simply sandwiched into a hearty thriller for the sake of standard romantic

---

*At least three theatrical-film versions of the tale were made (besides assorted video program variations), the most distinguished edition being the 1953 United Artists release, *Donovan's Brain*, with Nancy Olson in the female lead.

†Republic also called the film *Tiger Man*, while the British release title was *The Lady and the Doctor*.

‡In one of his more lucid moments, Arlen tells Vera's character, "Hey, you even look good in riding clothes."

§Otis L. Guernsey, Jr. *(New York Herald-Tribune)*, in dissecting the film, decided, "The picture's weakest point is the girl in the case, who is completely extraneous and who puts an annoying drag on the action whenever she appears." Even the song in the film was given to Janet Martin to sing in the cafe sequence, a Spanish rendition of "Yours."

interest, and, as indicated, the storyline set-up did not allow for much amorous interaction between her and increasingly "possessed" Arlen. Cinematographer John Alton, who did wonders with the sequence in which the brain comes to live and takes over control of Arlen, did his best to compliment Vera with soft-focus lighting, but much of his effort was vitiated by the odd assortment of waves styled into her lightened tresses by hairdresser Peggy Day. *

Yates, Republic, and the company stockholders must have been surprised to discover that *The Lady and the Monster* was considered one of the thriller-sleepers of the year. "This picture is definitely one of the season's most mature and engrossing mystery pictures" *(New York World-Telegram).* " . . . one of the most authentic hair-raisers screened this year at Broadway's horror house, The Rialto" *(New York Herald-Tribune).* John Baxter, in *Science Fiction in the Cinema* (1970), ranks this feature as "one of the Forties' most diverting horror films." But sadly, Vera did not share in the cornucopia of glory. "Miss Hruba, former ice-skating star, makes bid for dramatic buildup here, but is handicapped by her role" *(Variety).* A. Weiler *(New York Times)* politely suggested she is a "mite too lethargic."

Like many other economy-minded studios, Republic had a persistent habit of contracting performers and technical talent for packages of "quickie" pictures. Thus it was that (associate) producer-director George Sherman, and players Erich von Stroheim and Richard Arlen were rushed from *The Lady and the Monster* to give Vera support in *Storm over Lisbon* (Republic, 1944).† By 1944 the World War II spy-story genre had been drained of novelty, and if *Casablanca* (Warner Bros., 1943) is considered the apex of espionage films set in a city of intrigue filled with pro-Allies and Axis-loyal (counter) agents, then *Storm over Lisbon* might vie as ⌐being the nadir of the species.‡ "World events are gyrating too rapidly for so silly a spy picture," scoffed Howard Barnes *(New York Herald-Tribune).* The *New York World-Telegram* reviewer was even less polite, insisting that this Republic entry was "aimed at the readers of the cartoon books."

In *Storm over Lisbon,* von Stroheim is Deresco, an international spy mastermind, who has a fabulous castle overlooking the Lisbon harbor. Through his ownership of a bustling local gambling casino-cafe, he manages to traffick quite successfully in secret documents, selling to the highest bidder. Thus far the Lisbon police, trying to maintain the city's "neutrality," cannot directly connect von Stroheim with any particular illegal act. Suddenly two parties rush onto the scene, threatening to topple von

---

* James Agee, writing in *The Nation,* found Vera "unusually attractive."

† Rereleased in July 1950 as *Inside the Underworld.*

‡ Warner Bros. attempted to duplicate the success of *Casablanca* with the stale *The Conspirators* (1944), also set in Lisbon. At least it had excellent production values and a cast that included Hedy Lamarr, Paul Henreid, Sydney Greenstreet, Peter Lorre, et al. to compensate for the stale jumble of spying in the Portuguese capital.

Stroheim's apple cart. First, there is newspaperman John Craig (Arlen), who has escaped the Japanese with valuable military data. He soon finds himself caught in von Stroheim's clutches, with the latter anxious to extract the potentially salable information from the recalcitrant Arlen. Then there is exotic, mysterious ballerina Maritza (Vera), who is in the Portuguese capital just long enough to obtain a passport and then clipper plane passage to America. Until she can acquire her exit visa—however and from whomever—she accepts a post at von Stroheim's club, agreeing to put her dancing talents to use in entertaining the customers. Scattered into the eighty-six-minute story are Otto Kruger as a spy who has outlived his usefulness, Robert Livingston as the plane pilot, Eduardo Ciannelli and Mona Barrie as two of von Stroheim's chief helpers, and, for comedy relief, Alice Fleming and Sarah Edwards as two elderly tourists who crave excitement. If the latter two characters had only known about von Stroheim's penthouse prison and lethal elevator, or that Vera's Maritza was actually an Allies-loyal operative, they might have jumped for joy.

While *Storm over Lisbon* passed through the distribution circuit quickly and was soon forgotten in the wake of newer celluloid products, the critics did pause long enough to discourse on the dramatic growth of Yates's protégée. "If Miss Ralston had an easier command of the English language she would have been ideally suited to her role of international glamor girl, for she photographs well and is our idea of what a beautiful spy should look like" *(New York Daily News)*. "Attempts to make a dramatic actress out of . . . [Miss Ralston] aren't too successful, the actress being too wooden. She's highly attractive, though, and a seductive dancer in a ballet sequence" *(Variety)*. The *New York World-Telegram* delicately phrased it; "[She] is making heavy going of her transformation from dancer to movie actress."

Perhaps the highlight of *Storm over Lisbon,* which boasted far more lavish sets than were the usual Republic standard, was the utilization of music from Borodin, particularly the melody which later became famous as "Stranger in Paradise" in the Broadway musical *Kismet.* As for the performance of von Stroheim, the performer once billed as "The Man You Love to Hate," he gave a hammy, exaggerated performance, making it quite obvious what he thought of the film project and the unimaginative direction of Sherman.* When asked what she thought of acting with this stout, bald, humorless little man, Vera said of von Stroheim, "He was a little on the hard side to work with; he was very precisioned."

After this brief sojourn away from screen skating, Vera returned to the ice rinks in *Lake Placid Serenade,* which debuted at New York's Republic

---

*It is reputed that director Sherman so abhorred working on Vera's pictures that he quit the studio rather than be subjected to such a trying artistic situation again.

Theatre on December 25, 1944.* The storyline was geared to parallel Vera's own true-life experiences: Vera Haschek, the skating queen of Czechoslovakia, is invited to America, but once in this country, the changing course of European events prevents her from returning to the Continent. In desperation she seeks aid from her wealthy uncle (Eugene Pallette), now a naturalized citizen. He invites her to be his house guest, where she must vie with his two spoiled rich daughters (Ruth Terry, Stephanie Bachelor) for the affections of Robert Livingston, Pallette's junior partner. Later, after being named queen of the Lake Placid celebration, she agrees to star in a Madison Square Garden skating revue, but, because of her immigration and personal problems, she insists upon being billed as the "Cinderella Girl." Needless to say, all ends happily, even with her godfather (Lloyd Corrigan) arriving in America to share in her newfound joy.

As production-value-conscious *Variety* noted, "Studio didn't stint on this one." Reportedly, Republic spent a whopping $1.5 million on this musical extravaganza, a far cry from the usual budget allotted to the studio's typical Western or actioner, which for all their low production costs brought in many times over a steady profit. *Lake Placid Serenade* boasts a wide assortment of settings to properly display Vera's skating skills: from scenes of Vera skating in Czechoslovakia, to the Lake Placid backdrop, to the quiet-pond spread near Pallette's estate, to the elaborate theatre-stage interior for the revue-show sequences. Without question, most of the film's eighty-five minutes belong to Vera. She is shown participating in a native Czech dance. Later she performs ice-ballet dances to the melodies of "Deep Purple" and "Intermezzo," and on another occasion she executes an intricate Hawaiian hula dance on ice. For variety's sake, Janina Frostova and Felix Sadovsky did a skating routine to "Hey, Slovana," young Twinkle Watts (who many thought could be another Vera on ice) had a specialty number, and the skating corps had a precision drill sequence that would have pleased Radio City Music Hall audiences. Proving that Yates (and Republic) was sparing no effort to make this the studio picture of the year, the company's top attraction, Roy Rogers (without his faithful horse Trigger!), was "roped" into the picture to provide the film's only vocal, "Winter Wonderland." For comedy relief, and rural audiences doted on these sequences, there were Barbara Jo Allen (Vera Vague) as the "angel" of the big show, Walter Catlett as a pursuing promoter, William Frawley as a Damon Runyonesque publicity man, and, of course, oversized Pallette as the gruff but kindly uncle. To woo the big band enthusiasts, the film boasted Ray Noble and Orchestra and Harry Owens and his Royal Hawaiians.

*A. H. Weiler (*New York Times*) quipped that the film "is as seasonal as an eggnog but not nearly as exhilarating."

Lake Placid Serenade, despite all the gingerbread trimmings which Yates-Republic bestowed on it, was not the hit of the year, and found it tough sledding at the box office. It was simply too expensive a film to recoup its costs in the small-town theatres across the country. But the Steve Sekely-directed musical did provide ample opportunity for critical appraisal of Vera's celluloid ice skating. Lee Mortimer *(New York Daily Mirror)* was immediately attracted by "Vera's shapely flashing calves and thighs. There is something to be said for skating costumes at that." Other reviewers were more intent on comparing Vera's athletic talents with those of Sonja Henie, the latter having completed her Twentieth Century-Fox contract with the previous year's *Wintertime.* "Long, lean-limbed and extremely lovely in a wistful, unsmiling way, Vera tops Sonja at every turn in the personal physique department. When it comes to skating, however, the crown still belongs to smiling Sonja. Vera skates handsomely, but almost entirely without esprit. Despite every effort of script and production to make it appear otherwise, skating with Vera is clearly exhibition and seldom fun" *(PM).*

The war in Europe ended in May 1945, and the Russians "liberated" Czechoslovakia. Vera then had the first communication from her father since before the war. She learned that he had been confined for a year in a German concentration camp because "he was too much a good Czech; too much a democrat." The Germans released Rudolf, Sr., just prior to the Russian liberation, because the S.S. uncovered among Rudolf's effects photographs of Vera with the Fuehrer at the 1936 Olympics and assumed that this man was, after all, a pro-Nazi.

Vera set the wheels in motion at once, after the war, to bring her father to California. He arrived early in 1946, a very ill person who required a doctor's constant care for over a year. Meanwhile Vera purchased a home in Sherman Oaks, California, where the four Hrubas were once again a united family.

Vera's sixth film, and her only release of 1945, was *Dakota,* which first teamed her with John Wayne, long a stalwart of the Republic Pictures contract stable.* As the daughter of railroad tycoon Hugo Haas, she elopes with free-enterprising gambler John Devlin (Wayne) and convinces him they should head for North Dakota rather than the "rich" lands of California. Independent-natured Vera has a plan in mind, for she knows the railroad is planning to extend to Dakota and she wants to purchase land

---

*In an article for *Views and Reviews,* Harry Sanford reports director Joe Kane as stating that Wayne initially rejected the picture which was to co-star Vera. Then Yates, situated for the duration in New York City, ordered Kane, Wayne, producer Edmund Grainger, and scripter Lawrence Hazard to New York. Kane recalled, "The last thing Wayne said to me as he left to go in the elevator to see Yates was that he would *not* do the picture with Vera under any circumstances." By whatever means, Wayne's objection to the assignment was resolved behind a closed door in conference with Yates.

options and then resell to the train companies at a large profit. In the course of their trek westward they encounter Ward Bond and Mike Mazurki, the duo who rule Fargo, North Dakota, with an unjust iron hand, and salty old Captain Bounce (Walter Brennan), skipper of the vessel *River Bird*. Once in Fargo the land war begins, with Wayne joining forces with the wheat farmers against Bond and his gang. By the end of the film not only have the villains been routed, but the somewhat grasping Vera has softened her approach to life and seen the wisdom of her husband's scruples.

For a potentially rousing action film, *Dakota* had only a minimum of heavy-going action, the highlights being the prairie fire and the slug-fest between Wayne and the team of Paul Fix and Grant Withers. No matter how hard the studio's technical talent tried, it could not disguise the fact that "the production itself is somewhat shoddy, with faked backgrounds and drab surroundings" *(New York Herald-Tribune)*. As for Vera's second-billed presence in *Dakota, Variety* was quick to observe, "Vera Hruba Ralston, femme lead, comes through a river ducking, the fire and fights with every hair in place and not a single wrinkle."

Vera's next film, *Murder in the Music Hall* (Republic, 1946)*, returned her to the skating arena, with John English, more noted for directing Republic serials, helming the production.† A hated former producer-director and ex-convict is stabbed to death, thus establishing the title for *Murder in the Music Hall*. Contradictorily, however, the homicide actually transpires in a building next door to the Manhattan-sited music hall.‡ As Lila Layton, star of the Ballet on Ice, Vera makes her onscreen skating entrance to the accompaniment of an instrumental and choral arrangement of "My Wonderful One" and soon disappears into the dark night to the consternation of her friends. "From the way everyone is worrying about me," her character says, "you'd think I'd committed a crime." Of course, this is the established key red herring: that she will be (and is) murder suspect number one. *Murder in the Music Hall* has an excellent supporting cast, including Nancy Kelly, Helen Walker, Julie Bishop, and Ann Rutherford as four other suspects, William Gargan, the screen's former Ellery Queen, as the police inspector, and Jerome Cowan as a columnist. Fay McKenzie, as the singer in Ilka Gruning's cafe, handled the vocal numbers, providing a pleasant contrast to Vera's three skating routines.§

*Reedited and rereleased in 1950 as *Midnight Melody*.
†Director English reportedly informed Vera just what he thought of her acting talents. Not surprisingly, he soon departed from Republic Pictures.
‡The theatre in question was in no way supposed to be Radio City Music Hall.
§One scripting loophole of the film had the stage performers in the show-within-the-movie taking interminable intermission time, so that within the plot they might have the opportunity to solve the caper. With Vera rushing breathlessly hither and thither it was a wonder at all that she had the energy to perform her routines in the skating act revue-within-the-movie.

In ICE-CAPADES REVUE (Rep '42)

With Herbert J. Yates in 1943

With Richard Arlen in THE LADY AND THE MONSTER (Rep '44)

With Jack LaRue and Pierre Watkin in DAKOTA (Rep '45)

689

With Maria Ouspenskaya and William Elliott in WYOMING (Rep '47)

With Henry Travers in THE FLAME (Rep '47)

With John Wayne in THE FIGHTING KENTUCKIAN (Rep '49)

With Walter Brennan and William Ching in SURRENDER (Rep '50)

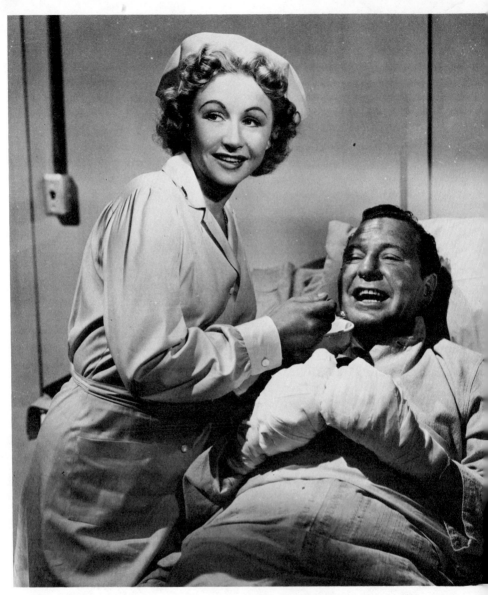

With Phil Harris in THE WILD BLUE YONDER (Rep '51)

With John Qualen, John
Carroll, and William Ching
in BELLE LE GRAND (Rep '51)

With John Russell in
HOODLUM EMPIRE (Rep '52)

With Fred MacMurray in
FAIR WIND TO JAVA
(Rep '53)

693

Dorothy Masters *(New York Daily News),* in her two-and-one-half-star review, noted of Vera, "she's a person of considerable interest thanks largely to a neatly dovetailed screen play."

Murder in the Music Hall represented two "lasts" for Vera. First, since skating required her to practice as much as six hours a day, thus cutting into her dramatic studies, Yates informed her that the time had come when she must choose between a skating career and an acting career.* Selecting the latter, Vera says, "I hung up my skates."† She was never to skate again, either professionally or for her own enjoyment. Second, when the film was completed, she decided to drop the use of Hruba from her professional name mostly because it was so often misspelled on theatre marquees, "and that can be dangerous." Then too, filmgoers and critics alike had difficulty pronouncing Hruba and, as a result, "Americans called it everything from 'Rhumba' to 'Rhubarb', and when someone actually pronounced it 'Rum-Bum', I knew it had to go."

In Los Angeles, on Tuesday, June 4, 1946, Vera became an American citizen. "It was the most exciting day of my life. I owe this country so much and it will always be my home." She celebrated the momentous occasion quietly with her family and then returned to her regimen as a film performer. The Hollywood community and the public at large were startled, to say the least, when Vera announced that same month that "I mean to start studying Shakespeare. . . . After all, with so many thee's and thou's, I should certainly overcome my weak point in pronunciation."

Despite her publicized interest in the Bard, stimulated by her visits to New York and evenings of watching the Old Vic Company performing, Vera was next cast in another Western, *Plainsman and the Lady* (Republic, 1946)‡ starring William Elliott, then regarded by the *Motion Picture Herald-Fame* poll as number-two "Western Money-Maker" lead in American motion pictures.§ This Western was conceived as an expansive period entry, detailing the history of the Pony Express as the two-thousand-mile route between St. Joseph, Missouri, and Sacra-

---

*According to on-the-spot participants, Yates once issued orders to Republic's music director, Cy Feuer, to record twenty minutes of soft waltz music with the full studio orchestra. Yates offered no explanation. Feuer did as he was instructed and late one evening, when most of the studio hands were at their homes, Yates and Vera were seen skating arm in arm on a stage ice-skating rink to the waltz music.

†Even Sonja Henie, after signing with RKO for the color skating picture, *It's a Pleasure* (1945), realized that the genre had run its course and there were no new variations to offer a jaded filmgoing public.

In an interview at the time Vera explained, "You see the skating must be kept—what is that word?—subordinate to the plot. That is not easy, to find good stories which can also use big ice spectacles."

‡Rereleased in 1954 as *Drumbeats over Wyoming.*

§The others for 1946 were: (1) Roy Rogers, (3) Gene Autry, (4) George "Gabby" Hayes, (5) Smiley Burnette, (6) Charles Starrett, (7) Johnny Mack Brown, (8) Sunset Carson, (9) Fuzzy Knight, (10) Eddie Dean. (Most of these top-ten attractions were Republic contract performers.)

694

mento, California was established in the pre-Civil War days.* With Elliott as a wealthy cattleman-rancher, Vera as banker Reinhold Schunzel's daughter, Joseph Schildkraut as the unscrupulous, oily stagecoach-line promoter, tough gunslinger Don Barry, and Gail Patrick as Vera's society-conscious sister, the vacuous film, with its elaborate ballroom scenes and outdoor sequences, tried to be a powerful, swashbuckling sagebrush tale. However, it was at heart "too muddled and too long" (Otis L. Guernsey, Jr., *New York Herald-Tribune*). If the incongruous blend of contrasting exotic foreign accents (Czechoslovakian Vera, German Schunzel, Austrian Schildkraut) could be overlooked, there was ample opportunity to note and perhaps agree with *Variety's* scribe who reported that Vera "is seen to excellent advantage whether in a party dress or riding togs. Incidentally she has developed into a first-rate thespian."

Convinced that he knew the motion-picture market best, Yates again cast Vera with "Wild Bill" Elliott in *Wyoming* (Republic, 1947), a film ballyhooed as "Rough, Roaring, Romantic, Big in Stars! Big in Action!" It was to be yet another historical "epic." In the course of the scenario, Charles Alderson (Elliott) migrates to the territory of Wyoming with his young wife (Vera) and Maria (Maria Ouspenskaya), the latter the life-long acquaintance of Vera's mother. Vera later dies in childbirth, but her baby survives and is raised by Ouspenskaya. Meantime, Elliott, aided by his pal Windy (George "Gabby" Hayes), consolidates a huge cattle empire. The little girl is later sent east for her education,† and by the time she returns a beautiful young woman (Vera), Wyoming has become a state and Elliott has fallen in love with Lila Regan (Virginia Grey), manager of the Great Northern Hotel. Nesters are encroaching on Elliott's grazing land, leading to growing tensions between the cattlemen and the farmers. Glenn Forrester (John Carroll), former lawyer and now Elliott's foreman, takes the farmers' side and walks out on Elliott. Vera, smitten with Carroll, takes his part, all of which leads Elliott to eventually perceive the error of his ways. Intertwined in this overly familiar tale‡ is Albert Dekker as the slick villain who pretends to be on the side of both factions.

---

*William K. Everson in *A Pictorial History of the Western Film* (1969) observes, "Having built Bill Elliott into a top Western star via a series of expert and fast-moving 'B's, they [Republic] changed Bill to William and promoted him to nine-reel historical western 'specials,' in which he was tied down by frock coats and silk shirts, reels of dialogue, studio 'exteriors' and back projection, and far too little fresh air, horses, and wagons. Expensive films like *In Old Sacramento* [1946] and the *Plainsman and the Lady* contained not a quarter of the action or appeal of his five-reelers . . ."

†Vera's "accent" is explained away in the script by having her sent to Europe to complete her finishing-school education. But the mixture of Vera's diction and Ouspenskaya's Russian accent was distracting in a story of the American Old West.

‡There are similarities to MGM's *The Sea of Grass* (1947), which, despite the presence of Spencer Tracy and Katharine Hepburn, was too expensive a programmer to recapture its production costs.

The film, directed by Joe Kane,* was considered pretty tame going by action fans, who would have preferred more brawls and gunplay in the yarn. The Vera of 1973 recalls that her dual role had its problems. "It was a little confusing there for a while because Bill was my lover in one picture [*Plainsman and the Lady*] and my father and husband in the next. . . . It could only happen in Hollywood." Vera photographed at her most attractive in *Wyoming*. Her hair was very blonde, which blended well with the gowns, several of which were white, designed by Adele Palmer. Unfortunately, looks alone were not enough to carry her part, which the *New York Times* labeled as "implausible."

By late 1947, Vera had completely won the heart of sixty-seven-year-old Yates. He separated from his wife of more than thirty years, and their four children (all of whom were adults by this time). He intended to marry the much-younger Vera as soon as an amicable divorce settlement could be arranged. However, this was not to occur for another five years. In the meantime, Vera continued with her career, particularly striving to rid herself of the telltale Czech accent. The latter was "something I just couldn't lose, no matter how hard I tried."

Vera's emoting showed definite improvement in her next vehicle, *The Flame* (Republic, 1947), the second of five pictures she would co-star in with ex-MGM performer John Carroll.† Unfortunately, it was one of those turgid triangular-love-story dramas, and *Cue* magazine advised, "*The Flame* is a good picture to stay away from, with or without a good book." The *New York Herald-Tribune*'s reviewer could not resist quipping, "Republic has attempted to make a blowtorch out of a birthday candle." Or, as Howard Thompson *(New York Times)* uncharitably phrased it, "The sole distinction of *The Flame,* a rambling inept bit of claptrap . . . is the bleakly amusing fact that most of the performers seem either bored or amused with the whole thing." The story, marred by flashback after flashback, concerned an overly ambitious French nurse (Vera) who weds supposedly fatally ill Robert Paige, so that when he dies, she can deliver her inheritance (a whopping insurance policy) to her lover, none other than Paige's corrupt brother (Carroll). Predictably, Vera falls in love with Paige, which requires—for plot purposes—an about-face of Carroll's nasty characterization (he reveals a hidden good streak by sacrificing his life to eliminate pushy blackmailer Broderick Crawford). *Vari-*

---

*Kane was one of Vera's favorite directors. "He is so gentle and so understanding—and I don't react well to temperamental people—directors, players or anybody else!" Director Kane, on the other hand, has said: "She really wasn't a bad gal personally. Everybody liked her, but the situation was next to impossible. She was not box office. Yates insisted on block sales, which meant a Vera picture. I could hardly ever get a big male star, because he knew if he signed, Vera most likely would be cast opposite him. Yates wouldn't let me cast a big female star in any picture because usually Vera wanted the role whether she was right for it or not."

†Vera and Carroll have remained good friends over the years. He is now a successful Florida businessman and, Vera says, "as handsome as ever."

ety observed, "Miss Ralston shows considerable improvement in her work."

Her next outing, *I, Jane Doe* (Republic, 1948), is Vera's favorite film. "I think it was my best because I had the materials and script to work with. It was right up my alley." This stark courtroom drama cast Vera as a French war bride who comes to America only to find that her spouse (John Carroll), a former U.S. pilot, is a two-timer and already wed to Ruth Hussey. She murders him and is placed on trial where, because she steadfastly refuses to reveal her true identity, she is referred to as Jane Doe. Her defense attorney is the philanderer's compassionate wife (Hussey), who later decides to reopen the murder case when Vera has Carroll's baby in prison. Lawrence Kimble's script strove for adult dialog but verged too often on corn,* and, with its overabundant reliance on flashbacks, so aggravated A. H. Weiler *(New York Times)* that he charged, "its sum total, sadly enough, is a combination of soap opera, tear-jerking and weak suspense." Another Manhattan critic spit forth, "Something tells us that, if *I, Jane Doe* is ever shown in Europe, it will not do much toward enhancing respect for American justice." Vera received what were becoming by now the customary "token" reviews by the majority of big-city critics. None of them wished to challenge her acting levels with the standards used for a Bette Davis. On the other hand, they wanted to give her more serious consideration than would be accorded a personality performer, such as Marie McDonald, or a band singer-dancer like Vera-Ellen. In *I, Jane Doe,* Weiler *(Times)* found Vera "merely lachrymose" and *Variety* tagged her "impassive."

Soon after the release of *I, Jane Doe,* Dore Schary, then vice-president in charge of production at RKO, asked to borrow Vera for the feminine lead in *The Set-Up* (RKO, 1949). Yates immediately refused to put her on loan, stating, "This is her home. Republic is where she works." Consequently, the meaty role went to Audrey Totter. "You know," Vera confides about that long-ago lost part, "Mr. Yates was—I guess—a little bit jealous. He was always around the sets when I worked and when anyone saw him heading my way, I was warned with 'Watch it, here comes Pop.'"

Cinematically, 1948 ended for Vera with what is possibly her most inferior film, *Angel on the Amazon,* her third and final professional association with associate producer-director John H. Auer. Once again Lawrence Kimble "created" the screenplay for a movie that, according to the *New York Herald-Tribune,* "comes close to winning the nod for

---

*At one point in the trial, Hussey, admitting that she would have killed Carroll if Vera had not, turns and points to the defendant, and says, "There but for the grace of God sit I." At another stage in the film, Vera's infant son catches a fever and dies in a nearby hospital. But after a brief recess, Vera, Hussey, the jury, and everyone concerned with the case have all forgotten about this "tragedy."

the worst film of the year." Today *Angel on the Amazon* can be considered high camp.

In this lackluster farrago, Vera is Christine Hidgeway, whose aging processes are in a state of arrest due to her once having been frightened by a panther. She is approaching old age, but younger George Brent does not know this and ardently woos her. Vera's husband, Brian Aherne, knows the shocking truth and is rightfully dazed by it, while Constance Bennett, as a psychiatrist, figures that the youthful "angel" is just plain nuts. Of this embarrassing—even by Republic's standards—production, Vera now says, "The whole thing was unreal."

Meantime, Vera's father, Rudolf, had recovered his health and returned to Prague to attend to what remained of his business affairs. Since he did not approve of Vera's close relationship with Yates, he chose to remain in his homeland and obtained a job there as a minor government official for the Communists. Marie Hruba Ralston filed for, and received, a divorce in 1948, for she had no intention of joining Rudolf in Prague under the existing political atmosphere. Rudolf, Sr., then took a new wife by whom he later had a son, also named Rudolf.*

For Christmas, 1948, the divorced Marie visited her two sisters in Prague. After a tour of Europe, Vera and Yates joined her there for a planned two-week holiday. Vera had earlier been informed by the U.S. State Department that her passage out of Czechoslovakia could not be guaranteed even though she was now a United States citizen. ("I'm such an outspoken witch and the Communists had no more love for me than I for them.") Vera, Yates, and Marie Ralston left Prague after only three days. "Czechoslovakia was so poor. It was heartbreaking to see little children without enough food to eat. I don't like to see my country again. I don't want to see the sadness." She did not return to her homeland thereafter, even though she and Yates annually traveled to Europe. "This is my country now," she says of the United States. "I love it. It has been very good for me and to me."

John Wayne was number-four box-office star in the United States in 1949, more as a result of his appearances in John Ford's *She Wore a Yellow Ribbon* (RKO) and Allan Dwan's *Sands of Iwo Jima* (Republic) than for his co-starring stint with Vera in *The Fighting Kentuckian* (1949). This latter film represents Wayne's debut as a film producer, and it is very likely that this golden opportunity, given to Wayne by Yates, induced him to play straight man in a second Vera Ralston vehicle. Not that Wayne was antithetical towards her. Socially they got along well together, and she always regarded him as one of her favorite leading men. However, Wayne was well aware that Yates's personal interest in Vera had blinded his business acumen and that Vera's films were generally overbudgeted

*Vera and the new Rudolf "write to each other to this day. I have been helping him financially. He is a nice boy."

in relation to the probable box-office return under the Republic small-town distribution-exhibition setup.

In *The Fighting Kentuckian,* scripted and directed by George Waggner, Vera is the dark-haired Fleurette, daughter of a French general (Hugo Haas) exiled from France to Alabama in 1819. She encounters Wayne while on a shopping spree in Mobile, and it is love at first glance. The many obstacles to be overcome before they can "get together" include the routing of culprits who yearn to evict the French from their lands, battling it out with wily rivermen, and getting Vera bathed in a tub with foam up to her lovely neck. The battle scenes in the film are lively and set to musical variations of "La Marseillaise." The picture benefits from an intriguing supporting cast. Corpulent Oliver Hardy, in a rare latter-day appearance without sidekick Stan Laurel, is Wayne's cohort; Marie Windsor is the scheming Ann Logan;* with Odette Myrtil as Vera's exiled mother, Philip Dorn as an ex-French army colonel, John Howard as the southern landowner determined to wed Vera, and Paul Fix as Windsor's associate in villainy.

The Fighting Kentuckian emerged as an oddball piece of entertainment. " . . . if it is history, it is obscure and unconvincing" (A. H. Weiler, *New York Times*). The film also lacked sufficient rough-and-tumble scenes, too much footage being devoted to Hardy's comedy relief, and, in particular, to the romantic clinches between Vera and Wayne, with Vera receiving a full share of close-ups. Vera, "who wears some pretty dainty apparel for a pioneer lady" (Weiler, *New York Times*), was given full rein to posture and dally as the film's focal point. Nevertheless, as Howard Barnes *(New York Herald-Tribune)* pointed out, she "plays the heroine with considerable restraint." It was predictable that this would be (and was) the final film Wayne would make with Vera.

Beginning in 1950, Hollywood's slogan was "Movies Are Better Than Ever," and Vera proved that she, too, was better with the release of *Surrender* (Republic, 1950). Again with black hair, she played a post-Civil War bitch, a girl named Violet Barton, from La Mirada, Texas. She is selfish and calculating, as well as being wanted by the Houston police for thievery. She tells her sister (Maria Palmer), "Money is the greatest thing in the world. I don't care who pays the bills," and "I'll use any man any way I wish." Without an iota of conscience, she weds wealthy newspaper editor William Ching for his money, but discovers that she really loves John Carroll, who is as dishonest as she. They decide to head for Mexico after Vera stabs to death her first husband (Francis Lederer), who had suddenly shown up on the scene. However, Vera and Carroll wind up being shot and

---

*Actress Windsor recently told the authors, "I always found Vera to be a charming and warm person with a delightful sense of humor. She was always extremely close to her family."

dying side by side, à la *Duel in the Sun* (1946). The film contains one song, also called "Surrender," written by Jack Elliott and John Carroll.

Although Otis L. Guernsey, Jr. (*New York Herald-Tribune*) stated that Vera "is something less than convincing as a femme fatale" (during the film's first half-hour her sidelong glances and eye rolling are disconcerting characteristics), her performance did improve as the movie progressed, with Vera the wench and Carroll the cad vying for honors as most unredeemable human being in the Old West. Much of the salvation of *Surrender* as a viable screen commodity goes to veteran director Allan Dwan, who also would helm Vera's next two Republic features.*

In *Belle Le Grand* (Republic, 1951), John Carroll and William Ching were again Vera's major vis-à-vis. In the title role, Vera was a lady gambler in rugged, silver-rich Virginia City. She has a yen for rambunctious gambler John Carroll, who has designs on her innocent sister (Muriel Lawrence). Noble-hearted Vera swaggered through the tale with her head high and her bustle rustling as she weds flashy Carroll to save Lawrence from a dire fate. Hope Emerson was thankfully on hand as the rowdy harridan Queen of the Comstock, and Stephen Chase was present as the sinister force. Lawrence, who was introduced to screen audiences in this feature, sang in her gooey, innocent style, "Voce di Primavera," and "Drink to Me Only with Thine Eyes." More demanding critics, like Otis L. Guernsey, Jr. (*New York Herald-Tribune*), passed off *Belle Le Grand* as "merely another pedestrian attempt to capitalize on a colorful period."

Then, in *The Wild Blue Yonder* (Republic, 1951), Vera offered what some critics call her worst performance, as an army nurse sought after by air force rivals Wendell Corey and Forrest Tucker. The real star of the World War II picture was the B-29 bomber (known as the Superfortress) and how its use by the Allied forces did so much to end the war. For comedy relief in *The Wild Blue Yonder* there was Phil Harris, who sang "The Thing." William Ching had his musical moment with "The Man Behind the Armored-Plated Desk," performed with a male quartet, and there were also renditions of the "Army Air Force Song" and "The Heavy Bomber Song." Today Vera can look back on this film and judge: "It was blah! It was almost a walk through. There was nothing to my part; I was only there for romantic interest in a man's action picture."

Prior to the national release of *The Wild Blue Yonder*, sequences from the film were heard on "Lux Radio Theatre" (September 24, 1951) when

*Dwan, who was a contract director at Republic between 1945 and 1953, and helmed fourteen films there, was a keen observer of the Vera Hruba Ralston star-building situation under Yates. He told Peter Bogdanovitch in *Allan Dwan* (1971) regarding *Surrender:* "I can't tell you what I think about it—it should be buried some place! Yates loaned Carroll some money and that was one way of getting it back—give him a lot of work."

Of *Belle Le Grand*, Dwan told Bogdanovitch, "Making allowances for the cast—Carroll and Vera Ralston again—it was a pleasant picture. Of course, she tried very hard and was a very nice girl. She just hadn't been trained to be an actress long enough to star in pictures. You can't just come off the ice and be a dramatic actress—unless you slide off with the right finish."

700

the dramatic anthology program presented *Movietime, U.S.A.* The Republic film was one of eight features to get a preview highlight treatment, and Vera, Corey, and Tucker were at the microphones to reenact snatches of scenes from the forthcoming air drama.

Perhaps Vera's finest screen performance was in *Hoodlum Empire* (Republic, 1952). In *fourth* billing she is a French peasant girl who is seen in a flashback sequence saving the life of John Russell from the Germans during World War II. She later marries him in the United States. Vera seemed very relaxed in this role, more so than in any other, and her voice was soft and at its most appealing. Her hair was blonde again, and her facial makeup blended well with the coloring. The screenplay by Bruce Manning, based on a Bob Considine story, revolved around a Senate investigation into the rackets and bore a tight resemblance to the actual Senator Kefauver probes of 1951. In *Variety*'s estimation, "the picture packs a wealth of exploitation values and rates as a stout box-office contender." The wise filmgoer could quickly parallel performances to reality, with Luther Adler as Frank Costello,* Brian Donlevy as Kefauver, Claire Trevor as Virginia Hill, Gene Lockhart as Senator Tobey, and so forth. Forrest Tucker was particularly effective as Adler's strong-arm underling. Some critics of *Hoodlum Empire* carped that because the actual thing (the Kefauver Hearings) was so spontaneous and powerfully real, the movie imitation seemed a pale carbon-copy at best, especially vitiated by the moralistic ending, which has the committee chairman within the film voice the plea that the cure for organized crime "rests with you, and you, and also you."

On Saturday, March 15, 1952, Herbert John Yates, as *Time* magazine put it, "signed a new contract with his favorite cinemactress." After obtaining a marriage license in Burbank, he drove Vera a few miles to North Hollywood where they were quietly married in the Little Brown Church in the Valley. With $50 worth of flowers adorning the altar, and Yates's first wife (!) and his secretary standing in as witnesses, Yates, at the age of seventy-two, took as his second wife, twenty-nine-year-old Vera Ralston. Vera admits to always being very much aware that their marriage provided a certain amount of amusement to Hollywood. She says: "Most people thought that I married him because I wanted to be in pictures and he was a millionaire. On the contrary, we were in love. To me, he was everything. He was my boy friend, my lover, my husband and my left hand." They played golf at 8:00 A.M. the day after their marriage and then honeymooned in Europe for three months.

According to Vera, her position as wife to the studio's president did not change the attitudes of her co-workers. "All of the people loved me because I never let them feel that I was *Mrs.* Yates. They never thought of me as the boss's wife—just as Vera!"

*George Raft, originally cast for the role, walked out of the project when his underworld pals suggested he not play the part.

Like the rest of the Hollywood film studios in the early 1950s, Republic was suffering from the economic pinch of the competing television industry and from the vast repercussions of the post-World War II governmental antitrust suits concerning block bookings, and illegal tie-ins of distribution-exhibition among the major motion-picture companies. In 1953, production at Republic was down to twenty-two features and two serials, less than half of what had been the company's annual output throughout the lucrative 1940s. But the studio, under Yates, struggled onward.* Republic's big picture of 1953 was *Fair Wind to Java*, a romantic adventure yarn based on the Garland Roark novel.† Vera, of course, was "selected" to star in this overly lavish production filmed in Trucolor,‡ and Fred MacMurray, then on the career skids, was hired at a relatively modest fee to portray her leading man.

In *Fair Wind to Java*, Vera appeared as Kim Kim, a Japanese dancer, a part reminiscent of those performed a decade earlier by Maria Montez and Dorothy Lamour. Carefree Kim Kim is purchased by Yankee sea captain MacMurray for entertainment purposes, but later he weds her. She is also the keeper of the secret of where a fortune in jewels is hidden, and both MacMurray and a bevy of villains (Robert Douglas, John Russell, Grant Withers, Buddy Baer) are most anxious to obtain possession of the fabulous loot.

From the film's opening, everything is geared for the "spectacular" finale, with the audience being informed that this is the year 1883, when the giant volcano on the Pacific island of Krakatoa exploded, with its rumbles heard three thousand miles away. As Joseph Kane guides the ninety-two-minute feature to its conventional plotline conclusion, one waits with eager anticipation for the explosive fireworks and tidal wave, counting on the studio's fabled special-effects team of Howard and Theodore Lydecker to provide their visual wizardry. Unfortunately, the Lydeckers, whether through last-minute budget limitations or a temporary loss of creativity, failed to make their Trucolor miniature effects live up to expec-

*One of the studio's more memorable "little" pictures of 1953 was John Ford's *The Sun Shines Bright*.

†*Fair Wind to Java* had originally been scheduled to star John Wayne, but he had quit the studio in a dispute over filming *The Alamo* (which he would make in 1960 for United Artists). Director Joe Kane would later recall to cinema historian Harry Sanford, "Truly it [this film] could have been called the *Kane Mutiny* and I even considered quitting the studio after 18 years. It got that bad. . . . the trouble started when we began to cast the picture. Guess who Papa Yates decided was to play the role [of fourteen-year-old Kim Kim]? Yep—Vera! I was ready to walk out." Kane also related that the studio junked most of the original book scenario to transform it into a nineteenth-century high seas yarn; that Yates rejected a Java location junket because he and Vera would then be unable to make their annual European trek; that instead half of a huge sailing ship was built on a soundstage and mounted on rockers with a very expensive painted backdrop; and that despite a crash diet, Vera was still far from suited to the part.

‡It was Vera's debut picture in color.

tations, leaving the lumbering romance story with a flat action finale.*
The film was not a financial success.

Dark-haired Vera is quite beautiful in native Javanese garb and darkened skin.† During the filming at Paradise Cove near Malibu Beach, California, a canoe carrying MacMurray, Victor McLaglen, and Vera capsized, throwing them into the cold waters of the Pacific Ocean. They had to swim a half-mile to shore into the waiting arms of panicked Republic brass. It was later learned that MacMurray, who suffered from a dread fear of water, literally swam for his life. Vera, by order of Yates as well as for insurance precautions, always had a double nearby to take over the strenuous physical requirements of a screen role. However, this time her double was on shore. Vera did her own swimming.

For her second 1953 release, Vera, who never really enjoyed making Westerns, let alone riding horseback, was back on the trail in *A Perilous Journey*, a journeyman actioner directed by production-line assembler R. G. Springsteen. Only moviegoers with the shortest memories could have failed to notice the great similarities between the plots of *A Perilous Journey* and Robert Taylor's far superior *Westward the Women* (MGM, 1951). In the Republic version, forty-nine women are heading to California to be mail-order brides for domesticity-hungry 1850s gold-miners.‡ The gals, under the chaperonage of rugged Hope Emerson, sail for the West Coast via Panama on a rigged vessel skippered by Charles Winninger. Vera, as Francie Landreaux, is hot on the trail of her gambler husband, who has deserted her. Once in California, she locates her spouse in David Brian's Sacramento saloon, but the erring man is shot down in cold blood. In the course of the "maze of hackneyed histrionics" (*Variety*), Vera sings "Bon Soir," one of the film's three songs.§ Virginia Grey, as a New England spinster lady daring to seek emotional fulfillment, was far more effective than Vera as the alleged femme fatale, who stirs both Brian and ex-cowboy-card-sharpie Scott Brady.

In May 1954, Republic released to the world "The greatest epic since *Gone with the Wind*," starring "the screen's most beautiful woman." *Jubilee Trail* (Republic, 1954) was based on a diverting best-selling novel by Gwen Bristow, and was adapted for the screen by Bruce Manning, who

---

Krakatoa, East of Java (Cinerama, 1969) relied on the same historic natural phenomenon for its wrap-up, and, as lensed in widescreen Cinerama, was an equal disappointment.

†According to Vera, Yates informed her, at the time of casting *Fair Wind to Java,* Unless you dye your hair [she had tried brunette wigs] I can't let you have the role." When the picture was completed, Vera told columnist Louella Parsons, "*Fair Wind* was the first time I ever had a chance to play a character part. I have always had to play blonde, goodie-goodie parts, and this gives me a chance to do something different."

‡The studio's ads proclaimed this film a story of "love-hungry women on a voyage no man dared to make."

§The other numbers were "On the Rue de la Paix" and "California."

should have omitted many of the talky sequences in favor of more action for Jack Marta's Trucolor cameras.

Again brunette, Vera is Florinda Grove, a New Orleans saloon entertainer who is wanted back in New York for murder.* She and a genteel widow friend (Joan Leslie) find themselves heading for California via St. Louis, Independence, and Santa Fe. Once in old Los Angeles, Leslie's fatherless baby becomes the kidnapping target of meanie Ray Middleton. The latter is eventually gunned down by drunken old doctor Pat O'Brien. Vera performed four songs in *Jubilee Trail*, "Saying No" (sung in French and English), "Jubilee Trail" (performed with Buddy Baer and the "boys"), "A Man Is a Man," and "Clap Your Hands" (performed with Baer and the boys). The *New York Times*'s Howard Thompson pointed out that Vera "sheds her rather flamboyant kittenishness for some good, straight emoting toward the last reel." This refers to the sequence in which Vera creeps into a secluded spot above the saloon and, while seated on the floor, offers her "first prayer, and if I do it badly, you'll [God] have to forgive me." She briefly describes her past wayward existences, admits her romantic feelings for Handsome Brute (Baer), and begs the Lord to protect Leslie and the child. She concludes the touching prayer with a simple "Florinda," as though signing a letter.

Jubilee Trail, despite its elaborate mountings and the fine Victor Young score, was met with general indifference by the public.† "Instead of red-blooded men and women, we see stock characters," grumbled Joe Pihodna (*New York Herald-Tribune*). When the picture crossed the Atlantic Ocean and was screened in London, the British *Monthly Film Bulletin* complained, "The action is slow and diffuse, and the film would greatly benefit by cutting. The Indian attack at the beginning, for instance, is unexplained, and seems superfluous." Ironically, although *Jubilee Trail* was and is considered a Vera Ralston screen vehicle, it was actually Joan Leslie who had the picture's focal female role,‡ thus making it all the more incongruous that the film's box-office failure should be thrust so completely on Vera's cinema track record.δ

*On this superexpensive production, the Republic publicity staff went hog-wild to please Yates and incidentally to induce a television-addicted public to return to the cinema. The promotional material described Vera's Florinda as "beautiful, courageous, gay, she was born to be adored by men and sees no reason why she shouldn't make the best of what she was born for."

†Director Kane had wanted to lens the picture in CinemaScope, which would have enhanced its market value, but Yates was feuding with the head of Twentieth Century-Fox, which then held the patent controls on the special equipment required.

‡The ex-Warner Bros. ingenue joined Republic in 1952 for *Toughest Man in Arizona* and made four additional pictures at the studio in the next two years.

*The exorbitant production costs for *Jubilee Trail*, considering the diminished film-rental revenues possible in the 1954 distribution market, would be a point of high contention during subsequent Republic stockholder suits lodged against Yates and his regime. It did not sit well with shareholders that Vera was "given" as keepsakes such expensive props from *Jubilee Trail* as the specially designed dangling earrings, or the 2½ x 4-foot oil painting of her in an Adele Palmer wardrobe.

While *Jubilee Trail* was in distribution, Vera and Yates made their annual European trek, accompanied by Marie Ralston. On this trip they obtained a special audience with Pope Pius XII in Vatican City. Vera has framed photographs of this special event, which hang on a wall of honor in her home. By this time, Vera and Yates had acquired a secluded, small estate in Santa Barbara, California, overlooking the sea.

Timberjack (Republic 1955) was Vera's only feature done on location away from the Hollywood area. "We traveled to Helena, Montana [Glacier National Park] and nearby Floodhead Lake with lovely bears outside; it was nice and cold at five o'clock in the morning, but gorgeous country." Again, she is cast as a brunette song-and-dance gal, this time as the owner of the Vermillion Belle, a deluxe cabaret which caters to the local loggers. David Brian, a standard villain in Republic Pictures of this vintage, is seen as the ruthless owner of the Talka River Logging Company, out to swindle Sterling Hayden,* Vera's childhood beau, of his rich virgin timberlands. With Howard Petrie, Jim Davis, and Elisha Cook, Jr., as Brian's toughie stooges, Adolphe Menjou as Vera's drunken old dad, and Hoagy Carmichael as "Jingles," the melancholy pianist at the Vermillion Belle, the picture lumbered along to its lethargic conclusion. ". . . the scenery is by far the most intriguing point in the movie, which can hardly command straight-faced comment on its acting and story" (Joe Pihodna, *New York Herald-Tribune*). Vera as a svelte Western saloon siren sang, among other tunes, "What Every Young Girl Should Know,"† while deadpan Carmichael, who performed like a second-rate Oscar Levant, croaked "My Dog," and the Lancers handled the title tune. For some strange reason, the usually expert cinematographer Jack Marta (or the Consolidated printing labs) ran afoul of the Trucolor cameras, and the onlocation coloring of the gorgeous scenery was murky.

Stockholders of Republic Pictures Corporation, at the annual meeting in New York in April 1955, were informed by Yates that the studio might actually cease making motion pictures for theatres and concentrate entirely on films for television, because regular movies were a losing proposition. When one stockholder inquired why Republic could not make profitable features when the other Hollywood studios seemed to be doing alright, Yates crustily replied, "We don't know how other companies keep their books." Stockholders Bernard E. Smith, Jr., and Harold Weill moved that a committee be formed to investigate the corporation's operations. Weill charged that reliable, unbiased information was probably not available because of the nepotism in the studio's upper echelons. "Favoritism," he stated, "extends even to Yates' actress wife." Yates later remarked of

---

*It would later be revealed in the above-mentioned stockholders' suit that thirty-nine-year-old Hayden had to be paid a special "bonus" inducement to appear in a Vera Ralston picture.

†Dubbed by Virginia Rees.

the committee: "I don't know what they're really after. But, if they want a proxy fight, we'll give them one."

Accused of Murder (Republic, 1956) returned Vera to a contemporary storyline. "There is some quite promising material in this thriller, adapted from a novel [*Vanity Row*] by W. R. Burnett, but the handling is too stereotyped to make much out of it, and the flat playing of the cast arouses little interest or sympathy for the characters" (British *Monthly Film Bulletin*). Filmed in color and Naturama (Republic's widescreen process), Vera was seen as Ilona Vance, a club singer accused on circumstantial evidence of murdering a gangland lawyer (Sidney Blackmer).* Police lieutenant David Brian is firmly convinced of Vera's innocence and spends seventy-four minutes pursuing the real culprit. In a plot twist— badly handled by director Joseph Kane—Vera admits that she actually did cause Blackmer's death, but that it was accidental since she was only trying to prevent him from committing suicide. The best performance in this programmer was given by reliable Virginia Grey, cast as a dance-hall girl who, after being beaten up by Warren Stevens, gives testimony that almost convicts "innocent" Stevens of Blackmer's death.

On October 29, 1956, two of Republic's minority Wall Street stockholders, Rose Steinberg and Irvin Amster, filed suit against Yates and his studio regime. The plaintiffs asserted that "since 1942 Mr. Yates for personal reasons has used and continues to use company assets to promote as a star Mrs. Herbert J. Yates, also known as Vera Ralston, to the loss and detriment of the company." Of two of Vera's films, the brief stated, "The male lead was played by John Wayne, an established box-office attraction. Yet these two pictures—unlike other pictures starring John Wayne in which the female lead was not played by Vera Ralston—failed to cover their costs." Steinberg and Amster, in their detailed allegations, further alleged that Rudy Ralston and Walter Titus, Yates's son-in-law, were given top Republic positions at salaries far beyond their possible industry worth.† Papers like the *New York Daily News* ballyhooed this ticklish legal case with such headlines as, "Suit Calls Film Tycoon's Wife 9-1 Floperoo." Justice Thomas A. Aurelio refused to dismiss the charges but asked that the two plaintiffs submit a "more definite" complaint.‡

Meanwhile, Vera continued to appear in Republic Pictures. She starred

---

*Vera was again blonde in this picture, but sporting an unbecoming short coiffure.

†Rudy Ralston, who held an engineering degree from Realka University in Prague, joined Consolidated Laboratories after World War II, and then was promoted to (associate) producer status at Republic, working on such films as *Hellfire* (1949), *The Last Bandit* (1949), *Buckaroo Sheriff of Texas* (1950), *Down Laredo Way* (1953), and Vera's last three films, *Gunfire at Indian Gap* (1957), *The Notorious Mr. Monks* (1958), and *The Man Who Died Twice* (1958).

‡Further stockholders' suits would be filed in 1958 asking for dissolution of the firm and the appointment of a receiver, claiming that Yates was continuing to operate the company "as though it were a private family-owned business" and that he was guilty of "seeking to unload family shareholdings for a premium over the market price with tax benefits to self and relatives."

in two of the company's twenty-seven 1957 releases. *Spoilers of the Forest* seemed like a sawdusty offshoot of *Timberjack*. Vera and her stepfather (Carl Benton Reid) own 64,000 acres of Montana timber land which grasping Ray Collins intends to control. Collins hires burly Rod Cameron to woo Vera and to convince her to sell out the precious natural resources on her land tract. Even at a brief sixty-eight minutes, the pacing was slow-going, save for one good action scene in which a huge truck loaded with logs goes out of control and races pell-mell down a steep gradient. Once more, the Trucolor-Naturama cameras focused more on the outdoor scenery than on the characters, and it was supporting player Hillary Brooke as Collins's ritzy, conniving wife who performed most engagingly. She was especially effective in the San Francisco scene in which she gives Vera her first taste of luxury.

Gunfire at Indian Gap (Republic, 1957), produced by Vera's brother, Rudy, was very much a second road-company rehash of John Ford's *Stagecoach* (1939), but without any of that classic Western's intrinsic values. However, Vera did offer a convincing job of acting as the Mexican-American girl who is persecuted unmercifully by the like of George Macready. She went brunette again for this black-and-white Western, set at the Eldorado Relay Station of the Arizona Stage Company, in which the assorted outlaws (John Doucette, George Keymas, and boss Macready) are out to capture a cache of money. Before the villains meet their just fate, Vera is nearly raped by Doucette, denounced by duplicitous Macready, and almost deserted by hero Anthony George.

Her initial 1958 release, *The Notorious Mr. Monks* (Republic, 1958), got scant bookings, as Republic was easing its way out of theatrical production, having already leased the bulk of its film library for television rental. Lensed in widescreen Naturama, Vera appeared as Angela Monks, the hard-hearted, world-weary, younger wife of Paul Fix, who is brought home drunk by a handsome hitchhiker (Don Kelly). She arranges for Kelly to work on the ranch and immediately begins making a play for the physically attractive stranger. As she paws his naked chest, she asks: "How old do you think I am? Being married to an old man—it makes me feel old." For the role, Vera's hair was lightened and hacked short. In attempting to come across as a tough babe, she resembled a more refined Shelley Winters, with her character insisting, "I'm a lady and should be treated like a lady." Midway in the Richard C. Sarafian screenplay, the story takes a sharp point of departure. Young hitchhiker Luana Anders turns up, attracts Kelly's attention, and later, after it is proven that Fix accidentally fell to his death, a suddenly remorseful widowed Vera offers her blessing as Kelly and Anders walk off into the sunset.

Vera's last feature film to date was unveiled in July 1958, a few months prior to Yates's relinquishment of all connection with Republic, its television company, and Consolidated Film Laboratories. In *The Man Who*

Died Twice (Republic, 1958), she is a nightclub singer, warbling within the picture two songs by Jerry Gladstone and Al DeLory, "There I Was in Love" and "One Step from Nowhere." Her husband in the film, Don Megowan, is the middle-man in a narcotics ring until he burns to death in an automobile explosion. Shortly after, Vera is witness to the murder of two narcotics investigators and suffers a nervous collapse. The dead man's brother (Rod Cameron) appears on the scene to assist the police and discovers that Megowan did not die after all and is the one who shot the two agents. Megowan tries to kill Vera because she was a witness to his homicidal deeds, but he is shot down in a rooftop chase. *Motion Picture Herald* credited the film with "some briskly-paced direction" by Joseph Kane.* In many cities, *The Man Who Died Twice* played on a double bill with MGM's programmer, *Andy Hardy Comes Home*.

In a retrospective glance at her screen career, Vera says, "I feel sometimes I didn't get the right parts and many of the scripts were bad." She offers as an analogy: "If you give a cook an egg and water what can she do with it? Not very much. It's the same thing with an actress. If it isn't there, there isn't very much you can do with it. I just don't think I was given the right chances at all." When asked her opinion of her own emoting, she replied, "I never considered myself a good actress—or a good skater either. I always belittle myself. . . . It keeps me regular." If given an opportunity to turn back the clock and start it all over again, she most would have liked to take a crack at the role of Loxi Claiborne in *Reap the Wild Wind* (Paramount, 1942), played by Paulette Goddard in the Cecil B. DeMille feature. "That part is *me*," Vera says.

After fifteen years of a daily studio schedule from eight in the morning till six at night, Vera suddenly found that she required a rest. She and Yates played golf every day and swam either in the pool at their Sherman Oaks home or in the ocean at Santa Barbara.† They endured the notoriety of a $20,000 jewelry theft from their home in May 1958, and then proceeded to make their annual trek to Abano, Italy, where Yates underwent a two-week hot springs treatment for arthritis. The couple enjoyed frequent excursions to Hawaii and Mexico. They derived most satisfaction, she says, from their home and garden in Santa Barbara.

Vera turned to interior decorating as a creative outlet and designed marble floors for both of their homes. "This way I save on carpets. The cost of things is terrible." The floors in Santa Barbara are black and white with a large circle in the entrance foyer. At the center of the circle is a *Y* with a *V* and an *R* on either side. The Yateses took regular hikes along the seashore, gathering shells and driftwood, which Vera incorporated into a seascape design and inserted into a glass-enclosed niche in the foyer.

In mid-June 1962, the Hollywood community was a bit astonished to

---

*Kane directed twelve of Vera's twenty-six features.

†When Yates relinquished his $178,000-a-year Republic post, he negotiated a very lucrative stock-deal compromise with the ousting faction.

learn that Vera and Yates were represented in Santa Monica superior court in a domestic estrangement suit, dating back to May of that year when they had separated. Vera requested a $4,400-a-month temporary alimony pending final divorce action. The case was soon thereafter dropped, with Yates announcing that he and Vera would be taking a second honeymoon. The reconciled Vera happily told the press, "I love my husband and he loves me."

In 1963, Vera was saddened to receive word from a cousin in Prague that her father had died. Then, in 1965, aboard the S.S. *Columbo* bound for Italy, Yates suffered the first of nine heart attacks. When he had two more heart seizures at Abano, Vera flew in her personal doctor from Hollywood, along with her brother, Rudy, and her mother, and she telephoned the news to the Yates children. When it was medically advisable, Yates was flown to a New York hospital and from there to St. Joseph's Hospital in Los Angeles. He died at their Sherman Oaks home on February 2, 1966, at the age of eighty-five. "My husband was a real fantastic man in every direction," Vera comments. "He was smart in business, and most of all, he was very honest and helped an awful lot of people. He was very well liked. The crew—they were crazy about him because he was just a regular man. I always thought I would go first. He was a young old man." Funeral services for Yates were held at St. Peter's Episcopal Church, Bayshore, Long Island, with the interment at the Oakwood Cemetery, Bayshore. In addition to Vera, he was survived by his daughter, two sons, a sister, thirteen grandchildren, and ten great-grandchildren.

Unknown to all but her mother and brother, Vera had a nervous breakdown soon after Yates's death. "For a year I was in such a state of shock that I couldn't walk or stand. I couldn't even shower without a nurse's help." Finally, with her mother and housekeeper as companions, she went to Hawaii to recuperate.

In October 1970, after a holiday trip to Mexico, Vera's mother had a heart attack and thereafter suffered a number of strokes. She was hospitalized for six months and then underwent a severe stroke requiring a prolonged hospitalization period of more than two years. During this time, Vera visited the bedside daily. "That's when I gained thirty pounds from no exercise. Oh, boy!" Marie Hruba Ralston died on January 24, 1973, in Los Angeles. Vera went into mourning, during which time she lost thirty-five pounds, bringing her weight down to an astonishing 111 pounds.

She then sold her Sherman Oaks home and resided exclusively in Santa Barbara with a Spanish-speaking maid and two very large and voracious watchdogs (Gypsy and Dino) as her sole companions. Because her maid understood no English, Vera enrolled in a Spanish class and added that language to the six already at her command. Vera's home, with twenty-four doors and an elaborate alarm system, is decorated with paintings, plants, flowers, and skating trophies, along with photographs of her various screen characterizations. Her favorite color is purple, and she prefers to write letters in ink of that color. She still receives a regular flow of fan mail and answers each letter personally.

A prerecorded interview with Richard Lamparski, author of the *Whatever Became of?* . . . series of books, was heard early in 1973 on Lamparski's New York radio program of the same name, and he included a chapter on Vera in the fourth volume of his series, published in October 1973.

Vera admits to receiving occasional television offers. During the period of her mother's illness she accepted none, but now, "If something good came along—who knows?" She adds: "But, I don't need to work, thank God. I'm very comfortable. I think if a person is on top and leaves the profession, it is better than to start all over and not be as good as before—don't you agree?" She wants to retain her youthful vitality by thinking young and to remain active even if it is only through knitting or crocheting or planting flowers. She does not believe in the currently fashionable women's lib because "We were born to be feminine. Men *like* feminine women." Her current mania is watching television. She thinks Lucille Ball is "tremendous," and she was delighted that Liza Minnelli won the Academy Award. She considers Peggy Fleming an excellent skater, "but there will never be another like Sonja Henie." Her response, when told of the Vera Hruba Ralston film cult, was "No kidding!" and "What is that word?—c-o-l-t?"

During the early spring months of 1973 Vera planted forty-nine avocado trees on her Santa Barbara estate, "and that was a little difficult," and "I had the whole house painted, which was another big project for a widow."

Then, on Saturday, June 16, 1973, she was married to Charles De Alva, a forty-one-year-old Santa Barbara businessman and buyer for a chain of retail stores. "He is very good to me," she wrote to this volume's co-author, Don E. Stanke, a few days after the wedding, "yet he is tall, dark and handsome. We like the same things—music, art, gardening and lots of home life. We kept it a secret; only two persons were invited to our wedding which was a Catholic ceremony in San Raque Chapel." As a wedding gift, Vera's groom gave her "the loveliest large, gold bonsai tree with cultured pearls. Wait 'til you see it."

More recently, Vera communicated, "So far we are having a lovely marriage and are still working with much gusto at the avocadoes."

Feature Film Appearances

As Vera Hruba:

ICE-CAPADES (Rep., 1941) 89 M.

Associate producer, Robert North; director, Joseph Santley; story, Isabel Dawn, Boyce DeGaw; screenplay, Jack Townley, Robert Harari, Olive Cooper: additional dialog, Melville Shavelson, Milt Josefsberg; art director, John Victor Mackay; music director, Cy Feuer; songs, Sol Meyer, George R. Brown, and Jule Styne; Duke Ellington; skating sequences stager, Harry Losee; wardrobe, Adele Palmer; camera, Jack Marta; supervising editor, Murray Seldeen; editor, Howard O'Neil.

James Ellison (Bob Clemens); Jerry Colonna (Colonna); Dorothy Lewis (Marie); Barbara Jo Allen (Vera Vague); Alan Mowbray (Pete Ellis); Phil Silvers (Larry Herman); Gus Schilling (Dave); Tim Ryan (Jackson); Harry Clark (Reed); Renie Riano (Karen Vadja); Carol Adams (Helen); Belita, Lois Dworshak, Megan Taylor, Vera Hruba, Red McCarthy, Phil Taylor, Jackson and Lynam, The Benoits, Dench and Stewart (Ice-Capades Performers).

ICE-CAPADES REVUE (Rep., 1942) 79 M.

Associate producer, Robert North; director, Bernard Vorhaus; story, Robert T. Shannon, Mauri Grashin; screenplay, Bradford Rogers, Gertrude Purcell; songs, Sol Meyer, George R. Brown, and Jule Styne; Meyer and Styne; Charles E. King; Meyer and Walter Scharf; Edmund L. Gruber; Robert Crawford; music director, Walter Scharf; music arrangers, Ken Darby, Marlin Skiles; skating sequence stager, Harry Losee; camera, John Alton; editor, Thomas Richards.

Ellen Drew (Ann); Richard Denning (Jeff); Barbara Jo Allen ([a.k.a. Vera Vague] Aunt Nellie); Jerry Colonna (Theophilus Twitchell); Harold Huber (Duke Baldwin); Bill Shirley (Denny); Marilyn Hare (Bubbles); Si Jenks (Homer); Charles Williams (Menkin); William Newell (Deakin); Sam Bernard (Snake Eyes); Pierre Watkin (Wiley Stone); Edward Keane (Gabby Haskoff); George Byron (Master of Ceremonies); Donna Atwood, Lola Dworshak, Vera Hruba, Morgan Taylor, Joe Jackson, Jr., Robin Lee, Rod McCarthy, Phil Taylor, Eric Waite, Jackson and Lynam, Pierre and Denise Benoit, Dench and Stewart (Ice Capades Skating Stars); Roy Butler, Harrison Greene, Broderick O'Farrell, Cy Ring (Creditors); Jimmy Conlin (Biddle); Mary McCarty (Miss Trent); Betty Farrington (Mrs. Trent); Elmer Jerome (Mr. Bixby); Hal Price, Lee Shumway, Stanley Blystone, George Sherwood (Cops); Dave Willock (Guide); Edwin Stanley (Otis); Frank Jaquet (Operator); Beatrice Maude, Kathryn Sheldon (The Two Hattie Williamses); Emil Van Horn (Gorilla); Jack Norton (Drunk); Irene Shirley (Mrs. Sawyer); Frank Brownlee (Mr. Sawyer). Television Title: *Rhythm Hits the Ice.*

As Vera Hruba Ralston:

THE LADY AND THE MONSTER (Rep., 1944) 86 M.

Associate producer-director, George Sherman; based on the novel *Donovan's Brain* by Curt Siodmak; screenplay, Dane Lussier, Frederick Kohner; art director, Russell Kimball; set decorator, Otto Siegel; assistant director, Bud Springsteen; music, Walter Scharf; sound, Earl Crain, Sr.; camera, John Alton; editor, Arthur Roberts.

Erich von Stroheim (Professor Franz Mueller); Vera Hruba Ralston (Janice Farell); Richard Arlen (Patrick Cory); Mary Nash (Mrs. Fame); Sidney Blackmer (Eugene Fulton); Helen Vinson (Chloe Donovan); Charles Cane (Grimes); Bill Henry (Roger Collins); Juanita Quigley (Mary Lou); Josephine Dillon (Mary Lou's Grandmother); Tom London (Husky Man in Tails); Sam Flint (G. Phipps, the Bank Manager); Edward Keane (Manning); Lane Chandler (White, the Ranger); Wallis Clark (Warden); Harry Hayden (Dr. Martin); Antonio Triano and Lola Montes (Dance Team); Maxine Doyle (Receptionist); Billy Benedict (Bellhop); Herbert Clifton (Butler); Harry Depp (Bank Teller); Lee Phelps (Headwaiter); Janet Martin (Cafe Singer); Frank Graham (Narrator).

STORM OVER LISBON (Rep., 1944) 86 M.

Associate producer-director, George Sherman; story, Elizabeth Meehan; adaptor, Dane Lussier; screenplay, Doris Gilbert; art director, Gano Chittenden; music, Walter Scharf; ballad music, Maurice de Packh; assistant director, Bud Springsteen; sound, Richard Tyler; camera, John Alton; editor, Arthur Roberts.

Vera Hruba Ralston (Maritza); Richard Arlen (John Craig); Erich von Stroheim (Deresco); Robert Livingston (Bill Flanagan); Otto Kruger (Alexis Vanderlyn); Eduardo Ciannelli (Blanco); Mona Barrie (Evelyn); Frank Orth (Murgatroyd); Sarah Edwards (Maude); Alice Fleming (Agatha); Leon Belasco, Vincent Girondo (Fado Singers); Bud Geary, Kenne Duncan, Roy Barcroft (Henchmen); Ruth Roman, Karen Randle, Annyse Sherman (Checkroom Girls); The Aida Broadbent Girls (Dancers); Marie Day (Maid); Lucien Prival, Muni Seroff (Men in Tails); Lester Sharpe (Overfelder); Kirk Alyn (Bandleader); Gino Corrado (Headwaiter); Jac George (Waiter); Will Kaufman (The Baron); Almeda Fowler (Woman); Alphonse Martell (Maitre d'Hotel); Louis Ludwig Lowy (Croupier); Manuel Paris (Roulette Dealer); Georgia Davis (Canteen Girl); Charles Wagenheim (Frustrated Man); Eula Guy (Hysterical Wife); George Derrick (Gigolo); Victor Travers (Man with Newspaper); Fred Rapport (Claim Check Man); Dick Alexander (Doorman); George Humbert (Italian Waiter); Georges Renavent (Secret Service Official); Jack Kirk (Driver).

LAKE PLACID SERENADE (Rep., 1944) 85 M.

Associate producer, Harry Grey; director, Steve Sekely; story, Frederick Kohner; screenplay, Dick Irving Hyland, Doris Gilbert; art director, Russell Kimball; set decorator, Earl Wooden; assistant director, Harry Knight; ice director, Arthur Vitarelli; music director, Walter Scharf; choreography, Jack Crosby; sound, Richard Tyler, Howard Wilson; special effects, Howard and Theodore Lydecker; camera, John Alton; editor, Arthur Roberts.

Vera Hruba Ralston (Vera Haschek); Robert Livingston (Jordan); Eugene Pallette (Carl Oermak); Barbara Jo Allen ([a.k.a. Vera Vague] Countess); Walter Catlett (Webb); William Frawley (Jiggers); Ruth Terry (Susan); Stephanie Bachelor (Irene); Lloyd Corrigan (Haschek); John Litel (Walter Benda); Ludwig Stossel

(Mayor of Lany); Andrew Tombes (Skating Club Head); Marietta Canty (Maid); Twinkle Watts, McGowan and Mack, Janina Frostova, Felix Sadovsky, Janet Martin, Ray Noble and Orchestra, Harry Owens and His Royal Hawaiians (Specialties); Roy Rogers (Guest Star); Mike Macy (Judge); Sewall Shurtz (Apprentice Boy); Janna De Loos (Friend at Lake); Demetrius Alexis (Tourist); Erno Kiraly, Hans Herbert (Judge); Ferdinand Munier (Kris Kringle); Nora Lane (Benda's Secretary); John Dehner (Radio Announcer); Frank Mayo, Pat Gleason, Dick Scott, Ernie Adams, Charles Williams (Reporters); Ruth O. Warren (Cleaning Woman); Bert Moorehouse (Photographer); Eric Alden, Stewart Hall, Craig Lawrence (Candidates); Geoffrey Ingham (Good Looking Man); John Hamilton (Hopkins); Eddie Kane (Desk Clerk); Chester Clute (Haines); Stanley Andrews (Executive); Virginia Carroll (Receptionist).

DAKOTA (Rep., 1945) 82 M.

Associate producer-director, Joseph Kane; story, Carl Foreman; adaptor, Howard Estabrook; screenplay, Lawrence Hazard; art directors, Russell Kimball, Gano Chittenden; set decorators, John McCarthy, Jr., James Redd; music director, Walter Scharf; choreography, Larry Ceballos; song, Andrew Sterling, Harry Von Tilzer; assistant director, Al Wood; sound, Fred Stahl; special effects, Howard and Theodore Lydecker; camera, Jack Marta; editor, Fred Allen.

John Wayne (John Devlin); Vera Hruba Ralston (Sandra "Sandy" Devlin); Ward Bond (Jim Bender); Walter Brennan (Captain Bounce); Mike Mazurki (Bigtree Collins); Hugo Haas (Marko Poli); Ona Munson (Jersey Thomas); Paul Fix (Carp); Nicodemus Stewart (Mose); Olive Blakeney (Mrs. Stowe); Robert Livingston (Lieutenant); Robert H. Barrat (Mr. Stowe); Pierre Watkin (Wexton Geary); Olin Howland (Devlin's Driver); Grant Withers (Slagin); Selmer Jackson (Dr. Judson); Claire Du Brey (Wahtonka); Jack LaRue (Slade); Jonathan Hale (Colonel Wordin); Roy Barcroft (Poli's Driver); Larry Thompson (Poli's Footman); Sarah Padden (Mrs. Plummer); George Cleveland (Mr. Plummer); Jack Roper, Fred Graham, Russ Kaplan, Cliff Lyons (Bouncers); Al Murphy (Trainman); Houseley Stevenson (Railroad Clerk); Bobby Blake (Boy); Paul Hurst (Captain Spotts); William Haade, Dick Wessel (Roughnecks); Rex Lease (Railroad Conductor); Eddy Waller (Stagecoach Driver); Betty Shaw, Martha Carroll, Adrian Booth, Linda Stirling, Virginia Wave, Cay Forester, (Entertainers); Eugene Borden, Peter Cusanelli, Hector Sarno (Italians); Michael Visaroff (Russian); Victor Varconi (Frenchman); Paul E. Burns (Swede); Arthur K. Miles (Ciano); Dorothy Christy (Nora).

MURDER IN THE MUSIC HALL (Rep., 1946) 84 M.

Producer, Herman Millakowsky; director, John English; story, Arnold Phillips, Maria Matray; screenplay, Frances Hyland, Laszlo Gorog; ice numbers director, Fanchon; music director, Walter Scharf; assistant director, Rollie Asher; art director, Russell Kimball; set decorators, John McCarthy, Jr., Earl Wooden; sound, Fred Stahl; special effects, Howard and Theodore Lydecker; ice sequences camera, John Alton; camera, Jack Marta; editor, Arthur Roberts.

Vera Hruba Ralston (Lila); William Marshall (Don); Helen Walker (Millicent); Nancy Kelly (Mrs. Asquith); William Gargan (Inspector Wilson); Ann Rutherford (Gracie); Julie Bishop (Diane); Jerome Cowan (George Asquith); Edward Norris (Carl); Paul Hurst (Hobarth); Frank Orth (Henderson); Jack LaRue (Bruce Wilton); James Craven (Mr. Winters); Fay McKenzie (Singer in Mom's Cafe); Tom London (Ryan); Joe Yule (Doorman); Mary Field (Waitress); Anne Nagel (Mission Attendant); Ilka Gruning (Mom); Inez Palange (Mrs. Aldine); William

Austin (Clerk); Spec O'Donnell, Billy Vernon (Ushers); Nolan Leary (Doctor); LeRoy Mason (Fingerprint Man); Brooks Benedict (Police Photographer); Lee Phelps (McCarthy); Virginia Carroll (Cashier); Lillian Bronson (Woman Cleaner); Wheaton Chambers (Evangelist Leader); John Wald (Radio Officer); James Farley (Police Sergeant).

As Vera Ralston:

PLAINSMAN AND THE LADY   (Rep., 1946) 82 M.

Associate producer-director, Joe Kane; story, Michael Uris, Ralph Spencer; screenplay, Richard Wormser; music, George Antheil; music director, Cy Feuer; choreography, Fanchon; assistant director, Nate Barrager; art director, Gano Chittenden; set decorators, John McCarthy, Jr., George Milo; sound, Richard Tyler; special effects, Howard and Theodore Lydecker; camera, Reggie Lanning; editor, Fred Allen.

William Elliott (Sam Cotten); Vera Ralston (Ann Arnesen); Gail Patrick (Cathy Arnesen); Joseph Schildkraut (Peter Marquette); Donald Barry (Feisty); Andy Clyde (Dringo); Raymond Walburn (Judge Winters); Reinhold Schunzel (Michael Arnesen); Paul Hurst (Al); Russell Hicks (Senator Twin); William B. Davidson (Mr. Russell); Charles Judels (Manuel Lopez); Eva Puig (Anita Lopez); Jack Lambert (Sival); Stuart Hamblen (Matt); Noble Johnson (Wassao); Hal Taliaferro (Pete); Lola and Fernando (Specialty Dancers); Byron Foulger (Simmons); Pierre Watkin (Senator Allen); Eddy Waller (Fred Willats); Charles Morton (Doctor); Martin Garralaga (Alvarades); Guy L. Beach (Bookkeeper); Joseph Crehan (Postmaster General); Grady Sutton (Male Secretary); Eddie Parks (Drunk); Norman Willis, Tex Terry, Chuck Roberson (Deputies); Rex Lease (Croupier); Henry Wills (Indian); Daniel Day Tolman (Young Clerk); David Williams (Clerk); Hank Bell (Yard Master); Roy Barcroft (Cowboy); Jack O'Shea (Bartender); Carl Sepulveda (Big Mex).

THE FLAME   (Rep., 1947) 97 M.

Associate producer-director, John H. Auer; based on a story by Robert T. Shannon; screenplay, Lawrence Kimble; music director, Cy Feuer; music, Heinz Roemheld; art director, Gano Chittenden; camera, Reggie Lanning; editor, Richard L. Van Enger.

John Carroll (George MacAllister); Vera Ralston (Carlotta Novak); Robert Paige (Barry MacAllister); Broderick Crawford (Ernie Hicks); Henry Travers (Dr. Mitchell); Blanche Yurka (Aunt Margaret); Constance Dowling (Helen Anderson); Hattie McDaniel (Celia); Victor Sen Yung (Chang); Harry V. Cheshire (Minister); John Miljan, Garry Owen (Detectives); Eddie Dunn (Police Officer); Vince Barnett (Stage Door Attendant); Hal K. Dawson (Telegraph Clerk); Jeff Corey (Stranger); Ashley Cowan (Page Boy); Cyril Ring (Mr. Moffett); Howard Mitchell (Doorman); Martha Holliday (Check Girl); John Albright (Youth); John Treback (Waiter).

WYOMING   (Rep., 1947) 84 M.

Associate producer-director, Joe Kane; screenplay, Lawrence Hazard, Gerald Geraghty; art director, Frank Hotaling; set decorators, John McCarthy, Jr., George Suhr; music, Nathan Scott, Ernest Gold; music, Nathan Scott, Ernest Gold; music director, Cy Feuer; assistant director, Virgil Hart; second unit director, Yakima Canutt; sound, Herbert Norsch; special effects, Howard and Theodore Lydecker; camera, John Alton; editor, Arthur Roberts.

William Elliott (Charles Alderson); Vera Ralston (Karen); John Carroll (Glenn Forrester); George "Gabby" Hayes (Windy); Albert Dekker (Lassiter); Virginia Grey (Lila Regan); Mme. Maria Ouspenskaya (Maria); Grant Withers (Joe Sublette); Harry Woods (Ben Jackson); Minna Gombell (Queenie); Dick Curtis (Ed Lassiter); Roy Barcroft (Sheriff Niles); Trevor Bardette (Timmons); Paul Harvey (Judge Sheridan); Louise Kane (Karen at Age Twelve); Linda Green (Karen at Age Three); Tom London (Jennings); George Chesebro (Wolff); Jack O'Shea (Bartender); Charles Middleton (Doctor); Eddy Waller (Grub Liner); Olin Howland, Charles King, Glenn Strange (Cowboys); Eddie Acuff (Homesteader); Marshall Reed (Man); Rex Lease (Clerk); Charles Morton (Settler); Tex Terry (Morrison); Dale Fink (Boy); Ed Peil, Sr. (Nester); Roque Ybarra, James Archuletta (Indian Boys); David Williams (Hotel Clerk); Lee Shumway (Rancher).

I, JANE DOE   (Rep., 1948) 85 M.

Associate producer-director, John H. Auer; screenplay, Lawrence Kimble; adaptor, Decla Dunning; art director, James Sullivan; set decorator, Charles Thompson; music, Heinz Roemheld; music director, Morton Scott; assistant director, Dick Moder; makeup, Bob Mark; costumes, Adele Palmer; sound, Vic Appel; camera, Reggie Lanning; editor, Richard L. Van Enger.

Ruth Hussey (Eve Meredith Curtis); John Carroll (Stephen Curtis); Vera Ralston (Annette Dubois, alias Jane Doe); Gene Lockhart (Arnold Matson); John Howard (William Hilton); Benay Venuta (Phyllis Tuttle); Adele Mara (Marga-Jane Hastings); Roger Dann (Julian Aubert); James Bell (Judge Bertrand); Leon Belasco (Duroc); John Litel (Horton); Eric Feldary (Robert Dubois); Francis Pierlot (Father Martin); Marta Mitrovich (Marie); John Albright (Reporter); Louis Mercier (Francois); Gene Gary (Degnan); Henry Rowland (German Lieutenant); Walden Boyle (Court Clerk); E. L. Davenport, Roy Darmour (Reporters); Ed Rees (Court Stenographer); Howard Mitchell (Bailiff); Nolan Leary (Jury Foreman); Eva Novak (Jury Woman); Martha Holliday (Trudy Marsh); Myron Healey (Interne); Charles Flynn, Harry Strang, Chuck Hamilton, Stanley Blystone (Policemen); Jack Clifford (Police Captain); Sonia Darrin (Nurse); Frank Reicher, Boyd Irwin (Doctors); Willy Wickerhauser, Frederic Brunn (Soldiers); Cliff Clark (City Editor); Jeff Corey (Immigration Officer); Frances Robinson (Dorothy Winston); Dave Anderson (Black Man); Sammy McKim, Bobby Stone, Ray Hirsch (Newsboys); James Dale (Assistant Editor); Jerry Lynn Myers (Baby).

ANGEL ON THE AMAZON   (Rep., 1948) 86 M.

Associate producer-director, John H. Auer; story, Earl Felton; screenplay, Lawrence Kimble; art director, James Sullivan; set decorators, John McCarthy, Jr., George Milo; music, Nathan Scott; music director, Morton Scott; assistant director, Lee Lukather; makeup, Bob Mark; sound, Victor B. Appel, Howard Wilson; special effects, Howard and Theodore Lydecker; camera, Reggie Lanning; editor, Richard L. Van Enger.

George Brent (Jim Warburton); Vera Ralston (Christine Ridgeway); Brian Aherne (Anthony Ridgeway); Constance Bennett (Dr. Karen Lawrence); Fortunio Bonanova (Sebastian Ortega); Alfonso Bedoya (Paulo); Gus Schilling (Dean Hartley); Richard Crane (Johnny MacMahon); Walter Reed (Jerry Adams); Ross Elliott (Frank Lane); Konstantin Shayne (Dr. Jungmeyer); Charles LaTorre (Waiter); Elizabeth Dunne (Housekeeper); Alberto Morin (Radio Operator); Dick Jones (George); Alfredo DeSa (Brazilian Reporter); Tony Martinez (Bellhop); Gerardo Sei Groves (Native); John Trebach (Waiter); Manuel Paris (Night Desk Clerk).

THE FIGHTING KENTUCKIAN (Rep., 1949) 100 M.

Producer, John Wayne; director-screenplay, George Waggner; art director, James Sullivan; set decorators, John McCarthy, Jr., George Milo; music, George Antheil; assistant director, Lee Lukather; makeup, Bob Mark, Webb Overlander, Don Cash, Cecil Holland; costumes, Adele Palmer; sound, Dick Tyler, Howard Wilson; special effects, Howard and Theodore Lydecker; camera, Lee Garmes; editor, Richard L. Van Enger.

John Wayne (John Breen); Vera Ralston (Fleurette DeMarchand); Philip Dorn (Colonel Georges Geraud); Oliver Hardy (Willie Paine); Marie Windsor (Ann Logan); John Howard (Blake Randolph); Hugo Haas (General Paul DeMarchand); Grant Withers (George Hayden); Odette Myrtil (Mme. De-Marchand); Paul Fix (Beau Merritt); Mae Marsh (Sister Hattie); Jack Pennick (Captain Dan Carroll); Mickey Simpson (Jacques); Fred Graham (Carter Ward); Mabelle Koenig (Marie); Shy Waggner, Crystal White (Friends).

SURRENDER (Rep., 1950) 90 M.

Producer, Herbert J. Yates; associate producer-director, Allan Dwan; story, James Edward Grant; screenplay, Grant, Sloan Nibley; art director, James Sullivan; set decorators, John McCarthy, Jr., Charles Thompson; costumes, Adele Palmer; music, Nathan Scott; special effects, Howard and Theodore Lydecker; camera, Reggie Lanning; editor, Richard L. Van Enger.

Vera Ralston (Violet Barton); John Carroll (Gregg Delaney); Walter Brennan (William Howard); Francis Lederer (Henry Vaan); William Ching (Johnny Hale); Maria Palmer (Janet Barton); Jane Darwell (Mrs. Hale); Roy Barcroft (Deputy); Paul Fix (Williams); Esther Dale (Aunt May); Edward Norris (Wilbur); Howland Chamberlin (Manager); Norman Budd (Carson); Nacho Galindo (Grigo); Jeff York (Canning); Mickey Simpson (Pete); Dick Elliott (Senator Clowe); Ralph Dunn (Jailer); Virginia Farmer (Mrs. Brown); J. Louis Johnson (Butler); Elizabeth Dunne (Elderly Woman); Cecil Elliott (Mrs. Schultz); Glenn Strange (Lon, the Deputy); Kenne Duncan (Rider); Paul Stader (Gentleman Gambler); Wesley Hopper (Barney Gale); Tex Terry (Shotgun Guard); Charles Morton (Doorman); Doris Cole (Colette); Al Rhein (Dealer); Al Murphy (Cashier); Tina Menard (Flower Vender); Frank Dae (Elderly Gentleman); Petra Silva (Maria); Tony Roux (Chocolate Vender); Shelby Bacon (Georgie); Fred Hoose (Assistant Editor).

BELLE LE GRAND (Rep., 1951) 90 M.

Producer, Herbert J. Yates; director, Allan Dwan; based on the story by Peter B. Kyne; screenplay, D. D. Beauchamp; art director, James Sullivan; set decorators, John McCarthy, Jr., George Milo; costumes, Adele Palmer; music, Victor Young; special effects, Howard and Theodore Lydecker; camera, Reggie Lanning; editor, Harry Keller.

Vera Ralston (Belle Le Grand); John Carroll (John Kilton); William Ching (Bill Shanks); Muriel Lawrence (Nan Henshaw); Hope Emerson (Emma McGee); Grant Withers (Shannon); Stephen Chase (Montgomery Crane); John Qualen (Corky McGee); Henry Morgan (Abel Stone); Charles Cane (Cal); Thurston Hall (Parkington); Marietta Canty (Daisy); Glen Vernon (Bellboy); Don Beddoe (Smith); Isabel Randolph (Woman); John Holland, Frank Wilcox, Paul Maxey, Pierre Watkin, John Hart (Men); Edward Keane (Carter); Russell Hicks (Chairman); Rodney Bell, Sam Flint, John Close, Edward Cassidy, John Vosper, John Hamilton, Howard Mitchell, Perry Ivins (Brokers); Jimmy Ogg (Newsboy); Sam

Sebby, William Schallert (Clerks); Maude Eburne (Woman Companion); Carl "Alfalfa" Switzer (Messenger Boy); Queenie Smith (Anna, the Maid); Joseph Granby (Hendrick); Jerry Miley (Bartender); Peter Brocco (Tyler); Keith Hitchcock (Butler); Hal Price, Abe Dinovitch, Heenan Elliott, George Slocum, Don Harvey, Jack Low (Miners); Dick Elliott (Hotel Clerk); Andrew Tombes (Cartright); Eddie Parks (Waiter); Fred Hoose (Doctor); John Wengraf (Sinclair); James Kirkwood (Judge); Howard J. Negley (Dan); Ruth Robinson, Edythe Elliott, Mary Alan Hokanson (Miners' Wives); Gino Corrado (Gamberelli); Thomas Browne Henry (Prosecuting Attorney); Jim Arness, Eddie Dunn (Guards); Emory Parnell (Fire Marshal); Chester Clute (Secretary).

THE WILD BLUE YONDER   (Rep., 1951) 98 M.

Producer, Herbert J. Yates; director, Allan Dwan; story, Andrew Geer, Charles Grayson; screenplay, Richard Tregaskis; art director, James Sullivan; set decorators, John McCarthy, Jr., Charles Thompson; costumes, Adele Palmer; music, Victor Young; songs, Robert Crawford; Young and Ned Washington; Young and Dwan; Charles R. Green; special effects, Ellis F. Thackery, Howard and Theodore Lydecker; camera, Reggie Lanning; editor, Richard L. Van Enger.

Wendell Corey (Captain Harold Calvert); Vera Ralston (Lieutenant Helen Landers); Forrest Tucker (Major Tom West); Phil Harris (Sergeant Hank Stack); Walter Brennan (Major General Wolfe); William Ching (Lieutenant Ted Cranshaw); Ruth Donnelly (Major Ida Winton); Harry Carey, Jr. (Sergeant Shaker Schuker); Penny Edwards (Connie Hudson); Wally Cassell (Sergeant Pulaski); James Brown (Sergeant Pop Davis); Richard Erdman (Corporal Frenchy); Phillip Pine (Sergeant Tony); Martin Kilburn (Peanuts); Hal Baylor (Sergeant Eric Nelson); Joe Brown, Jr. (Sergeant O'Hara); Jack Kelly (Lieutenant Jessup); Bob Beban (Sergeant Barney Killion); Peter Coe (Sergeant Pollio); Hall Bartlett (Lieutenant Jorman); William Witney (General Curtis E. LeMay); David Sharpe (Sergeant "Red" Irwin); Paul Livermore (Sergeant Harker); Jay Silverheels (Benders); Glen Vernon (Crew Man); Joel Allen (Chaplain Goodrich); Don Garner (George); Gayle Kellogg (Pilot); Gil Herman, Freeman Lusk, Reed Hadley (Commanding Officers); Richard Avonde (Joe Wurtzel); Robert Karnes (Co-Pilot); Kathleen Freeman (Nurse Baxter); Jim Leighton, Ray Hyke, (Lieutenants); John Hart, Paul McGuire, Robert Kent (Generals); Amy Iwanabe (Tokyo Rose's Voice); Andy Brennan (Orderly); Bob Morgan (Engineer Schiller); Steve Wayne (Sergeant); Stann Holbrook (Bombardier); Jack Sherman, Myron Healey (Tower Voices).

HOODLUM EMPIRE   (Rep., 1952) 98 M.

Associate producer-director, Joseph Kane; story, Bob Considine; screenplay, Bruce Manning, Considine; art director, Frank Arrigo; music, Nathan Scott; camera, Reggie Lanning; editor, Richard L. Van Enger.

Brian Donlevy (Senator Bill Stephens); Claire Trevor (Connie Williams); Forrest Tucker (Charley Pignatalli); Vera Ralston (Marte Dufour); Luther Adler (Nicky Mansani); John Russell (Joe Gray); Gene Lockhart (Senator Tower); Grant Withers (Reverend Andrews); Taylor Holmes (Benjamin Lawton); Roy Barcroft (Louie Draper); William Murphy (Pete Dailey); Richard Jaeckel (Ted Dawson); Don Beddoe (Senator Blake); Roy Roberts (Chief Tayls); Richard Benedict (Tanner); Phillip Pine (Louis Barretti); Damian O'Flynn (Foster); Pat Flaherty (Mikkelson); Ric Roman (Fergus); Douglas Kennedy (Brinkley); Don Haggerty (Mark Flynn); Francis Pierlot (Uncle Jean); Sarah Spencer (Mrs. Stephens); Thomas Browne Henry (Commander Mermant); Jack Pennick (Tracey); Dick

717

Wessel (Keiller); Paul Livermore (Mike); Fred Kohler, Jr. (German Soldier); Tony Dante (Tommy); Tom Monroe (Rocco); Leah Waggner (Billie); Betty Ball (Pearl); William Schallert (Inquiry Clerk); John Phillips (Radio Commander); Joe Bailey (Eckert of the FBI); Lee Shumway (U.S. Marshal); Charles Trowbridge (Commissioner Garrison); Elizabeth Flournoy (Miss Adams); John Halloran (Inspector Willard); John Pickard (Man); Gil Herman (Officer O'Neil); Mervin Williams (Floyd-Servant); Mikel Conrad (Chunce); Richard Reeves (Rollins); Matty Fain (Eddie Fostie); Stanley Waxman (Lonnie); Sydney Mason (Burns); Whit Bissell (Filby); Sid Tomack (Meyers); Eddie Foster (Doorman); Dick Paxton (Elevator Operator); Sam Scar (Sporty); George Volk (Finter); Don Michael Drysdale (Joe Gray's Boy); Andy Brennan (Taxi Driver).

FAIR WIND TO JAVA   (Rep., 1953) C—92 M.

Associate producer-director, Joseph Kane; based on the novel by Garland Roark; screenplay, Richard Tregaskis; art director, Frank Arrigo, music, Victor Young; special effects, Howard and Theodore Lydecker; camera, Jack Marta; editor, Richard L. Van Enger.

Fred MacMurray (Captain Bell); Vera Ralston (Kim Kim); Robert Douglas (Saint Ebenezer/Pulo Besar); Victor McLaglen (O'Brien); John Russell (Flint); Buddy Baer (Kung); Claude Jarman, Jr. (Chess); Grant Withers (Jason Blue); Howard Petrie (Reeder); Paul Fix (Wilsin); William Murphy (Ahab); Sujata (Dancer); Philip Ahn (Gusti); Stephen Bekassy (Lieutenant); Keye Luke (Pidada); John Halloran, Howard Chuman, Maicla Kalili, Al Kikume (Guards); Richard Reeves (Hoppo Two); Virginia Brissac (Bintang).

A PERILOUS JOURNEY   (Rep., 1953) 90 M.

Associate producer, William J. O'Sullivan; director, R. G. Springsteen; based on the novel *The Golden Tide* by Vingie Roe; screenplay, Richard Wormser; art director, Frank Arrigo; music, Victor Young; songs, Young and Edward Heyman; camera, Jack Marta; editor, Richard L. Van Enger.

Vera Ralston (Francie Landreaux); David Brian (Monty Breed); Scott Brady (Shard Benton); Charles Winninger (Captain Eph Allan); Hope Emerson (Olivia Schuyler); Eileen Christy (Susan); Leif Erickson (Richards); Veda Ann Borg (Sadie); Virginia Grey (Abby); Dorothy Ford (Rose, Singer); Ben Cooper (Sam Austin); Kathleen Freeman (Leah); Barbara Hayden (Cathy); Paul Fierro (Pepe); Angela Greene (Mavis); John Dierkes, Alden Aldrich (Mates); Fred Graham (Whiskers, Stowaway); Trevor Bardette (Whiskered Miner); Richard Reeves (Stewart, the Sailor); Bob Carney (Barfly); Charles Evans (Minister); Philip Van Zandt (Tout); Byron Foulger (Mr. Martin, the Desk Clerk); Denver Pyle (Bartender); Harry Tyler (Vagrant); Emil Sitka (Drunk); Jack O'Shea (Cook); Brandon Beach, Frank Hagney, Stanley Blystone (Ad Libs); Dick Alexander (Crying Miner); Charles Cane (Miner); Gloria Clark (Bride-to-Be).

JUBILEE TRAIL   (Rep., 1954) C—103 M.

Producer, Herbert J. Yates; associate producer-director, Joseph Kane; based on the novel by Gwen Bristow, screenplay, Bruce Manning; music-music conductor, Victor Young; songs, Young and Sidney Clare; choreography, Bob Mark; technical advisor, D. R. O. Hatswell; assistant director, A. J. Vitarelli; costumes, Adele Palmer; art director, Frank Arrigo; set decorators, John McCarthy, Jr., George Milo; sound, Earl Crain, Sr., Howard Wilson; camera, Jack Marta; editor, Richard L. Van Enger.

Vera Ralston (Florinda Grove [Julie Latour]); Joan Leslie (Garnet Hale); Forrest Tucker (John Ives); John Russell (Oliver Hale); Ray Middleton (Charles Hale); Pat O'Brien (Ernest "Texas" Conway); Buddy Baer (Nicolai Gregorovitch Karakozeff); Jim Davis (Silky); Barton MacLane (Deacon Bartlett); Richard Webb (Captain Brown); James Millican (Rinardi); Nina Varela (Doña Manuela); Martin Garralaga (Don Rafael Velasco); Charles Stevens (Pablo, a Peon); Nacho Galindo (Rico, Bartender); Don Beddoe (Mr. Maury, Hotel Manager); John Holland (Mr. Drake); William Haade (Jake, the Sailor); Alan Bridge (Mr. Turner); John Halloran, Sayre Dearing (Turner's Men); Stephen Chase (Mr. Forbes, an Admirer); Daniel M. White (Henry); Eugene Borden (Kimball, a Detective); Morris Buchanan (Waiter); Rodolfo Hoyos, Jr., Rico Alansiz (Spaniards); Bud Wolfe (Blandy); Paul Stader (Barbour); Marshall Reed (Detective); Maurice Jara (Vaquero); Rosa Turich (Señora Silva); Manuel Lopez (Señor Silva); Frances Dominguez (Woman); Richard Dodge (Sentry); Perry Lopez (Silva's Son); Claire Carleton (Estelle, the Madame); Peter Ortiz (Horseman); Victor Sen Yung (Mickey, the Chinese Man); Edward Colmans, George Navarro (Orosco Guests); John Mooney (Dan); Grant Withers (Major Lynden); Alma Beltran (Servant Girl); Anna Navarro (Conchita); Frank Puglia (Don Orosco); Pepe Hern (Ranch Hand); Glenn Strange (Tom Branders); Joe Dominguez (Ernesto); Felipe Turich (Pedro); Gloria Varela (Dolores); Linda Danceil (Rosita); Emil Sitka (Chair Bit); Brett Houston (Man at Bar); Bill Chandler (Handsome Man at Table); Norman Kent (Drunk at Table); Emmett Lynn (Drunk Mán with Little Hat); Joe Ploski (Pace Holding Bit); Tex Terry (Penrose); Rocky Shahan (Mexican Rider); Chuck Hayward, Bob Burrows (Velasco Riders); Pilar Del Rey (Carmelita Velasco); James Lilburn (Sergeant Aherne); Jack O'Shea (Corporal); Jack Elam (Sergeant); Tina Menard (Isabel); Raymond Johnson (Corporal); Manuel Paris (Mexican); Charles Sullivan (Card Player); Ralph Brooks (Bartender); Robert "Buzz" Henry, Ted Smile (Velasco's Sons).

TIMBERJACK   (Rep., 1955) C—94 M.

Producer, Herbert J. Yates; director, Joe Kane; based on the novel by Dan Cushman; screenplay, Allen Rivkin; music, Victor Young; songs, Paul Francis Webster, Johnny Mercer, Ned Washington, and Hoagy Carmichael; assistant director, Herbert Mendelson; choreography, Jack Baker; costumes, Adele Palmer; art director, Frank Arrigo; set decorators, John McCarthy, Jr., George Milo; sound, Roy Meadows; camera, Jack Marta; editor, Richard L. Van Enger.

Sterling Hayden (Tim Chapman); Vera Ralston (Lynne Tilton); David Brian (Croft Brunner); Adolphe Menjou (Swiftwater Tilton); Hoagy Carmichael (Jingles); Chill Wills (Steve); Howard Petrie (Axe-Handle Ole); Jim Davis (Poole); Ian MacDonald (Pauquette); Wally Cassell (Veazie); Elisha Cook, Jr. (Punky); Karl Davis (Red Bush); Tex Terry (Charley); George Marshall (Fireman).

ACCUSED OF MURDER   (Rep., 1956) C—74 M.

Producer, Herbert J. Yates; associate producer-director, Joseph Kane; based on the novel *Vanity Row* by W. R. Burnett; screenplay, Bob Williams, Burnett; music, R. Dale Butts; song, Herb Newman, Buddy Bregman; assistant director, Virgil Hart; art director, Frank Arrigo; camera, Bud Thackery; editor, Richard L. Van Enger.

David Brian (Lieutenant Roy Hargis); Vera Ralston (Ilona Vance); Sidney Blackmer (Frank Hobart); Virginia Grey (Sandra Lamoureaux); Warren Stevens (Stan Wilbo); Lee Van Cleef (Sergeant Emmett Lackey); Barry Kelley (Police

Captain Art Smedley); Richard Karlan (Chad Bayliss); Frank Puglia (Caesar Cipriano); Elisha Cook, Jr. (Whitey Pollock); Ian MacDonald (Trumble); Greta Thyssen (Myra Bayliss); Claire Carleton (Marge); Hank Worden (Les Fuller); Wally Cassell (Doorman); Robert Shayne (Police Surgeon); Simon Scott (Day Office Cop); John Damler (Night Office Cop); Gil Rankin (Fingerprint Policeman); Joseph Corey, Leon Tyler (Jitterbugging Sailors); Harry Lewis (Bartender); David Bair (Parking Attendant); Bill Henry (Walt, the Cop); Bob Carney (Waiter); Victor Sen Yung (Houseboy).

SPOILERS OF THE FOREST   (Rep., 1957) C—68 M.

Producer, Herbert J. Yates; associate producer-director, Joe Kane; screenplay, Bruce Manning; assistant director, Leonard Kennedy; costumes, Alexis Davidoff; art director, Frank Arrigo; music director, Gerald Roberts; camera, Jack Marta; editor, Richard L. Van Enger.

Rod Cameron (Boyd Caldwell); Vera Ralston (Joan Milna); Ray Collins (Eric Warren); Hillary Brooke (Phyllis Warren); Edgar Buchanan (Tom Duncan); Carl Benton Reid (John Mitchell); Sheila Bromley (Linda Mitchell); Hank Worden (Casey); John Compton (Billy Mitchell); Angela Greene (Camille); Paul Stader (Dan); Mary Alan Hokanson (Marie Milna); Raymond Greenleaf (Clyde Walters); Eleanor Audley (Mrs. Walters); Don Haggerty (Williams, the Ranger); William Haade (Loader); Jo Ann Lilliquist (Joan Milna as a Child); Bucko Stafford (Billy Mitchell as a Child); Robert Karnes, Ken Dribbs (Drivers); Rory Mallinson (Timber Cruiser); Virginia Carroll (Sarah, the Maid); John Patrick (Bartender); Bob Swan (Secretary); Mack Williams (Minister); Theresa Harris (Nancy, the Maid); Helen Wallace (Fainting Woman); Pauline Moore (Hysterical Woman); Judd Holdren (Mr. Peyton).

GUNFIRE AT INDIAN GAP   (Rep., 1957) 70 M.

Producer, Rudy Ralston; director, Joe Kane; screenplay, Barry Shipman; assistant director, Leonard Kunody; art director, Ralph Oberg; set decorator, John McCarthy, Jr.; assistant director, Leonard Kunody; makeup, Bob Mark; music supervisor, Gerald Roberts; costumes, Alexis Davidoff; sound, Weldon Coe; camera, Jack Marta; editor, Fred Knudtson.

Vera Ralston (Cheel); Anthony George (Juan Morales); George Macready (Pike [Mr. Jefferson]); Barry Kelley (Sheriff Daniel Harris); John Doucette (Leder); George Keymas (Scully); Chubby Johnson (Samuel); Glenn Strange (Matt); Daniel White (Moran); Steve Warren (Ed Stewart); Chuck Hicks (Deputy); Sarah Selby (Mrs. Moran).

THE NOTORIOUS MR. MONKS   (Rep., 1958) 70 M.

Producer, Rudy Ralston; director, Joe Kane; story, Peter Paul Fix; screenplay, Richard C. Sarafian; art director, Ralph Oberg; set decorator, John McCarthy, Jr.; costumes, Alexis Davidoff; makeup, Bob Mark; assistant director, Leonard Kunody; music supervisor, Gerald Roberts; sound, Earl Crain, Sr.; camera, Jack Marta; editor, Fred Knudtson.

Vera Ralston (Angela Monks); Don Kelly (Dan Flynn); Paul Fix (Benjamin Monks); Leo Gordon (Chip Klamp); Luana Anders (Gilda Hadley); Tom Brown (Neilson); Lyle Talbot (Leonardo); Emory Parnell (Cobus Anders); Fuzzy Knight (Tom); Hank Worden (Pete); Grandon Rhodes (Mr. Hadley).

THE MAN WHO DIED TWICE   (Rep., 1958) 70 M.

Producer, Rudy Ralston; director, Joe Kane; screenplay, Richard C. Sarafian; art director, Ralph Oberg; set director, John McCarthy, Jr.; songs, Jerry Gladstone and Al DeLory; assistant director, Leonard Kunody; makeup, Bob Mark; sound, Edwin B. Levinson; camera, Jack Marta; editor, Fred Knudtson.

Rod Cameron (Bill Brennon); Vera Ralston (Lynn Brennon); Mike Mazurki (Rak); Gerald Milton (Hart); Richard Karlan (Santoni); Louis Jean Heydt (Hampton); Don Megowan (T. J. Brennon); John Maxwell (Chief Hampton); Bob Anderson (Sergeant Williams); Paul Picerni (George); Don Haggerty (Frank); Luana Anders (Young Girl Addict); Jesslyn Fax (Sally Hemphill).

Publicity pose (1953) aboard the liner *United States*

With Herbert J. Yates in 1953

With Fred Graham in
A PERILOUS JOURNEY
(Rep '53)

With Chill Wills in
TIMBERJACK (Rep '55)

With Lee Van Cleef and
David Brian in ACCUSED
OF MURDER (Rep '56)

With John Doucette and Anthony George in GUNFIRE AT
INDIAN GAP (Rep '57)

With Paul Fix in THE NOTORIOUS MR. MONKS (Rep '58)

With Don Kelly and Leo Gordon in a publicity pose from
THE NOTORIOUS MR. MONKS

With husband Charles De Alva in 1973

The Production Crew for *The Glamour Girls*

JAMES ROBERT PARISH, New York-based biographer, was born near Boston. He attended the University of Pennsylvania and graduated as a Phi Beta Kappa with a degree in English. A graduate of the University of Pennsylvania Law School, he is a member of the New York Bar. As president of Entertainment Copyright Research Co., Inc., he headed a major researching facility for the film and television industries. Later he was a film interviewer-reviewer for *Motion Picture Daily* and *Variety*. He is the author of such books as *The Fox Girls, The Paramount Pretties, The RKO Gals, Actors' Television Credits, Hollywood's Great Love Teams,* and *The Great Movie Series.* He is co-author of *The Cinema of Edward G. Robinson, The MGM Stock Company, The Great Spy Pictures, Vincent Price Unmasked,* and others. Mr. Parish is also a film critic for national magazines.

* * *

A native of St. Paul, Minnesota, DON E. STANKE has lived for most of his adult life in or near San Francisco, California. For a number of years he was employed by the *San Francisco Examiner*, writing press releases and editing the publication's internal house organ. After further study of journalism at University of California night courses, he embarked on the avocation of interviewing show business personalities, leading to published career articles in various cinema periodicals. Mr. Stanke is employed full-time as Operations Manager of a medical X-ray firm located in San Leandro, California, but has found time to contribute to *The Real Stars #2* and with Mr. Parish, has co-authored two other Arlington House books, *The Debonairs* and *The Swashbucklers.*

* * *

T. ALLAN TAYLOR, godson of the late Margaret Mitchell, has long been active in book publishing and is presently production manager of one of the largest abstracting and technical indexing services in the United States. He has served as editor of such volumes as *The Fox Girls, The MGM Stock Company, Good Dames, Vincent Price Unmasked,* and *Hollywood's Great Love Teams.*

* * *

Brooklynite JOHN ROBERT COCCHI has been viewing and collecting data on motion pictures since childhood and is now regarded as one of the most thorough film researchers in the United States. He is the New York editor of *Boxoffice* magazine. He was research associate on *The American Movies Reference Book, The Fox Girls, The Paramount Pretties,* and many other volumes, and has written cinema-history articles for such journals as *Film Fan Monthly* and *Screen Facts.* He is the co-founder of one of Manhattan's leading film societies.

*　　*　　*

MICHAEL R. PITTS is the entertainment editor of the *Anderson* (Ind.) *Daily Bulletin* and holds a B.A. in history and an M.A. in journalism from Ball State University. He has been published in numerous cinema journals and is the co-author of such volumes as *Film Director's Guide*, *The Great Spy Pictures*, and *The Great Gangster Pictures*.

*　　*　　*

New York-born FLORENCE SOLOMON attended Hunter College and then joined Ligon Johnson's copyright research office. Later she was director of research at Entertainment Copyright Research Co., Inc., and she is presently a reference supervisor at ASCAP's Index Division. Ms. Solomon has collaborated on such works as *The American Movies Reference Book*, *TV Movies*, and *The Great Movie Series*. She is the niece of the noted sculptor, the late Sir Jacob Epstein.

*　　*　　*

RENÉ JORDAN has written extensively on films for many publications, including *Film Quarterly*, the *Village Voice*, *Films in Review*, *Cinema*, and *Film Ideal*. He is the author of *Clark Gable*, *Marlon Brando*, and *Gary Cooper* for the Pyramid Illustrated History of the Movies. He resides in New York City.

Index

Bruce, Nigel, 232, 486
Bruce, Virginia, 468
Brute Force, 142-43, 193
Bryan, Jane, 623
Brynner, Doris, 363, 364
Brynner, Yul, 363
Bubna, Ina, 36
Buccaneer's Girl, 149, 197
Buchanan, Edgar, 161
Buchman, Sidney, 630
Bulldog Drummond, 39, 94
Burke, Billie, 34, 80, 88
"Burke's Law," 174
Burks, Robert, 547
Burnett, W. R., 706
Burns, Marion, 49
Burr, Raymond, 91, 163, 165
Burton, Richard (actor), 360, 365, 434
Burton, Sir Richard (author), 473
Busch, Niven, 402
Bushell, Anthony, 41
Bushman, Francis X., 177
Butler, Ivan, 397
Butterflies Are Free, 93
By the Dawn's Early Light, 58
Byrd, Ralph, 393

Cabot, Bruce, 228
Cabre, Mario, 161
Caesar and Cleopatra (G. B. Shaw), 606
Cagney, James, 83, 235
Cahn, Sammy, 134, 254, 485
Cahoon, Wyn, 227
Calamity Jane and Sam Bass, 147, 195
Calhoun, Rory, 168, 169, 420
Callan, Michael, 277
Callejo, Cecilia, 228
Cameron, Kate, 57, 398, 473
Cameron, Rod, 139, 140, 146, 491, 707, 708
Campbell, Alan, 610
Canby, Vincent, 281, 436, 439
Cannon, Norman, 41
Cansino, Antonio, 218-19
Cansino, Eduardo, 219, 220, 221, 224
Cansino, Eduardo, Jr., 219, 283
Cansino, Margarita Carmen. *See* Hayworth, Rita
Cansino, Vernon, 219
Capote, Truman, 353, 425
Capp, Al, 532
Captain's Paradise, The, 130, 163, 200
Capucine, 364
Cardin, 352
Cardinal Richelieu, 601
Cardinale, Claudia, 280
Careless Lady, 47, 97
Carey, Macdonald, 134
Carey, Philip, 180
Carleton, George, 470

Carlisle, Mary, 51
Carmen Jones, 528
Carmichael, Hoagy, 634, 705
Carminati, Tullio, 334
"Carol Burnett Show, The," 281
Caron, Leslie, 319, 329-30, 332
Carradine, John, 176, 180
Carrie, 422-23, 446
Carillo, Leo, 486
Carroll, Earl, 132, 136
Carroll, John, 232, 695, 696, 697, 699, 700
Carroll, Kathleen, 363
Carroll, Leo G., 90
Carroll, Madeleine, 132, 134, 594
Carson, Jack, 235, 523
Carson, Johnny, 147, 178, 180
Casablanca, 401, 683
Casbah, 146, 194
Cass Timberlane, 408
Cassavetes, John, 273
Cassini, Igor, 266
Castiglione, La, 166, 201
Castle, Mary, 266, 521
Catch Me If You Can, 176
Catholic Legion of Decency, 558, 560
Catlett, Walter, 49, 685
Cavalcade, 597
Cavallaro, Carmen, 530
Cavan, Allan, 223
Ceiling Zero, 230
Chamberlain, Richard, 566
Chambers, Dorothy, 273
Chandler, Jeff, 533
Chaney, Lon, Jr., 52, 165, 175
Channing, Carol, 363
Charade, 355-56, 358, 373
Charisse, Cyd, 163, 180
Charlie Chan in Egypt, 221, 285
Charlot's Revue, 35
"Chase and Sanborn Hour," 73
Chase, Stephen, 700
Chatterton, Ruth, 51, 357, 609
Chayefsky, Paddy, 550
Cheers for Miss Bishop, 429, 627
Chevalier, Maurice, 347, 363, 469, 601
Cheyenne Autumn, 20
Chiang Kai-shek, Madame, 80
Children's Hour, The, 319, 354-55, 356, 373, 604
Ching, William, 699, 700
Chopin, Frédéric, 630, 631
Christian Century, 149
Christian, Paul, 494
Christopher, Jordan, 437
Christy, George, 530
Churchill, Winston, 635
Ciannelli, Eduardo, 684
Cini, Giorgia, 635
Circus World, 279, 304

733

738

743

745

746

748